ENCYCLOPEDIA of the HOLOCAUST

ENCYCLOPEDIA of the HOLOCAUST

Israel Gutman, Editor in Chief

Volume 1

Yad Vashem
The Holocaust Martyrs' and Heroes'
Remembrance Authority
Jerusalem

Sifriat Poalim Publishing House
Tel Aviv

MACMILLAN LIBRARY REFERENCE USA
Simon & Schuster Macmillan
NEW YORK

Simon & Schuster and Prentice Hall International
LONDON MEXICO CITY NEW DELHI SINGAPORE SYDNEY TORONTO

Macmillan Publishing Company
866 Third Avenue
New York, New York 10022
Collier Macmillan Canada, Inc.
Library of Congress Catalog Card Number: 89-13466
Printed in the United States of America

printing number
2 3 4 5 6 7 8 9 10

Library of Congress Cataloging-in-Publication Data

Encyclopedia of the Holocaust / Israel Gutman, editor in chief.
p. cm.
Includes bibliographical references.
ISBN 0–02–896090–4 (set)
Trade edition ISBN 0–02–546705–0 (set)
Two-volume edition ISBN 0-02-864527-8 (set)
1. Holocaust, Jewish (1939–1945)—Dictionaries. I. Gutman, Israel.
D804.3.E53 1990 89-13466
940.53'18'-03—dc20 CIP

Acknowledgments of sources
and permissions to use previously published materials
are made in Acknowledgments, page xix.

Complete and unabridged edition 1995

Contents

Editorial and Production Staff

Project Editor
Sylvia Juran

Editorial Consultants
Abraham J. Edelheit
Hershel Edelheit

Copy Editors
Eric L. Haralson David Olivenbaum

Proofreaders
Jeffrey P. Edelstein Emily Garlin Candice L. Gianetti Gloria Klatt

Production Director
Matthew M. Kardovich

Indexer
Cynthia Crippen

JERUSALEM STAFF

Translator into English
Mordechai Shalev

Illustrations Researcher
Moshe Shalvi

Illustrations Assistant
Yehudit Levin

Staff

Marianne Asaf Eitan Ben-Noah Shelly Berliner Daphna Blumert
Tamar Blumert Heftsibah Cohen Eva Condor Joan Hooper Tirza Lavi-Muttath
Stephanie Nakache Zvi Reiter Jacqueline Rokhsar Yaakov Stein Tsiporet Yagil

PUBLISHER
Philip Friedman

MANAGING EDITOR, ENCYCLOPEDIAS
Elly Dickason

Foreword

Auschwitz will remain as the darkest, the cruelest, the most incomprehensible—and yet also the most documented—event in history. Thanks to the testimonies of the victims, the confessions of the killers and their accomplices, and the research of historians, we are able to know its essential features. The meticulous preparations for the "Final Solution" of the Jewish question at the highest level of the Third Reich, the active collaboration of all its ministers, the pernicious role played by Nazi propaganda, by the army, and by Nazi science, the economy, industry, and medicine—anyone who wants to learn the facts needs only to look into the archives. They exist. The effort of the SS to destroy them failed. The enemy did not succeed in erasing the traces of his crimes. Thus he has been defeated in at least one domain, that of remembrance.

That his total war against the Jewish people was also a war to the death against Jewish memory is no longer doubted by anyone. His aim was not only to exterminate all the Jews on the planet but also to torment them, to torture them, to humiliate them, to drive them to despair and shame—in short, to dehumanize them before casting them into the shadows of history, from which they would never again emerge.

Why this cold and calculated hatred—both rational and irrational, and elevated to the status of a national, even a universal ideology—for an ethnic, social, and religious minority which, over the centuries, has contributed so much to civilization and its progress? Why did this hatred find such resonance in Germany itself and in most of the occupied countries? Why the Allies' conspiracy of silence and their indifference toward this war that the common enemy was fighting within the greater war?

A tragedy unlike any other, senseless, it defies answers. It could have been avoided; at least, its extent could have been diminished. We will never understand why the extermination of six million human beings was made possible. But we do know how. It is only necessary to read certain works of history, to study the documents, to investigate the accounts of witnesses. And to consult this monumental encyclopedia, on which the most knowledgeable specialists in the subject, under the editorship of Dr. Israel Gutman, the most eminent among them, have collaborated for many years.

Everything is here, in condensed form, of course. Cities and towns and villages, ghettos and prisons, important dates, reference books and statistics, massacres and revolts, names and pseudonyms, fighters and chroniclers, heroes and martyrs: do you want to know about their fate? You must. To turn one's back on this chapter of history means wanting to forget it. And he who forgets becomes an accomplice of the enemy. To forget the victims is to kill them a second time.

Certainly, we shall never understand either the dehumanized cruelty of the executioner or the human gentleness of his victims. Yet here it is not a question of understanding, but of knowing. To confess our incomprehension is a sign of humility; to refuse to learn the facts is a proof of arrogance. And of indifference.

That is the importance of this encyclopedia: the amount of knowledge accumulated in it is so extensive that it must be regarded as an indispensable source.

ELIE WIESEL
New York, September 1989
Translated from the French
by Sylvia Juran

Preface

The decades since the end of World War II have witnessed a growing awareness throughout the world of the significance of the Holocaust as a central event in the history of the Jewish people and of Western civilization. The purpose of this encyclopedia is to put at the disposal of teachers, students, and all those interested in the subject a comprehensive and up-to-date work on the Holocaust: its background, its history, and its impact, written by the leading scholars and experts in Holocaust studies from many countries. The encyclopedia deals in depth with the sources and motivations for all manifestations relating to or forming part of the Holocaust. They include:

1. The rise and growth of racist ideology and Nazi-style hatred of the Jews, promoted by Hitler and the Nazi party, which Germany adopted as official policy when it came under Nazi rule.

2. The discriminatory racist legislation under which the Jews were excluded from human society in Germany, and the relentless policy of stripping the Jews of all their economic assets and sources of livelihood and of gradually excluding them from the Nazi-created Third Reich.

3. The process, instituted against the Jews in Poland during the war, of oppression, terrorization, starvation, imprisonment in ghettos, and deportation. In the critical phase of the war—the attack on the Soviet Union—this process turned into mass murder and, subsequently, into a campaign that aimed at the total destruction of the Jews of Europe. The decision on this course of action was taken at the top level of the German state and the Nazi party, by the leaders who bore responsibility to the highest degree; the planning was put into the hands of a state apparatus, and the process was implemented by special murder squads and in killing installations.

The encyclopedia devotes a substantial amount of space to the Jews in Nazi-dominated Europe: their leadership and organizations, their misery, the extent of their knowledge about what lay in store for them, their activities as they confronted a hopeless situation, their stubborn struggle for life and survival, and the desperate means of resistance to which they resorted in the face of the inescapable death closing in on them. Much attention is devoted to the countries under German occupation or control and the degrees and stages of oppression they underwent, to the fate of other civilian population groups, and, in particular, to Soviet prisoners of war, who were tortured in the camps and murdered en masse. According to Nazi racist principles, the people in these groups were inferior beings, lacking full human worth and the right to exist. Another issue dealt with is the attitude toward Jews manifested by various occupied peoples, their resistance attempts, and the actions they took, if any, to save Jews who were being driven to their death. Other subjects examined include the position taken by the free democracies and the Jews living in them, as well as by the Jewish community in Palestine (then administered by the British Mandatory government), with regard to the anti-Jewish persecutions and, later, the "Final Solution." Also explored are the postwar influences of the Holocaust on ideological and political concepts, and on the positions and policies of the various religions and their institutions; the way in which the world regards the Jews and the Jews regard themselves in the postwar period; the treatment of the Holocaust in historiography; and the repeated attempts to deny the Holocaust or to distort its meaning and the responsibility of its perpetrators.

The basic approach taken by the editors of the encyclopedia is that the Holocaust was a historical and ideological event that must be examined in the historical context and with the historian's tools and methods. At the same time, the editors realized that any attempt to understand the factors leading to the Holocaust, the persons involved in it, and the lessons to be derived from it requires the contribution of scholars from other disciplines—political science, sociology, religion, psychology, law, medicine, literature, and the arts.

While the need for a basic work on the Holocaust in encyclopedia format was not in doubt, the decision to carry out this project was taken after much considered thought. The first question confronting the initial team of editors was whether the research on the Holocaust to date had covered the many aspects of the subject sufficiently to justify undertaking such a comprehensive project. Preliminary investigations showed a firm base for such an effort, and now that the work has been completed we believe that this original assumption is borne out by the results. Another question arose concerning the form that the work should take—its style and its terminology. The Holocaust is a subject laden with powerful emotions. It is not only Holocaust survivors and persons who suffered directly who are so emotionally involved that they are not always capable of approaching the subject objectively and analytically. Even intellectuals, such as George Steiner, have stated that the bestiality of the Holocaust does not lend itself to the normal linguistic and associative means of expression that belong to our ethical and cultural tradition; in the face of the Holocaust and its horror, we are therefore silent and paralyzed, and the only possible reaction is one of mute, frozen communion. In a letter, Nelly Sachs suggested that "an altar of silence be erected, made up of rocks—of unhewn words." Others have asserted that authors of fiction cannot cope with the challenge posed by the Holocaust. In many instances the diaries of victims and the memoirs of survivors create a more authentic picture of the Holocaust and make a stronger impact with the facts they describe and their distinctive power of expression than do the intuition and the imagery of the writer of fiction. It is not by chance that it was writers such as Tadeusz Borowski, Primo Levi, and Elie Wiesel who were able to give authentic articulation to the essence of the horror of the concentration camp universe, having themselves been prisoners in the camps; their personal experience of the war and the Holocaust constituted the motivating force and internal compulsion behind their literary work. The Israeli poet Abba Kovner, in a short essay, "Epilogue for Historians," warned of the natural inclination of historians to seek satisfactory answers to questions for which no answers exist: this may lead to a situation in which "the fog appears to lift and everything falls in place in accepted terms . . . and even the horror can be weighed and measured." Our work in the encyclopedia is based on criteria derived from conscientious and sound investigation. However, we had to retain at least a trace of the terrible shock that a person experiences when he or she touches on the Holocaust. We have also tried to avoid, as best we could, providing simple and clear-cut answers to complex and troubling issues, preferring to leave the questions partially unanswered, as food for thought and doubt, rather than trying to resolve them by smooth formulas that disregard facts.

The use of Nazi terminology was one of the problems we faced. Each case was decided individually, the criterion being how widely the name or term was used. We therefore chose to use the German terms *Kristallnacht*, *Judenrat*, *Selektion*, *Aktion*, *Arisierung*, *Anschluss*, and so on. These terms are unique in their Nazi context and lose much of their meaning in translation.

The very definition of the word "Holocaust" (in Hebrew, *sho'ah*) is not always uniform or generally accepted. Even scholars interpret it with different nuances. These differences apply not only to the term's origin and meaning; they also involve the categories of victims to which it relates. Throughout the course of human history, mass killings and bloodshed of other kinds have taken place during revolutions, social upheavals, civil wars, and retaliatory acts, especially in the twentieth century, and are subsumed under the term "genocide." Frequently, no distinction is made between these acts and the Holocaust carried out by the Nazi regime. As a result, such events as the Biafra tragedy or the mass killings in Cambodia are sometimes referred to as "holocausts"—a practice that blurs the uniqueness of the Holocaust. In our conception, the Holocaust in the Nazi period and during World War II was, above all, the process of the oppression and murder of some six million European Jews—the only one among Hitler's goals and war aims that he succeeded in accomplishing.

Several components of the persecution and murder campaign set the Holocaust apart from mass-murder phenomena of the past and of the twentieth century (even during World War II itself). The Holocaust did not originate in a real conflict between the German people and the Jews of Germany or the Jews of the world. In fact, the Jews of Germany were a loyal and devoted element of German society who made a great contribution to the development and flourishing of the country's economy, science, and culture. In many nations, especially in eastern Europe, Germany was highly esteemed among the Jews, who regarded it as an enlightened country that was tolerant toward its Jews. Quite often, the Jews of these countries were suspected of being loyal to Germany, and their Yiddish language (which is mainly based on a dialect of German origin) was sometimes thought to be an element used by the Jews to "Germanize" the non-Jewish population. Moreover, owing to such demographic processes as a low birthrate and rapid assimilation, the Jewish population of Germany was fast diminishing, and some were predicting its almost complete decline and its disappearance within a foreseeable period.

It follows that the discrimination against the Jews introduced by the Nazis in Germany, their efforts to drive the Jews out of the country, and their decision for the total physical destruction of the Jews did not result from any confrontation between Germany and the Jews or from any threat posed by the Jews to Germany. This was an annihilation operation that had its source in Nazi racist ideology and was decided upon on that basis. In the Nazi concept, not only were the Jews different because of their origin and certain alleged peculiar physical attributes, but the Jewish race as such, in its biological substance and its blood, was believed to embody noxious traits and hereditary characteristics that could not be changed by evolution, education, or integration. If Jews mixed with other races, it was held, these negative traits and characteristics would predominate and determine the image and nature of society.

Such claims contradict scientific fact as well as the basic and hallowed tenets of Christianity. But Nazi racist ideology did not confine itself to defining the Jew as having acquired inferior racial biological traits in a perversion of the process of natural selection, adaptation, and survival according to the Darwinist theory. The guidelines laid down by Hitler stated that the Jews were neither a religious nor a national group but an ambitious and well-organized subversive race. The Jewish race had set itself the aim of disrupting the natural dynamics among the human races, and through conspiracy and manipulation it exerted influence in the world and prevented the "master race" (*Herrenvolk*—that is, the Nordic Aryans) from taking its rightful place as the ruler and inaugurator of a new social order and new principles of existence. In short, the Jews were deemed an "anti-race," the complete opposite of the Germans. For this reason, a campaign—no less significant than any military confrontation—was being waged whose purpose was to change the course of history. The Aryan race, and in particular its purer and more determined German component, was engaged in a struggle with the Jewish threat. Such were the groundless claims on which was based the "war" against the Jews, a war that increased in ferocity until it reached the stage of relentless physical annihilation.

Some researchers have tended to disregard the racial elements in Hitler's and the Nazis' ideology or to discount its role, and to concentrate on what they regard as the political pragmatism of the Third Reich's course. This approach ignores the historical reality. The regime's policy toward the Jews, the measures taken against them, and the fate that they suffered in all the areas under Nazi rule, occupation, and influence were determined, in principle and practice, by the dictates of fanatic and unrestrained racism. This fact represents the very essence of the Holocaust.

The Holocaust, as it was carried out, strove to physically destroy a blameless people—an ethnic entity that was not a participant in the war. This drive had as its purpose the persecution of every person of Jewish descent (according to the Nazi racial definitions) and the tracking down of every Jew who tried to elude the fate planned for him by going into hiding or converting to Christianity. When such a Jew was caught, he was dealt with in the most inhumane and merciless fashion. The objective was to trap and kill every Jew, irrespective of age, gender, political view, occupation, or social status. To this end a state apparatus of civilians, diplomats, and security and military forces, as well as personnel specifically assigned to the job of killing, was spread all over Europe and charged with the planning, organization, and execution of the campaign. That apparatus knew that its task constituted the Führer's highest priority, and it was tireless in its efforts to ensure that no Jewish community and no individual Jews escaped the bitter end planned for them. Even when the Third Reich's unconditional surrender had become inevitable and the only surviving Jews in most of the German-occupied areas were slave-labor forces working for the Nazi war machine, the Nazis did not put a halt to the murder of those human beings, whose only crime was that that they were Jews.

The most radical consequence of Nazi racism, the Nazi murder machine with its use of lethal gas, was, for the most part, applied solely to the Jews. Other categories and ethnic groups, however, were persecuted and murdered as well, including Gypsies, members of the Polish intelligentsia, and Soviet prisoners of war. Millions from these groups were killed, because the Nazis regarded them as enemies, as socially disruptive, or as racially inferior. These victims too are often seen as victims of the Holocaust. To judge by the nature of the regime that the Nazis imposed on the occupied countries (especially the Slavic lands), and by General Plan East (*Generalplan Ost*), in which they outlined their future policy concerning these people, it can well be imagined how the Nazis would have treated the people that were "inferior" in their eyes, their opponents in other countries, and, indeed, all of mankind, had they succeeded in establishing their "New Order."

Nevertheless, a distinction must also be made between the Holocaust (which rested on the principles of racism and was expressed in the attempted total and immediate destruction of a people) and attacks on population groups that the Nazis considered harmful from the social, political, or military point of view and, consequently, expendable. No discriminatory legislation was enacted in the German Reich before the war against the Poles and the Russians, whom the Nazis considered to be racially inferior. Even during the war, Poles and Russians living in occupied countries such as France or Hungary were not persecuted or killed on account of their racial origin. There is, of course, no difference in the gravity of the crimes committed by the Nazis against the members of any people, as far as the individual victim is concerned, or the injury and sorrow inflicted on his family. It is when we define the Holocaust as a social, political, and historical phenomenon that a clear and fundamental difference emerges between it and all the other forms of persecution and mass murder committed by the Nazis.

The kind of antisemitism that spawned a negative image of the Jew on religious or other grounds did not arise during the Nazi period but preceded it. It is inconceivable that the Nazis could have succeeded in creating a hostile atmosphere against the Jews and in carrying out their design on the scale that they did—deporting and murdering Jews by the millions—had it not been for the distrust and hatred of Jews that antisemitism had legitimized and fostered over many generations. The Nazi experience proved in full, and in the most cruel manner, the rule that hatred based on religious and political grounds does not stop at the victim's doorstep but serves as a boomerang. Nazism was determined to wipe the Jewish people off the face of the earth, but it also attacked Western civilization, its norms of morality, and the political and social systems created and developed on the basis of those ethical concepts. In universal terms, Nazism was an attack that aimed at a total revolution: the uprooting of the standards of Western civilization, based on the Judeo-Christian tradition, and their replacement with a world in which racial criteria and a cult of raw, brutal power would hold sway.

The editorial board of the encyclopedia turned to experts in different parts of the world to contribute to the *Encyclopedia of the Holocaust.* On occasion, some contributors expressed views at variance with those of the board, but these were as a rule approved, out of the obligation to respect the contributors' right to express their ideas freely and to reflect as wide a range of theoretical approaches as possible. A determined effort was made to present major events and issues from a variety of different angles, and, above all, to base the material in the encyclopedia on the multifaceted sources at our disposal —German and Jewish, and from the occupied and Allied countries.

The encyclopedia's structure was based on a list of entries that included individual names, major events, the countries involved, the concentration camps, the ghettos, the extermination camps and murder sites, political movements and trends, and resistance movements. This list was made up of approximately one thousand entries that were classified in accordance with their relative importance and estimated length.

As in other encyclopedia projects, changes were made in the original structure of the work during the course of its preparation. Contributors were sometimes unable to keep to the allocated space and wrote at much greater length, involving the editors in a thankless job of cutting. At times it was felt that such reduction might impair the entry, and consequently the entire article was kept, in view of the importance and originality of the subject matter—even if this might lead to certain disproportions.

Collecting the vast reservoir of material and dealing with the complex problems presented in an encyclopedia of this size and standard was made possible by the systematic and ongoing research undertaken in many countries and in different languages. It included wide-ranging German studies of the historical background, the stages of Hitler's rise to power, and the structure of the Nazi regime and its components; examination by Polish scholars of the character of the occupation regime; research into the Holocaust conducted in Israel, which has provided monographs on ghettos, camps, and the resistance movement; analysis of the nature of totalitarian movements and of psychological and other effects of the Holocaust, centered in the United States; and the local research work that has been taking place in other countries. The works of such authors as Gerald Reitlinger, Léon Poliakov, Raul Hilberg, Nora Levin, Lucy Dawidowicz, Nathan Eck, and, most recently, Leni Yahil have been valuable contributions to the historical portrayal of the Holocaust in its various aspects. The major innovation and significance of the encyclopedia lies in the fact that it encompasses within a single work the Holocaust research of a great many authors, each writing in his or her area of expertise.

Almost every entry in the encyclopedia has a select bibliography attached to it, with preference given to books in English, but also listing basic books written in other languages. The encyclopedia also contains a great many photographs, maps, and diagrams. Among the appendixes are a glossary, a chronology, and a listing, by country, of the number of Jewish victims of the Holocaust. This enumeration is the first of its kind in that it represents not the calculations and assumptions of a single author, but the summing-up of data gathered by a group of experts.

The executive editorial board operated as a team, supervising the work in all its stages; the international board, serving as an advisory body, was of great help to the project in its execution. The initiative of the project was undertaken by the publisher, Sifriat Poalim, headed by Tsvi Raanan, who enlisted a team of technical and administrative personnel to help carry out the work of the encyclopedia. The work was done at the publisher's Jerusalem office and at Yad Vashem, without whose library, archive, collection of photographs, and staff the project could not have been accomplished.

Israel Gutman
Editor in Chief
Jerusalem, June 1989

Introduction

This encyclopedia seeks to provide, insofar as its format allows, the widest possible scope of information on what has justly been called the worst event in human history. Its nearly one thousand entries cover manifold aspects of the Holocaust—here defined as the Third Reich's attempt, during the period of Nazi power (1933–1945), to physically destroy the Jews of Europe—from its antecedents to its postwar consequences. A primary aim has been to make knowledge that was previously available mainly to scholars accessible to the educated public at large.

Entries are of many kinds and fall into many categories. Examples of the latter, to cite only a few, are *geographical:* regions; countries (many in the form of paired articles, detailing the history of the Holocaust period from both the non-Jewish and the Jewish point of view); cities and smaller places; Nazi camps; sites of massacres; *biographical:* Nazis and collaborators; partisans; Jewish and non-Jewish leaders and resisters; rescuers of Jews; persons who relayed to the free world the facts of the Holocaust; entries concerning the *postwar impact:* survivors; trials of war criminals; reflections in literature, films, art, and music; education on the Holocaust; documentation centers. A dozen or so entries are in multiple form (several related articles grouped together) in order to cover different aspects of a major topic; examples are Museums and Memorial Institutes and Youth Movements.

The blind entries, located alphabetically throughout the encyclopedia (such as Nazi Doctors. *See* Physicians, Nazi), direct the reader to topics sought, or to closely related topics. Entry titles are almost invariably in the foreign language of origin, but English translations of these names and terms appear as blind entries (for example, "Stab-in-the-Back" Myth. *See* Dolchstosslegende). Acronyms are avoided as entry titles, but they too are found as blind entries (UNRRA, OSI, and so on). Some lengthy blind entries, such as that for Camps, appear as small essays guiding the reader to many relevant entries.

The encyclopedia's articles are further linked by a comprehensive system of cross-references. When the reader of an entry encounters a name or term in small caps, he or she is being advised that the name or term is the title of another entry, as in this example:

> In BIAŁYSTOK, the first announcement made by the JUDENRAT (Jewish Council), on German orders, stated: "As of the morning of July 10, 1941, all Jewish men, women, and children aged fourteen and over must wear a white armband on their left sleeve, with a blue Star of David on it" (*see* BADGE, JEWISH).

Cross-references are also found at the end of many entries, such as [*See also* Propaganda, Nazi] at the end of the entry Goebbels, Joseph. The cross-references and blind entries are adjuncts to the detailed index in the fourth volume of the encyclopedia.

In the interest of accuracy and authenticity, original foreign-language names and terms are used almost exclusively, with English translations provided in parentheses; for well-known organizations, the foreign acronyms are also included, as Reichssicherheitshauptamt (Reich Security Main Office;

RSHA). Toward this same end, diacritics are provided for all Latin-alphabet languages. Thus, Bełżec and not Belzec, Ustaša and not Ustasha. For non-Latin-alphabet languages such as Hebrew and Russian, nonscholarly transliteration systems are used. With few exceptions, italics are limited to foreign words and terms as such: *Ostarbeiter* (eastern [slave] laborer), *rampa* (railway platform). The basic source for place-names was *Webster's New Geographical Dictionary* (Springfield, Mass., 1984); preference was given to the name most commonly used during the Holocaust period. Variant names appear as blind entries.

What made the events described here possible? The response "racist fanaticism, combined with unlimited opportunity" fails to satisfy. As Elie Wiesel has observed, the "why" cannot be answered; we can only learn the "how." How the worst—men without substance, but with limitless malevolent energy—gained power, how they infected some and aroused fear and hesitation in others. How they quickly and easily, well before initiating World War II, became professional thieves and killers. How they ranged as predators, hunting down guiltless men, women, and children in order to destroy them. How, free of restraints, they covered occupied Europe with a grotesque network of "camps," into which they drove and lured the immense numbers of people whom they had forced from their homes. How, in the most obscene manner, they robbed these human beings—already robbed of home, family, possessions, and strength—of all there was left to take, their lives. Such was the outcome of the racist lunacy that constituted the very center and foundation of Nazi ideology.

Can it be that these crimes took place not so many years ago, within the lifetime of many of us? But for an accident of geography or birth this could have been our parents, our brothers and sisters, ourselves. These were people like ourselves, with the same thoughts and feelings as our own. Yet each was an individual, unique, who suffered as an individual.

The facts are here, but they are only a beginning. It is for each reader to bring them to life in his or her own heart. Having thought, and reflected, and wept, we ask: In the face of this terrible lesson, what must we learn, and what can we do? What is our responsibility?

To ensure that this will never happen again.

Most importantly, to remember the victims. Each day, each hour, as best we can, in our own lives, let us speak up for those who were made silent.

Thanks are due to the many people in Israel and the United States who cooperated in the work of the encyclopedia. For all concerned, this was a deeply emotional involvement. Brigitte Goldstein was an infallible source of help in German-language matters, and Sylvia Kanwischer made thoughtful and valuable suggestions during the encyclopedia's early stages. Karin Vanderveer was a capable, efficient administrative assistant. The expertise and judgment of Abraham Edelheit and Hershel Edelheit were relied on throughout. Above all, thanks and gratitude are due to Israel Gutman, the encyclopedia's editor in chief, to Robert Rozett, the associate editor, and to Moshe Shalvi, the project coordinator. Their commitment, their knowledge, and their warm-hearted support were unfailing and indispensable.

SYLVIA JURAN
Project Editor
New York, October 1989

Acknowledgments

We would like to thank Martin Gilbert for his permission to use some of the maps from *The Macmillan Atlas of the Holocaust* (New York, 1982).

We also wish to express our thanks and appreciation to the various institutions and libraries that have kindly granted us permission to reproduce photographs in their possession. Appropriate credit lines appear with each such photograph. All photographs without attribution were provided by the Yad Vashem archives in Jerusalem.

Alphabetical List of Entries

C

F

H

I

J

L

M

N

O

P

Q

R

S

Directory of Contributors

A

MICHEL ABITBOL
Hebrew University of Jerusalem
Algeria
Libya
Morocco
Tunisia

SAMUEL ABRAHAMSEN
Brooklyn College
Norway

IRIT ABRAMSKI-BLIGH
Yad Vashem, Jerusalem
Husseini, Hajj Amin al-
Iraq
Libya: Forced-Labor and Internment Camps
Syria and Lebanon

UWE ADAM
Frankfurt am Main (deceased)
Anti-Jewish Legislation
Daluege, Kurt
Darré, Richard Walther
Frick, Wilhelm
Gas Chambers
Lammers, Hans Heinrich
Ley, Robert

JACQUES ADLER
University of Melbourne
Amelot
Conseil Représentatif des Juifs de France
Paris
Rayski, Abraham
Union des Juifs pour la Résistance et l'Entr'aide

MIKHAIL AGURSKY
Hebrew University of Jerusalem
Litvinov, Maksim Maksimovich
Molotov, Viacheslav Mikhailovich
Stalin, Joseph Vissarionovich

GABRIEL E. ALEXANDER
Jerusalem
Berlin

YITZCHAK ALPEROWITZ
Yad Vashem, Jerusalem (emeritus)
Bielski, Tuvia

DAVID ALTSHULER
Museum of Jewish Heritage, New York
Museums and Memorial Institutes: A Living Memorial to the Holocaust—Museum of Jewish Heritage

MORDECHAI ALTSHULER
Hebrew University of Jerusalem
Soviet Union

ZIVA AMISHAI-MAISELS
Hebrew University of Jerusalem
Art of the Holocaust

JEAN ANCEL
Yad Vashem, Jerusalem
Antonescu, Ion
Antonescu, Mihai
Bessarabia
Bogdanovka
Bucharest
Bukovina
Centrala Evreilor
Chernovtsy
Comisia Autonoma de Ajutorare
Cuza, Alexandru
Domanevka
Dorohoi
Edineti
Filderman, Wilhelm
Goga, Octavian
Iaşi
Iron Guard
Kishinev
Lecca, Radu
Marculeşti
Mogilev-Podolski
Odessa
Richter, Gustav
Romania: Jews during the Holocaust
Safran, Alexander
Secureni
Sima, Horia
Transnistria
Transylvania, Southern
Trials of War Criminals: Romania
Uniunea Evreilor Români
Vapniarka
Vertujeni

YITZHAK ARAD
Yad Vashem, Jerusalem
Aktion Reinhard
Bełżec
"Erntefest"
Extermination Camps
Family Camps in the Forests
Fareynegte Partizaner Organizatsye
Franz, Kurt
Gens, Jacob
Glazman, Josef
Jeckeln, Friedrich
Klooga
Kommissarbefehl
Kruk, Herman
Pechersky, Aleksandr
Ponary
Reichskommissariat Ostland
Sobibór
Treblinka
Vilna

SHLOMO ARONSON
Hebrew University of Jerusalem
Gestapo
Heydrich, Reinhard
Reichssicherheitshauptamt
SA
SS

HAIM AVNI
Hebrew University of Jerusalem
Spain: General Survey

GABRIEL BACH
Supreme Court of Israel
Eichmann Trial

ZVI BACHARACH
Bar-Ilan University
Funk, Walther
Galen, Clemens August Graf von
Grawitz, Ernst Robert
Hitlerjugend
Lichtenberg, Bernhard
Propaganda, Nazi
Wurm, Theophil

DAVID BANKIER
Hebrew University of Jerusalem
Baum Gruppe
Chamberlain, Houston Stewart
Deutscher Vortrupp, Gefolgschaft Deutscher Juden
Documentation Centers: Wiener Library
Four-Year Plan
Freemasons
Führerprinzip
Horst Wessel Song
Lebensraum
Mischlinge
Nazi Party
Nuremberg Laws
Reichsbund Jüdischer Frontsoldaten
Weltsch, Robert

AVRAHAM BARKAI
Tel-Aviv University; Leo Baeck Institute, Jerusalem
Arisierung
Boycott, Anti-Jewish
Schacht, Hjalmar
Warburg, Max

YEHUDA BAUER
Hebrew University of Jerusalem
Beriḥa
Gypsies
Joint Distribution Committee
Kasztner, Rezső
Mayer, Saly
Riegner Cable
Schwartz, Joseph J.
Totenkopfverbände
World War II

ARIE LEON BAUMINGER
Jerusalem
Bauminger, Heshek

MOSHE BEJSKI
Supreme Court of Israel
"Righteous among the Nations"

GRACIELA BEN-DROR
Moreshet Institute, Givat Haviva
Argentina

HEDVA BEN-ISRAEL
Hebrew University of Jerusalem
Great Britain: Appeasement of Nazi Germany
Munich Conference

ARIEH BEN-MENAHEM
Ramat Hasharon, Israel
Front of the Wilderness Generation
Grossman, Mendel

AVRAHAM BEN-YAKOV
Jerusalem
Bulgaria

SARAH BENDER
Tel-Aviv University
Białystok

MICHAEL BERENBAUM
United States Holocaust Memorial Museum
Museums and Memorial Institutes: United States Holocaust Memorial Museum

STEFAN BIERNACKI
Main Commission for Investigation of Nazi Crimes in Poland, Warsaw
AB-Aktion
Documentation Centers: Main Commission for Investigation of Nazi Crimes in Poland
Forster, Albert
Goeth, Amon Leopold

YSRAEL CH. BILETZKY
Bar-Ilan University
Literature on the Holocaust: Yiddish Literature

DANIEL BLATMAN
Yad Vashem, Jerusalem
Bund

SARA BLOOMFIELD
U.S. Holocaust Memorial Council, Washington, D.C.
U.S. Holocaust Memorial Council

NAHUM BOGNER
Yad Tabenkin Institute, Ramat Efal, Israel
Cyprus Detention Camps

JACOB BORUT
Yad Vashem, Jerusalem
Frankfurt am Main

STEVEN B. BOWMAN
University of Cincinnati
Athens
Corfu
Greece
Koretz, Zvi
Rhodes
Salonika
Thrace

RANDOLPH L. BRAHAM
City University of New York
Baky, László
Becher, Kurt
Brand, Joel
Cluj
Dej
Endre, László
Freudiger, Fülöp
Gendarmerie, Hungarian
Hungary: Jews during the Holocaust
Kállay, Miklós
Kamenets-Podolski
Kaposvár
Krumey, Hermann Alois
Munkács
Munkaszolgálat
Relief and Rescue Committee of Budapest
Satu-Mare
Sighet Marmaţiei
Stern, Samu
Strasshof
Szálasi, Ferenc
Sztójay, Döme
Tîrgu- Mureş
Transylvania, Northern

MARTIN BROSZAT
University of Munich (deceased)
National Socialism

CHRISTOPHER R. BROWNING
Pacific Lutheran University
Auerswald, Heinz
Deportations
"Final Solution"
Frank, Hans
Ganzenmüller, Albert
Killinger, Manfred von
Lösener, Bernard
Ludin, Hans Elard
Luther, Martin
Madagascar Plan
Neurath, Konstantin Freiherr von
Nisko and Lublin Plan
Rademacher, Franz
Rauff, Walther
Reichskommissariat für die Festigung des Deutschen Volkstums
Ribbentrop, Joachim von
Sajmište
Thadden, Eberhard von
Wagner, Horst
Wannsee Conference
Weizsäcker, Ernst von

YEHOSHUA R. BÜCHLER
Moreshet Institute, Givat Haviva
Buchenwald
Dora-Mittelbau

JOZEF BUSZKO
Jagiellonian University, Kraków
Auschwitz
Höss, Rudolf
Płaszów

DANIEL CARPI
Tel-Aviv University
Italy: Aid to Jews by Italians
Italy: Concentration Camps

SHALOM CHOLAWSKI
Kibbutz Ein Hashofet
Atlas, Yeheskel
Baranovichi
Belorussia
Derechin
Diatlovo
Gomel
Grodno
Kaplinski, Hirsch
Koldichevo
Lachva
Lida
Maly Trostinets
Minsk
Mir
Mushkin, Eliyahu
Nesvizh
Novogrudok
Partisans
Rufajzen, Oswald
Slonim
Volozhin
Zorin, Shalom

YEHOYAKIM COCHAVI
Bet Loḥamei ha-Getta'ot; Haifa University
Centralverein Deutscher Staatsbürger Jüdischen Glaubens
Goebbels, Joseph
Göring, Hermann
Hilfsverein der Deutschen Juden
Hirsch, Otto
Kulturbund Deutscher Juden
Mittelstelle für Jüdische Erwachsenenbildung
Museums and Memorial Institutes: Bet Loḥamei ha-Getta'ot
SD
Speer, Albert
Zentralausschuss der Deutschen Juden für Hilfe und Aufbau
Zentralstelle für Jüdische Auswanderung

ASHER COHEN
Haifa University
Arrow Cross Party
Budapest
Horthy, Miklós
Youth Movements: Hungary

NAVA COHEN
Hebrew University of Jerusalem
Medical Experiments

RICHARD COHEN
Hebrew University of Jerusalem
Arendt Controversy
Baur, André
Blum, Léon
Consistoire Central des Israélites de France
France: General Survey
France: Jewish Responses to Persecution
France: The Jews and the Holocaust
Helbronner, Jacques
Hirschler, René
Jarblum, Marc
Jefroykin, Jules
Lambert, Raymond-Raoul
Meiss, Léon
Saliège, Jules-Gérard
Union Générale des Israélites de France

JOHN S. CONWAY
University of British Columbia, Vancouver
Barth, Karl
Bonhoeffer, Dietrich
Christian Churches: General Survey

ABRAHAM COOPER
Simon Wiesenthal Center, Los Angeles
Museums and Memorial Institutes: Simon Wiesenthal Center

LEONARD DINNERSTEIN
University of Arizona
Displaced Persons, Jewish

BARBARA DISTEL
Dachau Museum, West Germany
Dachau
Kaufering

ELLY DLIN
Yad Vashem, Jerusalem
Education on the Holocaust: United States and Israel

ELIEZER DOMKE
Haifa
Hamburg

JUDITH E. DONESON
Clayton, Missouri
Films, Nazi Antisemitic
Films on the Holocaust

TADEUSZ DREWNOWSKI
University of Warsaw
Literature on the Holocaust: Poland

KRZYSZTOF DUNIN-WASOWICZ
Polish Academy of Sciences, Warsaw
Pawiak Prison
Stutthof
Warsaw: General Survey
Warsaw Polish Uprising

EUGENIUSZ DURACZYNSKI
Polish Academy of Sciences, Warsaw
Armia Krajowa
Delegatura
Gwardia Ludowa
Polish Government-in-Exile
Sikorski, Władysław Eugeniusz

BENYAMIN ECKSTEIN
Hebrew University of Jerusalem (deceased)
Ebensee
Gunskirchen
Gusen
Mauthausen
Melk

ABRAHAM J. EDELHEIT
Touro College, New York
Biltmore Resolution
Historiography of the Holocaust
Silver, Abba Hillel
White Paper of 1939

LEO SHUA EITINGER
Oslo University (emeritus)
Survivors, Psychology of: Survivors of Ghettos and Camps

ISRAEL ELDAR
Hebrew University of Jerusalem
Blum, Léon

ELIZABETH E. EPPLER
Jerusalem
Einstein, Albert
Goldmann, Nahum

SHAUL ESH
Hebrew University of Jerusalem; Yad Vashem (deceased)
Entjudung

ROBERT A. EVERETT
Fairleigh Dickinson University
Parkes, James William

ANDREW EZERGAILIS
Ithaca College
Latvia: General Survey
Latvia: The Fate of Latvian Jewry

SIDRA DEKOVEN EZRAHI
Hebrew University of Jerusalem
Literature on the Holocaust: United States

JEAN-CLAUDE FAVEZ
University of Geneva
Red Cross, International

HENRY L. FEINGOLD
City University of New York
American Jewry and the Holocaust
Bermuda Conference
McDonald, James Grover
Morgenthau, Henry, Jr.
Roosevelt, Franklin Delano
United States of America
Wise, Stephen Samuel

GILA FLAM
United States Holocaust Memorial Museum, Washington, D.C.
Music, The Holocaust in

EVA FOGELMAN
Jewish Foundation for Christian Rescuers/ADL, New York
Survivors, Second Generation of

JOHN P. FOX
Leicester University
Education on the Holocaust: Great Britain

JÖRG FRIEDRICH
West Berlin
Trials of War Criminals: Dispensation of Justice in Germany
Trials of War Criminals: Subsequent Nuremberg Proceedings

MARIAN FUCHS
Żydowski Instytut Historyczny, Warsaw
Music, The Holocaust in

YOAV GELBER
Haifa University; Yad Vashem, Jerusalem
Haavara Agreement
Jewish Brigade Group
Parachutists, Jewish
Prisoners of War: Jewish Prisoners of War

HAIM GENIZI
Bar-Ilan University
American Committee for Christian German Refugees
American Friends Service Committee
Bergson Group
Nonsectarian Refugee Organizations in the United States
United States Army and Survivors in Germany and Austria

SHARON GILLERMAN
Los Angeles
Education on the Holocaust: United States and Israel

SEEV GOSHEN
Haifa University
Kahn, Franz
Lidice
Rathenau, Walther

HELGE GRABITZ
Hamburg, West Germany
Law and Judiciary in Nazi Germany

GIDEON GREIF
Yad Vashem, Jerusalem
Fleischmann, Gisi
Reik, Haviva

WILLY GROAG
Kibbutz Givat Hayyim
Youth Movements: Bohemia and Moravia

LEO GROSS
Tufts University (emeritus)
Superior Orders

ISRAEL GUTMAN
Hebrew University of Jerusalem; Yad Vashem, Jerusalem
Anielewicz, Mordecai
Anschluss
Antisemitism
Arierparagraph
Axis
Badge, Jewish
Barasz, Efraim
Berman, Adolf Abraham
Blum, Abraham
Christian Churches: After the Holocaust
Czerniaków, Adam
Diaries, Holocaust
Dolchstosslegende
Dubnow, Simon
Edelman, Marek
Feiner, Leon
Gepner, Abraham
Ghetto
Gitterman, Yitzhak
Glazer, Gesja
Greiser, Arthur
Grosman, Haika
Hausner, Gideon
Holocaust, Denial of the
Kaplan, Chaim Aaron
Kaplan, Josef
Kapo
Kolbe, Maximilian
Korczak, Janusz
Kovner, Abba
Levi, Primo
Lubetkin, Zivia
Muselmann
Nossig, Alfred
Oneg Shabbat
Partisans
Poland: The Jews in Poland
Rasse- und Siedlungshauptamt
Ringelblum, Emanuel
Robota, Roza
Schiper, Ignacy
Stroop, Jürgen
Szlengel, Władysław
Third Reich
Umschlagplatz
Warsaw: Jews during the Holocaust
Warsaw Ghetto Uprising
Wdowinski, David
Wilner, Arie
Wittenberg, Yitzhak
Youth Movements: General Survey
Zagan, Shakhne
Zimetbaum, Mala
Zuckerman, Yitzhak
Żydowska Organizacja Bojowa
Żydowski Związek Wojskowy
Zygelbojm, Samuel Artur
Zyklon B

AMY HACKETT
New York
Physicians, Nazi

DAVID HADAR
Hebrew University of Jerusalem (emeritus)
Bernheim Petition
Glücks, Richard
Gustloff, Wilhelm
Hess, Rudolf
Hindenburg, Paul von Beneckendorff und von

LEAH HADOMI
Haifa University
Literature on the Holocaust: Germany

ESTHER HAGAR
Yad Vashem, Jerusalem
Dvinsk
Kaiserwald
Liepāja
Riga

EDDIE HALPERN
Israel Broadcasting Authority, Jerusalem
Music, The Holocaust in

JOSEPH HELLER
Hebrew University of Jerusalem
Jabotinsky, Vladimir
Loḥamei Ḥerut Israel

ESRIEL HILDESHEIMER
Jerusalem
Eppstein, Paul
Germany
Reichsvertretung der Deutschen Juden

MOSHE HOCH
Institute for Conservation and Research of Jewish Music of the Holocaust, Givatayim, Israel
Music, The Holocaust in

COLIN HOLMES
University of Sheffield
Great Britain: Fascism in Great Britain
Mosley, Sir Oswald

ARIEL HURWITZ
Kibbutz Galon
Fort Ontario
Intergovernmental Committee on Refugees
Jewish Labor Committee
United States Department of State
World Jewish Congress

EBERHARD JÄCKEL
Stuttgart University
Hitler, Adolf
Mein Kampf

YESHAYAHU JELINEK
Ben-Gurion University of the Negev
Bratislava
Europa Plan
Hlinka, Andrej
Hlinka Guard
Slovakia
Slovak National Uprising
Tiso, Jozef
Transcarpathian Ukraine
Ústredňa Židov

KAROL JOŃCA
University of Wrocław
Nacht und Nebel

PRISCILLA DALE JONES
Wolfson College, Cambridge University
Trials of War Criminals: General Survey
Trials of War Criminals: Subsequent British Trials

FELICJA KARAY
Tel-Aviv University
HASAG
Skarżysko-Kamienna

STEVEN T. KATZ
Cornell University
Jewish Philosophical and Theological Responses to the Holocaust

MENAHEM KAUFMAN
Hebrew University of Jerusalem
American Zionist Emergency Council
B'nai B'rith
Proskauer, Joseph Meyer

YITZCHAK KEREM
Yad Vashem, Jerusalem
Athens
Greece

NILI KEREN
Seminar ha-Kibbutzim, Tel Aviv
Korczak-Marla, Rozka

HILLEL KLEIN
Hebrew University of Jerusalem (deceased)
Survivors, Psychology of: General Survey

SHLOMO KLESS
Hebrew University of Jerusalem
Weissmandel, Michael Dov

BRONIA KLIBANSKI
Yad Vashem, Jerusalem
Plotnicka, Frumka
Relief Committee for the War-stricken Jewish Population
Tenenbaum, Mordechai

JOKE KNIESMEYER
Anne Frank Foundation, Amsterdam
Frank, Anne

LIONEL KOCHAN
University of Warwick (emeritus)
Abetz, Otto
Best, Werner
Blomberg, Werner von
Brack, Viktor
Canaris, Wilhelm
Clauberg, Carl
Dannecker, Theodor
Dibelius, Otto
Frank, Karl Hermann
Frank, Walter
Gerstein, Kurt
Globke, Hans
Globocnik, Odilo
Hassell, Ulrich von
Himmler, Heinrich
Krupp von Bohlen und Halbach, Gustav
Lenard, Philipp
Lohse, Hinrich
Ludendorff, Erich
Niemöller, Martin
Pohl, Oswald
Rauschning, Hermann
Röhm, Ernst
Rosenberg, Alfred
Rudel, Hans-Ulrich
Sauckel, Fritz
Schellenberg, Walter
Stahl, Heinrich
Stuckart, Wilhelm
Stülpnagel, Karl Heinrich von
Thierack, Otto
Veesenmayer, Edmund
Wirth, Christian

ARIEH JOSEPH KOCHAVI
Haifa University
United Nations Relief and Rehabilitation Administration

ALFRED KONIECZNY
University of Wrocław
Gross-Rosen
Organisation Schmelt

RYSZARD KOTARBA
Main Commission for Investigation of Nazi Crimes in Poland, Kraków
Płaszów

SHMUEL KRAKOWSKI
Yad Vashem, Jerusalem
Althammer
Auschwitz
Bełchatów
Bergen-Belsen
Biebow, Hans
Blechhammer
Bor-Komorowski, Tadeusz
Bothmann, Hans
Chełmno
Death Marches
Deutsche Ausrüstungswerke
Dora-Mittelbau
Eicke, Theodor
Fischer, Ludwig
Katyn
Koppe, Wilhelm
Kraków
Kramer, Josef
Krüger, Friedrich Wilhelm
Łódź
Lublin
Lublin-Lipowa
Mengele, Josef
Mikołajczyk, Stanisław
Narodowe Siły Zbrojne
Polnische Polizei
Poniatowa
Prisoners of War: Jewish Prisoners of War
Radom
Resistance, Jewish
Rowecki, Stefan
Rumkowski, Mordechai Chaim
Rzeszów
Stalingrad
Volksdeutsche
Werwolf

DAVID KRANZLER
Queensborough Community College, New York
Japan
Schonfeld, Solomon
Shanghai

BOGDAN KROLL
Archive for Recent Documents, Warsaw
Rada Główna Opiekuńcza

LESZEK KUBICKI
Institute of State and Law, Warsaw
Trials of War Criminals: Poland

OTTO DOV KULKA
Hebrew University of Jerusalem
Germany
Reichsvertretung der Deutschen Juden
Theresienstadt

ZBIGNIEW LANDAU
Warsaw
Forced Labor: Jews in Occupied Poland
Ghettos, Nutrition in

HAGIT LAVSKY
Hebrew University of Jerusalem
Displaced Persons, Jewish

LUCIEN LAZARE
Yad Vashem, Jerusalem
Alsace-Lorraine
Armée Juive
Cohn, Marianne
Darlan, François
Fédération des Sociétés Juives de France
French Police
Gamzon, Robert
Gaulle, Charles de
Glasberg, Alexandre
Lévitte, Simon
Lublin, Lucien
Oradour-sur-Glane
Polonski, Abraham
Rayman, Marcel
Veil, Simone
Weill, Joseph
Youth Movements: France

SINAI LEICHTER
Hebrew University of Jerusalem
Częstochowa
Kielce
Piotrków Trybunalski

DOV LEVIN
Hebrew University of Jerusalem
Adamowicz, Irena
Brizgys, Vincentas
Elkes, Elchanan
Estonia
Irgun Berit Zion
Kėdainiai
Kovno
Lietuviu Aktyvistu Frontas
Lithuania
Memel
Ninth Fort
Partisans
Policiniai Batalionai
Robinson, Jacob
Rumbula
Tallinn
Vaivara
Voldemaras, Augustinas
Yelin, Haim
Ziman, Henrik

YOSSEF LEWINGER
Tel-Aviv University (emeritus)
Bačka

HAYA LIFSHITZ
Yad Vashem, Jerusalem
Black Book of Soviet Jewry, The
Kutorgiene-Buivydaité, Elena
Šiauliai

ROBERT JAY LIFTON
City University of New York
Physicians, Nazi

GEORG LILIENTHAL
University of Mainz
Anthropology and National Socialism

DEBORAH E. LIPSTADT
Los Angeles
American Press and the Holocaust

FRANKLIN H. LITTELL
Temple University
Christian Churches: After the Holocaust
Niebuhr, Reinhold

YAACOV LOZOWICK
Yad Vashem, Jerusalem
Jäger, Karl

CZESŁAW LUCZAK
University of Poznań
Forced Labor: Fremdarbeiter
Haupttreuhandstelle
Umwandererzentralstelle
Warthegau

CZESŁAW MADAJCZYK
Polish Academy of Sciences, Warsaw
Generalgouvernement
Generalplan Ost
Museums and Memorial Institutes: Poland
Poland: General Survey

YITZCHAK MAIS
Yad Vashem, Jerusalem
HICEM

ZYGMUNT MANKOWSKI
University of Lublin
Majdanek
Sporrenberg, Jacob
Zamość

MICHAEL R. MARRUS
University of Toronto
Commissariat Général aux Questions Juives
Darquier de Pellepoix, Louis
France: The Jews and the Holocaust
Grynszpan, Herschel
Laval, Pierre
Pétain, Philippe
Refugees, 1933–1945
Statut des Juifs
Vallat, Xavier

FREDKA MAZYA
Kibbutz Haogen
Silesia, Eastern Upper

JACOB METZER
Hebrew University of Jerusalem
Menczer, Aron

MEIR MICHAELIS
Hebrew University of Jerusalem
Badoglio, Pietro
Ferramonti di Tarsia
Italy
Mussolini, Benito
Rome

ALAIN MICHEL
Centre Yair, Jerusalem
Eclaireurs Israélites de France
Les Milles
Oeuvre de Secours aux Enfants

DAN MICHMAN
Bar-Ilan University
Antwerp
Association des Juifs en Belgique
Belgium
Breendonck
Brussels
Mechelen

JOZEPH MICHMAN
Hebrew University of Jerusalem (emeritus)
Asscher, Abraham
Cohen, David
Hague, The
Joodse Raad
Mussert, Anton Adriaan
Nationaal Socialistische Beweging
Netherlands, The
Rotterdam
Seyss-Inquart, Arthur
Trials of War Criminals: The Netherlands
Visser, Lodewijk Ernst
Vught
Westerbork
Westerweel, Joop

SERGIO I. MINERBI
Hebrew University of Jerusalem
Kappler, Herbert
Pius XII

GEORGE L. MOSSE
University of Wisconsin, Madison
Racism

MARIAN MUSHKAT
Tel-Aviv University
Crimes against Humanity
Documentation Centers: Berlin Documents Center
Extradition of War Criminals
Genocide
Law Punishing Nazis and Nazi Collaborators
Lemkin, Raphael
Trials of War Criminals: Bergen-Belsen Trial
Trials of War Criminals: Norway
Trials of War Criminals: Nuremberg Trial
Trials of War Criminals: Zyklon B Trial
United Nations War Crimes Commission

TIKVA S. NATHAN
Haifa University
Survivors, Psychology of: Children of Survivors

SHLOMO NETZER
Tel-Aviv University
Będzin
Sosnowiec

FRANCIS R. NICOSIA
Saint Michael's College, Winooski, Vermont
Zionist Movement in Germany, 1933–1939

AKIVA NIR
Kibbutz Shomrat
Banská Bystrica
Nováky
Sered
Sixth Slovak Brigade
Slovak National Uprising
Youth Movements: Slovakia

DALIA OFER
Hebrew University of Jerusalem
Aliya Bet
Rescue Committee of the Jewish Agency in Turkey
Struma

Efraim Ofir
Kibbutz Shuval
Youth Movements: Romania

Wila Orbach
Yad Vashem, Jerusalem
Mińsk Mazowiecki

Harry Paape
Netherlands State Institute for War Documentation, Amsterdam
Documentation Centers: Rijksinstituut voor Oorlogsdocumentatie

Mordecai Paldiel
Yad Vashem, Jerusalem
Abegg, Elisabeth
André, Joseph
Baublys, Petras
Beccari, Arrigo
Benoît, Marie
Binkiene, Sofija
Bogaard, Johannes
Borkowska, Anna
Choms, Władysława
Deffaugt, Jean
Douwes, Arnold
Evert, Anghelos
Getter, Matylda
Grüninger, Paul
Hautval, Adelaide
Helmrich, Eberhard
Kowalski, Władysław
Le Chambon-sur-Lignon
Lipke, Janis
Lutz, Carl
N.V. Group
Nèvejean, Yvonne
Nicolini, Giuseppe
Overduijn, Leendert
Schindler, Oskar
Schmid, Anton
Sendler, Irena
Šimaite, Ona
Skobtsova, Elizaveta
Sousa Mendes, Aristides de
Sugihara, Sempo
Sztehlo, Gábor
Van der Voort, Hanna
Zabinski, Jan

Stanley G. Payne
University of Wisconsin, Madison
Spain: Spanish Fascism and the Jews

Yael Peled (Margolin)
Jerusalem
Draenger, Shimshon
Draenger, Tova
He-Haluts ha-Lohem
Liebeskind, Aharon
Montelupich Prison

Eli Pfefferkorn
Silver Spring, Maryland
Wiesel, Elie

Falk Pingel
Georg-Eckert-Institut Braunschweig; University of Bielefeld
Columbia Haus
Concentration Camps
I.G. Farben
Jehovah's Witnesses
Kogon, Eugen
Natzweiler-Struthof
Neuengamme
Oranienburg
Ostindustrie GmbH
Sachsenhausen
Wirtschafts-Verwaltungshauptamt

Cristian Popisteanu
Bucharest
Romania: General Survey

Dina Porat
Tel-Aviv University
Ben-Gurion, David
Gruenbaum, Itzhak
Joint Rescue Committee
Sereni, Enzo
Szenes, Hannah
"Tehran Children"
Yishuv

Teresa Prekerowa
Warsaw
Aid to Jews by Poles
Białystok
Grobelny, Julian
Hotel Polski
Kossak-Szczucka, Zofia
Wolinski, Henryk
Zegota

Tsvi Raanan
Kibbutz ha-Zorea
Bormann, Martin

Joseph Rab
Moreshet Institute, Givat Haviva
Łódź Ghetto, Chronicles of the

György Ranki
Hungarian Academy of Sciences, Budapest (deceased)
Hungary: General Survey

Hannu Rautkallio
Tampere University
Finland

Shimon Redlich
Ben-Gurion University of the Negev
Ehrenburg, Ilya Grigoryevich
Eynikeyt
Jewish Antifascist Committee

Jehuda Reinharz
Brandeis University
Weizmann, Chaim

Shalom Robinson
Talbiyeh Psychiatric Mental Health Center, Hadassah Medical School, Hebrew University of Jerusalem
Survivors, Psychology of: Survivors in Israel

Jacqueline Rokhsar
Yad Vashem, Jerusalem
Barbie Trial
Joyce, William
Norway: General Survey
Quisling, Vidkun
Stürmer, Der

AVIHU RONEN
Tel-Aviv University
Merin, Moshe
Silesia, Eastern Upper

HERBERT ROSENKRANZ
Yad Vashem, Jerusalem
Austria
Löwenherz, Josef
Vienna

LIVIA ROTHKIRCHEN
Yad Vashem, Jerusalem
Beneš, Edvard
Bohemia and Moravia, Protectorate of
Czechoslovak Government-in-Exile
Prague
Tuka, Vojtech
Wisliceny, Dieter

ROBERT ROZETT
Yad Vashem, Jerusalem
Auschwitz Protocols
Budapest
Debrecen
Horthy Offer
Kistarcsa
Komoly, Ottó
Košice
Lutz, Carl
Mach, Alexander
Miskolc
Oradea
Pracovná Skupina
Protocols of the Elders of Zion
Przemyśl
Railways, German
Resistance, Jewish
Slovakia
Slovak National Uprising
Szeged
Timişoara
Trials of War Criminals: Hungary
Uzhgorod
Vyhne

ADALBERT RÜCKERL
Ludwigsburg, West Germany (deceased)
Denazification
Kriminalpolizei
Ludwigsburger Zentralstelle
Ordnungspolizei
Trials of War Criminals: West Germany

ADAM RUTKOWSKI
Centre de Documentation Juive Contemporaine, Paris (deceased)
Documentation Centers: Centre de Documentation Juive Contemporaine
Drancy
Gurs
Institut d'Etude des Questions Juives
Vittel

SUZANNE D. RUTLAND
Sydney College of Advanced Education, Australia
Australia, Jewish Refugees in

NANA SAGI
Hebrew University of Jerusalem
Board of Deputies of British Jews
Brodetsky, Selig
Great Britain: Jewish Refugees
Reparations and Restitution

MICHELE SARFATTI
Centro di Documentazione Ebraica Contemporanea, Milan
Documentation Centers: Centro di Documentazione Ebraica Contemporanea

CHAIM SCHATZKER
Haifa University
Education on the Holocaust: West Germany
Youth Aliya
Youth Movements: Germany and Austria

PESACH SCHINDLER
Hebrew University of Jerusalem
Kiddush ha-Hayyim
Kiddush ha-Shem

KARL A. SCHLEUNES
University of North Carolina
Hitler, Adolf

GITTA SERENY
London
Stangl, Franz

MILTON SHAIN
University of Cape Town
Greyshirts
South Africa

ELISHEVA SHAUL
Yad Vashem, Jerusalem
Bartoszewski, Władysław
Bernadotte, Folke
Dvoretski, Alter
Grojanowski Report
Homosexuality in the Third Reich
Karski, Jan
Schwarzbart, Ignacy Isaac

MENACHEM SHELAH
Haifa University; Yad Vashem, Jerusalem
Belgrade
Chetniks
Croatia
Jasenovac
Macedonia
Pavelić, Ante
Rab
Sarajevo
Serbia
Tito
Ustaša
Yugoslavia

DAVID H. SHPIRO
Tel-Aviv University
Eisenhower, Dwight David
Joint Boycott Council

DAVID SILBERKLANG
Yad Vashem, Jerusalem
American Jewish Committee
American Jewish Conference
Boycotts, Anti-Nazi
Council for German Jewry
Hirschmann, Ira A.
Hull, Cordell
St. Louis

Shmuel Spector
Yad Vashem, Jerusalem
Abugov, Aleksandr
Aktion 1005
Babi Yar
Bach-Zelewski, Erich von dem
Bandera, Stefan
Berdichev
Blobel, Paul
Brest-Litovsk
Brunner, Alois
Budzyń
Demjanjuk Trial
Dirlewanger, Oskar
Dnepropetrovsk
Einsatzgruppen
Fegelein, Hermann
Fomenko, Witold
Frankfurter, David
Gas Vans
Gildenman, Moshe
Gräbe, Hermann Friedrich
Hahn, Ludwig
Hilfswillige
Karaites
Kharkov
Kherson
Knochen, Helmut
Koch, Erich
Koch, Karl Otto
Kovel
Kovpak, Sidor Artemevich
Krasnodar
Kremenchug
Krimchaks
Kube, Wilhelm
Liebehenschel, Arthur
Lutsk
Melnyk, Andrei
Mogilev
Nazi-Soviet Pact
Novak, Franz
Oberg, Carl Albrecht
Ohlendorf, Otto
Opole Lubelskie
Orhanizatsyia Ukrainskykh Natsionalistiv
Ostbataillone
Partisans
Pinsk
Poltava
Prützmann, Hans-Adolf
Pruzhany
Rasch, Emil Otto
Ravensbrück
Red Orchestra
Reichskommissariat Ukraine
Rostov-on-Don
Rovno
Russkaya Osvoboditelnaya Armiya
Simferopol
Smolensk
Sonderkommando
Stahlecker, Franz Walter
Starachowice
Trawniki
Trials of War Criminals: Krasnodar Trial
Tuchin
Ukraine
Ukrainische Hilfspolizei
Ukrainska Povstanska Armyia
Vinnitsa
Vitebsk
Vlasov, Andrei
Wolff, Karl
Yad Vashem
Zhitomir

Eliyahu Stern
Bet Loḥamei ha-Getta'ot
Danzig

Zeev Sternhell
Hebrew University of Jerusalem
Action Française
Fascism

Christian Streit
Mannheim, West Germany
Prisoners of War: Soviet Prisoners of War

Yehiel Szeintuch
Hebrew University of Jerusalem
Gebirtig, Mordecai
Glik, Hirsh
Kaczerginski, Shmaryahu
Katzenelson, Itzhak
Literature on the Holocaust: Yiddish Literature
Spiegel, Isaiah
Sutzkever, Abraham
Zeitlin, Hillel

Uriel Tal
Hebrew University of Jerusalem (deceased)
Holocaust

Jerzy Tomaszewski
University of Warsaw
Zbąszyń

Harold Troper
University of Toronto
Canada

Yehuda Tubin
Moreshet Institute, Givat Haviva
Museums and Memorial Institutes: Moreshet

Judith Tydor-Baumel
Bar-Ilan University
Great Britain: Jewish Refugees
Rescue of Children, United States

Michal Unger
Hebrew University of Jerusalem
Edelstein, Jacob

Joseph Walk
Yad Vashem; Leo Baeck Institute, Jerusalem
Baeck, Leo
Breslau
Documentation Centers: Leo Baeck Institute
Warhaftig, Zorah

Jehuda L. Wallach
Tel-Aviv University
Blitzkrieg
Jodl, Alfred
Keitel, Wilhelm
Manstein, Erich von
Reichenau, Walter von
Waldheim, Kurt

Charlotte Wardi
Haifa University
Literature on the Holocaust: France

DIRECTORY OF CONTRIBUTORS

HENRY WASSERMAN
Yad Vashem, Jerusalem
Munich
Nuremberg

ABRAHAM WEIN,
Yad Vashem, Jerusalem
Documentation Centers:
Żydowski Instytut Historyczny
Yizkor Book

DAVID WEINBERG
Bowling Green State University, Ohio
France: After the Holocaust

AHARON WEISS
Yad Vashem, Jerusalem; Haifa University
Berezhany
Biberstein, Marek
Brody
Chortkov
Drogobych
Gorodenka
Janówska
Judenrat
Jüdischer Ordnungsdienst
Katzmann, Fritz
Kolomyia
Lublin
Lvov
Nachtigall Battalion
Petliura Days
Rogatin
Sheptytsky, Andrei
Stanisławów
Stry
Tarnów
Ternopol
Zolochev

HANS-HEINRICH WILHELM
West Berlin
Abwehr
Ahnenerbe
Auslandsorganisation der NSDAP
Euthanasia Program
Kaltenbrunner, Ernst
Korherr, Richard
Müller, Heinrich
Nebe, Arthur
Oberg, Carl Albrecht
Organisation Todt
Papen, Franz von
Parteitage
Streicher, Julius
Wehrmacht

DAVID S. WYMAN
University of Massachusetts, Amherst
Auschwitz, Bombing of
Evian Conference
President's Advisory Committee on Political Refugees
War Refugee Board

LENI YAHIL
Haifa University (emeritus)
Denmark
Duckwitz, Georg Ferdinand
Eichmann, Adolf
Einsatzstab Rosenberg
Kristallnacht
Mauritius
Sprachregelung
Sweden
Switzerland
Wallenberg, Raoul

HANNAH YAOZ
Tel Aviv
Literature on the Holocaust: Hebrew Literature

JAMES E. YOUNG
University of Massachusetts, Amherst
Museums and Memorial Institutes: General Survey

RUTH ZARIZ
Bet Loḥamei ha-Getta'ot
Exchange: Jews and Germans
Luxembourg

IDITH ZERTAL
Tel-Aviv University
Exodus 1947

EFRAIM ZUROFF
Simon Wiesenthal Center for Holocaust Studies, Jerusalem
Kalmanowitz, Abraham
Office of Special Investigations
Rescue of Polish Jews via East Asia
Sternbuch, Recha
Va'ad ha-Hatsala
Wiesenthal, Simon

RONALD W. ZWEIG
Tel-Aviv University
Churchill, Winston Leonard Spencer
Eden, Sir Anthony
Great Britain: General Survey
Great Britain: Jewish Refugees

AB-AKTION (Ausserordentliche Befriedungsaktion; Extraordinary Pacification Operation), extermination campaign directed against Poles. The immediate objective of the AB-Aktion was to suppress Polish resistance and put fear into the hearts of the Polish population by liquidating persons who were capable of inciting or organizing Polish resistance to the Germans. In that respect, the AB-Aktion was a continuation of previous terror operations, such as the political purge carried out in 1939.

The Reich security organizations did not possess precise information on the growing resistance movement, but the possibility of an uprising was taken into account, and the Wehrmacht had in fact warned of it. The GENERALGOUVERNEMENT chief, Hans FRANK, was in favor of forestalling the threat by destroying the Polish leaders.

In February and March 1940, the Reichsverteidigungsrat (Reich Defense Council; the military planning committee) discussed the subject and drew up plans, based on past experience gained by the Reich. A decision was made to exterminate, at one blow, potential leaders of a resistance movement —identified as the activists among the Polish intelligentsia—and thereby also to intimidate the population. On May 16, 1940, a few days after the Germans had launched their offensive in western Europe, Frank gave the order for the AB-Aktion to begin. Approximately thirty-five hundred persons whom the Germans regarded as belonging to the leadership class, as well as three thousand suspected of criminal activities, were arrested in the Generalgouvernement and massacred (one of the sites of the massacres was the Palmiry Forest). The plan had been to bring the operation to an end by the middle of 1940, but it continued until the fall, most probably because of the success of the German offensive in the west.

The operation failed to achieve its objective of destroying the resistance movement. For a while, the resistance organizations (for example, the Związek Walki Zbrojnej, or Union for Armed Struggle) had their membership reduced by a third, but the movement recovered and accelerated its operations. The danger that the Polish population would become disillusioned with resistance following the defeat of France, which had been a real threat, did not materialize.

The AB-Aktion, and the crimes committed in the course of that operation, were among the charges raised at the NUREMBERG TRIAL and at the series of war crimes trials held by the Supreme People's Court in Poland.

BIBLIOGRAPHY

Broszat, M. *Nationalsozialistischer Polenpolitik, 1939–1945.* Stuttgart, 1964.

STEFAN BIERNACKI

ABEGG, ELISABETH (1882–d. after 1957), German Quaker who saved Jews in Berlin during World War II. Raised in Strasbourg (Alsace) when it was part of Imperial Germany, Abegg became involved in activities

Elisabeth Abegg.

for the Quakers when she moved to Berlin. A history teacher at the Luisen girls' school, she was dismissed in 1933 by the Nazi school director for her pronounced anti-Nazi views.

In 1942, at the age of sixty and while looking after her bedridden mother and sick elder sister, Abegg began using her home in the Tempelhof district as a temporary shelter and assembly point for many Jews. She created a rescue network made up of friends from the Quaker movement, pastors, and former students, and over a period of almost three years helped dozens of Jews escape deprivation and deportation. Her activities included sheltering Jews either in her own home (in a building that also housed several Nazi party members) or in temporarily empty adjoining apartments in her care. Abegg found safe and permanent refuges both in Berlin and in more distant locations such as Alsace and East Prussia; she sent provisions to enable those who escaped to survive and provided them with false identities. She helped still others to escape across the Swiss border, selling her jewelry and other valuables in order to finance this work. She also tutored Jewish children at her home to compensate for their not being able to attend school. Bringing false identification papers, money, and provisions, she visited her charges in various locations.

In a booklet dedicated to her on her seventy-fifth birthday in 1957, entitled "And a Light Shone in the Darkness," her former charges offered profuse praise of Elisabeth Abegg's dedication, care, and humanity.

BIBLIOGRAPHY

Leuner, H. D. *When Compassion Was a Crime.* London, 1966.

MORDECAI PALDIEL

ABETZ, OTTO (1903–1958), German ambassador to Vichy France during World War II. Abetz studied art and later taught drawing at a girls' school. His support for the Nazi party dates from 1931. In 1934, in addition to his teaching duties, he began to organize meetings of French and German ex-servicemen. In 1935, as a French expert, he entered the For-

Otto Abetz, Hitler's ambassador to Vichy France. [National Archives]

eign Office under Joachim von RIBBENTROP. He spent much time in France, but was expelled in 1939 in connection with the measures being taken against the Cagoulards, a secret fascist organization.

Abetz returned to France in 1940 and in August of that year was appointed ambassador to the Vichy government. He held this post for the next four years, advising the German military and police administration in Paris and dealing with all political questions in occupied and unoccupied France. In his efforts to secure complete French cooperation with Nazi objectives, Abetz enjoyed the support of Pierre LAVAL. As a party activist (he was appointed an SS-*Brigadeführer* in 1941), Abetz took a leading role in supporting the deportation of foreign Jews and then of French-born Jews, especially after the German occupation of southern France in November 1942. He was arrested after the liberation and in 1949 was sentenced by a military tribunal in Paris to twenty years' hard labor for war crimes, including the deportation of Jews and of French workers. He was found not guilty of complicity in the murder of Georges Mandel, the Jewish former minister of the interior.

Abetz served five years of his sentence. Released in 1954, he died four years later in a motor accident in the Rhineland.

BIBLIOGRAPHY

Browning, C. R. *The Final Solution and the German Foreign Office: A Study of Referat D3 of Abteilung Deutschland, 1940–1943.* New York, 1978.

Marrus, M. R., and R. O. Paxton. *Vichy France and the Jews.* New York, 1981.

Paxton, R. O. *Vichy France: Old Guard and New Order, 1940–1944.* New York, 1972.

LIONEL KOCHAN

ABUGOV, ALEKSANDR (b. 1913), Russian Jewish partisan commander. A native of Odessa, Abugov grew up in Kirovograd and became a locksmith. After his army service he studied at the Kharkov sports academy and worked as a fencing instructor.

When the Germans invaded the Soviet Union, on June 22, 1941, Abugov was called up and posted to the Ukrainian front, where he served as a second lieutenant in an armored-train unit. The unit was besieged and Abugov was taken prisoner of war. Seeing that the Germans were murdering the Jews among the prisoners, Abugov posed as an ethnic Russian. He passed through several prisoner-of-war camps—Uman, Vinnitsa, Shepetovka, Brest-Litovsk, and Kobrin—and finally reached the camp in KOVEL, from which he made his escape. He joined a partisan unit in the village of Dolsk, in Polesye. By September 1942, the group had grown in size and Abugov commanded its reconnaissance squad.

At the end of 1942 the unit moved east, where Abugov encountered Jews fleeing from the Serniki and Dubrovitsa ghettos. He was deeply moved by the difficult situation of the Jews and decided, with several friends, to leave his unit and together with Jewish youths to set up his own partisan unit. At the request of Gen. Vasily Begma, commanding officer of the two Rovno divisions, Abugov joined the Rovno division and was appointed commander of the reconnaissance battalion, a 400-man cavalry unit, with which he took part in the liberation of ROVNO in February 1944. On his discharge he became the district sports officer. He married one of the young women who had served with him and, together with other members of his family, moved to Poland. In 1949 he emigrated to Israel.

BIBLIOGRAPHY

Spector, S. *The Holocaust of Volhynian Jews, 1941–1944.* Jerusalem, 1986. (In Hebrew.)

SHMUEL SPECTOR

ABWEHR (full name, Amt Ausland/Abwehr im Oberkommando der WEHRMACHT; Foreign Bureau/Defense of the Armed Forces High Command), the German Reich's most important intelligence service in World War II. Established in 1938, the Abwehr was preceded by two intelligence branches, the Reichswehr Abwehr Abteilung (Army Intelligence Section) and the Abwehr Abteilung of the War Ministry. Until 1944 the Abwehr was headed by Adm. Wilhelm CANARIS. The navy and the air force each had an intelligence service as well. The civilian sector was the concern of the Foreign Ministry intelligence service; two intelligence services maintained by the SD (Sicherheitsdienst; Security Service), one headed by Walter SCHELLENBERG, dealing with foreign affairs, and the other, headed by Otto OHLENDORF, for internal affairs; and an intelligence service for economic affairs. The war zones had their own intelligence services: Fremde Heere–Ost (Foreign Armies–East; as of April 1, 1942, run by Reinhard Gehlen) and Fremde Heere–West, both of which were part of the Oberkommando des Heeres (Army High Command). On the lower command levels, the intelligence branches were frequently served by one and the same intelligence officer.

The effectiveness of the German military intelligence services in World War II is a highly controversial subject that has been embellished by many legends. The most successful spy operating on his own (his code name was "Max") has been identified by historian Herbert Rittlinger as "the Jew Klatt," a financier by profession, whom the Abwehr had inherited from the Austrian intelligence. "Max" is alleged to have had first-class connections in Moscow and the Balkan countries and to have been one of the most mysterious figures in modern espionage. Canaris's achievements as a military attaché in Madrid, Bucharest, Sofia, Ankara, Budapest, and other places cannot as yet be properly evaluated, since the relevant documents (assuming that they still exist) have not become accessible. It is known that until June 22, 1941, the day of the German attack on the Soviet Union, the German military intelligence's opinion of the Soviet military potential was so low that it bordered on the grotesque—an opinion, incidentally, that they shared with British and American intelligence. German radio intelligence was quite reliable, and its achievements were comparable to corresponding intelligence branches in other countries. During the course of the war, signals intelligence became the most important element of intelligence gathering.

The Abwehr made headlines mostly by virtue of the scandals and affairs in which it was involved, among them foreign-currency violations, corruption, diversion of funds to obscure purposes, passport violations, smuggling, and misuse of foreign army uniforms. There were instances when it failed to grasp enemy intentions in time; when its agents defected to the enemy at an opportune time; when it failed to detect double agents; and when treacherous disinformation agents talked too much and divulged true instead of misleading information. All these mishaps took place in the Abwehr and were regarded in professional German intelligence circles as hazards that were always present in intelligence work; the latter claimed that only to outsiders did they appear as unpardonable bungling.

More difficult to judge are the politically motivated "mistakes," "offenses," and failures to act. For example, did Canaris deliberately act against the interests of his employers when he recruited and surrounded himself with potential adversaries of the regime? These included members of the Freikorps, SA (Sturmabteilung; Storm Troopers) mercenaries, and National Bolsheviks serving in the special "Brandenburg" Regiment; Oberstleutnant Hans Groscurth, the pastor's son whom Canaris made head of the sabotage and subversion section; Generalmajor Hans Oster, an anti-Nazi whom Canaris appointed head of the central division and chief of staff of the foreign section; members of the anti-regime Bekennende Kirche (Confessing Church) whom Canaris used as couriers; Catholic priests, whom he trusted with secrets; and Ukrainian nationalists and Russian monarchists, whom he recruited to serve as a fifth column during the German attack on the Soviet Union. Was Oster betraying his country when he used various channels to transmit to the West in 1940 the presumed date of that attack, in such a way that nobody in the capitals concerned paid any heed to his warnings? Is it true that Canaris and Generalmajor Erwin Lahousen (Groscurth's successor) vigorously protested the slaughter of the Jews when, in the fall of 1941, they received the first detailed eyewitness account of the slaughter? By then, the fact that Jews were being murdered was undoubtedly known to both of them.

There is documentary evidence that the Geheime Feldpolizei (Secret Field Police), which was under the Abwehr's control, took active part in the murder of Jews in the Soviet Union. It has also been conclusively proved that Canaris forwarded to Joseph GOEBBELS a proposal made by the chief of the Abwehr's counterintelligence section, Generalmajor Franz Eccard von Bentivegni, to force all the Jews in Berlin to wear a sign identifying them as security risks, and to concentrate them in the eastern section of the capital.

The core of the resistance center that did exist in the Abwehr was smashed long before the July 20, 1944, abortive coup against Hitler. Hans von Dohnányi, Dietrich BONHOEFFER, Josef Müller (an eminent Munich lawyer and devout Catholic, who had been attached by Oster to the Abwehr and who had good connections with the Vatican), and Oster were under arrest on twenty-four-hour surveillance from April 1943; and Canaris was under house arrest from February 1944. The Abwehr was disbanded and incorporated into the REICHSSICHERHEITSHAUPTAMT (Reich Security Main Office; RSHA) as the Military Bureau, and Groscurth was taken prisoner by the Soviets on the Stalingrad front. Nevertheless, in April 1945, Canaris, Oster, Bonhoeffer, and Dohnányi, who at the time were imprisoned in the FLOSSENBÜRG concentration camp, were summarily tried, sentenced to death, and hanged by the Germans.

BIBLIOGRAPHY

Brissard, A. *The Nazi Secret Service.* New York, 1974.

Buchheit, G. *Der deutsche Geheimdienst: Geschichte der Militärischen Abwehr.* Munich, 1966.

Hoetl, W. *The Secret Front: The Story of Nazi Political Espionage.* New York, 1971.

Hohne, H. *Canaris, a Biography.* Garden City, N.Y., 1979.

Hohne, H. *The Order of the Death's Head: The Story of Hitler's SS.* New York, 1969.

HANS-HEINRICH WILHELM

ACTION FRANÇAISE, French radical right-wing antisemitic movement. Action Française was founded in 1899, when the Dreyfus affair was at its height, to counter liberal intellectuals who were rallying to the defense of the Jewish army captain charged with treason. The point of departure of the new movement was that the question of Dreyfus's guilt or innocence was irrelevant; at stake was the good of the nation and of the state, for which it was imperative that the army be free of all stain. The public interest was held always to take precedence over the interest of the individual—all the more so when that individual was a Jew, a foreign body in the French people.

Thereafter, until its formal dissolution at the end of World War II, Action Française was the spearhead of "integral nationalism," the nationalism of blood and soil. French "integral nationalism" regarded the nation as an organic entity, engaged in an unending struggle with four enemies that threatened to destroy it: Jews, foreigners, Protestants, and Freemasons. To defend itself and safeguard its survival, the nation had to fight all these elements and seek to banish them from its midst.

The central thesis of "integral nationalism" was that in order to put a stop to France's disintegration, the heritage of the French Revolution had to be discarded and monarchic rule restored. Nationalism—according to Charles Maurras (1863–1952), the founder and undisputed leader of Action Française—was not only a political value; it was also, perhaps above all, an aesthetic value. "Goddess France" was a creation unlike any other in the world, and the preservation of this unique entity required absolute national egotism; any element that weakened the body of the nation had to be destroyed. Heading the list of such elements was democracy, which was based on the principles of equality, individualism, and human rights, and which served as the arena for struggle among diverse interest groups and political parties.

Antagonism toward the Jews guided Maurras's actions throughout his life, and for nearly fifty years his movement was in the vanguard of French antisemitism. The history of the movement, in many ways, parallels Maurras's own life. Action Française derived its influence from his writings; Maurras was one of France's leading intellectuals and authors, a member (from 1939) of the Académie Française and a figure highly esteemed by many in the country's intelligentsia.

In World War II, Maurras led a virulent

campaign of anti-Jewish incitement and tried to gain recognition as the ideologue of the Vichy regime's "national revolution." He enthusiastically welcomed the racist laws introduced in October 1940. These laws were to serve the new regime's aim of removing the Jews from the life of the French people and thereby to erase 150 years of the country's history as a republic; this corresponded to the objectives of Action Française. Indeed, the movement had been founded for the purpose of liquidating the heritage and ideals of the French Revolution, which constituted the principles on which the Third Republic (1871–1940) was based.

When the war ended, Maurras was sentenced to life imprisonment for collaborating with the enemy. Action Française was always a small movement in size, but its intellectual influence was disproportionately large, not only in France, but also in Italy, Spain, Belgium, and countries of eastern Europe.

BIBLIOGRAPHY

Curtis, M. *Three against the Third Republic: Barrès, Maurras, Sorel.* Princeton, 1959.

Nölte, E. *Three Faces of Fascism: Action Française, Italian Fascism, National Socialism.* New York, 1966.

Sutton, M. *Nationalism, Positivism, and Catholicism: The Politics of Charles Maurras and French Catholics, 1890–1914.* Cambridge, 1982.

Weber, E. *Action Française: Royalism and Reaction in Twentieth-Century France.* Stanford, 1962.

ZEEV STERNHELL

ADAMOWICZ, IRENA (1910–1963), Polish liaison officer among various ghetto underground movements. Born in Warsaw, Adamowicz was a pious Catholic and a member of the leadership of the Polish scout movement. She graduated with a degree in social work at Warsaw University. In the 1930s she was greatly attracted by the Ha-Shomer ha-Tsa'ir movement and even participated in its social and educational work. In the summer of 1942, Adamowicz carried out many dangerous missions for the Jewish underground organizations in the ghettos of WARSAW, BIAŁYSTOK, VILNA, KOVNO, and ŠIAULIAI. In addition to the important information she conveyed, her visits to the isolated ghettos brought moral encouragement to those imprisoned there. With her help, contact was established between the Jewish underground organizations and the members of the ARMIA KRAJOWA (Home Army).

After the war, Adamowicz maintained close relations with the survivors of the pioneer Zionist movements in Poland and with her friends from those movements in Israel. For her unique activity in the war years she was awarded the "RIGHTEOUS AMONG THE NATIONS" medal by YAD VASHEM in Jerusalem.

BIBLIOGRAPHY

The Jewish Partisans. Merhavia, Israel, 1958. (In Hebrew.)

DOV LEVIN

AFRICA, NORTH. *See* Algeria; Libya; Morocco; Tunisia.

AFSC. *See* American Friends Service Committee.

AHNENERBE (lit., "ancestral heritage"), the Society for Research into the Spiritual Roots of Germany's Ancestral Heritage (Studiengesellschaft für Geistesurgeschichte Deutsches Ahnenerbe), founded in Berlin on July 1, 1935, by Heinrich HIMMLER, Richard Walther DARRÉ, and the German-Dutch lecturer Herman Wirth. The society published a magazine, *Germanien,* whose object was to broaden support for Wirth's cult of "Germandom." Shortly after Ahnenerbe was founded, however, the leading "scientific" role in the society was put in the hands of Walther Wüst, the Nazi-appointed dean of the faculty of philosophy at Munich University, since Wirth was found to have no standing among the academic community.

From its very inception, Ahnenerbe concerned itself with esoteric, mostly pseudoscientific, subjects. These included, in addition to ancient Germanic history, Hanns Hörbiger's universal ice theory (*Welteislehre*); the Atlantis myth; interpretation of the *Ex-*

ternsteine ("external stones," a peculiar outcrop of rock near Detmold, reputed to be the site of ancient pagan worship); revival of ancient Germanic customs; research into the runes (ancient Germanic letters of the alphabet); interpretation of symbols (such as the origin and meaning of the swastika); and promotion of the cult of the medieval German king Heinrich I (r. 919–936), "Conqueror of the Slavs," a fad of Himmler's that involved archaeological digs and memorial services at Quedlinburg (now in East Germany), where Heinrich I had resided.

Before long, Ahnenerbe branched out into various other fields, a process that was speeded up when Himmler took direct charge of the society in 1937 and eventually became its president. Ample funds now poured into Ahnenerbe's treasury. New projects undertaken by the society included a research expedition to Tibet; research into ancient forms of naturopathy; genealogical research; publications such as the *Atlas of German Folklore* and a book series, Forest and Trees in Aryan-German Thought and Culture; archaeological excavations at ancient settlements or at sites related to German legends, such as Altchristburg in East Prussia, Hohmichele near Sigmaringen, Haithabu in Schleswig, and Krimhildestuhl near Bad Dürkheim; speleological expeditions to the Altmühltal caves and Franconian Switzerland; research on the history of the Lombards; research on the art and culture of the Irish-Scottish Mission (sixth to ninth centuries); meteorological research; divination (by use of rods); reexamination of the occult sciences; research on astronomy; research on ownership marks and clan symbols; research on military geology (prospecting for war-essential metals); the study of paleontology; research on animal geography and history; and study of the development of a "national telescope." In the planning stage were expeditions to Hawaii, southern Nigeria, Manchuria, South America, Iceland, and Iran.

In 1939 Ahnenerbe launched its annual "Science Weeks," a lecture series at Salzburg. It also compiled and published lists of "Jewish scientists or scientists related to Jews by marriage" and confiscated libraries, such as the Jewish author Lion Feuchtwanger's Oriental-Semitic library and the library, consisting of 80,000 to 100,000 volumes, of the Salzburger Universitätsverein (Salzburg University Society), which had been disbanded by the Gestapo shortly after the ANSCHLUSS. Ahnenerbe representatives were sent to scientific congresses as observers; rival research organizations, such as the German Society of Celtic Studies and the Westphalian Native Lodge, were undermined to facilitate their takeover by Ahnenerbe, which also schemed against Alfred ROSENBERG, particularly Rosenberg's ambitious plan for establishing a *Hohe Schule* (academy of sciences) on the shore of Lake Chiem in Bavaria.

Many of these projects became outmoded as soon as the war broke out, and others were continued to enable the researchers to dodge military service. Soon, Germany's territorial expansion created new challenges, which Ahnenerbe was eager to tackle. Among these were the "recovery" of German church registers and archives in the Baltic states; the seizure of art treasures in Poland; the sifting of art collections in the museums of Kiev, Odessa, Rostov, and Novocherkassk; "archaeological excavations, on a larger scale" in the Dnepropetrovsk district; an investigation of Gothic memorial tablets in the Crimea; a study of the dialects of the Cimbri (an ancient Germanic tribe) in the South Tirol; folklore research in "Gottschee" (Kočevje, in Slovenia), Norway, and Flanders; historical research on the *limes* (ancient Roman imperial fortifications) and on Cossack life, designed to shore up Himmler's plans for the establishment of settlements populated by soldier-farmers; a plan for policy on science in the Greater German Reich; research into the history of the Mongols; a comprehensive exploration of Caucasia; and the breeding of a "superior steppe horse for use in war and agricultural colonization," by crossing the Przewalski and Gmelin wild-horse lines.

It was almost impossible to establish which projects were plain charlatanry, which were politically motivated research, and which were conventional scientific projects. Many projects never went beyond the preliminary stage, which was not surprising in view of the short time available, the lack of means, and the low regard of the scientific community for Ahnenerbe (the organization did not attract the better-qualified and established scientists).

In 1942 this obscure society was swallowed up by the *Reichsführer*'s personal staff. The fact that its very existence is still known is not because of any scientific achievement by its researchers but because of the evil experiments conducted under its auspices by the German air force medical officer Dr. Sigmund Rascher in DACHAU, and the skull collection created by Dr. August Hirt, professor of anatomy at the Reich University of Strasbourg, as of 1941. A favorite of Himmler's, Rascher most likely did not need his post at Ahnenerbe's Institute of Military-Scientific Applied Research (*Wehrwissenschaftliche Zweckforschung*) to conduct his carcinoma-test series and his experiments in high-altitude flights under conditions of low pressure and freezing temperatures. As an air force senior medical officer, he was acting on orders of Professor Erich Hippke, air force sanitation inspector; Professor Georg August Weltz of the Munich Institute for Air Force Medicine; and Dr. Siegfried Ruff of the Berlin Institute of Flight Medicine of the German Flight Research Institute; and with the knowledge of Erhard Milch, the inspector general of the air force.

In his freezing experiments, Rascher was assisted by Professor Ernst Holzlöhner, a Kiel physiologist acting on a research assignment from Hippke, and by Dr. E. Finke, another air force medical officer. All the machinery and installations required by Rascher for his experiments were provided by the air force. The Dachau concentration camp did not come under Ahnenerbe, and in his capacity as Ahnenerbe president, Himmler was not authorized to give instructions to the concentration-camp commandant. It was only as *Reichsführer*-SS and chief of the German police that Himmler was in a position to approve of Rascher's human experiments on prisoners in Dachau. Rascher's association with Ahnenerbe was therefore no more than a scientific cover for a favor that Himmler was doing for Hermann GÖRING's Luftwaffe. As far as Rascher's cancer research was concerned, Himmler had given his approval to Rascher himself, in a private capacity, as early as 1939.

Rascher's high-altitude experiments are reported to have been conducted on 180 to 200 prisoners, "mostly Jews, Germans, Russians, and Poles—including also some Christian clergymen," of whom about 80 perished as a result. In the freezing experiments, of which 400 were carried out, from 280 to 300 prisoners took part and between 80 and 90 of them died.

In 1945 Rascher was executed in Dachau by a shot in the neck, on Himmler's orders, as an accessory to at least eight cases of kidnapping children perpetrated by his wife; she was a close acquaintance of Himmler's and had falsely claimed to have given birth to children after the age of forty-eight. She was hanged in the RAVENSBRÜCK camp shortly before it was liberated, after attacking a female guard in the camp.

Hirt's skull collection, according to a memorandum he submitted to Ahnenerbe on December 10, 1941, was intended to close an existing gap:

> We have large collections of skulls of almost all races and peoples at our disposal. Of the Jewish race, however, only very few specimens of skulls are available and their processing cannot assure us of obtaining reliable results. The war in the east now presents us with the opportunity to overcome this deficiency. By procuring the skulls of the Jewish-Bolshevik commissars, who represent the prototype of the repulsive but characteristic subhuman, we have the chance now to obtain authentic scientific material.

In the future, all "Jewish-Bolshevik commissars" were to be handed over to the field gendarmerie, so as to enable medical students serving in the army to take the required anthropological measurements; then, after carefully severing the heads from the bodies, they were to dispatch the remains to Strasbourg in special lead containers filled with preservative fluid. Henceforth, Hirt's interests broadened: in November 1942 he was to receive "150 skeletons of prisoners, that is, Jews" from the AUSCHWITZ extermination camp for "certain anthropological examinations." Delivery of the order was delayed, however, and it was only in June of 1943 that Hirt was informed by one of his assistants of the receipt of "79 Jews, 2 Poles, 4 Central Asians, and 30 Jewesses, processed." In late

July and early August, 122 corpses (including the corpses of 29 females) were delivered, of persons whom the camp commandant had had killed in a special gas chamber, using for this purpose a chemical Hirt had selected.

A part of Hirt's skull collection is said to have been moved to the Mittersill castle in the fall of 1944. Hirt died in Schönenbach, in the Neustadt district (Black Forest), on June 2, 1945. He is presumed to have taken his own life.

[*See also* Medical Experiments.]

BIBLIOGRAPHY

Kater, M. H. *Das "Ahnenerbe" der SS, 1935–1945: Ein Beitrag zur Kulturpolitik des Dritten Reiches*. Stuttgart, 1974.

Mitscherlich, A., and F. Mielke. *Doctors of Infamy: The Story of the Nazi Medical Crimes*. New York, 1949.

HANS-HEINRICH WILHELM

AID TO JEWS BY POLES. A number of factors made it extremely difficult for Poles to come to the aid of the Jews in POLAND during World War II: the lack of contact between the Jews and the Polish environment; the antisemitism that spread in certain circles of Polish society; the regime of terror in Nazi-occupied Poland, which was aimed at the entire population, on a scale unparalleled in western Europe; and the death penalty the Nazis applied in Poland for giving aid to Jews.

Forms of Help. The most dangerous, and yet the most frequent, form of help given to the Jews was the offering of refuge in private dwellings. Most of the people who gave refuge to Jews also provided them with financial assistance. In the main the motivation for help was that of human compassion; devout Catholics felt obligated to abide by the commandment to "love thy neighbor." Others—chiefly among leftist and liberal circles—acted out of ideological and political considerations. Some of the Poles who gave help to Jews did so in return for financial reward, which was very high in certain cases. Those who gave help came from all walks of life. There were even a few cases in which antisemites helped Jews. Aid to Jews was extended mainly in two centers—WARSAW (where twenty thousand to thirty thousand Jews were in hiding) and KRAKÓW.

At a later stage, aid in organized form was given by underground organizations, trade unions, and political parties—Democrats, Socialists, and Communists. In most of these cases, the recipients of the aid were Jews who were members, or relatives of members, of the respective organization. Beginning in early 1943, these organizations (except for the Communists) were assisted by ZEGOTA (the Polish Council for Aid to Jews).

Some monasteries (primarily Franciscan) took in Jewish children; the Benedictine monastery near Vilna even extended aid to Jewish fighters. Several of the boy scouts from the underground Gray Ranks organization (Szare Szeregi, which was affiliated with the Home Army, or ARMIA KRAJOWA) cooperated with Ha-Shomer ha-Tsa'ir, acting as its intermediary between one city and another, and smuggling arms. It is difficult to estimate the extent of this kind of aid in figures.

According to postwar estimates by historians, several tens of thousands of Jews were saved by the local population. The number of "Aryans" who gave help to Jews (Poles and, in eastern Poland, also Belorussians and Ukrainians—the latter much more rarely) is variously estimated as ranging from 160,000 to 360,000, that is, 1 percent to 2.5 percent of the population. A list drawn up by the MAIN COMMISSION FOR INVESTIGATION OF NAZI CRIMES IN POLAND puts the number of non-Jews executed individually by the Germans for aiding Jews at 872, with several hundreds more murdered in mass executions (as when the Nazis burned down entire villages).

Military aid given to Jews was minimal. The information available concerning the earliest contacts with various groups is under dispute. These contacts were established by the ŻYDOWSKI ZWIĄZEK WOJSKOWY (Jewish Military Union), the second Jewish fighting organization in the Warsaw ghetto, whose nucleus consisted of members of the Revisionist Betar youth movement. It made contact with the Korpus Bezpieczeństwa (Security Corps; KB), an underground organization affiliated with the Armia Krajowa, which acted as a gendarmerie when the WARSAW POLISH UPRIS-

ING took place. It was only in the fall of 1942 that the ŻYDOWSKA ORGANIZACJA BOJOWA (Jewish Fighting Organization; ŻOB), after several abortive attempts, established links with Armia Krajowa headquarters, with the help of Henryk WOLINSKI. The Armia Krajowa planned an uprising against the Nazis that would take place only when the front line of battle was drawing near, since it did not believe that an earlier attempt stood any chance of success. The ŻOB, on the other hand, felt that the Jews had no time to lose and that a revolt had to be attempted even if it was hopeless. The Armia Krajowa, moreover, was not convinced that the ŻOB really meant to execute its schemes when it spoke of fighting the Nazis. For these two reasons, the quantity of weapons supplied to the ŻOB by the Armia Krajowa was very small.

During the WARSAW GHETTO UPRISING, the Armia Krajowa, the Gwardia Ludowa (later the ARMIA LUDOWA, or Polish People's Army), the KB, and the Socjalistyczna Organizacja Bojowa (Socialist Fighting Organization) carried out several actions to indicate their solidarity with the Jews and attacked German positions, losing men in these attacks. They also helped several groups of ghetto fighters to make their way through the Warsaw sewers to the city's "Aryan" side. At a later stage, when the question of establishing Jewish partisan units came up, the Armia Krajowa refused to cooperate, believing that such units would have a pro-Soviet orientation. The Gwardia Ludowa/Armia Ludowa gave the Jews some help, but the possibilities open to it were limited. In the Warsaw Polish uprising, in the summer of 1944, Jews fought in Armia Ludowa units.

A constant source of danger to the Jews who had gone into hiding was the so-called *szmalcowniki* (blackmailers)—gangs of robbers who roamed the countryside, blackmailed the Jews in hiding, and extorted ransoms from them, frequently also informing on them to the Germans. There were also instances when Poles who looked like Jews or gave help to Jews were blackmailed by the *szmalcowniki*.

These *szmalcowniki*, for the most part, came from the lower strata of the population. It was difficult to fight them, since only in rare instances was it possible for their victims to identify them. The *szmalcowniki* were also wanted by the Polish underground because they worked for the German police, and they were often sentenced to death by the underground tribunals. Several dozen such death sentences were carried out in 1943 and 1944, and as a result, the activity of the blackmailers diminished considerably.

Contacts Abroad. The Jewish underground's efforts to establish its own contacts with the outside world did not materialize. Beginning in 1942, however, the BUND and the Żydowski Komitet Narodowy (Jewish National Committee; the ŻOB's political arm) had the help of the DELEGATURA (the representative, in Poland, of the Polish government-in-exile), whose couriers carried letters back and forth between Poland and England and which also transmitted the two Jewish organizations' messages on current affairs by radio. The addressees in London were the Jewish representatives on the Polish National Council—Samuel ZYGELBOJM, and subsequently Emanuel Scherer and Isaac SCHWARZBART. Funds contributed in London by international Jewish organizations were transmitted to Poland (by parachute drops) together with funds for the Armia Krajowa and the Delegatura.

In 1940 the Polish underground also began transmitting to London reports on the situation of the Jews. Some historians believe that these reports were deliberately delayed, especially those concerning the deportation of the Jews from the Warsaw ghetto to the extermination camps. Other historians claim that the reports were transmitted promptly, and that it was the Allied governments who held them back. Ultimately, public statements made by the Polish government-in-exile and the testimony of emissaries from Poland—primarily that of Jan KARSKI—played an important role in dispelling the doubts of the free world about reports on the annihilation of European Jewry by the Germans.

BIBLIOGRAPHY

Bartoszewski, W., and Z. Lewin. *Righteous among Nations: How Poles Helped the Jews, 1939–1945.* London, 1969.

Datner, S. *Las sprawiedliwych: Karta z dziejów ratownictwa Żydow w okupowanej Polsce.* Warsaw, 1968.

Friedman, P. *Their Brothers' Keepers: The Christian Heroes and Heroines Who Helped the Oppressed Escape the Nazi Terror.* New York, 1957.
Gutman, Y. *The Jews of Warsaw, 1939–1943.* Bloomington, 1980.
Laqueur, W. *The Terrible Secret.* London, 1980.
Ringelblum, E. *Polish-Jewish Relations during the Second World War.* Jerusalem, 1974.
Tec, N. *When Light Pierced the Darkness: Christian Rescue of Jews in Nazi-occupied Poland.* New York, 1986.

TERESA PREKEROWA

AJ. *See* Armée Juive.

AJB. *See* Association des Juifs en Belgique.

AKIVA. *See* Youth Movements.

AKTION "ERNTEFEST." *See* "Erntefest."

AKTION 1005, code name for a large-scale activity that aimed to obliterate the traces of the murder of millions of human beings by the Nazis in occupied Europe. A decision to undertake this action was made in Berlin after news of the mass murders began to emerge in the Allied countries, and when the hastily buried corpses began to pose a serious health hazard in the early summer of 1942.

The operation's code name originated in an important letter from the Gestapo commander Heinrich MÜLLER to Martin LUTHER in the Foreign Office, who had forwarded an anonymous letter complaining about the corpses flooding the WARTHEGAU area. At the head of the letter, under the name of the ministry, appeared the number 1005 in brackets, and this became the code by which the operation was known. The units that put it into effect were called Sonderkommandos 1005.

The operation commenced in June 1942 with attempts to burn the corpses in the CHEŁMNO extermination camp. At the same time, SS-Standartenführer Paul BLOBEL was appointed head of Aktion 1005. He created a small staff in Łódź, and in an initial stage, between the summer of 1942 and that of 1943, supervised the burning of bodies in the AKTION REINHARD extermination camps (BEŁŻEC, TREBLINKA, SOBIBÓR), in the Chełmno camp, and at AUSCHWITZ (until the crematoria were installed there). An architect by profession, and a member of the engineering corps in World War I, Blobel developed systems for burning on pyres, installations for crushing bones, and methods of scattering ashes.

In a second stage, beginning in early June 1943, liquidation of the mass graves in areas of the occupied USSR and Poland began. The first site seems to have been the JANÓWSKA camp in Lvov, where the Sonderkommandos 1005 later employed in the other areas studied the methods used.

Each Sonderkommando 1005 consisted of several SD (Sicherheitsdienst; Security Service) and Sicherheitspolizei (Security Police; Sipo) officers, who supervised the work, and several dozen German policemen from the ORDNUNGSPOLIZEI (German regular police), who were charged with guarding the workers and the area. The labor was carried out by scores or hundreds of prisoners, mainly Jews. Pyres were built with long, thick wooden beams 23 to 26 feet (7–8 m) long, soaked with a flammable liquid, and the corpses were placed in layers between them. In the extermination camps, railway tracks were used for the foundation of the fire. The prisoners were divided into three groups: one opened the graves and exhumed the bodies, the second brought the corpses on stretchers and arranged them on the pyre, and the third was employed in sifting the ashes, crushing the bones, collecting any valuables overlooked earlier, and scattering the ashes. One or two prisoners were responsible for kindling the pyre and counting the corpses burned. The capacity of one pyre at Janówska was about two thousand bodies a day. Upon termination of work at the site, reconstruction was carried out, such as leveling the terrain, harrowing, and replanting. Since Aktion 1005 was defined as a "Reich secret" (*geheime Reichssache*), the Germans in the unit had to sign declarations promising secrecy, and the prisoners were killed on completion of their work.

AKTION 1005
USSR
front line in November 1942
front line in September 1943
Moscow
Klooga
ESTONIA
LATVIA
Riga
Salaspils
REICHSKOMMISSARIAT OSTLAND
Dvinsk
Vitebsk
Klaipėda (Memel)
LITHUANIA
Kovno
Vilna
PONARY
Tilsit
Orsha
Borisov
Molodechno
Minsk
Mogilev
Maly Trostinets
Bobruisk
Rogachev
Ozarichi
Gomel
Baltic Sea
Danzig
Augustow
Grodno
Skidel
Białystok
Grudziądz
Neustadt
Działdowo
Łomza
Stargard
Bromberg
Ciechanów
BELORUSSIA
Hohensalza
Konin
TREBLINKA
Kobrin
Pinsk
Berlin
CHEŁMNO
Zgierz
SOBIBÓR
Brest-Litovsk
Łódź
Lublin-Lipowa
Chełm
MAJDANEK
Borki camp
REICHSKOMMISSARIAT UKRAINE
BABI YAR
Kiev
GREATER GERMANY
AUSCHWITZ
Zamość
BEŁZEC
Berdichev
Kharkov
Drobitski Yar
PŁASZÓW
Lvov (Janówska camp)
Belaya Tserkov
Uman
Krivoi Rog
Dnepropetrovsk
Kamenets-Podolski
0 miles 200
0 kilometers 300
© Martin Gilbert 1982
Nikolayev
Sea of Azov
Black Sea
CRIMEA

In early November 1943, the prisoners of the Sonderkommando 1005 in Janówska saw that their work was drawing to a close, and planned to attack the police at night and escape. On November 19, their plan was partially carried out. Of the scores of Jews who fled, a few individuals survived, including Leon Weliczker, who had recorded his impressions when he was in the unit, and later published them.

After the German defeat at Stalingrad and the retreat from the Ukraine in the first half of 1943, Blobel sped to Kiev in order to organize the erasing of the mass graves there. It was Blobel who supervised the slaughter at BABI YAR near Kiev, at Drobitski Yar in KHARKOV, and in many other places. In the first half of August 1943, two units were formed in Kiev: Sonderkommando 1005-A and Sonderkommando 1005-B. SS-Sturmbannführer Hans Zohns was appointed to head the entire operation. On August 18, Sonderkommando 1005-A began to remove the bodies at Babi Yar; it received 327 prisoners for this task, including about 100 Jews. On September 29 the prisoners learned that they were to be put to death the next day. A group that sought to escape had prepared saws for their chains and a key to open the grille at the entrance to the dugout in which they were locked, and it was decided to break out that night. At midnight, under cover of darkness, a group of 25 shouting prisoners stormed the guards and took advantage of the confusion reigning among them; about 15 men reached freedom.

After Kiev, Sonderkommando 1005-A continued to burn bodies in Berdichev, in Belaya Tserkov, and in Uman. After a short holiday the unit worked at KAMENETS-PODOLSKI, until it was disturbed by the approach of the Red Army. It transferred to ZAMOŚĆ in the Lublin area, and finished in ŁÓDŹ, then accompanying the last of the Jews from the Łódź ghetto to Auschwitz.

Sonderkommando 1005-B supervised the burning of bodies in Dnepropetrovsk, in Krivoi Rog, and in Nikolayev and the surrounding area. On April 9, 1944, after a holiday, the unit was sent to RIGA. It established its base near the Salaspils camp, burned about twenty thousand bodies, and also operated in DVINSK and other places.

Aktion 1005 in Belorussia was divided into two units. In eastern Belorussia, which was under military rule, the *Aktion* was carried out by Sonderkommandos 7a and 7b and by Einsatzkommandos 8 and 9 under the command of a Dr. Siekel, an Einsatzkommando 8 officer. From the fragmentary information available, it is known that the activity was carried out in the districts of GOMEL (7.5 miles [12 km] northwest of the city, and near Ozarichi and Rogachev), Mogilev (near the villages of Pashkovichi and Pulkovichi), Bobruisk, and VITEBSK (near Orsha and Borisov). In October 1943 in western Belorussia, which was under civilian rule, Blobel's deputy, Arthur Alexander Harder, created Sonderkommando 1005 Mitte (Central), the base of which was in the SS camp MALY TROSTINETS, and which came under the command of Max Krahner.

Sonderkommando 1005 Mitte began its activity by burning the bodies of the forty thousand to fifty thousand Jews of MINSK and the Reich who had been killed and buried in the vicinity of Minsk. The unit continued its work in different towns in the area of Minsk and Molodechno, and from there it went on to the districts of Brest-Litovsk, PINSK, Kobrin, and Lomza. On August 16, 1944, this unit was transferred to Łódź to escort the transports of the Jews from the ghetto to Auschwitz.

In the Baltic countries, 1005 is known to have been active in Lithuania—in PONARY, near Vilna; and in the NINTH FORT in Kovno. The activity in these two vicinities began in September 1943, and in both, the Jewish prisoners organized an escape. In Kovno all seventy of the prisoners employed fled on December 24, 1943; only thirty-four of them survived, however. In Ponary the escape took place on the night of April 15, 1944, and of the forty prisoners who escaped, fifteen survived. The Sonderkommando 1005 organized in Tilsit (Sovetsk) burned thousands of corpses of Soviet prisoners of war near Pegegen in the Klaipėda (Memel) region. The operation in Latvia has been mentioned above. In Estonia the bodies were burned when the KLOOGA camp and its subcamps were liquidated at the approach of the Red Army. The Germans did not have time to set fire to all the pyres, and Red Army photographers filmed a pyre prepared for burning.

In the Białystok district, which was a separate administrative unit, a Sonderkommando 1005 was established and functioned from mid-May until mid-July 1944 in the towns of Augustów, Grodno, and Skidel, and the village of Grabowka. On July 13 the prisoners were brought to a pit where they were to be killed, but the forty-three Jewish prisoners took flight and eleven of them managed to escape.

In the GENERALGOUVERNEMENT, Sonderkommando 1005 was active in LVOV and the Lvov region, as noted above, and in Zamość in the Lublin district. In the same district a unit operated in the Borki camp near Chełm, using Jewish prisoners of war (formerly in the Polish army) from the LUBLIN-LIPOWA camp. The corpses burned were mainly those of Soviet and Italian prisoners of war. The Jewish prisoners planned an escape and hewed out a tunnel, and on the evening of December 24, 1943, ten of them fled. Four reached partisan units, and after the war they gave evidence on what they had seen at Borki.

As the Soviet army approached in mid-1944, the principal 1005 activity in the Generalgouvernement began. A meeting was convened by Wilhelm KUBE, the *Höherer SS- und Polizeiführer* (Higher SS and Police Leader) in Kraków, with the participation of all the SD and Sipo commanders and the police of the districts. Each commander undertook to establish a Sonderkommando 1005 in his area. A similar instruction came from Berlin to the SS and police leaders in the areas of Poland annexed to the Reich, where tens of thousands of Poles had been killed in the early days of the occupation in 1939. Sonderkommando 1005 units were active in Soldau (now Dzialdowo) in the Ciechanów region; in the Gau Danzig (Gdańsk) region in West Prussia in the towns of Graudenz (now Grudziądz), Bromberg (now Bydgoszcz), Stargard, Neustadt (now Nowe Miasto), Cronau (now Kronowo), and Kulm (now Chełmno); and in the Warthegau district in the vicinities of Konin, Zgierz (Gornau), and Hohensalza (Inowrocław).

Outside eastern Europe, Aktion 1005 activity was carried out in Yugoslavia near the village of Jajinci in the area of the SAJMIŠTE camp, where there were about eighty thousand corpses, including those of about eleven thousand Jews. The operation began on November 6, 1943, and up until the flight of one of the prisoners engaged in the activity, about sixty-eight thousand bodies were burned.

Most of the Germans employed in Aktion 1005 were not returned to their units but were assembled in early October 1944 in Salzburg, Austria. There they were formed into Einsatzgruppe "Iltis," for special tasks under the command of Paul Blobel, particularly to fight against the Yugoslav partisans in the region of Carinthia.

Although burning the bodies from the mass graves did not efface the Nazi crimes, it did cause difficulties in determining the facts of the crimes and in drawing up statistics on the number of victims. In many cases, the commissions investigating Nazi crimes in the USSR and in Poland found no trace of the mass graves, and they encountered difficulty in reaching estimates.

BIBLIOGRAPHY

Spector, S. "Aktion 1005 to Obscure the Murder of Millions during World War II." *Yahadut Zemanenu* 4 (1986): 207–225. (In Hebrew.)

Weliczker-Wells, L. *Brygada śmierci* (*Sonderkommando 1005: Pamiętnik*). Łódź, 1946.

SHMUEL SPECTOR

AKTION REINHARD, code name for the operation that had as its objective the physical destruction of the Jews in the GENERALGOUVERNEMENT, the territory in the interior of occupied Poland, within the framework of the "FINAL SOLUTION." The name was coined by the SS men in charge of the operation, several months after it had been launched, in memory of Reinhard HEYDRICH, the chief planner of the "Final Solution" in Europe, whom members of the Czech underground had assassinated on May 27, 1942. The aim of Aktion Reinhard was to kill the 2,284,000 Jews then living in the five districts of the Generalgouvernement—Warsaw, Lublin, Radom, Kraków, and Lvov (Eastern Galicia)—according to the German data as stated in the minutes of the WANNSEE

CONFERENCE of January 20, 1942.

Preparations for Aktion Reinhard began in October and November of 1941. Himmler appointed Odilo GLOBOCNIK, *SS- und Polizeiführer* (SS and Police Leader) in the Lublin district, to head the program, with Hauptsturmführer Hans Höfle as chief of operations, in charge of organization and manpower. The operational headquarters was in Lublin, and its tasks were as follows:

1. Overall planning of the deportations
2. Construction and operation of extermination camps
3. Coordination of the deportations from each of the five districts
4. The extermination process in the camps
5. Confiscation of the victims' possessions and valuables and their dispatch to the appropriate authority in the Reich.

For security reasons, Globocnik's orders on the extermination process were given to him orally. Deporting the Jews from the ghettos and escorting them to the extermination camps—an integral part of Aktion Reinhard—were the responsibility of the SS and police in the various districts, and were not under the direct authority of Globocnik and his staff.

The personnel who were put at Globocnik's disposal for the operation included a team of 450 Germans. At its core was a group of 92 men, headed by Kriminalkommissar Christian WIRTH, who had been assigned to Globocnik for the EUTHANASIA PROGRAM. That operation had been broken off in mid-1941, and for security reasons the men who had taken part were not posted to the front. Their assignment to Aktion Reinhard provided Globocnik with personnel who had gained experience in the use of gas as a means of killing people, as practiced in the Euthanasia Program. It was this group from which the key German staff was chosen for Reinhard, including the commanders of the extermination camps; each camp was allotted 20 to 30 German staff.

The Aktion Reinhard headquarters recruited a special auxiliary unit for its purposes, consisting of Ukrainian volunteers, most of them Soviet prisoners of war. They were billeted in the SS training camp at TRAWNIKI, where they were provided with black uniforms, given arms, organized into platoons and companies, and put through a brief training program. The platoon and company commanders were Germans, some of them VOLKSDEUTSCHE (ethnic Germans); the local population referred to them as "Trawniki men" or "Askaris." Each extermination camp was assigned from 90 to 120 Ukrainians; "Trawniki men" were also employed in deporting Jews from the ghettos and in escorting the transports on their way to the camps.

Three extermination camps were established under Aktion Reinhard: BEŁŻEC, SOBIBÓR, and TREBLINKA. A number of considerations determined the location of the camps. They had to be close to a railway, so that transportation would not pose a problem; for security reasons, they had to be in an isolated area, as remote as possible from population centers; and in order to lend a semblance of credence to the cover being used for the operation—that the Jews were being transferred to work "somewhere in the east," in occupied Soviet territory—the camps had to be near the eastern border of the Generalgouvernement.

The first camp to be set up, between November 1941 and March 1942, was the one in Bełżec, on the Lublin-Lvov railway line. The killings there began on March 17, 1942. The camp at Sobibór, east of Lublin, was constructed in March and April of 1942, and it began operations in early May 1942. The Treblinka camp, 50 miles (80 km) northeast of Warsaw, was established in June and July 1942, and the murder operations there were launched on July 23, 1942, coinciding with the start of the mass deportation from the Warsaw ghetto. The gas used in all three camps was carbon monoxide, generated by gasoline or diesel engines placed outside hermetically sealed gas chambers and pumped into them through a system of pipes. The Aktion Reinhard camps were not equipped for the cremation of bodies; the victims were buried in huge pits, and it was not until the end of 1942 and the beginning of 1943 that bodies were burned in huge pyres, the purpose being to erase evidence of the crimes that had been perpetrated there. The camps were constructed by Polish workers living in the area, augmented by Jews on forced labor, and the latter became the first victims.

For manual labor the camps used, by the hundreds, Jewish prisoners who were retained for this purpose from the transports that were put through the extermination process. As a rule, these prisoners were killed after working in the camps for several weeks or months, to be replaced by new arrivals from the transports. Only a few remained alive for any length of time.

The program of deportations to the extermination camps was based on the existing division of the Generalgouvernement into five districts, and the determining factor was proximity to a given camp and to the railway line that led there. Thus, Jews from the Kraków and Lvov (Eastern Galicia) districts were sent to Bełżec, from the Warsaw and Radom districts to Treblinka, and from the Lublin district to Sobibór. This pattern, however, was subject to change, and some of the Jews from the Lublin district were sent to Bełżec and Treblinka.

The method of deportation from the ghettos was uniform for most places in eastern Europe. Its principal elements were surprise, speed, terrorization, and keeping the victims unaware of their real destination. The authorities in charge of the deportation announced it the day before it was to take place, and at times without a single day's notice; the announcement was made to the local JUDENRAT (Jewish Council), which in turn had to pass it on to the ghetto population (the Judenrat was told that the Jews were being transferred to work camps in the east). At the same time the ghetto was encircled with a heavy guard of German security units, to prevent anyone from escaping. In the large ghettos, which contained tens of thousands or even hundreds of thousands of Jews, the deportation could not be completed in one day; therefore, in each separate *Aktion* the Judenrat was told to gather several thousand people for deportation. If the Judenrat was unable to supply the required quota, even with the help of the Jewish police at its disposal, German and Ukrainian reinforcements were sent in, to break into the houses and courtyards where the Jews were hiding and drag them out.

In the large ghettos, there were many *Aktionen* over a period of weeks and months, for as long as was necessary to clear the ghetto of all its inhabitants. In the small ghettos the *Aktionen* were a one-time operation, taking a day or two. Many persons were shot inside houses, in the street, or in the hiding places where they had taken refuge; among those shot were the elderly and the sick who were too feeble to walk on their own, as well as anyone who offered resistance.

Once they were removed from the ghetto, the Jews were taken to the railway station, usually by foot, where they were loaded into freight cars. The cars were crowded to suffocation, sometimes containing as many as one hundred and fifty persons each. The trip from the loading point to the extermination camp, which under normal circumstances lasted a few hours, sometimes took days, the trains being stopped for many hours en route, either in stations or on the railway line. Owing to the unbearable conditions in the cars—overcrowding, lack of water and sanitation, intense heat in the summer and cold in the winter—many died on the way; when the trains arrived at the death camp, there were often dozens or even hundreds of corpses aboard.

In order to ensure the exclusive and total control by the SS over the Jews in the "Final Solution" stage, and to raise the efficiency of the deportation process, the entire Jewish population of the Generalgouvernement was removed from the control of the German civil administration and placed under the authority of the SS, on June 3, 1942. When the Treblinka camp was put into operation in July of that year, deportations proceeded at a record pace, so much so that there were not enough trains available for the transports. At this time the German attack on Stalingrad and Caucasia was at its height, and the German army on the front was in urgent need of all the rolling stock that the railway administration had at its disposal. It required Heinrich HIMMLER's personal intervention with Theodor GANZENMÜLLER, the Transport Ministry's state secretary in charge of the German railways (Reichsbahn), for the required amount of rolling stock to be allocated to the deportation of the Jews.

In mid-July 1942, Himmler paid a visit to the Aktion Reinhard headquarters and to the camps under its control. Following his visit, on July 19, he issued an order according to which the deportation of the Jews in the Generalgouvernement to the extermination camps was to be completed by December 31, 1942. Beyond that date, only a few Jews were to be left whose retention was essential for the war effort, and these would be held in special work camps that were to be established in Warsaw, Kraków, Częstochowa, Radom, and Lublin.

The order, which called for deporting nearly the entire Jewish population from the ghettos, caused manpower problems for factories and workshops engaged in the war effort, and the military officials in charge of war production protested against this blow to the output of essential supplies needed by the armed forces. According to data submitted by the army, out of the 1 million workers employed in its plants in the Generalgouvernement, 300,000 were Jews, and of these one-third were skilled craftsmen. As a result of the army's appeal against Himmler's order, it was decided to keep some Jewish workers in several of the large ghettos until further notice.

The deportations continued, and, according to German data, by about the end of December 1942, 136,000 Jews in all remained in four of the Generalgouvernement districts; in the fifth, Lvov, 161,000 remained. The ghettos in these districts were liquidated in the period between January and June 1943 and the Jews in them removed; most were deported to extermination camps, while several tens of thousands, mostly young and skilled workers, were put in concentration camps and work camps.

In the last few months of 1942, when the deportations from the Generalgouvernement under Aktion Reinhard were coming to an end, the operation's scope was extended to include Jews from the Białystok district, numbering some 210,000. Most of the Białystok Jews were deported to Treblinka, and several transports went to Auschwitz; by August 1943 all the Jews of the Białystok district had been sent to extermination camps. From the Kraków district, the Jews were deported to Bełżec up to October 1942, and afterward to Płaszów and Auschwitz. Not all of the Jews in the Generalgouvernement found their end in the concentration and extermination camps; thousands were shot on the spot, where they lived. In the Lvov district alone, over 160,000 Jews were murdered in local *Aktionen*.

In the course of Aktion Reinhard, the Germans seized a huge amount of property, which the Jews of Poland had accumulated by hard work and manifold economic activities over the hundreds of years that they had been living in the country. This included real estate—houses, buildings, industrial plants, and land—the value of which cannot even be estimated in financial terms. In addition, an enormous quantity of movable property was left behind in homes and factories and was confiscated by the German authorities, although some of it fell into the hands of the non-Jewish local population. The Jews who were being deported took along those articles that they were allowed, including cash and valuables; all this accumulated in the camps where they were killed, and passed into German hands.

There was stiff competition over the control of Jewish property among the various official German bodies, especially between the civil administration of the Generalgouvernement, which regarded itself as the local government, and the SS with its several branches, which considered itself in charge of all aspects of the "Final Solution," including the property of the Jews. On September 26, 1942, the WIRTSCHAFTS-VERWALTUNGSHAUPTAMT (Economic-Administrative Main Office; WVHA) issued guidelines for the use of Aktion Reinhard headquarters and the commandant of the Auschwitz camp on the procedure to be followed in dealing with the money and valuables brought by Jewish victims to the extermination camps. According to these guidelines, all the cash and valuables accumulated in the camps were to be forwarded to the WVHA; other items, such as watches, clothing, eating utensils, and bedding, were to be distributed among the Economy Ministry, the army (for handing out to the troops), the SS workshops, and the *Volksdeutsche* in the occupied countries.

The Aktion Reinhard headquarters set up a special camp in Lublin, attached to the Majdanek camp, as a collecting center for the possessions left behind by the victims at Treblinka, Sobibór, and Bełżec. The site was an old airfield, and its hangars were used as warehouses for the loot. Jewish prisoners, mainly women, were employed in the warehouses. On December 15, 1943, the Aktion Reinhard headquarters submitted an account of the moneys, gold, and valuables taken from the Jews in the extermination camps for which the Reinhard headquarters was responsible. The figures were quoted in German marks (the rate of exchange of the reichsmark against the United States dollar at the time was 2.5 to 1). The report contains the particulars of the various categories: United States currency, about $1,100,000 in cash and $250,000 in gold coins; other foreign currency, from forty-eight countries; other gold coins, from thirty-four countries; 2,910 kilograms (6,415 lb) of gold bars; 18,734 kilograms (41,301 lb) of silver bars; diamonds totaling 16,000 carats. The report ends with the sum totals of the value of all the Jewish possessions collected.

Cash in Polish zlotys and German marks	RM73,852,080.74
Precious metals	8,273,651.60
Foreign currency, in cash	4,521,224.13
Foreign gold coins	1,736,554.12
Precious stones and other valuables	43,662,450.00
Textiles	46,000,000.00
Total	RM178,045,960.59

In addition, vast quantities of possessions were appropriated by German officials, SS men, Ukrainian camp guards, police, and local residents.

Aktion Reinhard, which began in mid-March 1942, continued until early November 1943, when the last Jews in the Majdanek, Poniatowa, and Trawniki camps were murdered; this operation was given the name "ERNTEFEST" ("Harvest Festival") by the Germans. In all, more than two million Jews of the Generalgouvernement were killed in Aktion Reinhard.

BIBLIOGRAPHY

Arad, Y. *Belzec, Sobibor, Treblinka: Operation Reinhard Death Camps.* Bloomington, 1987.

Gutman, Y., and L. Rothkirchen, eds. *The Catastrophe of European Jewry.* Jerusalem, 1976.

Hilberg, R. *The Destruction of the European Jews.* 3 vols. New York, 1985.

Reitlinger, G. *The Final Solution.* London, 1968.

YITZHAK ARAD

AKTION T4. *See* Euthanasia Program.

ALGERIA, republic in central North Africa; the largest of the Atlas Mountains states. Algeria was conquered by the French in the period from 1830 to 1847, and the Europeans who settled there—French, Italians, and Spaniards—were given the rights of citizens of FRANCE. In 1870 the Jews of Algeria also became French citizens, under a decree signed by the French minister of justice, Isaac-Adolphe Crémieux. On the eve of World War II the *colons* (French citizens in Algeria) accounted for nearly one-eighth of the total population.

Jews had been living in Algeria since the time of the Roman empire. In the fifteenth and sixteenth centuries they were joined by Jewish refugees from Spain. On the eve of World War II the Jewish population of Algeria was 120,000 (1.5 percent of the total, and

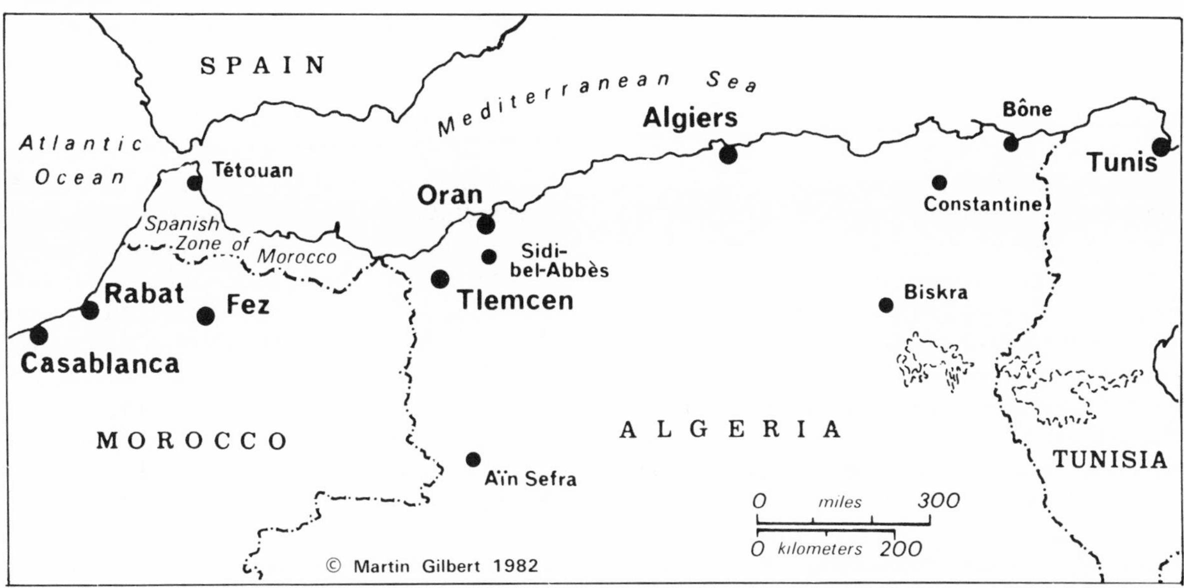

one-eighth of the number of French citizens). More than half of the Jewish population was concentrated in three large cities—Algiers, Oran, and Constantine.

Under Muslim rule the Jews had the status of *dhimmi* (protected people); that is, they were officially protected and tolerated, but also humiliated, discriminated against, and occasionally persecuted. Under French rule their economic and political situation improved greatly, especially when they acquired French citizenship, in 1870. Unlike the situation in TUNISIA and MOROCCO, which were French protectorates, in Algeria—which was originally a French colony and then officially became a part of France—French policy was designed to assimilate the Jews. This policy led first to the abolition of the traditional community organization and its replacement by a Consistoire (1845), in accordance with the French model, and then to the granting of citizenship to the Jews under the Crémieux Decree.

The improvement in the situation of the Jews was accompanied by a deterioration of their relations with the non-Jewish population. A wave of antisemitic violence and pogroms struck Algeria immediately after the Crémieux Decree and reached its climax in the 1880s, when antisemitic circles and political parties gained control of all the local European government institutions. A second wave came in the mid-1920s and lasted until the end of World War II. This wave also spread to Morocco and Tunisia, carrying along the Arab population, who were incited by propaganda beamed from Berlin and Rome and were also the objects of an anti-Zionist campaign promoted by the local Arab nationalists active on the eve of World War II.

Under the provisions of the French-German armistice of June 1940, North Africa was considered part of unoccupied France. The Germans had no foothold there until the Allied invasion of Algeria and Morocco in November 1942, to which the Axis powers reacted by occupying Tunisia. As in France itself, Marshal Philippe PÉTAIN and his Vichy regime enjoyed tremendous support among the European population of the Maghrib (Morocco, Algeria, and Tunisia), which welcomed the armistice and accepted the claim that France's defeat had been caused by the degeneration of France's republican regime. For this reason the Europeans in Algeria were not inclined to defend democratic institutions, and these were indeed abolished when the Vichy regime was installed. There was no need for Vichy to purge the French administration in North Africa, since most of the senior officials rallied to Pétain's side—either out of opportunism or out of conviction—

and diligently applied all the orders they received from Vichy, including those relating to the Jews.

In the sphere of anti-Jewish legislation, Algeria was singled out for special attention by the Vichy regime. Since Algeria was considered an integral part of France, all French laws and regulations applied to it; for the Jews of Algeria this meant that their legal status was similar to that of the Jews in unoccupied France. This fact alone, however, does not explain the special measures taken against the Algerian Jews, since the Vichy regime also persecuted, with no less determination, the Jews of Morocco and Tunisia, who were not French citizens but had the status of a subject people. Actually, the Vichy regime saw in the three countries a single geopolitical entity containing a large Jewish population, sandwiched in between a Muslim majority, whose loyalty to France was doubtful, and a European minority, which had adopted antisemitism as its political credo.

The anti-Jewish legislation was therefore applied to Algeria not only because it fitted in with the Vichy regime's ideological orientation. The Vichy authorities believed that it could also serve the double purpose of catering to the wishes of the Europeans and gaining for France the sympathy and support of Algeria's Muslim population. Under the "New Order" introduced by Vichy, a series of laws were enacted that discriminated against the Jews and set them apart both from the rest of the French population and from the general population of Algeria. The first step in this direction was the repeal of the Crémieux Decree, by an ordinance issued on October 7, 1940, that deprived the Jews of Algeria of their French nationality, except in a few cases, such as that of Jews who had been awarded military distinctions. In this way the regime complied with a demand that antisemitic circles had been making for seventy years. The ordinance was followed within a few days by another anti-Jewish decree, of even broader implications—the STATUT DES JUIFS (Jewish Law).

The Algerian version of the Statut des Juifs was identical with the French: it defined as a Jew any person who had three Jewish grandparents, or who had a Jewish spouse and two Jewish grandparents. It imposed various restrictions and prohibitions on the Jews—excluding them from the public service, the teaching profession, the courts, the local councils, the army, the media, the film industry, and the theater. In the following two years the COMMISSARIAT GÉNÉRAL AUX QUESTIONS JUIVES (General Office for Jewish Affairs) issued several more sets of anti-Jewish decrees, all of which were applied to Algeria as well as to Vichy France. Thus, an "Aryanization" office (*see* ARISIERUNG) was established in Algeria that was authorized to confiscate Jewish-owned property and was in charge of dismissing Jews from banks, insurance companies, and the stock exchange. A 2 percent *numerus clausus* (quota) was imposed on Jews in the professions—doctors, lawyers, druggists, registered nurses, and so on; the number of Jewish students at the University of Algiers was drastically reduced to 3 percent; and Jewish children were excluded from secondary and elementary schools (a measure that was not put into effect even in metropolitan France). In 1941 a general census of the Jews of Algeria was undertaken, and by 1942 preparations were under way to set up a JUDENRAT (Jewish Council) on the model of the UNION GÉNÉRALE DES ISRAÉLITES DE FRANCE (General Council of French Jews), but these were brought to a halt by the Allied invasion on November 8, 1942.

The extent of German involvement in Algerian affairs is unclear. While the WANNSEE CONFERENCE included North African Jews under the heading "France," these Jews did not attract the Germans' attention before the latter's occupation of Tunisia, in November 1942. But account must be taken of the atmosphere created by the antisemitic organizations in Algeria and the existence of dozens of labor camps on the southern border of Morocco, where thousands of Jews—mostly foreigners but including a number of native Jews—were held, having been charged with subversive activities or black-market operations. The Bedeau camp, near the town of Sidi-bel-Abbès, served as a concentration camp for Algerian Jewish soldiers, who had been formed into a special unit, the Groupement de Travailleurs Israélites (Jewish Workers' Group), and subjected to exceptionally hard forced labor under the command of Foreign Legion officers.

In general, it may be assumed that the Jews of Algeria, like their French counterparts, thought that German pressure was to blame for the racist laws that were introduced against them. As a result, despite their loss of status, property, and livelihood, they never abandoned their loyalty to France and would not believe that the "Jewish laws" were a French creation. This state of mind also explains the fact that hundreds of Algerian Jews flocked to the underground when it came into being in late 1940. Indeed, the preponderance of Jews in the underground was such that it could well have been regarded as a Jewish organization, although the motivation of those who joined it was in no way "Jewish."

The Algerian resistance movement had its start when a few young Jews, some of them former French army officers, organized into a self-defense unit, under the cover of a sports club. At the same time, unconnected with the "sports club," other Jewish resistance groups sprang up in Algiers and Oran, whose membership included scions of the Jewish social elite, headed by members of the Aboulker family in Algiers. In the course of 1942 the various Jewish organizations formed a link and established contact with some French politicians and senior officers of the French secret service, who had come to Algeria on their own initiative in order to prepare the ground for resuming the fight against the Germans. Though this group apparently shared Pétain's ideology and political views, the Jewish underground accepted their authority since it was only through them that it could establish contact with the United States.

At the end of October 1942 the Americans informed the Algerian resistance of their planned landings on the shores of Algeria and Morocco, requesting them to take an active part in the operation by seizing the strategic points in Algiers, Oran, and Casablanca in order to neutralize them for several hours until the Allied forces could make their entry into these cities. In Oran and Casablanca the resistance organizations failed completely in this mission, but in Algiers the underground accomplished its task in full, attaining all of its objectives efficiently and with perfect discipline. Of the 377 resistance members who seized control of Algiers during the night of November 7–8, 315 were Jews. The plan had been for the United States advance team to enter Algiers within two hours of the landings, but fierce opposition by the French coast guard delayed its arrival until the evening of November 8, leaving the resistance to fend for itself. However, the fighters held out, at great risk to their lives, maintaining control of most of the points they had seized for the whole day that elapsed before the Americans appeared on the scene.

In the meantime, the Americans entered into negotiations concerning a cease-fire with Adm. François DARLAN, the designated successor to Pétain, who had arrived in Algiers two days earlier under mysterious circumstances. Darlan agreed to the cease-fire, but only after he had been given assurances by the Americans that the Allies would permit the Vichy regime to stay and would not interfere with internal affairs in North Africa, such as the "Jewish question." Darlan was then appointed High Commissioner of North Africa. For the short while that he held that post—until he was murdered, on December 24, 1942—Darlan remained loyal to Pétain, adamantly refusing to abolish any of the racist laws. The Americans kept the agreement they had signed with Darlan and lent their protection to a regime that, in its ideology and practice, violated the principles of democracy. The Jews—especially those who had been members of the resistance—were sorely disappointed, having expected that the American conquest of Algeria would have an immediate beneficial effect on their condition. Not only did the Vichy regime stay in office, but in many places attacks on Jews became even more frequent, since they were now also accused of collaborating with the Americans.

Anti-Jewish incitement reached new heights in the wake of Darlan's assassination. All the former leaders of the Jewish underground were arrested on the charge of collaborating with the assassins. To their great surprise, the Jewish prisoners now found out that the order for their arrest had been given by none other than their former leaders in the resistance—the senior French officers who, on the day after the American invasion, had taken their places in Darlan's Vichy-style administration.

News of the Jewish leaders' arrest was brought to the knowledge of Robert Murphy, President Franklin D. ROOSEVELT's personal representative in North Africa. The American diplomat was preoccupied with his search for a replacement for Darlan and did not want the affair reported in the United States press. Newspapers were already expressing misgivings about the American moves in the area and publishing eyewitness accounts and background articles on the condition of the Jews in Algeria and the sufferings of concentration camp prisoners. Though Jews in the United States were far from indifferent to this state of affairs, they were cautious in expressing their dissatisfaction with the continued presence of the Vichy regime in North Africa, lest their attitude be misused by American isolationist elements. Their apprehension increased when Gen. Henri Giraud, Darlan's successor, appointed as governor-general of Algeria Marcel Peyrouton, who as minister of the interior in Pétain's first cabinet had signed the racist laws issued by Vichy in October 1940.

Pressure by the American media forced the United States government to ask Giraud to abolish the racist laws. Giraud agreed, but only when it was made clear to him that refusal to do so might mean that the military aid he had requested would be denied. Giraud annulled the racist laws on March 14, 1943, but on the same day he reinstated the law that had abolished the Crémieux Decree, on the pretext that the decree discriminated against Algeria's Muslims.

Thus, within a period of less than three years, Algerian Jews were twice deprived of their citizenship—once by Pétain and once by Giraud. The "repeal of the repeal" of the Crémieux Decree aroused much resentment among the Jewish organizations in the United States, leading them to renew their fight against the Giraud regime with increased vigor. While the United States government went out of its way to protect Giraud, Gen. Charles de GAULLE lent a receptive ear to the Jewish organizations, since his rivalry with Giraud over who was to be the leader of the struggle for the liberation of France was then at its peak. It was obvious that the outcome of the struggle between the two generals would have an impact on the fate of the Crémieux Decree. The Gaullist movement's growing strength inside France, however, dampened its enthusiasm to restore political rights to the Jews of Algeria. When de Gaulle took over in Algeria, on May 3, he refrained from officially canceling his predecessor's decision. Not until three months had passed from the date of that decision without any regulations being issued for its implementation, as required by law, did de Gaulle take advantage of this legal loophole to inform the leaders of Algerian Jewry that the Crémieux Decree was again in force. It took many more months, however, for the last vestiges of the Vichy period to disappear. Late in 1944 dozens of Jewish refugees were still imprisoned in concentration camps, and it took even longer to purge the Algerian administration fully of all the pro-Vichy elements, who, as long as they were in office, persisted in treating the Jews as though nothing had changed since November 1942.

BIBLIOGRAPHY

Abitbol, M. *North African Jewry during World War II.* Detroit, 1989.

Amipaz-Zilber, G. *The Jewish Underground in Algeria, 1940–1942.* Tel Aviv, 1983. (In Hebrew.)

Ansky, M. *Les Juifs d'Algérie du Décret Crémieux à la Libération.* Paris, 1963.

Danan, Y. M. *La vie politique à Alger de 1940 à 1944.* Paris, 1963.

Murphy, R. *Diplomat among Warriors.* London, 1964.

Szajkowski, Z. *The Jews and the French Foreign Legion.* New York, 1975.

MICHEL ABITBOL

ALIYA BET ("illegal" immigration), entry into Palestine during the period of the British Mandate by other than the official way—a permit issued by legal representatives of the authorities. The phenomenon was given different designations, each expressing a value judgment: (1) Aliya Bet (*aliya* in Hebrew means "immigration," and *bet* refers to "B," illegal, in contrast to "A," or legal, immigration); (2) *ha'apala* (lit., "climb," "struggle upward"); (3) independent immigration; and (4) illegal immigration. The first three were designations used by Zionist elements; two of them, Aliya Bet and Ha'apala, were current within the Labor movement and became the idiom in spoken and written Hebrew, while the third designation, "independent immigration," was used by the Revisionists and their activists. The fourth, "illegal immigration," was the term used by the British Mandatory authorities. The immigrants who entered Palestine by this method were called Ma'apilim (from Ha'apala) by the Jews in Palestine and "illegal immigrants" by the British.

There were several patterns of Aliya Bet: immigration undertaken by individuals on their own initiative, and immigration initiated by Zionist organizations that encouraged and assisted their members. The majority of these immigrants traveled by boat and tried to land in Palestine without being detected. The boats used for this purpose were antiquated freighters that were no longer in regular use; living conditions on these boats were difficult and at times quite unbearable. Some immigrants journeyed by an overland route, from eastern Europe to countries bordering on Palestine, and then tried to cross the border. Other "illegals" were persons who had entered Palestine legally, as tourists, and stayed on, without obtaining a residence permit from the authorities. Still another method was to use legal entry permits without being entitled to them, for example, through fictitious marriages contracted for this purpose, or by using forged entry visas.

All Aliya Bet movements had a common origin—a situation in which large numbers of Jews felt a growing urgency to depart from their countries of residence, at a time when the rate of authorized immigration did not keep up with the demand. The pressure for such departure, for political or economic reasons, became so strong that people were willing to take enormous risks, including the risk of running afoul of the law. Preceded by spontaneous attempts by individuals, organized Aliya Bet provided ideological motivation for people to leave their homes and make their way to Palestine by this method, and gave it the dimensions of a mass movement. Of the 530,000 immigrants who entered Palestine up to the establishment of the state of Israel, 25 percent—some 130,000 persons—came by way of Aliya Bet. Of these, 104,000 arrived by sea, in 136 boats; 52,000 of these were caught by the British and deported to internment camps in Cyprus (*see* CYPRUS DETENTION CAMPS).

Before World War II. Aliya Bet began before World War I with the modern settlement of Palestine by Jews, when the Ottoman rulers were obstructing the entry of Jews into the country. When World War I ended, the British military authorities who were then in control did not permit entry to anyone who had not lived in the country before the war, and this compelled a large number of young Jews to organize and enter Palestine in defiance of existing regulations. It is estimated that under the postwar military administration (1917 to 1920), two thousand immigrants entered Palestine either by posing as prewar residents or by jumping the border.

The first immigration law, enacted in the summer of 1920, established the criteria for the admission of immigrants to Palestine. In the summer of 1922, definitive laws and regulations on immigration were issued, and these remained in force until the publication of the British WHITE PAPER of May 1939, which severely restricted Jewish immigration. From 1922 on, the number of immigrants to be admitted into the country was an issue that put a constant strain on the relations between the British Mandatory government and the Zionist political leaders. In the 1930s, the authorities approved about one-third of the requests for immigration certificates submitted by the Jewish institutions. It was this gap between the number of requests submitted and the number approved by the British, reinforced by the rising pressure by Jews in Europe after the advent of Adolf Hitler to be permitted to emigrate to Palestine, that created the Aliya Bet movement under the British Mandate.

In the 1930s, Aliya Bet was a significant element in the growth of the Jewish population in Palestine. When the first international Jewish sports gathering, the Maccabiah, was held in Palestine in 1932, it attracted more than twenty thousand tourists to the country,

On facing page and above: arrival of the illegal ship *Haumot Hameukhadot* (The United Nations) at Naharia, Palestine, on January 1, 1948. Civilians waited on shore to mingle with the new arrivals in order to prevent them from being easily identified by British soldiers. Those who were caught were loaded onto British military trucks and transported to detention camps. One of the boats used to convey illegal immigrants from ship to shore bore the name of a member of the Ha-Irgun (Revisionist underground), Alexander Rot. [A Living Memorial to the Holocaust—Museum of Jewish Heritage, New York]

and about ten thousand of these visitors remained there after their visas had expired. There was also a rise in the number of fictitious marriages for purposes of immigration, and this ruse made it possible for two people to use one certificate.

In the latter half of the 1930s, most of the immigrants to Palestine arrived by ship. This method, for Aliya Bet purposes, was first employed in 1934 by Polish He-Haluts members in two voyages on a ship named *Vellos,* and by Betar members on a ship named *Union*. In both cases the immigrants were motivated by ideological and social considerations and felt that they could not wait until their turn came to be granted an official certificate.

The plight of Jews in Europe—especially the Nazi persecutions in Germany and Austria and the antisemitism in Poland—drove a growing number among the general Jewish public, as well as members of the Zionist movement and the youth movements, to participate in Aliya Bet in 1937 and 1938. In the summer of 1938, Vienna and Prague, after Warsaw and Berlin, were its centers. During the initial phase, the Aliya Bet ships left from Greek ports, with the immigrants arriving by train; later, the main route was by boat down the Danube, via the Black Sea to the Mediterranean. Aliya Bet was an ideological and social protest movement against the established Zionist leadership (which initially disapproved of this form of immigration) and against the British policy on Jewish immigration to Palestine. It was also a means of escape from Nazi-ruled and other endangered countries, and thus became part of the general movement of Jewish refugees fleeing from central and eastern Europe (*see* REFUGEES, 1933–1945).

By 1939 the Zionist movements had set up their own organizations for Aliya Bet, and the private operators also greatly extended the range of their enterprises. In that year, more than seventeen thousand Jews came to Palestine via Aliya Bet, while only eleven thousand arrived on official immigration permits. The New Zionist Organization (NZO), which had been established by the Revisionists, opened its own Immigration Center, with offices in Paris and London, and in Palestine the Mosad le-Aliya Bet (Organization for Aliya Bet, or Mosad for short) was created jointly by the Jewish Trade Union Federation, the Histadrut, and the underground Jewish defense organization, the Hagana. The two bodies assumed the overall task of organizing and planning Aliya Bet and making the decisions for implementation in various centers of Jewish population. Their emissaries in those centers had the job of selecting and organizing the immigrants, raising the required funds, and obtaining the agreement of the respective local authorities for the Jews to leave or to pass through the country; for this last purpose the emissaries had to cultivate local political elements.

The Immigration Center concentrated its efforts on unifying and organizing the Aliya Bet operations ("independent immigration," in Revisionist terminology) that members of the NZO had established in places with a significant Jewish population. The top leaders of the NZO—including its president, Vladimir JABOTINSKY—participated in establishing the center. In Jabotinsky's view, "independent immigration" represented the Jews' own way of battling Great Britain, and a means of recruiting masses of Jews to the movement that could arouse and activate the Zionist youth's potential. In fact, he had been propagating these ideas since 1932. The NZO leaders thought that the Immigration Center, by means of an agreed-upon policy, would be able to set up a system that would take into account the conflicting interests of Betar, the underground movement Irgun Tseva'i Le'ummi associated with them, and the Revisionist party, and would fix the order of precedence for their respective candidates for immigration, as well as mediate between the movement's activists in the various centers and coordinate their work. The actual result was that several Revisionist activists who had been organizing immigration—such as Paul Haler, Herman Flesch, and Avraham Stavsky—preferred to continue their work in a private capacity. Some of the activists felt that privately organized immigration was more efficient, and others regarded it as a potential source of considerable financial profit. These different attitudes caused friction between the Immigration Center of the NZO and the "independent immigration" offices of the private activists in the various countries.

Other private persons organized immigration on their own as well. One well-known figure among them was Dr. Baruch Confino, a member of the Zionist movement in Bulgaria, who is credited with having arranged the immigration of 3,000 persons. The Mosad le-Aliya, which took over the work of Aliya Bet from He-Haluts in Poland, operated as a centralized body. It was headed by a Hagana man, Shaul Meirov (later Avigur), who had a number of prominent He-Haluts activists working with him in the Mosad center in Paris. Some of the He-Haluts emissaries from Palestine in Europe became Aliya Bet orga-

The "illegal immigration" ship *Atrato VII*, which sailed from the Romanian port of Constanţa on the Black Sea with 390 Jewish refugees on May 20, 1939. Mosad le-Aliya Bet, the Jewish immigration authority in Palestine, organized the voyage. The ship arrived in Palestinian territorial waters on May 28 and was intercepted by the British navy. [Hagana Archives, Tel Aviv; Beth Hatefutsoth]

nizers in various Jewish communities (Moshe Averbuch-Agami in Vienna, Pino Ginzburg in Berlin, and Joseph Barpal and Ruth Klüger-Aliav in Romania). The candidates for immigration were selected from members of the youth movements and the veteran Zionists in the Jewish communities. The ships were chartered by persons who had this specific assignment, and places were allocated to the various communities on the basis of overall planning, coordinated with the emissaries in the communities. The raising and distribution of funds were also centralized. Most of the immigrants did not pay the full costs of the fare, but well-to-do immigrants from Germany and Austria were asked to pay more than their share, in order to help finance the passage of young people who had no means of their own. This system also came to be adopted by the Revisionist immigration organizers.

The Mosad did not have the full support of the Zionist organization's political leadership (contrary to the all-out support received by the Revisionist Immigration Center from its movement's political leaders). Members of the kibbutz movement, Ha-Kibbutz ha-Meuhad, gave Aliya Bet enthusiastic support, and most of the field operators were recruited from among its members. The labor leaders in the Jewish Agency Executive, such as David BEN-GURION and Eliezer Kaplan, at first were not in favor of Aliya Bet, and even when they changed their stand they differed with the Aliya Bet activists on the aims of the operation and the methods it was to employ. These differences were the result of their political approach, which saw mass immigration as the primary condition for the realization of the Zionist goals—a condition that could be achieved only in cooperation with Great Britain. As long as they believed such cooperation was possible, they were not prepared to give their support to operations that could create friction and sow the seeds of hostility between Palestinian Jewry and the British authorities.

It was only in late 1938 that Ben-Gurion became a supporter of Aliya Bet, after realizing that British policy was undergoing a radical change, switching from support of the Zionist enterprise to accommodation with the Arabs. At that point Ben-Gurion came to regard Aliya Bet as the major instrument that the Jews had at their disposal in the struggle for their future. The shift in the attitude of leading political figures strengthened the hand of those who supported Aliya Bet for moral reasons—saving Jewish lives and Jews' mutual responsibility for one another. This camp was led by the Labor leader, Berl Katznelson, who at the Zionist Congress in August 1939 depicted the refugee wandering from one end of the earth to the other as not only the symbol of Jewish distress, but also the banner and guide of Zionism in action.

Still, considerable opposition to Aliya Bet persisted in the Zionist organization, one of the opponents being Chaim WEIZMANN. Abba Hillel SILVER, the American Zionist leader, also expressed strong opposition to Aliya Bet at the congress. One reason for the continued opposition was the complaints circulating in the Zionist organization about the Revisionist and private Aliya Bet organizers, who were charged with exploiting the refugees' plight for the sake of easy profits.

In World War II. When the war broke out, Aliya Bet had to contend with new problems and uncertainties. Shipowners were expecting that the war would provide easier and more lucrative business opportunities, and they doubled and trebled the price for charters and also failed to keep their commitments. Governments, for their part, restricted the free use of vessels over which they had control. These difficulties, plus a lack of funds and a political reassessment of Aliya Bet, caused Zionist-organized Aliya Bet to slow down, and, in 1941 and 1942, to come to a complete halt.

There were second thoughts about continuing Aliya Bet in a war in which the Jewish people and Britain had an identical interest—to defeat the Nazis. The dilemma facing the Zionist leaders was how both to struggle against Britain and at the same time to cooperate with it. The Nazis were still permitting Jews to emigrate, whereas the British adhered to their tough policy on immigration, prohibited the entry of "enemy aliens," reduced legal immigration to a minimum, and found a new way of punishing the "illegal" immigrants when caught, by deporting them (to MAURITIUS). The quandary meant that no clear policy could be adopted on Aliya Bet, and in the absence of substantive support it became very difficult to cope with the problems involved in the operations. The Mosad made efforts to complete the processing of groups ready to leave, but did not always succeed in doing so. There was the case of the so-called Kladovo Group (Kladovo is a town in Yugoslavia on the Danube River, about 90 miles [145 km] southeast of Belgrade), which had left Reich territory and was stranded in Yugoslavia. The Nazis caught up with them in the fall of 1941 and murdered them on the spot. An example of the conflict, in moral and Zionist terms, between Aliya Bet operations and cooperation with the British was the case of the *Darien*, a ship that Mosad operators had purchased for the Kladovo refugees. In July 1940, when it seemed that the Kladovo Group could not be brought to the ship, the *Darien* was sold to the British, for joint British-Jewish sabotage operations. These operations, however, were delayed. In September 1940 the Mosad operators thought that they should use the ship for Aliya Bet, and they defied orders received from the Hagana chief, Eliyahu Golomb, to hand over the ship to Hagana men who were engaged in joint intelligence and aid operations with the British in Greece. Instead, they put 789 immigrants on board the ship, which reached the shores of Palestine in March 1941. These immigrants, however, were not the ill-fated Kladovo Group for whom the ship had originally been designated.

The leaders of the NZO also looked for ways to cooperate with the British in the war against the Nazis, and they had to face similar moral questions. NZO-organized immigration came to a halt about six months after the outbreak of the war, with the departure of the *Sakarya*, most of whose passengers had been ready to leave since the summer of 1939. The NZO thereafter never resumed "illegal" immigration on an appreciable scale.

"Private enterprise" Aliya Bet also came almost to a complete halt during the war, with the exception of Baruch Confino, who kept on sending boatloads of Jewish refugees from Bulgarian ports. Of the three boats at his disposal, one, the *Rudnichar,* made three successful trips to the shores of Palestine (September, November, and December 1939); another, the *Libertad,* made one such trip (July 1940); the third boat, the *Salvador,* sank in a storm in the Sea of Marmara and most of its 220 passengers drowned. Confino at this point suspended his operations, but he resumed them after the war. The largest group of immigrants to reach Palestine by private enterprise was that organized by Berthold Storfer, acting in behalf of the Vienna Jewish community, with the consent of the Nazi authorities; he dispatched three ships. Between November 1 and November 24, 1940, the three ships, *Pacific, Milos,* and *Atlantic,* arrived at the Haifa port, where they were impounded by the British and their passengers transferred to the *Patria* for deportation to Mauritius. The Hagana, with the help of the immigrants, sabotaged the ship to prevent its departure, but a miscalculation caused the *Patria* to sink, with a loss of 267 lives. The survivors were interned at the Atlit camp near Haifa, and 1,600 of the *Atlantic* passengers were deported to Mauritius on December 9, 1940, where they remained until the end of the war.

During 1942, following the sinking of the STRUMA, the Mosad reorganized its immigration operations. These were resumed in the spring of 1944. The new port of departure was Constanţa on the Black Sea, where the immigrants were put on small freighters, converted for passenger use, that sailed to Turkey. There they were issued immigration permits and resumed their trip, this time by train. The ships that were used did not meet the usual safety standards and could not be insured. They did not sail under the protection of the International RED CROSS or of a neutral country, and had not been assured of safe conduct by the Germans; this meant that they were in danger of warlike action from either side.

The resumption of immigration in this form was the result of a combination of several factors: a clear-cut decision by the Jews of Palestine, once they became aware of the meaning of the "Final Solution," to take up rescue operations; cooperation between Mosad le-Aliya, the representatives of the political department of the Jewish Agency in Turkey, and British intelligence agents; and the joint teams set up by the Jewish communities in Romania, with the help of the Palestinian Jewish representatives in Istanbul (*see* RESCUE COMMITTEE OF THE JEWISH AGENCY IN TURKEY). In addition, the operation benefited from the facts that the downfall of Nazi Germany was clearly drawing near and the United States was now taking political action in behalf of the rescue of Jews. From the British point of view this immigration was legal, in line with a British government decision, in July 1943, to issue an immigration permit to Palestine to any Jewish refugee reaching Turkey.

Up to the end of the war, ten groups took this route, totaling over three thousand persons; most of them were refugees from Poland, Hungary, and Transnistria. Much haggling and struggling went on before the final choice was made of the persons who were to join the trip, since many of those who wanted to felt that this was the only way to save themselves. The guidelines suggested by the Palestine Jewish organization on how the immigrants were to be chosen were not relevant to the actual conditions, and there were cases of persons of means being preferred. One of the ships, the *Mefkura,* sailing in August 1944, was sunk by a Soviet submarine by mistake, and only five of the passengers on board were saved.

In the immediate postwar years, Aliya Bet reached new records, as a result both of the pressure exerted by the She'erit ha-Peletah (Holocaust survivors) and of the excellent organization of the operation, which now enjoyed political support and priority. The Mosad le-Aliya, still headed by Shaul Avigur, became a highly efficient body with agents who were highly expert in their work. The ships acquired were manned by volunteers —officers and crews who were members of Palyam (the naval arm of the Hagana's striking force, the Palmaḥ) or Jewish sailors from the Western world (including 200 volunteers from the United States). Well-trained signal personnel on shore and on board the ships monitored the movement of the ships at sea in order to coordinate their time of arrival and ensure the safe landing of the passengers. On shore, experienced people awaited the new arrivals, to help them disembark and to distribute them as quickly as possible among the Jewish settlements, so as to prevent their detection by the British. On a budget of 7 million pounds, the Mosad moved 70,691 of these immigrants to Palestine on sixty-four ships. The British, however, caught most of the boats and deported their passengers to Cyprus.

Aliya Bet became the very heart of Zionist activity. It focused attention on the issue of rehabilitating the survivors of the Holocaust and assuring their future—an issue that had become a moral, political, and economic challenge for the nations of Europe—and presented the Zionist solution as the only possibility, in view of the complex relations between the Jews and European nations in the wake of the Holocaust. Support for Jewish immigration to Palestine became a political issue that enjoyed wide public sympathy and persuaded governments to favor the establishment of a Jewish state, despite Arab opposition. Aliya Bet also became a unifying factor in the Jewish world; it had the support of all the Jewish organizations once it became clear that masses of Jews, survivors of the Holocaust, were longing to get to Palestine. Aliya Bet was capable of fulfilling their desire, in numbers far exceeding the official rate of immigration permitted by the British—a meager 1,500 per month.

Immigration centers were set up all over Europe: in France, Italy, Yugoslavia, Greece, and other Balkan countries, staffed by fifty Mosad emissaries. It was only in 1946, however, that the Aliya Bet operation really resumed on a large scale; up to the end of 1945, only eight boats, with 1,022 passengers, were brought to Palestine in this way. In each Aliya Bet center the *modus operandi* was adapted to local conditions. In Italy, which was the point of departure for about half of all the sailings, the center was headed by Yehudah Arazi and Ada Sereni, who developed their own methods, concentrating on cultivating ties with political leaders, public figures, and intellectuals. In particular, Arazi attached great importance to the political goals of Aliya Bet, and he believed that these would be achieved only if there was an ongoing flow of ships en route to Palestine and if the number of passengers was large enough to impress public opinion.

The principal center of the Mosad's operations was in France. It was to France that Jewish children were brought from the Netherlands and Belgium (where they had been saved, many in convents), and France was the gathering point for Jews from the DISPLACED PERSONS' camps. In order to arrange for them to be able to depart for Palestine, political contacts had to be cultivated, a process in which the Mosad operators made use of the French officials' hostility to the British. Conditions in France for the Mosad's work were more difficult than in Italy, because of the greater efficiency of French central control. The EXODUS 1947 affair was linked to these operations in France, and the positive attitude of the French in that affair was an example of the effectiveness of the Mosad work there. The fate of this ship and its passengers, who were returned to Germany, galvanized world public opinion and dramatized the tragic plight of the Holocaust survivors and their desperate determination to get to Palestine.

Regarding Aliya Bet from eastern and southern Europe, there was concern that countries in these regions would close their borders and prohibit the exit of Jews (as was the case in the Soviet Union); the immigrants had to be ransomed to enable them to leave. Emigration operations from Romania and Bulgaria were complicated and extensive, with twenty-one thousand emigrants leaving these countries in five sailings. Of these, fifteen thousand were passengers on the *Pan Crescent* and *Pan York*, two ships that sailed straight to Cyprus, by prior agreement with the British. In Yugoslavia the Mosad operators had the benefit of sympathy for persecuted Jews among persons who were close to the ruling circles, and this enabled them to channel over eight thousand immigrants through that country, in four sailings.

In August 1946 the British had come to the conclusion that in order to hold down the flow of "illegal immigration" they had to revert to the deportation procedure, and they selected Cyprus as the place to which the "illegals" would be deported. This policy led to fifty-two thousand of the would-be immigrants being deported to Cyprus, from thirty-two ships that had tried to bring them to Palestine. In Cyprus the deportees were held in camps, most of them staying there until after the state of Israel was established.

BIBLIOGRAPHY

Avneri, A. *From Velos to Tauras: The First Decade of Jewish Illegal Immigration to Mandatory Palestine (Eretz Yisrael), 1934–1944.* Tel Aviv, 1985. (In Hebrew.)

Habas, B. *The Gate Breakers.* New York, 1963.

Hadari, Z. V. *Refugees Defeat an Empire: Chapters of Illegal Immigration, 1945–1948.* Tel Aviv, 1986. (In Hebrew.)

Kimche, J., and D. Kimche. *The Secret Roads.* London, 1954.

Ofer, D. *Illegal Immigration during the Holocaust.* Jerusalem, 1988. (In Hebrew.)

Zweig, R. W. *Britain and Palestine during the Second World War.* London, 1986.

DALIA OFER

ALSACE-LORRAINE, two provinces in northeastern FRANCE, bordering on Germany; a historical bone of contention between the two countries. France controlled Alsace-Lorraine during the seventeenth and eighteenth centuries. From 1871 to 1918 the area was held by Germany; in 1919 it reverted to France. It was again in German hands from 1940 until the fall of 1944, when it was returned to France following the Allied conquest.

Jews lived in Alsace-Lorraine from the ninth century. In 1939 the Jewish population was twenty thousand, the largest community being that of Strasbourg (Ger., Strassburg), followed by that of Metz. In the wake of the MUNICH CONFERENCE of September 1938, violent demonstrations took place in Alsace-Lorraine, in the course of which Jewish shops in Strasbourg and other places were attacked. Jewish youth movements in Strasbourg set up a coordinating committee for their struggle against the antisemitic elements. German agents and members of the Nazi party smuggled antisemitic propaganda into Strasbourg, which became a distribution center of such material for all of France. Jewish relief organizations were established in Strasbourg and Metz to facilitate the absorption of Jewish refugees from central and eastern Europe.

When World War II broke out in September 1939 the French authorities evacuated the inhabitants of the border areas, among whom were fourteen thousand Jews. They were moved to the central area of western France, in and around the cities of Poitiers, Limoges, and Périgueux. With the fall of France in June 1940, some five thousand Jews from Alsace-Lorraine fled to southern France, which was not under German occupation. The following month the Germans expelled the remaining Jews of Alsace-Lorraine, and the area was now *judenrein* ("cleansed of Jews").

It was in Strasbourg that Professor August Hirt, director of the Anatomical Institute at the local Reich University, set up a collection of Jewish skulls and skeletons for the study of the theory of race, as authorized by Heinrich HIMMLER. On June 21, 1943, seventy-three Jewish men and thirty Jewish women were moved from AUSCHWITZ to the NATZWEILER-STRUTHOF camp, where they were gassed to death; their corpses were handed over to Hirt's laboratory.

A large percentage of the Jews from Alsace-Lorraine, dispersed over various parts of France, were active in the Jewish resistance organizations. Some two thousand Alsace-Lorraine Jews perished in the Holocaust. When the war ended most of the remaining Jews of Alsace-Lorraine returned to their homes and reestablished Jewish communities and communal institutions.

BIBLIOGRAPHY

Marrus, M. R., and R. O. Paxton. *Vichy France and the Jews.* New York, 1981.

LUCIEN LAZARE

ALTHAMMER, concentration camp in Poland established in mid-September 1944 near Ruda Śląska, a town 10.5 miles (17 km) west of Katowice, as a satellite camp of AUSCHWITZ. There were about five hundred Jewish prisoners in the camp. Most were from the Łódź ghetto, and the rest were from Hungary and France, in addition to a few Greek Jews. The camp also had a small number of "privileged" German prisoners, all of whom were functionaries. The Althammer inmates were employed in the construction of a nearby power station. As a result of the harsh working conditions and starvation, a third of the camp population was sick. The camp commandant, SS-Oberscharführer Josef Mirbeth, acted with great cruelty, torturing the prisoners with his own hands and shooting some to death. On January 19, 1945, four hundred prisoners were put on a death march, in the direction of Gliwice; most of them were killed en route. Of the remainder—those who were sick and had stayed in the camp—the majority were murdered by the Germans before the retreat; the survivors reached the Nordhausen camp in Saxony. A few dozen prisoners succeeded in escaping and were liberated by the Red Army on January 27, 1945.

BIBLIOGRAPHY

Piper, F. "Podoboz Althammer." *Zeszyty Oświęcimskie* 13 (1971): 137–153.

SHMUEL KRAKOWSKI

AMELOT, Jewish organization established in June 1940 to coordinate assistance to the French Jewish community; it was situated in Paris on Rue Amelot, from which it took its name. On June 15, 1940, as the German troops entered Paris, some immigrant Jewish activists—members of the FÉDÉRATION DES SOCIÉTÉS JUIVES DE FRANCE (FSJF), Po'alei Zion, the BUND, and other groups—met and decided to pool their resources and reactivate communal institutions. With the return to Paris of David Rapoport, a central figure in the FSJF before the war, the amalgam was solidified. The FSJF's welfare organization, the Colonie Scolaire, became its center.

Amelot was reluctant to adhere to the Comité de Coordination des Oeuvres Israélites de Bienfaisance (Coordinating Committee of Jewish Welfare Societies), formed under Nazi pressure in January 1941, but it nevertheless joined the committee out of recognition of communal needs. However, increasing Nazi control over the committee led Amelot to resign from it in May 1941. From then on it followed its own line, although it was dependent on the committee.

In May and August 1941, when eight thousand Jewish men were interned, Amelot further extended its relief activities. When the UNION GÉNÉRALE DES ISRAÉLITES DE FRANCE (UGIF) was formed in January 1942, Amelot maintained its independence, with UGIF agreement. Since Amelot was an immigrant-based committee, the July 1942 mass deportations temporarily interrupted its activities, but by August, with the necessary UGIF protection, they were resumed.

Amelot also assisted Jews who had escaped deportation and could not be helped by the UGIF. Disregarding precautions, Amelot, under Rapoport's leadership, hid children and distributed forged papers. In June 1943, Rapoport was arrested and deported. Under Abraham Alpérine, a new leadership was established. Early in 1944, Amelot was a constituent member of the Comité Général de Défense in Paris, which united all Jewish resistance forces and campaigned for the UGIF's closure. Under the FSJF, Amelot maintained itself throughout the war and saved over one thousand children, helped thousands of adults, and through its four canteens distributed thousands of meals. From its inception it followed a policy of self-help, working with Communists and the UGIF when required. It made an important contribution to the survival of the Jews of Paris.

BIBLIOGRAPHY

Adler, J. *The Jews of Paris and the Final Solution.* New York, 1987.

JACQUES ADLER

AMERICAN COMMITTEE FOR CHRISTIAN GERMAN REFUGEES (ACCR), American Protestant relief agency that provided help to Christian refugees from Nazism in the United States. Many Protestants shared the generally apathetic attitude of the American people toward refugees from Nazism, in spite of the fact that one-third of those reaching American shores were Christian refugees who had fled Nazi-dominated countries on account of political, religious, and ethnic persecution. In order to alleviate the distress of German co-religionists by providing immediate relief and resettlement services, the American Committee for Christian German Refugees was established in February 1934. The committee had to struggle for years to maintain its existence, meeting with many disappointments. Because of Christian apathy, even toward the plight of Christian refugees, Jewish organizations came to the rescue of the ACCR in certain crises.

Although given only very limited support by the churches, the committee acted as an arm of the churches, mainly those affiliated with the Federal Council of Churches, for the purpose of refugee relief administration. Possibly owing to its close relationship with the liberal-minded Federal Council, the ACCR failed to gain the support of the conservative theological communities. Even liberal circles did not support the committee, because Protestants thought of themselves in denominational terms (such as Baptists, Methodists, or Lutherans), rather than in general terms, as Protestants or Christians. Therefore, the ACCR, as an interdenominational agency, was unable to attract widespread moral or financial support. Its poor resettlement record—three hundred persons between 1935 and 1945—is a proof of that failure.

Chronic shortage of funds and high overhead resulted in a weak organization with a limited program. However, the report of 1940, the busiest year of the committee, showed certain progress. With an annual income of $226,214 and a staff of thirty-three, the ACCR that year took care of 4,413 migration cases (not all of whom reached the United States), gave vocational advice to 678, granted scholarships to 38 students, located jobs for 256, and retrained 127 refugees.

With the establishment of the Committee on Foreign Relief Appeals in the Churches (1939), and mainly with the foundation of the Federal National War Fund (August 1943), the ACCR's financial problems were largely solved, and it gradually emerged as the nation's first and greatest Christian refugee agency. In the decade from September 1935 to December 1945, it expended $1,481,436 for services to approximately 15,000 refugees from forty-two countries. It gave advice, granted affidavits, secured jobs, settled newcomers, offered vocational training, and sent funds abroad to help European co-religionists. The moral support was sometimes as important as the practical aid. Bearing in mind the strong anti-alien atmosphere, Thomas Mann, a refugee himself, in 1945 summed up the ACCR's achievements, saying that the committee functioned as "the conscience of America."

With the termination of the National War Fund's support and the establishment, in 1946, of the Church World Service, which became the agent of the churches for relief work, there was no justification for the ACCR's continuing existence. Its diminished importance was also attested by the fact that from 1945 it brought into the United States only eight hundred displaced persons. In July 1947 the ACCR was liquidated, its sixty-one staff members were dismissed, and its cases were transferred to the Church World Service.

[*See also* Refugees, 1933–1945.]

BIBLIOGRAPHY

American Committee for Christian German Refugees. *Toward a New Life: Ten Years of Stewardship.* New York, 1945.

Davie, M. R. *Refugees in America.* New York, 1947.

Genizi, H. *American Apathy: The Plight of Christian Refugees from Nazism, 1933–1945.* Ramat Gan, Israel, 1983. See pages 96–136.

Nawyn, W. E. *American Protestantism's Response to Germany's Jews and Refugees, 1939–1941.* Ann Arbor, Mich., 1981. See pages 159–181.

Ross, R. W. *So It Was True: The American Protestant Press and the Nazi Persecution of the Jews.* Minneapolis, 1981.

HAIM GENIZI

AMERICAN FRIENDS SERVICE COMMITTEE (AFSC). The Society of Friends, or Quakers, constitutes one of the smaller religious groups in the United States. In 1933 they numbered 112,000 members. The Quaker belief that God is within every man leads to a respect for all men as individuals, thus precluding a resort to violence and war. Quakers believe that religious experience and social concern are inextricably related.

The American Friends Service Committee was established in 1917 with the dual purpose of giving Quakers an opportunity for constructive service to humanity and a means by which they could find their moral equivalent for military service during World War I. Through Quaker centers in different parts of the world they engaged in relief work, community development, educational programs, and social-action projects.

As its first project, the AFSC conducted a feeding program for 1.2 million German children suffering from World War I. Owing to this relief work, the Friends gained German appreciation, which, along with their nonpartisanship and dedication to human need, elevated them into a position to intervene more efficiently on behalf of victims of persecution than almost any other agency. Even the Nazis treated them with respect.

During the first years of Adolf Hitler's regime, the scope of the AFSC's activities on behalf of refugees was surprisingly small, unlike that of the European Quakers. This was probably the outcome of a dilemma faced by the Quakers as a result of the anti-Jewish measures in Germany. Some feared that supporting the Jewish cause would seriously compromise the Quakers' reputation in Germany. Their close relationship with Friends in Germany, whom they did not wish to offend or harm, also led to inaction. Therefore, American Quakers were almost completely silent publicly with regard to the Nazi anti-Jewish policy.

The institutionalized help of the AFSC appeared only after the KRISTALLNACHT pogrom of November 1938. A Refugee Division was established, with headquarters in New York City, that provided services only in certain fields not provided through other agencies. The Quakers were eager to go "beyond relief into the more far-reaching openings for reconstruction and rehabilitation." Through hostels, American seminars, college workshops, and other educational projects, the AFSC concentrated on orientation and Americanization. These were only small pilot projects that demonstrated to the large relief agencies "the Quaker way" in which refugees should be treated. Although members of the AFSC, under the leadership of Rufus M. Jones as chairman and Clarence E. Pickett as executive secretary, enthusiastically labored on behalf of refugees, the rank and file of Quaker communities in the United States failed to contribute to the cause either financially or by absorbing refugee families.

For the AFSC operations abroad, the picture was quite different. As a "foreign-minded" organization, the Foreign Service Section was much more effective than the Refugee Division. In response to a request from the American Jewish JOINT DISTRIBUTION COMMITTEE (JDC), the Quakers sent a commission to Germany in 1939 to ascertain the exact situation of Jews and Christians and to provide help if necessary. Indeed, from 1933 through the war, the warm relationship between the AFSC and Jewish agencies such as the JDC, HICEM, and OEUVRE DE SECOURS AUX ENFANTS was an example of interfaith cooperation on refugee matters. As a result of the division of work among the relief agencies, the AFSC devoted its major efforts to helping Christian refugees, but Quaker assistance to Jewish refugees in Paris, Marseilles, Lisbon, and Madrid was sometimes crucial. Feeding and rescuing children in France, helping refugees in neutral Portugal, and coordinating the activities of relief agencies in Spain were among the achievements of the AFSC. Over the course of a decade the scope of its services for victims of Nazi persecution was meaningfully expanded, from an expenditure of $17,000 in 1934 to $1,911,300 in 1944, with more than two hundred paid workers and many volunteers.

While during the Hitler era Jews and "non-Aryan" Christians were the main beneficiaries of AFSC help, after 1945 the Quakers focused their attention on helping Germans, Japanese, Indians, and Chinese, among others. Since 1948 the AFSC has been providing relief in Palestinian Arab refugee camps in the Middle East. In appreciation of its relief work for refugees during and after World War II, the AFSC, along with the British Service Council, received the Nobel Peace Prize in 1947.

BIBLIOGRAPHY

Byrd, R. O. *Quaker Ways in Foreign Policy*. Toronto, 1960.

Genizi, H. *American Apathy: The Plight of Christian Refugees from Nazism, 1933–1945*. Ramat Gan, Israel, 1983. See pages 172–214.

Pickett, C. E. *For More than Bread*. Boston, 1953.

Vining, E. G. *Friend of Life: The Biography of Rufus M. Jones*. Philadelphia, 1958.

HAIM GENIZI

AMERICAN JEWISH COMMITTEE (AJC), United States Jewish defense organization founded in 1906 with the aim of protecting the civil and religious rights of Jews anywhere in the world. The committee was oligarchic and until 1931 was limited to sixty members, all of German-Jewish origin and all from the upper socioeconomic stratum of American Jewry. Membership was expanded to 350 in 1931 and to thousands via chapter membership, introduced in 1944.

Cyrus Adler was the committee's president until his death in 1940. He was succeeded by Solomon Marcuse Stroock for one year, and then by Maurice Wertheim, who served until 1943. Wertheim was replaced by Judge Joseph M. Proskauer. Throughout this period, the committee followed a generally non-Zionist line in defining both its internal and American Jewish policies, in opposition to "Diaspora nationalism" and its stance vis-à-vis the Nazi regime. Whereas this policy-making became somewhat more pro-Zionist under Wertheim, it moved in an anti-Zionist direction during the first years of Proskauer's tenure.

The committee's approach to dealing with the Nazis was one of quiet diplomacy, in contrast to the protests and mass demonstrations undertaken by the American Jewish Congress and other organizations in the United States. In 1933 the committee, together with other organizations, approached President Franklin D. ROOSEVELT and Secretary of State Cordell HULL to request a State Department protest (*see* UNITED STATES DEPARTMENT OF STATE) to the German government regarding the treatment of the Jews in Germany. While the two leaders expressed their sympathy, they declined the request.

The committee sought to publicize information on Germany, but attempted to have this information and any protest action dealt with by non-Jews. Therefore, the AJC opposed the anti-Nazi rally sponsored by the American Jewish Congress in March 1933, and refrained from joining similar rallies afterward. Similarly, the committee opposed the anti-Nazi boycott movement (*see* BOYCOTTS, ANTI-NAZI) that developed during the early part of the Nazi regime.

During World War II, the committee maintained its prewar diplomatic policy, but its willingness to participate in joint protests with other groups increased after the United States entered the war in December 1941 and as information regarding the murder of the European Jews reached the United States. For nearly a year, from the late fall of 1942 to the early fall of 1943, the committee cooperated with the American Jewish Congress and other organizations to present current rescue projects and postwar proposals to the government. The AJC was one of eight organizations forming the Joint Emergency Committee on European Jewish Affairs, established in March 1943. This committee submitted a twelve-point rescue proposal to the BERMUDA CONFERENCE and organized mass meetings to inform the public of the Nazis' murder of the Jews.

In April 1943, the AJC agreed to join the AMERICAN JEWISH CONFERENCE to further American-Jewish unity in defining policy in face of the disaster in Europe. However, the conference's September 1, 1943, resolution calling for the establishment of a Jewish commonwealth in Palestine led the committee to withdraw from the conference in October 1943. In protest against this controversial move, 10 percent of its membership resigned from the committee.

The AJC continued its activities relating to postwar Jewish issues, and in 1944 established the Research Institute on Peace and Post-War Problems, directed by Dr. Max Gottschalk, to plan proposals for securing Jewish rights in the postwar world. The committee remained influential in government circles, and was one of the two American Jewish organizations (together with the

American Jewish Conference) designated by the State Department as consultants to the United States delegation at the San Francisco Conference, which founded the United Nations in April 1945. The AJC was also represented at the Paris Peace Conference in 1946.

BIBLIOGRAPHY

Cohen, N. W. *Not Free to Desist: The American Jewish Committee, 1906–1966.* Philadelphia, 1972.

Lazin, F. A. "The Response of the American Jewish Committee to the Crisis of German Jewry, 1933–1939." *American Jewish History* 68/3 (March 1979): 283–304.

DAVID SILBERKLANG

AMERICAN JEWISH CONFERENCE, American Jewish umbrella organization established in August 1943 in an attempt to unite American Jewry for planning Jewish postwar policy. At the initiative of Henry Monsky, the president of B'NAI B'RITH, representatives of thirty-two national Jewish organizations met in Pittsburgh on January 23, 1943, two months after the State Department (*see* UNITED STATES DEPARTMENT OF STATE) had confirmed to Stephen WISE reports of the Nazi plan to kill the European Jews (*see* RIEGNER CABLE). At the Pittsburgh meeting a resolution was made to convene a conference, to be named the American Jewish Assembly, with 500 delegates—375 elected and 12 appointed by cooperating organizations. A three-part agenda was to be addressed: (1) Jewish rights and status in the postwar world; (2) the implementation of Jewish rights regarding Palestine; and (3) the election of a delegation to carry out the assembly's program in cooperation with Jewish representatives around the world. The rescue of European Jewry was added to the agenda in late July of 1943, one month before the American Jewish Conference convened.

The AMERICAN JEWISH COMMITTEE (AJC) and the JEWISH LABOR COMMITTEE, which had declined Monsky's invitation to the Pittsburgh meeting for fear of Zionist domination, joined the conference in April and May, respectively. The effect of the negotiations leading to the AJC's joining was both to expand the conference and to weaken its authority, since complete freedom of action was guaranteed to each participating organization. As a result of these negotiations, the assembly was renamed a conference, in order to avoid Jewish nationalist overtones.

Rescue was the first of the three main topics (rescue, Palestine, and postwar issues) discussed at the five-day conference, but the resulting conclusion was in effect merely a reiteration of several earlier proposals by various American Jewish groups. Whereas the conference's discussion of rescue was lackluster, its treatment of the Palestine issue was electrified by Abba Hillel SILVER's impassioned speech of August 30, which called for the creation of a Jewish state to end "the immemorial problem of our national homelessness, which is the principal source of our millennial tragedy." Silver's passion swept the conference, and on September 1 a resolution calling for a Jewish commonwealth in Palestine was passed by a vote of 477 in favor, 4 against, and 20 abstaining.

The American Jewish Committee withdrew from the conference on October 24, 1943, citing the Palestine resolution as its reason, while other organizations gave only limited cooperation to the conference. The American Jewish Conference never succeeded in unifying American Jewry or in gaining acceptance by the United States government as the representative of American Jewry on rescue, postwar, and Palestine issues. In 1944 the conference was reconvened, and it was subsequently able to exercise limited influence on the United States government and the United Nations on postwar questions. But having failed in its attempt at unity, it gradually diminished its activities and declined in importance until it disbanded in 1949.

BIBLIOGRAPHY

Kohanski, A. S., ed. *The American Jewish Conference: Its Organization and Proceedings of the First Session, August 29 to September 2, 1943.* New York, 1944.

DAVID SILBERKLANG

AMERICAN JEWISH CONGRESS. *See* World Jewish Congress.

AMERICAN JEWISH JOINT DISTRIBUTION COMMITTEE. *See* Joint Distribution Committee.

AMERICAN JEWRY AND THE HOLOCAUST. During the 1930s, when American Jewry was compelled to confront the crisis befalling the Jews of Europe, it lacked organizational cohesiveness and could not speak to power holders with one voice. That internal division partly accounted for its ineffectiveness during the years of the Holocaust. But even had it been unified, it is unlikely that by itself it could have altered wartime priorities, in which the rescue of European Jewry had no place. No American ethnic group possessed the power to alter single-handedly the major priorities of public policy, especially during wartime. Jews, despite antisemitic depictions of them as wielding great behind-the-scenes power, were no exception to this rule.

The disunity within American Jewry was reflected first in its inability to reach a common ground for appraising the threat posed by the advent of the National Socialist regime in Germany in 1933. Organizations like the JEWISH LABOR COMMITTEE, representing the still-powerful elements of the democratic Left anchored in the Jewish labor movement, would have no dealings with the National Socialists. But elements farther to the left slavishly followed the Comintern line, which moved from a united-front strategy to its opposite, a nonaggression pact with Germany, signed in August 1939. The AMERICAN JEWISH

Anti-Nazi demonstration organized by the American Jewish Congress in New York City on May 10, 1933, to protest the Nazi burning of books written by Jewish and non-Jewish authors.

COMMITTEE—which represented the more Americanized, affluent, Germanic elements of the community—shared the erroneous but popular conventional wisdom which held that the responsibilities of power would tame Hitler and that the Germany of Goethe and Heine was only temporarily eclipsed. The committee preferred quiet behind-the-scenes diplomacy to ameliorate the deteriorating condition of German Jewry. In contrast, the American Jewish Congress, which represented the more liberal and relatively less Americanized eastern European Jewish immigrants and their offspring, was convinced that an aroused public opinion could improve the situation, and called for a continuing round of protest rallies. Neither agency's strategy proved effective. The National Socialist regime was as immune to moral suasion as it was to diplomatic.

These defense and community-relations agencies represented different constituencies in the Jewish community. What appeared ultimately as differing political ideologies was really the outer manifestation of different degrees of acculturation. Not only were the political assumptions of the committee and the congress different, but so were their approaches to the tenets of the Jewish faith. The committee was composed of wealthy, assimilated German Jews, who saw Judaism as a religion only. The congress was composed of poor and middle-class, partly acculturated eastern European Jews who, though no longer Orthodox, still saw Judaism as a cultural and "national" community, that is, as an ethos. Such disparities characterized the entire world of American Jewish organizations, so that it is difficult to speak of an American Jewish community in the 1930s and 1940s. The common base in culture, language, and experience that might have engendered such a sense of communalism was not yet in place. Instead, there were small communities loosely grouped together as Jewish. Only in the eyes of the American antisemites and in their rhetoric, which was strident during this period, were the Jews of America a single unified entity.

These constituencies, represented by their organizations, differed on all major issues: the nature of the Nazi threat, the efficacy of a boycott, the centrality of the YISHUV (the Jewish community in Palestine), the apportionment of philanthropic funds, the proper strategy against the 1939 British WHITE PAPER restricting immigration to Palestine, the desirability of a Jewish army, and even the advisability of Jews, as a group, advocating the removal of restrictive barriers to immigration into the United States. There were also considerable differences on domestic political issues generated by the welfare-state program and the foreign policy of the New Deal.

Voluntary Organizations. At the same time, changes developed in the 1920s in the way the community was led and how it influenced public policy. In the free voluntaristic environment of America, it was always difficult to say who was being represented by the various Jewish organizations. They had no legal basis for their actions, and their leaders operated in the capacity of interested individuals. Earlier, in the first part of the century, men like Louis Marshall, Jacob Schiff, and Justice Louis Brandeis had assumed leadership positions by means of these organizations and were so recognized by officials of the American government, who spoke to the Jewish community through them. During the 1930s this pattern changed, as many nominal Jews gained high places in the Roosevelt administration because of their prominence in one of the elite groupings of American society: the law establishment, organized labor, the business community, the news media, the universities, and the political parties themselves. Men like Sidney Hillman, a labor leader; Samuel Rosenman, a lawyer involved in Democratic politics; Justice Felix Frankfurter; Henry MORGENTHAU, Jr., who began his career with Franklin D. ROOSEVELT in New York state politics; and Herbert Lehman, an investment banker and governor of New York, were often marginally Jewish and sometimes unhappily so. Earlier leaders, raised in a more intact Jewish environment, had had no doubt about the responsibilities to the Jewish interest that wealth and position assigned to them. The newer people who had reached the top during the Roosevelt period considered themselves Americans who happened to be Jewish. They would not risk their careers for a Jewish need. Yet it was through these people, who were only tenuously connected to the Jewish community, that the needs of American Jewry were ad-

American Zionist leaders at the British embassy in Washington to protest against the White Paper (1940). (1) Solomon Matz; (2) Nellie Ziv; (3) Leon Gellman; (4) Isadore Breslau; (5) Solomon Goldman; (6) Hayim Greenberg; (7) Stephen S. Wise; (8) Louis Segal; (9) Herman Hollander; (10) Israel Goldstein. [Keren Hayesod–United Israel Appeal, Jerusalem]

dressed by the government. The amount of cooperation they gave varied with time and circumstance, but, except in the case of Morgenthau, it was rarely sufficient to fill the need. In a real sense the American Jewish community was leaderless, since people like Rabbi Stephen S. WISE could speak to the administration only through these nominal spokespersons. How different the case might have been is illustrated by the actions of Morgenthau in using his influence to establish the WAR REFUGEE BOARD, which marked the zenith of the American rescue effort in 1944.

Yet the picture was not totally gloomy. Despite its low level of leadership, the community was able to unify for limited objectives. The Jewish agenda was eventually made known to Roosevelt, and in the area of philanthropy a tenuous unity was achieved when the United Jewish Appeal was established in 1939. Most importantly, the American Jewish JOINT DISTRIBUTION COMMITTEE, known in the Jewish world as "the Joint," which was established in 1914 to extend relief to Jewish communities abroad, maintained the apolitical character mandated in its charter and was thereby able to avoid the contention dividing the remainder of the highly politicized community. It did loyal service for the beleaguered Jewish community, even providing supplemental allotments of kosher food for Palestinian Jews serving in the British army. At the same time the Joint, working through proxy agencies in Europe, financed the rescue and sheltering of thousands of Jews in the neutral countries. It was in philanthropy and rehabilitation rather than politics and power that the strength of American Jewry lay.

Economic Depression. The Great Depression and the domestic political and social condition it brought in its wake, rather than the disunity within American Jewry, were the principal factors in the Roosevelt administration's response to the Holocaust. The depression was the major preoccupation of government during the 1930s.

During the critical years between 1937 and 1941, just before America entered the war, the economy was still in decline. That condition not only caused policymakers to enforce the restrictive immigration laws, which were administered to curtail the flow of refugees, but it also created intergroup tensions within American society that made the role of rescue advocates more difficult.

The strident antisemitism of the 1930s traumatized the Jews of America. It had a paralytic effect that even the new visibility of Jews in high places in the Roosevelt administration did not allay. Many believed that the antisemitic rantings of demagogues like Gerald L. K. Smith and Father Charles Coughlin, who spoke to millions over the airwaves, were a portent that "it could happen here." As a group the Jews were emerging from the depression faster than any other ethnic group in the nation. This rapid recovery generated envy and resentment, especially among the Irish, who controlled the hierarchy of the Catholic church. The Jews had been welcomed into the ethnic urban coalition on which the strength of the Roosevelt administration was based, but within that coalition all was not in harmony. Without the support of key elements of that coalition, which might amplify Jewish political influence, the sheltering and rescue of European Jewry, a major item on the Jewish agenda, could not be achieved. Moreover, the antisemitism of the 1930s awakened the defense instinct of Jewish organizations like the American Jewish Committee, which channeled a great deal of energy and funds into fighting the domestic enemy and proportionately less into alleviating the danger faced by European Jewry. It was, of course, far more possible to influence opinion and policies at home than it was abroad.

Intracommunity disunity and strife were partly alleviated when news of the "FINAL SOLUTION" was received in the fall of 1942. But the AMERICAN JEWISH CONFERENCE, which was organized in 1943 by the major Jewish organizations to impose a policy of unified action, at least for limited objectives, foundered on the rift of community strife. The role of the BERGSON GROUP became a focal point of subsequent Holocaust dialogue.

The Bergson Group. It is too early to give a fair verdict on whether the activities of the Bergson group helped or hindered the rescue effort. The "Bergson boys," so called after their leader, Peter Bergson (a pseudonym of Hillel Kook), differed from other sources of disunity in that they were a group of Zionist Revisionists who came to the United States from Palestine, rather than an indigenous product of the American Jewish community. Under several different names, the group variously advocated the creation of a Jewish army of stateless and Palestinian Jews and a militant rescue program based on the strategy of separating the rescue issue from the issue of establishing a Jewish homeland in Palestine. The second issue was the centerpiece of the Zionists' BILTMORE RESOLUTION (May 1942), adopted by the American Jewish Conference in 1943.

The Bergson group never became a mass organization, but it skillfully utilized the media and cultivated political leaders to make its program known. It demonstrated a flair for publicity that became an annoyance to the mainline organizations. They tried to silence the new organization, and in one instance, Dr. Nahum GOLDMANN, acting for the mainline Zionist organizations, proposed to government officials that the group be deported to Palestine. So bitter did the strife become that it was carried to the secular press by means of expensive full-page advertisements in which each party accused the other of everything from draft dodging to misuse of funds.

Some historians believe that in their misunderstanding of how American Jewry operated and was managed, especially the notion of having a democratic mandate, the Bergson group aggravated disunity. Its rescue program was in any case mostly beyond the realm of political possibility. But there are others who think that it was precisely organizations like the Bergson group and the ultra-Orthodox Agudat Israel that had a more realistic understanding of the disaster. They saw the threat better because they were not locked into the secular assumptions of indigenous agencies. They understood that a "business-as-usual" attitude was not appropriate, given the scale of the catastrophe. Such researchers point out that virtually every step for rescue, including finally the creation of a special government agency with the specific objective of rescuing Jews (the War Refugee Board), was suggested and then initiated by the Bergson group. Whatever the case, the bitter conflict stands today as a monument to the tragedy of the American Jewish posture during the Holocaust.

Any fair examination of the role of American Jewry during that time must take great care not to read the contemporary condition of relative coherence and effectiveness back into the past. This is a comparatively new development, which, ironically, was accelerated by the bitter lesson that American Jews learned about the high price of disunity.

The basic truths of American politics have not been altered. One of the most basic is that a minority ethnic group or special-interest group may have "a voice but not a veto" in the shaping of public policy. During the years between 1933 and 1945, American Jewry had such a voice. Its message to decisionmakers was sometimes muddled, but the fact that it desperately wanted its European brethren to be saved was understood. The steps it proposed were interpreted as an interference with the major American aim, which was to win the war, and were rejected.

BIBLIOGRAPHY

Bauer, Y. *American Jewry and the Holocaust: The American Jewish Joint Distribution Committee, 1939–1945.* Detroit, 1981.

Bauer, Y. *Out of the Ashes: The Impact of American Jewry on Post-Holocaust Jewish Europe.* Oxford, 1989.

Feingold, H. L. "Courage First and Intelligence Second: The American Jewish Secular Elite, Roosevelt, and the Failure to Rescue." *American Jewish History* 72/4 (June 1983): 424–460.

Feingold, H. L. *The Politics of Rescue: The Roosevelt Administration and the Holocaust, 1938–1945.* New York, 1982.

Wyman, D. S. *The Abandonment of the Jews: America and the Holocaust, 1941–1945.* New York, 1984.

HENRY L. FEINGOLD

AMERICAN LITERATURE ON THE HOLOCAUST. *See* Literature on the Holocaust: United States.

AMERICAN PRESS AND THE HOLOCAUST. The treatment accorded by the American press to the destruction of the Jews during World War II can best be described as a "sidebar," the name given by journalists to a story that is ancillary to the main story. The press coverage of the Nazi persecution of the Jews paralleled United States policy regarding refugee rescue. It was not an issue of primary importance. The press's behavior reflected the United States' attitude of "rescue through victory." It was relatively rare for more than the isolated paper to call for action to assist Jews.

A great deal of information, including that about the "FINAL SOLUTION" and the systematic destruction of the Jews, was available long before the end of the war. Practically no aspect of the Holocaust remained unknown by 1945. However, significant information was often buried on the inside pages of newspapers. For instance, the June 1942 announcement that two million Jews had been killed as a result of planned annihilation was placed at the bottom of page 6 of the *Chicago Tribune* and given thirteen lines. The story was treated similarly by other major papers. Many readers probably missed this story and similar ones published well inside the paper. Those readers who did see it had cause to assume that the editors did not really believe it; had they believed it, a reader might have reasoned, they would have accorded it more prominent placement.

From the beginning of the Nazi regime, the press in the United States generally failed to take Hitler's prewar and, in certain cases, wartime threats against Jews seriously. It generally did not grasp that ANTISEMITISM was a, if not the, keystone of Nazism. Consequently, what was done to the Jews was often attributed to opportunistic and political motives or to war-related privations.

American reporters who were in Germany could transmit reports until December 1941 (some reporters were repatriated only in May 1942). Though their movements in Germany were stringently circumscribed, they were still able to send out significant information. Some reporters went to the railway stations in order to listen to the conversations of soldiers on their way home from the front. These reporters always faced the threat of expulsion.

After the United States entered the war, news of the fate of European Jewry was released primarily by governments-in-exile or Jewish sources. The press was inclined to discount this news because it came from "interested parties," that is, the victims. Ironically, news released by the perpetrators was treated with far greater credulity than that released by the victims, as was the case with the LIDICE story.

During World War I, reporters had been told atrocity stories about the Germans. These stories, which were the products of propagandists' imagination, had left their legacy. In World War II, reporters doubted the reports of German atrocities because they seemed too similar to exaggerated World War I reports. Sometimes reporters in Europe believed the news, while editors and publishers in the United States did not. Moreover, the number of victims made it more plausible for the press to dismiss the news as "beyond belief." Stories detailing the deaths of several hundred were sometimes given more credence than reports of the deaths of millions.

The press's behavior can be explained partly by the magnitude of the numbers, the absence of "independent" eyewitnesses, the inability to obtain confirmation from "impartial" sources, and the experience with World War I atrocity stories. Even when the news was confirmed by the Allies, reports were still buried in small articles on inside pages. The government's desire to ignore the story also kept the press from focusing on it.

While the unprecedented nature of the events made it easier, particularly at the outset, to discount this kind of news, by 1943 and certainly by the time of the destruction of Hungarian Jewry in 1944, a great deal of evidence had become available. Most reporters seemed to know about the Holocaust, and some papers published editorials lamenting what was happening. But they generally maintained their practice of placing the stories in inconspicuous places and reacting dispassionately. It is impossible, of course, to determine whether increased press attention would have prompted the government to follow a different policy.

Many Americans, including much of the press, felt that the Jews were continuously "wailing" about their fate and demanding special attention. Ironically, early reports sometimes received more attention than did later, more horrifying news of death and atrocities. By mid-1943 the news of the persecution of the Jews was regarded as an "old story," and therefore most newspapers carried it on inside pages.

There were, however, newspapers and magazines that pursued the story of the fate of the Jews with persistence and energy. Among them were a disproportionate number of liberal publications, including *P.M.*, *The New Republic*, *The Nation*, *Commonweal*, and the *New York Post*, as well as the liberal journalists Dorothy Thompson, William Shirer, Arthur Koestler, Sigrid Schultz, Freda Kirchwey, I. F. Stone, Max Lerner, and Alexander Uhl. The Hearst papers also focused on the story when they became strong supporters of the BERGSON GROUP, and repeatedly demanded action on behalf of the Jews. In marked contrast to the behavior and reaction of the general press, the Jewish press in the United States believed the stories that were coming from Europe and treated the news with urgency and concern.

BIBLIOGRAPHY

Laqueur, W. *The Terrible Secret: An Investigation into the Suppression of Information about Hitler's "Final Solution."* London, 1980.

Lipstadt, D. E. *Beyond Belief: The American Press and the Coming of the Holocaust, 1933–1945.* New York, 1986.

Wyman, D. *The Abandonment of the Jews: America and the Holocaust, 1941–1945.* New York, 1984.

DEBORAH E. LIPSTADT

AMERICAN ZIONIST EMERGENCY COUNCIL, coordinating body of United States Zionist organizations, originally (1939) called the Emergency Committee for Zionist Affairs. From January 1942 its name was the American Emergency Committee for Zionist Affairs, and from the fall of 1942, the American Zionist Emergency Council. The council was created by the Zionist Executive on the outbreak of World War II to represent the latter in the United States, given the possibility that restrictions might be placed on the activity of the Zionist leadership in London and Jerusalem as a result of the war.

One of the council's main tasks was to convince the American public of the centrality of Palestine in the future of the Jewish people. Its founding members were the senior Zionist leaders of America and representatives of the four major American Zionist bodies: the Zionist Organization of America, the Hadassah Women's Zionist Organization, the Labor Zionists, and Mizrachi, the religious Zionist movement. From 1939 to 1941, the council had no strong leadership and encountered severe organizational difficulties. It was most hesitant in its political activity against the British 1939 WHITE PAPER, which had restricted Jewish immigration to Palestine and land purchase there; and during the deportation of "illegal" Jewish immigrants to MAURITIUS. At this time the United States was still neutral, and the council shied away from publicly supporting the Zionist demand for the establishment of a Jewish army to combat the Nazis.

The Emergency Council did not focus its efforts on activity for the Jews persecuted under Nazi rule. By agreement among the American Zionists, this task was assumed in the main by the American Jewish Congress, most of whose members were Zionists and whose leaders, especially Stephen S. WISE, were heads of the Emergency Council. The council dealt only with problems related to Palestine and the Zionist movement, such as rescue immigration. Extended arguments with the American Jewish JOINT DISTRIBUTION COMMITTEE on financing such immigration led at times to delays and failures. In the winter of 1940 the Zionists of America were asked to raise the sum of $20,000 for purchasing a ship to transport to Palestine 1,150 young Jews stranded at Kladovo, Yugoslavia, on the frozen Danube River. The Emergency Council failed in this task, and the refugees were eventually massacred by the Germans.

In the area of rescuing Zionist activists from occupied Europe by obtaining immigration visas to the United States, the Emergency Council was forestalled by the JEWISH LABOR COMMITTEE and the VA'AD HA-HATSALA (Rescue Committee) of the Union of Orthodox Rabbis of the United States and Canada. Several Zionist activists were saved as a result of a change in the UNITED STATES DEPARTMENT OF STATE's visa policy. On the other hand, the Emergency Council financed the expenses of about one thousand agricultural pioneers from VILNA who immigrated to Palestine by way of the Soviet Union.

After the sinking of the STRUMA in February 1942, the Emergency Council sent protest cables to President Franklin D. ROOSEVELT and Prime Minister Winston CHURCHILL, but it did not organize demonstrations, since the British embassy had warned that it would see this as a "declaration of war against Great Britain."

In 1942 and 1943, the council participated in protest meetings organized by American Jewry against the "FINAL SOLUTION," but these activities had little influence on the events in Europe. Before the AMERICAN JEWISH CONFERENCE convened in August and September 1943, extensive discussions were held in the council. It had failed as an effective leadership for American Zionists, and even Chaim WEIZMANN, president of the World Zionist Organization, concluded that with its existing composition and structure, the council was not suited to political activity on the required scale. A reorganization was undertaken, and the American Zionist leader Rabbi Abba Hillel SILVER was appointed head of the board of directors of the council. The Holocaust of European Jewry was discussed at the American Jewish Conference, but no steps were resolved to further rescue work, and the debates focused on the postwar program for a Jewish commonwealth in Palestine.

Immediately after the war, under Silver's leadership, the Emergency Council became a pressure group. In the wake of the Holocaust, it waged a political struggle between 1945 and 1948, emphasizing the obligation of the United States to guarantee a home for the Holocaust survivors in a sovereign Jewish state. Despite the State Department's refusal to comply with the Zionist demands, the council convinced a large sector of American public opinion of the justification of these demands. The council continued assisting the "illegal" immigration of survivors to Palestine as well as the struggle for a Jewish state until the latter was established on May 15, 1948. In 1949, the Emergency Council was reorganized as the American Zionist Council.

BIBLIOGRAPHY

Halperin, S. *The Political World of American Zionism*. Detroit, 1961.

Silverberg, R. *If I Forget Thee O Jerusalem*. New York, 1970.

Urofsky, M. I. *American Zionism from Herzl to the Holocaust*. Garden City, N.Y., 1975.

MENAHEM KAUFMAN

ANCESTRAL HERITAGE. *See* Ahnenerbe.

ANDRÉ, JOSEPH (1908–1973), Belgian abbot who helped to rescue hundreds of Jewish children. In liaison with the Comité de Défense des Juifs, an underground Jewish organization searching for secure hiding places for Jews in distress, Abbé André coordinated his rescue activities out of his parish office, which was located next to the German military headquarters in Namur.

Abbé André found hiding places for many Jews. He kept an eye on all Jews whom he had directed to secure shelters. If convinced that a certain place had become unsuitable or that the treatment given was inadequate, he immediately took steps to have the Jew transferred to a new location. His role was especially significant in the rescue of children.

Traveling from place to place, he implored at monasteries, convents, and private homes that they take Jewish children under their protective wings. It did not take long for the Gestapo to realize that Abbé André was frustrating its designs for the deportation of all Belgian Jews, and they trailed his movements. He eventually became a marked man and had to go into hiding until the liberation of Namur by the United States Army in September 1944.

Abbé Joseph André, standing in the front row, fourth from the right. He is shown here with the people he saved during the Holocaust, at a tree-planting ceremony on October 30, 1968, at Yad Vashem, when he received his medal and scroll as a "Righteous among the Nations."

He then undertook the arduous task of gathering the children and returning them to their parents or to Jewish organizations. André never thought of trying to convert the children. On the contrary, he always emphasized the duty of maintaining every person's own faith, to the extent that many children under his care knew the "Hatikvah" (the Jewish national anthem).

Abbé Joseph André was recognized as one of the "RIGHTEOUS AMONG THE NATIONS" by YAD VASHEM in 1968.

BIBLIOGRAPHY

Friedman, P. *Their Brothers' Keepers*. New York, 1957.

MORDECAI PALDIEL

ANIELEWICZ, MORDECAI (1919 or 1920–1943), commander of the WARSAW GHETTO UPRISING. Anielewicz was born into a poor family living in a Warsaw slum quarter; he graduated from the Laor Jewish secondary school and joined the Zionist Ha-Shomer ha-Tsa'ir movement, where he distinguished himself as an organizer and a youth leader.

On September 7, 1939, a week after the outbreak of the war, Anielewicz fled from Warsaw and, together with the senior members of his movement, made his way to eastern Poland, assuming that the Polish forces would establish their defense line there. On September 17, however, eastern Poland was occupied by the Soviet army. Anielewicz reached the southern part of the Soviet-occupied area and tried to cross into Romania and establish a route for Jewish youth trying to get to Palestine. He was caught by the Soviets and put in jail; when he was released, he decided to return to Warsaw—by then under German occupation—and on the way he stopped at many towns and cities, visiting the Jewish communities. He stayed in Warsaw for a short while only and left for Vilna, which by then had been incorporated into Lithuania. It contained a large concentration of refugees from Warsaw, among them members of the youth movements and political parties. Anielewicz called on his fellow Ha-Shomer ha-Tsa'ir members to send a team of instructors back to German-occupied Poland, where they would resume the movement's educational and political activities in the underground. He and his friend Mira Fuchrer set an example by being the first to volunteer for this assignment.

By January 1940, Anielewicz had become a full-time underground activist. As the leader of the Ha-Shomer ha-Tsa'ir underground movement, he set up cells and youth groups, organized their activities, helped publish an underground newspaper, arranged meetings and seminars, and made frequent illegal trips outside Warsaw, visiting communities and his movement's chapters in the provincial ghettos. He also found time to study for himself, especially Hebrew, and read much history, sociology, and economics. It was in this period that, in his attempts to comprehend the situation, he crystallized his views, giving them expression in lectures and in articles that he published in the underground press.

Under the impact of the first reports of the mass murder of Jews in the east, following the German invasion of the Soviet Union in June 1941, Anielewicz revised his policy and concentrated on the creation of a self-defense organization in the ghetto. His first efforts to establish contacts with the Polish underground forces who were loyal to the POLISH GOVERNMENT-IN-EXILE in London were unsuccessful. In March and April 1942 he joined others in the formation of the Antifascist Bloc; the bloc, however, did not fulfill the expectations of its Zionist components, and after a wave of arrests, including those of Communist activists in the bloc, it ceased to exist.

Mordecai Anielewicz.

At the time of the mass deportation from Warsaw in the summer of 1942, Anielewicz was staying in Zagłębie (the southwestern part of Poland, which had been incorporated into Germany). There he worked at transforming the underground youth movements into an armed resistance movement. On his return to Warsaw after the mass deportation, he found that only 60,000 of Warsaw's 350,000 Jews were left in the ghetto, and that the small ŻYDOWSKA ORGANIZACJA BOJOWA (Jewish Fighting Organization; ŻOB) in the ghetto lacked arms and was in a dire situation, having suffered failures and lost members. Anielewicz embarked upon a determined drive to reorganize and reinvigorate the ŻOB and achieved rapid results; following the mass deportation, there was far more support in the ghetto than previously for the idea of armed resistance and its practical organization. Most of the existing Jewish underground groups now joined the ŻOB, and a public council, consisting of authorized representatives, was established in support of the ŻOB (the Żydowski Komitet Narodowy, or Jewish National Committee, and the Coordinating Committee, the latter also including the BUND). In November 1942 Anielewicz was appointed commander of the ŻOB. By January 1943 several groups of fighters, consisting of members of the pioneering Zionist youth movements, had been consolidated, contact had been established with the ARMIA KRAJOWA (Home Army) command, and a small quantity of arms had been obtained from the Polish side of the city.

On January 18, 1943, the Germans launched the second mass deportation from the Warsaw ghetto. Caught unawares, the ŻOB staff was unable to meet in order to decide on what action to take in response, but in one part of the ghetto the armed groups of ŻOB fighters decided to act on their own. There were two foci of ŻOB resistance, with Anielewicz commanding the major street battle. The fighters deliberately joined the columns of deportees and, at an agreed signal, attacked the German escorts at the corner of Zamenhofa and Niska streets, while the rest of the Jews fled from the scene. Most of the fighters belonging to the Ha-Shomer ha-Tsa'ir group fell in that battle. Anielewicz was saved by his men, who came to his aid in the close-quarters fighting. The resistance action taken on January 18 was of great importance, because four days later the Germans halted the deportation, a step that the ghetto population interpreted as meaning that the Germans were drawing back in the face of armed resistance by the Jews. The following three months, from January to April 1943, were used by the ŻOB for intensive preparations for the decisive test ahead, under the supervision of the organization's headquarters, led by Anielewicz.

On April 19, the eve of Passover, the final deportation of Warsaw Jews was launched, an event that served as the signal for the Warsaw ghetto uprising. In the first few clashes, the Jewish resistance fighters held the upper hand and the Germans suffered losses. The clashes and street fighting in the ghetto lasted for three days. The Germans introduced a large military force, against which the few hundred Jewish fighters, armed only with pistols, had no chance whatsoever; but the fighters did not surrender. Neither, for the most part, did the Jews who were in the bunkers; the appeals and promises they heard from the Germans did not lure them out of their hiding places, and the Germans had to burn down the ghetto, house by house, in order to destroy the bunkers. The fighting in the ghetto went on for four weeks, in the course of which the Germans and their helpers suffered constant losses. It was only on May 16 that SS-Brigadeführer Jürgen STROOP, the commander of the German force, was able to report that the *Grossaktion* ("major operation") had been concluded and the ghetto conquered.

In the first days of the fighting, Anielewicz was in command, in the midst of the main fighting forces of the ghetto. When the street fighting was over, Anielewicz, together with his staff and a large force of fighters, retreated into the bunker at 18 Mila Street. This bunker fell on May 8, and the main body of the ŻOB, including Anielewicz, was killed. In his last letter, of April 23, 1943, to Yitzhak ZUCKERMAN (a member of the ŻOB staff who was then on assignment on the Polish side), Anielewicz wrote:

> What has happened is beyond our wildest dreams. Twice the Germans fled from the ghetto. One of our companies held out for forty minutes and the other, for over six hours. . . . I have no words to describe to you the conditions in which the Jews are living. Only a few chosen ones will hold out; all the rest will perish sooner or later. The die is cast. In the bunkers in which our comrades are hiding, no candle can be lit, for lack of air. . . . The main thing is: My life's dream has come true; I have lived to see Jewish resistance in the ghetto in all its greatness and glory.

Kibbutz Yad Mordecai in Israel has been

named after Mordecai Anielewicz, and is the site of a memorial in his honor.

BIBLIOGRAPHY

Gutman, Y. *The Jews of Warsaw, 1939–1943.* Bloomington, 1980.

Gutman, Y. *Revolt of the Besieged: Mordehai Anielewicz and the Uprising of the Warsaw Ghetto.* Merhavia, Israel, 1963. (In Hebrew.)

Ringelblum, E. " 'Comrade Mordechai': Mordechai Anielewicz—Commander of the Warsaw Ghetto Uprising." In *They Fought Back*, edited by Y. Suhl, pp. 108–114. London, 1968.

ISRAEL GUTMAN

ANNE FRANK HOUSE. *See* Frank, Anne.

ANSCHLUSS, the takeover of AUSTRIA by Germany in March 1938 (the term is usually translated as "connection," "union," or "annexation"). The concept, denoting the inclusion of Austria in a united Greater Germany, entered German political terminology in 1918. Under the Treaty of St. Germain, the 1919 peace accord between Austria and the victorious allies, Austria was forbidden to join Germany and was made an independent republic. In the 1930s Engelbert Dollfuss, leader of the Christian Socialist party in Austria, set up a Fascist-style dictatorship, based on an alliance with Italy and opposed both to Austria's Social Democrats and to its Nazis. In July 1934 the Nazis made an attempt to seize power; they failed, owing to Italian intervention, but they did succeed in murdering Dollfuss in his chancellery office. Dollfuss's successor, Kurt von Schuschnigg, tried to reach an understanding with Nazi Germany, but Hitler would not settle for less than Austria's annexation to the Reich. As a result of the rapid rise of the Nazi movement in Austria, and the withdrawal of Italy's protection following the creation of the Rome-Berlin Axis, the Austrian regime lacked the strength to resist Hitler's pressure. The Anschluss, which took place on March 13, 1938,

In the days following the Anschluss (March 13, 1938), Jewish citizens of Vienna were forced to scrub away the election slogans of the Vaterländische Front (Fatherland Front, a party founded by Engelbert Dollfuss in 1933) from buildings and streets.

was in effect a dictate by Hitler, with massive support from the Austrian Nazis and with the agreement of Italy (which for Hitler was proof of Mussolini's loyalty and friendship). Britain and France went along with the Anschluss, despite the fact that it clearly violated a treaty that also bore Germany's signature.

BIBLIOGRAPHY

Kindermann, G.-K. *Hitler's Defeat in Austria, 1933–1934.* Boulder, 1988.

Luža, R. *Austro-German Relations in the Anschluss Era.* Princeton, 1975.

Schuschnigg, K. von. *The Brutal Takeover: The Austrian Ex-Chancellor's Account of the Anschluss of Austria by Hitler.* London, 1971.

Suval, S. *The Anschluss Question in the Weimar Era: A Study of Nationalism in Germany and Austria, 1918–1932.* Baltimore, 1974.

ISRAEL GUTMAN

ANTHROPOLOGY AND NATIONAL SOCIALISM. The strong desire of anthropologists and "racial hygienists" to put their concepts of population policy to practical use came to the fore in the 1920s. German anthropologists considered the Weimar Republic unwilling and ill suited to transform their concepts into official policies, and they expected Adolf Hitler to pave the way for their plans.

The anthropologists' urge for action was not exclusively motivated by "racial hygiene" (Ger., *Rassenhygiene*; the Nazi term for eugenics) but also had its sources in the demands of everyday life. Law courts, for example, were eager to base determinations of illegitimate paternity on reliable evidence. On the other hand, eugenicists found it unbearable that a relatively large group of persons was excluded from a selective population policy because their genetic value could not be determined, owing to their unknown paternity.

In 1926 Otto Reche, head of the Institute of Anthropology in Vienna, drew up the first genetic reports on disputed paternity. Independently of Reche, Otmar von Verschuer delivered his first reports in Berlin, in 1928, at the Kaiser Wilhelm Institute for Anthropology, Genetics, and Eugenics.

The reports were based on analyzing similarities of the phenotype (the visible characteristics). Between 120 and 130 features (for example, the ear, nose, eyes, hair, head, and fingerprints) of the mother, child, and assumed father were examined. After they had determined all the similarities between mother and child, anthropologists tried to identify as many characteristic features of the child as possible with those of the disputed father. Each statement was summed up in a final result, and was graded according to its probability.

This procedure was soon accepted in Austrian courts. In 1931 the Supreme Court of Vienna declared that a genetic examination in proceedings tracing paternity should be obligatory. In Germany, however, law courts took a skeptical view of this new evidence. There, the gradual public acceptance was closely connected with the antisemitic politics of the National Socialists. As part of the Law for the Restoration of the Professional Civil Service (*Gesetz zur Wiederherstellung des Berufsbeamtentums*) of April 7, 1933, all Jewish civil servants were removed from their places of work. This law served as a background for the legal definition of a Jew. Such a definition was given its final form in the first implementing order of November 14, 1935, which said that a Jew was a person descended from at least three fully Jewish grandparents. A "partial Jew" (*see* MISCHLINGE) was a person who had one or two Jewish grandparents. During the following years, special laws were enacted that systematically restricted the professional and social life of the Jews, and almost everywhere proof of one's "Aryan" identity, the *Ariernachweis*, was demanded.

The anti-Jewish legislation raised the problem of establishing racial descent. As a rule, such descent was proved by family documents. Sometimes, however, the necessary papers were not available. Proving descent was especially important to the Nazi authorities when Jewish descent was suspected, and it had to be determined whether the person in question was a "quarter Jew" (a *Mischling* of the second degree), a "half Jew" (a *Mischling* of the first degree), or a "full Jew" (*Volljude*). Therefore, the *Mischlinge,* whose officially estimated number varied between 115,000 and 750,000, became a focal point for the work of the Reichssippenamt (Reich Genealogical Office), which had been set up to clarify disputed cases of "Aryan" descent following the issuing of the Civil Service Law in 1933.

Only the Reichssippenamt was authorized to decide on "Aryan" descent, which was certified with a document, the *Abstammungsbescheid* (certificate of Aryan descent). First, the Reichssippenamt tried to establish a complete genealogy, with documentary evidence, of the person under investigation. This procedure, however, was prone to failure if birth or marriage certificates or entries were missing (usually in cases of illegitimate birth). In such cases the Reichssippenamt was entitled to draw upon "genetic and racial reports," if these concerned the "racial classification of individual persons." Such examinations functioned as a last resort and served as a basis for the *Abstammungsbescheid*, together with the previously obtained genealogical evidence.

Owing to its new function, the ordinary genetic report on disputed paternity developed into a "genetic and racial report." Its methodical basis remained principally unchanged: the genuine father was sought by means of genetic features. However, there were innovations. First, the purpose had changed. The object was not to unite an illegitimate child with its true father, in order to help it develop an emotional bond and to guarantee its rights, but to find out whether the offspring belonged by race to the German people, in order to determine whether or not the child should be granted its personal rights and liberty. The child's individual needs were of no importance. Second, the method suffered from its changed goal. Whereas the father was the center of attention in the former procedure, the emphasis now lay on the child. It was not as important to know the identity of the father of a child as it was to ascertain whether an offspring was of Jewish or German descent. Third, a racial classification was eventually made on the basis of alleged racial characteristics, and a largely intuitive racial analysis was carried out in search of Jewish features.

At first, only the Reichssippenamt had the right to conduct investigation about Jewish or non-Jewish descent, but beginning in 1938 law courts were also entitled to do so in certain cases. The public prosecutor was authorized to challenge the legitimacy of a child in the interest of the public, if its "racial classification" was disputed. In 1939, petitioning to determine one's blood relationship was allowed. Proceedings could be instituted if there was reasonable suspicion that legal and biological paternity were not identical. "Genetic and racial reports" became highly esteemed evidence, leading to a constantly increasing demand for them.

The genetic and racial tests were not conducted in the Reichssippenamt but exclusively in qualified institutions—mainly university institutes—whose directors were appointed by the Reich Ministry of the Interior as official experts. In a law of March 27, 1936, the Reich Ministry of Justice named nine such institutes, the majority of them institutes of anthropology and the rest institutes of genetics and racial hygiene. In 1943 the list of authorities that were entitled to issue such "genetic and racial reports" comprised twenty-two institutes and twelve individual experts. (The institutes were not obliged by the government to accept reports from the individual experts.) The institutes were as follows:

1. Berlin, Kaiser-Wilhelm-Institut für Anthropologie (Kaiser Wilhelm Institute for Anthropology; Prof. Dr. med. Freiherr Otmar von Verschuer [before 1942, Prof. Dr. med. Eugen Fischer])
2. Berlin, Institut für Rassenbiologie (Institute for Race Biology; Prof. Dr. phil. Wolfgang Abel)
3. Berlin, Institut für Rassenhygiene der Universität (University Institute for Racial Hygiene; Prof. Dr. med. Fritz Lenz)
4. Berlin, Erbpathologische Abteilung d. I. Medizinischen Klinik d. Charité (Heredity-Pathology Department of the First Medical Clinic of Charité; Prof. Dr. med. Friedrich Curtius)
5. Breslau, Anthropologisches Institut der Universität (University Anthropological Institute; Prof. Dr. phil.nat. Egon Freiherr von Eickstedt)
6. Cologne, Universitätsinstitut für Erbbiologie und Rassenhygiene (University Institute for Heredity Biology and Racial Hygiene; Prof. Dr. med. Ferdinand Claussen)
7. Frankfurt, Universitätsinstitut für Erb-

biologie und Rassenhygiene (University Institute for Heredity Biology and Racial Hygiene; Prof. Dr. med. Heinrich Wilhelm Kranz)

8. Giessen, Institut für Erb- und Rassenpflege (Institute for Heredity and Racial Cultivation; Prof. Dr. med. Hermann Boehm)
9. Greifswald, Institut für Menschliche Erblehre und Eugenik (Institute for Human Heredity Studies and Eugenics; Doz. Dr. phil. Fritz Steiniger)
10. Innsbruck, Erb- und Rassenbiologisches Institut der Universität (University Heredity and Racial Biological Institute; Prof. Dr. med. Friedrich Stumpfl)
11. Kiel, Anthropologisches Institut der Universität (University Anthropological Institute; Prof. Dr. rer.nat. Hans Weinert)
12. Königsberg, Rassenbiologisches Institut der Universität (University Racial Biological Institute; Dr. med. Bernhard T. Duis)
13. Leipzig, Institut für Rassen- und Völkerkunde an der Universität (University Institute for Race and Ethnology; Prof. Dr. phil. Otto Reche)
14. Munich, Anthropologisches Institut der Universität (University Anthropological Institute; Prof. Dr. med. Theodor Mollison)
15. Prague, Institut für Erb- und Rassenhygiene der Deutschen Karls-Universität (Institute for Heredity and Racial Hygiene of the German Charles University; Prof. Dr. med. Karl Thums)
16. Prague, Lehrstuhl und Institut für Rassenkunde der Deutschen Karls-Universität (Professorial Chair and Institute for Racial Studies of the German Charles University; Prof. Dr. phil. Bruno K. Schultz)
17. Strasbourg, Institut für Rassenbiologie der Reichs-Universität (Institute for Racial Biology of the Reich University; Prof. Dr. med. Wolfgang Lehmann)
18. Tübingen, Rassenbiologisches Institut der Universität (University Racial Biological Institute; Prof. Dr. phil. Dr. med. Wilhelm Gieseler)
19. Vienna, Anthropologisches Institut der Universität (University Anthropological Institute; Doz. Dr. phil. Karl Tuppa)
20. Vienna, Rassenbiologisches Institut der Universität (University Racial Biological Institute; Prof. Dr. med. Lothar Loeffler)
21. Weimar, Thüringisches Landesamt für Rassewesen (Thuringian State Department for Racial Knowledge; Prof. Dr. med. Karl Astel)
22. Würzburg, Rassenbiologisches Institut der Universität (University Racial Biological Institute; Prof. Dr. phil. Günther Just)

Among the individual experts allowed to issue such reports were:

1. Dr. Richard Günther, Vienna
2. Dozent Dr. phil.habil. Michael Hesch, Curator and Head of the Anthropological Department of the State Museum for Zoology and Ethnology, Dresden
3. Prof. Dr. phil. Dr. med.habil. Friedrich Keiter, University Racial Biological Institute, Würzburg
4. Dr. Werner Pendl, Vienna
5. Dr. Hella Pöch, Salzburg
6. Prof. Dr. med. Rudolf Polland, Director of the University Institute for Heredity Studies and Racial Hygiene, Graz
7. Prof. Dr. med. Dr. phil.nat. Andreas Pratje, University Anatomical Institute, Erlangen
8. Prof. Dr. med. Ernst Rodenwaldt, Director of the Hygienic Institute, Heidelberg
9. Dozent Dr. med. Dr. phil. Johannes Schaeuble, Head of the Department for Heredity and Race Lore of the Anatomical Institute, Freiburg im Breisgau
10. Dr. Josef Wastl, Custodian and Director of the Anthropological Department of the Natural History Museum, Vienna

After five years of their activities, and in view of the new legal regulations of 1938 and 1939, anthropologists and racial hygienists decided to meet at the Anthropological Institute of the University of Munich under the chairmanship of Otto Reche, on March 23, 1939. Most of the senior experts and their assistants attended the meeting, which served as an exchange of experience as well as of views.

Reche, in his dual function as rapporteur for the Munich conference and spokesman of the Rassenpolitisches Amt der NSDAP (Racial Policies Office of the Nazi Party), pointed out the aim of "genetic and racial reports" very clearly: "Only with this method is it possible to separate kinship and genetic lines and prevent foreign blood [*Rassenblut*] and hereditary diseases from being passed into the family. . . . Especially with illegitimate persons, the danger of hereditary taint and the infiltration of foreign blood is very great. It is well known, for example, that the Jews have given birth to many illegitimate half-castes."

The events of the KRISTALLNACHT pogrom in November 1938 did not prevent anthropologists and racial hygienists from using their science to determine the selection of Jews. The number of reports increased constantly during the Hitler period. For example, the Polyclinic of Genetics and Racial Hygiene in Berlin-Charlottenburg delivered 52 reports annually from 1935–1936 to 1937–1938, but its output of reports increased in 1938–1939 to 142, and in 1939–1940 to 314. The total number of all reports is unknown for the later years, but as of July 1942, ten out of twenty institutes delivered at least 3,700 reports.

At the end of 1942, the Reichssippenamt stated that applications for expert opinion had increased greatly, since applicants wanted to achieve a more favorable racial classification through genetic and racial examination. The increasing number of such applications was a decisive factor in the gradual fulfillment of the anthropologists' and racial hygienists' 1939 demand that new institutes be founded and that the group of experts be broadened.

The experts accepted the extension of ordinary genetic reports on disputed paternity to reports of racial descent, and they therefore also accepted the change in the aim, which was now that the true father of an illegitimate child should be determined in order to find out whether the candidate was a Jew or a *Mischling*. Anthropologists closed their eyes to the fact that Jewish descent could not be determined in the way that Negroid descent, for example, could be. Therefore, the Nazi laws now provided also for the determination of religious affiliation. A Jew continued to be a person who had at least three completely Jewish grandparents. His (or her) racial classification, however, derived from his affiliation to the Jewish religious community. Anthropologists did not make use of this fact to reject racial testimony because of its insufficient scientific basis. But even if Jewish descent could have been determined by genetic means, the aim would have remained immoral: first to deprive a human being of his rights, and, after 1941, to physically destroy him.

During World War II, the cooperation of anthropologists and racial hygienists with the Nazi party and government concerning their selection policies began to function less smoothly than previously. Appeals to courts in proceedings to determine Jewish descent had consequences that could not have been foreseen by their initiators. The appeals offered a final and very slim chance for Jews to escape persecution (and, eventually, death) with the help of the same bureaucracy that pursued their extermination. Thus, Jews increasingly contested the paternity of their legal and often legitimate fathers and claimed illegitimate descent from men of "German blood," in order to be classified as "Aryans" if they had been listed as *Mischlinge*, or to be accepted as *Mischlinge* if they had been listed as *Volljuden*.

In their desperation they sometimes tried to deceive the authorities. For example, the writer Rolf Italiaander, who was regarded as a *Mischling* by the Reichssippenamt, successfully concealed the Jewish descent of his grandparents on his father's side. First he declared his grandfather to be an illegitimate child of an Englishman. Then he found a photograph of an "Aryan"-looking man in a Berlin junk shop, soaked it in water, and rubbed it with cigarette ash to imbue the photograph with the patina of past decades. He then handed it in as a picture of his late grandfather. In addition, he destroyed the entry for the Jewish mother of his grandfather in the registration office of Düsseldorf, tearing it out of the entry list and swallowing it. Finally, his grandmother untruthfully affirmed that her husband had been the illegitimate son of an English sailor. In this way, Italiaander saved himself and forty members of his family from greater harm.

The authorities and party offices were not unaware of the attempts of Jews to disguise relationships with the help of these newly established legal possibilities in order to increase the chances of their survival. For this reason, from February 1943 on the Reich Ministry of Justice endeavored to limit the scope of courts regarding their decisions. Both the Reich Ministry of the Interior and the Reich Ministry of Justice tried to bind the authorities involved in the proceedings to the more rigorous antisemitic party line. Thus, the experts Rudolf Polland, Karl Tuppa, and Josef Wastl aroused the superior authorities' indignation because of reports they composed that were favorable to Jews.

Once the experts had accepted scientifically dubious evidence (such as yellowed photographs) to determine a candidate's descent, it was not far to actual manipulation, under the prevailing conditions. Thus, the anthropologists and racial hygienists had maneuvered themselves into a dilemma. Those who out of humanity manipulated the facts were, in official terms, deceivers—though morally they were justified. Those who worked objectively, at least from 1941 on, were accomplices to murder.

[*See also* Racism.]

BIBLIOGRAPHY

Grenville, J. A. S. "Die Endlösung und die 'Judenmischlinge' im Dritten Reich." In vol. 2 of *Das Unrechtsregime: Internationale Forschung über den Nationalsozialismus*, edited by U. Büttner, pp. 91–121. Hamburg, 1986.

Müller-Hill, B. *Murderous Science—Elimination by Scientific Selection of Jews, Gypsies, and Others: Germany, 1933–1945*. Oxford, 1988.

Noakes, J. "Wohin gehören die 'Judenmischlinge': Die Entstehung der ersten Durchführungsverordnungen zu den Nürnberger Gesetzen." In vol. 2 of *Das Unrechtsregime: Internationale Forschung über den Nationalsozialismus*, edited by U. Büttner, pp. 69–84. Hamburg, 1986.

Proctor, R. *Racial Hygiene: Medicine under the Nazis*. Cambridge, Mass., 1988.

Seidler, H., and A. Rett. *Das Reichssippenamt entscheidet: Rassenbiologie im Nationalsozialismus*. Vienna, 1982.

GEORG LILIENTHAL

ANTI-JEWISH LEGISLATION. More than two thousand anti-Jewish measures were enacted in Germany (in its January 1, 1937, borders) under Nazi rule. Owing to the federal structure of the Reich, it is difficult to ascertain their precise number. The figure cited here refers only to laws passed by the Reich and the larger *Länder* (states and provinces), and represents only a part of the total number of anti-Jewish regulations. If the smaller political units and the autonomous bodies are taken into account, the total exceeds three thousand.

The Nazi party program adopted in February 1920 contained four anti-Jewish objectives:

1. Jews should not be citizens, and should have the legal status of foreigners;
2. Jews should not be public officials;
3. Jews should be barred from immigrating into Germany;
4. Any Jew who is the owner or editor of a German newspaper should be removed from that position.

At the time these demands were not new, nor could they be regarded as particularly radical. They were no more than a repetition of the views advocated by all pre-1914 antisemitic parties and political groups, and corresponded to the ideas held by wide circles of the German population.

In retrospect, three distinct and separate waves of anti-Jewish legislation can be discerned. The first wave welled up in March 1933, and by April 7 had culminated in one of the major Nazi objectives—the enactment of the Law for the Restoration of the Professional Civil Service. This law authorized the dismissal of "non-Aryan" civil servants, except for those who had held that status since August 1, 1914, who had fought at the front for Germany in World War I, or whose father or son had been killed in action in that war. A "non-Aryan" was defined as a person "descended from non-Aryan, and especially from Jewish, parents or grandparents," even if only one parent or grandparent fitted that category.

This law became the model for measures excluding Jews from other occupations—for example, lawyers and tax consultants—and dismissing all "non-Aryan" employees; doctors and dentists were barred from the panels of social-medicine institutions. Under a law (the *Reichskulturkammergesetz*) that was passed on September 22, 1933, reestablishing a Reich Chamber of Culture, "non-Aryans" were removed from organizations and enterprises related to literature, the press, broadcasting, the theater, music, and art.

The legislation barring Jews from various professions and occupations was further augmented by measures designed to make these occupations inaccessible to them in the first place. The first such measure was the Law against the Overcrowding of German Schools and Institutions of Higher Learning (April 7, 1933), which restricted the admissible number of "non-Aryan" students to a certain percentage of the total. All regulations governing training and examinations for state-controlled occupations contained an ARIERPARAGRAPH ("Aryan clause"), which prohibited "non-Aryans" from sitting for final state examinations and thus closed all such occupations to them. The *Arierparagraph* was also introduced into the bylaws of professional organizations, societies, and clubs, and as a result it became increasingly difficult for Jews to protect their interests or take part in social activities.

Financial easements were denied to Jews: Jewish high school and university students were no longer eligible for reductions of school fees, scholarships, or any other kind of assistance; and newly married couples were not granted the usual matrimony loans if one of the partners was "non-Aryan."

Another category of laws and regulations was designed to discriminate against the Jewish religion and hamper observance of its practices and customs. Jewish ritual slaughter was outlawed as early as April 1933. Jewish judges could at any time be rejected, on grounds of bias. Local authorities, in ever-growing numbers, prohibited Jews from visiting public baths; Jewish students who did not attend classes on the Sabbath or Jewish holidays were penalized; and Jewish prisoners no longer had the right to receive kosher food. By mid-1935 these measures had severely restricted Jewish life in Germany. Jews, for the most part, maintained contact only with other Jews.

The second major wave of anti-Jewish legislation came on September 15, 1935, when the Reichstag, meeting in Nuremberg, passed two laws, drafted on short notice, that provided for the final legal and social separation between German Jews and the German people. Under the *Reichsbürgergesetz* (Reich Citizenship Law), the Jews were deprived of all voting rights and became *Staatsbürger 2 Klasse* (second-class citizens). One immediate effect of this law was the dismissal, by December 31, 1935, of all the Jewish civil servants, employees, and workers who still held their jobs. The broader function of the citizenship law was to serve as the legal basis for no fewer than thirteen further decrees, each relating to a different set of circumstances.

The other law passed that day was the *Gesetz zum Schutze des deutschen Blutes und der deutschen Ehre* (Law for the Protection of German Blood and German Honor), which forbade marriage between Jews and nationals of German or kindred blood. In the wake of that law, a complicated classification system was enacted defining various degrees of Jewishness, ranging from *Volljude* (full Jew) to *Geltungsjude* (person regarded as a Jew, even though he or she had two "Aryan" grandparents) to *Mischling* (partial Jew, i.e., a person of mixed blood), divided in turn into first and second degrees, with each degree having its own specified privileges, rights, and disabilities (*see* MISCHLINGE).

The third wave of anti-Jewish legislation related to the remaining sphere of Jewish activity: the economy. Though this wave began during 1936 and 1937, its timing was most directly connected to measures taken after the rioting on KRISTALLNACHT (November 9–10, 1938). In 1938 the status of the Jewish community as a recognized public authority entitled to subsidies and tax exemption was rescinded. On November 12, Nazi anti-Jewish legislation entered its final phase. A collective fine of 1 billion reichsmarks was imposed on the Jews as a body, as a penalty for the murder of a German diplomat in Paris, the ostensible impetus for the riots; in addition, they had to repair out of their own resources all damage they suffered in the rioting. The *Verordnung zur Ausschaltung der Juden aus dem deutschen Wirtschaftsleben* (Measure for the Elimination of Jews from the German Economy) completed the list of occupations from which Jews were already barred; as of January 1, 1939, there was no occupation a Jew could join or practice unless he dealt only with Jews.

In the period following November 9, 1938, more legislation was passed, in three different areas:

1. The seizure and confiscation of Jewish-owned assets (ARISIERUNG, or "Aryanization"), which was a legalized form of plunder by the state.

2. The separation of the Jews from the Germans, in both location and time: Jews were forbidden to enter certain places or show themselves in public at certain times. As of February 1939, for example, they could no longer enter railway sleeping or dining cars; in April 1939, local authorities were permitted to restrict Jews to specific houses or residential districts.

3. The concentration of all significant political affairs relating to "Jewish questions" in the hands of the SS organs, and the liquidation of Jewish institutions.

On November 9, 1938, Hermann GÖRING had succeeded in obtaining from Hitler authorization to deal with all Jewish political affairs. This enabled him, on January 24, 1939, to appoint Reinhard HEYDRICH as chief of the ZENTRALSTELLE FÜR JÜDISCHE AUSWANDERUNG (Central Office for Jewish Emigration), which in practice gave the SS the power of decision on all matters affecting the Jews. In legislative terms, this situation was expressed in the *Zehnte Verordnung zum Reichsbürgergesetz* (Tenth Implementation Decree under the Reich Citizenship Law) of July 4, 1939, which provided for the establishment of the Reichsvereinigung der Juden in Deutschland (Reich Association of Jews in Germany). This organization, responsible for the organization and implementation of emigration and all related matters, as well as for separate Jewish education and social welfare, was under the supervision and control of Heydrich in his capacity as chief of the Sicherheitspolizei (Security Police) and SD (Sicherheitsdienst; Security Service).

Even prior to the outbreak of war, German Jews were trapped in a legislative net that, by the sheer number of its component parts as well as by its single-mindedness, had no precedent in the history of the treatment of minorities. When war broke out, the existing regulations were extended in every possible direction and tightened up. Jews were forbidden to leave their residences after 8:00 p.m. (September 1, 1939); their radio sets were confiscated (September 20, 1939); their food rations were reduced (December 7, 1939), as were their other rations (January 23, 1940); their purchases were restricted to limited hours and to certain stores; their telephones were taken away (July 19, 1940). From the beginning of the war, the Jews were put on forced labor, with none of the provisions of labor legislation applicable to them. As of September 19, 1941, they had to wear the Jewish BADGE in public and, with a few exceptions, were not permitted to use public transportation. On October 23 of that year, Jewish emigration was prohibited.

The "FINAL SOLUTION"—launched in Germany with two transports of Jews to the east in October 1941—was reflected inside the Reich by the enactment of regulations that had the sole purpose of depriving the Jews of the last of their possessions, of discriminating against them in every possible way, and of taking from them whatever rights they still had left. The Jews who were deported to the east automatically lost their German citizenship (November 25, 1941). At the end of June 1942, the remaining Jewish schools were closed down. Germans who maintained friendly contacts with Jews ran the risk of having to spend three months in a concentration camp (October 24, 1941); German hairdressers were no longer permitted to attend to Jews (May 12, 1942); and Jews were no longer allowed to keep "German" house pets. The final anti-Jewish law, dated July 1, 1943, provided that when a Jew died, his estate would be forfeited to the Reich.

In the countries allied with Germany, or conquered and occupied by it, the extent and severity of anti-Jewish legislation depended on the regime and on the political and military pressure exerted by Germany—or, conversely, on the degree to which the country could convince Germany to respect its status under international law. Thus, after the annexation of Austria on March 13, 1938, no time was lost in applying Nazi racial legislation to Austria. The same applied, even more keenly and ruthlessly, to the Protectorate of BOHEMIA AND MORAVIA and the GENERALGOUVERNEMENT, the residual Polish "state," whose territory, as soon as it was seized, was used for the harshest and most brutal anti-Jewish measures, which were passed months and even years before they were applied in the Reich itself.

In the countries that were militarily defeated—France, the Netherlands, Luxembourg, Norway, Yugoslavia (Serbia and Croatia), and Greece—the local German military commander or the puppet regime generally introduced legal measures defining who was to be regarded as a Jew and eliminating Jews from the country's economic life. This also occurred in states allied with Germany (Italy, Slovakia, Bulgaria, Romania, and Hungary), although in such cases the Reich had to exert varying degrees of pressure to overcome the resistance shown by most of these governments. The only country under German control that enacted no anti-Jewish legislation was Denmark, whose situation and status saved it from German pressure, and which also succeeded in saving most of its Jewish population when the Germans finally resolved to deport that country's Jews in July 1943.

[*See also* Bernheim Petition; Entjudung; Law and Judiciary in Nazi Germany; Nuremberg Laws; Statut des Juifs.]

BIBLIOGRAPHY

Adam, U. D. *Judenpolitik im Dritten Reich.* Düsseldorf, 1972.

Adam, U. D. "An Overall Plan for Anti-Jewish Legislation in the Third Reich." *Yad Vashem Studies* 11 (1976): 33–55.

Hilberg, R. *The Destruction of the European Jews.* 3 vols. New York, 1985.

Schleunes, K. A. *The Twisted Road to Auschwitz: Nazi Policy toward German Jews, 1933–1939.* Urbana, Ill., 1970.

Walk, D., ed. *Das Sonderrecht für die Juden im NS-Staat.* Heidelberg, 1981.

UWE ADAM

ANTISEMITIC FILMS. *See* Films, Nazi Antisemitic.

ANTISEMITISM (Ger., *Antisemitismus*). The term "antisemitism," denoting opposition to and hatred of Jews, became widely accepted from the end of the 1870s. Principally it referred to the views at the core of the anti-Jewish political trends that appeared throughout Europe in the period following the Emancipation of the Jews in the nineteenth century. These were sociopolitical movements with nationalist and racist concepts, which placed opposition to Jews and to the threat which the Jews allegedly posed at the center of their outlook and activities. With the passage of time, "antisemitism" came to denote hatred of Jews in all its forms, throughout history.

The causes of antisemitism, as well as its enduring nature and intensity, are based primarily on the religious and spiritual creed of Judaism and on the role played by Jews in the economy and other spheres of life in the Western world. Furthermore, through the centuries the term "Jew" has been associated with concepts, stereotypes, images, and calumnies that together formed a negative composite image on both the conscious and the emotional level, often almost without any relationship to Jewish society as it really was.

Many believe that the principal roots and causes of antisemitism lie in the confrontation and antagonism between Christianity and Judaism. According to this view, the antipathy to Jews that existed in the Greco-Roman world, based on Jewish monotheism and different life-style, was of marginal and temporary significance, and it is from Christianity that antisemitism derives its real force and its continuity. The essence of the conflict between the two religions, which have a common root, is mainly theological, grounded in the issue of Jesus as the Messiah, and in the place of Judaism and the Jews in the Old and New Testaments. The Christian church ascribes to the Jews as such the guilt of deicide, and the inferior status to which Christianity relegated the Jews was interpreted not only as an expression of Christianity's superiority, but also as proof of its veracity, of the "victory of the Church over the Synagogue." Within these components of Christian dogma are to be found some of the bases of what became the cornerstones of antisemitism. The guilt ascribed to the Jews was a collective guilt; not only the Jews who lived at the time of Jesus' crucifixion were

A Hungarian antisemitic poster. The text reads: "Brother! If you want to have a change, join and fight with us, the Arrow Cross Party. Our leader is Count Sándor Festetics. Our district leader is István Fehér. The center: Szeged."

deemed guilty, but all the seed of Israel, for ever and ever. The distinction made between Christians, seen as personifying God's truth and mercy and representing the true Israel, and the Jews, seen as heretics wallowing in sin, developed into simplistic folk motifs in which the Jew is the embodiment of evil, the schemer and bearer of harm and disaster —that is, he is linked to and endowed with demonic powers.

In time the anxieties and fears, as well as the stereotypical image of the Jews, entered the folklore of Christian peoples, their cultural legacy, their literature, and their education, and were no longer mere components of religious thought but part of the general cultural background of Western society. Some of these concepts became rooted in antisemitism and accompanied it in all its forms. First, the wrongdoing of an individual Jew is not the manifestation of a personal flaw but an expression of the negative characteristics of all Jews, and the responsibility for such individual wrongdoing falls on all Jews. Second, the Jew is *eo ipso* to be suspected as having a hand in natural disasters, epidemics, and other crises, and there is no need to look for a rational explanation or pertinent evidence to prove his complicity in such events. Third, the Jews are a closed and unified community that formulates rules of morality and ethical standards for its own kind, different from those for outsiders. Out of the immense quantity and great variety of writings composed by the Jewish people in the course of its long history—sometimes in a spirit of openness and tolerance and sometimes reflecting the impact of outside pressure—the antisemites extracted those elements (especially from Talmudic literature) that could be misrepresented as proving Jewish hatred of and alienation from non-Jews, and identified as characterizing the Jews. Fourth, the Jews despise physical work, especially farming, and worship money and moneylending for interest; their role in human society is parasitic and unproductive. In some European languages the term "Jew" is synonymous with cheating and the extraction of usurious interest.

Modern antisemitism is a by-product of ideological and social developments during the period of the Enlightenment and the rise of the middle classes. In revolutionary FRANCE the "Jewish question" arose not as a separate issue but in connection with the now-accepted universalistic principle that equal civil rights should be granted to all men, regardless of religion or origin. In discussions in the National Assembly of France on the question of granting equal civil rights to Jews, the argument was raised that these rights should be denied to the Jews because they were not only a religious entity but a nation. Even the most ardent advocate of equal civil rights for Jews, Count Stanislas de Clermont-Tonnerre, declared, in December 1789, that "Jews should be given nothing as a nation, but everything as individuals." In the time of Napoleon, the questions put to the Sanhedrin (1807), a Jewish assembly convened in France by the emperor, were meant to inquire into Jewish observance and to ascertain whether the commandments of the Jewish religion stood in opposition to loyal citizenship and integration into the French nation. It is quite true that the granting of civil rights to Jews also posed difficult dilemmas and caused fierce arguments within the Jewish community, involving as it did the surrender by the Jews of the autonomous social frameworks that for many generations had been the foundation of the separate Jewish community, and the surrender of juridical and legal decisions according to Jewish law (*halakha*), the Sabbath as the day of rest, kosher food, and marriage within the Jewish community.

There were significant differences, however, between the granting of civil rights to Jews in France and the United States, and the process of the Jewish emancipation in GERMANY. In the United States, independence and the structure of national life were predicated on severance from the past, on founding the new nation on the basis of equality, and on the separation of church and state, which placed religion in a category that existed alongside the state structure. The different ethnic and national groups, living in a society that allowed much room for pluralism and recognized the right of entities to follow unique and diversified lines of development, were able to integrate into the national body and become partners in it.

This pluralism, to be sure, did not imply a partnership among equals, and from the first the white Anglo-Saxon Protestants dominated. The founders of the United States and their descendants determined the national challenges and norms of behavior and retained in their own hands the central positions of authority and the key economic positions. The problem of slavery confronted the American nation and society, and in its wake the problem of the blacks and the path toward its solution was strewn with internal strife and divisiveness. At times of turmoil, as during the Civil War or when the loss of hegemony by the ruling class and threats to its norms seemed to be in the offing, portents of antisemitism or restrictions on immigration (that is, quotas) appeared. Such a time of turmoil was the fateful period between the two world wars, when an anti-Jewish tendency appeared on the scene that had grave ramifications for the destiny of the Jews in Europe. Men of stature and influence in American culture, for example Henry Adams and Henry James, expressed antisemitic views in the face of the rapid urbanization and changes in American society that followed the Civil War. The noted anthropologist Madison Grant, in his book *The Passing of the Great Race* (1916), openly claimed that the flooding of the United States by great numbers of weak, broken, and mentally deficient people of all races, from the lowest strata of society in the Mediterranean countries and the Balkans to the wretched multitudes from the ghettos of Poland, endangered the American way of life and the "Nordic" racial structure of the people whose ancestors had founded America.

Nazi antisemitic poster in Polish, "The JEW is a swindler. Your only enemy." The tags read (from top to bottom): Meat, Water, Milk, Bread. The text reads: "Stop, dear reader, and see how the Jews cheat you. Instead of meat he [the Jew] grinds a rat; adds filthy water to the milk; and kneads the worm-infested dough with his feet."

After World War I, Henry Ford contributed his money and influence to further the distribution of the PROTOCOLS OF THE ELDERS OF ZION in the United States, and the book *The International Jew,* which appeared under his name, helped spread the ideas contained in the *Protocols* throughout the world. American antisemitism often took the form of social separation and rejection—the refusal to accept Jews into exclusive clubs and certain hotels, and the blocking of their paths to senior posts and leading positions in certain companies. Antisemitism was keenly felt in the United States during the twentieth century and was influenced from outside by various forces, including the Nazis. It continued to be felt keenly until after the end of World War II, but it never took on a generally brutal and violent character, and never led to the passage of restrictive national laws specifically against Jews. Even at the height of the Great Depression in the United States, whose source was the financial crisis that engendered massive unemployment, the Jews were never blamed for the situation, as had happened more than once in Europe during financial and economic collapses in such countries as France and Germany. Indeed, Jews took an active role in the economic recovery that President Franklin D. ROOSEVELT initiated, and his policies had the effect of broadening the spheres of American life in which Jews could participate. At no time did American antisemitism accrue political power as in Europe. The United States represents the kind of government and culture that, through a process of permutation, evolution, and material progress on a vast scale, has succeeded in integrating masses of people of different ethnic and religious backgrounds and cultures without destroying their identities, without oppression, and without abandoning the principles of democracy.

Germany passed through a process different from either the United States or France. A few of the Germans who tried to institute reforms in the social structure of the German states during the time of Napoleon's conquests supported improvement of the Jews' status. After Napoleon's defeat, however, such changes were regarded as part of the order imposed upon Germany by the enemy, and therefore were neither binding nor popular. The stages in the formation of the German nation were not motivated primarily by the adoption of revolutionary ideas advocating social change, but rather by the desire to unify the different parts of the German people into one strong national body. A prevailing goal was to derive inspiration and ideals from the German past and from spiritual and literary movements such as Romanticism, which embraced the traditions of medieval Germany. Whereas the character of the French and American revolutions allowed breadth of opportunity and belief in the perfectibility of man within the new laws and regimes, developments in Germany tended toward the suppression of outcasts and those who were different. The refusal to bestow equal rights in a single package and the fact that it took several generations before the process was fully accomplished also had a restraining influence, and heightened the unwillingness to accept the equality of the Jews, even when it had been legally granted.

Some well-known German philosophers expressed opposition to the integration of the Jews into the German nation. Among them was Johann Gottlieb Fichte, who enlisted his philosophy for the consolidation of the idea of modern German nationalism. In his view the Jews should be deprived of the right to belong to the German nation. He regarded Christianity as a basic component of German nationalism and asserted that the Jews are a nation within a nation, casting doubt on the possibility of changing the Jews and making them into an organic part of the German people. In Fichte's view, as human beings Jews must be given full rights, but not the privileges of citizenship. He saw only one way to make them worthy of such privileges: "to cut off their heads one night and replace them with new ones, free from all Jewish ideas."

Bruno Bauer, a philosopher and theologian of the Young Hegelian school of thought, published two essays in 1843 advocating that Jews should not be granted emancipation. According to Bauer, who identified with the trend calling for the end of the rule of religion over the thoughts of man, Christianity had arrived at the stage of development in which the state and the public had been freed from the chains of religion. In contrast, Judaism was a static and anachronistic religion, unable to adapt itself to changing times. Accordingly, Jews should not be granted emancipation, or, at least, emancipation should be withheld from them as long as they were not ready to abandon their religious beliefs. In his critique of Bauer, the young Karl Marx opposed the denial of emancipation for Jews. Marx differentiated between political and civil emancipation and human emancipation. The first was one of the distinguishing marks of the new state and freed the citizen from the yoke of state religion, a liberation that would also affect the Jews. The second was a higher state whose purpose it was to do away with the alienation and inequality that divide human groups from one another, especially because of the unequal distribution of wealth. With regard to progress toward full human emancipation, apart from equality as citizens, Marx viewed the Jews as an obstacle belonging entirely to the past; for him, Judaism and its commandments were egotistical. Through the Jew (and also by other means), money became material and gained control over the Christian people. Marx's conclusion was that "the social emancipation of the Jew is the emancipation of society from the Jew."

Frenchmen of the generation after the Revolution who had a radical socialist outlook, such as Charles Fourier, Alphonse Toussenel, and Pierre-Joseph Proudhon, were disappointed in the Revolution for not solving the troubling problems of society, and advocated diverse concepts. Some called for living in communes or cooperative communities (Fourier), while others had anarchic tendencies (Proudhon). Most, however, saw the main evil in the lack of equality in wealth and in the power of capital. Proudhon came out strongly against wealth that was not the product of a man's direct labor, but rather came from the exploitation of fellow men. He did not distinctly define the Jews, but the terms "nation" and "race" in references to Jews appear in his writings, and he saw in them the power behind the inequality and exploitation of society. In his view, "we are given into the hands of the Jews for good or for evil." The Jews, he said, are characterized by their unproductive parasitism, and a world plot connects them in the pursuit of their aims. Toussenel, who belonged to the school of Fourier and did not deal much with the subject of society, excelled in unbridled hatred of the Jews, writing a book titled *The Jews: Kings of the Period.*

From the time of the Congress of Vienna (1815) until the granting of full emancipation to the Jews (1871), expressions of antisemitism never disappeared in Germany. In 1819 the country was swept by the "Hep! Hep!" disturbances (the source of the cry is not fully clear), which caused material and physical damage, but not loss of life. Violently anti-Jewish writings continued to appear, such as those of Hartwig Hundt (known as Hundt-Radowsky), who called for the deportation or destruction of the Jews. Nor was there any lack of demagogues who advocated that the Jews return to their ghettos, wear a special badge, and pay special taxes. Even among the liberals who advocated the improvement of society, national unity, and changes in the government, there were severe critics of Jews

Nazi antisemitic poster in Polish, "Soviet Pyramid." The workers and peasants at the base of the pyramid are crushed by the Soviet army men above them, who, in turn, support the Jewish "bankers" conferring with Stalin.

and Judaism. Their accusations were based on analysis of the phenomena and characteristics ascribed to the Jews; the conclusions they arrived at sometimes generated wide repercussions, and in general constituted an attempt to halt the process of emancipation. The dominant personality and influence among them was the Heidelberg theologian Eberhard-Heinrich Paulus. Paulus engaged in a debate with Gabriel Riesser, a Jewish intellectual and ardent fighter for emancipation who played an important role in the Pan-German Parliament, held in Frankfurt during the revolutions of 1848–1849. According to Riesser, the Jews were a religious group similar to other religious groups. Paulus, however, saw Christianity as a religion that brings the believer to moral behavior, whereas Judaism is based on cult and on mechanical and abased ceremonies. He would grant equal rights only on condition that the Jewish commandments be abrogated. Paulus also maintained that Christian messianism had a universal appeal, whereas for the Jews messianism meant national salvation.

Notwithstanding these negative views, this period was marked by progressive and continuous evolution toward emancipation. The breaking up of the corporative frameworks, the desire to establish a unified German state, and developments in the economy and culture all contributed to this trend. Jews who left the ghettos achieved significant success in finance (the best-known example is the house of Rothschild) and in intellectual endeavors. Personalities like Heinrich Heine and the essayist and publicist Karl Ludwig Borne, although converts to Christianity, were influenced by Judaism in their creativity. An integral part of the progression toward equality was the abrogation of various prohibitions, such as those that forbade Jews to live in certain places or that limited them to certain professions. In 1830 the *Landtage* (state parliaments) enacted liberating laws, and a decisive stage was reached in the discussions and conclusions at the Pan-German Parliament. Jews and many gentiles believed that equality and the integration of the Jews into the German nation were inevitable and only a matter of time, and that the voices of the opponents and vilifiers, in the words of Borne, were no more than the last lingering shadows of the Middle Ages that were seeking to obscure—in vain—the dawn of a new age.

During the 1870s the granting of equal citizenship and legal rights to Jews was achieved throughout western and central Europe. With the completion of the cycle of emancipation, which appeared to signal general agreement for the integration of the Jews into the nation, antisemitism paradoxically appeared in a new form, which would bring disaster upon the Jews. It was not the antisemitism of the opponents of emancipation, even though that opposition, with its ancillary argumentation and demagoguery, was a factor in keeping antisemitism in the public eye. Neither was it a question of disappointment at the "reform" of the Jews (that is, at the attempt to end their isolation and wean them away from religious tradition, which many regarded as a precondition for emancipation), even though many who felt that improvements in the Jewish situation would lead to a general desertion from Judaism found their expectations unfulfilled.

The antisemitism in its new form, as it emerged from the 1870s, moved the allegations against the Jews and the concept of their innate disability into the national, and indeed the universal, social and political sphere. The Jews ceased being a separate category, judged through their behavior and deeds; the new antisemitism (the old antisemitism in its new guise) became a general ideology, a *Weltanschauung* with its own existence and at times without a real connection to Jews or Jewish society. It claimed to clarify the complex and troubling problems of modern man and to reveal the sources of economic crisis and poverty, of political conflicts, of societal ferment and war, and, in fact, of all the sicknesses that trouble mankind. The old antisemitism, in the view of the advocates of the new version, had been merely an impulsive emotion, whereas the new antisemitism was regulated and rational, based on objective scientific analysis that discovered the Jewish role in society. The very name of antisemitism, with which the advocates of the new version chose to define their ideology, was meant to emphasize the difference between it and earlier Jew-hatred. The name "antisemitism," which was taken from the Greek, was also intended to endow the ideology with a sort of scientific basis. In actuality, antisemitism was never directed against other "Semites," such as the Arabs, but only against the Jews. The new version of antisemitism was destined, in the twentieth century, to play a major and destructive role in the lives of Jews and all mankind. The German scholar Reinhard Rürup has stated that "Germany is the cradle of both the movement and the term antisemitism," from which they spread through countries in western, central, and eastern Europe. The question of whether one type of antisemitism spread generally, or whether indigenous varieties sprouted in each locality, has yet to be answered conclusively. It is reasonable to assume, however, that both general external and particular internal factors led to its spread.

It may be asked whether there was any connection between the early antisemitism, which from the mid-nineteenth century until the 1870s was marked by a significant retreat, and the antisemitism that emerged in Europe and became one of the dominant elements in the political, economic, and social struggle from the 1870s onward. Some have addressed themselves to this issue, such as the philosopher Jean-Paul Sartre, who tried to understand the meaning of the new antisemitism of the years from 1870 to 1944. He set forth his ideas in *Réflexions sur la question juive* (1946; published in English as *Anti-semite and Jew,* 1965). Sartre wrote that the essence of antisemitism is not grounded in historical fact relating to the Jews, but in the concept that the forces of history have created for themselves of the Jew. He emphasized that it is not the antisemite's personal experience with Jews that evokes his hatred toward them, but rather his tendency to see the source of his own personal failings in his abstract perception of Jews. Psychologists explain this type of antipathy in times of stress as a projection of the frustration of the modern anonymous masses and the consequences of this frustration on an object outside their circle. The Jew is the available scapegoat and meets these basically paranoid needs.

Hannah Arendt severed the new antisemitism from its past and claimed that in modern times, the Jews lost the support of rulers and protective regimes during and after the stage of the formation and acceptance of nationalism. As a result, the Jews were left with only the prop of money, which caused antipathy and left them vulnerable to attack. The importance Arendt ascribes to the Jewish role in the creation of the new antisemitism is schematic and simplistic and is not difficult to refute.

It is clear that even if the components of antisemitism in its new form are diverse and emanate from a new viewpoint, the old characterization of the Jew and the accompanying stereotypes have both played a part in the way that individuals and society as a whole conceive of the Jew. Moreover, even before the advent of political and racial antisemitism in Europe, the antisemitic factions, organizations, and claims, which at first had only a marginal influence, contained the potential to accrue power and momentum.

An important element in the new antisemitism is the identification of the Jew with modernism, capitalism, and urbanization. Social strata that were harmed by the swift changes in Germany during the last decades of the nineteenth century, as well as religious fundamentalists and conservatives, saw in modernization, capitalism, and urbanization a break away from tradition, the destruction of the traditional way of life, and the abolition of the framework that provided Germany with stability and its essential uniqueness. The Jews were regarded as the pioneers of change and the breakdown in tradition, and were seen as the principal beneficiaries of the new system. This found expression in the nationalist political *völkisch* movement, whose leading representatives opposed the industrialism and secularism that characterize modernity and that, in their view, undermine the foundations of the spiritual and cultural uniqueness of the German people. In the writings of advocates of the *völkisch* movement, much responsibility, or even the main responsibility, for undermining the German way of life can be ascribed to the Jews. The well-known biblical and Near Eastern scholar Paul Lagarde, who stood fast by his religious views and who hated liberalism, saw in the Jews a foreign and unifying force that bore within itself the germ of decay. In his view, "with germs one should not argue"; rather, they must be destroyed. Lagarde did not put forth a fully developed racist concept, but in his writings and in his refusal to consider conversion a solution to the "Jewish problem" can be seen the seeds of racism. One of his disciples, Ludwig Schemann, disseminated in Germany the ideas of the French racist Count Joseph-Arthur de Gobineau.

Another *völkisch* thinker was the cultural scholar Julius Langbehn, who was a generation younger than Lagarde and was active after the emancipation. Langbehn was an unstable megalomaniac who often changed his place of residence and area of study, yet he possessed great talent and intellectual curiosity. At one point he decided to devote himself to repairing the image of German culture, and his publications on the subject were widely read. Langbehn was willing to come to terms with traditional Jews, but he viciously lambasted the assimilated Jews. He opposed conversion, which he saw as merely a Jewish attempt at camouflage.

The challenge to emancipation focused on the negative characteristics and influence of Jews who became Germans by their own national self-identification. According to antisemitic arguments, these Jews were not satisfied with equality and did not integrate quietly into a working society. Instead, they aspired to take over wide areas of important but nonproductive branches of the economy, and to penetrate into science, art, literature, and the press, where they caused damage. According to their critics, the Jews destroyed good taste in Germany by engaging in imitation and dilettantism. Since their creativity was not deep-rooted and since they had no real contact with their new surroundings, they turned to radicalism and nihilism, which undermine patriotism and the national resilience. Even a composer of the stature of Richard Wagner, who during the revolutions of 1848–1849 was a radical liberal, changed his views; in his essay *Das Judentum in der Musik* (The Jews in Music), he accused the Jews of lacking original creativity and destroying artistic taste. Wagner's racism never reached full formulation. It was his son-in-law, Houston Stewart CHAMBERLAIN, who gave RACISM its character as a crystallized concept and lived to have contact with Hitler. Eventually, other intellectuals were harnessed to serve racism. Among them were scholars as eminent as the Nobel prize–winning physicist Philipp LENARD, who distinguished between "German physics" and "Jewish physics," the latter represented by Albert EINSTEIN and his theories.

The claim that the Jews were "a nation within a nation" was expanded. The more moderate of the new antisemites complained that the Jews had not fulfilled expectations and had not ended their national separatism. They did not identify unreservedly with the nation in the midst of which they lived, and they continued to maintain ties of communication and solidarity with Jews in other lands. According to the extreme antisemites, the Jews have an international leadership that functions in a secret fashion, similar to that of the FREEMASONS, intentionally entering the host nation and deliberately weaving a plot to take over other nations and eventually the entire world. The methods with which the Jews work, united in their secret international plot, are diverse and changing, but the Jews are not particular about the methods they use and keep their eyes on their final goal, of imposing their dominion over all mankind. In pursuit of this goal the Jews have concentrated capital in their hands and have turned it into a tool to promote their machinations. They have sought to inculcate political and social ideas in the guise of capitalism, liberalism, and socialism—ideologies that lead to national disintegration and direct men toward false universalistic concepts in the spirit of Judaism. Substantially there is no difference between these ideologies, because all of them are extensions of the one strategic plan of the Jews. Not only the traditional Jews but also the modern assimilated Jew is subject to the secret leadership, according to the antisemites, and supposed internal differences of opinion among the Jews are only a pretense to mislead non-Jewish society; the Talmudic dictum that the gentile world is to be hated must be followed by all Jews.

Blood libels (the accusation that Jews kill gentiles to obtain their blood for Jewish rituals) became numerous in the countries of western, central, and eastern Europe. Most infamous was the 1882 blood libel in the Hungarian village of Tisza Eszlar. During the trial the name of August Rohling, a professor of theology from Prague, also gained world attention. In 1871 Rohling published *Der Talmudjude* (The Talmud Jew) and offered to appear before a court to prove, using Talmudic sources, his claim that Jews use blood for ritual purposes. When it was demonstrated in Rohling's presence that he did not know how to read Talmudic sources and that his words were nothing but an evil libel, Rohling was forced to back down. As happens in such libels, however, sensational rumors proved to be hardier than the truth. The blood libel of which Mendel Beilis was accused in Russia and for which he was tried in 1913 also received worldwide publicity. Eventually the judges freed Beilis, but as in the Tisza Eszlar case, blood libel as such was not categorically denounced as a baseless invention.

According to extreme antisemites, a Jewish leadership working deep underground was orchestrating a long-range plan. At times certain institutions and organizations were said to be manifestations of this leadership. Among them were the Alliance Israélite Universelle, a Jewish philanthropic organization based in France that was devoted to spreading enlightened education to Jews in the Balkans, Asia, and North Africa. The Zionist Congresses were also tied to the leadership. In 1868 a novel, *Biarritz,* was published by Hermann Goedsche, under the pseudonym Sir John Redcliffe (Retcliffe). Its first chapter describes a secret meeting of the twelve Jewish tribes at night in the Prague Jewish cemetery. There, with the aura of an esoteric ceremony accompanied by prayer, oaths, and fire, those present survey the progress made by the Jews in their efforts to take over the Christian world, and formulate their future plans. This chapter went through different variations, all of which were presented as authentic. Redcliffe, who in reality was a post-office clerk, was described as a courageous man who had uncovered a Jewish plot that threatened the entire Christian world. In 1871 in Basel, Osman Bey's pamphlet *The Jewish Conquest of the World* was published, putting forth similar fabricated ideas.

Other variations on these themes appeared in different forms, but the version that became most important and influential, and that still continues to exert influence, is the *Protocols of the Elders of Zion.* The *Protocols,* which were disseminated in Russia from the beginning of the twentieth century, were a transparent plagiarism of a parody of Napoleon III by Maurice Joly, a long-forgotten French author. They were initially used by the Russian secret police to deflect political unrest toward the Jews. Remarkably, the *Protocols,* which were taken to the West by Russian emigrés at the time of the Bolshevik

An illustration from *Trau keinem Fuchs auf grüner Heid und keinem Jud bei seinem Eid* (Don't Trust a Fox in the Chicken Coop or a Jew at His Word), a children's book by Elvira Bauer published in Germany by Stürmer Verlag in 1936. [A Living Memorial to the Holocaust—Museum of Jewish Heritage, New York]

Revolution, reached Germany and other lands and were accepted by many as the truth. Even the London *Times* tended for a while to give credence to the *Protocols,* although later it exposed them as a forgery.

The success of the *Protocols* and similar works can be better understood against the background of the widely held accusation that Jews were among the leaders of the wave of revolutions that swept Europe during and after World War I; in particular, that they were among the leaders of the Bolshevik Revolution. The participation of Jews in these revolutions was prominent: personalities such as Leon Trotsky in Russia, Béla Kun in Hungary, and Rosa Luxemburg and Kurt Eisner in Germany were born Jews, although their politics and actions estranged them from Judaism. Nevertheless, their Jewish origins and those of other revolutionaries were emphasized everywhere, and aroused suspicions among many who had not previously been antisemitic.

Racial ideas also played a part in secular political antisemitism. The earlier vague antisemitism was superseded by claims supposedly based on objective scientific criteria. With the aid of caricatures projecting the ideas of ugliness, greed, and promiscuity, the image of the ugly Jew became established. The division of mankind by race, for which Gobineau had sought a basis, was originally conceived to give a foundation to the idea that the aristocracy, which had been displaced by the French Revolution, was really superior.

These ideas did not take root in France, but they did succeed in Germany. Those who hoped to divert dislike of Jews into a racial track found a sympathetic chord among many Germans. The Jews were virtually the only ethnic group dispersed throughout Europe on which an alien racial identity was pinned. The racial perspective allowed a mark to be placed on the Jew after all the other signs of stereotypical differences had virtually disappeared; the Jew now dressed like a German or Frenchman, behaved like a German or Frenchman, spoke impeccable German or French, and became a patron of music, art, and literature. The Jew-haters felt the need to transfer their hatred to an intangible and mysterious sphere, and racism fit the bill; if the Jew had characteristics that could not be changed, then it was justifiable to refuse to grant him equality. When the evil in the Jew, in all its aspects, was based on biology and blood, there was nothing different that was visible or could be erased; the cause was deeper. This held true for all Jews, whether traditional, assimilated, or converted to Christianity. In fact, the danger was seen as greater when Jews had acquired the language and outer appearance of Germans and had professedly left their own religion and race than when their Jewishness was transparent to all.

It is not incidental that an antisemite like Theodor Fritsch, who was known as a professional and eclectic antisemite (that is, one who was ready to adopt any and every reason or idea that would further his cause), in the end became a racist. Patriotism, which in the Second Reich (1871 to 1918) became strident nationalism, embodied by blood, war, and steel, reinforced by rapid industrialization, and translated into imperial designs, derided and detested tolerance and the values of equality. Heinrich von Treitschke, the ambitious historian and publicist of the Second Reich, who himself was a liberal in the days when liberalism flourished, claimed that the Jews were not completely loyal to Germany. He used the phrase "Die Juden sind unser Ungluck" ("The Jews are our misfortune"). His young pupil Heinrich von Class, who was active in reactionary right-wing circles during the Weimar Republic, went a step further, adopting racism and calling for the passage of discriminatory laws against the Jews.

Adolf Stoecker, a lay preacher who rose from humble beginnings to become the imperial court chaplain, was saturated with an anti-Judaism that was rooted in religion, and he imparted a public dimension to anti-Judaism. Stoecker tried to establish a Christian Socialist party to stop the growing Social Democrats, but when religious arguments did not work, he turned to antisemitism as a means of garnering mass support. Stoecker's antisemitism was still somewhat restrained, but that of Eugen Dühring, an eccentric philosopher with his own personal theory of socialism and a critic of the Christian church, was not restrained in the least. Dühring spoke clearly of a Jewish race that was totally evil. He advocated the abrogation of the Emancipation and the ousting of Jews from various spheres of life, and, finally, he viewed the deportation of the Jews as a desirable solution.

In periods of crisis, or in the face of failure or public outbursts of anger, an accusing finger was pointed at the Jews. Such was the case at the time of the *Gründerkrise* (the Founders' Crisis), which followed the prosperity after the victory over France in 1871 and the flow of reparations money; that prosperity led to the growth of speculative investments and profits, which in turn caused a crisis. Jews were at times represented as the cause of a calamity that at the same time struck other countries besides Germany. Men like Otto Glagua, who was among those badly hurt by the financial collapse, were not satisfied with accusing the Jews; they publicly aired the theory that Jews by nature turn to business, capital, and the stock market. In other words, said Glagua, the Jewish role in society is that of an unproductive parasite. Politicians and parties arose that exploited the circumstances and used antisemitism to pave their way to the Reichstag. In 1881, 300,000 people signed a petition calling for the expulsion of Jews from government jobs. During the 1880s in Germany antisemitic congresses were held that supposedly were international, but in reality the only non-Germans in attendance were from the Austro-Hungarian Empire, and their position was dictated by the Germans.

In the 1890s the antisemitic parties in Germany were in a state of decline. However, the right-wing conservative parties incorporated antisemitism as part of their platforms. With signs of defeat in World War I becoming apparent, strident antisemitism again became prominent. During the war, rumors were rife that Jews were not serving at the front but had infiltrated noncombat positions, and military leaders ordered that the matter be checked. Jews were also accused of fostering defeatism in the rear during the revolutionary period of 1918 and 1919. The frustration that came in the wake of the collapse of the war effort, the economic crisis during the Weimar Republic, and the revulsion felt by many toward the republic all engendered anti-Jewish ideas and feelings.

Political antisemitism was not only a German phenomenon but embraced all of Europe, and, as mentioned, it struck roots in France. There, during the last decades of the nineteenth century and the beginning of the twentieth, the Jewish issue was a component of the long debate between the republicans and royalists. The Dreyfus affair of the 1890s is seen as an anti-Jewish campaign that made a profound and stormy imprint on Europe. Eduard Drumont, the author of the book *La France juive* (Jewish France), whose anti-Jewish activities began before the Dreyfus affair and reached their apogee during it, has been appraised by the historian Jacob Katz as having expressed views as extreme and severe as those of the Nazis during the Weimar Republic.

Drumont raised the cry "France for the French." He wrote prolifically, published antisemitic books and newspapers, and was widely read. For a short time he also coordinated the antisemitic faction in the French parliament and led an antisemitic political party. French antisemitism sometimes dovetailed with the anti-Freemasonism that was fostered by the Catholic church. The connection between the Freemasons and the Jews did not exist to the same extent in Germany because there, Jews as a rule had not been admitted to Masonic lodges. Some believe that the reason why antisemitism in France did not reach the level of its German counterpart was that the Jews in France comprised a smaller percentage of the population than in Germany; and when the regions of Alsace and Lorraine were transferred to Germany after the German victory over France in 1871, a focal point and main arena of French antisemitism disappeared. In France several financial scandals contributed to antisemitism, such as the collapse of the Union Générale bank, which was under the aegis of Catholics and was a competitor of Jewish banks; the collapse of the stock of the Panama Canal company; and several instances of corruption in which Jews as well as some well-known members of the social elite and the regime were involved. However, racial Darwinist ideas were never widely accepted in France. In general, the "Jewish question" was not at the core of any of the powerful political factions. The "Jewish question" in France was often an issue of the differences between Jews: the Jews who had been in France for a long time, were rooted in its culture, and had contributed to the French war effort, as contrasted to recently arrived foreign Jews. The latter were the main object of discrimination and antipathy, especially between the two world wars. Léon Blum, as the leader of the Socialist party, and at times the premier, was a target for incitement and outbursts owing to his Jewish background, yet it is doubtful whether in this period a Jew in Germany could have risen to a similar position. The closest, Walther RATHENAU, who filled various crucial posts in Germany during World War I and whose outlook tended toward the right, was assassinated in 1922, not long after he became Germany's foreign minister.

The situation of Jews in states with one dominant nationality, like Germany and France, must be distinguished from that in states where the Jews were one of many large minorities. In AUSTRIA, the Germans after World War I lost the dominance they had held in the former large Austro-Hungarian Empire, and moreover remained isolated from other Germans. Antisemitism was strong there, with foundations both in popular culture and in a nationalist ideology. In MEIN KAMPF, Adolf HITLER claimed that VIENNA was for him a school in antisemitism. The effective and popular mayor of Vienna, Karl Lueger, was (in the late nineteenth century) the first person of high rank in the Austro-Hungarian Empire who openly expressed antisemitic ideas and knew how to sell them to the Catholic majority. Another antisemitic leader who influenced Hitler, according to the latter's writings, was Georg von Schönerer, an advocate of Pan-Germanism who was close to the nationalist racist concept but whose influence in Austrian politics was limited. Although antisemitism increased and was directed primarily toward Jews who came to Vienna from eastern Europe, it never played an important role in internal Austrian politics or Austrian foreign relations between the two world wars. Antipathy toward the Jews attained a brutal, totally unrestrained expression with the ANSCHLUSS in 1938, and more than one of the Nazi leaders who were extreme in the persecution and murder of the Jews were of Austrian origin.

In HUNGARY, and to some extent in POLAND during the 1860s and 1870s, the trend was to bring the Jews closer to the nationalist movement within the multinational state structure, to make them a part of the population that identified with Hungarian or Polish nationalist aims. In the last decades of the nineteenth century, political antisemitism with an ideological tone increased in both countries. Both had long-standing, brutal, and vulgar antisemitic traditions, as in Germany. In both, Jews constituted a relatively high percentage of the urban population and controlled a significant proportion of trade, finance, and the professions. Since the Jews were considered outsiders, and since they themselves often maintained their uniqueness and separateness from the gentiles (in particular in Poland and ROMANIA), to a certain extent there was in these countries a real conflict or problem with regard to the Jews. The dominant antisemite in Hungary before World War I, Victor Istoczy, defined himself as an advocate of sociopolitical antisemitism, and spoke of "defense" against the Jews. He was in contact with prominent antisemites in Germany and took part in the first antisemitic congress, in Dresden. Istoczy spoke of "racism," but it seems that racism did not play a significant role in his anti-Jewishness.

In Poland during the 1890s a national democratic movement, that of the Endeks, arrived on the scene and adopted a platform emphasizing antisemitism. The party's authoritarian leader and ideologist, Roman Dmowski, was an aggressive antisemite, and at times wielded great influence in the party. As early as 1907 Dmowski called the Jews an ethnic entity that was foreign to the Polish mentality, was not able to assimilate, and was likely to spread foreign and repulsive ways among the Poles. Therefore, he maintained, the assimilation of the Jews, except in a few cases, was not desirable. Later, Dmowski and his circle asserted that the Jews had allied themselves with Poland's historical enemies (Russia, Prussia, and Austria-Hungary) and had derived benefit therefrom. Moreover, he declared, they bore much of the responsibility for Poland's sorry state. In 1912 Dmowski organized an anti-Jewish boycott, and from then on the economic component in political anti-Jewish propaganda—"Jewish Bolshevism"—became more prominent in the party's platform and policy. Between the world wars, antisemitism became a significant component of public and government opinion.

Except for Czechoslovakia, the situation of the Jews deteriorated in the countries of central and eastern Europe that had been created after the end of World War I. Although these states signed minority treaties, it was not within their power to uphold them, especially with regard to protecting the Jews' rights. Moreover, the desire of the largest ethnic group in each state to impose its own stamp on the country harmed all the minorities, and the Jews as a weak minority suffered more than others. The Romanians succeeded in abrogating the rights of Jews in the territories that Romania had annexed, and conducted a fierce anti-Jewish propaganda campaign. During the White Terror in Hungary (1919–1920) the Hungarians avenged themselves on the Jews for their alleged role in the revolution, which was led by Béla Kun. Hungary became the first country to invoke a *numerus clausus* (quota) in institutes of higher education, restricting the number of Jews who could study in them. In Poland, anti-Jewish policy was applied primarily in the economic sphere. The economic difficulties that struck the countries of central and eastern Europe strengthened anti-Jewish attitudes. For the most part, antisemitism in these countries was not racial or biological.

Der
ewige Jude
GROSSE POLITISCHE SCHAU IM BIBLIOTHEKSBAU DES DEUTSCHEN MUSEUMS
ZU MÜNCHEN · AB 8. NOVEMBER 1937 · TÄGLICH GEÖFFNET VON 10-21 UHR

"Der ewige Jude" (The Eternal [or Wandering] Jew), a poster for the 1937 antisemitic exhibition arranged by the Nazis in Munich. The exhibition was also mounted in Vienna, on August 2, 1938. The text of the poster reads: "A large political exhibit in the library building of the Deutsche Museum in Munich from November 8, 1937. Open daily 10:00 to 21:00."

Among other reasons, the deep religiosity prevailing in them did not permit that kind of racist antisemitism to spread, and the relative isolation of the Jews prevented a search for ways of separating them out.

In the second half of the 1930s, after the 1933 Nazi rise to power, open and strident antisemitism received a great boost and legitimation as an acceptable policy. In Hungary and Romania fascist parties with a clear antisemitic tone were active. In Poland the right-wing parties and (after the death of the authoritative leader, Józef Piłsudski) the political camp in power supported a mass exodus of Jews. The extreme rightist movements wanted to speed up such an exodus by using violence and pogroms. The governing bloc, on the other hand, wanted to achieve this goal by political means. Hungary saw itself as an ally of Germany and a partner in territorial revisionism, and in 1938 and 1939 it passed antisemitic and racial laws. For a while in Romania pillaging, violence, and pogroms took place under government auspices.

The position of these peoples and nations during the period of Nazi rule and occupation is a separate and important chapter. The Poles did not take an active part in the annihilation of the Jews, but the dominant attitude of the population and the underground was one of indifference during the murder of the Jews, most of which, through no fault of the Poles, was carried out on their soil. The Romanians participated actively in the mass murder, but in the last stages of the war they recoiled from handing over Jews for total destruction. In Hungary the situation of the Jews during most of the war years was relatively tolerable, but with the German invasion of Hungary in March 1944 and the beginning of deportations to extermination camps, the Hungarian authorities helped in the work of annihilation, and much of the Hungarian population also played a shameful role.

Russian antisemitism has special characteristics. For centuries Russia was closed off to Jews. Jews were concentrated in the western district, which the tsarist empire had annexed from Poland and Romania. Stringent laws prevented Jews from leaving the area known as the Pale of Settlement to settle in the large cities of central Russia. The authorities attempted to break down Jewish separateness through administrative measures. For a long time antisemitism in Russia was government policy, and only small groups of Jews were permitted to play any part in the nation's economic development. Radical intellectuals viewed the antisemitism of the masses of peasants as a sign of their political awakening. The wave of pogroms that swept Russia during the 1880s, even when initiated not by the government but by extremist organizations close to it, was not opposed by the regime. These developments spurred the emigration of large numbers of Jews from Russia to countries overseas, especially to the United States. Only after the February 1917 revolution were Russian Jews granted equal rights. The wave of emigrés that left Russia after the 1917 revolution contributed to the spread of antisemitic ideas in the countries where they took refuge. Between the two world wars, antisemitism in the Soviet Union was illegal, and therefore hidden. The roles filled by individual Jews in the Soviet regime contributed to a new kind of antisemitism, one with new motives, which during World War II and the Holocaust had a deadly effect in the Nazi-occupied areas of the Soviet Union. In the opinion of some historians, Stalin's campaign against the old Bolsheviks was not free of an anti-Jewish motive.

In Germany, political antisemitism was first and foremost ideological in nature, claiming that the Jew played a key role in the confrontation between universalist philosophies and in current social and political conflicts. The brutality and violence of pogroms and persecutions that marked antisemitism in eastern Europe were not, at the beginning, part of German political antisemitism. However, the future would teach that a theory of racial antisemitism, which did not advocate force but rather spoke of "rational" solutions to the "Jewish question" as an answer to the problems of the nation and the entire world, contained within it sparks that would ignite a raging fire.

The division of people into races seemed to concur with the Darwinian interpretation of natural selection. It led to the conclusion that natural selection in nature (which balances or provides parameters for propagation, and improves through adaptation and survival those better suited to their surroundings) does not play a role in human society only because of artificial human intervention. Such intervention disrupts the process of evolution, which is based on competition and the elimination of the weak and unsuccessful. It is clear that this conclusion clashes with concepts that are rooted in religions ascribing to humans a special status as having been created in God's image.

A major place in the development of racism in Germany belongs to Houston Stewart Chamberlain, who added to it the dimension of historical evolution and the struggle within that evolution. Chamberlain was an Englishman who became Germanized and believed that he had a mission to the German people. According to Chamberlain, the Jews had declined over time. Neither King David nor Jesus was Jewish, and the great achievements ascribed to the Jews had actually been accomplished by gentiles. On the other hand, Chamberlain said, the Germans had developed into the elite Aryan race, and they enjoyed a spiritual singularity that enabled them to create great achievements. Chamberlain's book *Die Grundlagen des 19. Jahrhunderts* (The Foundations of the Nineteenth Century) was written to describe and explain this evolution and the racial struggle conducted throughout history. It was also written to make the Germans aware of the geographic expansion they deserved, and of the enemies surrounding them.

In Germany, racism, more than any other theory (aside from nationalism), was the substance of NATIONAL SOCIALISM. National Socialism did not adopt one anti-Jewish line, while abandoning the others. The authorities of the Third Reich were faced with the challenge of defining who was an Aryan and determining who was a Jew. They never attempted to define a person's race by means of elements in his blood, the shape of his skull or nose, his hair color or body type, and so on, realizing that such criteria would undoubtedly lead to many Nazis being defined as Jews and many Jews being considered pure Aryans. Therefore the Nazis turned to religion as the measurement of race, even though Hitler had claimed many times that the Jews did not constitute a religion but a race, and that it was race which determined their identity as Jews. The religious criteria that were instituted required that a check be made of the religious affiliation of persons who had abandoned Judaism or had intermarried. Some of the MISCHLINGE (people of mixed German and Jewish ancestry) were classified with the Jews, although they belonged to families that were German by any definition.

Long before the Nazi rise to power in Germany, it became clear that providing basic education to the masses and granting them political rights would not automatically strengthen liberalism, democracy, and mutual understanding among men and nations, as liberal and socialist circles had hoped and conservative nationalists had feared. It turned out that the superstitions and prejudices absorbed by popular culture over the course of generations had a firm hold on the people's soul and consciousness. Alongside innovative and progressive trends, another direction began to make headway, which opposed internationalism and socialism and claimed to have found the solution for the problem of the underprivileged in a national framework. This new direction, without being revolutionary in the accepted sense, manifested dynamism—albeit a nationalist dynamism—and the ability to capture and hold the imagination of the people. For the most part, antisemitism was an inseparable or dominant element in that trend and its motivation.

It has not been substantiated that antisemitism affected the entire German nation or even that the majority of Germans adopted an actively antisemitic outlook, and it would be wrong to make such a claim. From the mid-nineteenth century to the 1870s, emancipation and the ideas of liberalism had gained momentum in Germany and had made constant progress (which the antisemites and supporters of the old regime sought to stop). This situation changed, however, during the Second Reich. The liberal movement, which had come to be largely identified with Jews and which protected Jewish rights, weakened. Jews and non-Jews who opposed antisemitism had to organize in order to safeguard the rights already granted, and they were being put more and more on the defensive. The Social Democrats regarded Jew-hatred as an element undermining their ideological basis and found antisemitism to be the "socialism of fools," as the Social Democrat leader, August Bebel, put it. This recognition notwithstanding, the socialist camp tried not to be identified as defending the Jews, a position viewed as unpopular, and socialist propaganda was not above mentioning the connection that existed between Jews and capitalism.

Political antisemitism was a sign of the crisis that struck society and nationalism at the end of the nineteenth and in the first decades of the twentieth century. Countries in which democracy was rooted and flourishing—such as Great Britain, the Netherlands, and the Scandinavian nations—were not hurt much by the various radical movements and by antisemitism. The other countries, however, suffered great turmoil. The interwar period is regarded by many historians as an era in which fascism spread all over Europe. Yet these scholars tend to differentiate between National Socialism, which had antisemitism at the core of its ideology, and fascism in Italy and other countries of western Europe. The latter for a long time rejected antisemitism, and even when they accepted it, did not adopt racism as a main ideological component.

In Germany, the Jews had been asked to give up many elements of their tradition and organizational pattern in order to be worthy of equal rights and integration into German society. As a result, the greater part of German Jewry passed through a profound metamorphosis. The Jews, primarily urbanized and representing only about one percent of the population, adopted religious reforms that did away with many of their commandments and traditions, changed their marriage habits, and significantly reduced their birthrate. Many Jews turned to higher education and the professions to which it led, and tried to excel in them. Certain areas of advancement, however, remained closed to them, such as the officers' corps, and higher posts in the academic field and in the government administration. As a result, many Jews became concentrated in certain professions, including law and medicine, and also turned in significant numbers to the natural sciences, the press, and the arts. The number of German Jews who won Nobel prizes was many times greater than their proportion in the population. The Jews' drive to excel and their disproportionate numbers in some professions made them conspicuous and exposed them to suspicion and hatred. To escape from this hatred and to attain positions from which they were barred, many Jews converted; yet even then they did not cease to be Jews in the searching and watchful eyes of their professional rivals and the Jew-haters. In the opinion of sociologists and demogra-

Antisemitic graffito on a Jewish shopwindow in Germany (1938). The text is written in "pidgin German" to mock the "nonethnic" German Jew. It reads: "Am I not a good German?" [Bildarchiv Preussischer Kulturbesitz]

phers, the Jews of Germany would have disappeared within a few generations through assimilation and a declining birthrate, and it was only the influx of Jews from the east that slowed down this inevitable decline. Politically, most of the German Jews were liberals, and their first preference was for the further development of liberal policies. With the weakening of liberalism in Germany, the Social Democrats became a reliable barrier against antisemitism. Many Jews voted for the Social Democratic Party and supported it, even though they apparently did not fully identify with its ideology, and as a persecuted and besieged group were only looking for a helping hand. German Jews were great patriots, with a profound love for German culture and the German landscape. Even Orthodox Jews, who would never consider giving up their religious principles, were ardent German patriots. For many Jews, their world was destroyed when Germany turned its back on them and they found out that their love for their country had been a one-sided, unrequited love.

During the Nazi period "anti-Jewishness" became part of an overall outlook, in several ways. First, it was integral to the Nazi ideology, not as just one among many different concepts, but as a central element. Second, it was considered a powerful and effective propaganda weapon, used to explain all the existing inadequacies and failures and to shore up the opposition to the liberal parliamentary regime. Third, with Hitler's rise to power, anti-Jewish racism became a political component of the means employed by the government to implement its policies—of excluding the Jews from social, cultural, and economic life; separating them, insofar as possible, from the rest of the population; and, in the end, getting rid of them altogether in all the lands under German control.

Anti-Jewishness in the Nazi period followed the directives laid down by Hitler in the 1920s. It was not based on an emotional approach and did not take the form of outbursts, but constituted a consistent "rational" policy, grounded in legislation. The Nazi anti-Jewishness did not confine itself to any particular set of charges against Jews but made use of all the many and varied antisemitic calumnies and libels that had been thought up over the generations.

At one stage the Nazi state tried to replace the term "antisemitism" with "anti-Jewishness." This was done both for political reasons ("antisemitism" could be considered to apply to Arabs as well as to Jews) and because Jew-hatred was no longer a separate subject, but a fundamental part of a political ideology. Although this effort did not succeed and the term "antisemitism" remained in use, certain new terms did enter circulation, such as "Jewish blood" and, conversely, "German and related blood." The Nazis took pains not to speak of the export of racism, since according to the principles of the Nazi version of that ideology, the different peoples of Europe would not be promised equality and partnership with the German master race. To the extent that the Nazis did try to disseminate and export antisemitism, they did so in the belief that it would help obscure their long-term goals and deflect public attention abroad from the emerging Nazi threat.

Political antisemitism did not lead directly and inevitably to Nazism, and the Nazi takeover of Germany was not mainly a result of antisemitism. Nazism came to power as a form of German nationalism, aided by the prevailing circumstances of defeat and crisis. Yet antisemitism helped Nazis to gain power and win the hearts of the German masses. Even though the Nazis did not particularly emphasize antisemitism on the eve of their rise to power, it was a well-known element in their creed and action, and was no obstacle to their takeover. Nor did it engender very much opposition from the army, the churches, or German society as a whole.

Between the two world wars antisemitism was on the increase all over Europe, as an ideology and, in some countries, also as a practical policy applied to the Jews. This development derived from the growing influence of the Third Reich and the various fascist movements, and it was particularly strong in the countries of eastern Europe. The democracies did not accept antisemitism—indeed, they opposed it—but they preferred to downplay their disapproval so that their policies and actions would not be interpreted as a defense of persecuted Jews, since in the Nazi period such a "reputation" was unpopular and considered politically detrimental. In general, the Nazi policies against the Jews caused the Nazis only minor damage in the democratic and liberal countries, and except in extreme instances, such as the KRISTALLNACHT pogrom in November 1938, they did not encounter any real opposition. With the outbreak of the war it became clear that the Nazis were not confining their anti-Jewish policies to the territory of Greater Germany. They applied these policies with increasing severity against the Jews in every place they occupied and in every country where they attained political power and ideological influence.

The "FINAL SOLUTION" may be said to have been the all-out implementation of two closely related tendencies in the Nazi party and the Third Reich's ideology and policy: the Nazis' racist anti-Jewish ideology, which regarded the confrontation with the Jews as a struggle in which there could be no compromise; and the conclusion reached by the Nazis that the threat inherent in "Jewish blood" could be removed only by spilling that blood. The dynamics of the anti-Jewish policies and the relentless escalation of the methods applied by the Nazis reached the point where the only means left to be used was indiscriminate mass murder. It was this combination of ideology and its practical outcome that led to the "Final Solution." Undoubtedly, the crystallization of the diabolic plan was facilitated by the climate of resignation to the Third Reich's anti-Jewish policies and, at times, by the approval and collaboration that the Nazis found nearly everywhere they went, even at the stage of the "Final Solution" itself.

After World War II antisemitism was

An antisemitic parade (late 1930s) in Vienna. Twenty thousand National Socialists demonstrated against the treaties of St. Germain and Versailles and the "Jewish" press.

greatly weakened in the West, and the Western churches on many occasions admitted the fatal mistake they had made in cultivating the Christian aspects of antisemitism. In the Soviet Union and its satellites, however, strong expressions of antisemitism recurred a few years after the end of the war, and in times of crisis and change antisemitism was once again employed as a tactical tool. Not only was this a denial of the ideas and principles that the Soviet Union and socialism in general had adopted, but it was also a strange paradox. The state and the system that radical antisemites had claimed were a Jewish creation were now turning to the cynical and brutal exploitation of antisemitism. Over the years antisemitism began to appear under the guise of "anti-Zionism." The United Nations gave this development its blessing in a resolution, passed in November 1975, that equated Zionism with racism. The denial of the Holocaust (*see* HOLOCAUST, DENIAL OF THE) is also essentially a form of antisemitism, seeking to eradicate the truth in order to permit the resurrection of Jew-hatred as it existed in the past. There have been expressions of antisemitism in countries that have no Jews living in them; one such example was the widespread dissemination of antisemitic literature in Japan in the 1980s.

It is difficult to know or to predict whether, despite these various manifestations, antisemitism is in a process of decline or is only hibernating, waiting for some trauma to strike the world that will revive it and once again make it a powerful factor. Above all, it is clear that the struggle against antisemitism requires eternal vigilance and counteraction, not only to ensure that the genie does not escape from the bottle, but also to excise this disease from the body of mankind.

BIBLIOGRAPHY

Almog, S., ed. *Antisemitism through the Ages.* Oxford, 1988.

Davies, A. T. *Antisemitism and the Christian Mind: The Crises of Conscience after Auschwitz.* New York, 1969.

Ganger, J. G. *The Origins of Anti-Semitism.* New York, 1985.

Katz, J. *From Prejudice to Destruction: Antisemitism, 1700–1933.* Cambridge, Mass., 1980.

Massing, P. W. *Rehearsal for Destruction: A Study of Political Anti-Semitism in Imperial Germany.* New York, 1949.

Parkes, J. *Antisemitism.* Chicago, 1964.

Pinson, K. S., ed. *Essays on Antisemitism.* New York, 1946.

Poliakov, L. *Suicidal Europe, 1870–1933.* Vol. 4 of *The History of Anti-Semitism.* New York, 1985.

Pulzer, P. G. *The Rise of Political Anti-Semitism in Germany and Austria.* London, 1988.

Rürup, R. *Emancipation und Antisemitismus.* Göttingen, 1975.

Zimmerman, M. *Wilhelm Marr, the Patriarch of Anti-Semitism.* Oxford, 1986.

ISRAEL GUTMAN

ANTONESCU, ION (1882–1946), Romanian general and statesman; ruler of ROMANIA from 1940 to 1944. In World War I, Antonescu distinguished himself as a member of the general staff, and in 1933 he was appointed its chief. In 1937 and 1938 he was minister of defense in the cabinet headed by Octavian GOGA and Alexandru CUZA, the first Romanian cabinet that was outspokenly antisemitic. Antonescu did not belong to the antisemitic fascist movement headed by Corneliu Codreanu, but he did act as liaison between that movement and the traditional political establishment.

The fall of France in the summer of 1940 shattered Romania's political status, and it was forced to cede large parts of its territory to the Soviet Union, Hungary, and Bulgaria. During this severe national crisis—which threatened Romania's continued existence as an independent state—Antonescu was appointed prime minister by Prince Michael. Prior to this appointment, he had been confined on King Carol II's orders to a monastery after blaming the king and the military establishment for not preparing the Romanian army for war.

Upon being appointed prime minister, on September 5, 1940, Antonescu forced King Carol to abdicate in favor of his son Michael. Antonescu, however, was the real ruler. Together with Horia SIMA, chief of the IRON GUARD, Antonescu established the National Legionary Government, whose declared purpose was to draw close to Germany and Italy and to purge Romania of "foreign elements" and "foreign influence." Soon after assuming his post, he met with Hitler and gained his trust and esteem. Fearing that the Red Army was planning to seize the part of Moldavia still left in Romania's hands, Antonescu called on the German army to enter Romania, which it did in October of that year.

Soon after, Antonescu encountered problems with his Iron Guard partners, because of the violent and uncontrolled means they employed in seizing property—including the property of Jews—and in removing officials of the old regime from their posts, actions creating economic chaos and political unrest. In January 1941, the Iron Guard Legionnaires openly rebelled against Antonescu, who with Hitler's help was able to subdue them, henceforth ruling as dictator without setting up his own political party. Antonescu joined Germany in the invasion of the Soviet Union in June 1941 in order to recover BESSARABIA and northern BUKOVINA, which the Soviets had taken from Romania in June 1940. He also occupied TRANSNISTRIA, the considerable area of the Ukraine located between the Dniester and Bug rivers.

When he was in his thirties and serving as a military attaché in London, Antonescu had married a French Jewish woman, whom he later divorced; his stepmother too had been Jewish. Nevertheless, he was imbued with traditional antisemitic views and attitudes. These were based on economic and religious considerations according to which the Jews were exploiters who wanted to control Romania's economy, especially its commercial life, and therefore had to be removed from the villages and from economic positions. Antonescu, however, did not accept the racist Nazi-style doctrine, and throughout the war years he maintained public contact with representatives of Romania's Jewish community.

In his policy toward the Jews, Antonescu differentiated between Old Romania (the Regat, or pre–World War I Romania) and southern TRANSYLVANIA on the one hand, and Bessarabia and northern Bukovina on the other. In a secret draft order, he prepared for a purge of Bessarabia and Bukovina—extermination of the Jews in the rural areas, and imprisonment of the urban Jews in concentration camps and ghettos.

In Romania proper (Old Romania and southern Transylvania), Antonescu, on June 19, 1941, ordered the expulsion of 40,000 Jews from villages and towns to urban Jewish centers. He confiscated and nationalized Jewish property and imposed on the Jews a special levy of 4 billion lei (about $40 million). He did not, however, permit the 300,000 Jews of these areas to be handed over to the Germans or murdered.

Late in the summer of 1941, Antonescu ordered the expulsion of 150,000 Jews from Bessarabia, Bukovina, and the Dorohoi district, survivors of earlier massacres, to Transnistria. There, many of them were murdered, starved to death, or succumbed to disease and epidemics. For two years Antonescu stood firm in refusing to permit the return of the survivors from Transnistria, and it was only at the end of 1943 that certain categories of Jews, such as orphaned children, were permitted to go back to Romania. In the wake of an explosion on October 22, 1941, in the Romanian headquarters in ODESSA (which Romanian troops had occupied), Antonescu ordered punitive measures to be taken against Communists and Jews; for every Romanian or German officer killed, 200 persons were ordered to be killed, and 100 for every Romanian or German of other rank; 25,000 Odessa Jews were murdered in these retaliatory measures.

Although he had agreed to the German program for the "final solution of the Jewish question" in Romania, according to which all the Jews of his country were to be deported to the BEŁŻEC extermination camp in Poland, he hesitated in permitting its implementation and in the end withdrew his consent. For a while (until the spring of 1942) Antonescu permitted the Zionist movement to operate, in order to solve the "Jewish question" by emigration of the Jews from Romania; this policy was defeated by German pressure, and by the British refusal to permit Jews from an enemy country to enter Palestine.

On August 23, 1944, as the Soviet army was advancing into Romania, Antonescu was arrested on the order of King Michael. He was taken to the Soviet Union, and subsequently sent back to Romania to be tried there. Sentenced to death, he was executed as a war criminal on June 1, 1946.

BIBLIOGRAPHY

Ancel, J., ed. *Documents concerning the Fate of Romanian Jewry during the Holocaust.* 12 vols. Jerusalem, 1986.

Simion, A. *Preliminarii politico-diplomatice de insurectiei române din August 1944.* Cluj, 1979.

Yust, W., ed. *Eventful Years.* Vol. 3. Chicago, 1947. See pages 828–834.

JEAN ANCEL

ANTONESCU, MIHAI (1907–1946), Romanian political figure. Antonescu was a lawyer and served as a professor of international law in Bucharest. He was not a member of any antisemitic or fascist party; as a young man he had expressed disapproval of anti-Jewish discrimination at the universities.

During the period of King Carol's dictatorship (1938–1940), Antonescu struck up a friendship with Ion ANTONESCU (they were not related), based on mutual opposition to the king's policy. Mihai Antonescu was never known as a supporter of the IRON GUARD, but he also refrained from denouncing its actions in public. In September 1940, when Ion Antonescu formed his first cabinet, the National Legionary Government (Governul National-Legioner), Mihai Antonescu was appointed minister of propaganda. In the period immediately preceding his appointment to the cabinet, Mihai Antonescu, who until then had voiced anti-Nazi attitudes, switched to support of Nazi Germany and its policies.

As Ion Antonescu's closest confidant, Mihai accompanied the premier on his January 1941 visit to Germany and took part in talks with Hitler and other leading figures in the Nazi regime. Acting in behalf of Ion Antonescu, Mihai coordinated the tactical moves against Iron Guard chief and deputy premier Horia SIMA, and, following the suppression of the Iron Guard elements, became deputy premier and foreign minister (February 1941) and the Romanian dictator's closest adviser. Mihai Antonescu incurred the hatred of the Legionnaires (the Iron Guardsmen), and on several occasions they threatened his life.

Mihai Antonescu was put in charge of censorship, and he instructed the media, especially the veteran Romanian newspapers, to adopt a rabidly antisemitic line, thereby preparing the ground for the exclusion of the Jews from Romanian society. As deputy prime minister he also concentrated on drafting the laws for the dispossession of Jewish property; in March 1941, Jewish-owned property in the cities—buildings, apartments, stores, and so forth—was confiscated. Antonescu initiated laws and administrative regulations that further restricted the opportunities available for Jews to earn a livelihood, caused their dismissal from posts they held, barred them from certain occupations, and "purged" the civil and public administrations of their Jewish employees.

On the eve of the war against the Soviet Union, Mihai and Ion Antonescu drew up the *Curatirea Terenului* (Cleansing of the Ground) edict, for "purifying" BESSARABIA and BUKOVINA of Jews. In a cabinet meeting held on July 3, 1941, Mihai Antonescu openly discussed the plan. He chaired a meeting of the officials designated to head the civil administrations of Bessarabia and Bukovina, at which, *inter alia*, he ordered them to get rid of the Jews there, who, he charged, were traitors to Romania and supporters of communism and the Russians.

In the initial phase of the war, until October 1941, Mihai Antonescu ran the country because Ion Antonescu was preoccupied at the front, directing the Romanian forces fighting the Russians. It was in that period that the Jews of Old Romania (the Regat) suffered the worst blows: they were expelled from the towns and villages, confined to detention and labor camps, and robbed of their belongings. Worst of all was the pogrom in IAŞI, which began on June 29, 1941, and continued for several days. The degree to which Mihai Antonescu was directly involved in the pogrom cannot be determined. In meetings he had with Jewish community leaders in that period (until September 1942), Mihai Antonescu claimed that he took a "humane" approach, abhorred criminal action in all its forms, and was concerned solely with safeguarding the interests of the Romanian people. This, however, did not prevent him on occasion from issuing threats against the Jewish leaders, for example, Dr. Wilhelm FILDERMAN.

In talks with Hitler and other Nazi leaders, Mihai Antonescu praised the Nazis for the example they were giving the world on how to solve the "Jewish question." In November 1941 he consented to the request made by the German ambassador to Romania, Manfred von KILLINGER, to stop emigration of Jews from the country, and a few weeks later he agreed to withdraw the Romanian state's protection from Jews in the Nazi-occupied countries of Europe who had Romanian passports. As a result, most of these Jews were deported to extermination camps. Mihai Antonescu cooperated with Gustav RICHTER, the adviser on Jewish affairs in the German legation in Bucharest, and on Richter's demand he disbanded the Federatia Uniunilor de Comunitati Evreesti (Federation of Jewish Communities) and in its place established the CENTRALA EVREILOR (Jewish Center), a kind of JUDENRAT (Jewish Council). In the summer of 1942 Antonescu gave Richter written assurance on behalf of the government of Romania that the country's Jews would be deported to the extermination camps in Poland.

In the fall of 1942, under the impact of the sharp dispute with Hungary over northern Transylvania, the critical situation on the front, and the heavy economic and financial burden that Germany had imposed on ROMANIA, Mihai Antonescu began to look for ways to extricate Romania from the war and bring about a rapprochement with Britain and the United States. Ion Antonescu gave full support to these efforts, and resisted pressure by the Germans to dismiss the deputy premier from his post. The latter was convinced that the Jews would play an important role in

Mihai Antonescu during his trial in 1946.

influencing public opinion in the Allied countries.

Supported by orders from his chief, Mihai Antonescu embarked upon a new policy. He put a stop to the deportation of Jews from Romania and renewed contacts with the leaders of Romanian Jewry, especially with Filderman, Chief Rabbi Alexander SAFRAN, and the heads of the Zionist movement, Misu Benvenisti and Abraham Leib Zissu. Together with these leaders he explored possibilities for enabling as many Jews as possible to emigrate from Romania. With this end in mind, he agreed to the establishment of an emigration office and, in effect, to the resumption of the Zionist movement's activities. He put the diplomatic pouch at Filderman's disposal for communicating with the heads of the JOINT DISTRIBUTION COMMITTEE and other Jewish organizations in the free world, conducted the negotiations for the repatriation of orphans and other survivors of the deportations to TRANSNISTRIA, and alleviated some of the day-to-day burdens of the Jews. From mid-1943 his speeches had few antisemitic overtones and made no specific mention of the Jews.

In foreign policy, Mihai Antonescu attempted to persuade the Germans to bring the war in the West to an end and concentrate on the war against the Soviet Union and the Slav peoples. He failed in his attempt to extricate Romania from the war together with Italy, but protected the American ambassador's family after Romania severed relations with the United States at the end of 1941. He also protected the Italian ambassador himself when Italy surrendered to the Allies in September 1943. After the fall of Stalingrad, Mihai Antonescu tried to revise the documents that bore his signature and to destroy the written evidence of his criminal liability.

Mihai and Ion Antonescu were arrested on August 23, 1944; in 1946 they were sentenced to death and executed. Unlike Ion Antonescu, Mihai Antonescu behaved poorly during the trial. He tried to put the blame on others and to stress the modest steps he had taken to relieve the plight of the Jews.

BIBLIOGRAPHY

Ancel, J., ed. *Documents concerning the Fate of Romanian Jewry during the Holocaust*. Vols. 3, 5, 8, 9. Jerusalem, 1986.

Seton-Watson, H. *The East European Revolution*. London, 1961. See chapter 5.

JEAN ANCEL

ANTWERP, city in Flanders in northern BELGIUM, close to the Dutch border. Antwerp is Belgium's largest port and one of the major ports on the European continent. On the eve of the German invasion some fifty thousand Jews lived in Antwerp, of whom only 10 percent were Belgian nationals. Thousands of Jews fled Belgium at the time of the invasion; consequently, during the German occupation, the city had a Jewish population of about thirty thousand, representing 40.4 percent of the country's Jews, compared to the 51.4 percent of Belgian Jewry living in Brussels. Despite its smaller size, the Jewish community of Antwerp was the more prominent, by virtue of its distinct Jewish character and its range of activities. Antwerp had three separate Jewish communities: two Ashkenazic, named Maḥzikei Hadas and Shomrei Hadas, and one Sephardic. There were thirty-four synagogues and prayer houses; two comprehensive elementary schools (Yesodei ha-Torah and Taḥkemoni); four Hebrew schools; two rabbinical academies (yeshivas); twenty-two social organizations, including burial societies and foundations of various kinds (especially for mutual aid); and four aid organizations (Alliance Israélite Universelle, the Central Charity and Social Assistance Organization, the Committee for Jewish Refugees, and Tomkhei Aniyyim [Supporters of the Poor]). Six publications, in Yiddish, French, and Dutch (Flemish), appeared regularly. Several Zionist and non-Zionist political parties were active in the community, as were nineteen youth movements, six professional organizations, and three sports clubs.

The Antwerp Jewish community was of relatively recent vintage and for the most part consisted of immigrants from eastern Europe and, to a much lesser degree, from Germany. It was the eastern European style that determined the community's daily and organizational life. A substantial number of Jews were merchants and peddlers, but there was also a large Jewish proletariat. The diamond trade played a very important role in the life of the Jews and the general economic life of Antwerp. In the years just preceding the German occupation, there was an increase in the number of antisemitic incidents in Antwerp, which the Jews tried to cope with as best they could. The mayor of Antwerp, the Socialist Camille Huysmans, was friendly to the Jews and tried to be of help to them in various ways.

Under the German occupation, the fate of the Jews of Antwerp was essentially the same as that of the rest of Belgian Jewry, but a number of events and developments affected only Antwerp. During the fighting many Antwerp Jews tried to flee; some of them made their way to the south of France, but most had to turn back. Community life and the economic situation were partially restored, and for the first few months daily life was fairly undisturbed. Despite plans made before the German occupation to transfer the diamond industry to Britain, most of the diamond dealers and workers and the merchandise itself had remained in the city. The diamond industry was reactivated in the first phase of the occupation and even flourished for a while, especially the trade in industrial diamonds.

Following a German decree under which foreign nationals could be removed from the coastal area of Flanders, the Antwerp military command, on its own initiative, decided to apply the decree to Jews who had immigrated to Belgium after 1938. On December 23, 1940, a first group, consisting of 222 men and women and 21 children, left for the Limbourg province; as time went on, the number of expellees rose to 3,334. They were distributed over forty-five villages and towns, the local authorities providing them with accommodation in various places, and Jewish and other institutions helping them to maintain themselves. In March 1941 the expellees were able to return to Antwerp, in several groups, although some of them were detained for a few months in the Overpelt camp. By January 1942 all had returned.

Antwerp was the scene of the only pogrom against Belgian Jews under the occupation. On April 10, 1941—the eve of Passover—small numbers of members of right-wing groups incited riots in the Jewish quarter. Four days later, on April 14, the film *Der ewige Jude* (The Eternal Jew) was screened at a meeting of the Volksverwering (People's Defense; a pro-Nazi organization headed by the attorney René Lambrichts). When the meeting ended, some of the participants proceeded to break into two synagogues and into the residence of Rabbi Marcus Rottenberg, setting fire to Torah scrolls, other religious objects, and furniture. Members of other right-wing movements joined the rioters in the pogrom, among them the Flemish SS. The fire department and the police were ordered not to interfere. The pogrom was apparently initiated by the local German authorities, and the German military commanders in Belgium disapproved of it.

The economic situation of the Jews took a turn for the worse in the summer of 1941, when "Aryanization" was introduced in Belgium. In several instances, the German police broke into diamond-polishing plants and confiscated the merchandise. When the ASSOCIATION DES JUIFS EN BELGIQUE (AJB) was formed, late in 1941, a branch was also set up in Antwerp, and Nico Workum was appointed its chairman (in addition to his appointment as deputy chairman of the AJB). One of the branch's tasks was to enroll into local Jewish schools the Jewish children who had been evicted from the general public-school system.

Under the occupation, the Jewish political parties reduced their activities to a minimum, and when the deportations were launched even that minimum was abandoned, for all practical purposes. In contrast, the youth movements, especially the Zionist movements, resumed their operations and, for many Jewish youngsters, became a home away from home. They ran very active programs and took part in efforts to obtain food from nearby farms and distribute it among Antwerp Jews. In 1942 and 1943, the youth movements made various attempts to smuggle members into Switzerland and Spain. Scores of young people reached Switzerland (the exact number is not known).

At the time when Belgian Jews were being deported to northern France for forced labor there, four such deportations took place in Antwerp in the course of 1942—on June 13, July 14, August 15, and September 12. Deportations to the east commenced in early August 1942. Even earlier, at the end of July 1942, the first orders were issued for Jews from Antwerp to report to the Dossin camp in MECHELEN (Malines). This step was followed by mass arrests: on August 13, 1942, Romanian nationals were arrested, and on Sabbath eve, August 14, another large group of Jews was seized. On September 10, the eve of the Jewish New Year, Jews were apprehended in the streets of Antwerp. Only those who could prove their Belgian nationality were released, while the rest were taken to Mechelen. In the following months, individual arrests were made from time to time. One such arrest was that of Rabbi Rottenberg, who was later released from Mechelen, and then sent to the VITTEL camp in France; he met his death in AUSCHWITZ, to which he was deported at the end of 1944. The last arrests of Jews took place on the night of September 3–4, 1943, and this time it was Belgian nationals who were taken. From the end of 1942, only a handful of Jews were left in Antwerp, since the majority of the Jewish population had not been Belgian nationals. The school and welfare systems were sharply reduced and even so ran into great difficulties in trying to maintain their operations.

According to testimony given shortly after liberation, some three thousand Jewish men and women and three hundred children went into hiding in Antwerp and its vicinity; of these, some 30 percent were Dutch nationals. Later estimates came up with a lower figure, but precise data do not exist. Many Antwerp Jews were connected with the Comité de Défense des Juifs and took part in the committee's efforts to provide hiding places for Jewish children and adults; others belonged to various resistance movements, such as the Mouvement National Belge.

Following the liberation of Antwerp, on September 4, 1944, the surviving Jews orga-

Arnold and Lilian Buschel, who were deported from Antwerp to Auschwitz in September 1943.

nized an Aid Committee for Jewish War Victims (Hiso-Hulp aan Joodse Slachtoffers van de Oorlog), which assisted Jews who returned to Belgium, as well as others who were in need. Soldiers of the JEWISH BRIGADE GROUP also helped in the rehabilitation efforts. Some of the survivors of Antwerp emigrated and others helped restore prewar Jewish community life, albeit on a reduced scale. The number of Jews in Antwerp in 1969 was estimated at ten thousand five hundred.

BIBLIOGRAPHY

Brachfeld, S., ed. *Uit vervlogen tijden.* Herzlia, Israel, 1987.

Schmidt, E. *L'histoire des Juifs à Anvers (Antwerpen).* Antwerp, 1969.

Steinberg, M. *L'étoile et le fusil.* Vols. 1–3. Paris, 1983–1986.

Steinberg, M. "The Trap of Legality: The Association of the Jews of Belgium." In *Patterns of Jewish Leadership in Nazi Europe, 1933–1945.* Proceedings of the Third Yad Vashem International Historical Conference, edited by Y. Gutman and C. J. Haft. Jerusalem, 1979. See pages 353–376.

DAN MICHMAN

APPEASEMENT. *See* Great Britain: Appeasement of Nazi Germany.

ARCHIVES. *See* Documentation Centers.

ARENDT CONTROVERSY. Hannah Arendt (1906–1975) was a philosopher and political scientist whose study *The Origins of Totalitarianism* (1951) has become a classic. Her book *Eichmann in Jerusalem,* published in 1963, was the cause of a sharp public polemic. Arendt had been sent by *The New Yorker,* a weekly magazine, to cover the EICHMANN TRIAL in Jerusalem in 1961. Her report, first published serially in the magazine and then in book form, dealt with the process of destruction, Eichmann's role in it, and the trial's legal aspects. Among other subjects, she discussed the responses of the European Jewish communities to the Holocaust and the Nazi occupation, and the social and political implications of the trial in Israeli society. The account was written in a pungent style, giving the historical evidence a distinct theoretical conceptualization.

The major theses that provoked the controversy centered on Arendt's analysis of Adolf EICHMANN and her portrayal of Jewish behavior, based to a great extent on Raul Hilberg's study *The Destruction of the European Jews* (1961). Viewing Eichmann within the framework of a totalitarian society and a social structure that had consecrated evil, Arendt refused to see his participation in the "FINAL SOLUTION" as being anything more than normal and his actions and thoughts as reflecting the antisemitic ideology of National Socialism. Reduced to a Nazi bureaucrat and unmotivated by antisemitic feelings, Eichmann was seen as a paradigm of "the banality of evil." In contradistinction to her portrayal of Eichmann, Arendt assessed the Jewish communities in Europe, and especially their leadership, with a sterner moral yardstick. In the behavior of Jews across Europe she found a common denominator: a lack of moral responsibility that expressed itself most blatantly in the predisposition to protect vested elements in the community, often at the price of sacrificing others. Arendt summarized her conclusions in this regard with the statement that had the Jewish community been left leaderless and in a state of anarchy, "there would have been chaos and plenty of misery but the total number of victims would hardly have been between four and a half and six million people."

Eichmann in Jerusalem sparked a public airing of historical issues relating to the Holocaust in which laymen, journalists, intellectuals, jurists, social scientists, and historians, both Jewish and non-Jewish, took part. Not all of Arendt's critics were negatively inclined; some praised her essay as a brilliant exposition on man's predicament in the face of totalitarianism. Others condemned the work for what they considered its disrespectful treatment of the Jewish victims. Her critics generally posited that an inquiry into the Holocaust necessitated a knowledge of the facts, an understanding of the catastrophe derived from experience, and the avoidance of overly rationalistic interpretations. Moreover, it was felt that the "true nature" of the persecutors and their victims must be preserved, as well as a clear-cut delineation between them. Moral judgment also had its limits and restrictions: the Jews, the tragic victims of the Holocaust, were above reproach, and historians who had not experienced their suffering were expected to refrain from judgment. The opposite was true regarding the Germans. Here there existed a moral imperative for contemporary society to uncover and condemn the moral collapse of Germany during the war. An important element in facing the Holocaust required a constant evocation of German cruelty in order to avoid a further catastrophe.

Eichmann in Jerusalem provoked responses from survivors and interested observers in America, Europe, and Israel, many of whom related publicly to the Holocaust for the first time. As such, the polemic provides a unique perspective for evaluating the public conception of the Holocaust in the early 1960s. Moreover, although it originally aroused anger and resentment, Arendt's book eventually stimulated serious thought and historical scholarship.

BIBLIOGRAPHY

Barnouw, D. "The Secularity of Evil: Hannah Arendt and the Eichmann Controversy." *Modern Judaism* 3 (1983): 75–94.

Hausner, G. *Justice in Jerusalem.* New York, 1968.

Krummacher, F., ed. *Die Kontroverse: Hannah Arendt, Eichmann und die Juden.* Munich, 1964.

Muller, S. "The Origins of *Eichmann in Jerusalem*: Hannah Arendt's Interpretation of Jewish History." *Jewish Social Studies* 43 (1981): 237–254.

Robinson, J. *And the Crooked Shall Be Made Straight.* New York, 1965.

RICHARD COHEN

ARGENTINA. The years from 1930 to 1943 in Argentina are known as the "shameful decade." In 1930 the Nationalists seized power in a corporative and military revolution, but in late 1931 the neo-Conservatives promised the presidency to Gen. Agustín Pedro Justo. Justo's presidency, which lasted until 1938, was paved with electoral corruptions designed to maintain the Conservatives in power. The army and the church cooperated with the regime, the heads of the economy supported it, and, despite the ideological disagreements prevailing in the country, the government met with very little opposition.

In 1938, Roberto M. Ortiz became president. From a radical party background, Ortiz tried to reorganize the regime along democratic lines. Following the example of the United States and of other Latin American countries, Ortiz adopted a position of neutrality when war broke out in Europe. In May 1940, however, he stated in the Argentine Congress that neutrality does not mean passivity and insensitivity, and expressed sympathy for the victims of the Nazi occupation. In this respect, Ortiz appeared as a liberal tending toward support for the Allies. However, in September 1940, with Ortiz incapacitated by illness, the conservative and nationalist vice president, Ramón S. Castillo, became acting president, and his brand of neutrality in World War II was an expression of sympathy toward the Axis countries.

In World War II. In 1943, a group of generals seized control and established a military dictatorship with a strong Catholic orientation. The parties were disbanded, and Catholic education was introduced in the state schools. It was from this group of generals that the populist rule of Gen. Juan Domingo Perón, the future president of Argentina, emerged in 1946. Unlike most of the Latin American countries, Argentina continued its policy of neutrality. Only in January 1944 did it yield to American pressure and sever its relations with Germany. It declared war on Germany as late as March 1945, whereas most of the Latin American countries had done so in 1941 and 1942, after the United States entered the war. The belligerent neutrality of Argentina was anti-American, anti-democratic, and anti-Communist, matching the position of the Spanish dictator, Francisco Franco, and was considered desirable from an economic viewpoint.

At the outbreak of World War II, nationalist groups in Argentina supported a neutrality with a pro-German bias. Despite the small size of the Movimiento Nacionalista (Nationalist Movement) and its internal divisions, its extensive propaganda penetrated influential sectors in the country, including the army, the Catholic church, and many groups within the nationalist intellectual elite. The movement opposed liberalism, communism, and the democratic camp, and at times professed antisemitism. It apparently succeeded in implementing its goals, in anticipation of the military putsch of June 1943. Catholic circles in Argentina were split between a nationalist, antiliberal majority and a pro-Western democratic minority. A number of the nationalist, military-minded groups adopted the Nazi ideology and were financed by the German embassy in Buenos Aires.

Following disquieting reports of the penetration of Nazi propaganda in Argentina, a parliamentary inquiry commission was set up, and, on the basis of its conclusions, a number of German Nazi institutions working under the cover of cultural or commercial activity were declared illegal. Most members of the German community in the country openly supported Nazi Germany, teaching its racist ideology in the German schools and cultural institutions, and enjoying the support of nationalist bodies.

On the other hand, antifascist and antiracist groups also existed in Argentina, and in mid-1937 they had created the Committee against Racism and Antisemitism. In the wake of the German invasion of the Netherlands and Belgium, Acción Argentina was created by democratic and anti-Nazi intellectuals, who cautioned against the presence of a potentially treacherous "fifth column" in the country and strove for the severing of relations with Germany.

The Immigration Laws. A law dating from 1876 allowed free immigration to Argentina. As a result of the Great Depression of 1929, Argentina, like most of the Latin American countries, took steps to restrict immigration. On November 26, 1932, a government decree was issued according to which potential immigrants had to prove that they had a profession or a place of work guaranteeing their livelihood, given the difficulties caused by the rising unemployment in the wake of the world crisis. This was a turning point, concluding the period of mass immigration and inaugurating a policy of selective immigration. Immigration was still possible by virtue of the articles of the law providing for reunification of families or concerning agricultural settlement. However, the gates of the country were in the process of closing. A decree passed in October 1936 prohibited immigration stemming from ideological reasons, in order to curtail immigration of Communists and anarchists.

In July 1938, with increasing Nazi pressure for the emigration of refugees from the Reich following the German annexation of Austria (*see* ANSCHLUSS), the EVIAN CONFERENCE was convened on the initiative of the American president, Franklin D. ROOSEVELT. The Argentine representative at the conference promised to make every effort to help find a solution for the refugee problem. The Argentine government, however, after a reconsideration of its immigration policy, on July 28, 1938, passed a decree specifying new restrictions and placing stricter supervision along its borders to prevent illegal immigration, claiming that foreigners were infiltrating Argentina, particularly by way of Brazil and Uruguay. The reasons given in this decree point to its connection with the events in Europe and the fear of large-scale immigration. The stated focus of the problem was not the fear of unemployment but the "current international situation," as a result of which an immediate increase was expected in the number of people wishing to settle in Argentina. The toughening of the entry procedures was designed to give precedence to immigrants meeting the needs of Argentina's "society, culture, and economy." The word "Jews" was not explicitly mentioned in the decree, but is implied in the argumentation it contained, especially in face of the increasing applications by Jewish refugees and potential Jewish immigrants. Argentina's policy did not change even after the KRISTALLNACHT pogrom in Germany (November 9–10, 1938) and the widespread echoes of Nazi violence in the world press.

In early December 1938 the eighth Pan American Conference met in Lima, Peru, and approved a resolution against persecution carried out for reasons of race and religion. It also resolved that every country in the Western Hemisphere would try to absorb immigrants from any country of North and South America or of Europe in accordance with its internal needs and according to the characteristics and professions of the immigrants.

Argentina was very active at the conference, and frustrated American pressures for a binding resolution on immigration. Moreover, emphasis was placed on the continuation of selective immigration, which would prevent the entry of refugees forced to flee, in contrast to immigrants coming of their free choice. In addition, at a conference held by the finance ministers of Brazil, Argentina, Uruguay, and Paraguay, in February 1939, it was resolved to work to prevent the transit of people not possessing the required documents and visas, and the transit of people considered dangerous to public order, or undesirable by virtue of their past. These categories embraced refugees from the collapsing Spanish republic, as well as democrats, socialists, anarchists, and Jewish refugees who for various reasons had no documents. Argentine policy was influenced by this coordination among the four countries of the region, and Jewish refugees on thirty-five ships arriving in the Buenos Aires harbor in the years from 1938 to 1942 were refused entry. Most of them were sent back to Europe; a small minority found refuge in Chile and Curaçao.

Reactions of public figures and extensive press coverage alerted the public to the case of the Jewish refugees arriving in February 1939 on board the *Conte Grande,* and in October 1941 on board the *Cabo de Buena Esperanza*. But despite all the efforts on their behalf, they were not allowed to enter Argentina. Finally, passengers on board the *Conte Grande* were allowed to enter Chile, and those on board the *Cabo de Buena Esperanza* were allowed to enter Curaçao.

Throughout the war the closed-gates position continued. The local officials, the consuls in Europe, and the senior echelon of policymakers in Argentina all strictly enforced this position. Yet despite all the difficulties and restrictions, some 39,400 Jews arrived in Argentina during the Holocaust period, 26,500 legally and the rest illegally.

Thus, Argentina during the Holocaust period maintained a closed-gates policy vis-à-vis the Jewish refugees, notwithstanding its broad expanses of vacant territory and its need for development in a variety of fields. Support for the Jews by circles in the center and to the left of the political spectrum was of little avail, since they were unable to influence the government, which determined the immigration policy. In the decisive years, when chances of rescue still existed, there was an increasing disparity between the number of refugees applying for entry into Argentina and the limited number that Argentina was willing to absorb.

BIBLIOGRAPHY

Ebel, A. *Das Dritte Reich und Argentinien: Die diplomatische Beziehungen unter besonderer Berücksichtigung der Handelspolitik (1933–1939).* Cologne, 1971.

Frye, A. *Nazi Germany and the American Hemisphere, 1933–1941*. New Haven, 1967.

Nolberg, H. *Auslandsdeutschtum und Drittes Reich: Der Fall Argentinien*. Cologne, 1981.

Walter, R. J. *The Province of Buenos Aires and Argentine Politics, 1912–1943*. Cambridge, 1985.

GRACIELA BEN-DROR

ARIERPARAGRAPH ("Aryan clause"), regulation barring "non-Aryans" (that is, Jews) from membership in German political parties, economic establishments, various voluntary associations (especially student and sports groups), social clubs, and so forth. Clauses of this nature made their appearance in Germany during the nineteenth century in the bylaws of student societies and political and social organizations of a nationalist and racist character, and were applied by them to exclude Jews.

In the Third Reich the *Arierparagraph* represented a transitional stage. It was introduced in April 1933 in a number of laws enacted to provide for the "legal" purge of the Jews from various spheres of society, including the government and public sector, universities and other institutions of learning, and professional societies. The NUREMBERG LAWS, passed in September 1935, raised this anti-Jewish racist criterion to the status of a general, basic law.

[*See also* Anti-Jewish Legislation.]

BIBLIOGRAPHY

Schleunes, K. A. *The Twisted Road to Auschwitz: Nazi Policy toward German Jews, 1933–1939*. Urbana, Ill., 1970. See pages 92–120.

ISRAEL GUTMAN

ARISIERUNG ("Aryanization"), term used to denote the transfer of Jewish-owned independent economic enterprises to "Aryan" German ownership throughout the Third Reich and the countries it occupied. The process had two stages: "voluntary" sales of Jewish-owned businesses, in the period from 1933 to 1938, arising from the exclusion of Jews from the economic life of the country; and forced transfer, under law, in the final phase of the *Entjudung der deutschen Wirtschaft* ("de-Judaization" of the German economy), following KRISTALLNACHT, the November 1938 pogrom.

"Voluntary" Stage. At the beginning of 1933, there were some one hundred thousand Jewish-owned enterprises in Germany. About half of these were retail stores, dealing mostly in clothing, footwear, or furniture; the rest were factories and workshops of various kinds, publishing firms, newspapers, and independent practices of medicine, law, and other professions. In the early years of the Nazi regime, the economic boycott and exclusion process focused more on those fields of commerce that had a high proportion of Jewish-owned enterprises, and less on the Jewish firms that had international contacts and prestige. The "free professions" (those requiring higher education) were targeted as early as April 1933, when a special law was passed "for the restoration of the career public service" (*Gesetz zur Wiederherstellung des Berufsbeamtentums*); this was the first Nazi law to make Aryan descent a condition for public employment, and the condition also came to be applied to self-employed doctors and lawyers. The campaign against the Jewish-owned retail trade, on the other hand, was not at first based on formal legislation, and consisted mainly of boycotts and intimidation, inspired from above and often accompanied by violence (*see* BOYCOTT, ANTI-JEWISH). The government offices in Berlin, mainly the ministries of the economy and the interior, from time to time issued prohibitions of "partisan actions" (*Einzelaktionen*), and similar instructions were also put out by the central party institutions. These did not, however, stop the boycott propaganda and actions aimed at the exclusion of Jews from the country's economy. There were more and less harsh periods, but the process went on steadily, relentlessly, and most efficiently, so much so that by the spring of 1938, 60 percent to 70 percent of the Jewish enterprises in Germany had been liquidated.

The methods used in the boycott campaign included the publication of conspicuous street posters and newspaper advertisements denouncing any German who bought from Jews as a "traitor to his people." From time to time uniformed patrols were posted in front of Jewish stores threatening potential customers and keeping them out. Non-Jewish customers who were seen entering Jewish stores were photographed and had their pictures and names published in the local press or on special billboards (the latter also displayed copies of the antisemitic paper *Der* STÜRMER). In addition to such sporadic actions, administrative measures were taken by the authorities without legal basis; Jewish enterprises did not receive any orders from public institutions, even when they had won public tenders; Nazi party members were prohibited from buying in Jewish-owned stores (a prohibition that was broadened to apply also to employees of local government authorities); and welfare recipients were not permitted to use their food stamps for buying in Jewish stores. Local newspapers were forbidden to publish advertisements of Jewish enterprises.

The "creeping" boycott actions affected mainly the Jewish retail trade. Of the more than fifty thousand Jewish retail stores that existed in 1933, only nine thousand were left in 1938. On the other hand, factories and workshops, especially those that were labor-intensive or export-oriented, were able to sustain themselves during the first few years of the Nazi regime and even to some extent to thrive on the general boom of the German economy. This was also true of the private Jewish banks, even though they had long been the butt of Nazi propaganda against "international Jewish financial capital." The continued existence of some Jewish enterprises had a variety of causes: the Nazi regime's concern about unemployment, which was still rife up to 1936; the staying power of large industrial plants and stores; and, in the case of the banks, their international connections, which affected German exports and the influx of foreign currency (of which there was a shortage).

The *Arisierung* measures were orchestrated

by the *Gauwirtschaftsberater* (economic counselors) of the Nazi *Gauleiter* (district leaders) in close cooperation with the local chambers of commerce and industry, economic organizations, and local and central economic and tax authorities. The declared purpose of the joint apparatus was to make sure that veteran party members would get the best businesses. For this purpose, detailed and up-to-date files were kept in the offices of the economic counselors to keep track of the Jewish enterprises in their respective *Gau* (district), and every *Arisierung* deal had to be approved by the competent economic counselor. All available "persuasion" and pressure tactics were employed in order to prevail upon the Jewish owners to sell their enterprises at a fraction of their value, ranging from economic boycott to physical attacks and even imprisonment in concentration camps and accusations by the Gestapo of having committed various crimes. As a rule, measures of this kind were used against small and medium-sized enterprises. More sophisticated means were used on the owners of large businesses, as long as a semblance of legal procedure was still maintained. Such enterprises were acquired by large and prestigious companies, and sometimes arrangements were made that enabled the Jewish owner to receive at least a part of his capital. But there were also cases of wealthy owners being jailed or put in concentration camps and held until they agreed to give up their enterprises. In some well-known instances, huge plants were confiscated in favor of the Reich without any compensation being paid, as in the case of the Simson armament factory in Suhl (Thuringia) in 1935, and the Petschek family firm in the Sudetenland in 1938.

Compulsory Stage and Final Liquidation. The second stage, that of compulsory *Arisierung*, began immediately after the November 1938 pogroms; in large measure, it was the result of political developments and the war preparations. Compulsory *Arisierung* was one of the points in the legislation announced by Hermann GÖRING on November 12, 1938, in his program to "exclude the Jews from the economic life of Germany" (*Ausschaltung der Juden aus dem deutschen Wirtschaftsleben*). The new regulations prohibited all independent economic activity by Jews, except for certain services that they could continue to render to Jews only. Jewish enterprises that had not yet been sold were put under a government-appointed trustee (*Treuhänder*), whose task was to "Aryanize" the enterprise, for a fee that amounted to a substantial percentage of the price at which it was sold. A special regulation, which Göring enacted on December 10, 1938, provided for the first time that a part of the profits of *Arisierung* would go to the state. Compulsory *Arisierung* was applied to all Jewish businesses, factories, and workshops that were still in existence at the time; apartment houses, however, were explicitly postponed to a later date, apparently because of the impending plan to restrict Jews to living in Jewish-owned apartment houses (later known as *Judenhäuser*).

Compulsory *Arisierung* was the more conspicuous and drastic stage, but by that time the process of eliminating the independent economic activity of Germany's Jews was well advanced, and all that compulsory *Arisierung* accomplished was to liquidate the little that was left in a single stroke and within the space of a few weeks. The value of the property held by the Jews of Germany in 1933 had been estimated as in excess of 10 billion reichsmarks (RM). A census of Jewish property, in April 1938, within the borders of "Greater Germany," put its value at 8 billion RM; one-quarter of this property was in Austria. Only a little over 1 billion RM was classified in the census as working capital (*Betriebsvermögen*); 2.5 billion RM were said to be invested in real estate. A confidential Reich government document stated that 5 billion RM were liquid assets, available for immediate seizure. This last sum was made up for the most part of proceeds from the sale of enterprises in the earlier, "quiet" stage of *Arisierung*.

A census of Jewish holders of assets over 5,000 RM was one of several measures initiated at the end of 1937 that aimed to put an end to all remaining Jewish economic activity. Preparations had begun a year earlier by government departments in the wake of the FOUR-YEAR PLAN. This plan, which was derived from a secret memo of Hitler, was designed to prepare Germany's army and economy for war. From that point on, Göring, who headed the Four-Year Plan organization, was also in charge of the "purge of Jews from the German economy," the aim being to use the confiscated Jewish assets to finance the production of German armaments. Further measures included a census, taken in July 1938, of all Jewish enterprises still in existence; a law barring Jews from various branches of trade and brokerage; and the final annulment of all remaining licenses to practice held by Jewish doctors. Two months later, in September 1938, Jewish lawyers still in practice were also deprived of their licenses. Throughout 1938, pressure on Jewish enterprises, by boycott and harassment, increased and was extended to include industrial manufacturing enterprises. The process of "voluntary" *Arisierung* and liquidation of Jewish enterprises was correspondingly speeded up. No data are available as to which proportion of the Jewish enterprises were liquidated and which passed into "Aryan" German hands during the entire period of the two stages of the *Arisierung*. The more profitable and well-established of these enterprises were no doubt highly attractive prizes to large, well-known German firms, individual Nazis bent on getting rich, and ordinary Germans. Prominent among a variety of legal and administrative steps taken in preparation for the liquidation of the remnants of Jewish economic activity were the orders issued by Reinhard HEYDRICH to the banking system. In July 1938, in addition to his other posts, Heydrich was put in charge of the Devisenfahndungsamt (Foreign Currency Investigation Bureau). He gave the banks until the end of October to complete preparations for introducing special blocked accounts (*Sperrkonten*) for Jews, which would facilitate supervision of these accounts and restrictions on their use.

The final liquidation of economic activity by German Jews had been carefully prepared to go into effect immediately after the November 1938 pogroms. At a closed meeting held on October 14, 1938, Göring declared: "The time has come for the Jews to be driven out of the economic life, [and] their assets have to flow into the hands of the Reich . . . rather than serve as a source of riches for incompetent party members." The shots fired by Herschel GRYNSZPAN at the German diplomat Ernst vom Rath in Paris, and the pogroms that followed, were only welcome pretexts, used for propaganda purposes, to implement within a few weeks a program that had been planned and prepared for months.

The November 1938 pogroms marked the transition to open and undisguised robbery of Jewish property in Germany by official institutions of the Nazi regime. The first step was the imposition of a collective contribution, the so-called *Sühneleistung* ("atonement payment") in the amount of 1 billion RM. This penalty payment was promulgated in Göring's special decree of November 12, 1938, and took the form of a direct individual tax, in the amount of 20 percent of the declared capital, to be paid by every Jew who had assets of over 5,000 RM. In practice, the rate was raised to 25 percent, and 1.25 billion RM were collected. In addition, the Reich authorities confiscated 250 million RM in insurance money due to Jews as compensation for the material damage caused to them in the pogrom.

In the period from 1938 to 1941, 140,000 Jews were able to emigrate from Germany, leaving behind most of their property. Part of that property fell into the hands of the authorities on the spot, in the form of the *Reichsfluchtsteuer* ("escape tax") and other "legal" levies; the rest was kept in special blocked accounts in the name of the depositors. No precise figures are available, but there is no doubt that the Jews who emigrated were able to save only a small fraction of the 8 billion RM in assets that the Jews of Germany and Austria had declared in April 1938. As for the remaining Jews, their private assets, from early 1939, were kept in blocked accounts in special banks, from which the owners could draw only a fixed monthly sum, the minimum they needed for their living expenses.

From 1939 until the summer of 1943, when the deportations to the extermination camps were completed, some of the private Jewish property and the property of the Jewish communities and Jewish organizations in Germany was accumulating in the coffers of the Reichsvereinigung der Juden in Deutschland (Reich Association of Jews in Germany). On orders of the authorities, all the assets of Jewish communities that had been liquidated, or the proceeds from the sale of such assets, were turned over to the Reichsvereinigung, and the remaining communities functioned as branches of that (Nazi-controlled) body, which was also responsible for their financial administration. As long as emigration from Germany continued, the Jews who left the country were in effect forced to "donate" all their remaining property to the Reichsvereinigung. These funds were kept in a special "emigration account" that was under Gestapo control, and any withdrawal from it required Gestapo approval. Some of the money in that account was used to finance the operations of the Reichsvereinigung, as were the taxes and other compulsory payments that the Reichsvereinigung kept on collecting from Jews who still had some money left. The Reichsvereinigung used these funds to finance the community organizations, the schools, and the medical establishments—in effect, to maintain a growing proportion of the Jewish population, by welfare subsidies, old-age homes, and other social services. In addition to the expanding staff employed by community institutions, a self-contained Jewish economic sector existed, in which Jews supported themselves with their remaining assets and savings.

According to estimates made by the Reichsvereinigung, German Jews in October 1941—on the eve of the mass deportations—had in their possession private assets in the amount of 300 million RM; an additional amount of over 100 million RM was held by the Reichsvereinigung in its accounts. On orders of the Gestapo, the persons selected for deportation had to "donate" their remaining assets to the Reichsvereinigung, which in turn put the assets into a special account. The Jews who were earmarked for deportation to THERESIENSTADT had to sign a "home purchase agreement" (*Heimeinkaufsvertrag*) with the Reichsvereinigung. According to this agreement, the Reichsvereinigung undertook to take care of them for the rest of their lives, in exchange for their depositing a minimum of 1,000 RM, or, alternatively, their entire remaining assets, with the Reichsvereinigung.

During the deportations to the east, the entire property of the deportees, as well as the moneys held in the special blocked accounts of emigrants, was to be confiscated in favor of the state treasury, on the basis of Regulation 11 of the Reich Citizenship Law (*see* NUREMBERG LAWS) of November 23, 1941. In actuality, this was one of the Gestapo's manipulations designed to preempt the Finance Ministry's departments and acquire the remnants of Jewish property in the country. An explicit order by Heinrich HIMMLER declared that the proceeds of this property were to finance the costs of the "Final Solution," on which the Gestapo was the supreme authority. Although the Gestapo made use of the Reichsvereinigung accounts and staff to collect and temporarily hold Jewish property, it was clear that the Reichsvereinigung's ownership of these accounts was a fiction and that in practice it could not withdraw the smallest amount without the special permission of the Gestapo representative. No data are available on the amounts held in these accounts and their ultimate disposal following the dissolution of the Reichsvereinigung in July 1943. There are indications that certain sums were in fact transmitted to the Theresienstadt ghetto administration. It is not known how much of the money was finally passed on to the German state treasury and how much was kept by the Gestapo or by the SS and its commanders.

The deportees' apartments were handed over to the city governments, which arranged for transfer of the titles by the appropriate agency. The contents of the apartments and the valuables of the former owners were passed on to the Finance Ministry. Works of art, libraries, and especially Jewish traditional items were forwarded to the collection that Alfred ROSENBERG had set up, with the help of the EINSATZSTAB ROSENBERG staff.

BIBLIOGRAPHY

Barkai, A. *Vom Boykott zur "Entjudung": Der wirtschaftliche Existenzkampf der Juden im Dritten Reich, 1933–1943.* Frankfurt, 1988.

Genschel, H. *Die Verdrängung der Juden aus der Wirtschaft im Dritten Reich.* Göttingen, 1966.

Margaliot, A. "Trends and Courses in the Economic Struggle of German Jewry during the Period of Racial Discrimination." In vol. 2 of *Nation and History*, edited by S. Ettinger, pp. 339–355. Jerusalem, 1984. (In Hebrew.)

Schleunes, K. A. *The Twisted Road to Auschwitz: Nazi Policy toward German Jews, 1933–1939.* Urbana, Ill., 1970.

AVRAHAM BARKAI

ARMÉE JUIVE (Jewish Army; AJ), French Jewish resistance and fighting organization founded in Toulouse in January 1942. The initiative for creating the Armée Juive was taken by Abraham POLONSKI and Lucien LUBLIN, two militant Zionists who had made up their minds, at the beginning of the German occupation of FRANCE, to create a fighting force. Apart from the threat posed to the AJ by the Gestapo and the Vichy government, the organization also had to contend with distrust on the part of the Zionist leaders. The AJ recruited its members in secret, swore them in on the Bible and the blue-and-white Zionist flag, and began training them even before it obtained any weapons. There is no information available about the number of members recruited by the AJ.

In the fall of 1943 the AJ launched an operation in which it organized from among its members groups of trained men who crossed the Pyrenees into Spain—sometimes under unbelievably harsh conditions—in order to get from there to Palestine and join the Jewish forces attached to the British army. The total number of Jews that the AJ succeeded in transferring to Spain was 300; of these, 80 were He-Haluts members from the Netherlands who had fled to France. AJ squads of armed partisans took action against informers and Gestapo agents in Toulouse, Nice, Lyons, and Paris; in Nice, the partisans liquidated a particularly dangerous gang of "physiognomists" (informers capable of recognizing persons as Jews by their facial features and expression) who were working for the Gestapo.

The AJ group in Lyons distributed tens of millions of francs to rescue organizations and fighting units; the money had been allocated to the Jewish resistance movement by the Jewish Agency and the American Jewish JOINT DISTRIBUTION COMMITTEE and smuggled into France from Switzerland. In the Tarn department, the AJ formed a fighting unit, and AJ forces attached to the French Forces of the Interior (FFI) of the Montagne Noire (in the south of France, near Montpellier) raised the blue-and-white flag and took part in the heavy fighting that the FFI was conducting. Four AJ officers fell in Lyons and Toulouse.

The AJ suffered its heaviest losses in two Gestapo operations: in May 1944 the Gestapo traced five of the organization's members who were operating in Paris (belonging to the Dutch group), and in July 1944 it arrested twenty-five AJ fighters in Paris, thereby liquidating the AJ's French group in the capital. After being tortured, the AJ men were put on the last deportation train to leave the DRANCY camp (August 17, 1944). However, fourteen of the AJ prisoners jumped off the train and escaped. The AJ's French groups took part in the general uprising of August 1944 in Paris, Lyons, and Toulouse.

BIBLIOGRAPHY

Avni, H. "The Zionist Underground in Holland and France and the Escape to Spain." In *Rescue Attempts during the Holocaust,* edited by Y. Gutman and E. Zuroff, pp. 555–590. Jerusalem, 1977.

Latour, A. *Jewish Resistance in France (1940–1944).* New York, 1981.

Lazare, L. *La résistance juive en France.* Paris, 1987.

Poliakov, L. "Jewish Resistance in France." *Yivo Annual* 8 (1953): 252–263.

Steinberg, L. *Jews against Hitler (Not as a Lamb).* New York, 1974.

LUCIEN LAZARE

ARMIA KRAJOWA (Home Army; AK), the underground military organization in occupied POLAND, which functioned in all areas of the country from the fall of 1939 until its disbanding in January 1945.

The AK originated from the Służba Zwycięstwu Polski (Polish Victory Service), created in late September 1939 by Gen. Michael Torkarzewski-Karaszewicz. That December, Gen. Władysław SIKORSKI replaced this organization with the Związek Walki Zbrojnej (Union for Armed Struggle), which became the AK in February 1942. The AK's first commander was Stefan ROWECKI (known as Grot, or "arrowhead"), until his arrest; he was succeeded by Tadeusz BOR-KOMOROWSKI, from July 1943 until the latter's capture in September 1944. The last commander was Leopold Okulicki, known as Niedźwiadek ("bear cub").

The executive branch of the AK was the

operational command, which was composed of many units. Estimates of the AK membership in the first half of 1944 range from 250,000 to 350,000, with more than 10,000 officers. Most of the other Polish underground armies were incorporated into the AK, including the Bataliony Chłopskie (Peasants' Battalions), a large military organization of the Stronnictwo Ludowe (People's Party); the Socjalistyczna Organizacja Bojowa (Socialist Fighting Organization), established by the Polska Partia Socjalistyczna (Polish Socialist Party); the Narodowa Organizacja Wojskowa (National Army), established by the Stronnictwo Narodowe (National Party); and, from March 1944, part of the extreme right-wing organization, the NARODOWE SIŁY ZBROJNE (National Armed Forces).

The AK divided itself organizationally in Poland into sixteen regional branches, subdivided in turn into eighty-nine inspectorates, which were further divided into 278 districts. The supreme command defined the main tasks of the AK as preparation for action and, after the termination of the German occupation, general armed revolt until victory. Power was then to be seized in Poland by the DELEGATURA establishment, the representatives of the London-based POLISH GOVERNMENT-IN-EXILE; and by the government-in-exile, which would return to Poland.

While the AK did not engender a general revolt, its forces were responsible for intensive economic and armed sabotage. In 1944 it acted on a broad scale, one of its operations being the WARSAW POLISH UPRISING, which broke out on August 1, 1944, and was quelled by the Germans only on October 2. AK units carried out thousands of armed raids and daring intelligence operations, bombed hundreds of railway shipments, and participated in many partisan clashes and battles with the German police and Wehrmacht units.

In February 1942 the Operational Command of the AK Information and Propaganda Office created the Section for Jewish Affairs, directed by Henryk WOLINSKI. This section collected information about the situation of the Jewish population, on the basis of which reports were drafted and sent to London. It also centralized contacts between Polish and Jewish military organizations. Only a few Jews were accepted into the ranks of the AK, which generally turned down Jewish applicants. The AK provided the Warsaw ghetto with about sixty revolvers, several hundred hand grenades, and ammunition and explosives. During the WARSAW GHETTO UPRISING, AK units carried out holding actions outside the ghetto walls.

BIBLIOGRAPHY

Ciechanowski, J. M. *The Warsaw Rising of 1944*. Cambridge, 1974.

Gutman, I., and S. Krakowski. *Unequal Victims: Poles and Jews during World War II*. New York, 1986.

Korbonski, S. *The Polish Underground State*. New York, 1981.

Terej, J. J. *Na rozstajach dróg: Ze studiów nad obliczem i modelem Armii Krajowej*. Wrocław, 1978.

EUGENIUSZ DURACZYNSKI

ARMIA LUDOWA. *See* Gwardia Ludowa.

ARMY. *See* Armée Juive; Russkaya Osvoboditelnaya Armiya; Ukrainska Povstanska Armyia.

ARMY, JEWISH. *See* Armée Juive.

ARROW CROSS PARTY (Nyilaskeresztes Párt), Hungarian fascist party and movement created by Ferenc SZÁLASI in 1937. The name is also often used, inaccurately, to designate other parties (such as the party of the National Will and the Hungarian National Socialist party) that were also founded and led by Szálasi.

Szálasi labeled his theories *Hungarizmus*. They were a hardly intelligible mixture of romantic agrarian, anticapitalist, anti-Marxist, nationalist, and, above all, aggressively antisemitic ideologies. The movement's leadership, like Szálasi himself, came from the ranks of ex–army officers, journalists, and middle-ranking government and county officials. Popular support came mainly from officers, students, impoverished intellectuals, and the lowest classes of the urban and agrarian proletariat. In the 1939 national election, the only election in which the party took part, the Arrow Cross obtained over 25 percent of the vote (in Budapest it received 72,383 votes, compared with 95,468 for the government party) and became the most important opposition party.

Although the Arrow Cross advocated a consistent pro-German foreign policy, the party was not included in the pro-Nazi government, even after the German occupation of HUNGARY on March 19, 1944. Only after the deportation of Jews was stopped on July 7 and after Miklós HORTHY's attempt to make a separate armistice was aborted on October 15 was a coalition government led by the Arrow Cross formed, under German pressure. During the short Arrow Cross rule the deportation of Jews was resumed, and eighty thousand Jews were expelled from Hungary, most of them women, in a severe and murderous march to the Austrian border. Many of the deportees died en route. In Budapest during this time, several thousand Jews were murdered and their bodies thrown into the Danube. The government came to an end when the Red Army took Budapest in January 1945.

After the war, Szálasi and most of the prominent Arrow Cross leaders were tried as war criminals by the Hungarian courts. The majority of the party's rank and file were reintegrated into civilian life, many of them after joining the Communist party.

BIBLIOGRAPHY

Lacko, M. *Arrow Cross Men and National Socialists, 1935–1944.* Budapest, 1968.

Macartney, C. A. *October Fifteenth: A History of Hungary, 1929–1945.* New York, 1957.

ASHER COHEN

ART OF THE HOLOCAUST. Responses in painting and sculpture to the Nazi persecution of the Jews began in the early 1930s, when artists reacted to Adolf Hitler's rise to power and early discriminatory measures. They were continued during the period of the Holocaust, and they continue unabated to this day. The art involved can be divided into different categories, dependent on the status of the artist (inmate, survivor, liberator, refugee, nonparticipant, memorial builder), the goals set forth (witness report, depiction on the basis of photographs, personal expression, denunciation, affirmation of identity, symbolization, memorialization), and the style (realist, expressionist, surrealist, abstract).

One of the best known of these categories is the art produced by the inmates of the camps and ghettos under impossible conditions, often at the risk of their lives. Whereas some were involved in the production of "official art" for the Germans, most camp artists set themselves two major goals. First, their art was to serve as an eyewitness report of what went on in the camps, thus undermining the German wish for secrecy on the subject. They therefore depict every phase of camp life, from the cattle cars and *Selektionen*, through brutal labor, to the gas chambers and the stacks of dead left unburied toward the end of the war. These artists have stressed that their work, done for the most part in a realistic style, was to be judged not as art but as documentation. Second, but equally important, inmate art was a form of resistance to dehumanization in allowing the inmate both to retain a personality of his own and to be able to order his life, at least on paper. This affirmation of individual identity through the very act of creation gave the artist a reason to live. The combination of these two needs —to bear witness and to affirm life by resisting dehumanization—accounts for the many relatively idealized portraits that have survived, works that both bear witness to the individual subject's existence and show us the way he wished to be remembered, as healthy and full of life rather than starving to death.

A special place among inmate artists is held by the group of underground artists at THERESIENSTADT—Leo Haas, Bedrich Fritta, Karel Fleischmann, and Felix Bloch—who, aside from their realistic official art, secretly produced expressionistic works that stripped the veneer off the "model camp" and exposed the starvation and death that lay at its core. These drawings are radically different from those produced by other artists in the camps. However, the level of anger expressed in them and their expressionistic style can also be found in the works of artists such as Boris Taslitzky and Zoran Music, who were active during the last days of the camps, after discipline had broken down, and in the works of many artist-survivors after the liberation.

The final group of witnesses were the liberators who entered the camps and were confronted by conditions beyond their wildest nightmares, including gruesome piles of corpses and *Muselmänner* (*see* MUSELMANN) with no will to live. These liberators depicted the sights that met their eyes. They recorded the scenes objectively, as did Feliks Topolski, or obsessively, as did Corrado Cagli, and occasionally tried to reconstruct events in the camps by interviewing the inmates, as did Zinovii Tolkatchev.

It was the photographers among the liberators who had the most immediate impact on the public at large, flooding magazines and newsreels with their reports on the camps, and turning every bystander, no matter how far away, into an eyewitness. It is for this reason that among the most common images of the Holocaust in the public imagination are those of the mounds of corpses, the emaciated, bald survivors barely able to stand or move, and the inmates standing crowded together behind barbed wire, scenes that were recorded in countless photographs.

The corpses and the survivors were to enter art because of the powerful impression these photographs created on artists. In contrast, the depictions of people behind barbed wire represented the primal image of the camps that had emerged in art in the mid-1930s and that dominated it during the war years in all countries. This motif was based on the knowledge that the camps were surrounded by barbed-wire fences, and it remains a potent image to this day, reappearing in George Segal's *Holocaust* memorial as a clear symbol of the camps.

Other common motifs can also be discerned in non-inmate art, although none has remained as well known. Thus, for instance, images of refugees were extremely common in art from the late 1930s until 1948, as a reaction to the sights that artists in the Allied countries most frequently encountered. They expressed the problems of artists who were themselves refugees, and reflected the plight

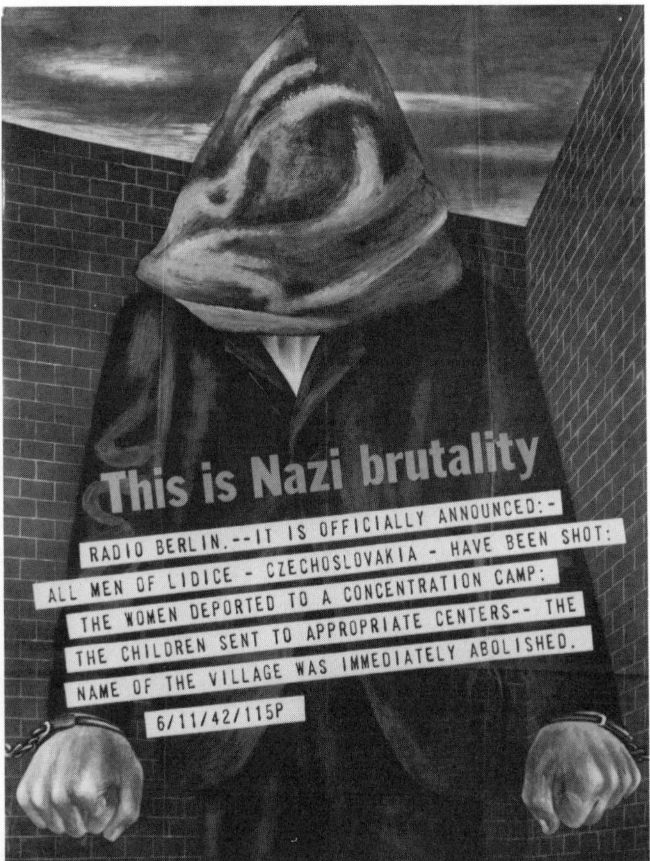

"This Is Nazi Brutality," a 1942 poster by New York artist Ben Shahn (1898–1969). Shahn was born in Kovno, Lithuania, and from 1942 to 1944 he worked as an artist in the Office of War Information, where this poster was printed. It protested the killing of 199 Czech men and boys by the Nazis in the mining village of Lidice, in reprisal for the assassination of SS general Reinhard Heydrich by two Czech patriots. [A Living Memorial to the Holocaust—Museum of Jewish Heritage, New York]

Overleaf: Four drawings by Helga Weissová-Hosková, a Czech artist now living and painting in Prague. In 1941 she and her family were deported to Theresienstadt. As a teenager there, she illustrated daily life in the ghetto. In one of the drawings, internees are cutting bunks down from three tiers to two, in anticipation of the 1944 inspection visit by the International Red Cross, whose standards for "humanitarian conditions" stipulated beds with no more than two tiers. [A Living Memorial to the Holocaust—Museum of Jewish Heritage, New York]

Koffer

L410
Helga Weissová 13 let
pokoj 24

Dh 924

422

"Throw away [down] your baggage and run to the trucks." Arrival at Auschwitz. A drawing by Alfred Kantor, who survived the Theresienstadt, Auschwitz, and Schwarzheide concentration camps. Other such sketches, with explanatory notes, give a graphic day-by-day picture of inmate life in the camps. They were later published in *The Book of Alfred Kantor* (1971). [A Living Memorial to the Holocaust—Museum of Jewish Heritage, New York]

of the survivors who became DISPLACED PERSONS after the war. The subject slowly disappeared from art after 1948, because the state of Israel was seen as a solution to this problem.

The same is true of themes of Jewish resistance, especially that of the WARSAW GHETTO UPRISING, which were immensely popular during and immediately after the war. Artists from William Gropper in New York to Lea Grundig in Palestine and Raphael Mandelzweig in eastern Europe characterized the Jewish nature of this resistance by adding a bearded Jew to the group of young men and women fighting the Nazis.

The image that created the deepest and most lasting impression—the mounds of corpses—was one that also posed the greatest aesthetic and emotional problems, especially for those artists who encountered it only in photographs. Haunted by this image, they sought ways to translate it into art, usually following the lead of Pablo Picasso, whose *Charnel*

House dealt with the theme by means of semi-abstraction, or by concentrating on isolated groups of corpses, as did Rico Lebrun, Hans Grundig, and Gerhart Frankl. The aim was to establish a human context and an emotional relationship with the spectator that would allow him to overcome his repugnance to the forms before his eyes long enough to take in the artist's message. Jews and Christians often handled this subject differently. Whereas the latter felt free to use the photographs as a basis for their art, Jewish artists usually felt unable to do so, and the images of death that obsessed artists such as Hyman Bloom and Leonard Baskin are drawn from other visual sources, or, when based on Holocaust photographs, as in the works of Ben Shahn, are used to express deaths ostensibly entirely unrelated to the Holocaust.

Other symbols of the camps were formed from single objects that one could more easily adapt to different contexts. For example, from 1945 on, the crematorium chimney became synonymous with the camps, and the placement of such a chimney in the background of the works of Cagli and Hans Grundig anchors the scene within a camp context. The same is true of the works of Samuel Bak, for whom the chimney is a literal stand-in for the camps, whether set on an island dominated by the dice of chance, in the desert, or protruding from a humanoid pear and feeding on its lifeblood. In like manner, when Friedensreich Hundertwasser decided to express his own Holocaust past, he did so by juxtaposing three symbols: the crematorium chimney, a garden of blood, and his own personal symbol of hiding, the labyrinth. The symbol of the chimney is so well known that it is constantly used or alluded to in monuments, and even Buky Schwartz's *Pillar of Heroism* at YAD VASHEM, although composed of three concave surfaces, is immediately perceived from the distance as a chimney.

Even more far-reaching and adaptable as a Holocaust symbol is barbed wire, a strand of which immediately conjures up images of human beings behind a barbed-wire fence. Barbed wire can be used alone in an abstract composition, as Igael Tumarkin used it in the early 1960s to give a specific Holocaust meaning to his work, or it can be set before or around a hand or another object, as in works by Chaim Gross. Its meaning is so clear-cut that it can be used in other contexts to make Holocaust analogies. Thus, a Russian artist, Marc Klionsky, wraps a strand of barbed wire around a Russian Jew to symbolize his imprisonment in Russia, which is likened to a concentration camp. On the other hand, Tumarkin in the 1980s wrapped barbed wire around a prayer shawl that covers a mound of earth, in order to protest the establishment of Israeli religious settlements in the West Bank. The settlement is thus compared to a ghetto behind barbed wire, divided from the land around it, and the image suggests the possible destruction of the settlement in the future.

All the above symbols were taken from the camp experience itself. But artists who were interested in learning moral lessons from the Holocaust had from the early 1930s employed other images culled from religion and mythology to convey their ideas. These revolve around three main themes, each standing for a protagonist in the drama, and each conveying several alternate messages.

For instance, resistance to Nazism after 1933 was usually suggested through the image of David killing a Nazi Goliath, or in more general terms by Prometheus slaying the vulture. Jacques Lipchitz popularized both images in this context, using the first to stress the Jewish element in the conflict, and the second to bring home to non-Jews that Nazism was a threat to everyone and not only to the Jews. By emphasizing in some statues the physical resemblance between Prometheus and the vulture, Lipchitz also suggested that Nazism was an evil within man that he must defeat.

The victim, on the other hand, had several biblical symbols, each containing different nuances of meaning. Several artists attempted to use the traditional image of the sacrifice of Isaac in a Holocaust context, an image that is particularly potent in literature. However, since the usual artistic image of the sacrifice depicts the moment when the angel *stops* the slaughter, only a few artists succeeded in using this image. Mordechai Ardon portrays Sarah crying out at God in anguish on beholding her son dead on the altar, while Frederick Terna, a survivor, has done a

Pablo Picasso, *The Charnel House,* 1944–1945. Oil and charcoal on canvas, 6′6″ × 9′½″. [Museum of Modern Art, New York]

series of works in which he shows the angel pushing the knife in Abraham's hand into Isaac, thus blaming God for the Holocaust; or Abraham aiming the knife at God or at himself, unwilling to perform the sacrifice. Job, too, was used to protest the Holocaust to God, as he demands an explanation for the crime. Ivan Meštrović's emaciated Job accuses God, while Nathan Rapaport's Job, with a number on his arm, retains his faith despite everything.

By far the most frequently invoked symbol of the Holocaust victim was the crucified Jewish Jesus, who often wears a prayer shawl to make his identity clear. Here the artist, be he Christian like Otto Pankok or Jewish like Marc Chagall, turns to address not God but the Christian world, pointing out to the Christians that they are slaying Christ again when they kill his brothers, the Jews. This imagery, which became dominant in the 1930s, was reinforced when cruciform corpses were discovered in the camps, inspiring artists such as Graham Sutherland to make a direct use of Holocaust imagery in his 1946 portrayal of Christ. Many of the artists who used this imagery, such as Giacomo Manzù, Ernst Fuchs, and Mauricio Lasansky, used it also to denounce the church for not doing enough to save the Jews, linking the church clearly with Christ's killers rather than with Christ himself.

The third protagonist of the Holocaust, the Nazi aggressor, posed many problems for the

Halina Olomucki, *Before the Roll Call at Auschwitz,* 1950. Pastel, 12.6″ × 13.65″ (26.5 × 35 cm). [Yad Vashem Museum]

artist. A few tried portraying him realistically, but were overwhelmed by the limited expressiveness of such images of the "banality of evil." Most artists therefore portrayed the Nazis as monsters and images of death, using images that had been developed by artists like John Heartfield and George Grosz in Germany in the 1920s as part of their battle against the Nazi party. After the Holocaust, artists came to the conclusion that, as Lipchitz had put it, there is an evil beast in all of us. Matta, Francis Bacon, Leon Golub, and others present ambiguous figures that combine victim and oppressor in a highly problematic manner, implying both an inability to draw a clear line between good and evil, and a pessimistic view of all mankind as tending toward the monstrous. This attitude is seen most clearly in the works of Maryan (Pinhas Burstein), a survivor of AUSCHWITZ. Embittered by his experience, he turned all of humanity into a monstrous race, exuding excrement from every orifice.

Maryan's extreme reaction brings up the problem of the art of the survivors. All of the artist-survivors, after the liberation, described their experiences in their art, and many of them felt that this therapeutic activity freed them from the weight of the Holocaust. Whereas some went on documenting the Holocaust, believing, as Halina Olomucki did, that it was their sacred duty to the dead to record their agony, most artists—Maryan included—turned their backs on their past and tried to become entirely engrossed in modern art. Some of these, such as Avigdor Arikha, maintain this position; having moved from abstract expressionism to realism, Arikha focuses on the individual object, refusing to recognize any reality beyond it. Most of the other artists, like Hundertwasser, Maryan, Erich Brauer, Isaac Celnikier, Yehuda Bacon, and Osias Hofstatter, returned at some point in their maturity to the Holocaust, expressing it in terms of the style and iconography they had meanwhile developed. Often this return was motivated by world events, such as the EICHMANN TRIAL, the wars of Israel, or the continuing massacres in a world that had learned nothing

Mordechai Ardon, *Sarah*, 1947. Oil on board, 54½″ × 42¾″ (138.4 × 108.6 cm). [Zvi Reiter]

from the past. Many of these artists feel threatened, and they take a highly pessimistic stance. Thus, Bak sees Judaism as a destroyed and patched-up reality that will never be the same, and Zoran Music states his lament in the titles of his paintings of the 1970s, which he based on his 1945 drawings of camp corpses: *We Are Not the Last!*

Other Jewish artists, who did not experience the Holocaust themselves, felt a need in its wake to relinquish in part their socialist or assimilationist views and to return openly to Judaism. This is particularly notable among American artists, including Shahn, Gropper, Max Weber, Jack Levine, who began painting Jewish subjects in the 1940s. These works included biblical themes, praying men, shtetl scenes, and Hebrew inscriptions. On the other hand, younger artists, such as R. B. Kitaj, returned to an affirmation of their Judaism, not by dealing with traditional Jewish themes but by working on pictures related to the Holocaust. This interrelationship between Jewish identity and the Holocaust is a growing phenomenon, especially among secular Jewish artists, whose only knowledge of Judaism is compounded of pogroms, persecutions, and the Holocaust.

A more positive view of events was generated by the creation of the state of Israel, which artists such as Chagall and Lipchitz immediately saw as an answer to their questions regarding the Holocaust and as a solution to the plight of the survivors still in displaced persons' camps. However, Israel's continuing wars, and especially the threats to its existence in 1967 and 1973, forced some artists to a more pessimistic expression; they saw in every conflict an inherent renewal of

Buky Schwartz, *The Pillar of Heroism*, 1967, at Yad Vashem. Stainless steel, height 68.9 feet (21 m). [Zvi Reiter]

Elsa Pollak, *Auschwitz*, 1985, at Yad Vashem. Bronze, height 9.8 feet (3 m). [Zvi Reiter]

the Holocaust. On the other hand, the relations between Jews and Arabs since 1967 have caused both left-wing artists like Matta and Israeli artists like Igael Tumarkin to adapt Holocaust imagery to the new conflicts, with the Palestinians replacing the Jews as the victims. This generalization of Holocaust imagery is, in fact, part of a wider phenomenon, in which these images are applied, especially by artists associated with the Communists, to any current conflict, from Korea to Vietnam. In these works, the Americans and their allies are given the role of Nazi murderers. The artists thus attempt to activate an inbred, unquestioning hatred against those who have been clothed in the despised Nazi images.

The anxiety felt by many artists—not only survivors—in the postwar world is often linked by Jewish artists to the Holocaust. This is especially evident in the works of Jonathan Borofsky, all signed with numbers rather than with his name. Several of these works reflect his fear of being victimized by a Hitler-like person or by Gestapo dogs. These fears have developed particularly in response to the millennial feeling that man is about to destroy himself. Artists like Robert Morris have joined survivors such as Music in depicting Holocaust corpses in an attempt to tell the world that catastrophe looms and that we can avert it if we act before it is too late.

A recent development has been the imagery created by the children of survivors, many of whom, like Yocheved Weinfeld, try to put themselves in their parents' place and imagine their own reactions had they been in the camps. On the other hand, young German artists, such as Anselm Kiefer, have begun to take tentative steps toward dealing with the past. Kiefer's art stresses the need to do so in order that healing may begin.

BIBLIOGRAPHY

Blatter, J., and S. Milton. *Art of the Holocaust.* New York, 1981.

Costanza, M. S. *The Living Witness: Art in the Concentration Camps and Ghettos.* New York, 1982.

Czarnecki, J. P. *Last Traces: The Lost Art of Auschwitz.* New York, 1989.

Frommhold, E. *Kunst im Widerstand.* Dresden, 1968.

Kampf, A. *The Jewish Experience in Twentieth Century Art.* South Hadley, Mass., 1984.

Museo Civico Bologna. *Arte e resistenza in Europa.* Bologna, 1965.

Novitch, M., L. Davidowicz, and T. L. Freudenheim. *Spiritual Resistance: Art from the Concentration Camps, 1940–1945.* New York, 1981.

Reith, A. *Monuments to Victims of Tyranny.* New York, 1969.

Roskies, D. G. *Against the Apocalypse.* Cambridge, Mass., 1984.

Thompson, V. *A Mission in Art: Recent Holocaust Works in America.* Macon, Ga., 1988.

ZIVA AMISHAI-MAISELS

ARYAN CLAUSE. *See* Arierparagraph.

"ARYANIZATION." *See* Arisierung.

ASIA. *See* Japan; Rescue of Polish Jews via East Asia; Shanghai.

ASSCHER, ABRAHAM (1880–1950), Dutch Jewish public figure. Asscher was proprietor and chief executive of the most important diamond firm in Amsterdam, a member of the Amsterdam chamber of commerce, and one of the leaders of the Liberal party, which he represented on the North Netherlands Regional Council from 1917 to 1940. He was active in many Jewish institutions and was a member of the Zionist movement. In 1932 he was elected chairman of the standing committee of the Union of Ashkenazic Communities and chairman of the Amsterdam Jewish Community Council. He thus became the outstanding personality of Dutch Jewry and its chief spokesman.

Together with his friend David COHEN, Asscher formed the Comité voor Bijzondere Joodse Belangen (Committee for Special Jewish Affairs) in reaction to developments in Germany, and was its head as long as it existed (it was dissolved in March 1941). Shortly after the occupation of the NETHERLANDS by the Germans in May 1940, Hermann GÖRING paid a visit to Asscher's diamond factory and purchased diamonds in the amount of 1.4 million guldens. On February 12, 1941, the German authorities asked Asscher to form a Jewish Council (JOODSE RAAD), which, together with Cohen, he did, and the two men served as the council's co-chairmen. Asscher took little part in the day-to-day operations of the Joodse Raad, but he chaired all its plenary sessions and did all he could to save Jews from deportation to Poland. The German Sicherheitspolizei (Security Police) granted Asscher certain favors, despite the fact that in his talks with the Germans he denounced the Nazi regime in no uncertain terms; many of his relatives and friends, for example, were spared and were not deported to Poland. By nature a tempestuous and courageous man, Asscher wanted to protest the German persecution of the Jews, but Cohen always managed to persuade him not to resign his position and to keep cooperating with the German authorities.

On September 23, 1943, Asscher, together with all the other members of the Joodse Raad, was arrested, sent to the WESTERBORK camp, and from there to BERGEN-BELSEN (the fate of the other Dutch diamond merchants as well). When the war was over and Asscher was free, he returned to the Netherlands. The Dutch government charged him with collaborating with the enemy, and Asscher was arrested; following an investigation, however, the file against him was closed. A Jewish tribunal acting on behalf of the Jewish communities found him guilty and barred him from participating in any form of Jewish communal activity. Asscher, however, did not acknowledge the tribunal's competence to judge him, and broke off all ties with the Jewish community. When he died, he was buried in a non-Jewish cemetery.

BIBLIOGRAPHY

Michman, J. "The Controversial Stand of the Joodse Raad in the Netherlands." *Yad Vashem Studies* 10 (1974): 9–68.

Michman, J. "The Controversy Surrounding the Jewish Council of Amsterdam." In *Patterns of Jewish Leadership in Nazi Europe, 1933–1945.* Proceedings of the Third Yad Vashem International Historical Conference, edited by Y. Gutman and C. J. Haft, pp. 235–258. Jerusalem, 1979.

Presser, J. *The Destruction of the Dutch Jews.* New York, 1969.

JOZEPH MICHMAN

ASSOCIATION DES JUIFS EN BELGIQUE (AJB; Flem., Jodenvereeniging van Belgie), the organizational framework forced upon the Jews of BELGIUM in World War II. The military administration introduced by the Germans in Belgium differed from that of neighboring occupied countries and left to the local authorities a considerable measure of freedom of action. However, a consistently hostile policy was pursued toward the Jews from the very beginning of the occupation in May 1940, starting with the introduction of anti-Jewish legislation and the elimination of the Jews from the economic life of the country. One measure considered was making the Jews a separate sector of the population, supervised by a special administration, to be headed by an appointed body.

As early as the fall of 1940, a coordinating committee—the Comité de Coordination des Communautés Israélites—was set up by the Jews, which, however, had no legal standing. In 1941, when the Nazi anti-Jewish policy took a turn for the worse in all parts of occupied Europe, the concept of central Jewish leadership crystallized, the idea being to establish it in every country, in accordance with local circumstances. In Belgium, the German Sicherheitspolizei (Security Police; Sipo) decided in the late spring and summer of 1941 to establish a compulsory countrywide Jewish organization. The form proposed was similar to that of organizations set up in Germany, France, and the Netherlands, but it took into consideration the special situation in Belgium, where, for all practical purposes, the Jews were concentrated in only four cities—BRUSSELS, ANTWERP, Liège, and Charleroi. The plan for their organization was submitted to the various branches of the German military administration in Belgium, and, after discussion, the order for the creation of the Association des Juifs en Belgique was published, on November 25, 1941.

The order, consisting of eight paragraphs, made it compulsory for all Jews (who came under the definition of that term, as promulgated on October 28, 1940) to belong to the association; established the association as a body recognized by public law; and imposed on it certain functions, including the encouragement of emigration and responsibility for educational and welfare institutions. Formally, the association was put under the Belgian ministries of health and the interior, but all its substantial decisions were subject to the approval of the German military administration. The association was empowered to collect money, and the Belgian government was made responsible for any deficit that it might incur.

The November 25 order emphasized the association's Belgian character, but this was not borne out in practice; its main function, in 1942 and 1943, was the registration of Jews for forced labor and for deportation to the extermination camps in eastern Europe.

An executive board was appointed on December 22, 1941. Rabbi Salomon Ullmann, a Belgian citizen whose parents had immigrated from Hungary, was appointed chairman. Ullmann had been the chief Jewish chaplain and had become chief rabbi in November 1940, replacing Josef Wiener, who had fled the country; in April 1941 the Germans had also appointed Ullmann chairman of the coordinating committee of Jewish communities. Nico Workum, of Antwerp, was appointed deputy chairman. Other members of the executive body were Salomon Van den Berg, Noë Nozyce, and Juda Mehlwurm—representing the Jewish communities of Brussels, Liège, and Charleroi, respectively—and Joseph Teichmann and Maurice Benedictus, who were both from Antwerp and had not previously been involved in Jewish matters. Benedictus eventually became the association's leading figure, first as its secretary and later as its executive director. Teichmann resigned after serving on the board for a while. Only three members of the executive board were native Belgians; this was an indication not only of the composition of Belgian Jewry, but also of a clear-cut German policy to separate the Jews, as a body, from the Belgian people. The association's executive board had four local committees working under it—in Brussels, Antwerp, Charleroi, and Liège—and a number of administrative departments.

From the AJB's inception, it was not widely trusted or respected by the Jews. This attitude was expressed in written material, as well as in the fact that thousands of Jews failed to report for registration in the association offices when ordered to do so in March and April of 1942. This attitude changed somewhat in the summer of that year, when Belgian Jews were being sent for forced labor in northern France. Working for the association was then regarded as an essential occupation, and persons listed as association employees were exempt from this forced labor. For this reason, many Jews applied for work in the association, which responded so liberally that eventually many of those listed as its employees did little real work; the list of employees came to include even intellectuals and underground members who were opposed to the association in principle.

German pressure on the association increased as the time for deportations to the east drew near, and this also meant a growing involvement of the Sipo in the association's affairs. When the wearing of the Jewish BADGE was introduced, by an order published on May 27, 1942, the association, of its own accord, helped in distributing the badge in its offices, so that the Jews could meet the deadline for wearing it (June 3). On July 15, Benedictus was put in charge of the "mobilization for work" operation; thus he became in effect personally responsible for the association's role in the deportation of the Jews.

On Saturday, July 25, 1942, a group of Jewish Communists, members of the underground, occupied the AJB's offices and burned the lists they found there. They told the association employees who happened to be there that they were causing harm to the Jews. The loss of the lists had no effect on the Germans' plans for the deportations since they had their own copies. But German pressure on the association grew, and the Germans now insisted on more direct cooperation by the association in preparing for the deportations. Benedictus was removed from his job as head of the section for work mobilization (*Arbeitseinsatz*), and his successor, Robert Holcinger, was more amenable to German demands for cooperation. The first call-up notices for "work" were sent out to Belgian Jews at the beginning of August, together with a circular from the association urging the Jews to respond to the order and warning them, "in view of the grave actions committed in the last few days," that "failure to comply with the order will lead to serious consequences for your families and indeed for the entire Jewish population in the country." But despite this warning, and assurances that the call-up was indeed for purposes of work, resistance among the Jews became more determined, although some Jews did report. On the night of August 15–16 the Germans launched raids against the Jews. That month saw the first five transports of Jews leave the MECHELEN (Malines) camp for AUSCHWITZ. Following another raid on the Jews, on August 28 and 29, a group of Jewish members of the underground "armed partisans" organization attacked and killed Holcinger.

The standing of the association in the eyes of the authorities and of the Jewish community, and in its own eyes, suffered greatly as a result of the assassination. A further deterioration took place in the wake of continued arrests and raids (the worst of these occurring on September 11 and 12, 1942—the eve and first day of the Jewish New Year). Rabbi Ullmann resigned from his post on September 8, and at the end of the month the Charleroi local association committee decided to disband. (Even before taking this step, the committee had been involved in underground activities.)

In an effort to exert pressure on the AJB, the Sipo's section for Jewish affairs summoned dozens of leading Jews to a September 24 meeting with the section chief, Kurt Asche. Asche uttered threats against the Jews assembled in his office and arrested six of them, including Rabbi Ullmann, Salomon Van den Berg, Alfred Blum, and Maurice Benedictus. They were sent to the BREENDONCK camp, but released after fifteen days, on the intervention of Cardinal Joseph-Ernst van Roey and in response to pressure by the military administration. The association emerged from these events as a more submissive—and weaker—organization. Its role in the arrest and expulsion of Jews was now mainly confined to providing food and clothes to Jews on the eve of their deportation and to those interned in Mechelen; to looking after the families left behind by the deportees; and to overseeing education and health.

The new chairman of the association was Marcel Blum, a native of Belgium, who was the president of the Brussels Jewish community; he was nominated for the post by the association and approved by the authorities (the candidate proposed by Asche having been turned down by the military administration). Another reorganization of the association's structure and operations took place in the wake of Operation "Iltis," on September 3 and 4, 1943, in which Belgian Jews were arrested. The Antwerp local committee was abolished and the Brussels local committee merged with the association's central office, its activities now consisting of the maintenance of several orphanages, welfare centers, and hospitals. Most of the Jews still legally left in Belgium were either employed by the association or housed in one of its institutions. In this period the association also served as a cover for illegal operations, many of its employees being members of the underground.

In the middle of August 1944, the AJB was ordered to submit an updated list and photographs of all of its personnel. It delayed its response as long as possible. On August 24, Rabbi Ullmann was arrested and sent to Mechelen. Four days later, on August 28, the association board held its last meeting and decided to close its offices and cease operations. Six hundred orphan children who had been housed in the association's institutions were put into hiding, in a special operation to save them from arrest.

The association had been in existence from the end of 1941 until a few days before the entry of Allied forces into Brussels on September 3, 1944. It disbanded of its own accord, rather than on German orders. Generally, it had been submissive to the German authorities, but it played much less of a role as an instrument in the deportation of Jews than did similar organizations in other European countries. This was due both to the fact that the Jewish community of Belgium disregarded its orders, and to the success of efforts by Jewish underground groups to undermine its authority. On the other hand, the existence of the association as a legal organization enabled it to provide welfare and educational services to the Jews up to the very last days of the German occupation.

BIBLIOGRAPHY

Schirman, I. *La politique allemande à l'égard des Juifs en Belgique, 1940–1944: Mémoire de licence.* Brussels, 1971.

Schmidt, E. *L'histoire des Juifs à Anvers (Antwerpen).* Antwerp, 1969.

Steinberg, M. *L'étoile et le fusil.* Vols. 1–3. Brussels, 1983–1986.

Steinberg, M. "The Trap of Legality: The Association of the Jews of Belgium." In *Patterns of Jewish Leadership in Nazi Europe, 1933–1945.* Proceedings of the Third Yad Vashem International Historical Conference, edited by Y. Gutman and C. J. Haft, pp. 353–376. Jerusalem, 1979.

DAN MICHMAN

ATHENS. When the Greek capital fell under Italian occupation in April 1941, its Jewish community numbered approximately 3,500, out of a total population of 1.5 million (including the port city of Piraeus). Some of the Athens Jews were descendants of Sephardic immigrants who had come from SALONIKA, Izmir, and Larissa in the nineteenth century. Others came later from Kastoria and Ioannina. All the Jews in Athens, however, were united around the central synagogue. Already Greek-speaking, they were little affected by the Hellenizing and nationalizing policies of the interwar period.

During the spring and summer of 1941, the Germans stripped all of occupied GREECE of its agricultural produce and industrial resources, plunging the country into a serious famine. Jews suffered greatly along with the general population during the harsh winter of 1941–1942. Estimates record three hundred famine-related deaths a day among the Greek population.

The Italian occupation effected no anti-Jewish measures. Gen. Carlo Geloso, the Eleventh Army commander of Italian-occupied Greece, was respected by the community for his civility, his friendship toward leading Athenian Jews, and his efforts to protect Jews and foil Gestapo efforts to implement Nazi anti-Jewish measures. Geloso's successor (after May 3, 1943), General Vecchiarelli, similarly refused to carry out German demands. The Italians could not, however, prevent the Germans from establishing a Gestapo office, which arrested the leaders of the community council and other important Jews, and confiscated libraries and the communal archives.

In the summer of 1941, Greek fascists formed the Ethniko-Socialistike Patriotike Organosis (ESPO), under Dr. Speros Sterodemas, whose youth movement persecuted Jews and ransacked the synagogue on Melidoni Street. Rabbi Eliahu Barzilai, who had been chief rabbi since 1935 and was made community president by the Gestapo on July 20, 1941 (he was confirmed as such by the Italian and Greek authorities on September 1), managed to save the building with the aid of the Italian police. Immediately afterward the Jewish community officially dissolved itself, but it set up a secret committee that assisted the resistance. On September 22, 1942, Kostos Perrikos blew up the ESPO center, killing Sterodemas and a number of German soldiers. During the Day of Atonement services the Gestapo took ten important Jews as hostages in retaliation (they were later released owing to Italian intervention).

Throughout the Italian occupation Jews escaped from the German and Bulgarian occupation zones of Greece, many with their families, to Athens, whose Jewish population consequently rose to some eight thousand to ten thousand. This haven became a potential trap after the fall of Italy in September 1943. On September 8 the German army occupied Athens, accompanied by EINSATZSTAB ROSENBERG. Dieter WISLICENY, from Adolf EICHMANN's office, went to Athens on September 20 and set up a JUDENRAT (Jewish Council). It was headed by Moses Sciaki, who was murdered in January 1944; his aide, Isaac Kabelli, succeeded him. (Kabelli survived the war and wrote prolifically on the role and fate of Greek Jewry, but he was ostracized as a collaborator by the survivors.) On September 21, 1943, Rabbi Barzilai was ordered to hand over the communal lists of Jews. He replied that the ESPO had destroyed them during their raid on the synagogue, but he was then ordered to produce new lists within twelve hours. The rabbi destroyed the extant lists and warned the community to flee. He himself was escorted (or kidnapped, according to Baruch Shibi of the resistance) by the partisan network to the mountains of central Greece. There he issued calls to the Western powers to aid the main Greek resistance group, the National Liberation Front (Ethnikon Apeletherotikon Metopon, or EAM), in its efforts to save Jews and fight the Germans.

On October 7, 1943, an order by SS general and police chief Jürgen STROOP, who had been transferred to Athens after his Warsaw assignment, appeared in the local newspaper *Eleftheros Vima,* instructing the Jews to register with the community; only two hundred did. Eventually, two thousand registered, including three hundred of Italian and two hundred of Spanish nationality. The following month all Jewish property was confiscated for the Greek state in retaliation for the poor registration showing.

Following a rumor that the Gestapo was distributing unleavened bread, Jews assembled at the Melidoni Street synagogue on March 24, 1944. About 350 were seized, and their families as well were soon arrested, bringing the total to 800. They were all imprisoned in the notorious Haidar prison, and on April 2 formed part of a Jewish transport going from Greece to AUSCHWITZ. Arriving nine days later, on April 11, 433 of the Athenians were selected for labor details; only about 40 of them survived the war. A further transport, arriving on June 6, contained Jews from CORFU and Athens.

There were numerous protests by Greek leaders to the Greek government and the Italian and German occupiers. One hundred and fifty Salonika lawyers, after an approach to Simonides, the Greek governor of Macedonia, appealed to the government in Athens to at least shift the deportations from Poland to a Greek island. The response was that the Germans would not allow it. Jewish refugees from Salonika in Athens, aided by Athenian Jews, tried to pressure the government. They were joined by the intellectual and religious leadership, especially Archbishop Damaskinos and the heads of the institutions of higher learning, who argued eloquently on behalf of the Jews. Dr. Constantine Logothetopoulos, the head of the government in 1943, had the idea of settling the Orthodox refugees of Bulgarian-occupied Thrace in the vacant Jewish quarters of Salonika. His halfhearted attempt to stop the deportations through a letter to Guenther Altenberg, the German plenipotentiary in Athens, on March 23, 1943, arrived too late. On March 29 Athenian nongovernment leaders made an appeal, unprecedented in occupied Europe, to halt the deportations of loyal Greek citizens. This too failed because Salonika was in the German zone. The government of Ioannis Rallis protested to the Gestapo over the deportations and helped to foster an atmosphere in which Greek Jews were assisted by the population. In particular, Professor Nikolaos Louvaris (the minister of education, and later of communications) expended considerable effort to save the Jews.

Some of the Jews of Athens, including those who took refuge there, survived with the support of the resistance, the police, the church, the intelligentsia, ordinary people, and the government. The metropolitan of Athens, Archbishop Damaskinos, called upon his church and the nation to protect the Jews. Some one hundred and fifty baptismal certificates were issued; hundreds of Jewish children were placed under church protection; the police issued numerous false papers; and individual gentiles in the resistance hid Jews, assisted them to escape to the free mountains, and ferried approximately one thousand to Turkey. The Phoenix Chapter of the Athens Masonic Order also assisted Palestinian Jews who had served in the British Expeditionary Force to escape from their German captors.

STEVEN B. BOWMAN

After the War. The Jewish population of Athens increased owing to immigration, primarily from Salonika, but also from cities like Chalcis, Ioannina, and Volos, where the Holocaust had left only a handful of Jews. The Jewish community revived with the help of the American Jewish JOINT DISTRIBUTION COMMITTEE. The Organization for the Assistance and Rehabilitation of Greek Jews was formed under Greek government supervision to administer property reparations. In 1945 the Jewish Board of Communities was established in Athens; it played a key role in rehabilitating the Jewish community of Athens and other Jewish communities, particularly in Thessaly. In the 1950s, ORT (the international organization for developing skilled trades and agriculture among Jews through training) set up a technical school in Athens, and the city's Jewish community continued to maintain its own elementary school. The community numbered slightly under three thousand at the end of the 1980s.

YITZCHAK KEREM

BIBLIOGRAPHY

Avni, H. "Spanish Nationals in Greece and Their Fate during the Holocaust." *Yad Vashem Studies* 8 (1970): 31–68.

Carpi, D. "Notes on the History of the Jews in Greece during the Holocaust Period: The Attitude of the Italians (1941–1943)." In *Festschrift in Honor of Dr. George S. Wise,* edited by H. Ben-Shahar et al., pp. 25–62. Tel Aviv, 1981.

ATLAS, YEHESKEL (Yehiel; 1913–1942), physician and partisan commander. Born in Rawa Mazowiecka, in the Warsaw district, Atlas studied medicine in France and Italy. The outbreak of war in 1939 found him in Kozlovshchina, near Slonim, in the area occupied by the Soviet army. His parents and sister died in the ghetto there on November 24, 1941, five months after the Germans had conquered the area. Atlas stayed on, serving the farmers of the neighborhood as a physician and giving medical assistance to Soviet troops who had survived in the forest. When the DERECHIN ghetto was liquidated, on July 24, 1942, Atlas organized those who escaped into a Jewish partisan company under his command. Numbering 120, the company was subordinated to a Soviet partisan leader named Bulat, who headed a battalion that fought in the Lipiczany Forest.

On August 10, Atlas initiated an attack on Derechin in which forty-four German policemen were captured and executed. Though the Soviet authorities wanted the "fighting doctor" to practice medicine for the partisans, after the Derechin attack the partisan leadership, recognizing his gifts as a tactician, did not want to lose him as a combat commander. Atlas and his men blew up a train on the Lida-Grodno line, burned down a bridge on the Neman River, and, on September 5, launched an attack on Kozlovshchina in which over thirty Germans were killed.

Yeheskel Atlas.

The company gained fame throughout the region for its daring exploits and was mentioned in dispatches for its role in the Ruda-Jaworska battle of October 10, during which 127 Germans were killed, 75 captured, and a considerable amount of much-needed war material seized. Atlas also assisted the family camp attached to his company that housed escapees from nearby ghettos. Following the second *Aktion* that took place at DIATLOVO, on August 6, its refugees too were helped by Atlas. His personality, military exploits, and acts of revenge made a profound impression on both the Jewish and non-Jewish partisans in the region.

On December 5, 1942, Atlas was wounded in a battle at Wielka Wola; after handing the command over to Eliyahu Lipshowitz, he died from his wounds.

BIBLIOGRAPHY

Eckman, L., and C. Lazar. "Dr. Yehezkiel Atlas." *Jewish Combatant* 1/2 (Fall 1980): 8–13.

Kahanovitch, M. "Organizers and Commanders." In *The Fighting Ghettos,* edited by M. Barkai, pp. 134–147. Philadelphia, 1962.

SHALOM CHOLAWSKI

AUERSWALD, HEINZ (b. 1908), Nazi official; German commissar of the WARSAW ghetto from May 1941 until November 1942. Auerswald was one of the "ghetto managers" in eastern Europe who worked to maintain the ghettos for the efficient and productive exploitation of Jewish labor in the period before the regime made its decision regarding the ultimate disposition of the Jews.

Auerswald was a lawyer by career. He

joined the SS in June 1933 but gained party membership only in the late 1930s. Performing his military service with the Schutzpolizei (the regular police), Auerswald was sent to Warsaw with a police battalion in the fall of 1939. He was soon transferred to the civil administration that was established to govern the occupied city. There he was in charge of VOLKSDEUTSCHE (ethnic Germans) affairs until his appointment as commissar of the Warsaw ghetto, with its population totaling at least 400,000 people.

In his new capacity, Auerswald sought to foster a growing ghetto economy on the one hand and to halt the spread of epidemics on the other. While the former involved a more rational use of Jewish labor and marginally better provisioning for the working segment only, the latter involved further constrictions of the ghetto boundaries—intensifying the existing overcrowding—and the imposition of the death penalty for Jews caught outside the walls. The diary of Adam CZERNIAKÓW, the head of the Warsaw JUDENRAT (Jewish Council), reveals that on at least one occasion Auerswald spoke with the Jewish leader as a fellow human being—treatment virtually without parallel in the history of the Holocaust. In the days immediately before the deportations began, however, Auerswald cynically denied to Czerniaków that any danger threatened the ghetto.

Following the mass deportations from Warsaw to TREBLINKA between July and September 1942, Auerswald became the district administrator (*Kreishauptmann*) in the Ostrów area in November 1942 and was drafted into the army the following January. He was investigated by German judicial authorities in the 1960s but was not indicted.

BIBLIOGRAPHY

Browning, C. R. "Nazi Ghettoization Policy in Poland, 1939–1941." *Central European History* 19/4 (December 1986): 343–368.

Gutman, Y. *The Jews of Warsaw, 1939–1943: Ghetto, Underground, Revolt.* Bloomington, 1982.

Hilberg, R., S. Staron, and J. Kermisz, eds. *The Warsaw Diary of Adam Czerniakow.* New York, 1979.

Trunk, I. *Judenrat: The Jewish Councils in Eastern Europe under Nazi Occupation.* New York, 1972.

CHRISTOPHER R. BROWNING

AUSCHWITZ (Pol., Oświęcim), largest Nazi concentration and extermination camp, located 37 miles (60 km) west of Kraków. Auschwitz was both the most extensive of some two thousand Nazi concentration and forced-labor camps, and the largest camp at which Jews were exterminated by means of poison gas.

On April 27, 1940, the head of the SS and German police, Heinrich HIMMLER, ordered the establishment of a large new concentration camp near the town of Oświęcim in Polish Eastern Upper SILESIA, which had been annexed to the Third Reich after the defeat of Poland in September 1939. The building of the camp in Zasole, the suburb of Oświęcim, was started a short while later. The first laborers forced to work on the construction of the camp were three hundred Jews from Oświęcim and its vicinity. Beginning in June 1940, the Nazis brought transports of prisoners into the camp. During the first period, most of them were Polish political prisoners. On March 1, 1941, the prison population was 10,900, most of it still Polish.

Very soon Auschwitz became known as the harshest of the Nazi concentration camps. The Nazi system of torturing prisoners was implemented here in its most cruel form. In one of the camp's buildings, the so-called Block 11, a special bunker for the severest punishments was erected. In front of that building stood the "Black Wall," where the regular execution of prisoners took place. Ironically, above the main gate of the camp was a large inscription that declared: "Arbeit macht frei" (Work leads to freedom).

In March 1941, Himmler ordered the erection of a second, much larger section of the camp, which was located at a distance of 1.9 miles (3 km) from the original camp. This was called Auschwitz II, or Birkenau. The original camp became known as the *Stammlager* (main camp)—Auschwitz I. In addition to the inhabitants of the Zasole suburb of Oświęcim, about two thousand Poles from the villages of Babice, Budy, Rajsko, Brzezinka (in German, Birkenau, which became the name for the entire camp of Auschwitz II), Broszkowice, Pławy, and Harmęże were expelled from their homes, which were destroyed in order to build these two parts of the Auschwitz camp. A large expanse of

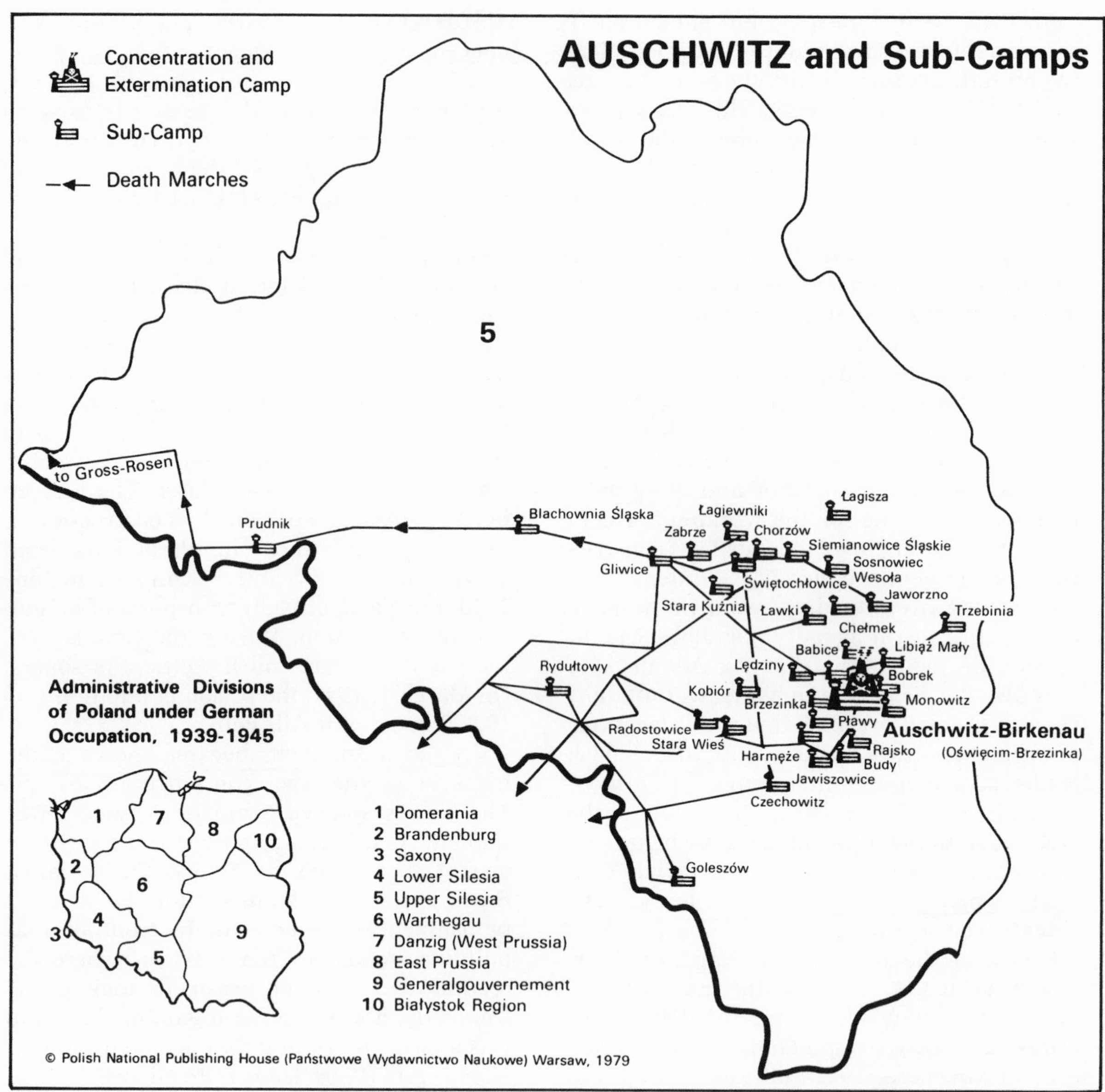

about 15.5 square miles (40 sq km) was declared a prohibited area.

In October 1941, intensive work on the construction of barracks and other camp installations started in Auschwitz II. In the final stage, Auschwitz II was composed of nine sub-units, which were isolated from one another by electrically charged barbed-wire fences. These components were designated as camps BIa, BIb, BIIa, BIIb, BIIc, BIId, BIIe, BIIf, and BIII.

In March 1942 a *Frauenabteilung* (women's section) was established in the main camp, Auschwitz I, but was moved on August 16, 1942, to a section of Birkenau. The first groups of women to be imprisoned in the section in Auschwitz I were 999 German women from the RAVENSBRÜCK camp, and an equal number of Jewish women from Poprad, Slovakia; by the end of March more than 6,000 women prisoners were being held in the new section. In nearby Monowitz (Pol., Monowice) a third camp was built, which was called Auschwitz III (Buna-Monowitz). The name Buna derived from the Buna synthetic-rubber works in Monowitz. Other subcamps affiliated with Monowitz were set up, and they too were included as part of

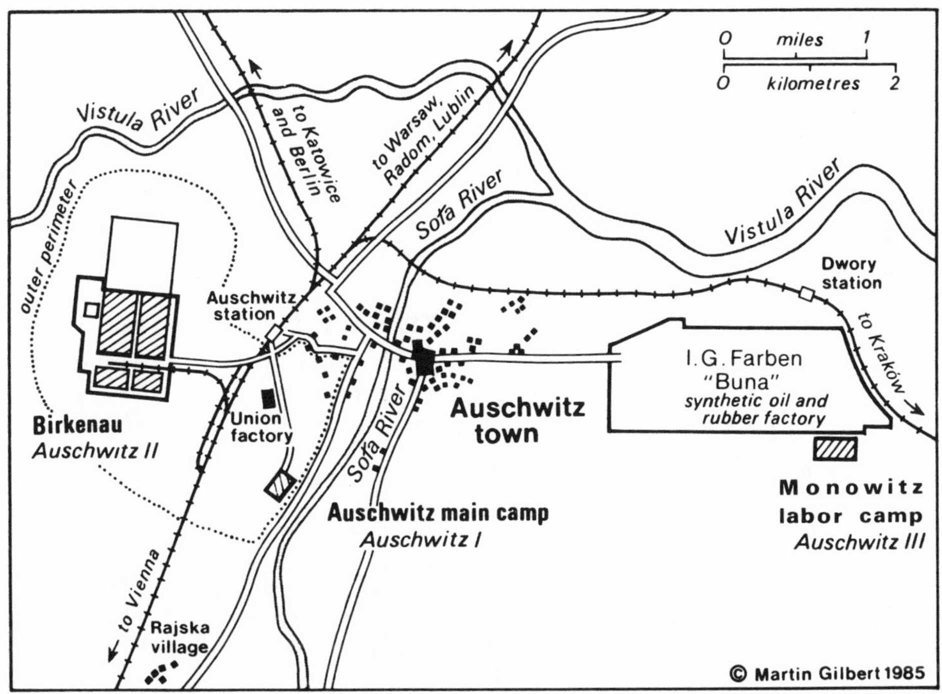

The three camps of Auschwitz.

Auschwitz III. In the course of time, another forty-five subcamps were built. Auschwitz II (Birkenau), which was the most populated camp of the Auschwitz complex, also had the most cruel and inhuman conditions. The prisoners of the Birkenau camps were mostly Jews, Poles, and Germans. For a time, the Gypsy family camp and the family camp of the Czech Jews were located there.

In Birkenau the gas chambers and the crematoria of the Auschwitz killing center operated. Auschwitz III (Buna-Monowitz and the other forty-five subcamps) were mainly forced-labor camps; the most important were Budy, Czechowitz (Czechowice), Gleiwitz (Gliwice), Rajsko, and Fürstengrube (Wesola). The inmates, chiefly Jews, were worked to the point of total exhaustion for German firms, among them I.G. FARBEN, Oberschlesische Hydriewerke, Deutsche Gasrusswerke, and Erdöl Raffinerie.

The Process. As the trains stopped at the *rampa* (railway platform) in Birkenau, the people inside were brutally forced to leave the cars in a great hurry. They had to leave behind all their personal belongings and were made to form two lines, men and women separately. These lines had to move quickly to the place where SS officers were conducting the *Selektion,* directing the people either to one side (the majority), for the gas chambers, or to the other, which meant designation for forced labor. Those who were sent to the gas chambers were killed that same day and their corpses were burned in the crematoria, or, if there were too many for the crematoria to process, in an open space. The belongings left in the cars by the incoming victims were gathered by a forced-labor detachment ironically called "Kanada" (so termed because Canada was a symbol of wealth to the prisoners). Under the strict supervision of the SS, those prisoners had to store the property in specially built warehouses, to be shipped later to Germany for the benefit of the Third Reich's coffers.

Those victims not sent to the gas chambers were sent to that part of the camp called the "quarantine." But first they were taken to the camp's bath, the "sauna." There their clothes and every last personal belonging were taken from them, their hair was shorn—men and women alike—and they were given striped prisoners' garb. In the quarantine a prisoner, if not soon transferred to slave labor, could survive only for a few weeks; in the forced-

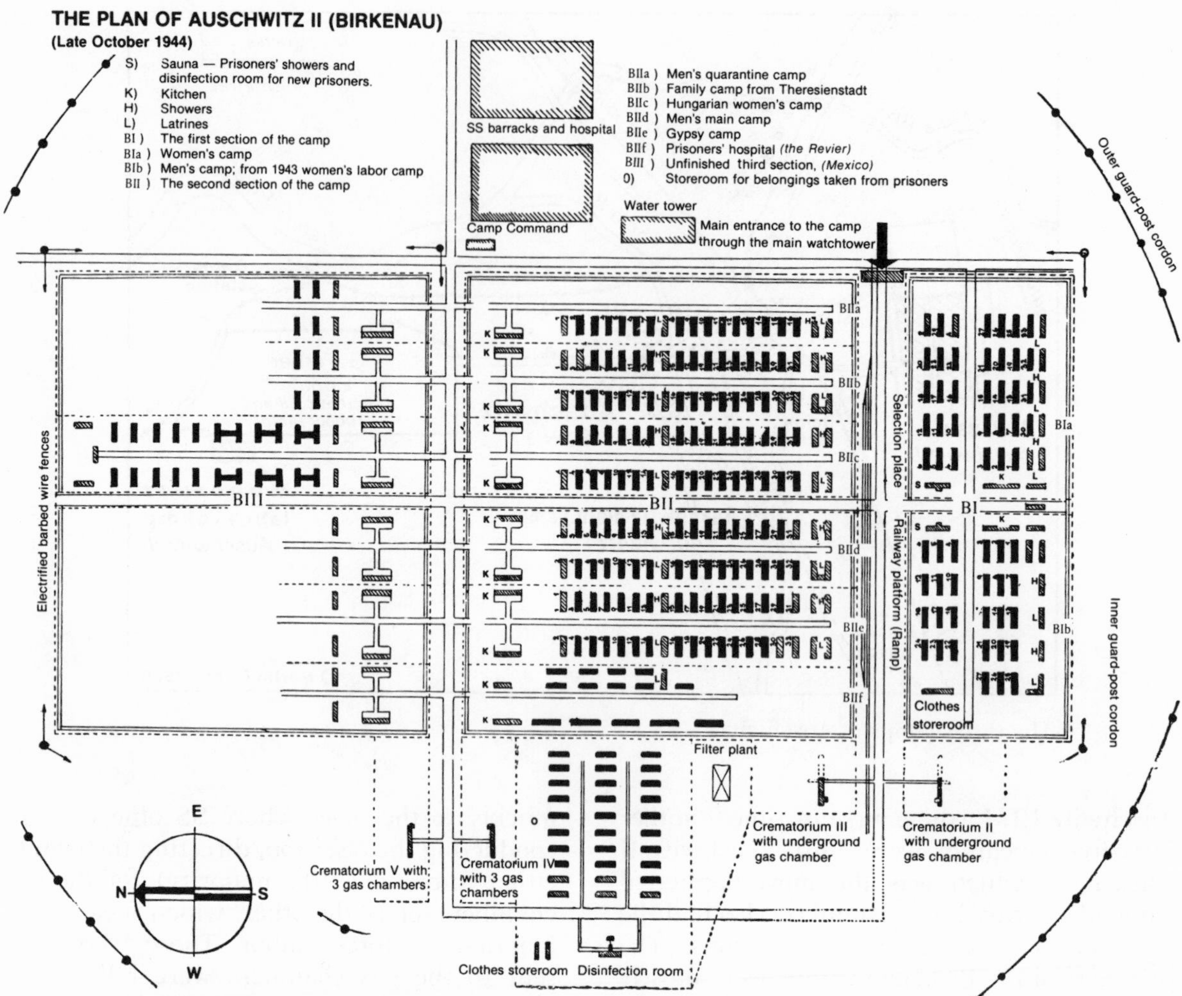

Plan of Auschwitz II (Birkenau), late October 1944. Adapted from *The Death Factory*, by Ota Kraus and Erich Kulka (1966).

labor camps the average life expectancy was extended to a few months. After that time, many of the prisoners became what was called in the camp jargon a MUSELMANN, a person so emaciated and weak that he could hardly move or react to his surroundings. It was no wonder that every prisoner tried to get out of quarantine as soon as possible.

Most of the prisoners were sent to Auschwitz subcamps or other concentration camps; some were directed to different work in Auschwitz I or III. One of the most dreaded institutions in Auschwitz was the roll call (*Appell*), which occurred early in the morning and in the late afternoon after the inmates had returned from their places of work, but sometimes also in the middle of the night. The inmates were made to stand to attention, motionless, usually sparsely clad, for many hours in the cold, in rain and snow, and whoever stumbled or fell was sent to be gassed. One of the most terrible tasks was that of the prisoners assigned to a special working group called the SONDERKOMMANDO. They were forced to work in the crematoria, burning the corpses of the victims who had been killed in the gas chambers on that day.

Prisoners were registered and received numbers tattooed on their left arm upon leaving the quarantine in Birkenau for forced labor in Auschwitz or in one of the subcamps. The same procedure applied to those prisoners who were directed straight to Auschwitz I; 405,000 prisoners of different nationalities were registered in this way. Not included in any form of registration were the vast majority of the Auschwitz victims, those men and women who, upon arrival in Auschwitz II, were led to the gas chambers and killed there immediately. Also not included in the registration were those prisoners who were sent to work in other concentration camps not belonging to the Auschwitz system, such as GROSS-ROSEN or STUTTHOF. Still another group of unregistered prisoners were those who were designated for execution after a short stay in the camp. That group consisted mainly of hostages, Soviet army officers, and partisans.

A day in the life of a prisoner, as many authors of concentration camp memoirs have so aptly described, is divided into a lengthy series of duties and commands. Some are dictated by camp routine, whereas others are unforeseen, a result of an order from above or an arbitrary outburst of violence on the part of the camp commandant. Some are directed against all the prisoners; others are aimed at an individual prisoner or a particular group of prisoners. All of the inmate's physical and mental capacities are unceasingly employed in an effort to get through the torturous stages that constitute an ordinary day—waking at dawn, straightening one's pallet, morning roll call, the journey to work, hours of hard labor, standing in line for a meal, the return to camp, block inspection, and evening roll call. "In camp, a small time unit," noted Victor Frankl, "a day, for example, filled with hourly tortures and fatigue, appeared endless." Any aberration or slip on the part of the prisoner—as a result of an incident in the work battalions or in the block, or a personal weakness or disease—very often meant death.

The "Kanada" slave-labor detachment.

Jewish brothers arriving at Auschwitz on a transport from Hungary in May 1944.

Besides those who were selected for forced labor upon arrival at the *rampa* in Birkenau, there was another, much smaller, group that was spared for the time being and not sent to the gas chambers. These were the people who were selected for pseudo-MEDICAL EXPERIMENTS. Many of these "experiments" were carried out on young Greek Jewish men and women. They underwent unbelievable suffering and torture. In July 1942, Himmler proposed instituting sterilization of Jewish women in Auschwitz. A German physician, Professor Carl CLAUBERG, who had the rank of SS-*Brigadeführer* and who had initiated such experiments with Himmler's permission at Ravensbrück, was given the task of establishing a similar experimental station for sterilizing women and for other criminal pseudomedical experiments in Block 10 of Auschwitz I. Among the victims selected for these experiments were groups of twins (including children) and dwarfs. Clauberg was assisted by a group of Nazi physicians who also usually conducted the *Selektionen* on the *rampa*

This photograph, as well as the next nine, is from *The Auschwitz Album*. They were probably taken by Ernst Hoffman, a German photographer working in the Identification Service at Auschwitz. The series of photographs shows the arrival at Auschwitz-Birkenau of a transport of Hungarian Jews from the Transcarpathian Ukraine in June 1944. Here, the transport arrives at the *rampa*.

in Birkenau. The best known of this group was Josef MENGELE, who earned the notorious nickname "the Angel of Death" in the camp. His own barbarous experiments were mainly carried out on infant and young twins and on dwarfs.

On January 20, 1944, the total number of prisoners in Auschwitz was 80,839: 18,437 in Auschwitz I; 49,114 in Auschwitz II (22,061 in the men's section and 27,053 in the women's section); and 13,288 in Auschwitz III (of whom 6,571 were in Monowitz). By July 12, 1944, 92,208 prisoners were being held, and by August 22, that number had risen to 105,168. In addition, 50,000 other Jewish prisoners were held in the satellite camps. The total number of prisoners in that period was 155,000. The prison population was constantly growing, despite the periodic changes resulting from mass deaths, and despite the high mortality rate caused by starvation, hard labor, contagious diseases, and the total exhaustion of the prisoners.

In his memoirs, Rudolf HÖSS explained how Auschwitz was established as a killing center:

> In the summer of 1941, I cannot remember the exact date, I was suddenly summoned to the *Reichsführer-SS*, directly by his adjutant's office. Contrary to his usual custom, Himmler received me without his adjutant being present and said, in effect:
>
> "The Führer has ordered that the Jewish question be solved once and for all and that we, the SS, are to implement that order.
>
> "The existing extermination centers in the east are not in a position to carry out the large actions that are anticipated. I have therefore designated Auschwitz for this purpose, both because of its good position as regards communications and because the area can easily be isolated and camouflaged."
>
> We discussed the ways and means of effecting the extermination. This could only be done by gassing, since it would have been absolutely impossible to dispose by shooting of the large numbers of people that were expected, and it would have placed too heavy a burden on the

Two lines: men; women and children.

> SS men who had to carry it out, especially because of the women and children among the victims. (Höss, pp. 183–184)

The first, relatively small gas chamber was built in Auschwitz I. Here the experimental gassing using ZYKLON B gas first took place, on September 3, 1941. The victims were 600 Soviet prisoners of war and 250 other prisoners chosen from among the sick. After that experiment, the firm J. A. Topf and Sons received a contract to build much larger, permanent gas chambers connected with very large crematoria in Auschwitz-Birkenau, where the mass exterminations were mainly carried out. Altogether four such installations—II, III, IV, and V—were built in Birkenau. Each had the potential to kill 6,000 persons daily. The gas chambers were built to resemble shower rooms. The arriving victims were told that they would be sent to work, but that they first had to undergo disinfection and to shower.

Electrically charged barbed-wire fences 4 meters in height were erected around both Auschwitz I and Auschwitz II. They were guarded by SS men, who staffed the many watchtowers, and were equipped with machine guns and automatic rifles. In addition, Auschwitz II was surrounded by a network of canals 8 miles (13 km) in length. The whole complex of Auschwitz I and II was, moreover, enclosed by a chain of guard posts, two-thirds of a mile (1 km) out from the system of barbed-wire fences. The chain, called the *Postenkette* (outposts), was guarded by SS men with dogs; this unit was known as the *Hundestaffel* (dog battalion).

Auschwitz I, II, and III and the forty-five subcamps were overseen by one staff residing at the main camp, Auschwitz I. The commandants of the camp were, successively, Rudolf Höss, Arthur LIEBEHENSCHEL, Richard Baer, and again Rudolf Höss. They had the rank of SS-*Obersturmbannführer*. The most important division, noted for the cru-

The *Selektion*.

elty of its *Kommandatur* (command), was the Politische Abteilung (Political Division). The whole system was guarded by a specially organized regiment of the SS TOTENKOPFVERBÄNDE (Death's-Head Units), an SS Totenkopfsturmbann (Totenkopf battalion) consisting of twelve guard companies, numbering at different times from twenty-five hundred to six thousand SS men.

The Nazi staff of the camp was aided by a number of privileged prisoners who were offered better food and conditions and more chances to survive, provided they helped to enforce the terror regime on their fellow prisoners. These prisoners were KAPOs (prisoner orderlies), *Blockälteste* (block elders, responsible for a certain block of prisoners' barracks), and *Vorarbeiter* (foremen, responsible for a group of prisoner workers).

As of March 1942, special trains organized by the REICHSSICHERHEITSHAUPTAMT (Reich Security Main Office; RSHA), containing Jews from the occupied countries in Europe, began arriving in Auschwitz-Birkenau almost daily. Sometimes several, usually freight trains, arrived on the same day. In each of these trains, from one thousand to several thousand Jewish victims were forcibly brought in by the Nazis from the liquidated ghettos in Poland and other eastern European countries, as well as from countries in the west and south. The trains stopped at a special siding track that had been built within the Auschwitz-Birkenau camp. Its platform, called the *rampa,* became the busiest railway station in all of Nazi-occupied Europe, with one particular difference—namely, that people only arrived there, and never left again.

The first victims of the mass murder in Birkenau were Jews from Silesia. At the end of March 1942, transports of Jews started arriving from Slovakia and France; in July, from the Netherlands; and in August, from Belgium and Yugoslavia. In October, transports from the THERESIENSTADT ghetto began arriving; in November, transports from Greece and from the Ciechanów and

Białystok regions of Poland followed. The first transport from Berlin arrived in January 1943. Throughout 1943, transports continued to arrive from various countries under Nazi rule. One transport, of September 8, 1943, contained over five thousand inmates from the Theresienstadt ghetto who, surprisingly, arrived as entire families; they were not led to the gas chambers but were interned in a section of Birkenau that came to be known as the Theresienstadt family camp. After a stay of six months in this camp the inmates were suddenly driven out to the gas chambers and killed. On May 2, 1944, the first transport of Jews from Nazi-invaded Hungary arrived, presaging the large wave that would begin arriving on May 16 and would continue until the second week of July. The transports from Hungary were followed by transports from Łódź, the last ghetto to be liquidated in Poland, which came to Birkenau throughout August 1944.

Not only Jews but also about twenty thousand GYPSIES were deported to Auschwitz-Birkenau by the RSHA's order of January 29, 1943. The vast majority of them were killed in the gas chambers. A few hundred Polish political prisoners were also murdered in the gas chambers.

Resistance. Despite the severe conditions, the prisoners offered constant resistance to their oppressors. It took various forms, the most common being mutual help. However, there were also many instances of physical resistance and sabotage. One unidentified Jewish woman, on arriving on October 23, 1943, in a transport from BERGEN-BELSEN together with women who were led to the gas chambers, pulled a pistol out of the hands of an SS man and shot two others, Oberscharführer Schillinger and Unterscharführer Emmerich. The other women also resisted; all of them were killed by the SS reinforcement that arrived immediately. A very common form of resistance was escape; 667 prisoners, most of them Poles, Russians, and Jews, escaped under the most difficult conditions. However, 270 of the escapees were caught not far from the camp and afterward executed. The best-known and most dramatic escape was that of a Polish-Jewish couple, Mala ZIMETBAUM and Edward Galinski. They were caught and executed on September 15, 1944, in front of other prisoners who were forced to watch.

A well-known successful escape was that of two young Jews, Alfred Wetzler and Walter Rosenberg (Rudolf Vrba), on April 7, 1944. The two managed to reach Bratislava and contact some of the Jewish leaders still remaining there. They wrote a very detailed report on Auschwitz that was smuggled out to the free world (*see* AUSCHWITZ PROTOCOLS).

In 1943 a multinational resistance organization was formed on the initiative of Austrian prisoners; its name was Kampfgruppe Auschwitz (Auschwitz Fighting Group). This group operated in the main camp and in Birkenau; Monowitz had a group of its own, and the two were in contact with each other. The resistance movement in the camp was active in many spheres: helping the prisoners with medicines and food; documenting the Nazi crimes against the prisoners; organizing escapes, sabotage, and political action; seeking to place political prisoners in positions of responsibility; and preparing for an uprising in the camp.

Jewish leaders in the free world demanded that the Allied powers bomb Auschwitz (*see* AUSCHWITZ, BOMBING OF). This could well have stopped the continuation of the mass murders. As early as the fall of 1943, the Allied air forces could have destroyed the death installations in Auschwitz without much difficulty, from their newly conquered bases in Italy. In fact, they conducted bombardments of industrial targets in the vicinity of the camp. The destruction of Auschwitz by the Soviet forces would have been even easier. From July 1944, the Soviet front line was no more than 93 miles (150 km) from Auschwitz.

None of the Allied powers did anything to stop the mass murder in Auschwitz. No gas chamber was destroyed by the Allied air forces. The prisoners of the Sonderkommando, however, organized an uprising that took place on October 7, 1944, and did destroy at least one of the gas chambers. All the participants of that uprising fell in battle. After the uprising, the SS discovered that it was a group of young Jewish women from the Monowitz camp, led by Roza ROBOTA, who had smuggled out and supplied to the Sonderkommando the gunpowder that had been used in the uprising. Four of these

"Able-bodied" men after the *Selektion*.

Non-"able-bodied" men after the *Selektion*.

Striped prisoners' uniforms.

women, including Robota, were executed on January 6, 1945.

Prior to the uprising, the prisoners of the Sonderkommando accomplished another very important act of resistance: some of them managed to keep diaries, in which they described in detail the events at Auschwitz. These diaries were hidden in the ground. Discovered after the war, they provide the most significant, terrible, and authentic documents on Nazi barbarity in Auschwitz (*see* DIARIES, HOLOCAUST). The most important of these diaries are those of Zalman Gradowski and Zalman Levental.

Last Months. Immediately after the Sonderkommando uprising ended, the killing in the gas chambers came to a halt, and Himmler gave orders to demolish the crematoria. During November and December 1944, the technical installations of the gas chambers and crematoria I and II were dismantled, so that they could be transferred to the Gross-Rosen camp. Special Sonderkommandos of male and female prisoners were formed whose task was to clean up the crematoria pits, which were then to be filled with the human ashes from the crematoria, covered with earth, and planted with grass. Some of the warehouses containing the goods stolen from the Jews were hastily emptied of their contents; the valuable items were sent to Germany by train, and the rest of the booty was destroyed. Between December 1, 1944, and January 15, 1945, no fewer than 514,843 items of men's, women's, and children's clothing and underwear were shipped from the camp.

In the middle of January 1945, the Soviet army started an offensive in the direction of Kraków and Auschwitz. The Nazis began a hasty withdrawal. The fifty-eight thousand prisoners, most of them Jewish, were driven out of the Auschwitz camps and put on DEATH MARCHES. Most of them were killed during these marches; others were murdered even before the camps were evacuated.

On January 27, in the afternoon, soldiers of the Soviet army entered Auschwitz. In Birkenau they found the bodies of 600 prisoners who had been killed by the Nazis hours before the camp was liberated. However, 7,650 sick and exhausted prisoners were saved: 1,200 in Auschwitz I, 5,800 in Auschwitz II–Birkenau, and 650 in Auschwitz

III–Buna-Monowitz. The haste in which they had to withdraw made it impossible for the Germans to force these last prisoners on the death marches. Their hurried retreat also prevented them from emptying the rest of the warehouses of the victims' plundered property. In the warehouses, the Soviets found 350,000 men's suits, 837,000 outfits for women, and large amounts of children's and babies' clothing. In addition, they found tens of thousands of pairs of shoes and 7.7 tons (7,000 kg) of human hair in paper bags, packed for shipping.

Auschwitz was the largest graveyard in human history. The number of Jews murdered in the gas chambers of Birkenau must be estimated at up to one and a half million people: men, women, and children. Almost one-quarter of the Jews killed during World War II were murdered in Auschwitz. Of the 405,000 registered prisoners who received Auschwitz numbers, only about 65,000 survived. Of the 16,000 Soviet prisoners of war who were brought there, only 96 survived. According to various estimates, at least 1,600,000 people were murdered in the killing center at Birkenau.

After the war, several trials were held in Poland and West Germany of German Nazis who had committed crimes in Auschwitz. The former camp commandant, Rudolf Höss, was tried in March 1947 in Auschwitz before a Polish court and sentenced to death on April 2, 1947. While in the Polish prison he wrote his memoirs, which were published in Poland in 1956; they appeared in English in 1959. In November and December 1947, another trial took place in Kraków before a Polish court. Of the forty Nazis from Auschwitz indicted, twenty-three were sentenced to death and sixteen were sent to prison. Between 1963 and 1966 the so-called Auschwitz Trials I, II, and III took place in Frankfurt am Main before a court of the German Federal Republic. These ended with prison sentences for the twenty-two defendants accused of committing crimes in Auschwitz. Nine were sentenced to life imprisonment, and the others to terms ranging from three to nine years.

The horrors of Auschwitz have become legendary, and the name itself has passed into international usage as a byword for all that is bestial in humankind.

"Able-bodied" women after the *Selektion*.

Non-"able-bodied" women and children after the *Selektion*.

Women with shorn hair after "delousing."

On the way to the gas chambers. "For these crimes, there is no adequate punishment . . . this kind of guilt, in contrast to all criminal guilt, goes beyond and destroys every system of law and justice. . . . And as non-human as this guilt is, so is the innocence of the victims. As innocent as the victims were in front of the gas chambers, no human being can ever be. . . . This kind of guilt . . . is beyond all crime" (Hannah Arendt in a letter to Karl Jaspers, 1946).

BIBLIOGRAPHY

Gilbert, M. *Auschwitz and the Allies.* New York, 1981.

Gutman, Y., and A. Saf, eds. *The Nazi Concentration Camps: Structure and Aims; The Image of the Prisoner; The Jews in the Camps.* Proceedings of the Fourth Yad Vashem International Historical Conference. Jerusalem, 1984.

Höss, R. *Commandant of Auschwitz.* London, 1959.

Kielar, W. *Anus Mundi: Fifteen Hundred Days in Auschwitz-Birkenau.* New York, 1980.

Kraus, O., and E. Kulka. *The Death Factory: Documents on Auschwitz.* New York, 1966.

Langbein, H. *Auschwitz-Prozess: Eine Dokumentation.* 2 vols. Vienna, 1965.

Langbein, H. *Menschen in Auschwitz.* Vienna, 1972.

Levi, P. *Survival in Auschwitz: The Nazi Assault on Humanity.* New York, 1981.

Lukowski, J. *Bibliografia obozu koncentracyjnego Oświęcim-Brzezinka.* 5 vols. Warsaw, 1970.

Mark, B. *The Scrolls of Auschwitz.* Tel Aviv, 1985.

SHMUEL KRAKOWSKI and JOZEF BUSZKO

AUSCHWITZ, BOMBING OF. By the spring of 1944, the massive killing operations under way at AUSCHWITZ were well known to the Allied governments (*see* AUSCHWITZ PROTOCOLS). By that time the Allied air forces controlled the skies of Europe and clearly had the range to strike Auschwitz as well as the railways leading to it. Yet no effort was made to bomb the gas chambers or the deportation railways, despite numerous requests for such action.

Great Britain's Prime Minister Winston CHURCHILL and Foreign Secretary Anthony EDEN supported a proposal made by the Jewish Agency for Palestine to bomb Auschwitz and the railways to it. But officials in the British Air Ministry and the Foreign Office managed, by stalling, to choke the plan to death, without ever looking carefully into its feasibility. The official British reply to the Jewish Agency dishonestly stated that "technical difficulties" made the proposed operations impossible (*see* GREAT BRITAIN).

The United States government also received requests, mostly from Jewish sources, to smash the Auschwitz killing installations and the railways to Auschwitz. These proposals became numerous in the spring of 1944, as the deportation of the large Hungarian Jewish community began. The first of the requests was turned down by the United States War Department in late June 1944 on the ground that "it could be executed only by diversion of considerable air support essential to the success of our forces now engaged in decisive operations."

In reality, the War Department's negative decision was not based on any analysis of air force operations. The department never looked into the feasibility of carrying out such bombing operations; it did not even consult the air force commanders based in Italy who were in the best position to strike Auschwitz.

What happened was that the War Department officials, when first confronted with the issue in June 1944, looked into their own files in Washington. There they found that several months earlier, the War Department had secretly established a policy of noninvolvement in rescue activities. This policy had come in response to President Franklin D. ROOSEVELT's formation of the WAR REFUGEE BOARD (WRB) in January of that year. The president's executive order establishing the WRB had specified that the State (*see* UNITED STATES DEPARTMENT OF STATE), Treasury, and War departments each had a special responsibility to help the WRB in its rescue endeavors. War Department officials, alarmed that this might mean that military forces would be diverted to rescue missions, unilaterally decided on a policy of noninvolvement in rescue. This was done despite awareness that it was in violation of the president's executive order. The policy was kept secret.

When the first bombing request came to the War Department, forwarded through the WRB, War Department officials checked their files and found the department's no-rescue policy. On that basis they decided against the proposal, without even looking into its feasibility. Obviously, they could not inform the WRB of the real reason for rejecting the bombing request. Instead, they used the best argument available: that it would divert military power from essential war operations.

Aerial bombing map of Auschwitz used to plan runs over Auschwitz by United States forces. The industrial areas were targeted, leaving the railway lines to the camp intact. [A Living Memorial to the Holocaust—Museum of Jewish Heritage, New York]

With this, the die was cast. Each of the several succeeding requests to bomb the gas chambers and the railways was rejected for the same reason as the first. The last such request was turned down in mid-November 1944. It is now known that these bombings were definitely within the capability of the United States Air Force based in Italy; in fact, they could have been accomplished in connection with essential war operations.

Because the Auschwitz complex included a major industrial area adjacent to the camp, Auschwitz itself was a military target. The primary objective there was a synthetic oil refinery. The Germans had seven other synthetic oil plants in the region, all based on the vast coal resources of Upper Silesia and all within 45 miles of Auschwitz. From July through November 1944, more than twenty-eight hundred American heavy bombers pounded the eight oil installations. En route to their targets, all these aircraft flew along or over key deportation railways. On two occasions (August 20 and September 13), large fleets of American bombers struck the industrial area at Auschwitz itself, less than 5 miles from the four huge gas chamber installations.

Yet on August 14, 1944, the War Department insisted, in a letter to Leon Kubowitzki (Aryeh Kubovy) of the World Jewish Congress, that bombing the Auschwitz killing installations and the deportation railways was not possible because such actions "could be executed only by the diversion of considerable air support essential to the success of our forces now engaged in decisive operations elsewhere." This was a word-for-word repetition of the June refusal. It was at variance with the facts and was no more than an excuse for inaction.

BIBLIOGRAPHY

Gilbert, M. *Auschwitz and the Allies.* London, 1981.

Wyman, D. S. *The Abandonment of the Jews: America and the Holocaust, 1941–1945.* New York, 1984.

DAVID S. WYMAN

AUSCHWITZ PROTOCOLS, two detailed reports about mass killings at AUSCHWITZ that were based on information provided by four escapees from the camp in the spring of 1944.

On April 7, 1944, with the help of the Auschwitz underground, two Slovak Jews, Rudolf Vrba (Walter Rosenberg) and Alfred Wetzler, began the steps that would lead to their escape from the camp. Members of the Auschwitz underground prepared a hideout for them in a gap in a woodpile that was located beyond the camp's inner perimeter. To confuse the dogs that would inevitably search for them, strong Russian tobacco that had been soaked in gasoline was spread around them. For three days and two nights Vrba and Wetzler waited for the search to end, and then fled toward Slovakia.

Two weeks later they arrived in Žilina, where they met Erwin Steiner, a representative of the Jewish Council. After hearing their story, Steiner contacted the Bratislava Jewish Council and spoke to Oscar Krasnansky on the phone. Krasnansky immediately arranged permission to travel by train to Žilina. At Steiner's house, he heard the two escapees' testimony and wrote a thirty-page report based upon it. Vrba and Wetzler described the workings of the camp, gave estimated statistics of Jews who had been killed (about 1.75 million), and warned that preparations were being made for the murder of the nearly 800,000 Jews of Hungary and the 3,000 Czech Jews who had been brought from THERESIENSTADT six months earlier.

In Bratislava, the report was passed on to Rabbi Michael Dov WEISSMANDEL of the PRACOVNÁ SKUPINA (Working Group) in Slovakia. A follow-up report was supplied by two more escapees, Czesław Mordowicz and Arnost Rosin, who reached the Slovak border on June 6, 1944, following their escape from Auschwitz on May 27. Meeting with Krasnansky, they added fresh information about Auschwitz. Among other things, they told of the arrival and murder of about three thousand Greek Jews, and the beginning of the murder of Hungarian Jews—90 percent of whom were killed immediately upon arrival. Their information was combined with the first report.

Attempts to smuggle the protocols abroad met with mixed results. First, the Pracovná Skupina tried to dispatch the Vrba-Wetzler report to Istanbul, giving it to a supposedly reliable courier. However, instead of passing it on to the representatives of the Rescue Committee of the Jewish Agency in Istanbul, the courier apparently handed over the report to the Budapest Gestapo. Rabbi Weissmandel then tried to use his contacts with Swiss Orthodox Jews to transmit it to the West. At first this channel failed him, but on May 16, 1944, the Pracovná Skupina sent a message that reached Isaac Sternbuch, the representative of the Orthodox Va'ad ha-Hatsala (Rescue Committee) in Switzerland. The message contained an abridged version of the Auschwitz protocols, and exhorted the Allies to bomb the extermination camp and the railway lines leading to it. In addition, the group suggested that Hungary be warned, the facts of the mass killings be publicized, the International RED CROSS be allowed into the camp, and money be provided to help rescue Hungarian Jews.

With the hope that it would later reach the free world, the report was also disseminated to key people in Bratislava. Krasnansky and Oskar Neumann (a member of the Pracovná Skupina) gave Rezső KASZTNER of the RELIEF AND RESCUE COMMITTEE OF BUDAPEST a copy of the Vrba-Wetzler report on April 28, 1944, when he visited the city. Apparently Kasztner brought it back to Budapest, but did not publicize it for fear the information would disrupt the rescue negotiations taking place between Hungarian Jewish leaders and the

Nazis. In mid-May, Rabbi Weissmandel also sent the report to Fülöp FREUDIGER (the leader of the Orthodox Relief and Rescue Committee in Budapest), specifically warning him that the Nazis were about to begin the liquidation of Hungarian Jewry. According to his testimony at the trial of Adolf EICHMANN, Freudiger forwarded the information to the Zsidó Tanács, the Jewish Council of Hungary; Angelo Rotta, the papal nuncio; and the Hungarian regent, Miklós HORTHY. The papal chargé d'affaires in Bratislava, Giuseppe Burzio, was also given the report and sent it to Rome on May 22, 1944. It is not known for certain when it reached the Vatican, but the notes on the Vatican's copy are dated October 22 and 25, 1944.

Following the arrival of the escapees Mordowicz and Rosin, the expanded report was sent to the West. Dr. Jaromir Kopecky, the Geneva representative of the CZECHOSLOVAK GOVERNMENT-IN-EXILE, received a copy from the Pracovná Skupina's courier on June 13, 1944. He informed Gerhart Riegner of the WORLD JEWISH CONGRESS, who in turn sent a telegraphic summary of the report (*see* RIEGNER CABLE) and a cover letter by Kopecky to Elizabeth Wiskemann of the British legation in Bern. She dispatched the information to Allen Dulles, the head of United States intelligence in Switzerland, who sent it to the American representative in Bern, Roswell McClelland, and he in turn forwarded it to the Department of State in Washington on June 16. Others received the report soon thereafter. The BBC broadcast some of the details on June 18, and the Swedes received a copy of the report on June 23, 1944. With the reception of the protocols in the West and the dissemination of the information contained in them, the true purpose of the Auschwitz extermination camp became clear to the free world.

BIBLIOGRAPHY

Gilbert, M. *Auschwitz and the Allies.* New York, 1981.

Mendelsohn, J., ed. *The Holocaust: Selected Documents in 18 volumes*. Vol. 11. New York, 1981.

Wyman, D. S. *The Abandonment of the Jews: America and the Holocaust, 1941–1945.* New York, 1984.

ROBERT ROZETT

AUSLANDSORGANISATION DER NSDAP (Foreign Organization of the NSDAP), organization founded in 1930 on the initiative of Bruno Fricke, from Paraguay, and Gregor Strasser, who at the time was in charge of the NAZI PARTY organization in Germany. Initially the organization had 300 members, residents of foreign countries. On August 7, 1931, the first Nazi party branch abroad, in Buenos Aires, was officially recognized. It was followed, on October 5, by a branch in Rio de Janeiro. On August 20 of that year the first nationwide organization was established, in Paraguay.

The Auslandsorganisation's first director was Hans Nieland, who was in charge of the Nazi organization in Hamburg and became a member of the Reichstag in 1930. Originally named Bund der Freunde der Hitlerbewegung (League of Friends of the Hitler Movement), for internal purposes its name was the Auslandsorganisation of the NSDAP. When the Nazis came to power in early 1933, over 160 local party branches were in existence in foreign countries, with 3,100 members. In the spring of 1933 Robert LEY appointed Ernst-Wilhelm Bohle to head the Auslandsorganisation. In his first report, submitted to the Nuremberg party rally at the end of August 1933, Bohle stated that since 1929, 230 local and countrywide branches had been set up in foreign countries. During the years that followed, Bohle's organization sought to enroll in the Nazi party the VOLKSDEUTSCHE (ethnic Germans) all over the globe; their number, in 1937, was estimated at 7 million. Nearly all of them, however, were assimilated into the society of the countries in which they lived, and the plan made little headway.

In 1937, Bohle was appointed head of the Auslandsorganisation section in the German Foreign Ministry, in order to improve coordination of the supervision of Nazi party members abroad. The staff of the Auslandsorganisation in Germany was estimated, in 1938, to number 800 (the figure apparently also included persons holding honorary posts); their assignment was to supervise 600 party cells and bases, local and countrywide branches abroad (consisting of 29,099 members), and 23,000 party members serving in the merchant marine. At that time the Foreign Ministry, headed by Joachim von RIBBENTROP, had a staff of 2,665 officers and employees serving abroad. Germans who were permanently resident abroad numbered over 500,000, of whom 6 percent were party members. The fourth convention of the Auslandsorganisation, held in Erlingen in September 1936, was attended by over 5,000 *Amtsleiter* (office managers) from all over the world. The fifth convention, held a year later in Stuttgart (which had been declared the "city of Germans residing outside Germany"), attracted over 10,000 Germans from abroad.

A highly significant event in the organization's history was the assassination of Wilhelm GUSTLOFF, the national director of the Auslandsorganisation in Switzerland, by a young Jew, David FRANKFURTER, on February 4, 1936. In his eulogy of Gustloff, Hitler compared Gustloff to the "martyrs" who had sacrificed themselves for the Nazi movement and called the deed "a declaration of war."

The foreign-trade section of the Auslandsorganisation and the "Germany" section of the Foreign Ministry opposed the HAAVARA AGREEMENT, the purpose of which was to facilitate the emigration of German Jews to Palestine. Until 1939, they had little success. They felt that the export of goods from Germany for which no payment was made in return and which would promote the establishment of a Jewish national state was against Germany's interests. In the period from 1933 to 1938, imports to Germany rose much faster than exports, and one of the Auslandsorganisation's goals was to promote exports. To this day there is no consensus on the importance of the role that the Auslandsorganisation played in the field of foreign affairs, but it seems to have been overrated. In November 1941 Bohle resigned from his post in the Foreign Ministry, an act that was regarded as an admission of the Auslandsorganisation's failure as far as Germany's foreign interests were concerned.

BIBLIOGRAPHY

De Jong, L. *The German Fifth Column in the Second World War.* London, 1956.

McKale, D. M. *The Swastika outside Germany.* Kent, Ohio, 1977.

HANS-HEINRICH WILHELM

AUSSERORDENTLICHE BEFRIEDUNGS-AKTION. *See* AB-Aktion.

AUSTRALIA, JEWISH REFUGEES IN. Adolf Hitler's assumption of power and the persecution of Jews in Germany after 1933 created a refugee problem for the British dominion of Australia that grew steadily worse throughout the 1930s. As each new crisis occurred, the Australian government was pressured to change its alien migration policies, and between 1936 and 1939 a more generous quota was gradually introduced.

In the 1930s, Australia was seen as a suitable place of refuge because of its small population, low birthrate, and democratic traditions. In both London and Australia, Jewish representatives requested the Australian government to permit more Jewish REFUGEES to settle in Australia, but until 1936 such requests met with a negative response. Only aliens possessing 500 pounds in landing money or dependent relatives of aliens already residing in Australia were allowed to enter. This policy of virtual exclusion meant that few Jewish refugees arrived before 1936.

Between 1936 and 1939, owing to the intensification of Nazi antisemitism and the slow improvement of economic conditions in Australia, there was a gradual relaxation of alien immigration policies. In 1936 the government reduced the landing-money requirement to 50 pounds and agreed that a responsible Jewish organization could act as guarantor. Aliens without a guarantor needed 200 pounds' landing money, and there was a quota system for the issue of landing permits. At the government's instigation, the Australian Jewish Welfare Society (AJWS) was formed in 1937, under the presidency of Sir Samuel Cohen, to coordinate efforts for Jewish refugees. This replaced the German Jewish Relief Fund, created in New South Wales in 1936 to raise funds to assist German Jews escaping from Nazism. In June 1938, at the EVIAN CONFERENCE, the Australian government announced that it would not increase its alien immigration quotas. After the devastation of the KRISTALLNACHT pogrom in Germany in November 1938, the government revised its policy. In a major ministerial statement on December 1, 1938, the minister for the interior, John McEwen, announced that Australia would admit 15,000 refugees over a period of three years, although this statement was not as liberal as it appeared on the surface since the Australian high commissioner in London, S. M. Bruce, had proposed a figure of 30,000. The outbreak of war in September 1939 ended the flow of refugees; by this time some 7,200 had arrived, 5,080 of them in 1939.

With the pressures of the arrival of the Jewish refugees, the AJWS grew rapidly by 1938 from a small organization run largely by volunteers to a large-scale association with fourteen full-time employees, located at the Maccabean Hall in Sydney. With financial assistance from the Refugee Economic Corporation, founded by American philanthropist Charles J. Liebman, the Mutual Enterprises organization was created to assist refugees to establish themselves in business, and Mutual Farms was founded to settle refugees on the land. A training farm was opened at Chelsea Park, Baulkham Hills, Sydney. These schemes operated in New South Wales, while in Victoria a Welfare Society also developed, under the leadership of Isaac Herbert Boas and in cooperation with the Melbourne Jewish Aid Society, which provided interest-free loans to newcomers.

The origins of Australian Jewry date back to Australia's foundation in 1788. Organized Jewish communities did not develop until the 1830s and 1840s, following the arrival of free English Jewish settlers. A number of German Jews settled in Victoria during the gold rushes of the 1850s, while a trickle of east European Jews arrived between 1880 and 1914; in the 1920s, about 2,000 Polish Jews settled in Australia, mainly in Melbourne. According to the census of June 30, 1933, the number of Jews in Australia was 23,553, or 0.36 percent of the population.

Most of the foreign Jews were absorbed into the Australian community and, until the 1930s, Australian Jewry remained Anglo-Jewish and very conservative in outlook. The community enjoyed a high economic and social status. The Jews were very Australianized, and responded to the refugees in a cold, unfeeling, and materialistic manner. Their social rejection of the newcomers, who were seen as a threat to Australian Jewry's social and civic status, was a result of fear and distrust and also of a sense of conformity in this isolated and parochial community. In addition, there was a language barrier, especially in New South Wales, where, before 1939, very few in the established Jewish community spoke German, Polish, or Yiddish. The refugees were instructed not to speak German in the streets or streetcars, and not to walk in groups "loudly speaking in a foreign language," because "the welfare of the old established Jewish community in Australia as well as of every migrant depends on your personal behavior." The Jewish refugees were encouraged to make themselves as inconspicuous as possible and to assimilate quickly into Australian society.

Most Australians favored migration from the British Isles and opposed admission of large groups of aliens. The refugees represented the intrusion of an alien way of life, and Australians generally could not understand their different behavioral patterns and mode of dress. Many Australians believed that European Jews were different in ethics and morality from the Anglo-Jews whom they respected and admired. There was also fear of economic competition and the undermining of living standards, especially during the time of economic hardship in the 1930s. These factors created a sense of hostility toward the refugees and led to mounting accusations of various malpractices and unsavory behavior. The accusations were used to justify anti-refugee feelings—despite the fact that the refugees contributed to Australia's industrial development by bringing new skills, and to its cultural development, especially in music.

A small group of Australians were influenced by fascist ideas, and a few right-wing fringe organizations were formed during the 1930s. Most important of these were the New Guard in New South Wales, under the leadership of Eric Campbell, and the Australia First movement, which adopted Nazi racial policies and published large tracts of Hitler's speeches in its newspaper, the *Publicist*. A German Nazi party was also formed in Australia. Nazi influence was increased by the activities of the German consul general, Dr. Rudolph Asmis. In addition, the Social Credit movement of Canada, founded on the financial theories of Maj. C. H. Douglas (a former British army officer who believed that poverty existed amid plenty because of the banks' monopoly over credit), established roots in Australia with antisemitic overtones. This was evident in its Victoria publication, the *New Times,* and in the activities of its correspondent, Eric Butler.

With the outbreak of war, Australia joined the Allied war effort, and Australian forces were sent to fight in France and the Middle East. Later some of these forces participated in the fighting in Italy (1943), Normandy (1944), and various sections of the eastern front. Members of the Australia First movement were interned.

During the war, the Australian Jewish community became aware of the Nazi destruction program. Following the Allies' joint announcement on December 17, 1942, of their recognition of the massacre of the Jews in Poland, the United Jewish Emergency Committee was formed in Sydney by Dr. Jona M. Machover, a leading Zionist, originally an emigré from the Russian Revolution who settled in London and was stranded in Australia during the war. In Melbourne, the United Jewish Overseas Relief Fund (UJORF) was founded, under the presidency of Leo Fink, to raise funds and collect goods to assist the suffering brethren in Europe. At the same time, the Palestine Jewish community cabled the Australian government, informing it of the slaughter of Polish Jews and appealing to it "to open the gates of free countries to those who seek refuge from that inferno on earth." By 1943, communal documents recorded the destruction of 3 million to 4 million European Jews, and in November of that year a resolution, endorsed by the Jewish communities in all the Australian states and referring to the parlous state of European Jewry, was presented to Prime Minister John Curtin. It urged him to support Jewish immigration to both Australia and Palestine, and to participate in "any international scheme for the provision of relief to the survivors of Nazi atrocities." Despite these developments, most people were not aware of the full extent of the Holocaust or the exact details of the extermination program until after the war, and the Australian government made no positive response to the appeals during the war years.

Lack of understanding of the plight of European Jews was evidenced in the fact that refugees from Germany, Austria, and later Hungary were labeled as "enemy aliens" and were required to report regularly to the local police, to obtain a police pass if they wished to travel outside their police area, and to surrender their radios. Some of these refugees were also interned initially at Hay in New South Wales and later at Tatura, Victoria. There they joined some two thousand four hundred refugee internees who had been sent to Australia by Britain on the *Dunera* in September 1940 and internees from Singapore and other parts of East Asia.

The story of the *Dunera* became particularly notorious in the wake of British hysteria about Nazi agents among refugees. The *Dunera* was dispatched to Australia with 2,542 men on board. Included in the transport were 200 former Italian Fascists and 251 German prisoners of war, mostly seamen. The overwhelming majority of the passengers were "C" class aliens, that is, those who had been classified as potentially least dangerous to British security.

The *Dunera* had been built to accommodate sixteen hundred passengers, and the resultant overcrowding of the ship led to insufferable conditions during the voyage. The food was inedible, and the crew often behaved with barbaric cruelty. Many refugees were beaten, and all had their belongings ransacked. The refugees tried to make the best of their situation. Lectures were given, Torah study groups formed, and a constitution was written. These activities continued in the Hay and Tatura camps. The constitution was refined, and a makeshift college was set up where camp inmates could study subjects ranging from mathematics to metaphysics, besides a great variety of languages. A theater company, a rabbinical academy (yeshiva), and Zionist study groups were also established. Many of the *Dunera* internees returned to Britain toward the end of the war. Around one thousand remained; most of them volunteered for service in the Australian military forces employment companies, which engaged them in essential nonmilitary wartime work.

The total number of Jewish refugees reaching Australia between 1933 and 1945 was eight thousand two hundred, and their status was eventually redefined as that of "friendly aliens." Of the three thousand five hundred male refugees between the ages of eighteen and forty-five, nearly every one volunteered for military service as soon as refugees were permitted to do so, and one thousand two hundred were accepted. Of the rest, most were engaged in industries classified as essential to the Australian war effort; Jewish refugees also contributed their scientific knowledge to the war effort.

Because of their sense of isolation during the internment period and their disillusionment at the lack of support from the established Jewish leadership, the refugees instituted their own separate organizations. In Melbourne the Association of Jewish Refugees was formed under the leadership of the dynamic liberal rabbi Dr. Herman Sanger, who had arrived from Germany in 1936. In Sydney the Association of Refugees, led by Dr. Max Joseph, followed suit.

During the war years the "thirty-niners," as the refugees who arrived in the late 1930s were called, provided the impetus and manpower to introduce significant changes into Jewish communal management. These affected every aspect of Jewish life in Australia, including the growth of orthodox and liberal Judaism, the establishment of the first Jewish day school, the North Bondi Jewish Kindergarten and Primary School in Sydney, the creation of B'nai B'rith, and the evolution of a more democratic communal structure through the Board of Deputies and the formation of the Executive Council of Australian Jewry in 1944. Attitudes toward Zionism, previously a fringe movement in the community, also changed as a result of the impact of the newcomers. After the war, the Jewish immigration increased. By 1954 the total number of pre- and postwar Jewish refugees settled in Australia was approximately 25,500, while the total Jewish population had increased to 48,436.

BIBLIOGRAPHY

Blakeney, M. *Australia and the Jewish Refugees, 1933–1948*. Sydney, 1985.

Kwiet, K., and J. A. Moses, eds. "On Being a German-Jewish Refugee in Australia." *Australian Journal of Politics and History* 31/1 (1985): entire issue.

Pearl, C. *The Dunera Scandal: Deported by Mistake*. Sydney, 1983.

Rutland, S. D. "The Coming of the Refugees." In *Edge of the Diaspora: Two Centuries of Jewish Settlement in Australia*. Sydney, 1988.

SUZANNE D. RUTLAND

AUSTRIA. The German core of the Austro-Hungarian Empire, Austria became a separate republic in 1918 when the empire broke up into its national components and Habsburg rule came to an end. The country has an area of 32,432 square miles (84,000 sq km), and its population in 1937 was 6,725,000. Jews are believed to have lived in Austria from Roman times; in the Middle Ages, periods when the Jews enjoyed material and cultural prosperity alternated with periods of persecution and expulsions. In the modern era, Austria was one of the centers of the Jewish modernization process and the integration of Jews into the country's overall culture. In 1849 the Jews were given the right to organize as a community, and in 1867 they

Courtyard of the central synagogue in Vienna on March 18, 1938, when the Gestapo closed the Jewish community offices and institutions and arrested the officers and leaders. Among the SS men is Adolf Eichmann (left, facing the camera).

were granted equality of rights. During the second half of the nineteenth century and the first few decades of the twentieth, the Jewish population of Austria grew rapidly as a result of immigration from all parts of the empire, the greater part of the newcomers converging on the capital, VIENNA.

Jews played an important role in the economic and cultural life of Austria, which became a center of Jewish culture and the cradle of Zionism. At the same time the country was one of the first and most virulent centers of modern antisemitism. The Jewish population in Austria reached its height during World War I, approaching 250,000, as a result of the influx of war refugees from Galicia and Bukovina. After the war the Jewish population declined, to 191,000 in 1934 (176,000 in Vienna) and 185,000 in 1938 (170,000 in Vienna, 8,000 in Lower Austria, 1,000 in Upper Austria, 2,000 in Styria, 3,200 in Burgenland, and a few hundred in other parts of the country).

The Anschluss. On March 11, 1938, Adolf Hitler sent his army into Austria and on March 13 the annexation (ANSCHLUSS) of Austria to the Reich was proclaimed in Vienna. Most of the population welcomed the Anschluss enthusiastically, and this fervor also expressed itself in widespread antisemitic rioting and an almost total absence of resistance to the Nazis. The Austrian Nazis lost no time in following the pattern, established by their fellow Nazis in Germany, of attacking Jews and expelling them from the country's economic, cultural, and social life—indeed, they outdid the German Nazis.

This greater scope of Nazi violence and brutality in Austria was also inspired from the top: on March 18, 1938, the German minister of the interior, Wilhelm FRICK, gave Heinrich HIMMLER extraordinary powers, enabling Himmler to operate in Austria beyond the limits set by law, in order to "preserve order and security." That same day Himmler set up a Gestapo headquarters in Vienna (in the Hotel Metropol, which had been confiscated from its Jewish owners), vesting in it political and police authority in Vienna and Lower Austria. The following day, Chief of Police Reinhard HEYDRICH empowered the chief of the Gestapo headquarters in Vienna, Franz Josef Huber, to establish Gestapo Lower Austria. The following day, Chief of Police Reinhard HEYDRICH empowered the chief of the Gestapo headquarters in Vienna, Franz Josef Huber, to establish Gestapo branch offices in Linz, Graz, Salzburg, Klagenfurt, Innsbruck, and Eisenstadt. By March 18, the offices of the Jewish community and the Zionist institutions in Vienna were closed down, and their officers were put in jail; 444

Jewish societies in Vienna and 181 in the provinces were forced to terminate their operations. A total of 110 public personalities, bankers, and businessmen were arrested and deported to DACHAU in the first two groups to be sent there from Vienna, on April 1 and May 15, respectively. In the first night following the Anschluss, March 13–14, the Gestapo launched an organized campaign of looting Jewish apartments, confiscating artworks, rugs, furniture, and other valuables, and shipping the loot to Berlin. The Gomperz and Rothschild art collections (their owners had been arrested) were transferred to the museum in Linz and to the private collections of Hitler and Hermann GÖRING. Göring was put in charge of Austria's economy on March 15, 1938.

In the very first week after the Anschluss, Jews were dismissed from their posts in theaters, community centers, and public libraries, and, on March 26, from employment in universities and colleges, and later in markets and slaughterhouses. Ritual slaughter was outlawed. On March 14, three Jews serving in the Austrian army refused to take an oath of loyalty to the Führer, and as a result all Jews were dismissed from the army. This step, however, did not absolve the Jews from having to go through the humiliating process of reporting for the draft when they reached conscription age, going through the medical examination, and then being rejected for service because they were Jewish.

In Graz the synagogues were desecrated and four Jews were killed, and in Vienna the main synagogue was used as a place where Jews were subjected to torture. All over Austria Jews were arrested and held in jail until they were ready to sign a statement that they were voluntarily giving up their property. In Graz, the Jews who were tortured and kept in jail for two months included Nobel prize winner Professor Otto Loewi and Chief Rabbi Professor David Herzog. The number of suicides monthly among Jews jumped from four in February 1938 to seventy-nine in March and sixty-two in April. The official reason given for the arrest of the Jewish community leaders and activists was that their names had been found on a list of contributors to the last election campaign of the Austrian chancellor. That same list also served as the pretext for the first "contribution" levied on the Jews of Austria, the sum of 500,000 marks.

Gauleiter Josef Burckel, whose job it was to implement Austria's unification with Germany, set up an office in Vienna for the seizure of Jewish property, with branches in the provincial capitals. Most of the 26,236 Jewish-owned businesses existing in March 1938 were modest enterprises, but they did not escape the furious "Aryanization" drive (*see* ARISIERUNG) that marked the first few weeks of the Anschluss, or the robberies that took place in full daylight, often with police protection. Among those affected were the large department stores, such as Shiffmann Brothers. When Walter Raffelsberger took over the Jewish-property office, the Vermögensverkehrstelle (Property Transfer Office), he introduced order into the ongoing removal of the Jews' belongings. According to figures he published on July 21, 1938, almost all the Jewish-owned property in the provinces and 30 percent of the property in Vienna had already been seized.

On June 29, all Jews and all partners in mixed marriages who were employed in the private sector—some forty thousand persons—were dismissed from their jobs. The number of German "supervisors" of Jewish property rose from 917 in July 1938 to 2,787 that November, and the number of businesses they were supervising rose from 1,624 in July to 5,210 in September. The drop in exports forced the Nazi authorities to keep Jews in key export branches temporarily in their posts, especially those branches that dealt with exports to southern and eastern Europe. By the summer of 1939, 18,800 Jewish enterprises had been closed down: 606 factories (out of 986), 8,145 commercial enterprises (out of 11,402), and 9,485 workshops (out of 13,046). According to Nazi estimates, the difference between the real value of the large Jewish-owned enterprises and the total sum that their Jewish owners were paid for them amounted to more than 35 billion reichsmarks. In one instance a business valued at half a million reichsmarks, with liabilities of 50,000 reichsmarks, was "bought" at a price of 20,000. The Jewish owner was arrested on a charge of negligence in running the business, since he was unable to come up with the 30,000 reichsmarks needed to cover the debt.

Emigration. The emigration of the Jews from Austria was handled by Adolf EICHMANN. At the first meeting Eichmann held with leaders of the Jewish community and the Zionist movements, a meeting held in the Palestine Office (which dealt with Palestinian affairs, including immigration) two days after the Anschluss, he pretended to have been born in Palestine and to be familiar with the practices of Judaism. The executive director of the Vienna Jewish community, Dr. Josef LÖWENHERZ, reorganized the work of the Jewish Community Office in accordance with instructions dictated to him by Eichmann. The office was reopened on May 2, 1938, with Löwenherz as executive director, assisted by a council of eight section chiefs. That August, a special section was added to deal with provincial affairs, the Provinzreferat. Dr. Eduard Pachtmann, who had no previous experience in the field, was appointed head of the Zionist organization, in place of Dr. Oskar Grünbaum (who was in jail). He was joined by Zionist Youth Union leader Georg Überall (later, in Israel, he took the name Ehud Avriel) and by representatives of the Zionist National Funds and the Women's International Zionist Organization.

The Palestine Office was headed by Dr. Alois Rothenberg, who joined forces with the He-Haluts pioneering Zionist organization, headed by Ze'ev Willy Ritter; the nonpartisan organized Zionists of the eighteen-to-thirty-five age group; the YOUTH ALIYA (the fifteen-to-seventeen age group); and the young religious Zionist pioneers. A bitter controversy broke out between Rothenberg, who wanted to allocate the limited number of immigration permits for Palestine to the veteran Austrian Zionists, and Ritter, who demanded that they all be reserved for He-Haluts members and organized young skilled tradesmen and professionals. The Vienna Jewish Community Office, the Palestine Office, and the provincial communities all had to submit periodic reports to Eichmann —biweekly, monthly, and bimonthly—with the emphasis on the progress being made in the emigration of the Jews.

In addition to pressure from the top, there was terror in the streets. Emigration, in all its aspects, was concentrated in Vienna, so that community representatives and individuals trying to obtain the required documents had to stay in Vienna and stand in long lines, night and day, in front of the municipal and police offices. There they were exposed to humiliation and tortures by Nazi party thugs, the HITLERJUGEND (Hitler Youth), and brutal security men. The Jews of Austria were not allowed to share in the arrangements made with the Jews of Germany, whom the German Foreign Office permitted to emigrate in an orderly fashion to Palestine and other countries, together with a portion of their assets, under the HAAVARA AGREEMENT.

In August 1938 the ZENTRALSTELLE FÜR JÜDISCHE AUSWANDERUNG (Central Office for Jewish Emigration) opened offices in the Rothschild palace, which the Nazis had confiscated. Eichmann was in charge, assisted by Rolf Günther, who made wide use of extortion in his work. By systematic bureaucratic methods the Jews emigrating from the country were automatically divested of all their assets. Most of the financing of the emigration was funded by the levy that every emigrant had to pay, in proportion to the assets that he declared. The American Jewish JOINT DISTRIBUTION COMMITTEE and the British COUNCIL FOR GERMAN JEWRY agreed to provide the foreign currency needed for travel expenses and for the sum that the emigrant had to have in his possession on arrival at his destination. This was on condition that Eichmann release an equivalent amount from the blocked account of the community, to be used for welfare services and for assistance to emigrants who did not have enough means of their own to finance their departure. In the period from May to July 1938, 25 percent of the emigrants required full or partial assistance from the community, the number rising to 33 percent from August to October, 50 percent in November and December, and 75 percent between February and May 1939. In the first two months of the Anschluss, some seven thousand Jews crossed the border to Switzerland or Italy, and when these borders were closed to them the Jews tried to make their way to countries in western Europe. Sometimes the border police of the country they tried to enter forced the Jews back into Germany.

In the November 1938 KRISTALLNACHT pogroms, Eichmann imprisoned Jews in concentration camps as a means of extorting money from them and forcing them to speed up their emigration. When such a detainee was released, he was given a time limit in which to make his emigration arrangements; if he was still there after the limit had passed, he was again imprisoned. As a result there were a growing number of instances when adults or heads of families emigrated and left behind elderly parents and children. The number of old and infirm persons who had no relatives to care for them grew to 25,000, and there was a comparative rise in the number of abandoned children. Following the November pogroms, countries of western Europe agreed to accept 10,000 children, but only 2,844 children, in forty-three groups, were able to make use of this offer from December 1938 to August 1939. Some of the children were later seized by the Germans when they occupied these countries, and perished. Most of the children—2,262 of them—went to Britain.

Styria. Special treatment was granted by Eichmann to the Jews of Styria, whose capital, Graz, was declared the capital of the Nazi uprising in Austria and therefore aspired to be the first Austrian city to become *judenrein* ("cleansed of Jews"). In order to achieve this coveted goal by April 20, 1939 (Hitler's birthday), the chairman of the Zionist organization in Graz, Elias Grunschlag, was permitted to work closely with the Gestapo and the customs authorities to speed up the liquidation of debts owed by would-be emigrants and to deal collectively with the passports and other documents required for emigration. Eichmann also agreed to apply to the Jews of Styria the Haavara provisions and enable them to export to Palestine property and machinery in the amount of 5 million reichsmarks. This arrangement, however, was not put into effect before November 1938, and thereafter its scope was greatly reduced. The *Gauleiter* in Linz, August Eigruber, also granted special dispensation to his former friend and business partner, Max Hirschfeld, giving him a free hand in arranging for the emigration of Jews. Hirschfeld made full use of this opportunity. A similar relationship existed in Klagenfurt, the capital of Carinthia, between the Jewish community chairman, Nathan Kriegsfuss, and the local Nazi authorities.

Burgenland. The Jews of the "seven communities" of Burgenland, which were centers of Jewish learning and had been inhabited by Jews for hundreds of years, were driven out of their homes in the first few months after the annexation. On the Sabbath, March 26, 1938, the Jews of Frauenkirchen, under threat of deportation, were forced to come up with a "contribution" of 80,000 reichsmarks. This did not, however, prevent the Nazis from deporting ten of the wealthy families and forcing them across the border, after first compelling them to confirm, in writing, that they were voluntarily abandoning their property and leaving penniless. In the course of 1938 all the Burgenland Jews were driven out, on the pretext that they were too close to the borders of Hungary and Czechoslovakia and their presence there was jeopardizing the security of the Reich. About half were expelled to Vienna, and the rest had to wander from one border to the other. On April 26, 1938, the secretary of the religious Jewish organization Agudat Israel, Julius Steinfeld, gave a written promise to arrange for the emigration of all the Burgenland Jews. This was accomplished, with the cooperation of the Vienna Jewish community, the Jewish Agency, and the Rabbinical Aid and Rescue Committee in Britain, and with the granting of emigration priority to the Burgenland Jews.

Persecutions. In the city of Wiener Neustadt, all "Aryan" landlords were ordered to evict their Jewish tenants from their apartments. In Horn, the tombstones in the Jewish cemetery were desecrated in May 1938, and on September 18 the Jews had to leave the city without a day's notice. The Jewish communities were impoverished to the extent that they had to close their rented prayer-houses, and on August 7 they informed the Vienna community that they were no longer able to take care of their needs. Social life among the Jews in all the provincial communities came to a standstill, except for Graz, where there was still an active community.

In the November 1938 pogrom it was primarily the synagogues and the purification rooms (for washing the dead before burial) that were desecrated. In Klagenfurt the synagogue furnishings were destroyed by axes and Jewish apartments were vandalized. The impressive Graz synagogue with its cupola was blown up, as was the purification room, and 300 Jewish males were deported to Dachau. The worst pogroms took place in Innsbruck, where all the Jews were beaten up, an elderly Jewish couple were drowned, and the Zionist organization chairman and a wealthy merchant were murdered.

The November pogrom accelerated the liquidation of the Jewish communities. By May 1939, twenty-seven out of a total of thirty-three communities were closed down. Their property was confiscated by Eichmann and transferred to the Emigration Office in Vienna. On February 23, 1940, the authorities officially withdrew their recognition of the provincial communities.

Prior to the outbreak of the war, 126,445 Jews emigrated from Austria. Of the 58,000 who were left, 32,000 required welfare assistance. Another 2,000 managed to emigrate in wartime to other European countries up until November 10, 1941, when emigration of Jews was finally banned altogether. Of the 55,505 Jews who emigrated from Austria to European countries, 30,850 went to Britain; 15,000 were caught by the Nazis in their western European conquests and deported to extermination camps. The number of emigrants to North America was 28,700 (82 to Canada); to Central and South America, 11,580; to Asia, 28,700 (18,120 to China, mainly Shanghai); to Palestine, 9,190; to Australia and New Zealand, 1,880; and to Africa, 650. All in all, 128,500 Jews emigrated from Austria, to eighty-nine countries.

With the outbreak of the war, preparations for emigration continued, and technical training in anticipation of a new life was maintained. More than five thousand children studied in educational institutions under the auspices of the Jewish communities. Provision was made for some twenty-four thousand aged and ailing people for whom emigration would not be possible. At the beginning of October 1939, after the conquest of Poland, 1,048 young and elderly people, some stateless and some with Polish nationality, were deported to BUCHENWALD, where they were killed. Later in October two more transports, totaling 1,584 people, were dispatched to Nisko (*see* NISKO AND LUBLIN PLAN) from Moravian Austria (Moravská Ostrava), in the vicinity of the Protectorate of BOHEMIA AND MORAVIA. Most of the deportees were expelled across the San River into the area conquered by the Soviet army; only 199 of the Austrian deportees employed in building the camp in Nisko later returned to Vienna.

During February and March 1941 about 5,000 Austrian Jews were deported to the KIELCE district in Poland, and were subsequently murdered in 1942 in the BEŁŻEC and CHEŁMNO camps. With the onset of the mass expulsions in mid-October 1941, 5,000 Jews were deported to Łódź, together with 5,000 GYPSIES from the Burgenland district of Austria. Later that year, more than 5,000 were sent to the Łódź ghetto and another 3,000 to ghettos in the Baltic area. Following the WANNSEE CONFERENCE in January 1942, the deportations were accelerated: 3,200 Jews were sent to Riga, 8,500 to Minsk, and 6,000 to the Lublin region. In the second part of 1942, almost 14,000—nearly all of them aged—were deported to the THERESIENSTADT concentration camp. When the Vienna community was dissolved in November 1942, only 7,000 Jews remained in Austria, most of them married to non-Jews. All those who were fit were put on forced labor. The community organization, the Kultusgemeinde, was replaced by the Ältestenrat (Council of Elders) in Vienna, which represented all of Austrian Jewry before the authorities and ran the Jewish hospital, the home for the aged, and a soup kitchen. Josef Löwenherz headed the council until the end of the war.

Deportations continued on a smaller scale and the community virtually disappeared. At the end of the war about 1,000 Jews survived in Vienna. Some were partners of mixed marriages, and the Gestapo employed a number of their offspring in sorting out the vast quantities of confiscated Jewish property. About one-third of the survivors remained alive by living under cover.

In the second half of 1944, tens of thousands of Hungarian Jews were deported to Vienna and Lower Austria for forced labor in building fortifications. About 8,000 Jews, scattered among small labor camps in Vienna, were assisted by the remaining staff of the Vienna Jewish Hospital, which even opened a maternity ward. It also maintained the last vestiges of organized Jewish religious ritual in Vienna. More than 65,000 Austrian Jews died in the ghettos and concentration camps of eastern Europe, from which only 1,747 returned to Austria at the end of the war. They were eventually joined by some of the Austrian Jews who had emigrated before the war, but the bulk of the postwar Austrian community consisted of Jews who arrived from other countries, mostly of eastern Europe, after the end of the war. This community became the center for the BERIḤA organization.

[*See also* Youth Movements: Germany and Austria.]

BIBLIOGRAPHY

Bauer, Y. *My Brother's Keeper: A History of the American Jewish Joint Distribution Committee, 1929–1939*. Philadelphia, 1974.

Fraenkel, J., ed. *The Jews of Austria*. London, 1967.

Gedye, J. E. R. *Fallen Bastions: The Central European Tragedy*. London, 1940.

Moser, J. "Die Verfolgung der Juden." In vol. 3 of *Widerstand und Verfolgung in Wien 1934–1945*, pp. 194–326. Vienna, 1975.

Oxaal, I., et al. *Jews, Antisemitism, and Culture in Vienna*. London, 1987.

Rosenkranz, H. *Verfolgung und Selbstbehauptung: Die Juden in Österreich 1938–1945*. Vienna, 1978.

HERBERT ROSENKRANZ

AXIS (Ger., *Achse*), the political, military, and ideological alliance of Nazi GERMANY and Fascist ITALY. In the first three years of Nazi rule (1933–1935), Italy's political interests and its concern over Nazi aspirations for territorial expansion prevented any alliance between the two regimes, despite their ideological affinity. Benito MUSSOLINI's policy of ensuring the independence of Austria so that it would serve as a buffer between Italy and Germany even led him, in April 1935, to reach an agreement with France and Britain that was clearly directed against the Third Reich. This agreement called for the maintenance of peace within the framework of the League of Nations, expressed the signatories' opposition to "any unilateral violation of treaties which would jeopardize European peace," and promised concerted action against such steps.

Mussolini's attitude changed in the wake of Italy's invasion of Ethiopia in October 1935. The League of Nations strongly opposed the invasion, and sanctions—albeit ineffective ones—were imposed on Italy, leading to a break between that country and Britain and France. The ensuing political crisis led to a rapprochement between Italy and Germany, a process that was accompanied by a virulent propaganda drive against the "degenerating democratic West." This rapprochement was accelerated and reinforced by the Spanish Civil War, which broke out in July 1936, with both Italy and Germany lending military support to the anti-republican side. After Mussolini first used the term "Rome-Berlin axis," in a speech at Milan in November 1936, it became widespread.

At first, the two countries stressed their joint political interest in opposing the democratic powers and their regimes; Mussolini and Italian Fascism still had reservations about racism in general and its antisemitic version in particular. It was only in 1938, when the relative international weight carried by the two dictators had shifted, the Third Reich had grown in power, and the international crisis had deepened, that Mussolini adopted racism and launched an anti-Jewish drive. In May 1939, following the dismemberment of Czechoslovakia and a few months before the outbreak of war, Germany and Italy concluded the so-called Pact of Steel. Earlier, in November 1937, Italy had joined the Anti-Comintern Pact. In September 1940, a tripartite alliance was forged between Germany, Italy, and Japan to which the three countries committed themselves for ten years; this was known as the Berlin-Rome-Tokyo Axis. During World War II the term "Axis countries" also came to be applied to other states allied with Germany that had joined the Anti-Comintern Pact: Hungary, Romania, Slovakia, and Bulgaria.

BIBLIOGRAPHY

Duroselle, M. *Les relations internationals de l'Allemagne et de l'Italie de 1919 à 1939*. Paris, 1967.

Petersen, J. *Hitler-Mussolini: Die Entstehung der Achse Berlin-Rom, 1933–1936*. Tübingen, 1973.

Wiskemann, E. *The Rome-Berlin Axis: A History of the Relations between Hitler and Mussolini*. London, 1949.

ISRAEL GUTMAN

B

BABI YAR, ravine, situated in the northwestern part of Kiev, where the Jews of the Ukrainian capital were systematically massacred. At the southern end of the ravine were two cemeteries, one of which was Jewish.

Kiev was captured by the Twenty-ninth Corps and the Sixth German Army on September 19, 1941. Of its Jewish population of 160,000, some 100,000 had managed to flee before the Germans took the city. Shortly after the German takeover, from September 24 to 28, a considerable number of buildings in the city center, which were being used by the German military administration and the army, were blown up; many Germans (as well as local inhabitants) were killed in the explosions. After the war, it was learned that the sabotage operation had been the work of an NKVD (Soviet security police) detachment that had been left behind in the city for that purpose.

On September 26, the Germans held a meeting at which it was decided that in retaliation for the attacks on the German-held installations, the Jews of Kiev would all be put to death. Participating in the meeting were the military governor, Maj. Gen. Friedrich Georg Eberhardt; the Higher SS and Police Leader at Rear Headquarters Army Group South, SS-Obergruppenführer Friedrich JECKELN; the officer commanding Einsatzgruppe C, SS-Brigadeführer Dr. Otto RASCH; and the officer commanding Sonderkommando 4a, SS-Standartenführer Paul BLOBEL. The implementation of the decision to kill the Jews of Kiev was entrusted to Sonderkommando 4a. This unit consisted of SD (Sicherheitsdienst; Security Service) and Sicherheitspolizei (Security Police; Sipo) men; the third company of the Special Duties Waffen-SS battalion; and a platoon of the No. 9 police battalion. The unit was reinforced by police battalions Nos. 45 and 305 and by units of the Ukrainian auxiliary police.

On September 28, notices were posted in the city ordering the Jews to appear the following morning, September 29, at 8:00 a.m. at the corner of Melnik and Dekhtyarev streets; they were being assembled there, so the notice said, for their resettlement in new locations. (The text had been prepared by Propaganda Company No. 637 and the notices had been printed by the Sixth Army printing press.)

The next morning, masses of Jews reported at the appointed spot. They were directed to proceed along Melnik Street toward the Jewish cemetery and into an area comprising the cemetery itself and a part of the Babi Yar ravine. The area was cordoned off by a barbed-wire fence and guarded by Sonderkommando police and Waffen-SS men, as well as by Ukrainian policemen. As the Jews approached the ravine, they were forced to hand over all the valuables in their possession, to take off all their clothes, and to advance toward the ravine edge, in groups of ten. When they reached the edge, they were gunned down by automatic fire. The shooting was done by several squads of SD and Sipo personnel, police, and Waffen-SS men of the Sonderkommando unit, the squads relieving one another every few hours. When the day

Babi Yar, where Sonderkommando 4a of Einsatzgruppe C carried out the mass slaughter of 33,771 Kiev Jews on September 29 and 30, 1941.

ended, the bodies were covered with a thin layer of soil. According to official reports of the Einsatzgruppe, in two days of shooting (September 29 and 30), 33,771 Jews were murdered.

In the months that followed, many more thousands of Jews were seized, taken to Babi Yar, and shot. Among the general population there were some who helped Jews go into hiding, but there were also a significant number who informed on them to the Germans and gave them up. After the war, the officer in charge of the Sipo and SD bureau testified that his Kiev office received so many letters from the Ukrainian population informing on Jews—"by the bushel"—that the office could not deal with them all, for lack of manpower. Evidence of betrayal of Jews by the Kiev population was also given by Jewish survivors and by the Soviet writer Anatoly Kuznetsov.

Babi Yar served as a slaughterhouse for non-Jews as well, such as GYPSIES and Soviet prisoners of war. According to the estimate given by the Soviet research commission on Nazi crimes, 100,000 persons were murdered at Babi Yar.

In July 1943, by which time the Red Army was on the advance, Paul Blobel came back to Kiev. He was now on a new assignment, in coordination with SS-Gruppenführer Dr. Max Thomas, the officer commanding the SD and Sipo in the Ukraine: that of erasing all evidence of the mass carnage that the Nazis had perpetrated. For this purpose, Blobel formed two special groups, identified by the code number 1005. Unit 1005-A was made up of eight to ten SD men and thirty German policemen, and was under the command of an SS-*Obersturmbannführer* named Baumann. In mid-August the unit embarked on its task of exhuming the corpses in Babi Yar and cremating them. The ghastly job itself was carried out by inmates of a nearby concentration camp (Syretsk), from which the Germans brought in 327 men, of whom 100 were Jews. The prisoners were housed in a bunker carved out from the ravine wall; it had an iron gate that was locked during the night and was watched by a guard with a machine gun. They had chains bolted to their legs, and those who fell ill or lagged behind were shot on the spot. The mass graves were opened up by bulldozers, and it was the prisoners' job to drag the corpses to cremation pyres, which consisted of wooden logs doused in gasoline on a base of railroad ties. The bones that did not respond to incineration were crushed, for which purpose the Nazis brought in tombstones from the Jewish cem-

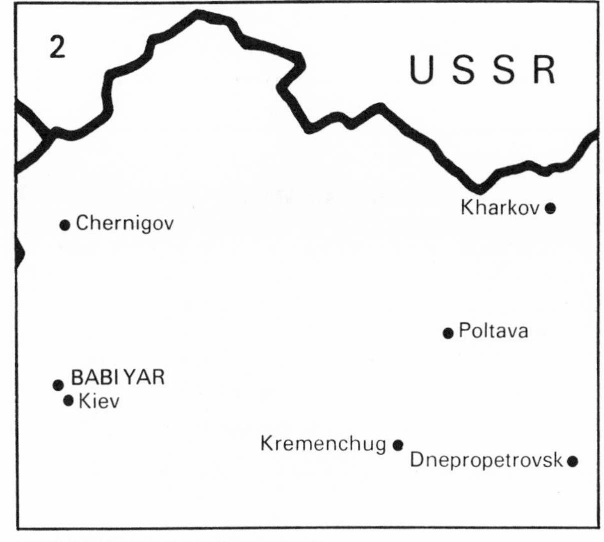

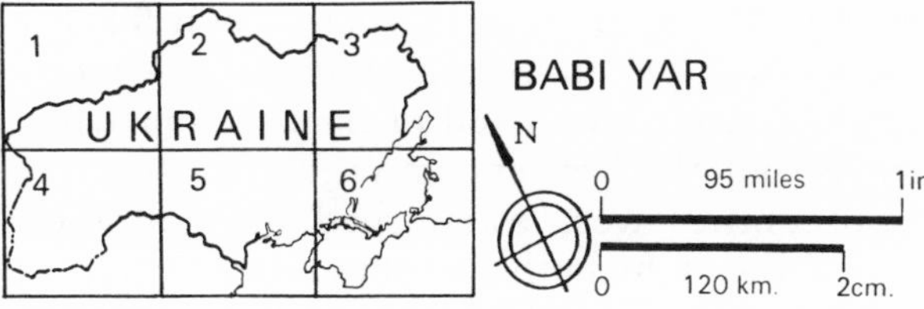

etery. The ashes were sifted to retrieve any gold or silver they might have contained. Cremation of the corpses began on August 18 and went on for six weeks, ending on September 19, 1943. The Nazis did their job thoroughly, and when they were through no trace was left of the mass graves.

On the morning of September 29, the prisoners learned that they were about to be put to death. They already had a plan for escape, and resolved to put it into effect the same night. Shortly after midnight, under cover of darkness and the fog that enveloped the ravine, twenty-five prisoners broke out. Fifteen succeeded in making their escape; the others were shot during the attempt or on the following morning.

It took a long time after the war for a memorial to be erected at Babi Yar. The demand for a memorial was first voiced during the "thaw" that set in during the Khrushchev regime, by which time Babi Yar had become a place of pilgrimage. Among those who made this demand were the writers Ilya EHRENBURG and Viktor Nekrasov, but their call was not heeded. In 1961, the poet Yevgeni Yevtushenko published a poem, "Babi Yar," which begins with the lines:

> No gravestone stands on Babi Yar;
> Only coarse earth heaped roughly on the gash:
> Such dread comes over me.

A year later, Dmitri Shostakovich set the poem to music, incorporating it into his Thirteenth Symphony. (Under pressure from the authorities, changes were made in the original text, and it is the amended text that is used today when the symphony is performed in the Soviet Union.) Both the poem and the musical setting had a tremendous impact in the Soviet Union, as well as beyond its borders. Demands increased for a memorial to be built at Babi Yar, but it was not until 1966 that architects and artists were invited to submit proposals, and it took eight more years for the memorial to be built. Since 1974 a monument stands in Babi Yar, but the inscription does not mention that Jews were among the victims there.

Monument erected in 1966 at Babi Yar. The Ukrainian text reads: "On this site there will be a monument for the victims of fascism during the German occupation of Kiev, 1941–1943."

BIBLIOGRAPHY

Ehrenburg, I., and V. Grossman, eds. *The Black Book of Soviet Jewry*. New York, 1981. See pages 3–12.

Korey, W. "Babi Yar Remembered." *Midstream* 15/3 (1969): 24–39.

Kuznetsov, A. *Babi Yar.* New York, 1967.
St. George, J. *The Road to Babi Yar.* London, 1967.

SHMUEL SPECTOR

BACH-ZELEWSKI, ERICH VON DEM (1899–1972), SS commander. Born in Lauenburg in Pomerania, Bach-Zelewski served as a private during World War I and then joined the police. He became a member of the Nazi party in 1930 and the following year enrolled in the SS.

After the Nazis' rise to power, Bach-Zelewski's career progressed rapidly, and in 1938 he was appointed SS commander in Silesia, with headquarters in Breslau (now Wrocław). After September 1939, the Polish part of Silesia was incorporated into his district of command and he was responsible for the expulsion of tens of thousands of Jews from the area. When the Germans invaded the Soviet Union on June 22, 1941, Bach-Zelewski became the Higher SS and Police Leader in central Russia, attached to the Central Army Group; in November of that year he was promoted to the rank of SS-*Obergruppenführer* and general of police. His duties also included command of Einsatzgruppe B, which mass-murdered Jews in Belorussia. In 1942, Bach-Zelewski was appointed Heinrich HIMMLER's representative in the fight against the partisans, and from January 1943 he was the commanding officer of all the forces fighting the partisans in eastern Europe. Between August and October 1944 he commanded the forces that suppressed the WARSAW POLISH UPRISING. Bach-Zelewski's units taking part in these operations became infamous for the mass murder of civilians and for the destruction of numerous villages and towns and of large parts of Warsaw. From the end of 1944 he was in command of various army corps.

After the war Bach-Zelewski appeared as a prosecution witness at the NUREMBERG TRIAL, before the American military tribunal there; at the Einsatzgruppen trial; at the trials of senior SS and army officers; and at the Warsaw trial of Ludwig FISCHER, who had been governor of the Warsaw district. Bach-Zelewski was held in prison; in 1951 he was given a ten-year sentence in a trial held in Munich, but was released after serving five years of his sentence. Re-arrested in 1958, he was sentenced at Nuremberg in 1961 to a further four and one-half years.

BIBLIOGRAPHY

Bartoszewski, W. *Prawda o von dem Bachu.* Warsaw, 1961.
Reitlinger, G. *The SS: Alibi of a Nation.* New York, 1956.
Zawodny, J. K. *Nothing but Honor: The Story of the Warsaw Uprising, 1944.* Stanford, 1978.

SHMUEL SPECTOR

BAČKA, district in YUGOSLAVIA that now forms the western part of the autonomous province of Vojvodina. Jews lived in Bačka in ancient times, but the first known organized Jewish communities were established there at the end of the eighteenth century.

Prior to the German invasion of Yugoslavia in April 1941, Bačka had a Jewish population of some sixteen thousand, representing 20 percent of Yugoslav Jewry and 2 percent of the district's population. There were seventeen Neolog communities, following a Conservative rite, and nine Orthodox communities. One-third of the Jews were engaged in trade and commerce, 20 percent were office workers, 10 percent were professionals (doctors, lawyers, and so on), and a similar number were skilled craftsmen and industrial workers. The Jewish community had a considerable impact on Bačka's cultural and educational life and on charitable activities. In the 1930s the Zionist movement gained the majority within most of the Jewish communities, and Zionist youth movements—Ha-Shomer ha-Tsa'ir (with twelve hundred members), Tekhelet Lavan (Blau-Weiss, with seven hundred), and Betar (with four hundred)—played an important role by running summer camps and *hakhsharot* (training schools for agriculture) and issuing their own regular publications. The clandestine Communist youth movement also had a substantial number of adherents among Bačka Jews. Some three hundred Bačka Jews had moved to Palestine, and Bačka communities helped tens of thousands of legal and "illegal" immigrants from

Germany and German-occupied countries to make their way to Palestine.

The anti-Jewish legislation introduced in Yugoslavia in 1940 generated resistance among Bačka Jews to the growing Nazi pressure. They supported the anti-Nazi coup of March 27, 1941, with most of the young Jewish men volunteering for the army in the April 1941 fighting. Several dozen were killed or wounded, or became prisoners of war.

When Yugoslavia was defeated and its territory carved up, Bačka was allotted to Hungary. Compared to the German occupation of neighboring SERBIA, the Hungarians were the lesser evil; but even in the early days of the occupation the Hungarians staged incidents to serve as an excuse for murdering thousands of Serbs and Jews. Many others were expelled and handed over to the Nazis; the leaders of the Jewish community and the Zionist movement were taken hostage; thousands of Jews were deprived of their citizenship and most of their possessions, by force or intimidation; and the communities had to pay a war levy. By May 1941, male Jews were being drafted for hard labor, in the course of which they were beaten up and tortured.

Terror against Jews and Serbs was stepped up in July 1941, when Hungary joined the war against the Soviet Union. Many Jews joined the TITO-led partisan movement, and the number of young Jews involved in the struggle against the Nazis was considerably larger than their proportion in the population. By the end of 1941 all male Jews, up to the age of sixty, were drafted into labor battalions (*see* MUNKASZOLGÁLAT) of the Hungarian army. For the most part they were posted to the Soviet front in the Ukraine, where they were worked to the bone, starved to death, left to freeze in the cold, or murdered by their guards. Some of the men managed to cross the lines, and it was these "deserters" who took the initiative to form the First Yugoslav Armored Brigade in the Soviet Union, which in the summer of 1944 was moved to the Serbian front.

In December 1941 and January 1942, incidents between a mobile partisan force and the Hungarian army served as a pretext for the slaughter of Serbs and Jews, under the cover of a *Razzia* (raid, roundup) that the Hungarian government had sanctioned on the recommendation of Hungarian and local Nazi elements. To carry it out, two special units were formed, under the command of Gen. Ferenc Feketehalmy-Czeydner, Col. László Deák, Maj. Gen. József Grassy, Capt. Márton Zöldi, and other Nazi agents. Over five thousand men were murdered in the course of January 1942, half of them Jews. Six Jewish communities were totally exterminated. Thousands were brought before "selection commissions" made up of Hungarians, which decided the way in which they were to be killed—by shooting, bayoneting, hanging, or other horrible methods. The city of Novi Sad was ransacked by units of the Second Combat Regiment, commanded by Grassy. On the very first day of the *Razzia,* dozens of Jews and Serbs were murdered; and on the third day, January 23, 1942, the gendarmes staged an incident that served as the excuse for mass slaughter; hundreds were murdered in the streets, the cemeteries, and the stadiums. The number of Jews murdered accounted for a third of the entire Jewish population in Bačka. The killing was stopped on the intervention of moderate elements, among them Endre Bajcsy-Zsilinsky, a member of parliament representing the Smallholders' party.

The massacre caused angry reactions among the Hungarian public and in neutral states, including Switzerland, Sweden, Spain, and Turkey. Miklós KALLAY, the Hungarian premier who had taken office in March 1942, had to admit that innocent people had been murdered. In the course of 1943 the men responsible for the carnage were put on trial but managed to flee to Germany, where they were given asylum. In March 1944, when the German army entered Hungary, the culprits in the Bačka crimes returned to the country and took part in the deportation of Hungarian Jews to extermination camps.

The situation of the surviving Jews of Bačka improved a little in 1943, but this did not prevent many young Jews from joining the mobile partisan units. Zionist functionaries took an active part in the rescue operations. Dr. Moshe Schweiger, a leader of the Ihud Olami (Zionist Labor) party in Bačka, took the initiative in setting up a committee in Budapest to care for the hundreds of refugees from Bačka in the Hungarian capital, to provide them with housing and employment, and to ensure that they would not be expelled. Dr.

Meir Weltmann-Tuval, an Ihud Olami member and leading Zionist, was very active in behalf of Bačka Jews at the Istanbul Jewish Agency office. He was joined by Dr. Francis Ofner, a Betar leader in Bačka, who had succeeded in escaping from the Hungarian murderers. Together, the two men arranged for dozens of Bačka Jews—children, youths, and adults—to make their way to Palestine.

After the Germans occupied Hungary, on March 19, 1944, German SS units, together with the Hungarian gendarmerie, came to Bačka and embarked on the deportation of the remaining Jews to extermination camps. Over a third of Bačka's Jews (which at the time numbered eight thousand) were deported to AUSCHWITZ and other extermination camps in May of that year. Of Bačka's prewar Jewish population of sixteen thousand, only twenty-five hundred survived to witness the liberation of the district. Many of these had volunteered for service in the Yugoslav army; some of Bačka's Jews fell in the final battles against the USTAŠA forces in Croatia, or even against SS units. The survivors reorganized themselves into ten communities, but eleven hundred went to Israel after the establishment of the state in 1948 and four hundred left for the West. Only a few hundred Jews were left in Bačka.

BIBLIOGRAPHY

Lewinger, Y. "Assassination of Jews in Bačka during the Police Raids, January 1942." *Studies on the Holocaust Period* 1 (1978): 189–212. (In Hebrew.)

Peric, M. *Demographic Study of the Jewish Community in Yugoslavia.* Belgrade, 1973.

YOSSEF LEWINGER

BADGE, JEWISH, distinguishing sign that Jews in Nazi Germany and in Nazi-occupied countries were compelled to wear to facilitate their identification as Jews. Such a distinctive sign had been imposed on Jews in ancient times, in the form of the color or shape of the clothes, shoes, hats, or scarves they were obliged to wear in order to differentiate between them and the rest of the population and humiliate them in other people's eyes. The first to introduce such a sign were the Muslims, who in the eighth century decreed that all the *dhimmi* (protected people)—Christians, Jews, and Samaritans—must wear clothes that set them apart from the Muslims. In Yemen such clothes were obligatory for Jews until the twentieth century. In Christian countries, distinctive signs for Jews were introduced on the basis of a canon issued by the Fourth Lateran Council in 1215, under Pope Innocent III (1198–1216), which laid down that Jews "of both sexes, in all Christian lands, shall be differentiated from the rest of the population by the quality of their garment." The form of this differentiation was not specified, but the decision makes it clear that its purpose was to prevent sexual intercourse between Jews and Christians.

The Lateran Council decision was not applied in all Christian countries at all times, or in a uniform manner, but the introduction of a "Jewish badge" did spread, and it became a means of shaming and humiliating Jews. The pointed hat, as a distinctive sign for Jews, is known to have been in use from the thirteenth century in various Germanic countries. Yellow as a distinguishing color for Jews had been decreed earlier, in Muslim countries, and the practice may have been taken over by Christian countries, though the reason for choosing this particular color is not clear.

A distinction must be made between the voluntary concentration of Jews in a certain part of a town and their forced confinement to a ghetto; between distinctive clothes and outward appearance that Jews adhered to of their own will, out of loyalty to their tradition, and the distinctive signs imposed on them by a hostile government for purposes of humiliation.

In modern times the Jewish badge was gradually abolished, disappearing altogether during the nineteenth-century Emancipation. Under the Nazis the term "yellow badge" first appeared in Robert WELTSCH's article "Tragt ihn mit Stolz, den gelben Fleck" ("Wear the Yellow Badge with Pride"), published in the *Jüdische Rundschau* on April 4, 1933, in reaction to the anti-Jewish boycott of April 1, 1933 (*see* BOYCOTT, ANTI-JEWISH). At that point no official Jewish sign was in existence and there were no plans to introduce such a sign. Weltsch was apparently referring to the slanderous and abusive inscriptions painted on the windows of Jewish-owned stores and businesses in "Operation Boycott" of April 1, and the relapse to medieval times that it signified. The proposal to impose a distinctive mark on the Jews was first made by Reinhard HEYDRICH at a meeting held in the wake of the KRISTALLNACHT pogrom, in November 1938.

At the height of the fighting in Poland, in September 1939, local German military and civilian authorities issued the first decrees ordering Jewish stores to be marked as such. Later decrees required Jews to wear a distinctive sign. In November 1939 the Jews of Lublin, for example, were ordered to wear a yellow badge on the left side of their breast, bearing the inscription *Jude*. On November 23, Hans FRANK, in one of the first regulations he issued as *Generalgouverneur*, stipulated that as of December 1, 1939, all "Jews and Jewesses" over the age of twelve living in the GENERALGOUVERNEMENT were to wear, on the right sleeve of their jacket or dress and on their overcoat, a white band at least 4 inches (10 cm) in width, with a blue Star of David inscribed on it. The Lublin order requiring a yellow badge was promptly withdrawn, and the Lublin Jews had to wear a white armband, like the Jews in the rest of the Generalgouvernement.

On November 14, SS-Brigadeführer Friedrich Übelhör, *Regierungspräsident* (administrative president) of the Kalisz district, issued an order for "all Jews, irrespective of sex or age, to wear a band 10 centimeters [4 inches] in width on the right arm, below the armpit, of Jewish-yellow color [*judengelber Farbe*]." On December 12, Übelhör issued a revised order: "Reichsstatthalter [Reich governor] Arthur GREISER has decreed that all Jews in the WARTHEGAU [must] wear a uniform distinctive sign. Accordingly, my order of November 14 under which Jews were obliged to wear a yellow band is amended, and I now order [that] Jews have to wear a yellow badge in the form of a Star of David, 10 centimeters in height, on the right side of their breast and on their back." In Zagłębie, a district that was also annexed to the Reich, like the Warthegau, the Jews were ordered to wear a band on the left sleeve, with a blue Star of David painted on it; this was later replaced by a badge.

When the Germans invaded the Soviet Union, in June 1941, they lost no time introducing into the newly occupied areas the various marks and methods used in Poland for differentiating between the Jews and the rest of the population. The guidelines on the treatment of Jews issued in 1941 by Hinrich LOHSE, the *Reichskommissar Ostland* (Reich Commissar of the Occupied Eastern Territories), contained the provision that "orders have to be issued that Jews be at all times identifiable as such by a yellow six-pointed star, clearly visible, at least 10 centimeters high, on the left side of their breast and on the back." In BIAŁYSTOK, which had its own civil administration, the first announcement made by the JUDENRAT (Jewish Council), on German orders, stated that "as of the morning of July 10, 1941, all men, women, and children aged fourteen and over must wear a white armband on their left sleeve, with a blue Star of David painted on it; the Star of David has to be 10 centimeters high and its outline at least 10 centimeters wide." The next order issued by the Białystok Judenrat, on July 11, 1941, however, spoke of "a yellow badge, as ordered"; the first order was presumably amended within a few days, and the armband was replaced by a yellow badge.

Forcing the Jews to wear a distinctive sign was one of the tactics of harassment that enabled the Germans to recognize Jews as such on sight, and was designed to create a gulf between the Jews and the rest of the population. The Jews were themselves responsible for acquiring the badges and distributing them. Even when the Jews were separated from the general population by being confined to ghettos, the orders requiring them to wear distinguishing signs remained valid and were strictly enforced. Jews who left the badge at home when they went out or whose badges did not meet the regulations were subject to fines and prison sentences. In WARSAW, warnings were posted in the hallways of apartment buildings, reminding Jews not to forget the badge when they went out. An announcement by the Białystok Judenrat of July 26, 1941, stated: "The authorities have warned that severe punishment—up to and including death by shooting—is in store for Jews who do not wear the yellow badge, on back and front."

In some ghettos various other distinctive badges were introduced—for identifying Jewish police, doctors, Judenrat employees, and people who held jobs in one of the many official factories. The purpose of these additional badges was to replace the Jewish badge and give the bearer a sense of being better protected and more favored than the anonymous masses in the ghetto. One of the Warsaw ghetto diarists drew up a list of nineteen different kinds of badges—in addition to the regular badge that all Jews had to wear—that were in use, at one time or another, during the existence of the ghetto. In May 1942 a decree was published in Warsaw forbidding the wearing of additional badges by the factory employees and confining the use of special badges to the Jewish police.

Frank's November 1939 decree on the wearing of distinctive signs in the Generalgouvernement was followed by a regulation issued by the governor of the Warsaw district, Hauptamtsleiter SA-Brigadeführer Dr. Ludwig Fischer; the regulation stipulated that the decree applied to Jews by "race" and was therefore also binding on converts to Christianity and their progeny. The converts living in Warsaw appealed to the RADA GŁOWNA OPIEKUŃCZA (Central Welfare Council; RGO), which was approved by the Germans, to intervene on their behalf so that they might be exempted from this shameful obligation. When the RGO applied to the Germans on the converts' behalf, the Germans requested a list of the persons to be exempted, but on receiving it, they rejected the RGO's request. In October and November 1940, when the Warsaw ghetto was set up, the Germans used the list to round up the converts and force them to enter the ghetto with the Jews.

Inside the Third Reich, the regulation requiring a yellow badge to be worn by the Jews (a *Judenstern*, or "Jewish star," in the regulation's wording) was promulgated in September 1941, that is, nearly two years after it had been imposed on the Jews of Poland. The regulation also applied to the Protectorate of BOHEMIA AND MORAVIA and officially also to the Polish areas that had been incorporated into the Reich, even though in the latter areas the practice had been introduced shortly after the German occupation of Poland. The September 1941 regulation required all Jews over the age of six to wear a yellow six-pointed star, the size of a fist, on the left side of the breast, with *Jude* inscribed on it in black. As in the other places where it was applied, the yellow-badge decree in the Reich and the areas annexed to it was one of a series of anti-Jewish measures and signified a further intensification of the anti-Jewish line. The distinctive mark imposed on the Jews in Germany became an integral part of the preparations for the "FINAL SOLUTION." That same month, restrictions were imposed on freedom of movement by the Jews in Germany; in October, emigration of Jews from Germany was prohibited; and this was followed in November by an announcement that Jews "who are not employed by factories essential to the country's economy" would be dispatched to the east in the next few months.

The Jewish badge was also adopted by Germany's satellite states. On September 9, 1941, a "Jewish code" became law in Slovakia, stipulating in part that the Jews of that country were to wear a yellow badge, and that only the president of the country could exempt certain individuals from this obligation. German authorities ran into difficulties when they tried to introduce the wearing of the badge in the occupied countries of western Europe and Vichy France. The opposition seems to have come both from local quarters that still wielded a measure of power in the internal administration of these countries

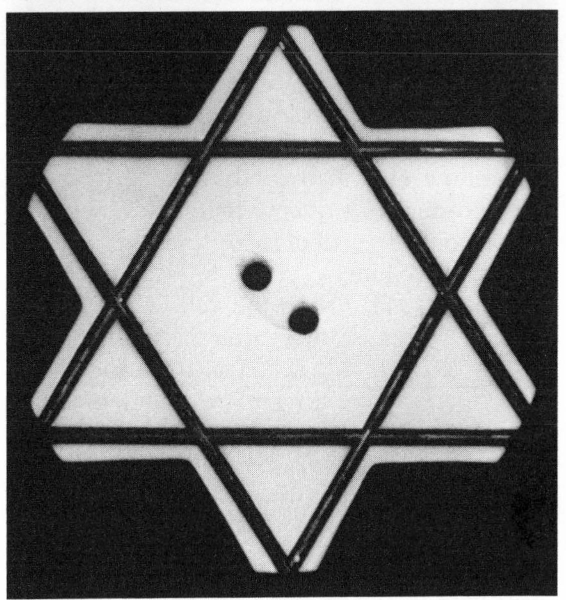

Three examples of badges worn by Jews. In France the yellow Star of David had the word *Juif* in Hebraic-looking letters at the center; in the Netherlands the word *Jood* figured on the badge. In Bulgaria a yellow-and-black button was sewn on clothing to identify Jews. [A Living Memorial to the Holocaust—Museum of Jewish Heritage, New York]

and, in rare instances, from German military authorities on the spot. In December 1942 the Germans began exerting pressure on the Vichy regime to impose the wearing of the yellow badge on the Jews of France—a preparatory step for the planned deportation and annihilation of the Jews of German-occupied western Europe. Adm. François DARLAN, Vichy premier at the time, rejected the German proposal, arguing that the anti-Jewish measures being applied in France were adequate and that a distinctive sign for Jews would come as a "great shock" to the French people. Adolf EICHMANN's office continued to press for the yellow badge to be applied in France, Belgium, and the Netherlands. In March 1942 the subject was discussed at meetings in Berlin and Paris, at one of which Helmut KNOCHEN, *Chef des SD und der Sicherheitspolizei* (Chief of the Security Service and the Security Police) for occupied France and Belgium, stated that in his opinion the yellow badge was "another step on the road to the final solution." The implementation of the yellow-badge decree was delayed, however, owing to the resistance shown by the French and the reservations raised by the German military administration, and also because the question of how to deal with Jews who were nationals of neutral countries or of Allied countries remained to be resolved.

In the Netherlands—where it was easier for the Germans to overcome resistance and obstacles—a decree was issued on April 29, 1942, according to which all Jews were obliged to wear a yellow star on the left side of their breast with the word *Jood* inscribed on it, in black ink. In Belgium the same decree was issued on May 27, 1942, to go into effect on June 3. In occupied France the decree was issued on June 7; it ordered all Jews aged six and over to wear a yellow star, the size of a clenched fist, on the left side of their breast, with the word *Juif* (Jew) or *Juive* (Jewess) inscribed on it. In the unoccupied zone of France the wearing of the yellow badge was not introduced, since the Vichy government persisted in its opposition to the measure. Some scholars of the Holocaust believe that the main reason for the Vichy regime's opposition—apart from concern over the reaction of the French public—was the fact that while the imposition of the yellow badge did not apply to Jews who were foreign nationals, Vichy authorities themselves would not be empowered to grant exemption from the badge to French Jews who had rendered distinguished service to France and French culture. In the end the Germans refrained from imposing the Jewish badge in Vichy France, even after November 1942, when they seized control of all of France, apparently because of the many manifestations of public opposition to the measure that they had encountered in occupied France.

In the satellite states and states that were otherwise dependent on Germany, the Nazis brought their power and influence to bear in order to have the Jewish badge adopted. In Hungary such pressure was applied in December 1942, but the government there was able to resist it. In March 1944, however, when the German army occupied Hungary, the first decision on Jewish affairs adopted by the new government under Döme SZTÓJAY, on March 31, was to impose the yellow badge on the country's Jews. Romania applied the yellow badge in the new territories that it occupied (BUKOVINA and BESSARABIA in July and September 1941, and TRANSNISTRIA in June 1942). The intention was to introduce the yellow star also in the Regat (the pre-1914 borders of the country), but Jewish intervention succeeded in foiling this design, except in Moldavia, in the final phase of the war (May 1944), when the yellow badge was applied "because the area is close to the battlefront." In BULGARIA, where there was strong opposition to anti-Jewish legislation and the persecution of the Jews, the government, in August 1942, decided to introduce a distinctive sign for Jews, in the form of a small yellow button. Even the wearing of that sign, however, was not strictly enforced, and most of the Jews in the country did not observe the order.

In DENMARK the German authorities considered introducing the yellow badge, but at no point did they dare risk making it mandatory. According to legend—which has also found its way into nonfictional writings—King Christian X threatened that if the Jewish badge were to be introduced in Denmark, he would be the first to wear one. While the king's opposition to anti-Jewish measures, like his personal courage, is unquestionable, he in fact never made such a declaration; the Germans, who were well aware of the Danes' unconditional resistance to anti-Jewish measures of any sort, never even attempted to force the yellow badge on Denmark.

The Jewish population's reaction to the yellow badge and the non-Jewish population's opposition to the measure in the German-occupied countries and in Germany itself were broadly as follows. In Poland, where a distinctive sign for Jews was first introduced, it initially had a considerable psychological impact, but further measures, much more severe in their effect on the Jews, overwhelmed this initial impact. Diaries from the period contain bitter and sarcastic references to the Jewish badge, such as one that compares the ghetto to Hollywood, because both are full of stars. The threat of severe penalties accounted for the almost uniform observance of the wearing of the Jewish badge; exceptions included members of the underground who served as illegal liaison officers among the ghettos, and Jews who had escaped from the ghetto to the "Aryan" side of the city.

In Germany the introduction of the Jewish badge was followed by a wave of suicides. Some Jewish sources report that there were a few instances of Germans' displaying solidarity with the Jews in the matter of the yellow badge. On the other hand, an internal SS report on the public mood, dated November 1941, includes an item to the effect that among the German population, surprise was voiced about the many Jews still to be found in Germany, as revealed by the yellow badges. The report mentions the special problem of persons classified as Jews under the Nazi racist legislation who were Christians by religion; congregants attending church services allegedly complained of having to sit next to persons wearing the yellow badge. Though Protestant clergymen were not prepared to exclude wearers of the yellow badge from services, they considered assigning them separate seating. Among the Catholic clergy, Cardinal Adolf Bertram in Germany and Cardinal Theodor Innitzer in Austria opposed such separation.

In western Europe many Jews defied orders and did not wear the yellow badge. In occupied France it had been estimated that more than one hundred thousand Jews would have to wear the badge, but in the weeks that followed the issuance of the order, only eighty-three thousand persons came to pick up the badges. Among the French population the yellow badge caused great dismay, and quite a few took effective steps against it. For example, yellow became a fashionable color, and some people wore stars or other items to express solidarity with the Jews. Even the French police, which had a poor record in its treatment of Jews, either found it difficult to overcome the defiance of the order to wear the yellow badge, or did not care to collaborate in this effort. Passersby who were asked to identify themselves because they looked Jewish sometimes turned out to be "proper" Frenchmen, and this experience too seems to have deterred policemen from trying to arrest violators of the yellow-badge decree. In the Netherlands there were many instances of demonstrative solidarity with the Jews. On May 1, 1942, a Dutch underground newspaper printed 300,000 stars bearing the inscription "Jews and non-Jews are one and the same."

In the Nazi concentration camps, prisoners were marked by triangular patches in various colors (in the case of Jews, by a Star of David consisting of two triangles in different colors) and by letters, the purpose being to indicate the ethnic and national identity of the prisoner and the prisoner's particular "offense." Poles brought to Germany on forced labor were marked by the letter *P*, and severe restrictions were imposed on them in their day-to-day contacts with Germans; but special distinctive marks, in all occupied countries or countries under the influence of the Third Reich, were applied only to Jews.

BIBLIOGRAPHY

Blau, B. "Der Judenstern der Nazis." *Judaica* 9 (1953): 34–47.

Friedman, P. "The Jewish Badge and the Yellow Star in the Nazi Era." In *Roads to Extinction: Essays on the Holocaust,* edited by A. J. Friedman, pp. 11–33. New York, 1980.

Kisch, G. "The Yellow Badge in History." *Historia Judaica* 4 (1942): 95–114.

Marrus, M. R., and R. O. Paxton. *Vichy France and the Jews.* New York, 1981.

Presser, J. *Ashes in the Wind: The Destruction of Dutch Jewry.* London, 1965.

ISRAEL GUTMAN

BADOGLIO, PIETRO (1871–1956), Italian soldier and statesman. Badoglio was made a marshal of Italy in 1926. He served as chief of staff of the Italian armed forces from 1925 to 1940; governor of Libya from 1928 to 1933; commander of the armed forces in East Africa from November 1935 to May 1936; and prime minister of Italy from July 25, 1943, to June 10, 1944, after Benito MUSSOLINI's downfall. Like most Italian officers, Badoglio accepted the Italian Jews as full members of the Italian nation; on the other hand, he was critical of the self-segregation of the Libyan Jews, who had not undergone a similar process of assimilation and "Italianization." When Mussolini adopted antisemitic policies, Badoglio proclaimed his support of Fascist racial programs, if only to curry favor with his master. After Mussolini's

Marshal Pietro Badoglio (right) talking with Gen. Werner von Blomberg. [National Archives]

downfall on July 25, 1943, he headed the new government but refused to repeal the anti-Jewish laws, having made a public pretense of continuing the war at Germany's side. Badoglio arranged an armistice with the Allies on September 3, 1943, and finally abrogated the anti-Jewish laws on January 20, 1944; by that time, however, he controlled only the smaller part of Italy, the rest of which was under total German control. He wrote *L'Italia nella seconda guerra mondiale* (Milan, 1946; published in English as *Italy and the Second World War,* 1988).

BIBLIOGRAPHY

De Felice, R. *Storia degli Ebrei italiani sotto il fascismo.* Milan, 1977.

Michaelis, M. *Mussolini and the Jews: German-Italian Relations and the Jewish Question in Italy, 1922–1945.* Oxford, 1978.

Zuccotti, S. *The Italians and the Holocaust: Persecution, Rescue, and Survival.* New York, 1987.

MEIR MICHAELIS

BAECK, LEO (1873–1956), rabbi, philosopher, and community leader. Born in Lissa, in the Posen province of Germany, Leo Baeck studied at the Jewish Theological Seminary in Breslau and the Hochschule für die Wissenschaft des Judentums (College for Judaic Studies) in BERLIN, where he was ordained a rabbi in 1897.

From 1897 to 1907 Baeck was rabbi of Oppeln, in Upper Silesia, and from 1907 to 1912, in Düsseldorf; from then on, until 1942, he was rabbi in Berlin, and a lecturer at the Hochschule. In World War I, he served as an army chaplain.

As early as 1897, Baeck demonstrated his intellectual integrity, when he refused to join the declaration against Zionism issued by a group of German rabbis (who came to be known as the "Protest" Rabbis). He gained a name for himself as an original scholar in 1905, with the publication of *Das Wesen des Judentums* (The Essence of Judaism; 1936), which was a response to the 1900 book by the Protestant theologian Adolf von Harnack, *Das Wesen des Christentums* (The Essence of Christianity). In the following years, Baeck published many articles on Jewish religion, dealing especially with the Second Temple period.

Rabbi Leo Baeck at Theresienstadt (1944).

In 1922 Baeck was elected chairman of the General Association of German Rabbis, and in 1924 and 1927 respectively, Grandmaster of the B'nai B'rith Lodge in Germany and member of the committee of the CENTRALVEREIN DEUTSCHER STAATSBURGER JÜDISCHEN GLAUBENS (Central Union of German Citizens of Jewish Faith). In 1920 he joined the executive board of the Palestine Foundation Fund (Keren Hayesod) as a non-Zionist; in 1926 he became a member of the Palestine Committee, and in 1929, of the committee of the newly founded Jewish Agency.

In 1933, when the REICHSVERTRETUNG DER DEUTSCHEN JUDEN (Reich Representation of German Jews) was established, Baeck became its president, by common agreement of the organization's founders. As such he had to preserve the internal unity of German Jewry and act as its accredited representative. He was twice arrested by the Gestapo, but each time he was released and reinstated in his position. Baeck refused to avail himself of opportunities to leave Germany, even when the situation of the Jews in Germany deteriorated and his own safety was threatened, and he remained at the head of the Reichsvertretung. In 1939 the Nazis changed its name to Reichsvereinigung der Juden in Deutschland (Reich Association of Jews in Germany), and it continued to function, under the supervision of the REICHSSICHERHEITSHAUPTAMT (Reich Security Main Office; RSHA), until June 1943, when it was dissolved.

At the beginning of 1943, Baeck was deported to the THERESIENSTADT ghetto, where he became a member of the Ältestenrat der Juden (Jewish Council of Elders) and with his sermons and speeches made a significant contribution to the morale of the ghetto population. Opinions vary, however, as to whether Baeck was justified in keeping to himself the information that reached him in the ghetto concerning the fate that awaited those Jews who were being deported to AUSCHWITZ. After the liberation of the ghetto and its dissolution in 1945, Baeck settled in London. There he devoted himself to public affairs, as chairman of the Council for Jews from Germany, and to teaching and research in Jewish institutions of higher learning in Britain and the United States.

Among the institutions commemorating Leo Baeck are the Seminar for Progressive Rabbis in London, the LEO BAECK INSTITUTE in Jerusalem, London, and New York, and a secondary school in Haifa, Israel.

BIBLIOGRAPHY

Adler, H. G. *Theresienstadt 1941–1945—Das Antlitz einer Zwangsgemeinschaft: Geschichte, Soziologie, Psychologie.* Tübingen, 1960.

Baker, L. *Days of Sorrow and Pain: Leo Baeck and the Berlin Jews.* New York, 1978.

Friedländer, A. H. *Leo Baeck: Teacher of Theresienstadt.* New York, 1968.

JOSEPH WALK

BAKY, LÁSZLÓ (1889–1946), Hungarian antisemite who was among those chiefly responsible for the destruction of Hungarian Jewry in 1944. Baky played a leading role in the Hungarian counterrevolutionary movement of the early 1920s and in many ultrarightist organizations. One of the most outspokenly antisemitic members of the Hungarian officers' corps, he retired as a major general from the gendarmerie in 1938 in order to devote his time to the extreme right. In May 1939 he was elected to the nation's parliament as a leading figure of the Hungarian National Socialist party (Magyar Nemzeti Szocialista Párt). Shortly after Hungary's occupation by the Germans on March 19, 1944, he became an undersecretary of state in the puppet government of Döme SZTÓJAY, a position he held until September 1. Following the ARROW CROSS PARTY coup of October 15, 1944, he played an active role in the Ferenc SZÁLASI regime as well. As undersecretary of state in the Ministry of the Interior, Baky was one of the leading architects of the deportation of the Jews from Hungary. He fled Hungary with the retreating Nazi forces, but was captured by the Americans, who extradited him to Hungary in October 1945. He was tried as a war criminal and executed.

BIBLIOGRAPHY

Braham, R. L. *The Politics of Genocide.* New York, 1980.

Katzburg, N. *Hungary and the Jews, 1920–1943.* Ramat Gan, Israel, 1981.

RANDOLPH L. BRAHAM

BANDERA, STEFAN (1909–1959), Ukrainian leader. Bandera was born in Eastern Galicia into the family of a priest of the Uniate church. When he was in his twenties he joined the ORHANIZATSYIA UKRAINSKYKH NATSIONALISTIV (Organization of Ukrainian Nationalists; OUN), and soon became one of the leaders of the national organization in the western UKRAINE. In 1932 and 1933 Bandera, along with his comrades Yaroslav Stetsko and Roman Shukhevich, gained control of the organization's national executive, which functioned clandestinely, dictated an extremist fascist-oriented nationalist policy, and called for an armed struggle. After the assassination of the Polish minister of the interior, Bronisław Pieracki, Bandera was arrested on January 13, 1936, and given a life sentence. When Poland was occupied by the Germans in September 1939, Bandera was released by the Russians and moved to German-occupied Poland.

Bandera brought about a split in the OUN

at its national conference in Kraków on February 10, 1940. The majority, led by him, was called the Revolutionary OUN (OUN-R), or the Bandera OUN (OUN-B). Prior to the German invasion of the Soviet Union in June 1941, Bandera helped the Nazis to set up two Ukrainian battalions, the NACHTIGALL BATTALION and the Roland Battalion, with the purpose of carrying out intelligence activities. The OUN-B organized "mobile units," which moved into the Ukraine with the German forces and established the local government and the UKRAINISCHE HILFSPOLIZEI (Ukrainian Auxiliary Police).

On June 30, 1941, Bandera's representatives in Lvov announced the establishment of an independent Ukrainian government, but since the Germans objected to this, Bandera was arrested, on September 15, 1941, and sent to the SACHSENHAUSEN camp. He maintained contact with the members of his organization throughout the Ukraine, and on his instructions the UKRAINSKA POVSTANSKA ARMYIA (Ukrainian Insurgent Army) was organized at the end of 1942. Bandera was released on September 25, 1944, and conducted negotiations with the Germans. At the end of the war he settled in Munich. From there he continued to lead the movement until he was shot and killed in 1959 by a Soviet agent.

SHMUEL SPECTOR

BANSKÁ BYSTRICA, town on the Hron River in SLOVAKIA. It had a population of thirteen thousand on the eve of World War II, of whom one thousand were Jews.

During the SLOVAK NATIONAL UPRISING in 1944, Banská Bystrica was the capital of the area liberated. When German forces marched into Slovakia in order to destroy the partisans, Gen. František Catlos, minister of defense in President Jozef TISO's government, ordered the country's armed forces to offer no resistance to the invaders. The headquarters of the field forces in Banská Bystrica, however, disobeyed this order and instructed the troops under its command to fight the Germans.

Banská Bystrica became the military, political, and administrative center of the Czechoslovak republic in the heart of Tiso's fascist Slovakia. It was the seat of the Slovak National Council (Slovenská Narodna Rada)—the government of the liberated area—the plenum of which functioned as the parliament. It was also the headquarters of the First Czechoslovak Army, the British, American, and Soviet military missions, and the Palestinian parachutists (*see* PARACHUTISTS, JEWISH). In addition, the trade unions had their head office in Banská Bystrica, and six newspapers were published in the town.

Jews from the areas invaded by the Germans took refuge in Banská Bystrica, their number estimated at five thousand. The team of parachutists from Palestine—Haviva REIK, Chaim Hermesh, Rafael (Rafi) Reiss, and Zvi Ben-Yaakov—were active among the Jews, with Abba Berdiczew serving in the British military mission. The parachutists arrived at a time when the battles were at their height, and the original plan of forming a fighting Jewish unit under their command was not feasible, since the Jewish fighters were dispersed among the various units in the field. The parachutists organized a relief committee for Jewish refugees, provided them with lodging and employment, and generally looked after them. Before the town fell into German hands, the parachutists retreated with a group of Jewish community leaders and members of youth movements.

The Germans broke the rebels' resistance by a concentrated attack involving seven divisions, and captured the town on October 27, 1944. President Tiso—who was a Catholic priest—then went to the town to offer a thanksgiving service.

Zvi Ben-Yaakov and Abba Berdiczew were taken to MAUTHAUSEN and killed. The Banská Bystrica jail was filled with fighters and other opponents of the regime, including Haviva Reik and Rafael Reiss; from the jail the prisoners were taken to nearby Kremnica, where they were killed.

A handful of Jewish refugees managed to flee into the mountains before the town's fall. Most of the Jews in the area that had been liberated were caught; some of them were murdered in Kremnica and Nemecka. The rest were taken to the SERED camp, from which they were then deported, primarily to THERESIENSTADT, SACHSENHAUSEN, and AUSCHWITZ.

BIBLIOGRAPHY

Lipscher, L. *Die Juden im slowakischen Staat, 1939–1945.* Munich, 1980.

Nir, A. *Paths in a Ring of Fire.* Merhavia, Israel, 1967. (In Hebrew.)

Venohr, W. *Aufstand in der Tatra: Der Kampf um die Slowakei 1939–1944.* Königstein, West Germany, 1979.

AKIVA NIR

BARANOVICHI (Pol., Baranowicze), city in Brest Oblast (district), Belorussian SSR. In the interwar period it was part of independent Poland; it was occupied by the Red Army in September 1939 and annexed to the Soviet Union, together with the rest of eastern Poland.

On the eve of World War II, 12,000 Jews were living in Baranovichi, constituting over half the town's population. When the Germans entered Baranovichi, on June 27, 1941, the Jewish population stood at 10,000. A JUDENRAT (Jewish Council) was set up, with Yehoshua Isikson, a prominent figure in the city, as its chairman. A few days after they had occupied the city, the Germans murdered 73 Jews on charges of being Communists. At the end of June 1941, Einsatzkommando 8 and Wehrmacht troops murdered 350 Jews. Some time later, 750 Jews were sent to their death at the KOLDICHEVO concentration camp.

The Germans demanded that Isikson provide them with a large number of Jews for forced labor, even those who were physically unfit, but Isikson refused to comply. On March 3, 1942, 2,300 Jews were murdered. Isikson and his secretary were forced to witness the killing and then they too were murdered. He was replaced as chairman of the Judenrat by Shmuel Yankelevits. Following the March 3 *Aktion*, Jews from various other places—Liakhovichi, Kletsk, Meitshet, Stolbtsy, and Gorodishche—were brought to Baranovichi.

In the spring of 1942, three underground organizations were formed in the ghetto, one headed by Eliezer Lidovski, another by Momeh Kopelovits, and the third by Zaritskevits. Lidovski's group was also joined by the Jewish ghetto policemen. After a while the three groups united into a single organization, with some two hundred members, most of them in the sixteen-to-thirty age group. Its members engaged in sabotage, accumulated arms, and established contact with partisans.

A heated debate went on in the underground as to whether the forthcoming battle should be fought in the ghetto or in the forests. It was decided that the uprising would take place in the ghetto, and July 19, 1942, was fixed as the date. A plan was worked out, with the ghetto divided into several sectors and a commander appointed for each sector. A considerable quantity of weapons was smuggled into the ghetto by the underground members, mostly from the German warehouses where they worked; by the fall of 1942 the ghetto had 70 rifles, 2 machine guns, 40 pistols, 15,000 rounds of ammunition, 500 hand grenades, and several cases of gunpowder. At the beginning of July, the underground command decided to put off the date for the uprising, mainly out of consideration for the rest of the ghetto population. From then on, the underground's main effort was directed at escaping from the ghetto.

On August 19, 1942, 700 young Jews were seized and sent to Molodechno, in the northwest of the Belorussian SSR. A second *Aktion*, launched on September 22, lasted for ten days and resulted in the killing of 3,000 Jews. Throughout the days that the *Aktion* was raging, the underground was debating whether to start an uprising. Its armed members had gone into bunkers but did not open fire. The young people in the ghetto demanded that a decision be made to escape into the forests. When the *Aktion* came to an end, groups of Jews began to flee the ghetto; some of those who took part in the escape returned to the ghetto to help more groups get out. On December 17, 1942, the Germans launched a third *Aktion*, murdering 3,000 Jews and liquidating the ghetto. Only three remaining locations still had a concentration of Jews, totaling 700: the ORGANISATION TODT forced-labor camp, the Feldbauleitung (field construction office), and the Gestapo offices, where Jews were used for cleaning and other services. In the course of the *Aktionen* there were instances of individual Jews defying the murderers and jumping off the trucks.

At least 450 Jews fled to the forests from the ghetto and the labor camps in Baranovichi. The uprising had been scheduled to take place when the underground members were certain that the final liquidation of the ghetto was being launched; but they were never sure that this was indeed happening, either during the second *Aktion* or the third. The rest of the ghetto population also withheld their support for an uprising as long as they felt that there was still a chance to live and that not all of the ghetto inhabitants were doomed.

BIBLIOGRAPHY

Baranowicze Memorial Book. Tel Aviv, 1953. (In Hebrew.)

Foxman, J. *Baranowich in Martyrdom and Resistance*. New York, 1964. (In Yiddish.)

Lidovski, A. *In the Forests*. Tel Aviv, 1946. (In Hebrew.)

SHALOM CHOLAWSKI

BARASZ, EFRAIM (1892–1943), executive director of the Jewish community in BIAŁYSTOK and chairman of the Białystok ghetto JUDENRAT (Jewish Council). Born in Volkovysk, Białystok district, into an affluent and prominent Jewish family, Barasz had both a Jewish and a general education, studying in Germany and earning an engineering degree there. He joined the Zionist movement while still in his youth. During World War I, he lived in Russia with his family, returning to Volkovysk at the war's end. He became a businessman, was active in many Jewish institutions, and chaired the local Zionist organization. Moving to Białystok in 1934, Barasz kept up his activities in Zionist affairs, and was appointed executive director of the Białystok Jewish community, a post in which he excelled because of his initiative and his organizational talents. He visited Palestine in the early 1930s, in order to prepare for his family's immigration there. His son, whom he had enrolled in the Hebrew University, joined the British forces in World War II and became one of the first Jewish fighter pilots from Palestine.

At the end of June 1941, following the German occupation of Białystok, Rabbi Gedaliah Rosenmann was appointed chairman of the Judenrat, but in actuality it was Barasz, the deputy chairman, who was in charge, both of the first Judenrat and its successor a month later. Many of the members of the Białystok Judenrat had previously held major posts in the organized Jewish community.

Efraim Barasz.

The ghetto in Białystok, established on July 31, 1941, held about thirty-five thousand Jews. Białystok came to be incorporated into a district that was joined to East Prussia. In the fall of 1942 the Białystok region was subjected to deportations and the liquidation of ghettos, although the Białystok ghetto itself was not affected. Barasz was aware of the mass murder of Jews by the EINSATZGRUPPEN, of the deportations, and of the destruction of Jewish communities, but he believed that work would "serve as a protective shield," as he put it: "Our main rescue effort has to be based on the establishment of a highly developed industry." Following this concept, Barasz did all he could to enlist the ghetto inhabitants in the work drive, issued stern warnings against sabotage acts, and even took part in the deportation of some of the ghetto population in February 1943 (in the course of which nine thousand to ten thousand Jews were driven out or murdered on the spot). At the same time, Barasz maintained close contact with the Białystok ghetto underground and, for a while, coordinated his activities with those of Mordecai TENENBAUM (Tamaroff), who later became the commander of the ŻYDOWSKA ORGANIZACJA BOJOWA (Jewish Fighting Organization; ŻOB) in Białystok and of the Białystok ghetto uprising. Barasz gained Tenenbaum's confidence, gave assistance to the commune of the He-Haluts Zionist youth movement that was set up in Białystok, provided the underground with laboratory facilities and experts for the manufacture of arms, and supplied it with funds for onward transmission to the ŻOB in Warsaw. Shortly before the ghetto uprising, however, Barasz's relations with the underground deteriorated and finally came to a complete break.

On the basis of his contacts with German officials, Barasz continued to believe that the German administration and police in Białystok wanted to keep the working ghetto in existence. He thought he could save the ghetto from total liquidation and the Jews from total annihilation.

The final phase of the liquidation of the ghetto came on August 16, 1943, and was followed by the uprising in the ghetto. Between August 21 and 27, twenty-five thousand Jews were deported to the TREBLINKA extermination camp, in five trains; several hundred Jews—Barasz, Rabbi Rosenmann, and other members of the Judenrat among them—were kept apart from the rest and put into a "small ghetto," the designation given to one of the streets of the former ghetto. In September the Jews from this "small ghetto," including Barasz, his wife, and the members of the Judenrat, were deported to the MAJDANEK concentration camp. From there the last of Białystok's Jews were apparently taken to the PONIATOWA camp, where all the Jewish prisoners were murdered, in November 1943. No precise details are available concerning the date and circumstances of Barasz's death.

BIBLIOGRAPHY

Blumenthal, N., ed. *Conduct and Actions of a Judenrat: Documents from the Białystok Ghetto.* Jerusalem, 1962.

Grosman, H. *People of the Underground.* Merhavia, Israel, 1965. (In Hebrew.)

Tenenbaum-Tamarof, M. *Pages from Fire.* Naharia, Israel, 1987. (In Hebrew.)

Trunk, I. *Judenrat: The Jewish Councils in Eastern Europe under Nazi Occupation.* New York, 1972.

ISRAEL GUTMAN

BARBIE TRIAL, criminal proceedings against former SS-Untersturmführer Klaus Barbie (b. 1913), held in Lyons, France, mainly between May 11 and July 4, 1987. Barbie joined the Nazi party in 1932 and the SS in 1935. He began working for the Gestapo in 1942, and in November of that year was posted to Lyons, where he served as the Gestapo chief for the next twenty-one months. During that period he directly committed or was responsible for numerous atrocities, earning him the nickname "the Butcher of Lyons." Among his most infamous acts was the torture of Jean Moulin, a hero of the French Résistance.

After the war Barbie became a counterintelligence agent for the United States in Germany. In 1951 he emigrated to Bolivia, settling in La Paz. He acquired Bolivian citizenship in 1957, under the pseudonym Klaus Altmann. In 1952 and again in 1954 Barbie was tried *in absentia* in France. Both times he was convicted of specific war crimes and sentenced to death. He was discovered in La Paz by the Nazi hunter Beate Klarsfeld in 1971. In the following years the French government requested his extradition many times, but it was only in 1983 that the Bolivians finally expelled Barbie and he was brought to France to stand trial.

Barbie was charged with crimes against humanity, which were not subject to the French statute of limitations. The specific charges were: responsibility for a raid on the headquarters of the UNION GÉNÉRALE DES ISRAÉLITES DE FRANCE on Rue Ste. Catherine in Lyons on February 9, 1943, where some 85

Jews were arrested and later sent to AUSCHWITZ; responsibility for the deportation of 44 Jewish children who were discovered by the Gestapo to be hiding in the village of Izieu, 43.4 miles (70 km) east of Lyons; and responsibility for ordering the last transport from Lyons to Auschwitz, on August 11, 1944. In all, Barbie was charged with responsibility for the deportation of 842 people from Lyons, about half of them Jews and half of them members of the French Résistance.

The Barbie trial was followed closely throughout the world. It aroused much controversy in France. Some Frenchmen feared it would raise questions on the French collaboration with the Nazis, especially regarding the arrest and killing of Jean Moulin. Others feared it might cause a new wave of antisemitism. Still others thought the trial might blur the distinctions between he Holocaust and other Nazi atrocities perpetrated during the war. In connection with the trial, neo-Nazis and some activists in Holocaust denial (*see* HOLOCAUST, DENIAL OF THE) tried to claim that Barbie's behavior was no different from that of many of the Allied forces during the war and of a number of nations after the war.

On July 4, 1987, Barbie was found guilty of crimes against humanity and was sentenced to life imprisonment, the maximum penalty under French law at the time.

[*See also* Trials of War Criminals.]

BIBLIOGRAPHY

Bower, T. *Klaus Barbie: Butcher of Lyon*. London, 1984.

Paris, E. *Unhealed Wounds: France and the Klaus Barbie Affair*. Toronto, 1985.

Ruzie, D. "The Klaus Barbie Case: War Crimes versus Crimes against Humanity." *Patterns of Prejudice* 20/3 (July 1968): 27–33.

Ryan, A. J., Jr., ed. *Klaus Barbie and the United States Government*. Frederick, Md., 1984.

JACQUELINE ROKHSAR

BARTH, KARL (1886–1968), Swiss Protestant theologian. Barth was the most prominent theologian in the Reformed (Calvinist) tradition in the first half of the twentieth century. He was educated in Germany, but in 1914 turned against his theological mentors because of their uncritical support of German nationalism and war aims. His commentary on the Epistle to the Romans (1919) was an outright attack on the "cultural Protestantism" of the nineteenth century and denied the identification of the Kingdom of God with human or national progress. Theology, for Barth, consisted not in man's attempt to find God, but solely in describing God's justification of man through faith. From 1921 to 1935, Barth was a professor of theology in Göttingen, Münster, and Bonn, establishing his school of "dialectical" theology, which looked to biblical revelation as the sole source of authority in the church and rejected any accommodation with nationalist or racial ideologies. From 1933 on, Barth was the theological leader of the German Confessing Church (Bekennende Kirche), in opposition to the pro-Nazi "German Christians"; he was the principal author of the 1934 Barmen Declaration, in which the supporters of the Confessing Church joined to defend their position against the totalitarian demands of the state. In 1935 he was expelled from Germany and returned to his native Basel, where he continued working on his unfinished major work, *Church Dogmatics* (13 vols.).

Barth's hostility to Nazi antisemitism was based on his biblical theology, though he did not at first recognize the need to make the "Jewish question" the central point of church resistance. Following his expulsion from Germany, he became more outspoken on behalf of the Jews, and from 1938 on his theology clearly affirmed the solidarity of Christians and Jews as the common heirs of biblical revelation. The second volume of *Church Dogmatics* (1942) contained a pointed chapter on the church's indissoluble dependence on and foundation in Israel. In later volumes of this work, he strongly criticized traditional Christian triumphalist attitudes, regarded Christian missionary activity to the Jewish people as theologically inadmissible, and repudiated the view that the Christian church had displaced Judaism as the sole channel of salvation. Despite his dogmatic views on modern Judaism and his exclusivist Christology, Barth's influence in the postwar period was significant, particularly in such bodies as the World Council of Churches, in rethinking the theological relationship between Christianity and Judaism.

Barth's writings that bear on such matters include *Church Dogmatics* (London, 1936–1969), *Der Römerbrief* (Oxford, 1933), and "The Jewish Problem and the Christian Answer," in *Against the Stream: Shorter Post-War Writings, 1946–1952* (London, 1954).

BIBLIOGRAPHY

Busch, E. *Karl Barth*. London, 1976.

JOHN S. CONWAY

BARTOSZEWSKI, WŁADYSŁAW (b. 1922), Polish anti-Nazi who aided Jews during the Holocaust. Bartoszewski was imprisoned in AUSCHWITZ from September 1940 to April 1941, and from 1942 to 1945 was a member of the ARMIA KRAJOWA (the Polish Home Army). He also belonged to the underground organization of young Catholics, the Front Odrodzenia Polski (Front for the Rebirth of Poland), and in September 1942 helped to set up a provisional committee that later became the ZEGOTA welfare organization. When the latter's permanent council was set up, on December 4, 1942, Bartoszewski became one of the two DELEGATURA representatives who regularly attended Zegota's board meetings. He was active in the underground and helped transmit to the POLISH GOVERNMENT-IN-EXILE reports on the Nazi terror against the Poles and on the situation of the Jews. In 1963 YAD VASHEM designated him a "RIGHTEOUS AMONG THE NATIONS."

Władysław Bartoszewski.

A prolific writer and historian, Bartoszewski has published a number of books, dealing mostly with the history of Warsaw during the war, the Polish Jews, and the rescue of Jews by Polish gentiles. They include *Warsaw Death Ring, 1939–1944* (1968) and *Righteous among Nations: How Poles Helped the Jews, 1939–1945* (1969). Bartoszewski is the president of the PEN Club in Poland, serves as a professor on the faculty of the Catholic University of Lublin, and frequently lectures in many countries.

ELISHEVA SHAUL

BAUBLYS, PETRAS (d. 1974), pediatrician and head of an orphanage in Kovno, Lithuania. Upon being contacted by an underground Jewish organization operating in the Kovno ghetto, Baublys agreed to use the orphanage facility (located in the Slobodka section of the city, where the ghetto was situated) as a temporary shelter and a conduit for transferring Jewish children to permanent, safe locations. Dozens of children and infants were accepted into the orphanage, some abandoned on the doorsteps by fleeing Jewish mothers. Children knowing a smattering of Lithuanian were kept within the orphanage compound for relatively longer periods; others, as well as children over the permissible age, were quickly spirited to hiding places with Lithuanian families, with Baublys providing free medical care for the sick children he visited. In order to minimize the danger of betrayal to the authorities, only a select group of the orphanage staff knew of this undertaking.

Baublys, his brother Sergejus, and his

sister-in-law Jadvyga (who hid a Jewish child in their home) were recognized by YAD VASHEM as "RIGHTEOUS AMONG THE NATIONS" in 1977.

MORDECAI PALDIEL

BAUM GRUPPE (Baum Group), clandestine anti-Nazi organization in Berlin, composed mainly of Jews who belonged to YOUTH MOVEMENTS and who during the Nazi rule joined the German Communist party or its youth organizations. Most of the group's members were Communists, but it also included Zionists, members of the left-wing Zionist youth movement Werkleute, and some who were recruited from Zionist youth movements such as Ha-Shomer ha-Tsa'ir and Ha-Bonim. Out of thirty-two militant members, only four were over the age of nineteen in 1933. The leaders of the group, Herbert Baum and his wife, Marianne, started their underground activity at the beginning of the Nazi regime.

Edith Fraenkel, a member of the Baum Gruppe, was sent to Theresienstadt and then to Auschwitz, where she died in 1944.

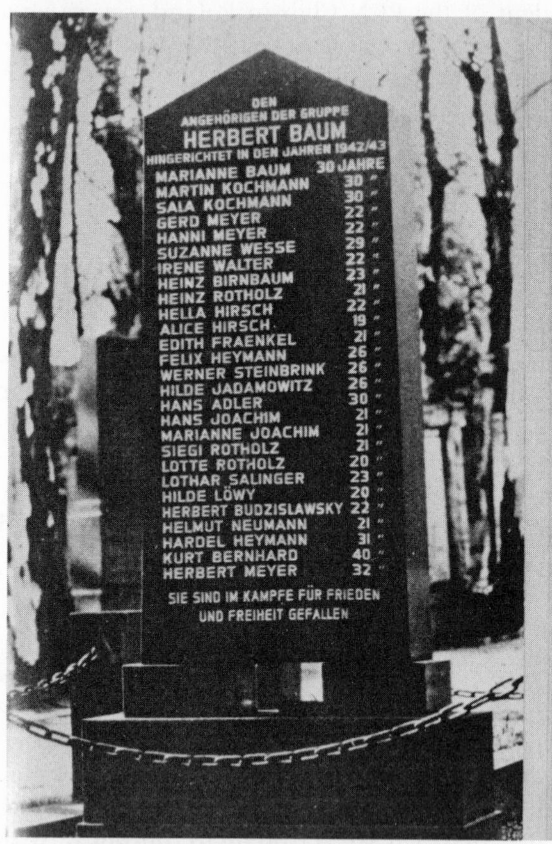

Monument to the Baum Gruppe in the Weissensee cemetery, East Berlin. The text reads (top): "To the members of the Herbert Baum group executed in 1942/43"; (bottom): "They fell in the battle for peace and freedom."

In 1936 the Jewish members were instructed by the Communist underground to set up an independent group and found Communist cells in Jewish youth organizations. Between 1937 and 1942, the activities of the group, which maintained links with all major similar groups in Berlin, included the distribution of illegal brochures and the organization of educational evenings, political training courses, and cultural events. The group also sought to strengthen the morale of Jews due to be deported to the east. On May 18, 1942, several members of the group set fire to different areas of *Das Sowjetparadies* ("The Soviet Paradise"), an anti-Bolshevik exhibit set up in Berlin by the Nazi Ministry of Propaganda; the group's action was considered a major anti-Nazi manifestation. Most members of the group were caught, either denounced by an informer planted by the Ge-

Heinz Birnbaum, one of the leaders of the Baum Gruppe.

Lotte Rotholz, a member of the Baum Gruppe. She died in Auschwitz.

stapo or because of their lack of training in conspiratorial work. Five hundred Berlin Jews were also arrested in revenge. Half of them were shot and the others sent to the SACHSENHAUSEN concentration camp and killed in the fall of 1942. Baum was tortured to death, and the other members were arrested and prosecuted in separate trials between July 1942 and June 1943; most of them were executed. Nearly all the other members were later deported to the east and died in AUSCHWITZ.

Werner Steinbrink, a leading member of the Baum Gruppe, was apprehended and executed on August 18, 1942.

BIBLIOGRAPHY

Eschwege, H. "Resistance of German Jews against the Nazi Regime." *Leo Baeck Institute Year Book* 15 (1970): 143–180.

Kwiet, K., and H. Eschwege. *Selbstbehauptung und Widerstand.* Hamburg, 1984.

Mark, B. "The Herbert Baum Group: Jewish Resistance in Germany in the Years 1937–1942." In *They Fought Back,* edited by Y. Suhl, pp. 55–68. New York, 1962.

Pikarski, M. *Jugend im Berliner Widerstand: Herbert Baum und Kampfgefährten.* Berlin, 1978.

DAVID BANKIER

BAUMINGER, HESHEK (Zvi or "Bazyli"; 1919–1943), one of the commanders of the Iskra (Spark) fighting organization in KRAKÓW. Bauminger, who was born in Kraków, received a Zionist religious upbringing and attended the Hebrew high school in Kraków. At the age of sixteen he joined Ha-Shomer ha-Tsa'ir, and he eventually became the head of the movement's branch in Kraków.

When World War II broke out he was drafted into the Polish army, ending up in Lvov. After the Germans invaded the Soviet Union on June 22, 1941, Bauminger was drafted into the Red Army and fell into German captivity. He managed to escape and make his way to Lvov, where fellow Ha-Shomer ha-Tsa'ir members provided him with Aryan papers. He then made his way back to Kraków on foot, reaching the ghetto in early 1942. There he met with the surviving members of his movement and with leaders of Akiva, reporting to them on the horrendous mass murders that the Germans had perpetrated on the Jews of Eastern Galicia and the Ukraine, and advocating an armed struggle against the enemy.

In mid-1942 a unified Jewish command, the ŻYDOWSKA ORGANIZACJA BOJOWA (ŻOB), was established; headed by Bauminger, it included members of Akiva, Dror, Iskra, and other organizations. Using hit-and-run tactics, each movement engaged in its own sporadic actions, but major operations were carried out jointly and directed by the unified command. The most important of these, con-

Zvi Bauminger.

ducted on December 22, 1942, was called the "Cyganeria Night" (Cyganeria being the name of the café that was the target). Nine German officers were killed in the attack and thirteen wounded; this was the first time that Kraków residents saw Germans killed and wounded. The escape plan was for the He-Haluts ha-Lohem fighters to make their way back to their headquarters at 24 Skavinska Street, while the Iskra fighters were to go to their headquarters in Czerwony Pradnik, a Polish workers' section of the city, several kilometers from the ghetto. The Germans, however, found out about the meeting at the He-Haluts ha-Lohem headquarters. They broke in, killing some of the members and capturing the rest.

Bauminger and his men continued fighting the Germans, carrying out acts of sabotage on German installations in and outside the ghetto. In March 1943 the Germans broke into the place where he lived. Bauminger fired at them, saving the last bullet to shoot himself in the temple.

BIBLIOGRAPHY

Bauminger, A. *The Fighters of the Kraków Ghetto.* Jerusalem, 1987. (In Hebrew.)

Bauminger, A., M. Bosak, and N. M. Gelber. *The Kraków Book: A Jewish Mother-City.* Jerusalem, 1959. See pages 381–429. (In Hebrew.)

Krakowski, S. *The War of the Doomed.* New York, 1984.

ARIE LEON BAUMINGER

BAUR, ANDRÉ (1904–1943), Jewish leader in Paris. Born in Paris, Baur was reared in a distinguished Jewish family of rabbis and community figures, and he himself became the president of the Paris Reform synagogue (on Rue Copernic) in the late 1930s. A well-to-do banker, Baur could easily have left Paris during the great exodus of Jews in 1940 but opted to remain and serve the community.

In March 1941 the Comité de Coordination, the recently established umbrella organization of Jewish welfare societies in Paris, was at a crossroads, and new responsible Jewish personalities were needed to invigorate it. Called upon by his uncle Julien Weill, who was the Chief Rabbi of Paris, Baur entered the Comité and tried to turn it in constructive directions and increase relief to the Jews of the occupied zone. Although he succeeded in bringing together reputable individuals to head the Comité, he was unable to obtain the suppport of the community for his welfare schemes.

In the fall of 1941, Baur held talks with Xavier VALLAT, head of the COMMISSARIAT GÉNÉRAL AUX QUESTIONS JUIVES (established by the Vichy government), on the creation of the UNION GÉNÉRALE DES ISRAÉLITES DE FRANCE (UGIF), and he became its vice president. From the outset of the UGIF's existence, Baur directed it to abide by legal methods of operation, and even in moments of great crisis (such as the mass arrest of Jews in Paris in July 1942), he adhered strictly to this outlook, hoping thereby to alleviate the plight of the Jewish community. Constantly concerned with the needs of Jews, Baur went to great efforts to guarantee the UGIF's resources, even to the point of proposing a more "harmonized" and authoritarian organization that would have eliminated the autonomous existence of UGIF-South, the UGIF division in the unoccupied zone. Baur fought valiantly to save his immigrant employees from dismissal in early 1943, but gave in to the German pressure when it threatened the UGIF's continuation.

Baur was a man of principle, deeply devoted to succoring the needy. His policy came to an impasse in July 1943, when SS-Hauptsturmführer Alois BRUNNER devised a scheme in which the UGIF would encourage relatives of interned Jews to voluntarily unite with their family members in DRANCY. With the full support of his council, Baur rejected turning the UGIF into a police arm of the SS and sought the intervention of Prime Minister Pierre LAVAL. As a result of his objection to carrying out Brunner's plan, Baur, his wife, and their four children were arrested and sent to Drancy. From there they were deported in December 1943 to AUSCHWITZ, where Baur perished.

BIBLIOGRAPHY

Adler, J. *The Jews of Paris and the Final Solution: Communal Response and International Conflicts, 1940–1944.* New York, 1988.

Cohen, R. I. *The Burden of Conscience: French Jewish Leadership during the Holocaust.* Bloomington, 1987.

Cohen, R. I. "The Jewish Community of France in the Face of Vichy-German Persecution, 1940–1944." In *The Jews in Modern France,* edited by F. Malino and B. Wasserstein, pp. 181–204. London, 1985.

RICHARD COHEN

BECCARI, ARRIGO, priest in Nonantola, near Bologna in northern ITALY, who together with Giuseppe Moreali, a local physician, saved the lives of 120 Jews, mostly children. In July 1942, an initial group of fifty Jewish children arrived in Nonantola, after having resided for a while in the Italian zone of occupation in northern Yugoslavia. They had earlier been separated from their parents, whose whereabouts remained unknown. With the increase of partisan activity in the Italian zone, the friendly Italian authorities suggested to Josef

Itai, the group leader, that he move his children to the safety of Italy proper (then at war on the side of Nazi Germany). With the aid of Delasem (Delegazione Assistenza Emigranti Ebrei), the Jewish welfare agency officially recognized by the Fascist government, the children were housed in Villa Emma, in the village of Nonantola. There they were joined by an additional fifty children, recent refugees from Nazi terror. When the Germans overran northern Italy on September 8, 1943, the children were no longer safe, and preventive measures had to be taken immediately to avoid their falling into German hands. Without seeking the approval of his superiors in Modena, Arrigo Beccari, an instructor in a nearby Catholic seminary whom Itai had earlier befriended, opened the seminary's doors to the children. Others were housed with surrounding villagers, while the food for all was prepared within the seminary walls. When the seminary rector first saw the children, who included girls, he crossed himself and exclaimed: "For a thousand years, a woman's foot has not trodden on these grounds, but let God's will be done."

With the Nazis intensifying their search for Jews in hiding, a plan was prepared to move the children and their adult caretakers, a total of 120 persons, out of the occupied zone. At first, the thought was to smuggle them across Allied lines south of Rome. But as this proved impractical, it was decided to transfer them to the Swiss border to the north. With the help of Giuseppe Moreali, the town doctor, false identities were provided and all 120 children and their caretakers were taken by train to the Swiss border, which they crossed on the eve of the Day of Atonement of 1943. The dangers attending the convoy of such a large group of children and their Italian guides on their trek to the Swiss border were great. The children, for instance, bore Italian names on their false credentials but were hardly proficient in that language.

Arrigo Beccari, left, and Dr. Giuseppe Moreali, right.

The Gestapo, belatedly discovering the children's flight, seized Beccari and interrogated him to elicit the names of persons involved in the rescue operation and the location of other Jews in hiding. Beccari withstood the terrible ordeal of Nazi torture and was released after many months of incarceration in a notorious Bologna prison.

Arrigo Beccari and Giuseppe Moreali were recognized by YAD VASHEM as "RIGHTEOUS AMONG THE NATIONS" in 1964.

BIBLIOGRAPHY

Zuccotti, S. *The Italians and the Holocaust.* New York, 1987.

MORDECAI PALDIEL

BECHER, KURT (b. 1909), Nazi official. Born in Hamburg, Becher arrived in Hungary with the rank of SS-*Obersturmbannführer* shortly after the German occupation on March 19, 1944, having served for several years on the Russian front. His alleged assignment from the SS headquarters was the procurement of horses and equipment for horse-drawn units of the Waffen-SS. Becher played a decisive role in the acquisition of German control over the giant Weiss-Manfred Works. He was also the chief SS negotiator with whom the RELIEF AND RESCUE COMMITTEE OF BUDAPEST, and especially Rezső (Rudolf) KASZTNER, had to deal. Becher was involved in the arrangement of the "Kasztner transport" and its eventual transfer from the BERGEN-BELSEN concentration camp to Switzerland. In this context he also met (having received Heinrich HIMMLER's consent) with Saly MAYER, the American Jewish JOINT DISTRIBUTION COMMIT-

TEE head in Switzerland, and with Roswell McClelland, the WAR REFUGEE BOARD representative, in Saint Gall on November 4, 1944. Considering the latter as "the personal representative of President Franklin Delano ROOSEVELT," Becher attached great importance to the meeting, transcending the rescuing of Jews.

A few months after Becher's promotion to SS-*Standartenführer* in January 1945, Himmler appointed Becher to serve as *Reichssonderkommissar für sämtliche Konzentrationslager* (Special Reich Commissioner for All Concentration Camps). Traveling in the company of Kasztner, Becher worked toward preventing the destruction of the camps in the last weeks of the war.

Becher was arrested by the Allies after Germany's surrender. He escaped prosecution as a war criminal, and was released from prison in Nuremberg on Kasztner's personal recommendation.

BIBLIOGRAPHY

Braham, R. L. *The Politics of Genocide: The Holocaust in Hungary.* New York, 1981.

Lévai, J. *A fekete SS fehér báránya.* Budapest, 1966.

Pintér, I. and L. Szabó, eds. *Criminals at Large.* Budapest, 1961. See pages 150–164.

RANDOLPH L. BRAHAM

BĘDZIN, town in the Katowice district in POLAND, founded in the Middle Ages. In the latter half of the nineteenth century, Będzin entered a stage of rapid development and attracted industry as a result of its location in an area rich in coal and iron ore. A Jewish community came into existence in Będzin in the late Middle Ages. In 1931 the Jewish population numbered 21,625 (45.4 percent of the total), and by the eve of World War II it had grown to approximately 27,000.

The German occupation of the city, on September 4, 1939, exposed the Jewish inhabitants of Będzin to maltreatment and harassment. On September 9 the Germans set fire to the main synagogue and fifty adjacent houses without giving the residents advance warning, and a number of Jews were burned to death. A series of anti-Jewish economic decrees was enacted, providing for the confiscation of Jewish property and the imposition of personal restrictions on the Jews.

The A. Rossner tailor shop in Będzin, which supplied uniforms for the Germans (March 4, 1941).

A JUDENRAT (Jewish Council) was established at an early stage of the occupation, headed by local Jewish public figures. After a while the local Judenrat was subordinated to the Judenräte center in SOSNOWIEC, and a new local Judenrat chairman, Chaim Molczadski, was appointed. The most difficult anti-Jewish decree ordered Jews to report for forced labor, which at times led to their being seized and deported to forced-labor camps in Germany. It soon became the Judenrat's task to organize these deportations. The Judenrat also helped establish workshops (known as "shops"), owned by Germans and using Jews as workers, on the assumption that by engaging in work benefiting the Germans, the city's Jews would be saved. The local Jewish YOUTH MOVEMENTS resumed their educational activities and also took on the teaching of children (who had been left without any schools) and vocational training, with an emphasis on agriculture. The Judenrat allocated a 100-acre (.404 sq km) plot of land at one end of the city to establish a *farma* (farm).

In May 1942, deportation of the Będzin Jews to the AUSCHWITZ extermination camp was launched, in the guise of "resettlement." The deportation reached its peak on August 12, when all the Jews of the city had to assemble on a central city plot, ostensibly in order to have their papers stamped. A *Selek-*

tion was made, and 5,000 Jews were dispatched to their deaths.

The youth movements intensified their operations, embarked on an anti-Judenrat information campaign, and cautioned the Jews not to report for the deportations. The *farma* was used as the site of clandestine meetings with leaders of the ŻYDOWSKA ORGANIZACJA BOJOWA (Jewish Fighting Organization; ŻOB). One of them was Mordecai ANIELEWICZ, the future leader of the WARSAW GHETTO UPRISING, who told the local youth movement activists about the extermination of Jews in the GENERALGOUVERNEMENT and helped organize a local resistance organization. The *farma* became the center of the youth movements' underground operations and the site of a defense headquarters, in which representatives of all the youth movements took part. The leadership consisted of Frumka PLOTNICKA (who had come from Warsaw), Zvi Brandes, Herschel Springer, Shlomo Lerner, and Ezriel ("Yozek") Koszok.

The Będzin Jewish underground made attempts to establish contact with the Polish underground, but these failed, as did the attempts to stage an armed uprising outside the ghetto. During a sortie that a fighting unit made from the ghetto, it was ambushed and killed. The underground concentrated its efforts on acquiring weapons, preparing for defense, and constructing bunkers; these efforts were accompanied by a debate among the youth movements, between those who demanded that the emphasis be on the struggle inside the ghetto walls and those who stressed the search for escape routes, mainly by way of the border with Slovakia.

In the spring of 1943, the Będzin Jews were confined to a ghetto that was set up in Kamionka, a suburb close to Środula, where the Sosnowiec Jews were held. On August 1, 1943, the final liquidation of the ghetto was launched. Youth movement members offered armed resistance in several bunkers. The operation took more than two weeks, the Jews being deported to Auschwitz. Some of the survivors in the ghetto escaped to Slovakia and Hungary, where they resumed underground operations. A handful of Będzin Jews returned to the city after the war, but the Jewish community was not revived.

BIBLIOGRAPHY

Brandes, A., and H. Reshef, eds. *Zvi Brandes: A Leader of the Zaglembian Haluts Underground.* Tel Aviv, 1972. (In Hebrew.)

Gilbert, M. *The Holocaust.* New York, 1985.

Mazia, F. *Comrades in the Storm: The Struggle of Zionist Youth against the Nazis.* Jerusalem, 1964. (In Hebrew.)

Rappaport, J. *Pinkas Zaglembie: Memorial Book.* Tel Aviv, 1972. (In Hebrew, Yiddish, and English.)

Stein, A. S., ed. *Pinkas Bendin: A Memorial to the Jewish Community of Bendin (Poland).* Tel Aviv, 1959. (In Hebrew.)

SHLOMO NETZER

BEŁCHATÓW, town in the Łódź district, Poland. On the eve of World War II it had six thousand Jews, comprising 60 percent of the total population. About one-third of the Jews left in the first few months of the German occupation. On March 1, 1941, a ghetto was set up in Bełchatów; in the fall of that year it took in the Jews of nearby towns—Zelów, Widawa, and Szczerców—as well as those from several villages who had been driven out of their homes. As a result, the ghetto was crowded to suffocation and sanitary conditions deteriorated.

Between August 1941 and April 1942, 1,950 men from the Bełchatów ghetto were transferred to forced-labor camps in the Poznań area, where they all met their death. The ghetto was liquidated from August 11 to 13 of that year by SS units stationed in the area, with the participation of the civilian German population led by the mayor, Josef Tramler, and the chief of the Łódź ghetto administration, Hans BIEBOW (who made a special journey to Bełchatów for this purpose). In the course of the liquidation, 5,000 Jews were deported to the CHEŁMNO extermination camp and were murdered there, 850 were transferred to the Łódź ghetto, and 150 managed to flee, although most of them were later caught and killed.

BIBLIOGRAPHY

Belchatow (In Memoriam). Buenos Aires, 1951. (In Yiddish.)

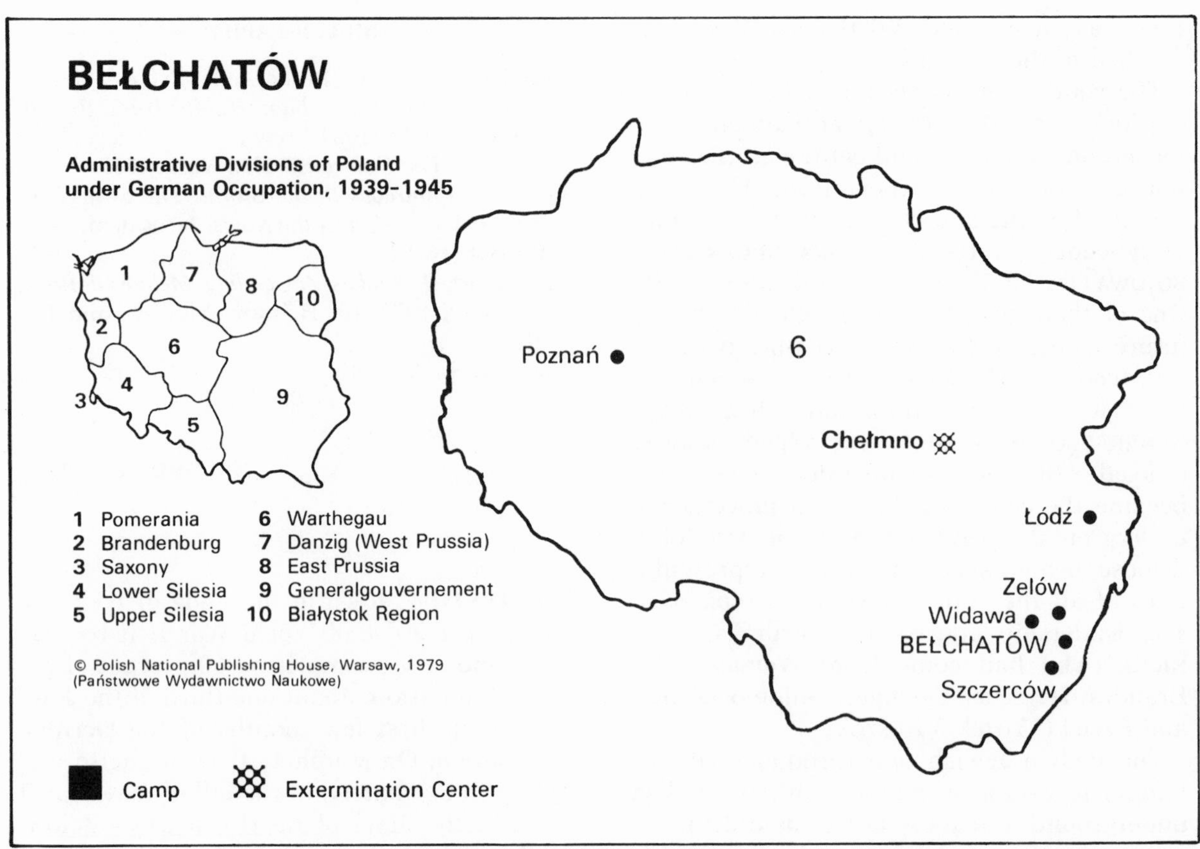

Dobroszycki, L. *The Chronicle of the Lodz Ghetto.* New Haven, 1984.

SHMUEL KRAKOWSKI

BELGIAN JEWS, ASSOCIATION OF. *See* Association des Juifs en Belgique.

BELGIUM. In the Middle Ages the area that is now Belgium had a small Jewish population, but in the fourteenth century the existing communities were liquidated. In the sixteenth century, Marranos (Jews concealing their Judaism) from Portugal settled in the Belgian cities, and by the seventeenth century a more or less overt Jewish community had come into being in Antwerp. During the eighteenth century Ashkenazi Jews also settled in Belgium, and by the century's end they had achieved equal rights. In 1830, when Belgium became an independent country, its Jewish population was a little over 1,000; by the end of the nineteenth century that number had greatly increased. During that period, however, Belgium was primarily a transit station for Jewish refugees from eastern Europe on their way to overseas destinations and, as a result, the Jewish community's size and institutions were not of a stable character. It was only from the early 1920s that Belgian Jewry steadily grew in size, with Jews arriving from the multinational countries that had been broken up (Russia and the Austro-Hungarian Empire) and, in the 1930s, from Nazi Germany. On the eve of the Nazi invasion Belgium had a Jewish population of 66,000 (out of a total of 8.3 million), but only 10 percent of the Jews were Belgian citizens.

The Jewish population was concentrated in four cities, Brussels, Antwerp, Liège, and Charleroi, but mostly in the first two. The official Belgian Jewish community was organized into a central Consistoire, but many of the immigrants formed their own communities, congregations, and associations, outside

BELGIUM

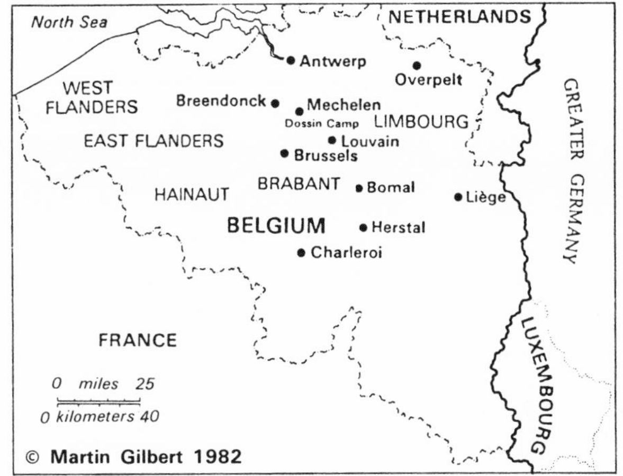

the Consistoire framework. The immigrants spoke Yiddish, but especially among the younger generation, French became the predominant language. All the shades of Jewish political opinion that had developed in Poland in the interwar period were present in Belgium, most prominently the socialist trends—Zionist and non-Zionist, including the BUND—and other, more radical leftist ideologies. This situation led to the development of very close ties between the Jews and the Belgian leftist movements, a factor that proved of great importance in the rescue efforts and the resistance during the Holocaust period.

German Occupation. German forces invaded Belgium on May 10, 1940, and on May 28, on the orders of King Leopold III, the Belgian army surrendered. The king stayed in Belgium, but the prime minister and some of the cabinet members fled the country, their first stop being France. After a great deal of internal discussion and controversy, a government-in-exile was established in London on October 31, 1940. As a result, two centers of official Belgian authority were now in existence, each with its own policy and objectives. The king, recognizing the new balance of power in the country, was inclined to cooperate with the Germans, and on one occasion even met with Adolf HITLER, but he refrained almost totally from overt activity. The government-in-exile supported the Allies, and neither of the two sides recognized the authority of the other. Hitler had no definite plans for Belgium's ultimate political status in the "New Order" that was to be established in Europe after a German victory, and the absence of such plans had a marked effect on the administration that the Germans installed in the occupied country.

The first four years witnessed a military administration (*Militärverwaltung*), under Gen. Alexander von Falkenhausen. In July 1944 a civil administration (*Zivilverwaltung*) took its place, the Germans now planning to turn Belgium into two *Reichsgaue* (territorial units) annexed to Germany: *Reichsgau* Flanders and *Reichsgau* Walonia; Josef Grohé was appointed *Reichskommissar* for Belgium. Under the military administration, a complex set of relationships existed between the administration and the other branches of the German government and Nazi party that had a foothold in Belgium: the Foreign Ministry and the SS in general, especially the REICHSSICHERHEITSHAUPTAMT (Reich Security Main Office; RSHA). The latter two bodies, which were both under Heinrich HIMMLER's authority, made strenuous efforts to expand their influence, while the military administration tried to curb them. The Belgian administration continued to function on a regular basis under the *secrétaires généraux* (principal secretaries), who held regular meetings to coordinate their activities and constituted a kind of mini-government; from time to time, personnel changes took place among the *secrétaires généraux*.

In early September 1944, Brussels and Antwerp were liberated by Allied forces, and by early November all of Belgium was set free. However, in the winter offensive that the Germans launched in the Ardennes in December 1944, they reoccupied areas in the southeast, and it was only in January 1945 that the last German troops were driven out.

According to data published in 1980, the Jewish population of Belgium at the time of the German invasion was 65,696 (not 90,000, as claimed in earlier studies); 34,801 Jews were imprisoned or deported, and of these, 28,902 perished, representing 44 percent of the total Jewish population. This was a lower percentage of Jews murdered than in the

Netherlands, mainly for three reasons: (1) the different kind of administration established by the Germans; (2) the different mentality of the Belgian Jews; and (3) the attitude of the local population.

In Belgium, German rule had all the attributes of Nazi anti-Jewish policy: eliminating Jews from all positions of influence, depriving them of their possessions and livelihood, putting them on forced labor, isolating them from the rest of the population, and, finally, deporting them to their death. Here, however, the German administration served as a restraining factor on the volume, intensity, and tempo of the anti-Jewish measures.

In the first two years of the occupation, before the deportations began, eighteen anti-Jewish decrees and regulations were issued, at relatively long intervals, creating the impression that the measures were on the whole quite moderate. On October 23, 1940, ritual slaughter was prohibited. Two decrees announced October 28 defined who was to be regarded as a Jew under the law, ordered the Jews to conduct a census and draw up a list of all their enterprises and occupations, and eliminated Jews from the public administration, the legal and teaching professions, and the media. On May 31, 1941, two decrees were issued, ordering Jews to display signs identifying their enterprises as Jewish and to declare their capital and other assets (including real estate), and restricting withdrawals by Jews from their bank accounts to a fixed monthly amount. On August 29 of that year Jews had their freedom of movement restricted; they were permitted to reside only in the four major cities, and they were subject to a nightly curfew, from 8:00 p.m. to 7:00 a.m.

A decree issued on November 25, 1941, established the ASSOCIATION DES JUIFS EN BELGIQUE (Association of Jews in Belgium; AJB), to which every Jew had to belong. Within a week, another decree ordered the expulsion of all Jewish children from the public-school system, and the AJB was required to set up its own elementary and secondary schools (the order was implemented only four months later). On January 17, 1942, Jews were forbidden to leave the country. A general labor draft issued on March 3 of that year was amplified by a decree dated March 11 that imposed special forced labor on the Jews. At the bidding of the RSHA, a decree was issued on May 27 ordering the Jews to wear the yellow badge (*see* BADGE, JEWISH). These orders and regulations were implemented by the military administration, which tried to restrict the influence of the SS and the RSHA and to stay in control. It was only when the "Final Solution" was initiated, in the spring of 1942, that RSHA and its various divisions became the predominant force controlling Jewish affairs. The differences of approach to the Jewish question are reflected in the reports submitted by Eggert Reeder, head of the military administration staff in the early stage of the occupation. They state that "Jewish influence in the economy is generally quite small, except for the diamond industry" (April 1941) and "the Jewish question . . . does not play the same role as in most other European countries" (July 15, 1941).

Deportation. In the summer of 1942 the deportation of Jews from Belgium was launched, in coordination with the deportations from the Netherlands and France. The preparations had been made by Adolf EICHMANN's section in the RSHA. At a meeting held in Eichmann's office in Berlin on June 11, 1942, the SS officials in charge of Jewish affairs in the Netherlands, Belgium, and France were ordered to prepare for the deportation of the Jews, to begin within a few weeks. Differences of opinion among the various branches of the regime delayed the beginning of deportations in Belgium, and they were begun only on August 4. On July 15, the AJB was ordered to set up a special bureau for coordinating the "labor draft" (*Arbeitseinsatz*) of the Jews. The deportations continued for over a year, coming to an end in September 1943 with "Operation Iltis," in which Jews of Belgian nationality were dispatched to the east (until then their deportation had been deferred).

The deportations were handled by a small staff in the Bureau of Jewish Affairs on Avenue Louise in Brussels; the roundup of Jews and their actual deportation was carried out, for the most part, by the German Feldgendarmerie (field police). By far the greater number of the deportees perished in AUSCH-

WITZ; some small groups were also sent to BUCHENWALD, RAVENSBRÜCK, and BERGEN-BELSEN. By an agreement between Himmler and Albert SPEER, the minister of armaments, groups of men were taken off the transports in late August and early September of 1942, to be put to work in Koźle (Cosel), a subcamp of the Auschwitz complex. The Belgian Jews in these groups manifested a better ability to survive under the horrible conditions than did the Dutch Jews.

Economic Measures. Economic measures against the Jews were introduced toward the end of 1940. In the early months of the occupation, no such measures had been taken, and for a while it even seemed that the Jews would be able to carry on a reasonable level of economic activity. Some Jews who had fled to France (mainly to southern France) when Belgium was occupied even returned to Belgium and resumed their economic activities there, especially in the diamond industry in Antwerp. But in November 1940 Hermann GÖRING ordered the Belgian economy to be "Aryanized," and as a result various German enterprises showed interest in acquiring Jewish businesses. In practice, "Aryanization" was launched only in late 1941, its "legal" basis being decrees of October 28, 1940, and May 21, 1941. The rate at which Aryanization proceeded was accelerated in March and April 1942, when the systematic liquidation of Jewish businesses in the textile, leather, and diamond industries was set in motion. The process of Aryanization, however, was never completed; according to a comprehensive survey drawn up by the Germans, the large Jewish enterprises stayed in existence and kept their assets intact. A similar situation prevailed with Jewish-owned real estate.

In 1942, several decrees dealing with economic affairs were enacted, requiring the confiscation of property owned by German Jews (decrees of April 22 and August 1), placing severe restrictions on the practice of medicine (June 1), and forbidding the sale of real estate without special permission (September 29) during the period when Jews were being deported to the camps.

German plunder of Jewish property also took the form of confiscation—of the property of Jews who did not return to their homes or were deported, and of Jewish institutions and art collections. This form of plunder was in the hands of EINSATZSTAB ROSENBERG (Operational Staff Rosenberg). When the deportations were in full swing, Einsatzstab Rosenberg handled only art collections and items of "ideological value" (such as Jewish religious and folklore objects and libraries). The confiscation of the contents of expropriated Jewish apartments "for the good of the German people" was left to the Reichsministerium für die Besetzten Ostgebiete (Reich Ministry for the Occupied Eastern Territories), also under Rosenberg, and to the military administration in Belgium. No estimate can be made of the value of the property seized by the Germans when they emptied the Jewish apartments of their contents. According to a figure given in August 1944, the sheer bulk of the furniture confiscated by the military administration was 3,531,450 cubic feet (100,000 cu m). Another stage in the theft of the Jews' possessions took place in the MECHELEN assembly camp, where they were stripped of any valuables still in their possession, such as watches and jewelry, just before boarding the deportation trains.

Forced Labor. The removal of the Jews from economic life was followed, beginning in June 1942, by their exploitation as a cheap source of manpower. There was no direct connection between the drafting of Jews for forced labor and the deportations (they involved different authorities), but because the drafting of Jews for forced labor and the deportation of Jews happened to coincide, they were seen as parts of the same operation. Actually, the forced-labor draft of Jews in Belgium was part of a drive that the Germans were carrying out in all the occupied countries of Europe. The Belgian Jews put on forced labor were employed primarily in the construction of fortifications along the coast of northern France, of which ORGANISATION TODT was in charge. A total of 2,252 Jews from Belgium were put to work there, setting out from Brussels, Charleroi, and Liège from June through August 1942, in seven groups. Other sources of employment for Jews on forced labor were German army construction projects and clothing factories in Belgium. Several groups of Jews also worked for short periods in the Fabrique Nationale d'Armes de

Guerre (F.N. Arms Factory) at Herstal, in stone quarries, and on soil amelioration. Forced-labor workers were given wages that were deposited in their name in a Brussels bank. This pay, however, was left in the bank up to the end of the war, either because the Jews in the forced-labor camps were deported to extermination camps (by way of the Mechelen or DRANCY camps) or because the Jews were afraid to claim it.

Relations between the Jews and the General Population. Relations between the Jews and the various components of the Belgian population were complicated, even before the German occupation of the country. There were a number of negative factors in this relationship: most of the population were Catholic; there was a language war between the Flemings and the Walloons; and most of the Jews were recent immigrants whose mentality was quite different from that of the native population. These factors, however, were balanced by the democratic character of the regime and by the rapid integration of the Jews in the economic life of the country and in some of its political movements. During the occupation, an important positive factor was the stand of the government-in-exile, which on January 10, 1941, issued a statement that declared all the decrees of the German military administration null and void and committed itself to restoring the stolen property to its rightful owners and to punishing Belgians collaborating with the Germans.

On October 10, 1940, the Germans asked the directors general of the Belgian governmental departments to take appropriate action to remove the Jews from the economic life of the country, but these officials refused to comply, citing legal grounds. The Germans did not press further, and published the anti-Jewish decrees on their own, with the Belgian administrative staff cooperating in the implementation of the decrees. Generally speaking, the reaction of the Belgian public to the anti-Jewish legislation in the first two years of the occupation was one of apathy. But there were exceptions: the anti-Jewish decrees of October 28, 1940, especially the one that ordered the elimination of Jews from public administration, aroused a negative reaction among the population; some official protests were even lodged. Prominent among these were the protests made by three senior Brussels jurists and by the Free University of Brussels, which had the largest number of Jewish lecturers. The Germans responded by reprimanding the university, but they took no further action; neither, of course, did the protests have any effect on German policy. Several radical right-wing Belgian organizations cooperated with the Germans—for ideological or economic reasons, or because they felt that there was no choice and that Nazi hegemony had to be recognized. These organizations included the Vlaams Nationaal Verbond (National Flemish Movement; VNV), headed by Staf de Clerq, and the Rexist movement, made up mostly of Walloons, and headed by Léon Degrelle. They also provided 400 volunteers for the SS, organized into two legions. These volunteers spread antisemitic propaganda and helped the authorities to implement their policies. In addition, Radio Bruxelles broadcast anti-Jewish propaganda quite often. The total effect of these organizations and institutions was not large, but it appears to have been enough to deter people, in a number of cases, from protesting the anti-Jewish policy. In 1941, a VNV member, Gerard Romsee, was appointed director general of the Ministry of the Interior, a post in which he helped apply the anti-Jewish legislation. On April 14, 1941, during Passover, a small group of Flemish antisemitic nationalists staged what came to be known as the "Antwerp pogrom" (apparently at the instigation of one of the local German agencies), in the course of which two synagogues and the house of Rabbi Marcus Rottenberg were damaged.

The introduction of the yellow badge, in a decree issued on May 27, 1942, led to a number of protests. The Greater Brussels city council refused to distribute the badge, and the AJB too declared that it was unable to undertake this task, but the councils of other cities with a Jewish population (such as Antwerp) did not react in the same manner. Most of the underground newspapers sharply denounced the decree and called upon the population to express its solidarity with the Jews. There was indeed much sympathy for the Jews among the population, and a number of people expressed their solidarity by wearing badges similar to the Jewish yellow badge. This reaction had no immediate effect on the situation, but some have seen it as a turning point, as a result of which the Belgian population was more inclined to help the Jews when the deportations were launched.

The stand taken by the Belgian population when the deportations began, in the summer of 1942, was of great importance. The Belgian resistance movement was not united and consisted of several groups, but there was wide support for resistance as such, and it was this general mood that made it possible, for example, for as many as 80,000 persons (non-Jews) to go into hiding and thereby avoid the forced-labor draft. An illegal press existed with a wide circulation. Some 70,000 people are estimated to have been organized in the resistance, out of a total population of 8 million. The Communist party played a central role in the resistance operations, despite its small size, and it was an important factor in the establishment, in March 1941, of the Front d'Indépendance, which became the largest resistance organization. The various resistance groups also had many Jews among their members. With the help of large sectors of the population, especially leftist party activists and church institutions (as well as individual Belgians not affiliated with any group), some 25,000 Jews were concealed from the Germans. Belgian Jews and Jews from the Netherlands passing through Belgium were helped to escape to France and Switzerland.

Concerning the participation of the Catholic church in providing hiding places for Jews, special mention must be made of Father Joseph André of Namur, of the regional seminary in Bastogne, and Bishop Louis-Joseph Kerkhofs of Liège; the bishop of Mechelen also provided refuge to many Jews. Cardinal Joseph-Ernst van Roey, the highest ecclesiastical authority in Belgium, took action on behalf of the Jews in several instances, although he was very careful about it. In the early phase of the deportations, van Roey intervened on behalf of Jewish converts and the Jewish partners of mixed marriages, as well as on behalf of Jews who were Belgian nationals, and obtained their release. A few weeks later van Roey acted similarly on behalf of Rabbi Salomon Ullmann and the AJB leaders who had been arrested and imprisoned in the BREENDONCK camp. On the other hand, van Roey's critics claim that by abstaining from a general protest and confining intervention to certain groups of Jews, the cardinal actually facilitated the deportation of the rest of the Jews. The queen mother, Elizabeth, also intervened on behalf of the Jews of Belgian nationality. On August 1, 1942, she met with three of the AJB leaders, and following that meeting she appealed to Hitler himself, through General von Falkenhausen.

The postponement of the deportation of Jews who were Belgian nationals, therefore, was achieved by a combination of intervention on their behalf by Belgian elements, a pragmatic approach on the part of the German military administration, and the consent, for the time being and for its own convenience, of the RSHA. Restricting protection to Belgian nationals, however, implied that the rest of the Jews (meaning most of the Jewish population of Belgium) could be abandoned. The Belgian Red Cross assisted many Jews by providing them with food parcels; in 1943, half the quantity of parcels earmarked for this purpose was distributed among the Jews who were in hiding. Side by side with many manifestations of aid to the Jews in the deportation period, however, there were also instances when Belgians informed to the authorities on Jews in hiding, and some radical right-wing organizations took up an active search for such Jews.

The Jewish Community. During the fighting in May 1940, many Jews tried to escape to France and to Britain. Some made their way to southern France or even to Spain; many others returned to their homes in Belgium after weeks of wandering. In the early months of the occupation, when no anti-Jewish action was taken, the Jews tried to rehabilitate their communal life; the first step in this direction was the formation of aid committees in Brussels and Antwerp.

This was followed by the renewal of activities in the communities and in some organizations, political parties, and youth movements. The flight of veteran leaders and of persons prominent in economic affairs had affected in particular the work of the Consistoire Central, several welfare organizations, and the Orthodox communities of Brussels and Antwerp. It was the leader of the General Zionists, Itzko Kubowitzki—the dominant figure among the remaining leaders—who sought to reorganize Jewish life and in the course of this effort helped integrate many Zionists into the representative bodies of Belgian Jewry. The Chief Rabbi (Grand Rabbin) of Belgium, Joseph Wiener, had fled during the fighting; in September 1940 he was replaced by Rabbi Salomon Ullmann, who in 1937 had become the chief Jewish military chaplain. (His father was the founder of one of the Orthodox congregations of Antwerp.) In addition to the existing organizations of Belgian and eastern European Jews, a committee was formed of German Jews who had settled in Belgium before its occupation and who now constituted 20 percent of the Jewish population. All these organizations underwent a decisive change in their operations when the AJB was formed, in late 1941. Some of the old organizations were integrated into the AJB, and others kept up their independent existence, officially or unofficially; but all of them were affected by the predominant role that was now being played by the AJB.

For a while, the elimination of Jews from jobs in the public administration was of no great consequence, since only a few Jews had held such positions. The same applied, temporarily, to the initial anti-Jewish economic decrees. When the general economic situation deteriorated, however, and Aryanization was launched in the summer of 1941, the effect on the situation of the Jews was marked, and the Jewish organizations were hard pressed to meet the community needs, especially for welfare. Nevertheless, up until the time of the deportations, the Jews were able to maintain a tolerable standard of living. At that point, a wide gulf opened between the Jews who had Belgian nationality and were protected and all the other Jews. Some contacts were maintained with the American Jewish JOINT DISTRIBUTION COMMITTEE, which transmitted financial aid to the AJB, and, later, to the Jewish Defense Committee (see below).

As a rule, the Germans did not interfere with Jewish religious life. The first anti-Jewish decree to be issued, however, outlawing *sheḥitah* (ritual slaughter) without first stunning the animal, discriminated against Jews observing their dietary laws; efforts were made to solve the problem by using electric stunning devices that the Dutch rabbis had sanctioned for this purpose. Orthodox Jewish families, more than the others, felt the impact of the worsening food situation, as of 1942. Jewish religious literary activity was kept up, and one interesting project was the translation of the Talmud into Yiddish, so as to facilitate its study by young students (the project was not completed, but a part of the translation was published after the Holocaust).

Education, in the initial phase, remained unchanged. Most young Jews did not attend Jewish schools and remained in the public school system until April 1942, when the decree expelling Jews from the general school system, issued in late 1941, was applied. The community lost no time in meeting the new need and established several schools and kindergartens, using for this purpose the premises of the Brussels Central Synagogue, among other places. In the 1942–1943 school year, which opened after the deportations had started, the AJB-maintained school network shrank considerably in size. During the 1943–1944 school year, classes were held only in the AJB orphanages, which had the official sanction of the German authorities. Religious schools *par excellence,* such as the yeshiva (rabbinical academy) at Heide, near Antwerp, remained open until the beginning of the deportations.

Zionist youth movements in Brussels and Antwerp (Ha-Shomer ha-Tsa'ir, Bnei Akiva, Maccabi ha-Tsa'ir, Gordonia and Betar) resumed their activities, albeit on a more modest scale, concentrating on educational training, cultural work, and mutual help, in cooperation with the official political parties and organizations. In their work they sorely missed the contact they had previously enjoyed with Palestine. The various youth movements cooperated with one another, the Antwerp religious Bnei Akiva and the Marxist Ha-Shomer ha-Tsa'ir joining in obtaining food in the city's hinterland and distributing it, and in running an agricultural training farm in Bomal, south of Liège.

Rescue Operations and the Underground. The Jews of Belgium were actively engaged in underground operations and efforts for their own rescue, often coming up with original ideas. It is a moot point among historians whether all actions in which Jews were involved can be classified as "Jewish," since many of these actions were initiated and carried out by organizations belonging to the Belgian Left. By 1940 and 1941 the Germans were arresting Jews active in Communist organizations of German emigrés. Numerous Communists were seized by the Germans in June 1941, following the German attack on the Soviet Union, and of these, a considerable number were Jews. Also arrested, in 1941 and 1942, were Jews who had worked in the general underground press. Jews played a dominant role in the RED ORCHESTRA, the spy ring operating for the Soviet Union, and they were among the members of the *Front d'Indépendance* (a Belgian organization, representing various groups, that called for armed resistance).

Specific Jewish acts of resistance first took place in late 1941. Shortly after the AJB was formed, several Yiddish-language underground newspapers made their appearance, published by the Bund and Po'alei Zion, and as late as 1944 a Communist-sponsored Yiddish newspaper was still being published. Two other Jewish papers—one in Dutch and one in French—also appeared. In late 1941 and early 1942 the Jewish underground press expressed opposition to the AJB and its operations.

In July 1942, in view of the deteriorating situation of the Jews, a joint underground Jewish defense organization was initiated called the Comité de Défense des Juifs (Jewish Defense Committee; CDJ). It began its activities in September 1942. The initiative for its creation was taken by Ghert Jospa (who established contact between representatives of the Jewish Communists and the Front d'Indépendance) and various Zionist activists—Abusz Werber, the leader of Po'alei Zion–Left; Edouard Rotkel and Benjamin Nykerk of the General Zionists; and Chaim Perelman, who had a Revisionist party background. Eugene Hellendael, a member of the Brussels local AJB, also joined the founding members of the CDJ. The CDJ had important ties with the general resistance organizations as well as with the AJB, and it played a central role in the rescue and resistance operations during the period from 1942 to 1944. It also had contacts with the Catholic church and various other bodies, and engaged in fundraising. The organization's main purpose was to find hiding places for Jews; its children's section, in cooperation with the Oeuvre Nationale de l'Enfance (National Children's Committee), headed by Yvonne NÈVEJEAN, succeeded in hiding four thousand children. Large numbers of Jewish adults also had the CDJ's help in finding a place to hide.

Jewish armed resistance operations (some of which had no connection with the CDJ) had some impressive successes. On two occasions, in the summer of 1942, the target was the AJB. In one instance, the purpose was to seize the card index that the AJB maintained in its office, and in the other the attack was directed at Robert Holcinger, the official in charge of sending out the call-ups for deportation. The single most significant resistance operation carried out by the Jewish underground was the attack on a deportation train, on the night of April 19–20, 1943, containing a transport of Jews from the Mechelen camp (Transport No. 20) headed for Auschwitz. A recent exhaustive study has shed much new light upon this operation, the only recorded instance of an armed attack in Europe on a train taking Jews to their death.

Individual escapes from the deportation trains originating in the Mechelen camp were quite frequent. Such an escape first occurred in Transport No. 16 on October 31, 1942. Of the 26,500 Jews who were deported from Mechelen, the total number of escapees was 571; of these, 539 escaped from transports 16 to 20. In the attack on Transport No. 20 itself, 231 Jews escaped, of whom 23 were shot to death by the train guards. Most of the escapees, some of whom were members of resistance groups, jumped from the train as soon as they could (a number had tried to escape from an earlier transport). One group of 17 Jews was saved by the outside help of three persons—none of them affiliated with any organization—headed by a Jew. This action was launched near the Mechelen camp, on the stretch between Mechelen and Louvain. The three tricked the train into coming to a halt and managed to open the door of one carriage; some of the Jews in the carriage jumped off, amid a hail of bullets from the train guards. This was not a large operation and it had only limited success, but it was linked to the other escapes and became a legend and a source of pride for the resistance movements. After the Holocaust, credit for this action was claimed by various elements.

In addition to offering resistance and going into hiding, hundreds of Jews attempted to flee to Switzerland and southern France, and from there to Spain. Many dozens of members of the Zionist youth movements succeeded in such attempts. In 1943, a few dozen Jews were saved from imprisonment and deportation because they were on the list of candidates for the exchange of Jews and Germans (*see* EXCHANGE: JEWS AND GERMANS). All in all, initiative on the part of Jews played a central role in the operations that enabled a relatively large proportion of the Jews of Belgium to be saved.

After Liberation. The rehabilitation of Belgian Jewry was a difficult and painful process. At first, the Belgian authorities did not want the Jews who had not been Belgian nationals before the war to remain in the country. The restitution of Jewish property also ran into difficulties. Another problem was the guardianship of the war orphans and the kind of upbringing they were to have; this issue caused friction among the various Jewish organizations, and also between the Jews and the Belgian authorities. The first attempt at reorganizing the Jewish community was made by Jews who came out of hiding after liberation; one body formed at this early stage was the Comité Central Israélite pour la Reconstruction de la Vie Religieuse en Belgique (Central Jewish Committee for the Reconstruction of Religious Life in Belgium). An important role was played in the first few months after liberation by the Jewish chaplains in the Allied forces and by the JEWISH BRIGADE GROUP, which was posted to Belgium in early August 1945, with bases at Tournai and Ghent. Soldiers of the brigade were involved in the renewal of Zionist activity and in the search for Jewish orphans and their return to the Jewish fold.

In the first postwar years the Zionist parties and youth movements were reestablished, amid a good deal of squabbling. The leftist Zionist parties gradually lost ground, and radical non-Zionist leftist parties did not make a comeback. Hundreds of war orphans and members of the Zionist youth movements left for Palestine, while others emigrated to other destinations. In Antwerp and Brussels, Jewish community life was restored, although on a much smaller scale than in the past; in other places, such as Liège, restoration occurred on a negligible scale.

On April 19, 1970, a memorial for the murdered Jews of Belgium was unveiled at Anderlecht, and on October 16, 1987, a memorial was dedicated in the Valley of the Destroyed Jewish Communities at YAD VASHEM in Jerusalem. Every year, survivors of the Holocaust and former resistance fighters hold a memorial march to the Dossin camp at Mechelen, the point of departure for the deportation of Belgian Jews to the extermination camps. Dozens of non-Jewish Belgians have been awarded the medal of "RIGHTEOUS AMONG THE NATIONS" by Yad Vashem for saving Jews during the war years.

In early 1981 a court in Kiel, Germany, tried Ernst Ehlers, the man who had been chief of the Sicherheitspolizei (Security Police) and the SD (Sicherheitsdienst; Security Service) in Belgium and northern France in the period from 1941 to 1944. Also tried were his successor in that post, Konstantin Canaris, and the head of the Jewish section in the Sicherheitspolizei and SD, Kurt Asche. Ehlers committed suicide before the trial opened, and Canaris was set free because of his poor health. Asche was found guilty as an accessory to murder and was sentenced, on July 8, 1981, to seven years for his part in the deportation of the Jews of Belgium.

BIBLIOGRAPHY

Gutman, Y., and C. J. Haft, eds. *Patterns of Jewish Leadership in Nazi Europe, 1933–1945.* Jerusalem, 1979. See pages 353–376.

Klarsfeld, S., and M. Steinberg. *Die Endlösung der Judenfrage in Belgien: Dokumente.* New York, 1980.

Ministère de la Justice, Commission des Crimes de Guerre. *Les crimes de guerre commis sous l'occupation de la Belgique, 1940–1945.* Liège, 1947–1948.

Steinberg, L. *Le Comité de défense des Juifs en Belgique, 1942–1944.* Brussels, 1973.

Steinberg, M. *Le dossier Bruxelles-Auschwitz: La police et l'extermination des Juifs de Belgique.* Brussels, 1981.

Steinberg, M. *L'étoile et le fusil.* 3 vols. Brussels, 1983–1986.

DAN MICHMAN

BELGRADE, capital of SERBIA in the nineteenth century and of YUGOSLAVIA from 1918. On the eve of World War II, Belgrade had three hundred thousand inhabitants. Jews are known to have lived in the city since the Middle Ages. On the eve of the German occupation of Yugoslavia, there were about eleven thousand Jews, mostly Sephardic (80 percent to 90 percent), in Belgrade, which was also the seat of the Federation of Jewish Communities in Yugoslavia.

On April 6, 1941, Germany, together with its allies Italy, Hungary, and Bulgaria, invaded Yugoslavia. Belgrade suffered heavy bombardment and about three thousand inhabitants were killed, including Jews. On April 13 the Germans occupied the city. A short while later, the authorities were instructed to carry out a census, and about nine thousand Jews were counted. Most of the Jewish men and some of the young women were organized into labor groups and employed mainly in clearing the ruins.

In the first months of the occupation, the military government issued many decrees aimed at harming the situation and livelihood of the Jews and restricting their contacts with the non-Jewish population. After the outbreak of the Serbian revolt against the Germans in July 1941, mass arrests of the Jewish males in Belgrade commenced, and until late August most were interned in the Topovske Šupe concentration camp on the outskirts of the city. From September to November of that year, the prisoners were put to death by firing squads of the German army, on the pretext (as recorded in German sources) that the Jews had participated in the opposition movement. In December 1941 all the Jewish women and children in Belgrade were arrested and taken to the SAJMIŠTE concentration camp near the city. In early March 1942 a gas van was sent from Berlin to Belgrade, and by early May all the women and children in Sajmište had been gassed to death. In August 1942 Dr. Harold Turner, head of the German civilian administration in Serbia, sent a report to his superiors in which he claimed: "Serbia is the only country in Europe in which the Jewish problem has been solved."

It is estimated that the Germans murdered about 90 percent of the Jews of Belgrade. After the war, about twenty-two hundred Jews returned to the city.

BIBLIOGRAPHY

Browning, C. *Fateful Months: Essays on the Emergence of the Final Solution.* New York, 1985. See chapters 2–4.

Ivanović, L. "Teror nad jevrejima u okupiranom Beogradu." *Godisniak grada Beograda* 13 (1966): 289–316.

MENACHEM SHELAH

BELORUSSIA (White Russia), Soviet republic in the western USSR. Until the thirteenth century the principalities of Belorussia were part of Kievan Russia; following the Mongol invasion of 1240, they became a separate entity. In the fourteenth century Belorussia was part of the principality of Lithuania, whose population, for the most part, was Belorussian and whose official language was also Belorussian. With the unification of Lithuania and Poland in 1569, Belorussia became part of the Polish kingdom.

In the seventeenth century Moscow seized substantial parts of Belorussia and, following the three partitions of Poland (in 1772, 1793, and 1795), it annexed the entire area of Belorussia. This was one of the most backward regions of European Russia: its population had no clear national identity of its own, it faced diverse and vexing social problems, 75 percent of its inhabitants worked on the land, and 71 percent were illiterate. During World War I Belorussia was a battle zone, and after the war it was the scene of fighting between the Soviets and the Poles. Under the Treaty of Riga (March 18, 1921) Belorussia was split up, the western part going to Poland and the eastern part becoming one of the Soviet Union's socialist republics. On September 17, 1939, the Red Army entered western Belorussia and incorporated it with all of its component districts into the Belorussian SSR. These districts were those of Vilna (Vilnius;

except for the city of Vilna and its environs, which were handed over to Lithuania), Novogrudok, BIAŁYSTOK, and Polesye.

Jewish communities were founded in Belorussia as early as the fourteenth century, in BREST-LITOVSK and GRODNO. After the unification of Lithuania and Poland, the authorities encouraged the settlement of Poles and Jews in Belorussia. When Belorussia was incorporated into tsarist Russia, it was included in the Pale of Settlement, the area where Jews were permitted to reside. Belorussian Jews suffered from all the tsarist anti-Jewish decrees and from persecution and pogroms. In the wake of the 1881 pogroms and the subsequent anti-Jewish measures, they emigrated to the West in large numbers.

Belorussia was a center of Jewish religious studies, as was Lithuania. The two Jewish communities were very similar in their way of life and creativity. Renowned rabbinical academies (yeshivas) were established, in VOLOZHIN, MIR, and many other centers. Belorussia was a center of the Hasidic pietistic movement and of the opponents of the Hasidim, known as the Misnagdim. A high proportion of Belorussia's Jews were manual workers, and a broad network of educational and mutual-aid institutions existed.

Western Belorussia. During the period following World War I the Jews of the western part of Belorussia, then under Polish rule, were hard hit by the anti-Jewish policies pursued in that border region by the Polish government. The effects of these policies hastened the pauperization process of the entire Jewish community.

The entry of Soviet forces into western Belorussia, on September 17, 1939, was a relief for the Jews, in view of the Nazi threat they had been facing, but it also aroused mixed feelings among large parts of the Jewish population. As it turned out, during the twenty-one months of Soviet rule the situation of the Jews in many respects underwent a rapid process of deterioration that eroded the very basis of Jewish existence. Many Jews lost their livelihood, Jewish public institutions were dissolved, and the anti-Jewish animosity of the population grew to unprecedented dimensions. The Soviet regime withheld from the Jews information on the basic elements of Nazi policy toward them.

On the eve of the German invasion of the USSR (June 22, 1941), the Jewish population of western Belorussia, including the Jews from western Poland who had taken refuge there, numbered 670,000. The German army advanced at lightning speed, occupying western Belorussia and reaching the old Polish-Soviet border within a week. A wave of pogroms, staged by the local population, swept over large parts of the region, much to the Germans' satisfaction. The Germans themselves, from the very beginning, launched one *Aktion* after another, in which 40 percent of the Jews of the Vilna, Novogrudok, and Polesye districts were murdered. In some places, the majority of the Jews were killed. Except for a part of the Jewish population of the Białystok district, the Jews of Belorussia were murdered in pits near the places where they had lived, and were buried on the spot. The first wave of *Aktionen* lasted until December 1941, and, as in other parts of the Soviet Union occupied by the Germans, they marked the beginning of the "FINAL SOLUTION." The *Aktionen* in this first wave were carried out by Einsatzgruppe B units: Sonderkommandos 7a and 7b, Einsatzkommandos 8 and 9, and units of Vorkommando Moskau, an advance detachment commanded by Franz Walter Six. At a subsequent stage, units of Einsatzgruppe A also participated in the slaughter. The mass murder came to a standstill in the winter of 1941–1942, because the Germans needed the manpower to help cope with the difficulties they were encountering in preparing for a long war, contrary to their earlier expectations. The economic situation in Belorussia and the harsh winter weather also obstructed the extermination program.

The second wave of mass murder began in the spring of 1942, and ended only with the total annihilation of the Jews of western Belorussia. The rise in partisan operations during that period prompted the Germans to accelerate the pace of extermination. According to German data, by the end of 1942 only thirty thousand Jews were left in Belorussia (excluding the Białystok district). In the course of that year most of the ghettos in western Belorussia were liquidated (*see* Table 1); the last to suffer this fate were the ghettos of Glubokoye (August 20, 1943) and Lida

TABLE 1. *Liquidation of Seventy-Four Ghettos in Western Belorussia*

PERIOD OF LIQUIDATION	VILNA DISTRICT	POLESYE DISTRICT	NOVOGRUDOK DISTRICT	TOTAL	PERCENTAGE
To end of 1941	3	1	2	6	8.0
From early to mid-1942	10		8	18	24.0
From mid-1942 to end 1942	5	17	14	36	49.0
From early to mid-1943	7	1	3	11	15.0
Second half of 1943	2		1	3	4.0
Total	27	19	28	74	100.0

(September 18, 1943). From the KOLDICHEVO camp, the last Jews fled on March 7, 1944.

The Jewish underground. The struggle of the Jews of Belorussia had various aspects: exerting a daily effort to stay alive in the ghettos, going into hiding, escaping from the ghetto, and joining armed undergrounds. Thousands of Jews went into hiding in bunkers and various other places of concealment; in the 16 ghettos for which data exist, twelve thousand six hundred persons hid in such places. Underground organizations were set up, following the first wave of *Aktionen*, in the Vilna, Novogroduk, and Polesye districts. In some instances these organizations were the continuation of the Zionist pioneering underground that had operated under the Soviet regime, from 1939 to 1941. In 94 out of 111 ghettos or other places with Jews in western Belorussia (not including the Białystok district and the city of Vilna), there were underground organizations and acts of resistance; 64 had an organized underground and in 30 other places there are recorded cases of resistance, although no organized underground is known to have existed in them. Members of the underground came from the Zionist youth movements Ha-Shomer ha-Tsa'ir, He-Haluts, He-Haluts ha-Tsa'ir, Betar, Ha-No'ar ha-Tsiyyoni, and Gordonia; from the Hebrew Tarbut (Zionist-oriented) schools and the Yiddish schools; and from adult groups. Forty-two of these underground groups had in their possession 500 rifles, 150 pistols, 35 machine guns, and 20 submachine guns. The number of Jews from the Vilna, Novogrudok, and Polesye districts who fled to the forests is estimated as at least twenty-five thousand.

The Jews of the Białystok district. The Białystok district was incorporated into East Prussia on July 17, 1941, thus becoming part of the Reich. Białystok itself had a Jewish population of sixty thousand to seventy thousand. When the Germans took the city in June of that year they launched an *Aktion* in which they murdered two thousand Jews, and several thousand more were killed in July. This was followed by a period of relative quiet in Białystok. In the provincial towns of the Białystok district, large-scale *Aktionen* took place; those who managed to escape from them took refuge in the city of Białystok. The extermination of the surviving Jewish population of the Białystok district was undertaken on November 2, 1942. At that point the number of Jews was still quite substantial. They were rounded up and put into transit camps, and in November and December were taken to the TREBLINKA extermination camp.

In early February 1943 a week-long *Aktion* was conducted in Białystok, in the course of which 12,000 Jews were murdered (2,000 were killed on the spot). Efraim BARASZ, the JUDENRAT (Jewish Council) chairman, continued to believe that the ghetto would not be liquidated, because the Germans needed the manpower it provided. On August 16, 1943, the Germans surrounded the ghetto. The uprising in the ghetto, commanded by Mordechai TENENBAUM, with the participation of the Dror, Ha-Shomer ha-Tsa'ir, Communist, and Betar movements, went on for several days, until the last of the fighters fell. Over 25,000 Białystok Jews were transported to Treblinka, and 1,200 children from Białystok were sent to AUSCHWITZ. Another 2,000 Jews, who had been in the "Small Ghetto," were sent to MAJDANEK. A few Jews from Białystok managed to escape and join the partisans; of these, 60 survived.

Eastern Belorussia. Large Jewish communities existed in the cities of eastern Belorussia. In the 1897 census, Jews had formed the majority of the population in these cities: in MINSK, 56.4 percent of the total; in MOGILEV, 54.3 percent; in VITEBSK, 56.3 percent; in GOMEL (Homel), 55.9 percent; in Orsha, 62.3 percent, and in Bobruisk, 63.1 percent. Because of emigration, however, and because Jews moved to other cities (including Moscow and Leningrad), the proportion of Jews in these cities went down, and in the 1926 census they no longer constituted the majority of these urban populations.

The October Revolution of 1917 posed new and basic problems for the Jews. As members of the middle class they found themselves deprived of their sources of livelihood, their employment and social status, and their traditional way of life. Jewish culture and education came under sharp attack. The autonomous Jewish community framework was dissolved, and the only official Jewish body permitted was the Communist party's "Jewish Section" (Yevsektsiya), which conducted an aggressive propaganda drive against traditional Jewish religious life. Jewish schools, academies, and synagogues were closed down. Many Jews however, continued to observe traditional customs in the privacy of their homes, and the Zionist youth movements Ha-Shomer ha-Tsa'ir and He-Haluts maintained their operations, clandestinely, until the late 1920s.

Minsk was the center of Yiddish culture and literature, and in the 1932–1933 school year, 36,650 Jewish children attended Yiddish schools. During the following years, however, a sharp turn was made as the Soviet purges were launched. In the mid-1930s the number of Jewish schools declined rapidly. The hundreds of clandestine Jewish schools that had been in existence were liquidated, and Jewish intellectuals were imprisoned, exiled, or executed.

In the 1926 census, 407,000 Jews were counted in eastern Belorussia (8.2 percent of the population). Minsk had a Jewish population of 53,686 (40.8 percent of the total); Gomel, 37,453 (43.7 percent); Vitebsk, 37,013 (37.5 percent); and Bobruisk, 21,558 Jews (42 percent of the total). In the 1939 census the number of Jews was down to 375,000, and on the eve of the German invasion in June 1941 it was 405,000, including Jewish refugees from western Belorussia and other parts of Poland.

With the outbreak of the war, the Germans speedily conquered eastern Belorussia. Minsk was taken on June 28, 1941, Vitebsk on July 11, and by July 16 German forces had reached SMOLENSK. Many Jews fled eastward to save their lives, but German forces dropped by parachutes barred the roads, and most of the refugees who had gone in the direction of Orsha and Moscow were intercepted and had to turn back. However, those who fled to the Gomel area made good their escape, since Gomel was taken by the Germans only on August 19. An estimated 120,000 Jews living in eastern Belorussia succeeded in escaping to the Soviet interior.

The Germans immediately began a program of mass murder, seeing the Jews of the Soviet Union as the personification of "Judeo-Bolshevism." The indifference of the majority of the population to the fate of the Jews encouraged the Germans to accelerate the massacres, and the difficulties they came to encounter on the front had the effect of increasing the rate at which the extermination proceeded. Jews living in small towns and villages were moved into larger ghettos. In some places, such as Bobruisk and Slutsk, the ghettos were set up in the open country. In Lepel the Jews had to vacate their homes and move into the ghetto at two hours' notice. They were left without water or food in houses without windowpanes, thirty to forty persons to each house, without fuel or warm clothing, and in a temperature of minus 77 degrees Fahrenheit (minus 25 degrees centigrade). Similar conditions prevailed in other ghettos in the area.

Reports submitted by the Einsatzgruppen accused the Jews of "maintaining contact with the partisans"; in some instances the reports cite reasons for killing the Jews: for "acts of sabotage," "refusal to obey orders," "offering resistance," and so on. Some of the reports contain figures for the number of partisans killed, in place of the figures for the Jews, and in others, "Jews and partisans" are lumped together.

By the end of 1941 the Jews of thirty-five ghettos had been murdered, among them those in the major cities, which contained the largest concentration of Jews—Gomel, Mogilev, Vitebsk, and Bobruisk. Together, they accounted for a third of the entire Jewish population of eastern Belorussia. In most of the ghettos the Jews had been killed by the end of October 1941. Only the Minsk ghetto, which with 100,000 Jews had the largest single concentration of Jews, remained in existence until October 1943.

The mass murder of Jews was carried out in huge pits that were prepared close to the ghettos. The Jews of Mogilev were murdered in Pashkovo, Pulkovichi, Smolevichi, and the Gorodishche Forest; the Jews of Cherven in Glinishche; those of Bobruisk in Kiselevich; those of Vitebsk in Ilov and Tserkoshchina; and the Jews of Minsk in MALY TROSTINETS. In Minsk, Pleshchenitsy, Gomel, Vitebsk, and Mogilev the Germans used GAS VANS (*dushkovki*). In the Minsk ghetto some ninety thousand Jews were murdered in consecutive *Aktionen*, five of them on a large scale, and several "interim" and "night" *Aktionen*. The killings were carried out by Einsatzgruppe B units, Sonderkommandos 7a and 7b, Vorkommando Moskau, Einsatzkommandos 8 and 9, Police Battalions 316 and 322, Lithuanian units, Belorussian police, and Ukrainian auxiliary units.

The Minsk ghetto had an underground organization that operated up to the very end. Approximately 10,000 Jews escaped from Minsk into the forest. In the period from November 1941 to October 1942, 35,442 Jews from the Reich and the Protectorate of BOHEMIA AND MORAVIA were also brought to Minsk to be killed. A transit camp was set up 5 miles (8 km) from Bobruisk, to which Jews from the west were brought. The first consignment, consisting of 960 Jews from Warsaw, arrived at the camp on May 29, 1942, followed on July 28, 1942, by another 500 Jews, and at a later date by more Jews from Warsaw. A total of 2,000 Jews were assembled in the camp; those who still survived in September 1943 were murdered that month. Mogilev was the site of a transit camp (*Dulag*, from *Durchgangslager*) for Jews and Communist party activists; 196 persons were murdered in that camp.

Belorussian Jews offered resistance in the various ghettos, and a small proportion escaped to the forests. Of the Jews surviving among the partisans in the forests, only a very few returned to their homes at the end of the war. Some five thousand Jews went back to Minsk, most of them from the forest. They were later joined by Jews who in the first few days of the war had fled to the Soviet interior, and Jews from other parts of the country. Throughout the war the majority of the local population evinced an unfriendly or even hostile attitude to the Jews; some, including Communist party activists, were extremely hostile. A very small minority showed a humane attitude, and some of these saved a few Jews.

The 1959 census reported 150,000 Jews in Belorussia, representing 1.9 percent of the total population; the 1970 census showed 148,000 Jews—1.64 percent of the total. Almost a third of all the Jews of Belorussia live in Minsk, the capital of the republic. In the Gomel and Mogilev districts the Jews represent 2 percent of the total population, in the Vitebsk district their proportion is 1 percent, and in the three remaining districts—Minsk, Brest-Litovsk, and Grodno—less than 0.5 percent.

BIBLIOGRAPHY

Cholawski, S. *The Jews in Belorussia (White Russia) during World War II.* Tel Aviv, 1982. (In Hebrew.)

Ehrenburg, I., and V. Grossman, eds. *The Black Book of Soviet Jewry.* New York, 1980.

Kalush, V. *In the Service of the People for a Free Byelorussia: Biographical Notes on Professor Radoslav Ostrovski.* London, 1964.

Krausnick, H., and H.-H. Wilhelm. *Die Truppe des Weltanschauungskrieges: Die Einsatzgruppen der Sicherheitspolizei und des SD.* Stuttgart, 1981.

Orbach, W. "The Destruction of the Jews in the Nazi-occupied Territories of the USSR." *Soviet Jewish Affairs* 6/2 (October 1976):14–51.

SHALOM CHOLAWSKI

BEŁŻEC, extermination camp in Poland. Bełżec was a small town in the southeastern part of the Lublin district, on the Lublin-Lvov railway line. In early 1940 the Germans set up a camp there for Jewish forced labor, which they used to build fortifications and dig antitank ditches along the demarcation line between German- and Soviet-occupied Poland. The camp was closed down at the end of the year. On November 1, 1941, as part of AKTION REINHARD, the Germans began construction of an extermination camp at Bełżec. The site they chose was near the Bełżec railway station, about 1,620 feet (500 m) away on a railway siding. It contained some of the antitank ditches that had been dug the previous year, and these were now destined to become mass graves for the Jews who were to be murdered in the camp.

Initially, the construction work was carried out by Poles from Bełżec, but these were later replaced by Jews from ghettos in the neighboring towns. Of the SS men who were in charge of the camp construction and operation, most had taken part in the EUTHANASIA PROGRAM, including the camp's first commandant, Polizeihauptmann and SS-Hauptsturmführer Christian WIRTH. When the camp was operating, its staff included twenty to thirty German SS men, who held the command and administration positions and oversaw the extermination program. There were also between ninety and one hundred twenty Ukrainian men from the TRAWNIKI camp—all of

them Soviet prisoners of war who had volunteered to serve the Germans—whose job it was to stand guard over the camp and the extermination process, quash any resistance from Jews being taken off the incoming rail transports, and prevent any attempts at escape. Among the Ukrainian group there were also Soviet VOLKSDEUTSCHE (ethnic Germans) who held junior command positions. The German staff had their quarters outside the camp, while the Ukrainians were housed inside. In addition to the German and Ukrainian staff, the camp used Jewish prisoners for various local jobs and services.

First Stage. In its first stage the Bełżec camp had three gas chambers, located in a 26-by-40-foot (8 × 12 m) barrack. The structure had double walls, with sand in between for insulation, and was divided into three rooms, each 13 by 26 feet (4 × 8 m). The floor of the gas chambers and the walls, up to a height of over 3 feet (1 m), were covered with tin sheets. A corridor led to the three doors of the gas chambers. Each door was 5 to 6 feet (1.8 m) high and 3.5 feet (1.1 m) wide, with rubber strips fastened to its sides so that when it was closed it sealed hermetically. The doors were made of hard wood, to resist pressure from inside the chambers, and could be opened only from the outside. Each gas chamber had an additional opening, for the removal of the corpses. There were pipes in the chambers through which the gas was pumped in.

By the end of February 1942, the gas chambers were ready for a test of their effective functioning. Several groups of Jews were brought in from Lubycze Królewska for this purpose and put into the chambers. The gas that was used (carbon monoxide) came in metal containers and was piped into the gas chambers. In addition to the Jews brought in from the outside, the Jewish prisoners who had been working on the construction of the camp were also gassed in this trial run. In the course of the initial testing, a 250-horsepower diesel engine was installed outside the gas chambers to generate the carbon monoxide gas and pump it into the pipes. This became the method that was to be used throughout the period of the camp's operation.

The Bełżec camp was relatively small, square in shape, with each side measuring 886 feet (270 m), and enclosed by a barbed-wire fence. To camouflage the inside of the camp, tree branches were affixed to the fence and trees were planted along the perimeter. There was a watchtower in each corner and one in the center of the camp, near the gas chambers. On the north side of the square was the gate through which the trains entered the camp area.

The camp was divided into two sections: the larger one in the northwestern part and the smaller in the eastern part. The former was named Camp I and contained the administration buildings, the staff quarters, the railway platform, and the track leading to it (which was long enough to hold twenty freight cars). The Jews who were taken off the cars were first concentrated in an adjacent lot in which there were two barracks; in one of them the prisoners had to take off their clothes, while the other served as a storeroom. The eastern part, named Camp II, contained the gas chambers and the antitank ditches. This extermination area was separated from the rest of the camp by a fence. Between the barrack in Camp I where the Jews took off their clothes and the gas chambers in Camp II was a path known as the "tube" (*Schlauch*), 6.5 feet (2 m) wide and several dozen yards long, fenced in on both sides. It was along this path that the Jews, now naked, were led to their death.

By March 17, 1942, the main installations had been constructed and tried out, and the mass extermination program was launched.

Mechanics of Extermination. From among the young males who arrived in the camp, some who were fit were selected and put to work. In the early stage, this "respite" delayed their death only by a day or two, or a few days at the most, until they too were sent to the gas chambers, and their places as workers taken by new arrivals. Later on, for the sake of greater efficiency, groups of men numbering from seven hundred to one thousand were kept alive for a longer period and forced to work in the extermination area. They were split up into work teams of various sizes, ranging from a few dozen to several hundred.

One of the teams was employed on the railway platform, where their job was to clean the freight cars from which the Jews had been forced, to take down those Jews who were unable to get off on their own, and to remove the corpses of the Jews who had not survived the train ride. Another team was assigned to the area where the victims had to undress and

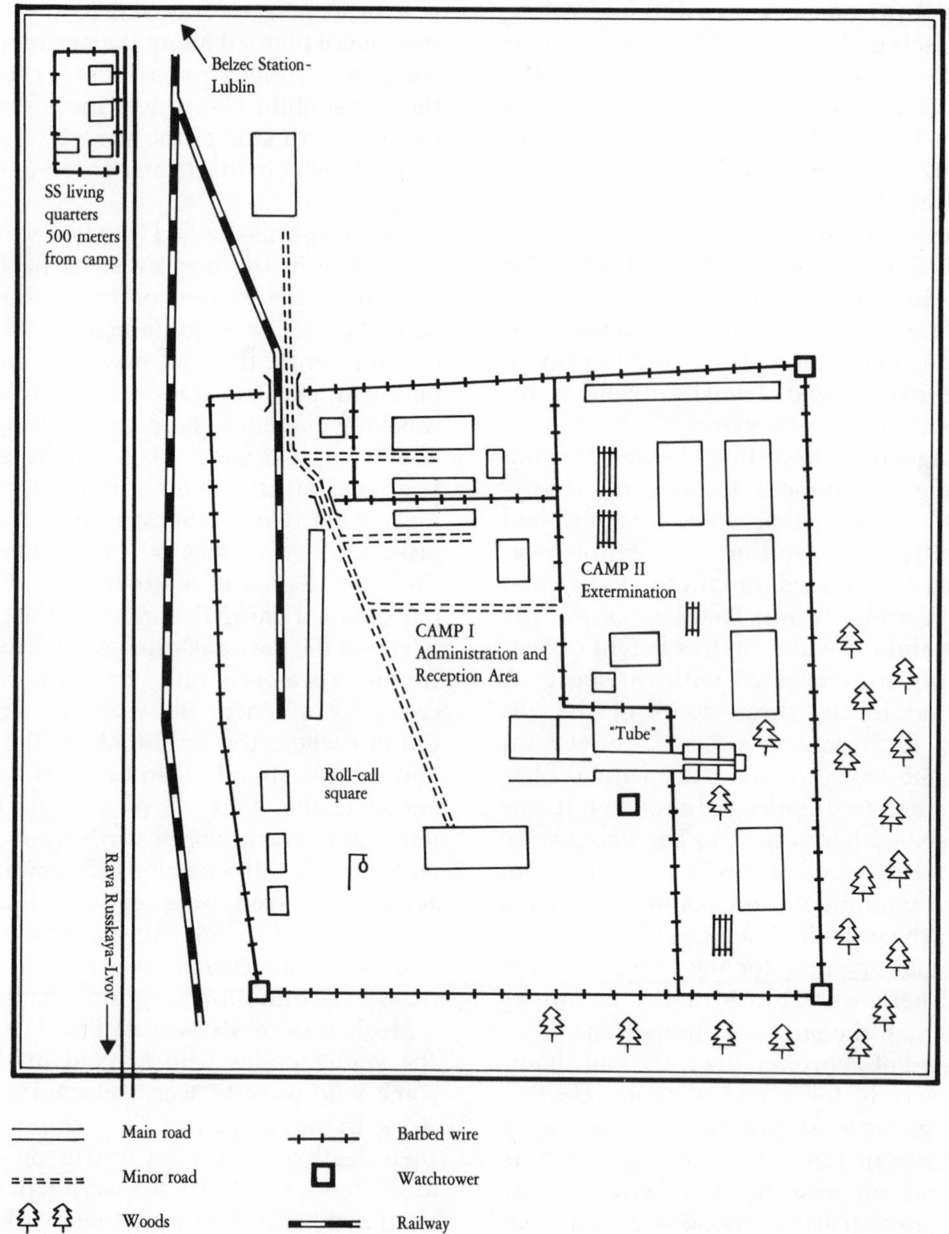

Plan of the Bełżec concentration camp.

leave their clothes and other belongings behind. This team was divided into several subgroups for specific tasks, such as collecting the discarded items, sorting them out, removing the yellow badges from the clothes, and making a search for money or valuables that the victims might have hidden in their clothes or other belongings. Another job for this team was to prepare all the clothes and other items for shipment to an outside destination. After a few months had passed, a new practice was introduced in the procedure leading to extermination: the women were shorn of their hair (which was to be used in the manufacture of felt footwear). This task too was allotted to one of the teams. The prisoners who made up the work teams were housed in several barracks in Camp I, together with a group of artisans—tailors, cobblers, carpenters, and so on—who worked for the camp staff.

Several hundred Jewish prisoners were allotted to Camp II, their assignment being to remove the corpses from the gas chambers and inter them in the burial pits. A special group, nicknamed "the dentists," had the job of extracting gold teeth from the mouths of the dead Jews.

At all times, the prisoners working in the camp were subject to maltreatment and cruelty, by both the Germans and the Ukrainians, and to *Selektionen,* which meant the immediate execution of those selected. Only a handful of prisoners held out for more than a few months. The murdered prisoners were replaced by other Jews chosen from the new arrivals.

In the first four weeks of operation, from March 17 to mid-April 1942, a total of about 80,000 Jews were murdered in the Bełżec camp: 30,000 from the Lublin ghetto, 15,000 from Lvov, and the rest from other ghettos in the Lublin district and Eastern Galicia.

The *modus operandi* of the Bełżec extermination machine, as devised by Wirth, was as follows. A train consisting of forty to sixty freight cars would arrive at the Bełżec railway station, after a trip lasting several hours—sometimes several days—under horrible conditions, with no water or toilet facilities, and with 100 to 130 Jews packed into each car. Many did not survive the trip and died en route. When the train came to a halt, twenty of the freight cars, with a total of 2,000 to 2,500 Jews aboard, were detached from the train and attached to a locomotive that pulled them into the camp. Once inside, the Jews were ordered out of the cars, and one of the German officers announced that they had arrived at a transit camp, for onward distribution to various labor camps. They were also told that they would now be disinfected and washed, for their own hygiene's sake, and that they had to hand over any money or valuables in their possession. The men were separated

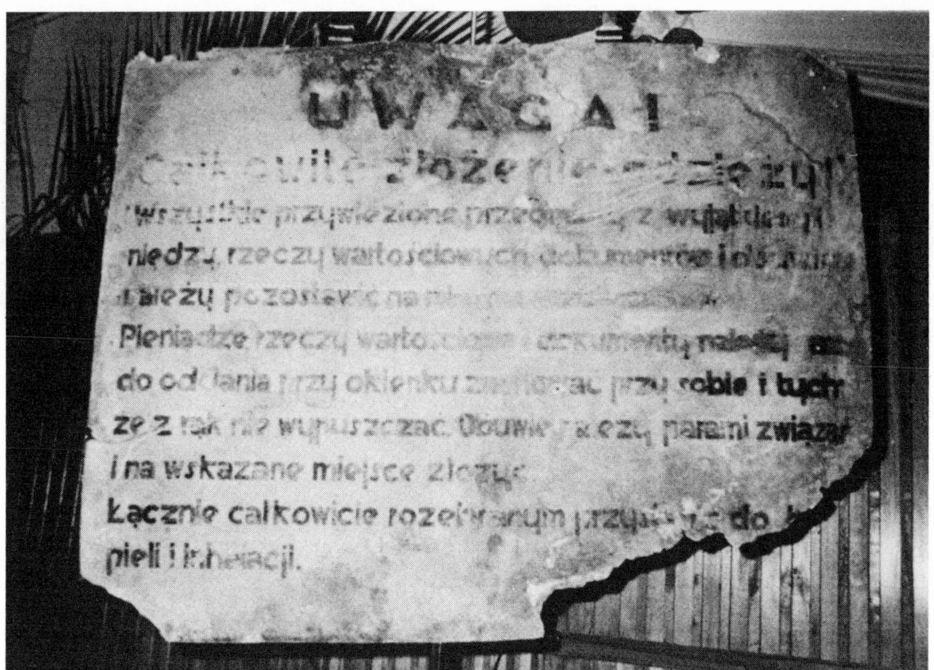

A sign from the Bełżec extermination camp. The Polish text reads: "ATTENTION. All belongings must be handed in at the counter except for money, documents, and other valuables, which you must keep with you. Shoes should be tied together in pairs and placed in the area marked for shoes. Afterward one must go completely naked to the showers."

from the women and children, and both groups were ordered to strip. With the Germans and Ukrainians shouting, threatening, and beating them, the Jews were rushed into the "showers"—that is, the gas chambers. As soon as they were locked in, the engine was started and the carbon monoxide began to flow into the gas chambers, killing all those inside within twenty or thirty minutes.

At first, the whole process, from the arrival of the cars in the camp to the removal of the corpses from the gas chambers, took three to four hours; as time went on, more efficient methods were introduced in the process and it took only sixty to ninety minutes. During the time that the twenty freight cars that had entered the camp were being cleaned and pulled out of the camp, twenty other cars took their place inside. The system was based on subterfuge and deception, to ensure that from the time the prisoners boarded the train to the moment the gas chamber doors closed behind them, they would believe that they were on their way to a labor camp.

Second Stage. In mid-April 1942, the camp ceased operating (the transports had temporarily halted) and was inactive for a month. The murder operation was resumed in May, and the transports that came in now also included Jews from the Kraków ghetto and the Kraków district. The German officers in charge had learned from experience that three gas chambers would not be enough to kill all the victims scheduled to be brought to Bełżec; a decision was therefore made to build larger gas chambers, and in order for this construction work to be carried out, as of mid-June the transports were discontinued for a month.

The existing gas chambers were demolished, and in their place a new building, made of brick and concrete and containing six 13-by-16-foot (4 × 5 m) cells, was erected. In the center of the building was a corridor with three doors on each side for entering the gas chambers. Each chamber had another opening on the outside wall, through which the corpses of the victims were later removed. The new gas chambers had a total capacity of 1,000 to 1,200 victims at a time, about half the number contained in twenty freight cars. Over the entrance to the building was a sign reading "Showers and Disinfection Rooms."

The transports were renewed in the second week of July and kept arriving on a regular schedule until the beginning of December. From July to October, about 130,000 Jews were brought to the camp from the Kraków district, and about 225,000 from the Lvov area in Eastern Galicia; there were also transports from the southern subdistricts of the Lublin and Radom districts. Some of the transports to Bełżec brought German, Austrian, and Czechoslovak Jews who had earlier been deported from their native countries to ghettos in Poland. The Germans were also planning to bring 200,000 Romanian Jews to Bełżec, but this plan was not carried out since the Romanian government refused to surrender Jews to the Germans.

The total number of murder victims in Bełżec was 600,000, virtually all Jews, with a few hundred (or at most a few thousand) Gypsies. This figure was confirmed by the Główna Komisja Badania Zbrodni Hitlerowskich w Polsce (MAIN COMMISSION FOR INVESTIGATION OF NAZI CRIMES IN POLAND) and was accepted by the judicial authorities of the Federal Republic of Germany.

Obliteration of the Camp. In December 1942, the transports to Bełżec and the extermination operation there came to an end. By this time most of the Jews of the GENERALGOUVERNEMENT had been killed, and the SS authorities in charge of Aktion Reinhard shut down the camp. SOBIBÓR and TREBLINKA, two extermination camps that had been constructed after Bełżec, continued to function, as did the AUSCHWITZ-Birkenau extermination camp.

Between December 1942 and spring 1943, the mass graves in Bełżec were opened and the bodies of the murder victims were exhumed and cremated. A special installation was put up to serve as a crematorium, made out of iron rails used for railways. Bones that resisted the flames were crushed, and these remains, together with the ashes, were buried in the ditches from which the corpses had been removed.

When the cremation of the bodies was completed, the camp was dismantled and all visible traces of the mass murder of which it had been the scene were removed. The Jewish prisoners, some six hundred in number, who had been kept behind in the camp were sent to Sobibór to be put to death there. In the final period, from the beginning of August 1942, the camp commander was SS-Hauptsturmführer Gottlieb Hering, who had replaced Christian Wirth. (Wirth had been appointed inspector of all the extermination camps set up under Aktion Reinhard.) After the camp was dismantled, the farmers in the area swarmed over the site, looking for money and gold that the Jews were rumored to have hidden there in the ground. To put an end to this, the Germans posted a Ukrainian guard, converted the grounds into a farm, and gave it to the guard. The area was plowed under and sown, and trees were planted on it. In the summer of 1944 the Bełżec area was liberated by the Red Army and the Polish army. It is now a national shrine.

Only a few individuals succeeded in escaping from Bełżec, and only one survived to tell the gruesome tale—Rudolf Reder, who spent four months in the camp and escaped in November 1942. After the war, Reder gave written testimony, which appeared in the form of a booklet, on what he had witnessed there. Apart from this one source, information on Bełżec has been difficult to come by, compared with evidence on the other extermination camps.

BIBLIOGRAPHY

Arad, Y. *Operation Reinhard Death Camps: Belzec, Sobibor, and Treblinka.* Bloomington, 1987.

Donat, A., ed. *The Death Camp Treblinka.* New York, 1979.

Reder, R. *Bełżec.* Kraków, 1946.

Ruckerl, A., ed. *Nationalsozialistische Vernichtungslager im Spiegel deutschen Strafprozesse: Belzec, Sobibor, Treblinka, Chelmno.* Munich, 1977.

Tregenza, M. "Belzec Deathcamp." *Wiener Library Bulletin* 30 (1977): 8–25.

YITZHAK ARAD

BENEŠ, EDVARD (1884–1948), Czech statesman. In prewar Czechoslovakia, Beneš was closely associated with his mentor, Tomáš G. Masaryk, founder of the Czechoslovak republic. Beneš headed his country's delegation to the Paris Peace Conference in 1919 and served as foreign minister of independent Czechoslovakia. His policy aimed at establishing a balance of power in eastern Europe; he negotiated treaties with Romania and Yugoslavia (the Little Entente) and counted on French hegemony as a spearhead against the German-Hungarian alliance. After the signing of a mutual pact with the Soviet Union in 1935, he also came to rely on that country as a safeguard against foes.

After President Masaryk's resignation in 1935, Beneš was elected as his successor. During the Sudeten crisis in September 1938, Beneš—abandoned by the Western allies—capitulated before Hitler's ultimatum and ceded the Sudetenland to Germany. He resigned on October 5 of that year and went into exile. After the outbreak of World War II, he established in France a Czechoslovak national committee, which moved to London in 1940, and he was recognized on July 21, 1941, as the president of the CZECHOSLOVAK GOVERNMENT-IN-EXILE.

Dr. Edvard Beneš, president of Czechoslovakia. [National Archives]

The Czech army intelligence and its network of agents in Europe had the reputation of being well informed. Consequently, Beneš was requested by the London office of the World Jewish Congress to verify the information about the Nazi extermination plan that reached Geneva in August 1942 (*see* RIEGNER CABLE). In his belated reply, Beneš claimed: "There seems to be no clear indication that the Germans are preparing for a wholesale extermination of all the Jews . . . although innumerable Jews are being severely persecuted and suffer from starvation." But shortly thereafter, the Jewish Agency announced that atrocity reports had been verified, and on December 15, 1942, the Beneš government strongly condemned the murder of Jews. Throughout the war years, Beneš maintained a close and friendly relationship with Jewish leaders and staunchly supported Jewish national aspirations in Palestine and the struggle for a Jewish state. He also took steps to minimize antisemitism in the Czechoslovak armed forces.

As head of the only eastern European government-in-exile allowed to return after the war, Beneš reestablished his government in Czechoslovakia in April 1945. After 1945 Czechoslovakia became a reunited country, and the Jews lost their status as a recognized minority group, having to declare themselves Czechs or Slovaks. In February 1948 Beneš succumbed to Communist demands by accepting a Communist-dominated cabinet, but he refused to sign the new constitution. Increasingly ill (he suffered two strokes in 1947), he resigned on June 7, 1948, and died a broken man in September of that year. His memoirs of the period of turmoil were published in 1954.

BIBLIOGRAPHY

Dagan, A. "The Czechoslovak Government-in-Exile and the Jews." In vol. 3 of *The Jews of Czechoslovakia*, edited by A. Dagan, pp. 449–498. New York, 1984.

Rothkirchen, L. "The Czechoslovak Government-in-Exile: Jewish and Palestinian Aspects in Light of the Documents." *Yad Vashem Studies* 9 (1973): 157–200.

LIVIA ROTHKIRCHEN

BEN-GURION, DAVID (1886–1973), prominent Zionist leader; first prime minister of Israel. Born in Płońsk, Poland, Ben-Gurion was a Zionist from his early youth and settled in Palestine in 1906. He was one of the founders of the socialist movement Po'alei Zion and subsequently of the Ahdut ha-Avoda and Mapai socialist political parties. In World War I he volunteered for the Jewish Legion, the volunteer formation in World War I that fought in the British army for the liberation of Palestine from Turkish rule. He was one of the founders of the Histadrut (the General Federation of Labor) and was its secretary-general from 1921 to 1935; in the latter year he became chairman of the Zionist Executive and of the Jewish Agency, holding both posts up to 1948. Ben-Gurion played a central role in the struggle for the establishment of a Jewish state, which he proclaimed on May 14, 1948. In the subsequent war he led both the political and the military struggles as prime minister and minister of defense, posts he retained until 1963.

Ben-Gurion's attitude toward European Jewry during the Holocaust period and the actions that he took for their rescue have been the subject of controversy. It has even been claimed that he consciously detached himself from the Holocaust events and concentrated on the building up of the YISHUV (the Jewish community in Palestine) and establishment of the state, almost to the exclusion of everything else. The views of scholars are divided: a minority holds that Ben-Gurion did in fact distance himself from the problem of European Jewry during the Holocaust; others maintain that from the early 1930s he was at all times preoccupied with the current and potential threats facing Jewish existence in Europe. Most scholars dealing with the general history of the Yishuv tend to take a more balanced view, and reject a one-sided approach.

The situation was, in any case, extremely complex. On the one hand, the conditions facing the Jews of eastern and central Europe in the 1930s deteriorated rapidly; on the other, there was a crisis in the relations between the Zionist movement and the British government. It reached a climax in May 1939, when the WHITE PAPER—limiting future

David Ben-Gurion (second from left) visiting Jewish survivors at Bergen-Belsen in November 1945. At a meeting in the camp he declared: "We shall not rest until every one of you who so desires joins us in the land of Israel in building a Jewish state."

Jewish development, including immigration, in the country—was issued. The combination of circumstances caused Ben-Gurion to conclude that Zionism had to blaze a new political trail. He spent much of the first two years of the war in the United States, in order to mobilize American Jewry's support for a far-reaching new program. It was ratified by a special Zionist conference held in New York in May 1942 at the Biltmore Hotel, hence its name, the BILTMORE RESOLUTION.

The resolution called for Palestine to be opened for large-scale Jewish immigration and, after the war, to become a Jewish commonwealth, under Jewish authority. In this way, it would provide a solution to the problems of the Jews (even if it could not absorb them all), and the mass immigration would also be the basis for its political and economic status. The political solution would be the concern of the Zionist movement, while Jewish organizations in the free world—who had financial means and access to the centers of political power—would have the task of providing immediate aid to the Jews of Europe, and first and foremost to Polish Jewry.

In May 1942, reports of the mass murder of the Jews began to be published, and when in October of that year Ben-Gurion returned to Palestine, he was already in possession of information concerning a German master plan for the systematic annihilation of the Jews. Thus, the millions of Jews for whom the Biltmore program had been conceived were being killed. Ben-Gurion, however, clung to his program, believing that "disaster is the source of strength" that would spur the Jewish people and the Zionist movement to action.

From the end of 1942, Ben-Gurion took part in organizing the Yishuv for rescue operations. He did not permit the establishment of a broad rescue committee under Jewish Agency auspices, since he felt that the Yishuv should have its own official committee; but he did leave political action in the hands of Jewish Agency departments, under the direction and watchful eye of his confidants, among them Shaul Meirov (Avigur), Eliyahu Golomb, and Zvi Yehieli. Ben-Gurion consistently had reservations about mass demonstrations, which were intended to rouse public opinion in the free world and influence Allied governments to help in rescue efforts, because he did not expect them to be effective while the war was in progress. He was against using "national funds" for rescue operations, but was in favor of collecting money for that specific purpose, and himself took part in such fund-raising.

Ben-Gurion's attitude and actions appear to have been based on his conviction that even if the Yishuv were to use its best people and all the resources at its disposal, it would not be able to save many lives, both because of the relentless German annihilation machinery and because the Allied powers, especially Britain, managed to thwart one rescue plan after the other. These included proposals for exchange of Germans for Jews; provision of protective documents to Jews; emigration; cessation of the extermination process in exchange for financial remittances (the EUROPA PLAN, for example); and the dispatch of PARACHUTISTS from Palestine.

Ben-Gurion's doubts about the chances of success for rescue efforts were further reinforced by the BERMUDA CONFERENCE of April 1943 and by various developments in 1944, such as the Allies' refusal to bomb AUSCHWITZ; the failure of the arrangement concerning Hungarian Jewry, proposed by Adolf EICHMANN and his aides, to exchange "blood for goods"; and, above all, Britain's attitude toward a plan on which Ben-Gurion had pinned great hopes —the rescue of thirty thousand Jewish children from German-occupied Europe. These disappointments led Ben-Gurion to concentrate on independent, smaller, and more realistic rescue programs.

This line of reasoning on Ben-Gurion's part and its practical consequences caused tension between him and a significant part of the Jewish population, and within the leadership itself. The approach was criticized not only by the opposition on the right but also by members of Mapai, Ben-Gurion's own party. Moreover, Ben-Gurion did not publicly reveal his analysis of the situation, the intuition that he had, and the way in which he reached his conclusions. The impression created was that he lacked compassion for the suffering of European Jewry and that his course of action was not affected by the Holocaust. In fact, he was deeply moved by the enormity of the tragedy, and his policies were molded by his determination to alleviate the suffering and its root causes by finding long-term solutions.

BIBLIOGRAPHY

Frieling, T. "Ben-Gurion and the Holocaust of European Jewry: A Sterotype Reexamined." *Yad Vashem Studies* 18 (1987): 199–232.

Gal, A. *David Ben-Gurion: Preparing for a Jewish State.* Sede Boker, Israel, 1985. (In Hebrew.)

Porat, D. "Ben Gurion and the Holocaust." *Zionism* 12 (1987): 293–314. (In Hebrew.)

Tevet, S. *David Ben-Gurion: The Burning Ground, 1886–1948.* Boston, 1987.

Tevet, S. *The Zeal of David: The Life of David Ben-Gurion.* Vol. 3. Jerusalem, 1987. (In Hebrew.)

DINA PORAT

BENOÎT, MARIE (b. 1895), French Capuchin monk who rescued Jews during the Holocaust. In the summer of 1942, Benoît was a resident monk in the Capuchin monastery in Marseilles, France. Witnessing the spectacle of Vichy authorities rounding up thousands of non-French Jewish refugees and handing them over to the Germans for deportation, Benoît decided to devote himself to helping Jews escape from France to either Spain or Switzerland, both neutral countries. Under his guidance, the Capuchin monastery was transformed into a nerve center of a widespread rescue network, in collaboration with frontier smugglers (*passeurs*) and in coordination with various Christian and Jewish organizations. A printing machine in the mon-

Father Marie Benoît in 1984.

astery's basement turned out thousands of false baptismal certificates, which the fleeing Jews needed in order to procure other necessary documents.

With the occupation of Vichy France in November 1942, the escape routes to Switzerland and Spain became more difficult to negotiate. The nearby Italian zone of occupation now became the principal escape haven. Journeying to Nice, Benoît coordinated plans with local Jewish organizations. Accompanied by Angelo Donati, an influential local Jewish banker in Nice, he met with Gen. Guido Lospinoso, the Italian commissioner of Jewish affairs (sent to Nice by MUSSOLINI, under German pressure, for the express purpose of instituting anti-Jewish measures), and convinced him that the rescue of the thirty thousand Jews in Nice and its environs was the divine order of the day. Benoît was promised that the Italian occupation authorities would not interfere. Not satisfied with this commitment, and harboring presentiments as to the ultimate fate of the Jews in Nice, Benoît continued on to Rome, and in an audience with Pope PIUS XII on July 16, 1943, he outlined a plan for transferring the majority of the thirty thousand Jews in the Nice region to northern Italy to prevent their falling into German hands. This plan was later expanded to provide for the Jews' transfer to former military camps in North Africa, now in Allied hands. The new Italian government of Marshal Pietro BADOGLIO (Mussolini had been deposed on July 25, 1943) was prepared to provide four ships for this giant undertaking, and ways were found to channel funds from Jewish organizations abroad. However, the premature publication of the Italian armistice on September 8 and the immediate German occupation of northern Italy and the Italian zone of occupation in France foiled this plan.

Benoît's activities now centered on helping Jews in Rome and its vicinity, with the Capuchin College inside the Vatican as his base of operations. To be able to deal effectively with the task of providing food, shelter, and new identities to thousands of Jewish refugees in Rome and elsewhere, he was elected a board member of Delasem (Delegazione Assistenza Emigranti Ebrei), the central Jewish welfare organization of Italy. When its Jewish president, Settimo Sorani, was arrested by the Germans, Benoît was nominated acting president; he chaired the organization's meetings, which were now held inside the Capuchin College. Benoît escaped several attempts by the Gestapo to arrest him, as his fame spread among Jews and non-Jews. He extracted letters of protection and other important documents from the Swiss, Romanian, Hungarian, and Spanish legations. These papers enabled thousands of Jews, under assumed names, to circulate freely in Rome. He also obtained a large batch of ration cards from the Rome police, ostensibly on behalf of non-Jewish homeless refugees stranded in the capital.

After Rome's liberation in June 1944, Benoît was hailed by the Jewish community at an official synagogue ceremony. With the war over and the Jews safe, he returned to his ecclesiastical duties. France awarded him various military decorations; Israel, through YAD VASHEM, conferred on him the title of "RIGHTEOUS AMONG THE NATIONS" in 1966.

BIBLIOGRAPHY

Grossman, K. R. *Die unbesungenen Helden: Menschen in Deutschlands dunkeln Tagen.* Berlin, 1961. See pages 242–284.

Morley, J. F. *Vatican Diplomacy and the Jews during the Holocaust, 1939–1943.* New York, 1980.
Rorty, J. "Father Benoit, Ambassador of the Jews: An Untold Chapter of the Underground." *Commentary* 2/6 (December 1946): 507–513.

MORDECAI PALDIEL

BERDICHEV, town in Zhitomir Oblast (district), Ukrainian SSR, known to have been in existence since the fourteenth century. Jews lived in Berdichev from the sixteenth century. The town became a center of Hasidism, the seat of the renowned rabbi Levi Yitzhak of Berdichev, and, in the nineteenth century, a center of Haskalah (Jewish Enlightenment).

Immediately prior to World War II, Berdichev had a Jewish population of over 30,000, out of a total population of 66,306. When the town was taken by the Germans on July 7, 1941, the Jewish population numbered 20,000. Three days later the military governor imposed a collective fine on the Jews of 100,000 rubles, in cash and valuables. Jews were harassed, some were murdered in groups, and synagogues were set on fire with the congregants inside at prayer.

On August 25, the Jews of Berdichev were ordered to move into a ghetto that had been set up in the poorest part of the town (if they did not live there already), which thus became unbearably congested. On September 4, on orders of the *Höherer SS- und Polizeiführer* (Higher SS and Police Leader) of the Ukraine, 1,500 young Jews were seized and taken out of town to be shot to death. A force of German and Ukrainian police surrounded the ghetto on September 15. Four hundred skilled craftsmen and their families, a total of 2,000 people, were set aside, and the rest, 18,600 persons, were taken out of town to pits that had been prepared in advance, to be shot to death.

Two thousand more Jews were murdered on November 3, leaving only 150 craftsmen alive. The following spring, on April 7, 1942, 70 Jewish women, who were married to non-Jews and lived outside the ghetto, were murdered together with their children. On June 16, the number of craftsmen was reduced to 60; and at the end of October 1943, when Soviet forces were approaching, those Jews who were still left alive were also murdered.

When Berdichev was liberated, on January 15, 1944, 15 Jews were found in the town.

BIBLIOGRAPHY

Ehrenburg, I., and V. Grossman, eds. *The Black Book of Soviet Jewry.* New York, 1981.

SHMUEL SPECTOR

BEREZHANY (Pol., Brzeżany), town in Ternopol Oblast (district), Ukrainian SSR, 31 miles (50 km) west of Ternopol. Between the two wars, Berezhany was part of Poland, and in September 1939 it was incorporated into the Soviet Union, together with the rest of eastern Poland. On the eve of World War II, Berezhany had a Jewish population of over four thousand.

On July 7, 1941, two weeks after the invasion of the Soviet Union, the Germans occupied Berezhany. The Ukrainians lost no time in attacking the Jews; on the morrow of the German entry, they killed three Jews, and a few days later, several dozen more, twelve of them in the Christian cemetery and others in the large municipal park. Various anti-Jewish measures were enacted, such as a dusk-to-dawn curfew, a ban on leaving the city, and the wearing of a Jewish BADGE (a band with a Star of David on the right arm). At the beginning of August 1941 a JUDENRAT (Jewish Council) was set up, consisting of twenty-four members, and its first task was to collect a fine of 300,000 zlotys from the community. The Judenrat also had to supply men for forced labor and to collect and hand over to the Germans valuables, goods, furniture, and household appliances owned by Jews.

On the eve of the Day of Atonement (September 30, 1941), all male Jews aged eighteen to sixty-five were ordered to assemble on the following day in the central town square. A *Selektion* was made that resulted in 700 men being taken to a nearby forest and murdered. On December 18 of that year, 1,200 Jews were moved out of the city, on the pretext that they were being transferred to nearby Podgaitsy. Along the way the German and Ukrainian escorts stopped the convoy and machine-gunned all the Jews to death. Toward the end of 1941, young Jews were seized and sent to labor camps in Zborov, Kamionka, and Hluboczek Wielki. Most of them met their death there, from hard labor, starvation, and the treatment meted out to them.

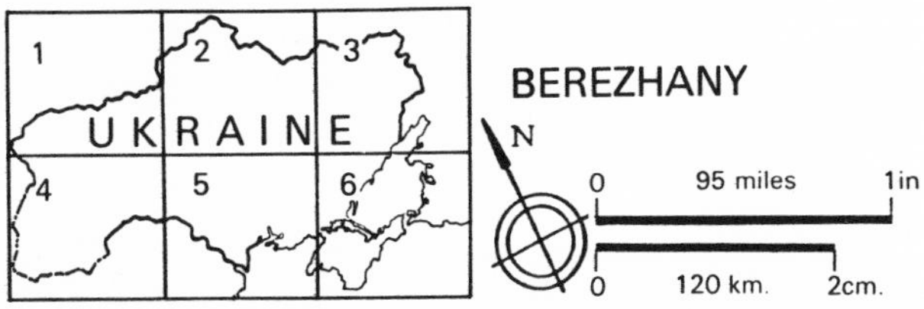

On February 17, 1942, several dozen Berezhany Jews were murdered in a place outside the town. In the spring of that year, Jews from neighboring villages were brought into the town. Additional dozens of Jews were murdered in June 1942. In a mass *Aktion* that took place on the Day of Atonement, September 21, fifteen hundred Jews were rounded up and deported to the BEŁŻEC extermination camp. On October 15, the remaining Jews of Berezhany were confined in a ghetto. Another *Aktion* took place on December 4 and 5, after which several hundred Jews were sent to their death in Bełżec. In that period a growing number of attempts were made to go into hiding in the ghetto or take refuge in the nearby forests.

In March 1943, twelve women were shot to death for having left the confines of the ghetto. At the end of that month and the beginning of April, the Germans and their Ukrainian helpers murdered two hundred men in the Jewish cemetery. In May, four hundred men were put into a work camp that was set up in the ghetto area. On June 12, 1943, the last of the Jews in the work camp and in the ghetto were murdered. Only a handful of the community members had remained in hiding and lived to witness the town's liberation in summer 1944.

BEREZHANY

BIBLIOGRAPHY

Katz, M., ed. *Brzeżany Memorial Book.* Haifa, 1978. (In Hebrew and English.)

AHARON WEISS

BERGEN-BELSEN, camp in the concentration camp system of Nazi Germany. Bergen-Belsen was located in Lower Saxony, northern Germany, near the city of Celle. The camp was officially established in April 1943 as an *Aufenthaltslager* (detention camp) for holding persons who were designated for exchange with German nationals in Allied countries whom the Germans wanted to repatriate. A prisoner-of-war camp on the site,

Stalag 311, was partially cleared to make room for the new camp.

From its inception, Bergen-Belsen came under the SS WIRTSCHAFTS-VERWALTUNGSHAUPTAMT (Economic-Administrative Main Office; WVHA), which was in charge of the administration of concentration camps. Its first commandant was Hauptsturmführer (later promoted to Sturmbannführer) Adolf Haas. Five hundred Jewish prisoners from the BUCHENWALD and NATZWEILER camps were taken to Bergen-Belsen to work on the construction of the camp; they were not candidates for exchange and belonged to the Baukommando (construction detachment), whose task was to construct facilities for the intake of the persons who, on the face of it, were candidates for exchange. In the course of the first eighteen months of the camp's existence, five satellite camps were set up, unconnected with one another, as follows:

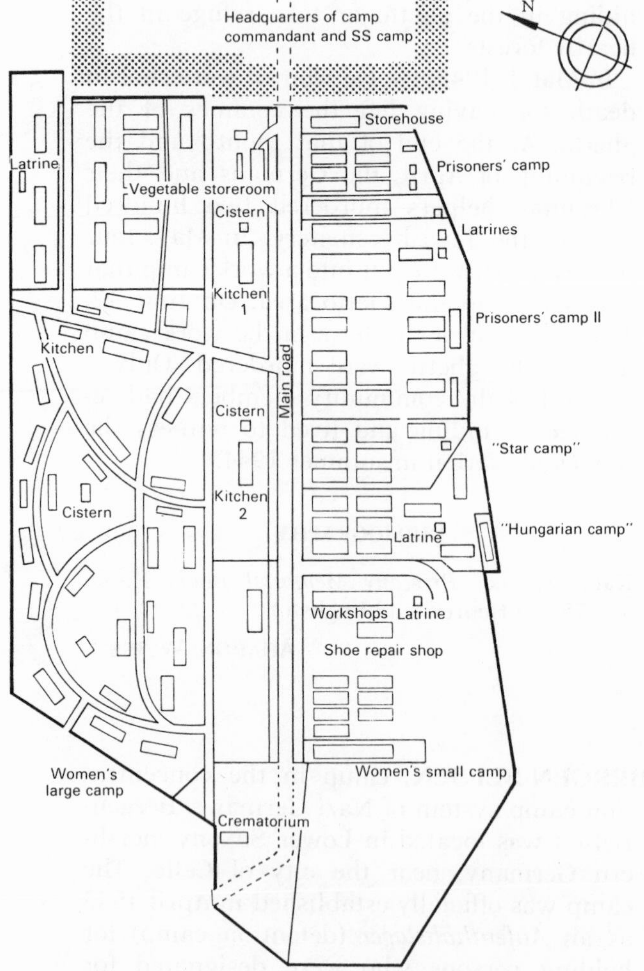

Plan of the Bergen-Belsen camp (February to April 1945). [From *Bergen-Belsen: Geschichte des Aufenthaltslagers 1943–1945;* Hannover, 1962]

1. A "prisoners' camp" (*Häftlingslager*) for the first 500 prisoners who had been brought in for construction of the camp. This was the first satellite camp to be built at Bergen-Belsen; conditions in the camp were among the worst possible, and the mortality rate was very high. The camp was closed on February 23, 1944, and the few surviving prisoners were transferred to SACHSENHAUSEN.

2. The "special camp" (*Sonderlager*). In mid-June 1943, two transports of Jews from Poland (mainly from Warsaw, Lvov, and Kraków), totaling 2,400 persons, were taken to this camp; these were Jews who had papers (*promesas*) in their possession, issued by various—mostly South American—countries. In late October 1943, 1,700 of these Jews were deported to AUSCHWITZ, where they were all immediately killed. Another 350 suffered the same fate in early 1944. This left 350 detainees in the camp, of whom 266 were in possession of immigration permits to Palestine, 34 were United States citizens, and 50 had South American papers. These prisoners were not assigned to work teams, and no contact was permitted between them and other groups of Bergen-Belsen prisoners.

3. The "neutral camp" (*Neutralenlager*). This camp contained two barracks in which 350 Jewish prisoners were housed from late July 1944 to early March 1945. The prisoners were nationals of neutral countries, among them 155 Spanish, 105 Turkish, 35 Argentine, and 19 Portuguese citizens. Conditions in this camp were better than in any other part of Bergen-Belsen. The prisoners here were not put to work, enjoyed better nourishment and sanitary conditions, and were treated by the SS with less cruelty than were prisoners in the other satellite camps.

4. The "star camp" (*Sternenlager*). This was the largest of the five satellite camps, containing eighteen barracks. It housed Jewish prisoners who ostensibly were designated for exchange (*Austauschjuden,* or exchange Jews). These prisoners did not wear the usual concentration camp uniform and were permitted to wear their own clothes, but they had to wear a yellow BADGE (a Magen David, or Star of David, from which came the name

Bergen-Belsen after the liberation of the camp by the British army on April 15, 1945.

"star camp"). Men and women lived in separate barracks, but members of the same family were able to meet. Most of the prisoners in the "star camp" were Jews from the Netherlands; in the period from January to September 1944, eight transports from the WESTERBORK camp in the Netherlands arrived in Bergen-Belsen, made up of 3,670 persons who were classified as *Austauschjuden*. In the first half of 1944, the "star camp" also took in small transports of Jews from various other countries. These included 200 Jews from Tunisia, Tripoli, and Benghazi who until then had been held in the Fossoli di Carpi camp in Italy; 200 Jewish women from the DRANCY camp in France, whose husbands were French prisoners of war being held by the Germans; and several hundred Jews from Yugoslavia and Albania. According to a count taken on July 31, 1944, the "star camp" contained a total of 4,100 Jewish prisoners classified as *Austauschjuden*.

5. The "Hungarian camp" (*Ungarnlager*), which was set up on July 8, 1944, and held 1,684 Jews from Hungary—the transport organized by Dr. Rezső (Rudolf) KASZTNER. Here, too, the prisoners wore their own clothes but were forced to display the yellow badge.

Only a few of the Jews who were brought to Bergen-Belsen as candidates for exchange were in fact set free in exchange deals (*see* EXCHANGE: JEWS AND GERMANS). On July 10, 1944, 222 Jews with immigration certificates to Palestine landed at the Haifa port. A few weeks later, on August 21, 318 Jews from the "Hungarian camp" reached Switzerland, followed by another 1,365 in December; on January 25, 1945, 136 Jews with South American papers also reached Switzerland.

Beginning in March 1944, Bergen-Belsen gradually became a "regular" concentration camp, the Germans transferring to it prisoners from other concentration camps who

Former SS women guards lowering the bodies of dead inmates into a common grave in Bergen-Belsen (April 1945).

were classified as ill and unfit to work (*Arbeitsunfähige*). The first such group came in late March 1944 and consisted of 1,000 sick prisoners from the DORA camp. They were put into a new section of the camp where the sanitary conditions were extremely poor; they received no blankets, no medical attention, and only minute food rations. Nearly all of them died within a short period; on the day of the camp's liberation, only 57 of the original 1,000 were still alive. More transports of prisoners "unfit for work" kept arriving from various camps, up to the end of 1944, most of them made up of Hungarian Jews. The majority were housed in the former "prisoners' camp", where conditions were at their worst and the mortality rate was the highest. Of the several thousand prisoners brought to this section of the camp in 1944 (the precise figure is unknown), 820 died in the period from April to June alone. Also transferred to this section of the camp were German convicts from the Dora camp, who were appointed "block elders" (*Blockälteste*) and Kapos (*see* KAPO), and who treated the Jewish prisoners under their authority with great brutality, causing their situation to deteriorate sharply. The prisoners also suffered from the sadistic practices of the camp doctor, Obersturmbannführer Dr. Karl Jäger, who forced them to keep running for long stretches of time. In summer 1944 some 200 prisoners were killed by phenol injections.

In August 1944 a new section was added, to serve as a women's camp, consisting of twelve barracks; 4,000 Jewish women prisoners from Hungary and Poland were brought there, but after a short stay they were sent on forced labor to the Buchenwald and FLOSSENBÜRG satellite camps. Most of the women were sent back to Bergen-Belsen, sick or exhausted by the hard labor that had been forced on them. In September and October of 1944, transports of Jewish prisoners from the PŁASZÓW camp, and 3,000 Jewish women prisoners from Auschwitz, arrived at Bergen-Belsen; they were housed in the "star camp" in new barracks put up for them, with no water, no beds, and no other facilities of any kind. Among these prisoners were Anne FRANK and her sister Margot; in March 1945 both girls succumbed to the typhus epidemic that was then raging in the camp.

On December 2, 1944, the camp commandant, Adolf Haas, was replaced by Hauptsturmführer Josef KRAMER. A census taken that day showed that the camp population was 15,257 persons, of whom some 8,000 were women. Kramer's first step was to convert Bergen-Belsen officially into a concentration camp. The residues of self-administration that still existed in the "star camp" were abolished, and the internal management of the camp was put into the hands of *Blockälteste* and Kapos, as was done in all the other concentration camps. A final and complete deterioration of the conditions under which the prisoners were living in the camp set in when tens of thousands of prisoners poured in—survivors of the DEATH MARCHES of prisoners who had been evacuated from camps in the east. These included 20,000 women prisoners from the Auschwitz and Buchenwald satellite camps, some of whom had passed through the GROSS-ROSEN camp on the death march to Bergen-Belsen.

Rabbi Leslie H. Hardman, British army chaplain, recites Kaddish at a common grave in Bergen-Belsen (April 1945).

In the period from January to March 1945 there were more death marches, which brought thousands of male prisoners from the Sachsenhausen and Buchenwald camps to Bergen-Belsen. The camp administration did not lift a finger to house the prisoners who were streaming in. Most of them had no roof over their heads, and were without water and food. There was now total chaos in the camps, and a typhus epidemic was at its height; in the month of March alone, 18,168 prisoners perished in the camp, and the number of deaths for the period from January to mid-April was 35,000.

On April 15, 1945, Bergen-Belsen was liberated by the British army. There were sixty thousand prisoners in the camp, most of them in a critical condition. Thousands of unburied bodies were strewn all over the camp grounds. The sight put the British sol-

Josef Kramer (seated), the commandant of Bergen-Belsen from December 2, 1944, was apprehended by the British army when it liberated the camp on April 15, 1945.

diers into a state of shock. The British had not anticipated the immediate rescue requirements, and in the first five days following liberation, fourteen thousand persons died; another fourteen thousand succumbed in the following weeks.

After liberation, Bergen-Belsen became the site of a DISPLACED PERSONS' camp, the British army medical corps helping in the physical rehabilitation of the former prisoners. The displaced persons' camp was in existence up to 1951, with the inmates, under the leadership of Josef Rosensaft, managing to organize a lively social, cultural, and political life in the camp.

The trial of forty-eight members of the staff of Bergen-Belsen, among them sixteen women, by a British military court was held in Lüneburg, Germany, from September 17 to November 17, 1945. Eleven of the accused—including the camp commandant, Josef Kramer—were sentenced to death, and on December 12, 1945, they were executed.

[*See also* Trials of War Criminals: Bergen-Belsen Trial; Appendix, Volume 4.]

BIBLIOGRAPHY

Bloch, S. E., ed. *Holocaust and Rebirth: Bergen Belsen, 1945–1965.* New York, 1965.

Hardman, L. H., and C. Goodman. *The Survivors: The Story of the Belsen Remnant.* London, 1958.

Kolb, E. *Bergen Belsen: Vom "Aufenthaltslager" zum Konzentrationslager, 1943–1945.* Göttingen, 1984.

Levy-Haas, H. *Inside Belsen.* Totowa, N.J., 1962.

Napora, P. *Death at Belsen.* San Antonio, Tex., 1967.

Phillips, R., ed. *The Belsen Trial: Trial of Josef Kramer and 44 Others.* London, 1949.

SHMUEL KRAKOWSKI

BERGEN-BELSEN TRIAL. *See* Trials of War Criminals: Bergen-Belsen Trial.

BERGSON GROUP, a group of members of the Zionist Revisionist movement active in the United States between 1940 and 1948. It supported the creation of a Jewish army to fight Nazi Germany, the rescue of Jews from the Holocaust in Europe, and the establishment of a Jewish state.

In the summer of 1940, Vladimir JABOTINSKY and Hillel Kook went to the United States in order to promote the creation of an independent Jewish army that would fight Adolf Hitler. They were joined by members of the Palestine underground group Irgun Tseva'i Le'ummi (Etsel), who had been there for some time, their original purpose being to raise funds for their organization. On Jabotinsky's death in August 1940, Kook took over the leadership of the group, assuming for this purpose the alias of Peter H. Bergson (hence the group's name). Samuel Merlin became Bergson's right-hand man. On December 4, 1941, the Bergson Group formed the Committee for a Jewish Army of Stateless and Palestinian Jews.

In November 1942, when Rabbi Stephen S. WISE made public a report on the systematic murder of several million Jews by the Nazis (*see* RIEGNER CABLE), the Bergson Group decided to concentrate all its efforts on the rescue of Europe's Jews and for the time being to shelve the campaign for a Jewish army. As Palestinian Jews, the members were not responsible to any local Jewish leadership or political group; they also did not have to account for their actions to Etsel headquarters in Palestine, to any community organization, or to the United States government; and they were not beset by any qualms about dual loyalty. This enabled them to use unconventional means in their operation. They disagreed with the American Jewish establishment, Zionists and non-Zionists alike, over the traditional ways of intercession—which they considered obsequious—with the authorities, and they were sharply critical of the paralysis that had taken hold of American Jews, out of the fear of increasing antisemitism.

Perturbed by the administration's reluctance to take action on behalf of Europe's Jews, the Bergson Group decided to make use of the power of public opinion in a democratic society to bring pressure to bear upon Washington to institute special measures in order to save Jews. Using methods of mass communication, such as full-page advertisements and mass demonstrations, the group appealed to the deep-rooted American religious and liberal tradition with outspoken and provocative slogans such as "The Jews don't want just to pray—they want to fight" and "Action, not mercy," which found a growing response among the public.

Launched in February 1943, the propaganda campaign gained in force with the help of a mass demonstration held at Madison Square Garden on March 9, which had at its center a pageant entitled *We Will Never Die*, composed by the author Ben Hecht in memory of the two million Jews known to have been murdered by that time. From New York, the pageant toured other cities throughout the country.

Following the failure of the BERMUDA CONFERENCE, which was to have come up with a solution of the refugee problem, Bergson convened an emergency conference (July 20 to 25, 1943) that called for stepped-up action in behalf of the rescue of Jews, and demanded that pressure be put on the Axis powers to permit the emigration of Jews, or at least to allow the Allies to supply the Jews in their countries with basic needs. The conference also called on the neutral countries to offer temporary asylum to refugees fleeing for their lives. It established the Emergency Committee to Save the Jewish People of Europe, which in turn resolved to devote its efforts to promoting a United States government agency whose sole concern would be to save Jews. The committee launched a two-pronged campaign—a national publicity drive to alert public opinion to the grave situation of European Jews, and the creation of a lobby, based on public support by both Jews and non-Jews, that would seek to convince the president and the Congress of the need to embark upon rescue operations. Emergency Committee members felt that the creation of a refugee council would lead to government recognition of the unique nature of the Jewish problem.

Journalists and intellectuals, such as Ben Hecht and Max Lerner, joined the publicity drive, and the committee's own magazine, *Answer*, also helped in spreading the Bergson Group's proposals. Leading public figures, such as the press magnate William Randolph Hearst, Secretary of the Interior Harold Ickes, New York mayor Fiorello La Guardia, and Will Rogers, Democratic congressman from California, were among the Emergency Committee's supporters and lent their names to its efforts. These included a pilgrimage of rescue to Washington, made by four hundred rabbis who marched on the White House on October 6, 1943, just before the Day of Atonement. President Franklin D. ROOSEVELT, however, arranged to be away from the White House so that he could avoid receiving the rabbinical delegation. On October 10, six thousand churches observed a "day of intercession" on which Christians offered prayers in behalf of "our brethren in Europe." The committee also began the collection of a million signatures on a petition that was to be presented to the president and Congress, calling for a government agency to be set up that would deal specifically with the rescue of Jews.

The attempts to gain the president's support were of no avail, but the lobbying in Congress did lead to some success. On November 9, 1943, two identical draft resolutions were introduced: in the Senate by Guy Gillette (Democrat from Iowa) and in the House by Will Rogers (Democrat from California) and Joseph Baldwin (Republican from New York). The resolutions called on the president to establish a government commission for the rescue of Europe's Jews. The public atmosphere engendered by the discussion of the draft in Congress, coupled with the intervention of Treasury Secretary Henry MORGENTHAU, Jr., may well have caused President Roosevelt to issue an executive order, on January 22, 1944, establishing the WAR REFUGEE BOARD, to deal with refugees of all religions. The campaign for a "free port" where refugees in danger of their lives would be given temporary refuge, which the committee had supported, met with partial success when the Oswego free port came into being (*see* FORT ONTARIO).

Once the War Refugee Board had been established, the Bergson Group turned its attention to issues that would arise when the war was over, and became active in behalf of a "Hebrew" state in Palestine. In May 1944, it set up the Hebrew Committee for National Liberation and a Hebrew Embassy in Washington.

The Bergson Group's independent line of action brought it into conflict with the Zionist leadership and with the American Jewish establishment. The conflict was exacerbated by the group's temporary shelving of the struggle for Palestine, and by the manner in which it once again took up the issue. Bergson himself demanded that the issue of rescuing Jews should be excluded from any controversy that might arise among Jewish political groups or between Zionists and non-Zionists. The omission of the name "Palestine" from the Gillette-Rogers draft resolution, and the Bergson Group's use of the term "Hebrew state" rather than "Jewish state," contradicted Zionist ideology. The Zionist establishment strongly criticized both Bergson's ideology and his strident tactics, and even asked the administration to take action against him and his men.

The Bergson Group took virtually no part in direct rescue or aid operations, but it did play an important role in bringing the Holocaust of European Jewry to the knowledge of the general public. It also prevailed upon public figures to pressure the American administration to take up rescue operations. Scholars are divided in their appraisal of the Bergson Group's contribution to the establishment of the War Refugee Board. Some (such as Lucy Dawidowicz and Jonathan Kaplan) belittle the group's role in this connection, while others (Sharon Lowenstein and Monty Penkower) stress the importance of that role. There seems to be general agreement, however, that the Bergson Group's organizations succeeded in increasing the pressure on key figures in the administration to search for means of rescuing Jews.

The evaluation of the Bergson Group's achievements seems to be linked to the assessment of the overall record of American Jewry during the Holocaust years. Those scholars (including Saul Friedman, Lowenstein, and David Wyman) who fault American Jews for their lack of initiative and their failure to act in behalf of European Jews extol the success scored by a handful of penniless youngsters, by means of unconventional methods, to arouse public opinion—and through it also the administration—to rescue action. Others (such as Yehuda Bauer, Dawidowicz, Henry Feingold, Leonard Dinnerstein, and Penkower) point to American Jewry's weak position at the time, because of which it could not have been expected to bring about a change in the general atmosphere of indifference and even hostility toward Jewish refugees then prevailing in the country. In their opinion, the current tendency to reproach American Jewry for its record in those years is based, in part, on the power that it attained only later.

BIBLIOGRAPHY

Dawidowicz, L. "Indicting American Jews." *Commentary* 75 (June 1983): 36–44.

Friedman, S. S. *No Haven for the Oppressed: U.S. Policy toward Jewish Refugees, 1933–1945*. Detroit, 1973.

Kaplan, J. "Rescue Activities of the Etzel Mission in the United States during the Holocaust." *Yalkut Moreshet* 30 (1980): 115–138; 31 (1981): 75–96. (In Hebrew.)

Lowenstein, S. R. *Token Refuge: The Story of the Jewish Refugee Center at Oswego, 1944–1946*. Bloomington, 1986.

Penkower, M. N. "In Dramatic Dissent: The Bergson Boys." *American Jewish History* 70/3 (March 1981): 281–309.

Wyman, D. S. *The Abandonment of the Jews: America and the Holocaust, 1941–1945*. New York, 1984.

HAIM GENIZI

BERIḤA (Heb.; "flight, escape"), the post–World War II movement of about 250,000 Jewish Holocaust survivors, mainly from eastern Europe, to DISPLACED PERSONS' camps in Germany, Austria, and Italy and to the West; the name applies both to the organization that directed the flow and to the mass movement that often outgrew the organization. The avowed aim was to reach the coasts, from which the wanderers could embark for Palestine.

The organized *beriḥa* began with groups of Jewish partisan survivors in the Vilna, Rovno, and Chernovtsy areas that initially had no contact with one another. They felt that they could not carry on life in their former homes, which had become Jewish graveyards. Many of the survivors had belonged to Zionist youth movements before the war, and their Zionist convictions had been strengthened by disillusionment with the Soviet regime; consequently, their natural path after the liberation was emigration to Palestine. They had heard that it could best be reached by way of Romania, and they therefore tried, each group separately at first, to make their way over the Romanian border. The groups coalesced, but their attempt to reach Romania failed, and they concentrated in Lublin, which had been liberated by the Red Army in July 1944. Here they were joined by a sizable group of their prewar comrades who had spent the war years as refugees in the USSR, mainly in central Asia; in January 1945, when Warsaw was liberated, the remnants of the ghetto rebels from Warsaw joined the group.

An incipient formal structure was created under Abba KOVNER, partisan and poet, and the leadership group made its way to Romania in March. Illegal transit points were established on the Polish border with Czechoslovakia and Romania, and by May about two thousand persons had reached Romania. On April 26, 1945, Kovner established the Organization of Eastern European Survivors, a semipolitical organization that was to unite the Jewish people beyond their party and political allegiances and help create a Jewish state that would be the last refuge for a nation for whom another Holocaust was predicted. The new group was soon to disintegrate, however, after contact with the lively and argumentative democracy of Palestine Jewry. It turned out that no immigration from Romania to Palestine was feasible, and the group turned west to Italy, where the Jewish Palestinian units of the British army (the JEWISH BRIGADE GROUP and others) were stationed. The soldiers had established a central organization for looking after Jewish survivors (Merkaz la-Gola, or Diaspora Center), led by an all-party coalition under Mordechai Surkis, Yehiel Duvdevani, and Aharon Hoter-Yishai.

As a result of the unification of the two elements in July 1945, the Beriḥa in Poland, now led by Moshe Meiri and Mordechai Rosman, directed the flow to Italy, by way of Budapest and Graz. By August 1945, roughly fifteen thousand Jews had reached Italy. However, there were only very limited ("illegal") opportunities for reaching Palestine at that time, and the difficult decision was reached to direct the increasing flow of survivors and returnees from the USSR to Poland, and from there to Germany, where, under United States Army rule, Jews were accepted into displaced persons' camps, housed, and fed. Transit to Italy from Germany and Austria all but ceased, and the soldiers took over some of the central positions, receiving the flow of people directed by the Polish Beriḥa.

In September and October 1945, the first emissaries sent by the Hagana (the Jewish underground in Palestine) arrived in Europe. Isser Ben-Zvi, Zvi Netzer, and Yohanan Cohen, among others, reached Poland and other places and integrated themselves into the loosely organized and illegal Beriḥa structure. The stream moved through various control points by way of the Polish-Slovak mountains, through Upper Silesia into the Náchod area in Bohemia, or by way of Szczecin into Berlin. Those who entered Czechoslovakia went either through Prague and then to Bavaria, or by way of Bratislava to Vienna, then to Salzburg, and on to either Germany or Italy. The Beriḥa activists were not paid, and necessary expenses were covered, often unwittingly but eventually with full knowledge, by the American JOINT DISTRIBUTION COMMITTEE as "transit" expenses for transport, food, and basic lodging. The small amount of property in the refugees' possession was scrupulously guarded, brought over the border by the Beriḥa workers, and delivered to the owners. Beriḥa had no central hierarchy; a coordination office in Bratislava—run by Levi Argov, an emissary from Palestine, more or less at his own initiative—worked out schedules for transports from Poland westward. Parallel points were set up in Hungary and Slovakia, again in coordination with Argov. In Austria another emissary, Arthur (Asher) Ben-Nathan, received the flow from Czechoslovakia and distributed it by way of Salzburg and Innsbruck.

The Soviets, whose control over eastern Europe was tightening, permitted the illegal flow in a halfhearted manner, although sometimes they suddenly pounced on the refugees and organizers and arrested them (some spent years in the Gulag, and a few were killed); but usually they turned a blind eye. The atti-

BERIḤA
North Sea
SWEDEN
Baltic Sea
BALTIC STATES
Kovno
Vilna
USSR
Hamburg
Stettin
POLAND
Białystok
Berlin
Warsaw
GERMANY
Náchod
Lublin
Prague
Kielce
Rovno
BOHEMIA
VOLHYNIA
FRANCE
Munich
SLOVAKIA
AUSTRIA
Vienna
UKRAINE
Salzburg
Bratislava
Innsbruck
Villach
Chernovtsy
BESSARABIA
Budapest
BUKOVINA
HUNGARY
Graz
Spezia
Sisak
Marseille
ROMANIA
YUGOSLAVIA
Ancona
Bucharest
ITALY
Adriatic Sea
Black Sea
Burgas
BULGARIA
Bari
GREECE
Athens
TURKEY
Mediterranean Sea
CYPRUS
British
0 miles 300
0 kilometres 500
PALESTINE
British Mandate
© Martin Gilbert 1982

Jewish refugees waiting at the Budapest train station to go to Italy; from there they made their way to Palestine (1945). [Zvi Kadushin; Beth Hatefutsoth]

tude of the British was predictably hostile, while the United States army, after some initial troubles, accepted the *beriḥa* flow because it was wary of a scandal with the administration and the public at home; in any case, it could not order soldiers to shoot at Jewish refugees, which was the only way it could have stopped them from coming.

Between August 1945 and the end of June 1946, Beriḥa figures show 48,106 refugees as having left Poland by means of the organization. If there is added an unknown number who came across without the help of Beriḥa, as well as similar movements of REFUGEES from Hungary and Czechoslovakia, a figure of some 60,000 to 65,000 transients is reached. The flight from Poland was mainly motivated by the murderous antisemitism there, exacerbated by the political struggle between the Communist regime and the strong opposition to it. The anti-Jewish action reached its climax on July 4, 1946, in the pogrom of KIELCE, following a ritual-murder accusation, with forty-two fatalities and a large number of injured. In the wake of the pogrom, 90,000 to 95,000 Jews fled from Poland between July and September 1946. Some of this flow was so sudden that the Beriḥa organization could not cope with it, and many fled across borders without any organized help. Later in that year the flow abated, and by early 1947 it became a trickle. During the summer and autumn of that year, the cooperation of the Polish and Czechoslovak governments in enabling the refugees to cross the borders was obtained, probably for a mixture of political and genuinely humanitarian reasons.

As the Beriḥa movements decreased in early 1947—a brief revival occurred from March through July, when some nineteen thousand Romanian Jews fled to Vienna by means of the Beriḥa to escape from a combination of hunger and political constriction—Beriḥa became hierarchically organized. Ephraim Dekel of the Hagana in Palestine became the organization's European leader, subject to the ALIYA BET immigration organization, headed by Shaul Avigur in Paris. But the transit points were slowly dismantled as activists moved to the coasts themselves, and in 1948, after the establishment of Israel, immigration became legal. Nevertheless, for countries from which no legal exit was possible, Beriḥa continued to maintain a skeleton framework under Meir Sapir in 1949.

The approximately 250,000 Jews who used the Beriḥa routes made it the largest organized illegal mass movement in modern times. No literature or propaganda of any kind was ever published by Beriḥa. It never needed to call on Jews to leave their homes; on the contrary, it often could not cope with the flow of people who wanted to escape. Thus, it was truly a service organization.

BIBLIOGRAPHY

Bauer, Y. *Bricha: Flight and Rescue.* New York, 1970.

Dekel, E. *B'richa: Flight to the Homeland.* New York, 1972.

YEHUDA BAUER

BERLIN, capital of Prussia and, from 1871 to 1945, of GERMANY. On the eve of World War II, Berlin's population was at its peak—4.34 million—and it was the second largest city in Europe.

Jews had been living in Berlin since the end of the thirteenth century; in 1573 they were expelled, and a hundred years later, in 1671, Jews again came to settle in Berlin. In the seventeenth and eighteenth centuries the Jewish population in Berlin kept growing—despite efforts by the kings of Prussia to limit their number—and by the middle of the nineteenth century it had risen to two thousand. Berlin was the first center of Haskalah, the Jewish cultural enlightenment movement; its most renowned exponent, Moses Mendelssohn, lived there. It was in Berlin, in 1778, that the Jüdische Freischule was established, the first Jewish institution of learning in which the German language was taught and general subjects were included in the curriculum.

In the nineteenth century and the early years of the twentieth century, the Jewish population of Berlin increased greatly—from 3,300 in 1812, to 36,000 in 1871, 94,000 in 1895, and 142,000 in 1910. The rapid rise was the result of a mass influx of Jews from the provincial towns; from the eastern provinces of Imperial Germany, especially from Posen (Pol., Poznań); and from eastern Europe. A high percentage of the Berlin Jewish population was therefore made up of *Ostjuden*—Jews from the east—a situation that had considerable impact on both the Jewish and the non-Jewish population of Berlin.

Jews in Berlin were prominent in various aspects of the city's economic, intellectual, and cultural life. The city was also the seat of the head offices of most of the national Jewish organizations—such as the CENTRALVEREIN DEUTSCHER STAATSBÜRGER JÜDISCHEN GLAUBENS (Central Union of German Citizens of Jewish Faith), the Ezra Society, the Zentralwohlfahrtstelle der Deutschen Juden (Central Welfare Organization of German Jews), and the Central Lodge of B'NAI B'RITH in Germany—and of most of the Jewish periodicals published in Germany.

Up to the end of World War I, control of the Jewish community was in the hands of wealthy liberals; after the war, the Jüdische Volkspartei, or Jewish People's Party—an alignment of the Zionists, including Mizraḥi and the Union of Eastern European Jewish Organizations—gained in strength in the Jewish community organization, and in 1928 a representative of that party, Georg Kareski, was elected president of the community. In 1930 the liberals were returned to power and Wilhelm Kleeman became president. The spokesman for the positions taken by liberal Jews was Leo BAECK, Berlin's leading liberal rabbi.

In 1923 the Berlin community took the initiative for the formation of a Preussischer Landesverband Jüdischer Gemeinden (Union of Jewish Communities in Prussia), in order to strengthen its own status among the other communities and to facilitate contacts with the government authorities. In the early 1930s Berlin is estimated to have had 115 Jewish houses of prayer. The community itself maintained 17 synagogues, with a seating capacity of 25,000; on the high holidays, extra halls were rented that doubled the available seating capacity, the services being either liberal or traditional. The community also supported dozens of religious congregations, including Orthodox prayer houses and a Sephardic synagogue. In the 1930s the community school system consisted of fifteen kindergartens, several elementary schools, two junior high schools, and one secondary school (*Gymnasium*). Adas Israel, the separatist Orthodox community, maintained its own elementary and secondary school and a girls' school. By the late 1920s one-seventh of all the Jewish children were attending Jewish schools. There were differences of opinion among the Jews concerning the educational role of the community—whether it should maintain a separate Jewish school system, based on Jewish values, or whether it should prefer a national German framework, with a minimum emphasis on Jewish elements. For the Jewish students attending the public schools, the community provided forty-eight *Religionsschulen* (Hebrew schools).

Jewish youth movements were active in Berlin, supported by the various Jewish politically oriented organizations. The community maintained youth centers, provided summer vacations in the country for thousands of children, arranged foster homes, and made vocational training facilities available. The Jewish youth had their own gyms and playgrounds. Bar Kochba was the leading sports club, and a Maccabi organization was established in 1921.

The Berlin community provided welfare services, with its institutions serving as a model for the entire country. The Jewish welfare office coordinated the operations of the various Jewish welfare organizations. The community maintained twenty four regional welfare and youth offices, an office for aid to the disabled, twelve orphanages, dozens of day nurseries for the infants of working mothers, poorhouses, a network of soup kitchens and school kitchens, and *Winterhilfe* (special aid in the cold season—initially as part of the overall organization and, after Hitler's rise to power, independently). The community also ran its own medical facilities, such as a 350-bed hospital (which operated throughout the war), a hospital for the disabled, two medical clinics, institutions for the blind, the deaf, and the mentally ill, and a training school for the staff of these establishments. The community also had loan institutions, a vocational training and counseling office, a section providing assistance to academically qualified persons, an employment office, and an emigration advisory office. The Jewish community was the largest Jewish employer, its annual budget for 1928 amounted to some 10 million marks, of which 30 percent was used for religious activities, 12 percent for education and vocational training, 30 percent for welfare and aid, and the remainder for maintenance and miscellaneous purposes. Revenue from taxes covered 60 percent of the expenditures. The separatist community, Adas Israel, in addition to its schools, provided welfare services and maintained its own cemetery.

In 1925, 50 percent of the breadwinners were salaried employees, of whom 80 percent were office workers, 18 percent manual workers, and 2 percent house servants. The economic depression of the early 1930s, coupled with the growing antisemitism, caused many Jews to apply to the Jewish employment office, with 50 percent of such applicants coming from the commercial sector, 25 percent from among the skilled workers, 15 percent from the ranks of unskilled workers, and 10 percent from the professional class.

In that same period a large number of Jews opted out of the organized Jewish community, either in order to convert (mainly to enter into a mixed marriage) or in order to avoid paying the community tax by turning *konfessionslos* (not belonging to any recognized religious denomination).

Under the Weimar Republic, Berlin was Germany's center of culture. Many Jews gained fame as theater directors, actors, playwrights, film producers, musicians, artists, and journalists. Despite the difficulties caused by the economic situation, Jews achieved success in the professions, many earning distinguished reputations in medicine, and held posts in the city's universities and academies. Jews were also prominent as entrepreneurs.

At the same time, however, Jews became the targets of antisemitic attacks. In the wake of the murder of two leaders of the leftist Spartacus League, Karl Liebknecht and Rosa Luxemburg (the latter a Jew, born in Poland), in January 1919, a wave of riots against *Ostjuden* was launched. Similar riots also occurred during the short-lived revolutionary attempt, the Kapp Putsch, in March 1920. In November 1923, an area in the eastern part of Berlin that was inhabited by Jews

Rosa Luxemburg, leader of the left-wing revolutionary Spartaksbund. She was killed by German army officers in January 1919 while being taken to the Moabit prison in Berlin. [Internationaal Instituut voor Sociale Geschiedenis; Beth Hatefutsoth]

from eastern Europe was the scene of a pogrom.

In 1926 Joseph GOEBBELS was appointed *Gauleiter* of Berlin and founded *Der Angriff* (The Attack), a Nazi party organ, which he used to spread Nazi antisemitism and incite the population against Berlin's "Jewish press." Goebbels exploited the February 1930 killing of Horst Wessel, an SA (Sturmabteilung; Storm Troopers) man in Berlin, to launch a campaign against the city's Jews. On the Jewish New Year of 1931, Jews on their way home from the synagogues were attacked on the Kurfürstendamm in western Berlin. The next year, 1932, saw a spate of attacks on Jewish university students and lecturers in the city. The election campaign that year served to intensify the antisemitic atmosphere. This was followed by a decrease in the number of Jews opting out of Berlin's Jewish community, and a rise in the community's tax revenue and in separate Jewish cultural activities.

In the September 1930 elections the Nazi party received 14.6 percent of the vote, four times as much as in the 1928 elections. The collapse of German democracy was accompanied by a crisis in the functioning of the Berlin city council. In the July 1932 elections the Nazis obtained 28.6 percent of the vote (as against 37.4 percent on the national level); in the November elections that same year, the Nazis lost some of their support and gained only 25.9 percent of the vote (33 percent in the whole of Germany).

On the night of January 30, 1933, the SA celebrated Hitler's appointment as Reich chancellor by staging a torchlight parade in the streets of Berlin. Jews who had been active in anti-Nazi political parties and organizations fled the city. It was at this point that the first wave of suicides hit the Jewish community, a phenomenon that was to repeat itself time and again for as long as the community continued to exist. On the night of the Reichstag fire (February 27, 1933), SA troops attacked the offices of the Centralverein.

The "Aryanization" of Jewish-owned enterprises began in 1933. As early as April 11 of that year, the newspaper announced that the businesses owned by its publisher, Rudolf Mosse, had been Aryanized. On August 1, the Berlin-Lichtenberg municipality revoked trading licenses that had been granted to Jews. On July 20, 1935, Berlin police closed down the Jewish-owned stores on the Kurfürstendamm. Until the KRISTALLNACHT pogrom, however, it was mainly the salaried employees who bore the brunt of Nazi policy in Berlin, as in all of Germany, whereas Jewish businesses continued to operate on the local as well as the international scene.

The Jewish leadership of Berlin made efforts to work out new principles that would assure the city's Jews a continued existence as a religious minority, within the framework of Nazi policies. The community bylaws were adapted to Nazi demands. A wall-to-wall coalition was formed, in which Alfred Klee, of the Jüdische Volkspartei, played a major role; Heinrich Stahl, of the Liberal (Reform Jewish) Association, was president of the community. At the end of 1933 an agreement was reached for the establishment of the REICHSVERTRETUNG DER DEUTSCHEN JUDEN (Reich Representation of German Jews), with its head office in Berlin.

There was an upsurge of Zionist activities in the Nazi period, in which the Zionist organ *Jüdische Rundschau,* edited by Robert WELTSCH, played a major part. He-Haluts and other Zionist youth movements gained substantial strength, and *hakhsharot* (agricultural training centers) were set up for their members, including those of the religiously observant youth organizations. Recha Freier founded YOUTH ALIYA, which aimed to take young Jews to Palestine. Zionist activists, aided by emissaries from abroad, helped organize "illegal" immigration to Palestine. Welfare agencies and educational institutions also greatly increased the scope of their operations; Jewish students from the public schools transferred to the community-maintained schools, and the Hochschule (from 1934, Lehranstalt) für die Wissenschaft des Judentums (College of Jewish Studies) expanded the range of its work. In response to the book burning staged by the Nazis in front of the Berlin Opera on May 10, 1933, the KULTURBUND DEUTSCHER JUDEN (Cultural Society of German Jews) was established, launching its activities in the fall of that year. The Jewish press improved the quality of its contents and raised its circulation. The Jews of Berlin turned inward, beginning a new life that saw the flourishing of Jewish culture.

Like the rest of German Jewry, the Jews of Berlin suffered from the Nazi restrictions and persecution campaign. The relaxation of anti-Jewish measures on the eve of the Olympic games in Berlin, in summer 1936, was of short duration, coming to an end as soon as the games were over. On May 30, 1937, a *Razzia* (raid) against Jews took place in the streets of Berlin, for all passersby to see.

The year 1933 also marked the beginning of a steady rise of Jewish migration, from all over Germany, including Berlin. Detailed figures on the movement of Jews to and from Berlin in the period 1933 to 1937 have not been preserved; of the 22,636 Jews who emigrated from Germany in 1937, 5,558 are known to have had their homes in Berlin. By the end of 1937 the Jewish population decreased to 140,000, and by September 1939 to 82,788—which was about 50 percent of the population figure in 1933. In Germany as a whole, the number of Jews in that period was reduced to approximately one-third of the number in 1933. This disparity between the rate of emigration from Berlin and that from the rest of the country may have meant that the Jews of Berlin felt more secure than other German Jews. In January 1939 the ZENTRALSTELLE FÜR JÜDISCHE AUSWANDERUNG (Central Office for Jewish Emigration) was set up in Berlin, on the model of an office that the Nazis had first established in Vienna.

On March 5, 1938, the Berlin Jewish community, like the other Jewish communities in Germany, was deprived of its status as a recognized public corporate body. In August 1939 it was reestablished as a "society" under the aegis of the Reichsvereinigung der Juden in Deutschland (the successor of the Reichsvertretung); in the interim period, between March 1938 and August 1939, the community was administered by an emergency committee of three (Heinrich STAHL, Moritz Henschel, and Herbert Selinger). From August 1939 on, the community was classified, in legal terms, as a "Jewish religious society," administered by a five-man committee and supervised by the Gestapo. Up to March 1940 Stahl was the chairman of the committee; he was followed by Henschel, who remained in office until February 1943, when the society was dissolved on Gestapo orders.

On *Kristallnacht* (November 9–10, 1938), most of the synagogues of Berlin were burnt down, and Jewish schools, the offices of Jewish public institutions, and Jewish medical clinics came under attack. Jewish department stores were stormed and ransacked, and the shattering of the shopwindows of the Jewish clothing stores on Leipzigerstrasse gave the pogrom its name. Dozens of Jews were murdered, and several thousand were arrested and taken to concentration camps (mainly to the ORANIENBURG camp). In the

A Jewish snowman in Berlin (1939). [Bildarchiv Preussischer Kulturbesitz]

wake of *Kristallnacht,* twelve hundred Jewish commercial enterprises in Berlin were put up for Aryanization; buyers were found for seven hundred, while the remaining five hundred were declared unsalable.

Other developments that followed *Kristallnacht* were the closing down, looting, and burning of dozens of Jewish institutions and the confiscation of their property, among them the Lehranstalt für die Wissenschaft des Judentums, the rabbinical seminary, the Jewish community library and museum, the archives of the community and of the Centralverein, and the library of the Adas Israel community. Also confiscated were the Jewish manuscripts, documents, and books in the libraries of Berlin universities, in the Bible Research Institute of the University of Berlin, in the Prussian State Archives (Geheimes Staatsarchiv), and in the Berlin city council archives. Religious services were permitted in four synagogues only (that number being increased to nine in early 1939). Only one Jewish newspaper, *Das Jüdische Nachrichtenblatt,* was allowed to be published in Berlin after November 1938.

As of December 3 of that year, Jews were no longer free to move about as they liked. Under the *Judenbann* (ban on Jews), they were prohibited from entering government office compounds. The Berlin police also prohibited Jews from using bathhouses and public swimming pools. During the war, the only place where the Jews were allowed to take walks was the Weissensee Jewish cemetery, but in May 1942 even that was put out of bounds.

Also in December 1938, the evacuation of Jews from residences in the prestigious parts of the city was launched, the official pretext being Albert SPEER's plans for the rebuilding of Berlin. At that point the Jewish community's housing advisory office—which was subject to city police orders—was given wide powers regarding the housing of Berlin Jews. In the final stage, when the community was being liquidated, the data accumulated by that office was a major source for drawing up the lists of Jews to be deported to their death.

In the post-*Kristallnacht* period, the Jewish community leaders saw their major task as facilitating the emigration from the Reich of the greater part of German Jewry, and, in the meantime, as creating temporary frameworks that would enable the Jews to hold out until their chance for emigration came.

At the outbreak of the war, an estimated 75,500 Jews were living in Berlin. The community employment office sought to find them productive job opportunities. In March 1941 Berlin Jews were also subjected to a labor draft; they were paid a wage from which various deductions were made, including a head tax that went to the community.

In early 1941 some 74,500 Jews were still living in Berlin; by October 1941 another 1,350 had emigrated, the last group of emigrants leaving the city on October 18 of that year. On October 23 further emigration of Jews from Germany was prohibited. It is known, however, that another 62 Jews managed to get out by December of 1941, and another 9 Jews left the country legally in the course of 1942. On September 19, 1942, the yellow badge (*see* BADGE, JEWISH) was distributed to the Jews in community offices, for which they had to pay ten pfennig. This well-organized distribution process enabled the community officials to carry out Gestapo orders to update the existing card index of Jewish residents of Berlin.

On the Day of Atonement in 1941, while Rabbi Leo BAECK was preaching, three top officials of the community (the president, Moritz Henschel; his deputy, Philip Kotzover; and the director of the housing office, Martha Mosse) were called out of the synagogue and summoned to Gestapo headquarters. There they were told of an impending operation under which a substantial number of Jews were to be evacuated from Berlin. The community was ordered to submit without delay up-to-date lists of the city's Jews, including their addresses, and to turn the Levetzow Street synagogue into a transit camp for one thousand evacuees. Later, other such assembly points, pending evacuation, were set up in such places as the Jewish home for the aged, the community office building, and the Jewish hospital.

The deportation of Jews, under the cover of evacuation of the apartments they were occupying, now became the established route. A few days prior to the date fixed for their reporting to the assembly place, deportees were advised that in view of their impending departure for emigration (*Abwanderung*), their apartment leases had run out; they were also ordered to submit to the community office a declaration containing a detailed list of all their property. This declaration was used by the community and the chiefs of the housing authority in Berlin in the liquidation of Jewish property in the city. (These lists have survived.) A JÜDISCHER ORDNUNGSDIENST—a form of Jewish police—was set up to make sure that the deportees would report at the appointed time.

Hundreds of Jews committed suicide rather than face deportation. In order to stem the panic, the publication of obituary notices was restricted, and a special section was formed in the Jewish hospital to handle the suicide cases. Some Jews tried to go underground (a number of them were helped by German organizations), and others tried to escape to neighboring countries. The Gestapo activated a network of Jewish informants that succeeded in locating many Jews who had gone underground.

The first transport left Berlin on October 18, 1941, taking some one thousand Jews to the Łódź ghetto, and from there to their deaths. Up to January 20, 1942, the day of the WANNSEE CONFERENCE, ten thousand Jews from Berlin were deported to their deaths, in nine transports, their destinations being RIGA, MINSK, KOVNO, and Łódź. The first transport for the THERESIENSTADT ghetto left Berlin on June 6, 1942; the first to go straight to AUSCHWITZ left Berlin on July 11 of that year.

In May 1942 the Jewish Communist underground exploded a fire bomb at the anti-Soviet exhibition "The Soviet Paradise"; as retaliation, 500 Jews were seized, of whom 250 were shot to death on the spot and the other 250 were deported to the Sachsenhausen camp. The Haluts underground in Berlin ordered its members to go into hiding. In June, the services provided by the Jewish community were curtailed; the schools were closed down, and some of the community staff were deported to the extermination camps. Alois BRUNNER—Adolf EICHMANN's deputy—was not satisfied with the rate at which the deportations were being carried out and took personal charge of the deportations in November and December of 1942. In December, when some of the Jews summoned for deportation had not reported, a corresponding number of Jews were seized in the Jewish community offices and put on the deportation train or shot to death on the spot. It is estimated that in the course of 1942 the number of Jews in Berlin was reduced from fifty-five thousand to thirty-three thousand.

On January 26 and 27, 1943, the senior officers of the Reichsvereinigung—Paul EPPSTEIN, Philip Kotzover, and Rabbi Leo Baeck—were deported to Theresienstadt. Until the beginning of 1943, Jews employed in the German armament industry were considered safe from deportation; however, on February 27 and 28 such Jews were rounded up at their place of work and taken straight to the assembly points. The large number of prisoners seized on this occasion required the use of improvised places of detention, including the Jewish community building and a concert hall. Among the Jews arrested were the spouses of Aryans, and those who had been exempt from wearing the yellow badge; some of these Jews were released, perhaps because of a demonstration that was staged by their wives.

On January 28, 1943, the Gestapo ordered the Berlin Jewish community legally liquidated, and a month later, on February 22, Henschel reported that the order had been carried out. Jews who were not subject to deportation were trained to take over various posts in the Jewish hospital and in the Rest-Reichsvereinigung (the "rump" association).

The great deportations of February and March 1943 had Auschwitz as their destination. The number of Jews left in Berlin in March of that year is estimated at 27,260, which by the following month had gone down to 18,300. Goebbels noted in his diary on April 11, 1943, that "Berlin's liberation from the Jews" was one of the regime's most important political achievements. In early June 1943 only 6,800 Jews were left in the city. On June 10, the offices of the Jewish community, as well as of all other Jewish organizations in Berlin, were closed down and the remaining employees were deported to their death. The capital of the Third Reich was declared *judenrein* ("cleansed of Jews").

The Jewish hospital, directed by Dr. Walter Lustig, was in operation up to the end of the war; it served mainly as an assembly camp for Jews from Berlin and other parts of Germany, pending their deportation to the extermination camps. The Jewish cemetery in Weissensee was also functioning. The last deportations from Berlin took place on January 5, 1945 (to Auschwitz); February 2, 1945 (to SACHSENHAUSEN and RAVENSBRÜCK); and March 27, 1945 (to Theresienstadt). A total of 63 deportation transports, carrying thirty-five thousand Jews, left Berlin for the various extermination camps, and 117 transports, consisting of a total of fifteen thousand Jews, went to the Theresienstadt ghetto.

It is estimated that forty-seven hundred Jews married to Aryans survived in Berlin, plus another fourteen hundred Jews who had gone into hiding; nineteen hundred Jews returned to Berlin from the extermination camps.

BIBLIOGRAPHY

Baker, L. *Days of Sorrow and Pain: Leo Baeck and the Berlin Jews.* New York, 1978.

Ball-Kaduri, K. J. "Berlin is 'Purged' of Jews: The Jews in Berlin in 1943." *Yad Vashem Studies* 5 (1963): 271–316.

Bendt, V. "Die Synagogen unter dem Nationalsozialismus." In vol. 2 of *Synagogen in Berlin*, edited by R. Bothe and V. Bendt, pp. 49–123. Berlin, 1983.

Offenberg, M., ed. *Adass Jisroel: Die Jüdische Gemeinde in Berlin (1869–1942): Vernichtet und vergessen.* Berlin, 1986.

Sellenthin, H. G. *Geschichte der Juden in Berlin und des Gebäudes Fasanenstrasse 79/80.* Berlin, 1959.

GABRIEL E. ALEXANDER

BERLIN DOCUMENTS CENTER. *See* Documentation Centers: Berlin Documents Center.

BERMAN, ADOLF ABRAHAM (1906–1978), psychologist, Zionist activist in the WARSAW ghetto underground, and one of the leaders of ZEGOTA (the Polish Council for Aid to Jews) in the Polish part of Warsaw. Berman obtained his D.Phil. degree at Warsaw University and was director of the Jewish center of psychological counseling clinics in Warsaw. He also taught in high schools and published articles dealing with social and educational psychology. From his early years, he was active in the Left Po'alei Zion. Under the German occupation, he was director of CENTOS (Federation of Associations for the Care of Orphans in Poland) in the Warsaw ghetto, a league affiliated with the Jewish self-help organization. Berman was active in the political underground and was one of the founders of the Antifascist Bloc, the precursor to the ŻYDOWSKA ORGANIZACJA BOJOWA (Jewish Fighting Organization; ŻOB) in the ghetto.

In September 1942, Berman moved to the "Aryan" side of Warsaw, together with his wife, Batya, who had been active in the ghetto underground as manager of a network of lending libraries. Posing as a Pole, Berman lived among the Poles up to the end of the war, making strenuous efforts to help the Jews, as representative of the Żydowski Komitet Narodowy (Jewish National Committee) and as secretary of Zegota. Owing to his connections and his non-Jewish appearance, he was able to move about freely and promote widespread efforts for the rescue of Jews surviving in Warsaw after the liquidation of the ghetto. He also helped to save the written records that had been hidden on the "Aryan" side, among them the last of the chronicles recorded by Emanuel RINGELBLUM. In January 1944, Berman fell into the hands of Polish blackmailers, but was freed by the help of his Polish friends and the payment of ransom.

When Poland was liberated, Berman became the chairman of the Central Committee of the Jews of Poland and a member of the Polish parliament. In 1950 he settled in Israel, was active in the leftist political camp, was elected to the second Knesset (Israeli parliament), and was involved in the activities of survivors' organizations and former underground fighters living in Israel. His underground and public activities during the Holocaust period are described in his two books, *The Underground Period* (1971) and *In the Place Where Fate Brought Me: With the Jews of Warsaw, 1939–1942* (1978; both in Hebrew).

BIBLIOGRAPHY

Kermish, J. "The Activities of the Council for Aid to Jews ('Zegota') in Occupied Poland." In *Rescue Attempts during the Holocaust,* edited by I. Gutman and E. Zuroff, pp. 367–398. Jerusalem, 1977.

ISRAEL GUTMAN

BERMUDA CONFERENCE, conference convened by the United States and Great Britain on April 19, 1943, ostensibly to find solutions for wartime refugees. In fact, it marked the high point of efforts by officials in both nations to thwart a move for more effective action to rescue European Jewry.

The idea of convening a refugee conference grew out of a need, felt first by British authorities in the final months of 1942, to defuse public protest after revelations were confirmed that the Nazi regime had actually begun a policy of systematic liquidation of Jews.

The British initiative rekindled a familiar diplomatic game between the two Allied governments. Diplomatic dispatches from both sides were prefaced with long recitations of the efforts they had undertaken in the rescue cause. The American dispatches even mentioned the internment of Japanese-Americans as evidence of the heavy burden the country was supporting. Resentful of the initiative's implication, American dispatches spoke of the forthcoming conference as if the idea had originated in Washington, much to the chagrin of the British, who hastened to correct the misimpression.

The site of the meeting also created some conflict, since neither side wanted to be linked directly to the refugee-rescue debacle—the lack of any serious effort to rescue Jews. Thus, Canada discouraged a suggestion that the conference convene in Ottawa, and the State Department (*see* UNITED STATES DEPARTMENT OF STATE) rejected Washington. Finally Assistant Secretary of State Breckinridge Long suggested the island of Bermuda, which, because of its inaccessibility during wartime, would allow both sides control of the press, and the conference itself could be kept free of the representatives of private agencies such as the JOINT DISTRIBUTION COMMITTEE (JDC) and the WORLD JEWISH CONGRESS.

As preparations for the conference developed, it was clear that both sides had set such severe limitations on what might be discussed and who might speak at the plenary sessions that the conference would have virtually nothing to show for its trouble. There was an insistence that the Jewish character of the problem be played down and a more universal approach assumed. The British, in the face of information that the Germans had earmarked the Jews for extinction, insisted that Jews were merely one of many victimized groups. The State Department continued to employ the term "political refugee," a euphemism to conceal the racial character of the refugee problem. In fact, neither side wanted to discuss the matter of the "Final Solution" but preferred to limit debate to the "refugee question." Even at that, the prohibition on circumventing American immigration laws that had been invoked at the EVIAN CONFERENCE remained in force. In the event (claimed as unlikely) that shipping should become available, the American delegation insisted that prisoners of war receive priority over refugees. Actually, there never was a shortage of ships with empty holds returning to American ports. Discussion concerning Palestine, the likeliest haven, was ruled out, as was the possibility of direct negotiations with Berlin. Not even the suggestion of sending food packages to concentration camp inmates was accepted for discussion, although the British themselves had established a precedent for such a policy by feeding the inhabitants of occupied Greece throughout the war. The conference found itself in the embarrassing situation of having little left to discuss.

MEMORANDUM

February 22, 1944

Memorandum of Myron C. Taylor re Bermuda Conference and the IGC. (Material obtained from file in Visa Division, State Department)

Myron C. Taylor addressed a memorandum on April 30, 1943, to Welles, Long, and Hull. The occasion was a wire from the Department to London requesting a meeting of the Intergovernmental Committee after the Bermuda Conference. A note in the file states that Mr. Taylor initialled the wire only on condition that his memorandum be presented to Mr. Long and the Secretary.

The text of the memorandum follows:

"Before any meeting is called the position of our own Government with respect to the refugee situation must be clearly developed. The Bermuda Conference was wholly ineffective, as I view it, and we knew it would be. What the IGC may be able to do, of course, is open to question, but with respect to anything that it may be able to do, it will require a commitment and large financial obligation if the plight of the refugees generally is to be relieved. The commitment also obligates this Government, if made, to find not only temporary places of refuge, but permanent places of settlement. It is my opinion, as it was before the Bermuda Conference, that the position of our Government and of the British Government must be thoroughly clarified and clearly understood in advance and if nothing constructive can be assured, such a meeting will only be another failure.

Myron C. Taylor"

The following penciled notation appears at the bottom: "Eu concurs with Mr. Taylor's memorandum. T.B.C.", and below this notation were several initials which could not be deciphered. Opposite Mr. Long's name at the top were the words, in ink, "I agree".

Memorandum from Myron C. Taylor, the principal American representative at the Evian Conference, to Cordell Hull, the secretary of state, and Sumner Welles and Breckinridge Long, assistant secretaries of state, regarding the failure of the Bermuda Conference.

The disparity in rank between the two delegations also caused unforeseen problems. Composed of Richard Law, son of a former prime minister and parliamentary undersecretary of state, and Osbert Peake and George Hall of the Home Office, the British delegation far outranked the American. This was especially so after Myron Taylor, President Franklin D. ROOSEVELT's personal emissary to the Vatican, and James G. MCDONALD, former League of Nations high commissioner for refugees from Germany, declined to head the American delegation. The State Department was compelled to settle for Harold Willis Dodds, president of Princeton University; Sen. Scott Lucas, Democrat of Illinois; and Rep. Sol Bloom, Democrat from Manhattan and chairman of the House Committee on Foreign Affairs. The last-mentioned, a Jew, was destined to become the most controversial member of the American delegation because Jewish rescue agencies found him unacceptable. Two of the technical experts supporting the American delegation, G. Robert Borden Reams and Robert C. Alexander, had earned similar reputations among rescue advocates for their adamant opposition to refugees. The only sympathetic member of the delegation was George Backer, whose leading positions in the Organization for Rehabilitation through Training (ORT) and the Jewish Telegraph Agency made him especially knowledgeable about the fate of European Jewry.

The composition of the American delegation; the refusal to include Joseph SCHWARTZ, head of the European branch of the JDC; the rejection of rescue suggestions by Joseph Proskauer, head of the AMERICAN JEWISH COMMITTEE, and by Rabbi Stephen S. WISE, head of the American and World Jewish congresses; and the fact that the State Department limited the number of press correspondents to five, representing the major news agencies, convinced even the most hopeful rescue advocates (mostly, but not exclusively, American Jewish groups) that the Bermuda Conference would be simply a ploy to deflect an aroused public opinion.

Yet even that objective eluded the conferees, who tried to find a strategy that could create the illusion of action while at the same time making certain that nothing untoward was in fact done. Much time was devoted to the notion of revitalizing the INTERGOVERNMENTAL COMMITTEE ON REFUGEES (IGCR), which was originally created at the Evian Conference in 1938 to enter into negotiations with Berlin on the refugee question. But the disinterring of the virtually defunct agency posed problems. Since negotiating with the Nazi regime had now been ruled out by the delegations, neither side was willing to fund the IGCR, and certainly the Jewish agencies, which had originally underwritten it, were reluctant to enter into an agreement that they felt was designed to thwart rather than to aid rescue. The second objective—to enhance the flow of refugees out of areas such as Spain and Switzerland, where they had found a precarious haven, by establishing a refugee camp in North Africa—offered more hope. But this suggestion, rather than dealing with the millions in the Nazi grip, focused on those whose lives, though uncomfortable, were at least not in danger. Moreover, there was much opposition by the United States War Department and the British Foreign Office to establishing such a camp in a Muslim area. It was not established until over a year after the conference ended, when it was too late to do any good.

An early press release, sounding a hopeful note, stated that all problems were being discussed openly and good progress was being made. In fact, both delegations manifested the fear that Berlin would "dump" refugees with the Allies and use them as a weapon to compromise the Allied drive for final victory. The conference was in danger of rejecting all proposals and thereby defeating its own goal of soothing an aroused public opinion. It was George Backer, speaking to the conference on April 25, who pointed out this danger. He observed that shipping was in fact available, and that by limiting its concern to those who had found haven in neutral nations the conference would have nothing significant to show. It should at least try, Backer urged, to rescue 125,000 Jews in eastern Europe who imminently faced certain death. Backer made a special plea to save the thousands of Jewish children who could assure a Jewish future despite the radical losses. But this plea too was rejected.

A brief optimistic news bulletin that spoke of the possibility of helping "a substantial number of refugees" marked the end of the conference, but a final report of the deliberations and conclusions was not published until December 10, 1943, eight months later. The public embarrassment that Backer had predicted came to pass. The American Jewish press was virtually unanimous in condemning the conference. Some spoke of it as a particularly cruel duplicity in the midst of a mass-murder operation. Public protest, rather than being stilled, reached new heights. Even the small camp established in North Africa in March 1944 housed only 630 refugees, and strict orders were issued by the State Department that there should be "a good mix" in selecting them.

The use of a conference to assuage an aroused public sentiment reveals much about the American aspect of the Holocaust. It illustrates that even when it was possible to arouse an otherwise lethargic public about the fate of European Jewry, government officials experienced few qualms in devising strategies to deflect its concern. Both the British and American governments were willing to go to extraordinary lengths to avoid doing what needed to be done. The episode gives historians a clue to the atmosphere and intentions surrounding the rescue of the Jews.

BIBLIOGRAPHY

Feingold, H. L. *The Politics of Rescue.* New Brunswick, N.J., 1970.

Wasserstein, B. *Britain and the Jews of Europe, 1939–1945.* Oxford, 1979.

Wyman, D. S. *The Abandonment of the Jews: America and the Holocaust, 1941–1945.* New York, 1984.

HENRY L. FEINGOLD

BERNADOTTE, FOLKE (1895–1948), Swedish statesman; count of Wisborg and nephew of King Gustav V. During World War II Bernadotte represented the Swedish RED CROSS in the exchange of prisoners between Germany and the Allies. In 1943 he became its vice president and in 1946 he was appointed its president. Bernadotte negotiated with Heinrich HIMMLER on behalf of the Swedish Red Cross, and in March and April of 1945 succeeded in persuading him to release more than seven thousand Scandinavian nationals who were being held in Nazi concentration camps; these included over four hundred Danish Jews imprisoned in THERESIENSTADT.

Following a meeting between Norbert Masur, the representative of the WORLD JEWISH CONGRESS in Sweden, and Himmler, Bernadotte also succeeded in arranging for the release of ten thousand women from the RAVENSBRÜCK concentration camp; two thousand of the women, who were nationals of various countries, were Jewish. Most of them were transferred to SWEDEN.

On May 20, 1948, the United Nations Security Council appointed Bernadotte as a mediator on its behalf between Israel and the invading Arab countries. He negotiated a four-week truce, beginning on June 11, 1948, but was unable to obtain from the Arab states an agreement for its extension. Bernadotte then worked out a plan for the settlement of the conflict based on Israeli concessions to the Arabs, but on September 17 of that year he was assassinated in Jerusalem by Hazit ha-Moledet (Fatherland Front), a group connected with the LOḤAMEI ḤERUT ISRAEL organization.

The Jewish National Fund planted a forest in the hills of Jerusalem in honor of Folke Bernadotte. His book, *Instead of Arms,* was published in 1949.

Folke Bernadotte.

BIBLIOGRAPHY

Hewins, R. *Bernadotte: Sein Leben und Werk.* Frankfurt, 1952.

Svenson, S. *Folke Bernadotte: Fredkämpe och folksforsonare.* Stockholm, 1949.

ELISHEVA SHAUL

BERNHEIM PETITION, petition against Nazi ANTI-JEWISH LEGISLATION presented to the League of Nations in May 1933. The Nazis came to power in January 1933 and in April of that year introduced anti-Jewish laws. The Jewish public outside Germany sought ways to protect the civil rights of German Jews. In their search, the Jewish activists cited the German-Polish Geneva Convention of 1922, under which both parties were committed to protect the minorities in Upper Silesia by safeguarding their equal rights and abstaining from any form of discrimination against them. That convention provided that in cases of differences in the interpretation of its provisions, the League of Nations Council would be the arbitrator, and that individuals or groups who felt that their rights under the convention were being violated would also have the right to petition the council. The Jewish activists decided to resort to this latter provision, basing themselves on a petition signed by Franz Bernheim, one of ten thousand Jewish residents of Upper Silesia, in which he complained of the anti-Jewish laws being applied in that area.

In May 1933, after the Bernheim petition had been presented to the council, the German representative informed the council that his government acknowledged that an international convention to which it had subscribed had priority over internal German legislation. On ending its deliberations, in June 1933, the council stated that the complaints raised in the Bernheim petition were valid and that Germany should abolish all discrimination against Jews in Upper Silesia.

The German government, which had reason to be interested in the full observance of the Geneva Convention, was forced to issue specific instructions to the authorities of Upper Silesia that invalidated the application of anti-Jewish legislation in that region. In addition, the German government ordered the country's central authorities to refrain from all anti-Jewish measures in Upper Silesia, and the Nazi party issued similar instructions. Finally, in September 1933, the German government submitted an explicit declaration to the League of Nations Council, in which it stated that all anti-Jewish legislation was null and void in Upper Silesia. The ongoing activities of the Comité des Délégations Juives (the international body set up after World War I to protect Jewish rights), and the measures that the Upper Silesian Jews took to organize themselves to protect their civil rights, also played a role in ensuring that these rights remained inviolate, up to May 1937, the terminal date of the German-Polish Convention. Until then, even the NUREMBERG LAWS were not applied.

Following the termination of the convention, the German and Polish governments signed a joint declaration concerning the protection of minority rights in their respective countries. This was a strictly bilateral statement that did not recognize any role for the League of Nations; in practice, the declaration meant that the Jews of Upper Silesia were being deprived of their rights.

From then on, the Nazi regime embarked upon a systematic policy designed to equate the status of Upper Silesian Jews with that of the Jews in the rest of Germany. The process was completed on March 31, 1938.

BIBLIOGRAPHY

Brugel, J. W. "The Bernheim Petition: A Challenge to Nazi Germany in 1933." *Patterns of Prejudice* 17/2 (1983): 17–25.

Feinberg, N. "Jewish Political Activities against the Nazi Regime in the Years 1933–1939." In *Jewish Resistance during the Holocaust.* Proceedings of the Conference on Manifestations of Jewish Resistance, pp. 74–93. Jerusalem, 1971.

DAVID HADAR

BESSARABIA, region situated between the Prut and Dniester rivers; the larger part is today in the Moldavian SSR and the smaller part in the Ukrainian SSR. Bessarabia was part of the principality of Moldavia until its annexation by tsarist Russia in 1812. In 1918 it was incorporated into ROMANIA, and on June 29, 1940, it was annexed to the Soviet Union, after the NAZI-SOVIET PACT and a Soviet ultimatum. In late June 1941, a few days after the German invasion of the Soviet Union, it again came under Romanian rule.

The Bessarabian Jews numbered about 205,000 in 1939. In June 1940, when the Romanian army retreated from Bessarabia, the Jews were accused of greeting the entering Soviet army as a liberator and of humiliating and striking the retreating Romanian soldiers. They were also accused of being hostile toward Romania, the Romanians, and the local inhabitants, and of collaborating with the Communist regime. In June 1941, shortly before the outbreak of the war between Germany and the USSR, the Soviet authorities deported between five thousand and ten thousand Bessarabian Jews, considered "enemies of the people," to Siberia and other remote regions. The number of Jews who succeeded in fleeing into the interior of the USSR in the first days of the German invasion was relatively small: the Soviet authorities prevented passage to the Ukraine and maintained guard units on the old border along the Dniester, and the German units swept rapidly from north to south on a wide front; within several weeks Bessarabia was in the rear. Some thirty thousand to forty thousand Jews fled, of whom twenty-five thousand were caught by the Soviet army and driven back to Bessarabia. Many escaped to ODESSA and were trapped in the siege there.

On the eve of the invasion of the Soviet Union, the Romanian dictator, Ion ANTONESCU, issued a secret edict, *Curatirea Terenului* (Cleansing of the Ground). It contained three sections, ordering on-the-spot physical extermination of all the Jews living in the villages; arrest of the Jews living in the cities and their concentration in ghettos; and detention of all the Communists and those who had served the Soviets during the year of Soviet rule in Bessarabia, with execution of those proved guilty of such collaboration. Units of gendarmes, who received the order prior to the outbreak of the war, participated in the massacre of Jews in the cities neighboring on the new border: Roman, Fălticeni, and Galaţi. The secret order for the army, code named *Ordine Speciale* (Special Orders), was transmitted to Gen. Ilie Seteflea by Ion Antonescu, and its execution was entrusted to the army administration known as Pretoria, headed by Gen. Ion Topor. The army units were ordered to help the soldiers actually engaged in the killings.

A special killing unit was hastily created from the Security Services, commanded by the deputy prime minister, Mihai ANTONESCU, and called the Esalon Special (Special Echelon). The unit, comprising about 160 soldiers, took part in the massacre of Jews and cooperated with the parallel German units. Together with the German army and Einsatzgruppe D, they massacred about 150,000 to 160,000 Jews during July and August 1941. The Romanians were responsible for most of these massacres, in which nearly all the village Jews were exterminated.

The second stage began in August 1941 with the creation of the camps and the ghettos in which the remaining Jews were concentrated. Most of the camps were established in Jewish villages such as VERTUJENI; in Jewish towns where most of the inhabitants had been killed by the Romanian army, such as MARCULEŞTI; and in Jewish quarters and ruined parts of cities and towns such as Bălţi, Soroca, and Khotin. In KISHINEV a ghetto was established in the poor and partially destroyed Jewish area, and 11,000 of the 50,000 Jews who had lived there before the war were forced into it. On September 4, 64,176 Jews still remained in all of Bessarabia, and on September 25, there were 43,397.

The third stage began on September 15, 1941, when Ion Antonescu ordered the deportation of all the Jews of Bessarabia to TRANSNISTRIA, the area of the Ukraine occupied by Romania. It took place chiefly on foot, by way of four crossing points: Atachi, Cosauti, Rezina, and Tiraspol. Most of the Jews were deported via Atachi, a Romanian village on the banks of the Dniester. According to an official estimate, about twenty-five thousand Jews were killed during the deportation, and tens of thousands were cast into an improvised communal grave in the Cosauti Forest in central Bessarabia, which was traversed by the convoys on their way to the crossing point. Tens of thousands were drowned in the Dniester River. For about a month convoys of Jews were transferred from place to place without planning or need, the principal aim apparently being to reduce the number of Jews. Anyone falling behind was shot by the Romanian escorts.

All the property of the Bessarabian Jews was plundered in several waves of "spontaneous," organized pillage. The inspectors of the Romanian National Bank "legally" confiscated valuables, jewels, and cash, and civilians and soldiers robbed the contents of

the deportees' homes and the belongings they had prepared to take with them. Because of massive corruption at all levels of government, only a small part of the "legally" confiscated property reached the coffers of the state treasury. Many acts of violence were committed by the general population, and far more by the Romanian soldiers. The homes, apartments, and business concerns of the Jews became state property (*averea statului*) and were handed over to the National Center of Romanization. The latter gave or sold them to Romanians, principally to ex-servicemen, widows, and Romanians from other regions.

In the census of "those of Jewish blood" conducted in May 1942, only 227 Jews were counted in the whole of Bessarabia, and most of these were Jewish only by virtue of the race laws. After the war, about 7,000 to 10,000 Jews who had fled into the Soviet Union or had been deported by the Soviet government before the war returned to Bessarabia. Some of the approximately 50,000 Jews liberated in Transnistria in the spring of 1944 had been among those deported from Bessarabia.

BIBLIOGRAPHY

Ancel, J. "The Romanian Way of Solving the 'Jewish Problem' in Bessarabia and Bukovina, June–July 1941." *Yad Vashem Studies* 19 (1988): 187–232.

JEAN ANCEL

BEST, WERNER (b. 1903), Nazi official; a senior member of the SS and Sicherheitspolizei (Security Police), and German plenipotentiary in occupied Denmark from 1942 to 1945. Born in Darmstadt to a family of officials, Best studied law and in 1929 was appointed *Gerichtsassessor* (judge) in the Hessian Department of Justice. He entered the Nazi party in 1930 and the SS in 1931. In 1933, very soon after the Nazi seizure of power, he was appointed state commissioner for the Hessian police force and police president for the province.

He progressed rapidly in subsequent years, becoming legal adviser to the Gestapo and deputy to Reinhard HEYDRICH and Heinrich HIMMLER. From 1935 to 1940 he was bureau chief in the head office of the SD (Sicherheitsdienst; Security Service) in Berlin. From September 1939 to June 1940 Best headed Section II of the REICHSSICHERHEITSHAUPTAMT (Reich Security Main Office; RSHA); it was for service in this capacity that he was later accused of complicity in the murder of Jews and members of the Polish intelligentsia in occupied Poland. He then served for two years (June 1940 to August 1942) as *Ministerialdirektor* of the military administration attached to the High Command in occupied France. His tasks included the suppression of the French Résistance and the "de-Judaizing" of France. From November 1942 until 1945, Best served as German plenipotentiary in occupied DENMARK. There is evidence that he tried to avert the impact of the "Final Solution" on the Danish Jews, almost all of whom escaped to Sweden.

In 1949 Best was sentenced to death by a Danish court, but this was commuted to twelve years' imprisonment. He was in fact released in 1951, whereupon he returned to Germany and became legal adviser to the Stinnes group of firms. A Berlin denazification court fined him 70,000 marks in 1958 as punishment for his role in the leadership of the SS. In 1969 he was arrested on charges of mass murder in Poland, but he was released on grounds of health in 1972. The charges were not formally withdrawn.

BIBLIOGRAPHY

Petrow, R. *The Bitter Years: The Invasion and Occupation of Denmark and Norway, April 1940–1945.* New York, 1974.

Yahil, L. *The Rescue of Danish Jewry: Test of a Democracy.* Philadelphia, 1969.

LIONEL KOCHAN

BETAR. *See* Youth Movements: General Survey.

BET LOḤAMEI HA-GETTA'OT. *See* Museums and Memorial Institutes: Bet Loḥamei ha-Getta'ot.

BIAŁYSTOK, city in northeastern POLAND, seat of the district of that name. Records of Białystok's existence date back to the fourteenth century. In 1807 it was handed over to the Russians; during the interwar period, it was part of independent Poland. The presence of Jews there is first mentioned in the mid-seventeenth century. The development of Białystok and of its Jewish community into a great center was the result of the growth of the textile industry in the nineteenth century. From a population of 400 at the beginning of that century, the city had grown to 61,500 by 1913; its Jewish population meanwhile ranged from 66 percent to 75 percent of the total (48,000 in 1913). In the interwar period the Jewish population went down to between 50 percent and 60 percent.

The first Jewish factory was established in 1850; by 1912, almost 90 percent of the textile factories in the city were Jewish-owned. In World War I most of the factories were destroyed; of the new factories and stores opened between 1921 and 1939, 75 percent belonged to Jews. The Jewish community had an intensive educational and cultural network.

Białystok was occupied by the Germans on September 15, 1939, but a week later, on September 22, it was handed over to the Soviet Union, which held it for the next twenty-one months. On June 27, 1941, the Germans took Białystok for the second time, and the same day, two thousand Jews were burned alive, shot, or tortured to death. That day, which the Jews came to call "Red Friday," marked the beginning of the end for the Jews of Białystok. In the first two weeks of the occupation the Jews were attacked repeatedly, and another four thousand were murdered in an open field near Pietraszek—members of the intelligentsia, Communists, and other political figures.

Two days after the occupation, the military commander of the city summoned Białystok's chief rabbi, Dr. Gedaliah Rosenmann, and the chairman of the Jewish Community Council, Efraim BARASZ, to his office and ordered them to form a JUDENRAT (Jewish Council). Within a day or two the Judenrat had come into existence, comprising twelve members, all of them veteran public figures. A month later a new Judenrat, twice the size of its predecessor, was established with Barasz as acting chairman. A ghetto was set up and, on August 1, 1941, fifty thousand Białystok Jews were confined there (including some from the Białystok district, outside the city itself). They were packed into a small area, a newly developed non-Jewish neighborhood which was split into two parts: east and west, divided by the Biała River. The ghetto's main gate was at 3 Upiecka Street; another gate was set up at 4 Jurowiecka, and there was eventually a third gate. The Judenrat had its offices at 32 Kupiecka, and most of its departmental offices, dealing with the ghetto's day-to-day affairs, were housed there as well.

The history of the Białystok ghetto can be divided into three periods: (1) from its occupation on June 27, 1941, until August 15, 1941, during which time the city was under military rule; (2) from August 15, 1941, to November 1942, when it was under a civilian district administration; (3) from November 1942 to the final liquidation of the ghetto in August 1943, when the Gestapo and the SS were in control.

The ghetto rapidly became a center of industry, a supply base for essential items required by the economic arm of the occupation authorities—and a constant target of German plunder and pillage. Most of the Białystok Jews worked in ghetto industries; a relatively small number were employed in German establishments outside the ghetto. The ghetto had about ten factories and a large number of newly established workshops, manufacturing numerous and diverse items. The Germans made up the orders for the items to be manufactured—the army's requirements figured prominently in these—and passed them on to the Judenrat for implementation. In addition to the "legal" manufacturing operations, which dealt exclusively with the needs of the occupation authorities, the ghetto also ran a variegated, clandestine "illegal" industry, which turned out products for the use of the ghetto inhabitants themselves. There was an open trade in clothes, leather goods, and textile products, as well as other items, which were exchanged for food. Other kinds of transactions also took place, based for the most part on smuggling. The Judenrat derived a handsome income from the tax that every shopkeeper had to pay it for wares sold. By mid-1942, however, the Gestapo ordered the Judenrat to put

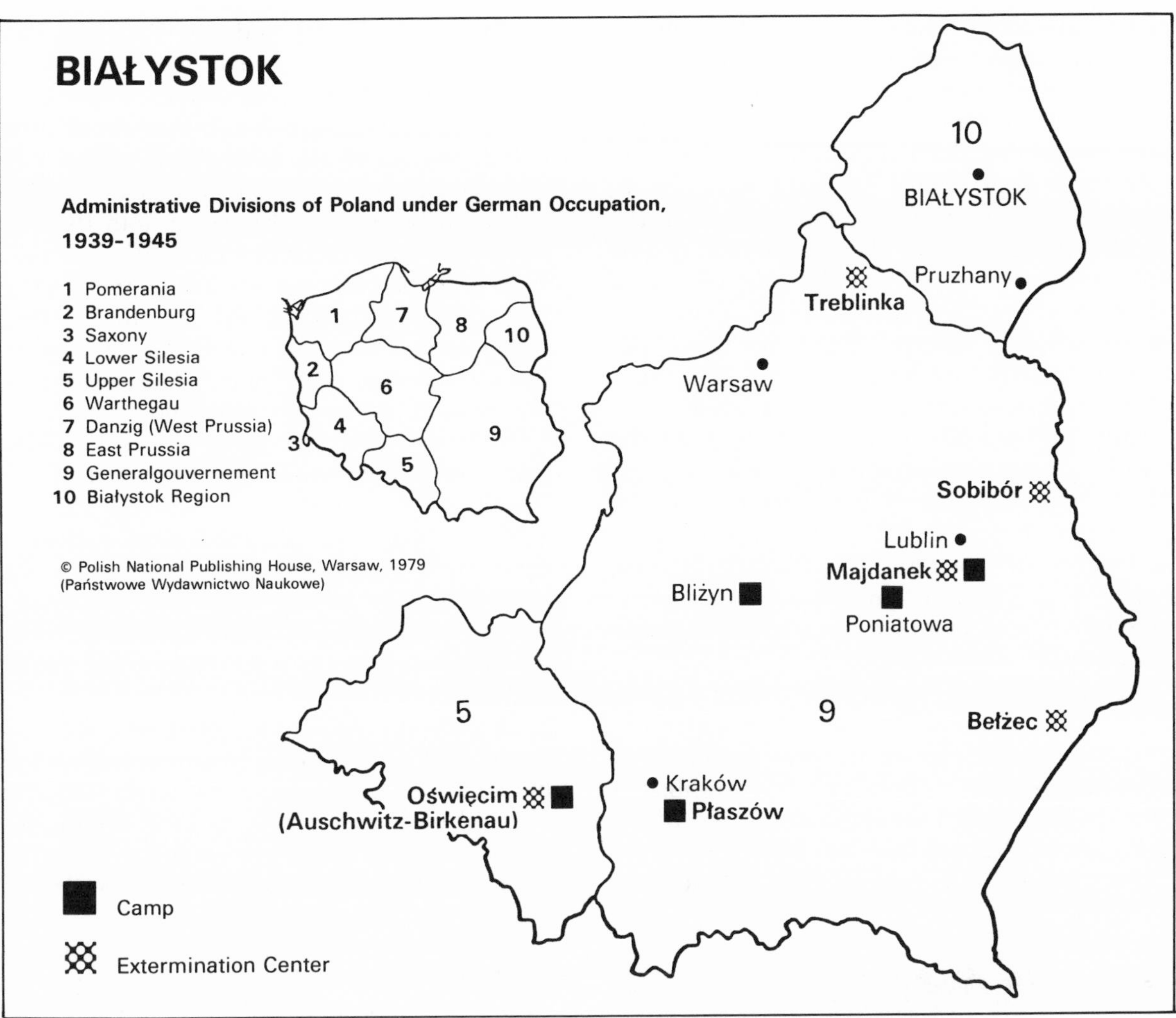

an end to the commercial activities in the ghetto.

The German civil administration supplied the ghetto population with its meager rations through the Judenrat. The flow of supplies, however, was irregular, except for bread, which did appear on a more or less regular basis. In order to increase the quantity of food available in the ghetto, the Judenrat encouraged inhabitants to grow vegetables and fruit on plots of land it owned (the former sites of buildings that had been destroyed and cleared of their ruins). These plots were dubbed "Judenrat gardens."

Between September 18 and October 21, 1941, on orders given by the German authorities, the Judenrat transferred 4,500 inhabitants of the ghetto to the town of PRUZHANY, some 62 miles (100 km) south of Białystok. These were the sick, the unskilled, and the unemployed—the poorest among the ghetto population. Some of them made their way back to Białystok, but most were killed when the Pruzhany ghetto was liquidated during the last four days of January 1943.

From the beginning, the various departments of the Judenrat had to deal with difficult and complex tasks. In the ghetto there were several soup kitchens, two hospitals, an outpatient clinic, a gynecological clinic, three pharmacies, a first-aid organization, two schools, a law court, and other institutions. A JÜDISCHER ORDNUNGSDIENST (Jewish police force) was also set up by the Judenrat, with a complement of 200 men.

Under the German occupation the Jewish youth movements, whose activities had come to an almost complete stop under the Soviets, resumed their operations. By early 1942, active cells of the various movements existed in the ghetto: the Communists, the BUND, and the Zionist youth movements He-Haluts–Dror, Ha-Shomer ha-Tsa'ir, Betar, and Ha-No'ar ha-Tsiyyoni. Also at that time, a group of Ha-Shomer ha-Tsa'ir activists came to Białystok from Vilna, with the assignment, *inter alia*, of creating a united front of all the youth movements in the ghetto. There was generally agreement that the goal of such a body was to wage armed struggle against the Germans, but several questions came up, apart from the existing rivalry and mutual distrust among the various movements (especially between the Communists and all the other groups). Would such a united front leave the ghetto for the forests to join the partisans in their fight? Or should its purpose be to prepare for fighting within the ghetto, and, if so, at what point and under what circumstances should an armed struggle be launched?

It was not until August 1942, following prolonged efforts made by two Ha-Shomer ha-Tsa'ir activists, Haika GROSMAN and Adek Boraks, that a headquarters was established for the first united underground in the Białystok ghetto. Named Bloc No. 1 or Front A, the headquarters represented the Communists, Ha-Shomer ha-Tsa'ir, and a part of the Bund. In November 1942, Mordechai TENENBAUM arrived in Białystok, on behalf of the Dror movement, and Bloc No. 2 then came into being, uniting all the other movements, with the Ha-Shomer ha-Tsa'ir members participating in both blocs. Efforts to join the two blocs in a single organization continued until shortly before the liquidation of the ghetto, but only in July 1943 did a united underground come into being, with Tenenbaum as its commander and Daniel Moszkowicz, a Communist, as deputy commander.

Deportation of Jews from Białystok.

On Tenenbaum's initiative a secret archive was established, under the direction of Zvi Mersik, on the model of the Warsaw ghetto's ONEG SHABBAT. The archive was in operation until April 1943, collecting testimonies and descriptions of events, as well as announcements issued by the Judenrat and reports of its meetings (which were channeled to the archive by Efraim Barasz). The documents, hidden on the Polish side of Białystok, were saved, and constitute an invaluable source of information. Barasz also made considerable sums of money available to Tenenbaum, but the latter's efforts to obtain arms from the Polish underground ARMIA KRAJOWA (Home Army) were all turned down.

From February 5 to 12, 1943, an *Aktion* was conducted in the ghetto, in the course of which two thousand Jews were shot on the spot and ten thousand were deported to TREBLINKA. Defense Bloc No. 1, with its meager resources, was activated and suffered many losses; other fighters, among them the Bloc commander Adek Boraks, were sent to Treblinka.

Barasz still believed that the thousands of Jews who had been deported from the ghetto would serve as scapegoats and that their sacrifice would save the remaining Jews, with the ghetto continuing to exist. In the course of the next six months, until the final liquidation of the ghetto—the threat of which was in the air throughout this period—Barasz made desperate efforts to ensure that the status quo in the ghetto was maintained, seeking to exploit the varied attitudes among the German authorities with this end in mind. The new orders that were coming in from the Wehrmacht reinforced his belief that the Białystok ghetto, which was now an important labor camp for the Germans, would not be liquidated. But this was not to be. Berlin issued the final order for the end of the ghetto, and in August 1943, Odilo GLOBOCNIK was assigned the task of its liquidation.

On the night of August 15–16, the Białystok ghetto was surrounded by three rings of German soldiers and SS men, armed with light and heavy arms, including artillery, and assisted by Ukrainian auxiliaries. One SS unit entered the ghetto and put the factories under guard. The previous night, Barasz had been summoned by the Gestapo. He was told that the ghetto inhabitants were going to be moved to LUBLIN and warned that the move had to proceed in an orderly fashion and that no resistance would be tolerated. Barasz tried in vain to have the order rescinded. The next morning, August 16, 1943, the ghetto population awoke to find the Judenrat's announcement posted on the walls, ordering it to report for immediate evacuation. The size of the ghetto population on the eve of liquidation was some thirty thousand.

At this moment—when tens of thousands of stupefied and exhausted Jews, with as many of their pitiful belongings as they could carry, were making their way to the assembly point on Jurowiecka Street—the underground rose in revolt. The precise moment was 10:00 a.m. According to a predetermined plan, the various cells of the underground took up their assigned positions, where they were to be issued arms and launch the attack. The plan was for the main force to attack the Germans along the Smolna Street fence, in order to breach the German lines and create a gap through which the fighters would make their escape to the forest. Diversionary attacks were to be made at four points, on Fabryczna, Nowogrodzka, Chmielna, and Ciepła streets, along the route where the Jews were making their way to the assembly point. The fighting was planned for the eastern side of the ghetto, where the command post of the revolt, as well as the arms cache and the fighters' bunker (at 7 Chmielna), were situated. Leaflets were passed out urging the population to disregard the evacuation order and not to proceed to the assembly point.

The fighting in the ghetto went on for five days, from August 16 to 20. The main battle in the first two days was fought over the Smolna Street fence. The fighters had only a few arms at their disposal, and over three hundred a day fell in battle. When the fighting was at its height, a large German force entered the ghetto, supported by armored cars and tanks. Realizing that the struggle inside the ghetto was lost, a group of fighters retreated into the Chmielna Street bunker, planning to make their way to the forest and continue the battle from there. On August 19, however, the Germans came upon the bunker and surrounded it, and all the seventy-two fighters in it (with one exception) were shot to death. The next day, which was the fifth day of fighting, the last defense positions—on Ciepła and Fabryczna streets—fell to the Germans. Mordechai Tenenbaum and Daniel Moszkowicz, who had led the uprising, were forced to retreat from the fighters' last stronghold, on Fabryzcna Street. There is no firm information on how they met their death, but it appears that they committed suicide.

The deportations from the ghetto began on August 18 and went on for three days, in the course of which the greater part of Białystok's Jews were deported. Some were sent to Treblinka, where they were murdered, and others to MAJDANEK, where they went through a *Selektion*. Those who were found fit were taken to the PONIATOWA camp the Bliżyn camp, or to AUSCHWITZ. A train with 1,200 Białystok children aboard was sent to THERESIENSTADT; a month later, these children too ended up in Auschwitz. In Białystok itself a "small ghetto" was left, containing 2,000 Jews, but three weeks later it too was liquidated and its occupants sent to Majdanek, among them Efraim Barasz, Gedaliah Rosenmann, and the commander of the Jewish police, Markus. They, too, were murdered in Majdanek, as were the remnants of Białystok's Jews, in the mass killing that took place in that camp on November 3, 1943 (*see* "ERNTEFEST").

In December 1942, small groups of armed men had escaped from the ghetto. By the summer of 1943, after the uprising, 150 fighters from the Białystok ghetto had joined the partisans. Several partisan units, especially the Forois (Yi., "go out") unit, which had merged with the "Jewish Group," engaged the Germans in a long series of raids. A number of young Jewish women, who had remained in Białystok posing as Aryans and had acted as couriers, maintained contact with these units. In some instances, partisan units made up of Białystok Jews received aid from the Polish and Belorussian population. In the spring of 1944, Forois linked up with Soviet partisans, at which time 60 of its Jewish partisans were still alive.

Some two hundred Jews from Białystok survived in the German camps, and several dozen were saved by hiding on the "Aryan" side of the city. Also saved were sixty fighters who had escaped to the forests and joined up with the partisans. Białystok was liberated by the Soviet army in August 1944.

BIBLIOGRAPHY

Blumenthal, N. *Conduct and Actions of a Judenrat: Documents from the Bialystok Ghetto.* Jerusalem, 1962.

Datner, S. *The Fight and Annihilation of the Białystok Ghetto.* Łódź, 1946.

Grossman, H. *The Underground Army: Fighters of the Bialystock Ghetto.* New York, 1987.

Klibanski, B. "The Underground Archives in the Bialystok Ghetto founded by Zevi Mersik and Mordecai Tenenbaum." *Yad Vashem Studies* 2 (1958): 295–330.

Schmulewitz, I., et al., eds. *The Bialystoker Memorial Book.* New York, 1982.

Sohn, D., Ed. *Bialystok: Photo Album of a Renowned City and Its Jews the World Over.* New York, 1951.

SARAH BENDER
and TERESA PREKEROWA

BIBELFORSCHER. *See* Jehovah's Witnesses.

BIBERSTEIN, MAREK (d. 1944), chairman of the JUDENRAT (Jewish Council) in KRAKÓW. Before the war, Biberstein was a prominent figure in the life of the city's Jewish community. When Kraków was occupied by the Germans, he was appointed chairman of the provisional community administration, which before long became a Judenrat, with Biberstein remaining at its head. In this capacity, he did a great deal to alleviate the lot of the community by organizing aid to those in need and by frequently intervening for the release of Jews who for one reason or another had been seized by the Germans. In June 1941, Biberstein was arrested on the charge of having violated foreign-currency regulations, but the real reason seems to have been the Germans' dissatisfaction with his conduct and their desire to remove him from his post. He was kept in prison in Tarnów until the end of July 1942, when he returned to the Kraków ghetto, a sick and broken man. A few weeks later Biberstein and his family were taken to the PŁASZÓW camp, where he perished on May 14, 1944.

BIBLIOGRAPHY

Bauminger, A., M. Bosak, and N. M. Gelber. *The Kraków Book: A Jewish Mother City.* Jerusalem, 1959. (In Hebrew.)

AHARON WEISS

BIEBOW, HANS (1902–1947), head of the ŁÓDŹ ghetto administration. Born in Bremen, Biebow was a businessman who had joined the Nazi party. When the ŁÓDŹ ghetto was established in the spring of 1940, Biebow was put in charge of its food and economic office (Ernährungs- und Wirtschaftsstelle für das Ghetto), which in October was redesignated the "ghetto administration" (Ghettoverwaltung). The office had a staff of 250 German officials. Thanks to his personal ties with Reinhard HEYDRICH, chief of the SD (Sicherheitsdienst; Security Service), and with Arthur GREISER, governor of the WARTHEGAU, Biebow enjoyed wide powers in administering the ŁÓDŹ ghetto. By exploiting the manpower in the ghetto factories that he established and by robbing the Jews of their property, Biebow was able to extract great profits. He personally made sure that the ghetto was hermetically closed and that the inhabitants would starve. He set up special warehouses in the town of Pabianice, where the personal possessions and clothing of the victims of the CHEŁMNO extermination camp were stored, sorted, and sent to Germany for use by the German population.

Biebow was among the officials who organized the transports to Chełmno from Łódź and from the ghettos in the provincial towns of the Warthegau. These transports began in

Hans Biebow (left), Nazi head of the Łódź ghetto administration.

December 1941 and continued throughout 1942. Biebow, however, did not want the ghetto administration to pass into the hands of the SS, and in order to maintain the flow of profits from the ghetto factories he ensured the ghetto's continued existence even after the 1942 deportations, up until the summer of 1944. Nevertheless, once it was decided that the ghetto would be liquidated, Biebow became very active in organizing transports to the Chełmno and AUSCHWITZ extermination camps, from June to August 1944, and in the ghetto's final liquidation. He excelled in deception tactics, convincing the Jews that the transports from the ghetto would take them to work camps attached to German factories. When the ghetto was liquidated in August 1944, Biebow remained in Łódź, and until January 1945 he supervised the removal to Germany of possessions left behind by the ghetto inhabitants. After the war, Biebow was tried by a Polish court in Łódź, sentenced to death, and executed.

BIBLIOGRAPHY

Trunk, I. *Judenrat.* New York, 1972.

SHMUEL KRAKOWSKI

BIELSKI, TUVIA (1906–1987), Jewish partisan commander. Bielski's family were farmers in Stankiewicze, near NOVOGRUDOK. At the age of seventeen he joined the Zionist pioneering movement, and in 1928 he was mobilized into the Polish army, where he rose to the rank of corporal. He married in 1930 and settled in the village of Subotnik, where he opened a textile store. In September 1939 the area was annexed to the Soviet Union.

With the German invasion of the Soviet Union on June 22, 1941, Bielski was mobilized. When the Germans invaded the region he fled to the forest, and from there to his village of birth. After their parents and other members of their family were slaughtered in the Novogrudok ghetto, Bielski and his brothers Zusya, Asael, and Aharon, escaped to the forests. Securing arms, they created a seventeen-member partisan core there, consisting mostly of members of Bielski's family. Elected as commander, Tuvia Bielski sent emissaries to the ghettos in the vicinity, inviting the inmates to join his group. Hundreds of the surviving Jews in the ghettos of the Novogrudok region—men, women, and children—streamed into Bielski's camp, and his partisan band grew daily.

Bielski learned to wage partisan combat, and he considered the saving of Jewish lives a supreme objective. His band inspired terror in the Novogrudok region as it took vengeance on the Belorussian police and on the farmers who massacred Jews. The German authorities offered a reward of 100,000 marks for assistance in capturing him.

With the creation of the band of Jewish partisans in the Naliboki Forest, Bielski won the trust of the Soviet partisan unit in the vicinity, and particularly of its commander, General Platon (Vasily Yehimovich Chernyshev). Bielski opposed the unit's intention of taking away his 150 fighters, leaving him with a civilian camp of refugees, and in order to frustrate this aim he made his camp a maintenance base for the Soviet fighters. His group was not a partisan band in the regular sense but a Jewish community in the forest, with a synagogue, a law court, workshops, a school, and a dispensary (*see* FAMILY CAMPS IN THE FORESTS).

In the summer of 1943, the Germans initiated a massive hunt through the Naliboki Forest in order to destroy the partisan forces, and in particular Bielski's band. The partisans retreated to the densest part of the forest, and the commander of Bielski's area or-

Asael Bielski (left) and Tuvia Bielski.

dered Bielski to pare down his unit to include only single people with arms; married men, women, and children were ordered to abandon the area where the unit had been staying and not follow the fighters to the center of the forest. Knowing that this instruction was a death sentence for the civilians in his group, Bielski disobeyed, retreating to the thickest part of the forest with his entire band. The fighters protected the civilians until they were able to emerge safely from the forest, evading the Germans who surrounded it. In the summer of 1944, with the liberation of the area, Bielski and his 1,230-strong partisan band, known as "Kalinin," marched into the town of Novogrudok. Asael Bielski was killed in battle as a soldier in the Soviet army at Königsberg in 1944.

After the war Bielski returned to Poland. That same year, in 1945, he immigrated to Palestine, and in 1954 he settled in the United States with his two surviving brothers.

BIBLIOGRAPHY

Ainsztein, R. *Jewish Resistance in Nazi-occupied Eastern Europe*. London, 1974. See pages 315–325.

YITZCHAK ALPEROWITZ

BILTMORE RESOLUTION, declaration adopted at a conference of American Zionists in 1942, explicitly advocating the establishment of a Jewish state in Palestine. In the spring of 1942, Zionist fortunes had reached their lowest ebb. Despite the dire straits of European Jewry, the cooperation of the YISHUV in the British war effort, and the collaboration of the Arabs with the Nazis, the British government adamantly refused to modify its WHITE PAPER OF 1939, which limited Jewish immigration into Palestine and contemplated a Palestinian state with an Arab majority. Furthermore, American Zionists had failed to mobilize the crucial support of either American Jewry or the administration of President Franklin D. ROOSEVELT. To counteract this situation, an extraordinary Zionist conference was called for May 10 and 11, 1942. Held in New York's Biltmore Hotel, it was attended by leading Zionist personalities, including Chaim WEIZMANN, Abba Hillel SILVER, Stephen S. WISE, David BEN-GURION, and Nahum GOLDMANN.

Despite the fact that no verified data existed at the time regarding the "FINAL SOLUTION," it was clear to those at the conference that European Jewry was in the throes of a great catastrophe. Article 2 of the resolution offered "a message of hope and encouragement to [our] fellow Jews in the ghettos and concentration camps of Hitler-dominated Europe, and our prayers that their hour of liberation may not be far distant." The resolution further offered warm greetings to Jewish fighting men and women, and sent a proposal of peace and goodwill to the Arabs. However, the conclusion of the resolution was unambiguous: "The conference declares that the new world order that will follow victory cannot be established on foundations of peace, justice, and equality unless the problem of Jewish homelessness is finally solved" (Article 8). Consequently, the resolution urged "that Palestine be established as a Jewish commonwealth integrated into the structure of the new democratic world."

Events in Europe were not yet sufficiently clear for American, or Palestinian, Zionists to fully comprehend. The RIEGNER CABLE was received in August 1942 and verified only late that November. Thus, the conference was responding to partial information and spoke of the need to relocate two million Jewish refugees at a time when nearly that number of Russian, Polish, and Romanian Jews had already been massacred. Even so, the resolution marked the first time that a majority of Zionists called openly for the establishment of Jewish sovereignty as the ultimate goal of Zionism. The resolution became central to the activities of Silver and Wise, as co-chairmen of the AMERICAN ZIONIST EMERGENCY COUNCIL. Indeed, although many non-Zionists in the United States (including those of the AMERICAN JEWISH COMMITTEE) did not support its statist demands, the resolution became the primary statement of Zionist goals until the United Nations opted for the partition of Palestine into separate Jewish and Arab states on November 29, 1947.

BIBLIOGRAPHY

Bauer, Y. *From Diplomacy to Resistance.* New York, 1973.

Shpiro, D. "The Political Background of the 1942 Biltmore Resolution." *Herzl Year Book* 8 (1978): 166–177.

Urofsky, M. *American Zionism from Herzl to the Holocaust.* New York, 1976.

ABRAHAM J. EDELHEIT

Sofija Binkiene.

BINKIENE, SOFIJA (1902–1984), rescuer of Jews in KOVNO, Lithuania. The widow of a well-known Lithuanian author, Binkiene lived near the Kovno ghetto. Although she had had no previous contacts with Jewish circles and was tending a sick husband, she helped Jews by offering them temporary shelter in her home. Many Jews, fleeing from the Kovno ghetto, found initial refuge in her home. At times, especially during the final liquidation of the ghetto in 1944, Binkiene roved the streets near the ghetto in the hope of bringing straggling Jews into the safety of her home. Many scores of Jews were thus helped and saved.

In 1967, Sofija Binkiene edited a book on Lithuanians who rescued Jews, *Ir be ginklo kariai* (Vilna, 1962). She was awarded the title of "RIGHTEOUS AMONG THE NATIONS" by YAD VASHEM in 1967.

MORDECAI PALDIEL

BIRKENAU. *See* Auschwitz.

BLACK BOOK OF SOVIET JEWRY, THE, a book of testimonies and documents (descriptions, letters, and excerpts from diaries) concerning Nazi crimes in the SOVIET UNION, the principal source of which were Jewish survivors and non-Jewish eyewitnesses. As stated in the subtitle, the book covers "the ruthless murder of Jews by fascist German invaders throughout the temporarily occupied regions of the Soviet Union and in the extermination camps of Poland during the war of 1941 to 1945." The *Black Book* was the work of the noted Soviet Jewish writers Ilya EHRENBURG and Vasily Grossman, with Soviet writers and poets, both Jewish and non-Jewish, among the contributors.

The idea of issuing such a book was conceived by Ehrenburg as early as 1943, and by the end of 1944 a first version was ready. At that point, Ehrenburg published excerpts in two volumes under the title *Merder fun Felker* (Murder of Peoples). At the beginning of 1945 the manuscript was given to the JEWISH ANTIFASCIST COMMITTEE in the Soviet Union on the instructions of committee member Shlomo Lozovski; there it was revised and emended. Copies of the manuscript were sent to the United States, Romania, and Israel in 1946. Excerpts from the manuscript were published in the United States in the English-language *Black Book*, which had as its subject the annihilation of the Jews in Europe as a whole. In Romania, the first part of the manuscript was published in 1946, under the title *Cartea neagra*. According to Ehrenburg, the book was printed in the Soviet Union by the publisher Der Emes, but the entire edition, as well as the manuscript, was destroyed in 1948, when the Jewish Antifascist Committee was liquidated.

The manuscript copy that had gone to Israel—in which the chapter on Lithuania is missing—was handed over to YAD VASHEM in 1965 by Shlomo Tsirulnikov, an activist in the V League (a wartime Soviet-YISHUV friendship league). Adapted and edited by Haya Lifshitz and Marek Kipnis, the book was published in Russian (Jerusalem, 1980), English (New York, 1981), and Yiddish (Jerusalem, 1984; this edition included a reconstructed version of the chapter on Lithuania). Among the material in the Ehrenburg archive that was opened to the public at Yad Vashem at the end of 1987 was an almost complete handwritten manuscript of the *Black Book*.

BIBLIOGRAPHY

Ehrenburg, I. *Men, Years, Life*. 6 vols. London, 1962–1968.

Sutzkever, A. "Ilya Ehrenburg: A Chapter of Memoirs from the Years 1944–1946." *Di Goldene Keyt* 61 (1967): 21–37. (In Yiddish.)

HAYA LIFSHITZ

BLECHHAMMER (Pol., Blachownia Śląska), concentration camp established in April 1942 near Koźle, a town 18.5 miles (30 km) west of Gleiwitz (present-day Gliwice). In its initial stage, Blechhammer was a forced-labor camp for Jews (a *Judenlager*). The first group of prisoners, numbering 350, were employed on the construction of the Oberschlesische Hydriewerke (Upper Silesia Hydrogenation Works), a chemical-products plant. After a short time a typhus epidemic broke out, and 120 prisoners who contracted the disease were sent to AUSCHWITZ, where they were killed. That June the remaining prisoners were transferred to a new and larger camp that had been built nearby. Most of the prisoners brought to Blechhammer were Jews from Upper Silesia, but there were other Jews as well, from fifteen different countries. The number of prisoners reached 5,500. They were housed in wooden barracks under appalling conditions, with no toilet or washing facilities. Some 200 female Jewish prisoners were put into a separate section of the camp. Hunger and disease were rife, especially diarrhea and tuberculosis. A crematorium was built, in which were cremated the bodies of 1,500 prisoners who had died from "natural" causes or had been killed.

On April 1, 1944, as part of a reorganization, the camp was put under the authority of the Auschwitz camp administration, and it became the satellite camp Auschwitz IV. Hauptsturmführer Otto Brossmann was the camp commandant until November 1944, when he was replaced by Untersturmführer Kurt Klipp. Throughout the camp's existence, Karl Demerer, a Viennese Jew, was the "camp elder" (*Lagerältester*). He had the courage to stand up to the camp authorities and in many instances was able to help the prisoners.

On January 21, 1945, 4,000 prisoners, including 150 women, were taken out of the camp and put on a death march lasting thirteen days. Some 800 prisoners were killed en route. On February 2, the survivors reached the GROSS-ROSEN camp, where they remained for five days before being moved to BUCHENWALD. Several dozen prisoners who tried to hide in Blechhammer during the evacuation were discovered and killed on the spot.

BIBLIOGRAPHY

Brown, J. *In Durance Vile.* London, 1981.
Piper, F. "Das Nebenlager Blechhammer." *Hefte von Auschwitz* 10 (1967): 19–40.

SHMUEL KRAKOWSKI

The Blechhammer concentration camp.

BLITZKRIEG (lit., "lightning war"), theory of the conduct of war, developed by the German armed forces in World War II, aimed at winning complete victory in as short a time as possible, measured in days and weeks rather than months and years. The term was first used in connection with the German attack on Poland in 1939. In the blitzkrieg, tanks and armored and other motorized vehicles for transporting troops were concentrated, and massive attacks by dive-bombers and self-propelled artillery were directed at selected enemy front-line positions. Dive-bombers also attacked vital enemy localities in the rear. These actions were calculated to create psychological shock and resultant disorganization in the enemy forces and to prevent any concerted reaction by the enemy high command.

The tactics of blitzkrieg were evolved by the German general Heinz Guderian (who drew most of his ideas from the writings of the British military theorists Basil Henry Liddell Hart and John Frederick Charles Fuller). They consisted of a splitting thrust by armored columns on a narrow front and complete disruption of the main enemy position at the point of attack, followed by wide-sweeping encirclement movements of fast-moving armored spearheads, thus creating large caldrons of entrapped and immobilized enemy forces.

The blitzkrieg method was successfully applied by the German Wehrmacht in the campaigns against Poland, France, Denmark, Norway, Yugoslavia, and Greece. However, after initial successes in the attack on the Soviet Union (Operation "Barbarossa"), its failure there in late 1941 was the turning point of World War II and heralded the doom of the Third Reich. The British also used the term "blitz" for the German terror air attacks on British cities from September 1940 to May 1941.

BIBLIOGRAPHY

Guderian, H. *Achtung Panzer.* Stuttgart, 1937.
Liddell Hart, B. H. Strategy: *The Indirect Approach.* New York, 1967.
Miksche, F. O. *Blitzkrieg.* London, 1941.

JEHUDA L. WALLACH

BLOBEL KOMMANDO. *See* Aktion 1005.

BLOBEL, PAUL (1894–1951), SS officer. Born into a Protestant family, Blobel attended a vocational school, where he learned construction and carpentry. In World War I he volunteered for the army and served in the engineering corps. After the war he resumed his studies, became an architect, and settled in Solingen. In the depression he lost his job and could not find any other employment. He

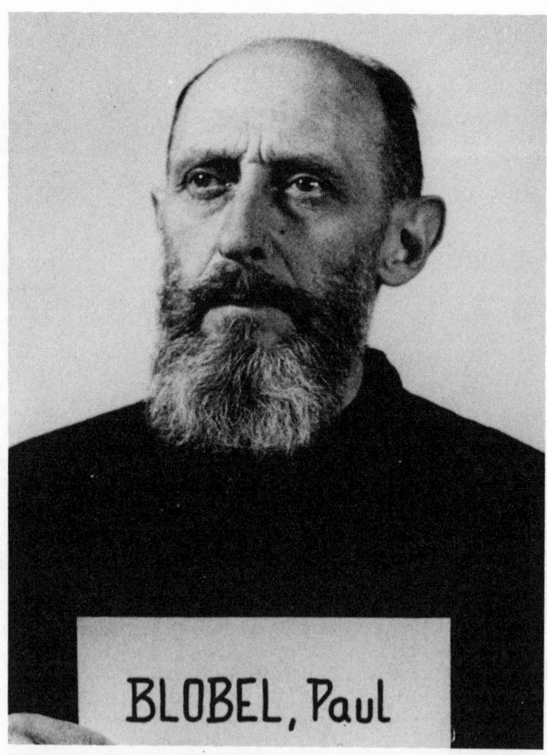

Paul Blobel, SS-*Standartenführer;* member of the SD; commanding officer of Einsatzgruppe C's Sonderkommando 4a. [National Archives]

joined the Nazi party in October 1931, and in January 1932 enlisted in the SS. In March 1933 he entered service with the Staatspolizei (Stapo) in Düsseldorf, and on June 1, 1934, he transferred to the SD (Sicherheitsdienst; Security Service) with the rank of *Untersturmführer* and was appointed SD officer for the Düsseldorf area. He advanced rapidly in the SS hierarchy and became a *Standartenführer* on January 30, 1941.

At the beginning of June 1942, Blobel was summoned to Pretzsch, a town on the Elbe northeast of Leipzig, where candidates for service in the EINSATZGRUPPEN were being assembled to be deployed in German-occupied territory in the Soviet Union. Blobel was appointed commanding officer of Sonderkommando 4a of Einsatzgruppe C, which was assigned to the Ukraine. At the head of this unit Blobel went from Sokal to Kiev by way of Volhynia, engaging in *Aktionen* along the route, in LUTSK, Dubno, ZHITOMIR, BERDICHEV, and other places. When Kiev fell, he entered the city and with his unit organized and carried out the murder of Kiev's Jews at BABI YAR, on September 29 and 30, 1941. His last *Aktion* in that area took place in KHARKOV, where his unit murdered 21,685 Jews in Drobitski Yar at the end of December 1941.

On January 13, 1942, Blobel was released from his post for reasons of health—he suffered from a liver ailment that was aggravated by his excessive drinking. When he recovered he was called to the REICHSSICHERHEITSHAUPTAMT (Reich Security Main Office; RSHA) and put in charge of AKTION 1005, an operation whose goal was to obliterate the traces of the mass murders committed by the Germans. Blobel established his headquarters in Łódź; his direct superior was the Gestapo chief, Heinrich MÜLLER, in Berlin.

Until the fall of 1943, the method Blobel used was to cremate the bodies on huge pyres. The first experiments to employ this method were carried out in CHEŁMNO. The permanent camps, such as AUSCHWITZ, were later equipped with crematoria. In the fall of 1943 Blobel set up special units, the Sonderkommandos 1005, for the specific task of disinterring and cremating the bodies from the mass graves in the German-occupied parts of the Soviet Union. These units were manned by Jewish and other prisoners who were killed when their work in a given place was done. Some of these prisoners, especially the Jews among them, succeeded in escaping, notably in Babi Yar, JANÓWSKA, the NINTH FORT in Kovno, PONARY, and Grabowka, near Białystok. At the end of October 1944, when their tasks were completed, the German personnel who had served in the Sonderkommandos 1005–men of the SD, Sicherheitspolizei (Security Police), and ORDNUNGSPOLIZEI (German regular police)—all joined Einsatzgruppe "Iltis," a new unit commanded by Blobel. It was posted to Carinthia, on the Austro-Yugoslav border, to take part in fighting against the Yugoslav PARTISANS.

Blobel was arrested after the war and was one of the principal defendants in The *Einsatzgruppen* Case (Trial 9) at the SUBSEQUENT NUREMBERG PROCEEDINGS. He was sentenced to death in 1948 and hanged at the Landsberg prison in Bavaria on June 8, 1951.

BIBLIOGRAPHY

Tenenbaum, J. "The Einsatzgruppen." *Jewish Social Studies* 17/1 (1955): 43–64.

SHMUEL SPECTOR

BLOMBERG, WERNER VON (1878–1946), German field marshal; minister of war from 1933 to 1938. Born into a military family, Blomberg joined the German general staff in World War I. During the period of the Weimar Republic he took part in the program of clandestine rearmament, especially in the training of officers and the formation of a covert general staff. As adjutant general, his duties took him to Russia and America. In 1932 he served as military adviser to the German delegation at the Geneva disarmament conference. He combined these duties with command of the army corps at Königsberg, and it was in this capacity that he first met Hitler, in 1931.

In 1933, upon the formation of the Hitler–von Papen government, Blomberg was appointed minister of war and enthusiastically supported Nazi rearmament. He strongly opposed Ernst RÖHM's plans to incorporate the SA (Sturmabteilung; Storm Troopers) into the German army, and in the ensuing putsch against Röhm played a central role in consolidating Hitler's power. On the death of President Paul von HINDENBERG in August 1934, Blomberg took a personal oath of loyalty to Hitler as Hindenburg's successor, thereby ensuring Hitler's control over the army. In 1935, Blomberg was appointed commander in chief of the new Wehrmacht. He cooperated in plans for the reoccupation of the Rhineland and was promoted to field marshal in 1936. Blomberg was reluctant to support Nazi war policy, and in 1938 was engineered out of office by Hermann GÖRING and Heinrich HIMMLER. His fall and that of Werner von Fritsch, the army commander in chief, shortly afterward, ensured that party control of the armed forces remained unhampered. Blomberg died in American detention at Nuremberg.

BIBLIOGRAPHY

Brett-Smith, R. *Hitler's Generals.* San Rafael, Calif., 1977.

Humble, R. *Hitler's Generals.* New York, 1974.

LIONEL KOCHAN

BLUM, ABRAHAM ("Abrasha"; 1905–1943), BUND leader and member of the ŻYDOWSKA ORGANIZACJA BOJOWA (Jewish Fighting Organization; ŻOB) in WARSAW. Blum was born in Vilna into a middle-class family, attended a Yiddish secondary school, and graduated with a degree in construction engineering from a Belgian institute. As a young man he became active in the Bund's youth movement. In 1929 he moved to Warsaw and became a full-time party activist. In the 1930s he was a member of the national board of the Bund youth movement, Zukunft (Future), and was active in the Bund-sponsored school network.

In the early days of World War II, Blum was one of the few Bund leaders who did not leave Warsaw. He played a central role in the Bund's clandestine operations as soon as they were launched, and helped run the party's soup kitchens, underground press, welfare services, and political indoctrination efforts.

In the underground's debate concerning the formation of a united fighting organization, Blum, as of the spring of 1942, supported the stand that called for the Bund to join with the Zionist groups in such an organization. Marek EDELMAN, in the report on the Bund's underground operations, *Getto Walczy* (The Ghetto Fights), published in 1945, described Blum as "the spiritual father of our resistance . . . the only person [in the Bund] able to control the situation [during the mass deportation from Warsaw]," and stated: "We owe it to him that we survived that terrible period." In October 1942 the Bund joined the ŻOB, and Blum was appointed the party's representative on the coordinating committee of the Bund and the Jewish National Committee (Żydowski Komitet Narodowy), the two bodies that formed the political leadership of the ŻOB. He rejected an offer to cross over to the "Aryan" side, despite the fact that his wife and children had gone into hiding there.

During the WARSAW GHETTO UPRISING in April 1943, Blum fought with a group of young people in the "Brushmakers" area. He was among the group that succeeded in escaping from the ghetto and reaching the Polish side by way of the city sewage system. For several days he was in hiding in the Kampinos Forest, and from there he returned to Warsaw. When his hiding place there was discovered, he tried to escape through a fourth-floor window by tying bed sheets together and climbing down, but the sheets tore; Blum fell and was injured. He was seized by the Germans and taken to the Gestapo, and all further trace of him was lost.

BIBLIOGRAPHY

Gutman, Y. *The Jews of Warsaw, 1939–1943.* Bloomington, 1980.

ISRAEL GUTMAN

BLUM, LÉON (1872–1950), premier of FRANCE on three occasions. Blum began his political career at the age of twenty-two as a member of the French Social Democratic party, to which he remained attached until the end of his life. From the close of World War I he supported Zionist aspirations in Palestine. Blum first came to power in 1936 at a most unpropitious moment for France, with respect to both domestic and foreign policy: it was faced with Germany's remilitarization of the Rhineland and with a deep internal economic crisis, and Blum had difficulty confronting these issues. With France rocked by mass waves of workers' strikes, Blum opted for far-reaching social and economic reforms, which further upset the internal equilibrium. During his term of office antisemitism grew, with Blum—France's first Jewish premier—at its center. He was forced out of office in early 1937 when he failed to receive the necessary support in the Chamber of Deputies. A short-lived return in 1938 exacerbated his relations with many elements of French society, which saw him as a symbol of all the negative attributes they associated with the Third Republic.

Léon Blum. [Beth Hatefutsoth]

Before World War II, Blum strongly opposed Hitler and National Socialism. His standpoint, however, was more reflective of a Social Democrat who opposed fascism than of a Jew who opposed racism. When attacking National Socialism, Blum did not address the treatment of the Jews in prewar Nazi Germany, but rather Nazi actions against Social Democrats and Social Democratic values. Nevertheless, in 1938, in the wake of the disappointing EVIAN CONFERENCE on refugees and the violent KRISTALLNACHT pogrom, Blum decried the idea of closing France to Jewish refugees from Nazism, and sharply criticized French Jews for supporting this position.

Arrested by the Vichy authorities on September 14, 1940, Blum, together with other French leaders of the Third Republic, was tried in the spring of 1942 at a show trial in Riom, which was never brought to a conclusion. On March 31, 1943, at the age of seventy-one, the former French premier was sent to BUCHENWALD. In early April 1945 he was removed from the camp, and after being shunted from one place to another was imprisoned in DACHAU. On April 28 he was transferred to the hands of the Wehrmacht. Blum was liberated on May 4, and within ten days arrived in Paris. In 1946 he returned to political activity and formed a socialist coalition government, which lasted only a month.

BIBLIOGRAPHY

Birnbaum, P. *Un mythe politique—La "République juive": De Léon Blum à Pierre Mendès-France.* Paris, 1988.

Colton, J. *Léon Blum: Humanist in Politics.* Durham, N.C., 1987.

Lacouture, J. *Léon Blum.* New York, 1982.

Léon Blum before His Judges. Foreword by C. R. Attlee. London, 1943.

RICHARD COHEN and
ISRAEL ELDAR

B'NAI B'RITH, international Jewish organization. Founded in New York in 1843, B'nai B'rith is the oldest secular Jewish organization in the United States, where most of its strength is concentrated. The B'nai B'rith Order was founded by Jewish immigrants from Germany as a "fraternal order," its structure and aims influenced by the FREEMASONS; it set itself the goal of blending humanistic Judaism with general human ideals. The order also assisted Jews in parts of the world where they were being persecuted. B'nai B'rith lodges and chapters sprang up in other countries, including Germany, where a B'nai B'rith order was established in 1882, in reaction to growing ANTISEMITISM in that country.

Reacting to manifestations of antisemitism in Europe, B'nai B'rith in the United States decided in 1913 to establish the Anti-Defamation League (ADL), a body that exists to this day. The ADL concentrated on gaining the support of public opinion. In the 1920s and 1930s it grew beyond the confines of B'nai B'rith and developed into a broadly based community organization, fighting Henry Ford's antisemitic campaign and the Ku Klux Klan. In the late 1930s the ADL worked against Nazi and fascist groups in the United States and became a prime source of information on their activities, to the extent that even the Federal Bureau of Investigation utilized the ADL files on these groups for its work.

B'nai B'rith was not always in accord with the activist line pursued by its offspring. In 1931, when Nazi thugs attacked Jews in the streets of Berlin, Rabbi Leo BAECK asked the president of B'nai B'rith, Alfred Cohen, to refrain from arousing public opinion in America against these acts in Germany. Even after Adolf Hitler's rise to power in Germany, Cohen continued to base his policy on Germany on Baeck's advice. (Baeck was concerned about possible Nazi reaction to a boycott movement of German goods among the Jews of America.) Opposing the stand taken by the Anti-Defamation League, Cohen refused to join the boycott of German goods, on the ground that such action would cause harm to the Jews of Germany, and particularly to B'nai B'rith in that country, which the Nazis permitted to function until 1937. An appeal by B'nai B'rith asking the United States government to protest to Germany against the persecution of the Jews was rejected by President Franklin D. ROOSEVELT, who at that point was not prepared to interfere in Nazi Germany's "internal affairs."

On April 9, 1937, the Gestapo seized all the B'nai B'rith chapters in Germany, arresting the officers and conducting searches of their residences, handcuffing the national B'nai B'rith officers, confiscating the order's assets, and liquidating all of its welfare institutions. A shocked Alfred Cohen appealed to Secretary of State Cordell HULL to protest to the German government on humanitarian grounds, but his appeal was turned down. Even at that time Cohen remained opposed to public protest and boycott, and still believed that "quiet diplomacy" could help the Jews of Germany.

In May 1938 Henry Monsky was elected president of B'nai B'rith, the first time that a Jew of eastern European origin had assumed this post. Monsky was a Zionist and his views were close to those held by the leaders of the American Jewish Congress; he supported the boycott of Germany and made it his policy to transform B'nai B'rith into a large-scale organization. A few months later, the KRISTALLNACHT pogrom took place in Germany (November 1938), followed by the total elimination of the Jews from the German economy and the liquidation of Jewish institutions. Even before that, the Jews of Germany had no place to go; but B'nai B'rith, fearful of arousing antisemitism in the United States—like most American Jews at the time—did not challenge the quota system of the 1924 Immigration Act and did not try to arouse public opinion against the administration's policy of not fully utilizing even the quotas provided by that act. In the wake of *Kristallnacht,* Monsky, together with other Jewish leaders, conveyed to the White House the concern of American Jewry over the existing state of affairs.

When reliable information was received concerning the "Final Solution," Monsky and the other Jewish leaders conferred with Roosevelt on ways of rescuing the Jews. Monsky sought to create unity in Jewish ranks and, with the support of the Zionists, established the AMERICAN JEWISH CONFERENCE, which set the rescue of European Jews as one of its goals. At the founding session of the conference, held in Pittsburgh in February 1943, Monsky formed an emergency committee for the affairs of European Jewry. The committee in turn drafted recommendations to be submitted to the BERMUDA CONFERENCE, and organized mass meetings. At the September 1943 meeting of the conference, the destruction of European Jewry was discussed; no one argued against Monsky's thesis that Jewish unity was a prerequisite for the rescue of Europe's Jews, but the meeting did not come up with a practical contribution to this end.

After the war, B'nai B'rith played an active role in addressing the problem of the Holocaust survivors. In 1946 Monsky testified before the Anglo-American Committee on Palestine, supporting the Zionist solution of the problem.

BIBLIOGRAPHY

Bisgyer, M. *Challenge and Encounter: Behind the Scenes in the Struggle for Jewish Survival.* New York, 1967.

Grusd, E. E. *B'nai B'rith: The Story of a Covenant.* New York, 1966.

Klutznick, P. *No Easy Answers.* New York, 1971.

Moore, D. D. *B'nai B'rith as a Challenge of Ethnic Leadership.* Albany, N.Y., 1981.

MENAHEM KAUFMAN

BOARD OF DEPUTIES OF BRITISH JEWS, the representative body of British Jewry, originating in 1760. Following the Nazi rise to power in Germany and the calamity that it represented for Germany's Jews, the Board of Deputies, then under the presidency of Neville Laski, was confronted by extremely serious issues on which it had to take a stand: the persecution of the Jews in Germany and, later, in the countries occupied by the Germans; the question of Jewish emigration from Germany to Britain; and the absorption and rehabilitation of these refugees. In those years—and even more so during the war—the board faced the problems of maneuvering between British loyalty and Jewish loyalty, and of deciding how to act when British interests did not coincide with, or even contradicted, the interests of the Jews.

The board appealed to the British government, and in particular to the Foreign Office, asking that it intervene with the Nazis to stop the persecution of the Jews, and raise the refugee problem at the League of Nations and other international forums. The British government, however, refused to take any step that could be interpreted as interference in the "internal affairs of Germany." This policy eventually became one of appeasement toward the Third Reich. The board confined itself to legal arguments and confidential, moderate steps, and did not put any public pressure on the government by alerting the Jewish community. It opposed and obstructed attempts by activist groups in the community to resort to more vigorous means. The board also resisted the boycott of Germany and the formation of a protest movement against the persecution of German Jewry.

In the summer of 1932, when Stephen S. WISE called for a preparatory meeting for the formation of the WORLD JEWISH CONGRESS, the board refused to take part and also stayed away from the preparatory meetings that followed; neither did the board join the World Jewish Congress when it was finally established. It did, however, participate with other leading Jewish organizations in the United States and Europe in sponsoring an international Jewish conference in London in October 1933 to deal with the situation of the German Jews and coordinate efforts to help them. The conference was a complete failure, mainly because of the isolationist tendencies of the United States organizations.

The board's position on combating the antisemitic campaign conducted by the British fascist movement under Sir Oswald MOSLEY (mainly in 1936) also displayed caution. It opposed any open clash with the fascists and rejected cooperation with anti-fascist movements. On this issue, as in the case of the boycott, ad hoc bodies sprang up that took energetic steps against the fascist threat. The Jews of London's East End, who had been personally affected by the fascists, were particularly active in these bodies and were angered by the board's failure to act. It was only in response to strong pressure that the board decided to establish a coordinating committee (later named the Defense Committee) whose task it was to counteract the fascist campaign against the Jewish community.

In 1939 a democratic changeover took place when Selig BRODETSKY, of eastern European origin, was elected to the presidency of the board, a position previously the preserve of members of old, established families in the community. With the election of Brodetsky, the strength of the Zionists on the board increased, and in 1943 they became the dominant force. As a result, the influence of the board with the British government lessened. During the war, the board submitted a series of requests and demands to the British government: to intervene in behalf of the Jews in the Nazi-occupied countries; to give wide publicity to Nazi anti-Jewish brutality, deportations, and murder; to issue declarations on the situation of the Jews; to provide assistance for the integration of the refugees in neutral countries or in GREAT BRITAIN; and to bomb AUSCHWITZ from the air. These requests and demands did not, however, meet with any response. As was the case with other Jewish organizations in Britain, the Board of Deputies of British Jews was unable to bring any meaningful influence to bear upon British policy concerning the Jews under Nazi persecution. Nor was the board able, despite all its efforts, to affect policy on such critical issues as the opening of the gates of Palestine to Jewish refugees, or the admission of Jewish refugees from Europe to Britain or other parts of the empire.

BIBLIOGRAPHY

Alderman, G. *The Jewish Community in British Politics.* Oxford, 1983.

Gould, J., and S. Esh, eds. *Jewish Life in Modern Britain.* London, 1964.

Sompolinski, M. "Anglo-Jewish Leadership and the British Government: Attempts at Rescue, 1944–1945." *Yad Vashem Studies* 13 (1979): 211–247.

Wasserstein, B. *Britain and the Jews of Europe, 1939–1945.* Oxford, 1979.

Wasserstein, B. "Patterns of Jewish Leadership in Great Britain during the Nazi Era." In *Jewish Leadership during the Nazi Era: Patterns of Behavior in the Free World,* edited by R. L. Braham, pp. 29–43. New York, 1985.

NANA SAGI

BOGAARD, JOHANNES ("Uncle Hannes"; 1891–1974), farmer in Nieuw Vennep (Haarlemmermeer), southwest of Amsterdam, who was responsible for the rescue of some three hundred Jews. Bogaard hid fugitive Jews on

Johannes Bogaard (center), planting a tree in the Garden of the Righteous at Yad Vashem, Jerusalem (1964).

his farm, as well as on the farms of relatives and friendly neighbors, for long periods of time. Born into a strict Calvinist family of limited means, he was taught by his father to respect the Jews as the people of the Bible. After the deportation of Jews from the NETHERLANDS began in July 1942, the entire Bogaard family of farmers devoted themselves to helping Jews escape the Nazi dragnet. When Jews were referred to Bogaard as being in need of help, Uncle Hannes ("Oom Hannes"), as he was affectionately known, traveled to Amsterdam once or twice a week to fetch the persons threatened with deportation and persuade them to follow him and place themselves under his care. Most were hidden in the vicinity of his farm, although at times there were up to one hundred Jews on his family's farm alone. He also collected money, ration cards, and identification papers from friends and acquaintances.

In November 1942 the Dutch Nazi police raided the Bogaard farm, capturing three Jews. Two more raids followed in the succeeding months, in which several dozen Jews were apprehended and a policeman was killed. Johannes's father, one of his brothers, and his own son Teunis were taken to a German concentration camp, where they perished.

By the end of 1943, Johannes Bogaard, until then operating largely on his own initiative, was able to link up with underground organizations, but most of his help still came from his own family. Alerted to the increased danger of detection by the authorities, most of the Jews in his charge were moved to other locations in the countryside for safe refuge. Bogaard probably saved more Jews, almost single-handedly, than any other person in the Netherlands. He was recognized by YAD VASHEM as a "RIGHTEOUS AMONG THE NATIONS" in 1963.

MORDECAI PALDIEL

BOGDANOVKA (Rom., Bogdanovca), extermination camp established in October 1941 by Romanian occupation authorities in the village of that name on the Bug River, in the Golta district of TRANSNISTRIA, on orders of Col. Modest Isopescu, the district commissioner. Most of the people deported to Bogdanovka—some forty-eight thousand—came from ODESSA, and about seven thousand from BESSARABIA. The last transport arrived at Bogdanovka on December 1, 1941; by then over fifty-four thousand Jews were being held there.

Several cases of typhus broke out in the camp in mid-December. In consultation with Fleischer, the German adviser to the Romanian administration of the district, Isopescu decided to kill the entire camp population and issued an order to this effect to Vasile Manescu, the military government official in charge of the district. Taking part in the operation were Romanian troops and gendarmerie, Ukrainian police, and civilians from the town of Golta brought in for this purpose, as well as local ethnic Germans (VOLKSDEUTSCHE). The chief of the Ukrainian regular police, Kazachievici, was in overall command.

The mass slaughter began on December 21, 1941. The sick and disabled prisoners, some 5,000 in all, were locked into two stables; layers of kerosene-drenched straw were spread over the roofs and set alight, and all the prisoners packed inside were burned to death. The rest of the prisoners, lined up in columns of 300 to 400 each, were marched to a nearby forest and driven to the banks of a watercourse (*garla mare,* "the great valley," as the Romanian camp commandants called it). They were ordered to remove their clothes, get on their knees, and lean over the valley, and were then shot in the back of

their necks with dumdum bullets or killed with hand grenades. The massacre went on for four days, in the course of which 30,000 Jews were murdered. The rest were left freezing in the cold, waiting on the banks of the river for their turn to die. With their bare hands they dug holes in the ground, packing them with frozen corpses and trying in this way to shelter themselves from the cold. Nevertheless, thousands of them froze to death. On Christmas Eve the killing came to a temporary halt, only to be renewed four days later, on December 28. By the end of the day on December 31, the remaining 11,000 Jews were also dead. Isopescu ordered all traces of the slaughter to be obliterated and the corpses to be burned. For two months, in January and February of 1942, 200 Jews who had been selected for this gruesome task were kept busy burning the corpses, piling them up in pyres with layers of straw and timber, and using gasoline to set the fire to the pyres. Of these 200 Jews, 150 died of cold and hunger or were shot to death by their Ukrainian guards.

In early 1945 Isopescu, Manescu, and the camp commandants were put on trial, in the first such proceedings against Romanian war criminals. The men responsible for the mass murder were sentenced to death (although the sentences were commuted to life imprisonment), and the other defendants were given long prison terms.

BIBLIOGRAPHY

Carp, M. *Transnistria.* Vol. 3 of *Cartea Neagră.* Bucharest, 1947.

Lavi, T., ed. *Rumania,* vol. 1. In *Pinkas Hakehillot; Encyclopaedia of Jewish Communities.* Jerusalem, 1969. (In Hebrew.)

JEAN ANCEL

BOHEMIA AND MORAVIA, PROTECTORATE OF, German protectorate proclaimed by Adolf Hitler on March 16, 1939, following the occupation of those territories by the Wehrmacht on the day before. The First Czechoslovak Republic had been established after World War I, on October 28, 1918, after the disintegration of the Austro-Hungarian monarchy. The Second Czechoslovak Republic, the rump state created in the wake of the MUNICH CONFERENCE (September 28–29, 1938) and the German annexation of the Sudetenland, came to an abrupt end. After the German invasion, Bohemia and Moravia, the heartland of the historic Czech lands, became part of the territory of the Reich.

Konstantin von NEURATH was appointed the Reich protector, Karl Hermann FRANK —leader of the Sudeten German party— became state secretary, and all other key positions were filled by Reich officials, who through the Landräte (local German councils) acquired control over the Czech provincial authorities. Nominally there remained the Czech president, Emil Hácha, and an "autonomous" Czech government, whose acts were nonetheless to be completely subordinate to the political, economic, and military interests of the Third Reich. Henceforward, the fate of the Jews differed in each of the former provinces of Czechoslovakia (*see* SLOVAKIA; TRANSCARPATHIAN UKRAINE).

On the eve of the German occupation, a total of 136 Jewish religious congregations existed in Bohemia, Moravia, and Silesia. The Jewish population numbered 118,310 persons, according to the criteria of the NUREMBERG LAWS.

Immediately after the occupation, a wave of arrests, coded Aktion Gitter (Operation Bars), was launched, mostly of emigrés from Germany, Czech public figures, and Jews. Jew-baiting became vociferous, the lead being taken by the most extreme of the fascist organizations, Vlajka (The Flag), which was especially active in Moravia. Anti-Jewish excesses began during the first days of the occupation: the synagogues of Vsetín and Jihlava (Iglau) were burned down. In other localities (Plzeň and Brno), Jews were rounded up in cafés and attacked on the streets under various pretexts.

In June 1939, Adolf EICHMANN arrived in PRAGUE and set up the ZENTRALSTELLE FÜR JÜDISCHE AUSWANDERUNG (Central Office for Jewish Emigration) to encourage large-scale emigration. It is estimated that before October 1941, when emigration was banned, 26,629 Jews managed to leave the country legally or illegally. Among these were 2,500 person who—under the HAAVARA AGREEMENT,

signed on January 13, 1939, between the Czechoslovak Ministry of Finance and the Jewish Agency—reached Palestine in three groups (March 1939, October 1939, and January 1940). Others emigrated to Great Britain, the United States, or South America, or escaped to neighboring Poland. Hundreds of children and young people were transferred by the He-Haluts and YOUTH ALIYA movements to Great Britain, Denmark, and the Netherlands for agricultural training. After the establishment of the Czech National Council in London (later, the CZECHOSLOVAK GOVERNMENT-IN-EXILE, under the leadership of Edvard Beneš, the second and last president of the republic), army reservists in Allied and neutral countries were called upon to enlist in the Allied armies. About 2,000 Czechoslovak Jews who reached Palestine joined the Czechoslovak army units, fighting at Dunkerque, and later as part of the Allied Middle East forces. In 1941 a Czechoslovak division, about 70 percent Jewish, was established in the Soviet Union.

Under a decree of June 21, 1939, Jews in the protectorate were ordered to register and subsequently to sell their gold, platinum, silver articles, and precious jewelry to the Hadega public purchasing agency and to deposit all their stocks, bonds, and securities in a foreign-currency bank. Fraudulent methods, threats, blackmail, and force were used to acquire Jewish enterprises through ARISIERUNG ("Aryanization"). The total value of Jewish assets expropriated by the Germans in the Protectorate of Bohemia and Moravia has been estimated as at least a half-billion dollars.

With the outbreak of war in September 1939, a reign of terror was unleashed. Ordinances were issued curtailing the freedom of movement of Jews. There were dismissals from employment, and certain rations (sugar, tobacco, and items of clothing) were denied to Jews. Hostages arrested, including numerous prominent Jews, were sent to concentration camps.

As early as October 1939, the first expulsion took place. Around three thousand men from Moravská Ostrava and Frýdek-Místek were dispatched to "retraining centers" in the Nisko settlement in the Lublin area (*see* NISKO AND LUBLIN PLAN). As of November 24, the bilingual weekly *Jüdisches Nachrichtenblatt–*

Židovske Listy made its appearance, censored by the Gestapo, as the organ of the Jewish Religious Organizations, and later of the Ältestenrat der Juden in Prag (Council of Jewish Elders in Prague). The expulsion of Jewish children from schools, and other restrictions, as on the use of telephones and public transportation, posed severe problems for the Jewish population; the burden fell upon the Jews to take care of education, social work, relief for the sick and aged, and, first and foremost, training in languages and new vocations to enable people to emigrate overseas.

The Jewish Religious Congregation (JRC) of Prague, subject to the authority of the Zentralstelle, was led by two members of the assimilationist Czech-Jewish movement: Dr. Emil Kafka, the chairman, and Dr. František Weidmann, the secretary, who, after Kafka's departure to London, was appointed chairman by the Zentralstelle. Jacob EDELSTEIN, the director of the Palestine Office in Prague, was appointed deputy chairman. Other leading members were Otto Zucker, Hanus Bonn, Marie Schmolka, Hanna Steiner, Dr. František Friedmann, Dr. Franz Kahn, Dr. Adolf Beneš, and Dr. Leo Janowitz.

The various departments of the JRC were gradually turned into unwilling tools of the German authorities, and their functions were redefined; tasks such as the liquidation of Jewish assets, consignment of Jews to forced labor, and assistance to deportees were imposed on their agenda. Any obstruction was regarded as sabotage punishable by death.

Early in September 1941, the JRC was ordered to take a census of the Jewish population. The 88,105 persons, identified in this census were ordered to wear the yellow Jewish BADGE and to live in complete isolation from the rest of the population. Shortly after Reinhard HEYDRICH was appointed acting

Deportation of Jews from Plzeň (Pilsen), 52 miles (83.6 km) southwest of Prague.

Reich protector, he called a meeting at Hradcany Palace to discuss the "solution of the Jewish problem." It was decided to concentrate the Jews of the protectorate in THERESIENSTADT and, after "their numbers have been considerably depleted by death," to send them to "the east."

First, five transports were sent from Prague to ŁÓDŹ, and one from Brno to MINSK and RIGA. These deportees were to share the fate of hundreds of thousands of Polish and Russian Jews: the greater part were annihilated in the camps of BEŁŻEC, CHEŁMNO, TREBLINKA, and Lublin (MAJDANEK). Some were massacred in the NINTH FORT in Kovno.

Between November 24, 1941, and March 16, 1945, 122 trains with 73,608 persons aboard were dispatched from the protectorate to Theresienstadt. A great majority of these people (60,399) were deported in the years 1942 to 1944 to AUSCHWITZ and other extermination camps; only 3,227 of them survived the war. As part of the retaliation campaign for Heydrich's assassination in Prague (May 27, 1942), a special transport of 1,000 Czech Jews was dispatched on June 10 to Poland; at Ujazd, they were ordered to dig their own graves before they were executed. The abandoned possessions of Jews, such as textiles, furs, furniture, and glassware, were stored by the Treuhandstelle (Trustee Office) set up by the Nazis in fifty-four warehouses. Eleven synagogues in the capital were utilized for this purpose.

On February 8, 1943, the JRC in Prague was reorganized as the Ältestenrat der Juden in Prag, headed first by Salo Krämer and his deputy, Herbert Langer. The last *Judenälteste* (head of the Jewish Council), from July 1943, was Dr. František Friedmann, and his deputy in charge of administration was Erich Kraus.

The final mass transport of "full Jews" (*Volljuden*) left Prague in the summer of 1943. After this transport, aside from the members of the Jewish Council and their families, only Jewish partners in mixed marriages were left in the protectorate. By December 31, 1944, their number amounted to 6,795. In late January and early February 1945, 4,243 persons were sent to Theresienstadt. On May 5, 1945 (the day of the liberation of Czechoslovakia), the total number of officially registered Jews in the Protectorate of Bohemia and Moravia was 2,803. It is estimated that of the 92,199 Jews living in Bohemia and Moravia before the start of the deportations, 78,154 perished and 14,045 survived the Holocaust.

Before their deportation to the extermination camps, the Jewish community leadership and cultural elite of Prague managed to save from destruction articles of the religious and cultural heritage of the Jews of Bohemia and Moravia. The Nazis intended to display this accumulation of items at a Central Museum of the Extinguished Jewish Race; instead it became the rich collection of Judaica exhibited in the Jewish Museum of Prague, a precious legacy of the 77,297 Jewish victims, whose names are inscribed on the walls of the Pinkas Synagogue.

[*See also* Youth Movements: Bohemia and Moravia.]

BIBLIOGRAPHY

Baum, K. "Nazi Anti-Jewish Legislation in the Czech Protectorate: A Documentary Note." *Soviet Jewish Affairs* 2/1 (May 1972): 116–128.

Dagan, A., et al., eds. *The Jews of Czechoslovakia: Historical Studies and Surveys.* Vol. 3. Philadelphia, 1984.

Duff, S. G. *German Protectorate: The Czechs under Nazi Rule.* London, 1970.

Mastny, V. *The Czechs under Nazi Rule: The Failure of National Resistance, 1939–1942.* New York, 1971.

Mastny, V., and R. Luza. *A History of the Czechoslovak Republic, 1918–1948.* Princeton, 1973.

LIVIA ROTHKIRCHEN

BOMBING OF AUSCHWITZ. *See* Auschwitz, Bombing of.

BONHOEFFER, DIETRICH (1906–1945), German Protestant theologian. Bonhoeffer's execution by the Nazis in the FLOSSENBÜRG concentration camp on April 9, 1945, in the closing stages of World War II, cut short his career as one of Germany's most significant twentieth-century theologians. After completing his studies at the University of Berlin (D.Phil., 1927) as a student of Adolf von Harnack, Germany's famous liberal theologian, Bonhoeffer became attracted to the more critical dialectical theology of Karl BARTH.

Early in his career he realized the dangers of the extremism and racist bias of Nazi ideology, and in 1933 he became an outspoken opponent of the German Christian (Deutsche Christen) faction of the German Evangelical Church (Evangelische Kirche), which lauded Adolf Hitler and gave its support to the rise of the Nazi party. Because of this opposition, Bonhoeffer was sent to be chaplain of the German church in south London from 1933 to 1935, but he was later recalled to lead an illegal training institute for ordination candidates of the anti-Nazi Confessing Church (Bekennende Kirche), until it was suppressed by the Gestapo in 1938. During the war, he was recruited by Adm. Wilhelm CANARIS, head of the ABWEHR (the Wehrmacht intelligence service), for secret contacts with foreign churches, but was arrested in April 1943 and imprisoned in Berlin and Flossenbürg until his execution.

Bonhoeffer came from a Christian tradition that saw the Jews as accursed, as stated in his April 1933 essay "The Church and the Jewish Question." However, he was the first theologian to recognize the implications for Christian theology of the Nazi persecution of the Jews, and in 1933 he warned his fellow churchmen of the perversion of the Gospels that these racist attacks implied. He subsequently became involved in efforts to assist Jews to escape from Germany, including a successful scheme in 1942 to smuggle a party of fifteen Jews to Switzerland, which led to his arrest. Bonhoeffer's sense of moral outrage against the Nazi treatment of Jews was a major factor in his support of the German resistance movement, in which various members of his immediate family were involved and for which they were later executed.

In his theology, Bonhoeffer addressed the deeper causes of the alienation between Judaism and Christianity, showing that all attempts to curtail the theological significance of the Jewish heritage must be regarded as heretical. In his unfinished work *Ethics,* he began to define the basis for a new understanding of the theological solidarity between Christians and Jews, which went beyond sympathy based on humanitarian feelings. He was continually disappointed by the timidity of the Confessing Church in facing its obligations to the Jewish people. But his involvement in conspiratorial activities after 1939 prevented him from publishing any more outspoken attacks on the regime. There are, however, hints of new approaches in the series of his letters that were smuggled out of prison between 1943 and 1945. A collection of them was first published in 1951, under the title *Widerstand und Ergebung* (Resistance and Surrender). It appeared in English translation in 1953 as *Letters and Papers from Prison* and was published in many subsequent editions.

Bonhoeffer's courageous opposition to the Nazi regime and his subsequent murder greatly enhanced his reputation in the postwar period, and his theological influence has been significantly instrumental in the post-Holocaust rethinking of Christian relationships with the Jewish people. His other major works include *Nachfolge* (1937; published in English as *The Cost of Discipleship*, 1948) and *Sanctorium Communio* (1929; *The Community of Saints*, 1963).

BIBLIOGRAPHY

Bethge, E. *Dietrich Bonhoeffer.* New York, 1977.

Bethge, E., ed. *Ethics.* New York, 1967.

Robertson, E. *The Shame and the Sacrifice: The Life and Martyrdom of Dietrich Bonhoeffer.* New York, 1988.

Willis, R. E. "Bonhoeffer and Barth on Jewish Suffering." *Journal of Ecumenical Studies* 24/4 (1987): 598–615.

Zerner, R. "Dietrich Bonhoeffer and the Jews: Thoughts and Action, 1933–1945." *Jewish Social Studies* 37/3–4 (Summer–Fall 1975): 235–250.

JOHN S. CONWAY

BOR-KOMOROWSKI, TADEUSZ (1895–1966), commander of the ARMIA KRAJOWA (Home Army) in WARSAW and of the WARSAW POLISH UPRISING in 1944. Bor-Komorowski was born in Lvov. His actual name was Komorowski, "Bor" being his later code name in the underground. In World War I he was an officer in the Austro-Hungarian army, and

Tadeusz Bor-Komorowski.

after the war served as an officer in the Polish army, in which he became a colonel. In 1939 he took part in the battle against the German invaders.

At the beginning of the German occupation, Bor-Komorowski was one of the organizers of the Polish underground in the Kraków area. In July 1941 he became deputy commander of the Armia Krajowa and two years later was appointed its commander, the POLISH GOVERNMENT-IN-EXILE promoting him to brigadier general. In his political views he was close to the National Democratic party (the "Endeks"). It was he who gave the order for the Polish uprising in Warsaw, which he led from August to October 1944. When the rebellion was put down, Bor-Komorowski became a prisoner of war. He was liberated at the end of the war and spent the rest of his life in London, where he was active among Polish emigrés. He wrote the story of his experiences in *The Secret Army* (1951), in which he told about the aid offered and the actions taken by the Armia Krajowa in the face of mass deportations and the killing of the Jews. His contentions, however, have no basis in fact.

BIBLIOGRAPHY

Korbonski, S. *The Polish Underground State: A Guide to the Underground, 1939–1945.* New York, 1969.

Zawodny, J. K. *Nothing but Honor: The Story of the Warsaw Uprising, 1944.* Stanford, 1978.

SHMUEL KRAKOWSKI

BORKOWSKA, ANNA (d. 1988), mother superior of a small cloister of Dominican sisters in Kolonia Wilenska, near Vilna, Lithuania. During the PONARY massacres of Jews in the summer months of 1941, Anna Borkowska agreed to conceal in her convent for brief periods seventeen members of Jewish Zionist pioneering groups, including Ha-Shomer ha-Tsa'ir. Later, she helped by smuggling weapons into the Vilna ghetto. Abraham SUTZKEVER, the Yiddish poet, related that the first four grenades received there were the gift of the mother superior, who instructed Abba KOVNER in their proper use. She later supplied other weapons.

As Nazi suspicions of her mounted, the Ger-

Abba Kovner, second from right, presenting Anna Borkowska with the Yad Vashem Righteous among the Nations medal and certificate in Warsaw (August 3, 1984). [Ma'ariv]

mans had Anna Borkowska arrested in September 1943, the convent closed, and the sisters dispersed. One nun was dispatched to a labor camp. In 1984, Anna Borkowska was recognized by YAD VASHEM as a "RIGHTEOUS AMONG THE NATIONS."

BIBLIOGRAPHY

Bartoszewski, W., and Z. Lewin, eds. *Righteous among Nations: How Poles Helped the Jews, 1939–1945.* London, 1969.

MORDECAI PALDIEL

BORMANN, MARTIN (1900–1945?), Nazi leader and close aide of Adolf HITLER. Bormann was born in Halberstadt into the family of a postal worker. Toward the end of World War I he interrupted his high school studies to enlist in the artillery, but the war ended before he reached the front. At the end of the war Bormann joined the Deutsche Freikorps, which carried out acts of violence along the Latvian border after Latvia declared itself independent. Subsequently, Bormann was active in the underground, paramilitary nationalist Frontbann organization, created by Ernst RÖHM, and participated in one of its political assassinations (*Fememorde*). In 1923 he was arrested for this, and sentenced to a year's imprisonment. In prison he became acquainted with Rudolf HÖSS, future commandant of the AUSCHWITZ extermination camp. After Bormann's release in 1925, he joined the Nazi party and the SA (Sturmabteilung; Storm Troopers) in Thuringia, and in 1926 was appointed head of Nazi press affairs and deputy SA commander of the region. In 1928 he rose to the rank of *Gauleiter* of Thuringia. Known in the Nazi party as an active fund-raiser, he was appointed treasurer at the party center in Munich.

With the Nazi rise to power in 1933, Bormann was elected to the Reichstag and became head of the office of Rudolf HESS, Hitler's deputy in the party. From this time Bormann remained at the center of Nazi power around Hitler and was responsible for all financial and administrative affairs. He was always in the shadow of the Führer, excelling as a planner and a behind-the-scenes man, but not as a public speaker.

After Hess's strange flight to Scotland in 1941, Bormann's power increased. In 1942 he was appointed head of the party secretariat and of the party staff, with the rank of *Reichsminister*, and in 1943 he became Hitler's secretary. In this capacity, Bormann also controlled Hitler's appointments calendar, sometimes preventing important figures such as Hermann GÖRING, Joseph GOEBBELS, Heinrich HIMMLER, and Albert SPEER from approaching the leader. He took notes on Hitler's speeches and monologues at luncheons with his favorites, the material known as Hitler's "table talks."

As the war continued and became Hitler's principal occupation, Bormann's status grew, since he was charged in Hitler's name not only with party affairs but with the domestic affairs of Germany. In particular, Bormann was active in fields such as the EUTHANASIA PROGRAM, the war against the church, the pil-

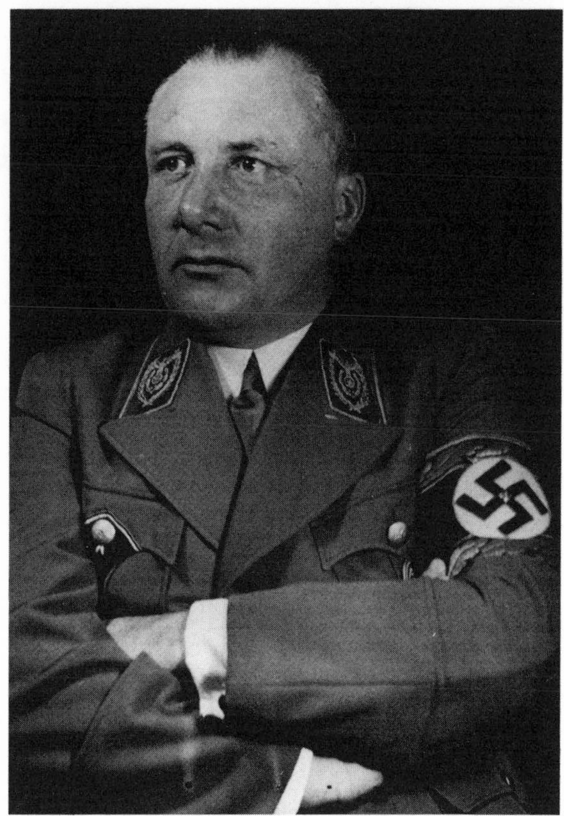

Martin Bormann, Nazi party secretary. [National Archives]

lage of art objects in the occupied countries of eastern Europe, and the expansion of forced-labor programs throughout Europe. Above all, Bormann, who was completely amoral, was the zealous executor of the racist plan of National Socialism and in particular of the persecution and extermination of the Jews. He signed the series of anti-Jewish edicts ordering the deportation of the Jews to the east, the concentration of power in Jewish affairs in the hands of the SS, and the concealment of the massacre as the "transfer of the Jews to labor in the east."

Bormann was appointed commander of the People's Army (Volkssturm), created toward the end of the war, in October 1944. His desire for greater personal power did not cease even after Hitler entered his bunker in Berlin. In the last stage of Nazi rule, Bormann tried to have Göring executed, was a witness to Hitler's marriage to Eva Braun a day before their suicide, and observed the suicide of Goebbels and his family. Before the surrender, it was Bormann who informed Adm. Karl Dönitz that Dönitz had been appointed the Führer's successor.

After Hitler's death, Bormann allegedly tried to conduct negotiations with the Soviets, but after becoming convinced that these were hopeless he gave the order to escape from the bunker. With that his trace vanished. On October 29, 1945, Bormann was indicted *in absentia* with the other Nazi leaders by the International Military Tribunal at Nuremberg, and on October 1, 1946, he was sentenced to death *in absentia*.

Bormann's fate is uncertain. According to unreliable testimony, he was killed by a Soviet shell or committed suicide, and according to rumors that spread in the 1960s he escaped to South America, perhaps to Paraguay. In early 1973 a West German forensic expert determined that one of two skeletons discovered in West Berlin during excavations in 1972 was almost certainly that of Bormann. On the basis of this determination, Bormann was officially declared dead.

BIBLIOGRAPHY

Lang, J. von, and C. Sibyll. *Bormann: The Man Who Manipulated Hitler*. New York, 1979.

McGovern, J. *Martin Bormann*. New York, 1968.

Wulf, J. *Martin Bormann: Hitlers Schatten*. Gütersloh, 1962.

TSVI RAANAN

BOSNIA. *See* Yugoslavia.

BOTHMANN, HANS (1911–1946), commandant of the CHEŁMNO extermination camp in central Poland. Bothmann joined the HITLERJUGEND (the Nazi youth movement) in November 1932 and the SS in June 1933. In September 1939, following the invasion of Poland, he was assigned to the Sicherheitspolizei (Security Police) in Poznań. He was appointed commandant at Chełmno in the spring of 1942, replacing Hauptsturmführer Herbert Lange, and he directed the mass killing operations in the camp until March 1943, when the transports of Jews to Chełmno were discontinued. The next month Bothmann, together with eighty-five members of the camp staff, was transferred to Yugoslavia, where he formed Sonderkommando Bothmann, which reinforced a company of gendarmerie attached to the "Prinz Eugen" Division of the SS. With these forces, Bothmann engaged in operations against the Yugoslav PARTISANS.

In the late spring of 1944, Bothmann and his unit were ordered back to Chełmno to renew the gassing operations, which continued through June and July. In August, Sonderkommando Bothmann took part in the liquidation of the ŁÓDŹ ghetto. It was then assigned to AKTION 1005, in which the corpses of the victims at Chełmno were burned to obliterate evidence of the killings that had taken place there.

In January 1945 Bothmann escaped to western Germany, where he was captured by the British; on April 4, 1946, he hanged himself in prison.

SHMUEL KRAKOWSKI

BOYCOTT, ANTI-JEWISH. The boycott of April 1, 1933, was the first national action against the German Jews after the Nazi seizure of power on January 30 of that year. The boycott was declared by the Nazi party on March 28, apparently after consultations with the top ranks of power at Hitler's residence in Berchtesgaden on the initiative of Propaganda Minister Joseph GOEBBELS. The declaration was described as an action of both reprisal and warning against world Jewry to cease what the Nazis called *Greuelpropaganda* (horror propaganda) and an economic boycott abroad against the "New Germany." The acts of terror committed by the SA (Sturmabteilung; Storm Troopers) against political rivals and Jews in the first months after the Nazi rise to power had indeed received extensive publicity and aroused public protests throughout the world, though Jewish institutions and organizations generally took a cautious line, fearing to harm German Jewry.

The boycott was organized initially as a Nazi party operation. Julius STREICHER was placed at the head of the organizing committee. Despite the apparently short period of preparation, everything was planned down to the last detail. At 10:00 a.m. on Saturday, April 1, the boycott was to begin simultaneously in every city and town, down to the smallest village. In fact, actions commenced in several places on the previous day or evening—a direct continuation of the harassment and confiscation that had been pursued continuously in the weeks preceding the "official" boycott. The pattern was the same, in accordance with the detailed instructions: guards of uniformed, sometimes armed, Nazis were placed in front of every store or other business owned by Jews, and their clients were prevented from entering. Trucks patrolled the streets with uniformed Nazis and members of the Stahlhelm organization, bearing signs and slogans proclaiming: "Ger-

Boycott of April 1, 1933, in Berlin. The sign in both windows reads: "Germans! Beware! Don't buy from Jews!"

mans! Defend yourselves! Don't buy from Jews!" In the main streets of the large cities an effort was made to avoid open violence, but in more remote places there were many incidents of shattered store windows, pillaging of stores, and physical assault of Jewish business owners. Despite the order not to harm the businesses of Jewish foreign nationals, many attacks did occur, especially on Jews of eastern European origin who lived together in poor sections of towns. An indication of such attacks is the complaints they engendered from diplomatic representations, particularly, in several cities, the representatives of Poland.

Besides retail stores, the liberal professions were a specific target for expropriation activities. Guards were placed at the doors of the offices of Jewish lawyers and doctors. In several cities, uniformed gangs of Nazis broke into law courts and forcibly expelled Jewish judges and prosecutors, both government employees and private lawyers. On the day before the boycott, the ministers of justice in Prussia and Bavaria had already sent the Jewish jurists "on vacation" and had forbidden them to enter the law courts "in order to guarantee their safety and to maintain public order."

The boycott declaration aroused a wave of protests and a series of interventions by government circles and both Jewish and non-Jewish businessmen abroad in an attempt to bring about its annulment. Jewish organizations in Germany and abroad published announcements rejecting the Nazi accusations of *Greuelpropaganda* and proclaiming an economic boycott against German exports. In Germany too the declaration of boycott aroused concern in economic circles over possible harmful consequences, in light of the unemployment and depression. On the afternoon of Friday, March 31, in a government consultation in Hitler's office in Berlin, the possibility had been discussed of annulling the boycott of the following day, on condition that the governments of Great Britain and the United States publish official announcements condemning the *Greuelpropaganda*. It was possibly because of these pressures that the boycott—initially declared for an unlimited period—ceased, by government announcement, after one day, while the hope was expressed that those spreading *Greuelpropaganda* abroad had learned their lesson. There was no conflict between the intentions of the party, which declared the boycott, and those of the government, which announced its cessation. Goebbels himself, the moving spirit in the organization of the boycott, declared at a party mass meeting on the evening of March 31 that the boycott would be stopped after one day and would be renewed on April 4 if the *Greuelpropaganda* abroad did not cease.

It is the opinion of several scholars that the Nazi leadership organized the boycott day as a "safety valve" for pressures from rank-and-file party members, in particular SA members, who demanded radical steps against the activity of the Jews in the economy, as promised in the Nazi party platform. According to this interpretation, the aim of the boycott was to allow postponement of these steps (1) until the stabilization of the Nazi regime and (2) because of Germany's uncertain financial situation and international position. Yet in fact the boycott was a clear and explicit starting signal for a process of harassment and oppression, designed to undermine the basis of the economic existence of Germany Jewry. Acts of terror, expropriation, and discrimination, which previously could have been interpreted as "individual" or "isolated" acts (*Einzelaktionen*) of violence on a local initiative, were legitimized through the boycott by the highest party and government institutions. In the boycott instructions, the initial and immediate targets of economic oppression were also clearly indicated: Jewish professionals and Jewish retail businesses. From this point of view, the April 1 boycott was the official opening for preparing the legislation passed on April 7 against Jewish professionals and government employees, and the administrative and propaganda campaign of repression against all economic activity among German Jewry.

BIBLIOGRAPHY

Adam, U. D. *Judenpolitik im Dritten Reich*. Düsseldorf, 1972.

Ball-Kaduri, J. *Das Leben der Juden in Deutschland im Jahre 1933: Ein Zeitbericht*. Frankfurt, 1963.

Barkai, A. *Vom Boykott zur "Entjudung": Der wirtschaftliche Existenzkampf der Juden im Dritten Reich, 1933–1943*. Frankfurt, 1988.

Schleunes, K. *The Twisted Road to Auschwitz: Nazi Policy toward German Jews, 1933–1939*. Urbana, Ill., 1970.

AVRAHAM BARKAI

BOYCOTTS, ANTI-NAZI, pre–World War II actions to boycott German goods in reaction to the Nazi persecution of the Jews. Following the Nazi rise to power in 1933, there were Jewish protests throughout the world against the policies of the new regime in Germany. These protests developed into boycott movements in many countries, most importantly in the United States.

On March 19, 1933, the Jewish War Veterans organization announced a boycott in the United States. Following the Nazi boycott of Jewish businesses (*see* BOYCOTT, ANTI-JEWISH) in Germany on April 1, 1933, additional boycott groups were formed in the United States and elsewhere. In May 1933, the Yiddish journalist Abraham Coralnik founded the American League for the Defense of Jewish Rights. He was succeeded six months later by Samuel Untermyer, who became a leading figure in the boycott movement until the United States entered World War II. Untermyer changed the organization's name to the Non-Sectarian Anti-Nazi League to Champion Human Rights, in order to emphasize the universality of the cause. In 1933, Untermyer and Coralnik organized the World Jewish Economic Conference in Amsterdam in an unsuccessful effort to coordinate an international Jewish boycott movement.

The American Jewish Congress (*see* WORLD JEWISH CONGRESS) issued its own boycott declaration in August 1933, and its JOINT BOYCOTT COUNCIL, formed in 1935 together with the JEWISH LABOR COMMITTEE's boycott movement, became one of the two leading boycott organizations in the United States. However, efforts to unify the boycott activities of Untermyer's League and the Joint Boycott Council were unsuccessful.

Support for the anti-Nazi boycott was widespread in the United States and elsewhere, but the movement never received the wholehearted backing of many important organizations and leaders, both among the American public in general and in the Jewish community. In the United States, the AMERICAN JEWISH COMMITTEE and B'NAI B'RITH were among the organizations opposing the boycott, while the BOARD OF DEPUTIES OF BRITISH JEWS in England and the Alliance Israélite Universelle in France opposed the movements in their respective countries.

In Britain, the Board of Deputies turned down a proposal to foster an economic boycott of Germany at a meeting held on July 23, 1933. Dissenting members of the board, including Lord Melchett (Henry Mond), formed the Jewish Representation Council. Together with an ad hoc committee, the Organization for Ending Hostilities to German Jews, this council strove to organize a boycott in Great Britain. Lord Melchett also played a role in convening the World Jewish Economic Conference in 1933. After 1934, however, the British boycott movement became splintered and lost most of its effectiveness.

Whereas several British and American organizations opposed international Jewish political activity in principle, the Jewish Agency found itself working against the boycott through the HAAVARA AGREEMENT (Transfer Agreement) reached with Germany. The agency's understanding of the practical necessities of aiding German Jews to leave Germany and emigrate to Palestine with part of their capital led to this conflict.

In January 1936, Simon Marks, Sir Herbert Samuel, and Lord Bearsted went to the United States from England to negotiate with American Jewish leaders on the creation of the COUNCIL FOR GERMAN JEWRY. However, they had to yield to American Zionist insistence that no scheme to transfer German goods out of Germany be considered.

The boycott met with limited success; the fur trade between Britain and Germany virtually ceased, and several American department stores, such as R. H. Macy and Gimbel Brothers, agreed to stop buying German goods. There is also some evidence that leading figures within the Nazi regime were at times concerned about the possible effects of the boycott movement on the German economy. However, the movement failed in its overriding goal of forcing Nazi Germany to change its Jewish policy.

BIBLIOGRAPHY

Gottlieb, M. R. *American Anti-Nazi Resistance, 1933–1941: An Historical Analysis.* New York, 1982.

Tenenbaum, J. "The Anti-Nazi Boycott Movement in the United States." *Yad Vashem Studies* 3 (1959): 141–159.

DAVID SILBERKLANG

BRACK, VIKTOR (1904–1948), senior SS officer (*Oberführer*) and one of the chief functionaries in the EUTHANASIA PROGRAM and the mass gassing of Jews in the EXTERMINATION CAMPS during World War II. The son of a physician, Brack studied economics in Munich. He was friendly with Heinrich HIMMLER and was his chauffeur before becoming liaison officer between the SS and the Führer's Chancellery (Kanzlei des Führers) in 1936. He rose to become deputy to Philip Bouhler, head of the chancellery, and Brack's office in the chancellery, known as T4, was responsible for the killing of more than fifty thousand Germans and Jews under the Euthanasia Program from 1939 to 1941. Brack himself personally interviewed the medical personnel employed in the program.

In the summer of 1941, when the "FINAL SOLUTION" was inaugurated, Brack made his experience available in the efforts to sterilize Jews in X-ray clinics and to exterminate them in the gas chambers of the camps in occupied Poland. As one of the accused in The Medical Case, tried at the SUBSEQUENT NUREMBERG PROCEEDINGS, Brack was sentenced to death by an American military tribunal in 1947 and executed in 1948.

BIBLIOGRAPHY

Lifton, R. J. *The Nazi Doctors: Medical Killing and the Psychology of Genocide.* New York, 1986.

Mitscherlich, A., and F. Mielke. *Doctors of Infamy: The Story of Nazi Medical Crimes.* New York, 1949.

Sereny, G. *Into That Darkness: From Mercy Killing to Mass Murder.* New York, 1974.

LIONEL KOCHAN

BRAND, JOEL (1907–1964), member of the RELIEF AND RESCUE COMMITTEE OF BUDAPEST (known as the Va'ada) during World War II. Born in Năsăud, Transylvania, then under Hungarian rule, Brand embraced Zionism after a stint in the radical leftist movement in Weimar Germany. He returned to Transylvania after Hitler's seizure of power but eventually settled in Budapest, where together with his wife, Hansi Hartmann Brand, he operated a medium-sized glove-manufacturing plant. After the Anschluss and especially after the outbreak of World War II, the Brands became interested in refugee affairs, organizing a variety of rescue and relief activities.

When the Va'ada was established in January 1943 to aid refugees who had escaped from or were seeking to escape from Slovakia

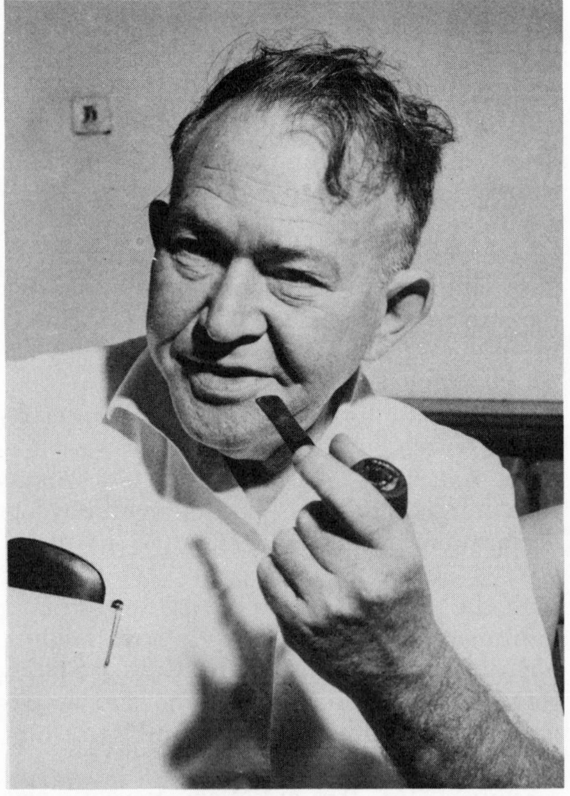

Joel Brand.

and Poland, Brand was chosen to head its Tiyyul (Trip) section, a border-crossing operation whose function was to smuggle Jews out of these countries.

After the German occupation of Hungary on March 19, 1944, the Va'ada's primary concern was the rescuing of Jews within Hungary. Brand was also engaged in the Re-Tiyyul (Return Trip) program, which enabled a number of Polish and Slovak refugees to return to Slovakia, where the situation of the remaining Jews was better, at least temporarily. While the first contact and rescue negotiations with the SS were established through Fülöp FREUDIGER, the Orthodox representative of the Jewish Council (Zsidó Tanács), and continued later by Rezső (Rudolf) KASZTNER, it was Brand whom Adolf EICHMANN summoned, on April 25, 1944, to offer his "Blood for Goods" arrangement. Under the arrangement, which was approved by the higher SS authorities, apparently including Heinrich HIMMLER, Eichmann expressed his readiness to exchange one million Jews for certain goods to be obtained from outside Hungary. These included 10,000 trucks that would be used for civilian purposes or only along the eastern front. Jews could not remain in Hungary, for he had promised to make the country *judenrein* ("cleansed of Jews"). But those covered by the bargain would be permitted to go into any Allied-controlled part of the world except Palestine, for the Nazis had promised the mufti of Jerusalem, Hajj Amin al-HUSSEINI, not to permit this. To effectuate the deal, Eichmann was ready to allow Brand to go abroad to establish contact with the representatives of world Jewry and the western Allies.

The true reason why Brand was chosen remains a mystery, but it appears that he had been recommended by Andor ("Bandi") Grosz, a doubtful character and minor intelligence agent who was in the service of anyone who paid him, including the Germans and the Va'ada. Grosz was reportedly employed by SS-Hauptsturmführer Otto Klages, the head of the SD (Sicherheitsdienst; Security Service) in Hungary; he was assigned to go together with Brand to establish contact with American and British intelligence officers in Istanbul and to discuss with them the possibility of a separate peace between Germany and the western Allies. Brand's mission, according to this scenario, was to camouflage Grosz's more important assignment.

Brand was informed about the completion of his travel arrangements on May 15, 1944, the day that mass deportations from Hungary began. Supplied with a German passport bearing the name Eugen Band, he left Budapest for Vienna in the company of Obersturmbannführer Hermann KRUMEY, a leading member of the Eichmann Sonderkommando, and Grosz left two days later. On May 19 Brand and Grosz arrived in Istanbul, where they were met by local representatives of the JOINT RESCUE COMMITTEE of the Jewish Agency. Since Brand had no Turkish visa, the details of his mission were revealed to Laurence Steinhardt, the American ambassador in Ankara, and to the leaders of the Jewish Agency in Jerusalem by the Agency's representatives in Turkey.

By the end of the month, the leaders of the American and British governments were fully informed about Brand's mission. Grosz was arrested by the British on June 1, shortly after crossing the Syrian border. Thus, he was unable to meet with authorized Jewish and non-Jewish representatives and to complete his assignment. Equipped with a British visa, Brand left—ostensibly for Palestine—on June 5, but was arrested by the British at Aleppo two days later. On June 10 he was given an opportunity (while under arrest) to reveal the plight of Hungarian Jewry and the details of his mission to Moshe Shertok (Sharett), head of the Jewish Agency's Political Department. Shertok was very favorably impressed with Brand, as was Ira A. HIRSCHMANN, the representative of the WAR REFUGEE BOARD, who interrogated him later in the month in Cairo. Before the month was over, Shertok and Hirschmann revealed the details of their interrogations to the YISHUV leaders and to top figures of the American and British governments.

In spite of pleas by the Yishuv leaders, the British decided against having any dealings "with the Gestapo" and even permitting Brand's return to Hungary. Their decision was based on many factors, among them the continuation of the "Final Solution" program in Hungary; the vehement opposition of the

Soviets (who were officially informed about the offer in mid-June) to any discussion on this matter with the Germans; and the concern of the British over acquiring responsibility for one million Jews in case the Nazis kept their side of the bargain. The Americans were more flexible, advocating that the negotiations be continued in the hope of saving lives. Whatever hopes the Jewish leaders of the free world had for Brand's mission dissipated on July 19, when the BBC brought it to public attention. The following day, the British press emphasized that the "monstrous offer" of the Germans to barter Jews was a loathsome attempt to blackmail the Allies.

Immediately after his June 10 meeting with Shertok, Brand was taken to Cairo, where he was intensively debriefed and treated as a "privileged prisoner" until October, when he was allowed to go to Palestine. A frustrated and dejected man, Brand felt for a long time that because of the failure and shortcomings of the Jewish leaders and the passivity and insensitivity of the Allies, the chance to save a million Jews had been missed. However, shortly before his death in Tel Aviv in 1964, Brand came to believe that he had made a "terrible mistake" in passing to the British the Eichmann offer, and that Heinrich Himmler had merely sought to sow suspicion among the Allies as a preparation for his much-desired Nazi-western coalition against Moscow.

BIBLIOGRAPHY

Bauer, Y. *The Holocaust in Historical Perspective.* Seattle, 1978. See pages 94–155.

Brand, J., and A. Weissberg. *Desperate Mission: Joel Brand's Story.* New York, 1958.

RANDOLPH L. BRAHAM

BRATISLAVA (Ger., Pressburg; Hung., Pozsony), city in Czechoslovakia; capital of SLOVAKIA. Bratislava dates back to the tenth century. From 1541 to 1784 it was the capital of Habsburg-ruled Hungary, and until 1848 it was the seat of the Hungarian parliament. In 1918 it became the capital of the Czechoslovak province of Slovakia, and from 1939 to 1945 it was the capital of the Slovak state. The presence of Jews in Bratislava is mentioned as early as the tenth century, but it was only in the seventeenth century that the Jewish community began to flourish. Rabbi Moshe Sofer (known as the Ḥatam Sofer; 1762–1839) established a large yeshiva (rabbinical academy), and the city became a great center of Orthodox Judaism. The Orthodox influence declined in the second half of the nineteenth century, when modern institutions of both a religious and a secular character were established. The city had an antisemitic tradition, which was expressed in anti-Jewish riots (in 1831, 1848, 1918, and 1937), during the Holocaust, and in the post–World War II period. In December 1940, Bratislava had a Jewish population of some fifteen thousand—about one-sixth of Slovak Jewry.

As a capital city, Bratislava was the seat of central Jewish organizations such as the ÚSTREDŇA ŽIDOV and the Union of Jewish Communities. It was also the home of nationalist bodies, such as the HLINKA GUARD, Hlinková Mladež (Hlinka Youth), the Freiwillige Schutzstaffel (Volunteer Battalions), and the German HITLERJUGEND. These organizations, together with urban mobs, frequently rioted against the Jews. Such riots began in October 1938, immediately after Slovakia was granted autonomy, and subsequently they were launched time and again. Bratislava's Jews—some of whom still lived in the Židovna, the old ghetto—were exposed to organized raids by rioters and to sporadic harassment. Following the attacks that took place in March 1939 to "celebrate" Slovakia's independence, a Jewish self-defense organization was formed in the Jewish quarter, its membership consisting of artisans, members of sports clubs, yeshiva students, and members of youth movements. The Jews defended themselves against sporadic attacks, and in a few instances the attackers had to pay with their lives.

The Bratislava Jews were quick to come to the aid of their brethren in an hour of need. The first to appeal for such help were the Jews of Austria, especially those who lived in the "Seven Communities" of Burgenland and were being persecuted by the SS, and Jewish residents of Slovakia whom the authorities had expelled to Hungary, claiming that they were Hungarian nationals. (The Hungarians had turned them back into the no-man's-land between the two countries.) For the latter, the Jewish organizations rented the premises of a factory that was no longer in operation—known as the "Patronka"—and put it in shape for lengthy occupation; this later became a place that the Jews mortally feared, since it was used as an assembly center prior to their deportation to the east.

Bratislava's port was the departure point for several "illegal" immigration boats that sailed for the Black Sea and the shores of Palestine. The passengers on these boats were refugees from neighboring countries as well as residents of Czechoslovakia; only some of them succeeded in reaching their goal.

The deportation of the Jews of Bratislava was preceded by their eviction from certain parts of the city—specific squares, streets, and quarters—and their removal to the provinces. This operation, known as the *dislokacia*, lasted from the fall of 1941 to the spring of 1942, and in its course 6,700 persons were moved out, that is, half the Jewish population of the city. Their property was confiscated by the authorities, and their apartments were handed over to other inhabitants. The official reason given for the *dislokacia* was the shortage of apartments for the city's growing population, but in fact the operation was a planned prelude to the deportations; the Jews were being gathered into a few places, to facilitate their eventual deportation to extermination camps.

When the deportations were launched, some of the victims were loaded into railway cars at Patronka, and sent straight to the east; others were first taken to assembly points selected for this purpose. In Bratislava the Jews continued to maintain their activities—legally, in the Ústredňa Židov, or illegally, in the PRACOVNÁ SKUPINA (Working Group). Following the SLOVAK NATIONAL UPRISING in 1944, the city came under German occupation. Many Jews who had not fled in time hid in city bunkers, a refuge for which, in most instances, they had to pay heavily: they were seized by raiding teams and sent to a camp in SERED, and from there to the extermination camps. When the number of Jews seized in this fashion declined, the Germans resorted to surprise checks in the street, often helped by tip-offs from informants and collaborators, Jewish and non-Jewish. At the beginning of the German occupation, several members of the Pracovná Skupina deluded themselves that they would be able to help the local Jewish population, but later they themselves were caught and taken to Sered. A Jewish underground, headed by Juraj Revesz, was also organized in the city, in order to give financial aid to the Jews in hiding; this group obtained money from the International RED CROSS delegate, Georges Dunand, and distributed it among those in need. Members of the underground who fell into German hands were used by the Gestapo as bait for other Jews roaming the streets; the latter knew these activists and turned to them for help. The result was that many of the Jews in hiding were discovered, along with their families. When the Soviets liberated Bratislava, in April 1945, only a few Jews were left.

Liberation did not put an end to pogroms. Particularly severe were the pogroms of the summer of 1946, when the Jewish hospital was among the places ransacked, and those of the summer of 1948. The latter were the last of the postwar attacks on the Jews of Bratislava, and in their course a self-defense group was formed that was able to capture the rioters. Most of the remaining Jews of Bratislava left in the great emigration wave of 1948 and 1949. Organized Jewish life, of modest dimensions, continues to function in the city.

BIBLIOGRAPHY

Dagan, A., ed. *The Jews of Czechoslovakia*. 3 vols. New York, 1968.

Dunand, G. *Ne perdez pas leur trace*. Neuchâtel, 1950.

Frieder, E. *To Deliver Their Souls: The Struggle of a Young Rabbi during the Holocaust*. Jerusalem, 1986. (In Hebrew.)

Grünhut, A. *Katastrophenzeit des slowakischen Judentums: Aufstieg und Niedergang der Juden von Pressburg*. Tel Aviv, 1972.

YESHAYAHU JELINEK

BREENDONCK, internment camp in Belgium, near the village of that name, south of the city of Antwerp. At the beginning of the century, a fortress was erected near the village, at the junction of the Antwerp-Brussels and MECHELEN-Dendermonde roads, as part of a chain of fortifications; this fortress, surrounded by a moat, consists of a building measuring 656 by 984 feet (200 × 300 m) and is still in existence.

At the end of August 1940 the Germans turned the fortress into a *Polizeihaftlager* (internment camp), and three weeks later, on September 20, the first group of detainees, numbering twenty persons, mostly "politicals" and Jews of foreign nationality, were brought to the camp. The camp was under the control of the Sicherheitspolizei (Security Police) and was run by SS men, with Wehrmacht personnel serving as guards. At the end of 1941 they were joined by Belgian SS men. The first commandant of the camp was Sturmbannführer Philip Schmitt, who was followed, in 1943, by an Austrian, Karl Schönwetter. The officer in charge of forced labor was Untersturmführer Artur Prauss,

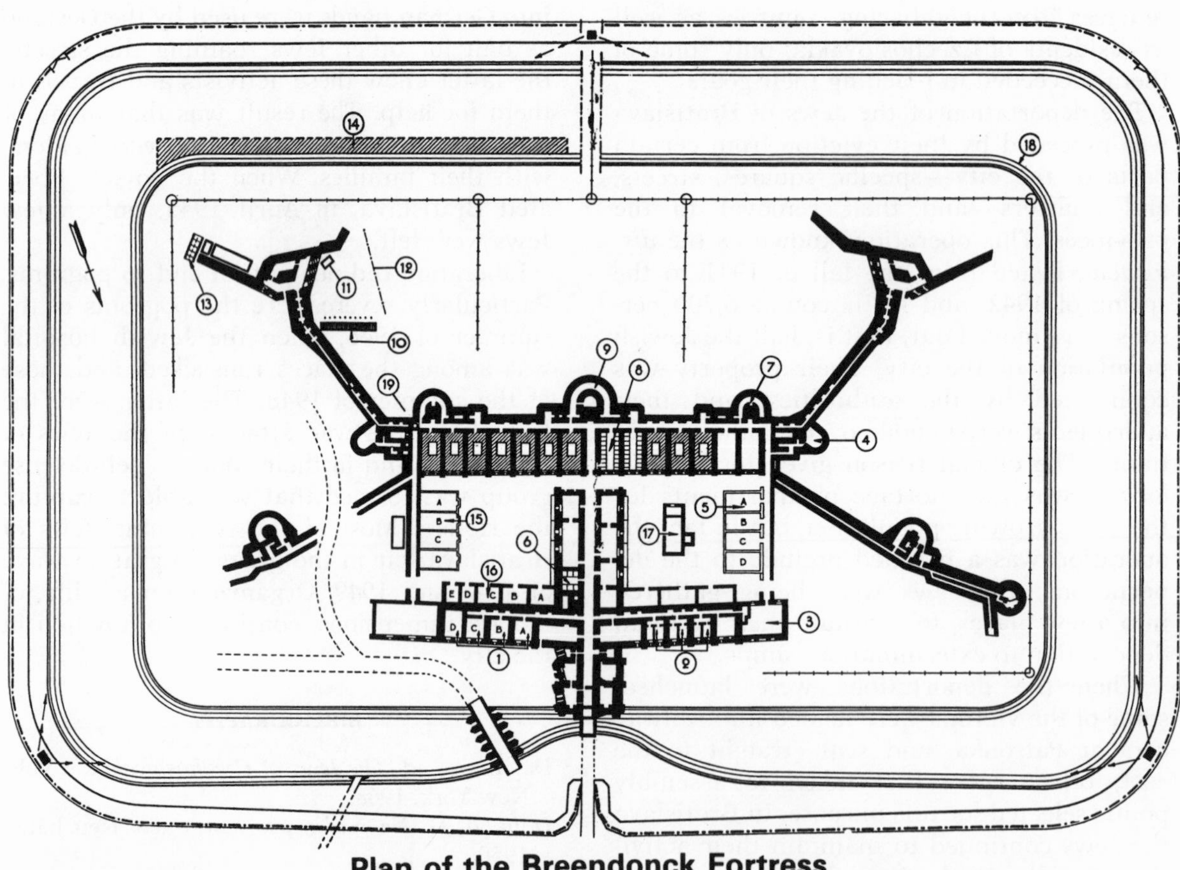

Plan of the Breendonck Fortress

1. SS offices
2. Gestapo preliminary interrogation office
3. Prisoner's latrines
4. Torture chamber
5. Wooden huts
6. Dark cells
7. Morgue (purported to be gas chambers)
8. Cells
9. Dome of the fortress
10. Execution site
11. Gallows
12. Wall for concealing torture area
13. Rabbit hutch where starved prisoners would try to steal the rabbit food.
14. Site where exhausted prisoners were thrown and they then drowned
15. Barracks
16. Storerooms
17. Printing shop
18. Site where prisoners were buried alive

Les Crimes de Guerre — Le Camp de Tortures de Breendonck, Liege 1948.

Plan of Breendonck.

who had the reputation of being the most cruel person in the camp staff. The camp commandant came directly under the authority of the Security Police chief for Belgium and northern France, Konstantin Canaris, and then of his successor, Ernst Ehlers.

In the early stage, conditions in the camp were quite tolerable, and the Jewish prisoners were not separated from the non-Jews. But at the end of 1940, the situation took a sharp turn for the worse; the "Aryan" prisoners were put into separate living quarters, although both groups continued to work side by side.

At first the Jews were in the majority, but during 1942, when the deportations from Belgium began, their numbers decreased. Almost all the Jews of Belgium were then put into the Jewish transit camp at Mechelen, and from there sent to extermination camps. The non-Jewish group consisted mostly of members of the underground (especially the leftist underground), hostages, and black-market operators. The total number of prisoners held in the camp is estimated as having ranged from 3,000 to 3,600 (of whom 7 percent were Jews), but no precise figures are available. Various sources have provided average occupancy figures (apparently for the end of each year):

	1940	1941	1942	1943	1944
Jews	40	200	180	50	45
Non-Jews	35	200	450	650	600

Some 300 persons perished in the camp from torture, harassment, and the harsh conditions; 450 were executed by shooting and 14 were hanged; 54 Jews were deported to AUSCHWITZ; and of the 165 others, 65 died in the camp.

Conditions were among the worst in the camps of western Europe: overcrowded and dilapidated housing, bad food, and harsh punishment; but worst of all was the violence. Prauss set the tone for the cruelty and brutality. One form of punishment used was to drown the prisoners, another to bury them up to the neck and then beat and kick them to death. Political prisoners were executed in groups from the end of 1942 onward, and especially on the eve of liberation in the summer of 1944.

The camp was made into a museum in 1948, and in 1954 a memorial, the work of the sculptor Idel Janchelevici, was erected at the site.

BIBLIOGRAPHY

Halkin, L. E. *Breendonck*. Brussels, 1946.

Ministère de la Justice, Commission des Crimes de Guerre. *Camp de tortures de Breendonck*. Liège, 1948.

Solonevitch, B. *Breendonck: Camp de tortures et de mort*. Brussels, 1944.

Wolf, J. *Le procès de Breendonck*. Brussels, 1973.

DAN MICHMAN

BRESLAU (Pol., Wrocław), city on the Oder River in Lower Silesia; it was part of GERMANY until 1945 and was annexed to Poland after World War II. Breslau was founded in the tenth century; Jews first settled there in the late twelfth century, and they lived there continuously after 1630. On the eve of World War II the city had a population of 630,000.

Breslau had one of the largest and most prominent Jewish communities in Germany. Several of the leading figures of the Wissenschaft des Judentums (the movement for the scholarly study of Judaism and Jewish history) were active there, among them Abraham Geiger, a leader of the Reform movement; Zacharias Frankel, leader of the Conservative trend; and the historian Heinrich Graetz. The Jewish Theological Seminary (Jüdisches Theologisches Seminar), the first modern institution of its kind in Germany, was founded in Breslau in 1854. Breslau was also an important center of Zionism in Germany; in 1912 the Blau-Weiss (Blue-White) Zionist youth movement was founded there.

After World War I a large number of Jews settled in Breslau from the districts of Poznań and southern Upper Silesia, which had been annexed to Poland. In 1925 the Jewish population of the city was 23,240 (4.2 percent of the total), making it the third largest Jewish community in Germany; in 1933 it declined to 20,202.

The period between the world wars saw a rise in antisemitism, which included the desecration of tombstones and the accusation that Jews had murdered a Christian child. In

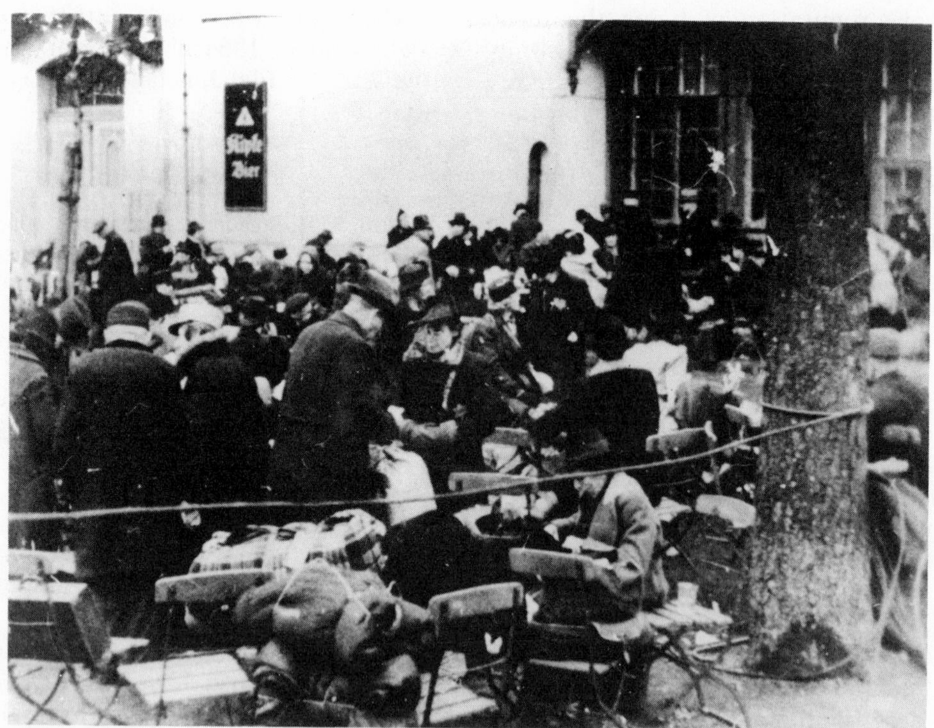

Jews rounded up in Breslau, awaiting deportation.

1932 the appointment of a Jewish lecturer at the University of Breslau led to riots, causing the university to cancel the appointment.

The Nazi rise to power led to more riots and to the murder of young Jews who were active in the Social Democratic party. Even before the anti-Jewish BOYCOTT of April 1, 1933, SA (Sturmabteilung; Storm Troopers) men stormed into the district courts and evicted the Jewish judges and lawyers. The discriminatory laws against Jews enacted by the central government were applied most severely in Breslau, and Jewish businessmen, under the impact of the official and unofficial boycott, were forced to liquidate their enterprises, or were deprived of them by the official policy of ARISIERUNG ("Aryanization"). In 1936 some four thousand Breslau Jews were in need of the aid offered by the nationwide Jewish relief campaign, the Jüdische Winterhilfe (Jewish Winter Relief). The Breslau Jewish community board did its best to solve the problems caused by the ongoing changes. It supported the actors and musicians who, having been dismissed from their jobs, joined the Breslau branch of the KULTURBUND DEUTSCHER JUDEN (Cultural Society of German Jews); it helped the sports clubs to set up a gym and a swimming pool for the Jewish population; and it expanded the existing *hakhsharot* (agricultural training centers) and vocational training centers in order to promote emigration and Aliya (immigration to Palestine).

During the KRISTALLNACHT pogrom all the synagogues in Breslau were destroyed except for the Orthodox Storch Synagogue, which was not set afire lest the fire spread to the adjoining buildings; however, the interior and the contents were severely damaged. As a result of the many arrests, the personal harassment, and the destruction of property, more and more Jews emigrated, so that by 1939 the Jewish population had dwindled to 10,309.

On March 31, 1941, the Jews in Breslau numbered 9,184. In September of that year Jewish apartments were confiscated and most of the Jews were relocated to special *Judenhäuser* (Jewish houses). In November, the first groups of Jews were sent to transit camps in Silesia (Riebnig, Grüssau, and Tomersdorf). Within a few days of their arrival at these camps, the deportations to the east began. Between November 25, 1941, and April 1944 the Jews of Breslau were deported in fifteen transports, primarily to THERESIENSTADT and AUSCHWITZ. The only Jews spared were 150 persons who were married to "Aryan" spouses.

Following the seizure of Breslau by the Soviet army and the annexation of the city to Poland, more than ten thousand Jews made their way to Breslau, most of them refugees from eastern Europe, and for a while the Jewish community institutions resumed operations. The Jewish community archive, one of the largest in Germany, was taken to Warsaw in 1945. At the end of the 1980s Breslau's Jewish population stood at less than seventy, not enough to maintain the community facilities and the cemeteries.

BIBLIOGRAPHY

Anders, G. *Besuch im Hades: Auschwitz und Breslau 1966.* Munich, 1979.

Polonski, F. "Holocaust we Wrocławiu/na Dolnym Slaku (1941–1944) w świetle dokumentów administracji skarbowej." *Dzieje Najnowsze* 18/3–4 (1986): 235–248.

Schwerin, K. "Die Juden in Schlesien: Aus ihrer Geschichte und ihrem Beitrag zur Wirtschaft und Kultur." *Bulletin des Leo Baeck Instituts* 19/56–57 (1980): 1–84.

Tausk, W. *Breslauer Tagebuch 1933–1940.* Berlin, 1975.

Walk, J., ed. *Als Jude in Breslau: Aus den Tagebüchern von Studienrat a. D. Dr. Willy Israel Cohn.* Gerlingen, West Germany, 1984.

JOSEPH WALK

The Germans handed Brest-Litovsk over to the Soviets on September 22, 1939. In the photo, Generaloberst Heinz Guderian is in the center. [Bildarchiv Preussischer Kulturbesitz]

BREST-LITOVSK (Brisk, in Jewish usage), administrative center of Brest Oblast (district) in southwestern BELORUSSIA. Brest-Litovsk has been known to exist since the eleventh century. It was there that the March 1918 peace treaty was signed between Soviet Russia and Germany. In the interwar period, Brest-Litovsk belonged to Poland.

Jews lived in Brest-Litovsk from the fourteenth century. Until the seventeenth century the city was the center of Lithuanian Jewry's spiritual life and religious scholarship. In 1897 Brest-Litovsk had over 30,000 Jews, constituting more than 75 percent of the total population. During World War I, however, many of the Jews were driven out and in 1931 its Jewish population was 21,440—44 percent of the total. The Jewish community maintained many public institutions, among them a Hebrew high school.

Soon after the beginning of World War II the Germans occupied Brest-Litovsk, on September 15, 1939, but they handed it over to the Soviets on September 22. In that one week the Germans arrested several prominent Jews and maltreated them. On June 23, 1941, a day after they had launched their invasion of the Soviet Union, the Germans occupied Brest-Litovsk for the second time; the town fortress, however, held out for another half year, until all of its defenders had fallen in battle. On June 28 and 29, Sonderkom-

mando 7b of Einsatzgruppe B went into action, rounding up five thousand men on the pretext that they were being drafted for work, taking them to the outskirts, and killing them all. In August of that year a twenty-member JUDENRAT (Jewish Council) was appointed, a Jewish police force set up, and a collective ransom payment of 5 million rubles imposed on the Jews. In November, orders were issued for the creation of two ghettos, known as the "small" and the "large" ghetto. A month later the ghettos were sealed off; the gates were guarded strictly and no food was allowed in. Jews in the ghettos were starving despite the efforts made by the Judenrat to help the needy through its welfare agencies. Workshops were set up in order to create employment for the ghetto population.

Early in 1942 a fighting underground with eighty members was established under the leadership of Aryeh Scheinmann. Those members of the underground who worked in the fortress or in the bombed-out airfield stole weapons and ammunition and smuggled them into the ghetto. Plans were made for a ghetto uprising. In late June, nine hundred skilled artisans were rounded up and sent on forced labor to the east. A few weeks later twelve of them came back; all the others had been murdered.

On October 15, 1942, the ghetto was cordoned off and its liquidation was launched. The Jews were rounded up and put on trains for the Brona Gora station, just north of Kobrin on the Brest-Litovsk–Baranovichi railway line. On arrival they were killed. Some of the Jews hid and others fled, but many days later they were apprehended and executed.

Prior to the liquidation of the ghetto the underground established contact with a group of alleged Russian partisans, and several armed groups left the ghetto to join these partisans in the forests. These so-called partisans, however, turned out to be gangs of robbers and murderers who killed the Jewish fighters and seized their possessions and weapons. On the day the ghetto was liquidated, two armed groups escaped from the ghetto, one consisting of thirteen fighters and the other of ten. While wandering in the forest, the smaller group encounted a "partisan" gang, which disarmed the Jewish fighters and murdered two of them; the others dispersed but some of them, too, were eventually killed. In the spring of 1943 Jewish fighters from Brest-Litovsk joined Soviet partisan units belonging to the Pinsk and Brest-Litovsk partisan formations.

Brest-Litovsk was liberated on July 28, 1944, and about ten Jews, who had been hiding, were found there. After a time some two hundred Jewish survivors of the Holocaust gathered in the city, including some from neighboring towns.

BIBLIOGRAPHY

Steinman, E., ed. *Brest-Litovsk.* Vol. 2 of *Encyclopedia of the Jewish Diaspora.* Jerusalem, 1958. (In Hebrew.)

SHMUEL SPECTOR

BRIZGYS, VINCENTAS (b. 1903), Lithuanian Catholic priest. Brizgys studied in Kovno and Rome. In the 1930s he was one of the leaders of the Center for Catholic Action (Kataliku

Veikimo Centras), a Lithuanian organization, and was appointed bishop of Kovno. During World War II he was auxiliary archbishop of that city.

At the end of June 1941, when LITHUANIA had fallen into German hands, Brizgys appended his signature to several statements thanking Nazi Germany for liberating Lithuania from the Soviet annexation and pledging loyalty to the new occupying power. Nevertheless, in the course of the Nazi occupation, Brizgys met several times with representatives of Kovno Jewry and expressed his sympathy with them. As the war went on, he displayed a benevolent attitude toward the rescue of the children in the Kovno ghetto. He did not, however, agree to intervene on their behalf with the Nazi authorities, claiming that by doing so he would jeopardize the position of the Catholic church in Lithuania. An internal German report, dated January 16, 1942, mentioned that Brizgys specifically prohibited the Catholic clergy from interceding on behalf of the Jews in any manner whatever. When the Germans retreated from Lithuania, in 1944, Brizgys left for Germany. After the war he moved to the United States, where he was active among Lithuanian emigrés.

BIBLIOGRAPHY

Garfunkel, L. *The Destruction of Kovno's Jewry.* Jerusalem, 1959. (In Hebrew.)

DOV LEVIN

BRODETSKY, SELIG (1888–1954), mathematician and Zionist leader. Born in the Ukraine, Brodetsky, while still a child, emigrated to Britain with his family. He studied at Cambridge and Leipzig, and on his return from Germany was appointed a lecturer in applied mathematics at Bristol University. From 1924 to 1949 he was a professor at Leeds University.

Brodetsky became a Zionist as a youth, and from 1928 until the establishment of the state of Israel in 1948, he was a member of the Jewish Agency executive committee and head of its political department in London. From 1939 to 1949, he was president of the BOARD OF DEPUTIES OF BRITISH JEWS, the first person

Selig Brodetsky. [Central Zionist Archives, Jerusalem]

to hold that post who was of eastern European origin and did not belong to the established Anglo-Jewish aristocratic families. His election was made possible by the growing strength of the Zionist element on the board, which succeeded in changing the board's composition and orientation. During Brodetsky's term of office, the board had to deal with fateful issues: aid to the Jews of occupied Europe during the war, postwar aid to the surviving refugees from the Nazi-occupied countries, and the struggle for Palestine. As a leader of British Jewry, Brodetsky bitterly attacked the policy of the British Mandatory government in Palestine, while at the same time emphasizing British Jewry's loyalty to the Crown. In January 1946 Brodetsky testified before the Anglo-American Commission, which was investigating the Palestine problem, denounced the WHITE PAPER policy, and demanded the immediate opening of the gates of Palestine for the entry of displaced persons.

From 1949 to 1951, Brodetsky was president of the Hebrew University in Jerusalem. His autobiography, *Memoirs: From Ghetto to Israel*, was published in 1960.

BIBLIOGRAPHY

Sompolinski, M. "Anglo-Jewish Leadership and the British Government: Attempts at Rescue, 1944–1945." *Yad Vashem Studies* 13 (1979): 211–247.

Wasserstein, B. *Britain and the Jews of Europe, 1939–1945*. London, 1979.

NANA SAGI

BRODY, town in Lvov Oblast (district), Ukrainian SSR. Founded in the sixteenth century, Brody was under Polish rule in the period from 1918 to 1939, and was annexed to the Soviet Union in September of that year. It was one of the important Jewish communities in Galicia, and for many years Jews constituted a majority of the population; in 1939, 9,000 Jews lived there. On July 1, 1941, the Germans occupied the town and lost no time in issuing anti-Jewish decrees: the Jews were ordered to wear an armband with the Star of David (*see* BADGE, JEWISH) and to make punitive payments; they were subject to forced labor; and were restricted in their movements. On July 15, 1941, a group of 250 intellectuals were summoned to the local Gestapo, where they were subjected to two days of torture and then murdered in ditches adjoining the Jewish cemetery. The JUDENRAT (Jewish Council) was ordered to supply hundreds of Jews daily for work on bridge repairs, on road building, and in military camps. By August, Jewish property was being plundered on a large scale by both Germans and Ukrainians. In December, the Germans began stopping Jewish youths in the street and transporting them to labor camps that had been set up in the area. In the first half of 1942, about 1,500 Jews were imprisoned in these camps. Their number dwindled sharply in the second half of 1942 and the beginning of the following year, owing to the high death rate caused by mistreatment, hard labor, starvation, and disease. In the summer of 1942 the Judenrat, on its own initiative, launched an effort to find jobs in areas that were considered vital to the German economy, in the hope that this would give protection, at least to some degree, from deportation to the labor camps.

On September 19, 1942, German and Ukrainian police arrested Jews on the streets or dragged them out of their houses and hiding places. When this *Aktion* was over, 2,000 Jews were taken to the BEŁŻEC death camp, while 300 were killed on the spot. In another *Aktion*, on November 2, another 2,500 people were sent to Bełżec. During the fall and winter of 1942, the German authorities brought into Brody remnants of other Jewish communities in the area, such as those of Sokolovka, Lopatin, Olesko, and Radechov.

In December 1942 the Germans announced the establishment of a ghetto in Brody, and by January 1, 1943, some six thousand persons had been gathered there, most of them from the vicinity. Many of the inmates died of starvation and typhus epidemics, and many others were shot by the Ukrainian police who guarded the ghetto perimeter. In March and April 1943 there were numerous *Aktionen*, as a result of which thousands of people were rounded up and put to death in the neighboring woods. Some of the young Jews who managed to escape from the ghetto into the forest formed groups and obtained arms with which they tried to resist their German and Ukrainian pursuers. The ghetto was liquidated on May 21, 1943. Over three thousand of its inmates were dispatched to MAJDANEK, and hundreds were murdered while still in the ghetto. In an effort to discover Jews still hidden there, the Germans and their Ukrainian helpers set the houses on fire, and many of those who had sought refuge found their death in the flames. The hunt for more Jews in hiding went on for many weeks; all those who were caught were murdered.

BIBLIOGRAPHY

Gilbert, M. *The Holocaust.* New York, 1985.

AHARON WEISS

BRUNACCI, ALDO. *See* Nicolini, Giuseppe.

BRUNNER, ALOIS (b. 1912), SS officer, one of Adolf EICHMANN's assistants. A native of Austria, Brunner joined the Nazi party in 1931 and the SS in November 1938. Following the German annexation of Austria, Brunner became a staff member of the Sicherheitspolizei and the SD (Sicherheitsdienst; Security Service) in Vienna. In August 1938 he became director of the Vienna ZENTRALSTELLE FÜR JÜDISCHE AUSWANDERUNG (Central Office for Jewish Emigration), which Eichmann had set up. In October and November of 1939, Brunner was in charge of the deportation of Jews from Vienna and Moravia to Nisko, in the Lublin district of Poland (*see* NISKO AND LUBLIN PLAN). In February and March of 1941 he organized the deportation of Viennese Jews to the Kielce area, and in October of that year he deported more Viennese Jews to the east. Later, in March 1943, Brunner was posted to Greece, to deal with the deportation of the Jews of SALONIKA and of Bulgarian-occupied THRACE and MACEDONIA; in July of that year he went to the region of southern France that until then had been under Italian occupation, to supervise the deportation of the Jews of Nice and other places in the area to AUSCHWITZ, by way of DRANCY. At the end of September 1944, he arrived in BRATISLAVA to complete the deportation of the Jews of SLOVAKIA.

Alois Brunner.

After the war, all trace of Brunner was lost. He was tried *in absentia* in Paris, and sentenced to death in 1954. Eventually he was given asylum in Syria, and has been living in that country under an assumed name.

BIBLIOGRAPHY

Felstiner, M. "Alois Brunner: Eichmann's Best Tool." *Simon Wiesenthal Center Annual* 3 (1986): 1–46.

Felstiner, M. "Commandant of Drancy: Alois Brunner and the Jews of France." *Holocaust and Genocide Studies* 2/1 (1987): 21–47.

SHMUEL SPECTOR

BRUSSELS. First mentioned in the tenth century, Brussels became the capital of Brabant in 1383, of the Low Countries in 1482, and later of the Spanish and Austrian Low Countries. Since 1830 it has been the capital of independent BELGIUM.

When the Germans occupied Belgium on May 17, 1940, thirty-three thousand Jews lived in Brussels, more than half the total Jewish population of the country. Most of them had immigrated to Belgium from eastern Europe and Germany after 1918, but Brussels also had the largest concentration of "veteran" Belgian Jews. They were well integrated into the city's social and economic life, and some held positions of prominence. Ninety-two percent of the Brussels Jews lived in the seven western quarters of the city, mostly in the area containing the main railway station and in the Anderlecht quarter.

Brussels was the location of the national

Jewish organizations: the Consistoire Central (Central Consistory), to which all Jews who held Belgian nationality belonged; the Chief Rabbinate; the Oeuvre Centrale Israélite de Secours (Central Jewish Relief Society; OCIS); and the HICEM office (which in Belgium bore the name BELHICEM), headed by Max Gottschalk, who was of great help to the refugees from Nazi Germany.

Brussels Jewry had its own philanthropic and communal organizations and professional unions, and it took an active part in political life. Among the Jewish umbrella organizations in Brussels were the Foyer Israélite de Bruxelles (Brussels Jewish Welfare Agency); the Conseil d'Associations Juives de Bruxelles (Brussels Council of Jewish Organizations), made up of thirty-three organizations of the lower middle-class Jews and headed by Leon Kubowitzki; and the Oeuvre de la Communauté du Travail des Juifs d'Allemagne (Association of German Jewish Laborers), comprising the Jewish refugees from Germany.

The immediate effect of the German occupation on the Jewish community was total chaos and the disruption of the community services and the work of the Jewish organizations. Many of the organizations' leaders fled while the fighting was going on; of the twelve board members of the official Jewish Community Organization, only one, Marcel Blum, stayed. Of the Orthodox Community Board, only the vice president, David Lazare (a Jew of Polish nationality), remained; and of the rabbis, only Abraham Joseph Feinburg, a Belgian national, stayed.

In the summer of 1940 several persons, on their own initiative, began to revive organized Jewish life in the city, with the emphasis on aid and relief. The OCIS resumed its work on a much larger scale than previously, since thousands of people were now in need. In the first five months of 1941, OCIS spent 220,000 Belgian francs on aid to the needy, and in 1941 as a whole, approximately 1 million francs. About 60 percent of this sum was contributed by the Brussels community, the rest coming from individual donors and the American Jewish JOINT DISTRIBUTION COMMITTEE. A special aid effort was made for the refugees from Germany, with Itzko Kubowitzki (Leon's brother) taking the lead, on behalf of groups of Brussels residents who were immigrants from eastern Europe. In September 1940 Rabbi Salomon Ullmann accepted the post of Chief Rabbi of Belgium, with his office in Brussels. On November 10 the Brussels Community Board resumed operations, its immediate task being to organize the Jewish population. Marcel Blum was elected president and Itzko Kubowitzki vice president; Edouard Rotkel, a Hungarian Jew who had come to Brussels in 1938, was elected secretary. Salomon van den Bergh, a wealthy furniture merchant, was also on the board. Anti-Jewish decrees issued on October 28, 1940, were met with criticism among some parts of the general population. Three senior jurists and the Université Libre de Bruxelles (Brussels Free University)—which had a larger number of Jewish lecturers on its faculty than any other Belgian university—issued protests against the anti-Jewish measures.

In early 1941 the Comité de Coordination (Coordinating Committee) was set up at the insistence of the Sicherheitspolizei (Security Police), but it did not become an important body. At the end of 1941 the ASSOCIATION DES JUIFS EN BELGIQUE (Association of Jews in Belgium; AJB) was established, with its head office in Brussels. The AJB took up the relief work that had previously been in the hands of OCIS; heading the AJB's social services, until the spring of 1943, was Professor Chaim Perelman.

In 1941 the economic situation of Belgium deteriorated, and the Jews were especially hard hit. As a result, the Jewish political organizations expanded their welfare operations. The relief organizations of the Zionist Po'alei Zion Left and those of the Communists—most of which had been in existence since before the occupation—enlarged the scope of their operations. Jews had been active in leftist organizations before the war, but under the Germans such activities were outlawed; many of the Jewish leftist activists were arrested between 1940 and 1942. From the end of 1941, in reaction to the creation of the AJB, specifically Jewish underground activity was launched. This activity also expressed itself in the publication of underground newspapers, such as Po'alei Zion's *Unzer Wort* (Our Word) and, later on, *Unzer*

Kampf (Our Struggle), the journal of the Brussels branch of the Communist party.

In April 1941 a decree on the expulsion of Jews from the general school system was put into effect, affecting three thousand Jewish children. This posed a particularly serious problem for Brussels Jewry because of the nearly total lack of teachers and school buildings for such a large number of children. University lecturers and students working for the AJB did, however, manage to set up an alternative Jewish school system, which functioned until the deportation of the Jews of Belgian nationality, in September 1943.

During the spring and early summer of 1942 economic pressure on the Jews grew stronger, as the liquidation and "Aryanization" (*see* ARISIERUNG) of Jewish enterprises were speeded up, especially in the textile and leather industries. The wealthy Jews tried to escape to southern France or Switzerland. This was also the time when the Jews were being drafted for FORCED LABOR. On June 26, 1942, a transport of Brussels Jews was sent to the labor camps of the ORGANISATION TODT in northern France. Thousands of other Jews worked for the Germans in various enterprises in Belgium itself.

A German order of May 27, 1942, obliged all Jews to wear the yellow badge (*see* BADGE, JEWISH), the distribution of which was imposed on the municipalities of greater Brussels; the order met with a hostile reaction on the part of the mayors. On June 5, J. Coelst, the acting chairman of the Conférence des Bourgmestres (Conference of Mayors), informed the German authorities of the mayors' refusal to cooperate in the distribution of the yellow badges. Since the AJB also refused to undertake this task, the German headquarters in Brussels had to use its own personnel for the job. Many of the city's residents expressed their solidarity with the Jews by wearing yellow badges similar to the ones that the Jews had been forced to put on.

In late July 1942 a roundup of the Jews was launched, pending their deportation. The Jews were issued summonses to report to the MECHELEN camp, but when an insufficient number turned up at the camp, the Germans began to look for Jews. From August 13 to 18, Jews were arrested in the streets of Brussels in large numbers, and on September 3, Jews were hunted down in the area of the main Brussels railway station. Many of the Jews who were arrested were taken to a school building in the Saint Gilles quarter and from there were transferred to Mechelen. More arrests were made in the months that followed, especially during the winter. The final roundup took place on the night of September 3–4, 1943, as part of Operation "Iltis"—the seizure by the Germans of all Jews of Belgian nationality, who a year earlier had been assured that they would not be deported. Out of the 975 "Belgian" Jews seized in this operation, 750 were from Brussels.

The arrest of Jews for forced labor, and the beginning of the deportation to eastern Europe, were met with increasing resistance on the part of the Jews of Brussels. On September 15, 1942, the Comité de Défense des Juifs (Jewish Defense Committee) was formed, with Jewish Communists and members of various Zionist organizations cooperating with one another. The committee made efforts to find hiding places for Jews, especially Jewish children, and also engaged in relief work; in February 1944 it was giving support to thirty-six hundred persons. The committee was also in touch with resistance fighters. Groups of Jews were active in Belgian resistance operations; most of them—about one hundred—belonged to the leftist partisan organizations, such as the Corps Mobile and the Corps de Bruxelles, which later united into one body. Many of the small resistance cells were made up exclusively of Jews. In the summer of 1942 two significant resistance operations took place in Brussels: in one, the AJB card index of Jews was destroyed by fire; and in the other, Robert Holcinger, the AJB official responsible for ensuring that Jews reported for deportation, was assassinated. Jews were also members of other underground groups, such as the Belgian resistance group Banco. Members of that group provided hiding places for several Jewish refugees from Germany. The refugees in their turn contributed by translating German informational material into French and Dutch, and French and Dutch material into German.

As many as twelve thousand Jews are estimated to have gone into hiding in various places in Brussels. One of them was the painter Felix Nussbaum, a refugee from Germany who eventually fell into German hands and was deported to AUSCHWITZ, where he perished. He left behind paintings in which he depicted his experiences; the largest collection of his work is to be found in the Museum of Cultural History of Osnabrück, his native city.

After the liberation, Brussels served as the center for the reorganization and rehabilitation of Belgian Jewry. The Consistoire and the Zionist Federation of Belgium were reconstituted. Together with the Aide aux Israélites Victimes de la Guerre (Aid Society for Jewish War Victims) and the Comité Central de Reconstruction Religieuse (Central Committee for the Restoration of Religious Life), they dealt with the special problems that arose at the time. These included the status of Jews who had been residents of Belgium before the war but did not hold Belgian nationality, the DISPLACED PERSONS who had reached Belgium, the restoration of Jewish property, and the care of Jewish war orphans.

In the late 1940s, the Jewish population of Brussels was estimated at twenty-seven thousand. Brussels served as the headquarters of the Union des Anciens Résistants Juifs de Belgique (Union of Veteran Jewish Resistance Fighters of Belgium) and the Union des Déportés Juifs et Ayant Droits en Belgique (Union of Jewish Deportees and Their Legatees Eligible for Pension Rights in Belgium). In 1970 a memorial for the victims of the Holocaust was erected in the Anderlecht quarter of Brussels.

BIBLIOGRAPHY

Communauté Israélite de Bruxelles. *La grande synagogue de Bruxelles: Contribution à l'histoire des Juifs de Bruxelles.* Brussels, 1978.

Ministère de la Justice. Commission des Crimes de Guerre. *La persécution antisémitique en Belgique.* Liège, 1947.

Steinberg, M. *L'étoile et le fusil.* 3 vols. Brussels, 1983–1986.

DAN MICHMAN

BRZEŻANY. *See* Berezhany.

BUCHAREST, capital of ROMANIA and before that of the principality of Walachia. Jews lived in Bucharest from the sixteenth century. It was the largest center of Romanian Jewry; during the twentieth century the number of Jews increased rapidly, reaching 76,480 by 1930 (twice as many as at the beginning of the century) and 102,018 by 1941. Several quarters in Bucharest, such as the Văcăresti-Dudest neighborhood and the "Blue Quarter," were considered Jewish areas. Throughout World War II Jewish refugees streamed into Bucharest from provincial towns, believing themselves safer in the capital and among many Jews. The central organizations of Romanian Jewry were in Bucharest, as well as Jewish schools, hospitals, and other institutions. However, Bucharest was also a center of the antisemitic IRON GUARD movement, and this had an effect on the situation of the Jewish community in the city.

As early as 1937, persecutions of Jews in professional, financial, and cultural fields commenced. Government offices and private institutions such as banks, factories, and publishing houses refused to employ them. In 1938, under the government of Octavian GOGA and Alexandra CUZA, Jewish businessmen were removed from the chamber of commerce. Most of the trade unions dismissed Jews from their ranks; the example was set by the Advocates' Association, which elected an antisemitic leadership on December 6, 1938. Many streets were dangerous for Jews.

With the establishment of the ANTONESCU government on September 6, 1940, members of the Iron Guard, known as Legionnaires, began to sow terror among the Jews of Bucharest. Jews were attacked in the streets, parks, and other public places; cars belonging to Jews were expropriated; many Jews were imprisoned and released only on payment of a ransom. The Legionnaires used the offices of the police, who were subordinate to them.

Antonescu failed in his attempt to deter the Legionnaires, to impose order in the capital, and to prevent the destruction of economic and productive life. On January 21, 1941, the Legionnaires rebelled, and attempted to remove Antonescu and seize power. During the revolt there were riots against the Jews of

Bodies of Jews killed in the Bucharest pogrom of January 1941.

Bucharest. Jews were seized in synagogues, on the streets, and in their homes, some according to lists drawn up in advance. About one hundred were placed on trucks and shot to death at various places in the vicinity of the city.

During the killings carried out by the Legionnaires, bands of ruffians attacked the Jewish quarters, plundering, raping, and destroying houses and shops. They were joined by mobs from the suburbs and Gypsies who took advantage of this opportunity to plunder. The riots lasted three days, and 127 Jews were murdered.

With the outbreak of war against the Soviet Union on June 22, 1941, the leaders of the Jewish organizations were declared hostages who would be put to death if the city's Jews worked against the authorities. On September 3 of that year the Jews were obliged to wear a "Jewish sign" (a black star on a white background), but after two days the president of the Federation of the Communities, Wilhelm FILDERMAN, managed to have the edict annulled. Various taxes were imposed on the Jews of Bucharest for the benefit of the army and the civil authorities; these included monetary "donations" and a onetime tax of several hundred million lei (April 1943).

In September 1942, a group of 395 Jews who in 1940 had asked to return to BESSARABIA after its annexation to the Soviet Union, as well as about 200 Jews considered to be Communists, were deported to TRANSNISTRIA. The deportees in the first group were killed by members of the SS in Transnistria. On Antonescu's order, all of the Jews who had settled in Bucharest after January 1, 1940, were deported from the city.

The policy of dispossession, expropriation, nationalization, and dismissals, together with the various levies and taxes, soon impoverished the Jewish population. By late 1941, a total of 8,234 Jewish wage earners had been dismissed. Recruitment of Jews for forced labor completed the process of pauperization. From the fall of 1941, Jews were employed in cleaning the streets and clearing them of snow. Forced-labor gangs were established

Annexations from June to September 1940: (1) Bessarabia and (2) N. Bukovina to USSR; (3) N. Transylvania to Hungary; (4) S. Dobruja to Bulgaria.

on August 1, 1941, and in 1942, 28,177 Jewish males were engaged in forced labor. Jews who did not present themselves for recruitment, or who fled from the labor gangs, were arrested and deported to Transnistria with their families. All Jewish youths between the ages of fifteen and eighteen were taken for forced labor in May 1943. In April 1944, when bombing of the city intensified, the local forced-labor gangs were brought to clear the ruins, take away the bodies of the dead, and remove unexploded bombs.

In addition to the national Jewish organizations, the institutions of the CENTRALA EVREILOR (Jewish Center) were also concentrated in Bucharest from February 1942. These included welfare institutions, in particular the Autonomous Aid Committee; the Palestine Office; the directors of the Zionist movement in Romania; the Jewish theater; two higher-education institutions created after the removal of Jewish students from the general system of higher education; and an orchestra made up of musicians who had been dismissed from Romanian orchestras. Until 1942 the journal of the Zionist movement, *Renasterea Noastra*, appeared in Bucharest, and after its closure by order of the authorities, the Jewish Center journal, *Gazeta Evreeasca*, appeared.

The Jews of Bucharest were saved from extermination on August 23, 1944, after the dictator, Ion Antonescu, was arrested by the king. The German forces close to the city did not succeed in entering it. Adolf EICHMANN, who was then in Budapest and was supposed to go to Bucharest to begin preparations for deporting the Jews, postponed his journey when he learned that the Romanians had broken off their alliance with Germany. The immediate opposition of the Romanian army, and the entry of the Soviet army into the city on August 30, 1944, prevented the Nazis from carrying out their scheme.

BIBLIOGRAPHY

Carp, M. *Pogromul dela Iaşi*. Vol. 2A of *Cartea Neagră*. Bucharest, 1948.

Lavi, T., ed. *Rumania*, vol. 1. In *Pinkas Hakehillot; Encyclopaedia of Jewish Communities*. Jerusalem, 1969. See pages 59–75. (In Hebrew.)

Pe Marginea Prapastiei, 21–31 Ianuarie 1941. Vol. 2. Bucharest, 1942.

Safran, A. *Resisting the Storm—Romania, 1940–1947: Memoirs*. Jerusalem, 1987.

JEAN ANCEL

BUCHENWALD, concentration camp, one of the largest on German soil, with 130 satellite camps and extension units. Buchenwald was situated on the northern slope of Ettersberg, a mountain 5 miles (8 km) north of Weimar, in Thüringen (now part of the German Democratic Republic). The camp was established on July 16, 1937, when the first group of prisoners, consisting of 149 persons, mostly political detainees and criminals, was brought to the site. The name "Buchenwald" was given to it by Heinrich HIMMLER on July 28, 1937.

Buchenwald was divided into three parts: the "large camp," which housed prisoners with some seniority; the "small camp," where prisoners were kept in quarantine; and the "tent camp," set up for Polish prisoners sent there after the German invasion of Poland in 1939. Besides these three parts were the administration compound, the SS barracks, and the camp factories. The commandants were SS-Standartenführer Karl KOCH (1937–1941) and SS-Oberführer Hermann Pister (1942–1945).

Large groups of prisoners began to arrive in the camp shortly after its foundation and by the end of 1937 their number reached 2,561, most of them "politicals." In the spring of 1938 the number of prisoners rose rapidly as a result of the operation against "asocial elements," the victims of which were taken to Buchenwald; by July 1938 there were 7,723 prisoners in the camp. Another 2,200 from Austria were added on September 23, 1938, all of them Jews. A further 10,000 Jews were imprisoned after KRISTALLNACHT (November 9–10, 1938), and at the end of November the camp prison population exceeded 18,000. By the end of the year, most of the Jewish prisoners were released, and the camp population had dropped to 11,000.

The outbreak of war was accompanied by a wave of arrests throughout the Reich, which brought thousands of political prisoners to Buchenwald. This was followed by the influx of thousands of Poles, who were housed in the tent camp. As of 1943, following the completion of armament factories in the vicinity of the camp, the number of prisoners grew steadily: to 63,048 by the end of 1944 and to 86,232 in February 1945. In the eight years of its existence, from July 1937 to March 1945, a total of 238,980 prisoners from thirty countries passed through Buchenwald and its satellite camps; of these, 43,045 were killed or perished in some other fashion there (the figure includes Soviet prisoners of war).

The first transports of German Jews arrived in the spring of 1938, followed by Austrian Jews and the *Kristallnacht* prisoners. The Jews were subject to extraordinarily cruel treatment, working fourteen to fifteen hours a day (generally in the infamous Buchenwald quarry) and enduring abominable living conditions. The Nazis' object at this point was to exert pressure on the Jews and their families to emigrate from Germany within the shortest possible time. Thus, in the winter of 1938–1939, 9,370 Jews were released after their families, as well as Jewish and international organizations, had made arrangements for their emigration. Of the *Kristallnacht* detainees, in the short while that these prisoners were held at Buchenwald, 600 were killed, committed suicide, or died from other causes. The number of Jewish prisoners rose again after the outbreak of the war, when Jews from Germany and the Protectorate of BOHEMIA AND MORAVIA were brought to the camp; in September 1939, the Jewish prisoners numbered some 2,700.

In accordance with an order issued on October 17, 1942, which provided for all Jewish prisoners held in the Reich to be transferred to AUSCHWITZ, the Jews in Buchenwald, except for 204 essential workers, were sent to that concentration and extermination camp. In 1944, transports of Hungarian Jews began coming to Buchenwald from Auschwitz; after a short stay in the main camp most of them were distributed among the satellite camps, where they were put to work in the armament factories. Beginning on January 18, 1945, when Auschwitz and other camps in the east were being evacuated, thousands of Jewish prisoners arrived in Buchenwald. The Auschwitz evacuees included several hundred children and youths, and a special barrack, which came to be known as "Children's Block 66," was put up for them in the tent camp. This block housed more than six hundred children and youths, most of whom survived. The Jewish prisoners were deprived of the privileges and exemptions granted to the other inmates, and Jewish prisoners were used for MEDICAL EXPERIMENTS.

Under United States military escort, German civilians were forced to view the evidence of atrocities at the Buchenwald camp. Here, they look at a truckload of dead Allied and political prisoners. [United States Army Signal Corps]

Resistance cells were formed in Buchenwald from the first years of its existence. In 1938 such a cell was established by members of the German Communist party in the camp, who included some of that party's most prominent figures. At first, the aim of the resistance cells was to plant their members in the central posts available to inmates, to support one another, and to have a say in developments in the camp. Up to the end of 1938 the internal administration of Buchenwald was, for the most part, in the hands of the criminal prisoners. When it was discovered that the criminals and some of the SS personnel were involved in corruption and stealing (from the *Kristallnacht* prisoners), the camp administration removed the criminal prisoners from most of their posts, and their influence gradually passed into the hands of the political prisoners. Some resistance cells, mainly those belonging to the Left, managed to plant some of their members in key positions held by prisoners in the internal camp administration, thereby facilitating their clandestine activities. Later, following the outbreak of the war and the influx into Buchenwald of political prisoners from the occupied countries, more resistance groups were formed, on the basis of nationality. In 1943 a general underground movement that included Jews came into being, called the International Underground Committee. The resistance movement in Buchenwald scored some impressive successes, primarily the acts of sabotage it carried out in the armaments works that employed Buchenwald prisoners. Underground members also smuggled arms and ammunition into the camp.

On April 6, 1945, the Germans began evacuating the Jewish prisoners. The following day, thousands of prisoners of various nationalities were evacuated from the main camps and the satellite camps. Of the 28,250 prisoners evacuated from the main camp, 7,000 to 8,000 either were killed or died by some other means in the course of the evacuation. The total number of prisoners from the satellite camps and the main camp who fell victim during the evacuation of Buchenwald is estimated at 25,500. In the final days of the camp's existence, resistance members who held key posts in the internal administration sabotaged SS orders for evacuation by slowing down its pace, and as a result the Nazis failed to complete the evacuation.

By April 11, most of the SS men had fled from the camp. The underground did not wait for the approaching American forces to take control but did so themselves, together with armed teams of prisoners, in the process trapping several dozen SS men left in the camp. On that day, April 11, some twenty-one thousand prisoners were liberated in Buchenwald, with four thousand Jews among them, including about one thousand children and youths.

In 1947, thirty-one members of the Buchenwald camp staff were tried for their crimes by an American court. Two of the accused were sentenced to death, and four to life imprisonment.

BIBLIOGRAPHY

Bartel, W., et al., eds. *Buchenwald—Mahnung und Verpflichtung: Dokumente und Berichte*. Berlin, 1983.

Briquet, G. *The Buchenwald Case*. Dachau, 1947.

Burney, C. *The Dungeon Democracy*. London, 1945.

D'Harcourt, P. *The Real Enemy*. New York, 1967.

Gutman, Y., and S. Avital, eds. *The Nazi Concentration Camps*. Jerusalem, 1984.

YEHOSHUA R. BÜCHLER

BUDAPEST, capital of HUNGARY. Budapest is situated on both banks of the Danube and consists of the united cities of Buda, Óbuda, and Pest; its population in 1941 was about one million, and in 1976 over two million. The first settlement on the site was the Roman colony of Aquincum. In 1872 the united city of Budapest was formed, and it became the capital of independent Hungary in November 1918.

A grave from the Roman period attests to a Jewish presence in Aquincum. From the twelfth century there was a constant Jewish presence in Buda, except for some short periods in the thirteenth century. Between the world wars, some 200,000 of Trianon Hungary's 450,000 Jews resided in Budapest, making it one of the most important urban Jewish population centers in Europe. It was the center of Hungarian Jewish life, and the Jewish presence in the culture, thought, politics, professions, and economy of the city was of great significance. During the years of restrictive anti-Jewish legislation (from 1938), the predominantly middle-class Jewish community suffered greatly, especially from unemployment. By 1940 the community supported 17,000 of its members with $100,000 in aid. Nonetheless, as the situation of the rest of European Jewry deteriorated during the course of World War II, Budapest Jewry lived in relative comfort and security until the German occupation in March 1944.

Some five thousand refugees from Germany, Austria, and later Poland began to arrive in Budapest in the late 1930s. The Hungarian Jewish relief organizations Magyar Izraeliták Pártfogo Irodaja (Welfare Bureau of Hungarian Jews) and Országos Zsidó Segito Akcio (National Hungarian Jewish Assistance Campaign), the RELIEF AND RESCUE COMMITTEE OF BUDAPEST (known as the Va'ada), and an Orthodox committee headed by Fülöp FREUDIGER, together with the Ameri-

Crowds of Jews in front of the Swiss embassy on Vadasz Street in Budapest, waiting to receive *Schutzpässe*.

can Jewish JOINT DISTRIBUTION COMMITTEE, assisted these refugees. The Joint provided $47,000 in aid during the first six months of the war. With the advent of deportations from SLOVAKIA in March 1942, significant numbers of Slovak Jews began escaping to Hungary. Most of the six thousand to eight thousand Slovak refugees eventually came to Budapest.

With the German occupation (March 19, 1944), the situation of Budapest Jewry deteriorated drastically. A central Jewish council, the Zsidó Tanács, was established under the Neolog leader Samu STERN. It was made responsible for governing Budapest Jewry and forwarding decrees to the provincial Jewish councils. Life was severely restricted in Budapest, as it was throughout Hungary, with orders such as the one calling for the closing of Jewish shops (March 22), which affected eighteen thousand Jewish stores in the capital. Hundreds of Jews were rounded up and interned in the KISTARCSA camp. Following Allied air raids in early April, the deputy interior minister, László ENDRE, ordered on April 12 that within twenty-four hours the Jewish community turn over 500 apartments to non-Jews who had been left homeless by the bombing. Before the day was over, Adolf EICHMANN, who was responsible for implementing the "Final Solution" in Hungary, had raised the quota to 1,500.

The provincial Jews were systematically concentrated and deported between mid-April and July, but the Jews of Budapest were not put into a ghetto during this, the first, wave of deportations from Hungary. The Hungarian authorities scattered the Jews about the city in 2,639 buildings, which were marked with a Star of David. The move to

Street scene in Budapest (1944).

these buildings, with their 33,294 apartments and 70,197 rooms, was made between June 17 and 24, 1944. Shortly thereafter, 17,500 Jews were dispatched from the outskirts of Budapest to AUSCHWITZ. On July 7 the Hungarian regent, Miklós HORTHY, ordered the stoppage of further deportations, saving the remaining Budapest Jews for the time being.

During the lull in the deportations, the Jews of Budapest continued as best they could, struggling to keep alive. Many looked for ways to protect themselves from renewed deportations. Most commonly, they tried to acquire baptismal certificates or applied for official government exemptions from all anti-Jewish statutes. Some groups, like the Relief and Rescue Committee and the Zionist youth movements, continued the rescue activities they had begun during the deportations. When Horthy announced that his government was withdrawing from the Axis with Germany on October 15, Budapest Jewry was exultant. But with the immediate fall of Horthy's regime and the establishment of a Nazi-backed government under Ferenc SZÁLASI, they began to face their gravest peril.

During the first days of the new ARROW CROSS PARTY's rule, some six hundred Jews were murdered in Budapest. Soon afterward, Jews were drafted to build fortifications. On November 8, deportations were resumed. Over seventy thousand Jews were taken to the Óbuda brickyards, and from there were marched out of the city on foot toward the Austrian border. The *Fussmarsch* (foot march), as this deportation was known, continued until December 24. In the meantime, on November 13, the Arrow Cross ordered the establishment of a ghetto, and by December 2 most of Budapest's unprotected Jews had been placed within its confines. The ghetto had four main entrances, on Wesselenyi, Nagyatadi Szabo, Nagydiofa, and Kisdiofa streets. It was divided into ten districts, each with a district commander. A ghetto police force was also established, but unlike other such forces under Nazi occupation, it never became enmeshed in the process of deportation. Public kitchens and a hospital also served the ghetto residents. During December 1944 and January 1945, random acts of Arrow Cross violence increased, and between ten thousand and twenty thousand Jews were shot along the banks of the Danube, their corpses making the river run red.

During the Szálasi period, the neutral diplomats—among them Friedrich Born (international RED CROSS), Raoul WALLENBERG (Sweden), Per Anger (Sweden), Carl LUTZ (Switzerland), Angelo Rotta (the papal nuncio), Valdemar Langlet (Swedish Red Cross), and Asta Nilsson (Swedish Red Cross)—exerted great efforts to rescue Budapest Jewry. In most aspects of their work they were joined by members of the Va'ada (especially Ottó KOMOLY); members of the Zionist youth movement; the Zsidó Tanács; and other nonaffiliated Jews. Christian organizations, notably the Jo Pasztor (Good Shepherd Society) under Gabor SZTEHLO, and a number of convents and monasteries, also aided Jews. The focus of the rescue was to ensure that the

Jews stayed out of the hands of the Nazis and Arrow Cross, and that they had sufficient food, shelter, and fuel to remain alive until the arrival of the Red Army.

The diplomats often protested to the government about the treatment of the Jews. With the help of the various Jewish rescuers, food, medicines, and fuel were obtained and distributed. Efforts were made to safeguard Jews from deportation by providing them with *Schutzpässe* (protective documents) in the name of the neutral governments and agencies. The Swiss issued 7,800, the Swedes 4,500, the Vatican 2,500, the Portuguese 700, and the Spanish 100; some 100,000 (mostly Swiss) were forged and distributed by the Zionist youth. The bearers of protective documents were placed under diplomatic protection, often taking up residence in the embassies and consulates and their annexes. The largest of these protected buildings was the "Glass House" on Vadasz Street and the annex next door, which were under the protection of the Swiss and housed over three thousand Jews. Special houses also were set up, in which between five thousand and six thousand children were protected from their planned transfer to the ghetto and from Arrow Cross rampages. In addition, the *Schutzpässe* were used to bring deportees back to Budapest before they reached the border. Frequently, bearers of false papers were assisted as well. In early November of 1944 a special "international ghetto" was set up for the bearers of the documents and their families. The extraterritorial status of the houses was not always honored, and many fell victim to Arrow Cross violence.

By December 26, 1944, the Soviets had completely encircled Budapest. On January 18, 1945, Pest was taken, and on February 13 Buda fell to the Red Army. Exact figures on the number of Jews in Budapest at the time of the Soviet entry are not available, but about 70,000 were in the ghetto, about 25,000 were under diplomatic protection, and another 25,000 were hidden, often with false "Aryan" papers—all told, some 120,000.

In the post–World War II period, Budapest remained the center of the diminished Hungarian Jewish community. As of the end of the 1980s, about sixty thousand of Hungary's eighty thousand Jews resided in the capital.

Moving into a Budapest apartment designated for Jews and marked with a Star of David (1944).

BIBLIOGRAPHY

Braham, R. L. *The Politics of Genocide: The Holocaust in Hungary*. New York, 1981.

Cohen, A. *The Halutz Resistance in Hungary, 1942–1944*. New York, 1986.

Lavi, T., ed. *Hungary*. In *Pinkas Hakehillot; Encyclopaedia of Jewish Communities*. Jerusalem, 1976. (In Hebrew.)

ASHER COHEN and
ROBERT ROZETT

BUDZYŃ, forced-labor and concentration camp in Poland. Budzyń was a village and estate in the Lublin district, 3 miles (5 km)

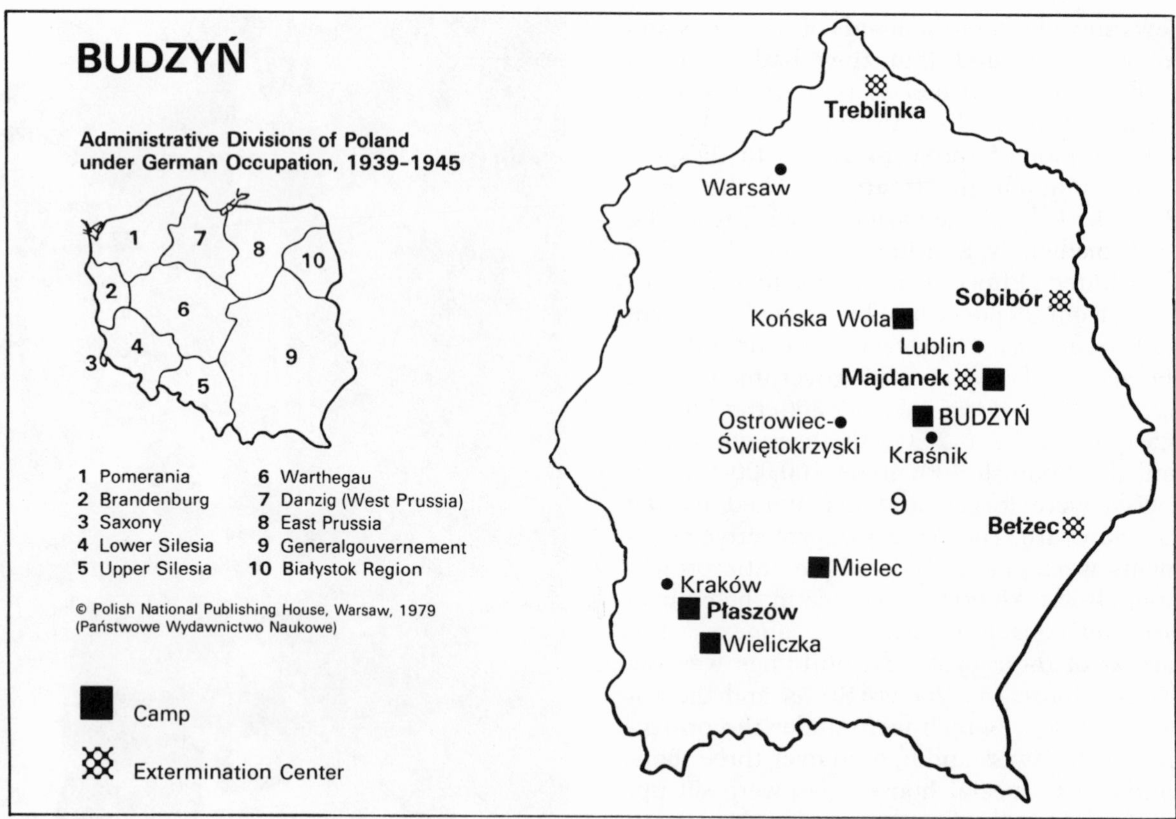

northwest of the town of Kraśnik. In the mid-1930s the Poles established a military-industrial combine on this site, including an aircraft industry. Following the German occupation of Poland, the military industries were taken over by the Hermann Göring Works, while the aircraft factory was operated by the Heinkel Company.

During the summer of 1942 a forced-labor camp was set up in Budzyń, and 500 Jews were brought in from the neighboring towns. In the fall, 400 prisoners of war were added from the Końska Wola camp and from the camp on Lipowa Street in LUBLIN. In May 1943, after the WARSAW GHETTO UPRISING had been suppressed, 800 Jews from Warsaw were brought in. By mid-1943 the camp had a prison population of 3,000, including 300 women and children. The prisoners were employed in the military factories, in construction, and in general services. The camp commandant, an SS officer named Feiks, mistreated the prisoners and from time to time killed some of them. In the fall of 1942 some 100 prisoners—sick or old persons, and children—had been taken to the BEŁŻEC extermination camp and murdered there. In August 1943 another 200 prisoners, classified as sick and unfit for work, were sent away, this time to MAJDANEK, to be killed. On October 22, Budzyń became a concentration camp and was attached to Majdanek. Late that winter, on February 8, 1944, dozens of prisoners were killed when the Ukrainian guards opened fire on them.

Owing to the influence exercised by the camp elder, Noah Stockman, a prisoner of war hailing from Brest-Litovsk, conditions in the camp were relatively bearable. In one instance, several groups of youngsters who came from the surrounding towns acquired weapons by stealing them from the military factories and escaped to the forests, where they joined the partisans. Stockman managed to persuade the camp administration to refrain from harsh retaliatory measures. For Passover 1944, again owing to Stockman's influence, unleavened bread was baked in the camp and a Seder ceremony was held. At the beginning of May of that year the evacuation of the camp began, and prisoners were sent in groups to Mielec, Ostrowiec, and Wieliczka, among other places.

BIBLIOGRAPHY

Freiburg, D. *Darkness Covered the Earth.* Tel Aviv, 1970. (In Hebrew.)

SHMUEL SPECTOR

BUKOVINA, historical name of the region covering the northeastern Carpathians and the plain at the foot of the mountains, bordering on the Dniester in the north. Up to 1774 the territory was part of the principality of Moldavia, then under Ottoman suzerainty. From 1774 to 1918 it was ruled by Austria, and during that period was called Bukovina. Many Germans and even more Ukrainians settled there, creating a difficult conflict of nationalities. By the end of the Austrian period the Ukrainians had become the largest nationality in northern Bukovina, although they were not a majority in all of Bukovina. Bukovina was incorporated into ROMANIA in 1918. In June of 1940, northern Bukovina—which had a Ukrainian majority—was annexed by the Soviet Union, following a Soviet ultimatum to Romania (an act that violated the NAZI-SOVIET PACT). A year later, in late June and early July 1941, in the wake of the German attack on the Soviet Union, Romania recaptured northern Bukovina.

Jews had settled in Bukovina in the thirteenth century. During the seventeenth century, Jews from Poland and the Ukraine entered the area in large numbers, and the influx increased sharply during the Austrian period. In 1890 Bukovina had a Jewish population of some ninety thousand. The Jews played an important role in the development of commerce and industry; the wealthy among them acquired landed estates, and some were even raised to the nobility. Under Romanian rule, between the two world wars, the situation of the Jews deteriorated: there was antisemitic rioting, Jews were driven out of various occupations, and their legal status was impaired. A law for the "reexamination of citizenship," passed by the government of

BUKOVINA, June 1940

Octavian GOGA and Alexandru CUZA in early 1938, deprived many Jews of their Romanian nationality.

During the Soviet annexation of northern Bukovina in June 1940 and the withdrawal of Romanian troops from that area, the Romanians vented their spite on the local population, especially the Jews, accusing them of being Communists and Soviet sympathizers and of armed acts of provocation against Romanian soldiers. At this early stage of the Holocaust, and without any connection to the Nazis, Romanian army units murdered hundreds of Jews and committed other grave crimes against them. Infantry Battalion 16, commanded by the antisemitic Maj. Valeriu Carp, killed dozens of Jews with indescribable tortures on its withdrawal from northern Bukovina in the direction of Fălticeni. The murders did not cease even when the withdrawal of the Romanian troops from Soviet-annexed northern Bukovina was completed, with the participation of a number of infantry battalions, in addition to the sixteenth. Jewish soldiers serving in the Romanian army were also the victims of humiliation and torture by Romanian troops, and a number of Jewish soldiers were murdered. Many Jews on their way to join their army units were thrown off the speeding trains.

The Soviet regime in northern Bukovina put an end to traditional Jewish cultural life and education and to the de facto autonomy enjoyed by the Jews under the Romanians. All non-Communist Jewish organizations were disbanded, and a campaign of harassment and arrests was launched against Zionist leaders and activists. On June 13, 1941, a drive was begun to deport to Siberia masses of Zionist leaders and activists, and anyone else who was regarded as an "enemy of the people." The expulsions into exile continued into the first few days of the war. From CHERNOVTSY (Rom., Cernăuţi; Ger., Czernowitz) at least four thousand Jews were exiled, as were hundreds of families from the provincial towns. This was accompanied by a campaign against persons of property and wealth, or against those whom the Soviets regarded as such; many Jews belonging to the middle class were affected, including professionals, whom the Soviets classified as "bourgeois."

Following the invasion of the Soviet Union by the Germans and their allies (which included Romania), on June 22, 1941, thousands of Jews were called up for service in the Red Army, but most of them remained where they were, since no special travel arrangements had been made for them. Only a few Jews were evacuated from Bukovina or managed to escape on their own into the Soviet interior, since many of the people trying to make their way eastward were intercepted by the German and Romanian armies. In many villages, pogroms against the Jews were launched as soon as the Soviet troops had withdrawn and before any Romanian army units had arrived. Organized gangs of peasants, mostly Ukrainians, robbed, tortured, raped, and murdered Jews by the hundreds and thousands. This was the case in Banila pe Ceremus, Sadagura, Rohosna, and other places. The Romanian army encouraged its troops to take "revenge" on the Jews, alleging that the Jews had aided the Soviet regime. In Ciudei, the first village in northern Bukovina that he captured, Major Carp ordered 450 Jews to be murdered. Between July 4 and 31, thousands of Jews were killed by Romanian troops in the villages they occupied.

Chernovtsy was occupied on July 5 and 6, by Romanian and German units. Together with them, Einsatzkommando 10a of Einsatzgruppe D entered the city. The Germans were not satisfied with the performance of their Romanian allies, who were also paying special attention to the removal of Ukrainians from northern Bukovina. Einsatzkommando 10a set an example to the Romanians when it carried out its first massacre in the city, murdering hundreds of Jews, mainly from the intelligentsia and the professional class. At the same time, German and Romanian units staged pogroms throughout the Chernovtsy district. In the Jewish-populated towns along the Dniester, hundreds of Jews were killed by Ukrainians from Galicia, and other Jews were killed on the northern bank of the river, having been forced across by Romanian and German troops. Approximately fifteen thousand Jews were killed in this wave of murder. On June 21, 1941, on orders of Ion ANTONESCU, the Jews living in the towns and villages of southern Bukovina were driven out. Local authorities interpreted the orders as they wished, and included the Jews of Siret in the expulsion. The old people and the women and children were for the most part sent to camps in southwest Romania. The small Jewish communities in the Olteni region were ordered to look after the Jews in the camps, a task they were incapable of carrying out.

In September and October 1941 the Jews in the camps of southwestern Romania were first freed, then "legally" fleeced, and then expelled to TRANSNISTRIA. In northern Bukovina, the Jews who had survived the pogroms and massacres were assembled into several camps and from there were transferred to ghettos, in Storojineti, Cotmani, Vizhnitsa (Vaşcăuti), and Lujeni. Many of them escaped or were transferred to Chernovtsy. On July 11 the Romanian civil administration took over in Bukovina, and Alexandru Rioşanu was appointed governor. The "Romanization" section of the civil administration was devoted to the confiscation of Jewish property. On July 30 a special decree was issued by the governor, ordering the Jews to wear the yellow badge (*see* BADGE, JEWISH). The military section attached to the governor's office, headed by Maj. Stere Marinescu, was responsible for the implementation of all anti-Jewish orders and regulations; it did so with great severity, adding further regulations of its own.

All the existing anti-Jewish laws and regulations in force in Old Romania (the Regat) were also applied in Bukovina. The Jews in Bukovina, however, were not allowed to maintain contact with their brethren in the rest of the country, the prohibition also applying to food shipments. On August 4 the first attempt was made to deport Jews from Bukovina to Transnistria, in a group consisting of Jews from Storojineti and its vicinity. Romanian gendarmes murdered 200 of these deportees by drowning them in the Dniester. On October 10, 1941, a secret order was received from Bucharest to expel all the Jews of Bukovina to the other bank of the Dniester. By then, all the Jews of northern Bukovina had been put into ghettos and camps. On October 11 a ghetto was established in Chernovtsy, and on the next day the deportation was launched. Some of the Jews were transported to Transnistria through the Atachi border crossing, but most of them were driven to hastily improvised camps in northern Bessarabia—SECURENI, EDINETI, and MARCULEŞTI—where many of them died. The survivors were deported to Transnistria between October 3 and 11, 1941. By November 15, when the deportation came to a stop, 57,000 Jews had been deported from Bukovina (including the southern part). The process was carried out in a most brutal manner, and many of the Jews were murdered en route to their destination. Jewish property left behind was pillaged at once by the local population, even though it was classified as property to be confiscated for the government. In Chernovtsy, only 20,000 Jews were left; 4,000 more were deported from there in June 1942.

As a result of efforts made by Jewish leaders in Bucharest, especially Dr. Wilhelm FILDERMAN and Chief Rabbi Alexander SAFRAN, the deportation was halted, the Jews having obtained an assurance from the deputy prime minister, Mihai ANTONESCU, that the Chernovtsy Jews required for the economy would be permitted to stay there. Ion Antonescu, the Romanian dictator, agreed to allow 10,000 Jews to stay, but in fact the number of Jews who remained in Chernovtsy for the rest of the war was 16,000, with several hundred refugees from Poland included in that figure. In October 1943 the wearing of the yellow badge was abolished, and Jews were again permitted to move about on the city streets. When the Red Army was drawing near, the Jews were afraid that the retreating Germans would take revenge on them. The Jews were not, however, permitted to move into the interior.

In February 1944 the Romanian army withdrew from Chernovtsy and the city was left in German hands; it was only the advance of the Soviet army and its swift occupation of the city that saved the Jews from extermination. In April 1945, when the Soviets permitted travel to Romania, most of the local Jews—the remnants of northern Bukovina's Jews—left Chernovtsy. Several thousand Jews, mainly individual survivors of the families that had been deported, returned to Chernovtsy in late 1944 and early 1945, from Transnistria. Most of them took up residence in the towns of southern Bukovina from which they had been driven out in 1941. A few years later the majority of them left Romania and settled in Israel.

BIBLIOGRAPHY

Ancel, J., and T. Lavi, eds. *Rumania,* vol. 2. In *Pinkas Hakehillot; Encyclopaedia of Jewish Communities.* Jerusalem, 1980. (In Hebrew.)

Levin, D. "The Jews and the Inception of Soviet Rule in Bukovina." *Soviet Jewish Affairs* 6/2 (October 1976): 52–70.

JEAN ANCEL

BULGARIA. Located in the Balkan Peninsula, Bulgaria has common borders with Romania, Yugoslavia, Greece, and Turkey. The Bulgarian people was formed by the integration of the Ugaritic Bulgars from the Volga region, who had conquered the area in the seventh century, with its original Slavic, Illyrian, Thracian, and Macedonian inhabit-

ants. The Bulgarian language belongs to the South Slavic group of languages, and most Bulgarians are Orthodox Christians.

From 1396 to 1878 Bulgaria was under Ottoman rule, and after gaining independence it continued to acknowledge Ottoman suzerainty, until 1908. In World War I Bulgaria fought on the side of the Central Powers; after the war it had to give up territory and make large reparations payments. Its regime was a constitutional monarchy, and it had a parliament (Narodno Sobranie, or National Assembly) in which leftist, centrist liberal-democratic, and right-wing nationalist parties were represented. In practice, however, it was the king who held power in the country.

In 1940 Bulgaria's population was 6.2 million, with 407,000 in the capital, Sofia. Up to the end of World War II, peasants constituted 80 percent of the population, and the economy was based primarily on agricultural production, its industry tiny even by eastern European standards. Eighty-five percent of the population were ethnic Bulgars, and the great majority, 87.5 percent, were Orthodox Christians. Muslim Turks accounted for 10 percent, and an additional 1.5 percent were Muslim Bulgars (Pomaks). There were also small groups of Catholics and Protestants. In 1943 there were 63,403 Jews in Bulgaria, about 1 percent of the population.

The earliest reports on the presence of Jews in the areas of what is now Bulgaria date back to the first century. During the Middle Ages the Jews had special privileges, and their situation in Bulgaria was better than in the other European kingdoms. Under Ottoman rule they were in the good graces of both the Bulgarian and the Ottoman authorities, who regarded them as a mediatory entity. When Bulgaria became independent in 1878, its Jews were granted full and equal rights.

Approximately 90 percent of Bulgarian Jewry descended from Jews who had been expelled from Spain in 1492 and had come to Bulgaria between the sixteenth and the nineteenth century, mostly by way of the SARAJEVO and SALONIKA Jewish communities; 10 percent of the Jews were Ashkenazic, of Austro-Hungarian and Romanian origin. In the interwar period some Ashkenazic Jews from Russia also took up residence in Bulgaria. Sephardic and Ashkenazic Jews lived in complete harmony, and at times the office of chief rabbi was held by an Ashkenazi. In the early twentieth century most of the Jews spoke Judeo-Spanish (Ladino), but over the course of time, with the growth of the Jewish intelligentsia, Bulgarian became the dominant language. Educated Jews were also fluent in German and French. Dozens of Jewish periodicals were published, in both Judeo-Spanish and Bulgarian. Zionism rapidly gained a predominant foothold in Jewish community life, and in 1918 it extended this foothold to the Consistory, the Bulgarian Jewish communities' central council.

The Jewish communities were autonomous financially and administratively. Jews lived only in the cities, and their main occupations were in the retail trade and the professions. They played no prominent role in the country's economy and had little influence on social and cultural life. The rural population scarcely knew the Jews, and it was only in Sofia, where half the retail trade was in Jewish hands, that their presence had an impact. As a result, Bulgaria was free of one of the usual factors contributing to the rise of antisemitism—Jewish competition in the economic sphere. Antisemitism never struck roots in Bulgaria; the Bulgarian people, itself of mixed origin, could not lay claim to "racial purity." During World War II some Bulgarians called for ethnic solidarity with the Japanese, because of the joint "Mongol" origin of the two peoples. After the war, certain ideologists denied that the Bulgarians had any link to the Mongol race, and claimed that they were pure Slavs, "brothers of the Russian people."

Karl Hoffmann, the representative of the REICHSSICHERHEITSHAUPTAMT (Reich Security Main Office; RSHA) in Bulgaria, in a letter to his superiors in Berlin dated April 5, 1943, stated: "Anybody who is familiar with conditions in Bulgaria must realize that as the time draws near for the 'transports' of the Jews, there will be problems. . . . The Jewish Question does not exist in Bulgaria in the sense that it does in Germany. The ideological and racial prerequisites for convincing the Bulgarian people of the urgent need for a solution of the Jewish Question as in the Reich are not to be found here."

This is not to say that there were never manifestations of antisemitism in Bulgaria. Occasional antisemitic incidents took place in the provincial towns and, more frequently, in Sofia. Three cases of blood libel (the accusation that Jews kill gentiles to obtain their blood for Jewish rituals) occurred in the late nineteenth century, and in the early twentieth century there were anti-Jewish riots in the Jewish quarters of several cities. In 1933 the Nazi-oriented nationalist Saiuz na Bulgarskite Natsionalni Legioni (Union of Bulgarian National Legions), known as the Legionnaires' Association, was formed. This was followed by the creation of a youth organization, Branik, modeled on the HITLERJUGEND, and a fascist organization, Ratnitsi Napreduka na Bulgarshtinata (Guardians of the Advancement of the Bulgarian National Spirit), known as the Ratnitsi, led by Petur Gabrovski.

In the 1930s Bulgaria again had close ties with Germany, its World War I ally. Its motivations were to regain the territories it had lost in 1918, to rid itself of the heavy reparations payments, and to free itself of the restrictions that had been imposed on the strength of its armed forces. In addition, Bulgaria's economy was becoming increasingly dependent on Germany, the volume of its trade with Germany rising from 29 percent of its total foreign trade in 1929 to 68 percent in 1939.

On February 15, 1940, King Boris III appointed the pro-German Professor Bogdan Filov (1883–1945) as prime minister. (Filov was sentenced to death after the war and executed.) On March 1, 1941, under an arbitration award made by Adolf Hitler, Bulgaria received back the southern Dobruja

(Dobrudzha) region from Romania. That day, Bulgaria joined the Axis; the following day, German forces entered Bulgaria, and in April Bulgaria took part in the Axis attack on Yugoslavia and Greece. In return it regained THRACE and MACEDONIA, as well as parts of eastern Serbia, thereby realizing its nationalists' dream of a "Greater Bulgaria." Bulgaria declared war on Great Britain and the United States, but not on the Soviet Union, and it did not send any of its forces to the eastern front—the only European member of the Axis to refrain from doing so. This was because King Boris felt he had to take into account the Slavophile sentiments of his subjects, who had not forgotten the role that Russia had played, in 1878, in helping Bulgaria gain independence.

Anti-Jewish Legislation. The rapprochement with Germany also had its effect on the Jewish issue. The German demands that Bulgaria enact anti-Jewish laws accorded fully with the antisemitic sentiments prevailing in Filov's cabinet. As early as July 1940, a government spokesman announced that Bulgaria was planning to "take steps that would restrict the activities of the Jews," and on October 7, 1940, the government approved the Law for the Protection of the Nation, which curbed the rights of the Jews. The chairman of the Jewish Consistory in Sofia, Josef Geron, together with other members of its executive board and Jewish activists, launched an information drive designed to make the government and the population aware of the grave damage that the anti-Jewish law would cause the Bulgarian people. The Consistory representatives also asked for the opportunity to present their case to the king, but he refused to receive them.

The struggle launched by the Jewish leaders had a positive impact on public opinion. In October 1940 a group of twenty-one leading writers sent a protest letter to the prime minister, the final passage of which read: "On behalf of civilization and on behalf of Bulgaria's good name, we beseech you not to accept the law, the repercussions of which would put a dark stain on our legislation and leave an intolerable mark upon our national memory."

The Bulgarian Medical Association lost no time in joining the writers' protest, using even stronger language, and the Bar Association followed suit, in yet more forceful terms. Political leaders from both left and right also appealed to the prime minister. Of special importance was the protest lodged by the Holy Synod (the supreme body of the Orthodox church) and the personal intervention of metropolitans Stefan of Sofia, Cyril of Plovdiv, Neofit of Vidin, and Sofroni of Vratsa.

The arousal of public sympathy for the Jews sparked off a reaction in the opposing camp. Fascist organizations such as the Federation of Reserve Officers (Saiuz na Zapasnite Ofitseri) and the Federation of Reserve Sergeants and Soldiers (Saiuz na Zapasnite Podofitseri i Voinitsi) distributed leaflets in support of the law. These bodies, known for their nationalist and revanchist attitudes, were joined by the Pharmacists' Association (Aptekarski Saiuz) and the Students' Union (Studenskata Organizatsia). Support for the anti-Jewish law was expressed by the Merchants' Association (Targovskoto Sdruzhenie), which had four thousand Jews among its membership. Despite these manifestations of support for the law, the majority of public opinion was opposed. The government, however, decided to adhere to its *Realpolitik* and persisted in its stand, motivated by opportunist political pragmatism rather than by racist antisemitic ideology: the anti-Jewish law was designed to pave the way for a further rapprochement with Germany. The protests against the law are of no avail, and on January 21, 1941, it passed parliament and was ratified by the king's signature that same day. The law provided the government with a legal basis for its anti-Jewish measures. The definition of "Jews" in the law was, basically, copied from the NUREMBERG LAWS, with some slight "improvement" on the Nuremberg text. In its introduction, the law stated that "the Jews are an evil and a foreign element among the Bulgarian People that acts against the State."

The law had three sections, as follows:

1. No branches of international organizations were permitted to exist in Bulgaria. This affected first the B'NAI B'RITH lodge

Members of the Jewish Consistory in Sofia, Bulgaria (1941).

and, a year later, the various component parts of the Zionist movement.

2. Jews could not be elected to public office and could not take part in a vote for such office; Jewish civil servants had to resign immediately; the *numerus clausus* (quota of Jews) was to be applied in the universities; mixed marriages between Jews and Bulgarians were prohibited; Jews were restricted to their current places of residence; and Jewish economic activities were severely restricted.
3. What was considered "anti-national" behavior by Jews and other foreign nationals was defined.

The authors of the law made attempts to conceal its antisemitic intent by applying it to all "foreigners." In February 1941, the Regulations for the Law for the Protection of the Nation were issued, which expanded the restrictions and applied only to Jews. These regulations, in effect, disenfranchised the Jews.

Commissariat for Jewish Questions. In August 1942 another regulation was issued, establishing the Commissariat for Jewish Questions (Komisarstvo za Evreiskite Vuprosi; KEV) in the Ministry of Internal Affairs. Its task was to apply the Law for the Protection of the Nation and the relevant regulations. Under those regulations, the Jewish community boards were stripped of their power and placed under the authority of the KEV. On September 30 of that year, Aleksander Belev (1900–1944) was appointed Commissioner for Jewish Questions. A pro-Nazi lawyer, Belev was one of the few Bulgarians who believed in antisemitism as an ideology. In September 1944, when the Soviet army entered Bulgaria, Belev tried to escape with the retreating Germans, but was caught by partisans and executed.

The August 1942 regulation also contained provisions for the financing of the KEV's wide range of operations. These expenses were to be covered by the blocked bank accounts of the Jews—a certain percentage of which would be set aside for this purpose—and by special fees that "persons of Jewish extraction" would have to pay for official documents issued to them. In other words, the Jews themselves would have to pay the enormous costs of their persecution: of the restrictions imposed on them in the initial stage, and of their eventual expulsion from Bulgaria. The various measures introduced by the KEV on the basis of the anti-Jewish law and regulations were intended as a prelude to the deportation of the Jews to the east. This was stated by Belev in no uncertain terms in a letter he addressed to the minister of internal affairs, Petur Gabrovski, on August 29, 1942: "The radical solution of our Jewish Question will be their emigration, which will have to proceed hand in hand with the confiscation of their property. . . . For the present, the possibility for such emigration does not exist, unless Germany were to agree to settle the Jews in Galicia or in another part of Russia. For the present, until such time as conditions arise that would enable the emigration of Jews to proceed, it is imperative to toughen the measures against them."

The "measures against the Jews" were taken during 1942. In the spring of 1943, the plan for the "solution of the Jewish Question" entered its final stage, that of their deportation from the country. First to be deported were the Jews of Thrace, Macedonia, and eastern Serbia, the territories that the Germans had handed over to Bulgaria. This was to be followed by preparatory steps for the deportation of all the Jews from Bulgaria.

Deportation. In November 1941 the Bulgarian foreign minister, Ivan Vladimir Popov, had a meeting with Joachim von RIBBENTROP at which the German foreign minister told him that, according to Hitler's decision, all the Jews would be expelled from Europe when the war ended. As a preliminary stage for the total removal of the Jews, their deportation to Poland was being planned. German Foreign Ministry officials kept a close watch on the development of the anti-Jewish policy in Bulgaria, and believed that they would have no problem in taking the Jews out of that country. On February 22, 1943, an agreement was signed in Sofia between Belev and Adolf EICHMANN's representative in Bulgaria, SS-Hauptsturmführer Theodor DANNECKER. The agreement provided that "as a first step, twenty thousand Jews will be deported to German territories in the east." The text that had been prepared for signature contained the words "from Thrace and Macedonia," but these words were struck out by Belev and Dannecker when they signed the document. A week later, on March 2, the Bulgarian government approved the agreement as it stood. Because of concern about possible adverse public reaction, a note was added to the official approval of the agreement stating that "the approval of this agreement does not require its publication in the official Gazette." (From most of the countries occupied by Germany, and even countries allied with it, such as Italy, Hungary, and Romania, the Jews were deported without any agreement being signed between the Reich and the local government.)

Two days later, on March 4, some 12,000 Jews from the Bulgarian-occupied territories of Thrace, Macedonia, and eastern Serbia were evicted from their homes. Allowed only some personal effects, they were put into concentration camps. They remained there for about a week in the custody of Bulgarian soldiers and police, who stole the Jews' belongings on the pretext of carrying out body searches. It was only when the Jews boarded trains that they were handed over to units of the German Wehrmacht. By the end of March the Bulgarian transports began moving north, with the Danube River port of Lom as their first destination. From there they proceeded on cargo boats to Vienna, where once again they were put on trains, which took them to their final destination, TREBLINKA. On March 20 and 21, 4,226 Jews from Thrace and the city of Pirot were deported, followed, from March 22 to 29, by 7,158 Jews from Macedonia (mostly from Skopje). The total number of Jews deported from the occupied territories was 11,384. Of these, 21 were reported by their escorts to have died en route, leaving 11,363 to be handed over to the Treblinka camp administration.

Reports on what had happened to the Jews of the occupied territories began to circulate among the Jewish communities in Bulgaria. The Bulgarian occupied territories were now emptied of their Jews, but Belev was still short of the 20,000 Jews stipulated in the agreement with Dannecker. Wanting to fulfill the agreement, he was forced to use Bulgarian Jews for this purpose. He chose to deport the Jews of Kyustendil, a town near the old border with Serbia. On March 5, 1943, the KEV representative in Kyustendil issued orders for the confiscation of water containers and other household utensils. The Jews of the town suspected that these items were to be used for a long train journey, and their fears were confirmed by a town official who leaked the information that a deportation order for Jews had been received.

The events that followed, however, were quite different from what might have been expected. Kyustendil became the occasion for an inspiring manifestation of the Bulgarians' solidarity with their Jewish fellow citizens and their determination to protect them. Bulgarian and right-wing Macedonian nationalist functionaries from the town sent a delegation to Sofia that arrived on March 8 and was joined by Dimitur Peshev, deputy speaker of parliament. The next day, the delegation held two meetings. At the first, held with the leaders of the Jewish Consistory, the delegation declared that they would do all in their power to prevent the implementation of the deportation order. The second was held with Minister of the Interior Petur Gabrovski. At this meeting, the Macedonian members of the delegation threatened the minister with "personal sanctions" (that is, assassination) if he did not call off the deportation. The deadline for the deportation was midnight, March 9–10, but Gabrovski agreed to its postponement. The delegation's prompt and determined intervention had achieved its purpose, and for the moment the Jews of Bulgaria were saved from deportation.

Peshev spent the following week, March 10 to 17, in talks with members of parliament, seeking to gain their support for a manifesto protesting the deportation of the Jews. On March 17 he submitted the manifesto to the speaker; it bore the signatures of forty-three parliamentarians. Its text included the following passage: "Such an act must not be permitted, not only because the persons affected have not been stripped of their citizenship and cannot legally be expelled from Bulgaria; an act of this sort would also have grave political consequences for the country as a whole." The government reacted angrily. On March 23, a majority in parliament reprimanded Peshev, who by now was isolated, and removed him from his post as deputy speaker. (After the war, Peshev was sentenced to fifteen years' hard labor as a war criminal, saved from a death sentence by his assistance to the Jews. His sentence was commuted and he lived the rest of his life in poverty.)

Following the postponement of the March 9 deportation, Belev resigned from his post. During April and May, the Jews of Bulgaria again had the threat of deportation hanging over them. The Germans maintained their pressure; on April 5, the German minister in Sofia, Adolf Beckerle, wrote to Berlin that it would not be long before the Jews would be deported from Bulgaria proper. At this point, however, the Bulgarian government was beginning to have its doubts, under the impact of the tumult in parliament and the mood of the people. A new plan was devised whereby 25,000 Sofia Jews would be exiled to the provinces, pending their deportation from the country. On May 22, 1943, a decree containing the new plan was published. The following day (the eve of a national holiday commemorating Saints Cyril and Methodius), the Jews of Sofia held a demonstration in the courtyard of the synagogue, and on May 24 there was a demonstration by Bulgarians, on the initiative of underground Communist groups. Militant Jews as well marched through the city. The police intervened, using brute force to break up both gatherings. The decree on the expulsion of the Jews from Sofia was put into effect, and within twelve days, 19,153 Jews were driven out of the capital and forced to live in some twenty provincial towns. Although this expulsion was the climax of Jewish persecutions, it also removed the threat of deportation to the extermination camps.

In the late summer of 1943, the political climate underwent a change. On August 28, King Boris III died under mysterious circumstances, following his return from a meeting with Hitler. In September, Italy surrendered, and the Allies kept up their advance. The Bulgarian government decided to adopt a more flexible policy. Petur Gabrovski was not reappointed to the cabinet; the United States sought to impress upon Bulgaria that it should change its policy, including its attitude toward the Jews; and in the fall of that year, the Germans stopped pressuring Bulgaria regarding the Jewish issue.

Further provisions of the Law for the Protection of the Nation stipulated that from 1941 all Jewish males between the ages of twenty and forty were to be drafted into special labor battalions. At first the Jews in these battalions worked side by side with Bulgarians, performing the same work and wearing the same uniforms. When the German Labor Service, the Reichsarbeitsdienst, protested against this equal treatment, the Jews were formed into separate units and assigned "very hard work" in the mountains and forests, under the same conditions as convicts sentenced to hard labor. In effect, the Jewish labor battalion camps became concentration camps. The upper age limit for the forced-labor draft was raised in 1943 to forty-six, and the workday was extended to twelve hours. Some twelve thousand Jews were drafted into the forced-labor battalions and put on extremely hard work, constructing new trails in the mountains, building new roads, and cutting trees in the forests.

The Law for the Protection of the Nation involved the same sort of restrictions and humiliations to which the Jews were exposed in other countries of occupied Europe: all Jews aged ten and above had to wear a yellow badge (*see* BADGE, JEWISH) on their clothing; every Jewish house or business had to display a sign identifying it as Jewish; Jews were dismissed from all posts in the schools and universities. The situation of the Jews in the provincial towns was exceptionally bad. The Jews exiled from Sofia were restricted to living only in Jewish houses, and were not allowed to take up employment; they lived in drastically overcrowded conditions, with as many as eight to ten persons to a room; they had only one hour a day in which to make their purchases in the public markets; and in some towns a permanent curfew was in force for Jews, except for one or two hours a day. Jews were prohibited from using the main streets, from entering certain kinds of business establishments, and from attending places of entertainment such as cinemas and cafés. Their radios, automobiles, and bicycles were confiscated, as were valuables such as jewelry and rugs.

The Bulgarian population was divided in its attitude toward the Jews. Some tried to enrich themselves at the expense of the latter, whereas others tried to help them by providing food supplies, by aiding the Jewish communities to maintain contact with one another, and by employing Jews illegally. It would be difficult to assess the precise proportion of the two groups in the population, but the Jews were under the impression that most Bulgarians remained faithful to their humane principles, were not infected by antisemitism, and had compassion for the Jews in their hour of need.

Rescue Efforts and Acts of Resistance. Prior to Bulgaria's alliance with Germany in April 1941, several attempts were made to save Jews without Bulgarian nationality, as well as groups of children and Zionist youth. "Illegal" immigration (ALIYA BET) ships left Bulgaria for Palestine. The first such ship, the *Salvador,* left Varna on December 4, 1940, only to sink twelve days later off the coast of Turkey because it was unseaworthy. Of the 335 refugees on board, 213 drowned, while 122 were saved and made their way to Palestine. Another 170 Jews from Bulgaria joined other Palestine-bound Jewish refugees on a Romanian ship, the *Dorian,* in late February 1941, and a month later a group of 65 children left for Palestine. From April 1941 until late 1943, the borders of Bulgaria were hermetically sealed for Jewish emigration.

In late 1943, Chaim WEIZMANN and Rabbi Stephen WISE, in London and Washington respectively, worked on plans for rescuing Bulgarian Jewry by transporting them to Palestine via Turkey. In Sofia, secret contacts concerning these plans were handled by the Swiss legation, and in Istanbul they were in the hands of Ira HIRSCHMANN, representative of the WAR REFUGEE BOARD. The fact that the Allied powers were taking interest in the fate of the Jews of Bulgaria induced the Sofia government to moderate its Jewish policy. Finally, in August 1944, it repealed the anti-Jewish legislation. On September 9, when the Soviet army entered Bulgaria, the new antifascist government that had by then been established declared war on Nazi Germany.

A few dozen Jewish youths joined the partisan units, and some of them fell in battles with the Bulgarian gendarmerie. Among those killed in action who had gained renown for their heroism were Emil Shekerdzhiiski, Violeta Iakova, Mati Rubenov, Menachem Papo, and Yosif Talvi.

The special situation in Bulgaria in those years has not been fully researched, and the question of who was responsible for saving the Jews has yet to be resolved. The Jewish community of DENMARK was the other community under the Nazis that was saved, but this was because they were moved to Sweden by a concerted effort of the Danish people. In Bulgaria the Jews survived in a country that was in the pro-German camp. Thus far, the answers given to this question have been colored by ideological bias and for the most part have not been based on reliable and conclusive evidence.

The official Communist version seeks to credit the Communists with saving Bulgarian Jewry. The Bulgarian Communist resistance did indeed demonstrate its concern for the Jews: its radio station in Moscow made several broadcasts condemning their persecution, and the Communist underground organization in Sofia took part in the May 24, 1943, demonstrations. These efforts, however, did not deter the Bulgarian government from expelling the Jews from the capital. The Communist version is unwarranted; as Nissan Oren has noted (1968), Communist propaganda during the war had no effect on the Bulgarian government.

Benjamin Arditi, one of the leaders of Bulgarian Jewry, has claimed that the Jews of Bulgaria were saved by King Boris's decisions, in March and May 1943, not to permit their deportation from the country. This version, too, does not present the complete story, and no original document exists to prove that the king made such a decision. On the other hand, Minister of the Interior Gabrovski would not have taken the risk of postponing the deportation decreed for March 9, 1943, without the king's authority. King Boris, moreover, was able to resist German pressure on an issue of immense importance: the demand by the Germans that Bulgarian forces join in the fighting against the Soviet army. No evidence has come to light to confirm the legend surrounding King Boris's mysterious death, according to which he was poisoned because he refused Hitler's demand for the surrender of Bulgarian Jewry. To date, the Bulgarian government has not granted scholars from the West access to the Royal Archives for that period. King Boris's acts and decisions on this issue are still shrouded in secrecy, and more research would be required to substantiate the claim that it was he who saved Bulgaria's Jews.

The question of how Bulgarian Jews were saved has two aspects: (1) Who gave the orders to postpone the deportations in March and May 1943, and to refrain from deporting the Jews in the fall of 1943? (2) What were the motives for these decisions?

Until his death on August 28, 1943, King Boris was the supreme authority in the country. The prime minister and all other members of the cabinet were absolutely loyal to the king and abided by his decisions. Not a single instance is known of the cabinet's disobeying the king or acting in defiance of his position. While the Reich representatives in Sofia had direct access to the cabinet, neither Filov nor Gabrovski would have dared to make a decision on such an important issue without the king's consent. It would appear, therefore, that it was the king who gave the orders. It must be borne in mind, however, that the ultimate decision for a moderate Jewish policy was made in September 1943; by then Boris was dead, his son, Simeon II, was a small child, and Filov was still the prime minister.

We may assume that the king had several motives for his decisions. First, the Soviet victory at Stalingrad in February 1943, the subsequent Soviet military advances, and the Allied victories in North Africa made it clear that the German chances of winning the war were growing slimmer. Second, Boris realized that because of the Allies' interest in the fate of the Bulgarian Jews it was worthwhile keeping them alive, as security to be redeemed after the war to expiate for Bulgaria's declaration of war on the United States and Britain in 1941. Fearing that the German forces stationed in Bulgaria might take action against him, Boris decided on a compromise solution for the Jewish problem. He deported the Jews from the newly occupied territories, promulgated anti-Jewish legislation, and expelled the Jews of Sofia to provincial towns, but he did not deport Bulgarian Jews from the country.

Once the drive for deportation lost its momentum, the post–May 1943 delaying tactics had the support of a variety of additional forces: the Holy Synod and the personal involvement of the metropolitans Cyril and Stefan; appeals by leaders of the entire political spectrum, from the Communists to the nationalist bourgeoisie, by various political organizations, and by the leadership of the country's Macedonian minority; the persistent and far-reaching campaign waged by the Consistory and by Jewish and Zionist leaders in the United States, who had the support of influential elements in the United States administration; and the tolerant and humane character of the majority of Bulgarians. A rare combination of international circumstances and internal pressures influenced the king's behavior. However, it would be difficult to assess the specific weight of each of these factors, which together saved the lives of fifty thousand Bulgarian Jews.

From 1948 to 1949, some forty-five thousand Jews—90 percent of the Jewish population—left Bulgaria to settle in Israel. Only a few thousand Jews remained. This phenomenon, of nearly the entire Jewish community's moving to the Jewish state, was based on the strong sense of Jewish national identity that Bulgarian Jewry had long fostered, on their unwillingness to live under a Communist regime, and on their memories of the Holocaust period.

BIBLIOGRAPHY

Chary, F. B. *The Bulgarian Jews and the Final Solution.* Pittsburgh, 1972.

Miller, M. L. *Bulgaria during the Second World War.* Stanford, 1975.

Oren, N. "The Bulgarian Exception: A Reassessment of the Salvation of the Jewish Community." *Yad Vashem Studies* 7 (1968): 83–106.

AVRAHAM BEN-YAKOV

BUNA-MONOWITZ. *See* Auschwitz.

BUND (Yidisher Arbeter-Bund in Russland, Lite un Poiln; League of Jewish Workers in Russia, Lithuania, and Poland), Jewish So-

A Bund May Day parade in Warsaw, May 1, 1936. The banner on the right reads: "Down with Militarism and Wars! Long live International Workers' Solidarity!" The banner on the left reads: "The Strike Is Our Weapon!"

cialist party. The Bund was founded in Vilna in September and October 1897. In its initial stage, the party's aim was to organize Jewish workers and strengthen their revolutionary ardor so that they would join the Russian Socialist movement in its struggle against the tsarist regime. The Bund was totally opposed to Zionism and to Hebrew culture and language, regarding Yiddish as the national language of the Jews of eastern Europe. It aspired to equal rights for Jews within the framework of a Socialist and democratic state in which the Jewish population would enjoy cultural autonomy, like all the other people in the state. After the Bolshevik Revolution in 1917, the Bund gradually ceased to exist in the Soviet Union; most of its members joined the Communist party, and those who did not were persecuted by the new regime.

In the interwar period, independent Poland became the major scene of the Bund's activities; small branches also existed in Romania, Lithuania, Belgium, and France, as well as in the United States. In Poland the party established a broad base of operations, including children's and youth organizations (SKIF and Zukunft, respectively), a sports movement, and a women's organization. The Bund was the moving spirit in the establishment of CYShO (Central Yiddish Schools Organization), the Yiddish school network, and was the leading political body among the Jewish workers' organizations. Two of its outstanding leaders, Henryk Erlich and Wiktor Alter, succeeded in consolidating the party and turning it into an important force among the Jewish population of Poland. After joining the Socialist International, the Bund established close relations with the Socialist parties in the West and with the Polish Socialist party. Between 1936 and 1939, the Bund led a determined drive against antisemitic elements in Poland, and did not hesitate from time to time to activate its party militia, which was formed in the 1920s to react to street attacks on Jews and assaults on Bund members by political rivals. During that period the organization gained substantial representation on city councils, especially in WARSAW, ŁÓDŹ, VILNA, PIOTRKÓW TRYBUNALSKI, and LUBLIN. In parts of Galicia and Upper Silesia, however, support for the Bund was conspicuously absent, especially in such important centers as LVOV and KRAKÓW. Moreover, despite continued efforts, the Bund never succeeded in having a candidate elected to the Sejm (the Polish parliament) or the senate.

When World War II broke out, most of the Bund's senior leaders left Poland. Most of the members of the party's Central Committee—Shlomo Mendelsohn, Emanuel Sherer, Vladimir Kossowski, Jekuthiel Portnoy (Noah), and Emanuel Nowogrodski—went to the United States, where they established an important center of support for party activities. The two top leaders of the party, Erlich and Alter, were arrested in the Soviet-occupied parts of Poland in September and October of 1939. The Bund made enormous and desperate efforts to have the two men released from Soviet imprisonment, for this purpose soliciting the help of leading personalities in the POLISH GOVERNMENT-IN-EXILE in London and the American labor movement. Their efforts were in vain, and in December 1941 both Bund leaders were murdered in the Soviet Union. In the eastern parts of Poland, which the Soviets had occupied—in Vilna, Białystok, Grodno, and other cities—most of the Bund members were arrested and exiled. In Warsaw, Bund members carried on underground operations. Until the beginning of the deportations to extermination camps, the Warsaw underground organization of the party issued publications that had a relatively wide circulation and were distributed in the provincial towns and cities of Poland. In June 1941 a Polish courier was caught with underground newspapers in her possession, as well as a list of Bund activists in various Polish cities. This led to the arrest and murder of a great number of party members in Piotrków Trybunalski, Kraków, Radom, and Tomaszów Mazowiecki.

The party leadership in Warsaw adamantly refused any political cooperation with Zionist parties or movements. In March 1942, when efforts were undertaken to form a united Jewish fighting organization, the Bund leader in Warsaw, Maurice Oisach, rejected the idea, saying that the Bund maintained ties with underground elements outside the ghetto. The party tried to set up a joint underground organization with the clandestine Polish socialist party, but the attempt failed. The Bund did not join the Antifascist Bloc that was created in the spring of 1942. One of the leaders of the Bund, the head of its youth faction, Abrasha Blum, did not agree with his elders and supported the establishment of a general Jewish organization. However, it was only in October and November of 1942—following the major *Aktion* in Warsaw—that the young Bund members, led by Blum, Berek Schneidemil, and Marek EDELMAN, joined the ŻYDOWSKA ORGANIZACJA BOJOWA (Jewish Fighting Organization; ŻOB), and even then, they refused to take part in the Żydowski Komitet Narodowy (Jewish National Committee) that had been set up. Therefore, a "Coordinating Committee" had to be established, in which both the Bund and the National Committee took part, as equals.

A similar situation existed in Vilna, where the Bund leaders, including Grisha Jaszunski, Berl Waydman, and Joel Fischmann, did not want to join the FAREYNEGTE PARTIZANER ORGANIZATSYE (United Partisan Organization), which was formed at the beginning of 1942. Here too, the young leaders, Abraham Chwojnik and Shmuel Kaplinski, were in favor of joining the Jewish fighting organization, and they did so, in the face of opposition by their elders. In both Vilna and Piotrków Trybunalski, the Bund was very influential in the Judenräte. Bund members Zalman Tennenberg and Yitzhak Samsonowitz headed the Judenrat in Piotrków Trybunalski—the only place where Bund members held these positions. In Vilna, Bund activists Jaszunski and Fischmann were on the Judenrat and wielded considerable influence there, but this came to an end when Jacob GENS became the head of the ghetto. The Bund was an important force in the struggle that the Łódź ghetto employees waged against Mordechai Chaim RUMKOWSKI for better living conditions.

In April 1942, Samuel ZYGELBOJM, a prominent Bund activist who had gone to the United States, was appointed to the Polish National Committee that had been set up in London. As a member of that committee, Zygelbojm was vehemently opposed to the Zionist bodies and their influence in London, and he refused to undertake joint action with the other Jewish member of the council, Ignacy Isaac SCHWARZBART. Two reports reached Zygelbojm—one sent in May 1942 and received the same month, and the other sent in August of that year and received in November—from a Bund activist in Warsaw, Leon FEINER, with detailed information on the annihilation of Polish Jewry. Zygelbojm thereupon sought to enlist the help of Polish authorities in London, the leaders of the major powers, and world opinion for the rescue of the Jews of Poland. Bitterly disappointed by the failure of his efforts, Zygelbojm, in despair, committed suicide in May 1943, as an act of protest against the indifference of the free world in the face of the murder of the Jews. His place on the Polish National Committee was taken by Emanuel Sherer, a Bund activist who went to London from the United States to take up his appointment.

The Bund took part in the WARSAW GHETTO UPRISING of April 1943, with four squads of its members joining in the fighting. In March 1944 the Polish government-in-exile in London awarded a medal of valor posthumously to Michael Kleppfisch, a Bund activist who had fallen in the uprising. Another Bund member, Marek Edelman, was one of the commanders of the ŻOB in Warsaw.

BIBLIOGRAPHY

In the Years of the Jewish Catastrophe: *The Voice of the Underground Bund*. New York, 1948. (In Yiddish.)

Johnpoll, B. K. *The Politics of Futility*: *The General Jewish Workers Bund of Poland, 1917–1943*. Ithaca, N.Y., 1967.

Kruk, H. "Diary of the Vilna Ghetto." *YIVO Annual* 13 (1965): 9–78.

Zygelbojm Book. New York, 1947. (In Yiddish.)

DANIEL BLATMAN

BUND DEUTSCHER MÄDEL. *See* Hitlerjugend.

C

CAMPS. [*The Nazis established a wide-ranging system of concentration, slave-labor, and extermination camps. Comprised of nearly three thousand camps, it crisscrossed Europe in a vast spiderweb of terror and mass intimidation. For an overview of this system of incarceration, see* Concentration Camps. *Prisoners detained while awaiting transfer to the "east" were held in assembly camps (Sammellager) and transit camps (Aufenthaltslager; Durchgangslager); see* Bergen-Belsen; Edineti; Gunskirchen; Kistarcza; Mechelen; Mogilev-Podolski; Secureni; Theresienstadt; Vaivara; Vertujeni; Vught; Westerbork. *In forced-labor camps (Arbeitslager or Zwangsarbeitslager), prisoners were worked to death; see* Blechhammer; Ebensee; Janówska; Klooga; Płaszów; Poniatowa; Trawniki; *see also* Forced Labor *and* Libya: Forced-Labor and Internment Camps. *Five camps were operated primarily as death factories, chiefly for Jews; see* Extermination Camps. *The Nazi camp system was rounded out by various prisoner-of-war camps and by the internment and detention camps run by some of Germany's client states (Croatia, Hungary, Italy, Romania, Slovakia, and Vichy France); see* Drancy; Ferramonti di Tarsa; Gurs; Les Milles; Vapniarka; Vittel. *After World War II, the British used detention camps on the island of Cyprus to keep Jewish "illegal" immigrants from reaching Palestine; see* Cyprus Detention Camps.]

CANADA. Just one week after the German invasion of Poland in September 1939, Canada joined the war effort against Nazi Germany. Second only to the Soviet Union in geographic area, Canada was economically and militarily unprepared for war. Nevertheless, this sparsely populated country eventually proved one of the leading military and economic mainstays of the Allied cause and a major contributor to the final defeat of Nazi Germany.

But if Canada was a stalwart of the Allied cause, it proved less than sympathetic to the mounting crisis of European Jewry. Most Canadians regarded the tragic plight of European Jews and their desperate need of a safe haven as an immigration problem best avoided. From Hitler's consolidation of power in 1933 to Nazi Germany's final surrender in the spring of 1945, Canada's doors remained closed to Jews. As a result, Canada had arguably the worst record among all the Western states in granting sanctuary to Jewish refugees from Nazi persecution.

Controls on Jewish admissions to Canada predate Hitler's rise. Prior to 1923, Jews entered Canada on equal terms with tens of thousands of other European immigrants. While preference was given to immigrants from Britain and the United States, the need for agricultural settlers to farm the vast Canadian prairies was so great that Canadian authorities actively recruited immigrants in eastern Europe. The Canadian public remained uneasy at the arrival of so many people of different ethnic and cultural origins. Nevertheless, the economic benefits of immigration were reassuring, as was the assumption that the immigrants would remain in rural Canada, where they and their children could gradually be assimilated.

Most Jews who came to Canada, however, seemed to defy the government's policy of agricultural immigration. Rather than go to rural areas or take up farm-based employment, they congregated in Canadian urban centers and competed with Anglo-Canadian artisans and professionals.

As the agricultural lands of western Canada filled with European settlers and anti-immigration sentiment grew stronger, the government restricted immigration. Barriers were raised against all eastern Europeans. However, especially harsh regulations restricted the entry to Canada of Jewish would-be immigrants, irrespective of country of origin (except those from Britain or the United States). After 1923 only those few Jews who had close family members in Canada or who could muster the political influence necessary to obtain a rarely issued entry permit were allowed into Canada.

When the depression of the 1930s deepened and rising European antisemitism sent many Jews in search of refuge, Canada's immigration regulations were further tightened and Canadian authorities turned a deaf ear to every plea on behalf of Jewish refugees. In this, Canadian officials reflected the prevailing national sentiment, which was steadfastly opposed to Jewish immigration. While this opposition was strong all across Canada, nowhere was it stronger than in rural, French-speaking, and Catholic Quebec, on which the government counted heavily for reelection. The government knew only too well that any concession on the Jewish refugee issue would cost it dearly at the polls.

In spite of this opposition, the small immigrant working-class Jewish community of Canada, constituting less than 1.5 percent of the national population and largely concentrated in Montreal and Toronto, lobbied in support of Jewish immigration. As the Nazi threat to European Jewry increased, the Canadian Jewish community, through its national umbrella organization, the Canadian Jewish Congress, also organized a national boycott of German-made goods. If the boycott had limited success, the prewar effort to open Canada's doors to Jewish refugees was a complete failure. Although Canada participated in the 1938 EVIAN CONFERENCE, it did so reluctantly and only to ensure that Canada did not become the focus of any Jewish refugee resettlement scheme which might be proposed.

With the outbreak of hostilities in 1939, Jewish community support for the national war effort was unreserved. But attempts to convince public servants and political leaders to admit those Jews of Europe who might still be rescued from the Nazis remained a Jewish priority. In spite of the determination of immigration authorities to hold the line against Jewish admissions, the Canadian Jewish Congress did wring several small and hard-won concessions out of the Canadian cabinet. In late 1941 the government approved the admission of 1,000 Jewish children from Vichy France whose parents had been transported to Poland. Unfortunately, this came too late. Before any of the children selected for Canada could be removed, the Nazis seized control of Vichy France. The children followed their parents to the death camps. Later in the war, the Canadian government, under renewed domestic Jewish and international pressure, permitted the entry of several hundred Jewish refugees who had found temporary sanctuary in Spain and Portugal.

Another group of Jewish refugees came to Canada, more by accident than design. After the fall of France in 1940, British fears of imminent invasion grew. So too did fears that German and Austrian refugees in Britain, including Jews, posed a fifth-column threat. Refugees were rounded up and interned pending determination of their loyalty. Individuals declared a national threat were to be imprisoned in Australia or Canada. By error, several thousand innocent young Jewish refugees were shipped to Canada, where they were initially held in prisoner-of-war camps. Long after the error was discovered and long after almost all the internees in Britain were released, Canada still refused to release those it held, for fear they they would want to stay. Canada wanted no Jewish refugees, and certainly not any who had entered through a back door. It took more than two years of pressure by the British government and prodding by the Canadian Jewish community before the young men were finally released to attend Canadian schools or undertake war-related work.

Canadian reluctance to permit the entry of Jewish refugees did not end with the Allied victory in 1945 or with revelations of the Holocaust. Canada, its prewar immigration regulations still intact, rejected any suggestion that it offer new homes to DISPLACED PERSONS, least of all to Jews. When acute labor shortages eventually forced Canada to admit displaced persons, the government devised schemes to permit the immigration of thousands of new settlers to waiting jobs, while keeping Jewish entries to a minimum.

Only in late 1947 did government policy begin to change. After much negotiation, the government reaffirmed its wartime pledge, allowing into Canada 1,000 Jewish children, now orphaned survivors of the Holocaust. At the behest of the largely Jewish-owned Canadian clothing industry, which claimed a shortage of skilled labor, the government also allowed limited recruitment of clothing and fur workers among Holocaust survivors. In addition, the government gradually enlarged the circle of those eligible for reunification with family members in Canada. But a more fundamental shift in policy was in the offing. As the total flow of immigrants grew so large that a gradually increasing number of Jewish displaced persons could hardly be noticed and the newly independent state of Israel promised to absorb the bulk of the remaining Jewish displaced persons, Canadian policy changed. In 1948 a new Immigration Act removed all discriminatory regulations against Jewish immigration.

BIBLIOGRAPHY

Abella, I., and H. Troper. *None Is Too Many: Canada and the Jews of Europe, 1933–1948.* Toronto, 1982.

Dirks, G. E. *Canada's Refugee Policy: Indifference or Opportunism?* Montreal, 1977.

Draper, P. J. "The Accidental Immigrants: Canada and the Interned Refugees." *Canadian Jewish Historical Society Journal* 2 (1978): 1–38, 80–112.

Troper, H., and M. Weinfeld. *Jews, Ukrainians and the Hunt for Nazi War Criminals in Canada.* Toronto, 1988.

HAROLD TROPER

CANARIS, WILHELM (1887–1945), German admiral; between 1935 and 1944 chief of the ABWEHR, the intelligence department of the Armed Forces High Command. Canaris was born at Aplerbeck, Westphalia, the son of a local industrialist. He entered the German navy in 1905 and during World War I served both in an intelligence capacity in Spain and as commander of a U-boat in the Mediterranean.

After the November 1918 revolution in Germany, Canaris participated in the Freikorps activity of the Marine Brigade and in 1919 was for a time adjutant of the Reichswehr (Armed Forces) minister, Gustav Noske. He continued to advance in his naval career, and by 1934 was commandant of the fortress at Swinemünde, northeast of Stettin, on the Baltic Sea. His earlier success in intelligence work secured Canaris the position of head of military intelligence (*Chef der Abwehrabteilung des Kriegsministeriums*) in 1935.

Canaris was a Nazi sympathizer, but he also developed contacts with the military opposition to Hitler, led by Generalmajor Ludwig Beck, chief of the General Staff from 1935 to 1938, and Generalleutnant Franz Halder, chief of the General Staff from 1938 to 1942. Canaris feared the outbreak of war, and sought to deter the regime through his intelligence reports. His protests against the brutalities perpetrated by the SS against the Polish intelligentsia, nobility, and clergy brought him into conflict with Reinhard HEYDRICH, who had been his subordinate as a trainee naval officer. Canaris also opposed Hitler's plans to bring Spain, then under Franco's rule, into the war.

Canaris's opposition to Hitler, combined with his fear of military defeat and Russian invasion, paralyzed to some extent his role in the resistance. After the assassination of Heydrich in 1942, friction increased between Canaris and both the SS and the new head of the REICHSSICHERHEITSHAUPTAMT (Reich Security Main Office; RSHA), Ernst KALTENBRUNNER. In January 1944 the arrest of Count Helmuth von Moltke, one of Canaris's co-conspirators, and the flight of two of Canaris's agents to the British in Turkey led to his dismissal the following month. Shortly after the July 1944 bomb plot against Hitler, Canaris was arrested. In February 1945 he

Adm. Wilhelm Canaris (right), chief of the intelligence service (Abwehr) of the Armed Forces High Command from 1935 to 1944. [National Archives]

was taken to the FLOSSENBÜRG concentration camp together with his longtime collaborator, Gen. Hans Oster, and was executed at Hitler's order on April 9, on charges of treason.

BIBLIOGRAPHY

Amort, C., and M. Jedlicka. *The Canaris File.* London, 1970.

Graml, H., et al. *The German Resistance to Hitler.* London, 1970.

Höhne, H. *Canaris: A Biography.* Garden City, N.Y., 1979.

LIONEL KOCHAN

CARPATHIAN RUTHENIA. *See* Transcarpathian Ukraine.

CATHOLIC CHURCH. *See* Christian Churches; Pius XII.

CDJC. *See* Documentation Centers: Centre de Documentation Juive Contemporaine.

CENTER OF CONTEMPORARY JEWISH DOCUMENTATION. *See* Documentation Centers: Centre de Documentation Juive Contemporaine.

CENTRALA EVREILOR (Jewish Center), Jewish institution in ROMANIA, similar to the JUDENRAT (Jewish Council), which the government of Ion ANTONESCU set up in February 1942, responding to pressure by the German legation in BUCHAREST. The Centrala took the place of the long-established Federatia Uniunilor de Comunitati Evreesti (Union of Jewish Communities), which had been disbanded in December 1941. The Centrala had the task of implementing all orders and decisions on Jewish affairs issued by the government and its various agencies, as well as acting as the representative Jewish body in all contacts with the authorities. Officially, the Centrala was not permitted to be in touch with any branch of the government except the office of Radu LECCA, the commissioner general for Jewish questions, who in turn took orders from Gustav RICHTER, the counselor on Jewish affairs at the German legation.

Heading the Centrala were persons who had previously not been active Jewish leaders. Its first chairman was Stefan Streitman, a convert from Judaism and a journalist by profession, but the real authority was in the hands of Nandor Ghingold, also a convert from Judaism, a physician with professional ties to some of the staff members of the German legation, who had recommended his appointment. One of the department heads was Adolf Willman, who was known to be a German agent, but there were also legitimate representatives of the Jewish population among the officers of the Centrala. Some of them had been kept on in the posts they had held in the federation, while the other officers included members of the Zionist movement who had joined in order to keep an eye on the Centrala and to take charge of the school system. At a later stage, members of the clandestine Communist party also joined the Centrala.

The two tasks assigned to the Centrala were, on the face of it, irreconcilable. On the one hand, it was to participate in preparations for the planned deportation of the Jews to the extermination camps in Poland, as demanded of the Romanian government by the Nazi representatives (headed by Richter). On the other hand, the Centrala was expected to cater to the Romanian authorities who sought to use it as an instrument for extorting money and property from the Jews, and as an agency that would supply forced-labor battalions. As long as the Romanian government agreed with the deportation plans, the Centrala did as the Nazis asked, making a census of the Jews (based on racial criteria) and a list of their addresses. It did not take Ghingold long to discover, as had Jewish leaders before him, that the corrupt regime could be softened by bribes. Ghingold promptly adopted this method, the bribes taking the form of contributions to Antonescu's wife, in her capacity as head of the Consiliul de Patronaj (Welfare Council), an umbrella organization of welfare institutions serving the soldiers and the surviving dependents of those killed in action. The total amount of these contributions to the Consiliul by the Centrala under Ghingold's administration exceeded the amount it spent on assisting the Jews who had been forced into the labor battalions or had been deported to TRANSNISTRIA.

The Centrala took no part in the struggle waged by the clandestine Consiliul Evreesc (Jewish Council), founded by Wilhelm FILDERMAN, against the implementation of the plans for the deportation of Romanian Jews to Poland, an issue that was coming to a head in the summer of 1942. The Romanian authorities, for their part, no longer considered Ghingold and his assistants to be genuine representatives of the Jews, and by June 1942, the minister of the interior, as well as other members of the cabinet, resumed the practice of consulting Filderman on all issues affecting the fate of the Jews.

When the threat of extermination by the Germans receded, Ghingold gradually came to change his attitude and was less and less inclined to assist the Zionist movement and the Jews in general. He had never thought of himself as representing the Jews, but rather as dealing with Jewish affairs on behalf of the Romanian government.

With the shift in Romanian policy on the Jews, the Centrala, in 1943 and 1944, increasingly assumed the traditional functions of the Union of Jewish Communities in organizing welfare operations and meeting the spiritual and material needs of the Jews, under the intolerable conditions created by the Romanian authorities. Under the law, the veteran Jewish leaders and institutions had to go through the Centrala; without it they could not send aid to the deportees in Transnistria or help the forty thousand Jews on forced labor and their families. When it became clear that a German defeat in the war was gradually becoming inevitable, more and more funds were made available for welfare operations, drawn from the various regular and special taxes and levies imposed on the Jews. In the Centrala, too, a growing number of officials were willing to be of help to the deportees and to divert funds for that purpose. Ghingold had an understanding of the situation and in general did not interfere with these efforts. On the other hand, he provided the impetus for Filderman's deportation to Transnistria, by transmitting to Lecca and Antonescu a memorandum that Filderman had addressed to him personally, protesting against the special levy of 4 billion lei ($35 million) that Antonescu had imposed on the Jews in May 1943—and against which Ghingold did not protest.

Under Ghingold's lead the Centrala retained power and influence among a part of the Jewish population, especially those Jews who were in need of the coveted certificate of exemption from forced labor. This was a way of extorting special payments from wealthy Jews and members of the professions, in exchange for enabling them to keep on earning a living and staying in their jobs. Using the Centrala staff, Lecca turned the exemption certificate into a lucrative source of income for himself and for the political figures and officials that he favored. Mihai ANTONESCU, the deputy prime minister, also ordered Lecca to provide funds for various purposes from this source. Other recipients of bribes from Lecca, from the same source—the Centrala—were staff members of the German legation. Ghingold himself never took a bribe, but he remained convinced that more money could be obtained from the wealthy Jews and that, willingly or unwillingly, they should contribute more, both for the welfare work of the Centrala and for the large payments that had to be made to the state treasury, or diverted to the pockets of government officials.

When it became obvious that the Centrala's days were numbered, Ghingold and his associates, like the rest of the Romanian establishment under Antonescu, collected recommendations for themselves certifying their "good conduct" and asserting that they had acted in behalf of the repatriation of the orphans and deportees. The Centrala executive officers were well aware of the bad reputation they had among the Jews, owing to the heavy payments they had extracted and their readiness to cooperate with the Romanian authorities.

In December 1944, after the liberation, the Centrala was disbanded and the Union of Jewish Communities was reinstated. The Centrala chiefs were put on trial and sentenced to long prison terms. Ghingold was released after ten years; he was rehabilitated, and until his death in 1988 practiced medicine on the staff of a leading Bucharest hospital.

BIBLIOGRAPHY

Ancel, J. *Romania.* Jerusalem, 1989.

Ancel, J., ed. *Documents concerning the Fate of Romanian Jewry during the Holocaust.* Vol. 7. Jerusalem, 1986.

JEAN ANCEL

CENTRAL COMMITTEE OF GERMAN JEWS FOR RELIEF AND RECONSTRUCTION. *See* Zentralausschuss der Deutschen Juden für Hilfe und Aufbau.

CENTRAL CONSISTORY OF FRENCH JEWS. *See* Consistoire Central des Israélites de France.

CENTRAL OFFICE FOR JEWISH EMIGRATION. *See* Zentralstelle für Jüdische Auswanderung.

CENTRAL OFFICE OF THE JUDICIAL ADMINISTRATIONS OF THE LÄNDER FOR INVESTIGATION OF NAZI CRIMES, LUDWIGSBURG. *See* Ludwigsburger Zentralstelle.

CENTRAL RESETTLEMENT OFFICE. *See* Umwandererzentralstelle.

CENTRAL UNION OF GERMAN CITIZENS OF JEWISH FAITH. *See* Centralverein Deutscher Staatsbürger Jüdischen Glaubens.

CENTRALVEREIN DER JUDEN IN DEUTSCHLAND. *See* Centralverein Deutscher Staatsbürger Jüdischen Glaubens.

CENTRALVEREIN DEUTSCHER STAATSBÜRGER JÜDISCHEN GLAUBENS (Central Union of German Citizens of Jewish Faith; CV), an organization, active between 1893 and 1938, that aimed to safeguard the civil and social equality of the Jews of GERMANY while fostering their German identity.

With the rise of the antisemitic movement in Germany in the last quarter of the nineteenth century, a central Jewish organization was founded to defend Jewish civil and social equality. At the time of its founding in 1893, the organization was accepted with reservations in the Jewish community; its ideas, however, were quickly absorbed. The number of members rose from 2,000 in 1894 to 72,500 in 1924. Many others belonged through the collective adherence of associated groups. At the peak of its activity the CV was the largest organization of German Jews, and regarded itself as their representative. Its first heads were Maximilian Horowitz (1893–1917) and Eugen Fuchs (1917–1919).

Until World War I the organization worked principally through legal channels and conducted information activity (called *Abwehrkampf,* "defense struggle"), mainly in an apologetic manner. In face of rising antisemitism after World War I, precedence was given to working through political channels. Contacts were made with parties and organizations supporting the republic and taking a stand against extreme German nationalism, especially Nazi nationalism. During the electoral campaigns, propaganda material was distributed in millions of copies. In 1929 a special archive was founded to collect the most complete information in Germany on Nazi activities and intentions. A special service placed material from that data bank at the disposal of newspapers and parties. Prior to the elections of September 1930, in which the Nazis made a decisive political breakthrough, the CV and the Zionists worked together, but the partnership was soon broken owing to doctrinal and practical disagreements.

Alongside this political activity, the CV's information activity expanded. Its monthly journal, *Im Deutschen Reich,* which had appeared since 1894, merged in 1922 with the long-standing Jewish journal *Allgemeine Zeitung des Judentums* and subsequently became a weekly called *Zeitung-CV,* which was also distributed to non-Jewish subscribers. An ideological and literary biweekly, *Der Morgen,* served the intelligentsia. The prominent leaders of the CV between the two world wars were Julius Brodnitz, Ludwig Holländer, and Alfred Wiener.

The CV placed stress on fostering German awareness and saw Jewry as a religious and spiritual group only; consequently, it adopted a negative attitude toward Zionism. At the same time some of its leaders, particularly the younger ones, demanded that the CV view the settlement enterprises in Palestine positively, if only because of the obligation of Jewish solidarity. Eventually most of the CV representatives at the head of the central institutions of German Jewry came from this pro-Palestine circle.

With the Nazi rise to power, the "defense" activity became insufficient, and the CV had to adapt to the new conditions. The *Zeitung-CV* attempted to continue its defense policy through declarations, such as "We shall be on our guard and firmly defend ourselves, in accordance with the constitution, against any effort to encroach on our rights." It continually reminded President Paul von HINDENBURG and the German conservatives participating in Hitler's government of their duty to defend the rights of all citizens without religious differentiation. At the same time, a legal office was established under CV direction, since the organization clearly recognized that only through legal channels could the rights of the Jews still be defended.

The CV launched a comprehensive information campaign, both within its own organization and on the invitation of Jewish communities. Tens of thousands of German Jews, avid for encouragement and guidance, came to hear the heads of the CV, most of whom tried to soothe the community and encourage its attachment to the German homeland. But when Nazi attacks persisted, and particularly after the blow of the anti-Jewish BOYCOTT of April 1, 1933, a new policy was adopted that encouraged independent Jewish organization and activity. CV members also helped sponsor the REICHSVERTRETUNG DER DEUTSCHEN JUDEN (Reich Representation of German Jews), created in September 1933, relying on cooperation between the various Jewish organizations. The CV organized independent educational and religious activities, and for a short time even hoped that this could constitute the basis for an arrangement with the government, a second "emancipation" (the first being the civil and political emancipation, culminating in 1871, of Germany's Jews) that would establish recognition of the Jews of Germany as a separate group in the country. These hopes were shattered by the new government's unrelenting hostility. The CV's change of attitude toward independent Jewish activity could be seen in the *Zeitung-CV*, which expanded, added sections, and began to publicize German Jewish activities in all fields.

In the fall of 1935, after the promulgation of the NUREMBERG LAWS, the CV was obliged to change its name to Centralverein der Juden in Deutschland (Central Union of Jews in Germany). After 1935 the organization increasingly recognized emigration and vocational training as its chief priorities. At the same time, the ideological and organizational struggles with other viewpoints (principally Zionism) continued, both in the CV publications and in the local and national institutions. With the passage of time, however, those disputes were restricted more and more to the theoretical sphere. In 1936 the CV changed its name to the Jüdischer Centralverein. The organization's last chairman, Ernst Herzfeld, stated in 1937 that the only difference of opinion between its members and the Zionists was whether emigration to countries other than Palestine should be welcomed or merely accepted as a necessary evil.

The CV ceased to exist as an independent group after the KRISTALLNACHT disturbances of November 1938. Like other Jewish bodies, it was incorporated into the compulsory new central organization, the Reichsvereinigung der Juden in Deutschland (Reich Association of Jews in Germany), established on July 4, 1939 (*see* Appendix, Volume 4). Its representatives continued to occupy central positions in the leadership of German Jewry.

BIBLIOGRAPHY

Hirschberg, A. "Der Centralverein Deutscher Staatsbürger Jüdischen Glaubens." In *Festschrift für Leo Baeck*. Berlin, 1970.

Paucker, A. *Der Abwehrkampf gegen Antisemitismus und Nationalsozialismus in den letzten Jahren der Weimarer Republik*. Hamburg, 1969.

Paucker, A. "Jewish Self-Defence." In *The Jews in Nazi Germany, 1933–1943*, edited by A. Paucker. Tübingen, 1986.

Reinharz, J. *Fatherland and Promised Land: The Dilemma of the German Jew, 1893–1914*. Ann Arbor, 1975.

Schorsch, I. *The Jewish Reaction to German Antisemitism, 1870–1914*. New York, 1972.

YEHOYAKIM COCHAVI

CENTRAL WELFARE COUNCIL. *See* Rada Główna Opiekuncza.

CENTRE DE DOCUMENTATION JUIVE CONTEMPORAINE. *See* Documentation Centers: Centre de Documentation Juive Contemporaine.

CENTRO DI DOCUMENTAZIONE EBRAICA CONTEMPORANEA. *See* Documentation Centers: Centro di Documentazione Ebraica Contemporanea.

CERNĂUŢI. *See* Chernovtsy.

CFGJ. *See* Council for German Jewry.

CGQJ. *See* Commissariat Général aux Questions Juives.

CHAMBERLAIN, HOUSTON STEWART (1855–1927), racial ideologist and major figure in modern ANTISEMITISM. An Englishman who opted for German nationality, Chamberlain is important for his role as an ideological link between older racist theories and Nazism (*see* RACISM). His book *Die Grundlagen des 19. Jahrhunderts* (The Foundations of the Nineteenth Century; 1899) combined racial theory with a vitalist philosophy and cultural criticism, creating a universal world view with markedly conservative traits.

Holding physical and moral inequality to be the basis of human existence, Chamberlain saw all of Western history in terms of a race struggle. He maintained that Jesus' "Aryan doctrine" had been racially poisoned by Judaism. This deformation of an "Aryan religion" by the Jew Paul in the racial chaos of the Roman empire had determined all of Euopean history and constituted what Chamberlain called "the foundation of the nineteenth century." Since then a constant war had been waged that, he wrote, had still not reached its end. The Germans, the legitimate rulers of the world as the last branch of the Aryan tree, had not attained their goal: the radical suppression of Judaism and redemption of the world from racial chaos. Only the Aryans were capable of a "creative culture," and therefore their intermingling with "inferior races" would lead to decline and degeneration.

Chamberlain's writings are a mixture of Richard Wagner's race mysticism, the racial theories of Joseph-Arthur de Gobineau and Paul de Lagarde, the biblical and philological studies of Julius Wellhausen, popular Darwinism, the vulgar empiricism of Ernst Haeckel, and other contemporary trends. He appealed to the Nazis because of his optimistic historical perspective on Germany's mission to liberate mankind from the Jewish race. Chamberlain rejected Gobineau's racial pessimism and the scientific natural monism of Social Darwinists, whose theories, he thought, led to a passive attitude of resignation toward the inevitable and deterministic process of decay. His racial theories exerted a deep influence on his contemporaries, including Emperor Wilhelm II, who was one of Chamberlain's devoted readers, corresponding with him and awarding him the Iron Cross for his publications; Alfred ROSENBERG's *The Myth of the Twentieth Century* was based largely on his ideas. Chamberlain saw in Adolf HITLER the man who would implement his theories.

BIBLIOGRAPHY

Field, G. G. *Evangelist of Race: The German Vision of Houston Chamberlain.* New York, 1981.

Mosse, G. *Towards the Final Solution: A History of European Racism.* New York, 1980.

Stackelberg, R. J. "Houston S. Chamberlain: From Monarchism to National Socialism." *Wiener Library Bulletin* 31/2 (1978): 118–125.

DAVID BANKIER

CHAMBON-SUR-LIGNON. *See* Le Chambon-sur-Lignon.

CHEŁMNO (Ger., Kulmhof), the first Nazi camp in which mass executions were carried out by means of gas, and the first site for mass killings within the framework of the "FINAL SOLUTION" outside the area of Nazi occupation in the USSR. The camp was destined to serve as a center for the extermination of the Jews in the ŁÓDŹ ghetto and the entire WARTHEGAU region, which had been annexed to the Third Reich. It was located in the Polish village of Chełmno, 47 miles (70 km) west of Łódź, in the Koło district. A total of 320,000 people were put to death there.

The camp was set up on two sites, 2.5 miles (4 km) apart: (1) the camp in the Schloss, an old palace inside the village, which served as a reception and extermination center for the victims and as a residence for the camp staff; and (2) the Waldlager, a camp in the adjacent Rzuwowski Forest, in which mass graves and cremation ovens were later found.

To administer and operate the camp, a special unit was set up, called Sonderkommando Kulmhof, also known as Sonderkommando Lange and, later, Sonderkommando Bothmann, after its first commandant, Hauptsturmführer Herbert Lange and, from March 1942, Hauptsturmführer Hans BOTHMANN.

Sonderkommando Kulmhof consisted of members of the Sicherheitspolizei (Security Police; Sipo) and the Schutzpolizei (regular uniformed police). Twenty members of Sipo held central posts in the camp. Some one hundred and twenty Schutzpolizei were divided into secondary units: the Transportkommando, the Schlosskommando, and the Waldkommando.

The Transportkommando operated mainly at the nearby Powiercie railway station, to which most of the victims were brought. Its function was to reinforce the German guard that had accompanied the deportees and to transport the latter in trucks to the Schloss camp.

The Schlosskommando guarded the palace camp and participated in the killing process. The Waldkommando, which operated in the forest camp, formed two cordons whose purpose was to ensure that no one approached the camp or saw what was happening inside. This unit also supervised the unloading of the victims' corpses, their burial, and, later, their cremation.

Sonderkommando Kulmhof was directly subject to the REICHSSICHERHEITSHAUPTAMT (Reich Security Main Office; RSHA) in Berlin. However, the governor of the Warthegau region, Arthur GREISER; the SS commander in the Warthegau, Wilhelm KOPPE; and the head of the Łódź ghetto administration, Hans BIEBOW, all concerned themselves with the affairs of the camp as well. Members of the camp staff received for their services a special increment of twelve to fifteen reichsmarks in their wages.

The deportees were generally brought in freight trains, to the Koło junction. From there they were transferred to another train, running on a narrow-gauge track, which proceeded to the Powiercie station. Sometimes the victims were taken in trucks straight from their dwelling places to Chełmno. Throughout the journey, the transports were always heavily guarded by German police. For example, transports from the Łódź ghetto went in a twelve-car train accompanied by a special unit consisting of 155 German police.

Jews of Sompolno, a town 90 miles (145 km) west of Warsaw, waiting to be transported to the Chełmno extermination camp (beginning of February 1942).

The victims were first concentrated in the courtyard of the Schloss, where they were reassured that they were being sent to a work camp and were to wash while their clothes were being disinfected. They were then taken in groups of fifty—men, women, and children together—to the ground floor of the Schloss, where they were told to strip. Here their valuables were collected in baskets that would supposedly be marked with their names.

The victims were then taken to the cellar, past signs reading "To the Washroom" hung on the passage door and stairway. From there they were brought to an enclosed ramp made of boards and slanted downward. At the end of the ramp stood a gas van with its doors open. The moment the victims entered the ramp, the Germans forced them, with blows, to run toward the bottom and into the van. They had no alternative other than to enter it.

Beginning in December 1941, three gas vans were operated in the Chełmno camp. They were Renault trucks, two of medium size and one larger, hermetically sealed inside and with double back doors. On the outside they looked like furniture delivery vans. The enclosed space within the van was from 13 to 15 feet (4 to 5 m) long, 6.75 feet (2.2 m) wide, and 6.5 feet (2 m) high; fifty to seventy people were crammed into each van, which was lined inside with galvanized tin. On the tin floor a wooden lattice was laid, under which a hole had been drilled and a metal pipe soldered into the hole. On the outside of the truck, the other end of this pipe was connected to a flexible exhaust pipe, through which carbon monoxide was pumped into the enclosure within the van.

After the van had been filled with people, the driver closed and locked the doors, entered the truck's cab, and switched on the motor. For ten minutes the victims within suffocated from the gas. Once they were dead, the pipe was detached from its connection

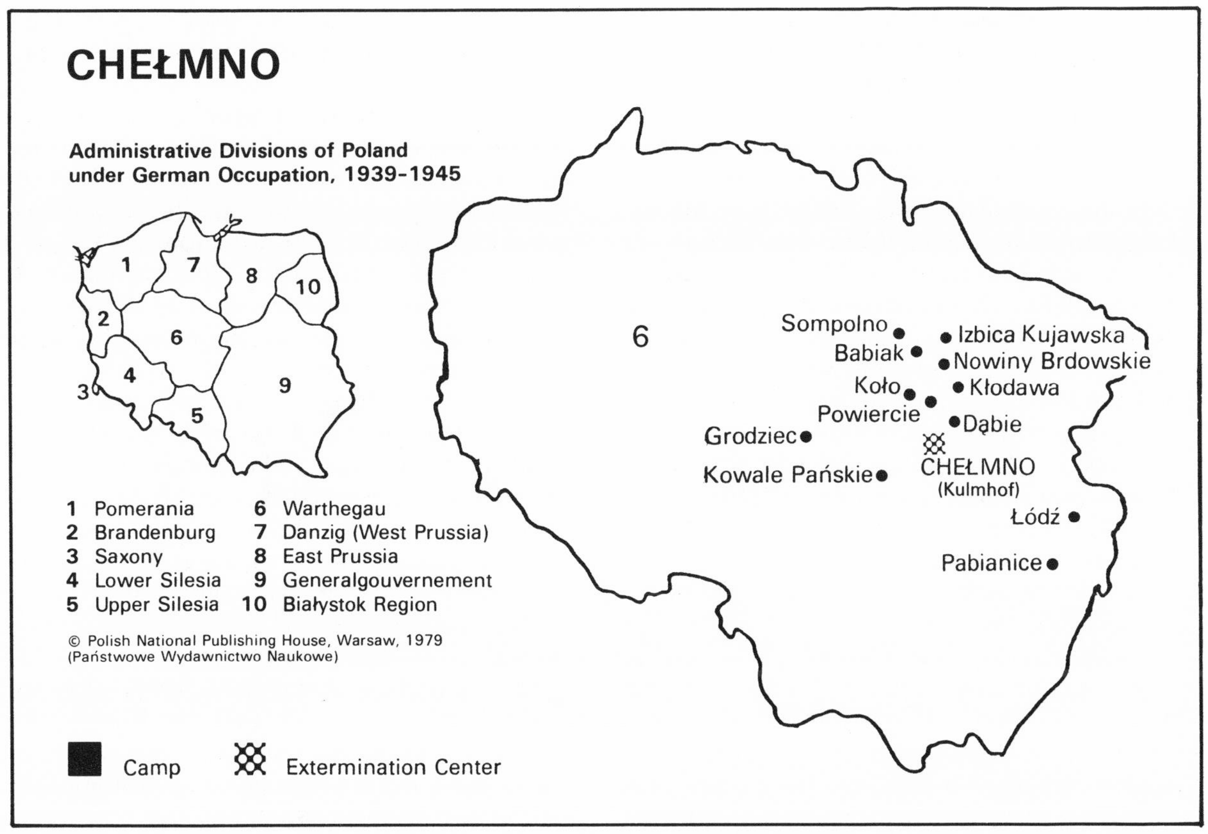

with the vehicle, which proceeded to the Waldlager. Here there were three clearings, separated by avenues of trees, in which four mass graves were located. Here, as of the summer of 1942, there were also two crematoria, 32.5 feet (10 m) long and 16 to 19 feet (5 to 6 m) wide.

From among the batches of deportees who reached Chełmno, a few men were selected to replenish a group totaling thirty to forty who were compelled to work as gravediggers; the weakest among them were regularly shot. This group had to take the fresh corpses out of the gas vans and bury them in the mass graves in the clearing (and, later, burn them in the cremation ovens). At nighttime the gravediggers were taken back to the Schlosslager and held in a locked room under heavy guard. These prisoners made many attempts to escape, and two of them succeeded, Moroka Podchlebnik and Jacob GROJANOWSKI (this may have been a pseudonym). Grojanowski, who arrived at Chełmno on January 6, 1942, escaped on January 19. At the end of that month he managed to reach the WARSAW ghetto, where he gave very detailed information on what was happening in the camp to ONEG SHABBAT, the underground archive headed by Emanuel RINGELBLUM. Grojanowski's report was passed on to the Polish underground, which sent it to the POLISH GOVERNMENT-IN-EXILE. In this manner, all the details about the Chełmno camp were known in London by June 1942.

The first transports to Chełmno began on December 7, 1941, and the camp began to operate on the following day. The first victims were Jews from the communities in the area: Koło, Dąbie, Sompolno, Kłodawa, Babiak, Dęby Szlacheckie, Kowale Pańskie, Izbica Kujawska, Nowiny Brdowskie, and Grodziec. The early victims also included five thousand GYPSIES who had been imprisoned in a separate section of the Łódź ghetto.

In mid-January 1942, the deportations from the Łódź ghetto began. Between January 16 and 29, 10,003 Jews were taken from the ghetto and killed at Chełmno; from February 22 to April 2, 34,073; from May 4 to 15, 11,680; and from September 5 to 12, 15,859. These numbers included Jews from Germany, Austria, Czechoslovakia, and Luxembourg who had first been expelled to the Łódź ghetto. In addition, 15,000 Jews sent from the Łódź ghetto to forced-labor camps in the Warthegau region were put to death.

In the course of 1942, Jews from all the other thirty-six places of Jewish settlement in the Warthegau region were transported to Chełmno for extermination. A few hundred Poles were also sent there, as well as Soviet prisoners of war and eighty-eight Czechoslovak children from the village of LIDICE.

The possessions and clothes brought by the victims to Chełmno were shipped to warehouses established in the town of Pabianice by the Nazi administration of the Łódź ghetto, headed by Hans Biebow. These articles were then distributed or sold to the German population of the Warthegau.

In March 1943 the transports to Chełmno came to an end, since the entire Jewish population of the Warthegau, except in the Łódź ghetto, had been exterminated. The Nazi authorities dismantled the camp, and the Schloss was demolished. The camp staff was transferred to Yugoslavia and incorporated into the "Prinz Eugen" Division of the Waffen-SS, which fought the Yugoslav partisans.

In April 1944, in connection with the planned liquidation of the Łódź ghetto, the Nazis decided to renew their extermination activities at Chełmno. Hans Bothmann and other members of Sonderkommando Kulmhof were brought back from Yugoslavia for this purpose and were joined by new camp staff, including Walter Piller, who was appointed deputy commandant. The camp was reconstituted in the former Waldlager. Here, two huts, each 66 feet (20 m) long and 33 feet (10 m) wide, were built to receive the victims, in addition to two new crematoria.

On June 23, 1944, transports to Chełmno from the Łódź ghetto began anew, and by July 14, 7,176 persons had been killed. The system was similar to that previously used: the victims, brought by truck, were told that they were going to work in Germany and that they must wash themselves while their clothes were being disinfected. Assembled in groups of seventy to ninety, they stripped, then went through a door with the sign "To the Washroom" on it, to a passageway 78 feet (25 m) long, fenced off on both sides. The passageway led to a slope, at the end of which stood a gas van.

In mid-July, to accelerate the pace of liquidating the Łódź ghetto, the Nazis halted the transports to Chełmno and began to send the ghetto's surviving residents to AUSCHWITZ, where the pace of extermination by ZYKLON B gas was ten times faster. Sonderkommando Kulmhof was transferrred to Łódź and, together with other German units, was occupied until the end of August 1944 with the final liquidation of the ghetto and the deportations of its inhabitants to Auschwitz. At the beginning of September 1944, Sonderkommando Kulmhof returned to Chełmno. Together with Sonderkommando 1005, it oversaw the exhumation and cremation of the corpses, since a decision had been made to obliterate all signs of the mass murders. The work was done by a group of fifty Jewish prisoners.

On the night of January 17, 1945, when the Red Army was approaching, the Nazis abandoned Chełmno. As they were executing the forty-eight Jewish prisoners remaining in the camp, the latter resisted, and three managed to escape. The others were killed.

After the war, a detailed description of the camp, what happened there, and the daily life of the Nazi staff was given to the American authorities in West Germany by Heinrich May, a former Nazi who was *Forstmeister* (forest inspector) in Precinct 77 of the Warthegau during Chełmno's existence.

From 1947 to 1950, trials were held in Poland of two staff members of the camp, Walter Piller and Hermann Gielow. Both were sentenced to death. Later, from 1962 to 1965, a trial of twelve of the camp's staff was held in West Germany. Three of them were sentenced to thirteen years' imprisonment, and one to seven years'; the others received only light punishment.

BIBLIOGRAPHY

Bednarz, W. *Obóz stracen w Chełmnie nad Nerem.* Warsaw, 1946.

Gutman, Y., and A. Saf, eds. *The Nazi Concentration Camps: Structure and Aims; The Image of the Prisoner; The Jews in the Camps.* Proceedings of the Fourth Yad Vashem Historical Conference. Jerusalem, 1984.

Krakowski, S. "In Kulmhof stationierte Gaswagen." In *Nationalsozialistische Massentötungen durch Giftgas,* edited by E. Kogon, H. Langbein, and A. Rückerl, pp. 110–145. Frankfurt, 1983.

SHMUEL KRAKOWSKI

CHERNOVTSY (Rom., Cernăuţi; Ger., Czernowitz), district center of Chernovtsy Oblast and former capital of BUKOVINA. Up to 1918, Chernovtsy was under Austrian rule; from 1918 to 1940 it was part of Romania. Its Jewish population in 1930 was 46,000, 40 percent of the total. In June 1940, Chernovtsy was incorporated into the Soviet Union. At first many Jews welcomed the Soviets, in the hope that they would put an end to antisemitic persecution, which had become much worse in the final phase of the Romanian regime's control of the province. The Soviets, however, brought Jewish national life to an end, and their policy of confiscating property and other assets severely affected the Jews. On June 13, 1941, some ten thousand Jews were arrested, most of them from Chernovtsy, and exiled to Siberia—among them community and Zionist leaders, persons who had owned property, and others who were seized at random. Many of these deportees were to perish in the camps from cold, starvation, and disease.

On June 30, 1941, eight days after the German invasion of the Soviet Union, the Soviets evacuated Chernovtsy after setting fire to several public buildings, thereby causing fires in the city center. Earlier, many Jews had been drafted into the Soviet army and moved from the city. Romanian and German troops who entered Chernovtsy, as well as local Romanian and Ukrainian inhabitants, systematically ransacked Jewish houses, murdered Jews, raped Jewish women, and abused the Jews in various ways. A large number of Jews were arrested, and some six hundred were killed by Einsatzkommando 10b and its Romanian helpers.

Einsatzgruppe D moved its headquarters into Chernovtsy on July 10, and on the insistence of its commander, Otto OHLENDORF, even more stringent measures were adopted against the Jews. Approximately 1,500 Jews were seized by Einsatzkommando 10b, most of them young people and intelligentsia, and murdered with the help of the Romanian police. The chief rabbi, Dr. Abraham Mark, was among the victims; the Great Synagogue was also set on fire on this occasion. In early August, Einsatzkommando 10b murdered another 682 Jews. The Romanian authorities, who had been given full control of the city, introduced various discriminatory measures: Jews had to wear the yellow badge (*see* BADGE, JEWISH), Jewish houses had to bear the sign *Jude* on them, Jews were prohibited from moving about at certain hours and in certain districts, and they had their food rations reduced, were put on unpaid FORCED LABOR, and were used as hostages.

On October 11, 1941, all the Jews in the city, over fifty thousand in all, were concentrated in a small area consisting of a few side streets; their property and assets were confiscated in favor of the Romanian National Bank. This action was taken on the order of the Romanian governor, Corneliu Calotescu, despite the opposition of the mayor, Traian Popovici. Most of the Romanian government officials were antisemites, supporters of the movements led by Alexandru CUZA and the IRON GUARD. On October 10 the local authorities were told of the order given by Ion ANTONESCU, the Romanian dictator, to deport the city's Jews to TRANSNISTRIA. The order was transmitted verbally, by two high-ranking officers of the Romanian general staff, to ensure that no written evidence of it would remain.

During the Festival of Tabernacles (October 12, 1941), the deportation to Transnistria began. The first transport consisted of 6,000 Jews, who were taken away in cattle cars. Heading the column of deportees were Rabbi Mordechai Fridmann of Boian and Rabbi Eliezer Hager; they carried Torah scrolls in their arms and were surrounded by Hasidim. The second transport left on October 17. The transports continued until November 15, when Antonescu ordered a halt. A total of 28,391 Jews were deported in October and November 1941 to Transnistria, by way of the MARCULEŞTI camp in Bessarabia. The 20,000 Jews left in Chernovtsy had been issued special permits certifying that they were "useful" for the economy. In the hope that this would save them from deportation,

CHERNOVTSY

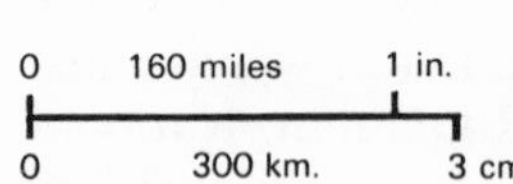

Annexations from June to September 1940: (1) Bessarabia and (2) N. Bukovina to USSR; (3) N. Transylvania to Hungary; (4) S. Dobruja to Bulgaria.

1,500 Jews converted to Christianity, but the authorities strongly disapproved, and many Jews were put on trial and sentenced to prison for having gone through a mock conversion. On June 4, 1942, the transports were resumed: 2,000 Jews were deported to Transnistria by way of the Atachi border post. Some were handed over to the SS and taken across the Bug River, where most of them were murdered. A second transport left on June 13 with 200 Jews aboard, some of them mentally ill; a third transport left on June 28. Altogether, 5,000 Jews were deported to Transnistria in the three transports, and by November 1943, 4,500 were dead. The mortality rate among the children deported to Transnistria was 100 percent, and among adults it reached 70 percent.

While the transports were leaving Chernovtsy, and for some time thereafter, Romanians from all over the country—businessmen and others—flocked into the city and seized control of the industrial plants and commercial enterprises that the Jews had left behind or that had been confiscated from them; some of the plants were dismantled and moved to the interior of the country. The sixteen thousand Jews left in Chernovtsy were in dire straits, most of them having taken on any work that could save them from deportation. In October 1943 the yellow badge and the restrictions on movement in the city were abolished. When the Red Army was approaching, the authorities barred the Jews from leaving the city as the Romanian residents were doing. Early in February of 1944, Chernovtsy was under the control of the German army, and it was only the city's swift liberation by the Soviet forces that made it impossible for the Germans to liquidate the remnants of the Jewish community. In April 1945 all but two thousand of the surviving native Chernovtsy Jews left the city and, by way of Romania, made their way to Palestine.

BIBLIOGRAPHY

Ancel, J., and T. Lavi, eds. *Rumania,* vol. 2. In *Pinkas Hakehillot; Encyclopaedia of Jewish Communities.* Jerusalem, 1980. See pages 487–511. (In Hebrew.)

Carp, M. *Transnistria.* Vol. 3 of *Cartea Neagră.* Bucharest, 1947.

Mircu, M. *Pogromurile din Bucovina si Dorohoi.* Bucharest, 1945. See pages 66–96.

Yavetz, Z. "Youth Movements in Czernowitz." *Jewish Heritage* 14 (Spring 1972): 9–18.

JEAN ANCEL

CHETNIKS (Serb., Četniki, from *četa,* "platoon"), Serbian guerrilla units that fought against the Turks and, in World War I, against Austro-Hungarian and German forces. In World War II, the Chetniks were armed bands of Serbs active in YUGOSLAVIA during its occupation (1941–1945). They had in common their loyalty to the Yugoslav royal house, aiming to restore it to the throne after the war, and their commitment to a relentless struggle against the partisan forces led by TITO.

The first Chetnik units came into being shortly after the Yugoslav army's surrender to the Germans in April 1941, on the initiative of Col. Draža Mihajlović, an officer of the Yugoslav general staff. Mihajlović gathered around himself Yugoslav soldiers fleeing the Germans and began to organize them in the Fruska Gora Mountains of central Serbia.

Mihajlović's men in Serbia took part in the uprising against the Germans in July and August of 1941, even cooperating with the partisans under Tito. The uprising was suppressed by the Germans with unspeakable cruelty, causing many deaths and widespread destruction. This brought the Chetniks to three conclusions: (1) there was no point in waging a hopeless armed struggle against the Germans, a struggle that would threaten the very existence of the Serbian people; (2) the proper course was to organize and gain strength, so as to be ready for an Allied invasion of the Balkans; (3) the pro-Communist partisans were the most dangerous enemy of all, and it was the struggle with them that would decide Yugoslavia's fate after Germany was defeated.

These conclusions exacerbated the differences between the partisans and the Chetniks, which before long turned into a civil war. The Chetniks' struggle with the invaders came to a complete stop at the end of 1941, and gradually evolved into cooperation with the Italians and the Germans against Tito.

At first, the western Allies had viewed the Chetniks as the core of the resistance movements in Yugoslavia against the invaders. But reports from British parachutists who had joined the fighting forces in Yugoslavia began to reach the West, indicating that the Chetniks' policy was to fight the partisans under Tito, rather than the Germans and their allies. Consequently, the attitude of the western Allies underwent a change in the second half of 1942, and they switched their aid to the partisans who were fighting the Germany enemy. By the end of 1943, the break between the West and the Chetniks was complete. The Chetniks had become collaborators and had joined the forces fighting the partisans. After the occupation of Serbia by the partisans and the Red Army, the Chetniks were hunted down. Shortly after the end of the war, Mihajlović and his men were captured and brought before a Yugoslav national tribunal; most were hanged.

At the initial stage, there were some Jews among the Chetniks, but when it turned out that the Chetniks were not fighting the invaders and their collaborators, and in fact were inclined to cooperate with them, the Jews switched to the ranks of the partisans. As the Chetniks increased their cooperation with the Germans, their attitude toward the Jews in the areas under their control deteriorated, and they identified the Jews with the hated Communists. There were many instances of Chetniks' murdering Jews or handing them over to the Germans.

BIBLIOGRAPHY

Millazzo, M. *The Chetnik Movement and the Yugoslav Resistance.* Baltimore, 1975.

Tomasevich, J. *The Chetniks: War and Revolution in Yugoslavia, 1941–1945.* Stanford, 1975.

MENACHEM SHELAH

CHILDREN. *See* André, Joseph; Beccari, Arrigo; Frank, Anne; Korczak, Janusz; Nèvejean, Yvonne; N.V. Group; Oeuvre de Secours aux Enfants; Rescue of Children, United States; "Tehran Children"; Union des Juifs pour la Résistance et l'Entr'aide; Van der Voort, Hanna.

CHILDREN'S AID SOCIETY. *See* Oeuvre de Secours aux Enfants.

CHIŞINĂU. *See* Kishinev.

CHOMS, WŁADYSŁAWA (1891–1966), Polish rescuer of Jews during the Holocaust. Choms headed the Lvov branch of ZEGOTA (the Polish Council for Aid to Jews), a Polish underground organization based in Warsaw. Before the war, in Drogobych, Eastern Galicia, where she headed the municipal welfare department, and in Lvov, where she was active in combating antisemitism, she showed a particular concern for the welfare of the Jewish people. With the German occupation of Lvov in June 1941, she became wholeheartedly involved in charitable work on behalf of destitute Jews. Collecting jewelry and money from wealthy Jews, she created a fund for extending aid to Jews, and rallied around her a group of devoted persons.

Aid came in various forms: the forging of false documents for Jews living outside the restricted ghetto perimeter; provision of money, food, and medical care for Jews inside and outside the ghetto; and the removal of Jewish children and adults from the ghetto

Władysława Choms in the Hall of Remembrance at Yad Vashem, Jerusalem, on May 22, 1963, when she received her award as a "Righteous among the Nations." She is in the front row, fourth from the left. To the right is the Eternal Flame.

to secure shelters in convents and with private families. Some sixty Jewish children were under her personal supervision.

Sought by the Germans (her officer-husband and son had fled to England and were known to have enlisted in the struggle against Nazi Germany), Choms was constantly on the move, ever changing names and addresses. In November 1942, while supervising a well-established rescue network in Lvov, she was elected by the Warsaw-based Zegota to establish and head a local branch in Lvov. Nicknamed the "Angel of Lvov" by her Jewish beneficiaries, she continued her charitable activities until November 1943, when, with the increasing threat to her personal safety, she was dispatched to Warsaw by her underground superiors.

After the war, Choms learned that her son, a pilot in the Royal Air Force, had been shot down and killed in 1941. She was recognized as a "RIGHTEOUS AMONG THE NATIONS," and planted a tree at YAD VASHEM in Jerusalem in 1963.

BIBLIOGRAPHY

Bartoszewski, W., and Z. Lewin, eds. *Righteous among Nations: How Poles Helped the Jews, 1939–1945*. London, 1969.

MORDECAI PALDIEL

CHORTKOV (Pol., Czortków), city in Ternopol Oblast (district), Ukrainian SSR. Until 1918, Chortkov belonged to Austrian-held Eastern Galicia, and in the interwar period to independent Poland. In September 1939, together with the rest of eastern Poland, Chortkov was occupied by the Red Army and annexed to the Ukrainian SSR.

Jews had been living in Chortkov since the sixteenth century. In the nineteenth century it was a center of Hasidism and the residence of a Hasidic rabbi. On the eve of World War II its Jewish population numbered six thousand.

The Germans took the city on July 6, 1941. On July 10 the Ukrainians, with German help, staged a pogrom, seizing Jews in the streets and murdering 300 of them in the city jail. On July 28 German police killed 150 Jews in the adjacent Czarny Las (Black Forest). Various decrees were enacted against the Jews, restricting their economic activities and freedom of movement and drafting them for forced labor. At the end of July a JUDENRAT (Jewish Council) was appointed, and on August 20 a 25,000-ruble collective fine was imposed on the Jews. Some members of the Judenrat, including the chairman, were arrested on October 12 and were murdered a few days later. On October 15 the Germans seized 200 Jews, mostly professionals, and murdered them in the Czarny Las.

Over a period of two months, beginning in the middle of November, groups of Jews were sent for forced labor to the Kamionka, Hluboczek, Borki Wielkie, and Stupki camps, and even as far as the JANÓWSKA camp in Lvov. In April 1942 a ghetto was established in Chortkov. Many of its inhabitants fell victim to the overcrowding, the lack of sanitation, and the epidemics that broke out. On August 27 an *Aktion* was carried out in which some six hundred Jews were murdered in the streets. It was followed by a *Selektion* that resulted in the deportation to the BEŁŻEC extermination camp of 2,000 Jews, most of whom were not in possession of work passes. In September the ghetto area was further reduced and conditions deteriorated even more. A second *Aktion* took place on October 5 that led to the sending of five hundred Jews to Bełżec.

On December 15 the Germans set up a work camp in Chortkov, populating it with over five hundred artisans and putting them to work,

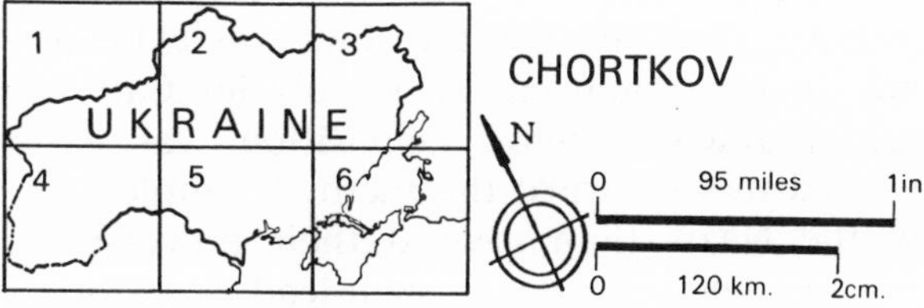

mainly for the German army. During the rest of 1942 and the early part of 1943, the Germans murdered many dozens of Jews from the work camp. Most of the camp's remaining inmates were killed on June 23, 1943, in a forest on the road to Jagielnica; the rest were transferred to the Hluboczek labor camp and to a farm at Swidowa. In September of that year the liquidation of the ghetto was complete.

During the ghetto's existence, attempts were made to organize an underground. A group of young people, led by Reuven Rosenberg, managed to obtain several handguns, and in the spring of 1943 they escaped to a forest in the area. Before long the Germans and their Ukrainian helpers discovered the group. In the ensuing clash most of the group's members were killed, while the rest continued to roam in the forest and fight the Germans. Another underground group in the ghetto was led by Meir Wassermann. Acquiring weapons, they escaped from the ghetto and operated against the Germans in the forests between Tluste and Jagielnica. Most members of this group fell in battle against the Germans and their Ukrainian collaborators.

On March 23, 1944, Chortkov was liberated by the Soviets, but the Germans launched a counterattack and the Soviet forces withdrew, together with about one hundred Jewish survivors from the city. It was only in the summer of 1944, when the Soviets returned to Chortkov, that the Germans were driven out from the entire sector.

BIBLIOGRAPHY

Austri-Dunn, Y. ed. *Memorial Book of Czortków.* Haifa, 1967. (In Hebrew and English).

AHARON WEISS

CHRISTIAN CHURCHES. [*The two articles in this entry survey the major developments taking place in Jewish-Christian relations during the Holocaust and afterward. For discussion of these relations in specific national settings, see the entries for those countries; see also under* Rescue.]

General Survey

Christian anti-Judaism derives from the earliest years of the Christian community, when the majority of Jews refused to accept the supernatural claims made for the person of Jesus of Nazareth. Its character changed in the fourth century, by which point most Christians were gentiles and Christianity became the state religion of the Roman empire. The theologians of the fourth and fifth centuries codified and extended anti-Judaic hostility by claiming that all Jews, as a community, shared the blame for the crucifixion of Jesus, that the destruction of Jerusalem in the year 70 was a divine punishment, that the Jewish people were to be treated with severity because of their obstinate blindness in refusing the promises made in their own traditional scriptures, and that the church had now superseded Judaism as the vehicle for salvation. These themes became the basis of traditional Christian teachings for many centuries, providing theological justification for repeated acts of persecution and violence. Despite the fact that successive popes issued edicts that Jews were to be considered witnesses of the original truth of divine relation to man—and, as such, regarded as potential converts—the triumphalist and monopolistic views of orthodox Christianity led to the imposing of social and physical segregation on the Jewish communities in ghettos or as minorities throughout Christian Europe; to widespread expulsions of Jews from Christian countries such as Spain and England; and to the repressive and often murderous policies of the Catholic Inquisition.

The influence of Martin Luther, especially in his rabid diatribes against the Jews at the end of his career, carried over the same theological antipathies into Protestantism, and contributed to the frequent persecution and the expulsions of Jews from German territories and city-states during the Reformation. Some of the followers of John Calvin, however, demonstrated a warmer sympathy for the Jews as the originators of Hebraic morality and of the sacred scriptures.

The rise of secularist thought in the eighteenth century, and of romanticism in the nineteenth, led to increasing skepticism in western Europe about traditional Christian dogmatic teachings, including Christian attitudes toward Judaism. The ingrained religious prejudices, however, remained entrenched in popular culture, especially in eastern Europe. Other forms of antisemitism, based on social, economic, or national ideas, increasingly came to overlap and supersede theological antipathies, adapting the stereotypes of earlier centuries and infusing the religious vocabulary with political and racist connotations. This incremental process was notable in the antisemitic propaganda of the early twentieth century, and in the formation of explicitly antisemitic political parties in Germany, France, and Austria. Only isolated Christian protests were voiced against the extremism of these racist views—notably the writings of the Protestant theologian Karl BARTH and Pope Pius XI's 1938 statement, "Antisemitism is inadmissible. We are all spiritually Semites." But the prevalence of dogmatic Christian attitudes, coupled with xenophobia and heightened ethnocentricity, prevented the growth of any more positive stance toward Judaism and the Jews. Christian theology provided no adequate defense against the escalating violence and mass murders of the Holocaust.

Roman Catholicism. Catholic attitudes toward the Nazi persecution of the Jews were ambivalent throughout the period of the Third Reich. The new Nazi regime's signature of a Reich Concordat with the Vatican in July 1933, and German Catholic support for its authoritarian and nationalist stances, gave rise to widespread illusions about the nature of Hitler's rule, illusions that were to be much criticized in the aftermath. This early collaboration preempted the possibility of mobilizing German Catholic opposition to the regime, even when the Nazis' pursuit of their totalitarian goals led to the increasing abrogation of the Concordat and persecution of the church. Despite the condemnation of Nazi ideology and RACISM in general in the papal encyclical *Mit brennender Sorge* (With Burning Concern) of March 1937, German Catholic sympathy for the Jews was evident only in individual cases, notably for Catholics of Jewish origin. Opposition was expressed more toward the methods employed by the Nazis than toward their repressive policies. The attitudes of such leading Catholics as the presiding bishop, Cardinal Adolf Bertram of Breslau, were characterized by deep-rooted hostility to the Jews, strong expressions of national loyalty, and the desire to protect their own church institutions. They led to silent acquiescence in face of the NUREMBERG LAWS of 1935 and the KRISTALLNACHT pogrom of 1938.

The episcopate's continued attempts to reach a workable compromise with the Nazi regime inhibited any forcible protests against the "FINAL SOLUTION." During the war, the German Catholic bishops took no clear stance in support of the Jews, in striking contrast to their strong protests against the Nazi EUTHANASIA PROGRAM. Reports of atrocities in eastern Europe and of the mass murders of Jews were disbelieved or were regarded with indifference. Limited support was given to the St. Raphael's Society (St. Raphaelsverein), which promoted emigration, principally for Catholic converts, and protests were made against the Nazi plans to annul marriages between Christians and Jews; these protests did secure protection for a few of those living in so-called mixed marriages.

The Vatican's policy under Pope PIUS XII (1939–1958) was dominated throughout the war years by the pursuit of a peaceful settlement by diplomatic means. Early illusions about the tractability of the Nazi leadership were shed only reluctantly, when the ineffectiveness of all protests to Berlin against Nazi persecution measures became clear. The reluctance of the German bishops to challenge the Nazi government, and the weakness of the papal nuncio in Berlin, contributed to the Vatican's passivity in face of the Nazi crimes. Stronger interventions on behalf of the victims of the war were, however, made to other governments more amenable to papal pressures, as in Slovakia, Hungary, and Romania. The Vatican condemned the antisemitic legislation passed in these countries, protested the deportations of Jews, whether converts to Catholicism or not, and demanded that the rights of all Catholics, including those of converts from Judaism, be respected. These efforts contributed to saving a minority of the Jewish populations in these states. Direct assistance by the Vatican in securing entry visas to Catholic countries (in Latin America, for example) was only modestly successful, and no efforts were made to cooperate with other relief agencies, either Protestant or Jewish. In Italy, a Vatican protest against German deportations of Italian Jews was lodged only after the initial roundup of Jews in Rome in October 1943. Similar interventions in Yugoslavia were limited in their success.

Pope Pius's pronouncements about the sufferings of the war victims were general in tone, and omitted any direct condemnation of the perpetrators, in the continuing but contentious belief that diplomatic representations would be more effective than open protest. The exaggerated belief in the efficacy of Vatican diplomacy led to the maintenance of a prudent reserve, which in hindsight has been vigorously criticized. The subsequent frustration of the Vatican's humanitarian moves by all the combatant powers induced a sense of pessimism and caution, and revealed the restricted influence of the Catholic church on national wartime policies. In the claustrophobic atmosphere of the Vatican, the unwillingness to admit the Church's impotence was accompanied by a failure to grasp the extent of Nazi atrocities against the Jews, as evidenced by the lack of sympathy for Zionist plans to secure a haven for Nazi victims in Palestine.

Throughout Nazi-occupied Europe, Catholic reactions were highly varied. In Italy itself, the Vatican and Catholic clergy played a significant role in helping and hiding Italian Jews. In France, traditional anti-Judaic antipathies combined with xenophobic resentment against the influx of foreign Jews to produce indifference to their plight; on the other hand, many younger clergy regarded assistance to the Jews as part of their resistance to the German invader. The French Catholic hierarchy was notably divided. More sympathetic attitudes were displayed after the first deportations of the Jews in the summer of 1942 and the occupation of Vichy-controlled southern France in November of that year. Significant support was given in the diocese of Lyons by Cardinal Pierre Gerlier, with the clandestine publication of the journal *Témoignage Chrétien* and the founding of the organization L'Amitié Chrétienne. A strong protest was issued in 1942 by Archbishop Jules-Gérard SALIÈGE of Toulouse. Numerous individual efforts were made to hide Jews, especially children, or to organize escape routes to Spain or Switzerland.

In Poland, the Nazi campaign of terrorization and persecution included measures designed to exploit the widespread Catholic antipathy to the Jews. The initial territorial separation and later annihilation of the Jews, on the one hand, and the decimation of the Catholic clergy and suppression of Catholic organizations, on the other, precluded any public protest. Nevertheless, a number of rescue attempts were made, particularly efforts by religious orders to save children. In Slovakia—whose president, Jozef TISO, was a priest, and whose parliament included numerous members of the clergy—harsh antisemitic measures, including deportations, were approved by the government in 1941 and 1942. Not until later in 1942, under pressure from the Vatican, did Slovak Catholic attitudes demonstrate more sympathy for the plight of the Jews. In Hungary, widespread indifference marked the stance of the Catholic population, and no public protests from the Catholic hierarchy were issued, although individual exemptions, were obtained, mainly for Jewish converts to Catholicism. In the Netherlands, a resolute protest by the Catholic bishops in 1942 led to an intensification of measures against Dutch Catholic Jews, which intimidated further public steps but also resulted in numerous rescue efforts on an individual basis. In Belgium, too, the Catholic clergy took many steps to help Jews.

The long centuries of being taught contempt for the Jews had inured Catholics to regarding the Jewish people as outside their circle of obligation. In the circumstances of Nazi persecution and annihilation, assistance to Jews was prompted more by the dictates of Christian charity than of solidarity. The events of the Holocaust did not lead at the time to any revision of Catholic theological doctrines, but the impact of the Holocaust was to produce major changes in Catholic attitudes toward the Jews from the Second Vatican Council Declaration on the Jews (1965) onward.

Protestantism. The main branch of Protestantism to give support to the Nazi ideological campaign against the Jewish people was the so-called German Christian movement, which formed the radical wing of German Lutheranism. This movement's enthusiastic support for Hitler personally, and its appeal to the latent antisemitism of Lutheran churchmen, resulted in its victory in the church elections of July 1933. The movement's attempts to reconcile Christian doctrine with its nationalist and political sympathies for Nazism—such as their claim that Jesus must have been of "Aryan blood"—led to the demand for the removal of all Jewish elements from Christian liturgy and practice, including the Testament and the teachings of the "rabbi" Paul. These excesses were quickly condemned as theological heresies by the conservatively orthodox members of the rival Confessing Church (Bekennende Kirche), which repudiated all Nazi efforts to control its teachings or to expel converted Jews from church office or membership. The German Christians movement was soon discredited, and it cannot be seen as influential in the implementation of the Nazis' plans to eradicate Jews.

But despite the Confessing Church's refusal to accept the tenets of Nazi ideology or to abandon the Jewish scriptures as a source of revelation, leading figures, such as Martin NIEMÖLLER and Otto DIBELIUS, still maintained the traditional Lutheran antipathy to the Jews on theological and social grounds. The majority of German Protestants did not challenge the right of the state to enact discriminating legislation against the Jews, and raised no objections to the initial Nazi measures taken against non-Christian Jews, though many shared the widespread public feelings of outrage against the excesses of the *Kristallnacht* pogrom. Their illusions about the nature of the Nazi regime, as well as their national and political loyalties, meant that protests were made solely in defense of the church's autonomy, or on behalf of Jewish converts. During the war, these feelings were only heightened. The young theologian Dietrich BONHOEFFER was virtually alone in recognizing the centrality of the Jewish persecution as an issue for Christians (although he too never abandoned theological anti-Judaism), and he was active in organizing efforts to enable a limited number of Jews to escape into exile.

The Confessing Church also sponsored the work of Pastor Heinrich Grüber in establishing a relief organization, principally to promote emigration of Jewish Protestants, that was tolerated if not approved by the Nazis. Grüber was, however, sent to a concentration camp in 1940, and further limited rescue efforts had to be undertaken clandestinely, notably in Württemberg, where a group of Confessing Church pastors offered sanctuary. In 1943 the bishop of Württemberg, Theophil WURM, though still denying any philosemitic tendencies, made a strong if belated series of protests against the mass murders without trial of Jews and members of other nations. In particular, he urged the abandonment of plans to deport and annihilate those Jews who still remained in Germany as partners or children of Christian Germans. The sense of moral outrage against these annihilations was a factor in the cre-ation of the ill-fated German resistance movement, led mainly by Protestants, although the traditional antisemitism of these conservative circles was reflected in their fragmentary plans for postwar reconstruction. Above all, the absence of any widespead public protest against the "Final Solution" indicated the success of the Nazi attempt to invalidate the Jews as an object of concern for the German churches.

The Reformed, or Calvinist, churches of France, Switzerland, the Netherlands, and

Hungary were more sympathetic to Judaism on theological grounds. In addition, their own history of resisting tyrannical persecutions led to a sense of identification with the Jewish victims of Nazism. In France, leading Protestants protested against the anti-Jewish measures of the Vichy regime. Relief efforts in concentration camps, such as GURS, and escape routes to Spain and Switzerland, were organized by CIMADE (Commission Inter-Mouvements auprès des Evacués), a French Protestant youth movement. Thousands of Jewish refugees were hidden in remote Protestant villages such as LE CHAMBON-SUR-LIGNON.

In Switzerland, the Geneva headquarters of the nascent World Council of Churches became a center for courier activities and relief efforts to aid Jews escaping from other parts of western Europe. The council also cooperated closely with Jewish organizations in informing Protestant communities worldwide about the extent of the Nazi atrocities. The Dutch and Danish Protestant churches actively assisted in rescue efforts. In Britain, strong leadership was given by the archbishop of Canterbury, William Temple, and by Bishop George Bell of Chichester. Both aroused public concern for the Jews' fate and urged the government to make more generous provision for the admission of refugees, whether Christian or not, and for their friendly reception in Britain. Wartime restrictions and the refusal of the British government to alter its policy on immigration into Palestine revealed the limitations of these representations.

The Protestant churches were slow to find an adequate response to the Nazi persecution of the Jews. The failure of the German Protestants to take a stronger stand, and the absence of a well-organized international Protestant agency, hampered relief efforts. Only after 1938 were effective international measures taken, and these were curtailed by the outbreak of war. The recognition that Protestant indifference was due largely to the survival of prejudicial stereotypes and the absence of a sense of theological affinity became the chief incentive in the postwar Protestant reassessment of Christian relations with the Jewish people.

BIBLIOGRAPHY

Busch, E. *Juden und Christen im Schatten des Dritten Reiches.* Munich, 1979.

Conway, J. S. *The Nazi Persecution of the Churches, 1933–1945.* London, 1968.

Friedlander, S. *Pius XII and the Third Reich: A Documentation.* London, 1966.

Gutteridge, R. *Open Thy Mouth for the Dumb: The German Evangelical Church and the Jews, 1879–1950.* Oxford, 1976.

Hay, M. *The Roots of Christian Anti-Semitism.* New York, 1981.

Kulka, O. D., and P. R. Mendes-Flohr, eds. *Judaism and Christianity under the Impact of National Socialism.* Jerusalem, 1987.

Lewy, G. *The Catholic Church and Nazi Germany.* New York, 1964.

Morley, J. F. *Vatican Diplomacy and the Jews during the Holocaust, 1939–1943.* New York, 1980.

Rengstorf, K., and S. von Kortzfleisch, eds. *Kirche und Synagoge: Handbuch zur Geschichte von Christen und Juden.* 2 vols. Stuttgart, 1968, 1970.

Scholder, K. *The Churches and the Third Reich: Preliminary History of the Time of Illusions, 1918–1934.* Vol. 1. London, 1987.

Snoek, J. M. *The Grey Book: A Collection of Protests against Anti-Semitism and the Persecution of the Jews, Issued by Non–Roman Catholic Churches and Church Leaders during Hitler's Rule.* Assen, Netherlands, 1969.

JOHN S. CONWAY

After the Holocaust

Since the collapse of Adolf Hitler's Third Reich there has been increased sensitivity in the Christian churches to the problem of ANTISEMITISM. Modern antisemitism, that is, antisemitism used as a political and ideological tool, has been widely condemned by church assemblies and courts of justice. There is also an emerging realization that the river of modern antisemitism has been fed by ancient streams of theological and cultural Jew-hatred.

The river reached flood proportions in the German Third Reich, when streams of ethnic (*völkisch*) racism and pseudoscientific racial anthropology combined with motives of blatant economic pillage and political expediency. The river of anti-Jewish violence then overflowed the familiar channels of nonviolent discrimination and occasional mob violence that had long carried the ill will of Christendom toward Jews. The force of the flood was not accidental, however: its power was purposefully harnessed to rational engines of destruction intended to wipe Jewry from the face of the earth.

Since the end of World War II, Nazism and political antisemitism have been readily condemned in most Western churches, along with other forms of racial prejudice (there has been no parallel development in the Eastern churches). Although the number of books and articles on the subject has greatly increased since the 1960s, still comparatively rare is evidence that the churches' officials and courts have come to terms with Christianity's own contribution to the attempted destruction of the Jews. The greatest progress has been made in local centers.

Even resolutions against "antisemitism" and "racism" are usually cast in such form as to make it clear that the unpleasant acts were something that was done by other people. Still protected from radical surgery, still unthreatened by any deep and insightful repentance, both theological and cultural antisemitism are alive in most of the Christian world—including circles that readily condemn what they call "racial prejudice," "anti-Judaism," or "anti-Semitism" (that is, political antisemitism).

Nevertheless, in contemporary theological writing the focus is on the frontier between the Christian churches and the Jewish people. The acid tests as to whether hierarchies and churches have made the pilgrimage of faith in the shadow of Auschwitz are three: (1) the attitude toward teaching the Holocaust and the lessons of the Holocaust; (2) the attitude toward a restored Israel; and (3) the attitude toward organized missions to the Jews (*Judenmissionen*). The red thread that ties these three issues together is the response to the question, "How do you stand on the question of the survival of the Jewish people?"

The major centers of theological change have been in West Germany, the Netherlands, and the United States.

Germany. German leaders in such change have been well aware that the Barmen Declaration (May 1934) of the Confessing Church (Bekennende Kirche), the cornerstone of Christian resistance to Nazism, condemned the idolatry of the dictatorship (*Führerstaat*) but did not deal with antisemitism. Dietrich BONHOEFFER—later to be martyred by the Nazis for complicity in the July 20, 1944, attempt on Hitler's life—tried to induce the Christian resistance to give attention to the importance of the *Judenfrage* ("Jewish question"), but he was unsuccessful. As church leaders such as the theologian Karl BARTH and Martin NIEMÖLLER later confessed with regret, they did not at the time see the significance for Christians of the assault on the Jewish people.

Neither did the Stuttgart Declaration of Guilt (October 1945)—adopted in the presence of foreign church delegates by leading German churchmen who had been opponents of Nazism and who earnestly repented of the churches' weakness in the face of the Third Reich's violation of human rights—mention what had happened to the Jews. The first postwar conferences and synods of the churches in Germany, as well as Christian consultations elsewhere in the world, regretted whatever injustices may have occurred and reaffirmed the traditional approach to the evangelization of the Jews. The issue of Jewish survival had not yet penetrated the thinking of ecclesiastical circles.

The mystery of Jewish survival was working, nonetheless, in the spiritual undertow of Christian thought. At a Protestant rally (*Kirchentag*) of 275,000 people in Berlin in 1961, some 28,000 participants flooded discussion sessions on "The Christian Obligation to the Jews." Out of this came Working Group (*Arbeitsgemeinschaft*) VI, which has since sponsored dozens of conferences and the publication of many collectively and individually written volumes. A chief center has been the Arnoldshain Adult Education Academy, near Frankfurt.

The first German Conference on the Holocaust and the Church Struggle was held in Hamburg in June 1975, under the joint sponsorship of the Gesellschaften für Christlich-Jüdische Zusammenarbeit (Societies for Christian-Jewish Cooperation), the National Council of Christians and Jews (United States), and the International Council of Christians and Jews.

The cooperative work with colleagues in

other churches, especially in America, has been important for German developments. A large German delegation participated in the International Theological Symposium on the Holocaust held in Philadelphia in 1978, returning home to press more vigorously for a reform and reconstruction of official teaching. In January 1980 the Synod of the Church of the Rhineland issued a powerful statement calling for basic changes. Co-responsibility for the Holocaust was accepted, theological antisemitism was condemned, the state of Israel was affirmed, and targeting Jews for conversion was repudiated. Although some units—conspicuously the Theology Faculty at the University of Bonn—reacted conventionally, the Rhineland Declaration gained widespread attention and approbation in Germany and in the ecumenical world.

The Netherlands. In 1961 an important initiative was undertaken in Israel by a committee of Dutch Protestants. Believing that remorse was not enough and that action was called for, under the leadership of Johan Pillon they founded Nes Ammim, a Christian *moshav* (cooperative settlement) in western Galilee. Nes Ammim has outlived the suspicion of missionary intention and has contributed worthily to the fraternal goal of helping to build up the land.

Postwar Dutch theology has been deeply influenced by the Leerhuis (House of Study) movement, centered in lay Bible study, which owes much to the Jewish thinkers Franz Rosenzweig and Martin Buber. Also important have been the *Vormingscentren* (theological training centers), fraternally related to the German *Evangelische Akademien* (evangelical academies). The first center, Kerk en Wereld (Church and World), was founded by Hendrik Kraemer, a close associate of Karl Barth and other leaders of theological renewal and resistance to Nazism. Kraemer—like Bonhoeffer, Barth, Reinhold NIEBUHR, and others close to Wilhelm Adolf Visser 't Hooft and the World Council of Churches in Process of Formation (from 1938 until the founding Assembly in Amsterdam in 1948)—combined the theme of biblical theological renewal with opposition to Nazi idolatry and antisemitism.

By 1970 both of the major Dutch Protestant churches, the Reformed and the Christian Reformed, had adopted official statements condemning antisemitism, affirming the importance of Israel—people, land, and state—and withdrawing from the traditional line on missions to the Jews.

The United States. During World War II the only American Christian theologian of rank to point to the theological significance of the Nazi assault on the Jews, and one of the very few to assay the meaning of the church struggle against idolatry, was Reinhold Niebuhr. His students have in their generation constituted the major Protestant phalanx leading the reform and reconstruction of preaching and teaching in the shadow of the Holocaust.

On the Roman Catholic side, the primary impulse to change has come from the conciliar reforms initiated by Pope John XXIII. On October 28, 1965, Vatican II issued *Nostra aetate* (Declaration on the Relation of the Church to Non-Christian Religions), in spite of desperate diplomatic efforts by Arab governments to prevent any change in the church's traditional teaching of contempt of the Jews. Followed a decade later by "Guidelines for Catholic-Jewish Relations" and twenty years later by "Notes on Jews and Judaism in Preaching and Catechesis," the directives of the Vatican have moved steadily toward greater recognition of the continuing indebtedness of Christians to their Jewish heritage, the sinfulness of antisemitism, and the Jewish right to self-definition. Nowhere has Vatican II had greater response than among American Catholics.

Landmarks in opening a deeper level of self-examination on the part of the churches in America were two self-study projects reported in Bernhard Olson's *Faith and Prejudice* (1963): a study of four publishers of Protestant church school lessons, and John T. Pawlikowski's book *Catechetics and Prejudice* (1973), an examination of the Roman Catholic church's teachings about Jews, Protestants, and racial minorities based in part on unpublished research conducted during the 1960s. Both books were distinguished by the way they revealed the layers of Christian theological antisemitism.

The year 1967 was a turning point in the preaching, teaching, and public alignment of American Jews, Protestants, and Roman

Catholics. American Jews responded to the perceived threat of a "second Holocaust" in the Six-Day War with greatly increased financial and political support of Israel. Against the background of a thunderous silence on the part of church bureaucrats, a number of Protestant conservatives, Protestant liberals, and concerned Roman Catholics launched three agencies that since that time have had increasing influence in the seminaries and congregations. The three were founded within a few weeks of each other.

One was Christians Concerned for Israel, which in 1978 expanded into a federation of many groups called The National Christian Leadership Conference for Israel. Its literature, newsletters, and advertisements have helped to educate the churches in articulate support of Israel and to make clear to political leaders of both parties that millions of church people of many denominations are united in a commitment to Jewish survival. The federation's predecessor organization was important in causing Christian congregations to observe Holocaust Memorial Day annually from 1972.

The second agency was the Israel Study Group, consisting of ten Roman Catholic and ten Protestant theologians, meeting in seminar three times a year to read and discuss theological papers on a restored Israel and related issues, such as the Holocaust, antisemitism, the Christian meaning of Jewish survival, and basic Christian dogmas in the shadow of Auschwitz. Now called the Christian Study Group on Israel and the Jewish People, the seminar has resulted in several major books and many articles, and has influenced denominational statements (Episcopal, Presbyterian, and United Church of Christ) reworking official stands on Christian-Jewish relations.

This study group has provided an important testing ground for the work of such Roman Catholic leaders as Father Edward Flannery (*The Anguish of the Jews*, 2nd ed., 1985) and Dr. Eugene Fisher (*Faith without Prejudice*, 1977) of the United States Catholic Conference, and of such Protestants as Roy Eckardt and Alice Eckardt (*A Long Night's Journey into Day*, 2nd ed., 1988) and Paul van Buren (*A Theology of the Jewish-Christian Reality*, 4 vols., 1980–).

The third new foundation was an interfaith, international, and interdisciplinary conference of college, seminary, and university people that became the Annual Scholars' Conference on the Holocaust and the Church Struggle. Meeting the first weekend in March of every year, the Scholars' Conference has brought together hundreds of professors, graduate students, and public educators and has led to the publication of a host of articles and several dozen books.

In July 1988 an international conference, Remembering for the Future, was held in Oxford and London, with 650 educators from twenty-four nations present. The first of two themes was "Christian-Jewish Relations during and after the Holocaust." The chairperson of the conference was Dr. Elisabeth Maxwell. Two of the six members of the executive committee were leaders in all three of the agencies mentioned above, and over half of the registrants at Oxford were alumni of the Annual Scholars' Conference (USA).

The prominence of Americans in these efforts, which are often carried on in close cooperation with colleagues in Israel, reflects the degree to which religious liberty and pluralism are accepted facts of life in the United States. The Jewish, Roman Catholic, and Protestant communities are all of great strength and their members are equally entitled to citizens' rights before the law.

This parity of strength and legal status has practical consequences in terms of sharing mutual concerns. One of the two oldest centers of Holocaust education in the United States, the Anne Frank Institute of Philadelphia (formerly the National Institute on the Holocaust), is independent of any single denominational or faith alignment and is strictly interfaith in its programs. The largest department of religion in the country, that of Temple University in Philadelphia, is oriented toward interfaith dialogue rather than seminary or divinity school apologetics. Its *Journal of Ecumenical Studies* is the preeminent quarterly journal in the field.

When Holocaust Memorial Day became a public calendar event in America, all chaplains of the army, air force, and navy were sent the book *Liturgies on the Holocaust*, by M. S. Littell (1986), and regardless of their own denominational affiliation were expected to lead services of participation in remembering the Holocaust and its lessons for all persons of conscience. Just as those reforming and reconstructing the churches' preaching and teaching about the Jewish people have looked to Jewish teachers for counsel and encouragement, so Jewish leaders, remembering the heavy losses of their people in an age of genocide, have been able more and more to look to the churches for participation in services of mourning and healing.

During the German church struggle those who opposed Nazism found support at the parish level, not in the hierarchies. In the reform of church preaching and teaching about the Jewish people carried out in Germany, the Netherlands, and the United States, with few exceptions the strongest impulses have continued to come from the parish and congregational levels rather than from the front offices.

FRANKLIN H. LITTELL

Poland. In Poland, the Catholic church had historically played a significant part in the spread of antisemitism. During World War II Polish priests helped to save Jews, and the Catholic church in Poland itself suffered a great deal from Nazi persecutions. Hundreds of Jewish children were given refuge in convents and church-sponsored children's asylums, although the church itself did not engage in an organized massive effort of saving Jews.

In the initial postwar phase, especially after the KIELCE pogrom of July 4, 1946, the hesitant and ambiguous attitude of Polish church leaders came in for a good deal of censure, but as time went on a change took place in the attitudes of many of the leaders, as well as of the entire Catholic public. An important contribution to this development was made by *Tygodnik Powszechny,* a leading Catholic weekly published in Kraków, which took a consistent position against antisemitism and gave the subject prominent space in its columns. The public appearances of Pope John Paul II also had an effect on the ongoing process of change in the influential sector of the Catholic population. Among the Catholic intelligentsia there is a growing interest in the history of the Jews and the relations between Jews and Poles, and from the mid-1980s there has been some soul-searching and an effort to analyze the complicated pattern of that relationship. This process has been furthered by numerous meetings of Jewish and Polish scholars at Oxford and in Poland, and by the studies in this field that have been published. In 1987 *Tygodnik Powszechny* published an article by a noted literary scholar, Jan Blonski, that raised the painful issue of the relations between Poles and Jews in a courageous and candid form. This article aroused much interest in Poland. In addition, the Polish Catholic periodicals *Znak* and *Wieża* have published special issues on Judaism in general and on the question of the Jews in Poland.

ISRAEL GUTMAN

BIBLIOGRAPHY

Cargas, H. J. *A Christian Response to the Holocaust.* Denver, 1981.
Fasching, D. J. *The Jewish People in Christian Preaching.* New York, 1984.
Fisher, E. "The Holocaust and the State of Israel: A Catholic Perspective." *Judaism* 75: 16–24.
Gerlach, W. *Als die Zeugen schwiegen: Die Bekennende Kirche und die Juden.* Berlin, 1987.
Littell, F. H. *The Crucifixion of the Jews.* Macon, Ga., 1987.
Littell, F. H., and H. G. Locke. *The German Church Struggle and the Holocaust, 1933–1945.* Detroit, 1974.
Littell, M. S., ed. *Liturgies on the Holocaust.* New York, 1986.
Osten-Sacken, P. von der. *Christian-Jewish Dialogue: Theological Foundations.* Philadelphia, 1986.
World Council of Churches. *The Theology of the Churches and the Jewish People.* Geneva, 1988.

CHRONICLES OF THE ŁÓDŹ GHETTO. *See* Łódź Ghetto, Chronicles of the.

CHURCHILL, WINSTON LEONARD SPENCER (1874–1965), British statesman and wartime leader. Churchill's political career, which extended from 1900 to the mid-1950s, spanned a period of tumultuous developments within the Jewish world: the growth of the Jewish national home in Palestine, the Holocaust, and the creation of the state of Israel. His political responsibilities during this period, as well as his personal pro-

Zionist sympathies and his imperial perspective, ensured him a central role in twentieth-century Jewish history.

During 1921 and 1922, as secretary of state for the British colonies, Churchill was closely involved with the formative years of the British Mandate in Palestine and with the early development of post–World War I Jewish settlement there. Firmly committed to the concept of a British Empire as vital to the interests of the United Kingdom, Churchill looked to the growing Jewish national home as a pro-British bastion. He was a leading opponent of Prime Minister Neville Chamberlain's foreign policy of APPEASEMENT (1937–1939), and called constantly for an active rearmament program against Adolf Hitler's Germany. He was also the leading parliamentary opponent of the 1939 WHITE PAPER, which limited Jewish immigration to Palestine and the purchase by Jews of land there; he supported continued Jewish immigration to Palestine.

When Britain declared war against Germany in September 1939, Churchill joined Chamberlain's government as First Lord of the Admiralty. From within the War Cabinet, Churchill tried to induce the government to abandon the White Paper. In January 1940, he convinced the cabinet to accept a *modus vivendi* whereby the White Paper would remain in force but nothing would be done that would prejudice a reconsideration of Palestine policy after the war. In effect, this meant that the constitutional provisions of the 1939 policy would be frozen.

This compromise agreement remained in force, even after Churchill succeeded Chamberlain as British prime minister in May 1940. Although Churchill attempted a number of times during the war years to propose alternative policies that would permit the creation of a Jewish state, his pro-Zionist stand was firmly opposed by the other members of the cabinet and by the British senior civil service. On each occasion, Churchill informed his colleagues of his intention to support the creation of an independent state with "three or four million Jews" after the war against Germany had been won. Only in 1943, following the final elimination of the Axis threat to the British position in the Middle East, did Churchill decide to confront the supporters of the White Paper and advocate new discussions on the political future of the Palestine Mandate. A Cabinet Committee on Palestine was formed which ultimately recommended that Palestine be partitioned between Jews and Arabs. This decision was accepted by the British cabinet in January 1944, and active planning for the partition began. However, the November 1944 assassination in Cairo of Lord Walter Moyne by members of the LOḤAMEI ḤERUT ISRAEL underground led Churchill to suspend any further deliberations until after the end of the war. The defeat of Churchill's Conservative party in the elections of 1945 meant that the wartime partition proposal was not revived.

Churchill's views regarding the future of the Jews in Palestine, together with the absolute primacy he gave to winning the war, deflected any concern for the immediate circumstances of European Jewry under the Nazis. Although he was sympathetic to Jewish matters, he was only rarely consulted regarding the fate of Jewish communities in occupied Europe. He consistently supported efforts to liberalize British restrictions on Jewish immigration into Palestine (one of the main avenues of escape from Europe), but he did nothing to foster active British support for programs of rescue. Despite his outspokenly pro-Jewish stance, there was no British equivalent of the American WAR REFUGEE BOARD. In a letter of February 1943 (drafted by the Foreign Office but signed by Churchill), the prime minister set out the reasons why Britain would not take an active role in rescue: transport was a major problem; the lines of escape passed through areas of vital military importance and would disrupt the war effort; and it would not be possible to rescue Jewish refugees while abandoning the far greater number of Allied citizens in German-occupied areas.

In July 1944, Churchill and Anthony EDEN both endorsed the appeals by the Jewish Agency that Auschwitz be bombed (*see* AUSCHWITZ, BOMBING OF). Nevertheless, neither intervened with sufficient force to overcome the obstacles created by British bureaucracy, and no bombing mission ever took place.

The Jewish issue remained a marginal one for British leaders. Although he was sympa-

Prime Minister Winston Churchill and Madame Chiang Kai-shek (Soong Mei-ling, sister-in-law of Sun Yat-sen), wife of Generalissimo Chiang Kai-shek, at the First Cairo Conference, November 25, 1943.

thetic to Jewish concerns and actively supported Zionist aspirations, Churchill shared the official British consensus that the rescue of European Jewry could only be achieved by the total defeat of Nazi Germany.

[*See also* Great Britain.]

BIBLIOGRAPHY

Cohen, M. J. *Churchill and the Jews*. London, 1985.

Gilbert, M. *Winston Churchill*. Vols. 6, 7. London, 1983, 1985.

Zweig, R. W. *Britain and Palestine during the Second World War*. Woodbridge, England, 1986.

RONALD W. ZWEIG

CLAIMS CONFERENCE. *See* Reparations and Restitution from Germany.

CLAUBERG, CARL (1898–1957), SS physician infamous for his experiments in sterilizing Jewish women at the AUSCHWITZ extermination camp during World War II. Clauberg was born at Wupperhof and served in the infantry during World War I. He later studied medicine at the universities of Kiel, Hamburg, and Graz, qualifying as a doctor in 1925. He had a successful medical career and in 1937 was appointed professor of gynecology and obstetrics at the University of Königsberg. At the same time he was chief doctor at a women's clinic in Upper Silesia and published numerous papers in his specialty. Clauberg was an enthusiastic Nazi, joining the party in 1933 and rising to the rank of *Brigadeführer* in the SS.

The sterilization program was initiated in 1941, and in 1942 Heinrich HIMMLER entrusted Clauberg with its experimental implementation at Auschwitz. He had the cooperation of internee doctors there (including the Polish camp doctor, Władysław Dering, whose experiments were later the subject of a famous libel case in England in 1964). The experiments at Auschwitz lasted until 1944; they involved sterilization by means of injections into the womb, which caused unimaginable suffering to the victims, Jewish and Gypsy women. Clauberg conducted similar experiments in the women's concentration camp of RAVENSBRÜCK in 1945.

Arrested by the Russians at the end of the war, Clauberg was tried in 1948 for his role in the "mass extermination of Soviet citizens." He was sentenced to twenty-five years' imprisonment, but was released in 1955 under the German-Soviet prisoner repatriation agreement. Clauberg showed no regrets for his experiments, and even boasted of his "scientific achievements." At the initiative of the Central Council of Jews in Germany, an action to prosecute Clauberg was undertaken in the West German courts. The council accused Clauberg of "having caused severe bodily harm" to Jewish women. The Kiel police put him under arrest, but he died in a hospital shortly before the date of the trial.

[*See also* Medical Experiments; Physicians, Nazi.]

BIBLIOGRAPHY

Lifton, R. *The Nazi Doctors: Medical Killing and the Psychology of Genocide.* New York, 1986.

LIONEL KOCHAN

CLERGY IN NAZI GERMANY. *See* Bonhoeffer, Dietrich; Christian Churches; Dibelius, Otto; Galen, Clemens August Graf von; Lichtenberg, Bernhard; Niemöller, Martin; Wurm, Theophil.

CLUJ (Cluj-Napoca; Hung., Kolozsvár; Ger., Klausenburg), capital of Cluj county and of Hungarian-ruled northern TRANSYLVANIA (1940–1944). In 1941, Cluj had a population of 110,956, of whom 16,763 were Jewish. The Jewish community was one of the largest in the province, with a well-developed network of educational, cultural, and charitable institutions. It boasted many politically active Zionist leaders, including Hillel Danzig and Rezső (Rudolph) KASZTNER. The last head of the Orthodox community was Zsigmond Léb; that of the large Neolog (Conservative) community was Dr. József Fischer, Kasztner's father-in-law, who during the pre-1940 era also served in the Romanian parliament as a representative of the Jewish party.

The ghettoization of the Cluj Jews began on May 3, 1944, and was completed within a week. The Jews were concentrated in the Iris brickyard in the northern part of the city. Consisting mostly of shacks used for drying bricks and tiles, the ghetto had practically no facilities for the approximately eighteen thousand Jews who were assembled there from Cluj county. The concentration of the Jews was carried out by the local administrative and police authorities with the cooperation of SS advisers, including SS-Hauptsturmführer Dieter WISLICENY. The ghetto was under the command of László Urbán, the city's police chief. Its internal administration was entrusted to a JUDENRAT (Jewish Council), whose members included Fischer (as head), Rabbi Akiba Glasner, Rabbi Mózes Weinberger, and Ernö Marton. As in all the other ghettos in Hungary, the local brickyard also had a "mint," a special building where the gendarmes and police tortured Jews into confessing where they had hidden their valuables.

Kasztner, who had been in the midst of controversial negotiations with the Eichmann Sonderkommando on a rescue arrangement, visited the city on May 4 and 5. Shortly thereafter, 388 Jews, including many of Kasztner's relatives and closest friends,

Annexations from June to September 1940: (1) Bessarabia and (2) N. Bukovina to USSR; (3) N. Transylvania to Hungary; (4) S. Dobruja to Bulgaria.

were taken out of the ghetto and transferred to Budapest. From there, together with some 1,300 other Jews, they were eventually taken to Switzerland via BERGEN-BELSEN—a rescue mission that engendered great controversy (*see* RELIEF AND RESCUE COMMITTEE OF BUDAPEST).

The Cluj ghetto was liquidated through the deportation of the Jews to AUSCHWITZ in six transports between May 25 and June 9, 1944. After the war, the city reverted to Romania. In 1947, it had a Jewish population of close to sixty-five hundred, including not only survivors but also some who moved there from other parts of Romania.

BIBLIOGRAPHY

Braham, R. L. *Genocide and Retribution*. Boston, 1983. See pages 24–27, 123–141.

Carmilly-Weinberger, M., ed. *Memorial Volume for the Jews of Cluj-Kolozsvár*. New York, 1970. (In English, Hebrew, and Hungarian.)

RANDOLPH L. BRAHAM

COHEN, DAVID (1882–1967), Dutch Zionist leader and public figure. Born in Deventer, Cohen was an expert in papyrology and became a professor of ancient history, first in Leyden and then in Amsterdam. He was active in Jewish affairs from an early age, joined the Zionist movement in 1904, and held key posts in it. He was one of the sponsors and organizers of the Zionist Students' Union and the Jewish Youth Federation. In World War I Cohen was active in providing assistance to Jewish refugees, mainly from Germany, and became the secretary of the Committee for Refugees. He was a member of the Jewish Council in The Hague and then in Amsterdam, and in 1934 was elected to the Standing Committee of the Union of Ashkenazic Communities. In 1933, when the Nazis rose to power in Germany, it was on Cohen's initiative that the Comité voor Bijzondere Joodse Belangen (Committee for Special Jewish Affairs) was established, and he became the executive chairman of its subcommittee on refugees.

Following the German occupation of the NETHERLANDS in May 1940, Cohen was among the sponsors of the Jewish Coordinating Committee set up in December of that year. On February 12, 1941, Cohen, together with Abraham ASSCHER, formed the JOODSE RAAD (Jewish Council) at the "suggestion" of the Germans. He was one of the council's two chairmen (the other being Asscher), taking part in its daily operations and determining its policy toward the Germans. During the war years the Joodse Raad came under severe attack from Lodewijk Ernst VISSER and from the Dutch government-in-exile for its policy of cooperation with the Germans. This was the background for Cohen's conflict with Visser, who was opposed to such cooperation. In the Joodse Raad itself there was also opposition to Cohen's policy, but he was always successful in overcoming this resistance and obtaining majority support for his position in the Coordinating Committee.

On September 23, 1943, Cohen was arrested, together with the other members of the Joodse Raad who were still in Amsterdam, and taken first to WESTERBORK and from there to THERESIENSTADT. When he came back to the Netherlands after the war, the Dutch government instituted judicial proceedings against him, charging him with collaborating with the enemy. Cohen was arrested, but after an investigation the file was closed. In 1947 Cohen was also charged before a Jewish community tribunal, where he put up a passionate defense of his policy during the war; but he was found guilty and was barred from holding office in any Jewish institution. In 1950 the sentence was annulled; Cohen returned to his university post, but did not again become active in Jewish public life. In 1955 he published his reminiscences, *Zwervend en Dolend* (Fugitive and Vagabond).

BIBLIOGRAPHY

Michman, J. "The Controversial Stand of the Joodse Raad in the Netherlands." *Yad Vashem Studies* 10 (1974): 9–68.

Michman, J. "The Controversy Surrounding the Jewish Council of Amsterdam." In *Patterns of Jewish Leadership in Nazi Europe, 1933–1945*. Proceedings of the Third Yad Vashem International Historical Conference, edited by Y. Gutman and C. J. Haft, pp. 235–258. Jerusalem, 1979.

Michman, J., H. Beem, and D. Michman. *The Neth-*

erlands. In *Pinkas Hakehillot; Encyclopaedia of Jewish Communities*. Jerusalem, 1985. (In Hebrew.)

Presser, J. *The Destruction of the Dutch Jews*, New York, 1969.

JOZEPH MICHMAN

COHN, MARIANNE (1924–1944), French Jewish underground activist. Born in Mannheim, Germany, Cohn was a member of the ECLAIREURS ISRAÉLITES DE FRANCE (French Jewish Scouts) and in 1942 joined the Mouvement de la Jeunesse Sioniste (Zionist Youth Movement). She belonged to the underground sponsored by both organizations, which smuggled into Switzerland Jewish children whose parents had been expelled from France. On June 1, 1944, Cohn was seized by a German patrol, together with a group of twenty-eight children, and all were imprisoned in the town of Annemasse. The underground succeeded in establishing contact with Cohn and devised a plan to get her out of jail, but she was not prepared to escape, fearing that the children would suffer if she were to do so. On July 8, two members of the Nazi-sponsored French militia broke into the prison, took Cohn out, and killed her with an ax. The children were all saved.

Marianne Cohn.

BIBLIOGRAPHY

L'activité des organisations juives en France sous l'occupation. Paris, 1947.

Hammel, F. C. *Souviens-toi d'Amalek: Témoignage sur la lutte des Juifs en France (1938–1944)*. Paris, 1982.

Latour, A. *The Jewish Resistance in France, 1940–1944*. New York, 1981.

LUCIEN LAZARE

COLLABORATORS. *See* Hilfswillige; Nachtigall Battalion; Ostbataillone; Policiniai Batalionai; Quisling, Vidkun; Ukrainische Hilfspolizei; Vlasov, Andrei; *see also under* Police in Occupied Countries.

COLUMBIA HAUS, concentration camp in Berlin, used mainly for detaining the victims of Nazi persecution who were under interrogation by the GESTAPO at its headquarters on Prinz-Albrecht Street. In the late summer of 1933, the basement of the Gestapo headquarters building was equipped with cells, but these could hold only about fifty prisoners at most. Many of the prisoners in "protective custody" were also held in the police jail on Alexanderplatz for their questioning by the Gestapo. Beginning in early 1934 (no exact date is available), the Gestapo also utilized Columbia Haus—a concentration camp set up by the SS—to hold prisoners who were under direct Gestapo investigation. Columbia Haus, located near the Tempelhof airfield, had originally served as a military prison. Like the Gestapo headquarters itself, it was loathed for the torture methods employed there. Owing to its close connection with the SA (Sturmabteilung; Storm Troopers) and, later, with the SS and Gestapo headquarters, Columbia Haus, instead of being disbanded when the initial 1934 persecution phase came to an end, was taken over by the Inspectorate of Concentration Camps. A Gestapo headquarters circular dated January 8, 1935, stated that henceforth "Columbia Haus

Prison" was to be designated "KL [*Konzentrationslager*] Columbia Haus"; at that time, it appears, Columbia Haus came administratively under the direct control of the Gestapo.

In late 1935, the Gestapo decided to increase its headquarters' prison capacity, and by fall 1936 the planned additional cells were ready for occupation. At that time the SS was in the process of liquidating all the camps it had been using in the first few years following the Nazi seizure of power—with the exception of DACHAU—and constructing new and larger concentration camp complexes. Columbia Haus was no longer needed. On November 5, 1935, the camp was closed.

BIBLIOGRAPHY

Krausnick, H., et al. *Anatomy of the SS State.* London, 1968.

FALK PINGEL

COMISIA AUTONOMA DE AJUTORARE (Refugee Aid Committee), organization established in BUCHAREST to render assistance to Jews in ROMANIA who underwent suffering under the Ion ANTONESCU regime. The committee was formed at the end of January 1941, following the suppression of the IRON GUARD revolt and the pogroms in Bucharest (January 21 to 23, 1941). It was founded on the initiative of leading figures in the Federatia Uniunilor de Comunitati Evreesti, or Union of Jewish Communities (Wilhelm FILDERMAN, Fred Saraga, and Emil Costiner); representatives of the Zionist movement (Misu Benvenisti and Dr. Cornel Iancu); businessmen; and a group of women who had already achieved a reputation for extending aid to Jews victimized by the regime. The committee, headed by Arnold Schwefelberg, a lawyer, collected funds and supplies needed by the victims of the Bucharest pogroms. Subsequently, it concentrated its efforts on alleviating conditions for the forty thousand Jews who had been expelled from their homes in towns and villages and were being detained in camps in various parts of the country. Sometimes the aid provided consisted of no more than a meal or a piece of clothing—just enough to keep the refugees alive. After the German (and Romanian) invasion of the Soviet Union, on June 22, 1941, and the mass deportation of Jews to TRANSNISTRIA, the committee—a voluntary body—could no longer cope with the growing needs, and schoolchildren and additional volunteers from all sectors of the Jewish population joined in helping its operations.

These activities, and the initiatives undertaken by the committee's leaders, reflected the disasters that befell Romanian Jewry: the IAŞI pogrom and the deportations that cost the lives of twelve thousand Jews from Iaşi in the period from June 29 to July 8, 1941; the camps, especially at Calaras-Ialomita, to which the survivors were taken; the removal of the Jews from the city of Constanţa to the Osmancea camp; and the transfer of Jews from small villages to large population centers. All these developments created an urgent need for financial and material aid to ensure at least the bare existence of the victims.

In the spring of 1941, before the outbreak of the war against the Soviet Union, the committee launched a major campaign for contributions. This was necessitated by the rapid impoverishment of new sectors of the Jewish population as a result of anti-Jewish measures undertaken by the Antonescu regime—the confiscation of houses and other properties, the imposition of special levies, the expulsion of Jews from villages, and, particularly, the dismissal of Jews from their posts and their exclusion from various professions. Sufficient money was collected in this drive to cover the needs. The committee also provided tools, money, food, kitchen utensils, and drugs to the Jews drafted into forced-labor battalions, and it tried to help the families of these draftees as best it could.

Filderman made efforts to channel aid to the Jews of BESSARABIA and BUKOVINA in the first few days of the murder campaign conducted by Romanian and German forces in July and August of 1941, but they were all rejected by the Romanian authorities. On December 17, 1941, the Union of Jewish Communities was disbanded, and on the same day permission was granted to provide aid to the Jews who had been deported to Transnistria. In place of the union the authorities installed the CENTRALA EVREILOR (Jewish Center), which was also supposed to take over the functions of the Refugee Aid Committee. The center, however, was not permitted to aid the Jews deported to Transnistria; its operations were restricted to the Jews in Romania proper. The committee kept up its work, but it added the term "autonomous" (*autonoma*) to its title, to distinguish it from the Jewish Center's aid committee, under whose auspices it formally operated.

In the fall of 1942 the committee was called upon to extend aid to new categories of deportees to Transnistria: Jewish political prisoners suspected of Communist activity; Jews who in the summer of 1940, following the annexation of Bessarabia and northern Bukovina by the Soviet Union, had applied—in vain—to return to the Soviet Union; and Jews who had violated the laws and regulations concerning forced labor. From 1942 to 1944 the committee was able to aid the deportees in Transnistria in various ways, in most instances helping to save their lives. In 1942 the committee also sent work tools to Transnistria to aid the cooperative societies that had been set up in the ghettos and camps of the region. In early 1943, after long and persistent efforts, the committee was permitted to send a delegation (headed by Fred Saraga) to visit several ghettos in Transnistria. This visit, coupled with those of representatives of the International RED CROSS and of the papal nuncio in Bucharest, Archbishop Andrea Cassulo, expedited the provision of relief to the deportees and the establishment of orphanages in Transnistria.

At the end of 1943 permission was granted for the repatriation of the Jews from Transnistria. The committee organized the return of six thousand Jews from the DOROHOI district and of four thousand orphaned children, providing food and clothing and arranging for rail transportation. The repatriation operation was halted in April 1944, following the liberation of northern Romania and northern Transnistria by the Soviet army and the seizure of the Dniester crossings by German forces. Many of the Jews who had not yet been repatriated were killed by the Nazis. The committee provided temporary housing and upkeep for the returnees. As of late 1943, the committee was receiving funds from the JOINT DISTRIBUTION COMMITTEE, transmitted to it by the International Red Cross.

The committee's operations grew in size after the fall of the Antonescu regime, and it began extending aid to thousands of Jews who had been released from forced-labor battalions, detention camps, and prisons, in addition to the returnees from Transnistria. At the end of 1944 and the beginning of 1945, Jewish Communists seized control of the committee, incorporating it into the Comitetul Democrat Evreesc (Jewish Democratic Committee). Although the Refugee Aid Committee's operations did not come to an end overnight, they were soon phased out, and what remained of the committee ceased to exist. A substantial part of its assets was diverted by the Jewish Communists for aid to Romanian gentiles.

BIBLIOGRAPHY

Ancel, J., ed. *Documents concerning the Fate of Romanian Jewry during the Holocaust*. Vols. 5, 8. New York, 1987.

JEAN ANCEL

COMMISSARIAT GÉNÉRAL AUX QUESTIONS JUIVES (Office for Jewish Affairs; CGQJ), agency established by the Vichy government in March 1941 to coordinate French anti-Jewish policy and to prepare and administer legislation in this field.

During his first contacts with the French authorities on the "Jewish question," in early 1941, Adolf EICHMANN's Paris representative, Theodor DANNECKER, advised Adm. François DARLAN, the head of the Vichy government, of the Nazis' intent to sponsor a Zentraljudenamt (Central Jewish Office) for the occupied zone. Consistent with their opposition to the division of their country, the French proposed instead a French-directed agency whose jurisdiction would extend to both zones. Technically, therefore, French sovereignty would be preserved. Delighted with the French willingness to cooperate, Dannecker agreed. Darlan established the new agency on March 29, 1941, and named the French war veterans' leader, Xavier VALLAT, a rabid antisemite but also an anti-German, to be its head.

Under Vallat, the CGQJ attempted to codify an anti-Jewish policy in the French national interest. The idea was to unify anti-Jewish actions throughout both zones, and to do so energetically and efficiently. Implicit in Vallat's approach was the hope that the Germans would gradually withdraw from this field, leaving the task to the French alone. Dissatisfied with the existing STATUT DES JUIFS (Jewish Law), Vallat put forward a new law on June 2, 1941, that aimed to define the Jews and to intensify Vichy's anti-Jewish program. All loopholes were to be closed. Basing itself on this second *Statut des Juifs*, the CGQJ soon prompted a flurry of decrees drastically limiting the number of Jews in commerce and the professions. On June 2, another law announced a forthcoming detailed census of Jews in the unoccupied zone—a grave step that profoundly shocked Jewish opinion and that was to have fatal consequences later, when Jews in France were rounded up and deported. Finally, by a law of July 22, 1941, the CGQJ launched a vast process of "Aryanization" (*see* ARISIERUNG)—the confiscation of Jewish property—in the unoccupied zone.

"Aryanization" became one of the major tasks of the CGQJ. Eager to ensure that Jewish property did not find its way to the Reich, the French government designated the CGQJ as the agency to take charge of confiscating Jewish property throughout France. Vallat entered into complex negotiations with the Germans, consulted with ministries, industrialists, and businessmen, and administered a complicated bureaucracy of inspectors and trustees. The goal was to liquidate or sell all Jewish holdings for the benefit of France. The vast scale of this project, which eventually involved more than forty-two thousand Jewish enterprises, drained the legislative and administrative energies of the CGQJ. Corruption and inefficiency followed, despite Vallat's efforts to combat both.

Because of his relatively moderate approach, the German authorities finally replaced Vallat, in May 1942, with Louis DARQUIER DE PELLEPOIX. An outsider at Vichy and far more at home in the pro-German milieus of Paris, Darquier did not have the legalistic or technical scruples of his predecessor. He and his staff increasingly went their own way, clashing with various ministries and indulging their taste for brutality and personal enrichment. Propaganda and repression assumed far more importance than under Vallat. The CGQJ spawned a parapolice organization, the Sections d'Enquête et de Contrôle. Darquier and his lieutenants were not averse to working with the Nazis, notably when roundups and deportations were conducted throughout France in the summer of 1942. When possible, the Vichy leaders kept the CGQJ at arm's length; Marshal Philippe PÉTAIN himself allegedly referred to Darquier as *Monsieur le tortionnaire* ("Mr. Torturer"). But the anti-Jewish machinery continued to function, and even to accelerate the rate of persecution.

In late 1943 the Germans pressured Vichy to drop Darquier, recognizing that he was unable to bring the Vichy government fully into line with Nazi policy. Darquier was succeeded in February 1944 by Charles Mercier du Paty de Clam, an undistinguished civil servant descended from the famous officer who arrested Alfred Dreyfus in 1894. Du Paty de Clam seems to have made efforts to reverse the Commissariat's anti-Semitic orientation, with some minor success. With the end of the war in sight, du Paty de Clam took leave from his office in May. Pierre LAVAL, who sought until the end to maintain control and government continuity in this sphere as in others, named Joseph Antignac, one of Vichy's top officials and most virulent antisemites, to head the Commissariat. Remarkably, "business as usual" remained the policy of the CGQJ even after the Allies went ashore in Normandy. When France was liberated, the agency, along with the rest of the Vichy administration, ceased to exist.

BIBLIOGRAPHY

Billig, J. *Le Commissariat Général aux Questions Juives (1941–1944).* 3 vols. Paris, 1955–1960.

Knobel, M. "C.-M.-V. du Paty de Clam, commissaire général aux questions juives." *Le Monde Juif* 117 (1985):18–24.

Marrus, M. R., and R. O. Paxton. *Vichy France and the Jews.* New York, 1981.

MICHAEL R. MARRUS

COMMISSAR ORDER. *See* Kommissarbefehl.

COMMITTEE FOR THE JEWS OF OCCUPIED EUROPE. *See* Joint Rescue Committee.

CONCENTRATION CAMPS (Ger., *Konzentrationslager;* KZ), camps in which persons are imprisoned without regard to the accepted norms of arrest and detention. Although the term "concentration camp" is sometimes used as a generic term for Nazi camps, not all the camps eventually established by the Nazis were designated as concentration camps proper. Their extensive camp system also included labor camps (*Arbeitslager*), transit camps (*Durchgangslager*), prisoner-of-war (POW) camps (*Kriegsgefangenlager*), and extermination camps (*Vernichtungslager*). This entry focuses on the network of concentration camps.

Concentration camps were an essential part of the Nazi regime of oppression. The regime imprisoned in such camps political adversaries and persons considered socially or racially undesirable. Forced labor performed by the prisoners became a central element of the imprisonment. During World War II the concentration camps also played a part in the Nazi fight against the resistance

CONCENTRATION CAMPS

Corporal punishment by whipping at the Buchenwald concentration camp.

movements, and some camps (such as AUSCHWITZ and MAJDANEK) were centers for the systematic extermination of Jews, GYPSIES, Soviet PRISONERS OF WAR (POWs) and other groups in the Reich and the occupied territories.

The history of the concentration camps can be divided into three periods: (1) 1933 to 1936; (2) 1936 to 1942; and (3) 1942 to 1944–1945.

From 1933 to 1936. In the earliest period, the concentration camps were used primarily for incarcerating internal political adversaries from the left and liberal circles, as well as members of the proscribed German labor movement organizations. Special places of detention for political prisoners came into being in the wake of the *Razzien* (raids) that were carried out after the Reichstag fire of February 28, 1933 (*see* LAW AND JUDICIARY IN NAZI GERMANY). The main categories taken into "preventive protective custody" (*vorbeugende Schutzhaft*) were Communist party members, as well as members of the trade unions and the Social Democratic party after these were outlawed on May 2 and June 21, 1933, respectively. At the end of July, when the first wave of arrests came to an end, a total of twenty-seven thousand persons were being held in "protective custody." To cope with this large number of political detainees, Germany's police and juridical authorities, as well as the SA (Sturmabteilung; Storm Troopers) and SS, established special detention centers (their precise number cannot be determined). In Prussia alone there were twenty separate detention camps for *Schutzhaft* prisoners. In the spring of 1934 these camps were put under the authority of Heinrich HIMMLER, who was also in charge of the political police in the various states of the Reich. This meant that the regular police, the juridical authorities, and the SA no longer exercised any control over the concentration camp prisoners, who passed to the control of the SS.

On July 4, 1934, Himmler appointed Theodor EICKE, the commandant of the DACHAU concentration camp, as *Inspekteur der Konzentrationslager und SS-Wachverbände* (Inspector of Concentration Camps and SS Guard Units). These guard units became known as SS TOTENKOPFVERBÄNDE (Death's-Head Units), after the death's-head symbol they wore on the collar of their uniforms. Eicke fixed the prisoners' daily routine, the methods of punishment, and the duties of the SS guards. He stressed what he considered to be the proper relationship between the guards and the prisoners, calling the latter "the enemy of the people." Eicke's system was accepted, with variations, in all the concentration camps, and in the course of time many of his subordinates occupied key positions in the camps. From the organizational aspect, the inspectorate of concentration camps came under the SS Main Office (SS-Hauptamt), headed by SS-Gruppenführer August Heissmeyer, but for the most part it acted on its own. Most of the small "protective custody" camps established in 1933 were now abolished. In September 1935 the official concentration camps were Dachau, Lichtenburg (on the Elbe, in the Prussian province of Saxony), Sachsenburg (in the state of Saxony), Esterwegen (in eastern Friesland, Prussia), and ORANIENBURG and COLUMBIA HAUS (near Berlin). A total of about six thousand prisoners were held in these camps.

Beginning in the autumn of 1933, persons other than "political" prisoners were also put into concentration camps. They included tramps and beggars, who in the Nazi jargon were dubbed "asocial elements," as well as persons with several previous criminal convictions, the *Berufsverbrecher* (habitual criminals). This reduced the percentage of political prisoners to about 75 percent by 1936. At a certain stage, a discussion was held in the Nazi hierarchy on whether the camp system should be continued, in light of the consolidation of the regime. Hitler decided the argument by supporting those who favored the continuation of the camps. The number of detainees fell in 1935 and 1936, but later grew again as new categories of prisoners, such as the asocials, were imprisoned.

From 1936 to 1942. The war preparations and the war itself led to an expansion of the concentration camp system. Except for Dachau, the camps established in the initial period were dissolved or put to other uses, and new and larger concentration camps were set up in their place: SACHSENHAUSEN (1936), BUCHENWALD (1937), MAUTHAUSEN and Flossenbürg (1938), RAVENSBRÜCK, the concentration camp for women (1939), Auschwitz (1940), and NATZWEILER (1941). In June 1940 NEUENGAMME, which until then had been a Sachsenhausen satellite camp, became an independent camp, and in May of 1941 GROSS-ROSEN as well became independent. In February 1942, STUTTHOF, which had been under the authority of the police and SS chief in Danzig, became a regular concentration camp. At the beginning of the second period, the Dachau camp's capacity was enlarged to accommodate six thousand prisoners.

In addition to these detention installations, which were officially designated as concentration camps, there were also hard-labor and "reeducation" camps, run by the Sicherheitspolizei (Security Police; Sipo), the Ministry of Justice, and even private enterprises. Late in 1941 CHEŁMNO began operating as an extermination camp, and in the spring of 1942 the extermination camps TREBLINKA, SOBIBÓR, and BEŁŻEC were established as part of AKTION REINHARD. Auschwitz-Birkenau (Auschwitz II) and Majdanek, which were existing concentration camps, had extermination centers established within them as well. These sites became the main places in which the Jews of Europe were killed. Chełmno and the three Aktion Reinhard camps were not part of the concentration camp system, whereas Auschwitz and Majdanek were both concentration camps and extermination centers. All the prisoners who were not killed immediately upon arrival in these two camps were considered concentration camp inmates.

In June 1936 Himmler assumed the newly created position of *Reichsführer-SS und Chef der Deutschen Polizei* (Reich Leader of the SS and Chief of the German Police). Three years later, in October 1939, the criminal police (KRIMINALPOLIZEI; Kripo) and the political police (the GESTAPO, which was responsible—among other things— for making arrests and transferring concentration camp prisoners) were both incorporated into the REICHSSICHERHEITSHAUPTAMT (Reich Security Main Office; RSHA). In his capacity as chief of the German police, Himmler was able to increase the number of nonpolitical prisoners incarcerated in concentration camps, especially habitual criminals, tramps, beggars, and Gypsies, and also HOMOSEXUALS and convicted prostitutes.

In taking charge of nonpolitical prisoners in such large numbers (which reached their

The remains of the Majdanek concentration camp have been preserved as a Polish national memorial. In the photo are prisoners' three-tier wooden bunks.

height in 1937 and 1938), the SS chiefs also had economic considerations in mind. The implementation of the FOUR-YEAR PLAN, whose objective was to prepare the army and the economy for war, led to a labor shortage especially in the area of construction. For this reason the SS sought to exploit the concentration camp prisoners for military and civil construction projects, and thereby to reinforce its own standing. Camps that were established from 1937 on had a quarry or brickyard near them, where the prisoners were put to work. The SS also set up its own factories for this purpose. Beginning in the summer of 1938, and reaching a peak in the wake of the KRISTALLNACHT pogrom, Jews were interned in the camps solely because they were Jews.

The rise in the number of nonpolitical prisoners, together with the general intensification of persecution during the period of war preparations, led to a constant increase in the number of concentration camp prisoners during the second period. When the war broke out there were about 25,000 prisoners in the camps; thereafter, there was a steep rise in their number, far exceeding the camps' capacity, as a result of which congestion in them took on catastrophic proportions. At the end of 1941 the concentration camps contained some 60,000 prisoners.

In the wake of the ANSCHLUSS in March 1938, prisoners from Austria, and later from the annexed areas of Czechoslovakia, were sent to the concentration camps. Prisoners from all the occupied countries followed, although the great majority were from Poland. These were primarily political and Jewish prisoners. However, the raids against actual or presumed resistance fighters (especially in Poland) were so sweeping that all segments of the population were affected, regardless of political convictions or involvement with concrete political actions.

With the expansion of the war into the Soviet Union, the concentration camp population was swelled by Russian POWs. Most of them were soon killed in the KOMMISSARBEFEHL extermination operations, for which special installations were put up where the prisoners were shot to death. By the spring of 1942, in Buchenwald and Sachsenhausen alone, about 21,500 Soviet POWs were shot to death. In the meantime a small gas chamber had been built in Auschwitz I (the main Auschwitz camp), and experiments with ZYKLON B gas were carried out in it. Some 600 Soviet POWs and 250 other prisoners were killed during the course of these experiments. All told, by May 1942 approximately 15,000 additional Soviet POWs had died in Auschwitz and in the SS POW camp at Lublin, having either been shot to death or perished from the intolerable conditions prevailing there.

From 1942 to 1944–1945. In the third period, concentration camp prisoners were systematically drafted for work in the armaments industry. The great losses suffered by the Germans in the fighting, especially on the eastern front, forced the Nazi leadership to draft growing numbers of Germans from the labor force into the army. Their places were mostly taken by forced labor from the occupied territories and, to a lesser degree, by concentration camp prisoners. Previously, forced labor in the concentration camps had been a method of punishment and persecution intended to humiliate the prisoners and lead to their deaths through overwork. Now, through an arrangement made by the SS with Minister of Armaments Albert SPEER, concentration camp prisoners were to be put at the disposal of state-owned and private companies that were in need of manpower for arms production. The newly created SS WIRTSCHAFTS-VERWALTUNGSHAUPTAMT (Economic-Administrative Main Office; WVHA), especially in 1943 and 1944, established, in the vicinity of industrial plants, a large number of satellite camps, which were put under the control of the existing main camps.

Speer's reorganization of the armaments industry also led to a corresponding change in the SS structure. Its two central departments, Haushalt und Bauten (Budget and Construction) and Verwaltung und Wirtschaft (Administration and Economy) were merged into the WVHA, with Oswald POHL in charge. The concentration camp inspectorate was also taken over by this office as its Section D, headed by Richard GLÜCKS. Section D was largely independent of the WVHA and had its offices at a considerable distance from it (at Oranienburg, near Sachsenhausen).

In the third period the SS did not establish any additional central concentration camps, but a number of existing camps that hitherto had not been under the control of the concentration camp inspectorate were taken over and run as such. These included the small Niederhagen camp, whose inmates were drafted to enlarge the Wewelsburg assembly site for the SS elite; the VUGHT and PŁASZÓW camps; the KAISERWALD camp; Majdanek, which had previously been the SS POW camp in Lublin; and the BERGEN-BELSEN camp for Jewish internees. In October 1944 Dora, which had been a Buchenwald satellite camp, became an independent camp, DORA-MITTELBAU (Nordhausen). The prisoners in Dora were employed in the production of V-2 rockets.

In the meantime, the Auschwitz and Majdanek camps were integrated, in 1942, into the systematic extermination of Jews. The SS oversaw the installation of gas chambers there, and most of the Jews deported to these camps were killed on arrival, especially children, women, the old, and the weak. Entire communities of Jews were brought to Auschwitz: from the Netherlands in 1942 and 1943, from Slovakia between 1942 and 1944, from Greece in 1943, and from Hungary and various parts of Poland, Germany, France, Belgium, and other countries in 1944. In Auschwitz the Jews were sent to the new section, Birkenau, which originally had been planned to house Soviet POWs; a large area there was used for female prisoners. Only a few of the other concentration camps had gas chambers installed in them. These were used for a limited time only and on a much smaller scale than in Auschwitz and Majdanek. By far, most of the prisoners in the third period were Jews, Poles, and Soviets. A large proportion of the Soviets had first been drafted as forced foreign laborers (*see* FORCED LABOR: FREMDARBEITER). Their presence in the concentration camps was a punishment for violating the exceptionally harsh rules that were applied to the *Ostarbeiter* (workers from the east). Next, by number, were the French, the Italians (after Italy's surrender), and the Yugoslavs. In the fall of 1944, as the war fronts were drawing near, the camps were gradually closed and the prisoners sent on long DEATH MARCHES to other camps still in existence.

Conditions. Living conditions in the concentration camps varied greatly among the camps and from one period to another. In the first period, prisoners were rarely incarcerated longer than a year, and the housing, food, and working conditions were tolerable, compared to the later years. The deaths that occurred were usually the result of deliberate maltreatment, or of SS and SA men shooting to death prisoners against whom they had a personal grudge.

In the second period the mortality rate rose as a result of maltreatment, the kinds of work the prisoners were assigned, the more primitive working conditions that prevailed, and the physical exertion called for in the quarries, as well as undernourishment and overcrowding in the barracks. Most of the victims were Poles, Russians, and Jews, but the so-called Spanish fighters—men who had fought on the republican side in the Spanish Civil War—also had only a very slight chance of surviving between 1940 and 1942, especially in Mauthausen. Up to the outbreak of the war in September 1939 the best conditions (relatively) were to be found in Dachau; the worst in Mauthausen. Between October 27, 1939, and February 18, 1940, Dachau was cleared of prisoners and served as a training camp for the Waffen-SS. After that it took in chiefly prisoners from other camps who were in poor physical condition, and as a result the mortality rate rose rapidly there too.

In 1943 living conditions for most concentration camp prisoners improved slightly, notwithstanding the large new intake, and the differences among the camps were less pronounced. The demands of the armaments industry and the wish to exploit the labor potential of the prisoners more rationally forced the SS, and the companies involved, to improve their treatment of the prisoners and provide them with adequate nourishment. Such improvement, however, applied only to places where the prisoners' work required technical knowledge and skill; in the construction projects—of which there were many—the general decrease in the mortality rate was not felt. In Auschwitz and Majdanek, the decrease did not apply to every sector: at Auschwitz-Birkenau, which contained the Jewish prisoners, the mortality rate remained at an extremely high level, whereas in the Auschwitz camp as a whole it decreased from 15 percent in March 1943 to 3 percent in August. In the liquidation phase of the camps, however, the rate rose again, to unbelievable heights.

The total number of people who perished in the concentration camps, not including those sent directly to extermination centers, can only be guessed at. Existing documentation accounts for more than 450,000, but the real number may be assumed to have been from 700,000 to 800,000. Eugen Kogon's estimate in *The Theory and Practice of Hell* of 1.2 million seems too high. On the other hand, his figure for the total number of concentration camp prisoners, 1.6 million, appears reliable. As far as is known, the highest total number of prisoners held at any given time was 714,211, the figure registered by the SS in January 1945.

Camp Routine. The prisoners had little choice in their daily actions. The SS dictated the day's course of events, down to the smallest detail. Violations of orders in the camp were severely punished—by flogging, solitary confinement, withholding food rations, and so forth. Some prisoners were assigned positions supervising their fellow inmates and working in the camp administration, as room, block, and camp "elders" and as KAPOs, who were in charge of work crews. Prisoners also worked in the camp kitchen, in the hospital, and in the office. The way these prisoners carried out their jobs was of great importance for the prison population as a whole. Some were just as brutal as the SS and exploited their positions for their own benefit only. Others made efforts to mitigate the SS terror regime and to protect prisoners who were in danger. The role played by functionaries among the prisoners is evaluated in widely divergent ways in Holocaust memoirs, and depends to a considerable degree on the personal experiences of the author.

The prisoners were categorized by the SS according to their national origin and the grounds for which they had been put into the concentration camps. Each category had its own conditions of imprisonment, which in turn affected the chances of survival. The different categories were identified by the color of the badges worn by the prisoners on their clothes. The prisoners—especially the "politicals" (the "reds") and the criminals (the "greens")—competed with one another for the assignments that carried influence. As a

Survivors of the Flossenbürg concentration camp after their liberation by the American army on April 23, 1945.

rule, German prisoners held the top posts; in Auschwitz, the Polish prisoners also played an important role. Soviet prisoners and Jews (irrespective of their nationality) had very little chance of obtaining any appointment. The criteria applied by the SS to the different categories were determined by its racist ideology.

Composition of Prisoners. In the first period the composition of the prison population was relatively homogeneous; most were anti-Nazis. It was therefore much easier for prisoners at that time to establish solidarity among themselves than in the following years. In the second period, the struggle for survival encouraged the emergence of cliques, who cheated and fought one another in efforts to obtain a share of the little food and inadequate accommodation available. On the other hand, there were also illegal groups of prisoners who organized mutual help; the first to do so were the German Communists in the camps. The influence exercised by these illegal groups increased in the third period, during which living conditions in the camps underwent temporary improvement. They managed to smuggle their members into important assignments and into the camp administration. Other groups, especially those made up of Soviet POWs, engaged in sabotage in the arms factories. In some camps, underground "international" prisoners' committees were set up, which made it their task to prepare for their self-liberation when the front line came closer.

The fate of the prisoners depended to a large extent on their practical skills, ideological views, and past social ties. Most of the newly arrived prisoners had to fend for themselves. From the SS they could expect harsh punishment and maltreatment if they committed an error. Only in rare instances was it possible for the other prisoners to help the new arrivals, or at least to sympathize with them. There was also a certain understandable tension between newcomers and old-timers familiar with the conditions, who had undergone a long period of adaptation and survival to attain a certain status in the camp.

For the new prisoner the first shock was usually his (or her) total humiliation as a human being: he had to relinquish all personal possessions, his hair was shorn, and he was tattooed with an identification number. This, added to the strenuous physical labor, the terrible living conditions, and the brutality of those in charge, made the danger to his life greatest in the first few months, when many perished. If, on the other hand, the prisoner had skills that could be put to practical use and was therefore attached to a work gang with a relatively easy assignment, or if he belonged to a social or ideological group that kept together in the camp (such as the Communists, JEHOVAH'S WITNESSES, or the conservative national resistance groups among the Polish prisoners), he had a chance of finding protection, escaping harassment, and becoming acquainted with appropriate conduct in the camp.

Some camps, such as Auschwitz-Birkenau and Stutthof, contained separate sections for women, and Ravensbrück was entirely a women's camp. The humiliation, loss of personal identity, absence of the most elementary sanitary conditions and of any privacy, and the cutting off of their hair had an especially damaging effect on the women prisoners, and led to a high rate of collapse and death among them. Sometimes there were children and youth in the camps. Their distress was especially intense, but often the hardest and most veteran prisoners took pity on them and tried to protect them.

Jews in the Camps. There were also tensions between the different ethnic groups, with Jews at the bottom of the ladder. During the first period the Jews were a relatively small group in the camps. In Dachau, for example, only 10 percent of the prisoners were Jews. Most of them belonged to the outlawed organizations of the labor movement or had been taken into "protective custody" because of their political activities. This situation changed in the second period, and as a result of the *Razzien* against "asocial" elements ordered by Himmler in 1936, as many as one-third of the persons taken to the camps were Jews. This was one of a series of intensified anti-Jewish measures introduced that year, resulting in a rapid deterioration of the situation of the Jews in Germany. Beginning with Dachau, the number of Jews in the concentration camps rose to between 15 percent and 20 percent of the camp population. A new height was reached in the wake of the November 9, 1938, *Kristallnacht* pogrom, when within a few days thirty-six thousand Jews were detained in the Reich (including Austria). Of these, eleven thousand were taken to Dachau, between ten thousand and twelve thousand to Buchenwald, and about six thousand to Sachsenhausen, creating catastrophic congestion in these camps. No single group underwent such sufferings in the period before the war as did the Jews on that occasion.

From the very beginning, the treatment meted out to Jews was worse than that given other prisoners. As early as 1933, the Jewish share in the prisoners' mortality rate at Dachau was disproportionately large. In the second period, conditions in the camps for Jewish prisoners deteriorated drastically. Following the mass influx of Jews in November 1938, the overall mortality in all the concentration camps multiplied rapidly, and most of the victims were Jews. The SS exploited the terrible conditions in the camps to force the Jews to emigrate from Germany. As a rule, at that time any Jewish prisoner who could produce an emigration visa was set free, and by the spring of 1939 most of the Jews who had been brought to the camps in November 1938 had been released.

Once the war broke out, Jews taken to concentration camps had little chance of survival. The groups of Polish Jews imprisoned in Buchenwald and in Mauthausen were nearly all annihilated within a few months. In the fall of 1941, when a medical commission carried out a selection of certain categories of prisoners in the camps, weeding out the feeble, the sick, and the "politicals" (whom the SS particularly disliked) to send them to gas chambers under the EUTHANASIA PROGRAM, the percentage of Jewish prisoners among those selected was extremely high. In the conditions prevailing during the second period, Jewish prisoners were rarely able to form groups of their own. Many, especially the German Jews, had the word *Jude* stamped on their clothes by the SS. For the individual Jewish prisoner this mark of identification had a variety of social and ideological meanings: some of the Jews among the prisoners were Social Democrats or Communists who were divorced from Jewish religious practice and faith; others had been close to traditional right-wing parties and were rooted in national bourgeois ideology; still others were strictly Orthodox Jews.

Even before the arrival of the Polish Jews, the German Jewish prisoners had a varied social background. This was now reinforced by the "national" differences between the two communities, the Polish and the German. At first the strongest bond between them was the persecution from which they all suffered. The perilous conditions of life and the careful watch kept by the SS over the Jewish prisoners during the second period as a rule precluded the emergence among the Jews of the kind of group cooperation and core associations that the "politicals" and the "criminals" had managed to create. Nevertheless, in some of the concentration camps, and also in Auschwitz, illegal Jewish groups engaged in mutual assistance and in activities of a political nature. Even among the SONDERKOMMANDO prisoners in Birkenau, who were part of the concentration camp but worked in the extermination center, an underground group was organized, and in October 1944 a revolt broke out in the camp.

In the third period, the deportation of the Jews from the Reich to ghettos and camps in the east also had its consequences for the Jews in the concentration camps in Germany. An order issued by the WVHA on October 5, 1942, called for all the concentration camps on the soil of the Reich to be made *judenfrei* ("free of Jews"). The Jewish prisoners were deported mostly to Auschwitz and Lublin (Majdanek), where they suffered the same fate as the other Jews sent to those camps. It was not until 1944 that some of Hungary's deported Jews, instead of being sent to extermination camps, were put on a march to the Reich for forced labor there. The majority of them were caught up in the chaos of the evacuation marches.

Once liberated, many former prisoners were unable to free themselves from the anguish of their experience in the concentration camps. Months, and often years later, they still felt the detrimental effects on their mental and physical health, which in some cases was irreparably damaged. Among the symptoms were a frequent inability to establish close contact with others, to hold a regular job, or to sustain a marital and family relationship, in addition to sleep disorders, anxiety attacks, body tremors, and gastritis. Some of the more typical of these symptoms have been described in the medical literature as the "concentration camp syndrome," although its precise manifestations and frequency of occurrence remain in dispute.

Effects of the Camps. Research on the effects of imprisonment in concentration camps—some of it based on personal experience—has, for the most part, taken the form of psychoanalytical studies. These seek to analyze the behavior of concentration camp inmates and to explain such phenomena as the formation of groups and the rivalry among them, emotional insensitivity, and the adoption of patterns of behavior that might aid in survival. Best known is *The Informed Heart*, by Bruno Bettelheim, who maintains that the prisoners adopted the standards of the SS, or at least had to build up a kind of schizophrenic conscience in themselves. From the beginning, however, there were also studies based on the sociological method (Kogon), which were later expanded by behavioral studies. While the rules laid down by the SS in the camps had to be observed by the prisoners to ensure their survival, there always existed groups of prisoners who adhered to their own set of standards and behaved accordingly. They often had to restrict such behavior to underground and "illegal" activities, with the result that not all their fellow prisoners were aware that such standards of behavior did indeed exist in the camps.

[*See also* Italy: Concentration Camps; Muselmann; Survivors, Psychology of; *see in addition under* Camps.]

BIBLIOGRAPHY

Bettelheim, B. *The Informed Heart: The Human Condition in Modern Mass Society.* London, 1961.

Des Pres, T. *The Survivor: An Anatomy of Life in the Death Camps.* New York, 1976.

Gutman, Y., and A. Saf, eds. *The Nazi Concentration Camps: Structure and Aims; The Image of the Prisoner; The Jews in the Camps.* Proceedings of the Fourth Yad Vashem International Historical Conference. Jerusalem, 1984.

International Tracing Service. Records Branch. *Catalogue of Camps and Prisons in Germany and German-occupied Territories, September 1939–May 1945.* 2 vols. Arolsen, West Germany, 1949–1950. Supplement, 1951.

Kogon, E. *The Theory and Practice of Hell: The German Concentration Camps and the System behind Them.* New York, 1950.

Pawelczynska, A. *Values and Violence in Auschwitz: A Sociological Analysis.* Berkeley, 1979.

Pingel, F. "The Concentration Camps as Part of the National-Socialist System of Domination." In *The Nazi Concentration Camps: Structure and Aims; The Image of the Prisoner; The Jews in the Camps.* Proceedings of the Fourth Yad Vashem International Historical Conference, edited by Y. Gutman and A. Saf, pp. 3–18. Jerusalem, 1984.

Rousset, D. *The Other Kingdom.* New York, 1947.

Segev, T. *Soldiers of Evil: The Commandants of the Nazi Concentration Camps.* New York, 1987.

FALK PINGEL

CONFERENCES. *See* Bermuda Conference; Evian Conference; Munich Conference; Wannsee Conference.

CONFISCATION. *See under* Expropriation.

CONSEIL REPRÉSENTATIF DES JUIFS DE FRANCE (Representative Council of French Jews; CRIF), umbrella organization of French Jewish societies, founded in January 1944. CRIF's foundation ended the long-standing divisions in FRANCE between French-born and immigrant Jewish associations, which were motivated by two factors: the fate of the remaining Jews, and postwar considerations. Joseph Fisher (later Ariel), president of the Zionist Federation, was instrumental in its establishment. From mid-1943 Fisher pursued a policy of unification, and by August 1943 he had succeeded in uniting the immigrant organizations into the Comité Général de Défense (CGD). Fisher pursued, however, a much broader objective: the unification of the immigrant organizations and the CONSISTOIRE CENTRAL DES ISRAÉLITES DE FRANCE (CC), the representatives of French Judaism. The divisions by then were more superficial than real; previous political obstacles, the evaluation of Vichy's policy, and the CC's perception of its role, which had hindered French Jewry's unity, had been overcome.

The CC and the CGD entered into negotiations in December 1943, and by early 1944 the broad principles of the CRIF were accepted. Shortly thereafter, debates developed concerning its charter. They ranged over three issues: the closure of the UNION GÉNÉRALE DES ISRAÉLITES DE FRANCE (General Council of French Jews; UGIF); resistance; and postwar policy on the establishment of a Jewish national home in Palestine. Questions of resistance and the UGIF were partly resolved. Divergences developed over the issue of Palestine: Communists and Bundists demanded a binational home, and the CC was concerned about the implications of too firm a commitment. A general consensus, however, overrode the differences. The CRIF was formed, with Léon MEISS as president. At liberation, it represented all the political tendencies and organizations, and it was able to act on behalf of a united community and to present the Jewish case to the provisional government.

BIBLIOGRAPHY

Adler, J. *The Jews of Paris and the Final Solution: Communal Response and International Conflicts, 1940–1944.* Oxford, 1987.

Conseil Représentatif des Juifs de France. *C.R.I.F.: Vingt-cinq années d'activités, 1944–1969.* Paris, 1970.

JACQUES ADLER

CONSISTOIRE CENTRAL DES ISRAÉLITES DE FRANCE (Central Consistory of French Jews), the hierarchical religious organization of French Jewry, established in 1808. During the 1930s, in the face of rising antisemitism, the Consistoire cautioned against overt public demonstrations and tried to curb the political activism of immigrant Jews. With the fall of FRANCE, the Consistoire's leadership relocated from Paris to Lyons, in the unoccupied zone.

Slow in responding to the catastrophe befalling French Jewry, the Consistoire began to function under the new circumstances in the spring of 1941 under the presidency of Jacques HELBRONNER, a sixty-eight-year old member of the Conseil d'Etat (Council of State). Following closely the Consistoire's traditional course of diplomacy, Helbronner advised the Jewish community to observe the anti-Jewish restrictions and thus to maintain the honor of French Jewry. On the community's behalf, the Consistoire filed numerous solemn protests against the Vichy racial legislation, and Helbronner intervened with Marshal Philippe PÉTAIN on many occasions. In this vein, the Consistoire led the campaign against the creation of the UNION GÉNÉRALE DES ISRAÉLITES DE FRANCE (UGIF) and tried to uphold its own unique position in French Jewry. Not disbanded by the Vichy law establishing the UGIF, the Consistoire remained responsible for Jewish religious life, maintaining open synagogues until the end of the war and involving itself in welfare projects through the work of the Aumônerie Générale Israélite (Jewish Chaplaincy) and the Chief Rabbi's Fund. As the historical representative of French Jewry, the Consistoire continued to advocate moderation even after the deportations of the summer of 1942, although it registered a most vehement protest to Vichy.

After the German occupation of the south in November 1942 and the mass deportations from Marseilles in January 1943, the Consistoire withdrew its opposition to the UGIF, and on several occasions they jointly determined Jewish responses. However, a major change in the Consistoire's orientation ensued only after Helbronner was deported in October 1943, during the all-out effort of the SS to round up French Jews. Under the leadership of Helbronner's successor, Léon MEISS, the Consistoire undertook discussions with all elements of the community, including the Communist factions, in an effort to establish a united Jewish position against the renewed German drive. Resistance groups and official representatives of established Judaism eventually set up the CONSEIL REPRÉSENTATIF DES JUIFS DE FRANCE, an all-encompassing Jewish organization that was to direct French Jewry from early 1944 until the liberation of France. At the head of this unique body was the president of the Consistoire, Léon Meiss.

BIBLIOGRAPHY

Adler, J. *The Jews of Paris and the Final Solution.* New York, 1987.

Cohen, R. I. *The Burden of Conscience: French Jewish Leadership during the Holocaust.* Bloomington, 1987.

Cohen, R. I. "French Jewry's Dilemma on the Orientation of Its Leadership (From Polemics to Conciliation: 1942–1944)." *Yad Vashem Studies* 14 (1981): 167–204.

Szajkowski, Z. "The French Central Jewish Consistory during the Second World War." *Yad Vashem Studies* 3 (1959): 187–202.

RICHARD COHEN

CORFU, northernmost Greek island in the Ionian Sea. Massive emigration from Corfu beginning after 1891 had reduced its Jewish population from five thousand to two thousand. Many of the older inhabitants spoke Italian, attesting to the long cultural and occasional political influence of Italy. The Italians occupied the island in April 1941, but after the Italian surrender to the Allies on September 8, 1943, the Germans conquered the island from its Italian garrison. The Jewish quarter was heavily bombed in mid-September and several Jews were killed.

Corfu's Jews had been convinced that the Germans would not cross from occupied Epiros to their island. They knew of German antisemitism, but, ignorant of the Holocaust, they did not feel threatened, and ignored warnings to flee given by the Italians, whose occupation had been relatively mild. The Germans quickly closed the Jewish school and instituted measures to keep the Jewish population under their control.

The commander of Corfu, Karl JÄGER, reported to his headquarters in Ioannina that the deportation of the Jews was not feasible under the circumstances, citing logistic problems, the presence of the Red Cross, and the potential intervention of the local population. On June 9, 1944, 1,795 Jews were arrested by German military police units from Ioannina and by local Greek police, assisted by the Jews Ino Recanati and Joseph Recanati of Athens, and were interned in the old fortress. At least 30 Jews escaped and were hidden by their Christian neighbors or reached Epirus, where they joined the partisans or were protected by them. After a tortuous seven-day journey to Athens, during which several young men escaped, later to fight with the resistance, the Jews were transported to AUSCHWITZ, where two-thirds were killed on arrival (June 30, 1944); only some 200 returned to Corfu. During the deportations, much of the Greek population showed considerable sympathy, especially in Lefkas; others, however, engaged in looting after Jewish shops and homes were systematically stripped by the Germans.

BIBLIOGRAPHY

Gilbert, M. *The Holocaust.* New York, 1985. See pages 698–699.

STEVEN B. BOWMAN

COUNCIL FOR AID TO JEWS. *See* Zegota.

COUNCIL FOR GERMAN JEWRY (CFGJ), British Jewish organization established in 1936 with the goal of aiding German Jews to leave GERMANY in coordinated emigration. Organizationally, the CFGJ succeeded and absorbed the Central British Fund for German Jewry (CBF), established in May 1933, and occupied the same premises in Woburn House, in London. Many of the CBF's officers became officers of the council as well, and the CBF became the council's financial arm.

In reaction to the NUREMBERG LAWS of September 1935, British Jewish leaders held a number of meetings at the Rothschild home at New Court, London. Through long discussions and consultations with German Jewish leaders, a consensus was reached between Zionists and non-Zionists in December 1935 in the form of an outline for an emigration plan. A delegation consisting of Sir Herbert Samuel, Lord Bearsted, and Simon Marks traveled to the United States in January 1936 with the aim of establishing a partnership with American Jewry in order to raise $15 million to assist in the emigration of 100,000 German Jews aged seventeen to thirty-five. Half of the emigrants would settle in Palestine, and the other half in other countries around the world. It was hoped that the young emigrants would quickly succeed in finding employment and would then bring their families out of Germany. In addition, it was hoped that another 100,000 German Jews would emigrate without assistance, thereby ensuring the emigration of a large part of German Jewry in a brief time.

Personal and organizational differences nearly prevented the formation of a joint council. American Zionist and non-Zionist leaders distrusted each other, and each organization was reluctant to yield any of its independence to the proposed umbrella group. The American Jewish organizations did not wish to submit their allocations of funds to British scrutiny.

The council's executive board held its first meeting in London on March 15, 1936, but the two major American groups, the JOINT DISTRIBUTION COMMITTEE and the United Palestine Appeal, joined formally only in August. The council never achieved the stature its British founders sought, since it lacked the power to make independent decisions. The coordination achieved succeeded in funding numerous vocational-training programs in Germany and elsewhere, as well as in assisting approximately 100,000 Jews to emigrate by the outbreak of World War II. More than $15 million was raised in this period, but events quickly overtook the council's plans and work, leaving the self-help aspect of the plan largely unrealized. British immigration policies in Palestine, emigration obstacles in Germany, and the growing impoverishment of German Jewry combined to limit severely the council's success.

The ANSCHLUSS of Austria, creating more potential refugees, and the heightened persecution of German Jewry in 1938 (*see* KRISTALLNACHT), threw the council's emigration plan into a shambles. Organized and planned emigration now became subsidized flight. With the outbreak of World War II, the council was forced to limit its activities to refugees in Britain, and its name was changed accordingly, to the Central Council for Jewish Refugees. Following the war, the needs of DISPLACED PERSONS and REFUGEES brought another reorganization and name change, to the Central British Fund for Relief and Rehabilitation. This organization still exists at Woburn House.

[*See also* Great Britain.]

BIBLIOGRAPHY

Bauer, Y. *My Brother's Keeper: A History of the American Joint Distribution Committee, 1929–1939*. Philadelphia, 1974. See pages 151–160.

Bentwich, N. *They Sought Refuge: An Account of British Jewry's Work for Victims of Nazi Oppression*. London, 1956.

Stiebel, J. "The Central British Fund for World Jewish Relief." *Transactions of the Jewish Society of England* 27 (1978/80): 60–61.

DAVID SILBERKLANG

CRACOW. *See* Kraków.

CRIF. *See* Conseil Représentatif des Juifs de France.

CRIMES AGAINST HUMANITY. Article 6 of the charter of the International Military Tribunal (IMT), which was to conduct the NUREMBERG TRIAL, empowered the IMT to try the major war criminals of the European Axis countries for three categories of crimes: crimes against peace, war crimes, and crimes against humanity.

Among the crimes defined as war crimes were violations of the laws or customs of war, such as murder, ill-treatment, deportation, forced labor, or wanton destruction not justified by military necessity. The IMT found that such acts, including also ill-treatment of civilian populations and prisoners of war, had been committed by the Führer and his cohorts in total disregard of the fundamental principles of international law, and had been based instead on cold-blooded, criminal considerations. The IMT therefore decided to deal with the entire category of war crimes in great detail and to determine the individual defendants' guilt for such crimes. Included in the tribunal's deliberations were acts of murder and ill-treatment of prisoners of war and civilian populations, especially the persecution of Jews.

Such acts of persecution were also defined as crimes against humanity, even if they were committed before the war but were connected to preparations for the war. Article 6(c) of the IMT charter defines crimes against humanity as "murder, extermination, enslavement, deportation, and other inhumane acts committed against any civilian population, before or during the war; or persecution on political, racial, or religious grounds in execution of or in connection with any crime within the jurisdiction of the tribunal, whether or not in violation of the domestic law of the country where perpetrated." It follows from this that the IMT was empowered to try crimes against humanity only if they were perpetrated in the execution of or in connection with war crimes or crimes against peace. Some of the acts defined as war crimes—such as murder, ill-treatment, and deportation—were also defined as crimes against humanity. These acts, however, were deemed war crimes only when they were a violation of the laws and customs of war, affecting the rights of fighting forces and the civilian population in occupied territory or in the course of warlike actions. Crimes against humanity, on the other hand, were defined as applying to acts against any civilian population—including the population of the country that commits the acts, and commits them on its own soil—at any time, in times of peace as well as in times of war. The latter feature—application to acts committed both in times of peace and times of war—also appears in the definition of crimes against peace, a category that includes not only the initiation and conduct of war, but also acts committed in times of peace, such as planning and preparation of aggression.

A corollary of this is that it is neither the time in which the act is committed nor the act itself that constitutes the exclusive characteristic of a crime against humanity and sets it apart from the other crimes defined in the IMT charter. What distinguishes crimes against humanity from other crimes are the extraordinary brutality and diversity of means that the Nazis employed to commit these crimes, the unprecedented policy of persecution and extermination on which they were based, and the fact that while initially they were related to a policy of aggression, they exceeded by far the definition of war crimes in the traditional sense. Among the victims of the Nazi crimes against humanity were populations for which the laws and customs of war provide no protection—such as nationals of neutral countries, stateless persons, nationals of countries that were partners in the Axis, and, of course, nationals of Germany itself. Above all, most of the victims of the Nazi crimes against humanity were Jews, who, prior to the Nuremberg Trial, were not deemed to have protection based on international law.

There is some substance to the view that the introduction of the category of crimes against humanity was designed to serve as a support to the categories of war crimes and crimes against peace, or to cover a side effect related to these two categories. Crimes against humanity related to acts committed in times of peace as well, in the framework of planning and preparation for war, and on the territory of the aggressor or any other territory (not necessarily Nazi-occupied areas), against the aggressors' own nationals, the nationals of countries that were not at war with Germany, or stateless persons. Since these acts were related to preparations for war, the persons responsible for them could not be convicted under the laws and customs of war, which deal with situations involving actual warfare. The separate category of crimes against humanity also seeks to take into account another element: while the crimes to which it refers affect various populations —groups that were persecuted on national, racial, and religious grounds—the crimes all have in common the element of "inhumanity": the cruel methods that were employed, and the unprecedented purpose of mass extermination of victims simply for belonging to a certain group (or being classified, by the criminals, as belonging to that group), without the victims' having committed any offense whatsoever.

Every crime is an offense not only against the victim, but also against the established order of the country in which it takes place—the country as a social organization that includes all its citizens, irrespective of color, political views, and origin. Similarly, every international crime, especially when it is a crime against humanity, is an attack on the international community as a whole, threatening the safeguards of its peace, and indeed its very existence. Nevertheless, what distinguishes crimes against humanity from the other categories of crimes is their "inhumanity," rather than the injury they inflict upon "humanity" as a worldwide community; this was why they were designated as crimes against "humanity" in the abstract sense of the term. However, acts defined as crimes against peace or war crimes can also be regarded as crimes against humanity, since the planning and carrying out of aggression prepares the conditions for inhumane offenses against human rights.

The element of humanity and the condemnation of and punishment for inhumane acts are not recent innovations in international law, the dictates of human conscience having long been regarded as one of international law's sources. Thus, the Petersburg Declaration of 1868 stated that the dictates of humanity must take precedence over the needs of war; and the fourth Hague Convention (1907) specified that in situations not specifically provided for in the convention, the civilian population and the fighting forces would also be protected by the principles of humanity and the dictates of society's conscience. This principle has since been reconfirmed time and again in various international treaties and conventions, such as the 1949 Geneva Convention and the 1977 Supplementary Protocols.

The IMT extended this principle to apply also to criminal acts that are not war crimes, in order to provide protection to every civilian population and to every individual, irrespective of his nationality and his country's policy and laws. Evidently, the principle is valid under all circumstances and takes precedence over every national law and every bilateral or multilateral international agreement; it is a universal and cogent principle, which is not subject to challenge and cannot be deviated from by unilateral decision; it can be changed or replaced only by a humanitarian principle that is of an even higher order (as stated in the 1969 Vienna Convention on Treaties). This means that, in formal terms, the definition of inhumane acts as being criminal in nature does not depend on the legal system or established policy of the country in which such acts occur. In this respect, too, crimes against humanity are *sui generis*, different from other criminal acts.

The criminal nature of crimes against humanity is far worse and of a totally different order than that of any other criminal act defined as such by the criminal codes of all civilized nations. This criminal practice was demonstrated in its most radical form by the Nazi policy and acts of brutal mass murder and extermination of entire peoples and population groups (*see* GENOCIDE). The unique character of a crime against humanity can also be recognized in other acts that in the European continental system of law have long been classified as inherently criminal (*malum per se*), and that in Soviet legal terminology constitute a threat to society and public order.

These aspects of crimes against humanity and crimes against peace are disregarded by those who have challenged the justice and the very nature of the Nuremberg Trial because it included these categories in the stated principles upon which it based the indictment. Such acts, so their argument goes, were political acts, for which those who committed them cannot be held accountable, as heads of sovereign entities who were not subject to any other entity or to any law other than a law declared as valid by their own state. It is true that in a certain respect the crimes defined by the IMT charter are of a political character, since their planning, preparation, and execution were possible only in the framework of operations, guidelines, initiatives, and decrees emanating from and authorized by the political administration of a state. This, however, is no reason to treat the persons responsible for these crimes as political criminals in the accepted sense of that term, since their acts were linked to the theory of RACISM and to other inhumane concepts that have no precedent in the annals of mankind. Thus it was declared, in legal theory and practice, that such criminals may be tried by any country that does not want to, or has no reason to, extradite them for trial in other countries or by international tribunals.

Furthermore, their status is like that of other categories of criminals to whom the principle of universal jurisdiction and punishment applies. Nor may these criminals seek to justify their acts by claiming that they were performing their official duties or acting on orders from their superiors. One restriction that the IMT charter did impose was that in order for crimes against humanity to be tried, they had to be related to war crimes or crimes against peace, either as side effects of such crimes or in support of them.

Many legal experts and human-rights activists seek to abolish this restrictive condition in the codification of international criminal law. They point out that while this condition applied to those tried at the Nuremberg Trial and the Tokyo trial of major Japanese war criminals, it should not be applicable to other criminals charged with crimes against humanity, and consequently their prosecution should not be linked to war crimes or crimes against peace. Indeed, such a link is conspicuous by its absence in Allied Control Council Law No. 10, of December 20, 1945, and in the laws of other countries, among them Israel's Nazis and Nazi Collaborators (Punishment) Law 5710-1950.

It is true that in most of the trials the Allies held in their zones of occupation in Germany, the judges preferred to follow the IMT precedent and held defendants responsible for crimes against humanity only when the acts were committed in the preparation of aggression or in violation of the laws and customs of war. This was so in the SUBSEQUENT NUREMBERG PROCEEDINGS, held by the Americans, in which the Nuremberg Military Tribunals tried Nazi judges, industrialists, and Einsatzgruppen personnel, among others. Those who call for the complete separation of the concept of crimes against humanity from war crimes and crimes against peace do so in order to endow this concept with the status of a human-rights principle that would protect all human beings at all times and under all conditions, completely independent of warlike events.

[*See also* Trials of War Criminals.]

BIBLIOGRAPHY

Falk, R. A., B. Kolko, and R. J. Lifton. *Crimes of War: A Legal, Political, Documentary, and Psychological Inquiry into the Responsibility of Leaders, Citizens, and Soldiers for Criminal Acts of War.* New York, 1971.

Goldstein, A. "Crimes against Humanity: Some Jewish Aspects." *Jewish Yearbook of International Law* 1 (1948): 206–225.

Schwelb, E. "Crimes against Humanity." *British Yearbook of International Law* 23 (1946): 178–228.

MARIAN MUSHKAT

CROATIA (Nezavisna Država Hrvatska, or Independent State of Croatia; NDH), puppet state in YUGOSLAVIA, established during World War II, that was in existence from April 1941 to May 1945. Its area—which underwent many changes owing to annexations—consisted of what are today the Federative Republic of Croatia and the Federative Republic of Bosnia and Herzegovina, a total of approximately 38,600 square miles (100,000 sq km). Its capital was Zagreb; it had a population of 6.3 million, of whom 3.3 million were Catholic Croats, 1.9 million Orthodox Serbs, 700,000 Muslim Croats, 170,000 Germans, 75,000 Hungarians, 40,000 Jews, 30,000 Gypsies, and 100,000 members of other minorities.

Serbian Minority. Croatia was set up by the Germans and the Italians on April 10, 1941, as part of their plan for the dismemberment of Yugoslavia. Ante PAVELIĆ, leader of the secessionist USTAŠA movement, was made head of state. Shortly after taking control, the Ustaša, with the support of many Croatians, embarked upon what it called "the purge of Croatia from foreign elements," which had as its main purpose the elimination of the Serbian minority. In a brutal terror campaign, more than half a million Serbs were killed, a quarter-million expelled, and two hundred thousand forced to convert to Catholicism. The Ustaša regime in Croatia, and particularly this drive in the summer of 1941 to exterminate and dispossess the Serbs, was one of the most horrendous episodes of World War II. The murder methods applied by the Ustaša were extraordinarily primitive and sadistic: thousands were hurled from mountaintops, others were beaten to death or had their throats cut, entire villages were burned down, women raped, people sent on death marches in the middle of winter, and still others starved to death.

Jews. The Jews of Croatia lived mainly in the larger cities: Zagreb (11,000), Sarajevo (10,000), Osijek (3,000), and Bjelovar (3,000). Sixty percent are estimated to have been Ashkenazim and the rest Sephardim. Most of the Jews belonged to the middle class; they were civil servants, merchants, and professionals such as doctors and lawyers. Zionists controlled the communities. Croatian Jewry carried on a wide range of activities; it had its own school network, weekly newspaper, welfare institutions, and youth movements. The NDH regime categorized the Jews as one of the "foreign elements" that had to be purged, and the Ustaša's German patrons encouraged it in its drive against the Jews. In pursuing this course, the Ustaša was motivated by desires to please the Germans and to acquire the Jews' property, rather than by ideological antisemitism. Three government departments were involved in Jewish affairs. The Ministry of the Interior, with Andrija Artuković as minister, dealt with anti-Jewish legislation; the security police (Ustaška Nadzorna Služba), under Eugen Dido Kvaternik, arrested, imprisoned, and murdered Jews, and ran the concentration camps; and the Ministry of Finance, under Vladimir Kosak, was charged with the depredation of Jewish property.

Anti-Jewish legislation. A few days after taking control, the Ustaša enacted anti-Jewish legislation, most of it based on the precedents set in the Third Reich, the GENERALGOUVERNEMENT, and SLOVAKIA. It included racial statutes on the model of the NUREMBERG LAWS, which defined who was a Jew and stripped the Jews of their civil rights. But there was an innovation in these laws—a paragraph empowering the head of state to bestow the title of "Honorary Aryan"—which provided an opportunity for corrupt practices. Most of the legislation dealt with economic affairs: Aryan trustees

were appointed to take over Jewish businesses; Jewish factories, enterprises, and real property were "nationalized"; Jewish civil servants were dismissed; and Jewish professionals (lawyers, doctors, veterinarians, and so on) were prohibited from dealing with non-Jewish clients. Collective fines, which had to be paid in gold or its equivalent, were imposed on the Jewish communities. Overnight, a pseudolegal expropriation drive was launched, which before long turned into an unbridled countrywide campaign of plunder and pillage in which everyone who stood to profit took part—trade unions, youth organizations, sports clubs, the armed forces, and government officials of all ranks. Ordinary citizens also took part in this campaign wherever they could; indeed, the share of "private" elements in the plunder was enormous—at least half of the property of which the Jews were robbed apparently never reached the state treasury but remained in the hands of individual Croatians. According to an estimate by the Ministry of Finance published in 1944, the value of the Jewish property it acquired was 25 billion dinars ($50 million, according to the prewar rate of exchange). Presenting the state budget for the 1942–1943 fiscal year, the minister of finance, Vladimir Kosak, said that the deficit would be covered by proceeds from the sale of Jewish property.

In the first few months of Ustaša rule, various other decrees were passed, mostly by local authorities, designed to restrict the Jews' freedom of movement and the places where they could live, and thereby to isolate them from the rest of the population. In May 1941 an order was announced under which the Jews had to wear the yellow Jewish BADGE with the letter *Ž* (from *Židov*, "Jew") prominently displayed on it.

Roundup, incarceration, and murder. The first arrests made among the Jews were part of a general preventive measure to forestall the rise of any anti-government organiza-

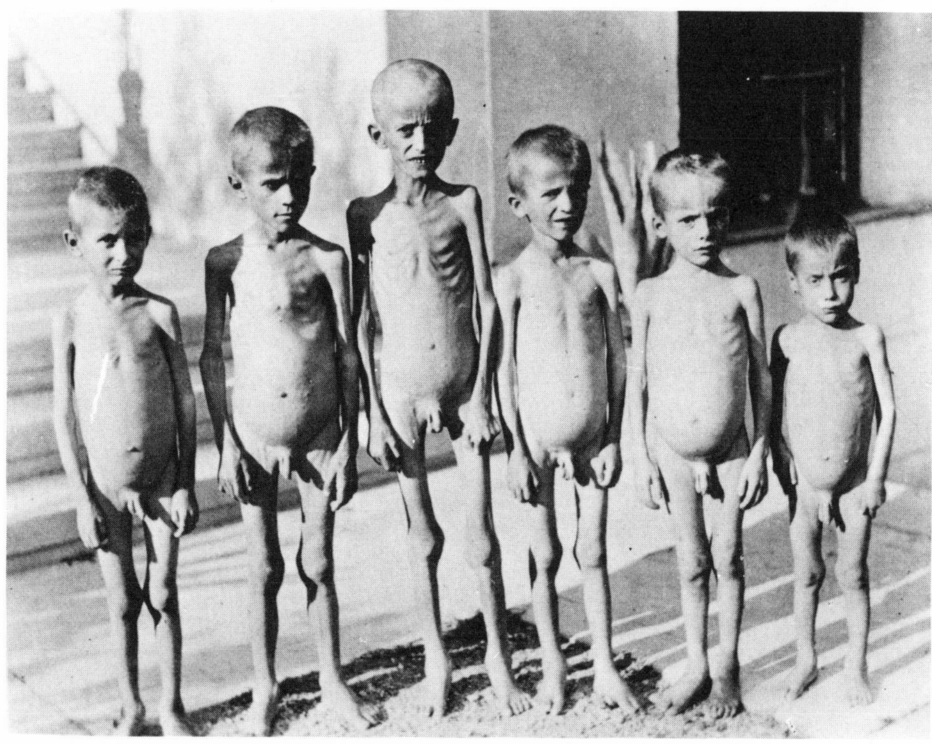

Children liberated from a Croatian concentration camp.

tions. It affected the active members of left-wing parties, Serbian parties, democrats, and left-wing intellectuals. Included in that wave of arrests were some one hundred Jewish youngsters who had been active in Zionist youth movements in Zagreb, as well as the Jewish lawyers in that city; both groups were taken to concentration camps that had been established in the country, where most of them were killed. Following the German invasion of the Soviet Union in June 1941, the incidence of sabotage acts in Croatia rose sharply and the situation of the Jews deteriorated further, as acts of sabotage led to retaliatory measures in which many Jews were executed (with the authorities stressing their Jewishness). The mass arrest of Jews was set in motion with a decree issued by Ante Pavelić on June 26, 1941, that accused the Jews of spreading lies in order to incite the population and of interfering with the orderly supply of essential commodities, "well-known black-marketeers that they are. . . . I declare that the Jews are collectively guilty and order them to be imprisoned . . . in concentration camps."

The onslaught on the Jews of Zagreb had begun a few days earlier, on June 22. By the end of the month several hundred Jewish families had been seized and, for the most part, put into the Pag and Jadovno concentration camps. In July it was the turn of the smaller communities, such as Varaždin, Koprivnica, Ludbreg, Karlovac, and Bjelovar. The prisoners were first assembled in the former trade-fair grounds in the heart of Zagreb and from there dispatched to various camps.

This was followed, at the beginning of August, by a drive against the Jews of Bosnia and Herzegovina. In the first stage, those living in small towns were arrested; at the end of the month, it was the turn of Sarajevo, where the roundup of the Jews took longer than expected and was completed only in November 1941. The concentration camp of JASENOVAC was constructed in August 1941, and after its completion most arrested Jews were sent there. Some Jewish women of Sarajevo were imprisoned in a special women's camp that had been set up in the town of Djakovo for lack of space in the other camps.

By the end of 1941, two-thirds of Croatian Jewry had been taken to Croatian concentration camps; most were killed on arrival or soon after. The Jews who had not yet been imprisoned were regarded as indispensable to the state's economy, were married to non-Jews, or had personal ties to members of the ruling clique. Some Jews also managed to flee to the Italian zone of occupation. In an interview with a German newspaper at the end of the summer of 1941, Pavelić declared: "The Jews will be liquidated within a very short time."

Jews were imprisoned in the following concentration camps:

1. Danica, near Zagreb. This camp was established in April 1941 and was disbanded at the end of the year. Most of the inmates were political prisoners; the Jewish lawyers of Zagreb were also incarcerated here.

2. Jadovno, in the Velebit Mountains. Established in May 1941 and disbanded in August of that year, when the area was about to be handed over to the Italians. It was here that the Jewish youngsters from Zagreb were imprisoned and murdered.

3. Pag, on Pag Island in the Adriatic. Established in June 1941 and dismantled by the end of August of that year. In the few weeks of its existence, hundreds of people were murdered in this camp. An inquiry commission set up by the Italian army when it took control of the area in August 1941 reported that shocking acts had been committed there. Among the murder victims were many of the people who had been seized in the first wave of arrests.

4. Kruscica, in Bosnia. Established at the beginning of August 1941 and disbanded by the end of the following month. This was mainly a transit camp for the Jewish women arrested in Bosnia and Herzegovina.

5. Loborgrad, in northern Croatia. Set up in September 1941 and dismantled in October 1942. It served as a camp for women and children and was run by VOLKSDEUTSCHE (ethnic Germans). In May 1942 the women and children prisoners were deported to AUSCHWITZ.

6. Djakovo, in southeast Croatia. Established in December 1941; in existence until June 1942. This was another camp where women and children were imprisoned. Several hundred prisoners died in a typhus epidemic that broke out there; the rest were transferred, in the summer of 1942, to Jasenovac, where they were killed on arrival.

7. Tenje, near Osijek. Set up in March 1942 and disbanded in August of that year, when all its prisoners were deported to Auschwitz to be gassed.

8. Jasenovac, 62 miles (100 km) from Zagreb. Established in August 1941; in existence until April 1945. This was the largest and best-known concentration camp in Croatia, the place where most of its Jews went to their death. It was also in Jasenovac that hundreds of thousands of people belonging to other nationalities were killed—Serbs, GYPSIES, and various non-Jewish opposition elements.

German role in deportation and extermination. Croatian Jews, for the most part, were murdered by fellow Croatians, but there is no doubt about the role played by the Germans. From the beginning of Ustaša rule, it was the Germans who supervised the "solution of the Jewish question." An SS officer named Müller was posted to Zagreb in May 1941 and took charge of the "solution." In Sarajevo, it was SS-Sturmbannführer Dr. Alfred Heinrich who handled the Jews. A major role was also played by the German ambassador in Zagreb, SA-Gruppenführer Siegfried Kasche, a veteran member of the diplomatic corps and a zealous antisemite. It was Kasche who pressured and exhorted the Croatian leaders to lose no time in killing all the Jews in the country, and who urged his colleagues in Berlin to make sure that the Jews in the Italian-occupied zone were seized and subjected to the same fate as their brethren in the other parts of Croatia. Kasche's right-hand man on Jewish affairs was SS-Sturmbannführer Hans Helm, who served as the embassy police attaché and belonged to the staff of the REICHSSICHERHEITSHAUPTAMT (Reich Security Main Office; RSHA).

As long as the Croatians continued to kill Jews, the Germans did not interfere, but German involvement grew at the beginning of 1942, when it appeared that the Croatians might call a halt to the killing. At the WANNSEE CONFERENCE of January 20, 1942, it was decided that the Germans would propose to the Croatians that they transfer the Jews

The Jewish Rab battalion, formed after the prisoners of the Rab internment camp were liberated in September 1943.

of Croatia to eastern Europe. In the negotiations that followed, Hans Helm, who was an expert on Yugoslav affairs, represented the German side, while Dido Kvaternik, chief of security services, was the Croatian representative. The Germans may have decided to take over the murder of Croatian Jews because the Croatians had lost some of their enthusiasm following the successes of the Red Army in the winter of 1941–1942. In the spring of 1942 the two sides agreed on the deportation of Croatian Jews to the east; the Croatian government undertook to arrest the Jews, take them to the railheads, and pay the Germans 30 reichsmarks per person for the cost of transporting the prisoners to the extermination camps. In return, the Germans agreed that the property of the Jewish victims would go to the Croatian government.

SS-Hauptsturmführer Franz Abromeit, an "expert" on the staff of Adolf EICHMANN's section, was sent to Zagreb to take charge of the deportation. Between August 13 and 20, 1942, five trains left Croatia for Auschwitz with 5,500 Jews aboard, half from the Tenje concentration camp and the rest from the Loborgrad camp and from Zagreb and Sarajevo. In May 1943, while Heinrich HIMMLER was on a visit to Zagreb, another series of deportations to Auschwitz was conducted, with the Germans joining the Croatians in drawing up the list of deportees. In two trains on May 5 and 10, a group of 1,150 Jews was deported, including the leaders of the Zagreb and Osijek Jewish communities. Of the thousands of Croatian Jews who were deported to Auschwitz, only a few dozen survived. In Croatia itself, a mere few hundred Jews remained alive, most of them because they were protégés of Croatian political leaders or were married to non-Jews.

Italian protection. Most of the Croatian Jews who survived owed their lives to the Italians. In their zone of occupation (the Dalmatian coast, Albania, and Montenegro), the Italians resolutely protected the Jews; some five thousand Jews were saved by the Italians in Yugoslavia.

In the summer of 1943 all the Jewish refugees in Dalmatia were put into a camp in RAB. Following the Italian surrender in September 1943, the area was liberated by the partisans, and most of the Jews were moved to liberated areas in the center of the country. Those who were fit to bear arms or perform other military service joined the partisan army, while the others were given the protection of the fighting forces.

Catholic Church. In the interwar period the Catholic church in Croatia had been a staunch supporter of Croatian nationalism, and it welcomed the establishment of the Croatian state. The Vatican had always supported the stand of the Croatian church and had encouraged Croatian separatism. The Ustaša extermination drive against Serbs, Jews, and Gypsies presented the church with a dilemma.

Many Catholic priests, mainly of the lower rank, took an active part in the murder operations. Generally speaking, the reaction of the Catholic church was a function of military and political developments affecting Croatia; when the standing of the NDH regime was weakening and the war was drawing to an end, protests by the church against Ustaša crimes became more and more outspoken. This was not the case in the earlier stages. A bishops' conference that met in Zagreb in November 1941 was not even prepared to denounce the forced conversion of Serbs that had taken place in the summer of 1941, let alone condemn the persecution and murder of Serbs and Jews. It was not until the middle of 1943 that Aloysius Stepinac, the archbishop of Zagreb, publicly came out against the murder of Croatian Jews (most of whom had been killed by that time), the Serbs, and other nationalities. The Vatican followed a similar line. In the early stage, the Croatian massacres were explained in Rome as "teething troubles of a new regime" (the expression of Monsignor Domenico Tardini of the Vatican state secretariat). When the course of the war was changing, the leaders of the Catholic church began to criticize the Ustaša, but in mild terms; it was only at the end, when Allied victory was assured, that Vatican spokesmen came out with clear denunciations. In some instances, Croatian clerics did help Jews. Their main effort was to save the lives of the Jewish partners in mixed marriages, and most of these did in fact survive. The church also extended help to the Zagreb Jewish community in providing food, medicines, and clothing for Jews in the concentration camps.

Communities. Jewish communities in Croatia were severely restricted in their activities during the Holocaust, mainly because most of them were liquidated at an early stage. Of the three major communities, that of Sarajevo ceased functioning at the beginning of 1942 and the Osijek community by the middle of that year. Only the Zagreb community remained in existence throughout the war.

The Zagreb community was the center of all Jewish activities. It stayed in touch with the Jewish institutions in Hungary (the RELIEF AND RESCUE COMMITTEE OF BUDAPEST), Switzerland, and Turkey; it received financial aid from abroad; and its representatives negotiated with Croatian government officials and others. Until the last deportation to Auschwitz, in May 1943, the community was headed by the Chief Rabbi of Zagreb, Dr. Shalom Freiberger, and the secretary, Aleksa Klein. Thereafter, the few Jews left in the city dealt mainly with the dispatch of food parcels to Jewish prisoners in concentration camps and with extending aid to the needy.

It is estimated that thirty thousand Jews were murdered in Croatia—80 percent of its Jewish population.

BIBLIOGRAPHY

Hory, L., and M. Broszat. *Der kroatische Ustacha Staat, 1941–1945*. Stuttgart, 1964.

Jelić-Butić, F. *Ustaše i N.D.H.* Zagreb, 1977.

Lederer, Z., ed. *The Crimes of the Germans and Their Collaborators against the Jews of Jugoslavia.* Belgrade, 1953.

Morley, J. F. *Vatican Diplomacy and the Jews during the Holocaust, 1939–1943.* New York, 1980. See pages 147–165.

MENACHEM SHELAH

CRYSTAL NIGHT. *See* Kristallnacht.

CULTURAL SOCIETY OF GERMAN JEWS. *See* Kulturbund Deutscher Juden.

CUZA, ALEXANDRU (1857–1946), founder of modern antisemitism in ROMANIA. A professor of economics at the University of Iaşi, Cuza propagated racist views of Jew-hatred and general xenophobia, accusing the Jews of having taken over Romania's cities and deprived them of their Romanian character, and of aiming to seize control of the entire country. In 1895 Cuza, together with Nicolae Jorga (a historian, writer, and political figure) and the Frenchman J. de Biez, established an international antisemitic organization, the Alliance Antisémitique Universelle. In 1910 Cuza and Jorga formed the National Democratic party, a protofascist political party based on Christian national ideas, whose main platform was the removal of the Jews from the professions and the army and a ban on their settlement in villages. Under Cuza's leadership the city of Iaşi, and especially its university, became the country's center of antisemitic activities. In 1923 he set up a fascist organization, the Liga Apararei Nationale Crestine (League of National Christian Defense), with Corneliu Codreanu as its secretary. Codreanu left the league in 1927 and established the IRON GUARD, in its initial form.

Cuza called for the imposition of a *numerus clausus* on Jews, that is, their restriction to a specific quota at the universities and in all other spheres—in effect, their removal from any position of influence in the cultural, intellectual, and literary life of the country. His fascist and antisemitic ideas preceded Nazi influence in Romania by many years, and he was able to boast that he had sounded the alarm of the Jewish "peril" much earlier than Hitler.

In 1935 Cuza and Octavian GOGA joined in forming the National Christian party by merging Cuza's league with the National Agrarian party headed by Goga. Goga came to power in 1937, with Cuza's help, and formed an outspokenly antisemitic government, the second of its kind in Europe. It remained in power for only forty-four days, but in that short time it succeeded in stripping a quarter-million Jews of their Romanian citizenship, and in ideological terms it paved the way for Ion ANTONESCU's dictatorship. The Communist authorities who assumed power after the liberation of Romania in 1944 did not take any action against Cuza and did not put him on trial "because of his advanced age."

BIBLIOGRAPHY

Ancel, J., ed. *Documents concerning the Fate of Romanian Jewry during the Holocaust.* Vols. 1, 5. Jerusalem, 1986.

Fischer-Galati, S. "Fascism, Communism, and the Jewish Question in Romania." In *Jews and Non-Jews in Eastern Europe, 1918–1945,* edited by B. Vago and G. L. Mosse, pp. 157–175. New York, 1974.

Weber, E. "Romania." In *The European Right: A Historical Profile,* edited by H. Rogger and E. Weber, pp. 501–574. Berkeley, 1966.

JEAN ANCEL

CYPRUS DETENTION CAMPS, transshipment and detention camps on the Mediterranean island of Cyprus in which the British authorities held Jewish "illegal" immigrants, most of them European survivors of the Holocaust trying to enter Palestine. On August 7, 1946, the British government made a decision to detain these Jews in Cyprus, hoping that this deterrent would put an end to Jewish immigration. The decision was geared to the British policy of breaking the power of the "Hebrew resistance movement" in Palestine. But before long the British came to realize that detention was not achieving the desired aim; the would-be immigrants continued their attempts to reach Palestine despite vio-

The former Canadian corvette (escort ship) *Josiah Wedgwood,* sailing under Panamanian flag from Italy with 1,259 Jewish refugees. It was intercepted by British warships on June 27, 1946, off the coast of Haifa in Palestine. The refugees were taken into custody by the British and then deported to the Cyprus detention camps.

lent clashes with British troops and transshipment to Cyprus. By December 1946 the British government, under pressure from the Jewish Agency and in view of the rapid rise in the number of people interned in the Cyprus camps, was allotting half the legal immigration quota (that is, 750 visas, or certificates, a month) to the Cyprus detainees.

The use of the Cyprus detention camps began on August 13, 1946, and ended on February 10, 1949, when the last group of detainees left for what had become the state of Israel. During this period, fifty-two thousand Jews passed through the Cyprus camps, having been taken off thirty-nine boats in their attempts to get to Palestine. To this number must be added twenty-two hundred children who were born in the camps. Some of the detainees spent only a few months in Cyprus, but many were held there for a year and longer. Responsibility for setting up the camps and for their administration and security was that of the British army in Cyprus, which handled the camps as though it were dealing with prisoners of war and according to the rules applicable to prisoner-of-war camps.

There were two kinds of camps. The "summer camps," of which there were five, were located at Kraolos, near Famagusta, and the detainees in them were housed in tents. The seven "winter camps" were located at Dekalia, north of Larnaca; here the housing consisted of tin huts and some tents. Conditions in the camps were quite harsh, especially for mothers of children and babies. The tents and barracks were overcrowded. there was no privacy, and families had to share accommodations with single persons. There were no partitions, no lighting fixtures, and no furni-

"Illegal immigrants" detained by the British in one of the "winter camps" in Cyprus (1947). [Bet Loḥamei ha-Getta'ot]

ture except beds. The food supplied by the British army was of poor quality; because of the inadequate facilities in the field kitchens, some of it was wasted and people went hungry. The detainees also suffered from a lack of shoes and clothing, which the British supplied only in limited quantities, from army surplus. The insufficient supply of water, particularly in the hot summer months, caused sanitary conditions to deteriorate and led to skin diseases and infections. Most of the British officers and troops in charge of the camps carried out their duties indifferently or unwillingly. Some, for humanitarian reasons, wanted to ease the refugees' lot, but they had little authority or resources. The British administration in Palestine, which was charged with establishing and maintaining the camps, had to bear the costs out of its budget, which in any case showed a deficit, and it sought to put the responsibility for the welfare of the detainees on the Jewish Agency and the JOINT DISTRIBUTION COMMITTEE (also known as the Joint).

This put the Jewish Agency in a dilemma. It did not recognize the legality of the detention, nor did it want to relieve the British authorities of their responsibility for the maintenance of the camps and the detainees' state of health. The Agency therefore asked the Joint Distribution Committee to take on responsibility for the welfare of the camp population, which the Joint readily did. As early as September 1946, a few weeks after the camps were set up, the Joint was already engaged in welfare operations there, which they maintained throughout the camps' existence.

The Joint greatly reduced the hardships from which the refugees suffered. It recruited medical and welfare teams in Palestine to run nurseries and clinics in the camps, it improved the quality of food rations for those in special need and supplemented the basic food supplies of the general camp population, it catered to religious requirements, and it set up a bureau for the search of missing relatives. The provision of educational facilities for the children and teenagers (of whom there were large numbers in the camps, most having been orphaned in the Holocaust) was yet another task taken on by the Joint, in partnership with YOUTH ALIYA. The majority of the youngsters were put into one camp, Camp 65, which became a kind of youth village. There, Youth Aliya educational teams established a school system based on the few teachers found among the refugees. The welfare teams recruited in Palestine included Jewish Agency–appointed emissaries of various political movements. Morris Laub, the Joint's director in Cyprus, became the spokesman and representative of the detainees vis- à-vis the British authorities on the island.

The detainees in the Cyprus camps were relatively young, with 80 percent of them between the ages of thirteen and thirty-five. Thus, they were among the more spirited and lively survivors of the Holocaust. They came to the camps as members of YOUTH MOVEMENTS, immigration groups, and political parties imbued with a strong Zionist ideology. Their ideology and self-discipline enabled them to adapt to the conditions in the camps.

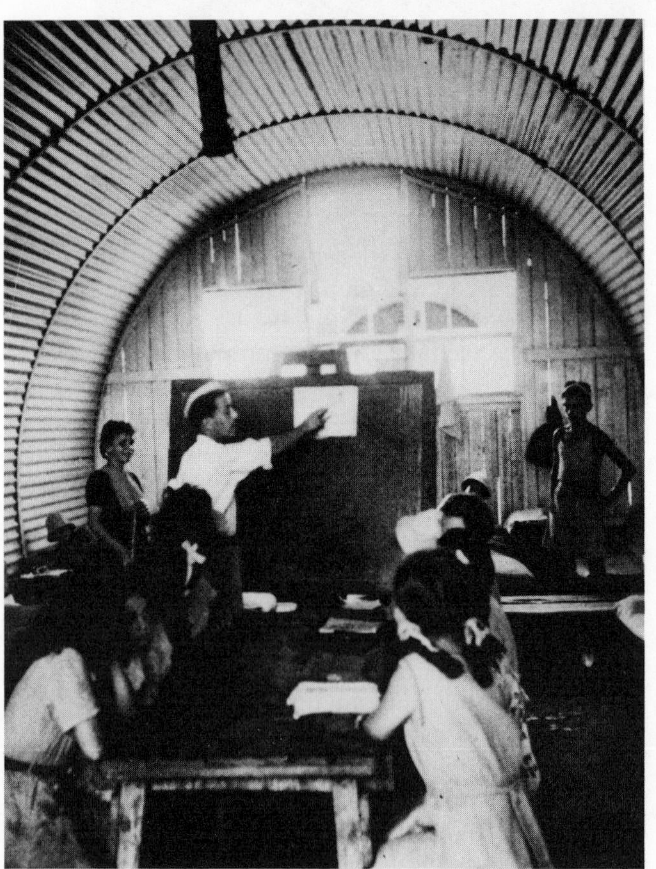

Refugee children learning Hebrew in one of the Cyprus detention camps (1947). [H. Fin]

In addition to being deprived of their liberty and exposed to harsh physical conditions, the detainees also suffered greatly from the enforced idleness of the camps. Efforts to keep them busy with cultural activities met with difficulties, owing to lack of means and scarcity of qualified personnel. An important contribution was made by emissaries from Palestine who lived with the refugees in the camps. Some of these were "legal": representatives of the various Zionist movements, welfare workers under Joint auspices, and teachers dispatched to Cyprus by the Rutenberg Teachers' Seminary. Others were "illegal"; they had been sent to Cyprus by the Palmah, the underground strike force of the Hagana (the Yishuv's underground military organization), to provide the young people in the camps with military training and prepare them for service with the Hagana when they arrived in Palestine. Living among the detainees and sharing their lot, these emissaries had great influence; they represented the Jewish national institutions and were the link between the refugees and the Jewish population in Palestine.

A few of the refugees who had second thoughts applied to the British authorities to return to the country from which they had set out. But generally, despite all their suffering, the Cyprus detainees displayed impressive moral strength and staying power during their internment. Though there were no written laws and no real sanctions that could have been applied, not a single criminal act was recorded among the detainees.

BIBLIOGRAPHY

Laub, M. *Last Barrier to Freedom.* Berkeley, 1985.

Oren, M. *You May View the Land from a Distance: Education of Youth in Cyprus.* Tel Aviv, 1987. (In Hebrew.)

Schaary, D. *The Cyprus Detention Camps for Jewish "Illegal" Immigrants to Palestine, 1946–1949.* Jerusalem, 1981. (In Hebrew.)

NAHUM BOGNER

CZECHOSLOVAK GOVERNMENT-IN-EXILE. After the MUNICH CONFERENCE (September 29–30, 1938), the president of Czechoslovakia, Edvard BENEŠ, resigned and went into exile. Following the outbreak of World War II, he established in France a Czechoslovak National Committee, which, after moving to London in 1940, functioned as a government-in-exile, one of several such London-based governments-in-exile of European countries that had been overrun by Hitler.

The government-in-exile was recognized by the Soviet Union and by the British government (July 21, 1941). From its establishment, President Beneš's main objective was to gain international recognition for the legal continuity of the Czechoslovak republic and its pre-Munich boundaries. One of its first moves was the setting up of a State Council (Statni Rada), a quasi-provisional parliament to act as a unifying body for resistance activities in exile. The Czechoslovak government-in-exile conducted extensive negotiations with the POLISH GOVERNMENT-IN-EXILE under Władysław SIKORSKI in order to obtain a far-reaching agreement, but the mutual efforts were unsuccessful. Jewish refugees from Czechoslovakia who reached Poland, the Soviet Union, Palestine, France, and Great Britain constituted a high percentage (estimated at 50 percent) of the Czechoslovak army units formed in exile. Members of the intelligentsia who managed to escape to Britain before the outbreak of the war, and who had a working knowledge of English, made themselves available to the government-in-exile for various services, particularly the information service and the Foreign Ministry.

Ernst Frischer, former head of the Jewish party in Czechoslovakia (1935–1939), was appointed the representative of the Jewish national group on the State Council. He developed a network for rescue activities and assistance and—together with the government's representatives in Geneva, Stockholm, and Lisbon—organized the sending of food parcels, medicine, and funds to the concentration camps, especially the ghetto of THERESIENSTADT. The official line of the government-in-exile on resistance inside Czechoslovakia was that no hazardous ventures should be undertaken that might entail the sacrifice of hundreds or thousands of lives. Yet a spectacular anti-Nazi action, conceived in London and eventually costing some five thousand lives, was the assassination, on May 27, 1942, of Reinhard HEYDRICH, the acting Reich Protector of BOHEMIA AND MORAVIA. It led to German retaliation in the form of mass murder, with the destruction of two villages in Bohemia (LIDICE and Lezaky) and the killing of their entire male population.

The flow of information between Prague and London, and the informants employed in the Protectorate by the Czech army intelligence in London, enabled the Czech government to furnish important information to the Allies. When asked by the WORLD JEWISH CONGRESS in August 1942 to confirm information regarding the German extermination plan (resulting from the RIEGNER CABLE), Beneš's belated response of November 1942 omitted mention of the wholesale deportations of Jews taking place in the Protectorate. However, the president and the government cooperated closely with the Jewish leadership in the free world and in Palestine. They made several diplomatic moves, including intervention with the Vatican and the Allied governments on behalf of persecuted Jews, and they openly condemned antisemitism. Foreign Minister Jan Masaryk was especially active on the Jewish issue, and his addresses over radio and at rallies were most sympathetic to the Jewish plight. It was the representative of the government at Geneva, Dr. Jaromir Kopecky, who in mid-June 1944 transmitted to the free world the so-called AUSCHWITZ PROTOCOLS, which reached him from Bratislava through underground channels and contained information on the annihilation process at AUSCHWITZ-Birkenau.

The Czechoslovak government-in-exile, the only one of its kind in eastern Europe to be allowed to return after the war to its native country, implemented some radical changes in its minority policy, with the objective of making the republic as nationally homogeneous as possible. The German minority and part of the Hungarian minority were transferred to their homelands (the TRANSCARPATHIAN UKRAINE was annexed to the Soviet Union according to the Czechoslovak-Soviet Treaty of June 29, 1945). The Jewish remnants in Czechoslovakia were given the option of declaring themselves either of Czech or of Slovak nationality.

BIBLIOGRAPHY

Dagan, A. "The Czechoslovak Government-in-Exile and the Jews." In vol. 3 of *The Jews of Czechoslovakia,* edited by A. Dagan, pp. 449–498. Philadelphia, 1984.

Rothkirchen, L. "The Czechoslovak Government-in-Exile: Jewish and Palestinian Aspects in the Light of Documents." *Yad Vashem Studies* 9 (1973): 157–199.

LIVIA ROTHKIRCHEN

CZECHOSLOVAKIA. *See* Bohemia and Moravia, Protectorate of; Slovakia; *see also* Czechoslovak Government-in-Exile.

CZERNIAKÓW, ADAM (1880–1942), head of the Warsaw JUDENRAT (Jewish Council). Czerniaków was born in WARSAW to a middle-class assimilationist family. He completed his chemical engineering studies in 1908. Later, he taught at the Jewish community's vocational school in Warsaw and served in various posts in independent Poland.

For many years Czerniaków represented Jewish artisans in several Polish organizations. From 1927 to 1934 he was a member of the Warsaw Muncipal Council, and in 1931 he was elected to the Polish Senate. Before World War II, he was a member of the executive council of the Jewish community. But in his public career between the wars Czerniaków was not regarded as a leader by the Jews, since he was not a member of any political party and had trouble expressing himself in Yiddish.

During the first week of the war, Maurycy Mayzel, chairman of the Jewish community's council, was one of the many who fled Warsaw. On September 23, in the midst of the siege of the city, Czerniaków noted in his diary that Stefan Starzynski, the mayor and commissar for civil defense, had appointed him "head of the Jewish religious community in Warsaw." On October 4, a few days after the city's surrender and the beginning of the German occupation, Czerniaków wrote: "I was taken to Szucha Avenue, where I was ordered to add twenty-four people to the community council and to serve as its head."

The official titles used by Czerniaków until the middle of 1941 were Head of the Judenrat and President of the Jewish Religious Community of Warsaw. From the middle of May 1941, his functions and authority were defined in the ghetto as corresponding to those of the mayor in the Polish part of the city.

The first Judenrat, established in October 1939, consisted of twenty-four members, including persons of recognized stature within Jewish society and outstanding figures in political organizations. Among them were the Zionist leader Maximilian Hartglas; Samuel ZYGELBOJM, a leader of the BUND; Isaac Meir Levin, the outstanding figure in Agudat Israel; and Abraham Weiss, a leading member of Mizraḥi. Most of the party activists included in the first Judenrat left Warsaw and traveled abroad during the first month of the occupation, when it was still possible to leave. Czerniaków too had this opportunity, but he refused to leave and sharply criticized the leaders who fled the city claiming that they would secure aid in the free world for the masses suffering under the heel of the Nazi conqueror.

However, even after a number of the Judenrat members had left, there still remained in it persons with wide experience in public work, among them Abraham GEPNER; Joseph Jaszunski, the director of ORT in Poland; and Stanisław Szereszewski, the chairman of TOPOROL, an association that promoted agriculture.

The Jewish community in Warsaw during the interwar period had provided for religious and educational needs and for relief work. After the ghetto was established, in October 1940, the scope of the Judenrat's activities widened considerably, and it had to deal with matters of food, work, health, housing, and sanitation—functions normally carried out by the municipality and the state authorities. The structure and bureaucracy of the Judenrat also broadened considerably. At one point during the ghetto period it had twenty-five different departments and 6,000 workers, as compared to 530 in the prewar Jewish community.

The Judenrat clerks, particularly in the higher administration and the police force, included agents planted by the German authorities and opportunists prepared to collaborate at any price. Czerniaków despised these people, but he realized that they were a necessary evil. Groups arose in the ghetto that for various reasons tried to oust Czerniaków, and some of them, like the one led by Abraham Gancwajch, had the support of members of the German police and the SD (Sicherheitsdienst; Security Service). All these attempts failed since Czerniaków was supported by the civil authorities in the GENERALGOUVERNEMENT. The Jewish underground severely criticized Czerniaków and the Judenrat's policy. At a certain stage in the ghetto's existence, public control committees were set up to strengthen supervision of the Judenrat and to improve the functioning of its personnel, but they brought no real results.

In studies of the Warsaw ghetto, much attention has been devoted to evaluating Czerniaków's activities. An analysis of this material shows that Czerniaków endeavored to prevent the direct intervention of the German authorities, and sought to organize the internal affairs of the Jews with a minimum of outside involvement. This approach made possible clandestine economic activity, the illegal smuggling of food, and so on. At the same time, there is no proof that Czerniaków maintained contact with the Jewish underground or sided with secret political activities. On the other hand, he persistently promoted education for the ghetto's children, and strove to save Jews in danger of being put to death.

During the years of Czerniaków's tenure as Judenrat head, he came into daily contact with the German police and the civil authorities, who changed five times until the mass deportation of the summer of 1942. In particular, from May 1941 onward, Czerniaków maintained constant contact with Max Bischoff, the German official in charge of moving merchandise in and out of the ghetto.

Until the ghetto was set up, Czerniaków was permitted to maintain contact with the Poles in the Warsaw municipality, chiefly the Polish mayor, Julian Kulski. In his contacts with the Germans, Czerniaków sought ways to influence them and arouse some sort of sensitivity to and consideration for the ghetto situation. These attempts were of no avail. He was twice beaten up by the Germans and

Adam Czerniaków.

suffered many insults. Czerniaków gained a certain measure of understanding through his ties with the ghetto commissar, Heinz AUERSWALD, but Auerswald too misled Czerniaków in the end by hiding from him the real facts of the mass deportation.

Chroniclers and diarists of the Warsaw ghetto are divided as to Czerniaków's personality and characteristics. Some, such as Emanuel RINGELBLUM and Itzhak KATZENELSON, both with a public background and close to the underground, were severely critical, seeing in Czerniaków an assimilator who mixed with assimilators, a man lacking close contact with the Jewish masses, who tended toward self-esteem and absurd public ceremonies in the midst of the grim reality of the ghetto. However, people who worked with Czerniaków praised the man and his qualities. He did indeed place assimilators in key positions, as when he made Joseph Szerynski (a police officer who had converted to Christianity) commander of the ghetto police, a choice considered miserable by all. But the accusation of a tendency toward self-aggrandizement and hollow ceremony is unfounded. It is generally accepted that Czerniaków had great personal decency and good intentions. A member of the underground and a leader of the ghetto fighters, Mordechai TENENBAUM (Tamaroff), noted in his diary that there were only three truly honest persons among the heads of the Judenrat, one of them being Czerniaków. Unlike the Judenrat leaders Mordechai Chaim RUMKOWSKI and Jacob GENS, Czerniaków was not at all guided by personal ambition, and was willing to cooperate with the Nazis only up to a point.

Refusing to help in the roundup of Jews destined for deportation, Czerniaków committed suicide at 4:00 p.m. on July 23, 1942. According to one version, a note was found on his desk addressed to his wife, saying: "They are demanding that I kill the children of my people with my own hands. There is nothing for me to do but to die." His death was interpreted as the protest of a man who was not prepared to cross the line between conducting ghetto activities and handing over Jews.

In the mid-1960s, YAD VASHEM received Czerniaków's wartime diary, which he kept regularly from September 6, 1939, until the day of his death. It consists of eight notebooks with 1,009 small pages in chronological order. The fifth notebook, covering the period between December 14, 1940, and April 22, 1941, has been lost. Czerniaków's diary, published in Hebrew, English, German, and Polish, is one of the most important surviving documents from the period of the Holocaust. It casts light on the man who stood at the head of the Warsaw Judenrat, provides a wealth of information about people and events, and reveals many details concerning the nature of the German rule over the Jews.

BIBLIOGRAPHY

Gutman, Y. "Adam Czerniaków: The Man and his Diary." In *The Catastrophe of European Jewry*, edited by Y. Gutman and L. Rothkirchen, pp. 451–489. Jerusalem, 1976.

Hilberg, R., S. Staron, and J. Kermisz, eds. *The Warsaw Diary of Adam Czerniakow: Prelude to Doom.* New York, 1979.

Tartakower, A., and K. R. Grossmann. "Adam Czerniakow the Man and His Supreme Sacrifice." *Yad Vashem Studies* 6 (1967): 55–67.

ISRAEL GUTMAN

CZERNOWITZ. *See* Chernovtsy.

CZĘSTOCHOWA, Polish city located about 124 miles (200 km) southwest of Warsaw, famed for Jasna Góra (Bright Mountain), the church containing a shrine with the icon of the Black Madonna of Częstochowa, revered all over Poland.

The Jewish community in Częstochowa was founded in 1765, when it numbered 75. It grew to 500 by 1808, and fifty years later there were 3,000 Jews, forming a third of the total population. When World War II broke out, 28,500 Jews lived in the city. In the Częstochowa area, on the banks of the Warta River, there are rich deposits of ores, forming the basis for steelworks. Częstochowa became a wealthy industrial center in the nineteenth century with the construction of roads and railways in the area. Jews took an active part in all the industries, as well as in banking, domestic and international trade, and crafts. A Jewish agricultural training farm and a trade school operated in Częstochowa during the interwar years, in addition to networks of religious and secular Jewish schools, as in most large Jewish communities in Poland.

The Germans entered Częstochowa on Sunday, September 3, 1939, the third day of the war, and persecution of its Jews began at once. More than 300 Jews were killed on the following day, which became known as "Bloody Monday." On September 16 a JUDENRAT (Jewish Council) was formed, headed by Leon Kopinski. Confiscation of Jewish property and household effects, beatings, mockery, and degradation went on incessantly. In August 1940, 1,000 young Jews were rounded up and sent to the Ciechanów forced-labor camps; very few survived.

A ghetto was established on April 9, 1941, by order of the *Stadthauptmann* (city commissioner), SS-Brigadeführer Dr. Richard Wendler, in the eastern, old part of the city. The ghetto was sealed off on August 23. Some

twenty thousand Jews from other cities (Łódź, Płock, Kraków) and villages were sent to the Częstochowa ghetto, which eventually held more than forty-eight thousand persons. The main places of work outside the ghetto were the German Metallurgie military factories on Krótka Street.

In preparation for the forthcoming liquidation of the ghetto, in May 1942 the Germans seized and killed the Jewish social, cultural, and political activists. Large-scale *Aktionen* began on September 22 and lasted until October 8. In each deportation, some eight thousand Jews were packed into sixty freight cars. A total of thirty-nine thousand Jews were sent in this way to the TREBLINKA extermination camp. Elderly people in the home for the aged and the children in the orphanage were killed on the spot. About two thousand Jews managed to escape or to hide in the city.

After the deportations, the northeastern part of the ghetto, called the "small ghetto," held some five thousand able-bodied Jews with skills or professions. On September 2, a privately owned German munitions factory (*Apparatenbau*) belonging to the HASAG network was established in the suburb of Stradom. This forced-labor camp existed for two years, and a total of three thousand Jews from Poland, Germany, and Austria passed through it. When a typhoid epidemic broke out the camp was closed (January 16, 1945), and the surviving inmates were deported to an unknown destination.

In June 1943, the HASAG Rakow steel mill was opened, in which five hundred to one thousand Jews from Slovakia and Poland were exploited. It was closed on January 16, 1945, and the workers sent to the BUCHENWALD and RAVENSBRÜCK camps. The largest camp in the Częstochowa area was HASAG Pelzery, which functioned from June 1943 until January 16, 1945. This was a munitions factory employing, at any given time, about five thousand Jews, from Poland, Germany, Austria, and Bohemia. Finally, there were an average of three thousand Jews working in the munitions factories of Warta and Częstochowianka.

In December 1942 the ŻYDOWSKA ORGANIZACJA BOJOWA (Jewish Fighting Organization;

Jewish slave laborers from Częstochowa (c. 1940 or 1941).

ŻOB) created a resistance unit in Częstochowa, with some 300 participants. They maintained contact with the Warsaw center. In January 1943 this group, under the leadership of Mendel Fiszlewicz, offered armed resistance to a German *Aktion*. During the clash 251 Jews were killed; the rest were deported to Radomsko and from there to Treblinka. The reprisals that followed included the murder of 127 of the Jewish intelligentsia, and 250 children and elderly people. In other resistance groups there were two relatively large units of partisans, who were killed by Polish rightist partisans, and several small units that joined the leftist Polish partisans. On June 25, 1943, another ŻOB group tried to resist the liquidation of the small ghetto. When the Soviet army liberated Częstochowa, there were still some 5,000 Jews in the area. In June 1946, 2,167 Jews were living in Częstochowa. After the KIELCE pogrom on July 4, many of them joined the BERIḤA for Palestine.

BIBLIOGRAPHY

Glicksman, W. M. "Daily Record Sheet of the Jewish Police (District I) in the Czestochowa Ghetto (1941–1942)." *Yad Vashem Studies* 6 (1967): 331–358.

Glicksman, W. M. *A Kehillah in Poland during the Inter-War Years*. Philadelphia, 1969.

Schutzmann, M. *The Czestochowa Book*. 2 vols. Jerusalem, 1967, 1968. (In Hebrew.)

Tenenbaum, J. *Underground*. New York, 1952.

SINAI LEICHTER

CZORTKÓW. *See* Chortkov.

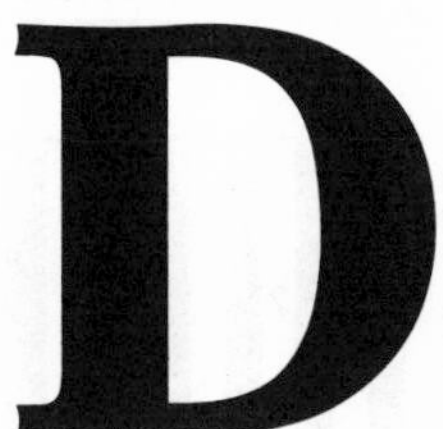

DACHAU, one of the first Nazi CONCENTRATION CAMPS, located in the small town of Dachau, about 10 miles (15 km) northwest of Munich. Dachau was chosen because it was the site of an empty munitions factory from World War I, which provided the needed space. The opening of the camp, with a capacity for 5,000 prisoners, was announced by Heinrich HIMMLER at a press conference held on March 20, 1933.

The first group of so-called protective-custody prisoners, consisting mainly of Communists and Social Democrats, was brought to Dachau on March 22, 1933. They were guarded by Bavarian state police until the camp was taken over by the SS on April 11.

On becoming commandant of the camp in June 1933, Theodor EICKE set up a scheme of organization with detailed regulations for camp life. Later, when Eicke was appointed inspector general for all concentration camps, these regulations were used, with local variations, elsewhere. With Dachau as his model, he developed an institution that was intended, by its very existence, to spread fear among the populace, an effective tool to silence every opponent of the regime. Dachau became a useful training ground for the SS. There, its members first learned to see those with different convictions as inferior and to deal with them accordingly, not hesitating to kill when the occasion arose. In later years, the members of the SS TOTENKOPFVERBÄNDE (Death's-Head Units) were able, without a thought, to annihilate many hundreds of thousands of people in GAS VANS and GAS CHAMBERS. The transformation of the terror system of National Socialism into bloody reality began in the Dachau concentration camp. Besides the guards and SS camp personnel, large numbers of SS military units were trained and instructed there.

When the camp opened, only known political opponents of the Nazis were interned. Communists, Social Democrats, and a few monarchists, who had passionately opposed one another (as well as the Nazis) before 1933, now found themselves together behind barbed wire. From about 1935, it was usual for all persons who had been condemned in a court of law to be taken automatically to a concentration camp after they had served their prison sentences. The first Jewish prisoners came as known political opponents of the Nazis. At Dachau, as elsewhere, they received even worse treatment than the other prisoners. Gradually, more and more groups were interned: JEHOVAH'S WITNESSES, who resisted the draft; GYPSIES, who, like the Jews, were classified as racially inferior; clergymen who resisted the Nazi coercion of the churches; HOMOSEXUALS; and many who had been denounced for making critical remarks of various kinds.

The number of Jewish prisoners increased with the systematizing of the persecution of the Jews. After KRISTALLNACHT (November 9–10, 1938), more than ten thousand Jewish citizens from all over Germany were interned in Dachau. Those who could prove their intention to leave Germany were released, and indeed most of them were released within a few months of detention. When systematic extermination of the Jews began in 1942, the

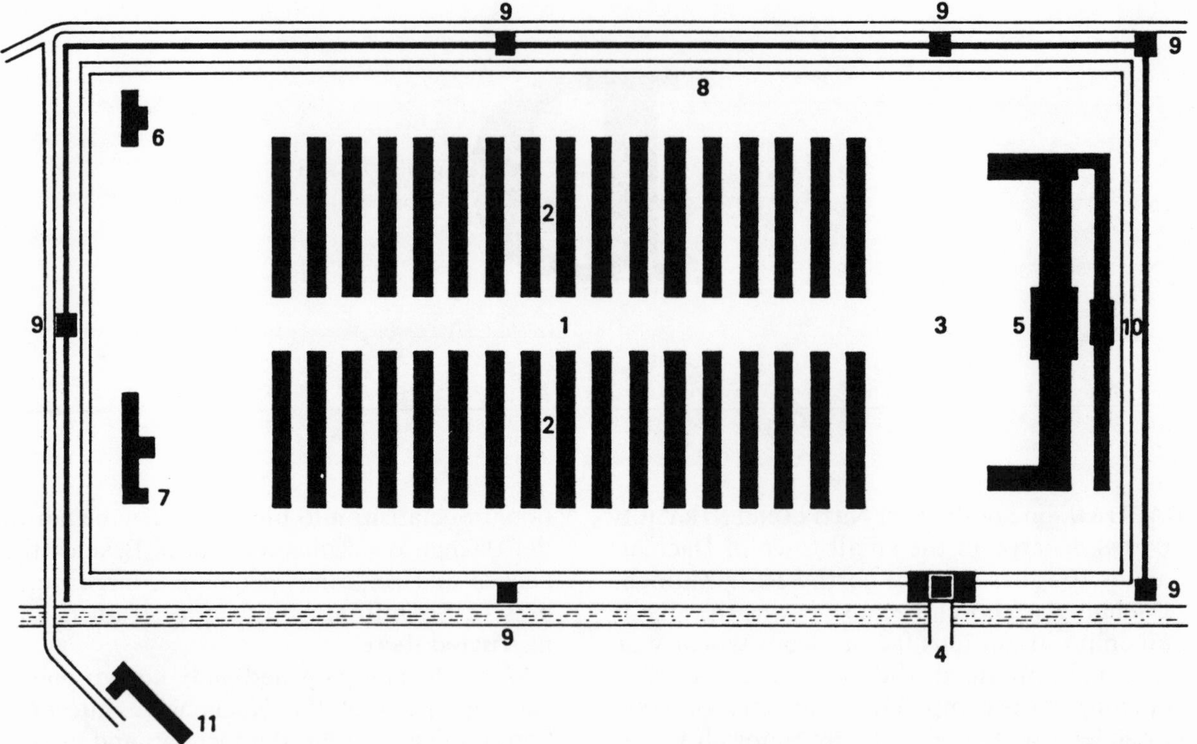

1. *Lagerstrasse* (main road)
2. Barracks
3. Parade ground for roll call
4. *Jourhaus* (entrance to the camp and guard room)
5. *Wirtschaftsgebäude* (kitchen, laundry, showers, etc.)
6. Disinfection hut
7. Vegetable garden
8. Ditch with live barbed-wire fence and camp wall
9. Watchtowers
10. *Bunker* (prison block)
11. Crematorium

Plan of the Dachau concentration camp.

Jewish prisoners were transported from Dachau and the other camps within the German Reich to the mass extermination camps in occupied Poland. When, during the summer and fall of 1944, additional subsidiary camps were installed near armament factories to increase production there, thousands of Jewish prisoners, mostly from Hungary but also from Poland, Czechoslovakia, Romania, and the USSR, were brought to the Dachau subsidiary camps. At the liberation of Dachau and its subsidiary camps in April 1945, about 30 percent of the total number of inmates were Jewish.

During its twelve-year existence, Dachau was always a "political camp": the political prisoners, who had been there first and knew the conditions best, held most of the key positions in the so-called prisoners' internal government, which had been instituted by the SS. Since this body organized the daily life in the camp, it could prevent criminal prisoners from reaching positions that would give them power over the others—power that criminal prisoners in other camps often misused for their own advantage. In 1937 and 1938, a new camp was built by the prisoners alongside the old buildings of the munitions factory: thirty-two barracks; the camp entrance building, containing the offices of the SS administration; the *Wirtschaftsgebäude* ("farm buildings," containing the kitchen, workshops, showers, and so on); and a camp prison. The camp was enclosed by a water-filled ditch, fortified by an electrified barbed-wire fence, and surrounded by a wall with seven guard towers.

During the summer of 1938, several thousand Austrian prisoners were brought to Dachau. Their arrival marked the beginning of the deportations that would reflect the course of the war: transports were sent to Dachau from each country as it was invaded by the German army. Prisoners included resistance fighters, Jews, clergymen, and others who refused to collaborate with the occupation. At the liberation, inmates from more than thirty countries were found in Dachau, with Germans forming only a minority.

All prisoners underwent the same fate when they entered the camp. They left all legal status behind, their remaining possessions were confiscated, their hair was shaved off, and they were dressed in striped fatigues. They were allocated a number as well as a colored triangle indicating the category of prisoner to which they belonged. The daily routine was filled with work, hunger, exhaustion, and fear of the brutality of the sadistic SS guards. The value of the cheap labor that the prisoners provided (the only cost involved was that of their miserable food rations) was quickly recognized and ruthlessly exploited.

At first, besides being employed in camp management and maintenance, the Dachau inmates worked in handicraft industries set up within the camp itself, as well as in so-called branch detachments outside the camp. They built roads, worked in gravel pits, and drained marshes, rehabilitating them as arable land. Initially, production in the camps was directly under the control of the individual camp commandant. But as the camps continued to grow, the range of production expanded, and the SS industries that were served by the camp labor were centralized under their main office in Berlin. In the first winter of the war, 1939–1940, the Dachau camp was used to set up the SS Totenkopf-Division. During this time the prisoners were sent to the camps at BUCHENWALD, FLOSSENBÜRG, and MAUTHAUSEN, where they had to work in quarries under the harshest conditions without any safety precautions whatever.

In the course of the war, the work force of the concentration camps became increasingly important for the German armaments industry. The network of camps, which gradually extended over the whole of central Europe, took on gigantic proportions. Dachau alone had, besides numerous smaller camps, thirty-six large subsidiary camps in which up to thirty-seven thousand prisoners worked almost exclusively on armaments. Private firms had the opportunity to hire slave laborers from the camps. For the prisoners, who worked under SS guard, they paid a daily rate to the SS WIRTSCHAFTS-VERWALTUNGSHAUPTAMT (Economic-Administrative Main Office; WVHA). The prisoners, however, received nothing. Those who fell ill were sent back to the main camp; this usually meant death. The firms received new, healthier laborers until these too could no longer meet the demands of their employers.

In Dachau there was no mass extermination program with poison gas. But out of the total number of 206,206 prisoners registered there were 31,591 registered deaths, most of them during the war. However, the total number of deaths in Dachau, including the victims of individual and mass executions and the final death marches, will never be known.

In Dachau, as in other Nazi camps, MEDICAL EXPERIMENTS were performed on helpless inmates. Himmler provided the opportunity for

Prisoners of the Dachau concentration camp (June 28, 1938).

SS physicians to use prisoners as guinea pigs. Dr. Sigmund Rascher played a key role in the "decompression" or "high-altitude" experiments. The alleged purpose was to examine the effect of a sudden loss of pressure or lack of oxygen, such as that experienced by army pilots whose planes were destroyed and who had to make parachute jumps at great heights. From mid-March to mid-May 1942, about 200 inmates were used for these experiments; according to the eyewitness testimony of the prisoners' nurse, Walter Neff, out of this number at least 70 or 80 died. Rascher was also responsible for the series of "freezing experiments," which were carried out from the middle of August to October 1942. Their ostensible object was to determine how pilots shot down at sea who suffered from freezing could be quickly and effectively helped. The air force expressed its readiness to conduct these experiments under the direction of Dr. Ernst Holzlöhner, who worked with a Dr. Finke and Dr. Rascher in Dachau. Holzlöhner and Finke broke off their work after October 1942, and Rascher continued alone until March 1943. According to the testimony of witnesses, from a total of 360 to 400 prisoners used in these experiments, 80 to 90 died.

Professor Dr. Claus Schilling, a well-known researcher in tropical medicine, opened a malaria experimental station in the Dachau camp. He hoped to discover possible methods of immunization against malaria, and for this purpose had about 1,100 inmates infected with the disease. The exact number of fatalities from these experiments cannot be determined, since the survivors returned to their previous work in the camp after the disease had subsided and many, physically weakened, then fell victim to other illnesses.

Besides these, a variety of other medical experiments were performed on Dachau prisoners. There was a tuberculosis experimental station; sepsis and phlegmon (purulent inflammation) were artificially induced in a group of prisoners to test and compare the effects of biochemical and allopathic remedies. In addition, there were attempts to make seawater drinkable and experiments with medications to stop bleeding.

The systematic killing within the concentration camp of people who were sick and incapable of work began after the official termination of the EUTHANASIA PROGRAM on September 1, 1941. In the summer of 1941, the camp physician at Dachau was commanded to register those prisoners who were sick or unable to work. Some weeks later, a medical commission from Berlin arrived to pass judgment, and during the winter of 1941–1942 "invalid transports" departed from Dachau in quick succession to the Hartheim castle, near Linz, which had served as an asylum for the insane before the war. There, 3,166 inmates from Dachau were gassed. In 1942 a gas chamber was built in Dachau, but it was not put into use. It was located within the camp's second crematorium, erected when the first crematorium, with only one incinerator, proved inadequate.

From 1934, when the leaders of the SA (Sturmabteilung; Storm Troopers) and opponents of National Socialism were murdered, Dachau was also used as an execution site. In addition, mass shootings of Soviet PRISONERS OF WAR took place there from October 1941 to April 1942, on an SS shooting range located outside the camp grounds. The exact number of these victims cannot be determined, since they were not listed in camp files. Later, Soviet prisoners of war were incorporated instead into the powerful forced-labor system and set to work for the armaments industry. Executions thereafter were carried out individually until the end of the war.

During the last months before the liberation, the prisoners at Dachau had to live under extremely inhuman conditions, which even they would not have been able to imagine. The gigantic transports continually arriving from other Nazi camps evacuated in the face of the advancing Allies brought human beings who were, for the most part, reduced to skeletons and exhausted to the point of death. During this period up to 1,600 prisoners were crowded into barracks intended for 200. In early 1945, over 100 inmates daily, and for a time over 200, fell victim to the typhus epidemic that had been raging in many of the camps since December 1944. An underground camp committee was organized to try to ensure the survival of the prisoners and, if necessary, to organize resistance to SS plans of action.

A memorial, *Dachau*, by the Yugoslav sculptor Nandor Glid, erected at Yad Vashem, Jerusalem, on April 24, 1979. The Yad Vashem memorial is a copy of the one erected on the site of the roll-call area at Dachau in 1967. Bronze, 21 × 52 feet (6.3 × 16 m).

On April 26, 1945, there were 67,665 registered prisoners in Dachau, among them 22,100 Jews; on this day more than 7,000 of them were forced, under SS guard, to march south. During the march anyone who could continue no longer was shot, and many others died from hunger, cold, or exhaustion. At the beginning of May, American troops overtook the remnants of those columns on the march; the SS guards had disappeared shortly before. After the war, it was revealed that plans had existed to kill all the inmates by bombs and poison.

On April 29, 1945, the camp was liberated by the Seventh Army of the United States armed forces. Forty former members of the camp's SS staff were tried by an American court at Dachau between November 15 and December 14, 1945. Of the forty accused, thirty-six were sentenced to death.

BIBLIOGRAPHY

Benz, W., ed. *Dachau Review*. Vol. 1. New York, 1987.

Berben, P. *Dachau, 1933–1945: The Official History*. London, 1975.

Konnilyn, F. *Hitler's Death Camps*. New York, 1981.

Wallner, P. *By Order of the Gestapo*. London, 1941.

BARBARA DISTEL

DALUEGE, KURT (1897–1946), Nazi official. In 1916, Daluege volunteered for army service and became a lieutenant. He was a member of the notorious Rossbach Freikorps, which conducted partisan activity against France. He studied engineering at the Berlin Technical College, and from 1924 worked for the Berlin garbage-disposal department as a construction and civil engineer. Daluege joined the SA (Sturmabteilung; Storm Troopers) in Berlin in 1926 and transferred to the SS in 1928, having been appointed commander of SS Group East. On January 12, 1933, he became a member of the Reichstag; that May he was named chief of the police department of the Prussian Ministry of the

Kurt Daluege (far left), general of the German police. [National Archives]

Interior, with the rank of *Ministerialrat* (senior counselor).

Daluege was short on intellectual ability (his nickname was "Dumm-Dummi") but possessed organizational talent. With no interest or personal involvement in ideology, he served as a willing instrument for the automatic execution of orders; he had little interest in racial issues and left "Jewish affairs" in the hands of Reinhard HEYDRICH.

Under Daluege's direction, the Prussian police was infiltrated with SS men. Following the RÖHM putsch (the action against the SA on June 30, 1934), Daluege was promoted to SS-*Obergruppenführer*, and when Heinrich HIMMLER became chief of the German police, Daluege was appointed head of the Hauptamt Ordnungspolizei (the main office of the regular uniformed police). After Heydrich was assassinated in June 1942, Daluege became acting *Reichsprotektor* of the Protectorate of BOHEMIA AND MORAVIA, a post he held for a year, during which time the LIDICE massacre was perpetrated. For this and other crimes, Daluege was executed in 1946 in Czechoslovakia.

BIBLIOGRAPHY

Wistrich, R. *Who's Who in Nazi Germany.* New York, 1982.

UWE ADAM

DANNECKER, THEODOR (1913–1945), SS officer who specialized in organizing the deportation of Jews from Nazi-occupied Europe. Born in Tübingen, Dannecker was a lawyer by training but in 1937 became a member of Adolf EICHMANN's staff and later an essential collaborator in carrying out the "FINAL SOLUTION." He was sent to Paris in 1940 by Eichmann's bureau (IV B 4) as head of its French branch. In this capacity, Dannecker worked directly under Eichmann and supervised the preparation of lists of French Jews whose arrest followed in May and August of 1941. The following year, Dannecker prepared a set of rules governing the deportation of French Jews and "stateless" Jews in France not effectively protected by a foreign power. He constantly urged the Vichy government to accelerate the deportations to the east, surprising even Vichy officials by the vehemence of his hatred for Jews.

Eichmann recalled Dannecker to Berlin at the end of 1942 for abuse of office, and in January 1943 he was transferred to Bulgaria, where he organized the deportation of eleven thousand Jews from Macedonia and Thrace. In October 1944 Eichmann appointed him Jewish Commissioner in Italy, where he remained until the end of the war. He committed suicide in an American prison camp at Bad Tölz in December 1945.

BIBLIOGRAPHY

Hilberg, R. *The Destruction of the European Jews.* 3 vols. New York, 1985.

LIONEL KOCHAN

DANZIG (Pol., Gdańsk), city on the shores of the Baltic Sea, held alternately over the centuries by Germany and Poland, with both claiming sovereignty over it. This rivalry became dangerous after World War I, when Danzig was made a "free city" under the auspices of the League of Nations, thus providing Poland with access to the Baltic Sea via a corridor that cut off East Prussia from the Reich. Ninety-six percent of the city's population were Germans wanting to be reunited with their fatherland. Their militant nationalism contained elements of antisemitism.

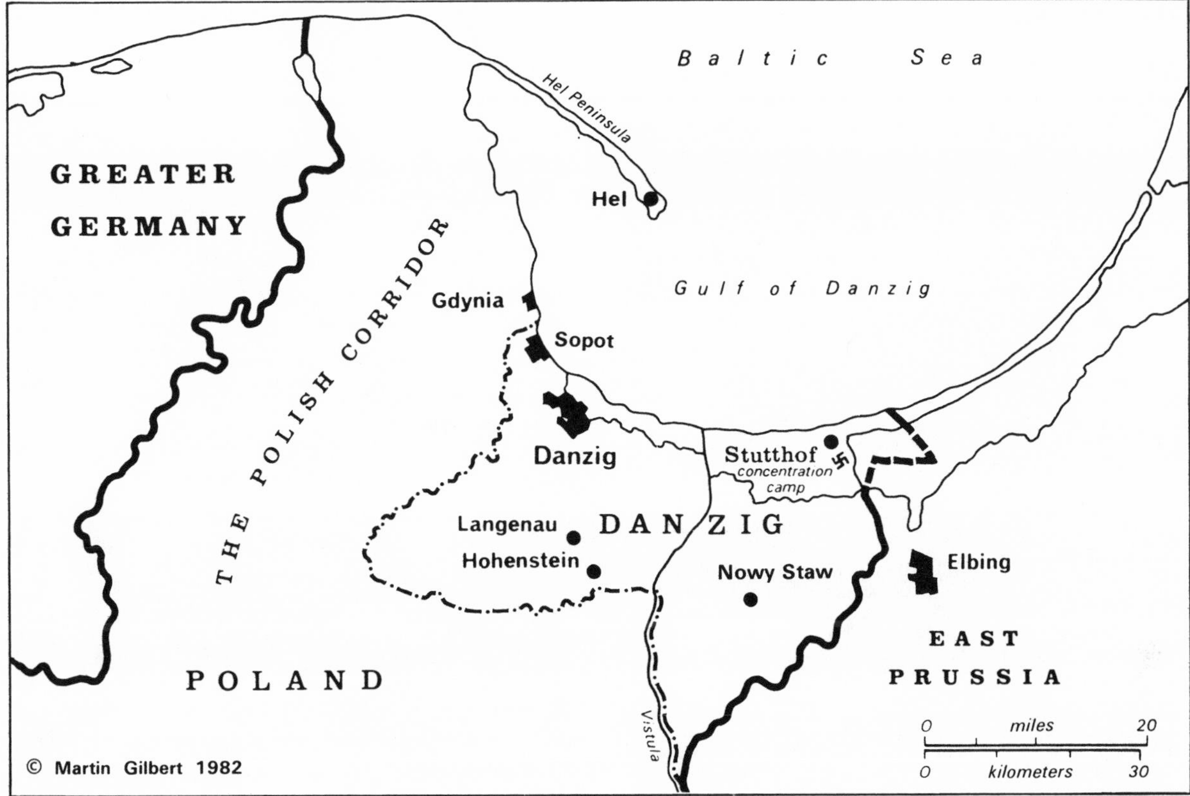

Since entrance to the free city was not restricted, tens of thousands of Jews fleeing from war, revolution, and pogroms passed through it on their way to countries abroad, and thousands of these refugees settled in Danzig, increasing the local Jewish population from twenty-five hundred to twelve thousand. Entrepreneurs among them contributed considerably to the city's industrial development and its transit trade. This economic impact, combined with Poland's protection of its citizens, strengthened the Jews' position, and their struggle for equal rights was also supported by the League of Nations as the guarantor of Danzig's democratic constitution. The League's presence was manifested by a high commissioner who acted on its behalf.

In the 1920s the governing body, the senate, was dominated by a coalition of parties from the Center and the Right, but in the elections of May 1933 the National Socialists became the leading power, winning more than 50 percent of the votes. The Christian conservative Hermann RAUSCHNING became head of the senate. For practical as well as ideological reasons he was opposed to racial antisemitism, one of the subjects he covered in his book *Gespräche mit Hitler* (1939; published in English as *Hitler Speaks*, 1939).

In November 1934, however, Rauschning was dismissed by the head of the Nazi party, Gauleiter Albert FORSTER, who named the veteran Nazi Arthur GREISER head of the senate. Greiser, like his predecessor, felt himself compelled to honor Danzig's international obligations and to refrain from complete identification with the politics of Nazi Germany. Even though the senate had already, in the 1920s, curtailed the Jews' civic rights —hampering their economic activities; preventing their naturalization; expelling foreign Jews; and discriminating against German Jews, who were not allowed to become officials—Greiser promised to safeguard the Jews' civic equality and to restrain the boycott propaganda. These promises were not kept.

The Jewish community, fighting for its rights, appealed in 1935 to the League of

Danzig grüßt seinen Führer!

"Danzig Salutes Its Führer!" Hitler (standing in front car) in a triumphant procession passing through Danzig on September 19, 1939. Albert Forster, the local *Gauleiter,* had declared the union of Danzig with Germany on September 1.

Nations through the offices of its high commissioner in Danzig, the Irishman Sean Lester, but since the impact of the League was already weakened, this proved of little avail. However, although the NUREMBERG LAWS had been promulgated in Germany in 1935, the Jews' situation in Danzig did not significantly change; in 1937 they still numbered twelve thousand, maintaining their key positions in the transit trade. The high commissioner from 1937 to 1939, Carl Jacob Burckhardt of Switzerland, tried to postpone actions against the Jews in order to avoid international complications, telling the Nazi government that he was acting for its benefit. In September 1937, he even obtained Hitler's consent to postpone the promulgation of the Nuremberg Laws in Danzig for reasons of foreign policy. Nevertheless, from October 20 to 23, 1937, a pogrom broke out, affecting mainly the Jewish traders and shopkeepers. In the following weeks the terror increased, and the government started to intensify the process of ousting the Jews from the economy and confiscating their property. On November 21, 1938, following KRISTALLNACHT, the Nuremberg Laws were promulgated, with certain local modifications.

In the meantime the Jewish community had shrunk to about four thousand, mainly through emigration, and the threats on the lives of those who remained increased. Under the circumstances, the board of the Jewish community proposed to evacuate the remaining Jews through emigration, or, if there was no other alternative, by organizing illegal immigration to Palestine. In the arrangement concluded with the senate, the latter agreed to stop the terror and facilitate the issuing of passports and the obtaining of visas in return for a public announcement by all the Jews that they were willing to leave the city. This announcement was made at a meeting of the entire community on December 17, 1938. Because of the difficulties in implementing the plan, however, sixteen hundred Jews, many of them elderly people, still remained in Danzig when war broke out in September 1939. The board continued its efforts to organize illegal immigration, and the last group of Jews sailed on the *Patria*, which was blown up in the Haifa harbor. At the end of February 1941, the government started to deport the remainder of the Jewish population, six hundred in number, to Poland and THERESIENSTADT.

Even though a number of the city's Jews were eventually murdered, the community's agreement with the senate saved thousands of Danzig's Jews from expulsion and death.

BIBLIOGRAPHY

Levine, H. S. *Hitler's Free City: A History of the Nazi Party in Danzig, 1925–1939*. Chicago, 1973.

Lichtenstein, E. *Die Juden der Freien Stadt Danzig unter der Herrschaft des Nationalsozialismus.* Tübingen, 1973.

Stern, E. *The Jews of Danzig, 1840–1943: Integration, Struggle, Rescue.* Tel Aviv, 1983. (In Hebrew.)

ELIYAHU STERN

DARLAN, FRANÇOIS (1881–1942), French admiral and statesman. In 1939 Darlan was appointed commander of the French fleet. When the Vichy government was established under Marshal Philippe PÉTAIN, Darlan joined it and held several portfolios in the cabinet. In 1940, after Pierre LAVAL's ouster, Pétain appointed Darlan prime minister. Darlan, pressured by the Germans as well as for internal reasons, in March 1941 created the COMMISSARIAT GÉNÉRAL AUX QUESTIONS JUIVES (General Office for Jewish Affairs). He introduced legislation under which all existing Jewish organizations were closed down and dissolved, to be replaced, late in that year, by the UNION GÉNÉRALE DES ISRAÉLITES DE FRANCE (General Council of French Jews; UGIF). Darlan, however, rejected the German demand that the Jews of France be forced to wear the yellow badge (*see* BADGE, JEWISH).

On April 14, 1942, Laval was reappointed prime minister, in response to German pressure. Darlan became the French government representative in North Africa a few days before its invasion by the Allies (November 8, 1942), and he persuaded the French army commanders on the spot to offer no resistance to the invading forces. President Franklin D. ROOSEVELT recognized Darlan as chief of state in French North Africa. Darlan retained the Vichy legislation, including the laws against the Jews. However, he was opposed both by the supporters of Pétain, who regarded him as a traitor, and by de GAULLE's Free French, who did not acknowledge the authority of the Vichy regime. On December 24, 1942, Darlan was killed by an anti-Vichy assassin.

Adm. François Darlan of France visiting Hitler at Berchtesgaden. [National Archives]

BIBLIOGRAPHY

Lacouture, J. *Le rebelle.* Vol. 1 of *Charles de Gaulle.* Paris, 1984.

Marrus, M. R., and R. O. Paxton. *Vichy France and the Jews.* New York, 1981.

LUCIEN LAZARE

DARQUIER DE PELLEPOIX, LOUIS (pseud. of Louis Darquier, 1897–1980), French coordinator of Vichy's anti-Jewish program from 1942 to 1944. A notorious antisemitic rabble-rouser, Darquier was chosen to head the Vichy government's COMMISSARIAT GÉNÉRAL AUX QUESTIONS JUIVES (Office for Jewish Affairs) in

May 1942, succeeding Xavier VALLAT, whom the SS in France found too moderate. At this point, the Nazis were about to begin the massive deportation of Jews from France to AUSCHWITZ. Darquier helped coordinate these deportations, and worked closely with the German authorities in PARIS. Quite apart from its brutality and its persecution based upon biological racism, which had hitherto been de-emphasized, Darquier's administration was characterized by corruption and incompetence. The Germans requested his removal, and he left office in February 1944. Darquier fled to Spain, where he lived until his death.

BIBLIOGRAPHY

Laloum, J. *La France antisémite de Darquier de Pellepoix.* Paris, 1979.

Marrus, M. R., and R. O. Paxton. *Vichy France and the Jews.* New York, 1981.

MICHAEL R. MARRUS

DARRÉ, RICHARD WALTHER (1895–1953), German *Reichsbauernführer* (Reich Farmers' Leader) as of April 1933, and *Reichsminister für Ernährung und Landwirtschaft* (Reich Minister of Food and Agriculture) from June 1933 to May 1942. Darré was born of German parents in Argentina. He studied at a high school in England and volunteered for army service in World War I, after which he pursued his studies in agriculture. He was regarded as one of the Nazi ideologists. Darré, a longtime friend of Heinrich HIMMLER—also a farmer —joined the Nazi party and the SS in 1930. In 1931, with Himmler's cooperation, he established the SS RASSE- UND SIEDLUNGSHAUPTAMT (Race and Resettlement Main Office). He was the author of *Das Bauerntum als Lebensquell der nordischen Rasse* (The Peasantry as the Life Source of the Nordic Race; 1928) and *Neuadel aus Blut und Boden* (The New Aristocracy of Blood and Soil; 1930), in which he opposed further urbanization and industrialization and developed a *Lebensraumprogramm* (Program for Living Space). The peasant was at the center of Darré's ideology, and he believed in a mythical connection between the blood of the German race and the soil (*Blut und Boden,* or "blood and soil"; Blubo). His abstract approach and his inability to cope with problems of war supplies led to a rift with Himmler and, before long, also with Hitler, and Darré was removed from his posts. At the SUBSEQUENT NUREMBERG PROCEEDINGS, the Nuremberg Military Tribunals (the Ministry Case, November 15, 1947, to April 14, 1949) sentenced him to five years' imprisonment, but he was released in 1950.

Richard Walther Darré testifying at his trial before the Nuremberg Military Tribunals.

BIBLIOGRAPHY

Farquharson, J. E. *The Plough and the Swastika: The NSDAP and Agriculture in Germany, 1928–1945.* London, 1976.

UWE ADAM

DAUGAVPILS. *See* Dvinsk.

DAW. *See* Deutsche Ausrüstungswerke.

DEATH CAMPS. *See* Extermination Camps.

DEATH MARCHES (Ger., *Todesmärsche*), forced marches of long columns of prisoners under heavy guard, over long distances, and

DEATH MARCHES
0 miles 300
0 kilometers 400
GREATER GERMANY
SWEDEN neutral
Kaiserwald
Riga
Moscow
German Front Line November 1942
DENMARK
Copenhagen
Baltic Sea
Memel
Kovno
Vilna
North Sea
Palmnicken
Lebork
Seerappen
Schippenbeil
Minsk
USSR
POMERANIA
Danzig
Heiligenbeil
Stutthof
BELORUSSIA
Bydgoszcz
Thorn
Sachsenhausen
Oranienburg
Biala Podlaska
Amsterdam
Neuengamme
Gardelegen
Ravensbrück
Warsaw
Kutno
Berlin
NETHERLANDS
Bergen-Belsen
Magdeburg
Halberstadt
Lublin
Kiev
Dora-Mittelbau
Majdanek
Nordhausen
Buchenwald
Rehmsdorf
Gross-Rosen
Ohrdruf
Blechhammer
BELGIUM
Lvov
Theresienstadt
Reichenau
Auschwitz
UKRAINE
Flossenbürg
Prague
Wodzisław
GALICIA
TRANSNISTRIA
LUXEMBOURG
SLOVAKIA
BUKOVINA
BESSARABIA
Natzweiler-Struthof
Gusen
Mauthausen
OCCUPIED FRANCE
Gunskirchen
TRANSYLVANIA
Dachau
Vienna
Odessa
Eisenerz
Budapest
CRIMEA
Flintsbach-am-Inn
HUNGARY
SWITZERLAND
ROMANIA
VICHY FRANCE
Fossoli
CROATIA
Belgrade
Bucharest
NICE AND SAVOY
Black Sea
YUGOSLAVIA
SERBIA
Bor
ITALY
BULGARIA
Adriatic Sea
Sofia
© Martin Gilbert 1985

Hungarian Jews in Austria, victims of the notorious death march from Budapest in November 1944.

under intolerable conditions, in the course of which the prisoners were brutally mistreated and many killed by their escorts. The term was coined by prisoners in the Nazi CONCENTRATION CAMPS and was later used by historiographers of the Nazi regime.

Death marches are known to have taken place especially in the final stage of the war, when concentration camps were being evacuated, but they were a fairly frequent phenomenon throughout the war period. The first death march organized by the SS took place in Poland, in mid-January 1940. On January 14 of that year, eight hundred Jewish prisoners of war from the Polish army were removed from their camp on Lipowa Street in Lublin, and a few days later, escorted by a troop of mounted SS men, they were marched in bitter cold to Biała Podlaska, a distance of approximately 62 miles (100 km). All along the route the Nazis killed prisoners, individually and in groups, and only a few dozen survived to reach their destination.

Following the German invasion of the Soviet Union in the summer of 1941, hundreds of thousands of Soviet PRISONERS OF WAR were moved along the highways of the occupied Ukraine and Belorussia while being transferred from one camp to another, and murdered in their masses en route or at prearranged slaughter sites. In July and August 1941, tens of thousands of Jews from BESSARABIA and BUKOVINA were marched to TRANSNISTRIA, with thousands shot to death along the way by their German and Romanian military and gendarmerie escorts.

Tens of thousands of Jews were also forced on marches when the ghettos of eastern Europe were being liquidated in 1942 and 1943. Many of them were the inhabitants of small ghettos who were moved to larger ghettos or other collection points many miles away—for the most part, their last steps before they were deported to the EXTERMINATION CAMPS. On the way, many of the Jews were murdered by their German escorts or by auxiliary police (Ukrainians, Lithuanians, and others).

The liquidation of the concentration camps began in the summer of 1944, during the great Red Army offensive in the east and the Allied landings in the west. The first camps to be evacuated were those in the Baltic states and in eastern and central Poland; in the west, the NATZWEILER camp was emptied at this time. Most of the moves were made by rail and, in the case of the KAISERWALD camp, also by boat, but some of the prisoners were forced on foot marches.

The first major death march began on July 28, 1944, when the camp on Gesia Street in WARSAW was evacuated. This camp had been established on the ruins of the Warsaw ghetto as an extension of the MAJDANEK camp network. At the time it was evacuated the camp held some 4,400 Jews from various countries, most from Greece and Hungary. About 3,600 prisoners were forced to march to Kutno, a distance of 81 miles (130 km). During the march, anyone too weak to keep up the pace was shot by the Nazis. No food was supplied to the marchers, nor were they allowed to stop for a drink of water. About 1,000 prisoners were murdered on the march to Kutno. When the remainder reached their destination they were put on a freight train, 90 persons to a car; several hundred died on the train, and the rest—who now numbered fewer than 2,000 —arrived at DACHAU on August 9.

Even harsher and longer was the march from the Bor camp in Yugoslavia. About four thousand Jewish prisoners were taken out of that camp, put on the road to Belgrade, and marched for eight days, during which they received hardly any food. From Belgrade they proceeded to Hungary, also on foot. Most of the prisoners were killed on the way and no more than a few hundred survivors were left when the column reached Hungary, where they were dispatched to the ORANIENBURG camp by train. One of the prisoners murdered on this death march was the Hungarian Jewish poet Miklós Radnoti, who composed his last poems on the march.

The death march from Budapest began on November 8, 1944, and lasted an entire month. In that march seventy-six thousand Jews—men, women, and children—were made to walk to the Austrian border, es-

The American military authorities ordered the German civilians of the town of Schwarzenfeld, 25 miles (40 km) north of Regensburg, to dig a huge grave for the bodies of concentration camp prisoners who were shot by SS troops on a death march (April 25, 1945). [United States Army]

corted by Hungarians. Thousands were shot to death en route, and thousands more starved to death or succumbed to cold and disease. Several hundred were saved by neutral diplomats such as Raoul WALLENBERG, who pulled Jews out of the columns, put them under their protection, and escorted them back to Budapest. On the Austrian border the Germans took over, leading the columns to various concentration camps, primarily Dachau and MAUTHAUSEN.

The Jewish concentration camp inmates lived with the constant fear that the German exploitation of their labor was a temporary measure which would terminate at the end of the war, when they would all be murdered. In November 1944 Himmler ordered the cessation of murder by gas at AUSCHWITZ, a turning point in the Nazi policy toward the Jews, attributed to Germany's imminent defeat in the war. The Jews were, therefore, included among the other camp inmates in the continuous evacuation operation.

In the wake of the renewed Soviet offensive in mid-January of 1945, the Nazis undertook the evacuation of the remaining concentration camps in Poland. In that month large death marches were launched, primarily from Auschwitz in the south and STUTTHOF in the north. The Germans began evacuating Auschwitz and its satellite camps on January 18, 1945; sixty-six thousand prisoners, mostly Jews, were marched to Wodzisław (Ger., Loslau). There they were put on freight trains and transported to various concentration camps, principally GROSS-ROSEN, BUCHENWALD, Dachau, and Mauthausen. At least fifteen thousand perished in that march.

On January 21, 1945, four thousand prisoners, most of them Jews, left the BLECHHAMMER camp on foot. On February 2 they reached Gross-Rosen, and after staying there five days, left for Buchenwald by train. During the foot march, at least eight hundred prisoners were murdered; the commander of the escort, an SS-*Untersturmführer* named Klipp, excelled in his cruelty.

The evacuation of the Stutthof camp complex was exceptionally brutal and tragic. On the eve of the evacuation, in the middle of January 1945, these camps had a prisoner population of 47,000, over 35,000 of them Jews, of whom most were women. On January 20, the Seerappen camp in East Prussia, a satellite of Stutthof, was evacuated; 1,400 Jewish women and 100 Jewish men were put on the road. The next day they were joined by convoys from other satellite camps in the area (Jessau, Heiligenbeil, and Schippenbeil), making a total of 7,000 Jews—6,000 women and 1,000 men. The march took ten days, and during its course 700 Jews were murdered. On January 31 the convoy arrived at Palmnicken, on the shores of the Baltic. The same day, the Nazis drove all the prisoners into the sea and machine-gunned them. Only 13 persons are known to have survived this massacre.

The first evacuation of the main Stutthof camp was launched on January 25, 1945. That facility contained twenty-five thousand prisoners, half of whom were Jewish women. Another twenty thousand were in various Stutthof satellite camps in Pomerania; most of these were included in the death marches. The main route led from Stutthof to the town of Lebork (Lauenberg), where the convoy halted because the area was encircled by Red Army troops. The surviving prisoners were sent back to the main camp. The large satellite camps in Pomerania were Thorn (Pol., Torun) and Bromberg (Bydgoszcz), containing six thousand Jewish women prisoners; of these, 90 percent were murdered on the death marches following the evacuations.

The evacuation of the main camp of Gross-Rosen and its satellites began in early February 1945. A total of forty thousand prisoners were moved out; thousands were murdered en route, and the remainder were put into the Mittelbau, FLOSSENBÜRG, Buchenwald, Mauthausen, Dachau, BERGEN-BELSEN, and SACHSENHAUSEN camps. Of the twenty thousand Jewish prisoners employed as forced laborers in the Eulengebirge camps, nearly all were killed, most of them either just before the evacuation or during the death march in February 1945.

In the course of March and April 1945, when the American and British armies were advancing in the west and the Red Army in the east, the Germans evacuated one concentration camp after the other, moving the prisoners into the territory still under their control. In mid-March, Nazi Germany still held seven hundred thousand prisoners in concentration camps, among them two hundred thousand women. Approximately forty thousand SS men were still employed in running the concentration camps, guarding the prisoners, and escorting the death marches. In those last two months of the Third Reich's existence, at least a quarter-million prisoners, men and women, were sent on death marches, some of which lasted for weeks. The graves of the murder victims and the others who perished on the highways were spread over central Germany and western Austria. In that final phase, the evacuation of the camps was generally a combined operation: the prisoners made their way partly on foot and partly by train. The train trip was no less harsh or cruel than the foot march; the prisoners suffered from intolerably foul air in the cars, which held an average of seventy persons each, and from lack of food and water.

Some of the death marches in the final months of the war were particularly brutal. In late March and early April 1945, masses of prisoners were moved out of the main Buchenwald camp and its satellites and were sent on long-distance marches in which they incurred heavy losses. Thus, on April 3 and 4 a convoy of prisoners from the Nordhausen camp was forced to march to Flintsbach-am-Inn, a distance of 549 miles (885 km); another convoy originating in Nordhausen marched to Bergen-Belsen, 214 miles (345 km) away; and a group from Ohrdruf was sent to Dachau, a march of 245 miles (395 km). On April 4, a convoy left Halberstadt for Giessen, 316 miles (510 km) away; on April 7, another group from Halberstadt was dispatched to Appendorf, a distance of 327 miles (527 km); and on April 8, a third Halberstadt convoy was sent 162 miles (262 km) to Burstendorf.

In the evacuation of the main Buchenwald camp, the first convoy left on April 6. It consisted of 3,100 Jewish prisoners, of whom 1,400 were murdered on the way. In the next few days, April 7 to 10, some 40,000 prisoners left the camp, of whom 13,500 were murdered during the march. Twenty-one thousand prisoners remained in Buchenwald, among them a few Jews. Rehmsdorf was one of the last of the Buchenwald satellite camps to be evacuated, on April 13; 4,340 Jewish prisoners left the camp, but no more than 500 reached their destination, THERESIENSTADT, the rest being murdered en route or perishing from other causes.

The evacuation of the DORA-MITTELBAU camp started on April 1, with most of the prisoners marched to Bergen-Belsen, a march lasting about two weeks. In one of the convoys the prisoners were forced into a barn that was then set on fire; the next day, when the American forces reached the site (near the town of Gardelegen), they found hundreds of burned corpses.

On April 25, 1945, there were about forty-five hundred prisoners in Stutthof, among them seventeen hundred Jews, when the final evacuation of the main Stutthof camp began. It was the continuation of the January death marches from the Stutthof satellite camps. Since the area of the camp was surrounded by Red Army forces, the prisoners were removed by sea, on ferryboats; two hundred Jewish women prisoners were first driven to the seashore and shot to death. Prisoners who tried to hide in the barracks were forced out and the barracks were set alight. Of the four thousand prisoners who left on five ferryboats, two thousand drowned or were shot to death by the Germans on the open sea. In the two evacuation operations of the Stutthof camps and the ensuing death marches, twenty-six thousand prisoners perished.

At the end of April, about two weeks before Nazi Germany's final surrender, death marches were launched from Flossenbürg, Sachsenhausen, NEUENGAMME, Magdeburg, Mauthausen, RAVENSBRÜCK, and several of the Dachau satellite camps. The marches of these last two weeks are believed to have cost the lives of tens of thousands of prisoners. On one short stretch alone, between Gunskirchen and Mauthausen, a distance of 37 miles (60 km), thousands of prisoners were buried, most of them Jews from Hungary. In another spot, near the town of Eisenerz, a mass grave was discovered after the war containing the bodies of thirty-five hundred prisoners who were on a death march to Mauthausen.

The evacuations and death marches were kept up literally until the Third Reich's last day. The final camp from which prisoners were sent on a death march was at Reichenau, in the Sudetic Mountains; this took place on May 7, the day on which Germany surrendered to the Allies.

Approximately a quarter of a million prisoners of the Nazi concentration camps were murdered or otherwise died on death marches between the summer of 1944 and the end of the war.

BIBLIOGRAPHY

Bauer, Y. "The Death Marches, January–May 1945." *Modern Judaism* 3/1 (February 1983): 1–21.

Krakowski, S. "The Death Marches in the Period of the Evacuation of the Camps." In *The Nazi Concentration Camps: Structure and Aims; The Image of the Prisoners; The Jews in the Camps.* Proceedings of the Fourth Yad Vashem International Historical Conference, edited by Y. Gutman and A. Saf, pp. 475–491. Jerusalem, 1984.

Strzelecki, A. *Ewakuacja, likwidacja, i wyzwolenie KL Auschwitz.* Oświęcim, 1982.

SHMUEL KRAKOWSKI

DEATH'S-HEAD UNITS. *See* Totenkopfverbände.

DEBRECEN, third largest city in HUNGARY, located in the northeastern part of the country on the Nagy Alfold (Great Plain), near the present-day Romanian border. Debrecen is a major center of Hungarian Calvinism. In 1941, 9,142 Jews lived there, comprising 7.3 percent of the population. An officially recognized Jewish community existed in the city from the mid-nineteenth century.

Like the other Jews of Hungary, the citizens of Debrecen were greatly affected by the first and second Hungarian anti-Jewish laws (1938 and 1939), which severely limited Jewish participation in economic life. Many Debrecen Jews became destitute. One reaction of the community was to turn inward, and as a consequence, Jews gravitated toward Zionism or sought solace in exploring their Jewish heritage more deeply.

Jewish men from Debrecen were drafted into the MUNKASZOLGÁLAT (Labor Service System) shortly after its creation in the summer of 1939. By 1941 the rate of conscription had increased significantly, and most of the area's Jews were sent to the Ukraine, from which few returned. Gen. Károly Beregffy, known to be particularly antisemitic, was the head of the Debrecen area draft board for the labor units and commander of the sixth labor camp, located near the city in the town of Hajdúbőszőrmény. In the fall of 1944, he served as a minister in Ferenc SZÁLASI's ARROW CROSS PARTY regime, for which he was hanged in 1945.

During the period of German occupation, the Jews of Debrecen, like those of SZEGED, were assigned to the fourth anti-Jewish operation zone (for the purpose of deportation, Hungary had been divided into six zones). For the city's Jews, the road from occupation to extermination was short and direct. German soldiers entered Debrecen on March 20, 1944. They promptly ordered the disbanding of the Jewish community and forced it to reorganize as a Zsidó Tanács (Jewish Council), under the leadership of Rabbi Pal (Meir) Weisz. A Jewish police force was set up under a former army captain, Béla Lusztbaum. On the last day of March a decree called for Jews to wear the Jewish BADGE. Early in April, Jewish automobiles were confiscated and Jewish telephones disconnected. On April 8 (during Passover), a handful of Jewish leaders were taken hostage by the authorities and imprisoned at nearby Hajdúszentgyorgy. Eventually, three hundred Jewish notables from the Debrecen area were confined there. On April 21, Jewish stores were forcibly closed. The following week witnessed a public burning of books considered "Jewish" or too liberal for the Hungarian right wing; it was directed by the antisemitic newspaper editor Mihály Kalosvari Borsca.

On April 28, 1944, the order to set up a ghetto was issued by the mayor, Sándor Kolcsey. Ironically, Kolcsey and the city secretary, József Zold, voiced their opposition to erecting a ghetto; this led to their ousting by Lajos Bessenyei, the Debrecen area chief magistrate. Lajos Csoka became the new mayor. On May 9, the boundaries of the ghetto, which was to be established in the western side of the city, were set. It had two parts, known as the "large" and the "small" ghetto, which were divided by Hatvan Street. The Jews of the city were forced to build the wall of the Debrecen ghetto, which stood 8.9 feet (2.7 m) high. On May 15 the ghetto was declared completed. A handful of Jews refused to enter it and hid in bunkers until the Soviet army arrived that fall. Local Hungarian police guarded the ghetto, whereas the Jewish police were charged with keeping order within the walls and were ordered to hand over those Jews whom the authorities wished to interrogate. Each Jew was allocated 43 square feet (4 sq m) of space, which meant that most rooms contained at least one entire family and often more. On June 7, all traffic in and out of the ghetto was ended, including that of Jews leaving the ghetto for work.

Two weeks later, on June 21, 1944, Hungarian gendarmes entered the ghetto and removed the Jews to the nearby Serly brickyards. There they joined the Jews from the neighboring communities of Balmazújvaros, Hajdúböszörmény, Hajdúdorog, Hajdúhadház, Hajdúnánás, Hajdúsamson, Hajdúszoboszló, Teglas, and Vamospercs—altogether, 13,084 Jews. At the brickyards, the Jews were stripped of their remaining valuables. A small group was sent to Hajdúszentgyorgy, from where the Jews were deported beginning on June 26. The first two trains, with 6,841 relatively fortunate passengers, were sent to STRASSHOF, in Austria, where the deportees were dispersed and put to work in agricultural and other enterprises for ORGANISATION TODT. Most of the other Jews from Debrecen were deported to AUSCHWITZ, where they arrived on July 3. About half of the Debrecen contingent of the Strasshof group survived the war. Among those killed in the Strasshof group were 233 Debrecen Jews, supposedly on their way to THERESIENSTADT; they were shot by SS men in Bratislava in May 1945.

During the period of ghettoization and deportation, news of the so-called Kasztner train (*see* KASZTNER, REZSŐ) reached Debrecen via messengers from the Zionist youth movement who posed as gentiles. They told the leader of the Orthodox community, Shlomo Strasser, that anyone from Debrecen could be included in the designated quota for the city. During the deportations, ten families, including those of Rabbi Weisz, Rabbi Strasser, and Zionist leaders, were taken to the Columbus Street camp in Budapest. Soon thereafter they embarked on the Kasztner train, which eventually brought them to freedom in Switzerland. A handful of Zionist youth activists led by Dr. Adoniyahu Billitzer also escaped from Debrecen. They reached Budapest, where they took part in rescue and defense activities.

Debrecen was taken by the Soviet army on October 20, 1944, and became the administrative center of the antifascist provisional government. Some four thousand Jews from Debrecen survived the war. In 1970, twelve hundred Jews were living there.

BIBLIOGRAPHY

Braham, R. L. *The Politics of Genocide.* New York, 1981.

Gonda, M. E. *A Debreceni Zsidok szasz eve: A martirhalalit halt Debreceni es kornyekbeli Zsidok emlekere.* Tel Aviv, 1970. (In Hebrew and Hungarian.)

Lavi, T., ed. *Hungary.* In *Pinkas Hakehillot; Encyclopaedia of Jewish Communities.* Jerusalem, 1976. (In Hebrew.)

ROBERT ROZETT

DEFFAUGT, JEAN, mayor of Annemasse, a French town on the Swiss border, where many clandestine escape routes for fleeing Jews converged. Deffaugt took it upon himself to visit Jews who were caught by the Germans while trying to cross the border and incarcerated in an annex of the Pax Hotel, where they had to withstand brutal interrogation of the Gestapo. He collected food, medicines, blankets, and other supplies,

Jean Deffaugt and his wife.

which he brought to the Gestapo prison to deliver to the inmates. Deffaugt pleaded with the Gestapo on behalf of the imprisoned Jews. As he later reminisced, "I was afraid, I admit. I never mounted the Gestapo stairways without making the sign of the cross, or murmuring a prayer." On one occasion, the Gestapo agreed to release into Deffaugt's care a group of children under the age of eleven, arrested while on their way to the border, on the basis of the following statement: "I, Jean Deffaugt, mayor of Annemasse, acknowledge receiving from Inspector Mayer, chief of the Security Services, eleven children of Jewish faith, whom I pledge to return at the first order." Deffaugt soon placed them in the hands of a Father Duret, who hid them in Bonne-sur-Menoge until the Allied liberation in the following weeks.

With the liberation of Annemasse by the United States Army, all the children were reunited by Deffaugt and turned over to Jewish hands. Jean Deffaugt was recognized by YAD VASHEM as a "RIGHTEOUS AMONG THE NATIONS" in 1965.

BIBLIOGRAPHY

Lazare, L. *La résistance juive en France.* Paris, 1987.

Minc, R. *L'enfer des innocents—Les enfants juifs dans la tourmente nazie: Recits.* Paris, 1966. See pages 132–137.

MORDECAI PALDIEL

DE GAULLE, CHARLES. *See* Gaulle, Charles de.

DEGESCH. *See* Trials of War Criminals: Zyklon B Trial; Zyklon B.

DEJ (Hung., Dés), former capital of Szolnok-Doboka county, in northern TRANSYLVANIA; part of the territory acquired by Hungary from Romania in September 1940. According to the census of 1941, the city had a population of 16,353, of whom 3,719 (19.3 percent) were Jews. The overwhelming majority of the Jews belonged to the Orthodox community; many of these were Hasidim. Between 1862 and 1944, the community had many well-established denominational and ecclesiastical institutions, which were under the overall leadership of the Paneth rabbinical dynasty. The last spiritual leader of the community was Rabbi Jacob Elimelech Paneth. Its secular head was Ferenc Ordentlich, who also served as head of the local branch of the Zsidó Tanács (Jewish Council), formed after the ghetto was established on May 3, 1944.

The ghetto was located in the nearby Bungur Forest, where most of its 7,800 Jews, including those brought in from the rural communities in the county, lived under the open sky, without shelter from the elements. Surrounded by barbed wire, the ghetto was guarded by the local police and a gendarme unit brought in from the nearby district of Zilah. The wealthier elements of the Dej community were subjected to particularly cruel treatment by the gendarmes, who were in pursuit of Jewish wealth.

The Jews in the ghetto were deported to AUSCHWITZ in three transports between May 28 and June 8. During the period immediately following the war, Dej, which had reverted to Romania, had a Jewish population of 1,020 (1947). This consisted of the local survivors, as well as those who had moved into the city from neighboring villages and from other parts of Romania.

BIBLIOGRAPHY

Braham, R. L. *Genocide and Retribution.* Boston, 1983.

Singer, Z., ed. *Volt egyszer egy Dés. . . .* Tel Aviv, 1970.

RANDOLPH L. BRAHAM

DE-JUDAIZATION. *See* Entjudung.

DELEGATURA, the POLISH GOVERNMENT-IN-EXILE underground representation in POLAND in the period from 1940 to 1945. Heading the Delegatura were a *delegat* (the government representative, who in 1944 was given the rank of deputy prime minister) and three deputies (who were given the rank of minister). The *delegaty*, in order of succession, were Cyril Ratajski, Jan Piekalkiewicz, Jan Jankowski, Stefan Korbonski, and Jerzy Braun. Assisting the *delegat* was a committee made up of representatives of the four political parties on which the government-in-exile was based. By decision of the four coalition partners, the Polish government-in-exile issued two declarations of principle, as well as several appeals to the Polish people and to the world.

The committee, which was an advisory as well as a decision-making body, had various names at different times: Polityczny Komitet Porozumiewawczy (Coordinating Political Committee; 1940–1943), Krajowa Reprezentacja Polityczna (National Political Representation; 1943), and Rada Jedności Narodowej (National Unity Council; as of January 1944). Its last chairman was Kazimierz Puzak, of the Polish Socialist party. In July 1945, when the Provisional Government of National Unity was established, the Delegatura and the council went out of existence.

The central structure of the Delegatura, which was an executive body, consisted of numerous sections. Their assignments corresponded to the departments of a regular administration. The Delegatura also established provincial, district, and municipal missions, the entire system amounting to an alternate government, rivaling the occupation authorities—an "underground state," with its own systems of education and law and its own armed force, the ARMIA KRAJOWA.

Until 1943, the Delegatura did not concern itself with the problem of Jews in occupied Poland, nor did it establish an organization for this purpose. Early that year a Jewish-affairs bureau was set up, headed by Witold Bienkowski, with Władysław BARTOSZEWSKI as his deputy, within the internal-affairs department. The task of this bureau was to organize the Delegatura's activities with regard to the Jewish population, to keep in daily touch with ZEGOTA (the Polish Council for Aid to Jews), and to process material on the fate of the Jews, for transmission to the Polish government-in-exile in London. The *delegat* himself also dealt with these subjects, as did the Civil Struggle Directorate (Kierownictwo Walki Cywilnej), which had been set up under his auspices. The latter's task was to coordinate popular resistance to the occupying power, and it frequently came out with denunciations of the Nazi crimes against the Jewish population. Thus, in a statement published on September 17, 1942, the Civil Struggle Directorate declared:

> For nearly a year now, in addition to the tragedy of the Polish people, which is being slaughtered by the enemy, our country has been the scene of a terrible, planned massacre of the Jews. This mass murder has no parallel in the annals of mankind; compared to it, the most infamous atrocities known to history pale into insignificance. Unable to act against this situation, we, in the name of the entire Polish people, protest the crime being perpetrated against the Jews; all political and public organizations join in this protest.

BIBLIOGRAPHY

Bartoszewski, W., and Z. Lewin. *Righteous among Nations: How Poles Helped the Jews, 1939–1945.* London, 1969.

Duraczynski, E. *Między Londynem a Warszawa, VII 1943–VII 1944.* Warsaw, 1986.

Engel, D. *In the Shadow of Auschwitz: The Polish Government in Exile and the Jews, 1939–1942.* Chapel Hill, 1987.

Gutman, Y., and S. Krakowski. *Unequal Victims: Poles and Jews during World War Two.* New York, 1986.

Korbonski, S. *The Polish Underground State: A Guide to the Underground, 1939–1945.* New York, 1981.

EUGENIUSZ DURACZYNSKI

DEMJANJUK TRIAL, trial held in the Jerusalem District Court; the second trial in Israel in which the death penalty was imposed under the Nazis and Nazi Collaborators (Punishment) Law 5710-1950 (the first was the EICHMANN TRIAL).

In 1975, information reached the United States Department of Justice that John Iwan Demjanjuk, a resident of Cleveland, Ohio, had collaborated with the Nazis as a member of the SS, and had served as a guard in the SOBIBÓR camp. His photograph, taken from an immigration application form he had filled out in 1951, was sent to Israel and was shown to survivors of the TREBLINKA extermination camp. All those who saw the photograph identified it conclusively as being that of a Ukrainian SS staff member at Treblinka who, because of his fearful cruelty, was called "Ivan the Terrible." A short time later the same survivors were shown a photograph taken in 1942, removed from an identification card used in the TRAWNIKI training camp for SS guards, and it too was identified as the same individual from Treblinka.

At the end of August 1977 the Cleveland state prosecutor submitted a request to the local district court asking for the annulment of Demjanjuk's citizenship, granted on November 14, 1958, on the ground that in his immigration application he had concealed the fact that he had been a member of the SS and a guard in the above extermination camps. On June 23, 1981, after a series of trials, Frank Batisti, senior judge of the Northern District Court of the State of Ohio, ruled that Demjanjuk had lied when filling out the immigration application form in 1951, had concealed his membership in the SS, had been in the Trawniki SS training camp, and had served in the Treblinka and Sobibór extermination camps. The judge ruled that Demjanjuk's American citizenship be annulled, in effect sentencing him to deportation from the United States. In October 1983, after Demjanjuk's appeals against the sentence had failed, the state of Israel submitted an extradition request for him to stand trial under the Nazis and Nazi Collaborators (Punishment) Law 5710-1950. At the end of 1985, after further hearings on the extradition, Israel's request was granted, and on February 28, 1986, Demjanjuk was taken to Israel and imprisoned there.

On February 16, 1987, the trial of Demjanjuk began in the Jerusalem District Court, before Supreme Court Judge Dov Levin and the Jerusalem District Court judges Dalia Dorner and Zvi Tal. The prosecution was represented by the attorney general, Yona Blattman, and the attorneys Michael Shaked, Michael Horowitz, and Dafna Beinwall, supported by a number of expert assistants. The defense consisted of the attorneys Mark O'Connor, John Gill, and Paul Chumak from the United States, and Yoram Sheftel of Israel. The prosecution charged Demjanjuk under the 1950 Punishment Law and under Clause 300 of the 1977 criminal law, on a number of counts: crimes against the Jewish people, crimes against humanity, war crimes, crimes against persecuted individuals, and murder.

Demjanjuk was born in 1920 in the village of Dub Makarenzi, in the Kazatin subdistrict of Kiev Oblast (district). In 1940 he was recruited into the Soviet army and from June 1941 fought against the Germans. He was wounded and hospitalized, returned to service, and during the battle in the Kerch region of the eastern Crimea in May 1942, was taken prisoner by the Germans. At the beginning of July he was brought to the prisoner-of-war camp in Chełmno, near Lublin. Soon afterward, in mid-July, Demjanjuk volunteered for service in the SS auxiliary units and was sent to the SS training camp at Trawniki, where he was trained as a concentration camp guard. At the beginning of October, Demjanjuk was posted to the Treblinka extermination camp, where he supervised the gas chambers and operated the machine that circulated the gas into the chambers. He forced the victims into the gas chambers with the utmost cruelty, flogged them with a whip or an iron pipe, slashed and stabbed them with a sword or dagger, and shot others. He served in Treblinka until September 1943, except for a short period during which he was in Sobibór.

The prosecution called sixty witnesses, among whom were many survivors of Treblinka, as well as criminal-identification experts, police investigators, historians, legal interrogators from Israel and West Germany, and experts from the United States. With the aid of these witnesses the prosecution described AKTION REINHARD (the extermination of Polish Jewry), the annihilation operation in the extermination camps, and the events of the Treblinka camp.

The defense did not deny what had taken place during the Holocaust, and especially the killings in the Treblinka camp, but it repudiated the identification of the defendant, claiming that John Demjanjuk was not "Ivan the Terrible" of Treblinka. The defense attorneys argued that the identification of the accused was erroneous from the outset, because it had been made by survivors many years after the events described by the prosecution, and the accuracy of their memory could not be relied upon. The defense also argued that Demjanjuk's identification card from Trawniki (the "Trawniki document"), which had been received from the Soviet Union, was a forgery made by the Soviet security services, and that Demjanjuk had never been in either Trawniki or the Treblinka and Sobibór extermination camps. It claimed that at the beginning of 1944 Demjanjuk had been sent from the Chełmno prisoner-of-war camp to Graz in Austria, to join the First Ukrainian Division under the command of Gen. Pavlo Shandruk; he was transferred from there, several weeks later, to Heuberg in Bavaria, to the camp of Gen. Andrei VLASOV's army, where he remained until the end of the war.

With the aid of psychological experts, the prosecution refuted the argument that the human memory could not be relied upon after such a long time; by means of the testimony of experts in criminal identification it rejected the argument that the "Trawniki document" was a forgery; and with the aid of historians it refuted Demjanjuk's alibi. On April 18, 1988, the judges found Demjanjuk guilty of all the charges in the indictment and sentenced him to death. The defense lodged an appeal in the Israeli Supreme Court.

[*See also* Trials of War Criminals.]

BIBLIOGRAPHY

Wagenaar, W. A. *Identifying Ivan: A Case Study in Legal Psychology.* Cambridge, Mass., 1988.

SHMUEL SPECTOR

DENAZIFICATION, the process of expurgating Nazism and its influence and punishing its practitioners. At the Yalta Conference, held in February 1945, six months before World War II ended, the three participants —Franklin D. ROOSEVELT, president of the United States; Winston CHURCHILL, prime minister of Britain; and Joseph STALIN, leader of the Soviet Union—in a joint statement announced that they were "determined to wipe out the Nazi party, Nazi laws, organizations, and institutions, remove all Nazi and militarist influences from public office and from the cultural and economic life of the German people, and take such other agreed measures in Germany as may be necessary for the future peace and safety of the world." Whereas the Moscow Declaration by the Allied powers (November 1, 1943) had spoken of the punishment of individuals responsible for Nazi crimes, the Yalta statement signified that the Allies were aiming, above all, at a radical reform of Germany's political institutions by the systematic elimination of all their Nazi and militarist elements.

The Potsdam Agreement, signed on August 2, 1945, by the leaders of the United States, Britain, and the Soviet Union, contained the following declaration:

> All members of the Nazi party who have been more than nominal participants in its activities and all other persons hostile to Allied purposes are to be removed from public or semi-public office and from positions of responsibility in important private undertakings. Such persons shall be replaced by persons who by their political and moral qualities are deemed capable of assisting in developing genuine democratic institutions in Germany.

By the time the Potsdam Agreement was signed, a large number of persons who were to be removed from office according to the above declaration were already being held in custody. Long before the occupation of Germany had been accomplished, the Supreme Headquarters of the Allied Expeditionary Forces had drawn up lists of persons who were subject to "mandatory arrest," on the assumption that they had taken part in Nazi crimes. When the war ended, these lists were extended to include persons thought to be particularly dangerous because of their prominent positions in Nazi organizations, the Wehrmacht, the administration, and the economy. A total of 178,000 persons were placed under "mandatory arrest" by the three western Allies and put into internment camps—95,000 in the American zone, over 64,000 in the British zone, and 19,000 in the French zone. In the Soviet-occupied zone, more than 67,000 persons were detained.

In German resistance circles, it had also been agreed as early as 1943 that in principle, when the war was over and the Hitler dictatorship had collapsed, all Nazi elements would have to be eliminated from public life, and that persons who had taken part in the crimes of the Nazi regime would be put on trial. Shortly after the Allied occupation of Germany, German opponents of the Nazi regime began to organize in various places to undertake such "self-purge" operations on their own; these attempts, however, were stifled by the western Allies' military administrations. Only the Soviets, for a short while, permitted feelings of loathing and resentment to be expressed in their zone by spontaneous lynch trials.

Neither the Yalta statement nor the Potsdam declaration contained any guidelines for implementing the announced policy of ridding Germany of Nazism and militarism. The result was that each zone had its own policy in this area, depending on the specific interests and goals of the occupying power.

In the American zone, two influences were at work among the military administration: on the one hand, a desire to reeducate the German people for life in a democratic society; and on the other hand, a belief in collective German guilt and, as a corollary, a general distrust of Germans that did not differentiate between supporters and opponents of the Nazi regime. The requirements of the economy and proper administration were given little weight; American officers, even of higher rank, who employed German experts with a Nazi past in the management of local institutions, were suspended on the spot.

In the British zone, the prevailing inclination was to institute a radical purge of Nazi and militarist influences. This zone, which contained the Ruhr district, had the highest population density, and in the war its housing, transportation, and manufacturing facilities had sustained greater damage than any other part of Germany. In this situation the British were soon ready to pursue a pragmatic policy and seek compromise, out of concern that life would break down completely if Germans familiar with local conditions and problems were to be excluded from employment in responsible posts. Under the Nazi regime all leading officials in the economy and administration, even those on a middle or lower level, had belonged to some sort of a Nazi organization, at least nominally. In these circumstances, the British occupation authorities felt forced to make use of persons who, by the criteria in force at the time, were to be regarded as politically incriminated. German antifascists protested strongly against this practice, but to no avail.

France—which had not taken part in either the Yalta or the Potsdam conference—also subscribed to the principle that Nazi elements had to be removed, but in the French zone the issue was never accorded the degree of importance that it had in the American or even in the British zone. France's goals were to weaken Germany, its "traditional enemy," by decentralizing Germany's political framework, and also to exploit the resources still to be found in the French zone of Germany for the restoration of the French economy, which had declined sharply as a result of the war. The French not only were ready to retain in their posts persons who were incriminated by activities in Nazi organizations, but often went so far as to engage German experts from other zones who had been dismissed from office for that very reason.

In the Soviet zone, from the start, denazification measures were designed to serve the Soviets' main objective—restructuring society in accordance with Communist principles. Leaders of industry and large landowners were dispossessed without hesitation. In many instances, property of the middle class was also nationalized, if the owner was regarded as having been a Nazi sympathizer. All key positions in the administration, the economy, and cultural life were staffed by Communists loyal to the official line, without consideration for their professional qualifications. Jurists who had served under the Nazi regime as judges or state attorneys were dismissed, with hardly any exceptions. Persons suspected of having taken part in Nazi crimes were taken into custody, and some were exiled to the east; but most of the rank-and-file members of Nazi organizations were not affected by the denazification measures—provided they showed that they were prepared to participate in the creation of a Communist society, as by joining the Communist party.

In order to avoid too great divergences in their respective denazification policies, the four powers, through the Allied Control Council for Germany, issued a regulation

(No. 24, dated January 12, 1946) that provided uniform guidelines to be applied in all the zones of occupation. Attached to the regulation was a list of offices and positions from which former Nazis were barred. Had these guidelines been observed, the denazification measures would have been much harsher than they were in practice. However, it was too late for that; developments had reached the point where the trend toward moderation could no longer be reversed by a Control Council regulation, especially in the French and British zones.

Another Control Council regulation, No. 38 (of October 12, 1946), required that former Nazis be classified in one of five categories:

1. Major offenders
2. Offenders (activists, militarists, profiteers)
3. Lesser offenders
4. Followers
5. Persons exonerated

Persons in categories 1 to 4 were subject to punishment or some form of "reparation": detention in a labor camp, for terms ranging from two to ten years (major offenders); banning from employment; confiscation of property; loss of pension rights; special deductions from current income; restriction of voting rights. Persons in category 4 who were born after January 1, 1919, were exempt from reparation in a "youth amnesty." In the French zone, other amnesties were announced in 1947 and 1948 affecting persons in category 4.

The basis for the classification was a questionnaire that had to be filled in by the person to be denazified, in which he had to give his personal data and divulge his activities during the Nazi regime and his association with Nazi organizations. If the questionnaire showed grounds for incrimination, the case came before a panel of three (one professional jurist, as chairman, and two lay judges) for decision. The Control Council regulation provided for the presumption of guilt, and it was up to the person so affected to prove his innocence; this resulted in many instances of similar cases leading to totally different outcomes.

In view of the difficulties encountered by the denazification procedure, the occupying powers soon sought to transfer its implementation to the Germans. At the Four-Power Foreign Ministers' Conference, which took place in Moscow in the spring of 1947, it was decided to recommend to the military commanders in the different zones that they transfer the responsibility for implementing Control Council regulations 24 and 38 to the Germans, and that they leave it up to the German authorities to decide on the measures required for such implementation; the occupying power, however, would retain its supreme authority on the subject. In the wake of this recommendation, denazification was handed over to the German authorities in 1947 and 1948.

The change in the international climate and the ensuing deterioration in relations between East and West reduced the interest of the powers in denazification. In March 1948, denazification was brought to an abrupt end in the Soviet zone. On October 15, 1950, the Bundestag (the West German parliament) recommended to the German states that they suspend current classification procedures affecting categories 3, 4, and 5; abstain from introducing any new procedures; and abolish the existing bans on practicing certain professions, on the blocking of bank accounts or other assets, and on the restriction of voting rights. The Bundestag also recommended the granting of pardons to most of the persons who had been sentenced to serve in labor camps. The German states complied with these recommendations by various laws enacted in the period from 1950 to 1954, and they thereby brought denazification to an end.

According to an (incomplete) table made by the West German Ministry of the Interior at the end of 1949, 3,660,648 persons had by then been processed in the three western zones; 1,667 had been classified in category 1 (major offenders); 23,060 in category 2 (offenders); 150,425 in category 3 (lesser offenders); and 1,005,874 in category 4 (followers). A total of 3,410,728 sentences of punishment and reparation were imposed.

Denazification had been launched with great zeal, but it ran out of steam when neither the procedures laid down nor the authorities charged with its implementation proved adequate for the task. Nazi activists who had committed the gravest crimes in the occupied countries did not, needless to say, admit to them in their questionnaires, and more often than not passed unharmed through the denazification process. On the other hand, it was not rare for persons who had been only nominal party members—who had succumbed to pressure from superiors in order to hold on to their jobs and had only held minor "honorary" posts in the party—to have severe sanctions applied to them. Numerous questionnaires were forged, and discrimination, as well as denunciations, occurred quite frequently. Since the motivation in these cases was based on personal and economic rather than political grounds, denazification was put in an even more questionable light. Moreover, depending on which occupation zone was responsible, similar cases were given quite different treatment, a situation that was naturally regarded as unfair and unjust. The less serious cases were dealt with in an early stage of the occupation, when the sentences imposed were relatively severe, whereas the more serious cases were put off. By the time they reached trial, the Allies were no longer as concerned about denazification as previously, with the result that the offenders escaped relatively lightly.

In the end, it was not only those subjected to denazification who opposed it; the process itself came to be rejected, even by opponents of the Nazi regime.

BIBLIOGRAPHY

Bower, T. *The Pledge Betrayed: America and Britain and the Denazification of Postwar Germany*. Garden City, N.Y., 1982.

Friedmann, W. *The Allied Military Government of Germany*. London, 1947.

Fuerstenau, J. *Entnazifizierung: Ein Kapitel deutscher Nachkriegspolitik*. Neuwied, West Germany, 1969.

Griffith, W. E. *The Denazification in the United States Zone of Germany*. Cambridge, Mass., 1966.

Johnson, J. *Dilemmas of Postwar Germany*. New York, 1948.

Lenz, H. *Der Schlusstrich: Gedanken zur Entnazifizierung*. Cologne, 1948.

Niethammer, L. *Entnazifizierung in Bayern: Säuberung und Rehabilitierung unter amerikanischer Besatzung*. Frankfurt, 1972.

ADALBERT RÜCKERL

DENMARK, the southernmost of the Scandinavian countries. Jews settled in Denmark in the late seventeenth century; in 1814 they were granted citizenship, and in 1849, under the constitution adopted that year, they received full rights. Denmark's Jews belonged to the lower and upper middle class; many made a name for themselves in science, literature, the arts, and journalism, or held senior posts in banking and the administration. The rate of mixed marriages was among the highest in the world. In the twentieth century most of Denmark's six thousand Jews lived in the capital, Copenhagen.

During the 1930s the Jewish community of Denmark, like that of every country bordering on Germany, was called upon to assist Jewish refugees. In 1940 a special body, the May Fourth Committee, was established by the community to care for the refugees, which it did in cooperation with several non-Jewish committees that had been formed for the same purpose. One special project was an agricultural-training program set up in coop-

eration with the Zionist pioneering movement He-Haluts, in which the Ministry of Agriculture issued a special permit enabling fifteen hundred youngsters to work on farms and some of them to engage in fishing as well. Shortly before the outbreak of World War II, YOUTH ALIYA groups from Germany, Austria, and Czechoslovakia came to Denmark, thanks to the efforts of Danish women's organizations.

On the whole, however, Danish policy on refugees was reserved; as in other European countries, it differentiated between "political" refugees and other kinds—the "other kinds" being the Jews. Political refugees—most of whom were Social Democrats or Communists—were taken care of by the Danish Social Democrat party's Matteotti Foundation, and were given preference as far as residence and work permits were concerned. On behalf of the government, the relevant ministries, mostly the Ministry of Justice and the Ministry of Social Affairs, handled refugee affairs.

Between 1934 and 1938 the laws and regulations applying to refugees became increasingly restrictive, and non-Scandinavians encountered great difficulties in entering the country and even more so in trying to obtain work permits. Most of the Jewish refugees who did succeed in reaching Denmark—their number is estimated at forty-five hundred—did not remain, and left the country for overseas destinations. When the Germans occupied Denmark in 1940, fifteen hundred Jewish refugees were still in the country, including several hundred *halutsim* (agricultural pioneers) and Youth Aliya children. During the 1930s, the Rigsdag (the Danish parliament) debated government policy on the refugees, with the conservative parties calling for a reduction in their number and a ban on further entries into the country, while the liberal groups expressed disapproval of government policy on the issue. Both the government and the general public expressed their opposition to antisemitism and joined the Jewish community in combating its manifestations.

In the first years following the German occupation (on April 9, 1940), the situation of the Jews remained unchanged—unlike that

One of the Danish boats used to ferry Jews from the town of Gilleleje to fishing boats at sea, which then brought them to safety in Sweden (October 1943). This boat is on permanent display at Yad Vashem in Jerusalem.

in other countries occupied by the Nazis. The Danes (in contrast to the Norwegians) did not offer any real resistance to the Germans, and reached agreement with the German government on the continued operation of the country's democratic administration. They followed a so-called policy of negotiations, under which the Danish government, and even the Danish army, remained in existence; only the conduct of foreign affairs was no longer in Danish hands. Relations between the two countries were still on a diplomatic basis, with the German minister to Copenhagen, Cecil von Renthe-Fink, staying in his post. The agreement between the Danish government and the occupation authorities contained a provision committing the Germans to refrain from causing harm to the Jews. The protection of Danish Jews by the Danish government remained in force even in times of crisis between the government and the Germans, and the Danish people resolutely resisted occasional German pressure on the Jewish issue, as well as the efforts of the small Danish Nazi party to stir up antisemitism. In the winter of 1941–1942, a public debate was held on the "Jewish question," in which the moderator, Hal Koch, a professor of theology, called on the Danish people to reject out of hand any suggestion that they discriminate against the Danish Jews, not only because justice and honor demanded it, but also because it was a prerequisite for preserving Danish liberty and the rule of law.

The steadfast stand on this issue by the Danish people and the Danish government persuaded the Germans that for the time being it would be preferable not to touch the Danish Jews; at the WANNSEE CONFERENCE, Martin LUTHER, representing the German Foreign Office, proposed that the Scandinavian countries be excluded for the time being from the "FINAL SOLUTION" because of the attitude of the local populations toward the Jews, and the small number of Jews in those countries. The Germans took it for granted that the issue would be resolved after victory had been achieved. This policy remained in force when von Renthe-Fink was replaced, in the fall of 1942, by Dr. Werner BEST.

A change came in the spring of 1943. With the growing strength of the Allied forces on the battlefronts, Danish resistance operations gathered momentum (in the early stage of the occupation such resistance had hardly existed). The strikes and sabotage acts created tension between the Danes and the Germans, and the "Jewish question" was put on the agenda. Throughout this period, and from the beginning of the occupation, the Jewish community had kept a low profile and its quiet life was not seriously disturbed. He-Haluts, however, showed greater sensitivity, became aware of the changing situation, and made plans for escaping from the country. An attempt by some of the young people to reach the coast of southern Europe by hiding under train carriages failed; on the other hand, a group of He-Haluts fishermen on Bornholm Island obtained a boat and used it to flee to Sweden. The Germans learned of the escape and issued a stern warning to the Danish government, which passed it on to the Jewish community. This incident caused friction between the Jewish community—which bore part of the cost of maintaining the Zionist training farms—and the He-Haluts trainees, with the community leaders threatening to take action if such attempts were repeated.

In late August 1943, a crisis erupted between the German authorities and the Danish government when the latter refused to accede to new demands made by the Germans. The Danish government resigned, and the German military commander in Denmark declared a state of emergency. Werner Best regarded this as an opportune moment for proposing to Berlin that the Jews of Denmark be deported; he probably felt that his proposal would bring German police reinforcements to Denmark and that this would have the effect of bolstering his own position, which had suffered as a result of the crisis. Best himself, it turned out, was not sure that his proposal should be carried out, fearing that his own relations with the Danes would be compromised.

On the night of October 1–2, 1943, the German police began arresting Jews. Reports of the planned deportation of the Jews were leaked to various Danish circles by several German sources, the most important of which was the German legation's attaché for shipping affairs, Georg Ferdinand DUCKWITZ. The reaction was spontaneous. The Danes alerted the Jews, helping them move into hiding places and from there make their way to the seashore, and, with the help of Danish fishermen, cross into Sweden. At first this was an unorganized and spontaneous operation, but soon the Danish resistance joined in and helped to organize the massive flight that followed the Swedish government's proclamation that it was ready to take in all the refugees from Denmark. In Denmark, all groups of the population went into action in order to save the Jews. Dozens of protests poured into the offices of the German authorities from Danish economic and social organizations; King Christian X expressed his firm objection to the German plans; the heads of the Danish churches published a strong protest and used their pulpits to urge the Danish people to help the Jews; and the universities closed down for a week, with the students lending a hand in the rescue operation. The operation went on for three weeks, and in its course seventy-two hundred Jews and some seven hundred non-Jewish relatives of theirs were taken to Sweden. The costs of the operation were borne partly by the Jews themselves and to a large extent by contributions made by the Danes. The Danish resistance movement grew in size and strength as a result of the successful rescue effort and was able to keep open a fairly reliable escape route to Sweden.

Rolf Günther—Adolf EICHMANN's deputy, who had come to Copenhagen in order to organize the deportation of the Jews—failed in his mission; the Danish police not only refused to cooperate with Günther but also helped the rescue operation. An order was also issued prohibiting German police from breaking into apartments in order to arrest Jews. Despite all these efforts, some five hundred Jews were arrested, including some *halutsim* and Youth Aliya children, and sent to THERESIENSTADT. The Danish public and the administration (which continued to function after the government had resigned) did not give up their concern for the fate of their Jewish countrymen in Theresienstadt. They sent food parcels to them and had the Danish Foreign Ministry bombard the Germans with warnings. The ministry also put forward a demand that a Danish delegation be permitted to visit the detainees in the Theresienstadt camp. Eichmann exploited this Danish demand by setting up a fake "model ghetto" in Theresienstadt when a Danish delegation, together with International RED CROSS representatives, visited Theresienstadt in the summer of 1944. However, the fact remains that the Danish Jews were not deported to AUSCHWITZ, and in the end were included in a Swedish Red Cross operation, carried out under Count Folke BERNADOTTE, in which Scandinavian nationals were transferred from concentration camps to Sweden, in the spring of 1945, before the war came to an end.

The Danish people's resolute refusal to discriminate against their Jewish fellow citizens and to surrender them, or the refugees among them, to the Germans; the rescue operation launched to transfer the Jews to a safe haven in Sweden; and the unwavering support and protection they gave to the Theresienstadt deportees—all represent an exercise of high moral and political responsibility, outstanding and exceptional for the time in which it took place. It has aroused profound admiration, and its echo reverberates to this day.

BIBLIOGRAPHY

Goldberger, L., ed. *The Rescue of the Danish Jews: Moral Courage under Stress.* New York, 1987.

Petersen, H. U. "Die dänische Flüchtlingspolitik 1933–1941." In *Deutschsprachiges Exil in Dänemark nach 1933: Zu Methoden und Einzelergebnissen; Vorträge des Kolloquiums am 1. und 2. Oktober 1984*, edited by Ruth Dinesen et al., pp. 73–94. Copenhagen, 1986.

Petrow, R. *The Bitter Years: The Invasion and Occupation of Denmark and Norway, April 1940–May 1945.* New York, 1974.

Valentin, H. "Rescue and Relief Activities in Behalf of Jewish Victims of Nazism in Scandinavia." *YIVO Annual of Jewish Social Science* 8 (1953): 224–251.

Yahil, L. *The Rescue of Danish Jewry: Test of a Democracy.* Philadelphia, 1969.

LENI YAHIL

DENYING THE HOLOCAUST. *See* Holocaust, Denial of the.

DEPARTMENT OF STATE. *See* United States Department of State.

DEPORTATIONS. As early as September 1919, Hitler wrote of the need for systematic measures in Germany to achieve "the removal of the Jews altogether." Thus, from the beginning, the physical removal of the Jews from Germany in one way or another was basic to Hitler's approach to the "Jewish question." But it was not until the mid-1930s that at least one party organization, Reinhard HEYDRICH's SD (Sicherheitsdienst; Security Service), a branch of Heinrich HIMMLER's SS, began to formulate policy based on this axiom by articulating as the final goal of Nazi Jewish policy a Germany "cleansed" or "free" of Jews (*judenrein; judenfrei*). This was to be achieved through intensifying pressures for emigration. It was with the annexation of Austria in March 1938 that the SD was first able to experiment freely in this regard, when Adolf EICHMANN established the ZENTRALSTELLE FÜR JÜDISCHE AUSWANDERUNG (Central Office for Jewish Emigration) in Vienna. However, Eichmann's methods still constituted forced emigration or expulsion rather than deportation.

The first experiment in actual mass deportation of Jews was carried out in the fall of 1938. In March of that year, Poland had decreed that Polish citizens living abroad who did not have their passports renewed with a special stamp by October 31 would be denationalized. The Germans realized that they would soon have on their hands as many as seventy thousand resident Polish Jews, who, without valid passports, would be unable either to return home or to emigrate further. As the deadline approached, Foreign Minister Joachim von RIBBENTROP urged the police to take preventive action. The Gestapo rounded up about seventeen thousand Polish Jews on the night of October 28, 1938, in order to deport them to Poland. The Poles closed their border on October 31, trapping most of the unfortunate deportees in a no-man's-land in the area of ZBĄSZYŃ, and their fate became the subject of prolonged German-Polish negotiations. Deportation without control of the area of reception had proved to be a fiasco.

The conquest of Poland in September 1939, however, offered the shapers of Nazi Jewish policy precisely what they had lacked the previous year. Almost immediately, plans emerged for large-scale deportations of Jews from the ever-expanding Third Reich into German-occupied Poland—to a Lublin Reservation, in particular (*see* NISKO AND LUBLIN PLAN). The first such deportations, in October 1939, were organized by Eichmann and involved five trainloads of Jews from Vienna; Mährisch-Ostrau, in the Protectorate of BOHEMIA AND MORAVIA; and Katowice, in the newly incorporated territory of Eastern Upper Silesia. They were transported to a transit camp at Nisko, on the San River, from which most

Deportations from Würzburg, Germany.

of the deportees were chased over the demarcation line into the Soviet zone.

However, Jewish deportations were only part of a much vaster scheme of demographic engineering approved by Hitler at that time, involving the resettlement of ethnic Germans (VOLKSDEUTSCHE) from the Soviet sphere and the deportation of all Poles from the incorporated territories as well. Eichmann was named the SS expert in charge of "Jewish affairs and evacuations," coordinating the outgoing deportations of Poles and Jews. Amid the chaotic conditions, "wild deportations" (the Nazis' term), and conflicting priorities that characterized German-occupied Poland, systematic deportation of the Jews proved once again unrealizable. Eichmann's Nisko operation was canceled, and the deportation of Jews from the incorporated territories into the GENERALGOUVERNEMENT was repeatedly postponed. Most of those deported by the Germans at this time—over 380,000 into the Generalgouvernement by March 1941, according to SS statistics—were Poles rather than Jews. In addition, several hundred thousand Jews—stripped of their homes, livelihood, and human dignity—fled eastward on their own.

In the summer of 1940, MADAGASCAR replaced the Lublin Reservation as the prospective goal of Jewish deportation, but this plan too proved impracticable. Jewish deportations remained sporadic and tied to other population movements. When more than 70,000 "undesirable" Frenchmen (including, of course, French Jews) were deported from Alsace-Lorraine into Vichy France, the *Gauleiter* (district leaders) of neighboring Baden and Saarpfalz exploited the opportunity to make their own territories *judenfrei* by deporting their 6,500 German Jews there as well, on October 22 and 23, 1940. And when a renewed wave of deportations into the Generalgouvernement was undertaken in early 1941, 5,000 Jews from Vienna and some 4,000 from the incorporated territories were included, until the whole resettlement action was suspended during preparations for the invasion of the Soviet Union. Thus, although total removal of the Jews through deportation was the centerpiece of Nazi expectations in the first eighteen months of the war, in reality such moves comprised only a small fraction of

Nazi deportation programs in this period.

With the invasion of the Soviet Union and the EINSATZGRUPPEN massacres of Soviet Jewry, Nazi Jewish policy shifted from expulsion to mass murder. But the mobile firing-squad methods used in the Soviet Union could not be employed on European Jews. They could not be shot down in the streets of Amsterdam, Paris, or Salonika as they were behind the front in the Soviet Union. Hence the Nazis came to a decision that Jewish deportations would be not an end in themselves, but the means of bringing the Jews to killing centers in the east. However, in late September 1941, before these centers were constructed, Hitler ordered that Germany be cleared of Jews by the end of the year. Between mid-October and mid-December, some fifty thousand German Jews were deported either to ŁÓDŹ or to the occupied areas of the Soviet Union. Many of the latter group were shot on arrival in Riga or Kovno; meanwhile, space was made in the overcrowded Łódź ghetto when deportations of its inhabitants to the first extermination camp, at nearby CHEŁMNO, began in December 1941. But a deportation program on the scale necessary to clear Germany, Poland, and other European countries of their Jews could not begin until the major extermination camps (BEŁŻEC, SOBIBÓR, TREBLINKA, AUSCHWITZ, and, later and on a much smaller scale, MAJDANEK) were ready to go into full operation, between March and July of 1942.

The intended victims (*see* WANNSEE CONFERENCE) were scattered throughout Europe in countries with varying degrees of sovereignty, many of them not under German occupation. The victims in Poland were already ghettoized and under total German control, but deportation of Jews from other parts of Europe would be a far more complex problem. Eichmann had gained considerable experience in both "Jewish affairs" and "evacuations," and his department, Section IV B 4 of the REICHSSICHERHEITSHAUPTAMT (Reich Security Main Office; RSHA), became the coordinating center of these deportations to the extermination camps. Eichmann had only a small staff directly under him (twelve to thirteen officials plus secretarial help in the Berlin office), but it was nonetheless a far-reaching network. The German embassies in many vassal and

The last Jewish families of Hohenlimburg (near Essen) in Germany being deported to a concentration camp (April 23, 1942).

allied states already had "Jewish advisers" who were in close contact with Eichmann. Himmler had also established his own police networks in areas under German military control, and here Eichmann had direct access to the local Sicherheitspolizei (Security Police; Sipo). The task of Eichmann's small outfit was to get others to perform the functions vital to the deportation program; thus a number of other agencies were of great importance.

Vital logistic support was provided by the Transport Ministry; the German RAILWAYS (Reichsbahn) under its jurisdiction, supervised by State Secretary Albert GANZENMÜLLER; and the Reichsbahn's Polish auxiliary, the Ostbahn. Securing "special trains" (*Sonderzüge*) for the Jews despite the immense demands made on German rail capacity throughout the war was crucial. For deportations within Poland, the local Sipo made arrangements directly with the Ostbahn. For all other deportations in Europe, Eichmann's deputy Rolf Günther and Eichmann's transportation expert, Franz NOVAK, worked with Reichsbahn authorities. The Jews were booked as passengers (one-way group fares, children half price, and infants under four free) but were transported for the most part as cargo, that is, in freight cars. In the end the railways carried nearly three million people to six obscure destinations in Poland and the incorporated territories, from which clothing and luggage, but no people, returned.

Another important agency in the deportation program was the Foreign Office. Its Jewish desk had long offered advice concerning the foreign-policy implications of Nazi Jewish programs, especially when foreign Jews were involved. Now it secured the right to be consulted by the SS concerning the "FINAL SOLUTION" in all European territories of the German sphere where foreign-policy considerations still had to be taken into account. The Jewish desk of the Foreign Office worked zealously to facilitate the frictionless implementation of the deportation program in many ways: urging preparatory anti-Jewish legislation, on the German model; negotiating agreements on the fate of Jewish property; exercising diplomatic pressure to assist Eichmann's representatives in attaining final agreement for the deportations, local help in conducting roundups, and in some cases even money to pay for deportation costs; and smoothing out complications arising from the presence of large numbers of Jews with foreign citizenship, who required special consideration if embarrassing incidents were to be avoided.

The actual deportations required the involvement of many other elements. In Poland, special ghetto-clearing units had to be mobilized and assembled for each operation. Even a single deportation from a German city was a major undertaking. The entire police force was mobilized; a large assembly area, usually the cargo depot, was taken over and sealed off for the day. Large numbers of municipal officials were involved: representatives of the Finance Office collected property inventories, liquidated property, and turned the proceeds over to officials of the Tax Office; personnel of the Labor Office collected workbooks; and those from the Housing Office collected keys and disposed of vacant apartments. In foreign countries the process was even more complicated, because allied and satellite governments had to be persuaded to perform not only all these essential functions of the deportation itself but also the preliminary steps of definition, registration, marking, expropriation, and concentration.

By the spring and summer of 1942, the extermination camps were ready and the full-scale deportation program of the "Final Solution" commenced. The onslaught against the Polish ghettos began in southern Poland in March, continued in Warsaw in July, and reached a climax in the fall, when the extermination camps (some of them now equipped with new, larger gas chambers) were virtually flooded with deportees beyond their killing capacity. In the WARTHEGAU, deportations from Łódź were carried out from mid-January until mid-May and again in September, while in the intervening summer months all the other ghettos of the Warthegau were systematically liquidated. By fall, only those Jews capable of physical labor were still alive in the Warthegau.

Added to this stream of victims sent from the ghettos to the extermination camps were the first deportations from other parts of Europe. In mid-February 1942 the Slovak government was approached with a request for 20,000 strong, young Jews for labor in the east, a proposal it eagerly accepted. In March, Eichmann requested the deportation initially of 1,000 and then of an additional 5,000 French Jews; this too encountered no difficulties. Full-scale deportations then quickly followed, as Germany informed Slovakia of its willingness to take all of the remaining Slovak Jews, of whom 58,000 were deported by the end of the summer. In July 1942, mass deportations began from France, Belgium, and the Netherlands, at first composed primarily of foreign Jews in order to facilitate local cooperation and acquiescence. In August, some 5,500 Croatian Jews were added to the deportations, though most of the Jews in Croatia were in fact killed locally by the native fascist USTAŠA. And in November, over 500 Norwegian Jews were rounded up and deported.

A second wave began in early 1943. Deportations continued from France, Belgium, and the Netherlands, along with a trickle from Norway and Croatia, but the center of German attention shifted to the Balkans. Through the efforts first of the Foreign Office and then of Eichmann's traveling representative, Theodor DANNECKER, an agreement was reached with Bulgaria, which rounded up and handed to the Germans over 11,000 "alien" Jews from Macedonia and Thrace. Plans to deport native Bulgarian Jews as well foundered, however, as domestic opposition emerged and Germany's prospects for victory began to dim after the defeat at STALINGRAD in February 1943. Indeed, wherever Germany had to rely on foreign collaborators, its leverage in extracting cooperation in deporting Jews began to weaken in the post-Stalingrad era. While Romania had cooperated with the operations of Einsatzgruppe D along its Russian front and had carried out its own deportation of the "alien" Jews of Bessarabia and Bukovina to Transnistria, where most of them perished, the Romanians now backed out of deporting their "own" Jews. The Jews in the Italian occupation zones of coastal Croatia, southern Greece, and southern France were similarly protected from the German onslaught by the Italian authorities. But the majority of Greek Jews lived in SALONIKA, in northern Greece. This region was occupied by the German military, which provided all the help Eichmann and his local representatives, Dieter WISLICENY and Alois BRUNNER, needed to deport 46,000 Greek Jews between March and May of 1943. The attempt to deport Jews from Denmark in October 1943 failed when the local population first hid the Danish Jews and then smuggled them to nearby Sweden. In the same month, however, following the German occupation of Italy, 1,000 Jews were deported from Rome to Auschwitz.

In 1944, even when the war was clearly lost, deportations continued from western Europe, northern Italy, and the former Italian occupation zone in Greece. Deportations were also resumed in 1944 from Slovakia and from the last remaining ghetto, in Łódź. But all of this was dwarfed by the single largest deportation operation of the "Final Solution"—the attempt to destroy Hungarian Jewry. Following the German occupation of Hungary in March 1944, Eichmann mobilized his entire team of experts and descended on Budapest. Once again willing collaborators were found, who helped to concentrate and deport 437,000 Jews between mid-May and early July of that year, before the head of state, Miklós HORTHY, reasserted himself and brought an end to the deportations, which could proceed only with Hungarian cooperation.

Ultimately, a great part of the victims of the Holocaust fell prey to starvation and disease in the ghettos, to German mobile firing squads, or to brutal murder by local fascists. But for the majority, deportation was the essential step that brought them to their death in the Nazi gas chambers and labor camps.

BIBLIOGRAPHY

Browning, C. R. *The Final Solution and the Foreign Office.* New York, 1978.

Hilberg, R. *The Destruction of the European Jews.* 3 vols. New York, 1985.

Hilberg, R. *Sonderzüge nach Auschwitz.* Mainz, 1981.

Reitlinger, G. *The Final Solution.* New York, 1953.

CHRISTOPHER R. BROWNING

DERECHIN (Pol., Dereczyn), town in the Belorussian SSR. Between the two world wars, Derechin was part of independent Poland. In September 1939, together with all of eastern Poland, it was occupied by the Red Army and annexed to the Soviet Union. On the eve of World War II, four thousand Jews lived in the town. Following the occupation by the

Germans on June 25, 1941, Jews from the nearby towns of Kholinka and Kolonya were deported to Derechin.

A ghetto was established, and all the "useless" Jews were moved into it. Artisans initially lived outside the ghetto. When rumors of the murder of Jews in SLONIM reached Derechin, the town's Jews began to talk about escaping to the nearby forests. The "useful" Jews opposed this, believing that their usefulness would save their lives and that escape would place them in danger. A youth underground arose; its aims were to escape to the forests and to offer resistance in the ghetto if its members were surrounded there before leaving. The young people smuggled twenty guns and automatic firearms, as well as ammunition, out of the Germans' munitions stores and hid them outside the town.

In the spring of 1942, partisan activity increased, and the police stations in Kholinka and the Puzeviche labor camps were attacked. The Jews of the ghetto began to hope that the partisans would reach Derechin as well. In July of that year, the first Jews left the ghetto and went to the Borelom Forest.

On July 24 an *Aktion* was carried out in the ghetto. Jews who had prepared bunkers went into hiding; some took axes with them to attack anyone breaking into the hiding place. About three hundred Jews fled to the surrounding forests, some to Borelom. Among those who fled to the forest were several who subsequently became well-known partisans, including Eliyahu Lipszowicz, a platoon leader in the unit of Dr. Yeheskel ATLAS. Lipszowicz's brothers Chaim Yehoshua and Gershon; his sister Taiba; the brothers Benjamin and David Dombrowski; Chaim Szelkowicz; and the brothers Moshe Chaim, Miszka, and Shalom Ogolnik were known in the forest as partisan fighters. Some who escaped to the forest were organized into a "family camp," with the aid of the partisan commander Boris Bulat.

On August 10, 1942, 120 partisans, headed by Atlas and Bulat, attacked the German garrison in Derechin. Jewish partisans led the attackers. The Belorussian and Polish police who were caught were shot next to the Jewish communal grave. In that battle three Jewish partisans from the town were killed. Sixty-four Jews who had escaped from Derechin fell in combat in the forest.

Derechin was liberated in mid-July 1944. Over two hundred of its Jews survived.

BIBLIOGRAPHY

Bornsztejn, S. *The Doctor Atlas Brigade: The Story of a Jewish Partisan.* Tel Aviv, 1965. (In Hebrew.)

Raban, Y., ed. *Deretchin: Memorial Book.* Tel Aviv, 1972. (In Hebrew and English.)

SHALOM CHOLAWSKI

DÉS. *See* Dej.

DEUTSCHE AUSRÜSTUNGSWERKE (German Armament Works; DAW), one of the SS's most important economic enterprises, established in May 1939, with headquarters in Berlin; Standartenführer Walter Salpeter was appointed as its head. DAW assumed control of the production plants that the SS had established in order to exploit the labor of inmates of the DACHAU, SACHSENHAUSEN, BUCHENWALD, and, later, AUSCHWITZ concentration camps. As time went on, more such factories were set up, in the LUBLIN, Puławy, STUTTHOF, Fürstenwalde, RAVENSBRÜCK, and NEUENGAMME camps. The number of prisoners employed in these plants rose from 1,220 in 1940 to 15,500 in 1943. The largest factories were in the JANÓWSKA concentration camp in Lvov and the Jewish prisoner-of-war camp in LUBLIN-LIPOWA, which together employed some 8,000 Jews. Most of the prisoners who worked in the DAW factories perished, either through the policy of *Vernichtung durch Arbeit* (extermination through work) or by mass-slaughter *Aktionen.* The largest *Aktion* was the murder of 2,000 Jewish prisoners of war, who were removed from Lublin-Lipowa on November 3, 1943, and taken to the crematoria at MAJDANEK, where they were shot to death.

[*See also* Forced Labor.]

BIBLIOGRAPHY

Ennos, G. "Die wirtschaftlichen Unternehmungen der SS." *Schriftenreihe der Vierteljahresheft für Zeitgeschichte* 7 (1963).

Hilberg, R. *The Destruction of the European Jews.* 3 vols. New York, 1985.

SHMUEL KRAKOWSKI

DEUTSCHER VORTRUPP, GEFOLGSCHAFT DEUTSCHER JUDEN (German Vanguard, German Jewish Adherents), organization founded in February 1933 by a group of Jewish university students in GERMANY led by a student of religion, Hans Joachim Schoeps. It started with about one hundred and fifty members, and its membership declined gradually until it was dissolved by the Gestapo in December 1935.

The organization represented an odd attempt to retain Jewish religious identity while stressing its profound links with German culture. Wishing to participate as a Jewish political movement in the "German national regeneration," it advocated an authoritarian leadership within the Jewish community. As a group of ultrapatriotic Germans, the Deutscher Vortrupp had a highly negative attitude toward eastern European Jews and opposed Zionism, Marxism, and liberalism. Jewish religious observance, however, was part of its program. It opposed Zionism as a form of assimilation because of the Zionist goal of becoming "a nation like all nations"; and it believed that Jews belong to the German *Volk*, having no more than a religious specificity. Schoeps, who was the group's leading figure, was deeply influenced by proponents of a conservative revolution and defined himself as a conservative Prussian Jew. Grounding his world view in the writings of the conservative German Jewish statesman Friedrich Julius Stahl and the philosopher Franz Rosenzweig, he maintained that Prussianism and Jewish religion were based on common values. Schoeps developed a German conservative and nationalist ideology into which Judaism was fused. Failing to comprehend the racist basis of Nazism, he believed that the Third Reich would develop as a corporate state, allowing the Jews to integrate into it. Politically, the Deutscher Vortrupp allied itself with the REICHSBUND JÜDISCHER FRONTSOLDATEN (Reich Union of Jewish Frontline Soldiers) in a common anti-Zionist front. Fearing arrest, Schoeps left Germany for Sweden in 1938. In the war years he maintained a correspondence with German conservative political circles in exile, in which he proposed the establishment of a *numerus clausus* (the quota permitted) policy for the Jews after their return to Germany as the only way to guarantee their proper integration once Germany had been liberated.

BIBLIOGRAPHY

Grossman, K. "Zionists and Non-Zionists under Nazi Rule in the 1930s." *Herzl Year Book* 4 (1961/1962): 329–344.

Rheins, C. J. "Deutscher Vortrupp, Gefolgschaft Deutscher Juden: 1933–1935." *Leo Baeck Institute Year Book* 26 (1981): 207–229.

DAVID BANKIER

DIARIES, HOLOCAUST. The extensive literature about the Holocaust, written in many languages, takes various forms, the most important being diaries, personal memoirs, and fiction. For the purpose of documentation, the diaries are the most valuable: as on-the-spot compositions or notes written at the time of, or shortly following, the events they describe, they can serve the historian as an authentic and reliable source of information. In some cases, memoirs or diaries reconstructed *post factum* by survivors also contain significant information and faithfully depict the reality of the Holocaust and the atmosphere prevailing in it. But a clear distinction must be made between diaries kept while the writers were in direct contact with the horror and the uncertainty, and memoirs written after liberation, which inevitably bear the marks of hindsight.

The Jews have a long and deep-rooted tradition of recording their tribulations. At times of distress and persecution, as during the Crusades and the 1648–1649 Chmielnicki massacres in southern Russia, Jews poured out their hearts in chronicles, descriptions of the events they were witnessing, so that the memory of these events could be kept alive for the future.

However, never has so much been written by Jews who were incarcerated, tortured, and doomed as during the Holocaust. Emanuel RINGELBLUM, in his description of the ONEG SHABBAT Archive in Warsaw, relates that when the first fearful months of the German occupation had passed, the Jews came to realize that "while the Nazi authorities selected entire groups and sectors of the population for harassment, they paid no attention to what the individual Jew was doing in the privacy of his home. And so the Jew began to write; everybody was writing—journalists, writers, teachers, public figures, the teenagers, and even the children. Mostly they kept diaries, in which they described the tragic events unfolding before their eyes as the personal experiences that they indeed were."

It has since become known that the Jews wrote in every place—in the occupied countries, in the camps, and in their hideouts among the non-Jewish population. Whatever their age, the Jews wrote—both those who were writers by profession, and ordinary people for whom this was the only writing they had ever attempted. The urge to write seems to have been prompted by two motives: the need to find an outlet to express, in free and unfettered writing, the helplessness of their condition, their persecution and humiliation; and, for many Jews, wittingly or unwittingly, the sense that what they were recording might well be the only evidence, the only indictment that would be left behind, of their fate, which would perhaps also serve as a deterrent for the future. Many of the diarists were Jews who were hiding among the Christian population or under their protection (as was the case of Anne FRANK), and the isolation and quarantine in which they lived prompted them to give written expression to the stark tragedy they were experiencing.

Many of the diaries and other writings composed during the Holocaust have been lost. It is therefore impossible to estimate how much was written, its quality, and the number of persons writing at a particular time or over a prolonged period. Even so, a tremendous amount of material has been preserved. In the Warsaw Jewish Historical Institute (ŻYDOWSKI INSTYTUT HISTORYCZNY), which has a large collection of diaries, 272 items are listed under "diaries," 65 of them from the Warsaw ghetto, in Polish and Yiddish. Most of these diaries were written during the war and were saved as a result of coincidental circumstances. A relatively large number of important diaries were rescued as part of the Ringelblum Archive. Of the 65 manuscripts from the Warsaw ghetto classified as diaries at the Warsaw Jewish Historical Institute, only 8 were dictated or written about the time of the liberation; all the others are documents dating from the Holocaust period. So rich is the Warsaw diary collection in both quantity and quality, regarding the life of the Jews in the ghetto, the structure of the ghetto with its various institutions, and a range of details, that a day-by-day history of the Warsaw ghetto can be reconstructed based on this material alone.

The diaries can be classified according to several distinct categories: day-by-day records of events; public diaries; private diaries; and teenagers' and children's diaries.

1. The diaries that contain a daily record of events are devoid of personal observations or interpretations by the person or persons who kept them. The most significant example of this category is the chronicles of the ŁÓDŹ GHETTO, in which the staff of the JUDENRAT (Jewish Council), following instructions of the Judenrat members, recorded current events in the ghetto from January 1940 to July 1944. The Łódź chronicles have the disadvantage of being an officially inspired document, but their continuity, the wealth of events and developments they contain, and the information they provide combine to present a detailed picture of a major aspect of life in the Łódź ghetto.

2. Among the diaries of a public character, two different types can be distinguished. One is similar in its makeup to a chronicle and has as its major purpose the recording of general events as they occur, but it puts the emphasis on details that the author considers important, interpreting and evaluating them and describing their impact on the Jewish population. This pattern is found in the diaries of the historian Emanuel Ringelblum in the Warsaw ghetto and of Herman KRUK in Vilna. Both these diaries reveal their authors' sense of history; indeed, the writers may have planned to use the original material as the basis for an eventual broader historical treatment of the era. Similar to these records in style and relative importance are the diaries of Adam CZERNIAKÓW, head of the Warsaw ghetto Judenrat, and Ludwik Landau, who lived on the Polish side of Warsaw. Czerniaków's diary contains a concise account of his actions from the beginning of the occupation until the great deportation in the summer of 1942, the period in which he headed the largest ghetto in Europe. The account is interspersed with comments that reveal the author's state of mind. Landau, by profession an economist, devotes most of his comprehensive diary to the events on the Polish side and among Polish society, but he also deals extensively with the Jewish aspect. Of a similar nature are the diaries of Raymond-Raoul (Heshel) LAMBERT, a leading figure in the UNION GÉNÉRALE DES ISRAÉLITES DE FRANCE (General Council of French Jews), and Eliezer Yerushalmi of the ŠIAULIAI (Shavli) ghetto in Lithuania. Two other diaries that concentrate on public affairs—and shed light on important episodes in the story of the Jewish underground and armed resistance movement—are those that were kept by two prominent figures in the underground in Poland. One was Mordechai TENENBAUM, a founder of the Vilna underground and of the ŻYDOWSKA ORGANIZACJA BOJOWA (Jewish Fighting Organization; ŻOB) in Warsaw, and head of the Białystok Fighting Organization and uprising. The other was Tova DRAENGER (*Justina's Diary*), a leader of the Akiva movement and the Fighting Haluts movement in Kraków.

Many diaries are a combination of the public and the private. Their authors devote a great deal of attention to public affairs, but also record their personal experiences and make subjective, critical comments on the course of events. Such are the important diaries of two Warsaw teachers, Chaim Aaron KAPLAN and Abraham Lewin; the Yiddish cultural scholar and YIVO (Institute for Jewish Research) leader Selig Kalmanowitz, of Vilna; the engineer Henryk Brisker of Warsaw; Jakub Poznański of the Łódź ghetto; two Jewish police officers in Warsaw, Stanisław Adler and Stefan Ernst; and the Piotrków rabbi, Shimon Huberband (who at one point joined the inner circle of the Oneg Shabbat Archive in Warsaw).

3. Personal or private diaries are those in which the authors concentrate on their own or their relatives' experiences, conduct a kind of dialogue with themselves, and at best give only a patchy description of current events or restrict themselves to those happenings in which they were themselves involved. Examples of this kind are the diaries of Ruth Leimanson-Engelstern and Naomi Schatz-Weinkranz, two Jewish women who had gone into hiding in Poland among gentiles.

4. The diaries of teenagers and children have a special place among the private diaries. These are very moving writings and impressive human documents, some with literary value. In a number of these diaries the authors lay bare their souls and cry out against mankind and the world, which have ceased to protect them and have abandoned them to the hands of wicked people whose intentions and evil designs they do not understand. The most famous of these diaries is the one by Anne Frank, written in a hideout in Amsterdam where she was living with her own and one other Jewish family. This description of a gifted girl growing into maturity while shut off from the world, suffering from shortages, and with a constant threat hanging over her head, is a gripping literary creation. David Rubinowicz, a village boy living in the Kielce district, was twelve years old when he began recording in a school notebook the sufferings that his family and neighbors were experiencing. David Shrakovik, a diarist in the Łódź ghetto, was a few years older. Sarah Pishkin of Rubevichi in Belorussia, who began her diary when she was fifteen, expresses the pain and tribulations of a girl who has based her hopes on religious faith and is now beset by doubts and despair. David Flinker, a boy living in Brussels, is firm in his religious beliefs, and his mature thoughts are concerned with a search for the meaning of the disaster that has struck the Jewish people. Yitzhak Rudaszewski, a boy from Vilna, describes the general feeling of helplessness that prevails in the ghetto, yet his diary abounds with references to public life and to the interest that he takes in his studies and in the youth movement's program of activities. Eva Heyman, a Hungarian girl, was thirteen in February 1944 and far removed from Jewish life, absorbed by her own and her family's pursuits; her diary records her sudden descent into an atmosphere of catastrophe, from which there is no escape. The diary of Tamara Lazarson, of Kovno, depicts a girl from an assimilated Jewish family who, under the impact of persecution and destruction, discovers her people and comes to believe in its future.

Diaries written in concentration camps

have an enormous value. Some were discovered in the ruins of the AUSCHWITZ-Birkenau crematorium; their authors were men of the Sonderkommandos, who were in daily contact with murder and with the victims who were being led to their deaths. These diaries, and other notes found in Birkenau, were kept by Polish Jews from religious backgrounds—Zalman Gradowski, Zalman Levental, and Leib Langfuss. Full of horror and pain, they also appeal to the world to understand how they had been forced to take part in such awful abominations. These diaries contain revealing details about the preparations for the Sonderkommando uprising in Birkenau and about the uprising itself, an event on which hardly any reports from other primary sources exist.

The diaries and notes kept by Jews who were experiencing the reality of the Holocaust constitute an authentic historical documentation of great importance. They reveal the inner world and thoughts of human beings in extreme distress and under constant tension, and provide an insight into the complexity of the predicaments, the problems, and the decisions faced by the organized Jewish population and its leaders.

[*See also* Literature on the Holocaust.]

BIBLIOGRAPHY

Adler, S. *In the Warsaw Ghetto: Memoirs of Stanislaw Adler.* Jerusalem, 1982.

Czerniakow, A. *The Warsaw Diary of Adam Czerniakow.* New York, 1979.

Dawidsohn-Draengerowa, G. *Pamiętnik Justyny.* Kraków, 1946.

Fishkin, S. "Excerpts from the Diary of Sarah Fishkin." *Yalkut Moreshet* 4 (July 1965): 21–35. (In Hebrew.)

Frank, A. *Diary of a Young Girl.* New York, 1967.

Grynberg, M., ed. *Pamiętniki z getta warszawskiego: Fragmenty i regestry.* Warsaw, 1988.

Heyman, E. *The Diary of Eva Heyman.* Jerusalem, 1974.

Kaplan, C. A. *Scroll of Agony.* New York, 1965.

Lambert, R.-R. *Carnet d'un témoin (1940–1943).* Paris, 1985.

Landau, L. *Kronika lat wojny i okupacji.* 3 vols. Warsaw, 1962.

Lazarson-Rostowski, T. *Tamara's Diary: Kovno, 1942–1946.* Tel Aviv, 1975. (In Hebrew.)

Lewin, A. *A Cup of Tears: A Diary of the Warsaw Ghetto.* Oxford, 1988.

Mark, B. *The Scrolls of Auschwitz.* Tel Aviv, 1985.

Poznanski, J. *Pamiętnik z getta łódzkiego.* Łódź, 1960.

Ringelblum, E. *Notes from the Warsaw Ghetto: The Journal of Emanuel Ringelblum.* New York, 1958.

Rubinowicz, D. *The Diary of David Rubinowicz.* Edmonds, Wash., 1982.

Rudashevski, Y. *The Diary of the Vilna Ghetto, June 1941–April 1943.* Naharia, Israel, 1973.

Wajnkranc, N. S. *Przemineto z ogniem.* Warsaw, 1947.

Yerushalmi, E. *Pinkas Shavli: A Diary from a Lithuanian Ghetto (1941–1944).* Jerusalem, 1958.

ISRAEL GUTMAN

DIATLOVO (Pol., Zdzięciół; Yi., Zhetl), town in Grodno Oblast (district), Belorussian SSR. In the interwar period it belonged to Poland, and in September 1939 it was annexed to the Soviet Union. Diatlovo had a Jewish population beginning in the sixteenth century, and by the end of the nineteenth century a majority of its inhabitants were Jewish. On the eve of World War II, 4,000 Jews lived in the town. From 1939 to 1941, Jews from German-occupied western Poland took refuge there.

The Germans entered Diatlovo on June 30, 1941. On July 15, 6 Jews who had been betrayed as Communists were put to death, and on July 23, 120 Jewish intellectuals were executed. That winter, on December 15, 400 Jews were sent to a work camp in Dvorets. To Diatlovo itself the Germans sent Jews from the towns of Kozlovshchina, Novoyelnia, and Bielitsa. A ghetto was established, in which all the Jews were concentrated, and a JUDENRAT (Jewish Council) was appointed.

At the end of 1941 an underground was formed in Diatlovo on the initiative of Alter DVORETSKI, the Judenrat's deputy chairman and leading personality, that included Moshe Pozdunski, Eliyahu Kowenski, Shalom Gerling, and Joseph Bitenski. Of the sixty members of the underground, ten were induced by Dvoretski to join the ghetto police, whom Dvoretski formed into a self-defense unit.

The underground set itself the goal of organizing the ghetto so as to stage an armed uprising in the event of an *Aktion* and thereby facilitate escape into the forest. It also sought to arouse anti-German feelings among the non-Jewish population. Using the Judenrat's

funds, Dvoretski acquired arms, and in January 1942 he smuggled two rifles into the ghetto, as well as a submachine gun and ammunition. Opinions in the underground differed on whether to fight in the ghetto or in the forest; the decision would determine where the arms were to be hidden. Dvoretski was in favor of fighting inside the ghetto.

In the spring of 1942, groups of Soviet partisans made their apppearance in the Diatlovo neighborhood. Dvoretski then resolved that the underground should aim at escaping to the forest. On April 20, 1942, following the arrest of Shalom Fyolvn, an underground member who had been caught in the act of trying to purchase arms, Dvoretski escaped from the ghetto together with a group of other members. The Germans put a price of 25,000 reichsmarks on his head.

On April 30, 1,200 Jews were taken from the ghetto and put to death. Dvoretski and his comrades did not attempt to attack the Germans while this *Aktion* was under way because the Soviet partisans refused to take the risk. Dvoretski now sought to accomplish two objectives. The first was to form a large force of Jewish partisans, made up of inhabitants of the Diatlovo ghetto and other ghettos nearby, in order to fight the Germans and save the lives of the Jews remaining in the ghettos. The other was to forge an alliance with Soviet partisan units in order to build up a large force that would seize control of the area and fight the Germans. But the partisans in the forests had no such ideas in mind. Returning from a conference with them, Dvoretski and Pozdunski fell into an ambush set by non-Jewish partisans and were killed in the ensuing fight.

In the wake of this incident, the escape of the Diatlovo Jews into the forests came to a halt, and they concentrated on constructing bunkers and hiding places. A second *Aktion* was launched on August 6, 1942, but this time the streets of the ghetto were empty since the Jews had taken refuge in the places prepared earlier. That morning, three Jewish partisans were on their way to the ghetto to lead Jews out to the forest, but they were killed as they tried to break through the cordon that had been placed around the ghetto. A group of 50 Jews, led by Hirsch KAPLINSKI, managed to escape into the forest. Altogether, about 600 Jews broke out of the Diatlovo ghetto and tried to reach the forests in the area. Those who succeeded were among the founders of such partisan groups as the ATLAS and BIELSKI units.

About three hundred and seventy Jews from the Diatlovo ghetto survived the war, 90 percent of them by escaping into the forests. One hundred and sixteen Diatlovo Jews fell while fighting in the forests or in the ranks of the Red Army.

BIBLIOGRAPHY

Kaplinski, B. *Zhetel Record: A Memorial to the Jewish Community of Zhetel.* Tel Aviv, 1957. (In Hebrew.)

SHALOM CHOLAWSKI

DIBELIUS, OTTO (1880–1967), Protestant bishop, theologian, and member of the German church resistance to the Nazis. Born in Berlin, Dibelius studied theology there and at Edinburgh, and was later pastor and, from 1925, general superintendent of the Evangelical (Lutheran) church in the Kurmark diocese in Prussia. Dibelius was always a German nationalist, and when the Nazis came to power his sermon at the inaugural service for the 1933 Reichstag in the garrison church at Potsdam was cautiously benevolent, although he also emphasized the irreconcilability of totalitarianism and the will of God. He was dismissed from his post and turned to the Confessing Church (Bekennende Kirche), founded by his close associate Martin NIEMÖLLER. Together they confronted the theory of the "total state" and the Nazi-organized "German Christian" movement.

During World War II Dibelius fought for freedom of religious expression and opposed Nazi church policy. On a number of occasions he was arrested and forbidden to preach. He was also in touch with some of the participants in the abortive plot against Hitler in 1944, but took no active part in the conspiracy. Though made aware by Kurt GERSTEIN of the mass killing of Jews at Bełżec and other extermination camps in Poland, Dibelius did not openly protest, always remaining within the limits of what was ecclesiastically legitimate. After the war he was appointed bishop of Berlin-Brandenburg. He was the first German to become a president of the World Council of Churches.

BIBLIOGRAPHY

Gutteridge, R. *Open Thy Mouth for the Dumb.* Oxford, 1976.

Littell, F. H., and H. G. Locke, eds. *The German Church Struggle and the Holocaust.* Detroit, 1974.

LIONEL KOCHAN

DIRLEWANGER, OSKAR (1895–1945), senior SS officer and war criminal. Dirlewanger was born in Würzburg, studied political science, and specialized in commerce; he was an officer in World War I and was wounded and awarded the Iron Cross. From 1919 to 1921 he served in various units of the Freikorps, which led to his arrest on two occasions. In 1923 he joined the Nazi party for the first time; in 1926 he joined it once more, and on March 1, 1932, he made it final. He was arrested in July 1934 for indecent behavior and sentenced to two years in prison. From 1937 to 1939 he served as a volunteer in the German "Condor" Legion, which fought on Franco's side in the Spanish Civil War.

In July 1940 Dirlewanger was accepted by the SS with the rank of *Obersturmführer*, and at his own suggestion, he set up and trained a special detachment (Sonderkommando) within the SS TOTENKOPFVERBÄNDE (Death's-Head Units), made up of persons who had been convicted of poaching and other offenses. In early 1941 Dirlewanger and his special SS battalion (SS-Sonderbataillon Dirlewanger) were posted to the Lublin district and attached to Odilo GLOBOCNIK's command. Here Dirlewanger became commandant of a Jewish labor camp in Dzikow, supervised the construction of fortifications on the Bug River in the BEŁŻEC region, and then fought against the Polish partisan movement in the GENERALGOUVERNEMENT. In late February 1942 he and his unit were posted to Belorussia to combat the partisans in that area. In Belorussia, Dirlewanger and his men outdid the other Nazis in the mass murder of the civilian population and the havoc and destruction they wrought upon many places of habitation. Because of these extraordinarily brutal activities, an investigation was launched against Dirlewanger and its findings were submitted to an SS court, but he was not put on trial.

In March 1944 Dirlewanger was promoted to SS-*Standartenführer* in the Waffen-SS, and in August of that year he was posted to Warsaw to help quell the WARSAW POLISH UPRISING, where he again made a name for himself by his great brutality; that same month he was promoted to SS-*Oberführer*. Late in 1944 he was posted to Slovakia with his unit to suppress the SLOVAK NATIONAL UPRISING. In June 1945 Dirlewanger died in Althausen under mysterious circumstances.

BIBLIOGRAPHY

Reitlinger, G. *The SS: Alibi of a Nation.* Englewood Cliffs, N.J., 1981.

SHMUEL SPECTOR

DISPLACED PERSONS, JEWISH. At the end of World War II, the Allied powers found approximately 7 million to 9 million people in Europe who had been uprooted by the war. Before the end of 1945, more than 6 million had been repatriated, leaving 1.5 million to 2 million displaced persons (DPs) who refused to return to their prewar homes, either out of free choice or because they feared retribution, economic deprivation, or annihilation.

On VE Day, May 8, 1945, the DPs included 200,000 Jews—survivors of the forced-labor camps, concentration camps, extermination camps, and DEATH MARCHES. Many Jewish survivors and REFUGEES were not prepared to resume their lives in Holocaust-haunted Europe, especially in antisemitic eastern Europe. Most of these survivors gathered in displaced persons' (DP) camps and organized as a group with its own national consciousness and political objective—to be enabled to emigrate from Europe, primarily to settle in Palestine. The Jews organized under the Hebrew name She'erit ha-Peletah ("surviving remnant"; 1 Chr. 4:43), existing as such from the end of the war in Europe in 1945 until December 1950, when this organization's Central Committee went out of existence.

Many thousands of Jews were at the very end of their strength by the time they were liberated, and died from exhaustion, disease, and also from the shock of liberation and from the effects of eating food that their emaciated bodies were not able to assimilate. Others, by the thousands, made their way to their countries of origin, within the Allies' repatriation program, or left for ports in southern Europe in the hope of being able to continue from there to Palestine. The rest of the Jewish survivors, about 50,000 persons, converged on camps in the Allied zones of occupation in Germany and Austria, mainly in the British zone in the north and the American zone in the south. Before long they were joined by a great number of Jewish refugees fleeing from eastern Europe with the BERIḤA (the organized exodus). These were mostly Jews from Poland, including repatriates from the Soviet Union, and refugees from Czechoslovakia, Hungary, and Romania. At the end of 1946 the number of Jewish DPs was estimated at 250,000, of whom 185,0000 were in Germany, 45,000 in Austria, and 20,000 in Italy.

The DPs were largely Jews from eastern Europe, primarily Poland, whereas most of the survivors from western Europe returned to their countries of origin. The great new influx changed the demographic composition of the DP population. At the time they were liberated, they consisted exclusively of persons who had been in and had survived the Nazi hell, as individuals, with no children or elderly people among them. At the end of 1946 about two-thirds of the DPs were "refugees," that is, they had not themselves had immediate experience of the Holocaust. Many were repatriates from the Soviet Union, and they included a larger number of family units and children, as a result of the Beriha and the marriages that had taken place among the original survivors.

Political Struggle. The existence of the She'erit ha-Peletah organization stemmed from nationalist Jewish motives and from external factors, the latter including the very limited number of emigration opportunities available in overseas countries and the British policy of keeping the gates of Palestine closed, as laid down in the 1939 WHITE PAPER. The struggle for a solution of the DP problem was therefore part and parcel of the Zionist struggle for the immigration of Jews to Palestine and for the establishment of a Jewish state there. The She'erit ha-Peletah played an active and important role in that struggle, together with the greater part of the Jews in the world, led by American Jewry. The following are the stages in the struggle.

1. The mission of Earl G. Harrison, the special envoy whom President Harry S. Truman appointed in the summer of 1945, to inquire into the conditions of the Jews in the DP camps in the American zone in Germany. Harrison was convinced that the only solution to the problem was the emigration of the Jewish DPs to Palestine, and he recommended that the British be asked to issue, without delay, 100,000 entry permits ("certificates"), without waiting for the overall settlement of the Palestine question. The Harrison mission was a decisive turning point, both because of the effect it had on the living conditions of the DPs, and because it resulted in President Truman's involvement in the struggle for the opening of the gates of Palestine.

2. David BEN-GURION's visit to the camps in Germany late in October 1945, in his capacity as chairman of the Jewish Agency. That visit strengthened and consolidated the joint political struggle being waged by the She'erit ha-Peletah, by the Jews of Palestine, and by Jews elsewhere. It persuaded the American occupation authorities to direct the Beriḥa into the American zone, facilitated the refugees' absorption in the camps, and made the camps a focus of Zionist political pressure.

3. The Anglo-American Commission of Inquiry's visit to the DP camps in February 1946. The commission included the DP problem in its investigation of the Palestinian question, and it too reached the conclusion that the great majority of the Jewish DPs wanted to settle in Palestine. It recommended the immediate settlement in Palestine of 100,000 refugees from Germany and Austria. The commission's recommendations were rejected by Britain, and the political struggle thereafter used different channels. The She'erit ha-Peletah concentrated on organizational affairs, education, and preparations for immigration to Palestine; the last also included efforts for "illegal" immigration continued in the face of mounting difficulties and the British decision, in August 1946, to deport the "illegal" immigrants to camps in Cyprus (*see* CYPRUS DETENTION CAMPS).

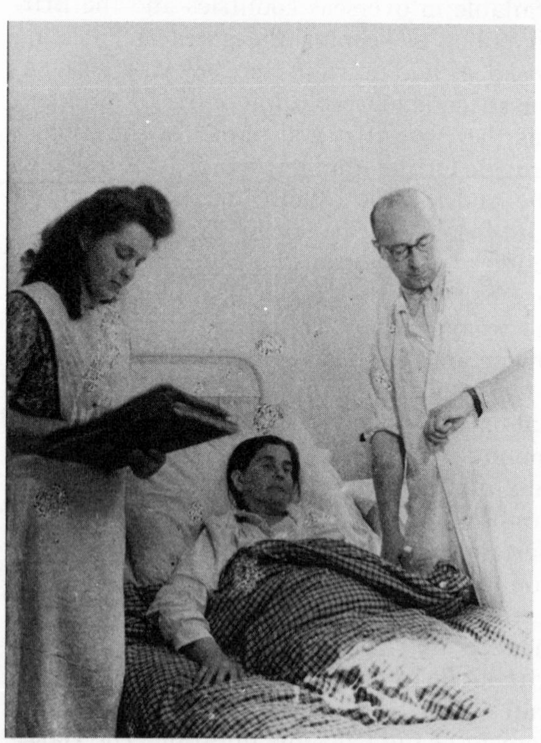

Sanatorium for displaced persons, Bad Wörishofen. [Collection of Toby Knobel Fluek, photograph courtesy A Living Memorial to the Holocaust—Museum of Jewish Heritage, New York]

Life in the DP Camps. When the war ended, most of the Jewish DPs were in the British zone in northern Germany and the American zone in the south. They lived behind barbed wire in dozens of severely overcrowded former labor or concentration camps, together with non-Jewish DPs. They were guarded and were exposed to humiliating treatment and, at times, to antisemitic attacks. Nutrition, sanitary conditions, and accommodation in the camps were poor, although they differed from one place to another. Better conditions prevailed, for example, in the Saint Ottilien convent near Munich, where the DPs themselves had set up a hospital soon after VE Day, and in several large camps, containing four thousand to six thousand DPs each, in Feldafing, Landsberg, and Foehrenwald, also in the American zone. Most of the survivors in the British zone were concentrated in the former BERGEN-BELSEN camp. In both zones, however, DPs were also lodged in residential houses in cities that the occupation authorities had requisitioned for this purpose, as well as in public buildings.

Following the Harrison mission and the subsequent implementation of his recommendations, living conditions in the American zone improved considerably, compared to those that continued to prevail in the British zone. In the American zone, the Jewish DPs gained recognition as a special ethnic group that had its own requirements. They were put into separate camps, where they had a wide degree of autonomy; at their request, they were allowed to live outside the camps, and German properties were set aside to be used for their accommodation; and the large Jewish welfare agencies, based in the United States, were able to expand their operations. A special adviser on Jewish affairs was appointed to American military headquarters in Germany, and living conditions in the camps were greatly improved.

Further improvements took place in the wake of Ben-Gurion's visit in October 1945, and the influx of refugees into the American zone was permitted to continue. In the course of 1946, wave after wave of refugees from the east converged upon the American zone, and by the end of the year by far the greatest number of DPs was to be found there. In the British zone, on the other hand, for quite a while the Jews continued to live with the non-Jewish DPs, political activities were restricted, and, in December 1945, the further entry of refugees was prohibited. As a result, only a small proportion of the DPs lived in that zone.

Employment presented a special problem. It was not essential, since the basic necessities of life were provided by the UNITED NATIONS RELIEF AND REHABILITATION ADMINISTRATION (UNRRA) and the welfare agencies, but it was required for other aspects of the rehabilitation of the DPs. Some of the adults were employed in camp services, or in vocational and agricultural training establishments. Only a few DPs were prepared to take up employment in German or Austrian economic enterprises, or were capable of doing so. The refusal of the Jewish DPs to manufacture goods and supply them to the German market, or to integrate in some other way in German economic life, presented a serious obstacle to the effort to engage the DPs in productive occupations. Other factors—such as the psychological effects of their past experience, the uncertainty about their future, the welfare regime under which they lived (which included the supply of items that they could trade in), and the general condition of the postwar German economy—were all good excuses for idleness and black-market activities, which took place despite the efforts of the various organizations to suppress such manifestations.

External Welfare Agencies. The DP camps were under the control of the military authorities, and the care of the DPs was entrusted to UNRRA (which had been set up as far back as 1943) and, as of July 1947, the International Refugee Organization (IRO). UNRRA supplied the basic necessities of life and also acted as the principal coordinating and supervisory agency of the nongovernmental welfare agencies.

A considerable number and variety of Jewish agencies were active among the DPs. First to reach the Jewish survivors were the Jewish military chaplains, and it was they who established the first link between the survivors and the outside world. Of special importance was the work of Abraham Klausner, who introduced a system for locating survivors, publishing lists of their names and where they were to be found, under the title *She'erit ha-Peletah* (the first volume of which appeared in June 1945). Klausner also helped to establish the Central Committee of the She'erit ha-Peletah and to organize the Jews in the DP camps.

In June 1945 a delegation of the JEWISH BRIGADE GROUP, headed by Aharon Hoter-Yishai and Yaakov Lifshitz, arrived in the DP camps—the first group of Palestinian Jews to establish contact with the survivors. They came from Treviso, Italy, where the brigade was stationed. The meeting with Jewish soldiers, serving in a Jewish military formation and wearing Jewish insignia on their uniforms, was a moving experience for the survivors. Men of the brigade assisted in transferring survivors and refugees to ports in southern Europe, and also helped organize schooling and welfare in the camps.

The American Jewish JOINT DISTRIBUTION COMMITTEE (known as the Joint), headed by its European director, Joseph J. SCHWARTZ, sent its first teams to the camps in June 1945. By August 1945 its operations gained official recognition and were expanded. The Joint augmented the DPs' rations, financed the greater part of their welfare and educational activities in the American zone, and took upon itself other assistance programs, such as those for psychological therapy and legal aid. It also contributed financially to the costs of emigration and of immigration to Palestine. It kept in close touch with refugee organizations, the Zionist Organization, the Central Committee of the She'erit ha-Peletah, and the camp committees. The Jewish vocational education organization, ORT, took on the task of establishing an employment and vocational training network for youths and adults.

The appointment of a special adviser on

Ceremonies at Bremerhaven, July 13, 1949, marking the departure of the 50,000th displaced person to the United States. [Collection of Ben Kaplan, photograph courtesy A Living Memorial to the Holocaust—Museum of Jewish Heritage, New York]

Jewish affairs to work with the American military headquarters—one of the results of the Harrison mission—was designed to facilitate ongoing contact with the Jewish DPs and consideration of their problems, as well as to advise the American military authorities and UNRRA on policy regarding them. The office was held by prominent American Jewish personalities, selected by a board representing the five major Jewish organizations: the AMERICAN JEWISH COMMITTEE, the Joint, the AMERICAN JEWISH CONFERENCE, the American Jewish Congress, and the Jewish Agency for Palestine. The office remained in existence until the end of 1949.

In the British zone, a Jewish Relief Unit, sponsored by British Jewry, was engaged in welfare operations. The Jewish Agency's Palestinian delegation, headed by Chaim Hoffman (Yahil), established itself in Germany in December 1945. In its initial stage it consisted of a staff of twenty made up, in effect, of representatives of Jewish political parties in Palestine. The delegation concerned itself with educational and cultural activities among the DPs, the organization of political work, counseling, and representational functions.

Also active in the DP camps were emissaries of Jewish YOUTH MOVEMENTS and agricultural settlement organizations from Palestine; a teachers' delegation (arriving in 1947), also from Palestine; and a variety of other Jewish aid, educational, and migration bodies such as the OEUVRE DE SECOURS AUX ENFANTS, the United HIAS Service, and the religious women's educational organization, Beis Yaakov.

Internal Organizations, Institutions, and Movements. From the very beginning, the internal organizations of the Holocaust survivors bore a distinctly Zionist character, for a number of reasons. Taking the lead in organizing the survivors were wartime leaders of the Zionist youth movements and fighters of the Jewish underground, who were highly respected and wielded great influence. The survivors, including those who had not been Zionists in the past, found in Zionism the only acceptable answer to their hopes and demands for the future, both as individuals and as victims of the Holocaust. Most of the survivors who were opposed to Zionism (mainly members of the BUND) were among those repatriated to their countries of origin; the ultrareligious anti-Zionists did not arrive in the camps in large numbers until a later stage, and even then they had to cooperate with the Zionist Beriḥa organization in order to get there. Above all, the Zionist solution appeared to be the only one that held out the hope of realizing the goal on which all the Jewish DPs agreed: to abandon blood-drenched Europe and open a new chapter of Jewish life, based on justice and independence rather than charity and subservience. The lack of emigration opportunities, and the anti-Zionist policy and actions of the British government, only served to reinforce the Holocaust survivors' support of Zionist goals and demands. In addition to its other activities, the She'erit ha-Peletah sought to achieve a greater unity among Zionists; to track down relatives among the survivors; to assist in bringing Nazi criminals to trial; and, owing to its strong sense of history, to participate in the efforts to document the Holocaust and commemorate its victims.

The first steps to establish a general survivors' organization were taken as soon as some of the survivors were liberated. In Bergen-Belsen, which was in the British zone, a provisional committee was set up as early as April 1945, chaired by Joseph (Yossele) Rosensaft. In Munich, in the American zone, a festive concert was arranged on May 27, 1945, to celebrate the liberation. It took place in the Saint Ottilien convent, which had been converted into a hospital.

The Central Committee. The survivors' organization in the American zone was initiated by the survivors themselves, with the support of American Jewish army chaplains and soldiers of the Jewish Brigade Group. The goal was to unite all the DPs under a single umbrella organization. On June 20, 1945, in Freimann-Flakkaserne, the First Congress of Zionists in Bavaria was held, at which the bylaws of the Union of Jewish Survivors in the American Zone of Bavaria were adopted. Under the charter, the union's major tasks were to represent the DPs and safeguard their interests. The charter contained a paragraph that called for close cooperation with the Zionist Organization, and henceforth the two bodies in large measure overlapped. A twenty-one-member council was elected, with Samuel Gringauz as chairman and Rabbi Abraham Klausner as honorary chairman; also elected was a small executive committee, with Dr. Zalman Grinberg as its director.

The committee established offices in the German Museum in Munich and set up various departments to deal with DP interests. On July 25, 1945, a conference of Jewish survivors in Germany was held in Saint Ottilien, attended by ninety-four representatives delegated by forty-six groups of survivors in Austria and Germany, including those at Bergen-Belsen. The conference's purpose was to establish a comprehensive organization of all DPs. Present were American army officers, newspapermen, and the head of the Jewish Agency's Immigration Department, Eliyahu Dobkin, who was the first official agency representative to visit the DPs. The overriding tone of the deliberations was one of activist Zionism. Clear-cut demands were formulated for organizing the survivors' life in Germany for as long as they had to stay there, especially with regard to educational facilities and vocational and agricultural training, and a DP Central Committee was formed. It soon transpired that a single survivors' organization for both the American and British zones was not feasible, and the new Central Committee was confined to the Jewish survivors in Bavaria. With the rapid growth of the number of Jews in the American zone, however, the Central Committee gradually became the DPs' principal representative body. In the second half of 1946 the Central Committee was officially recognized by the Americans as the authorized representative of the Jews in the American zone. Officials were elected at each of the three congresses held by the Central Committee: in January 1946, February 1947, and March and April 1948.

In the British zone, the provisional committee elected in Bergen-Belsen was active, and in addition a Central Committee of Jewish Survivors in the British Zone was formed, with Rosensaft serving as chairman of both organizations. Elections of officers were held at two conferences, in September 1945 and in the summer of 1947. The first of these was attended by Professor Selig BRODETSKY, member of the World Zionist Executive; representatives of the Jewish Brigade Group; and many guests. The committee also acted as the representative of the Jews in the British zone of Germany.

Once the Jewish survivors were separated from the others and had their own autonomous camps (in the summer of 1945), each camp elected a camp committee. While they did not have a budget of their own, the committees were supported by the Joint and the Jewish Agency emissaries and assumed responsibility for the camps' internal administration, including hygiene and sanitation, cultural activities, and education and religious life.

As soon as the war ended, the drive to unify the Zionist movement among the groups organized by the surviving partisans and ghetto fighters of eastern Europe gained momentum. One such group was formed in Bucharest, under the leadership of Abba KOVNER; another was the Partisans-Pioneers (it later added "Soldiers" to its title), formed by the Zionist youth movements Dror and Ha-Shomer ha-Tsa'ir.

On December 11, 1945, the United Zionist Organization, with the linked United Pioneer Youth Movement, was formed at a meeting in Landsberg, Germany. The two organizations, however, had only brief life spans as "united" bodies. Party and movement loyalty, nurtured by the movements' eastern European tradition; the party divisions existing

Representatives of the Jewish Committee and the Va'ad he-Haluts in Hannover, Germany. They were arrested on November 11, 1945, because they organized a meeting to protest recent British actions in Palestine.

in Palestine; and the psychological needs of the survivors for a proxy home and family all proved stronger than the drive for unification. The two bodies became identified with Mapai, the socialist party in Palestine.

In addition to the Zionist parties, there were the non-Zionist ultrareligious movements, Agudat Israel and Po'alei Agudat Israel. Their numbers grew when refugees from Hungary and Romania began to flow into the camps, but their political influence was limited, and they were active primarily in education, vocational training, and the publication of newspapers.

Education and Agricultural Training. An elaborate school system was established in the camps, initiated under great difficulties by the survivors. The system, assisted by Jewish Brigade Group soldiers, by emissaries of the Jewish Agency and of the Palestine Jewish community, and by the different welfare agencies, grew rapidly. It consisted of nursery schools; elementary schools; two high schools, one in Munich and one in Bergen-Belsen; educational institutions for the ultrareligious, such as Beis Yaakov girls' schools, teachers' seminars for women, and several Talmudic academies (yeshivas); and a vocational training network run by ORT. The formal educational institutions were complemented by "children's houses" and "kibbutzim," established mainly by the Zionist pioneering youth movements, which often took the place of the family structure. The formal educational system suffered from a shortage of instructors and textbooks, and the complementary institutions were hampered by partisan rivalries. It was only in 1947 that the Central Committee, the Jewish Agency, and the Joint set up an autonomous educational system.

Despite all the difficulties and shortcomings, the dedicated teachers and instructors coped successfully with the extraordinary problems of the mental and emotional rehabilitation of the children of the Holocaust. The educational institutions and kibbutzim were the centers of cultural life in the camps. The kibbutzim, moreover, became the main instrument for preparing the youth for immigration to Palestine, by means of the agricultural training they established on farms that the authorities requisitioned for this purpose. In the American zone, at the end of 1946, forty-two such farms were in operation, on which 3,500 youngsters were undergoing training. The first such model was "Kibbutz Buchenwald," formed as early as the beginning of June 1945. Its first group of graduates left for Palestine that August.

Newspapers and Documentation. The acute and highly developed political sense of the DPs found its expression in more than seventy newspapers that they published, some in Hebrew but most in Yiddish. Noteworthy were *Ha-Nitsots—Bita'on ha-No'ar ha-Leumi* (The Spark—Organ of the National Youth), which had begun to appear as early as the final days of the war in the Dachau concentration camp, and the mimeographed *Tehiyyat ha-Metim* (Resurrection of the Dead), which came out from early May 1945 in Buchenwald. The organ of the Central Committee in the American zone was *Unzer Veg* (Our Path). Of special importance, because of the role it played in molding public opinion, was the *Landsberger Lager-Zeitung* (Landsberg Camp News), later renamed *Yiddishe Zeitung* (Jewish Newspaper). In the British zone the major periodical was *Unzer Shtimme* (Our Voice). Most of the other newspapers were put out by political parties or *Landsmanshaften* (societies made up of persons from the same town or district). The majority were Zionist, but some were published by Agudat Israel.

Commemoration and documentation projects included the work of the Tsentraler Historisher Komisiye (Central Historical Commission), established in December 1945 by the Central Committee in Munich, to assist in bringing Nazi criminals to trial. A network of regional committees was set up under the commission's auspices whose task it was to take evidence and collect documentary material, including material on the DPs. In August 1946 the commission published the first issue of the monthly *Fun Letzten Hurban* (Concerning the Last Holocaust).

The DP chapter came to an end with the establishment of the state of Israel, when the survivors living in the camps in Europe and in Cyprus began to converge en masse on the Jewish state. About two-thirds of them made their way to Israel after the long struggle; the rest emigrated to the United States, which was now relaxing its immigration regulations. In late 1949 and early 1950 the Adviser on Jewish Affairs, the Jewish Agency mission, and the Central Committee, one by one, wound up their operations; in 1953 the last Jewish DP camp in existence in Germany was disbanded.

HAGIT LAVSKY

Attitude of the United States. At the end of the war, the primary burden of the care of the DPs fell upon the United States military, with Great Britain and France assuming responsibility for smaller numbers. Eighty percent to 90 percent of these refugees were Christians, the rest Jews. The relatively small number of Jews received disproportionate attention because they had been treated more brutally during the war and because their co-religionists in the United States, Great Britain, and Palestine lobbied their respective governments for more humane treatment. They also helped publicize the ways in which the world's two leading democracies—the United States and Great Britain—were failing to help rehabilitate the Holocaust survivors and relocate them to places where they could begin new lives. The problems created by the inability of Great Britain and the United States to agree on a common plan strained the relationship between these nations and exacerbated the difficulties of Europe's surviving Jews.

The problem of DPs had been anticipated. The Allies had established UNRRA in 1943 to help the DPs until they could be sent on their way. In addition, DP centers were established by the American, British, and French armies. (The Soviet government did not admit to having a DP problem in its zone of occupation.)

At first the military assumed that UNRRA would adequately administer and supplement the social services required by these DPs. The Supreme Headquarters of the Allied Expeditionary Forces (SHAEF) and UNRRA then signed a pact outlining their mutual responsibilities, but without any assurance that UNRRA personnel would be utilized. UNRRA functioned as an administrative and subordinate branch of the military. According to these agreements, the army would provide food, shelter, clothing, medical supplies, and security to the assembly centers housing the DPs; UNRRA's responsibilities included administering the camps and providing additional supplies, as well as recreational facilities, health and welfare services, and amenities such as tobacco and toilet articles. Self-help programs and vocational guidance also came under UNRRA. Furthermore, UNRRA claimed that it would provide the necessary professional and technical staff personnel, and give emotional sustenance while the DPs awaited repatriation. Another agreement, concluded in 1946, required UNRRA to operate a records office and tracing bureau, to prepare statistics and research reports, and to supervise educational programs; the army retained ultimate responsibility for DP care, movements of United Nations citizens and DPs, and overall management of the camps.

After the war ended in May 1945, hundreds of thousands more DPs remained in Germany and Austria than had been anticipated. Assembly centers that were established to hold 2,000 to 3,000 people contained more than 10,000. Former New York governor Herbert H. Lehman, the director general of UNRRA, hoped for 5,000 to 6,000 workers to process the DPs that summer, but only 2,646 were on the job in July.

Hurriedly recruited and poorly trained, too many of the original UNRRA workers lacked competence. Confused policies, inadequate supervisors, uncoordinated programs, generally poor administration, and conflicts with the military left a stigma that UNRRA never overcame. A Canadian major representing the organization in SHAEF was virtually ignored by superior officers in the rank-conscious military environment. Individual teams found themselves directionless, broken up and reshuffled, used and then unused. Many of the most efficient UNRRA personnel came from France, England, the Netherlands, Norway, and Poland, where they had experienced the savageries of Nazism and war, and understood the problems of the DPs. The least competent officials did not speak any of the DP languages, knew nothing of the DPs' background, and even profiteered from black-market activities. By December 1945, more than one thousand of the original employees were dismissed for a variety of reasons, including incompetence, inefficiency, lack of adaptability, and misconduct. The quality of operations began to improve thereafter, but the situation remained somewhat chaotic.

Word about the problems at the assembly centers soon reached American and British government officials. Jewish leaders, in particular, complained about the desperate position of their co-religionists in the DP camps. Thousands of Jews in the United States felt themselves morally bound to lead and finance the work of rehabilitating and resettling the Holocaust survivors. The continued maltreatment of their co-religionists grieved them deeply. After several requests, the army finally allowed the Joint to enter the DP centers, in June 1945, to minister to those in need.

Europe had been torn asunder during the war, and the DPs first and foremost needed new homes. However, most countries of the world snubbed European refugees fleeing totalitarianism and communism, and few were willing to harbor foreign immigrants. Everyone knew, of course, that the United States was the only nation that could probably absorb all of the DPs with little difficulty, but rigid immigration restrictions precluded the admission of more than a few thousand. Moreover, Zionist activity in both the United States, where Jews had some political influence, and Great Britain, where they had less, focused on Palestine as the only home for European Jewish survivors who wished to leave the Continent. The British government refused to countenance such an idea. It was keenly aware that the Arabs opposed entry of more Jews, and to keep its options open for Middle Eastern oil, strategic ports, and waterways, it tried to straddle the issue. At the conclusion of the war the British relented somewhat on the number of Jews who might go to Palestine (1,500 a month), but they refused to bend to further pressure from either the United States or the Zionists.

As a result of their stance, the British took other unfortunate and inhumane positions. Despite all that the Jews had suffered during World War II, the British refused to acknowledge in the fall of 1945 that Jews were living under worse conditions than any other victims of Nazi persecution. This situation was made clear in Earl Harrison's report, which concluded: "We appear to be treating the Jews as the Nazis treated them, except that we do not exterminate them."

Harrison and his entourage had toured more than thirty DP camps during July 1945. His mission had been endorsed by President Truman after the State and Treasury departments, as well as several members of Congress, had heard complaints about the desperate conditions plaguing the war's survivors following their liberation from the concentration camps. Truman thought that accurate information was necessary before proceeding further and for that reason he had appointed Harrison to undertake an inspection.

The findings of Harrison and his associates proved to be a devastating indictment of the Allied military policies in force immediately after the war ended:

1. Jewish DPs lived under guard, behind barbed-wire fences, in centers that included former concentration camps. In some instances, concentration camp victims were housed together with their former guards and tormentors.
2. Housing, medical, and recreational facilities were inadequate, and nothing was being done to improve the quality of life or to rehabilitate the inhabitants.
3. Two months after the war had ended DPs still wore their old concentration camp uniforms because no other clothes had been issued.
4. No efforts were being made to reunite families or to help survivors look for lost relatives. In fact, the army did not allow the survivors to help themselves, since they could neither send nor receive mail.
5. Many army officers and soldiers believed that the survivors must be criminals, since otherwise they would not have been locked up in this fashion. Some army personnel even told Harrison that perhaps Hitler had been right in his treatment of the Jews.

Apart from urging admission to Palestine for those Jews wanting to settle there, Harrison recommended that the United States and other countries should take some of them as immigrants. The Harrison Commission report led to significant changes in the administration of the American DP centers, and it also prompted President Truman to write to British Prime Minister Clement Attlee, urging him to open the gates of Palestine to Jews wanting to go there. (Truman conveniently ignored the suggestion in the report that the United States also take some of the DPs.) Truman's petition was not warmly received in Britain.

Attlee cautiously informed Truman that his cabinet would look into the matter. The decision that the British cabinet reached in October of 1945 was to launch a joint Anglo-American inquiry into the problems and to seek eventual settlement of the displaced persons. Truman agreed, the commission was established, and the investigation began in January 1946.

The committee's ten-point report, which recommended several solutions to the Arab-Jewish conflict in Palestine, was delivered to the president and the prime minister at the end of April 1946. The British and American governments responded differently to the conclusions. Truman pounced on the statement that 100,000 Jews should immediately be admitted to Palestine and ignored the nine other recommendations. Attlee, on the other hand, emphasized the conclusions in the report that called for the nations of the world, and not just Palestine, to admit the DPs, and that appealed for the suppression of violence and terrorism in Palestine. Publicly, Attlee commented that the British would not implement the recommendations unless (1) the United States provided financial and military assistance; and (2) the illegal armies (that is, the Hagana) in Palestine disbanded.

In private, Attlee was even more vitriolic. Neither he nor the members of the cabinet had anticipated a unanimous committee report or a recommendation that 100,000 Jewish displaced persons be admitted to Palestine. The cabinet had hoped to inveigle the United States into joint action, but had never quite made the point directly.

During the summer of 1946 the increased influx from eastern Europe into the DP camps hardened the British against allowing more Jews into Palestine, and forced Truman to reconsider ways of handling the DP situation. The DP centers became more crowded, and the army felt helpless because it lacked the facilities for dealing with all the additional refugees, yet Truman, because of Jewish pressure at home, refused to allow the camps to be closed to them.

While the exodus of Jews from Poland was taking place in 1946, an American and British delegation was once again trying to work out a plan that would bring 100,000 Jewish DPs into Palestine. The plan formulated by this new group would have divided Palestine into Arab and Jewish sections, with the Arabs receiving three times as much land as the Jews. Although Truman was ready to accept the compromise, pressure from American Jews once again forced him to reject the new plan.

Another event during the summer of 1946 that helped propel Truman into action was a Jewish dissident underground group's bombing of the King David Hotel in Jerusalem, in which ninety-one people lost their lives. This hardened British attitudes toward Jews. Truman finally announced, in August, that he would recommend to Congress that legislation be passed admitting some of the DPs to the United States. He was deliberately vague, and suggested no specific number that he thought should be admitted. This was the first time, however, that any responsible American official had made such a recommendation publicly.

The reaction within the United States to Truman's announcement was mixed, but among the majority of the Jews it was tepid. Most American Jews wanted to see a Jewish homeland established in Palestine; they believed that efforts to bring displaced Jews to the United States would dilute the problem in Europe and weaken the Zionist cause. On the other hand, they did not lack sympathy for the survivors of the Holocaust, and did not want to do anything to harm their chances for resettlement in any place.

The primary role, therefore, in bringing displaced Jews to the United States was assumed by the two leading non-Zionist American Jewish organizations, the American Jewish Committee and the anti-Zionist American Council for Judaism. The former provided the executive and staff leadership, and the president of the latter organization, Lessing Rosenwald, supplied most of the funds.

Most members of the American Jewish

Committee and the American Council for Judaism, as well as other Jews, feared to act openly on behalf of their European coreligionists. Antisemitism and opposition to bringing more Jews to the United States were quite open. Because of the strong prejudices, the leaders of these organizations joined to establish the Citizens' Committee on Displaced Persons, a nonsectarian group chaired by Earl Harrison.

The Citizens' Committee functioned as a lobby to inform the public and Congress of the plight of the DPs, and it urged appropriate legislation. At the outset, its leaders emphasized that 80 percent of the approximately 1 million DPs in Europe were Christian, which was not widely known at the time. The committee tried to awaken an apathetic nation to the facts that most DPs had no place to go and that out of humanitarian concerns the United States should take its fair share of these people.

This publicity helped develop a climate of favorable opinion for concrete legislation. To this end, the Citizens' Committee prepared a bill, based on recommendations made by the American Jewish Committee, providing that the United States would accept 400,000 DPs. Leaders of the Citizens' Committee had decided earlier that to receive the widest possible support, their legislation should be presented by a member of the majority party from the isolationist Midwest. They approached Republican senators Homer Ferguson and Arthur H. Vandenberg of Michigan, and Robert Taft of Ohio, but each refused to sponsor the measure. They then turned to the House of Representatives, where William G. Stratton, congressman-at-large from Illinois, who not only sympathized with their objectives but also saw an opportunity to develop a national reputation, agreed to sponsor it. On April 1, 1947, Stratton introduced a bill that would allow 400,000 DPs, in addition to those who entered under the immigration quotas, to enter the United States during the next four years.

Most congressmen knew little about DPs, could not understand why they had not gone home after the war, and feared a depression or a glut on the labor market if a large number of immigrants began coming to the United States. Hearings on the Stratton measure were held in the summer of 1947, but no bill was presented on the floor of the House of Representatives. President Truman, first in January 1947 and again in July, called upon Congress to produce suitable legislation to aid DPs but did not endorse the Stratton bill.

The key to the passage of DP legislation lay in the Senate. The House of Representatives was not prepared to pass any bill unless favorable action seemed likely in the upper house. After an initial period of hesitation, during which it appeared that no bill would be passed, propaganda from the Citizens' Committee, letters to representatives and senators, and newspaper editorials urging action began to take effect. Congress received more mail, most of it favorable, on assisting the DPs than on any other subject since Prohibition.

Unfortunately for the DPs, Senator Chapman Revercomb of West Virginia chaired the Immigration Subcommittee of the Senate Judiciary Committee, and his views were anything but favorable toward helping them. He had made a study of the DPs for the Republican Steering Committee in December 1946. His conclusions were negative and showed contempt for those who had suffered most from the war and during its aftermath, whom he characterized as "imbued with a communistic line of thought." When the Senate appeared ready to consider DP legislation in the summer of 1947, Revercomb urged his colleagues to schedule a Senate inspection tour of the camps in Europe before taking action. After lengthy debate the Senate agreed to this proposal, and Revercomb was appointed to head the tour.

In the fall of 1947 both the House of Representatives and the Senate sent committees to investigate the DP camps. The Citizens' Committee sponsored an inspection tour of the camps by Commander Paul Griffith of the American Legion, who thereafter changed his position and endorsed emergency legislation to aid DPs. Both the House and Senate committees also reached the conclusion that something should be done for the people in the camps. The House report noted: "If the Jewish facet of the problem could be cleared up, the solution of the remainder of the problem would be facilitated. The opening up of Palestine to the resettlement of Jewish displaced persons would break the logjam." Around the same time, the governors of several Midwestern states established local commissions to study the possibilities of resettling DPs in their midst. Finally, and perhaps most important for the future passage of legislation, Robert A. Taft, the Republican leader of the Senate, called for "immediate action" to help the DPs. As winter began it seemed likely that Congress would act.

In the second session of the Eightieth Congress, Frank Fellows of Maine, chairman of the Subcommittee on Immigration of the House Judiciary Committee, proposed a measure calling for the admission of 200,000 DPs from among those who had registered by April 21, 1947, with the DP camps. The DPs admitted were to be charged against future immigration quotas for their countries of origin. In the Senate, Revercomb's committee proposed legislation that would admit 100,000 DPs over a two-year period, confine eligibility to those who had been in the DP camps on or before December 22, 1945, and reserve 50 percent of the visas for agricultural workers. It also suggested that 50 percent of those admitted come from the nations of Europe that had been annexed by the Soviet Union after the war.

These restrictions alarmed American Jews. First, most of the Jews who had been in the DP camps in 1945 had meanwhile gone elsewhere—to Palestine, to the United States, and to other countries. Second, the mass exodus of Polish Jews to West Germany took place in 1946, and none of them would be eligible if the December 22, 1945, cutoff date remained. Third, very few Jews came from "annexed territories," by which the senators meant Estonia, Latvia, and Lithuania, which had been absorbed by the Soviet Union. And finally, very few Jews were agricultural workers. Adherents of a generous immigration bill considered the Revercomb bill a disaster.

The Revercomb proposal reached the Senate floor in May 1948. Two significant amendments to the bill passed. One increased the total number of DPs to be admitted to the United States to 100,000 per year for two years, and the other, proposed by Senator William Langer of North Dakota, gave preference to the VOLKSDEUTSCHE (ethnic Germans), those Germans expelled from eastern Europe after the war. Langer, the only member of the Senate Judiciary Committee to oppose the Revercomb plan in a committee vote, believed that the *Volksdeutsche* were worse off than other DPs, especially the Jews, all of whom he assumed had relatives in New York City.

The measure passed the Senate by a vote of 63 to 13. Harrison urged the House to reject the Fellows bill, which discriminated on religious, national, and occupational grounds. He considered the clause on the *Volksdeutsche* "a mockery of American justice" that was tantamount to accepting Nazi racial doctrine. Harrison's statement did not dissuade the House of Representatives from passing the Fellows bill essentially as presented, by a vote of 289 to 91. The two houses of Congress then selected conference committees to reconcile the bills.

The Senate conferees included Revercomb, Ferguson, Harley Kilgore of West Virginia, James Eastland of Mississippi, and Forrest Donnell of Missouri. In the conference, Revercomb, Eastland, and Donnell remained adamant against accepting provisions that might help Jewish DPs. They gave the House members an ultimatum: either the Senate measure or nothing. As a result, the conferees went along with modified aspects of the worst features of both the House and Senate bills. Consequently, DPs had to have arrived in Germany, Austria, and Italy by December 22, 1945, to be considered eligible for admission to the United States, whereas *Volksdeutsche* qualified if they had arrived by July 1, 1948.

The report so displeased some of the conferees that four refused to sign it. Despite the fact that many members of Congress believed that the bill was deliberately intended to exclude Jews, President Truman reluctantly signed it, while denouncing the measure as antisemitic and anti-Catholic. It was the former, but not the latter; Catholics predominated among both the DPs and the *Volksdeutsche.*

Jews and Jewish groups were incensed. Many Jewish groups wanted the act vetoed by the president, but on this point there was no unity. Truman appointed three liberals—Ugo Carusi, Edward M. O'Connor, and

Harry N. Rosenfield—to head the Displaced Persons' Commission in August 1948. Their interpretation of the Displaced Persons' Act was so broad, and their acceptance of questionable documents so frequent, that they undermined the thrust of the bigoted legislation, and more Jews entered the United States than had been anticipated. When Senator Pat McCarran of Nevada, a conservative Democrat, investigated the Displaced Persons' Commission in 1949, he accused it of lax procedures that allowed Communists and other subversives into the United States (the senator did not mention fascists or Nazis, since their admission apparently did not upset him). The frightened commissioners thereupon began adhering to the letter of the law. They also led the campaign to liberalize the Displaced Persons' Act of 1948, which Congress did in June 1950. Thereafter, the DPs ceased being a significant concern of America's Jews or of Congress.

By 1950, those Jews who had wanted to eliminate what they considered to be the specifically antisemitic provisions of the 1948 Displaced Persons' Act had accomplished their purpose. Congress changed the cutoff date to 1949 and did away with the preferences for agricultural workers and persons from annexed territories. Furthermore, by 1950 most of the Jewish DPs had left the assembly centers for Israel, the United States, or other nations.

On the international scene, the formation of the International Refugee Organization (IRO) in 1947, an agency designed to help resettle the DPs still in Europe (numbering over a million), helped to unplug the bottleneck in the DP centers and promoted the exodus to other countries. By 1947, in fact, several of the world's nations, realizing that they needed able-bodied people, sought DPs from the European assembly centers. Most countries wanted young, strong gentiles; none expressed a preference for Jews. Belgium selected twenty thousand Balts and Ukrainians to work in its mines, and the British took about thirty thousand single adults for agriculture, mining, and domestic tasks.

After the establishment of Israel in 1948, most of the Jewish DPs thought that the IRO would facilitate their movement there. However, more than 200 of the IRO's 435 administrative officers were British, and the agency reflected Britain's hostility to Israel. Consequently, it took the position that it could not send people to any place that had not been recognized by all of the United Nations. And, since the Arabs had attacked Israel as soon as the new nation came into being, it could not send DPs to "belligerent" countries in the Middle East. Thus, the European Jews made their way to Israel without the assistance of the IRO, but often with the overt aid of American army officials and the Beriḥa. For their part, the non-Jews had no difficulty being taken into Canada, Latin America, and the European nations.

Between 1945 and 1952, the United States accepted about 400,000 DPs, of whom perhaps 20 percent were Jewish. (Exact figures are impossible to obtain.) Great Britain admitted about 100,000 people, but figures are not available for the percentage of Jews. Some 136,000 Jewish DPs went to Israel, but here again statistics are only estimates.

The problem of the DPs need not have lasted as long as it did. Great Britain, however, was slow to realize that it would have to relinquish control of Palestine, and the United States was even slower in realizing that unless it made some attempt to receive DPs, the problem simply would not go away. All nations looked to America to take the lead. The fact that so many DPs were Jews also complicated the matter. The world did not want them. With the establishment of Israel in 1948, Jews were at last able to go there.

[*See also* Survivors, Psychology of; United States Army and Survivors in Germany and Austria.]

LEONARD DINNERSTEIN

BIBLIOGRAPHY

Abzug, R. H. *Inside the Vicious Heart: Americans and the Liberation of Nazi Concentration Camps.* New York, 1985.

Bauer, Y. *Out of the Ashes.* Oxford, 1989.

Dinnerstein, L. *America and the Survivors of the Holocaust.* New York, 1982.

Marrus, M. R. *The Unwanted: European Refugees in the Twentieth Century.* New York, 1985.

Proudfoot, M. J. *European Refugees, 1939–1952: A Study in Forced Population Movement.* Evanston, Ill., 1956.

Wilson, F. M. *Aftermath.* London, 1947.
Ziemke, E. F. *The U.S. Army in the Occupation of Germany.* Washington, D.C., 1975.

DNEPROPETROVSK, district capital in the Ukrainian SSR. On the eve of World War II, Dnepropetrovsk had a Jewish population of some 80,000, out of a total of 500,662. As the German armies approached on August 5, 1941, the evacuation of the city was begun and some 60,000 Jews left. The Germans took the city on August 25. In the first few days of the occupation, the Ukrainian population was extremely hostile to the Jews, plundering their property and informing on many of them to the Germans. The Jews were ordered to wear a Jewish BADGE (a blue Star of David on a white background) and to elect a committee that was referred to as the "community leadership." Its first chairman was a lawyer named Gorenberg. House managers were ordered to provide the command headquarters in the city with a list of their Jewish tenants, and the military administration made preparations to establish a ghetto for Dnepropetrovsk's Jews.

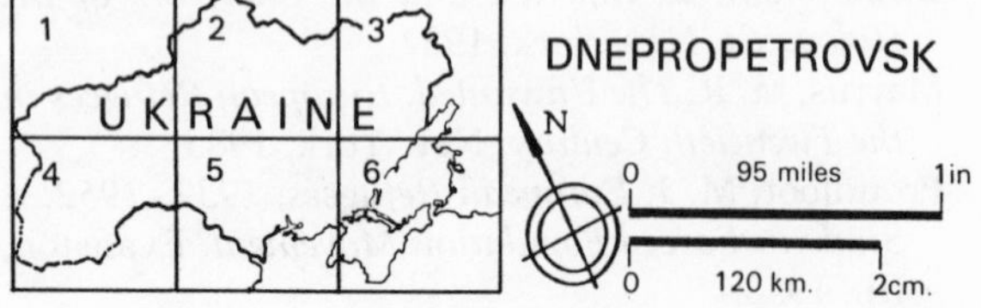

On October 8, 1941, the military governor imposed a collective fine of 30 million rubles on the city's Jews. On October 13, even before the fine was collected, Einsatzkommando 6 (of Einsatzgruppe C) began rounding up the Jews and confining them in a large department store in the city; from there the Jews were taken in groups to a nearby ravine, to be murdered. A total of fifteen thousand Jews were killed in this operation, which was followed at a later stage by the killing of the remaining five thousand Jews.

When Dnepropetrovsk was liberated by the Red Army on October 25, 1943, only fifteen Jews were left alive in the city.

BIBLIOGRAPHY

Ehrenburg, I., and V. Grossman, eds. *The Black Book of Soviet Jewry.* New York, 1981.

SHMUEL SPECTOR

DOCTORS, NAZI. *See* Physicians, Nazi.

DOCUMENTATION CENTERS. [*This entry consists of eight articles that describe major centers for the documentation of the Holocaust*:

Berlin Documents Center
Centre de Documentation Juive Contemporaine
Centro di Documentazione Ebraica Contemporanea
Leo Baeck Institute
Main Commission for Investigation of Nazi Crimes in Poland
Rijksinstituut voor Oorlogsdocumentatie
Wiener Library
Żydowski Instytut Historyczny

See also Yad Vashem *and the articles under* Museums and Memorial Institutes.]

Berlin Documents Center

The Berlin Documents Center is an archive consisting of material discovered by the United States Army in a Munich paper factory (where it was scheduled to be recycled), as well as papers that the Nazis had hidden in the mountains of the Harz and the Tirol. The center, situated in the Dahlendorf district of West Berlin, is to this day under guard by a United States military unit. Access to it is controlled and restricted to authorized representatives of governments and to scholars who show proof that the material they are looking for is essential to their research. Even for such requests, the center prefers to reply in writing, which is the usual practice when requests either are made for documents containing personal data, pension rights, and so on, or emanate from courts of law, official investigation agencies, or DENAZIFICATION proceedings.

The center contains some 30 million files, information sheets, and questionnaires on the persons who set up the Third Reich and ran it —from the lowest echelon up to the very top —and especially on the leaders of the Nazi regime, such as Joseph GOEBBELS, Hermann GÖRING, Julius STREICHER, and Joachim von RIBBENTROP. The center has 10.7 million individual sheets on members of the National Socialist party, over half a million files on SS members, and a similar number of files on SD (Sicherheitsdienst; Security Service) personnel. These files include questionnaires that the subjects themselves had filled in, information on disciplinary proceedings and district court proceedings against them (115,000 of the latter category), and correspondence of Nazi party and government offices ranging from the *Gaue* (the territorial units into which the Reich was divided for Nazi party purposes) all the way up to the Reich chancellery; also included in this category of files are the documents of the People's Court, the party's—and the Reich's—supreme court.

Other categories of papers include those containing data on Nazi doctors (forty thousand) and on teachers and university lecturers (several thousand); documents of the SS RASSE- UND SIEDLUNGSHAUPTAMT (Race and Resettlement Main Office), which dealt with the "Germanization" of occupied territories (2.5 million documents); and papers concerning the Reichskulturkammer (Reich Cultural Affairs Office) and other offices that decided on important appointments in all spheres of life. The material is stored in wooden boxes and in files that bear the relevant names and numbers.

The following are some of the most interesting documents held by the center, both in political terms and for research purposes:

1. A letter from Adolf HITLER, written in his own hand at 4:00 p.m. on April 29, 1945, in which he declares that he and his wife have decided to choose death rather than suffer the shame of defeat, and asks to be buried in the place where he had spent most of the last twelve years of his life;

2. The cable that the Nazi film director and photographer Leni Riefenstahl sent Hitler when France was conquered, expressing her joy and congratulations on the accomplishment of this task, "one of the most significant in human history";

3. Information that was used to identify a body, found on a South American seashore, that was said to be that of Josef MENGELE; the file describes Mengele as an honest, trustworthy, consistent, steady, and disciplined person, who meticulously carried out the orders he was given and remained loyal to his task even under the most trying circumstances;

4. The file on Adolf EICHMANN, in which he is described as a "perfect Nordic type"—a friendly, trustworthy, and ambitious person, who acts properly under all circumstances, is endowed with a lively intellect and a strong will, and conducts his work in accordance with the principles of National Socialism.

The Berlin Documents Center is one of the most important sources of archival material for the study of the structure of the Nazi regime and the way its staff was selected and behaved. SS men who wanted to marry had to produce documentary evidence, going back two hundred years, on their "pure" racial descent; the women had to produce documents and testimonies on their racial "purity," their moral standards, love of children, state of health (including the most intimate physical details), their suitability to be the mothers of a racially improved generation, and hair and skin color.

The center's material provides information not only on the Nazi ideological indoctrination and the persons in charge, but also on the steps that were taken to ensure that the Nazis possessed the biological and physical properties required for the planning of the right type of future generation. Those who did not possess these qualifications were entered on blacklists of the disqualified. Sometimes persons who had merely played pool or other games with Jews, or had spoken with Jews in their youth, had their names entered on these lists.

In the postwar period, most of the Germans who had served under the Nazi regime as district attorneys, judges, teachers, university lecturers, and government officials kept away, as best they could, from the center, in an effort to forget the past and to ease their reabsorption into German society as it had emerged from the defeat. As the United States high commissioner for the American zone of occupation, John J. McCloy, stated in a 1978 television interview, he at times had to bar access to the center's information to avoid embarrassing former Nazis who had assumed positions in the new German regime.

The Berlin Documents Center is financed by the West German government out of funds allocated for the maintenance of the offices of the Allied occupation authorities.

MARIAN MUSHKAT

Centre de Documentation Juive Contemporaine

The Centre de Documentation Juive Contemporaine (Center of Contemporary Jewish Documentation; CDJC) is an institution created in France to preserve the evidence of Nazi crimes for future generations. Established clandestinely in Grenoble in 1943 by Isaac Schneersohn and a team representing various Jewish organizations, it embarked upon the task of collecting and protecting documents relating to the fate of the Jews under German occupation.

The liberation of France in August 1944 enabled CDJC to operate openly and, thanks to the hasty departure of the Germans and their Vichy French collaborators, to collect a large quantity of files, with the assistance of the new regime.

Now located at 17, Rue Geoffroy-L'Asnier, the CDJC building was erected in 1956 on a plot of land allotted by the Paris city council, which is also the site of the Memorial for the Unknown Jewish Martyr. CDJC's rich archive contains documents of the German and French authorities relating to the history of the Jews in France during World War II; documents of the SD (Sicherheitsdienst; Security Service) and Sicherheitspolizei (Security Police), including lists of names of all persons deported to the extermination camps of AUSCHWITZ-Birkenau and SOBIBÓR; and the files of Alfred ROSENBERG and of the COMMISSARIAT GÉNÉRAL AUX QUESTIONS JUIVES (General Office for Jewish Affairs). The Rosenberg files are among the most important sources for the study of the organization and activities of the Third Reich and the Nazi party.

The research carried on in CDJC concentrates on four objectives: conducting basic research; disseminating information; bringing Nazi criminals to justice; and seeking indemnification for all categories of Nazi victims. CDJC has provided documents and legal opinions to establish the rights of the victims of the Nazi occupation.

Apart from its collection of documents, CDJC possesses a library of over twenty thousand volumes dealing with the Holocaust period, Nazi and neo-Nazi publications, speeches prepared for Nazi and neo-Nazi spokesmen, and an important collection of periodicals put out by French collaborators with the Nazis (including *Le Cahier Jaune, Le Franciste,* and *L'Action Française*).

Since 1946 the center has published *Le Monde Juif* (The Jewish World), a quarterly containing research studies, documents, commentaries, and book reviews.

CDJC has published over fifty books, most of them based on the documentary material contained in its archives. The center also organizes panel discussions, roundtable talks, and lectures dealing with the persecution of the Jews, their sufferings, and resistance activity during the German occupation in France and other countries. CDJC has mounted exhibitions, including "Auschwitz," "Bergen-Belsen," "Life and Revolt in Warsaw and Other Ghettos in Eastern Europe," and "The Jewish Fight against Hitlerism" (the last on permanent display).

BIBLIOGRAPHY

La France de l'Affaire Dreyfus à nos jours: Catalogue no. 1. Paris, 1964.

La France, Le Troisième Reich, Israel: Catalogue no. 2. Paris, 1968.
Le Monde Juive 80 (October–December 1975): entire issue.
Ten Years of Existence of the Jewish Contemporary Documentation Center, 1943–1953. Paris, 1953.

ADAM RUTKOWSKI

Centro di Documentazione Ebraica Contemporanea

The Centro di Documentazione Ebraica Contemporanea (Center for Contemporary Jewish Documentation; CDEC) was established to study the role of Jews in the Italian resistance movement and the history of the persecution of the Jews by the Fascists and the Nazis. It was founded in Venice in 1955, and later moved to Milan.

Over the course of time the center's tasks expanded broadly, and it now deals with three separate, but interconnected, fields, as follows.

1. Historical archives: the collecting of documentation on the Jews in Italy from the end of the nineteenth century until the present day, with special emphasis on the period of persecution from 1938 to 1945. The center conducts independent research on the latter subject.
2. Antisemitism in contemporary Italy: the center collects testimonies and documentation, undertakes research, and supports independent studies on the subject.
3. The collecting of books and periodicals in Italian and other languages on the persecution of the Jews from 1938 to 1945, contemporary antisemitism, the history of the Jews in Italy and the world, and Jewish culture and tradition.

In these three fields the center is the principal scholarly institution in Italy for Italian and foreign scholars. In the years since its founding the center has issued ten publications. It is preparing a memorial book on the Jews deported from Italy in World War II.

MICHELE SARFATTI

Leo Baeck Institute

The Leo Baeck Institute (LBI) is a research institute concerned with the history of the Jews in Germany and of German-speaking Jewish groups in other countries, from the time of the Emancipation of the Jews in the nineteenth century. The LBI collects documentary materials, and it sponsors and advances research in this field.

The LBI was founded in Jerusalem in 1955 by the Council of Jews from Germany. Its founders included major figures from the last generation of German Jewry, including Martin Buber, Siegfried Moses, Ernst Simon, and Gershom Scholem. The institute is named after Rabbi Leo BAECK (1873–1956).

It was not the institute's original intention to include within its scholarly work the history of German Jewry after the Nazi rise to power. Nevertheless, many studies published by the institute deal with Jewish life during the period of the Third Reich, covering among other things the REICHSVERTRETUNG DER DEUTSCHEN JUDEN (Reich Representation of German Jews), educational and cultural activities, the organization of mutual aid, and the policy of emigration, including the HAAVARA AGREEMENT. Studies on the history of the Jews under Nazi rule have also been published in the *Leo Baeck Institute Year Book* and in the institute's *Bulletin,* which since 1957 has appeared three times a year in German. The LBI has also published the memoirs of public figures who were active under the Third Reich, and of people from all sectors of the population between 1780 and 1945, together with historical and sociological surveys of those years. The growing emphasis of the institute on research into the history of German Jewry under the Nazis was reflected in particular in an international symposium, the first of this kind to be sponsored by the LBI. Held in 1985 in Berlin, it was devoted to the topic of "Self-Assertion in Adversity: The Jews in National Socialist Germany, 1933–1939"; among the participants were German historians.

The LBI has branches in the three principal centers of immigration of German Jewry—Israel, the United States, and Great Britain. The archives and library of the New York institute are among the largest and most comprehensive on the subject of German Jewish history. The editorial board of the English-language *Year Book,* which was headed by Robert WELTSCH from its foundation until 1978, is located in London. Since 1978 the

Year Book has been edited by Dr. Arnold Paucker. The Jerusalem institute publishes the German-language *Bulletin* and Hebrew translations of the classical works of Jewish thinkers in Germany. Representatives of the three branches meet at regular intervals under the chairmanship of the president of the institute, in order to coordinate their activity and in particular their research programs. The first president of the LBI was Leo Baeck (until his death in 1956), and the second was Dr. Siegfried Moses. After Dr. Moses's death in 1977, Rabbi Max Gruenewald became president.

BIBLIOGRAPHY

Moses, S. "Leo Baeck Institute of Jews from Germany." *Leo Baeck Institute Year Book* 1 (1956): xi–xviii.

Schorsch, I. "The Leo Baeck Institute: Continuity and Desolation." *Leo Baeck Institute Year Book* 25 (1980): ix–xii.

JOSEPH WALK and
OTTO DOV KULKA

Main Commission for Investigation of Nazi Crimes in Poland

The Main Commission for Investigation of Nazi Crimes in Poland (Główna Komisja Badania Zbrodni Hitlerowskich w Polsce; GKBZHwP) was created by the Polish National Council on March 29, 1945, as part of the Ministry of Justice; it was headed by the minister of justice. The commission's aims are to investigate Nazi crimes committed in Poland or perpetrated on Polish citizens outside Poland's borders; to cooperate with and provide legal aid to tribunals and bodies dealing with pursuit of Nazis in other countries; to conduct research into the occupation period; and to collect documentation and maintain a special archive.

A reform of April 6, 1948, established the Instytut Pamięci Narodowej (Institute of National Remembrance), whose members are chosen from outstanding experts on Nazi crimes and the period of the Nazi occupation. The institute's rich archival collections are available for scholars from Poland and abroad. By 1989, 382 volumes of its bulletins and books had been published.

STEFAN BIERNACKI

Rijksinstituut voor Oorlogsdocumentatie

The Rijksinstituut voor Oorlogsdocumentatie (Netherlands State Institute for War Documentation) is an official research institution, records depot, and library in Amsterdam devoted to the history of World War II, administered by the ministry of education and sciences. The institute was founded on May 8, 1945, after preparations for it had been made in the German-occupied country since 1943 with the moral support (since the spring of 1944) of the Dutch government-in-exile in London. Its directors have been Louis de Jong (1945–1979) and Harry Paape (since 1979), and it has thirty staff members.

By 1987, the Rijksinstituut had published sixty-two volumes: monographs, source publications, and miscellaneous works, as well as over 160 mimeographed reports on a great variety of subjects. Its Holocaust publications include B. A. Sijes's *The Strike of February 25–26, 1941* (1954), J. Presser's *The Destruction of the Dutch Jews* (1969), D. Giltay Veth and A. J. van der Leeuw's *The Weinreb-Report* (1976), and Harry Paape, Gerrold van der Stroom, and David Barnouw's *The Diaries of Anne Frank* (1986). Louis de Jong also paid much attention to several aspects of the Holocaust in his series The Kingdom of the Netherlands in the Second World War, which he was commissioned to write in 1955. The first volume appeared in 1969, and members of the institute's staff have participated in the preparation of this definitive study. The series will consist of fourteen parts (twenty-eight volumes), covering some sixteen thousand pages. It was completed in 1989.

The records depot contains several hundred archives and collections of documents. Those on the Holocaust include the archives of the Comité voor Joodsche Vluchtelingen (Committee for Jewish Refugees), the JOODSE RAAD (Jewish Council), the WESTERBORK transit camp, the VUGHT concentration camp, the IV B 4 section (the section dealing with Jews) of the REICHSSICHERHEITSHAUPTAMT (Reich Security Main Office; RSHA) branch in The Hague, the ZENTRALSTELLE FÜR JÜDISCHE AUSWANDERUNG (Central Office for Jewish Emigration) in Amsterdam, the Omnia Treuhandgesellschaft (Trust Company), whose branch in The Hague dealt with the ARISIERUNG ("Aryanization") of Dutch Jewish enterprises, and many other public and private collections.

The Rijksinstituut's special collections include more than 1,200 private diaries; 120,000 photographs; 200 films; 2,000 drawings; underground newspapers, pamphlets, poems, and doggerels; Allied and German propaganda leaflets; and 5,000 posters. The library of the institute contains about 45,000 titles.

Important tasks in the fields of education and social welfare (especially on behalf of survivors of the Holocaust, resistance fighters, and victims of acts of war), as well as general information, have been entrusted to the institute. It was also responsible for compiling and designing permanent exhibitions in the Netherlands War and Resistance Museum, the State Museum in Auschwitz, and the Westerbork Remembrance Center. The institute publishes annual reports in Dutch and progress reports in English.

HARRY PAAPE

Wiener Library

A research center on Nazism, the Wiener Library was founded by the CENTRALVEREIN DEUTSCHER STAATSBÜRGER JÜDISCHEN GLAUBENS (Central Union of German Citizens of Jewish Faith; CV) and originally operated clandestinely to accumulate material about the Nazi party. The only archive of its kind in the Weimar Republic, it was administered in cooperation with other German organizations and utilized for anti-Nazi propaganda. With Hitler's rise to power, the archive had to be destroyed.

Alfred Wiener (1885–1964), the general secretary of the CV, who had been very active in the fight against antisemitism, emigrated from Germany in 1934 and founded the Jewish Central Information Office in Amsterdam. This office gathered material on the situation in the Third Reich in order to provide information to all those interested in fighting Nazism. With the help of Dutch and other antifascists, Dr. Wiener collected the available press reports and Nazi literature stemming from Germany. By 1938 the office already had more than eight thousand books and some ten thousand press clippings, with sets of Nazi and anti-Nazi periodicals. The following year, the office was transferred to London and served as the basis of the Wiener Library.

During World War II, the materials were used by various British governmental departments, especially the Ministry of Information. The library became a leading research center on Nazism, fascism, and other totalitarian movements. It came to hold a vast collection of books, eyewitness reports, forty thousand prosecution documents from the International Military Tribunal of the NUREMBERG TRIAL, over a million newspaper clippings, and other archival material, mainly on twentieth-century antisemitism and, especially, Nazism. In 1980, most of the books and the original archival material were transferred to Tel Aviv University; microfilmed copies of the material remain in London.

BIBLIOGRAPHY

Weltsch, R. "About Alfred Wiener." *Leo Baeck Institute Year Book* 9 (1964): 29–30.

Wiener Library. *The Wiener Library: Its History and Activities, 1934–1945*. London, 1946.

DAVID BANKIER

Żydowski Instytut Historyczny

The Żydowski Instytut Historyczny (Jewish Historical Institute) is a research institute in Warsaw focusing on the history of the Jews of Poland, primarily during World War II and the Holocaust period. The institute is an autonomous unit within the Polish Academy of Sciences and is subject to the academy's scholarly supervision (and, according to Polish practice, also the academy's political and ideological supervision). Because of its special character, it has shared the vicissitudes of the Jewish community of Poland and of its cultural and public organizations. The work it has carried out, as well as its methods, have reflected the condition of the surviving Jewish remnants and the Polish regime's attitude toward the country's Jewish population.

The institute has its origins in the Central Jewish Historical Commission, founded in Lublin in 1944 (as soon as the city was liberated from the Germans). The commission moved in 1945 to Łódź, and, at the end of 1947, to Warsaw. It had branches, or at least representatives, in provincial towns and cities with a Jewish population, the largest such branch located in Kraków. The institute's activities involved primarily the collection of historical documentation, mainly on the Jews of Poland during the Holocaust; the collection of Jewish books and art that survived the war; and the taking of testimonies from Holocaust survivors. The commission also embarked upon the publication of collections of documents, diaries, and testimonies, and on research into the history of Polish Jewry in World War II. In 1948 it became the Jewish Historical Institute of Warsaw.

In the several decades of the institute's (and its predecessor's) existence, vast treasures have accumulated in all branches of its activities, and the research conducted by its staff has been an important contribution to Jewish historiography. The largest and most important collection is that of documents and papers from the Holocaust period, including the ONEG SHABBAT Archive (the Ringelblum Archive), which was found in the ruins of the Warsaw ghetto; documents from various ghettos—sometimes only fragments—such as those of Warsaw, Białystok, Łódź, Radom, Będzin, Sosnowiec, and Zamość; col-

The Oneg Shabbat (Ringelblum) Archive, which was hidden in metal containers in Warsaw and discovered in two parts, in September 1946 and December 1950. It is being examined by members of the Jewish Historical Institute.

lections of documents of German institutions from the Holocaust period; a collection of about 250 diaries, most dating back to the Holocaust period; some 7,000 testimonies taken in the period from 1944 to 1970 (the greater part from 1944 to 1947); important collections of notes written by prisoners in concentration and extermination camps; and a card index of Jewish prisoners of war, beginning in 1939.

Also of importance are collections that belonged to Jewish communities during the war period, and to Jewish organizations and institutions that went into operation as soon as Poland was liberated but were liquidated between 1948 and 1951. The institute also has sixty thousand books in various languages, dealing with the different branches of Judaica; some seven thousand pre-1800 printed items; twenty-five hundred periodicals; and a collection of manuscripts, some originating between the eleventh and the eighteenth century.

Research works published by the institute (or by the commission) include more than forty books and collections of documents. The institute staff also publish their research papers in learned journals, including the *Bleter far Yidishe Geshichte* (Pages of Jewish History), which the institute has been producing since 1948 and which by the end of 1986 had reached No. 137–138. The commission, and subsequently the institute, has been headed by the historians Philip Friedman, Nachman Blumenthal, Bernard Mark, Artur Eisenbach, and, most recently, Maurycy Horn. Its research scholars have included Joseph Kermish, Isaiah Trunk, Tatjana Bernstein, Szymon Datner, Franciszek Kupfer, Abraham Wein, and Rata Sakowska, to name only a few.

During the waves of Jewish emigration from Poland, most of the scholars who had been working at the institute left the country, resuming their work in their new places of residence, mainly in Israel.

BIBLIOGRAPHY

Wein, A. "The Jewish Historical Institute in Warsaw." *Yad Vashem Studies* 8 (1970): 203–214.

ABRAHAM WEIN

DOHMEN, NICO. *See* Van der Voort, Hanna.

DOLCHSTOSSLEGENDE ("stab-in-the-back" myth), fabricated version of the German defeat in World War I that gained popularity under the Weimar Republic. It claimed that the German army had not been defeated on the field of battle but rather that the home front had forced the military leaders to lay down their arms, as a result of the defeatist actions taken by the liberals, the Socialists, and the Jews. This fabrication was without any basis in fact, but it provided motivation for the Freikorps, the paramilitary organizations that sprang up. Both in the Weimar Republic and in the Third Reich, it was the version accepted by nationalist circles and by all those who sought revenge for Germany's defeat in the war and for the peace agreement that Germany had been compelled to sign.

Much of the support for this falsehood and its propagation came from Gen. Erich LUDENDORFF, one of the outstanding German commanders in World War I, who in fact had taken the lead in pressing the German government to ask for an immediate cease-fire in the fall of 1918.

BIBLIOGRAPHY

Bauer, Y. *A History of the Holocaust.* New York, 1982. See pages 73–76.

ISRAEL GUTMAN

DOMANEVKA, county seat in the Golta district of TRANSNISTRIA, 77.5 miles (125 km) northeast of Odessa. Domanevka was the site of one of the three mass-murder camps established in October 1941 in the Golta district, on orders of the district governor, Col. Modest Isopescu. In the period from November 1941 to January 1942, twenty thousand Ukrainian Jews and Jews who had fled from BESSARABIA were brought to Domanevka from Odessa, Ochakov, and Berezovka, all of them survivors of the massacre campaign conducted by Einsatzgruppe D.

In December of that year, Isopescu issued

DOMANEVKA

the order for the murder of these Jews, and they were shot to death in groups of five hundred. Taking part in the massacre were Romanian gendarmes and troops, as well as Sonderkommando R, made up of Germans living in nearby villages. The latter were attached to the VOLKSDEUTSCHE MITTELSTELLE (Ethnic Germans' Welfare Office), which had organized all the VOLKSDEUTSCHE living outside the borders of Germany, and which in 1941 had been attached to the SS. Also participating in the mass murder were Ukrainian militiamen. Some eighteen thousand Jews were murdered, after they had been robbed of their belongings. Their bodies were left lying in the fields, to fall prey to dogs. The murder drive came to an end in February 1942, and the transports coming to Domanevka after that date, consisting of Jews from Odessa and its environs, escaped immediate death. Another sixty Jews from Bessarabia were also seized and taken to Domanevka in this period. There were no more murders, but starvation, diseases, and exposure to the cold took a fearful toll among those who had survived the first wave of massacres.

Some two thousand to three thousand prisoners were now left in the camp. They were crowded into two broken-down stables, pigsties, and several roofless houses. They were not permitted to leave their filthy quarters, and only those who were fit for work were sent on forced labor and were given a small amount of food. The rest were simply left to starve to death, and every day several dozen died. The prisoners looked so terrible—sick, naked, ravaged by worms and rats—that when the governor of Transnistria, Gheorghe Alexianu, was scheduled to visit the camp in the summer of 1942, the Jews were removed so that he would not see them.

Control of the camp was in the hands of Romanian gendarmes. When the snow melted, a group of sixty Jews was charged with burning the victims of the great massacre, for fear of epidemics. It took two months to burn the bodies, layer upon layer, in fires fed by timber and petroleum. One guard unit of Sonderkommando R asked the Romanian gendarmes for permission to kill Jews, which was granted, and they thereupon murdered hundreds of Jews in the vicinity of the camp.

By the end of 1942 about one thousand Jews were left in Domanevka, the majority of them women. At the end of 1943 most of these were transferred to the Akhmetchetka camp, where they were murdered, as were two hundred and fifty Jews—including fifty children—who had managed to escape the deportation. At the beginning of March an SS unit crossed the Bug and killed several dozen Jews from the Ukraine.

On March 28, 1944, the Soviet army liberated Domanevka; about five hundred Jews were still alive, mostly expellees from Romania. A people's tribunal sentenced Isopescu to death, but the sentence was commuted to life imprisonment.

BIBLIOGRAPHY

Ancel, J., ed. *Documents concerning the Fate of Romanian Jewry during the Holocaust.* Vol. 6. Jerusalem, 1986. See pages 57–113.

JEAN ANCEL

DORA-MITTELBAU (also known as Dora-Nordhausen), concentration camp in the Harz Mountains, 3 miles (5 km) from Nordhausen, Saxony (now in East Germany). The Dora-Mittelbau camp was first mentioned on August 27, 1943, as an external unit of the BUCHENWALD concentration camp. On October 28, 1944, it became a major concentration camp under its own name, with twenty-

One of the underground tunnels where V-2 missiles were manufactured in the Dora-Mittelbau concentration camp.

three branches, most of them in the vicinity, inside a restricted military area.

In the second half of 1943, thousands of prisoners were transferred to Dora-Mittelbau, mostly from Buchenwald, and put to work excavating underground tunnels that were to serve as the site of a huge plant for the manufacture of V-2 missiles and other arms. Until the plant was put into operation (in the late spring of 1944), the ten thousand prisoners working on the site had no living quarters and were housed inside the tunnels under unbearable conditions, deprived of daylight and fresh air for weeks at a time. They had to work at a murderous pace, in twelve-hour shifts. The unspeakable sanitary conditions and lack of security precautions led to a mortality rate much higher than that in any other concentration camp in Germany. Only after production began was a camp of wooden barracks constructed in Dora-Mittelbau, to which the prisoners were transferred in the summer of 1944. That fall, when maximum production was attained in the camp, Dora-Mittelbau had a permanent prison population in the main camp of over twelve thousand, with another twenty thousand in the satellite camps.

When construction was completed and the plant went into operation, thousands of Jewish prisoners from various countries were brought to Dora-Mittelbau. They were treated with great brutality and were assigned the most physically exacting jobs; their mortality rate was higher than that of any other group of prisoners. Jewish prisoners who were exhausted and could not keep pace with the work were sent to AUSCHWITZ and MAUTHAUSEN in special transports, to be killed there.

The first group of prisoners sent to Dora-Mittelbau from Buchenwald included several individuals who had been active in the underground organization in that camp. Together with other groups of prisoners of various nationalities, they formed an underground while Dora-Mittelbau was still under construction, in order to sabotage the work and slow it down. When production began in 1944, the sabotage operations were intensified, seriously damaging the manufacturing process and upsetting the timetable for the delivery of the weapons so sorely needed by the Nazis in the final months of the war. Large numbers of prisoners were jailed on charges of sabotage; many were killed during their interrogation or were subsequently executed. More than two hundred prisoners suspected of sabotage, including several of the underground leaders, were hanged in public.

On April 1, 1945, the Nazis began the evacuation of the camp. Within several days most of the prisoners had been taken out, with the majority transferred to BERGEN-BELSEN. Thousands were murdered en route; at one point, near the village of Gardelegen, several thousand prisoners—mostly Jews—were crowded into a barn that was set afire, burning them all to death. Others succumbed to disease after they reached Bergen-Belsen, on the very eve of liberation. On March 25, 1945, Dora-Mittelbau and its satellites contained 34,500 prisoners. The camp was liberated on April 9 by United States forces, who found only a few prisoners there.

Between August 7 and December 31, 1947, an American military tribunal, which was independent of the International Military Tribunal at Nuremberg, tried nineteen former staff members of the Dora camp; fifteen were found guilty. The protective-custody camp leader, SS-Obersturmführer Hans Karl Moeser, was sentenced to death by hanging. In his trial statement he said: "The same way, with the same pleasure as you shoot deer, I shoot a human being. When I came to the SS and had to shoot the first three persons, my food didn't taste good for three days, but today it is a pleasure. It is a joy for me." The other defendants received sentences that ranged from five years to life imprisonment.

BIBLIOGRAPHY

Aalmans, W. J., ed. *The 'Dora'-Nordhausen War Crimes Trial.* N.p., 1947.

Bornemann, M., and M. Broszat. "Das KL Dora-Mittelbau." In *Studien zur Geschichte der Konzentrationslager,* pp. 154–198. Stuttgart, 1970.

Caspiva, J., F. Giessner, and K. Pelny. *Geheimwaffen in Konstein: Lager Dora.* Nordhausen, East Germany, 1964.

Diekmann, G., and P. Hochmut. *KZ Dora-Mittelbau.* Nordhausen, East Germany, 1971.

YEHOSHUA R. BÜCHLER and SHMUEL KRAKOWSKI

DOROHOI, town in ROMANIA, in northern Moldavia, bordering on BUKOVINA. In 1930, Dorohoi had a Jewish population of 5,820. Its Jews suffered more in World War II than others living in the Old Kingdom (Romania in its pre-1918 borders) because the town was near the new border with the Soviet Union, established at the end of June 1940 when the Soviets annexed northern Bukovina, and also because it was a Jewish center in northern Moldavia.

On July 1, 1940, Dorohoi was the scene of the first outbreak of violence against Jews in Romania, when a Romanian army unit that was withdrawing from Bukovina shot to death dozens of Jewish soldiers in its ranks and murdered Jewish inhabitants of the town, including women and children; a total of 200 Jews were killed. This took place before Romania had allied itself with Nazi Germany and before a single German soldier had set foot on Romanian soil. In June 1941, when Romania joined Germany in its invasion of the Soviet Union, a new drive of anti-Jewish persecution was launched. Jews from the nearby towns of Saveni, Darabani, Mihăileni, and Rădăuţi were expelled from their homes and forced into Dorohoi; at the same time, 300 Jews from Dorohoi—among them the community leaders—were interned in camps in western Romania (mostly in Tîrgu-Jiu), on suspicion of being Communists. In Dorohoi the Jews were forced to wear the yellow badge (*see* BADGE, JEWISH). At the end of August and the beginning of September 1941, 2,000 Jewish males from other places in the district were brought to Dorohoi; at the same time, the 300 Jews who had been interned in western Romania were permitted to return. All the Jews in the town were forced to subscribe to the war fund.

On November 5, 1941, the authorities informed the community leaders that an order had been issued for the expulsion of the Dorohoi Jews from their hometown. For this purpose, the Dorohoi district was administratively attached to Bukovina, the province from which all the Jews were expelled to TRANSNISTRIA. The expulsion order had in fact originated in Bucharest, and was part of a plan designed to thin out the Jewish population of northern Moldavia. The Jews were forced to "sell" their property to the Central Bank of

DOROHOI

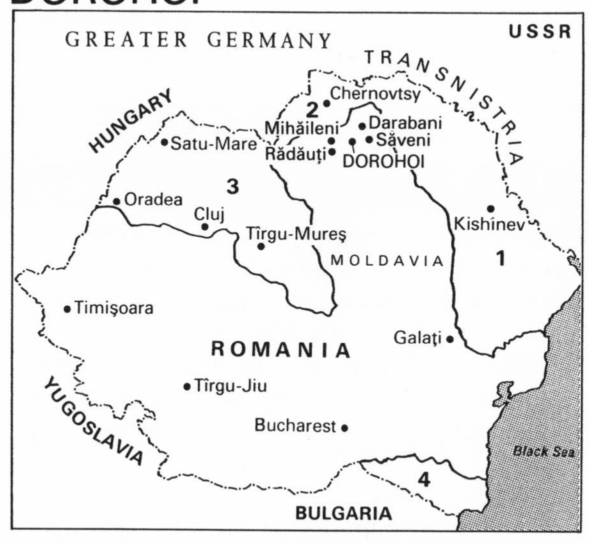

0 160 miles 1 in.
0 300 km. 3 cm.

Annexations from June to September 1940: (1) Bessarabia and (2) N. Bukovina to USSR; (3) N. Transylvania to Hungary; (4) S. Dobruja to Bulgaria.

Romania, and their houses were plundered by their Romanian neighbors.

On November 7 the Jews of Darabani and Rădăuţi were expelled, followed the next day by the Jews of Mihăileni and Saveni. The expulsion of the Dorohoi Jews began on November 12. Some four hundred and fifty Jews had obtained (through bribery) permits to stay in the town, ostensibly as being essential to the economy; even some of these, however, joined in the general expulsion, since they did not want to be separated from those members of their families who were not included in the residence permits. Eight thousand Jews were expelled from Dorohoi and the neighboring area in two transports. Many of them died en route, even before they had crossed the Dniester. In many families only the women and children were sent to Transnistria, with the men kept behind in Romanian forced-labor camps.

The Jews who remained in Dorohoi set up a new community leadership, and its members, together with the leaders of Romanian Jewry, made strenuous efforts to have the Dorohoi district reincorporated in the Old Kingdom and thereby to facilitate the return of the Jews from Transnistria. In the end, their efforts succeeded; the required authorization was given when the Soviet army was making its advance. A delegation of the Jewish Aid Committee was able to go to Transnistria in order to make arrangements for the repatriation of the Jews who had been expelled there. At the end of December 1943, 6,053 Jews from the Dorohoi district, out of the 10,368 who had been expelled from it, returned, together with 2,000 out of the 3,074 expelled from the town of Dorohoi. The local authorities continued to harass the returnees, and only after Dorohoi was liberated by the Red Army in April 1944 did their sufferings at Romanian hands come to an end.

BIBLIOGRAPHY

Carp, M. *Transnistria.* Vol. 3 of *Cartea Neagră.* Bucharest, 1947.

Lavi, T., ed. *Rumania,* vol. 1. In *Pinkas Hakehillot; Encyclopaedia of Jewish Communities.* Jerusalem, 1969. See pages 104–110. (In Hebrew.)

JEAN ANCEL

DOUWES, ARNOLD (b. 1906), Dutch rescuer of Jews during the Holocaust. The son of a pastor in the Dutch Reformed church, Douwes joined the Dutch underground and devoted himself to the rescue of Jewish adults and children. At first, he worked under the guidance of Johannes Post (an important underground figure who aided Jews), who was shot by the Germans. Douwes enlarged the scope of his mentor's rescue operations. Jewish families who had received notification to report for deportation to the WESTERBORK camp were referred to him by the Dutch underground. He concentrated his activities in the vicinity of the town of Nieuwlande, in the northeastern province of Drenthe. There, almost every household sheltered a Jewish person. Douwes looked after all the needs of these Jews, helping to supply them with food and other necessities, false identification papers, and financial support (through the underground). Together with Max Leons (nicknamed "Nico"), a Jew who posed as a Protestant colleague and friend of Douwes, he scoured the countryside and enlisted several hundred Dutch families in their mutual rescue activities.

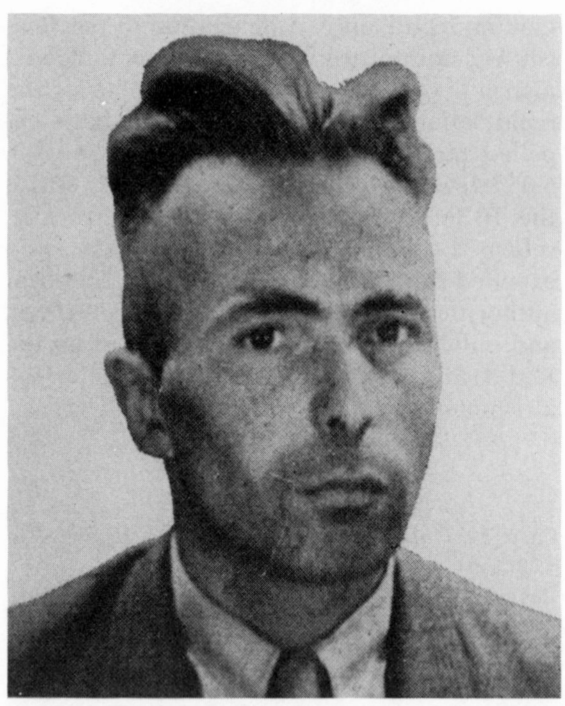

Arnold Douwes, from a photograph on a German "Wanted" poster of May 21, 1942.

Douwes personally met the children in Amsterdam, or at the train station upon their arrival in the Drenthe district. When the Germans staged raids in the vicinity, Douwes went for nocturnal rides on his bicycle, moving Jews—under the very noses of the Germans—to safer locations.

An operation of this magnitude could not go undetected for long, and Douwes was wanted by the authorities. To avoid arrest, he changed his appearance, growing a mustache and wearing a hat and eyeglasses. In spite of these precautions, he was apprehended in January 1945 and imprisoned in Assen, where he awaited his execution. The underground, however, succeeded in freeing him before that could take place. After the war, Douwes lived for a time in South Africa and then moved to Israel in 1956.

Arnold Douwes was responsible for saving the lives of hundreds of Jews, including some one hundred children. In 1965 he was recognized as a "RIGHTEOUS AMONG THE NATIONS" by YAD VASHEM. More than two hundred residents of the Nieuwlande area were later awarded the title as well.

BIBLIOGRAPHY

De Jong, L. *Het Koninkrijk der Nederlanden in de Tweede Wereldoorlog.* Vols. 6, 7. The Hague, 1975–1976.

MORDECAI PALDIEL

DRAENGER, SHIMSHON (1917–1943?), underground leader. Draenger, who was known as Simek, was born in Kraków. At the age of thirteen he joined the Akiva movement, and later became one of its main leaders. Until the outbreak of World War II he edited the movement's journal, *Divrei Akiva,* and the weekly *Tse'irim,* a newspaper for young people. On September 22, 1939, a short time after the German occupation of Kraków, Draenger was arrested because of the articles of Irene Harand, an Austrian anti-Nazi, that he had published in *Divrei Akiva.* Together with his future wife, Gusta Dawidson (*see* DRAENGER, TOVA), who was arrested at the same time,

Shimshon Draenger.

Draenger was held at the prison camp in Troppau, Czechoslovakia. Following his release in December 1939, he reassembled his followers under the guise of educational activity, thereby reconstructing the Akiva cell in Warsaw. At the beginning of the war Draenger tried, unsuccessfully, to save the members of his movement by smuggling them into Slovakia. From December 1941 to August 1942 he managed a training farm at Kopaliny, which was a cover for Akiva and its underground activity.

Draenger was one of the youth movement activists who from the beginning of the war maintained that the Jews had no chance of survival under the Nazi occupation, and this approach dictated his radical position and methods of activity. In August 1942 he helped found HE-HALUTS HA-LOHEM, a combat organization of Jewish pioneer youth, and was a member of its command. He set up the organization's Technical Office, which forged permits for the members giving entry to and exit from the ghetto, and sold these permits to finance arms purchases. He also edited the underground journal *He-Haluts ha-Lohem.*

In January 1943 Draenger was seized and was imprisoned in the MONTELUPICH PRISON, where he organized Bible and other study circles for his friends in jail. On April 29 of that year he escaped and was reunited with his wife, Gusta, who had also escaped from Montelupich. Both became partisans in the Wiśnicz Forest. There Draenger also resumed publication of *He-Haluts ha-Lohem*, exhorting the Jewish youth remaining in the forest to resist the Germans actively, urging the last residents of the ghetto to flee for their lives, and appealing to the Poles not to betray Jews to the authorities. His articles also sketched the history of the pioneer underground.

On November 8, 1943, Draenger was apprehended by the Germans and, presumably, was killed.

BIBLIOGRAPHY

Ainsztein, R. *Jewish Resistance in Nazi-occupied Europe.* London, 1974.

Dawidson, G. *Justina's Diary.* Tel Aviv, 1978. (In Hebrew.)

YAEL PELED (MARGOLIN)

DRAENGER, TOVA (1917–1943?), underground member and chronicler. Draenger's maiden name was Gusta Dawidson. Born in Kraków, by 1938 she was one of the leaders of the Akiva movement there. Together with Shimshon DRAENGER (who became her husband early in 1940), she edited *Tse'irim*, a weekly for young people. During the Nazi occupation she was one of the founders of HE-HALUTS HA-LOHEM, an underground combat movement in Kraków, and played an active role in its operations.

On September 22, 1939, she was arrested, together with Shimshon Draenger, and charged with belonging to the Austrian anti-Nazi Irene Harand group. In December 1939 they were released from the prison camp in Troppau, Czechoslovakia, where they had been interned. They resumed their activities in Kraków and Warsaw and, in 1940, reorganized Akiva in both cities.

In He-Haluts ha-Lohem, Draenger's main task was, with her husband, to produce forged documents for the organization's use. On January 18, 1943, having learned that her husband had been arrested, she surrendered to the Gestapo, as she and her husband had pledged to do if either was seized. She was put in the MONTELUPICH PRISON and, while there, until April 29 of that year, wrote her memoirs in the form of a diary, her purpose being to record the story of the final uprising in Kraków. Years later, these memoirs were published under the title *Justina's Diary*. She wrote on toilet paper, in several copies, helped by fellow members of the underground who shared the cell with her. The diary presents, in Draenger's own words, "the true story of the last and most daring revolt of the young fighters," and deals with the history of Akiva and He-Haluts ha-Lohem between April 1941 and March 1943. Miraculously, fifteen of the diary's twenty chapters were preserved, covering the period from August 23 to November 26, 1942.

Draenger escaped from prison on April 29, 1943, and, together with her husband, resumed underground activities, this time in the Wiśnicz Forest. The two also recommenced publication of *He-Haluts ha-Lohem*, the underground movement's journal.

On November 9 of that year, following her

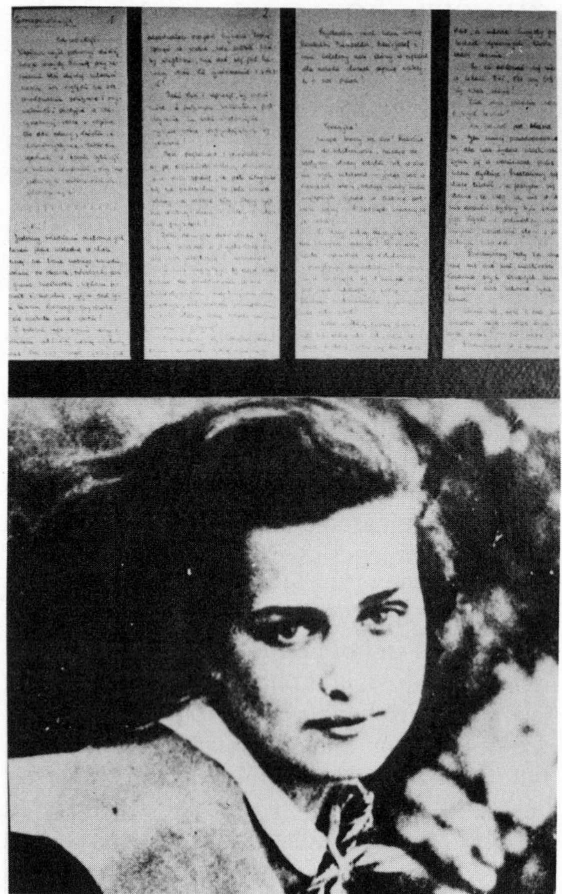

Tova Draenger and pages from her diary.

husband's arrest, Draenger again surrendered to the Nazis. Nothing is known of the subsequent fate of either, and it is assumed that they were both executed.

BIBLIOGRAPHY

Dawidson, G. *Justina's Diary.* Tel Aviv, 1978. (In Hebrew.)

YAEL PELED (MARGOLIN)

DRANCY, assembly camp (*Sammellager*) and detention camp for the Jews of FRANCE, from which they were sent to forced-labor and extermination camps. The camp was established in August 1941 in the northeastern Paris suburb of Drancy. It was situated in an oblong, reinforced concrete four-story building, which before the war had served as a gendarmerie barracks. The camp area covered 656 by 131 feet (200 × 40 m), with a 10-foot (3-m) lookout tower at each of its four corners. The camp was under twenty-four-hour guard by French gendarmes armed with machine guns. The outer road had a barbed-wire fence on each side. Four satellite camps were added to the camp, as part of the EINSATZSTAB ROSENBERG operation, to serve as depositories for artworks, valuable furniture, household goods, and books that had been confiscated from the homes of Jews who had been arrested, imprisoned, and deported. The camp was able to hold 4,500 prisoners; in the period from August 21, 1941, to August 17, 1944 (liberation day), some 70,000 prisoners passed through it. Its organization and structure were modeled along the lines of Nazi CONCENTRATION CAMPS.

The Drancy camp went through two distinct periods, one lasting from August 21, 1941, to July 1, 1943, when it was administered by the French, and the other from July 2, 1943, to August 17, 1944, during which it was run by the Germans. In the first, "French" period, three high-ranking French police officers named Savart, Laurent, and Gilbert succeeded one another in running the camp, although it was at all times under the control of the German Sicherheitspolizei (Security Police) and SD (Sicherheitsdienst; Security Service) commanders in France.

On July 2, 1943, Alois BRUNNER took over command of the camp, removing from their posts all the Vichy-appointed French commanders and running the camp with the help of four SS officers. The period was marked by a severe deterioration of the inmates' conditions and an intensive effort to deport a larger number of Jews to Auschwitz. Under Brunner's administration, prisoners were assigned functions previously performed by the French police. From August 25, 1942, when they took over from the French gendarmerie, the members of this internal police service (known as Membres du Service d'Ordre) played an important role in the life of the camp.

On June 22, 1942, the first transport, consisting of 1,000 Jews, left Drancy for AUSCHWITZ-Birkenau; the last such transport left Drancy on July 31, 1944. Between these two dates a total of sixty-four transports left Drancy, with 64,759 Jews aboard; of these, sixty-one transports, with 61,000 persons, went to the Auschwitz extermination camp, and three transports, with 3,753 persons, were sent to the SOBIBÓR extermination camp. Of the 65,000 Jews who went to their death from Drancy, more than 20,000 were French (born in France), 15,000 were Polish, and 6,000 were German nationals.

Solidarity and mutual help became the rule among the Drancy prison population, and this conduct was the first manifestation of resistance in the camp. The first escape took place within ten days of the camp's establishment. From August 21, 1941, to August 17, 1943, there were forty-one successful attempts to escape, and an untold number of unsuccessful attempts. In September 1943 the prisoners developed and began working on a plan for digging an escape tunnel, through which all the prisoners would be able to disperse. Running 4.5 feet (1.4 m) below the surface, the tunnel had its starting point underneath the camp commandant's office, and from there it passed under the barbed-wire fence. The planned place of exit was an underground air-raid shelter beyond the camp perimeter. Seventy prisoners worked in three shifts on the tunnel, day and night, beginning on September 15, 1943. On November 8, 1943—when no more than 98 feet (30 m) remained to be excavated (a day's work)—the Germans discovered the tunnel. As punishment, many prisoners were sent to their death, among them the leader of the camp underground, Robert Blum.

At the beginning of August 1944 the Allied forces reached Paris, and on the night of August 15–16 the Germans in Drancy hastily burned all the camp documents. The next day they fled, leaving 1,542 prisoners behind them. On August 17, the consul general of Sweden, Raoul Nordling, took over control of the camp and asked the French Red Cross to care for the inmates; the camp was now liberated.

Until November 15, 1942, food rations in the camp were tiny, and the prisoners were severely undernourished. The shortage of food was a constant feature, with the daily ration ranging from six hundred to eight hundred calories per person; 800 cases of edema and cachexia were recorded. The situation improved after mid-November, with the help of French Jewish organizations and the Red Cross; food parcels were also received in the camp from the families of the prisoners. However, after the advent of Brunner, there was a turn for the worse in this regard as well.

Cultural and religious life persisted in Drancy despite the difficult conditions. Jewish religious customs were observed, and hundreds of prisoners attended prayer services and religious ceremonies. The Jewish New Year (Rosh Hashanah) and the Day of Atonement (Yom Kippur) were celebrated in the synagogue, established in September 1941, and many prisoners also attended regular Sabbath services. On July 20, 1942, the Germans prohibited any further Jewish religious observance, but as late as the fall of 1943 the high holidays were still being celebrated, according to both the Ashkenazic and the Sephardic ritual. Many cultural activities took place in the camp; concerts and literary evenings of a wide variety were held. Books were smuggled into the camp, and a school was set up for the children. The school continued to function, clandestinely, even after January 1943, when it was officially closed down on German orders.

Men, women, and children were among the

Deportation of the Brin family from Drancy.

prisoners detained in Drancy and deported from there, among them some famous people: the French poet Max Jacob, who died in the camp in 1944; Pierre Masse, a senator who had been a member of Clemenceau's cabinet; the ballet director René Blum, the brother of Léon BLUM; the writer Tristan Bernard; Marcel Dassault, the aircraft constructor; Simone VEIL; Itzhak KATZENELSON; and Jankiel Handelsman (Snopek) and Joseph Dorembus (also known as Jacques Warszawski), later among the organizers of the Sonderkommando mutiny in Auschwitz-Birkenau, on October 7, 1944.

After the war a monument was erected, at the place where the camp's front gates once stood, to commemorate the Jews who were deported to the extermination camps from Drancy.

BIBLIOGRAPHY

Darville, J., and S. Wichens. *Drancy la Juive; ou La 2e Inquisition.* Paris, 1945.

Felstiner, M. "Commandant of Drancy: Alois Brunner and the Jews of France." *Holocaust and Genocide Studies* 2/1 (1987): 21–47.

Klarsfeld, S. *Le mémorial de la déportation des Juifs de France.* Paris, 1978.

Marrus, M. R., and R. O. Paxton. *Vichy France and the Jews.* New York, 1981.

Rutkowski, A. "Les déportations des Juifs de France vers Auschwitz-Birkenau et Sobibor." *Le Monde Juif* 26/57–58 (1970): 33–75.

Wellers, G. *L'étoile jaune à l'heure de Vichy: De Drancy à Auschwitz.* Paris, 1973.

ADAM RUTKOWSKI

DROGOBYCH (Pol., Drohobycz), city in Lvov Oblast (district), in the Ukrainian SSR. Now an oil-industry center, Drogobych is an old city that from 1772 to 1918 belonged to Austrian-held Galicia, and in the interwar period was part of Poland; between 1939 and 1941 it was in Soviet hands. Jews had lived intermittently in Drogobych since the fifteenth century, and on the eve of World War II the community numbered some fifteen thousand, over 40 percent of the city's population. In September 1939, hundreds of Jews who had escaped from German-occupied parts of Poland found refuge there.

Following the German invasion of Soviet Russia on June 22, 1941, groups of young Jews tried to flee from Drogobych to the east, and many were killed in the attempt, either during German air attacks or at the hands of Ukrainian nationalists who were active in the area. German forces entered the city on June 30 and the next day a pogrom took place. It lasted for three days, and over its course Ukrainians, assisted by Wehrmacht soldiers, murdered over three hundred Jews. In July, various measures against the Jews were introduced. Jews were seized at random and made to perform forced labor; the movement of Jews in the main streets was restricted; many Jews were compelled to vacate their apartments so that German officers could move in; Jews were banned from the city market; and they had to wear on their right-hand sleeve a white band with a blue Star of David.

The JUDENRAT (Jewish Council), which was set up in July, sought to reach an agreement with the German authorities regarding forced labor by Jews; in order to avoid the random seizures, it undertook to supply fixed quotas of laborers. These efforts, however, met with only limited success. The Judenrat also opened soup kitchens that dispensed meals to the needy.

In September and October of 1941, several dozen Jewish intellectuals were arrested and all trace of them was lost; later it became known that they had been tortured and then murdered in a forest near the city. On November 30 over three hundred Jews were murdered in the Bronica Forest outside Drogobych. That winter, many Jews died of starvation and a typhoid epidemic. In the spring of 1942 the Judenrat set up workshops to create employment for the Jewish population in the hope that this would save them from being sent to the work camps that had been set up nearby, where harsh conditions caused the death of many of the inmates. Hundreds of the city's Jews were also employed in local oil refineries and in the processing of oil products.

At the end of March 1942 an *Aktion* took place that resulted in 2,000 Jews being sent to their death in the BEŁŻEC extermination camp. A second large *Aktion,* launched on August 8, lasted until August 17. *Selektionen* were made at the various assembly points and only workers with employment cards from essential jobs in the oil industry were permitted to remain free. Germans and Ukrainian collaborators hunted down Jews in hiding and anyone they found was murdered. More than 600 Jews were killed in the city's courtyards and alleys, and over 2,500 were deported to Bełżec.

At the beginning of October 1942 a ghetto was established in which 10,000 Jews were confined, among them the remnants of Jewish communities in the vicinity. Another *Aktion* took place on October 23 and 24; 2,300 Jews were sent to Bełżec and 300 patients in a Jewish hospital were killed. Still another *Aktion* was launched in November and went on uninterruptedly for an entire month. Ten days after it began, 1,000 Jews were taken to Bełżec by train, and a few days later several hundred more. Hundreds of others were killed in the ghetto. At the end of 1942 and the beginning of 1943, the Jews who worked in the oil industry were put into separate work camps.

On February 15, 1943, 450 Jews were taken out of the ghetto to the Bronica Forest, where they were murdered. The liquidation of the ghetto began on May 21 and was completed by June 10. At the same time the Judenrat ceased to function. Many of the ghetto houses

Deportation of Jews from Drogobych.

were set on fire in order to force out any Jews who had hidden inside. The last Jews found in the ghetto were put on trucks and taken to the Bronica Forest, where they were killed and buried in pits. The destruction of the ghetto was followed by the murder of the Jews in the work camps, with only the most essential workers left alive. Following the Soviet advance of April 1944, these workers were sent west, to the PŁASZÓW camp. When the Soviet army entered Drogobych in August 1944, 400 Jewish survivors emerged from hiding places.

BIBLIOGRAPHY

Gelber, N. M., ed. *Memorial to the Jews of Drohobycz, Boryslaw, and Surroundings.* Tel Aviv, 1959. (In Hebrew.)

Gilbert, M. *The Holocaust.* New York, 1985.

AHARON WEISS

DROR (DEROR). *See* Youth Movements.

DUBNOW, SIMON (1860–1941), one of the great Jewish historians and thinkers of modern times and one of the founders of Autonomism, the movement that advocated Jewish national autonomy in the Diaspora. Dubnow was born in Mstislavl, Belorussia, received a traditional Jewish education, and acquired a broad general education on his own; he was close to the circle of the Jewish Enlightenment in Russia. Dubnow's first works on Jewish history were published in the 1880s. His greatest achievement was his pioneering approach to the study of the history of the Jews in eastern Europe and their spiritual and religious movements. In his research work, Dubnow stressed the periods of Jewish autonomy in Poland and Lithuania and the history of Hasidism. His major work was the ten-volume *Weltgeschichte des jüdischen Volkes* (World History of the Jewish People), which traced the history of the Jews from their beginnings to modern times; it was first published in its German translation between 1923 and 1929, and then in other languages, including the original Russian.

In his early work as a historian, Dubnow followed the trail of the nineteenth-century German Jewish historian Heinrich Graetz, but he later discarded the view that saw the Jewish people as a unique phenomenon in history with its own spiritual and religious mission. He adopted instead a secular concept, which regarded the Jews as a national entity that, despite the passage of generations and the rise and fall of its "centers of hegemony," has preserved its autonomous spiritual framework. In Dubnow's view, it was the spiritual and cultural elements that represented the highest degree of a people's development. Since the Jews, thanks to their unique history, had retained their specific spiritual essence more than any other people, they were ripe to assume this highest level of a people in progressive human society.

Simon Dubnow.

This was the source of Dubnow's political philosophy, which regarded the Emancipation as a turning point in Jewish history and called for the granting of spiritual and cultural autonomy to the Jewish populations of Europe. Dubnow regarded such a grant of autonomy as providing the basis for national Jewish existence and for the realization of Jewish strivings, especially in the countries of eastern Europe. This political concept was the ideological base upon which Dubnow and his associates established the Jewish People's Party (Volkspartei) in 1906.

In 1922 Dubnow succeeded in leaving the Soviet Union and settled in Berlin. When Hitler came to power, Dubnow moved to Riga, the capital of Latvia, and continued his work. When Riga was occupied by the Germans in early July 1941, the eighty-one-year-old scholar was put in the city's ghetto, and his library was confiscated. In his final days he reportedly told the people he met, "Jews, make sure that everything is written down and recorded." According to one account, Dubnow was sick and feverish when he was shot to death while being taken out of the ghetto, in December 1941.

BIBLIOGRAPHY

Pinson, K. S. "Simon Dubnow: Historian and Political Philosopher." In *Nationalism and History: Essays on Old and New Judaism, by Simon Dubnow,* edited by K. S. Pinson. New York, 1970.

Rawidowicz, S., ed. *Simon Dubnow in Memoriam: Essays and Letters.* London, 1954. (In Hebrew.)

Steinberg, A., ed. *Simon Dubnow: The Man and His Work.* Paris, 1963.

ISRAEL GUTMAN

DUCKWITZ, GEORG FERDINAND (1904–1973), German diplomat, one of the "RIGHTEOUS AMONG THE NATIONS." Duckwitz was born in Bremen, the son of a prominent merchant family, and in the early 1930s was a businessman in Copenhagen. He joined the Nazi party in 1932, and from 1933 to 1935 served in Alfred ROSENBERG's foreign-policy office, but left that post of his own accord and took a civilian job in a shipping firm.

At the beginning of World War II, Duckwitz was posted to DENMARK by the ABWEHR, the German intelligence organization. When Denmark was occupied by the Germans, Duckwitz was appointed shipping attaché at the German mission in Copenhagen. He established ties with the leaders of the Danish Social Democrat party and gained their trust. When the Germans were about to deport the Jews of Denmark to Nazi camps in the east at the beginning of October 1943, Duckwitz informed his Danish contacts of the German plans. It was mainly this advance warning that enabled the Danes to organize the operation that saved the Jews by smuggling them out to Sweden. Duckwitz even went so far as to travel to Sweden, where he met with the prime minister, Per Albin Hansson, who promised that the Swedish government would help in the effort to rescue Denmark's Jews.

After the war, Duckwitz remained in the foreign service of the Federal Republic of Germany (West Germany), and from 1955 to 1958 he served as the German ambassador in Denmark. His last post was that of director-general of the Foreign Ministry. For Duckwitz's share in the rescue of the Jews of Denmark, YAD VASHEM awarded him the title of "Righteous among the Nations."

BIBLIOGRAPHY

Kirchhoff, H. *Georg Ferdinand Duckwitz: Skitser til et politisk portraet.* Lyngby, Denmark, 1978.

Yahil, L. *The Rescue of Danish Jewry: Test of a Democracy.* Philadelphia, 1969.

LENI YAHIL

DÜNABURG. *See* Dvinsk.

DUTCH NATIONAL SOCIALIST MOVEMENT. *See* Nationaal Socialistische Beweging.

DVINSK (Latv., Daugavpils; Ger., Dünaburg), city in southeast LATVIA, on the Western Dvina (Daugava) River. In 1935 Dvinsk had a Jewish population of 11,116, out of a total of 45,160. In June 1940, together with the rest of Latvia, it was incorporated into the Soviet Union; and on June 26, 1941, four days after their invasion of the Soviet Union, the Germans occupied the city.

At some point between June 29 and July 2, all the Jewish males aged sixteen to sixty were assembled in the main square and from there were taken to prison. For a week they were subjected to torture, humiliation, and forced labor, and then the Germans began killing them. By July 16, according to official

German accounts, 1,150 Jews had been murdered. The rest underwent the same fate as time went on, with the exception of a few physicians and skilled workers who were released and some young Jews who managed to escape. Those Jews who had not been imprisoned also suffered from maltreatment, had their property confiscated, were thrown out of their homes, and were put on forced labor. Latvian police and volunteer helpers burned down the synagogues—sometimes while Jews were inside or after they had been forced in—and only two synagogues were left intact. In the second half of July, a decree was issued requiring the Jews to wear a yellow badge (*see* BADGE, JEWISH).

During the last week of July, the Jews were put into a ghetto; the site chosen for this purpose was the Latvian cavalry barracks on the banks of the Dvina, north of the city. The place was unfit for human habitation: it had no running water or other sanitary facilities, and was much too small for the number of Jews crowded into it. A few days later, thousands of other Jews were brought into the ghetto from the neighboring towns of Griva, Krāslava, Preiļi, Viski, and Līvanī. By early August, fourteen thousand to sixteen thousand Jews were packed into the ghetto, living there under unspeakable conditions. A JUDENRAT (Jewish Council) was put in charge, and its various subcommittees tried to improve the housing and sanitary conditions. The ghetto had a Jewish police force, a hospital staffed by fifteen doctors and a substantial number of auxiliary personnel, a pharmacy, an orphanage, and a burial society; in the course of time, many workshops were established.

Having set up the ghetto, the Germans embarked upon the systematic murder of its population, with the assistance of the Latvian auxiliary police. In late July or early August 1941, several hundred elderly Jews were murdered; a short while later, thousands of Jews from the neighboring towns were shot to death in pits that had been prepared in the Pogulanka Forest, 5 miles (8 km) from the city (Operation Province). In *Aktionen* that took place on August 8 and 9 and on August 18 and 19, thousands of Dvinsk Jews were murdered in the Pogulanka Forest, including 400 children from the ghetto orphanage. According to official German accounts, 9,012 Jews were killed in the period from July 13 to August 21. By the end of August 1941, 7,000 Jews were left in the ghetto, most of them workers employed by the German army or surviving members of the Jewish police force with their families, in addition to a small number of ghetto staff and workshop employees.

On November 7, 1941, a major *Aktion* was launched that lasted until November 9. In its course three thousand to five thousand Jews were murdered at Pogulanka. The first to be killed were the old, the ill, and the orphans, followed by persons who were unemployed or whose work was not essential in German eyes. "Essential" workers had been issued special pink passes (*Scheine*) on the eve of the *Aktion*, but their families were not spared, their turn coming at the end of the *Aktion*. In late November, the ghetto was put under strict quarantine because of a typhus epidemic that had broken out. The quarantine was in force for four months, and while it lasted, the ghetto was cut off from its supply sources and suffered from starvation, as a result of which more people died.

When the quarantine was lifted, in the spring of 1942, 1,000 Jews had survived—the ghetto staff, holders of the pink passes and some members of their families, plus a few who had managed to escape the *Aktion*, among them children hidden by local farmers. Half of these Jews lived in the ghetto and the others in their place of work. On May 1 the ghetto and all its institutions were liquidated, and the several hundred Jews who were in it at the time—among them members of the Jewish Council and the Jewish policemen—were killed. In Dvinsk itself, 450 Jews were left, mostly young men and women with no family ties, and a few unattached children. Many of the young people acquired arms and practiced using them, and some tried to escape in order to join the partisans in Belorussia, but these attempts, for the most part, were unsuccessful. In late October 1943 the Germans moved the surviving Jews of Dvinsk to the KAISERWALD camp; some of the young Jews resisted arrest with the arms they had, but only a few managed to escape. Several dozen Jewish craftsmen were left in the city, working for the security police, and on the eve of the German withdrawal in 1944, they too were taken to the camps. In April of that year, in the course of AKTION 1005, the Germans opened the mass graves in the pits at Pogulanka and other places, and burned the corpses in an effort to obliterate the traces of their crimes.

On July 27, 1944, the Red Army occupied Dvinsk. About twenty Jews were found there, having survived by hiding. By 1946, two thousand Jews had gathered in the city. They established an official Jewish community organization that maintained a cemetery, a synagogue, a Yiddish drama circle, and a Jewish (Yiddish) culture society.

In the course of the following years, the Jewish community in Dvinsk dwindled in size and its cultural activities were discontinued; in 1972 the Jewish cemetery was closed. A memorial for the Nazi victims, which the authorities put up in the city, makes no mention of Jews.

BIBLIOGRAPHY

Levin, D. *With Their Back to the Wall: The Armed Struggle of Latvian Jewry against the Nazis, 1941–1945.* Jerusalem, 1978. (In Hebrew.)

Levin, D., ed. *Latvia and Estonia.* In *Pinkas Hakehillot; Encyclopaedia of Jewish Communities.* Jerusalem, 1988. See pages 98–105. (In Hebrew.)

ESTHER HAGAR

DVORETSKI, ALTER (1906–1942), partisan commander. Dvoretski was born in DIATLOVO (Zhetl), studied law at the University of Vilna, and was admitted to the bar in 1938. He was a member of Po'alei Zion, where his main interest was sports activities. Under the Soviet regime (1939–1941) he practiced law in Novogrudok, in the Belorussian SSR.

At the beginning of the German occupation in 1941, Dvoretski settled in Diatlovo and was appointed chairman of its JUDENRAT (Jewish Council). Under the impact of the events he witnessed, he issued a call for rescue and revenge and organized an underground partisan group in the Diatlovo ghetto, with himself at the helm. He devised a plan to arm the Jewish youth in the surrounding towns and take them to the densely wooded Lipiczany Forest, in order to fight the Germans from there; this plan was also to be a means for saving Jews who were physically unfit for fighting.

Alter Dvoretski.

Dvoretski met with the Germans from time to time, while organizing the acquisition of arms and smuggling them into the ghetto. At all times, he carried a loaded pistol so as to be prepared for any eventuality. He provided weapons to a group of Soviet prisoners of war who had escaped from the camps in which they had been held, and steered them to the Lipiczany Forest. Another group of Jewish youth—refugees with no local family ties or property—also made its way out of the ghetto with Dvoretski's support in the form of advice, arms, and clothing.

Dvoretski worked out a detailed plan for armed resistance in case the Germans tried to carry out a massacre in the ghetto, but the plan was foiled by an act of betrayal. When Dvoretski himself went to the forest, he tried to implement his daring plans of rescuing the Jews of Diatlovo and the neighboring ghettos, and he dreamed of forming Jewish partisan regiments. What he found in the forest, however, were small groups of Soviet partisans—former prisoners of war—who had few arms in their possession and were not prepared to take the initiative in genuine attacks on the Germans. They had no contact with Moscow, lacked a proper command, and were altogether undisciplined; many had antisemitic tendencies. Dvoretski pressured the commander of several partisan groups to agree to launch an attack on the Diatlovo garrison in order to liberate the Jewish youth who were confined in the ghetto.

On the night of April 29, 1942, the partisan group made its way to Diatlovo, coming to a halt at the Christian cemetery on the outskirts of the town. A local peasant was sent to reconnoiter, and he returned with a report that a strong German detachment had come to the town in order to massacre the Jews on the next day, April 30. The Soviet partisans were not ready to risk an attack, and made their way back to their refuge in the forest. The plan for saving the Jews of Diatlovo had been frustrated. The commanders of the various partisan groups treated Dvoretski's proposals with a mixture of fear and envy; in the end, the partisans set an ambush and murdered Dvoretski and one of his comrades.

Dvoretski's activities in the ghetto enabled more than six hundred Jews from Diatlovo to flee during the liquidation of the ghetto on August 6, 1942, and to make their way to the Lipiczany Forest. There they formed a fighting battalion of partisans, commanded by Hirsch KAPLINSKI. This battalion eventually became a Jewish company (the third such) in the Soviet Orlianski-Borba battalion.

BIBLIOGRAPHY

Kahanovich, M. *The Fighting of the Jewish Partisans in Eastern Europe.* Tel Aviv, 1954. (In Hebrew.)

Kaplinski, B., ed. *Zhetel Record: A Memorial to the Jewish Community of Zhetel.* Tel Aviv, 1957. (In Yiddish.)

ELISHEVA SHAUL

ENCYCLOPEDIA of the HOLOCAUST

ENCYCLOPEDIA of the HOLOCAUST

Israel Gutman, Editor in Chief

Volume 2

Yad Vashem
The Holocaust Martyrs' and Heroes'
Remembrance Authority
Jerusalem

Sifriat Poalim Publishing House
Tel Aviv

MACMILLAN LIBRARY REFERENCE USA
Simon & Schuster Macmillan
NEW YORK

Simon & Schuster and Prentice Hall International
LONDON MEXICO CITY NEW DELHI SINGAPORE SYDNEY TORONTO

Macmillan Publishing Company
866 Third Avenue
New York, New York 10022
Collier Macmillan Canada, Inc.
Library of Congress Catalog Card Number: 89-13466
Printed in the United States of America

printing number
1 2 3 4 5 6 7 8 9 10

Library of Congress Cataloging-in-Publication Data

Encyclopedia of the Holocaust / Israel Gutman, editor in chief.
p. cm.
Includes bibliographical references.
ISBN 0-02-896090-4 (set)
Trade edition ISBN 0-02-546705-0 (set)
Two-volume edition ISBN 0-02-864527-8 (set)
1. Holocaust, Jewish (1939–1945)—Dictionaries. I. Gutman, Israel.
D804.3.E53 1990 89-13466
940.53'18'-03—dc20 CIP

Acknowledgments of sources and permissions to use previously published materials are made in Acknowledgments, page xix.

Complete and unabridged edition 1995

E

EAST ASIA. *See* Japan; Rescue of Polish Jews via East Asia; Shanghai.

EASTERN BATTALIONS. *See* Ostbataillone.

EAST INDUSTRY, INC. *See* Ostindustrie GmbH.

EBENSEE, subcamp of the MAUTHAUSEN concentration camp, created on November 18, 1943, about 2.5 miles (4 km) from the town of Ebensee in the Salzkammergut district of Upper AUSTRIA, at the foot of the Alps. The purpose of the camp was to provide labor for the construction of a system of tunnels in the side of a mountain to house a rocket-research factory. The small section of the tunnels that was completed went down 76 feet (250 m) into the mountain, was coated with concrete, and was several stories high.

The camp consisted of thirty-two dwelling huts and service buildings, including a crematorium. Most of the prisoners arrived from the main Mauthausen camp and its other satellites. At the height of occupancy, there were 18,437 prisoners in Ebensee. The first camp commandant was SS-Obersturmführer Otto Riemer, who in May 1944, while drunk, fired on a group of prisoners returning from work, killing 9 of them. After his subsequent removal from office, the position was occupied by SS-Hauptsturmführer Anton Ganz. The *Lagerälteste* (camp elder) was a German criminal offender named Magnus, who had occupied this office previously at the main Mauthausen camp. With his two assistants, also criminal offenders, he instituted a rule of terror among the prisoners. The camp registrar, who recorded the list of those who died at Ebensee, was Camille Scholtes, a prisoner from Luxembourg. The prisoners were of many nationalities, in particular Russian, Yugoslav, and French. Some staff positions were held by Germans, Spaniards, and Czechs.

In early June 1944 the first Jews arrived in Ebensee. As a result of the particularly difficult conditions and the cruel treatment meted out to them, their mortality rate was far higher than that of the non-Jewish prisoners. Early in 1945 the pace of work in digging the tunnels was intensified, and additional consignments of prisoners, including many Jews, were brought in. In mid-April of that year, inmates who had been transferred from the evacuated satellite camps to Mauthausen were sent to Ebensee; three consignments of 7,401 prisoners from MELK arrived.

The increased overcrowding in the camp brought with it a vast deterioration in the conditions of sanitation and a reduction in the food rations. In Block 23, where feeble prisoners were assembled, instances of cannibalism occurred. About eighty corpses were removed from that block daily. The mortality rate in the camp increased so greatly that the crematorium could not burn all the corpses. The sick were obliged to dig pits, into which the corpses were thrown; the bodies were then covered with a thin layer of earth. In April alone, 4,547 out of the 16,000 prisoners then in Ebensee died.

On April 30, most of the German prisoners were released and forced labor ended. At the roll call on May 5, the camp commandant, Ganz, asked the prisoners to go into Tunnel No. 5 so that they would not be wounded by the firing from the battles. When the prisoners refused, Ganz and his escort, followed by all the SS personnel, left the camp; its command was handed over to a local guard unit. On the following day, May 6, an American army unit arrived at Ebensee and the camp was liberated. At the entrance to Tunnel No. 5 a locomotive was found, with its water tank full of explosives. Apparently, it was intended to blow up the tunnel in which all the prisoners were to be assembled.

It is estimated that about eleven thousand persons died at Ebensee.

BIBLIOGRAPHY

Eckstein, B. *Mauthausen: Concentration and Annihilation Camp.* Jerusalem, 1984. (In Hebrew.)

Le Chêne, E. *Mauthausen: The History of a Death Camp.* London, 1971.

Marsalek, H., and K. Hacker. *Kurzgeschichte der Konzentrationslager Mauthausen und seiner drei grössten Nebenlager Gusen, Ebensee, und Melk.* Vienna, n.d.

BENYAMIN ECKSTEIN

ECLAIREURS ISRAÉLITES DE FRANCE

(French Jewish Scouts; EIF), pluralist and traditionalist scouting movement founded by Robert GAMZON in 1923. By 1939 the EIF was established in the Paris region, in the east of FRANCE, and in several other communities. From September 1939, it set up children's homes in the southwest of the country. After the armistice with Germany in June 1940, the movement redeployed in the unoccupied zone while continuing to function in Paris, despite the German prohibition against scouting. Together with the children's homes, which began to take in the children of Jews interned in camps, the movement organized in the south of France a number of rural groups made up partly of young foreign Jews. Although the EIF was a full member of Scoutisme Français (the French scout movement), established under the auspices of the Vichy government in October 1940, it was nevertheless forced to join the southern branch (UGIF-South) of the UNION GÉNÉRALE DES ISRAÉLITES DE FRANCE, the compulsory Jewish organization, at the end of 1941. The position of the EIF was somewhat enhanced when Gamzon was appointed to the administrative council of the UGIF, and the Eclaireurs constituted the latter's Fourth Section, which dealt with issues concerning young people.

The first deportations of Jews from France in March 1942 and the massive roundups that summer led to the creation of EIF's social service, La Sixième (The Sixth). Originally under the cover of UGIF, and later functioning entirely in the underground, La Sixième developed a rescue network that provided, essentially for children, false identities, placement among non-Jews, and transportation across the French borders. Despite the dissolution of the Fourth Section by the COMMISSARIAT GÉNÉRALE AUX QUESTIONS JUIVES (General Office for Jewish Affairs) in January 1943, EIF's educational activities continued until the following autumn, when the centers began to disband. During that winter an EIF fighting underground came into being, called the Compagnie Marc Haguenau, after the leader of La Sixième, who had committed suicide when captured by the Gestapo. Incorporated into both the Organisation Juive de Combat (Jewish Fighting Organization) and the Armée Secrète (Gen. Charles de GAULLE's underground faction), the company took part in the liberation of the southwest of France. One hundred and fifty members of the EIF, chiefly in La Sixième, lost their lives. The organization succeeded in rescuing several thousand Jews.

BIBLIOGRAPHY

L'activité des organisations juives en France sous l'occupation. Paris, 1947.

Michel, A. *Les Eclaireurs Israélites de France pendant la Seconde Guerre Mondiale.* Paris, 1984.

Pougatch, I. *Un bâtisseur: Robert Gamzon.* Paris, 1971.

ALAIN MICHEL

ECONOMIC-ADMINISTRATIVE MAIN OFFICE. *See* Wirtschafts-Verwaltungshauptamt.

EDELMAN, MAREK (b. 1921), a commander of the WARSAW GHETTO UPRISING. A native of Warsaw, Edelman was a member of Zukunft, the youth movement affiliated with the Jewish Socialist party, the BUND, and was one of its activists in the ghetto underground. When the relative standing of the young people in the underground gained in strength, Edelman became a member of the Bund's central institutions. In November 1942 he joined the ŻYDOWSKA ORGANIZACJA BOJOWA (Jewish Fighting Organization; ŻOB) and shortly afterward was appointed as his movement's representative in the organization's command.

In the Warsaw ghetto uprising of April 1943, Edelman was at first in charge of the "Brushmakers" area in the ghetto; following the withdrawal of the ŻOB forces, he and his men joined the group centered on 30 Franciszkanska Street. Edelman was among the last group of fighters to hold out in the ŻOB headquarters at 18 Mila Street, and he then crossed over to the "Aryan" side of Warsaw by way of the sewers, on May 10. In August 1944 Edelman served in the ranks of the ŻOB company that took part in the WARSAW POLISH UPRISING.

After the war, in 1945, Edelman published *The Bund's Role in the Defense of the Warsaw Ghetto*, in Polish and Yiddish. He also published *The Ghetto Fights* (1946), a short history of the uprising, in Polish, Yiddish, and English. He studied medicine and practiced it, remaining in Poland. From the early 1980s he was active in the Solidarity trade union movement.

BIBLIOGRAPHY

Krall, H. *Shielding the Flame: An Intimate Conversation with Dr. Marek Edelman, the Last Surviving Leader of the Warsaw Ghetto Uprising.* New York, 1986.

ISRAEL GUTMAN

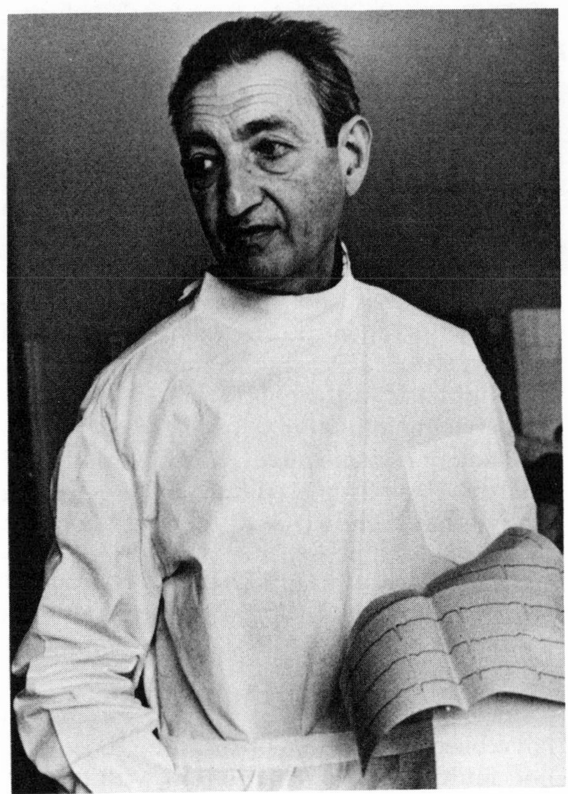

Marek Edelman.

EDELSTEIN, JACOB (1903–1944), chairman of the JUDENRAT (Jewish Council) in the THERESIENSTADT ghetto. Edelstein was born in Gorodenka, Galicia, and received a religious Zionist upbringing. During World War I his family moved to Brno (Ger., Brünn), the capital of Moravia, and from 1926 he was active in the Tekhelet-Lavan and He-Haluts Zionist youth movements. In 1929 he was elected Tekhelet-Lavan representative at the He-Haluts main office, and in 1933 he was appointed head of its Palestine Office in Prague. In the summer of 1937 Edelstein immigrated to Palestine and for three months worked there for Keren Hayesod (the Palestine Foundation Fund), but he was disappointed with that situation and decided to return to Prague, where he resumed his work as director of the Palestine Office.

On March 15, 1939, the day the Germans marched into Prague, the members of the Zionist leadership of Czechoslovakia held a meeting at which they decided that it was their duty to stay on and not abandon the Jewish population at a time of crisis. Edelstein became the leading personality in the

Jacob Edelstein.

Zionist leadership, was put in charge of emigration to Palestine, and before long became the official representative of the Jews in contacts with the Germans.

Until he was sent to Theresienstadt on December 4, 1941, Edelstein left the country for several trips abroad, with the Gestapo's permission, in order to look for ways and means to speed up the emigration of Jews. In May 1939 he visited Palestine, in November he was in Trieste, and at the end of that month he was in Vienna; in February 1940 he spent two days in Geneva and from there went to Berlin. He visited Bratislava in the fall of 1940, and in March 1941 he went to Amsterdam. In each of these places Edelstein met with the Jewish community leaders and the Zionist leadership, shared his information with them, and warned them of possible future developments. He had several opportunities to stay abroad rather than return to Czechoslovakia, but he always went back to Prague.

On October 18, 1939, Edelstein, with a group of a thousand men from Moravská Ostrava, left for Nisko, on the San River, south of Lublin, in connection with a German plan for the "resettlement" of Jews in the Lublin district (*see* NISKO AND LUBLIN PLAN). This plan ended in failure, and some of the deportees were returned to their place of origin. Edelstein went back to Prague in November 1939. His Nisko experience gave him an idea of the conditions in the east and of what was happening there. He decided to do everything in his power to ensure that the Jews of Czechoslovakia would not be dispatched to Poland, since he doubted whether they could hold out in the harsh conditions prevailing in German-occupied Poland. It was now his major concern to persuade the Germans to let the Jews stay in the Protectorate of BOHEMIA AND MORAVIA and to utilize them as manpower. Jewish labor as a means of saving Jewish lives became the core of Edelstein's policy, and this prompted him time and again to make proposals for the German exploitation of Jewish manpower.

In October 1941 the Germans decided on the establishment of the Theresienstadt ghetto as a temporary solution for the Jews of the Protectorate and a base for their future deportation to the east. The Jewish leadership, with Edelstein at its head, saw in the founding of Theresienstadt a personal achievement and the success of their efforts to gain permission for the Jews to stay in the Protectorate. They did not know that Theresienstadt was only a temporary arrangement. Edelstein arrived at Theresienstadt on December 4, 1941, and became the first chairman of its Judenrat. He was assisted by a deputy, Otto Zucker, and a council of twelve. The emphasis in the ghetto was on education of the young and on making the ghetto into a productive establishment. In January of 1943 Edelstein was dismissed from his post, on the charge that there was a discrepancy between the registered population of the Theresienstadt ghetto and the actual figure. On December 18, 1943, he was deported to AUSCHWITZ, where he and his family were shot to death, on June 20, 1944.

Edelstein's activities in Theresienstadt have been the subject of dispute. Those who find fault with him charge him with cooperating with the Nazis and with misreading the facts of the situation; their criticism is directed at his policy, but no doubt has been cast on his personal honesty and integrity. Others regard Edelstein as a hero who sacrificed himself for the sake of his people.

BIBLIOGRAPHY

Adler, H. G. *Theresienstadt, 1941–1945; Das Antlitz einer Zwangsgemeinschaft: Geschichte, Soziologie, Psychologie.* Tübingen, 1960.

Bondy, R. *"Elder of the Jews": Jakob Edelstein of Theresienstadt.* New York, 1989.

Lederer, Z. *Ghetto Theresienstadt.* London, 1953.

Rothkirchen, L. "The Zionist Character of the Self-Government of Terezin (Theresienstadt): A Study in Historiography." *Yad Vashem Studies* 11 (1976): 56–90.

MICHAL UNGER

EDEN, SIR ANTHONY (1897–1977), British statesman. A member of the Conservative party, Eden held a number of ministerial posts during the 1930s, and in 1935, at the age of thirty-eight, he was appointed foreign secretary. Eden was a strong supporter of the League of Nations and the concept of collective security. He resigned from the government of Neville Chamberlain in 1938, primarily because he did not support the policy of appeasing Fascist Italy. In the months prior to the outbreak of World War II Eden was, together with Winston CHURCHILL, an opponent of the foreign policies of his own party in government. When war broke out, Eden was offered the post of secretary of state for the British dominions, although not a seat in the War Cabinet. In May 1940, when Churchill became prime minister, Eden was appointed secretary of state for war. That December he was appointed foreign secretary and began to play a central role in the conduct of the war.

Despite the potentially vast influence of his office, and regardless of his close relationship with Churchill, Eden made little personal contribution to British policy, either on Palestine or concerning the fate of European Jewry. He showed little interest in either problem, and faithfully adopted the policies of his senior advisers in the Foreign Office. The specific terms of the WHITE PAPER on Palestine of 1939 were of little interest to the Foreign Office, but the redirection of Palestine policy that it represented (against the growth of the Jewish national home and in favor of Arab demands on the future of the Palestine Mandate) was a major cornerstone of British Middle East policy. The internal British dissension during the war on the fate of the White Paper policy caused the Foreign Office to oppose any proposal, including relief and rescue plans, that would have singled out Jews as victims of Nazism. The Foreign Office feared that such measures would strengthen Jewish group identity and further the interests of the Zionists. According to Eden's private secretary, Oliver Harvey, the foreign secretary expressed on at least two occasions a definite dislike for Jews (and a strong preference for Arabs). But this attitude was so widespread within the Foreign Office that it is doubtful whether Eden personally contributed anything unique to the general indifference to the Holocaust. The exceptions were his statement in Parliament on December 17, 1942, which described and condemned Nazi atrocities against Jews and promised punishment of the perpetrators, and his endorsement, in July and August 1944, of Jewish Agency requests that Auschwitz be bombed (*see* AUSCHWITZ, BOMBING OF). However, Eden's staff managed to deflect his concern, and since he was distracted by other foreign-policy issues, he did not pursue the bombing proposal.

In his subsequent career, Eden was prime minister when the Anglo-French-Israeli Sinai campaign was undertaken in 1956.

BIBLIOGRAPHY

Carlton, D. *Anthony Eden: A Biography.* London, 1981.

James, R. R. *Anthony Eden.* London, 1986.

Wasserstein, B. *Britain and the Jews of Europe, 1939–1945.* Oxford, 1979.

Zweig, R. *Britain and Palestine during the Second World War.* London, 1986.

RONALD W. ZWEIG

EDINETI (Russ., Edintsy), town in northern BESSARABIA; site of a transit camp. On the eve of World War II, Edineti had a Jewish population of fifty-three hundred, 90 percent of the total. In June 1940 Edineti, with the rest of Bessarabia, became Soviet territory, but a year later, following the German invasion of the Soviet Union, the Romanian army reoccupied the area. Some one thousand Jews were killed by the Romanian troops, assisted by the local population; the rest were expelled to TRANSNISTRIA, after having wandered all over Bessarabia amid great suffering. Following the expulsion of the local Jewish population, Edineti became the site of a transit camp for Jews from BUKOVINA, pending their deportation, and Jews from Banila, Vaşcăuti, Jadova, Vizhnitsa (Vijniţa), Ciudei, and Lujeni, as well as from Herta in Moldavia, were sent there. These were remnants of the Jewish communities in those places, survivors of massacres conducted by the Romanian forces and by local Romanian and Ukrainian inhabitants; before being taken to Edineti they had been held in the Storojineti ghetto.

Also brought to Edineti were Jews from Bessarabia whose deportation to Transnistria, in August 1941, had been interdicted by the German authorities. The first of these groups of Jews arrived in Edineti on August 20, 1941. They were crowded into stables and cattle sheds, behind barbed-wire fences, many living without a roof over their heads. Except for small quantities of water, the Romanians did not supply the Jews with any rations, and every day seventy to one hundred of them died from starvation and exhaustion. Anyone trying to escape ran the risk of being put to death. The mayor of the town was bribed by some Jews, and permitted them to purchase food. A Romanian army medical officer was also bribed, and as a result twenty-five hundred Jewish prisoners in Edineti were allowed to move into abandoned Jewish school buildings situated outside the camp. All the male prisoners were put to work on road building.

More and more groups of deportees converged upon Edineti, their total number amounting to twenty-three thousand. Worst off were the Jews from Bessarabia, who had been on the road for a long time, had gone through much suffering, and were completely destitute. The mortality rate was extremely high, and in October 1941, 85 percent of the children in the camp died. A typhus epidemic broke out in the camp, and for lack of medicine and food many of the prisoners fell victim to the disease.

On October 11, 1941, the camp was evacuated. The prisoners were divided into two groups. The first was dispatched to MARCULEŞTI, Bessarabia, and from there to Transnistria, hundreds being murdered en route by their military escorts. The second group was left in a field out in the open, with no shelter from the rain and snow. Five hundred of that group, mostly women and children, died during the following night, and the rest were deported to Transnistria by way of the Atachi border post.

On the way to Atachi, all the Jews who could not keep up with the pace of the column were murdered on the spot. A total of eight hundred Jews perished in this second group.

The number of Jews who survived Edineti and the subsequent stay in Transnistria is not known. Most of the prisoners of the Edineti camp were killed either before its evacuation or on the way to Transnistria.

BIBLIOGRAPHY

Ancel, J., and T. Lavi, eds. *Rumania,* vol. 2. In *Pinkas Hakehillot; Encyclopaedia of Jewish Communities.* Jerusalem, 1980. (In Hebrew.)

Reicher, M., and Y. Magan-Shitz, eds. *Yad L'Yedinits: Memorial Book for the Jewish Community of Yedinits-Bessarabia.* Tel Aviv, 1979. (In Hebrew.)

JEAN ANCEL

EDUCATION ON THE HOLOCAUST. [*The attempt to translate the Holocaust experience into a teaching environment is the subject of this entry, which is divided into three articles:* Great Britain; United States and Israel; *and* West Germany.]

Great Britain

The tremendous interest manifested by the British in the history of modern wars beginning in the eighteenth century is hardly surprising, given Britain's role in most of them. There has been particular interest in World War II, its outcome having rightly been seen as decisive for the survival of the island kingdom in the twentieth century. This is reflected in the great demand for books, films, and television documentaries on all aspects of the war, especially where Britain was concerned in any way.

What is true in British society overall is similarly reflected in the educational system. The study of British history (including participation in the major international and imperial wars) takes priority at the primary (ages five to eleven) and secondary (ages eleven to sixteen, and up to eighteen) levels of education, and even at polytechnics and universities. The British approach to history (as to much else) can well be described as "insular."

It follows, then, that in Britain today the academic study of the Holocaust—at whatever level—is minimal, or even nonexistent. Whereas some small change has been noticeable at the end of the 1980s, there is little widespread interest in the Holocaust in British society, and, consequently, it is not studied systematically and in depth in the educational system as a whole.

British society's rejection of the subject is reflected in the academic response. Both seem to dislike intensely what they see as a Jewish "preoccupation" with the suffering endured by Jews during the war. Its extent is still acknowledged, but society and the academic world believe that it should be set within the wider context of the overall suffering that the war produced. Today, the Holocaust is regarded by most (but not all) British people and academics as being very largely a "Jewish" subject of interest.

One could argue that since so-called Christians committed the crime of the Holocaust, the subject actually "belongs" more to them than to the victimized Jews, since the burden of "coming to terms" with that deliberate and systematic exercise of terror is firmly in the Christian court. But in a supposedly Christian country like Britain, this approach causes tremendous religious and psychological problems. Yet that is only the half of it. At the heart of the Holocaust lie human prejudice and the practical execution of the murderous irrationality that is present in all human beings. As elsewhere in the world, in Britain people simply cannot face up to the uncomfortable question that any study of the Holocaust is bound to pose: was the Nazi experience really that "unique," given that the executioners were human beings and not monsters from another planet?

In Britain, the reservations and rejections concerning the Holocaust are rationalized thus: "Why don't the Jews forget all about it?"; "It all happened such a long time ago"; and—more perniciously, in the academic world, because historically incorrect—"The Holocaust does not deserve any special study since it was only a small part of the war."

A survey conducted in Great Britain in 1987 and 1988 under the auspices of the United Kingdom Yad Vashem Academic and Educational Sub-Committee (Fox, 1989) covered the teaching of the Holocaust at the university and polytechnic level, at teacher-training colleges, and at secondary schools in the state and private systems. The attitude of most respondents to the survey was rather positive, but less so in the case of the universities. Many replies from the latter were somewhat negative, and some verged on the hostile.

Where the replies were positive—in the sense that particular teachers or lecturers expressed regret that they were unable to devote more time to the subject—it was remarkable how often the diary of Anne FRANK (in book, film, or exhibit form) was quoted as having been the inspiration for their own interest and that of their students. Other sparks igniting interest were the American television series "Holocaust" and the British film series "The World at War."

Most of the negative replies objected to the Holocaust being studied as a special subject, that is, in depth and systematically, in its own right. The gist of the negative replies, mostly from the universities, was that any elevation of the subject to such a "special" status would tent to "distort" its role in the war. Yet Yehuda Bauer and Lucy S. Dawidowicz, among others, view the key to understanding Hitler's imperatives for war up to 1939 and beyond as his determination to exterminate Russian and then European Jewry, within the context of a war for *Lebensraum* in the east at Russia's expense. Given the pan-European nature of the Nazis' systematic collection and slaughter of Europe's Jews during the war, it is nonsense to suggest that the subject was of "secondary" importance at the time.

In Britain there are no university chairs in Holocaust studies (compared to the plethora of those in history), nor are there likely to be, because the general lack of interest is compounded by the total reluctance—of Jews and gentiles alike—to fund such professorships. Indeed, there is only one university, that of Leicester, which has actually presented a special course (as part of a bachelor's degree program) on the Holocaust. A Centre of Holocaust Studies has now been established there, with the aim of developing a wider interest in the subject.

But in most other British institutions of higher learning, the picture is a dismal one. In the main, the subject is touched upon in more general courses on twentieth-century European history, or in more specific courses on Nazi Germany. Again, in the abovementioned survey, some replies asserted that there was so little time to cover everything that any more time devoted to the Holocaust would "distort" the history courses presented to the students. Given the almost total freedom that British universities and polytechnics have to devise their own courses, such an attitude is disappointing, the more so since present-day research and publications on the Holocaust in all its aspects far outnumber those on more "conventional" facets of World War II.

The situation is somewhat different, however, for the secondary schools. In British schools, when European or world history is dealt with, students are expected to have a much wider and more general education than at the post-secondary level. The schools, too, have virtually no freedom in devising examination syllabuses, which are determined largely by the examination boards throughout the country, although in 1989 the introduction by the government of a national curriculum was planned.

The lack of any specialized teaching on the Holocaust at the secondary level is, therefore, more understandable. On the other hand, it is encouraging that questions on Nazi Germany and, indeed, on the Holocaust, have begun to appear in some advanced-level (pre-university) examination papers. This forces teachers to pay more attention to the subject in the classroom, generating—as many admitted in their replies to the survey—greater interest among pupils and students.

Not all the results of the survey were negative. It disclosed, for example, that many departments of religious studies—at schools, teacher-training colleges, and even polytechnics and universities—dealt with the subject of the Holocaust in one way or another. Even departments of psychology and sociology were prepared to confront issues lying at the heart of the Holocaust, especially if they had a contemporary relevance. This was found to be so more frequently at the school level, where often (it was admitted) the Holocaust was studied less for its own sake than as a means to promote antiracist education in Britain's increasingly multi-ethnic society.

This brings up the question of whether the Holocaust should be studied as a special subject in its own right, or subsumed within antiracial studies. One cannot entirely deny the validity of the second approach, which constitutes another way of keeping the subject of the Holocaust alive and generating interest in it. The latter point is especially important with regard to the education of sixteen-to-eighteen-year-olds, and even a single question on the Holocaust in their public examinations is a positive step forward in furthering their knowledge of it. Yet a more specialized historical approach seems desirable: not only is the Holocaust insufficiently known about in Britain and in the British educational system, but its intrinsic importance and the scholarly apparatus available for its close investigation make it imperative that it be studied more widely, in Britain as elsewhere.

BIBLIOGRAPHY

Fox, J. P. *Report on 1987 Survey of United Kingdom Teaching on "The Holocaust" or "Nazi Final Solution of the Jewish Question" and Related Subjects.* Leicester, England, 1989.

JOHN P. FOX

United States and Israel

Holocaust education encompasses a very diverse range of activities in formal and informal teaching environments where the history of the racist anti-Jewish ideology and mass murder of the Jews during World War II is presented, and lessons and meanings are drawn from it. Isolated pockets of teaching about the Holocaust exist in Europe, South America, Australia, and South Africa, many of them under the rubric of Jewish education in a particular institution or school. However, in relative terms these are quite limited. Holocaust education is most advanced and widespread in the United States and Canada, and in Israel.

United States. The underlying aim of Holocaust education in the United States is to direct students to confront the past in order to recognize their individual responsibilities to act morally. Therefore, educators generally give much weight to the issues that relate to the participants in murder and to the bystanders. The major questions raised in connection with the perpetrators—the Nazis and their helpers—are: How were intelligent and cultured people turned into mass murderers? Could a similar event happen again? Could it happen to us? What must I, personally, do in order to sensitize myself to this potential danger? As to the bystanders, the aim is to grapple with such questions as: How could the average good people of the world have done so little to stop these horrors? Did they not know? Did they not care? What role was played by the Allied governments, especially the United States administration? What did the churches do in response? What are the implications for today in the light of news reports about world events?

Teaching about the Holocaust and its background (such as antisemitism and the pre-Holocaust history of European Jewry) helps strengthen that part of America's civic legacy which stresses the values of democracy, pluralism, and the responsibility of the individual for shaping society. The methodologies used most commonly in American schools tend to rely heavily on literature (particularly fiction), film, open-ended discussions on how students feel as they "relate" to this material, and role-playing and other techniques from the social sciences.

Isolated public-school educators began teaching about the Holocaust during the late 1950s, but significant interest in the subject was first expressed only in the early 1970s. The treatment of Nazism and its victims in public-school textbooks, however, had been systematically observed for over three decades. The earliest studies, carried out in 1961, showed that the basic facts of the Holocaust were glossed over and Nazi persecution of the Jews was greatly minimized. If the Holocaust was mentioned, the few lines devoted to it often created a distorted and misleading picture. By 1978, the record had hardly improved.

Aside from any earlier initiatives undertaken by individual teachers in their classrooms, the first single official program of instruction on the Holocaust in a public-school setting was launched in 1972 in Barrington, Massachusetts. In 1975, Philadelphia and New York City became the first public-school systems to pioneer systemwide curricula. Several years later the Baltimore school system became the first to mandate teaching of the Holocaust. Not so long afterward, non-Jewish parochial schools began to incorporate Holocaust teaching into their school programs.

The development and spread of teaching programs did not proceed without resistance. Some American ethnic minorities feared that Holocaust teaching units would turn public opinion against their national groups. The New York Association of Black Educators argued the irrelevance of Holocaust studies for blacks. Even some Jews opposed its teaching in public schools, fearing trivialization of the subject and a possible upswing of antisemitism.

Holocaust curricula designed for public schools were conceptualized in accordance with the needs of the participating school or school district, or in response to larger trends in education and society. New York City's curriculum was developed against the background of ethnic tension between blacks and Jews. The study of the Holocaust was to be taught not as a period in Jewish history but as a case of monumental bigotry, and thus a key topic in values education. In a similar vein, the Baltimore school system developed its curriculum as part of a commitment to stressing multicultural realities with the aim of reducing prejudice.

The extent to which the subject is being introduced and taught within American public secondary schools today is difficult to determine. Individual states continue to pass laws mandating Holocaust instruction, and many city- and state-sponsored curricula are now being written. Still, with no central organ for the dissemination of materials, efforts to provide teachers with materials and training are haphazard. Despite growing public awareness, the advances do not appear to have spread uniformly across the nation. According to one survey in 1983, fewer than three hundred secondary schools out of thirty thousand in the United States incorporated Holocaust studies into their curricula. Another small-scale survey conducted the same year indicated that 95 percent of the administrators, teachers, and students interviewed from public and private schools believed adequate coverage of the Holocaust in their school curriculum was lacking.

In the United States, informal education on the Holocaust is, by its very nature, broader, and is consequently varied, fluid, and extremely uneven in quality. It includes a myriad of activities in community centers, synagogue groups, afternoon and Sunday schools, church programs, youth groups, and adult-education centers. The range and type of programs are limited only by the imagination of those who initiate them.

Jewish education in the United States followed its own path of development with regard to the teaching of the Holocaust. Whereas the EICHMANN TRIAL (1961–1962) marked a turning point in Holocaust awareness for Israeli educators, it was mainly the occasion of the twentieth anniversary of the WARSAW GHETTO UPRISING (1963) that brought the Holocaust into the consciousness of American Jewish educators. The National Council of Jewish Education at its 1963 conference discussed the subject. Some conference participants explained their avoidance of the Holocaust as a response to parental fears for their children's emotional well-being, while others held that Judaism should only be a joyful experience for the students. More prevalent was the anxiety of both parents and educators that children would develop feelings of insecurity and fear that they themselves might become victims.

As of 1964, throughout the United States only two local Jewish education agencies had prepared guidelines for teaching the Holocaust. Between 1964 and the end of the decade, outlines for teachers were produced by the Bureaus of Jewish Education in New York, Los Angeles, and Philadelphia.

Educators began articulating goals for teaching the Holocaust, but the content and tone of their discussions, particularly in the 1960s, emphasized the emotional meaning of the Holocaust for students. Since students had no personal experience or memory of the events themselves, one of the tasks of the educator was to employ an intensive educational program to evoke pain. This often entailed the use of simulations, or an emphasis on horrors and atrocities. Almost overnight, it seemed, educators went from an initial concern about the negative effects of the Holocaust on Jewish identity to making the strengthening of Jewish identity into a nearly universal article of faith for Holocaust education. It was hoped that studying the Holocaust, like other periods in Jewish history, would link students to the Jewish past and future; by remembering those who were lost in the Holocaust, students would develop a strengthened feeling of solidarity with other Jews and a deeper commitment to the survival of the Jewish people.

With few conceptual precedents to go on, Jewish educators in the United States had to construct their own frameworks from which to view and make meaning of the Holocaust. Perhaps the most natural response was to examine the event through the traditional lens of Jewish experience, by seeking to build the Holocaust into contemporary Jewish consciousness through language, ritual, and prayer. The Holocaust was also shown to be instructive for dealing with the issues of the day. Jews, knowing the dangers of RACISM and intolerance better than anyone, had a special responsibility to help advance the frontiers of civil rights and social equality. The ideals they espoused were universal, but the authority of the universal message was drawn from the Jewish historical experience.

By the mid-1970s, there was a discernible attempt to break the particularist view of the Holocaust held by Jews. Some teachers argued that unless political, theological, and philosophical issues were addressed by Holocaust curricula, the subject would never penetrate the public-school arena. The materials used and produced during this period reflect a trend toward viewing the Holocaust within a framework of universal values. Without excluding the goal of strengthening Jewish identity, the vision for Holocaust education in some sectors was broadened to include cultivation of a commitment to universal moral principles among both Jewish and non-Jewish students.

In the late 1970s some prominent American Jews began lamenting the exaggerated place of importance the Holocaust had assumed in Jewish life. They felt that the event was becoming the strongest focus of Jewish identity and was being substituted for real Jewish learning and identity. The more recent curricula reflect this new attitude, which defends the importance of teaching the Holocaust while recognizing the necessity of restoring it to its proper historical perspective. The impression of increased Holocaust coverage in Jewish schools is confirmed by the few systematic surveys available. A 1973 survey conducted in the United States and Canada found that 276 out of 354 schools taught about the Holocaust, and approximately a quarter of them offered it as a separate course. In 1981, a mini-survey conducted among Jewish educators indicated that almost all schools offered a Holocaust course of twenty-five to thirty hours of instruction.

Israel. The situation in Israeli schools is different in many respects. Since the autumn of 1982, the study of the Holocaust has been a compulsory subject in the history syllabus of government high schools (both state secular and state religious schools). It is mandated to be taught for thirty instructional hours in the eleventh or twelfth grade, depending on the preference of the local school. The methodological approach is historical. Primary sources are presented, and the instruction emphasizes factual information, the complexities of the historical situation, and the difficulties involved in attempting to arrive at generalizations or conclusions.

The focus of the subject matter is also different. While in the United States the issues seen to be most relevant are those related to the perpetrators and the bystanders, Israeli students concentrate their attention on the Jewish victims. The aim is to raise questions about the meaning of the Holocaust in the framework of Jewish history and as Jews living in Israel after the Holocaust: Why were the Jews murdered? Must they always be victims? What can the Jews do about their circumstances? In sharp contrast to the situation described above, where the meanings and implications of the Holocaust are mostly comprehended on an individual level, the most critical search for answers in Israel is a collective, national one: What is the central lesson of the Holocaust for Israeli society today? Is there a danger of Jews again becoming victims of genocidal slaughter? Or is the danger that Jews, forced to be militarily strong, are also becoming morally weak, and increasingly desensitized to the suffering of others?

These differences in what is seen to be the core of this history are significantly manifested in the controversy over the place and meaning of the Holocaust in human history. One extreme focuses on the evil that men do and places the context for the Holocaust in "man's inhumanity to man" and the universal lessons that can be learned from this extreme case study. Naturally, there is an emphasis on the parallels between this event and other examples of genocide and selective mass murder that have occurred in the past.

On the other extreme the focus is on the specific victims, the Jews, and the context is the long history of antisemitic persecutions, the particular situation of the Jews, and their unique position in this history (as compared with other victims of mass persecution). The emphasis is on those elements that distinguish the Holocaust from all other events in history. Between these extremes each educator finds his or her place.

Higher Education in the United States and Israel. Every tertiary institution in Israel that teaches the humanities offers an extensive range of courses on the Holocaust, either in a separate department or as part of a larger field of study, such as contemporary Jewish history or German history. To be certified to teach history in high school, education students must take at least one university course on the Holocaust.

The situation on American campuses is different. Naturally, Jewish history occupies a much more marginal place, and as a rule very few courses in it are offered at the average university. Nonetheless, in many places where little is taught about how Jews lived for thousands of years, there is an isolated course on how they were murdered in World War II. Teaching the Holocaust without the context of Jewish history may risk skewing the focus of the topic. Another serious problem is that alongside some highly qualified scholars who teach at North American universities, including two who hold full chairs in the field, a majority of those who teach Holocaust courses on the tertiary level are lecturers without specialized knowledge in this area of Jewish and general history who have transferred from another discipline in order to fill this gap.

BIBLIOGRAPHY

Friedlander, H. "Postscript: Towards a Methodology of Teaching about the Holocaust." In *The Holocaust—Ideology, Bureaucracy, and Genocide: The San Jose Papers*, pp. 323–345. Millwood, N.Y., 1981.

Gutman, Y., and C. Schatzker. *The Holocaust and Its Significance*. Jerusalem, 1984.

Pate, G. S. *The Treatment of the Holocaust in United States History Text Books*. New York, 1980.

Schatzker, C. "Teaching of the Holocaust: Dilemmas and Considerations." *Annals of the American Academy of Political and Social Science* 450 (July 1980): 218–226.

Strom, M. S., and W. Parsons. *Facing History and Ourselves: The Holocaust and Human Behavior*. Watertown, Mass., 1982.

ELLY DLIN and SHARON GILLERMAN

West Germany

When World War II ended, the schools in Germany were without history textbooks. The Allies who had occupied Germany and were administering the country had removed all books dating from the Nazi period, and it was about ten years before new history textbooks became available. Until the 1950s the Holocaust, and how to confront it, was not a subject raised in German schools.

A wave of swastika graffiti and desecration of synagogues that swept Germany toward the end of 1959 impelled the authorities, the churches, and the student and teachers' organizations to inquire about the extent to which the Holocaust was being taught in German schools, and how it was being presented in textbooks.

Each of the states comprising the Federal Republic of Germany has its own curricula and textbooks. Surveys, comparative studies, and other projects have considered the problems of teaching the Holocaust, and a German-Israeli conference was held that examined the history textbooks and submitted recommendations for improvements. However, no survey has been made of the actual teaching of the Holocaust in West Germany, and it is difficult to define how it is being taught, since every teacher is free to supplement or detract from the official curriculum or textbook contents as he or she sees fit.

In the chapters on Jewish history and the Holocaust in the West German history texts, it was found that three general approaches exist: (1) teaching the Holocaust as a moral obligation, in view of the crimes that were committed; (2) teaching the Holocaust as part of civic and political education; and (3) teaching the Holocaust as a basic element in history, indispensable for the study of Western civilization and German history. The Holocaust is described in detail in all the textbooks, and the charge that had been made, that knowledge of the Holocaust was being withheld, had no basis in fact.

On the other hand, most of the textbook descriptions of the Holocaust do not place it in the context of Jewish history, before or after the Holocaust, or in the continuity of European and German history. The majority of the textbooks limit themselves to a narrative description of the events, with expressions of dismay and shock added; no attempt is made to analyze the roots of antisemitism and its place in Nazi ideology and the Third Reich. Most of the books also avoid any serious in-depth consideration of the question of responsibility and culpability for the Holocaust, and of those who bore that responsibility, aside from mentioning Adolf Hitler, a handful of other leading figures, and the murderous personnel who perpetrated the actual killings. The greater part of the information and findings brought to light by Holocaust research in the past few decades has not found its way into the textbooks.

BIBLIOGRAPHY

Quenzer, W. "Young Germans' View of Auschwitz." *Patterns of Prejudice* 14/4 (October 1980): 10–17.

Renn, W. F. "Confronting Genocide: The Depiction of the Persecution of the Jews and the Holocaust in West German History Textbooks." In *Contemporary Views of the Holocaust,* edited by R. L. Braham, pp. 157–180. Boston, 1983.

Schatzker, C. "Die Juden in den deutschen Geschichtsbüchern: Schulbuchanalyse zur Darstellung der Juden, des Judentums und des Staates Israel." *Schriftenreihe der Bundeszentrale für Politische Bildung* 173 (1981): 1–188.

CHAIM SCHATZKER

Ilya Ehrenburg (center) with Jewish partisans from Vilna (1944).

EHRENBURG, ILYA GRIGORYEVICH (1891–1967), Russian Jewish writer and journalist. Ehrenburg lived abroad for many years, mostly in Paris, and was a foreign correspondent for Soviet newspapers. After the German invasion of France in 1940, he returned to the Soviet Union. Although Ehrenburg was an assimilated Jew and was steeped in Russian culture, his writings often dealt with Jewish subjects. During World War II he became increasingly conscious of his Jewish identity and expressed these feelings in his publications. In *Padenie Parizha* (The Fall of Paris; 1941) he denounced fascism and antisemitism, and in a poem written in 1940 he lamented the Nazi persecution of the Jews. During the war years he was a correspondent for *Krasnaia Zvezda* (Red Star), the newspaper of the Red Army, and played a leading role in anti-Nazi propaganda in the Soviet Union and abroad.

Ehrenburg was one of the most prominent personalities to be appointed to the JEWISH ANTIFASCIST COMMITTEE. In the committee's meetings and consultations he stressed the need to publicize the Jewish role in the war effort against the Nazis, and openly criticized manifestations of antisemitism among the Soviet population. He was one of the first in the Soviet Union to encourage the collection of documentary evidence on the murder of the Jews and on active Jewish resistance to the Nazis. Ehrenburg was the editor of *Merder fun Felker* (Murderers of Peoples; 2 vols., 1944–1945). Together with Vasily Grossman, he edited *Chernaya kniga* (The BLACK BOOK OF SOVIET JEWRY), a collection of documents on the Holocaust in the Soviet Union. He also co-sponsored *Krasnaya kniga* (The Red Book), which documented Jewish participation in the Red Army, the partisan movement, and the resistance to the Nazis in the ghettos. These books, however, were not released for publication, since it became Soviet policy to throw a veil over the Holocaust, a policy that became increasingly pronounced after the war. In the spring of 1945, official criticism was voiced against Ehrenburg's extreme anti-German stand.

The fate of the Jews during the war continued to preoccupy Ehrenburg in the postwar years. An abridged English translation of *Chernaya kniga* was published in New York in 1946, and the full version (which was smuggled out of the USSR), in 1980. Six volumes of his memoirs were serialized in the journal *Novyi Mir* between 1960 and 1965 under the title *Lyudi, gody, zhizn* (Men, Years, Life); at his death he was working on the concluding volumes. Ehrenburg bequeathed his entire archive to YAD VASHEM, including a complete, uncensored edition of *Chernaya kniga* and many personal letters from survivors.

BIBLIOGRAPHY

Goldberg, A. *Ilya Ehrenburg—Revolutionary, Novelist, Poet, War Correspondent, Propagandist: The*

Extraordinary Epic of a Russian Survivor. New York, 1984.

SHIMON REDLICH

EICHMANN, ADOLF (1906–1962), Nazi official who played a central role in organizing the anti-Jewish policies culminating in the "FINAL SOLUTION." Eichmann was born in Solingen, in the Rhineland; his father was an accountant. His mother died when he was eight years old, and the family—the father and five children—moved to Linz, Austria. Eichmann did not complete secondary school, nor did he finish the course in mechanics at the vocational school that he attended for two years. After holding several different jobs he became a traveling salesman for an American oil company, Vacuum Oil; using a motorcycle for his rounds, he had an accident in which he was seriously injured. In 1933 he was dismissed from his job. The previous year an acquaintance, Ernst KALTENBRUNNER, had persuaded Eichmann to join the Austrian National Socialist party, and eventually also the SS. When the latter was outlawed in Austria in 1933, Eichmann, now unemployed, moved to Germany. There he enlisted in the Austrian unit of the SS, where he also went through military training. He then served for a while in the DACHAU concentration camp.

In October 1934 Eichmann volunteered to work in the central office of the SD (Sicherheitsdienst; Security Service), then headed by Reinhard HEYDRICH, and moved to Berlin. At the time, Heinrich HIMMLER was chief of police in the SD. Eichmann first worked in the section that dealt with the FREEMASONS, and in 1935 he was moved to a new intelligence section, the Jewish section, then under Herbert Hagen. Henceforth Eichmann regarded the solution of the "Jewish question" in the Third Reich as his life mission.

Eichmann was now one of the chief planners of the anti-Jewish operations undertaken by the SS; before long, he was also responsible for their execution. At this time the SD and the Gestapo joined in an effort designed to speed up the emigration of the Jews from Germany, as part of which Hagen and Eichmann were sent in 1937 to Palestine and Egypt on a fact-finding mission. Eichmann's conclusion was that increased immigration of Jews into Palestine was not desirable, since the establishment of a Jewish state was not in the interest of the Third Reich.

Following the annexation of Austria to Germany in March 1938 (*see* ANSCHLUSS), Eichmann was sent to Vienna to organize the emigration of the Jews. It was here that he first revealed his organizational talent and his ability to put the anti-Jewish aims of the Nazis into practice. It was Eichmann who evolved a method of forced emigration, consisting of three elements: undermining the economic condition of the Jews by confiscation of their property; putting fear into their hearts by the use of terror; seizing control of Jewish communal institutions and forcing their leaders to cooperate (a foretaste of the JUDENRAT). In August 1938, in order to streamline the Jewish emigration process, Eichmann set up the ZENTRALSTELLE FÜR JÜDISCHE AUSWANDERUNG (Central Office for Jewish Emigration), whose purpose was to strip the Jews of all their belongings and leave them with no option but to seek emigration to some other country and to get there with the help of some Jewish organization (mainly the JOINT DISTRIBUTION COMMITTEE). Eichmann also took direct action to expel Jews, by pushing some of them into a no-man's-land across the Austrian border. Contrary to his previous reservations concerning Jewish immigration into Palestine, he now cooperated with the Jewish organizations that were running ALIYA BET ("illegal" immigration). When the Germans seized control of BOHEMIA AND MORAVIA, Eichmann introduced the system of forced emigration to PRAGUE, and, in the summer of 1939, he established in the Czech capital a Central Office for Jewish Emigration, on the model of the Vienna office. The pattern established by Eichmann had been adopted by the Reich leaders even earlier, in the wake of KRISTALLNACHT, and on January 24, 1939, on Hermann GÖRING's order, the Reichszentrale für Jüdische Auswanderung (Reich Central Office for Jewish Emigration) was set up in Germany under Heydrich in the Ministry of the Interior.

During 1938 and 1939, Eichmann's authority over Jewish policies grew rapidly; when war broke out, his area of operations was greatly widened and his own position strengthened. Following Himmler's creation in September 1939 of the REICHSSICHERHEITSHAUPTAMT (Reich Security Main Office; RSHA), under Heydrich, Eichmann was appointed head of the Jewish section in the Gestapo, whose chief at the time was Heinrich MÜLLER. Eichmann's authority exceeded that of a section chief. In practice he came directly under Heydrich, but from time to time he was also called in by Himmler. In 1939 and 1940 Eichmann played the central role in the expulsion of Poles and Jews from the Polish areas that had been incorporated into the Reich (*see* DEPORTATIONS). By that time Eichmann had already established, in coordination with Müller, the pattern for the mass expulsion of Jews in an operation in which Jews from Vienna and Czechoslovakia were deported to Nisko (*see* NISKO AND LUBLIN PLAN). On the basis of this pattern, the methods were developed for mass deportations throughout the Nazi period. The Nisko operation served as a precedent for the attempt to concentrate all the Jews of the Reich in the Lublin Reservation—the first phase in the Nazi leaders' search for a total solution to the "Jewish question." After Nisko, further attempts were made, under Eichmann's supervision, to expel Jews from several places in Germany itself, but they met with opposition in Germany and elsewhere, and the Lublin Reservation plan was rescinded.

In October 1940, Eichmann in person led the expulsion of 6,500 Jews from Baden-Pfalz and the Saar district to the south of France. The operation may have been connected with the MADAGASCAR PLAN; while this plan was being prepared by the German Foreign Ministry, Eichmann was working out his own detailed program for the creation of a huge police-controlled ghetto on that tropical island off the coast of Africa. Eichmann was, by this time, in undisputed control of the Jewish populations of Germany, the Ostmark (Austria), and the Protectorate of Bohemia and Moravia. From time to time he summoned the leaders of these Jewish populations to his office in Berlin to give them his orders, especially concerning the issue of forced emigration—orders that were then carried out under the watchful eye of Eichmann's representatives in the respective capitals. He had a network of officials in most of the German-occupied countries and in the satellite states, where they served as "advisers" to the governments, their task being to promote the implementation of anti-Jewish policies. The more prominent of these representatives were Alois BRUNNER, Theodor DANNECKER, Dieter WISLICENY, and Rolf GÜNTHER (Eichmann's deputy).

A significant change in Eichmann's activities came with the decision to execute the "final solution of the Jewish question," together with the war against the Soviet Union. The final form of the Jewish section in the RSHA had been laid down in March 1941, and henceforth the section bore the designation IV B 4. Eichmann now gave orders on various occasions prohibiting the emigration of Jews from the European continent, and he ceased cooperating with the organizers of the "illegal" immigration into Palestine. His operations reached their full extent after Himmler's order of October 1941 prohibiting the emigration of Jews, which coincided with the start of transports of Jews from Germany to the east. Preparations for mass murder had begun even earlier, in the summer of 1941, at which time Eichmann, on Himmler's order, held talks with Rudolf HÖSS, the commandant of AUSCHWITZ, on the practical details of the mass murder.

In October 1941 Eichmann took part in more discussions on the subject, conducted by those charged with the implementation of the "Final Solution." At this point, he was promoted to *Obersturmbannführer* (lieutenant colonel). Since Eichmann was the officer in charge of transporting the Jews of Europe to the extermination sites, Heydrich asked him to prepare the WANNSEE CONFERENCE, where the implementation of the operation was outlined, with the participation of all government bodies that had a part in the "Final Solution." It was Eichmann who sent the invitations to the various officials, drafted Heydrich's address to the conference, and took down the minutes. Following the conference, he called in his representatives from the various countries to plan the operation. In 1942 and 1943, the years in which Jews from all over Europe were being deported to the extermination camps in Poland, it was from

Eichmann's office that the orders went out for the time and place of departure of the transports, the number of deportees, and so on. The schedules were coordinated with the railway authorities in each country; Eichmann was also in close contact with Martin LUTHER of the German Foreign Ministry. Rules were laid down on rounding up the Jews, seizing their homes, and confiscating their property; Eichmann saw to it that in Germany itself, his section would benefit from the booty.

Eichmann made every effort to solve problems in a way that ensured the maintenance of a regular timetable for the deportation trains going to the extermination camps. He made several visits to the camps and was well versed in the murder procedure. Eichmann was not directly involved in the extermination actions in Poland or the areas that had belonged to the Soviet Union, nor did he take any part in the EINSATZGRUPPEN operations, but through his representatives, he was active in all the other European countries from which Jews were being sent to their death. Only the Scandinavian countries—Denmark, Norway, and Finland—had no Eichmann representatives. One of the problems that confronted Eichmann and his associates was the treatment of the partners of mixed marriages and their progeny (*see* MISCHLINGE); there were many discussions on the subject, but the issue was never completely resolved.

A special place in Eichmann's actions was held by the THERESIENSTADT ghetto, which served first as a concentration camp for Jews from Czechoslovakia and Vienna, and later also for Jews of privileged status (mainly from Germany) and those over sixty, of whom it could not be said that they were being sent to the east to work. In practice, the "ghetto for the aged" was no more than a transit camp, from which a great many trains left for the extermination camps. Eichmann also tried to project Theresienstadt as a "model ghetto" by showing it to RED CROSS commissions—after first altering its appearance with temporary improvements—in order to refute published reports of the atrocities that the Nazis were committing.

Only in HUNGARY was Eichmann personally in charge of the deportations. Immediately after the occupation of the country by German forces on March 19, 1944, Eichmann arrived in Hungary, accompanied by a large team of aides, which he had assembled at the MAUTHAUSEN camp in preparation for the invasion. In Hungary, Eichmann put to full use all the experience he had gained; within a short period—from May to early July—he succeeded in deporting some 440,000 Jews from all the provinces that were then part of Hungary. This was made possible by the cooperation of the Hungarian authorities. Even after the Hungarians stopped the deportations in early July, Eichmann tried, by deceptive tactics, to have additional thousands of Jews deported from Budapest. But it was only in October 1944, following the ARROW CROSS PARTY coup d'état in Hungary, that he was able to resume his murderous operations. By now it was no longer possible to send the Jews to Auschwitz by train, since the murders in the gas chambers there had stopped and the eastern front had drawn near. Eichmann's answer was to put 76,000 Jews on DEATH MARCHES to Austria, from where they were to be sent to forced-labor camps in Germany.

In Hungary, Eichmann encountered various efforts to rescue the Jews; among these was the rescue work carried out by Raoul WALLENBERG, in conjunction with other representatives of neutral countries, which persisted despite all that Eichmann tried to do to thwart it. Eichmann played a major role in the "Blood for Goods" plan, which led to the Joel BRAND mission to Istanbul, with a proposal to set Jews free in exchange for a supply of trucks and other goods needed by the Germans. He was also involved in the EUROPA PLAN conceived in Slovakia, according to which Jews were to be released in return for a large payment in United States dollars. On various occasions Eichmann intervened in order to foil opportunities that presented themselves for saving Jews and removing them from German control, as in negotiations with BULGARIA and ROMANIA. In two instances Eichmann was forced to agree to the liberation of some Jews: in the "Repatriation" plan, which primarily affected Jews of Spanish origin trapped in Greece, and in the program for the exchange of Jews and Germans (*see* EXCHANGE: JEWS AND GERMANS).

When the war ended, Eichmann went into hiding and then, like other SS men, fled to

Argentina with the help of the Vatican. He lived there with his family until May 1960, when he was captured by the Israeli Security Service and brought to Israel. In April 1961 he was put on trial before the district court in Jerusalem (*see* EICHMANN TRIAL). He was found guilty and sentenced to death; the Israeli Supreme Court, sitting as a court of appeals, upheld the sentence, and on June 1, 1962, Eichmann was executed by hanging. His body was cremated and the ashes scattered over the sea.

The trial engendered a debate about Eichmann's character. Some, headed by Hannah Arendt (*see* ARENDT CONTROVERSY), argued that Eichmann was a very ordinary individual, who was not motivated by any special hatred of Jews, and that all he did—as he himself claimed—was to carry out the orders received from his superiors, within the general framework of Nazi bureaucracy. Others believe that Eichmann was the personification of the spirit of inhumanity in Nazism, the regime that nurtured the rise of destructive drives and created the conditions for mass murder and the execution of the "Final Solution." What cannot be doubted is that Eichmann served the Nazi program for exterminating the Jewish people with zeal and efficiency.

BIBLIOGRAPHY

Arendt, H. *Eichmann in Jerusalem: A Report on the Banality of Evil.* New York, 1964.

Aronson, S. *Reinhard Heydrich und die Frühgeschichte von Gestapo und SD.* Stuttgart, 1971.

Harel, I. *The House on Garibaldi Street.* New York, 1975.

Kempner, R. M. W. *Eichmann und Kumplizen.* Zurich, 1961.

Levai, J. *Eichmann in Hungary: Documents.* Budapest, 1961.

Robinson, J. *And the Crooked Shall Be Made Straight: The Eichmann Trial, The Jewish Catastrophe, and Hannah Arendt's Narrative.* Philadelphia, 1965.

LENI YAHIL

EICHMANN TRIAL. The trial of Adolf EICHMANN, held in Jerusalem in 1961 and 1962, riveted the attention of the Israeli public and aroused great interest the world over. This was the first time that the Holocaust was presented to a competent judicial body in full detail, in all its stages and from all its aspects. Journalists from many countries converged upon Jerusalem to cover the trial, and international public opinion followed its course with concentration; the trial gave rise to discussions on a great variety of subjects, on the legal, social, educational, psychological, religious, and political levels.

In May 1960 Eichmann was kidnapped in Argentina by Israeli agents, taken to Israel, and handed over to the Israeli police. On May 23, 1960, the prime minister of Israel, David BEN-GURION, announced in the Knesset (the Israeli parliament): "Adolf Eichmann . . . is under arrest in Israel and will shortly be put on trial." A magistrate issued an order for Eichmann's arrest and remanded him for trial, the order being renewed from time to time. The police investigation was put into the hands of a special unit established for this purpose (Bureau 06), which took nine months to complete its task.

When the investigation was completed, on February 21, 1961, the attorney general, Gideon HAUSNER, signed the bill of indictment against Eichmann and submitted it to the district court in Jerusalem (which marked it Criminal File 40/61). The indictment consisted of fifteen counts of "crimes against the Jewish people," "crimes against humanity," "war crimes," and "membership in a hostile organization"—that is, the SS, SD (Sicherheitsdienst; Security Service), and GESTAPO, all three of which had been declared "criminal organizations" by the International Military Tribunal at the NUREMBERG TRIAL, in a judgment rendered on October 1, 1946.

The crimes against the Jewish people with which the accused was charged consisted of all aspects of the persecution of millions of Jews, including their arrest and imprisonment in concentration camps, their deportation to extermination camps, their murder, and the theft of their property. The charges did not, however, confine themselves to Eichmann's participation in crimes against the Jewish people; they also included crimes against other peoples, such as the mass expulsions of Poles and Slovenes; the seizure, deportation to extermination camps, and murder of tens of thousands of GYPSIES; and

The Eichmann trial. Supreme Court Justice Moshe Landau is at top center; Eichmann is in the questioning box. Robert Servatius, the defense attorney, is at the bottom, second from left, and Attorney General Gideon Hausner is third from left.

the deportation and murder of some one hundred children from the village of LIDICE in Czechoslovakia, in revenge for the killing of Reinhard HEYDRICH. All the counts related to offenses under the Nazis and Nazi Collaborators (Punishment) Law 5710-1950.

The trial, conducted by the District Court in Jerusalem, began on April 10, 1961. It took place in a Jerusalem community center that had been adapted for this special purpose. The court consisted of Supreme Court justice Moshe Landau (who presided), Jerusalem District Court president Benjamin Halevi, and Tel Aviv District Court judge Yitzhak Raveh.

The public prosecution was represented by a team headed by Attorney General Hausner, and the defense team was headed by Dr. Robert Servatius, a German lawyer who had served as attorney for the defense of several of the accused in the Nuremberg trials of major war criminals.

When the trial began, the defense lawyer raised several preliminary arguments, questioning the court's competence to try his client for the charges contained in the bill of indictment. His major arguments were: (1) there was reason to doubt whether the three judges, who were Jews and citizens of the state of Israel, were able to give the accused a fair trial; (2) the trial must not be held, because the accused had been kidnapped from his place of residence in Argentina and illegally taken to Israel; (3) the Nazis and Nazi Collaborators Law 5710-1950 was a *post factum* law and therefore wrong and unjust; and (4) the offenses listed in the bill of indictment had been committed outside the borders of the state of Israel and before the state's establishment.

All these arguments were rejected by the court. On the contention that the judges might lack objectivity, the court stated: "When a judge sits on a bench, he does not cease to be flesh and blood with human emotions; but he is bidden by law to overcome these emotions. If this were not so, no judge would ever be qualified to sit in judgment in a criminal case evoking strong disgust, such as a case of treason or murder or some other heinous offense."

Concerning the principle that no criminal laws should be passed that were of retroactive validity, the court stated that the principle was not legally binding; it was rather a principle of justice, since the natural sense of justice is generally outraged by a person's being punished for a deed that was not illegal at the time it was committed. The situation with regard to the offenses that were being charged in this case, however, was quite different: the Nazis and Nazi Collaborators Law (like similar laws enacted by various countries after the war) did not introduce new legal norms; all it did was to make it possible to bring persons to trial for committing offenses that were known to be against the law at the time they were committed, in every place in the world, including Germany—the illegality of which these persons were well aware. Owing to the illegal regime that was in power in Nazi Germany, the perpetrators of these crimes were not punished for them at the time; but it was precisely the sense of natural justice that called for the establishment of a forum where the persons suspected of these crimes could be brought to trial.

With regard to the argument concerning Eichmann's kidnapping in Argentina and the manner in which he was brought to Israel against his will, the court, quoting precedents of United States and British courts, found that jurisdiction to try an accused person depends only on the essence of the criminal law cited in the bill of indictment and its applicability to the offenses with which the accused is charged; a court is not entitled to examine in what manner an accused was brought into the sovereign territory of the state in which he is to stand trial.

The court further found that the date on which the state of Israel was established was of no relevance to the court's competence to try Eichmann; moreover, the plan for the destruction of the Jewish people was also meant to include Jews who at the time of World War II were residents of Palestine. Undoubtedly, there was a strong connection between the existence of the state of Israel and the objective of ensuring that persons who committed "crimes against the Jewish people" be brought to trial for those offenses.

After the court's rejection of the preliminary arguments, the accused was ordered to state how he pleaded on the counts as enumerated in the indictment. Eichmann's answer, on each count, was: "In the sense of the indictment, not guilty."

This was followed by the body of evidence being presented to the court. By means of more than one hundred witnesses and some sixteen hundred documents—many of them bearing Eichmann's own signature—the prosecution presented to the court the full account of all the events related to the Holocaust of European Jewry, or the "FINAL SOLUTION of the Jewish question," as the Nazis called it. In great detail the prosecution furnished the court with proof of the persecution of the Jews in all its stages: the anti-Jewish legislation; the incitement among the general population of hostility to the Jewish minority; the plunder of Jewish property; and, worst of all, the searching out of the Jews in every European country under German occupation and in the satellite states, their imprisonment, under inhuman conditions, in ghettos and concentration camps, where they were harassed and humiliated, and, finally, their systematic mass murder, with the aim of completely destroying the Jewish people. The prosecution demonstrated what had happened to the Jews of Europe, country by country and camp by camp; it proved the personal involvement of Eichmann, as the head of section IV B 4 (the Gestapo section for Jewish affairs), in every

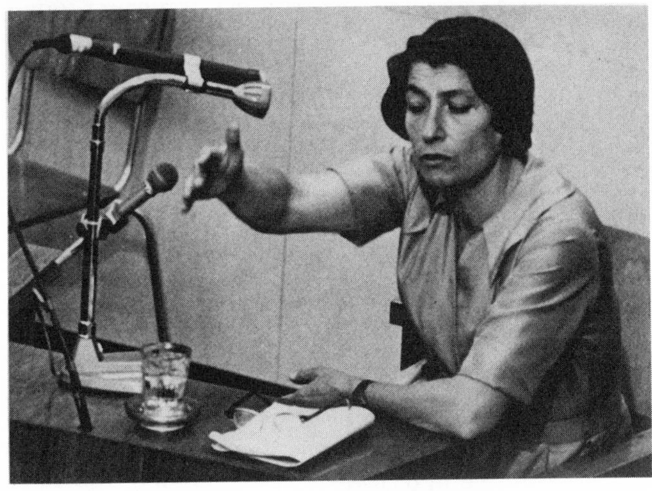

Zivia Lubetkin testifying at the Eichmann trial in Jerusalem (1961).

stage of the heinous operation, and that, in fact, Eichmann was in charge of all the steps taken to implement the plan for the "Final Solution."

The defense did not really question the facts related to these events, or challenge the authenticity of the documents proving Eichmann's involvement in the crimes. The systematic defense line was to play down Eichmann's role in the whole process by depicting him as a small cog in the machinery of murder, an underling who had no choice but to carry out the orders he was given by his superiors. The court rejected this claim. The trial proved that mentally and emotionally, Eichmann fully identified with his task; indeed, the evidence presented to the court—which included official documents from German sources—showed that in the final stages of the war, Eichmann's desire to come as close as possible to the complete and total destruction of the Jews became an obsession. This was demonstrated with particular force in Hungary, where Eichmann was sent by Heinrich HIMMLER in 1944 to take personal charge of the deportation of that country's Jews to the extermination camps in Poland.

The court also found that the claim made by the defense that Eichmann was only acting under orders was of no avail to him, from the legal standpoint; this claim was also disproved in fact, as the court was persuaded that Eichmann had done everything in his power to interpret and implement the orders he received in as extreme and harsh a manner as possible. Accordingly, the court found Eichmann guilty on all counts (with some unimportant changes) and, on December 15, 1961, sentenced him to death.

Eichmann lodged an appeal against the verdict that was heard by the supreme court sitting as a panel of five justices, with the president of the supreme court, Justice Yitzhak Olshan, presiding. On May 29, 1962, the supreme court announced its rejection of the appeal and confirmed the judgment of the lower court. Following the denial by the president of Israel, Itzhak Ben-Zvi, of Eichmann's request for clemency, Eichmann was executed by hanging at midnight between May 31 and June 1, 1962. It was the only instance in the annals of the state of Israel of a death sentence being carried out. Eichmann's body was cremated and the ashes scattered over the sea, beyond Israel's territorial waters.

In general, the trial was well received around the world and seen as the embodiment of historical justice. It also had various positive side effects. The citizens of Israel, particularly the youth, learned for the first time, from the mouths of numerous witnesses, how the brutal and inhuman methods employed by the Nazis made it possible for millions of people to be exterminated without having any chance of offering effective resistance, and they came to understand that there was no reason for this phenomenon to arouse in themselves feelings of guilt and inferiority. On the other hand, the heroism displayed by the Jews during the WARSAW GHETTO UPRISING and in other revolts evoked their admiration and pride.

The Eichmann trial also led to increased interest in Holocaust research and to a chain reaction in the investigation and trial of Nazi war criminals. In Germany particularly, the investigation of charges of complicity in Nazi crimes was intensified, and many of the trials that were subsequently held in Germany against Nazi criminals can be traced to the Eichmann trial and the shock it had upon the German people.

BIBLIOGRAPHY

Arendt, H. *Eichmann in Jerusalem: A Report on the Banality of Evil.* New York, 1964.

Harel, I. *The House on Garibaldi Street.* New York, 1975.

Hausner, G. *Justice in Jerusalem.* New York, 1966.

Kempner, R. M. W. *Eichmann und Komplizen.* Zurich, 1961.

Pearlman, M. *The Capture and Trial of Adolf Eichmann.* New York, 1963.

Robinson, J. *And the Crooked Shall Be Made Straight: The Eichmann Trial, The Jewish Catastrophe, and Hannah Arendt's Narrative.* Philadelphia, 1965.

Von Lang, J., ed. *Eichmann Interrogated.* New York, 1983.

GABRIEL BACH

EICKE, THEODOR (1892–1943), commandant of concentration camps and of SS

TOTENKOPFVERBÄNDE (Death's-Head Units). Born in Hüddingen, Eicke served in the German army from 1909 to the end of World War I and then became a police informant. He joined the Nazi party and the SA (Sturmabteilung; Storm Troopers) in 1928, and in 1930 transferred to the SS. Eicke was close to SS chief Heinrich HIMMLER and rose rapidly in the formation's chain of command. In June 1933 he was appointed commandant of the DACHAU concentration camp, with the rank of *Oberführer.* In this post he introduced his own methods in the administration of the camp, the torture of prisoners, and the manner in which the Totenkopfverbände camp guards conducted themselves. These methods, which were exceptionally cruel, became standard for all the concentration camps in Germany. Eicke played a key role in the "Night of the Long Knives" (*Nacht der langen Messer*) on June 30, 1934, when the top echelon of the SA was liquidated, and it was he who shot the SA chief, Ernst RÖHM, after the latter refused to commit suicide. The following month, Eicke was appointed chief of the concentration camps' administration and of the SS guard formations, and was promoted to the rank of *Brigadeführer.*

In November 1939 he became commander of the "Totenkopf" Division of the Waffen-SS. Under his command, it took part in the fighting in France and on the eastern front and had a great many crimes on its record; its first criminal action was the murder of some one hundred British prisoners of war in France on May 26, 1940. Eicke was killed on the eastern front on February 16, 1943, while serving as an SS-*Obergruppenführer* in the Waffen-SS.

BIBLIOGRAPHY

Berber, P. *Dachau.* London, 1975.

Krausnick, H., et al., eds. *Anatomy of the SS State.* London, 1968.

Sydnor, C. W., Jr. *Soldiers of Destruction: The SS Death's Head Division, 1933–1945.* Princeton, 1977.

SHMUEL KRAKOWSKI

EIF. *See* Eclaireurs Israélites de France.

EINSATZGRUPPEN (full name, Einsatzgruppen des Sicherheitsdienstes [SD] und der Sicherheitspolizei [Sipo]; Operational Squads of the Security Service and the Security Police), task force of mobile killing units operating in German-occupied territories during World War II. Einsatzgruppen made their first appearance during the ANSCHLUSS, the incorporation of Austria into the Reich in March 1938. These were intelligence units of the police accompanying the invading army; they reappeared in the invasion of Czechoslovakia, in March 1939, and of Poland, on September 1 of that year.

In the invasions of Austria and Czechoslovakia, the task of the Einsatzgruppen was to act as mobile offices of the SD and the Sipo until such time as these formations established their permanent offices; they were immediately behind the advancing military units, and, as in the Reich, they assumed responsibility for the security of the political regime. In the Sudetenland, the Einsatzgruppen, in close cooperation with the advancing military forces, lost no time in uncovering and imprisoning the "Marxist traitors" and other "enemies of the state" in the liberated areas.

Six Einsatzgruppen were organized on the eve of the Polish invasion; five were to accompany the invading German armies, and the sixth was to operate in the Poznań area, which was to be incorporated into the Reich as the WARTHEGAU. Each Einsatzgruppe was subdivided into several Einsatzkommandos, one each to an army corps. There were fifteen Einsatzkommandos, each with a complement of one hundred twenty to one hundred fifty men. Einsatzgruppe personnel were recruited from among the SD, Sipo, and SS, on a regional basis. During the invasion of Poland, the Einsatzgruppen were disposed as shown in Table 1.

The Einsatzgruppen did their work in accordance with policy lines for foreign operations issued by the Sipo and SD. These policy lines had been laid down as early as August 1939 by Reinhard HEYDRICH, head of the REICHSSICHERHEITSHAUPTAMT (Reich Security Main Office; RSHA), and by Generalquartiermeister Eduard Wagner, the Wehrmacht representative in that office. The basic instruction was to combat, in enemy countries, elements in the rear of the frontline units

TABLE 1.

EINSATZGRUPPE	COMMANDING OFFICER	ATTACHED TO ARMY	NUMBER OF COMMANDOS
I	Brigadeführer Bruno Streckenbach	Fourteenth	4
II	Obersturmbannführer Dr. Emanuel Schäfer	Tenth	2
III	Obersturmbannführer Dr. Ludwig Fischer	Eighth	2
IV	Brigadeführer Lothar Beutel	Fourth	2
V	Brigadeführer Ernst Damzog	Third	3
VI	Oberführer Erich Naumann	Posen	2

who were hostile to the Reich and to Germans.

A more detailed description of the Einsatzgruppen's mission is contained in an order of the day issued by the Eighth Corps: "To conduct counterespionage, to imprison political suspects, to confiscate arms, and to collect evidence that is of importance to police intelligence work." In practice, "combating hostile elements" was given a broad interpretation and became terror operations on a grand scale against Jews and the Polish intelligentsia, in which some fifteen thousand Jews and Poles were murdered.

On September 21, 1939, Heydrich sent a high-priority note to the Einsatzgruppe commanders giving instructions for the treatment of Jews in the conquered territories. The Jews were to be rounded up and concentrated in large communities situated on railway lines; Judenräte (Jewish councils; *see* JUDENRAT) were to be established; and operations against the Jews were to be coordinated with the civil administration and the military command.

On November 20 of that year, on orders from Berlin, the Einsatzgruppen's operations were terminated and their personnel were absorbed by the permanent SD and Sipo offices in occupied Poland. When the plans were drawn up for the attack on the Soviet Union, ample use was made of the experience these men had gained, and four Einsatzgruppen were reestablished as A, B, C, and D.

Invasion of the Soviet Union (June 1941). In briefing sessions with the German army commanders on the planned Operation "Barbarossa," Adolf Hitler emphasized that the impending war with the Soviet Union would be a relentless struggle between two diametrically opposed ideologies. Its success would be determined not only by military victories, but also by the ability to root out and destroy the propagators of the rival ideology and its adherents. Hitler entrusted this job, of liquidating the personnel of the Soviet political and ideological apparatus, to Heinrich HIMMLER, chief of the SS and of all German police formations (*Reichsführer-SS und Chef der Deutschen Polizei*). Decree 21, Hitler's order for Operation "Barbarossa," in the section "Instructions for Special Areas," states:

> In areas where military operations are being conducted, the *Reichsführer-SS*, in the name of the Führer, will assume the special duties required for setting up the political administration. . . . In the discharge of these duties the *Reichsführer* will operate independently and on his own authority. . . . The *Reichsführer* will ensure that the pursuit of his objectives will not interfere with military operations. Details will be worked out directly between the High Command and the *Reichsführer-SS*.

After consultations between Heydrich (acting as Himmler's representative) and Eduard Wagner, Gen. Walther von Brauchitsch, the commander in chief of the army, issued an order stating that for the fulfilling of special security police assignments that went beyond the scope of military operations, special units of the SD would be employed in the army's operational area. These units were to proceed according to the following guidelines: "The special units will operate in the rear of the fighting forces and their task will be to seize archives, to obtain lists of organizations and anti-German societies, and to look for individuals such as exiled former political leaders, saboteurs, and the like; they will uncover any existing anti-German movements and liquidate them; and they will coordinate their activities in these areas with the military field-security apparatus." The order adds that while the Sipo and the SD (including the Einsatzgruppen) would be operating on their own responsibility, as far as logistics were concerned they would be attached to the armed forces and would depend upon the latter for housing, rations, transport, communications, and other matters. To ensure the proper coordination, representatives of the SD and Sipo would be attached to corps and army headquarters. In its concluding section, the order provides that the special units were empowered to take administrative action against the civilian population, on their own responsibility but in cooperation with the military police, and with the approval of the local Wehrmacht commander. (For example, the extermination of the Kiev Jews at BABI YAR was decided on at a meeting held in the office of the military governor of the city, General Eberhardt, with the general attending and concurring in the decision.)

By this order, which faithfully reflects the agreement arrived at by Heydrich and Wagner, the Wehrmacht relieved itself of the task of carrying out mass murder, and restricted its involvement to logistics. However, under the conditions that developed in the occupied areas of the Soviet Union, the cooperation between the Wehrmacht and the Einsatzgruppen from time to time went beyond the provisions of the agreement, as when military units were deployed to stand guard over individuals or groups of persons who had been condemned to die, or over the area designated for their execution.

Organizing and Training the Einsatzgruppen. Early in May 1941, the men who had been chosen as candidates for the Einsatzgruppen were assembled in the training school of the German border guard in Pretzsch (a town on the Elbe River, northeast of Leipzig). The school did not have enough space to hold all the candidates, and some had to be quartered in the neighboring towns of Duben and Bad Schmiedeberg. Most of the candidates had come from the RSHA, whose manpower division had ordered the SD and the Sipo to select suitable men for this purpose. Another group of candidates came from the Sipo senior officers' training school in Berlin; yet another group, of 100 men, had been attending an officer candidates' school of the KRIMINALPOLIZEI (Criminal Police), and were dispatched from there to join the Einsatzgruppe candidates at Pretzsch.

The commanding officers of the Einsatzgruppen, the Einsatzkommandos, and the Sonderkommandos were chosen by Himmler and Heydrich from a list prepared by Section I of the RSHA; most had been serving as senior officers of the SD (*see* Appendix, Volume 4). The technical staff of the Einsatzgruppen—radio operators, clerks, interpreters, drivers, and others—were recruited from among the staff of the RSHA and the SS. Three of the Einsatzgruppen—B, C, and D—had attached to them companies of Reserve Police Battalion No. 9, later replaced by men from Battalion No. 3, as well as companies of the Waffen-SS, for special duties.

Each of the reestablished Einsatzgruppen had sub-units, usually called Einsatzkommandos or Sonderkommandos. In theory, the Einsatzkommandos were to be attached to the armed forces behind the lines and the Sonderkommandos to those forces at the front. In practice, however, the Einsatzgruppen and their sub-units were deployed according to geographic sectors and not according to rear or frontline areas. The distinction between the Einsatzkommandos and the Sonderkommandos evaporated. Both the Einsatzkommandos and the Sonderkommandos also had temporary sub-units, usually referred to as Teilkommandos (lit., "part commandos"). When they were charged specifically with entering a town or city, they were sometimes called Vorkommandos (forward commandos).

The composition of the Einsatzgruppen was as follows:

1. Einsatzgruppe A consisted of Sonderkommandos SK1a, SK1b; and Einsatzkommandos EK2, EK3.
2. Einsatzgruppe B consisted of Sonderkommandos SK7a, SK7b; Einsatzkommandos EK8, EK9; and Vorkommando (V-KO) Moskau (SK7c).
3. Einsatzgruppe C consisted of Sonderkom-

mandos SK4a, SK4b; and Einsatzkommandos EK5, EK6.

4. Einsatzgruppe D consisted of Sonderkommandos SK10a, SK10b; and Einsatzkommandos EK11a, EK11b, EK12.

The first commander of Einsatzgruppe A, SS-Standartenführer Dr. Franz Walter STAHLECKER, had about one thousand men at his disposal. Einsatzgruppe A was attached to Army Group North; its area of operations covered the Baltic states (LITHUANIA, LATVIA, and ESTONIA) and the territory between their eastern borders and the Leningrad district.

The first commander of Einsatzgruppe B, SS-Brigadeführer (later Gruppenführer) and Generalleutnant der Polizei Arthur NEBE, had 655 men under his command. The Einsatzgruppe was attached to Army Group Center, and its operational area extended over BELORUSSIA and the SMOLENSK district, up to the outskirts of Moscow. The sub-unit of Einsatzgruppe B that was deployed toward Moscow was called Vorkommando Moskau. When the German forces began their withdrawal from Moscow, the Vorkommando was disbanded.

The first commander of Einsatzgruppe C, SS-Standartenführer Dr. Emil Otto RASCH, had seven hundred men under his command; the Einsatzgruppe was attached to Army Group South and covered the southern and central Ukraine.

Einsatzgruppe D, commanded by SS-Standartenführer Professor Otto OHLENDORF, had a complement of six hundred men. It was attached to the Eleventh Army and operated in the southern Ukraine, the Crimea, and Ciscaucasia (the Krasnodar and Stavropol districts).

On the face of it, the units, relatively small in size, had a very large area to cover. However, when they were engaged in mass-murder operations, the Einsatzgruppen were assisted by large forces of German police battalions and local auxiliary police battalions —Ukrainian, Belorussian, Latvian, or Lithuanian. At times they also had rear echelon troops at their disposal, such as garrison battalions, military gendarmeries, or even soldiers of the ORGANISATION TODT.

In early June 1941, Bruno Streckenbach, head of Branch I of the RSHA, came to Pretzsch in order to explain, on behalf of Himmler and Heydrich, Hitler's orders concerning the liquidation of the Jews. After the war, Ohlendorf gave evidence on the meeting with Streckenbach before the Nuremberg Military Tribunals, at the SUBSEQUENT NUREMBERG PROCEEDINGS, as did Dr. Walter Blume, who had been the commanding officer of Sonderkommando 7a. In his statement, Blume declared that in June 1941 Heydrich and Streckenbach had briefed them on their assignment of exterminating Jews, and had explained the ideological background. A large number of Einsatzgruppe, Einsatzkommando, and Sonderkommando commanders had taken part in the briefing sessions. Another such session, attended by the commanders of all units and sub-units, took place on June 17, 1941, in Heydrich's office in Berlin. At this time, Heydrich set out in detail the policy that was to guide the Einsatzgruppen in carrying out their assignments, among them the implementation of the Führer's order to liquidate the Jews. A third such meeting, also very close to the date of the invasion of the Soviet Union (June 22, 1941), was held in the office of the chief of the ORDNUNGSPOLIZEI, Kurt DALUEGE. It was attended by the senior SS and police officers who had been designated to act as Einsatzgruppe commanders in the various parts of the Soviet Union, when these were occupied by the German army. On July 2, 1941, these officers also received written instructions from Heydrich, which contained the following passage:

> The following is the gist of the highly important orders that I have issued to Einsatzkommandos of the Sipo and the SD, with which these two services are called upon to comply. . . .
>
> 4) *Executions.*
>
> The following categories are to be executed:
>
> Comintern officials (as well as all professional Communist politicians); party officials of all levels; and members of the central, provincial, and district committees;
>
> people's commissars;
>
> Jews in the party and state apparatus;
>
> and other extremist elements (saboteurs, propagandists, snipers, assassins, agitators, etc.).

The order affecting the "Jews in the party and state apparatus" encompassed, in prac-

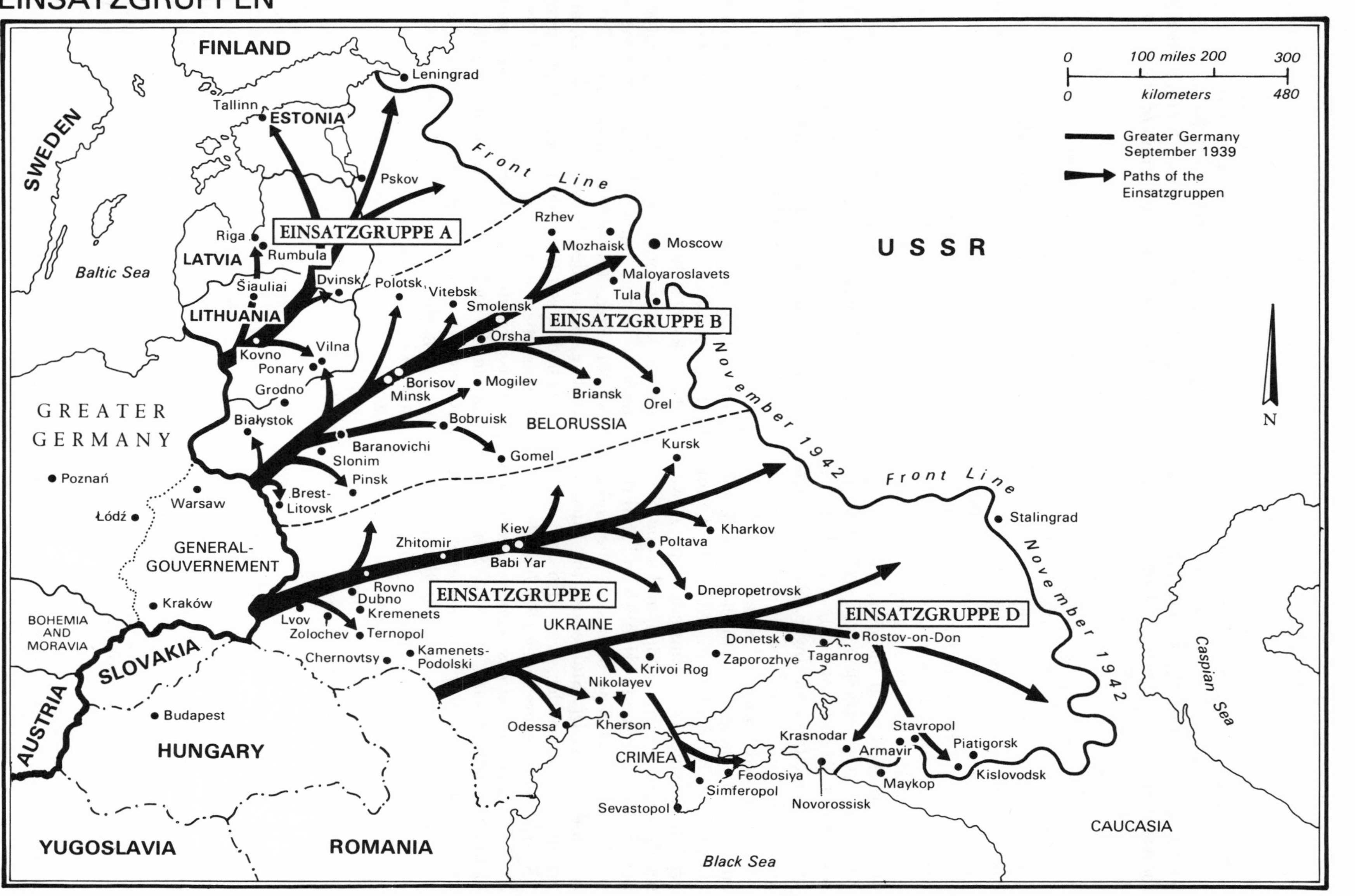
EINSATZGRUPPEN
0 100 miles 200 300
0 kilometers 480
Greater Germany September 1939
Paths of the Einsatzgruppen
N
USSR
Front Line
November 1942
Front Line
November 1942
EINSATZGRUPPE A
EINSATZGRUPPE B
EINSATZGRUPPE C
EINSATZGRUPPE D
FINLAND
SWEDEN
Baltic Sea
Leningrad
Tallinn
ESTONIA
Pskov
Riga
LATVIA
Rumbula
Šiauliai
LITHUANIA
Dvinsk
Polotsk
Vitebsk
Smolensk
Orsha
Rzhev
Mozhaisk
Moscow
Maloyaroslavets
Tula
Kovno
Ponary
Vilna
Grodno
Białystok
Borisov
Minsk
Mogilev
Briansk
Orel
Bobruisk
BELORUSSIA
Baranovichi
Slonim
Gomel
Kursk
Pinsk
Brest-Litovsk
GREATER GERMANY
Poznań
Łódź
Warsaw
GENERAL-GOUVERNEMENT
Kraków
Zhitomir
Kiev
Babi Yar
Kharkov
Poltava
Dnepropetrovsk
Rovno
Dubno
Kremenets
Lvov
Zolochev
Ternopol
UKRAINE
Chernovtsy
Kamenets-Podolski
BOHEMIA AND MORAVIA
SLOVAKIA
AUSTRIA
Budapest
HUNGARY
Donetsk
Zaporozhye
Taganrog
Rostov-on-Don
Krivoi Rog
Nikolayev
Odessa
Kherson
CRIMEA
Feodosiya
Simferopol
Sevastopol
Krasnodar
Armavir
Stavropol
Piatigorsk
Kislovodsk
Maykop
Novorossisk
Stalingrad
Caspian Sea
CAUCASIA
Black Sea
YUGOSLAVIA
ROMANIA

tice, all the Jews in the Soviet Union. Einsatzgruppe Report No. 111 of October 12, 1941, did in fact make it perfectly clear that the purpose was to kill all Jews.

The Einsatzgruppen's Itineraries. With these orders in mind, the Einsatzgruppen began their march into the Soviet Union, in the footsteps of the German army. Einsatzgruppe A started out from East Prussia, and its units—the Sonderkommandos and Einsatzkommandos—rapidly spread out across Lithuania, Latvia, and Estonia. On June 25, Einsatzgruppe A headquarters entered Kovno at the same time as the advance formations of the army, and at the beginning of July it moved to RIGA. The local auxiliary police (made up of Lithuanians or Latvians), together with the Einsatzgruppe's various units, embarked upon the massacre of Jews, mainly in VILNA (PONARY), KOVNO (the NINTH FORT), and Riga (RUMBULA), as well as in many other cities and towns. Next, Einsatzgruppe A and several of its sub-units advanced toward Leningrad, so as to be able to enter the city together with the "Totenkopf" Division of the Waffen-SS. When the Leningrad front stabilized, Einsatzgruppe A was for the most part disbanded, and some of its personnel were used to establish and staff the regional SD and Sipo offices. At the end of September 1941 Dr. Stahlecker, the Einsatzgruppe A commander, was also appointed SS and Sipo commander (*Befehlshaber der Sicherheitspolizei und des Sicherheitsdienstes*) of REICHSKOMMISSARIAT OSTLAND. Small and mobile sub-units of Sonderkommandos 1a and 1b continued to "clean up" the area between the Baltic states and the eastern front.

Einsatzgruppe B had WARSAW as its starting point; some of its units passed through Vilna and GRODNO on the way to MINSK, where they arrived on July 5, 1941. Other units belonging to Einsatzgruppe B passed through BREST-LITOVSK, SLONIM, BARANOVICHI, and Minsk, and from there proceeded to southern Belorussia: MOGILEV, Bobruisk, and GOMEL, advancing as far as Briansk, Kursk, Orel, and Tula. Along their route, in all the places through which they passed, they murdered masses of people—Jews, GYPSIES, Communist activists, and prisoners of war. At the beginning of August 1941, Einsatzgruppe B headquarters moved to Smolensk, and some of its units were deployed in northern Belorussia, in places such as Borisov, VITEBSK, and Orsha. Two months later the headquarters moved again, to Mozhaisk, while its special advance unit, Vorkommando Moskau, established itself in Maloyaroslavets; both expected to enter Moscow with the Fourth Panzer group of the German army.

Einsatzgruppe C made its way from Upper Silesia to the western Ukraine, by way of KRAKÓW. Two of its units, Einsatzkommandos 5 and 6, went to LVOV, where they organized a pogrom against the Jews with the participation of Ukrainian nationalists. Sonderkommando 4b organized the mass murders at TERNOPOL and ZOLOCHEV, and then continued on its way to the east. Einsatzgruppe C headquarters and Sonderkommando 4a went to ZHITOMIR, by way of Volhynia, with 4a carrying out massacres en route, in Dubno and Kremenets. On September 29 and 30, Sonderkommando 4a, commanded by Paul BLOBEL, perpetrated the mass slaughter of Kiev Jews at Babi Yar. This unit was also responsible for the murder of KHARKOV's Jews, in early January 1942. Einsatzkommando 6 marched to the east and undertook the liquidation of the Jews of Krivoi Rog, DNEPROPETROVSK, and Zaporozhye, proceeded to Stalino (Donetsk), and reached ROSTOV-ON-DON. Einsatzkommando 5 was then broken up into SD and Sipo teams to staff local offices of the two organizations in such cities as Kiev and ROVNO. In Rovno, the capital of REICHSKOMMISSARIAT UKRAINE, these teams launched a large-scale *Aktion* at the beginning of November 1941, in which most of the Jewish inhabitants were murdered.

Einsatzgruppe D, as mentioned, was attached to the Eleventh Army. During its advance it carried out massacres in the southern Ukraine (Nikolayev and KHERSON), in the Crimea (SIMFEROPOL, Sevastopol, Feodosiya, and other places), and in the KRASNODAR and Stavropol districts (Maykop, Novorossisk, Armavir, and Piatigorsk).

By the spring of 1943, when the Germans began their retreat from Soviet territory, the Einsatzgruppen had murdered 1.25 million Jews and hundreds of thousands of other Soviet nationals, including prisoners of war.

Jewish prisoners of war were separated from the rest and put to death at an early stage, in the advance transit camps. The method that the Einsatzgruppen employed was to shoot their victims in ravines, abandoned quarries, mines, antitank ditches, or huge trenches that had been dug for this purpose. The killing by shooting, especially of women and children, had a devastating effect on the murderers' mental state, which even heavy drinking of hard liquor (of which they were given a generous supply) could not suppress. This was among the primary factors that led the RSHA in Berlin, in August 1941, to look for an alternative method of execution. It was found in the form of GAS VANS—heavy trucks with hermetically sealed vans into which the trucks' exhaust fumes were piped. Within a short time these trucks were supplied to all the Einsatzgruppen.

The Einsatzgruppen performed their murderous work in broad daylight and in the presence of the local population; only when the Germans began their retreat was an effort made to erase the traces of their crimes. This was the job of Sonderkommando 1005 (*see* AKTION 1005): to open the mass graves, disinter the corpses, cremate them, and spread the ashes over the fields and streams.

In practice, the Einsatzgruppen left behind an immense record of their deeds, in the form of summary reports drawn up in Berlin on the basis of detailed reports submitted by the various units in the field. Among the most comprehensive of these summary reports was the *Ereignismeldung der UdSSR* (Report of Events in the USSR), which was first issued on June 23, 1941, and was continued until Report No. 195, dated April 24, 1942. Next, and in continuation, came the *Meldungen aus den besetzten Ostgebieten* (Reports from the Occupied Eastern Territories), which began on May 1, 1942, and were kept up until May 21, 1943. In addition, there were the reports on the operations and the situation of the SD and Sipo in the USSR, covering the period from June 22, 1941, to March 31, 1942.

After the war, the Einsatzgruppe leaders were tried at the SUBSEQUENT NUREMBERG PROCEEDINGS, in the ninth trial conducted by the Nuremberg Military Tribunals. The trial, *The United States of America* v. *Otto Ohlendorf et al.*, was presided over by Judge Michael A. Musmanno. It began on July 3, 1947, and ended on April 10, 1948; there were twenty-four defendants. Fourteen of them were sentenced to death, seven to periods of imprisonment ranging from ten years to life, and one to the time already served; two were not tried or sentenced. Four of the defendants were actually executed, and sixteen had their sentences commuted or reduced to periods extending from the time already served to life imprisonment. One defendant was released, one died of natural causes, one committed suicide, and the execution of one was stayed because of the defendant's insanity.

Following the establishment of the Zentrale Stelle der Landesjustizverwaltungen (Central Office of the Judicial Administrations of the *Länder*) at Ludwigsburg, West Germany (*see* LUDWIGSBURGER ZENTRALSTELLE), over one hundred more indictments were handed down against Einsatzkommando commanders, officers, noncommissioned officers, and privates. In the ensuing trials no death sentences were passed, since the Federal Republic of Germany had abolished capital punishment.

[*See also* "Final Solution."]

BIBLIOGRAPHY

Hilberg, R. *The Destruction of the European Jews.* New York, 1985.

Krausnick, H., and H.-H. Wilhelm. *Die Truppe des Weltanschauungskrieges: Die Einsatzgruppen der Sicherheitspolizei und des SD 1938–1942.* Stuttgart, 1981.

Krausnick, H., et al. *Anatomy of the SS State.* London, 1968.

Lozowick, Y. "Rollbahn Mord: The Early Activities of Einsatzgruppe C." *Holocaust and Genocide Studies* 2/2 (1987): 221–241.

SHMUEL SPECTOR

EINSATZKOMMANDOS. *See* Einsatzgruppen.

EINSATZSTAB ROSENBERG (Operational Staff Rosenberg), organization for the plunder of the cultural and artistic treasures of the Jews, created by Alfred ROSENBERG in order to "secure ownerless cultural property of Jews." The unit's first activity of this kind was carried out in France by the Sonderstab Bildende Kunst (Special Operational Staff for the Arts), created by order of Hitler on September 17, 1940. Immediately after the occupation of France in June 1940, Hitler had expressed his desire to take possession of the artistic treasures of the Jews. Members of the unit carried out a thorough search operation in the collections of the Rothschild family and among the treasures of other Jewish collectors, in order to expropriate works of art remaining after the deportation or flight of their owners. They also attempted to discover storehouses and hiding places where works of art had been hidden, and searched the freight of overseas removal companies, claiming that they wished to prevent art treasures from being smuggled out of France. The operation was carried out with the aid of the French police and the German Sicherheitspolizei (Security Police), and with the active support of the German embassy in Paris.

Nonetheless, Rosenberg complained that the French authorities intrigued against the searches and that the French administrators responsible for Jewish property concealed works of art. According to the report summarizing the results of the operation in France between 1940 and 1944, the plundered works of art were transferred to Germany in twenty-nine consignments, in 137 freight cars holding 4,174 crates. They included nearly twenty-two thousand items: paintings, furniture—some antique—and objets d'art of all kinds from different periods, from all over the world. Besides the unique works of art that found their way to the homes of Hitler, Hermann Göring, and other leaders of the Third Reich, other items (principally furniture) were placed at the disposal of different Reich authorities, or were stored in different hiding places in Germany.

Concurrent with the activity in France, Einsatzstab Rosenberg carried out a furniture expropriation action (Möbel Aktion) in the Netherlands and in Belgium, such as that which Rosenberg had begun previously in Germany. Furniture was removed from tens of thousands of apartments of Jews who had emigrated or been deported to eastern Europe, and was given to Germans whose apart-

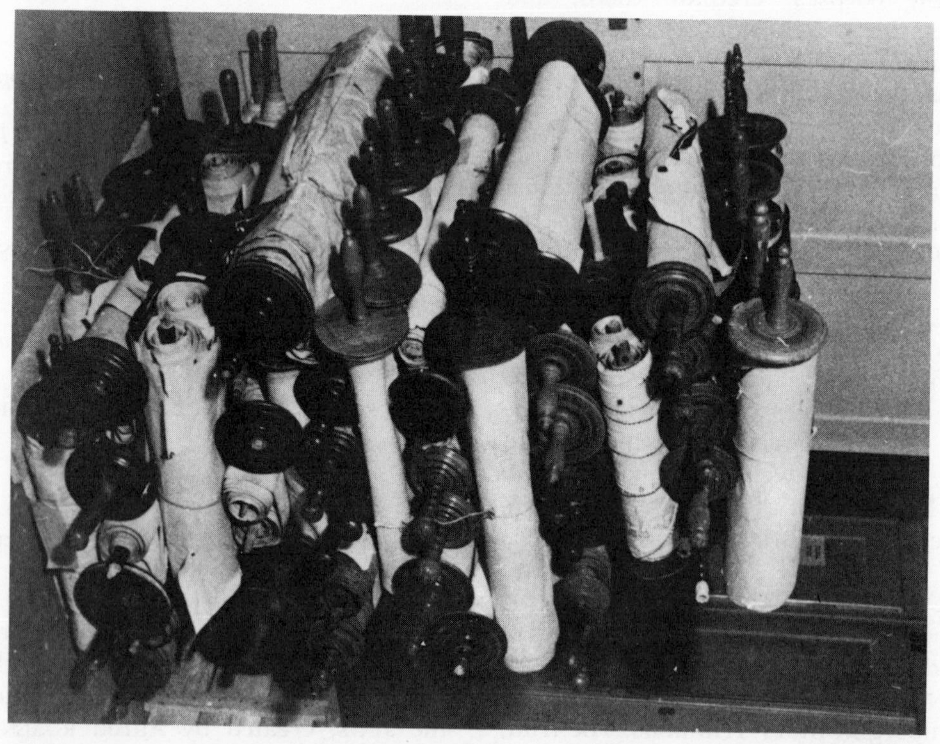

Some of the six hundred Torah scrolls plundered by the Nazis from synagogues in Germany.

Books and other archival material looted by the Nazis, later collected by the United States Army and brought to the Offenbach Archival Depot.

ments had been damaged by bombs. The property was transferred in 735 freight trains. Some of the pillage from the Netherlands, including clothing and linen, was transferred on rafts along the Rhine. On October 3, 1942, Rosenberg reported to Hitler that 40,000 tons of furnishings had been brought to Germany in the Möbel Aktion.

In eastern Europe the activity was less organized and controlled but no less comprehensive. In addition to the theft of works of art, there was large-scale plunder of ritual articles. In all the occupied countries, the Jewish libraries, including the ancient and valuable libraries of the Netherlands and Salonika, were looted. The plunder was one of the matters brought up on various occasions during the NUREMBERG TRIAL.

BIBLIOGRAPHY

Poliakov, L. *Harvest of Hate.* New York, 1979.

LENI YAHIL

EINSTEIN, ALBERT (1879–1955), physicist. Einstein was born at Ulm, Germany, of an assimilated Jewish family. While working in a patent office in Bern, Switzerland, he published in 1905 three revolutionary papers; one of them, on his special theory of relativity, gained him international fame. He then taught physics at the universities of Bern, Zurich, and Prague. In 1914, Einstein was appointed professor of physics at the Berlin Academy of Science and the Kaiser Wilhelm Institute of Physics, where he published in 1916 an extended version of the theory of relativity. In 1921, he was awarded the Nobel prize in physics. When Hitler came to power in 1933, Einstein happened to be out of Germany; he never set foot in that country again. He resigned from the Prussian Academy of Science and eventually emigrated to the United States, where he worked at the Institute for Advanced Studies in Princeton, New Jersey, for the rest of his life.

By his very nature Einstein was a fierce enemy of Nazism and all totalitarian regimes. Thus, in January 1933 he wrote: "My great fear is that this hate and power epidemic will spread throughout the world. It comes from below the surface like a flood, until the upper regions are isolated, terrified, and demoralized and then also submerged." The Nazis canceled his honorary citizenship (held from 1914, in addition to his Swiss citizenship), confiscated his property, and put a price of 50,000 reichsmarks on his head. In a statement to the Swiss press, he said: "As long as I have the choice, I shall live only in a land where political freedom, tolerance, and equality of all citizens reign."

In the United States, Einstein took part in Jewish rescue efforts, and in 1941 he tried in vain to influence President Franklin D. ROOSEVELT by writing to Eleanor Roosevelt, drawing her attention to the policy of the State Department, "which makes it all but impossible to give refuge in America to many worthy persons who are victims of the Fascist cruelty in Europe." Though Mrs. Roosevelt was ready to raise the issue with her husband, nothing came of it. After the war, Einstein also expressed criticism of SWITZERLAND's policy toward REFUGEES, stating that the country "behaved with unjust brutality . . . even towards those [refugees] whom it has allowed to enter its territory."

It was his hatred of Nazism that motivated Einstein, despite his pacifism, to warn Roosevelt, in August 1939, concerning the possibility that Germany might acquire sufficient quantities of uranium in the recently incorporated territory of Czechoslovakia to produce "extremely powerful bombs of a new type" that "might well destroy [a] whole port together with some surrounding territory." Einstein therefore recommended that the United States acquire uranium from the Belgian Congo. When the letter reached Roosevelt after the outbreak of the war, in October 1939, the National Research Defense Committee began to organize production of the atom bomb. In May 1946, after the war and the dropping of the first atom bombs, Einstein, presiding over the National Commission of Nuclear Scientists, declared: "The release of atom power has changed everything except our way of thinking, and thus we are being driven unarmed towards a catastrophe. . . . The solution of this problem lies in the heart of humankind."

BIBLIOGRAPHY

Clark, R. W. *Einstein: The Life and Times.* New York, 1971.

Frank, P. *Einstein: His Life and Times.* New York, 1948.

Seelig, K. *Albert Einstein: A Documentary Biography.* London, 1956.

ELIZABETH E. EPPLER

EISENHOWER, DWIGHT DAVID (1890–1969), military leader and thirty-fourth president of the United States. In World War II, Eisenhower was the architect and commander of the Allied invasion of Europe (June 6, 1944) and commander in chief of the Allied Expeditionary Forces in Europe up until the surrender of Germany (May 8, 1945). When the war ended, he became commander in chief of the American occupation forces in Europe until his appointment, later in 1945, as chairman of the United States Joint Chiefs of Staff, a post he held until 1948. From 1950 to 1952 he was commander in chief of the North Atlantic Treaty Organization (NATO). He served as president of the United States from 1953 to 1961.

The forces under Eisenhower's command liberated tens of thousands of Jews from concentration and forced-labor camps. Eisenhower himself visited several concentration camps as soon as they were liberated and, at news conferences and over the radio, expressed feelings of revulsion and shock at the atrocities that had been committed. He ordered that as many American soldiers as possible be taken to the camps to see for themselves the evidence of the unspeakable crimes that the Nazis had perpetrated.

Three years later, in his book *Crusade in Europe* (1948), Eisenhower recorded his impressions of his first visit to a concentration camp.

> The same day I saw my first horror camp. It was near the town of Gotha. I have never felt able to describe my emotional reactions when I first came face to face with Nazi brutality and ruthless disregard of every shred of decency. Up to that time I had known about it only generally or through secondary sources. I am certain, however, that I have never at any time experienced an equal sense of shock. I visited every nook and cranny of the camp because I felt it my duty to be in a position from then on to testify at first hand about these things in case there ever grew up at home the belief or assumption that "the stories of Nazi brutality were just propaganda."

To accelerate a solution to the problem of Jewish DISPLACED PERSONS (DPs), Eisenhower created the post of adviser on Jewish affairs to the supreme commander of the Allied forces. The first person to hold the post, army chaplain Rabbi Judah Nadich, made a deep

Gen. Dwight D. Eisenhower, commander in chief of the Allied forces in Europe, views the charred bodies of prisoners at the Ohrdruf camp in Germany (April 4, 1945). The camp was liberated by advance troops of the Fourth Armored Division of the Third Army. Second from the left is Gen. George S. Patton; at Eisenhower's left (arms akimbo) is Gen. Omar N. Bradley. [United States Army Signal Corps]

impression on Eisenhower; under his influence Eisenhower approved the establishment of separate Jewish DP camps in the American zone of Germany, in order both to keep the Jews apart from the many Nazi collaborators who had infiltrated the camps and to facilitate the physical, social, and moral rehabilitation of the survivors of the Holocaust. This action made it possible for the She'erit ha-Peletah (the "surviving remnant" of Europe's Jews) to organize as an autonomous body. Later, Eisenhower ordered the admission into the DP camps of the thousands of Holocaust survivors smuggled by the BERIḤA movement from eastern Europe into the American zone in Germany and Austria.

In October 1945, Eisenhower met with David BEN-GURION and agreed to his request that Hebrew teachers and agricultural instructors from Palestine be permitted to operate in the DP camps. This opened the door for the implementation of an extensive program of activities among the She'erit ha-Peletah by representatives of the YISHUV (the organized Jewish community of Palestine) and its underground armed force, the Hagana.

BIBLIOGRAPHY

Eisenhower, D. *Eisenhower: At War, 1943–1945.* New York, 1986.

Nadich, J. *Eisenhower and the Jews.* New York, 1953.

DAVID H. SHPIRO

ELKES, ELCHANAN (1879–1944), physician and chairman of the Ältestenrat (Council of Elders) in the KOVNO ghetto in Lithuania.

Elkes was born in the Lithuanian village of Kalvarija, close to the German border. He received a traditional Jewish and Hebrew education. While still a youngster, he was sent to Kovno to attend school. He completed his medical studies in Königsberg, Germany, and for seven years was village doctor in Berezino in Belorussia. During World War I, Elkes served as a medical officer in the Russian army, and he received numerous decorations. From the early 1920s, he headed the internal-medicine department in the Bikkur Holim Jewish hospital in Kovno. Reputed to be one of the best doctors in Lithuania, he numbered heads of state and diplomats among his patients.

Elkes was a Zionist, active on the Jewish cultural scene, and close to members of He-Haluts, the association of pioneering Zionist youth. During the period of Soviet rule (1940–1941), he used his contacts as physician to Moscow's representative in Lithuania to help obtain exit permits for thousands of Polish Jewish refugees who were stranded in Lithuania.

On June 24, 1941, the Germans captured Kovno, and thousands of Jews were arrested and murdered by the invaders and their Lithuanian collaborators. The remaining thirty thousand Jews were ordered to move into a ghetto and to choose a head for the Ältestenrat. On August 4 an emergency meeting was called, and was attended by twenty-eight leading personalities from all walks of Jewish life in the city. At this meeting, the last of its kind in the Kovno Jewish community, Elkes was nominated unanimously for the position and, with a heavy heart, he accepted the nomination. He was sixty-two years old and in failing health.

Elchanan Elkes (left), chairman of the Ältestenrat (Council of Elders) in the Kovno ghetto, with Dr. Moshe Berman. Berman was the head of the new hospital in the ghetto, opened at the end of 1941 after the Germans burned the old one in October. The photograph was taken by Zvi Kadushin, the Kovno photographer whose clandestine camera recorded life in the ghetto.

Elkes headed the Ältestenrat from its establishment until it was disbanded. All who came into contact with him attested to his impressive moral stature and devotion to the Jewish cause, his courage and dignity in his dealings with Nazi officials, his simplicity of manner with his fellow Jews, and his modest way of life. This was in sharp contrast to the corruption and haughtiness manifested by some of the Ältestenrat personnel. For these qualities he was held in high regard by the Jewish ghetto population. Elkes looked favorably on the anti-Nazi underground activity in the Kovno ghetto. Despite the danger involved, he was asked to organize supplies for the members of the General Jewish Fighting Organization (Yidishe Algemeyne Kamfs Organizatsye; JFO) who left the ghetto to fight as partisans in the forests. He declared: "Every opportunity for resistance should be exploited, especially in matters of honor." Elkes's stand influenced other members of the Ältestenrat to support the JFO.

At the beginning of July 1944, with the Red Army not far from Kovno, the Nazis proceeded to liquidate the ghetto and transfer its inhabitants to Germany. Elkes, at the risk of his life, appeared before the ghetto commandant, Obersturmbannführer Wilhelm Göcke, and suggested that Göcke drop the transfer plan, saying that this act would be held to his credit. Göcke refused bluntly, but allowed Elkes to leave unharmed. A few days later the ghetto was evacuated, and Elkes was transferred, with many of the surviving Jews, to the Landsberg concentration camp in Germany, where he was put in charge of the hospital hut. Soon afterward he fell ill, and died on October 17, 1944.

On October 19, 1943, while still in the ghetto, Elkes sent his children in England a final testament in Hebrew. He wrote: "With my own ears I have heard the awful symphony of weeping, wailing, and screaming from tens of thousands of men, women, and children, which have rent the heavens. No one throughout the ages has heard such a sound. Along with many of these martyrs I have quarreled with my Creator, and with them I cried out from a broken heart, 'Who is as silent as you, O Lord' " (a bitter allusion to a well-known prayer, "Who can compare to you, O Lord").

BIBLIOGRAPHY

Garfunkel, L. *The Destruction of Kovno's Jewry.* Jerusalem, 1959. (In Hebrew.)

Gutman, Y., and C. Haft, eds. *Patterns of Jewish Leadership in Nazi Europe, 1933–1945.* Proceedings of the Third Yad Vashem International Historical Conference. Jerusalem, 1979. See pages 93–112.

DOV LEVIN

EMERGENCY COMMITTEE FOR ZIONIST AFFAIRS. *See* American Zionist Emergency Council.

EMIGRATION. *See* Aliya Bet; Beriḥa; Council for German Jewry; Haavara Agreement; HICEM; Hilfsverein der Deutschen Juden; Madagascar Plan; White Paper of 1939; Zentralstelle für Jüdische Auswanderung.

ENDLÖSUNG. *See* "Final Solution."

ENDRE, LÁSZLÓ (1895–1946), one of the leading figures of Hungarian Nazism. Endre played a prominent role in many ultrarightist organizations and was the founder of the "Race-protecting Socialist Party" (A Fajvédő Szocialista Párt). In 1919 he was appointed constable and in 1923 chief constable of Gödöllő, a position he held until the end of 1937, when he became deputy prefect of Pest county. He had intimate contacts with the German Nazis, and began a close personal relationship with Adolf EICHMANN after Hungary's occupation by the Germans on March

László Endre (left).

19, 1944. As undersecretary of state in the Döme SZTÓJAY puppet government's Ministry of the Interior, a position he held between April 9 and September 5, 1944, Endre was among those chiefly responsible for the destruction of Hungarian Jewry. He fled with the retreating Nazi forces, but was captured by the Americans and extradited to Hungary in October 1945. Tried as a war criminal, he was hanged on March 29, 1946.

BIBLIOGRAPHY

Katzburg, N. *Hungary and the Jews: Policy and Legislation, 1920–1943.* Ramat Gan, Israel, 1981.

Macartney, C. A. *October Fifteenth: A History of Hungary, 1929–1945.* New York, 1957.

RANDOLPH L. BRAHAM

ENGLAND. *See* Great Britain.

ENTERDUNGSAKTION. *See* Aktion 1005.

ENTJUDUNG (lit., "de-Judaization"), term put into use in Nazi ANTI-JEWISH LEGISLATION. It is found in Eugen Dühring's infamous work on the "Jewish question," *Die Judenfrage als Rassen- Sitten- und Kultur-Frage* (1881), in the chapter "Early Steps and Ultimate Goals," in which he speaks of the *Verjudung* ("Judaization," or "corruption by Jews") of the nations and all they stand for. "This," he writes, "is a fact; the challenge now is *Entjudung* ['removal of the Jews']." It was clear to Dühring that this challenge could not be met all at once, and he therefore recommended *Entjudungsprozeduren*—"procedures, ways and means, of getting rid of the Jews."

In the Nazi period the term was used exclusively in an economic context and meant the removal of the Jews from economic life. As such, it appears for the first time in Nazi legislation in a decree by the minister of the interior, dated February 6, 1939. This makes it possible to determine with a high degree of accuracy the emergence of the term in that sense. The need for it arose when the term ARISIERUNG ("Aryanization" [of Jewish businesses]) was found to be no longer suitable; that term had previously been used even in official communications, although the word *arisch*—"Aryan"—and its derivatives disappeared from the terminology of German legislation after the NUREMBERG LAWS. The new expression, with its negative connotation, put a greater emphasis on the desire to remove the Jews from the body politic.

The decree of February 6, 1939, was named *Einsatz des jüdischen Vermögens* (meaning, in effect, "confiscation of Jewish assets"), which was also the name under which its better-known predecessor (which it complemented), the decree of December 3, 1938, was known. It points out the earlier decree "complements in a decisive manner previous instructions concerning the *Entjudung*—the removal of the Jews—from the German economy and provides a comprehensive legal basis thereto." The important innovation is that, according to the decree, "henceforth, *Entjudungen* [the plural of *Entjudung*] may also be carried out by the use of force," although "for the time being there should be no forceful *Gesamtentjudung* [total de-Judaization] of real property that is not being used for agriculture or afforestation." The term *Entjudung* also appears in the other parts of that decree and its appendixes.

2. *Entjudung von gewerblichen Betrieben* (removal of Jews from industries);
3. *Entjudung des Grundbesitzes* (removal of Jews from the ownership of land);
4. *Erfassung ungerechtfertigter Entjudungsgewinne* (seizure of illegitimate profits derived from *Entjudung*);
5. *Beteiligung der Parteistellen an dem Entjudungsverfahren* (participation of Nazi party offices in the *Entjudung* process).

Later on, the *Entjudung* operation was referred to as the *Entjudungsgeschäft* ("de-Judaization business"). For example, on June 10, 1940, the Reich minister of economic affairs issued an "Order for the Investigation of *Entjudungsgeschäfte*" whose purpose was to reimburse the Reich (and not, of course, the original owners whose property had been confiscated) for "unreasonable profits" made on such transactions after January 30, 1933. Further instructions on this aspect were issued in 1941.

The term *Entjudung* also appears in a 1944 document containing a list of "privileged" Jews who were deported from the Netherlands to the "model camp" of THERESIENSTADT; listed among them are also "persons" (in a second document, "Jews") who had bought this status in the *Entjudung der Niederlande* ("removal of the Jews from the Netherlands").

BIBLIOGRAPHY

Esh, S. "Words and Their Meaning: Twenty-Five Examples of Nazi-Idiom." *Yad Vashem Studies* 5 (1963): 133–167.

SHAUL ESH

EPPSTEIN, PAUL (1901–1944), a leader of German Jewry under the Third Reich. Eppstein was born in Ludwigshafen, and he majored in sociology at Mannheim University, where his teachers were Max Weber, Karl Jaspers, and Karl Mannheim.

At the age of twenty-six he became a lecturer in sociology at the business college in Mannheim. In 1929 he was appointed principal of the city's adult education college (*Volkshochschule*), which in less than four years developed into one of the most important institutions of its kind in Germany. When Hitler came to power in 1933, the college was closed down. Eppstein was asked to come to Berlin to participate in community activities on behalf of German Jewry, activities that under the new circumstances were in need of expansion and reorganization. His first appointment was with the ZENTRALAUSSCHUSS DER DEUTSCHEN JUDEN FÜR HILFE UND AUFBAU (Central Committee of German Jews for Relief and Reconstruction) and the Union of Jewish Communities of Prussia.

That same year, Eppstein was invited to join the board of the REICHSVERTRETUNG DER DEUTSCHEN JUDEN (Reich Representation of German Jews), in which he was primarily occupied with administration and social activities. Following the KRISTALLNACHT pogrom in 1938, Eppstein was invited to England to lecture in sociology, but he refused to leave Germany so long as the remaining Jews were in need of his services. He kept up his work in the new Reichsvereinigung der Juden in Deutschland (Reich Association of Jews in Germany; 1939–1943); indeed, the scope of his responsibilities was enlarged, especially as regarded day-to-day contact with the authorities and his work in connection with emigration. As of the end of 1940, following the arrest of Otto HIRSCH, Eppstein was the organization's sole executive director, under its presiding officer, Rabbi Leo BAECK.

In the years that he worked for the Reichsvereinigung, Eppstein was arrested several times by the Gestapo. One such arrest took place in the summer of 1940. When he was released, in October of that year, the REICHSSICHERHEITSHAUPTAMT (Reich Security Main Office; RSHA) ordered him to desist from any further activity related to emigration, and henceforth he concentrated on administrative affairs. Late in January 1943, about six months before the abolishment of the Reichsvereinigung, Eppstein was expelled to the THERESIENSTADT camp, together with Leo Baeck. On his arrival, he was appointed chairman of the Ältestenrat der Juden (Council of Jewish Elders), together with Jacob EDELSTEIN but in fact replacing him. Opinions vary on the way Eppstein carried out his task in Theresienstadt. In some quarters he has been criticized for not standing up to the German ghetto administration and for will ingly submitting to its demands, as well as for alienating his fellow prisoners and standing aloof from them; others believe that he was a staunch spokesman for the Jews, both in Germany and in Theresienstadt. Eppstein was imprisoned in the summer of 1944, because (according to one version) the Germans found fault with a speech he had made before the ghetto prisoners. The day after the Day of Atonement, 1944, Eppstein was executed.

Paul Eppstein (left) at Theresienstadt (1944). [Leo Baeck Institute, Jerusalem]

BIBLIOGRAPHY

Adler, H. G. *Theresienstadt, 1941–1945*. Tübingen, 1955.

Ehrmann, F., ed. *Terezin, 1941–1945*. London, 1965.

Lederer, Z. *Ghetto Theresienstadt*. London, 1953.

ESRIEL HILDESHEIMER

"ERNTEFEST" ("Harvest Festival"), code name for the operation to exterminate the last surviving Jews of the TRAWNIKI and PONIATOWA labor camps and the MAJDANEK concentration camp (all in the GENERALGOUVERNEMENT area of Poland). The date fixed for the operation (known as Aktion "Erntefest") was November 3, 1943, timing that was apparently influenced by the uprising of the Jewish prisoners in the SOBIBÓR extermination camp a few weeks earlier, on October 14. Heinrich HIMMLER, concerned that there might be more uprisings in the Generalgouvernement area, gave the order to kill all the Jews employed there on forced labor. The task of implementing the order was entrusted to Jacob SPORRENBERG, the *Höherer SS- und Polizeiführer* (Higher SS and Police Leader) of the Lublin district. "Erntefest" was carried out as a military operation, with thousands of SS and police, including Waffen-SS units, mobilized for it from all over the area. In order to forestall any acts of resistance, the operation was accomplished at top speed simultaneously in all three camps, and came as a complete surprise. On the eve of the operation, Poniatowa held some fifteen thousand Jews; Trawniki had eight thousand to ten thousand, including women and children, most of them brought there from the Warsaw ghetto, during and after its liquidation.

On November 3 at dawn, the Trawniki and Poniatowa camps were surrounded by SS and police forces. The Jews in the camps were taken out in groups and shot to death in pits that had been prepared for this purpose near each of the camps. In Trawniki the shooting was accompanied by background music blaring forth from loudspeakers, set up for this specific occasion in order to drown out the sound of the shooting. In Majdanek, the Jews were separated that day during the morning parade from the rest of the prisoners; they were then taken to pits that had been dug next to the camp's southern fence a few days earlier, and shot to death. Two powerful loudspeakers had been set up nearby to broadcast loud dance music. On the same day, Jews from other labor camps in Lublin —from the old airfield, the armament workshops, and elsewhere—were brought to Majdanek and shot to death next to the same pits. A total of seventeen thousand to eighteen thousand Jews were murdered in Majdanek on that day.

In Poniatowa, a Jewish underground group offered resistance when they were about to be taken to the pits, and set fire to some barracks. Their resistance was crushed. In all three camps Jews tried to take refuge in hiding places in the barracks, but they were all caught, either on November 3 or on the days that followed, and put to death. Hundreds of Jews were left behind in each camp in order to burn the bodies of the victims. They, too, were murdered when the job was done.

A total of forty-two thousand to forty-three thousand Jews were murdered in the "Erntefest" operation. This was the final *Aktion* to take place in the Generalgouvernement area, bringing AKTION REINHARD to an end.

BIBLIOGRAPHY

Arad, Y. *Belzec, Sobibor, Treblinka: Operation Reinhard Death Camps.* Bloomington, 1987.

YITZHAK ARAD

ESCAPE. *See* Beriḥa.

ESTONIA, Soviet republic in the northwestern USSR. Estonia is the northernmost of the three Baltic republics and the smallest; in 1939 its population was 1,133,917. At the end of 1917, after some two hundred years of Russian tsarist rule, Estonia declared its independence. Early in World War II it was forced to accept Soviet bases on its soil (September 29, 1939), and in August 1940 it was annexed to the USSR as a Soviet republic. In July 1941 the Germans, assisted by units of the Estonian nationalist group Omakaitse, conquered Estonia. During the three years of Nazi rule, Estonia was an administered area (Generalbezirk Estland) included in REICHSKOMMISSARIAT OSTLAND. The Estonians were granted self-rule under Hialmar Mae, leader of the extreme nationalist movement VAPS. When the Red Army returned in September 1944, Estonia once again became a Soviet republic.

Estonia's first Jewish communities arose in the middle of the nineteenth century. Between the two world wars, some forty-five hundred Jews (0.4 percent of the entire population) lived in Estonia, half of them in the capital city, TALLINN, and the rest in the towns of Tartu, Valga, Pärnu, Narva, Viljandi, Rakvere, Voru, and Nõmme, and in smaller settlements. Like the country's other national minorities, the Estonian Jews enjoyed broad cultural and educational autonomy, including the provision of Hebrew and Yiddish government schools. From the mid-1930s, as the extreme nationalist Omakaitse adherents gained power, demands increased to reduce the Jewish role in Estonia's economy and to limit the number of Jewish university students.

In the year of Soviet rule (1940–1941), the Jews' factories and businesses were nationalized along with those of the rest of the Estonians. Many Jewish breadwinners were absorbed into the nationalized economy, but the system of autonomy was canceled and the Jews' educational and religious activity curtailed. At the same time, however, Jews were appointed to government economic and security positions. During the waves of arrests visited on the Estonian population, the Jews suffered badly in proportion to their numbers because of economic activity discountenanced by the Soviet regime as well as Zionist political activity. On June 14, 1941, eight days before the German invasion of the Soviet Union, some ten thousand Estonians, including five hundred Jews (5 percent of the total), were exiled to Siberia. Most of the Jews managed to flee the country before the German conquest; some two hundred and fifty of them were conscripted into the Estonian Corps of the Red Army, where they constituted 0.8 percent of the soldiers; some one thousand Jews remained in Estonia under Nazi rule.

During the first weeks under the Germans, the Jews were subjected to many limitations and decrees. They were forced to wear the yellow badge (*see* BADGE, JEWISH) and forbidden to walk on sidewalks or use public transportation; their property was confiscated. The Jews of Estonia were in fact at that time already doomed. Sonderkommando 1a (SK1a; a division of Einsatzgruppe A), under SS-Obersturmbannführer Dr. Martin Sandberger, was placed in charge of their extermination. Omakaitse units assisted the Sonderkommando in the killing. First, the

ESTONIA on the Eve of WW II

Omakaitse arrested and murdered hundreds of youths and men aged sixteen and older. The remaining men, along with the women and children, were herded into school buildings; some were sent to perform forced labor. Later they were all interned at the Harka labor camp near Tallinn.

On October 12, Sandberger reported to his superiors that all Jewish men aged sixteen and over, except doctors and the "Jewish elders" appointed by the Germans, were being executed by the Estonian "self-defense" units, under the supervision of Sonderkommando 1a. They had already killed 440 Jews. The operation was continued in and around Tallinn, where Jews in hiding had not yet been captured. During the last weeks of 1941, the rest of the Jews, mostly women and children, were executed by the Sonderkommando and the Omakaitse. According to the report issued by Einsatzgruppe A, 936 Jews had been killed in Estonia by January 1942. On the regional map attached to that report, it was noted that Estonia was "free of Jews" (*judenfrei*). This fact was also announced at the WANNSEE CONFERENCE, held on January 20 of that year.

Starting in the fall of 1942, tens of thousands of Jews were sent to Estonia from other areas under Nazi rule: from THERESIENSTADT, from the Lithuanian ghettos of VILNA and KOVNO, Bistrița in Transylvania, and the KAISERWALD camp in Latvia. They were concentrated in twenty labor camps and forced to mine oil shale for the production of synthetic fuel, dig antitank ditches, build bunkers, and perform other military work. The main camp was VAIVARA. When these Jews weakened and could no longer work, many of them were killed; others died of disease, hunger, and torture. In the fall of 1944, faced with the advance of the Red Army, the Germans hurriedly removed the remaining Jews from the camps and transported them across the Baltic Sea to the STUTTHOF concentration camp. On September 18 and 19, 1944, most of the Jews were killed in the Lagedi and KLOOGA camps. Fewer than ten survived.

Between 1944 and 1950 some fifteen hundred Estonian Jews—survivors of the thousands who had fled to the Soviet interior in 1941—returned to Estonia. Eventually, the survivors of the Siberian exile were also allowed to return.

BIBLIOGRAPHY

Dworzecki, M. *The Jewish Camps in Estonia, 1942–1944.* Jerusalem, 1970. (In Hebrew.)

Dworzecki, M. "Patterns in the Extermination of Estonian Jewry." *Yalkut Moreshet* 11 (November 1967): 135–147. (In Hebrew.)

Kruus, R. *People, Be Watchful.* Tallinn, 1962.

Levin, D. "Estonian Jews in the U.S.S.R., 1941–45." *Yad Vashem Studies* 11 (1976): 273–297.

Levin, D. "The Jews of Estonia in the First Year of the Soviet Regime (1940–1941)." *Behinot Studies on the Jews in the USSR and Eastern Europe* 7 (1976): 73–84. (In Hebrew.)

DOV LEVIN

ETHNIC GERMANS. *See* Volksdeutsche.

EUGENICS. *See* Anthropology and National Socialism.

EUROPA PLAN, plan devised by the PRACOVNÁ SKUPINA (Working Group) in SLOVAKIA for saving the Jews of Europe from extermination, by the payment of ransom.

In the summer of 1942, a group of activists within the ÚSTREDŇA ŽIDOV (Jewish Center) in Slovakia sought to end the deportation of Slovak Jews to extermination camps. One of the people the activists tried to influence was Dieter WISLICENY, the SS officer who served as adviser on Jewish affairs to the government of Slovakia, whom they planned to bribe with a substantial sum of United States dollars. The deportations did in fact come to an end after the group had reached agreement with Wisliceny on the sum to be paid (between $40,000 and $50,000). There is no evidence that it was Wisliceny's intervention that brought the deportations to an end, or that there was any such intervention on his part, but the members of the group believed that this was the case. Encouraged by what the group regarded as a success, one of its leading members, Rabbi Michael Dov WEISSMANDEL, suggested trying to end the extermination process in the camps in Poland, and to provide aid to the Jews who had already been deported. On the basis of ties that two members of the group —Gisi FLEISCHMANN and Andrej Steiner—had with Wisliceny, by way of Karol Hochberg, a plan was worked out. It was given various names: the Europa Plan, since it aimed to save the Jews of Europe; the Rabbis' Plan, because the letters dispatched to Jewish organizations abroad in relation to the plan were signed by two rabbis, Weissmandel and Armin-Abba Frieder, who was also a member of the Working Group; and the Great Plan, because it involved the rescue of Jews from all over Europe, compared with the Small Plan, which involved only the rescue of Slovak Jews. The substance of the plan was that in exchange for the Germans' bringing the deportations and exterminations to a stop, the Jews of the free world would pay them a large sum in hard currency—2 million to 3 million United States dollars, according to one version.

Negotiations on the plan continued for nearly a year, from the fall of 1942 until August 1943, when Wisliceny brought them to an end. In the course of the negotiations, the Working Group made attempts to save the Jews of Greece with the help of Wisliceny, and to establish contact between the SS and several leaders of Hungarian Jewry.

The Working Group members were convinced that the reason the Europa Plan failed was that the required funds were not provided. The replies received by the group from Jewish organizations and institutions in Switzerland and Istanbul stated that the money was not available, and that the transfer of funds to Axis countries was prohibited. The negotiations conducted by the Germans in Hungary concerning the rescue of Jews—"Blood for Goods" (*see* BRAND, JOEL)—were a direct sequel to the Europa Plan. To this day the plan has remained the subject of searching debate. No clearcut evidence has been found that would prove that the SS was indeed ready to make a deal with the Jews in exchange for money; all that exist are the testimonies given by the Working Group members and by Wisliceny. On the other hand, the appeals and entreaties of the group were sometimes met with disdain, derision, and callousness. Subsequently, the surviving members of the Working Group smarted under feelings of frustration and bitterness.

BIBLIOGRAPHY

Bauer, Y. *American Jewry and the Holocaust: The American Jewish Joint Distribution Committee, 1939–1945.* Detroit, 1981.

Bauer, Y. *The Jewish Emergence from Powerlessness.* Toronto, 1979.

Fuchs, A. *The Unheeded Cry.* New York, 1986.

YESHAYAHU JELINEK

EUTHANASIA PROGRAM. The term "euthanasia" is generally used to describe "mercy killings," but it was employed by the Nazis to describe their systematic killing of various groups of individuals.

Before 1933, a certain tradition appears to have existed in Germany of helping to bring about death in certain borderline cases, especially in hospitals and nursing institutions. Doctors and nurses with strong conservative-nationalist or religious convictions ignored the unequivocal provisions of criminal law and "assisted death," and not just in rare cases.

When Hitler came to power in 1933, it was soon apparent that what the Nazis had in mind when they used terms like "the nation's health" and "racial hygiene" was the creation of a homogeneous *Herrenvolk* (master race), exuding health, and superior in mind and body to all other peoples: a people that had the right to claim world rule for itself for all time to come. This goal was to be achieved by multiplying those who belonged to the *Volksgemeinschaft* ("folk community") and were regarded as healthy and racially superior, and by getting rid, as fast as possible, of all those who belonged to foreign races, those who were not needed for the superior development of the German people, and of the sick and weak. Hitler wanted the Hitler Youth to be "as hard as steel, as strong and pliant as leather, and as fast as greyhounds." He was less concerned about the mental superiority of the "people of poets and thinkers" presumably because he regarded it as a natural attribute of the Germans, and therefore allowed himself, now and then, to ridicule the "decadent intellectualism" of German intellectuals.

As long as the Nazis confined themselves to the forced sterilization of "Rhineland bastards" (the children fathered by black troops serving in the post–World War I occupation forces), the "hereditary diseased," and "habitual criminals," the resistance they encountered was remarkably small. Neither was there any objection to the forcible confinement of "asocial elements," the disabled, "idiots," and "shirkers." When the war broke out there was no protest against the field hospital that military doctors were setting up to filter "war neurotics," or against the formation of battalions made up exclusively of persons suffering from diseases of the ear, the heart, or the kidneys. "Malingerers" were threatened by doctors that they would be put into concentration camps or "probation units" (made up of convicted criminals who had been pardoned so that they could be sent to the front). Such threats were actually carried out. When the battle of Stalingrad was drawing to its end, only front-line troops had food rations delivered to them, and some thirty thousand to forty thousand wounded and sick troops were not given medical treatment.

The critical point came when doctors and medical aides were asked, unequivocally, to participate in the murder of at least some of their patients. This was the meaning of the Euthanasia Program that Hitler entrusted to Reichsleiter Philip Bouhler, Dr. Karl Brandt, and doctors of their choice, for implementation in the late fall of 1939, with retroactive authorization as of September 1, 1939. "Manslaughter on request" accounted for very few of the killings performed under the Euthanasia Program; this was Social Darwinism on a grand scale, carried out without constraints in the T4 institutions. (T4 was the code name of the Nazis' "euthanasia" killing measures, derived from the address in Berlin—Tiergartenstrasse 4—where the Euthanasia Program, under the aegis of the Reich Chancellery, had its headquarters.) Later, in 1941 and 1942, the T4 specialists were transferred to the east, where they could practice the skills they had acquired in gassing and other forms of mass murder, on a truly immense scale in the extermination of Jews.

The Euthanasia Program, to judge by available records, encountered astonishingly few misgivings on religious, moral, or legal grounds. This may well have been due to a sophisticated personnel policy, the cunning *modus operandi*, and the mentality of the men in charge of the institutions, who were not inclined to lodge public protests or to take part personally in the operation. Disciplinary problems were avoided by spreading the assignments over a relatively large number of staff. There was ample opportunity for relaxation and entertainment to enable staff members to take their mind off their work, and a strong effort was made to keep the operation secret. To blunt any remaining humane feelings, hard liquor was always available in ample quantities. Frequent vacations were granted at choice resorts in Austria, free of charge, for the staff members together with their families; there were special allowances and bonuses and various other perquisites. The result was that the turnover of personnel in the T4 institutions was extraordinarily small, and no serious conflict ever developed between management and staff. Institutions whose managements were loath to cooperate in the operation had their patients transferred elsewhere, where no such difficulties were encountered.

The Euthanasia Program, even under the conditions prevailing at the time, was an illegal enterprise, and its implementation cannot therefore be explained by the high respect for authority and discipline that German officials were trained to observe. On the contrary, the bureaucrats' legalistic inertia caused them to oppose this innovation of the state going on a rampage against the weakest elements of the population, for whose welfare it was responsible. The euthanasia doctors, Karl Brandt and his team, who made ample use of the authorization they had been given by Hitler and, for the most part, knew their patients only from their files, were all of the type that is ready to take risks and is not bothered by legal niceties. They trusted their intuition; they were career-minded and flexible, venal, and unscrupulous.

It is estimated that up to 1939, some 200,000 to 350,000 persons were sterilized; of these, beginning in 1939, many fell victim to the Euthanasia Program. Some of them escaped that fate, either because it was felt that their sterilization had rendered them harmless or that they could still be useful as manpower, or because their families had made special efforts to bring them home before it was too late. On the other hand, many of the victims of the program who were gassed, shot to death, or killed by lethal injections had not been previously sterilized; these included children and patients found in hospitals and various other institutions in territories occupied at a later stage.

The first large-scale euthanasia action seems to have taken place in Pomerania and western Prussia shortly after the Polish campaign. During 1940, four euthanasia institutions went into operation: Grafeneck, in January; Brandenburg, in February; Hartheim, in May; and Sonnenstein, in June. In the first half of the year, 8,765 persons were gassed in these four institutions, three-quarters of them in May and June, a time when world attention was focused on the Battle of France. By the end of 1940, a total of 26,459 patients had been put to death, and in the first eight months of 1941, an additional 35,049 were "disinfected." These were the figures given by the accounting section of T4's head office.

Growing criticism of the Euthanasia Program—such as a sermon given by Bishop Clemens GALEN in Münster on August 3,

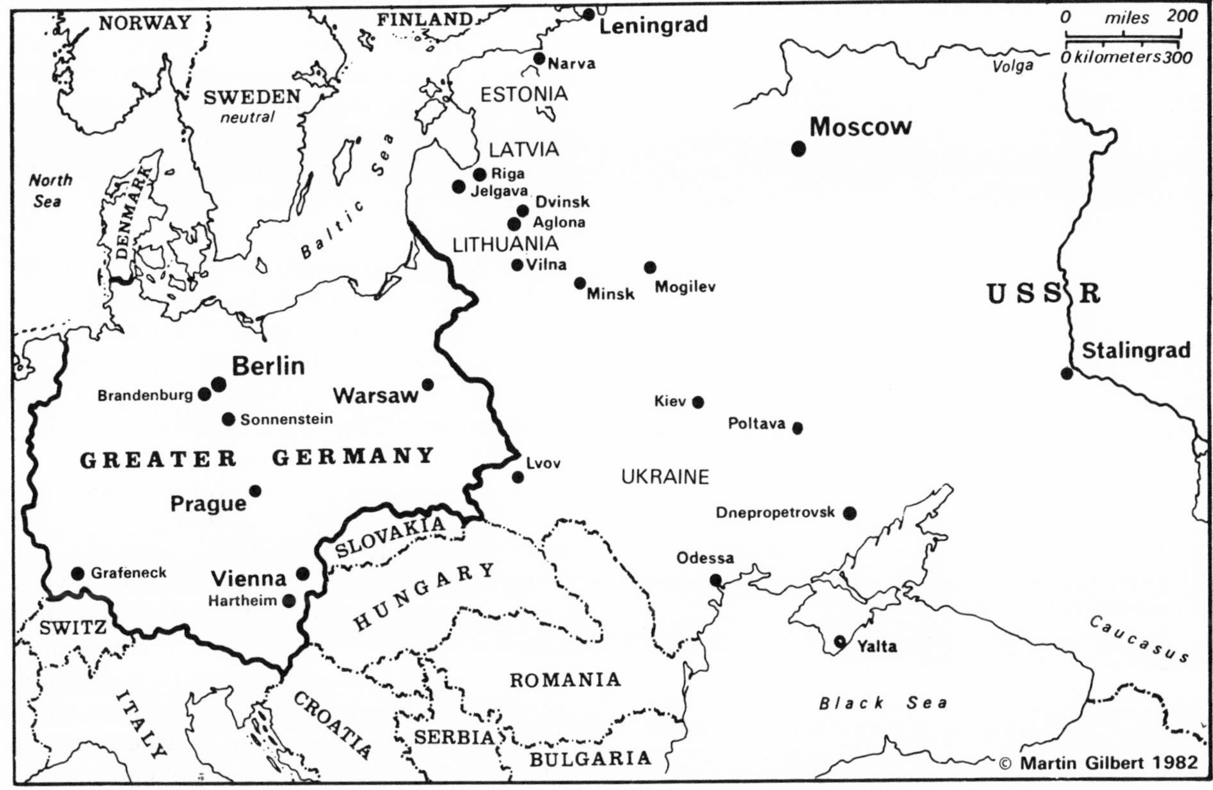

1941—caused Hitler to bring it to an official end. In practice, however, the operation was continued up to the end of the war, under a more effective camouflage. By September 1, 1941, the date of its official termination, 70,273 people had been "disinfected," according to T4 figures. Another figure given by T4 was the number of beds that had been made available for other purposes up to the end of 1941: 93,521.

This has led Ernst Klee (1985) to the conclusion that by then, as many as 33 percent of all the beds that had been occupied by the mentally ill in the prewar period had been made available. A large number of mentally ill persons were also killed in the occupied areas in the east: in Riga, Jelgava (Mitau), and Dvinsk (Dünaburg), 1,800 to 2,200; in Aglona, 544; in Poltava, 545; in Minsk and Mogilev, 836; in Dnepropetrovsk, 1,500; in Markayevo, 240; in Kiev, 360; and so on.

Following the transfer of the Euthanasia Program staff to AKTION REINHARD, its functions were taken over, temporarily, by different institutions. In one place, Meserlitz-Oberwald, 18,000 patients are said to have been killed between 1942 and 1945, mostly by lethal injections; among the victims, according to evidence given shortly before the end of the war, were sick German soldiers. Available data do not permit a precise figure to be given for the total extent of the Euthanasia Program. Its victims included the inmates of homes for the aged, homosexuals, the residents of welfare institutions, foreign workers, and concentration camp prisoners. As early as August 1942, Bishop Ludwig Sebastian of Speyer, in notes prepared for a conference of bishops held in Fulda that month, stated: "Far more than 100,000 people have been the victims of euthanasia. Men over seventy are no longer to receive medicine. Who is worth being kept alive at all? Only a Nazi." In the NUREMBERG TRIAL, the number of euthanasia victims was estimated at 275,000. It may be assumed that in the strict sense, 200,000 persons were murdered in the Euthanasia Program.

Mention should also be made of the role played by the Catholic and Evangelical churches in the period that led up to the Euthanasia Program and during its operation. Before embarking upon the program, Hitler held consultations on the reaction that he could expect from the two churches. With a few exceptions, his expectations of lack of opposition were borne out by the facts.

[*See also* Anthropology and National Socialism; Medical Experiments; Physicians, Nazi.]

BIBLIOGRAPHY

Klee, E. *"Euthanasie" im NS-Staat: Die Vernichtung "Lebensunwerten Lebens."* Frankfurt, 1985.

Lifton, R. J. *The Nazi Doctors: Medical Killing and the Psychology of Genocide.* New York, 1986.

Mielke, F. *Medizin ohne Menschlichkeit: Dokumente des Nürnberger Ärzteprozesses.* Frankfurt, 1960.

Nowak, K. *"Euthanasie" und Sterilisierung im Dritten Reich: Die Konfrontation der evangelischen und katholischen Kirche mit dem Gesetz zur "Verhütung erbkranken Nachwuchses" und der "Euthanasie"-Aktion.* Göttingen, 1978.

Wuttke-Groneberg, W. *Medizin im Nationalsozialismus: Ein Arbeitsbuch.* Rottenburg, 1982.

HANS-HEINRICH WILHELM

EVERT, ANGHELOS (1894–1970), head of the Athens police during 1943. Inspired by Metropolitan Damaskinos's public denunciation of the persecution of Jews, Evert ordered that new and false credentials be issued by the police to all Jews requesting them. Hundreds of such credentials were thus made available to needy Jews, some of them personally issued by Evert (such as those of Haim Efraim Cohen, an attorney, to whom Evert personally handed a new identity card with the name Pavlos Georgiou Panopoulos). Thanks to this courageous decision by Evert (which, owing to his personal involvement, placed him in jeopardy of arrest and severe punishment by the Germans, in the event of disclosure), countless Jews were able to ride out the German occupation undetected, under new identities. For this deed, Anghelos Evert was recognized by YAD VASHEM as a "RIGHTEOUS AMONG THE NATIONS" in 1969.

MORDECAI PALDIEL

EVIAN CONFERENCE, conference on the problem of Jewish REFUGEES that was held in Evian, France, on the shore of Lake Geneva, in July of 1938. From 1933 through 1937, about 130,000 Jews fled Germany. For the most part, this outflow was orderly; refugees were still able to take some property with them, and places for resettlement were generally available.

The extreme persecution that came in the wake of Germany's annexation of Austria in March 1938 rapidly erased all order from the refugee exodus. Within eleven days of the annexation, President Franklin D. ROOSEVELT proposed an international conference, (1) to facilitate the emigration of refugees from Germany and Austria; and (2) to establish a new international organization to work for an overall solution to the refugee problem. A primary motivation for the UNITED STATES DEPARTMENT OF STATE, which had first suggested the conference, was to blunt pressures in the United States for more liberal immigration legislation. Roosevelt made it clear from the start that no country would be expected to change its present policies significantly. The United States, he pointed out, contemplated no increase in its immigration quotas; but the German and Austrian quotas —until then far undersubscribed—would soon be opened for full use.

From July 6 to 15, 1938, delegates from thirty-two countries (the United States, Great Britain, France, six smaller European democracies, Canada, the Latin American nations, Australia, and New Zealand) met at the French resort town of Evian. In the opening public speech of the conference, Myron C. Taylor, the American delegate, stated that the United States' contribution was to make the German and Austrian quota of 27,370 per year fully available. As the sessions proceeded, delegate after delegate excused his country from accepting additional refugees.

The British representative declared that the overseas British territories were already overcrowded, were not suited to European settlement, or were unable to accept many refugees because of political conditions. Some areas, such as parts of East Africa, might offer possibilities, but only for limited numbers. He excluded Palestine from the

Evian discussion entirely. England itself, being fully populated and in the throes of the current unemployment problem, was not available for immigration. The delegate from France stated that his country would do what it could, but it had already reached "the extreme point of saturation as regards admission of refugees." The Belgian emissary reported that the same situation prevailed in his nation. The Netherlands could receive more immigrants only as refugees presently there moved on to lands of final settlement.

Australia could not encourage refugee immigration because, "as we have no real racial problem, we are not desirous of importing one." New Zealand's representative maintained that on account of economic problems, only a limited number could be accepted into his land. He went on to characterize the Evian Conference as a "modern 'wailing wall.' " Because of the depression, Canada had almost no room for immigrants. For the Latin American countries, unemployment was the main factor in the need to keep immigration at a low rate. The tiny Dominican Republic, one of the last countries to report, alone offered encouragement, volunteering to contribute large but unspecified areas for agricultural colonization.

An American news correspondent accurately reflected the tenor of the conference: "Myron C. Taylor . . . opened proceedings: 'The time has come when governments . . . must act and act promptly.' Most governments represented acted promptly by slamming their doors against Jewish refugees."

Before adjourning, the Evian Conference established the INTERGOVERNMENTAL COMMITTEE ON REFUGEES (ICR) and commissioned it to negotiate on two fronts. One task was to "approach the governments of the countries of refuge with a view to developing opportu-

The Evian Conference was held in July 1938. James McDonald (seated, second from right) was one of the American delegates.

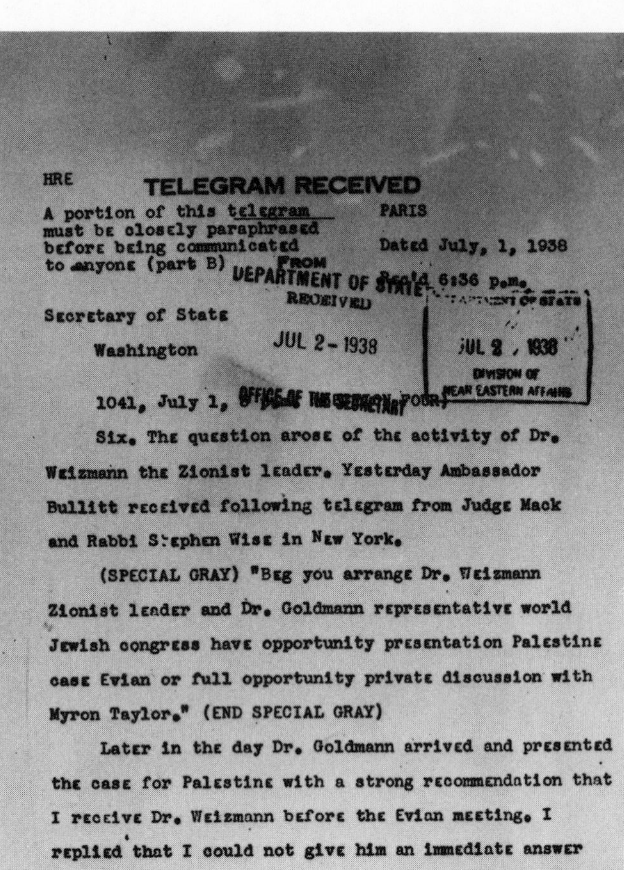

HRE

TELEGRAM RECEIVED

A portion of this telegram must be closely paraphrased before being communicated to anyone (part B)

PARIS

Dated July, 1, 1938

Rec'd 6:36 p.m.

FROM DEPARTMENT OF STATE RECEIVED JUL 2 - 1938 OFFICE OF THE SECRETARY

DEPARTMENT OF STATE JUL 2, 1938 DIVISION OF NEAR EASTERN AFFAIRS

Secretary of State

Washington

1041, July 1, [illegible] FOUR)

Six. The question arose of the activity of Dr. Weizmann the Zionist leader. Yesterday Ambassador Bullitt received following telegram from Judge Mack and Rabbi Stephen Wise in New York.

(SPECIAL GRAY) "Beg you arrange Dr. Weizmann Zionist leader and Dr. Goldmann representative world Jewish congress have opportunity presentation Palestine case Evian or full opportunity private discussion with Myron Taylor." (END SPECIAL GRAY)

Later in the day Dr. Goldmann arrived and presented the case for Palestine with a strong recommendation that I receive Dr. Weizmann before the Evian meeting. I replied that I could not give him an immediate answer and discussed the position with Palairet who said that his government would naturally prefer that this meeting should not take place. I said there would be opportunity for Dr. Weizmann to present his case privately at Evian if he so desired and that I would not see him before the conference met.

Seven

Part of a telegram sent by Myron Taylor, the American representative at the Evian Conference, to Secretary of State Cordell Hull and Under Secretary Sumner Welles on July 1, 1938. Sir Michael Palairet was the second British delegate at this conference on the emigration and resettlement of refugees from Germany and Austria. [U.S. National Archives and Records Service]

nities for permanent settlement." The other step aimed at persuading Germany to cooperate in establishing "conditions of orderly emigration," which particularly meant to permit removal from the Reich of a reasonable amount of refugee property.

The ICR, however, received little authority and almost no funds or support from its member nations, and it had virtually no success in opening countries to refugees. The coming of war in September 1939 cut short its efforts to arrange with Germany for refugees to bring some property out with them, and the committee soon slipped into inactivity.

Many months before the demise of the ICR, it was evident that the Evian Conference had accomplished virtually nothing. Even as the conference closed, most observers agreed that it had failed in its main task, of finding places where the refugees could go. An immediate consequence of the conference was that it crushed the hopes of hundreds of thousands of European Jews, people who had been looking to the nations at Evian to save them from an increasingly impossible situation.

The Evian Conference stands in historical perspective as a critical turning point. At the conference the Western democracies made it clear that they were willing to do next to nothing for the Jews of Europe. Soon afterward, KRISTALLNACHT, which took place in the autumn of 1938, signaled to the world that Jews could no longer live where the Nazis ruled. At Evian, the world had shown that it would not make room for those Jews. Thus 1938 became the crucial year in the coming of the Holocaust. By its end, the world knew the Jews had to leave. Germany was still pressing the Jews to leave, and the Jews themselves were now anxious to do so. But the world's doors, closed at Evian, remained shut throughout World War II.

In the midst of the Holocaust, the United States and Great Britain held another conference to consider helping the Jews of Europe. The delegates to the BERMUDA CONFERENCE of April 1943 knew clearly that the Jews were being systematically exterminated. They too decided to do next to nothing.

BIBLIOGRAPHY

Abella, I., and H. Troper. *None Is Too Many: Canada and the Jews of Europe, 1933–1948.* New York, 1983.

Feingold, H. L. *The Politics of Rescue: The Roosevelt Administration and the Holocaust, 1938–1945.* New Brunswick, N.J., 1970.

Katz, S. Z. "Public Opinion in Western Europe

and the Evian Conference of July 1938." *Yad Vashem Studies* 9 (1973): 105–132.

Marrus, M. R. The *Unwanted*. New York, 1985.

Stein, J. B. "Great Britain and the Evian Conference of 1938." *Wiener Library Bulletin* 29/1 (1976): 40–52.

Wyman, D. S. *Paper Walls: America and the Refugee Crisis*. Amherst, Mass., 1978.

DAVID S. WYMAN

EVREISKI ANTIFASHISTSKI KOMITET. *See* Jewish Antifascist Committee.

EXCHANGE: JEWS AND GERMANS. During much of World War II, an agreement between the Nazis and the Allies permitted small numbers of Jews to be exchanged for Germans living in Palestine or other countries of the British Empire. The Jews involved either were of Palestinian nationality, possessed immigration visas ("certificates") to Palestine, or had a valid claim thereto. The origin of the exchange lay in the fact that when the war broke out, some two thousand Germans were living in Palestine (descendants of Knights Templar who had settled in Palestine in the nineteenth century), while there were British nationals in Germany and German-occupied Poland whom the British government sought to repatriate to Britain. These British subjects included Jews from Palestine who were stranded in Poland at the outbreak of the war.

This led to lengthy negotiations for the exchange of their respective nationals between the two warring countries. In the initial stage the negotiations were conducted by way of the United States embassy in Berlin. In June 1941, when the United States recalled its ambassador in Berlin, Switzerland became the go-between. As time went on, the Germans were eager to increase the number of Germans who would be exchanged and were prepared to exchange them for Jews who were not Palestinian nationals and only had immigration visas in their possession.

Developments in the exchange issue can be divided into three phases:

1. The first phase, which lasted from the beginning of the war up to the second half of 1941, saw efforts being made from several quarters for an exchange to be arranged. In Palestine, pressure was brought on the Jewish Agency to intervene with the British authorities on behalf of relatives of Palestinian Jews who had been stranded in Germany or Poland. In the British Parliament, members frequently put questions to the government concerning the fate of Palestinian nationals stranded in Poland. At the same time, the families of German nationals in Palestine applied to their government for action to be taken to bring their relatives to Germany. Both governments were highly suspicious of each other, and as a result negotiations on the subject did not begin. The German attitude changed in July 1940, when the Spanish consul in Jerusalem (who represented German interests in Palestine) informed the German government that seven hundred German nationals, men, women, and children, had been notified that they were going to be transferred from Palestine to another destination. Subsequently, these Germans were deported to camps in Australia. This caused the German government to step up the pace of the negotiations, and coincided with increased pressure in Britain on the Foreign Office to effect an exchange.

2. The second phase lasted from mid-1941 to February 1943, and in that period three groups of exchangees arrived in Palestine. The first group, consisting of 46 persons (29 women, 16 children, and 1 man), arrived in December 1941, having been exchanged for 69 Germans. The second group arrived in Palestine in November 1942 and was made up of 139 British subjects, of whom 69 were Palestinians. They were exchanged for 305 Germans. This group of Palestinian residents had been staying in Poland at the time of the major *Aktionen* in the Polish ghettos and their reports deeply influenced the YISHUV and its rescue efforts. Another group, numbering 15 persons, arrived in February 1943. Both the Germans and the British made sure that only persons who answered the conditions of the agreement would be exchanged. With respect to Palestinians, those whom the British regarded as meeting the conditions were (a) holders of British passports; (b) women who had acquired Palestinian nationality in Poland by marriage prior to August

1939, and their children; (c) women and children who had gone abroad from Palestine before the war broke out; or (d) wives and children of residents of Palestine who were not Palestinian nationals.

The punctilious British observance of these conditions, in addition to the fact that many of the potential exchangees were no longer alive or could not be traced in the ghettos and camps, meant that in this period the number of Germans exchanged was twice as high as that of Palestinian Jews. There were also various obstacles to be overcome, created by the mutual suspicion of the two governments and requiring very precise timetables and details of the exchange method, by means of intermediaries.

3. In the third phase, which lasted from February 1943 to April 1945, positions on the exchange issue underwent a change; there was a trend to widen the range of categories that would qualify for exchange, both among German official circles and Jews in Nazi-occupied countries, and among Jewish organizations and institutions in Palestine and neutral countries. The deep impact of the exchange that had taken place in November 1942 persuaded Jewish Agency officials in Palestine and Switzerland that this method offered a crumb of hope. As Eliyahu Dobkin, head of the Immigration Department of the Jewish Agency, stated at a meeting held on October 8, 1943: "There was a time when we deluded ourselves that the Allied powers would be ready to propose an exchange plan to the Germans—hundreds of thousands of Jews, for German nationals in the democratic countries."

At this time also, the Jewish Agency's Palestine Office in Geneva distributed hundreds of letters stating that the bearer of the letter was a candidate for exchange. These letters had the effect of preventing, or at least postponing, the deportation of Jews to extermination camps, especially from the Netherlands and Belgium. For their part, Jews in the Netherlands and Belgium applied to Geneva for written confirmation that they had been granted immigration "certificates" as a means of saving themselves.

For several months in 1943, leading officials in the German government entertained the idea that preparations should be set in motion for a large-scale exchange. Top officials in the German Foreign Ministry believed that it would be possible to repatriate a large number of Germans from Palestine and various other countries in the British Empire and South America, in exchange for Jews in German-occupied countries. The German foreign minister, Joachim von RIBBENTROP, proposed that thirty thousand Jews be assembled for this purpose to serve as candidates for such an exchange. In a letter dated May 14, 1943, Eberhard von THADDEN, head of the German Foreign Ministry section dealing with Jewish affairs, wrote: "Since the British have more Germans in their hands than we have British, in this special case Jews could also be used for exchange." Heinrich HIMMLER agreed, but reduced the proposed number to ten thousand, and a special camp was put up at BERGEN-BELSEN to take in the candidates for exchange. In July 1943, several Jews who had been staying at the HOTEL POLSKI in Warsaw were sent to Bergen-Belsen and assured that they were candidates for exchange. Most of them were cheated and sent to the AUSCHWITZ extermination camp; a few did get to Bergen-Belsen and were saved. At the end of 1943 and the beginning of 1944, some four thousand Jews from the WESTERBORK concentration camp in the Netherlands were sent to Bergen-Belsen. In August 1943, twelve hundred children from the BIAŁYSTOK ghetto were sent to THERESIENSTADT for a temporary stay; they, too, were candidates for exchange, but in the end they were sent to Auschwitz and killed there. The negotiations with the British were conducted by Switzerland, as the power representing Britain's interest in contacts with Germany. The plan did not materialize. The Germans labored under two illusions: (1) that there were many Germans who wished to return to Germany, whereas in fact this was true of only a few; and (2) that the British were willing to go to great lengths in order to rescue Jews.

As 1943 drew to an end, the Germans no longer expected a large-scale exchange to take place. Negotiations with the British were kept up, but the purpose was to maintain a channel of communication. In January 1944, conditions were ripe for another exchange. In that month the United States established its

WAR REFUGEE BOARD, and a genuine effort was launched to rescue Jews from the Nazis' clutches. In March 1944 Ira HIRSCHMANN, as representative of the board, established himself in Istanbul and began negotiations from there, through the International RED CROSS; another board representative, Roswell McClelland, went to operate in Geneva with the same objective. In April 1944 a representative of Switzerland went to Berlin for negotiations on an exchange. These negotiations dragged on, and only on June 26, 1944, did an exchange take place, the fourth of its kind. A total of 283 Jews were exchanged, 222 from Bergen-Belsen and 61 from the VITTEL concentration camp in France. None of the Jews was a Palestinian national. All were taken to Vienna and from there went to Palestine, by way of Turkey. In exchange, 150 Germans were returned, 74 of them from South Africa. The deal took into account the larger number of Germans that had been permitted to leave in the previous exchange transactions.

Another exchange was made in March 1945, this time with Sweden acting as the intermediary. It affected 99 Jews from Bergen-Belsen and 38 from the RAVENSBRÜCK concentration camp. Ostensibly, the group was made up of Jews who were Turkish nationals, but this was not true of the majority. They boarded a ship in Sweden and went to Turkey, and from there to Palestine. When the war ended, some 600 to 700 Jews in Bergen-Belsen were in possession of immigration certificates and were candidates for exchange. It is not known how many of these starved to death in the final days of the war.

The number of Jews who were exchanged, in the five groups, is shown below.

December 1941	46
November 1942	69
February 1943	15
June 1944	283
March 1945	137
Total	550

The saving of 550 Jews was in itself important, but the exchange operation had an effect that was over and above these results, in three respects:

1. The rescue of persons who held Palestinian nationality or immigration visas to Palestine.

2. The saving of hundreds of Jews because they were in possession of a paper certifying that they would be granted immigration visas to Palestine and were therefore not sent to extermination camps. Some of these were sent to Bergen-Belsen; others stayed where they were. Many held out to the end of the war and were thus rescued.

3. The information supplied by the exchanges. This was particularly important in the case of those exchanged in November 1942, who had left Poland after the large *Aktionen* of the summer and fall of 1942. Theirs was the first testimony of the dimensions of the Nazi extermination operations, and it aroused in the YISHUV an awareness of the urgency of rescue efforts.

BIBLIOGRAPHY

Adler, H. G. *Der verwaltete Mensch.* Tübingen, 1974.

Barlas, C. *Rescue during the Holocaust.* Tel Aviv, 1975. (In Hebrew.)

Eck, N. "Jews in Exchange for Germans." *Studies in Holocaust and Resistance* 2 (1973): 23–49. (In Hebrew.)

From Bergen-Belsen to Freedom: The Story of the Exchange of Jewish Inmates of Bergen-Belsen with German Templars from Palestine. Jerusalem, 1986.

Kolb, E. *Bergen-Belsen: Geschichte des "Aufenthaltslagers," 1943–1945.* Hannover, 1962.

Wasserstein, B. *Britain and the Jews of Europe, 1939–1945.* Oxford, 1979. See pages 222–235.

RUTH ZARIZ

EXHUMATION OPERATION. *See* Aktion 1005.

EXODUS 1947, an "illegal immigration" ship that became the symbol of the struggle for the right of free Jewish immigration into Palestine.

Zionist policy, as it came to be formulated in the fall of 1945, regarded the Holocaust survivors and the DISPLACED PERSONS in Europe as the major force in the political struggle for the establishment of a Jewish state and for the continuation of ALIYA BET ("illegal" immigration)—the major arena of the struggle at the time. In November 1946 the Mosad le-Aliya Bet, the main Aliya Bet agency, acquired an American ship, the *President Garfield*. Originally an excursion ship for cruises in rivers and coastal waters, the *President Garfield* during the war had been converted to serve navy requirements. It had room for 4,000 passengers and was the largest ship ever used by the Mosad up until then. By organizing this voyage, the Mosad people sought to relieve the pressure by the Jewish displaced persons in Germany to leave the camps, and also to launch an "illegal immigration" operation, unprecedented in size, that would be covered by the media and draw the attention of the members of the United Nations Special Committee on Palestine (UNSCOP), then visiting Palestine on a fact-finding mission.

In early July 1947, within seven days, 4,500 Jewish refugees, equipped with a Colombian collective-transit visa, were moved from camps in Germany to the south of France. There they boarded the *President Garfield*, lying at anchor in the old port of Sète, near Marseilles. With discreet help from cabinet members of the French Socialist government and the French security agencies who supported the Jewish and Zionist cause (help that caused a sharp confrontation in the cabinet with the ministers who supported the British position), this logistically complicated operation was launched, with far-reaching political implications.

On July 11, at dawn, the ship departed for the shores of Palestine. Once it was on the high seas, the ship changed its name to *Exodus 1947*. The 4,500 "illegal" immigrants aboard the ship, made up of organized groups and individual refugees, maintained impressive internal discipline throughout the voyage, despite the overcrowding and shortages from which they suffered. During the voyage the ship was under the surveillance of the British fleet, and even before it had entered Palestine's territorial waters, British destroyers closed in on *Exodus 1947* and forced it to proceed to the Haifa port. There, the British used force to remove the passengers from the ship; the refugees offered strong resistance, and in the ensuing clash three Jews were killed and many were wounded.

On July 20 the *Exodus 1947* refugees were put on board three British deportation vessels, which were to take them back to their port of departure in France. This was an innovation in British policy; since August 1946, "illegal" immigrants who were apprehended had been deported to Cyprus. On this occasion, the British decided to take the Jewish refugees back to the country that had enabled them to leave the Continent, hoping thereby to prevent that country from giving further aid to the Zionist struggle.

Emil Sandström, the Swedish judge who was chairman of UNSCOP, with two other members of the committee, was present in the Haifa port when British soldiers were dragging the resisting Jewish refugees on board the deportation ships. One of the two other members, in an on-the-spot opinion, said that the scene they were witnessing was the most convincing evidence that had yet been brought before the committee of the need for a Jewish national home. The report presented to the United Nations by the committee in September 1947, recommending that the British Mandate be terminated and a Jewish state be established in a part of Palestine, did indeed reflect the impact of the *Exodus* affair and of the post-Holocaust situation of the displaced Jews of Europe.

For an entire month, the three British deportation vessels lay at anchor off Port-de-Bouc, a French port in the Mediterranean. The thousands of Jewish refugees aboard the ship suffered from incredibly overcrowded conditions, poor sanitary arrangements, and the scorching summer heat. The French authorities refused to accede to the British demand that they force the refugees to land in France, but they offered asylum to any refugee who wanted to stay in France. The Mosad people on board and the leaders of the organized and well-disciplined groups among the passengers arranged for all of the thousands of Holocaust survivors to go on a hunger strike and thereby rivet world attention to their plight. Finally the British, at the proposal of Foreign Secretary Ernest Bevin, decided that the refugees would be taken back to the camps in Germany—a decision that raised the anger even of United States President Harry S. Truman and Secretary of State George Marshall, who, while trying to help the Jewish refugees, had until then stayed out of the *Exodus* affair.

Among the Zionist leaders a sharp debate developed as to how the affair should be resolved. When it first became known that *Exodus* refugees might be sent back to Germany, Chaim WEIZMANN and others felt that it would be preferable for the refugees to disembark in France. David BEN-GURION, however, was adamantly opposed, and insisted that the Zionist Executive adopt a unanimous stand rejecting all proposals that might wreck or weaken the strategy on which the Zionist struggle was based.

On September 8, 1947, British troops in the port of Hamburg, Germany, forcibly removed the refugees from the ship. Each refugee was dragged off the ship by a team of steel-helmeted soldiers, in full view of the hundreds of newspapermen from all over the world who were covering the event. The refugees, for the most part, stayed in the camps in Germany for over a year, and reached Israel only after the state was established, the last arriving in 1949. The *Exodus 1947* episode was the climax of the drama of the "illegal immigration" to Palestine, and even while it was being enacted, it turned into a test of strength between the British and the Jews of Palestine.

BIBLIOGRAPHY

Bauer, Y. *Flight and Rescue: Bricha.* New York, 1970.

Druz, J. *The Exodus Incident in a New Light.* Tel Aviv, 1971. (In Hebrew.)

Gruber, R. *Destination Palestine: The Story of the Haganah Ship Exodus 1947.* New York, 1948.

Holly, D. C. *Exodus 1947.* Boston, 1969.

Schaary, D. *The Cyprus Detention Camps for "Illegal" Immigrants to Palestine, 1946–1949.* Jerusalem, 1981. (In Hebrew.)

IDITH ZERTAL

EXPROPRIATION. *See* Arisierung; Einsatzstab Rosenberg; Haupttreuhandstelle Ost.

EXTERMINATION CAMPS (Ger., *Vernichtungslager*), Nazi camps in occupied Poland in which a huge number of Jews were killed, as part of the "FINAL SOLUTION of the Jewish question in Europe." These camps had a single goal: the blanket murder of the Jews, irrespective of age or sex. In contrast to the procedure at other camps, no *Selektionen* took place (with some exceptions in AUSCHWITZ-Birkenau); everyone brought to an extermination camp, including persons fit for work, was murdered. For this reason, such camps have sometimes been called "death factories."

The systematic mass murder of Jews began when the Germans invaded the Soviet Union, on June 22, 1941. In the first phase, carried out primarily by the SS EINSATZGRUPPEN, hundreds of thousands of Jews were shot to death. This method of killing, however, proved too slow for the Germans, and the considerable manpower required made it difficult to keep the project secret. Thus, senior SS officers devised a different murder technique, that of gassing. Experience in the lethal use of gas had been gained in the institutions involved in the mass murder of the EUTHANASIA PROGRAM.

An experiment in murdering human beings with poison gas was made on September 3, 1941, in the main camp of Auschwitz. A group of 600 Soviet prisoners of war was put in a hermetically sealed cell into which crystals of ZYKLON B gas were thrown; all the prisoners were soon dead of asphyxiation. Following this successful experiment, and others, in Auschwitz and elsewhere, the SS authorities in charge of the "Final Solution" planned to construct extermination camps that would use gas for the murder operations.

Thus, instead of killing the Jews where they lived throughout Europe, the Germans decided to bring them to extermination camps, all in occupied Poland: Auschwitz-Birkenau (Auschwitz II), CHEŁMNO, BEŁŻEC, SOBIBÓR, and TREBLINKA. Auschwitz-Birkenau was also a concentration camp; here, in some cases, *Selektionen* were made among the incoming transports, with some of the arrivals "selected" for work or for onward dispatch to other camps. Some scholars classify the MAJDANEK concentration camp as an extermination camp because there was a period when transports arriving there were handled as they were in Auschwitz, and murdered by gassing. The first extermination camp, at Chełmno, in the Łódź district, was put into

operation on December 8, 1941. In that camp the victims were killed in GAS VANS; the operation functioned uninterruptedly until April 1943, was then closed for over a year, and reopened for a short while in the summer of 1944. Some 320,000 people are estimated to have been murdered there.

Auschwitz-Birkenau began operating as an extermination camp in March 1942. At its height, it had four gas chambers using Zyklon B, as well as crematoria. Until it was closed in November 1944, up to 1.5 million Jews were murdered there, as were tens of thousands of GYPSIES and Soviet prisoners of war.

Bełżec, Sobibór, and Treblinka were established in the framework of AKTION REINHARD, the murder operation aimed at the Jews of the GENERALGOUVERNEMENT, in Poland. These extermination camps used carbon monoxide gas generated by a gasoline or diesel engine. Bełżec was in operation from March to December 1942, and some 600,000 Jews were murdered there; Sobibór, from April 1942 to October 1943, with 250,000 murdered; and

Treblinka, from July 1942 to August 1943, with 870,000 victims.

The existence of the extermination camps and their operations were classified as top secret in the Third Reich, with the SS coordinating an elaborate system of diversion and deception around them. The camps were concealed, first of all, from the prospective victims, but also from the local population and from German authorities not directly involved in the "Final Solution." From the outside the sites had the appearance of labor or concentration camps, and the gas chambers looked as though they contained showers and disinfection rooms. The Jews who were to be sent to the camps were told that they were going to labor camps somewhere in the east; when they arrived at their destination, they were informed that they had come to a transit camp or labor camp, and that they were to take a shower while their clothes were disinfected. As a further means of hiding the truth, the women and children were separated from the men. The actual murder operation lasted fifteen to thirty minutes. The bodies of the victims were removed from the gas chambers by crews of Jewish prisoners and cremated.

There were audacious attempts by Jews to escape from the extermination camps. Most of these ended in failure, but a few succeeded, and the survivors revealed the truth about the camps to the outside world. Uprisings took place in Treblinka on August 2, 1943, and in Sobibór on October 14 of that year; in each instance, hundreds of prisoners fled the camps. On October 7, 1944, Jews of the Auschwitz-Birkenau SONDERKOMMANDO, who worked in the gas chambers and crematoria, revolted. The majority of those who escaped during these outbreaks were captured and killed.

The extermination camps were under the jurisdiction and administration of the SS. Auschwitz-Birkenau was attached to the WIRTSCHAFTS-VERWALTUNGSHAUPTAMT (Economic-Administrative Main Office; WVHA), which controlled most of the concentration camps in the Third Reich. The other extermination camps were administered by the SS chiefs in their respective districts: Bełżec, Sobibór, and Treblinka came under the SS and Police Leader (*SS- und Polizeiführer*; SSPF) of the Lublin district, and Chełmno under the SSPF of the WARTHEGAU. Command, administration, and guard duties within the camps were in the hands of the SS (in Bełżec, Sobibór, and Treblinka, the guard unit was made up of Ukrainian volunteers, most of them Soviet prisoners of war). Manual labor in the camps, which included the removal of corpses from the gas chambers and their interment or cremation, was carried out by Jews selected from among the arrivals to the camps.

A total of some 3.5 million Jews were murdered in the extermination camps, as well as tens of thousands of Gypsies and Soviet prisoners of war.

[*See also* Genocide.]

BIBLIOGRAPHY

Arad, Y. *Belzec, Sobibor, Treblinka: Operation Reinhard Death Camps.* Bloomington, 1987.

Arad, Y. *Treblinka: Hell and Revolt.* Tel Aviv, 1983. (In Hebrew.)

Broad, P. *KZ Auschwitz: Reminiscences of Perry Broad, SS-Man in the Auschwitz Concentration Camp.* Oświęcim, Poland, 1965.

Feig, K. *Hitler's Death Camps.* New York, 1981.

Gutman, Y., and A. Saf, eds. *The Nazi Concentration Camps: Structure and Aims; The Image of the Prisoner; The Jews in the Camps.* Proceedings of the Fourth Yad Vashem International Historical Conference. Jerusalem, 1984.

Kraus, O., and E. Kulka. *The Mills of Death: Auschwitz.* Jerusalem, 1961. (In Hebrew.)

YITZHAK ARAD

EXTRADITION OF WAR CRIMINALS. In the Moscow Declaration of November 1, 1943, the three principal powers in the anti-Nazi alliance—the United States, the USSR, and Great Britain—solemnly committed themselves to bring to trial those major war criminals whose crimes were not confined to any particular geographical location. Such trials were to be conducted within a framework that the three powers would agree upon. It was under this commitment that the Nuremberg and Tokyo International Military Tribunals were set up (*see* NUREMBERG TRIAL).

The declarations issued by the three major powers and their allies stated that each member of the alliance would try the war criminals who had committed crimes on that member's territory or against its nationals. It was further agreed, especially in the 1945 Potsdam Agreement, that war criminals would also be tried by tribunals that the major powers would establish in Germany, in their respective zones of occupation.

Like arrangements made to facilitate the extradition of Nazi war criminals in cases where a country had a particular interest in holding the trial, such declarations established the principle of universality of punishment applied to war criminals. This was the same principle applying to piracy on the high seas and other grave crimes and obliging every country that holds a person wanted for such crimes either to try or to extradite that person.

It follows from this that in the case of the trial and punishment of Nazi war criminals the rule that extradition depends on the existence of an extradition agreement between the two countries concerned does not apply. In practice, the principle of the universality of punishment of war criminals was recognized and enforced only before the cold war; specifically, until March 31, 1948, when the UNITED NATIONS WAR CRIMES COMMISSION ceased operating.

For political motives (especially their desire to exploit the information possessed by some Nazi war criminals for intelligence purposes or their expertise for military research projects), the Western powers stopped complying with the rules established by the United Nations War Crimes Commission. Under these rules, every person whose name appeared in the United Nations Commission's lists of war criminals had to be put on trial or extradited. The Soviet Union similarly ceased prosecuting Nazi war criminals, and failed to respond to Western requests for their extradition.

The result was that a large number of Nazi criminals escaped without being tried or extradited. They included Dr. Josef MENGELE, Klaus Barbie (*see* BARBIE TRIAL), and Alois BRUNNER. The Polish War Crimes Commission, which was attached to the United States military headquarters in the American zone of occupation in Germany, discovered Mengele in a prisoner-of-war camp and requested his extradition to Poland. Holocaust-survivor organizations in Germany, as well as other Jewish and non-Jewish bodies, urged speedy compliance with the request made by Col. Marian Mushkat, the head of the Polish War Crimes Commission, for Mengele's extradition. Their efforts, however, were in vain; the Nazi criminal disappeared, and, as was subsequently discovered, was even helped to escape to South America.

At about the same time, a French commission located Klaus Barbie in an American camp for prisoners of war. Its request to extradite Barbie to France was denied, and it was only years later that he was found to be living in Bolivia. After extended negotiations with the Bolivian government, Barbie was extradited to France in February 1983.

Alois Brunner has been in Damascus since 1954, and arrest warrants have been issued by France, Austria, and the Federal Republic of Germany. A request to the Syrian authorities for extradition, made by West Germany in 1984, has so far brought no response.

[*See also* Wiesenthal, Simon.]

BIBLIOGRAPHY

Mushkat, M. "The Mengele File." *International Problems* 45 (1985): 25–31. (In Hebrew.)

Robinson, J. *And the Crooked Shall Be Made Straight.* Philadelphia, 1965. See chapter 2.

Ruzie, D. "The Klaus Barbie Case: War Crimes versus Crimes against Humanity." *Patterns of Prejudice* 20/3 (July 1986): 27–33.

MARIAN MUSHKAT

EYNIKEYT (Unity), Yiddish-language newspaper of the JEWISH ANTIFASCIST COMMITTEE that appeared from 1942 to 1948. The committee, which was organized by the Soviet government, was made up of Jewish representative figures and intellectuals in the USSR; its purpose was to gain world Jewry's support for the Soviet Union and Soviet policy. *Eynikeyt* first came out in Kuibyshev, where government offices had been relocated when the German siege of Moscow began, in October 1941, and it was later published in Moscow. Originally, it came out once every ten days. The first editor was Shakhno Epshtein, the committee's secretary; after his death, in 1945, he was replaced by G. Zhits. *Eynikeyt* was directed primarily at Yiddish-reading Jews in the United States and other countries, and it was also read by Jews in the Soviet Union, at home and at the war front. At its height, it was printed in ten thousand copies, and as of July 1943 it was appearing weekly. Both during and after the war, *Eynikeyt* published news reports and articles on Jewish subjects, such as the Nazi killings of Jews, Jews and their distinguished service in the Red Army and the partisan movement, and attempts at revolt in the ghettos—all topics that were barely mentioned in the regular Soviet press.

There is evidence that *Eynikeyt* created a great deal of interest among Soviet Jews; in a single year, five thousand letters to the editor were received. The paper had correspondents in the centers of Jewish population in the Soviet Union, as well as on the various fronts. It took special interest in the western areas of the country when these were liberated, seeking to gather information on the extermination of Jews and on Jewish survivors. In December 1943, the Soviet writer and journalist Vasily Grossman published in *Eynikeyt* an article titled "The Ukraine without Jews."

After the war, *Eynikeyt* reported on attempts at Jewish resettlement in Palestine and on the revival of Jewish culture in the Soviet Union. It appeared three times a week. The Jewish Antifascist Committee made efforts to turn it into a daily and increase its distribution, but these were unsuccessful—in the war years because of the shortage of paper, and after the war as a result of government policy against manifestations of Jewish culture. As of the autumn of 1946, *Eynikeyt* became increasingly critical of Jewish nationalist expressions and Jewish issues. In November 1948, when the Jewish Antifascist Committee was disbanded, *Eynikeyt* ceased publication.

BIBLIOGRAPHY

Redlich, S. *Propaganda and Nationalism in Wartime Russia: The Jewish Antifascist Committee in the USSR, 1941–1948*. Boulder, 1982.

SHIMON REDLICH

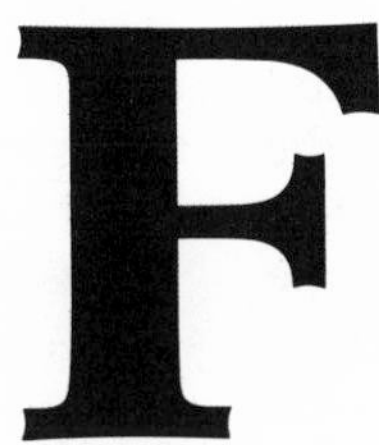

FAMILY CAMPS IN THE FORESTS, groups of Jews—men, women, and children, and families of various age groups—who took refuge in forests in the Holocaust period, struggling to save their lives. Such camps existed in the forests of eastern Poland, western Belorussia, and the western Ukraine. In size the camps ranged from those consisting of a few families only, to camps in which many hundreds of Jews gathered. As a rule, each camp had a group of armed men who defended the camp and obtained food for its inhabitants. The emergence of family camps coincided with the rise of the Jewish partisan movement (*see* PARTISANS), and indeed the two phenomena were interconnected; in most places in the forests with a concentration of Jewish partisans, a family camp existed. Sometimes partisan units were combined with family camps. The main difference between the two was that whereas the family camp's primary purpose was to save lives, with fighting the enemy secondary, for the partisans the priorities were reversed.

Family camps could exist only in areas with large forests, which in eastern Europe meant mainly Belorussia, Polesye, and northern Volhynia. For this reason most of the camps, and the largest, were situated in the Naliboki Forest of western Belorussia—for example, the camp commanded by Tuvia BIELSKI, with twelve hundred people, and Shalom ZORIN's camp, with eight hundred. A few family camps, with dozens of families each, also existed in Eastern Galicia and the Lublin district. The great majority of the family-camp population were Jews from towns and villages located in the vicinity who were no strangers to the forest or to the conditions prevailing in it. But Jews from MINSK, VILNA, BARANOVICHI, Sarny, LIDA, and similar places were also to be found in the camps.

Some individual Jewish families appeared in the forests as early as the latter part of

1941, but most of the family camps were made up of refugees from the Nazi extermination drive that swept western Belorussia and the western Ukraine in the spring and winter of 1942. The flight of Jews into the forest camps kept up until the spring of 1943. Among those who took this route of escape were the survivors of uprisings in various ghettos, such as those of LACHVA, TUCHIN, and NESVIZH, who made their own way to the camps after the fighting was over and the ghetto had been set on fire.

Daily Life. The routine of life in the family camps was determined by the security problem; the need for mobility (that is, for moving quickly to another location when this was necessitated by information received in the camp or when military operations were being carried out by Germans or their collaborators); the search for food; and the difficulties posed by the climate and the general harsh conditions prevailing in the forest. The acquisition of food required military action by armed groups of men belonging to the camp who broke into the villages near the forest and seized foodstuffs by force; in some cases, fights broke out and shots were exchanged with the police and local security men, leading to casualties and loss of life.

For security reasons the camps were situated deep in the forests and in swampy areas. In summer, the people lived in lean-tos made of tree branches; in winter they built wooden huts, embedding them deep in the ground. Whenever there were indications that the existence and location of a camp had been discovered, it would be moved elsewhere. In most cases the local population was hostile to the Jews in the family camps, their age-old antisemitism being reinforced by Nazi propaganda and by the raids made by Jews from the camps on the farmers' food supplies. On occasion, local peasants who had discovered the location of a family camp informed the German military and police of their find and led them to the scene, and as a result many of the camp inhabitants were murdered. But in some places the family camps were given help by the local population. Most of the forests in which the Jewish family camps were situated also contained Soviet partisans, who had to contend with the same enemies as the Jews and also had to get their food from the villages in the area. This created a mixed

Jews in the Tuvia Bielski family camp in the Naliboki Forest (May 1944).

relationship of interdependence and competition between the camps and the partisans, in which the partisans were the predominant factor. As a result, the attitude of the Soviet partisans influenced the fate of the Jews in the family camps and the number of Jews whose lives were saved.

Whenever encouraging reports were received about the family camps and the rescue opportunities they offered, Jews from ghettos still in existence tried to make their way there. In contrast, reports of a hostile attitude displayed by the local population or the partisans, and of the murder of Jews in the forests, had a deterrent effect on people who had been considering the risk of breaking out of the ghetto. Until the end of 1942, Soviet partisans in western Belorussia and the western Ukraine were still in the initial stage of organization. The existing units were relatively small and in some cases had no regular contact with the headquarters of partisan movements operating in the east and in areas closer to the front line. Discipline in such units was poor. These circumstances provided a fertile ground for the emergence of criminal elements in the forests that, under the guise of being partisans, engaged in pillage and murder. Jews in the family camps suffered greatly from attacks by this kind of gang, which robbed them of their clothes, boots, and other belongings, and also murdered them. The situation of the family-camp Jews improved in 1943, during the course of which the Soviet partisan movement was organized and gained in strength. In some places the family camps were incorporated into partisan brigades and had tasks assigned to them—maintenance jobs, tailoring and shoe repairs, arms repairs, and the baking of bread for the fighting units. The large Bielski and Zorin camps were turned into maintenance units serving the partisan brigades deployed in their area.

Persecution. The family camps in the Lublin, Białystok, and Grodno districts were in the most difficult situation. The partisans active in these areas belonged to the Polish ARMIA KRAJOWA (Home Army) or NARODOWE SIŁY ZBROJNE (National Armed Forces). As anti-Soviet groups, they viewed the Jews in the forests as a pro-Soviet element and persecuted them; many Jews fell victim to these Polish partisans. In the western Ukraine, the situation of the Jews was still worse; this was the area in which groups of Ukrainian nationalists (BANDERA men, "Bulbowcy," and others) operated and murdered Jews in the forest camps or on their way there.

Apart from these enemies, the Jews had other dangers to face. Many died from starvation and disease. But the worst threat was the antipartisan raids staged by the Germans. From 1942 to 1944, such German raids took place in nearly every forest in which there were Jewish family camps. When such a raid occurred, thousands of German troops and collaborators would surround the forest to make sure that nobody could escape while other forces were combing the interior. The family camps suffered the most from these raids; their mobility was restricted, they had women and children to take care of, and they had no advance notice that would have enabled them to flee the area before the enemy forces closed in. The only way they could save themselves was by hiding in swampy areas deep in the forest, or in underground bunkers, prepared in advance and well camouflaged.

No exact data or credible estimates are available of the number of Jews who took refuge in the family camps and the number of those who survived. The most that can be said is that the number of Jews who were saved in the family camps did not exceed ten thousand.

BIBLIOGRAPHY

Arad, Y. "Jewish Family Camps in the Forests—An Original Means of Rescue." In *Rescue Attempts during the Holocaust.* Proceedings of the Second Yad Vashem International Historical Conference, edited by Y. Gutman and E. Zuroff, pp. 333–353. Jerusalem, 1977.

Barkai, M., ed. *The Fighting Ghettos.* Philadelphia, 1962.

Bornstein, S. *The Doctor Atlas Brigade: The Story of a Jewish Partisan.* Tel Aviv, 1965. (In Hebrew.)

The Jewish Partisans. Vol. 1. Merhavia, Israel, 1958. (In Hebrew.)

YITZHAK ARAD

FAR EAST. *See under* East Asia.

FAREYNEGTE PARTIZANER ORGANIZATSYE (United Partisan Organization; FPO), Jewish anti-German underground organization in the VILNA ghetto. In July 1940, when Lithuania—including Vilna—was occupied by the Soviet Union, the existing Zionist youth organizations had to go underground. When the city was taken by the Germans on June 24, 1941, the Zionist organizations preserved their underground framework. In the first few months of the German occupation, their efforts concentrated mainly on saving their members from the extermination *Aktionen* that were then being conducted in Vilna by the EINSATZGRUPPEN. At that time there was discussion in the Zionist underground groups about whether they should continue their underground activity in the Vilna ghetto, where most of the Jews had been murdered, or move to ghettos in Belorussia or the GENERALGOUVERNEMENT, where at the end of 1941 the Jews were still living in relative quiet. All the movements, except for He-Haluts ha-Tsa'ir–Dror, headed by Mordechai TENENBAUM (Tamaroff), were in favor of remaining.

On New Year's Eve, December 31, 1941, 150 members of the Haluts (Pioneer) youth movements in the ghetto attended a meeting, where for the first time Abba KOVNER's appeal "Not to Go like Sheep to the Slaughter" was read. Kovner declared that all the Jews who were taken from Vilna were murdered at PONARY, and called upon the Jewish youth to organize for armed struggle against the Germans. On January 21, 1942, representatives of the Zionist youth movements—among them Kovner of Ha-Shomer ha-Tsa'ir, Nissan Reznik of Ha-No'ar ha-Tsiyyoni, Josef GLAZMAN of Betar, and Yitzhak WITTENBERG of the Communists—held a meeting at which they decided to establish a united resistance movement, to be called the Fareynegte Partizaner Organizatsye. He-Haluts ha-Tsa'ir–Dror was absent, as was its leader Tenenbaum, who had left Vilna for the Warsaw and Białystok ghettos. Wittenberg was elected the commander of the FPO, with Kovner, Glazman, and Reznik serving on his staff.

The organization's aim was to prepare for armed resistance in the event of the ghetto's being in danger of liquidation, and also to spread the idea of resistance to other ghettos. The BUND, which had not taken part in the founding meeting, joined the FPO in the spring of 1942. Members of He-Haluts ha-Tsa'ir–Dror who had stayed in the ghetto established their own underground group, under the leadership of Yechiel Scheinbaum, calling themselves "Yechiel's Combat Group." The FPO divided itself into underground cells, with five to a cell, based on their places of residence in the ghetto; three such cells made up a platoon and six to eight platoons formed a battalion. The FPO had two battalions, each composed of one hundred to one hundred and twenty fighters. In addition, there were units that were subordinate to headquarters. The FPO headquarters included representatives of all the parties and YOUTH MOVEMENTS that had united to join in underground activities.

The FPO sent emissaries to the Grodno, Białystok, and Warsaw ghettos in order to establish contact with them, propagate the idea of resistance and rebellion, and inform them of the mass extermination of the Jews in Vilna and the rest of Lithuania. Attempts were also made to establish ties with the Polish underground army (ARMIA KRAJOWA) in Vilna, but these efforts failed. There was contact with a small non-Jewish Communist group that was active in Vilna, and the ghetto underground lent its aid to this group. An attempt was also made to send women emissaries through the front lines to the Soviet Union, to tell the world of the mass extermination of the Jews and to appeal for help. These emissaries were stopped by Germans near the front lines, but they managed to escape and make their way back to Vilna.

The FPO's most pressing problem was to obtain arms. Only a few possible sources existed. Weapons could be purchased from the local population, and members of the underground working in the German captured-weapons depot at Borbiszki were able to smuggle out some weapons and give them to the FPO. Primitive hand grenades and Molotov cocktails were manufactured in the ghetto itself. The weapons that the underground managed to acquire consisted primarily of pistols, plus a small number of rifles, hand grenades, and submachine guns; they

Jewish partisans from the Fareynegte Partizaner Organizatsye who left the Vilna ghetto and escaped to the Rudninkai Forest return to Vilna after the liberation in July 1944.

were kept in a cache in the ghetto. At its height, the FPO had some three hundred organized members, and for each a weapon of some sort was available. The FPO carried out acts of sabotage outside the ghetto—such as mining the railway used by trains heading for the front lines, or sabotaging equipment and arms in German plants in which underground members were employed.

The chairman of the Vilna JUDENRAT (Jewish Council), Jacob GENS, knew of the underground's existence and maintained contact with its leaders. In the spring of 1943, when the small ghettos and labor camps in the Vilna area were liquidated, the FPO intensified the smuggling of arms into the ghetto and contacted the partisans active in the forests of western Belorussia. Several groups of young people who were not FPO members headed for the forests, and partisan emissaries came to the ghetto. The Judenrat, warned of these activities by the German authorities, regarded them as endangering the continued existence of the ghetto, and this led to friction between it and the FPO. At the same time, the Communist underground became more active in the city of Vilna, and its ties with the FPO grew stronger; the FPO commander, Wittenberg, was also a member of the Vilna Communist underground committee.

Acting on information that was passed on to them, the Germans arrested the members of the Vilna Communist underground committee and demanded from Gens that Wittenberg be handed over to them; otherwise the ghetto and its entire population would be liquidated. On July 15, 1943, Gens invited the FPO command to his house and arrested Wittenberg on the spot. As German security police were leading Wittenberg to the ghetto gate, they were attacked by FPO members, and Wittenberg was set free. The FPO mobilized its members and took up positions in several of the ghetto houses. On the following day there was a confrontation between the FPO and the ghetto police, in which many of the ghetto inhabitants sided with the latter and demanded that Wittenberg be handed over, in order to save the ghetto from the Germans. To avoid a bloody battle among the Jews, Wittenberg gave himself up to the Germans, and that same night he committed suicide. Abba Kovner was elected to take his place as the FPO commander. For the FPO the affair served as a warning, and it decided to establish a partisan base in the forest that would be available as a place of refuge for FPO members should the need arise.

On July 24, 1943, a group of FPO men, headed by Glazman, left the ghetto for the Naroch Forest. On September 1, when the Germans launched the deportation *Aktion* to Estonia, which was a step in the ghetto's liquidation, the FPO mobilized its members, took up positions in one section of the ghetto, and called on the Jews not to report for deportation and to rebel. The ghetto inhabitants did not respond to the call, believing that this time they were being sent away for work elsewhere and that they were not destined for extermination. On the evening of that day there was an armed clash between underground members and the German forces combing the ghetto; in the clash, Yechiel Scheinbaum, who was cooperating with the FPO at the time, was killed. When darkness fell, the Germans left the ghetto and did not return to it for the duration of the *Aktion,* which lasted until September 4. Gens, the Judenrat chairman, had promised to provide the Germans with the required quota for Estonia. In the wake of the *Aktion,* the FPO gave up the idea of an uprising, since the ghetto inhabitants had not heeded its call, and began moving its members out, to the Naroch and Rudninkai forests.

On the day the ghetto was liquidated, September 23, 1943, the last group of FPO members, numbering eighty to one hundred persons and headed by Abba Kovner, left the ghetto by way of the city sewers and made their way to the Rudninkai Forest. Most of the five hundred to seven hundred FPO members escaped to the forests and joined the PARTISANS, forming themselves into Jewish battalions as part of the Soviet partisan movement. Altogether, about six hundred to seven hundred young people left the Vilna ghetto for the forests and joined the partisans. Some of the Jewish units, however, were disbanded and their members absorbed, and others were joined by non-Jewish partisans, in line with Soviet partisan headquarters policy, which opposed the existence of separate Jewish units. Partisans from the Vilna ghetto fought in the forests until the Soviet army reached them, and they took part in the liberation of Vilna, on July 13, 1944.

BIBLIOGRAPHY

Arad, Y. *Ghetto in Flames: The Struggle and Destruction of the Jews of Vilna in the Holocaust.* Jerusalem, 1980.

Dworzecki, M. *Jerusalem of Lithuania in Revolt and Holocaust.* Tel Aviv, 1951. (In Hebrew.)

Korchak, R. *Flames in Ash.* Merhavia, Israel, 1946. (In Hebrew.)

YITZHAK ARAD

FASCISM, an intellectual, cultural, and political phenomenon in twentieth-century Europe. Fascism, in form and ideology, ruled ITALY in the period from 1922 to 1945, but in its broad sense the term came to be applied to similar regimes and ideologies in other countries.

Fascism has its roots primarily in the twentieth century. Its emergence was an expression of the accelerated modernization processes that the European continent experienced in the final few years of the nineteenth century and of the social changes and the intellectual revolution that occurred in the Western world at that juncture. Fascism, as an ideology and a mass movement, was not a regrettable accident that Europe encountered in the preceding generation; it was an organic part of Europe's culture, its social fabric, and its intellectual and political patterns of development.

The form in which fascism crystallized in the quarter of a century preceding World War I, and developed further in the interwar period, represents a synthesis of organic nationalism and anti-Marxist socialism, a revolutionary ideology whose principal elements are the repudiation of liberalism and Marxism, as well as democracy. In its essence, fascist ideology is the negation of materialism, and it considers liberalism, Marxism, and democracy to be nothing but different aspects of that "materialist" malady. On the basis of that repudiation of materialism, fascism pretends to have produced a total spiritual revolution. Fascist activism, which prides itself on its elitism, calls for absolute political rule, unfettered by the principles of democracy. The state is the expression of national unity and represents society with all its classes. Planning, a directed economy, and corporatism are the main elements of fascism, the concrete expressions of the victory of politics over economics, and, in the final analysis, represent the transfer to central control of society and the economy to the state. As an ideology of outright disassociation and rebellion, fascism rejects the political culture rooted in the eighteenth century and the French Revolution; it seeks to create a new community-based and anti-individualist civilization which, in the opinion of its followers, is the only kind of civilization that can assure the continued existence of human society. All sectors and classes of the population will find their place in this society, which is the natural framework of a harmonious and organic community, a nation that has been purified and strengthened and revitalized, and in which the individual is no more than a cell in the collective entity.

As an ideology that rejects rationalism, individualism, and the materialist and utilitarian concepts of society and state, fascism refuses to regard social organization as an artificial construction, the work of human beings who maintain frameworks of cooperation for the sole purpose of serving the interests of the individual. It totally negates the theory of "natural rights" and the individualist and mechanist views of society. In the fascist view, man is not a creature that takes precedence over society, a creature with rights of its own as a rational and moral being, or as a being created in the image of God; on the contrary, man is a social being, an integral part of an organic entity, which owes its very existence to the social entity. This is why fascism opposed the ideologies of liberalism and Marxism, which were prevalent in Western society around 1900. Liberalism and Marxism have a common root: they are both comprehensive systems based on nineteenth-century rationalism, which regards man as taking precedence over society. In both the liberal and Marxist views, society's sole purpose is to serve the needs of man, although the two systems differ over the methods by which this purpose is to be achieved. For the fascist ideologists, both those from the beginning of the twentieth century and those of the 1930s, liberalism and Marxism are ideologies of social warfare. Both systems destroy the organic unity of the nation and undermine the foundations of tribal solidarity, without which no historical-cultural and biological entity is capable of waging the struggle for survival. Fascism's proclaimed purpose is to restore society's solidarity and unity.

Notwithstanding its origin as a repudiation of liberalism and Marxism, fascism arose out of a profound awareness of the social problem. The nation will not become a unit so long as the proletariat is not absorbed into it as an integral part, so long as the incessant struggle among economic, social, and political forces continues and no way is found to harness them all to a joint effort for the general good. Ever since the last decade of the nineteenth century, fascism has claimed that it represents a new type of social radicalism and socialism, a national socialism that is non-Marxist, anti-Marxist, and, in many respects, post-Marxist.

Fascism, however, is not only a political movement; it is also a cultural phenomenon, with its roots in the technological and intellectual revolution of the end of the nineteenth and the beginning of the twentieth century. Accelerated economic growth and technological progress brought in their wake tremendous changes in the pace and way of life and the standard of living. Antirational values and a cult of the emotions, the inner drives, and spontaneity became the fashion of the times. The rational and "mechanist" view of the world, a trend prominent in western European thought since the seventeenth century, was replaced by the "organic" view. The emphasis was now on a variety of historical values and idealistic directions, a trend that tended to undermine the adherence to rationalism and individualism. There was a growing belief in the individual's subordination to society and to the judgment of history. Thus, in the eyes of intellectuals of the 1890 generation such as Gustave Le Bon, Maurice Barrès, Georges Sorel, and Georges Vacher de Lapouge, society was not simply the arithmetical sum of individuals, driven by the liberal society's intellectual individualism and the "utilitarianism and materialism" by which it was ruled. The more profound fascist intellectuals of the interwar period considered these attitudes, which came to the fore as early as the first decade of the twentieth century, to have been the roots of fascism, with Giovanni Gentile, the leading philosopher of Italian Fascism, defining fascism as a revolt against positivism.

This new world view led to glorification of the nation, and to the emergence of nationalism as a political system based on an array of filter devices and defense mechanisms whose purpose was to safeguard the integrity of the "tribe." An ideological movement came into being that shook up not only the entire set of values bequeathed by the eighteenth century and the French Revolution, but also the Christian concept of morality. As Vacher de Lapouge put it, "A morality that believes in natural selection puts the obligation to the race in the highest place—the place in which Christianity puts obedience to God."

Here it is important to stress one element that is significant for the understanding of later developments. The reaction against rationalism in the form of democracy and Marxism was not just the result of literary neoromanticism or a new fashion in art; it was science that led the great attack on democracy and Marxism. This is the real meaning of the intellectual revolution of the end of the nineteenth and the beginning of the twentieth century. The new life sciences and social sciences—Darwinian biology (in its popular interpretation); history as taught by Heinrich von Treitschke, Ernest Renan, and Hippolyte Taine; social psychology according to Le Bon; and the Italian school of political sociology (Wilfredo Pareto, Gaetano Mosca, Robert Michels)—all rose up against the basic assumptions of liberalism and democracy. On the basis of the new social sciences (especially social anthropology and psychology), which adopted many aspects of Social Darwinism, a new theory of political behavior came into being. Thus it was that the new branches of science contributed to the rise of an intellectual climate which undermined the very foundations of democracy and in large measure facilitated the emergence and spread of fascism.

It is the rational explanation of the irrational, as contained in the elitist theory, that provides the link between the social sciences' rules and fascism's practice. This explanation, as put forth by the Italian school of political sociology, played a role in the rise of revolutionary syndicalism, but it also contributed to the rise of nationalism as a political ideology, and in many ways represents the point at which the two movements meet.

It thus happened, at the beginning of the twentieth century, that the new social sciences—primarily psychology and anthropology, which also fed sociology, political science, and the new studies of history—provided the conceptual framework for the antiliberal reaction. These sciences also enabled contributions from theorists of the 1850 generation—Charles Darwin, Joseph-Arthur de Gobineau, and Richard Wagner—to fuse with contributions of the 1890 generation. The ancient romantic element, the old trends of historicity, the theory of the origin of the nation in antiquity, the search for the vital forces that are "the soul of the people" —all of these were now endowed with the sanction of science. The idea that emotions and the subconscious were more important in politics than reason became increasingly accepted, leading as a logical conclusion to the growing disdain for democracy and for its institutions and agencies.

Biological and psychological determinism, which represent the core of the writings of Le Bon, Vacher de Lapouge, Edouard-Adolf Drumont, and even Hippolyte Taine, and which filled the pages of countless publications in every field of intellectual endeavor, in the end became the source from which the theory of racism was nourished. This is the background against which the new nationalism arose and was consolidated at the end of the nineteenth century, a nationalism that did not change up until World War II. Tribal nationalism, based on biological determinism and Social Darwinism—the nationalism of blood and soil—was not a German invention, nor was it confined to Germany. It flourished in France at the turn of the century, and in many respects it was France that served as the real ideological laboratory of fascism in those years. In Italy the growth of fascist ideology lagged behind that of France by fifteen to twenty years, and it was only at the end of the first decade of the new century that the gap was closed.

It was Barrès, one of France's outstanding writers at the beginning of the twentieth century, more than any other European thinker, who reflected the European cultural predicament on the eve of World War I. Barrès was among the first of the philosophers to use the term "national socialism," even before the end of the nineteenth century. This term for a new brand of socialism assumes that the continued existence of the nation depends upon reconciliation between the proletariat and society as a whole. This solution, which Barrès proposed in France, was raised in Italy by Enrico Corradini in the early years of the twentieth century. Corradini's idea was to base intersocial relations in Italy on a kind of family compact among the various sectors. He assigned two goals to national socialism: to make peace between the proletariat and the nation, and to make the Italians conscious of the fact that Italy, in both material and moral terms, was a "proletarian nation." The term was coined by Corradini, and it meant that the whole nation had to prepare for the struggle for existence—the natural state for the ongoing struggle among the nations.

The other basic element of fascism is the revision of Marxism. The challenge to the Hegelian, rational content of Marxism is identified with Georges Sorel and the Italian revolutionary syndicalists. "Sorelianism" did in fact blaze a new path of revolution. Contrary to Leninism, which has as its aim a revolution by and for the proletariat—albeit sponsored by an elite vanguard—Sorelianism lays the foundations of a revolution for and on behalf of society as a whole, including all its sectors and classes. Contrary to the French and Bolshevik revolutions, which, in different degrees of extremism, changed the social order, the new Sorelian revolution was to be a political, national, cultural, psychological, and moral revolution. Such a revolution becomes feasible when psychology takes the place of the rationalist and Hegelian elements of Marxism. This new socialism—vitalist and voluntarist in nature—represents a philosophy of action, based on intuition and the cult of energy, violence, and the myth of violence. Violence, in Sorel's view, is a permanent value and the wellspring of morality. Sorelian socialism sought to destroy Western culture—that materialist, individualist, and humanist culture; he rejected Cartesian rationalism, the theory of "natural rights," Immanuel Kant, and Jean-Jacques Rousseau.

That was the basis on which the fascist synthesis was created, a synthesis of tribal nationalism and a new kind of socialism that was revolutionary, antibourgeois, and anti-Marxist in character. This socialism replaced class as the subject of the revolution, and despised democracy, parliaments, political parties, and pressure groups. It regarded the rules of the game as practiced in a democracy as the source of corruption, decadence, and moral decay. Such a synthesis, which emerged in France and Italy, was unrelated to the events that took place in Europe beginning in the summer of 1914. It was around 1910 that the theoreticians of revolutionary syndicalism met the theoreticians of integral nationalism, a meeting that found its expression in publications such as *La Lupa* in Italy and *Cahiers du Cercle Proudhon* in France. In France the development had taken place earlier, but Italy caught up in the immediate prewar period. The disciples of Sorel and Charles Maurras in France, and the followers of Corradini and the revolutionary syndicalists (Arturo Labriola, Robert Michels, Sergio Panunzio, Paolo Orano, and Angelo Oliviero Olivetti), developed the socialist-nationalist synthesis into a genuine political force. During the war itself, revolutionary syndicalism turned into national syndicalism and fascism.

At this time the nonconformists of the Left were joined by one of their old followers, Benito MUSSOLINI. Mussolini had ties to revolutionary syndicalism as early as 1902, when he was a contributor to *Avanguardia Socialista*, Arturo Labriola's publication. Although Mussolini was not a revolutionary syndicalist in the precise sense of the term, intellectually and emotionally he did belong to that movement. Between 1909 and 1914 he and his revolutionary syndicalist mentors parted ways, in political terms, but the differences between them were tactical and temporary rather than substantive and basic. From the beginning of his political career up to the consolidation of the Fascist movement, Mussolini adhered to the basic principles of revolutionary syndicalism and took an active part in the process that led it to national syndicalism and from there to Fascism. As indicated, in taking this course Mussolini was preceded by the revolutionary syndicalists, and it was they who made the breakthrough to the Fascist synthesis. Mussolini followed them when he joined the camp that supported Italy's entry into the war in the fall of 1914, putting an end to their differences (in 1911, he had opposed the war with the Ottoman empire over Libya). In Mussolini's eyes World War I was conclusive proof that the revolutionary syndicalists were right. It demonstrated the sweeping power of nationalism and provided the opportunity to put into practice a heroic, vitalist socialism, the foe of bourgeois values. Once Mussolini and his erstwhile intellectual mentors were reunited, the emerging ideology of Fascism had found its leader, and the war provided the cadres and created the social and psychological conditions for its practical application.

The basic principles of that ideology, which had been established prior to August 1914, reemerged in the 1920s and 1930s, having in the meantime been steeled in the crucible of World War I. It was not the war, however, which produced fascism; it was the modernization of Europe that brought it about. But for that generation, the war provided the laboratory tests that proved the theses propounded by Le Bon, Michels, Pareto, and Sorel: the masses are conservative, they long for authority, and they behave irrationally; democracy is a luxury suitable for an era of peace and prosperity, and its restrictions can easily be dispensed with, even in countries that have a tradition of political freedom. Most importantly, the war revealed two facts of overriding significance: (1) it provided the definitive answer to the great question of modern history and proved that in industrialized countries nationalism—a sweeping force and the focus of solidarity—has absolute superiority over class; and (2) it revealed the immense power of the modern state.

World War I opened up new vistas for the functions of the state, for the controls that it could exercise, and for its driving power. It proved that the state was able to control the economy, the means of production, and labor relations, and that it was capable of dictating the basic elements of economic planning and mobilizing all sections of society for a concentrated national effort. The war also revealed the great extent to which people were prepared to accept state authority, to forego their freedoms, to accept what was in effect a dictatorship, and as far as the majority of the population was concerned, even to sacrifice their lives, on a scale that could not have been imagined. In other words, total war demonstrated that the national state was able to control the individual in every domain of his life, and that totalitarianism—whose initial ideological features had been outlined by theorists of the 1890 and 1910 generations—could really exist. Italy's revolutionary syndicalists were not the only ones to learn the lesson, but they were the first to have the opportunity to translate that lesson into terms of political victory and the seizure of power—an opportunity given to them by the social and political circumstances prevailing in their country at that time.

Fascism was a phenomenon that was to be found throughout Europe, although it differed from place to place, depending on the different cultural, social, and political circumstances. However, even the vast differences between the industrial centers of northern and central Europe and the peripheral areas of southern and eastern Europe could not obscure the common denominator of fascism in all these countries. The basic principles of fascism in Italy, France, Britain, Belgium, Spain, and Romania were identical. In France the term "fascist" applied to Georges Valois, who in 1925 founded the first fascist movement outside Italy; Marcel Déat and Gustave Hervé, who had come from socialism; Jacques Doriot, an erstwhile Communist; Bertrand Jouvenel, a former liberal; and the former right-wing nationalists Pierre Drieu La Rochelle and Robert Brasillach. In Italy it was true of the Hegelian philosopher Giovanni Gentile, the famous jurist Alfredo Rocco, the nationalist ideologue Corradini, and the revolutionary syndicalists Panunzio, Olivetti, Michels, Agostino Lanzillo, Paolo Mantica, Micele Bianchi, Edmondo Rossoni, Umberto Pasella, and Ottavio Dinale. In Britain it applied to Oswald MOSLEY; in Spain to José Antonio Primo de Rivera; in Belgium to Léon Degrelle; and in Romania to Corneliu Zelea Codreanu. All of these men entered upon the same struggle against the same divisive elements, on behalf of the same organic unity of the nation.

Fascism came up with two instruments of its own in order to maintain "the unity of the nation"—corporatism and the totalitarian state. Corporatism is fascism's original contribution to the emergence of a "third way," a way that is neither liberalism nor Marxism, and it symbolizes the fascists' belief in the power of politics to dominate market forces and class interests. The corporatist system is designed to enable the authoritarian state to plan the economy and settle labor relations and the differences between social classes. Once political and personal rights and freedoms are abolished, the workers' right to organize is also canceled. Corporatism puts an end to the legitimacy of special interests and subordinates the social and economic system to the state; it represents the real basis on which the totalitarian state rests.

As a historical phenomenon, fascism exists on three levels—as an ideology, a movement, and a form of government. Before fascism came to power anywhere (which it eventually did only in Italy, and for a short while during World War II in Romania), the corporate state served as the model of a solution that would enable all sectors of society to be mobilized by the state, in the service of the nation. But as soon as this ideology was applied, the result, in concrete terms, was that the class interests of the proletariat were set aside for the sake of the interests of the bourgeoisie, these latter being regarded as identical with the national interest. This had not been the goal of revolutionary-syndicalist ideology, the original backbone of fascism, but this was the result, in practice, of subordinating social relations in the authoritarian regime by means of the corporatist system.

The authoritarian state seeks to control every sphere of life—politics, the economy, society, and culture. It does away with all institutions or organizations that express a pluralism of ideas and beliefs—parliaments, political parties, a free press, and a choice of educational opportunities. It demands not only discipline but also identification and unconditional readiness for sacrifice.

Indeed, totalitarianism is the cornerstone of the fascist revolution's ideology. For Gentile, Mussolini, and Primo de Rivera the totalitarian state signifies the beginning of a new era, an era in which the commonwealth has absolute priority over the individual. The individual exists only to perform his duty and is only a means to an end—the state's achievement of the goals it sets itself. This means the end of liberal culture. It follows that the fascist revolution is a total revolution, a moral and spiritual revolution, which creates a new order for all sectors of society.

Mussolini, in his definitive work on fascism, *The Fascist Doctrine* (on which he collaborated with Gentile), leaves no doubt that the state embraces all spheres of human activity, organizes them, and determines what their content should be; there is no aspect of society's life that is not political, and there is therefore none that may be excluded from the state's grip.

In this sense, fascist ideology was truly revolutionary. It was unwavering in its resolve to dissociate itself from the established order, and it provided a complete alternative answer, in the political as well as the moral and aesthetic spheres. Fascism's idealism and appeal to the emotions provided the instruments for a total revolution, the sole revolution that was devoid of any elements of a class war. This revolution of the spirit, the will, and the instincts has a unity of purpose: to create a new man, inextricably tied to the nation and promoting the values of violence, heroism, and sacrifice. Such a cult of unity, altruism, and youth had a tremendous appeal in those days all over Europe, among young people who had only contempt for the bourgeois world of their parents. This was the great secret of the attraction—overt or covert—that fascism exerted for large sections of the young generation in the interwar period. In fact, the influence of fascist ideology went far beyond the hard core of its founders and devoted followers. Much wider circles, to one degree or another, were drawn to its promise of a violent rebellion of spiritual forces and basic instincts, of primitive and unrestrained reaction against the routine and conventional essence of bourgeois civilization. Even more widespread was the contempt for the clash of interests, the compromises, the give-and-take of liberal democracy. For many, dictatorship was a more natural form of government than one based on a social compact.

Although the fascist revolution was put into power in one country only, its impact was felt all over Europe. Like any other ideology, fascism ran into a constant struggle with reality. It soon turned out that it was extremely difficult to overcome social and economic interests and the influence of the traditional centers of power—the monarchy, the church, and high finance. Like every other movement, fascism was also forced into various compromises, which saved Italy from becoming an entirely totalitarian state. Nevertheless, in the case of Italian Fascism, the correlation between ideology and practice was very high. No one can claim that Stalinist terror was the fulfillment of Marxism, or that the social reforms introduced by Léon Blum were the realization of socialism, but fascism's practice was a direct projection of its ideology. The development of Italy into a totalitarian state, although never fully implemented, was based on the inner logic of the fascist ideology, and there was nothing improvised about it. The abolition of parliamentary and democratic institutions, along with fascist violence, political murder, and the physical or political liquidation of the opposition, were all expressions of the fascist system's essential character. The mobilization of the masses—the marches, the mass rallies, the militias, and the uniformed youth movements—was an effective translation into practice of the theories of the nature of man as they had been taught by some of Europe's greatest scientists. Thus a new political culture was born, in which the state took precedence over the individual and could demand of the individual whatever sacrifice it wanted. Such a political culture rejects the power of reason to conduct the life of society and transfers the emphasis to the sphere of the emotions and instincts.

This political culture spread all over Europe, and in the depressed conditions that prevailed in the 1920s and the 1930s it gathered destructive force, on an unprecedented scale. No society was invulnerable to it, and the inroads it made were not a function of social class, educational level, age, religion, or origin. Everywhere, in all sectors of society and in all religious groupings, people were to be found who were ready to accept fascism as a legitimate and original third way, with a stature equal to that of Marxism and liberalism.

ANTISEMITISM was not an integral and essential element of fascist ideology. This was the great difference between fascism and Nazism. Nazi ideology was based on the doctrine of biological determinism, in which antisemitism was a central, indispensable pillar. In fascism, on the other hand, antisemitism differed from place to place and from one trend to another. In principle, fascism was receptive to antisemitism or to creating its own version, based on its own component of integral nationalism. Organic nationalism, the nationalism of blood and soil, was by far the most fertile ground for antisemitism. In fascism, the extent of the antisemitic dimension was determined by the pervasiveness of the racist element within the nationalist ideology, but even there the versions differed greatly. Italian Fascism, in its early period, was generally free of antisemitism, which developed in its later stages, gradually and often as a result of external events. The 1938 Italian racist legislation resulted from the growth of extremist nationalist trends in Italian Fascism and the eradication of the original element of revolutionary syndicalism, as well as from Italy's rapprochement with Nazi Germany.

In France there were fascist groups (for example, ACTION FRANÇAISE) whose ideology differed only slightly from that of Nazism, and others that were practically untouched by antisemitism. As World War II approached, however, the antisemitic dimension in French fascism increased in strength, and by October 1940 the Vichy government, which was not formally a fascist government, introduced racist laws closely resembling the NUREMBERG LAWS. British fascism was extremely antisemitic, as was fascism in Belgium, Romania, and Hungary. Spanish fascism, in contrast, was free of antisemitism. In Italy, despite the official anti-Jewish policy that prevailed following the introduction of the racist legislation, and despite manifestations of antisemitism in the Fascist party, the persecution and hatred of Jews never came close to that in central and eastern Europe.

[*See also* Great Britain: Fascism in Great Britain; Racism; Spain: Spanish Fascism and the Jews.]

BIBLIOGRAPHY

Gregor, A. J. *Young Mussolini and the Intellectual Origins of Fascism.* Berkeley, 1979.

Hamilton, A. *The Appeal of Fascism: A Study of Intellectuals and Fascism, 1919–1945.* New York, 1971.

Laqueur, W., ed. *Fascism: A Reader's Guide; Analyses, Interpretations, Bibliography.* London, 1979.

Larsen, S. U., et al., eds. *Who Were the Fascists? Social Roots of European Fascism.* Oslo, 1980.

Mosse, G. L. *Masses and Man.* New York, 1980.

Mussolini, B. *Fascism: Doctrine and Institutions.* New York, 1968.

Nolte, E. *Three Faces of Fascism: Action Française, Italian Fascism, National Socialism.* New York, 1969.

Payne, S. G. *Fascism: Comparison and Definition.* Madison, Wis., 1980.

Turner, H. A., Jr., ed. *Reappraisals of Fascism.* New York, 1975.

Weber, E. *Varieties of Fascism.* New York, 1966.

ZEEV STERNHELL

FÉDÉRATION DES SOCIÉTÉS JUIVES DE FRANCE (Federation of French Jewish Organizations; FSJF), umbrella organization of *Landsmannschaften* (fraternal lodges made up of Jewish immigrants in FRANCE from eastern and central Europe on the basis of common geographical origin—the same town, city, or region), established in 1913. In the late 1930s the FSJF was chaired by Marc JARBLUM, a Socialist Zionist leader. At the time it consisted of over two hundred societies and, for the first time in its history, lent its support to the Zionist movement. The very existence of the FSJF, and its comparative strength, reflected the problems affecting the relations between Jewish immigrants in France and the native-born Jews. The umbrella organization of the latter was the CONSISTOIRE CENTRAL DES ISRAÉLITES DE FRANCE (Central Consistory of French Jews), for which being Jewish was based exclusively on religious affiliation, and which did not take kindly to the existence of *Landsmannschaften.* For this reason, the immigrant activists did not find a place for themselves in the long-established Jewish organizations.

Under the Nazi occupation, several FSJF leaders in Paris established a clandestine committee, code-named AMELOT, which set up and ran welfare institutions for needy Jews. The Amelot committee continued to function as an underground organization even when the Gestapo ordered the closing down of all existing Jewish bodies and their replacement by a single central institution, the UNION GÉNÉRALE DES ISRAÉLITES DE FRANCE (General Council of French Jews; UGIF).

The leaders of the FSJF, however, had fled to Vichy-controlled southern France, together with more than half of the Jewish population that had been living in the German-occupied sector. Despite pressure from French authorities and Jewish leaders, Jarblum refused to accept membership in the UGIF, and instead created an underground FSJF committee in many places where Jews lived. These local committees undertook the care of tens of thousands of Jews, and provided them with forged "Aryan" identity papers. Funds that the American Jewish JOINT DISTRIBUTION COMMITTEE (known as the Joint) had previously given to the UGIF were now channeled to the FSJF. At the end of 1942, after the German occupation of Vichy France, the FSJF established an absorption center in the Italian-occupied zone of France, where the Italian authorities protected the Jews from persecution by the Nazis and Vichy officials.

On February 9, 1943, the Gestapo, under the command of Klaus BARBIE, raided the FSJF offices in Lyons, seized eighty-six Jews whom they found there, and deported them to extermination camps. Jarblum himself was not caught, and in the wake of the Gestapo raid he was smuggled into Switzerland. The FSJF, now led by Reuben Grinberg and Leo Glaser, kept up its work. From Geneva, Jarblum passed on instructions to the FSJF, as well as substantial amounts of money that he obtained from the Joint, the WORLD JEWISH CONGRESS, and the Jewish Agency. The FSJF also financed Jewish youth organizations that were smuggling children across the border into Switzerland, and the movement of young fighters to Palestine by way of Spain. In addition, it formed partisan units in several cities and in the Maquis.

The FSJF played the leading role in the establishment of the Comité Général de Défense (Jewish Defense Committee) in August 1943, in which all Jewish underground organizations—including the Jewish Communists—took part; FSJF leader Glaser was appointed its secretary-general.

Many FSJF activists were caught and murdered. This was also Leo Glaser's fate after he was arrested in Lyons, in June 1944.

BIBLIOGRAPHY

L'Activité des organisations juives en France sous l'occupation. Paris, 1947.

Adler, J. *The Jews of Paris and the Final Solution: Communal Response and International Conflicts, 1940–1944.* Oxford, 1988.

Klarsfeld, S. *Vichy-Auschwitz: Le rôle de Vichy dans la solution finale de la question juive en France, 1942.* Paris, 1983.

Lazare, L. *La résistance juive en France.* Paris, 1987.

LUCIEN LAZARE

SS-Oberführer Hermann Fegelein, Hitler's brother-in-law. [National Archives]

FEGELEIN, HERMANN (1906–1945), senior SS officer; confidant of Adolf HITLER. Fegelein was born in Ansbach. He served in the Rossbach Freikorps, in the Reichswehr cavalry, and then in the Bavarian police. After the Nazi rise to power he became director of the SS riding academy in Munich. In occupied Poland, Fegelein first had the assignment of setting up SS cavalry units, which were then formed into a cavalry brigade, under his command. When the Germans invaded the USSR, the brigade was sent to the east and, in July and August 1941, it "purged" the Pripet Marshes of whatever remnants of Red Army units it found there; in the course of this operation its men murdered some twenty thousand Jews.

From May to December 1942, Fegelein was inspector of cavalry in the REICHSSICHERHEITSHAUPTAMT (Reich Security Main Office; RSHA); in December 1942 he was promoted to SS-*Oberführer* and put in command of a task force (Kampfgruppe Fegelein) that operated on the central front. In September 1943 Fegelein was wounded and posted to the rear, and in January he was appointed Heinrich HIMMLER's and the SS's liaison officer in Hitler's headquarters. He married Gretel Braun, the sister of Eva Braun, Hitler's companion, and joined Hitler's inner circle. In June 1944 he was raised to the rank of SS-*Gruppenführer* in the Waffen-SS.

In the final days of the Reich, Fegelein was in Hitler's bunker. Wanting to escape from Berlin, he left the bunker without telling anyone, returned to his home, and changed into civilian clothes. At this point Hitler found out about Himmler's negotiations with Folke BERNADOTTE, the representative of the Swedish Red Cross, which in Hitler's eyes amounted to treason. Hitler therefore accused Fegelein too of having committed treason, and also of desertion, and on April 27 ordered his arrest. Fegelein was stripped of his rank and, on April 28, was executed. Eva

Braun, who was to marry Hitler the following day, did not intercede to save her brother-in-law's life.

BIBLIOGRAPHY

Trevor-Roper, H. R. *The Last Days of Hitler.* New York, 1947.

SHMUEL SPECTOR

FEINER, LEON (1888–1945), BUND activist and member of the Jewish underground in Poland. Feiner was born in Kraków and studied law at the Jagiellonian University there. As a longtime member of socialist movements and a Bund activist in independent Poland, he frequently defended leftist political activists in court. Feiner came from an assimilated background and was well versed in Polish culture, but his loyalty to the Bund, as well as the increasingly anti-Jewish policy that Poland was pursuing, brought him closer to the Jewish masses and made him want to share their fate. In the second half of the 1930s he was imprisoned in Bereza-Kartuska, a Polish concentration camp in which a large number of opposition figures, of various shades of political opinion, were held.

Leon Feiner.

When the war broke out, Feiner fled to the Soviet-occupied part of Poland, only to be put in prison. Following the German conquest of the area in 1941, he escaped and made his way back to Warsaw, where he lived under an assumed identity on the Polish ("Aryan") side of the city and was an underground representative of the Bund and of the Jews in the ghetto. When the Bund joined the ŻYDOWSKA ORGANIZACJA BOJOWA (Jewish Fighting Organization; ŻOB), Feiner was appointed Bund representative on the "Aryan" side, and together with Abraham BERMAN (who represented the Żydowski Komitet Narodowy, or the Jewish National Committee), formed the coordinating committee for contacts with the Polish underground. In the fall of 1942 Jan KARSKI, a member of the Polish underground who was sent to London in its behalf, took a message from Feiner addressed to Samuel ZYGELBOJM, for transmission to all the Jews in the free world. Feiner asked Zygelbojm to tell the Jews "to lay siege to all important offices and agencies of the British and the Americans, and not to move from there until these Allied powers give guarantees that they will embark upon the rescue of the Jews. They [the demonstrators] should abstain from food and water, waste away before the eyes of the apathetic world, and starve to death. By doing so they may perhaps shock the conscience of the world." It was Feiner who drafted and forwarded to their destinations most of the Bund's reports and messages to London and the United States.

In the last few months of 1942, Feiner helped establish a Polish organization for giving aid to Jews and trying to rescue them, a project that had been initiated by various Polish circles—Catholics, liberal intellectuals, and representatives of political parties (mostly of the Center and the Left). From January 1943 to July 1944 Feiner was deputy chairman of ZEGOTA, the Polish Council for Aid to Jews, and was its chairman from November to December 1944, until the liberation of Warsaw in January 1945.

After the liberation, Feiner, who was suffering from a malignant disease, was transferred to Lublin, the temporary seat of Poland's new regime. A month later he died.

BIBLIOGRAPHY

Neustadt, M., ed. *Destruction and Rising: The Epic of the Jews in Warsaw.* Tel Aviv, 1946. (In Hebrew.)

ISRAEL GUTMAN

FERRAMONTI DI TARSIA, internment camp (officially designated "concentration camp") for Jews near Cosenza in Calabria (southern Italy); the largest of the fifteen internment camps established on Benito MUSSOLINI's orders between June and September 1940.

Construction of the camp was started on June 4, 1940, six days before Italy's entry into the war; arrests of Jews, both foreign and Italian, commenced on June 15, and arrestees began arriving at Ferramonti on June 20. Between June 1940 and August 1943 there were 3,823 Jewish internees at Ferramonti; 3,682 were foreigners and 141 were Italians (Jews of Italian nationality were not interned unless guilty or suspected of anti-Fascist activities). The commandant of the camp, a commissioner of public security, was assisted by an official of the Ministry of the Interior, ten policy agents, and seventy-five Fascist militiamen commanded by a *centurione* (captain).

Moshe Sharett (Shertok), head of the political department of the Jewish Agency and later prime minister of Israel, visiting former inmates at the Ferramonti di Tarsia camp in Italy (April 1944). Sharett is standing at the center. [Eliyahu Ben-Hur]

Living conditions at the camp, acceptable at first, became increasingly difficult as the situation of the Jews deteriorated. Even so, Ferramonti was never a "concentration camp" in the German sense of the term. The internees were not maltreated, and they were allowed to receive food parcels, to visit sick relatives, and to engage in cultural activities; nor were there periodic "selections" to swell the columns on their way to the gas chambers in Poland. Four weddings and twenty-one births took place at the camp. Relations between the internees and the camp authorities were tolerable throughout the camp's existence; there were no mutinies or revolts, and very few breaches of discipline. On September 4, 1943, six weeks after Mussolini's downfall, the BADOGLIO government released the internees.

BIBLIOGRAPHY

Zuccotti, S. *The Italians and the Holocaust: Persecution, Rescue, and Survival.* New York, 1987.

MEIR MICHAELIS

FIGHTERS FOR THE FREEDOM OF ISRAEL. *See* Loḥamei Ḥerut Israel.

FIGHTING ORGANIZATION OF PIONEER JEWISH YOUTH. *See* He-Haluts ha-Lohem.

FILDERMAN, WILHELM (1882–1963), Romanian Jewish leader. Filderman was born in Bucharest. He studied law in Paris, earning a doctorate. In 1912 he was one of the few Jews granted Romanian nationality; this enabled him to earn his livelihood by practicing law. In the interwar period Filderman was a member of the Romanian parliament, and he served as chairman of most of the important Jewish organizations in the country, among them the Federatia Uniunilor de Comunitati Evreesti (Federation of Jewish Communities), the Uniunea Comunitatilor Evreesti din Regat (Union of Jewish Communities in the Regat [the Old Kingdom; Romania in its pre–World War I borders]), the UNIUNEA EVREILOR ROMÂNI (Union of Romanian Jews), the JOINT DISTRIBUTION COMMITTEE's office in ROMANIA, and the Consiliul Evreesc (Jewish Council).

In the years following World War I, Filderman was active on behalf of the granting of Romanian nationality to the Jews of the Regat and in assisting the Jewish refugees from the Ukraine. He also aided in the preservation of Jewish rights in the face of the prevailing antisemitism in Romanian political and economic life, which also had its effect on Jewish religious life and education. Filderman persisted in this struggle even during the IRON GUARD's regime of terror (September 6, 1940, to January 24, 1941) and during Ion ANTONESCU's dictatorship, notwithstanding the fact that Antonescu dissolved the existing Jewish organizations and in their place set up the CENTRALA EVREILOR (Jewish Center). These activities finally led to Filderman's expulsion to TRANSNISTRIA in May 1943; the immediate cause was his opposition to the collective ransom of 4 billion lei (about $40 million) that Antonescu imposed on Romanian Jewry. Even in Transnistria, however, Filderman maintained his activities, and in August of that year he was permitted to return from exile.

Throughout the war years Filderman maintained contact with senior officials, cabinet ministers, and Premier Ion Antonescu and his close associate, Mihai ANTONESCU (who also held senior cabinet posts). The Romanian leaders were forced to accept Filderman as the authentic representative of the Jews (most of the leaders of the Jewish Center were Jewish converts to Christianity or collaborators who did not represent the Jews and had been appointed to their posts on the recommendation of the German legation). Filderman also earned the respect of Romanian opposition leaders, who cooperated with him; they included such renowned figures as Iuliu Maniu, head of the Peasants' Party (Partidul National Taranesc), and Dinu Bratianu, head of the National-Liberal Party (Partidul National-Liberal). During the spring and summer of 1942 Filderman formed a clandestine Jewish leadership, the Jewish Council, composed of representatives of the Zionist Organization and other Jewish bodies. The Jewish Council sought to save the Jews of Romania from deportation to Poland and to alleviate the daily life of the Jewish population, then suffering from the effects of countless antisemitic laws and regulations.

In the fall of 1941, when he was still chairman of the Federation of Jewish Communities, Filderman failed in his efforts to prevent the deportation to Transnistria of the Jews of BESSARABIA and BUKOVINA. He played a decisive role, however, in foiling the plans to deport the entire Jewish population of Romania to the EXTERMINATION CAMPS in Poland in the fall of 1942, and in preventing the expulsion of Jews from neighboring countries who had taken refuge in Romania. In August and September of 1941, as a result of Filderman's intercession with Ion Antonescu, the decree on wearing the yellow badge (*see* BADGE, JEWISH) was abolished in the Regat. For two years, from the end of 1941 to the end of 1943, Filderman persisted in a struggle for the right to send aid to the Jews who had been deported to Transnistria, and he followed up by campaigning for their repatriation to Romania, meeting with partial success.

After the fall of the dictatorial regime in August 1944, Filderman continued his public activities. In the following three years, from 1944 to 1947, he fought for the restoration of Jewish rights and Jewish property, and against the drafting of Jews into the ranks of the antisemitic Romanian army. In pursuing his aims, Filderman exploited every available legal loophole, and he also lobbied in the senior echelons of the regime. He saved the Romanian Jews from deportation to the extermination camps by making this a national Romanian issue and by persuading the leaders of the regime that compliance with the German demand for deportation would be a violation of Romanian sovereignty.

After the war, the Jewish Communists campaigned against Filderman, as part of their efforts to gain control of the Jewish organizations in Romania. Filderman was forced to resign from all his positions of leadership, and in early 1948 he fled to France, where he remained for the rest of his life.

BIBLIOGRAPHY

Ancel, J., comp. *Yad Vashem Central Archives: The Dr. W. Filderman Archives.* Jerusalem, 1974.

Safran, A. *Resisting the Storm: Memoirs, Romania, 1940–1947.* Jerusalem, 1987.

JEAN ANCEL

FILMS, NAZI ANTISEMITIC. Film played an integral role in the dissemination of Nazi ideology. Anti-Jewish characters and themes recur throughout the cinema of the Third Reich, although only a minimal number of these films focus on antisemitic themes.

In the fall of 1938, the Propaganda Ministry sent a request to German film companies to begin the production of explicitly antisemitic films. Major themes to be developed were the world Jewish conspiracy, *völkisch* ideology, and pseudo-anthropological theories based on blood and physiognomy. It was felt that if these ideas were portrayed effectively in film and other media, they could help prepare the German people for a "solution" to the Jewish problem.

The first two anti-Jewish films, *Robert und Bertram* (Robert and Bertram; director, Hans Heinz Zerlett) and *Leinen aus Irland* (Linen from Ireland; Heinz Helbig), appeared in 1939 and used comedy to caricature the subhuman Jew. Both films rely on negative physical stereotypes, and both expose the Jew's tendency to infiltrate Aryan society, as well as the Jewish male's desire for the pure, blonde, Aryan female. In the end, no matter how cunning he is, the Jew is always foiled.

The major cinematic attack on the Jews occurred in the late summer and the fall of 1940. Two feature films, *Die Rothschilds* (The Rothschilds; Erich Waschneck) and *Jud Süss* (Jew Süss; Veit Harlan), and one so-called documentary, *Der ewige Jude* (The Eternal Jew; Fritz Rippler), were to be shown successively over a short period of time.

Die Rothschilds was both antisemitic and anti-British, using the historic backdrop of the Napoleonic wars to portray the financial control and cunning of the Rothschild banking family. The Rothschilds are depicted as having made their fortune from the blood of the Germans, with England appearing as a decaying society dominated by Jews. The final scene shows a flaming Star of David superimposed over a map of England. The film was unsuccessful and was withdrawn from circulation shortly after its premiere in the summer of 1940. It was shown later as *Die Rothschilds Aktien von Waterloo* (The Rothschilds' Stock since Waterloo).

Jud Süss appeared in September 1940. It focuses on the rootlessness of the Jew and his ability to penetrate Aryan society. Apart from the assimilated Süss, the Jewish characters are dirty, hook-nosed, or without scruples. One actor plays three Jewish characters, thereby depicting the eternal nature of the Jew. It is said that 120 Jews from the Lublin ghetto were used as extras in the film.

The story is set in eighteenth-century Württemberg. Süss Oppenheimer wields enormous power as financial adviser to the reigning duke, convincing him to allow Jews to enter Stuttgart. Süss rapes the blonde Aryan Dorothea while having her Aryan husband tortured. Tainted for life, Dorothea drowns herself. The duke dies; now powerless, Süss is arrested, tried, and publicly hanged. The Jews are exiled from the city with the hope, as the film notes, that this lesson "will never be forgotten."

Jud Süss was extremely successful. Heinrich HIMMLER ordered all members of the SS and police to see it. It was also viewed by concentration camp guards. Witnesses saw a HITLERJUGEND (Hitler Youth) group in Vienna trample a Jewish man to death after seeing the film. It was shown in small towns in Poland prior to deportations of the Jews in order to prevent help being given to them by the local population. The director, Veit Harlan, was tried for crimes against humanity at Nuremberg, but the case was dismissed because of the difficulty in obtaining evidence.

The most vile of the three films, *Der ewige Jude,* premiered in November 1940. It embodies the full gamut of Nazi antisemitic ideology in the style of Julius STREICHER's *Der* STÜRMER. In a "documentary" manner, it depicts the "filthy" ghettos of the Jews; the uncreative Jewish parasite; Jewish control of world finance, politics, and the arts; and the Jew as a homeless, rootless cosmopolite who infiltrates Aryan society. The final sequence depicts a Jewish ritual slaughter scene in a particularly cruel manner. "Authenticity" is provided by the use of maps and statistics to verify statements. The central aim of the film is to create the image of a wandering pest who must be exterminated. *Der ewige Jude* was not successful, the German public having had their fill with *Jud Süss.* Clearly, though, the appearance of these three films in 1940 was not coincidental but rather part of an overall plan connected with the destruction of European Jewry.

[*See also* Antisemitism; Propaganda, Nazi.]

BIBLIOGRAPHY

Hull, D. S. *Film in the Third Reich: A Study of the German Cinema, 1933–1945.* Berkeley, 1969.

Leiser, E. *Nazi Cinema.* New York, 1975.

Taylor, R. *Film Propaganda: Soviet Russia and Nazi Germany.* London, 1979.

Welch, D. *Propaganda and the German Cinema, 1933–1945.* Oxford, 1983.

JUDITH E. DONESON

FILMS ON THE HOLOCAUST. Both fiction and nonfiction films have helped to shape attitudes and stereotypes concerning the Holocaust. As a medium capable of educating as well as entertaining, film often establishes how this tragedy represents itself as history in the minds of people. Despite the diversity of subjects and themes (and without regard to aesthetic quality), it is possible to discern several general areas that provide insight into the scope and content of films on the Holocaust.

Among the earlier fiction films, many come from countries that suffered heavily under Nazi domination, especially in eastern Europe. Examples include two films from Poland, *Border Street* (1948; Aleksander Ford), about the Warsaw ghetto, and *The Last Stop* (1948; Wanda Jakubowska), filmed at AUSCHWITZ; and one film from Czechoslovakia, *Distant Journey* (1949; Alfred Radok), about a Jewish family deported to the THERESIENSTADT ghetto.

In the 1950s, Andrzej Wajda began his trilogy on the war and the postwar period in Poland. *Generation* (1954) portrays life in occupied Warsaw in 1942, and *Kanal* (1956) tells of Poles escaping from the Nazis via the city's sewers. These were followed by *Ashes and Diamonds* (1958). The persecution of the Jews plays a minor role in the trilogy. Wajda's 1961 film *Samson* depicts a Jew's inability to function in Warsaw during the war. *The Passenger* (1962; Andrzej Munk) relates the meeting of a woman once imprisoned in Auschwitz with her former guard, as she recalls her experiences in flashbacks.

A number of Czech films appeared in the 1960s: *Sweet Light in a Dark Room* (1960; Jiri Weiss), about a Czech boy hiding a Jewish girl from the Nazis; *Diamonds of the Night* (1964; Jan Nemec), depicting two boys who escape from a transport as they are chased by hunters in the woods; *The Shop on Main Street* (1965; Jan Kadar and Elmar Klos), which relates the crisis of conscience of a Slovak Christian in the face of the deportation of the town's Jews; and *And the Fifth Horseman Is Fear* (1968; Zbynek Brynych), a tale of frightened Jews and Czech informers.

A look at a cross-section of films from the late 1940s through the 1980s helps to illustrate how the Holocaust often plays a secondary role to the central story of the film. *Distant Journey* and *The Last Stop* are two examples. Others include *Judgment at Nuremberg* (United States, 1961; Stanley Kramer), a dramatization of the trial of German judges at Nuremberg; *Ship of Fools* (United States, 1965; Stanley Kramer), which tells in hindsight of a ship's passengers returning to Germany in 1932; *Landscape after Battle* (Poland, 1970; Andrzej Wajda), which focuses on attempts to return to normalcy in a DISPLACED PERSONS camp after the war; *Cabaret* (United States, 1972; Bob Fosse), set in Weimar in 1932, on the eve of Nazi rule; *Seven Beauties* (Italy, 1975; Lina Wertmüller), which tells of an Italian soldier who is without scruples in his attempt to survive a concentration camp; *Julia* (United States, 1977; Fred Zinnemann), based on the friendship of two women and set against the backdrop of the Nazi period; and *The Tin Drum* (West Germany, 1979; Volker Schlöndorff), the story of a young man in Danzig during the war who refuses to

The Diary of Anne Frank (United States, 1959; George Stevens). [Israel Film Archive, Jerusalem]

grow up in order to avoid entering the absurd world created by adults.

Though fewer in number, films that focus on Jewish characters provide insight into the problems confronted by European Jewry during the war. Representative of these are *The Diary of Anne Frank* (United States, 1959; George Stevens), demonstrating how Anne's diary became one of the first universal symbols of the Holocaust; *Kapo* (Italy, 1960; Gillo Pontecorvo), about a Jewish KAPO in a concentration camp; *The Two of Us* (France, 1966; Claude Berri), which portrays a breakdown of Jewish stereotypes; *The Garden of the Finzi-Continis* (Italy, 1970; Vittorio De Sica), the story of the deportation of the Jews of Ferrara; *Voyage of the Damned* (United States and Great Britain, 1976; Stuart Rosenberg), about the ship ST. LOUIS, with its Jewish refugees who sought a safe haven in Cuba and the United States, only to be refused and sent back to Europe; and *Jacob the Liar* (East Germany, 1978; Frank Beyer), the story of a Jew in a ghetto who keeps hope alive among his fellow Jews by telling them that the Germans are losing the war. Included here are post-Holocaust films about the adjustment of survivors, such as *The Pawnbroker* (United States, 1965; Sidney Lumet) and *Madame Rosa* (France, 1977; Moshe Mizrahi).

The French film *The Sorrow and the Pity* (1970; Marcel Ophuls) demonstrates how film can participate in the historical discourse. This documentary, four and a half hours in length, touched a nerve in France as it destroyed the popular myth of the French as a nation of resisters and aggravated the wound made by the many French who collaborated with the Nazis. The controversy was pursued in a series of French fiction films, including *Lacombe, Lucien* (1974; Louis Malle), the story of collaboration as a tale of the banality of evil; *Black Thursday* (1974; Michel Mitrani), about the July 1942 roundup of Jews in Paris by the French police; *Mr. Klein* (1976; Joseph Losey), concerning the case of a man willing to capitalize on the plight of Jews fleeing from the Nazis, until he himself is mistaken for a Jew; and *The Last Metro* (1980; François Truffaut), a more gentle answer to the films that preceded it, which tells of a theatrical troupe that continues performing during the occupation, guided by its Jewish director, who is hidden in the cellar below the stage.

Turning to nonfiction films, it must be recognized that archival film footage on the Holocaust is either Nazi anti-Jewish propaganda film or footage shot by the liberating armies. This imposes obvious limitations on any interpretation of the Holocaust through archival film. Some films that utilize archival footage are *Night and Fog* (France, 1955; Alain Resnais), which depicts the world of the concentration camp; *Warsaw Ghetto* (Great Britain, 1968; BBC/TV); *Genocide* (Great Britain, 1973; Michael Darlow), from the Thames Television series *The World at War*; and *The Liberation of Auschwitz* (West Germany, 1986; Irmgard von zur Muehlen).

Topics portrayed in nonfiction film are broad and varied, from studies of the rise of fascism to the Allies' refusal to bomb Auschwitz. Among these are *The Illegals* (United States, 1947; Meyer Levin), showing the illegal immigration of refugees into Palestine; *Genocide* (United States, 1981; Arnold Schwartzman), which won an Oscar for the best documentary film; and *Who Shall Live and Who Shall Die?* (United States, 1981; Laurence Jarvik), which explores American guilt for not having done more to save the Jews of Europe. Marcel Ophuls's lengthy documentary *Hotel Terminus* (1988) traces the life of Klaus Barbie, the "butcher of Lyons" (*see* BARBIE TRIAL).

A docudrama nine and a half hours long that was made for American television, *Holocaust* (United States, 1978; Marvin Chomsky for NBC/TV), became the catalyst for an unprecedented public response to the period of the "FINAL SOLUTION." Telecast throughout Europe and the United States, and considered by many critics to be a soap opera and a

The Garden of the Finzi-Continis (Italy, 1970; Vittorio de Sica). [Israel Film Archive, Jerusalem]

trivialization of the Holocaust, this American miniseries elicited national discussions of the Holocaust in West Germany, France, and Switzerland, as well as in the United States. It also paved the way for other television dramas and films, making the subject acceptable for public consumption. One of these was the epic *War and Remembrance* (United States, 1988–1989; Dan Curtis for ABC/TV), which made an impressive attempt to portray the horror of Auschwitz.

After *Holocaust,* a number of interesting fiction films appeared on the "Final Solution." Examples are *The Boat Is Full* (Switzerland, West Germany, and Austria, 1980; Markus Imhoof), a story of Jewish refugees denied asylum in Switzerland; *Charlotte* (the Netherlands and West Germany, 1981; Franz Weisz), the story of Charlotte Salomon, a young Jewish artist deported and killed in Auschwitz; *The Revolt of Job* (Hungary, 1981; Imre Gyongossy and Barna Kabay), which tells of a Jewish couple who adopt a gentile boy and teach him the ways of Judaism; *Sophie's Choice* (United States, 1982; Alan Pakula), the story of a Polish survivor of Auschwitz and her ill-fated choices; *Angry Harvest* (West Germany, 1985; Agnieszka Holland), the portrait of a lonely Polish man who falls in love with the Jewish woman he is hiding during the war; and *Elysium* (Hungary, 1986; Erika Szanto), the tale of a young Jewish boy arrested in the streets of Budapest and taken to a camp where medical experiments are performed on children.

Shoah (France, 1985; Claude Lanzmann). [Israel Film Archive, Jerusalem]

Claude Lanzmann's *Shoah* (France, 1985) was eleven years in the making. It does not use a single frame of archival footage. Rather, through interviews with the perpetrators, survivors, and bystanders involved in the Holocaust, the film mercilessly explores, in more than nine and a half hours of film, the process that led to the death of six million European Jews. *Shoah* is a film that forces the viewer to confront and to attempt to understand, at some level, what was the Holocaust.

BIBLIOGRAPHY

Avisar, I. *Screening the Holocaust: Cinema's Images of the Unimaginable.* Bloomington, 1988.

Bettelheim, B. *Surviving and Other Essays.* New York, 1979. See pages 274–314.

Diamond, S. A. "'Holocaust' Film's Impact on Americans." *Patterns of Prejudice* 12/4 (July–August 1978): 1–9.

Doneson, J. E. *The Holocaust in American Film.* Philadelphia, 1987.

Doneson, J. E. "The Jew as a Female Figure in Holocaust Film." *Shoah: A Review of Holocaust Studies and Commemorations* 1 (1978): 11–13.

Friedman, R. M. "Exorcising the Past: Jewish Figures in Contemporary Films." *Journal of Contemporary History* 19/3 (July 1984): 511–527.

Insdorf, A. L. *Indelible Shadows: Film and the Holocaust.* New York, 1983.

Langer, L. "The Americanization of the Holocaust on Stage and Screen." In *From Hester Street to Hollywood: The Jewish American Stage and Screen,* edited by S. B. Cohen. Bloomington, 1983. See pages 213–230.

Liehm, A. J. *Closely Watched Films: The Czechoslovak Film Experience.* White Plains, N.Y., 1974.

Stoil, J. M. *Cinema beyond the Danube: The Camera and Politics.* Metuchen, N.J., 1974.

JUDITH E. DONESON

"FINAL SOLUTION" (Ger., *Endlösung*), the Nazis' comprehensive program to solve their "Jewish question" by murdering every Jew in Europe. Initiated by Adolf HITLER in the summer of 1941 in the euphoria of his greatest successes and his seemingly imminent victory over the Soviet Union, the "Final Solution" was the culmination of a long evolution of Nazi Jewish policy—from Hitler's earliest articulation of a solution to the "Jewish question" in 1919, through the Nazi attempts to coerce Jewish emigration in the 1930s, to the schemes for mass expulsion after the outbreak of war, and, finally, the leap to mass murder with the EINSATZGRUPPEN assault on Russian Jewry in 1941. The emergence of the "Final Solution" as both concept and program was a complex phenomenon conditioned by Hitler's ideology and manner of governing, by the nature of the Nazi regime, and by the changing circumstances in which the Nazis found themselves.

In the very earliest document of Hitler's political career, a letter written on September 16, 1919, in reply to a query from Adolf Gemlich (a former agent of Hitler's superior, Capt. Karl Mayr), he articulated the view that the "Jewish question" would be solved not through emotional antisemitism and pogroms but only through an "antisemitism of reason" that would lead to a systematic legal struggle to deprive the Jews of their privileges and classify them as foreigners. "The final goal, however, must steadfastly remain the removal [*Entfernung*] of the Jews altogether." The "Jewish question" remained central for Hitler in the 1920s. For Nazis, he declared, the "Jewish question" was the "pivotal question" (*Kernfrage*), and the party was therefore determined to solve it "with well-known German thoroughness to the final consequence." For the most part the "final consequence" was expressed in terms such as "removal" (*Ausweisung*), "expulsion" (*Austreibung*), and "exclusion" (*Ausschaltung*). Occasionally, however, his language became more ominous, particularly when he made the analogy between the tuberculosis bacillus, which had to be destroyed (*vernichtet*), and the Jew—the "racial tuberculosis" (*Rassentuberkulose*) of peoples who had to be removed if the German *Volk* were to recover its health. On one occasion in 1922, he fantasized about publicly hanging every Jew in Germany and leaving the bodies dangling until they stank.

Such statements indicate the depth of Hitler's obsession with the Jews as the source of all of Germany's historical misfortunes and current problems, indeed as the "greatest evil"; his determination to seek an uncompromising and comprehensive solution to this "Jewish question" by getting rid of the Jews one way or another; and his violent and murderous predisposition. They do not, however, constitute a grand design, blueprint, or decision for the "Final Solution" of 1941 to 1945: the comprehensive and systematic mass murder of all European Jewry.

In the early 1930s, between the Nazis' electoral breakthrough and Hitler's assumption of power, there was little or no preparation in the party for its subsequent Jewish policy. In the years immediately following the attainment of power, various Nazi factions pursued different and often conflicting policies, with Hitler generally favoring the approach of systematic legislative discrimination—the "antisemitism of reason" of the Gemlich letter—over the public violence of pogroms and "wild actions." Lacking at this time, however, was any articulation of what had been so common in Hitler's statements during the early 1920s, namely, the determination of the final goal of Nazi Jewish policy. Few Nazis seemed to be looking ahead to where the persecution of the Jews might lead. In the SS, however, as early as 1934 a report for Heinrich HIMMLER on the "Jewish question" emphasized the need to work toward a total emigration of German Jewry.

While emigration became the centerpiece of SS Jewish policy thereafter, this remained a "voluntary solution" until the ANSCHLUSS with Austria in March 1938. The Jewish expert of Reinhard HEYDRICH's SD (Sicherheitsdienst; Security Service), Adolf EICHMANN, was then sent to Vienna, where he organized assembly-line procedures for expediting and coercing Jewish emigration.

The year 1938 was a turning point for Nazi Jewish policy in other ways as well. Expulsion began to characterize Nazi Jewish policy throughout Germany, as Soviet Jews were ordered out of the country in the spring, followed by Polish Jews in the fall. Hermann GÖRING began the systematic ARISIERUNG ("Aryanization") of Jewish property, which threatened to pauperize the Jews of Germany within months and make emigration even more difficult. Joseph GOEBBELS made his bid for power over Nazi Jewish policy by instigating the KRISTALLNACHT pogrom of November 9 and 10, 1938.

In the wake of Kristallnacht, the Nazis finally moved to coordinate the disparate and often conflicting Jewish policies pursued by the regime until then. Göring announced Hitler's instructions to the Nazi leaders gathered before him on November 12, 1938:

> The Jewish question is to be summed up and coordinated once and for all and solved one way or another. . . . If the German Reich should in the near future become involved in conflict abroad then it is obvious that we in Germany will first of all make sure of settling accounts with the Jews. Apart from that, the Führer is now at last to make a major move abroad, starting with the powers that have brought up the Jewish question, in order to get around to the Madagascar solution. He explained this to me in detail on November 9. There is no longer any other way.

In the following months Hitler approved the negotiations between Hjalmar SCHACHT and George Rublee for the resettlement of German Jewry, and Göring established the Reichszentrale für Jüdische Auswanderung (Reich Central Office for Jewish Emigration) on the model of Eichmann's Vienna experiment. The office was placed under Heydrich's control, with the charge that the "emigration of the Jews from Germany [was] to be furthered by all possible means."

Hitler himself spoke before the Reichstag on January 30, 1939, reiterating the two themes of Jewish emigration and of the dire consequences of war that Göring had summarized earlier. He chided those states that criticized Germany's treatment of its Jews for their own reluctance to accept Jews: "The world has sufficient space for settlements." If, however, war broke out first, "then the result will not be the Bolshevization of the earth, and thus the victory of Jewry, but the annihilation of the Jewish race in Europe."

Should Hitler's threats at this time be seen as a literal statement of his clear intention to kill the Jews upon the outbreak of war? They may have had other motives: on the one hand, a desire to exercise diplomatic blackmail against governments presumed to be under Jewish influence to accept Germany's impoverished Jewish refugees and not thwart its imminent destruction of Czechoslovakia; on the other, a wish to impart to Hitler's followers the notion that a policy more radical than emigration would be needed after the outbreak of war to solve the "Jewish question." Several facts support the latter interpretation. First, less than two weeks before the Reichstag speech, Hitler made the same threat to the Czech ambassador, František Chvalkovsky—an unlikely person in whom to confide premeditated mass murder, but an entirely appropriate target for diplomatic pressure. Second, when war did break out in September 1939, Hitler did not immediately initiate the systematic mass murder of the Jews under German control. Instead, with his clear approval, Nazi Jewish policy became radicalized in a different way; solving the "Jewish question" still meant removing the Jews one way or another.

The conquest and partition of Poland brought an additional two million Jews into the German sphere, including more than one-half million in the "incorporated territories" annexed directly to the Reich. In addition, however, some seven million Poles resided in the incorporated territories. If the "Jewish question" was one major obsession in Hitler's world view, the conquest of *Lebensraum* ("living space") in eastern Europe was the other. Poland thus presented a major challenge to the Nazis, not only in the new magnitude of the "Jewish question" its conquest entailed but also in the extent of territory inhabited by Poles that was to be transformed into German "living space." According to a plan approved by Hitler in late September 1939, the Poles and Jews of the incorporated territories were to be expelled into the GENERALGOUVERNEMENT, and the very concept of Polish nationhood was to be eradicated through the "liquidation," including physical destruction, of the Polish intelligentsia, deemed the bearers of Polish nationalism. The incorporated territories were to be repopulated with ethnic Germans (VOLKSDEUTSCHE) evacuated from the Baltic states and eastern Poland, areas that had been surrendered to the Soviets as the price of the Nazi-Soviet non-aggression pact of August 1939 (*see* NAZI-SOVIET PACT). As for the Jews, they were to be expelled not just from the incorporated territories but from all of the Third Reich into a reservation on the outer edge of the German empire, at that time the Lublin region on the demarcation line with Soviet-occupied eastern Poland.

The Nazis set in motion a massive demographic upheaval, but the overall plan could not be realized. Very quickly, Jewish deportations from within prewar German boundaries were prohibited. Deportations of Jews from the incorporated territories were scaled down, while precedence was given to deporting Poles, whose farms, businesses, and homes could be turned over to incoming *Volksdeutsche*. By the spring of 1940, Hitler let it be known that the Lublin Reservation was no longer the target of a solution to the "Jewish question" (*see* NISKO AND LUBLIN PLAN). There was not enough territory in Poland to spare for the Jews.

Himmler was receptive to this hint, and in late May 1940 he presented Hitler with a memorandum on the treatment of the populations of eastern Europe that included the notion of expelling all the Jews to some colonial territory in Africa. Other eastern Europeans not suitable for "Germanization" were to be turned into slave laborers. Concerning this systematic eradication of the ethnic composition of eastern Europe, Himmler concluded: "However cruel and tragic each individual case may be, this method is still the mildest and best, if one rejects the Bolshevik method of physical extermination of a people out of inner conviction as un-German and impossible." Hitler judged Himmler's proposals "very good and correct." Within weeks, this notion of expelling the Jews overseas was concretized in the form of the MADAGASCAR PLAN, which Hitler discussed approvingly with Mussolini in late June. Until the German defeat in the Battle of Britain in September 1940 rendered its imminent realization impossible, the Madagascar Plan was briefly the centerpiece and preoccupation of Nazi Jewish policy.

However ephemeral and unrealized the Lublin Reservation project and the Madagascar Plan proved to be, they represented an important stage in the evolution of Nazi Jewish policy. Shortly before the war a Foreign Office circular had noted, in reference to the large Jewish populations in Poland, Hungary, and Romania: "Even for Germany the Jewish question will not be solved when the last Jew has left German soil." With direct control over much of Europe and a growing list of unequal alliances with states not directly occupied, the Nazis considered the "Jewish question" no longer a German but rather a European issue; German domination of the Continent imposed the obligation to solve this problem in a fundamental way. The removal of the Jews altogether, once Hitler's prescription for Germany, was now the unquestioned premise of the Nazis' commitment throughout Europe. Clearly, with notions such as the Lublin and Madagascar programs, the Nazis had already accustomed themselves to the idea of an unprecedented loss of life and population decimation among the Jews.

This changing mentality among the Nazis was reflected in their increasing references to a "final solution to the Jewish question." In June 1940, Heydrich referred to the Madagascar Plan as a "territorial final solution." Beginning in September 1940, Eichmann's staff routinely referred to "the doubtless imminent final solution to the Jewish question" (*die zweifellos kommende Endlösung der Judenfrage*) when refusing to permit Jewish emigration from any country in Europe other than Germany, so that the latter would be the first *judenrein* ("cleansed of Jews") nation in Europe. By 1940, therefore, even before mass murder became the goal of Nazi Jewish policy, the Nazis were already committed to a way of thinking about the "Jewish question" that precluded any solution that was less than both "final" and trans-European.

At the same time, large-scale, systematic mass murder as a method of problem-solving was becoming commonplace. It was already established that the denationalization of Poland was to be achieved through the systematic liquidation of the Polish intelligentsia. Simultaneously, Hitler initiated the killing of mentally and hereditarily ill Germans, deemed "unworthy of life." This was euphemistically referred to as the EUTHANASIA PROGRAM, although it had nothing to do with any voluntary request of the victim to be released from his suffering. In its personnel, technology (including the use of carbon monoxide in gas chambers), and bureaucratic mode of operation, this murder program in particular foreshadowed the mass murder of the Jews that was soon to follow.

Hitler's decision to invade the Soviet Union

and the ensuing preparations for it in the spring of 1941 were especially significant in the accelerating movement toward the mass murder of European Jewry. The invasion of the Soviet Union promised to aggravate the conditions of the vicious circle in which the Germans had entrapped themselves, for each new military success increased the number of Jews under their control whom they were committed to get rid of through a "final solution" of one kind or another. The campaign against Russia, as Hitler made clear to his generals, was to be not a conventional war, but a war of destruction against National Socialism's racial and ideological enemies. Not only was *Lebensraum* to be conquered, but Bolshevism and its Jewish progenitor were to be eradicated. With the formation of the Einsatzgruppen, systematic mass murder as a method of solving the Nazis' self-imposed "Jewish question" began.

Even then, however, the evolution to the "Final Solution" was not yet complete. The Einsatzgruppen were targeted against Jews in the newly occupied territories only, and moved into their tasks gradually as their commanders tested the limits of their men and of army cooperation, as well as the usefulness of local collaboration. Only in late July or early August 1941 did all the mobile killing units begin the systematic mass murder of all Jews in the Russian territories, including women and children.

At this point, Hitler stood at the pinnacle of his success. The German army had torn through Soviet defenses, encircled huge numbers of Soviet troops, destroyed most of the air force, and rampaged through two-thirds of the distance to Moscow. Victory seemed imminent, and Hitler faced the intoxicating prospect of having all of Europe at his feet. In the euphoria of the conquest of Poland, he had approved plans for a massive demographic reorganization on Polish territory, including the expulsion of Jews to the Lublin Reservation. With victory over France, he had approved the Madagascar Plan. Now, with the seeming victory over Russia, the last inhibitions fell away. Precisely when and how instructions were given is not known, but Göring, Himmler, and Heydrich now knew what Hitler expected of them. On July 31, 1941, Heydrich visited Göring and had him sign an authorization to prepare and submit "an overall plan of the organizational, functional, and material measures to be taken in preparing for the implementation of the aspired final solution of the Jewish question."

If the notion of the "Final Solution" was now clear to the leading Nazis, the means of its implementation were not. The Einsatzgruppen had encountered numerous problems, most importantly the lack of secrecy, the psychological burden on the killers, and the logistic inadequacy of the killing methods in relation to the number of intended victims. If unsatisfactory for the Soviet Union, the firing-squad method was even less suitable for murdering the rest of European Jewry. The Nazis chose to become pioneers of mass murder in an uncharted land. The past offered no suitable landmarks, but in the fall of 1941 new killing techniques were improvised. The perverse organizational genius of the Nazis was now revealed, as they merged elements of their past programs in order to create something entirely new.

The physical setting of the concentration camp, the killing methods of euthanasia, and the deportation techniques of the population-resettlement programs were combined to create a system of EXTERMINATION CAMPS. In relative secrecy, a small number of camp personnel using assembly-line techniques could kill millions of victims, brought trainload by trainload, day after day, to these factories of death. A bureaucratic apparatus, detached from direct contact with the killing process but long inured to the notion that the Jews had to be removed one way or another, could perform on a business-as-usual basis all the diverse functions necessary to uproot and ship to their death millions of people. The German population in general, accepting the notion of the Jew as an enemy against whom it was legitimate for the state to take preventive measures, looked on with indifference.

In the fall of 1941, steps were taken to turn the conception of a "final solution to the Jewish question" into reality. The deportation of the German Jews was sanctioned by Hitler in late September and began in mid-October. The first gassing experiment was conducted in AUSCHWITZ in early September, and construction of two extermination camps at BEŁŻEC and CHEŁMNO began in late October or early November. The first mass murder of German Jews took place in KOVNO and RIGA in late November and early December, and the first extermination camp, at Chełmno, began full-time operations also in early December. The last step in turning the idea of the "Final Solution" into reality was the WANNSEE CONFERENCE of January 20, 1942. At this conference, Reinhard Heydrich and his Jewish expert, Adolf Eichmann, met with the state secretaries of the ministerial bureaucracy. Most of those attending were already aware that Jews were being killed, but the full scope of the mass murder program was only now revealed. Eleven million Jews, from Ireland to the Urals and from Scandinavia to Spain, were the intended victims—in short, every Jew in Europe. Heydrich requested the support of the state secretaries, and was pleasantly surprised by their enthusiasm for the project.

Though initially conceived as a program to be carried out following Germany's expected victory over the Soviet Union, the "Final Solution" henceforth endured through Germany's changing fortunes of war. In 1942, with victory postponed, the Nazis made a virtue of necessity, proclaiming that the "Final Solution" had to be effected during the war to avoid an outcry from abroad. In 1944, with their fortunes in decline, they rushed to finish their gruesome task—to achieve a victory in their racial war that imminent military defeat could not undo. Nazi Jewish policy was shaped by a number of factors and evolved toward the "Final Solution" in fits and starts over many years, but this in no way detracts from the fact that in the end it was the most important legacy, indeed the epitome, of National Socialism.

[*See also* Deportations; Genocide.]

BIBLIOGRAPHY

Adam, U. D. *Judenpolitik im Dritten Reich.* Düsseldorf, 1972.

Browning, C. R. *Fateful Months: Essays on the Emergence of the Final Solution.* New York, 1985.

Browning, C. R. "Nazi Resettlement Policy and the Search for a Solution to the Jewish Question, 1939–1941." *German Studies Review* 9/3 (1986): 497–519.

Hilberg, R. *The Destruction of the European Jews.* New York, 1985.

Jäckel, E., ed. *Hitler: Sämtliche Aufzeichnungen, 1905–1924.* Stuttgart, 1980.

Jäckel, E. *Hitler's Weltanschauung: A Blueprint for Power.* Middletown, Conn., 1972.

Mayer, A. J. *Why Did the Heavens Not Darken? The "Final Solution" in History.* New York, 1989.

Schleunes, K. A. *The Twisted Road to Auschwitz: Nazi Policy toward German Jews, 1933–1939.* London, 1972.

CHRISTOPHER R. BROWNING

FINLAND. In 1939, about two thousand Jews lived in Finland, including some three hundred refugees from Germany, Austria, and Czechoslovakia. The local community was composed mostly of Jews who had come from Russia during the nineteenth century, and had been made equal citizens of independent Finland in 1917. Jews lived in Helsinki, Turku, and Viipuri (Vyborg).

Before and during World War II, antisemitism in Finland was virtually nonexistent and the Finnish government resisted the spread of Nazi ideology. As Finnish citizens, Jews fought the Red Army in the Winter War toward the end of 1939. During the one hundred days of fighting, the Jewish casualty rate was proportionately higher than that of the rest of the population; fifteen Jewish soldiers were killed and many wounded. Following the German invasion of the country in 1941, Finland was involved in the war against the Soviet Union, and at least three hundred Jews fought in Finnish uniforms. Many Jewish women were active in the civil-defense corps, and eight Jewish soldiers lost their lives. Speaking of these events in 1944 at the Helsinki synagogue, the marshal of Finland, Carl Gustaf Emil Mannerheim, extolled the Jewish contribution to the national defense.

Although at the WANNSEE CONFERENCE the Jews of Finland were included in the plans for the "FINAL SOLUTION," Finnish Jewry came through the war unscathed. The Nazis did not press the Finns very strongly regarding the "Jewish question," because they feared alienating them and losing the much-needed Finnish military presence on the eastern front. When Heinrich HIMMLER raised the issue during a visit to Finland in the summer of 1942, he was rebuffed by Prime Minister Johann Wilhelm Rangell. Rangell later wrote:

> Himmler asked: "How is the situation with the Jews in Finland?" I said to him that in Finland there are roughly a couple of thousand Jews, decent families and individuals whose sons are fighting in our army like the rest of the Finns and who are respected citizens as all the rest. I concluded my statement with the words, *"Wir haben keine Judenfrage"* (We have no Jewish question), and I said it with such a clarity that the discussion of the matter ended then and there. The Jewish question was not discussed with Himmler any other time.

Later the same year, however, in correspondence with the Gestapo chief, Heinrich MÜLLER, the head of the Finnish State Police (Valpo), Arno Anthoni, agreed to deport eight Jewish refugees whose names had appeared on the Valpo's extradition lists. The total number of prisoners handed over to the German authorities in TALLINN on November 6, 1942, was twenty-seven. Nineteen were non-Jewish citizens of the Soviet Union and the republic of Estonia. Five were Jewish prisoners, one of whom was accompanied voluntarily by his wife and minor son, and another by his son. One of the eight Jews survived the ordeal.

In his trial after the war, Anthoni explained the action as simply a police measure. The Valpo's extradition lists contained the names of more central European Jewish refugees, but this deportation remained the only one.

The story of the Jewish-refugee extradition was blown up by Swedish and Finnish newspapers in early December 1942 into a major scandal. The resignation of Karl August Fagerholm, minister of social affairs and a leading Social Democratic politician, was also connected with this issue. Eventually, in the spring of 1944, the Swedish government accepted a Valpo recommendation that it receive about one hundred and sixty of the Jewish refugees still remaining in Finland. The rest of the Jewish refugees in Finland survived the war, along with all the Finnish nationals of the Jewish faith.

FINLAND

BIBLIOGRAPHY

Mikola, K. J. "Finland's Wars during World War II." In *Finland's War Years: A List of Books and Articles concerning the Winter War and the Continuation War, Excluding Literature in Finnish and Russian,* edited by K. Nyman, pp. iii–xxxii. Mikkeli, Finland, 1973.

Rautkallio, H. *Finland and the Holocaust: The Rescue of Finland's Jews.* New York, 1987.

HANNU RAUTKALLIO

FISCHER, LUDWIG (1905–1947), governor of the Warsaw district in occupied Poland. Born in Kaiserslautern, in the Rhine district of Germany, Fischer became a member of the Nazi party in 1926 and joined the SA (Sturmabteilung; Storm Troopers) in 1929, rising to the rank of *Gruppenführer.* In 1937 he was elected to the Reichstag. He was appointed governor of the Warsaw district in October 1939, and remained in that post until the

German withdrawal from Warsaw in January 1945. In April and May of 1943 he was also acting governor of the Lublin district. Fischer was responsible for the establishment of the Warsaw ghetto in November 1940, as well as of other ghettos in the Warsaw district. He was heavily involved personally in organizing terror operations against Jews and Poles in his district and in the liquidation of the ghettos during 1942 and 1943. Fischer was arrested in West Germany after the war and in 1946 was extradited to Poland, where he was tried for his crimes, sentenced to death, and hanged.

BIBLIOGRAPHY

Gutman, Y. *The Jews of Warsaw, 1939–1943.* Bloomington, 1982.

Raporty Ludwiga Fischera gubernatora dystryktu warszawskiego. Warsaw, 1987.

SHMUEL KRAKOWSKI

FLEISCHMANN, GISI (1897–1944), Zionist activist in SLOVAKIA; leader of the Women's International Zionist Organization and of the PRACOVNÁ SKUPINA (Working Group).

When the ÚSTREDŇA ŽIDOV (Jewish Center) was established in Slovakia in 1940 on order of the authorities, Fleischmann was appointed head of its Aliya (immigration to Palestine) section. This section became the cover for the continuation of Zionist activities among the youth and of the *hakhshara* (agricultural training) network; it also provided vocational training.

Among Gisi Fleischmann's early achievements was the aid she helped organize for 326 Jews from Prague. These men had been interned in a camp in Sosnowiec, Poland, and had made their way to Slovakia early in 1940. Fleischmann managed to convince the Slovak government to allow the men to remain in Slovakia temporarily while she searched for a more permanent haven for them. They were housed in a camp at VYHNE. With the help of Richard Lichtheim (the Jewish Agency representative in Geneva) and Henry Montor (of the United Palestine Appeal in New York), she found safer places for them. Eventually, al-

Gisi Fleischmann.

most all of the men reached Palestine or other free countries before the deportations from Slovakia began in the spring of 1942.

Early that spring, a group of Slovak Jewish leaders had come to the conclusion that in order to help rescue the Jewish population in Slovakia and other occupied countries, underground methods would have to be employed. Fleischmann was one of the early founders of this "Working Group," as it came to be called. After the deportation of Slovakia's Jews began, in March 1942, the Working Group tried to stop it by bribing Adolf EICHMANN's representative in Slovakia, Dieter WISLICENY. In order to raise the required funds, the group entered into an exchange of letters with Nathan Schwalb of the American Jewish JOINT DISTRIBUTION COMMITTEE's office in Geneva. When the first wave of deportations ceased (there were to be none from October 1942 to the fall of 1944), the Working Group was greatly encouraged and came up with an even bolder proposal, the EUROPA PLAN. This called for the cessation of deportations from all parts of German-occupied Europe in exchange for foreign currency or goods that would be transmitted to the Germans by Jews in free countries. The proposal was submitted to Wisliceny. Fleischmann played a major role in formulating the plan, in bringing it to fruition, and in establishing contacts for this purpose with individuals and organizations abroad. Not taking the proper precautions, she was arrested by the Gestapo and held in prison for four months, rejecting all efforts made in this period to enable her to leave Slovakia. On her release she resumed her previous work.

After the SS entry in force into Slovakia in the summer of 1944 and the suppression of the SLOVAK NATIONAL UPRISING in October of that year, Fleischmann sought to obtain an appointment with Alois BRUNNER, another representative of Eichmann. She also tried to persuade Kurt BECHER to discontinue the deportations; both these efforts were unsuccessful. Fleischmann turned down an offer to be hidden from the Germans in a Bratislava bunker.

On September 28 of that year, most members of the Working Group, including Fleischmann, were arrested during an SS raid. They were all taken to the SERED labor camp except for Fleischmann and one other member of the group, who were permitted to stay behind in Bratislava to take care of the needs of the detainees and to close down the Jewish Center's affairs.

At the beginning of October 1944, Fleischmann was deported to AUSCHWITZ in one of the last transports of the war, with a special instruction to the Auschwitz authorities labeling her as "RU" (*Rückkehr unerwünscht*, "return undesirable"). She was gassed on arrival in the camp.

BIBLIOGRAPHY

Campion, J. *In the Lion's Mouth: Gisi Fleischmann and the Jewish Fight for Survival.* Lanham, Md., 1987.

Fuchs, A. *The Unheeded Cry.* New York, 1984.

Neumann, Y. O. *Gisi Fleischmann: The Story of a Heroic Woman.* Tel Aviv, 1970.

GIDEON GREIF

FLIGHT. *See* Beriḥa.

FLIGHT OF NAZI CRIMINALS. *See* Extradition of War Criminals.

FMZ. *See* Front of the Wilderness Generation.

FOMENKO, WITOLD (1905–1961), a "RIGHTEOUS AMONG THE NATIONS." Born in Warsaw into a Ukrainian family, Fomenko was still a child when he moved with his family to Chełm, where he grew up in a Jewish neighborhood, learning to speak and write Yiddish. In 1924 the family moved to LUTSK, where Fomenko played in a military band and gave music lessons. Many of his students were Jewish, and through them he came to know the Stoliner Rebbe, Rabbi Yohanan Perlov, and composed tunes for Perlov's Hasidic songs. In the mid-1930s, Fomenko had to give up his musical activities on doctors' orders, and with the help of Jewish friends he learned to be a barber.

In 1941, following the occupation of Lutsk and the establishment of a ghetto in the city, Fomenko began providing help to the Jews, bringing into the ghetto food, medicines, firewood, and other supplies, mainly for the soup kitchen where the needy received their meals. Fomenko paid for these purchases with his own income from the large barbershop he had opened, which had Jews among its employees. Whenever he visited the ghetto he tried to raise the morale of the Jews by telling them jokes and good news, and by singing anti-Nazi songs he had composed.

On the eve of the liquidation of the Lutsk ghetto, Fomenko began helping Jews to leave the ghetto and providing them with false "Aryan" documents that he had acquired or had had his Christian friends prepare for him. Following the arrest of a Jewish woman who had one of these documents in her possession and was tortured by her captors, Fomenko and his father were arrested, but the military commander of the city, who was a customer of Fomenko's, intervened on their behalf and they were released. Fomenko kept up his aid and rescue efforts even after the ghetto's liquidation, for those Jews who were being held in a labor camp in the city. When that camp was also liquidated, in December 1942, Fomenko concentrated on finding hiding places for Jews with Christian families in Lutsk, in most cases paying the families for their trouble. He also provided refuge for many Jews in his own house and among the members of his family in the city. Not all the Jews whom Fomenko helped survived the war—only thirty-six of them were still alive on the day the city was liberated.

After the war, Fomenko married one of the Jewish women he had saved, and with her made his home in Israel. He was awarded the Righteous among the Nations medal of YAD VASHEM, and planted a tree on Righteous among the Nations Avenue on Remembrance Hill in Jerusalem.

BIBLIOGRAPHY

Sharon, N., ed. *Sefer Lutsk*. Tel Aviv, 1961. (In Hebrew.)

Spector, S. *The Holocaust of Volhynian Jews, 1941–1944*. Jerusalem, 1986. (In Hebrew.)

SHMUEL SPECTOR

FORCED LABOR. [*This entry consists of two articles. The first,* Fremdarbeiter, *deals with the Nazi policy of using within the Reich forced labor from occupied countries. The second,* Jews in Occupied Poland, *surveys the use of Jewish slave labor in the ghettos and labor camps in Poland. For different aspects of the Nazis' exploitation of labor, see* Deutsche Ausrüstungswerke; HASAG; I.G. Farben; Munkaszolgálat; Organisation Schmelt; Organisation Todt; Ostindustrie GmbH.]

Fremdarbeiter

Laborers from Germany's satellites or occupied territories brought to work in the Reich were called *Fremdarbeiter* (foreign workers). The idea of using foreign workers for forced labor in the Third Reich was conceived in Berlin even before the September 1939 attack on Poland. It was first put into practice in Austria, after the ANSCHLUSS, in March 1938. Some 100,000 Austrian civilians, including 10,000 engineers, were taken to work in Germany, and by August 31, 1939, 70,000 workers from the Protectorate of BOHEMIA AND MORAVIA had gone the same route.

The German victories in the first phase of World War II and the ensuing occupation of many lands gave the Germans large reservoirs of manpower for their exploitation. Accordingly, the central German authorities in charge of employment policy worked out a detailed program for the drafting of these human resources. The plan provided for extremely harsh methods of recruitment to be applied in Poland and the occupied Soviet areas, whereas in the other countries under German occupation or in the satellite countries, far more lenient methods were to be used.

The first contingents of *Fremdarbeiter* were meant to replace the millions of Germans who had been taken out of the work force to be drafted into the army, and to spare the Germans the need to impose emergency labor drafts on their own population. When the BLITZKRIEG failed to achieve its purpose and the war dragged on with no end in sight, the German authorities needed the foreign workers to enable them to intensify recruitment for the armed forces and provide for the growing needs of the armaments industry.

Initially, the Germans tried to persuade people in the occupied countries to volunteer for work in Germany. To those who were ready to do so—mostly among the unemployed and those refugees who were in dire economic straits—the Germans promised all sorts of material benefits. At no time, however, did the number of volunteers fill the quota of workers required by the German economy.

Starting immediately after the outbreak of the war, the Germans used prisoners of war (POWs) on jobs in support of the German economy, contrary to international law on the subject. As early as the autumn of 1939, 340,000 Polish POWs were put to work on the land.

In the spring of 1940 the Germans decided to introduce in the GENERALGOUVERNEMENT various compulsory measures, such as conscriptions for work, seizures of persons who

Ukrainian women and girls waiting to be sent as forced laborers to Germany (1942).

did not possess papers exempting them from such conscription, and withholding of food rations from persons refusing to work. In August 1942 a decree was enacted imposing FORCED LABOR (*Zwangsverpflichtung*) in all occupied countries and POW camps. In western European countries, the local authorities on occasion cooperated with the Germans in their recruitment drives, in exchange for the release of POWs by the Germans or for a change in the status of POWs to that of foreign workers in Germany.

By 1942, the German drive for the recruitment of foreign workers had become a sophisticated and brutal manhunt, which also met with growing opposition and was an important element in the rise of organized resistance movements in Nazi-occupied Europe. Although millions of persons were conscripted for work in Germany between 1942 and 1944, the gap between the quotas set by the Germans and the actual number of workers who were brought to Germany grew apace. Reports on the poor working conditions in Germany and the treatment of foreign laborers, together with the growing signs of an impending German defeat, made it increasingly difficult for the Germans to obtain the help of local collaborators and overcome the general opposition of the local populations to working in Germany. The German retreat in the east and the shrinking area under their control also had the natural effect of reducing the reservoir of manpower available to them.

The great majority of foreign laborers were brought from Poland and the Soviet Union. In early 1941 there were 800,000 Polish foreign workers in Germany, representing 55 percent of the total foreign labor force in Germany at the time. From June 1941, when Germany invaded the USSR, German-occupied areas of the Soviet Union became the major source of foreign laborers. In September 1944 the total number of foreign workers in Germany was 5.5 million, to which must be added another 2 million POWs. Of the total number of 7.5 million foreign workers, 38 percent belonged to Soviet peoples, and 20 percent were Poles. The rest of the foreign laborers were drafted in France, Czechoslovakia, the Netherlands, Belgium, and Norway. Among the satellite countries and Germany's allies, Italy was the only one to provide foreign workers in significant numbers. The percentage of foreign workers employed by the German economy never came up to German expectations, but it grew all the time. In May 1940 foreign laborers were only 0.8 percent of the total work force; by May 1941 that percentage had risen to 8.4, and in September 1944, foreign laborers represented 20.8 percent of the total work force in Germany. By late 1944 the number of foreign laborers had risen to 8 million, and together with the POWs, it amounted to approximately 9 million. One out of five workers in Germany was a foreigner, and one out of every four tanks and every four aircraft manufactured in Germany was produced by foreign workers.

There were differences of opinion in the top Nazi echelons in charge of the work force and the economy concerning the policy to be followed in exploiting the manpower available and the foreign laborers. Albert SPEER, who in February 1942 was appointed *Reichsminister für Bewaffnung und Munition* (Minister of Armaments and War Production), was an efficient administrator who sought to put the emphasis on raising war production, both in Germany and in the occupied countries. Fritz SAUCKEL, on the other hand, who in March 1942 became *Generalbevollmächtigter für den Arbeitseinsatz* (Chief Plenipotentiary for the Labor Effort), made it his goal to accelerate the conscription of foreign laborers. Sauckel prided himself on the large number of workers he had brought to Germany from other countries, enabling Germany to avoid taking drastic measures to recruit workers among the German population, even if this did not always coincide with efficiency and the requirements of production.

The people responsible for the work force and production were well aware that the conditions under which the foreign laborers were living, the wages they were paid, and the treatment they were given had a direct bearing on the results of the recruiting drives of foreign laborers and on their productivity. In most instances, however, the supervision of the laborers was in the hands of the police—the Sicherheitspolizei (Security Police) and the Ausländische Arbeiter (Foreign Workers) section of the GESTAPO—and they were guided by racist principles, partisan considerations, and xenophobia. The situation of the laborers from eastern Europe, in terms of their living conditions and the attitude toward them, differed sharply from that of the laborers from western Europe. Poles and Russians were regarded as inferior—in racist terms, they were *Untermenschen,* or "subhumans"—and as a rule, they were put on hard physical labor and were subjected to harsh control, humiliation, and severe penalties. They had to wear an identifying sign on their clothes, *P* for Poles and *Ost* (east) for the

Ukrainian women and girls waiting to be sent to Germany as forced laborers (1942). They are being photographed and registered before their departure.

Russians. They were not permitted to leave their lodgings after working hours; to use public transportation; to attend cultural events, places of entertainment, or restaurants attended by Germans; or even to participate in church services together with Germans. The pay they received for their work was especially low. Germans were warned not to have any social contact with Poles or Russians and, above all, to abide by racial purity, that is, to shun sexual intercourse with them. Germans who did have sexual intercourse with foreign workers were charged with *Rassenschande* (race defilement), which carried the sentence of death.

The conditions for foreign workers from the west were much better, but they, too, complained of being treated like slaves. The employers, and especially the farmers who had foreigners working for them, did, however, often disregard the strict rules on the treatment of foreign laborers laid down by the Nazi party, since these laborers were indispensable to them. Moreover, the defeats suffered by the Nazis on the war fronts created a need for an increased work force and led them to consider improving the treatment of foreign laborers, as well as some changes in policy toward other sources of potential labor. Eventually, some changes were implemented.

The racist policy and the policy of mass killings applied to laborers caused much damage to the Reich's total war effort. Racist considerations precluded the sending of Jews to Germany as foreign workers. The few Jews who did infiltrate the ranks of workers coming to Germany from various countries made every effort to avoid identification as Jews. At a time when Germany was suffering from a severe shortage of manpower, millions of Russian POWs were dying of starvation, ill-treatment, and deliberate murder; and masses of Jews who were working as forced laborers in the occupied countries or as prisoners in concentration camps were taken away from their places of work and deported to the extermination camps.

BIBLIOGRAPHY

Billstein, A. *Fremdarbeiter in unserer Stadt, 1939–1945.* Frankfurt, 1980.

Evrard, J. *La déportation des travailleurs français dans le IIIe Reich.* Paris, 1972.

Ferencz, B. *Less than Slaves: Jewish Forced Labor and the Quest for Compensation.* Cambridge, Mass., 1979.

Homze, E. L. *Foreign Labor in Nazi Germany.* Princeton, 1967.

Luczak, C. *Polscy robotnicy przymusowi w Trzeciej Rzeszy podczas II Wojny Światowej.* Poznań, 1974.

Luczak, C., ed. *Położenie polskich robotników przymusowych w Rzeszy, 1939–1945.* Poznań, 1975.

Pfahlmann, H. *Fremdarbeiter und Kriegsgefangene in der deutschen Kriegswirtschaft, 1939–1945.* Darmstadt, 1968.

CZESŁAW LUCZAK

Jews in Occupied Poland

The forced labor for which the Jews of occupied POLAND were drafted took various oppressive forms and lasted from the beginning of World War II until its end. As soon as the German army entered Poland in September 1939, individual Jews and groups of Jews were forced to clear roadblocks and debris and to pave roads. Units of the Wehrmacht played an active role in forcibly recruiting Jews for such work, seizing them at random on the streets or dragging them out of their homes, and maltreating them while they were at work. Often the only purpose for subjecting Jews to forced labor was to degrade them, by compelling them to carry out hard physical tasks that had no practical purpose at all, while subjecting them to beatings and to harassments such as cutting off their beards; or by making them do physical exercise.

On October 26, 1939, compulsory labor was introduced in the GENERALGOUVERNEMENT by law, applying to Jewish males aged fourteen to sixty; implementation was put into the hands of the SS command. Subsequently the law was extended to apply also to women, and to children aged twelve to fourteen. In the period from October to December 1939 compulsory labor was also introduced by locally issued decrees for Jews living in those parts of Poland incorporated into the Reich.

On January 13, 1940, orders were issued by Generalgouverneur Hans FRANK for the implementation of the October 26, 1939, law. The decrees provided for compulsory service, in the form of labor, by all Jews, men and women alike, from the ages of fourteen to sixty, whether or not they had employment of their own. The compulsory service was scheduled to extend over two years, but it could be prolonged "in case the desired reeducational goal had not been achieved in that period." To facilitate the imposition of the law, the Germans ordered all Jews aged fourteen to sixty to register; this process was to be enforced by the Judenräte (Jewish Councils; *see* JUDENRAT) under the supervision of the mayors. The Jews registered were divided into six categories, based on their professional or trade qualifications. In addition, in measures unrelated to the registration, Jews were forced into temporary labor assignments, such as removing snow, loading goods the Nazis had confiscated from Jews, and building walls around areas earmarked as ghettos.

As time went on, special labor camps were put up for Jews, who were summoned by name to report to them. In these labor camps the Jews were quartered in barracks and had to work under very harsh conditions. In the Lublin district, twenty-nine such camps were in operation by July 1940. In August of that year twenty thousand Jews in the nineteen to thirty-five age group were ordered to report to labor camps. Many chose to disregard the call-up, despite the heavy risks involved, because of the intolerable conditions of life and work in the camps, where the inmates were also exposed to such torments as pursuit by vicious dogs, humiliation, and beatings. Frequently the men on forced labor had no living quarters assigned to them, did not receive minimal food rations, and had to sleep under the open sky; those working on land amelioration projects sometimes had to stand in water during their work. Many people perished in the camps; others were completely exhausted when they returned and were permanently disabled. One vivid illustration of conditions in the camps is the fact that out of six thousand men from the WARSAW ghetto sent to the labor camps, one thousand were no longer fit for work within two weeks. In certain ghettos (for example, that of ŁÓDŹ) the entire population was on forced labor and the ghettos, in effect, became labor camps.

In addition, Jews in large numbers also worked in German factories in Poland and in ghetto "shops" (workshops), especially during the last stage of the ghettos' existence. At the end of 1940 over 700,000 people were on forced labor in Poland. That number dropped to 500,000 in 1942 and a little over 100,000 in mid-1943; the reasons for the decrease were the high mortality rate in the ghettos and the destruction by the Nazis of the Jewish population. Conditions of work in places other than labor camps differed from one to the other; all had in common a ten- to twelve-hour workday and the total absence of social benefits and vacations.

From the beginning, the forced-labor operation was administered by the SS. In the areas that were incorporated into the Reich, the SS remained in charge of forced labor up until the total annihilation of the Jewish population, but in the Generalgouvernement responsibility for the project was taken over by the Ministry of Labor, in July 1940. Two years later, on June 25, 1942, the forced-labor administration was again changed, and this time the Sicherheitspolizei (Security Police; Sipo) took over. In practice, the remuneration paid to persons on forced labor was tiny

Jewish men and boys rounded up in Warsaw for forced labor.

Jewish forced labor in Będzin, Poland.

or nonexistent. The rule concerning Jews was that their pay had to be lower than that of other nationalities. Even when minimum wages were paid, substantial deductions were made for various purposes, as determined by the Germans. In Białystok, for example, the deductions amounted to 50 percent of the total, and for the work on the Frankfurt-Posen highway, as much as 80 percent was deducted from the pay.

The following figures, relating to Warsaw, illustrate the extent to which forced labor was not remunerated: out of 2 million workdays by persons on forced labor in the period from October 21, 1939, to November 15, 1940, nearly three-quarters (1.44 million) were not paid at all. Where wages were paid, they were so low that the recipients could not buy any extra food on the black market—which meant that they starved like all the others. It follows that the German policy on forced labor by Jews, and on the wages for such labor, contributed directly to the physical destruction of the Jews.

When the great majority of the Jews had been killed, those remaining in the ghettos were forced to keep on working—in the "shops"; in sorting out for the Germans the possessions of the murdered Jews; and in various institutions and factories serving the needs of the Reich. Factories employing Jews had to pay substantial sums to the Sipo. The Jews in turn had to pay bribes in order to obtain employment—which they sought to do by any means, in the belief that this would save them from deportation to the extermination camps.

In mid-1942 and in April and May of 1943, some of the Jews in the Generalgouvernement ghettos were taken to labor camps at TRAWNIKI and PONIATOWA, where they were put to work in various workshops. In November 1943 the Germans murdered forty thousand Jews in these camps (*see* "ERNTEFEST"). In Łódź, forced labor was kept up longer than anywhere else, until the ghetto was liquidated in August 1944.

BIBLIOGRAPHY

Ferencz, B. *Less than Slaves: Jewish Forced Labor and the Quest for Compensation.* Cambridge, Mass., 1979.

ZBIGNIEW LANDAU

FOREIGN ORGANIZATION OF THE NSDAP. *See* Auslandsorganisation der NSDAP.

FORSTER, ALBERT (1902–1948), German politician and Nazi official. Forster was born in Fürth, Bavaria, and became a tradesman. In 1923 he joined the Nazi party, and in 1930 was elected to the Reichstag; that same year he also became *Gauleiter* of DANZIG, then a free city. When Adolf Hitler came to power, Forster was charged with the Nazification of Danzig and was one of the persons responsible for the actions taken against the Poles and Jews in the city. When the Germans occupied Poland in September 1939, Forster was appointed *Chef der Zivilverwaltung* (head of the civil administration) of the Pommern (Pol., Pomorze) district. He later became the Reich governor (*Reichstatthalter*) of Danzig and *Gauleiter* of Danzig and West Prussia.

Forster was responsible for the extermination of entire populations; mass deportations; deportations for forced labor; the forced "Germanization" of Poles; and the destruction of Polish cultural treasures. When the war ended he was captured by the Allies and in 1946 was extradited to Poland. There he was tried by the Supreme National Tribunal, sentenced to death, and hanged, on April 28, 1948.

BIBLIOGRAPHY

Jastrzebski, W., and J. Sziling. *Okupacja hitlerowska na Pomorzu Gdańskim w latach 1939–1945.* Gdańsk, 1979.

STEFAN BIERNACKI

FORT ONTARIO, so-called free port for REFUGEES in the United States proposed by the United States WAR REFUGEE BOARD (WRB). The idea, modeled on the pattern of customs-free ports, was to bring imperiled refugees from Europe to shelters in the United States, where they would be held without legal status until the war's end, at which time they would be returned to their countries of origin.

The idea of a free port, originally proposed and supported by both the BERGSON GROUP and the WORLD JEWISH CONGRESS, was offi-

Albert Forster, *Gauleiter* of Danzig, reviews a parade of the Danzig SS-Heimwehr (Home Guard) in August 1939.

Eleanor Roosevelt with the director of the Fort Ontario Refugee Center, visiting the shelter at Oswego, New York (September 20, 1944). [Franklin D. Roosevelt Library]

cially put forward by John Pehle, director of the WRB, in February 1944. Many important individuals in both the State Department and the War Department opposed the idea. A bill introduced in Congress to establish free ports died in committee.

In the midst of his 1944 re-election campaign, President Franklin D. ROOSEVELT announced his plan to create a free port at Fort Ontario in Oswego, New York. His announcement did not presage any major change in the president's refugee policy. The creation of the free port was only a token act; Roosevelt made it clear that it would serve only 1,000 refugees, who would be returned to Europe at the termination of hostilities. The president also instructed his assistants to make sure that the group would contain others besides Jews. In fact, refugees brought to Oswego came not from Nazi-occupied zones but from liberated areas, and did not therefore face imminent death.

The refugees, once settled in the shelter, were not permitted to work in town or to leave the camp, and a great deal of tension arose among them. At the end of the war there was an attempt, supported by Congress and important elements of the administration, to have the refugees sent back to Europe. Other elements, however, prevailed, and the refugees interned at Fort Ontario were permitted to remain in the United States.

BIBLIOGRAPHY

Gruber, R. *Haven: The Unknown Story of 1,000 World War II Refugees.* New York, 1983.

Lowenstein, S. *Token Refuge: The Story of the Jewish Refugee Shelter at Oswego, 1944–1946.* Bloomington, 1986.

Strum, H. "Fort Ontario Refugee Shelter, 1944–1946." *American Jewish History* 73/4 (June 1984): 398–421.

ARIEL HURWITZ

FOUR-YEAR PLAN (*Vierjahresplan*), Nazi economic program. The memorandum for the establishment of the Four-Year Plan was written by Adolf HITLER himself in August 1936 and kept secret because of possible opposition from economic circles. It was seen as a watershed in the German economy, marking Hitler's first intervention in German economic policy, and for the first time stating his war aims and a self-imposed timetable of intensified rearmament.

In the memorandum, Hitler set a twofold task: to make the German army operational and the German economy fit for war within four years. To achieve this goal, the plan aimed at creating a self-sufficient and independent German economy and particularly at protecting German agriculture against war conditions, making it able to withstand a blockade to the maximum. Hitler sought the goal of self-sufficiency through the pursuit of an expansionist policy and through stress on making Germany less dependent on outside raw materials.

For this purpose, the Göring Reich Works (Reichswerke Hermann Göring) were founded and refineries and aluminum works established. The plan also promoted the development of a synthetic-materials industry in order to replace raw materials and control the allocation of labor. Hermann GÖRING, in spite of his ignorance of economic affairs, was nominated as commissioner for the implementation of the plan, receiving extraordinary general powers in the economic sphere. During the war, these powers were extended to the economic structure of the occupied countries so as to extract everything possible from them in a policy of ruthless plundering. Göring also directed the deportation of millions of people from the occupied territories for FORCED LABOR.

The increased self-sufficiency of Germany had a direct effect on the potential for speeding up the Reich's antisemitic policy. In order to begin Germany's economic mobilization, Hitler had the thought of issuing a law making the whole of Jewry liable for all the damage allegedly inflicted by individual Jews upon the German economy.

BIBLIOGRAPHY

Barkai, A. *Das Wirtschaftssystem des Nationalsozialismus: Der historische und ideologische Hintergrund 1933–1936*. Cologne, 1977.

Eicholtz, D. *Geschichte der deutschen Kriegswirtschaft 1939–1945*. Berlin, 1985.

Petzina, D. *Autarkiepolitik im Dritten Reich: Der nationalsozialistische Vierjahresplan*. Stuttgart, 1968.

Speer, A. *Inside the Third Reich: Memoirs*. London, 1970.

Treue, W. "Hitlers Denkschrift zum Vierjahresplan 1936." *Viertel-jahrshefte für Zeitgeschichte* 3/2 (April 1955): 184–210.

DAVID BANKIER

FPO. *See* Fareynigte Partizaner Organizatsye.

FRANCE. [*This entry consists of four articles. The first is a general survey of French history during the Vichy regime and the Nazi occupation. The second,* The Jews and the Holocaust, *reviews the Nazi efforts to carry out the "Final Solution" in France with the assistance of French collaborators, and the third,* Jewish Responses to Persecution, *is an inquiry into the Jewish reactions in France to these efforts. The fourth article,* After the Holocaust, *surveys the recovery of French Jewry after the end of the war. See also* Action Française; Fédération des Sociétés Juives de France; French Police; Youth Movements: France.]

General Survey

From the 1870s until 1940, France was governed as a republic, which had been instituted by the National Assembly. Designated as the Third Republic, it never had a constitution, and instead was governed by constitutional laws. After the fall of France to the German army in June 1940, and the signing of the armistice with Germany, the National Assembly voted in July to suspend the constitutional laws of the Third Republic. Marshal Philippe PÉTAIN was granted full powers as head of state by the National Assembly, and a new regime was set up at the spa town of Vichy, in the south of France.

The French defeat had immediate consequences for the nature of French society. Desirous of ending the war as rapidly as possible and returning to a normal way of life, the new French government entered into hurried negotiations with Germany to obtain an armistice. By the end of June 1940, the armistice was already taking effect. France was divided into two areas: the occupied zone, under German rule and occupation, and the unoccupied zone, under the new Vichy regime. The occupied zone, which included PARIS, encompassed the entire Atlantic and Channel coasts and contained the more fertile regions in western, northern, and eastern France. The armistice and the official division of France left millions of Frenchmen in a quandary as to whether their hurried exodus to the south at the beginning of the German invasion had been a necessary precaution. French officials, and above all Pétain, urged them to return to their homes and allow France to emerge from the ravages of war and begin the process of reconstruction. Hundreds of thousands of Frenchmen heeded the call and returned to the occupied north before the borders between the zones were more firmly instituted in late September 1940.

Beyond the geographic rearrangement of France, a major upheaval in France's social and political orientation was engendered by the lightning defeat. Following the dissolution of the Third Republic and its liberal principles, the Vichy regime embarked on a policy of returning the country to the hallowed ideals of prerevolutionary France. The regime, which was generated by internal disenchantment with republican ideals and by the turbulent xenophobic atmosphere of the 1930s, replaced the principles of *liberté* (liberty), *égalité* (equality), *fraternité* (fraternity) with *travail* (work), *famille* (family), and *patrie* (homeland). Riding on the nationalist appeal to bring France back to the French, a common refrain of those years, Vichy methodically went about curbing the influence of foreigners in the country and harassing the rights of Jews and various refugee groups. Vichy read French public opinion well. Following the trauma of defeat, the deflated

French temperament eagerly awaited a national renewal. Pétain's nomination as the head of the new French state was a source of renewed pride and hope. His call for a "new order"—a collective submission to authoritarianism and to the exalted sources of authority (*travail, famille, patrie*)—was resoundingly welcomed by almost all elements of French society.

Opposition to Pétain during his first year in office came from a very small segment of French society, while sincere enthusiasm for his attempts to save France from reliving the hardships of World War I emanated from diverse corners of the French political and cultural spectrum. For example, the Catholic church in France, which had been in constant conflict with the Third Republic, could not remain unresponsive to Pétain's efforts to bring France back to what the church regarded as pure Christian principles. The marshal was seen as the redeemer of France and the church, and loyalty to him and his policies was the order of the day.

This adulation went further and penetrated into political circles of opposing ideologies. Thus, when the Pétainist mystique was at its height and a sense of *attentisme* ("wait and see") prevailed, open resistance of the kind advocated by Charles de GAULLE attracted few. This, notwithstanding Vichy's concerted efforts and strategy to court Nazi Germany and procure a more tenable arrangement with the German authorities. Minister of State Pierre LAVAL, who had been most active in this direction, worked diligently behind the scenes to bring Pétain and Hitler together. Their eventual meeting at Montoire from October 22 to 24, 1940, provided sufficient evidence that Vichy's "national revolution" included a policy of collaboration. France, under the "new order," was to become part of the New Europe under Hitler's tutelage. Laval's negotiations with the Germans eventually backfired and he was removed from office at the end of 1940, to be replaced by Adm. Jean-François DARLAN, commander in chief of the French navy. Darlan too was convinced that France's best interests were served by an accord with Germany. In May 1941 he met with Hitler at Berchtesgaden and granted the Germans military facilities in North Africa and Syria, in return for which the French received virtually no German concessions in the area that counted the most—in the terms of the armistice.

French society began to show increasing signs of displeasure and opposition to the Vichy regime from the summer of 1941, in part owing to the German invasion of the Soviet Union. Communist and socialist elements in France, which had been reticent to engage in resistance activity against Vichy, declaring themselves to be in favor of "neither Pétain nor de Gaulle," were now provoked to increased action. This was still far from a total break with Pétain, but it was nonetheless a significant step forward.

The growing internal fissure in French society failed to convince Vichy to change its goal of rapprochement with Nazi Germany—indeed, almost the contrary could be claimed. In April 1942, Laval succeeded in maneuvering himself back into power, replacing Darlan, and he openly declared his support for a Nazi victory to withstand Bolshevik world domination. Although the Nazi leadership paid little attention to these statements, Vichy proceeded, hoping to strengthen its bond with Germany. As part of this new drive, Laval agreed to send more French laborers to Germany and to enact intensified anti-Jewish legislation in the occupied zone. French officials were instructed to grant the German occupying forces all the assistance necessary in their plans for mass roundups of Jews in the summer of 1942. Laval's concerns at this juncture necessitated harmony with the country that demanded French forced labor and that was building a New Europe, free of communism. However, Vichy's image emerged tainted from the collaboration. More and more Frenchmen raised their voices in protest against their government, among them leading figures in the Catholic and Protestant churches. Resistance activity of various orientations, spurred on by increasing German repression and French concessions, grew considerably.

The rather peaceful occupation of the Vichy zone by the German and Italian forces in early November 1942 put an end to the euphemistically named "free zone." Italy began a liberal and humane occupation of eight southern departments east of the Rhône that lasted until September 1943. It was the German occupation and Vichy's acquiescence that heightened the internal decay in the country. The hope of improved living conditions through a policy of collaboration had proved to have no solid foundation. The French population felt itself increasingly taxed by the armistice agreement as occupation costs rose to approximately 500 million francs a day. The financial exploitation of France included a constant siphoning-off of French foodstuffs and raw materials, but more critical and alienating was the growing number of French workers in Germany, which by 1943 had reached some 700,000. All this did not convince Laval to reappraise his gamble on a German victory.

In September 1943, Germany hastened to fill the vacuum left after the fall of Benito MUSSOLINI and the Italian armistice agreement with the Allies by occupying the Italian zone in southern France. On the horizon, however, loomed the growing strength of the Résistance, which in the same month liberated Corsica. From that point on, Maquis fighters (the name came from Corsican Résistance units that fought in wild terrain) became an ever-present nemesis to Vichy and the German occupation. They were not alone. De Gaulle's Free French organized militarily and politically for a takeover of France, and when the time came they were able to fill a void in the French administration. The Allied landing in Normandy on June 6, 1944, signaled the end of the occupation. The liberation of France came two months later, and as de Gaulle marched triumphantly into Paris, Pétain, Laval, and other Vichy officials fled ignominiously to Germany. They would later be returned to Paris and tried for treason.

BIBLIOGRAPHY

Kedward, H. R., and R. Austin, eds. *Vichy France and the Resistance.* New York, 1985.

Whitcomb, P. W., trans. *France during the German Occupation, 1940–1944.* 3 vols. Stanford, 1959.

RICHARD COHEN

The Jews and the Holocaust

Evidence of a Jewish presence in France exists from the first century A.D. From 465,

A trial of members of the French Résistance by a German military court in Paris between April 7 and 14, 1942. The defendant in the photograph is a Jewish woman, Simone Schloss.

the Jewish population in a number of French towns increased considerably. France became a center of Jewish learning from the eleventh century. However, one hundred thousand Jews were expelled from the country in 1306. This mass expulsion was followed by a decree of Charles VI in 1394 stipulating that Jews would no longer be tolerated in the kingdom of France, and by subsequent expulsions from other French provinces.

On the eve of the French Revolution, the Jewish community in France numbered forty thousand. The largest concentration was in Alsace-Lorraine, where Ashkenazic Jews had established themselves. Some three thousand Portuguese Jews had settled in the south, and they were the first to receive full emancipation, on January 28, 1790. The Ashkenazic Jews were granted full civil rights on September 27, 1791.

Jewish integration into French society proceeded more or less smoothly, notwithstanding occasional antisemitic occurrences; the most serious among them was the Dreyfus affair at the end of the nineteenth century. Throughout that century, in a spirit of modernization and urbanization, Jews migrated in large numbers to Paris, making it the center of Jewish life in France. Jews developed a deep-seated attachment to France and French culture, attested by the large migration from Alsace-Lorraine after its annexation to Germany in 1870. Moreover, France continued even after the Dreyfus affair to appear as the land of liberty and equality in the eyes of world Jewry. In the interwar period, immigrants from eastern Europe flocked by the tens of thousands to Paris, while thousands of Jewish refugees from Germany sought refuge in the city in the 1930s. On the eve of World War II Paris contained two-thirds of French Jewry, and this group had become a vibrant institutional and cultural community.

In the 1930s the Third Republic began to reassess its open-door policy of the preceding decade. Increasing voices called for a hold on Jewish immigration and an abrogation of Jewish emancipation. Yet, though stringent restrictions against refugees were gradually introduced and internment camps were set up for them, Jewish emancipation remained in force until the fall of France and the establishment of the Vichy regime.

RICHARD COHEN

In the summer of 1940, about 350,000 Jews lived in France, more than half of whom were not French citizens. Among these were tens of thousands of Jewish REFUGEES from Belgium, the Netherlands, and Luxembourg, some of whom had fled the Reich several years earlier. Persecution of these Jews began almost immediately, both in the German-occupied zone and in the zone left under French control.

The unusual context of the Holocaust in France is the considerable degree of autonomy accorded the French during the Nazi occupation. In this respect France differed substantially from fully occupied countries like Belgium, the Netherlands, and Denmark, or puppet states like Norway. Notably, throughout the entire period of the deportations of Jews, France had a French government, based in Vichy; a head of state (Marshal Pétain); an administration at least nominally responsible for the whole of the country; and a powerful police force. Even after the Nazis moved across the demarcation line, in November 1942, the French government remained formally in charge of the nation and retained a substantial degree of authority.

The Germans needed and received a great deal of assistance from the French to carry out their plans. After the war, defenders of Vichy claimed that the work of this government limited the damage, preventing even higher numbers of deportees from France. German documents lend a superficial plausibility to this notion, for it is plain that the Nazis in charge of the "FINAL SOLUTION" had hoped to do better in France, envisioning a completed task by the end of 1943. The SS in charge of the deportations failed to meet their own quotas, and Vichy claimed the credit for this failure. However, close examination of the German record, as well as research on the role of Vichy and its agencies, tells a different story.

The deportations of 1942 to 1944 (see below) did not begin in a political vacuum. The dispatch of the Jews "to the east" was, rather, the culmination of two years of aggressive legislation and persecution, including the passage of laws defining who was to be considered Jewish, isolating Jews in French society, taking away their livelihood, interning many, and registering them with the police. In the German-controlled zone the SS in France, under Obersturmführer Helmut KNOCHEN, set the apparatus of persecution in place. Matters concerning Jews were assigned to SS-Hauptsturmführer Theodor DANNECKER, who reported directly to the office of Adolf EICHMANN in Berlin.

Remarkably, however, the Vichy government too moved against the Jews, taking the initiative to issue the comprehensive STATUT DES JUIFS (Jewish Law) in October 1940, and to establish a central agency for coordinating anti-Jewish legislation and activity in March 1941, the COMMISSARIAT GÉNÉRAL AUX QUESTIONS JUIVES (General Office for Jewish Affairs; CGQJ). In November 1941, moreover, Vichy established the UNION GÉNÉRALE DES ISRAÉLITES DE FRANCE (General Union of Jews of France; UGIF), a Jewish agency operating under Vichy authority that was intended to control Jewish activities and communal affairs. During the two years following France's defeat, the French government deliberately incorporated antisemitic activity into its *révolution nationale*—the officially declared policy of turning France in an authoritarian, nationalist, and corporatist direction.

The French government considered it extremely important that its laws should apply throughout the entire country, in the occupied as well as the unoccupied zone; through the enforcement of such measures, Vichy assumed it was strengthening French sovereignty and hastening the day when full French sovereignty would be restored. Vichy's leadership believed that the Germans would be grateful to the French for pursuing their own anti-Jewish policy, and would respond by yielding greater control over this and other spheres of national policy. In addition, the French were anxious to see that the property confiscated from the Jews did not fall into the hands of the Germans. Vichy inaugurated an extensive program of "Aryanization" in July 1941, with the important objective of maintaining formerly Jewish property in France. In practice, "Aryanization" simply meant the confiscation of Jewish possessions by the state. It developed into a vast property transfer, involving some forty-two thousand Jewish businesses, buildings, and other properties. For their part, the Nazi occupation authorities engaged in a subtle form of entrapment. Nudging Vichy ever deeper into measures against the Jews, and withholding serious pressure on the French for about a year, the occupation relieved itself of much of the trouble of antisemitic persecution while drawing the French into areas where even some Vichyites showed signs of discomfort.

All Jews suffered grievously from the first two years of persecution, except for a tiny handful of well-established French Jews who received exemptions from the Vichy government. In legal terms, the way was cleared for persecution without limits, using the powerful judicial and administrative apparatus of the French state. The confiscation of Jewish property and the elimination of Jews from professions and the government service transformed thousands into penniless refugees in France. Foreign Jews were particularly vulnerable, and were especially victimized by both the Germans and Vichy. Thousands were forced into labor camps or interned, often in conditions that approached the Nazi concentration camps of the 1930s. The first victims of the Holocaust in France died in these camps, their number eventually totaling about three thousand.

Following the WANNSEE CONFERENCE of January 1942, the Nazis began to prepare for the deportation of Jews from France and other western European countries. They proceeded slowly and methodically, for the task was enormous and the German personnel that could be spared for the operation were relatively few. In particular, the Nazis did their best to ensure the cooperation of the French government and administration.

The spring and summer of 1942 were turning points. At the end of April, Pierre Laval, who was committed to intensifying collaboration with Germany, became head of the French government under Marshal Pétain. In May the legalistic and anti-German Xavier VALLAT was replaced at the head of the CGQJ by the racist collaborator Louis DARQUIER DE PELLEPOIX. Darquier had no scruples about

The concentration camp at Le Vernet in the south of France, about 31 miles (50 km) south of Toulouse. [JDC Archives, New York]

extending full support to the Nazis in their murderous enterprise. Simultaneously, the Wehrmacht yielded authority over repressive activity in France to the SS, now headed there by Höherer SS- und Polizeiführer (Higher SS and Police Leader) Carl Albrecht OBERG. The French police under René Bousquet worked out an arrangement with the SS whereby the former were given an important degree of autonomy, in exchange for agreeing to work against the enemies of the Reich. In their own zone the Germans cleared the way for deportations by imposing the wearing of a yellow star by all Jews (June 7), rounding up large numbers, and controlling the movements of the rest.

On June 11, a decisive meeting took place in Berlin at which arrangements were made for regular deportations of Jews from France, Belgium, and the Netherlands. Demands for cooperation now rained down on Vichy. After deliberations, Laval and the French cabinet agreed to help. Throughout the summer and fall of 1942, roundups of Jews took place in both the occupied and unoccupied zones. Most of the work was done by the French police. On July 16 and 17, in one of the most cruel and spectacular operations, they rounded up 12,884 Jews in Paris, some 7,000 of whom—families with small children—were crowded for days in the Vélodrome d'Hiver sports arena with no food, water, or sanitary facilities. Elsewhere, parents were torn from their children, with the victims unceremoniously packed into cattle cars and shipped to the transit camp at DRANCY, just outside Paris. In all, 42,500 Jews were sent eastward in 1942, perhaps one-third of them from the unoccupied zone.

The cover-up of the Germans, which Laval agreed to repeat, was that the Jews were being sent to work camps "in the east." Officially, Vichy would only report that the victims had gone "to an unknown destination." In fact, the end of the line was AUSCHWITZ, where most of the deportees were immediately killed.

The deportations of the summer and fall of 1942 stirred the first serious opposition to Vichy among certain segments of French opinion. The roundups of Jews could scarcely be concealed, and the cruelty of the separation of families was heavily criticized. A split developed in the Catholic church, hitherto solidly behind Pétain and the *révolution nationale.* Highly placed clergymen now made their first open protest against the anti-Jewish activity of the regime. For Vichy, the deportations signaled the failure of its strategy on the Jewish issue. Far from winning greater independence, the French were now being heavily importuned by the Germans. After November 1942, with Nazi troops in the formerly unoccupied zone, this worsening situation was obvious to all.

Difficulties arose as the deportations gradually included French Jews as well as outsiders. Having agreed to the deportation of foreign Jews from both zones, the Vichy authorities found themselves drawn into satisfying the Nazis' deportation quotas, which were fixed by the available railway transport from Drancy to Auschwitz and not by technicalities such as nationality. As early as January 1943, when massive deportations from both zones resumed, the Germans reported that the French police were no longer as reliable as they once had been in assembling and dispatching the Jews. Even Laval dragged his feet—refusing, in August 1943, to agree to strip French Jews of their citizenship so as to facilitate their deportation.

Yet despite occasional protests and difficulties, the deportations continued, the last convoys leaving France in the summer of 1944. Laval, Pétain, and the government would not change course. To the end, Vichy enforced the extensive apparatus of anti-Jewish laws that legitimized the deportations in the eyes of some, and it certainly facilitated the process of deportation. Some Jews managed to escape for a time, by fleeing to the Italian-occupied zone of France. There the Italian Fascist troops provided a remarkable sanctuary—not only against German demands for deportations, but against the application of Vichy antisemitic laws as well. This protective screen was shattered in September 1943 when the Italians surrendered to the British and Americans. Other Jews escaped to SPAIN or to SWITZERLAND, although passage across either frontier was not normally permitted by the host countries and was fraught with danger from the German and Vichy police.

Thousands of Jews were assisted by a small but sympathetic element in the French population, often at great risk to those providing rescue or aid. Such Frenchmen were to be found among all groups but particularly among Protestants, many of whom by tradition also felt themselves to be a beleaguered minority in France. Help and sanctuary came from a variety of other sources: the Quakers, the American Jewish JOINT DISTRIBUTION COMMITTEE (known as the Joint), the YMCA, the Catholic Témoignage Chrétien, and Jewish resistance networks. An outstanding example was the Protestant village of LE CHAMBON-SUR-LIGNON, which became a kind of underground railway, smuggling several thousand Jews to safety.

In all, over 77,000 Jews from France were either killed in concentration camps in Poland or died while in detention. Approximately 70,000 went to Auschwitz, and the rest to other camps—MAJDANEK and SOBIBÓR, and a few dozen to BUCHENWALD in August 1944. Of all these Jews, about one-third were citizens of long standing; 8,700 were sixty years of age or over, 6,000 were under thirteen, and 2,000 were under the age of six.

The "Final Solution" in France was a Nazi project from beginning to end. Few Frenchmen advocated massacre, and only a small number of extreme collaborationists in Paris ever carried antisemitism to the murderous conclusions of Hitler and his associates. However, it seems highly unlikely that the Germans would have been capable of deporting large numbers of Jews from France without the help provided by the French authorities. Two years of persecution by the French government and administration helped snap the bonds that bound Jews to French society, leaving many helpless once the Nazis' machinery of destruction turned to France.

It is true that the final toll—about one-fifth of the country's Jews were killed—seems less, proportionately, than in many other countries, but the circumstances the Nazis faced in France must be taken into account and the considerable difficulties they had to overcome noted. Unlike Belgium or the Netherlands, where Jews were concentrated in a few urban areas and were therefore easy to capture, those in France were scattered about a large country in thousands of localities. Many were living in the countryside, where only the local authorities could keep track of them and round them up. (This had been the case since the collapse of the French armies in 1940 and the scattering of the French population to the south and east. The Germans themselves had contributed to the dispersion, by not allowing Jews back into the occupied zone after the armistice.) Unlike Poland, where there was always a heavy German police presence, there were few men to spare for France—only three battalions for the occupied zone, for example, or about three thousand men.

There is no evidence, on the other hand, that Vichy authorities attempted in a concerted way to limit the deportations. No models for alternative strategies occurred to Vichy leaders, and they seem to have considered the entire question of Jewish persecution as of secondary importance. Like everyone else, the Vichy leadership was slow to fathom the "Final Solution," despite the Nazis' repeated declarations that all the Jews would be deported, and despite the periodic hints of the slaughter in Poland. Most of the officials at Vichy seem to have shared in the widespread anti-Jewish mood of 1940, and many agreed with the legalistic antisemitic strategy of Vallat. Others were indifferent, kept their views to themselves, and carried out the anti-Jewish legislation in their sphere of authority. Recent research, therefore, rejects the theory of a consciously plotted strategy to save as many Jews as possible.

MICHAEL R. MARRUS

BIBLIOGRAPHY

Billig, J. *Le Commissariat général aux questions juives (1941–1944)*. 3 vols. Paris, 1955–1960.

Hyman, P. *From Dreyfus to Vichy: The Remaking of French Jewry, 1906–1939*. New York, 1979.

Klarsfeld, S. *Le mémorial de la déportation des Juifs de France*. Paris, 1978.

Klarsfeld, S. *Vichy-Auschwitz: Le rôle de Vichy dans la solution finale de la question juive en France, 1942*. 2 vols. Paris, 1983, 1985.

Marrus, M. R., and R. O. Paxton. *Vichy France and the Jews*. New York, 1981.

Paxton, R. O. *Vichy France: Old Guard and New Order, 1940–1944*. New York, 1982.

Rutkowski, A., ed. *La lutte des Juifs en France à l'époque de l'occupation (1940–1944)*. Paris, 1975.

Szajkowski, Z. *Analytical Franco-Jewish Gazetteer, 1939–1945*. New York, 1966.

Tint, A. "The Jews of France in the Last Half Century." *Jewish Journal of Sociology* 1/1 (April 1959): 127–131.

Weinberg, D. *Community on Trial: The Jews of Paris in the 1930s*. Chicago, 1977.

Wellers, G., A. Kaspi, and S. Klarsfeld, eds. *La France et la question juive, 1940–1944*. Paris, 1981.

Jewish Responses to Persecution

When the Germans struck at France in May 1940, the Jewish community sensed an immediate blow to its security. Together with millions of Frenchmen, it took part in a massive exodus to the unoccupied southern zone. More than 100,000 Jews took to the roads in those panic-stricken days, among them Jewish leaders and rabbis, stripping occupied France of experienced leadership and rabbinical guidance. After the armistice was signed on June 22 and the French leadership called on Frenchmen to return to the north, as many as 30,000 Jews are reported to have returned there, trusting the new agreement, and raising the Jewish population in the Seine region to almost 150,000. During the initial months of turmoil and indecision after the armistice, some 30,000 Jews were successful in crossing the southern French border in the hope of finding refuge abroad.

The process of reorganizing the community slowly began to unfold in the fall of 1940 amid contradictory assessments as to the possibility of Jewish life under Nazi occupation and Vichy rule. Jews in France were not alone in this quandary. French people of opposing political and social views tended to favor a quick return to normal life rather than venture into a period of constant struggle with the authorities. Indeed, a certain resignation set in, as well as a desire to see France return to a more nationalist outlook. Jews in France shared some similar sentiments, yet their situation was confounded by the Nazi threat. Inevitably within this crucible, the tensions that had prevailed in the Jewish community during the 1930s between leaders of the native Jews and the eastern

European immigrants surged to the surface and prevented a united stand, both in the northern occupied region and in the southern unoccupied zone.

In the north, prior to the Vichy STATUT DES JUIFS, immigrant Jewish leaders had established in Paris a special clandestine committee, known as AMELOT, to coordinate relief activity in the community. Its attempt to involve native French Jews in the enterprise failed to materialize owing to their trepidation at cooperating with immigrant Jews at a time when French nationalism and xenophobia were at their height. Without the support of the more established community, Amelot's efforts were necessarily limited. As for the native Jews, a sense of organizational disarray was apparent in the summer of 1940, although the return of Rabbi Julien Weill, the Chief Rabbi of Paris, to the city in August improved the situation somewhat.

Dannecker entered into this vacuum of communal leadership. He met with various Jewish leaders, native and immigrant, and after several months of pressure and threats, and of intercommunal disagreement, succeeded in cajoling them into joining together to form an umbrella organization in January 1941, to be known as the Comité de Coordination des Oeuvres Israélites de Bienfaisance (Coordinating Committee of Jewish Welfare Societies). Uppermost in the minds of the leadership when it succumbed to this unprecedented decision were concern and awareness of the growing pauperization of the community as a result of the extensive economic problems. Members of the CONSISTOIRE CENTRAL DES ISRAÉLITES DE FRANCE (Central Consistory of French Jews)—the official Jewish community—were now openly participating with members of the immigrant community to improve and coordinate relief activity; only the Jewish Communists aligned in Solidarité (*see* UNION DES JUIFS POUR LA RÉSISTANCE ET L'ENTR'AIDE) were excluded from this organization. Although the body was established "voluntarily," it probably would not have come into existence without German pressure. However, the unification that Dannecker sought was not forthcoming, and his continuous, devious efforts to consolidate the Coordinating Committee were counterproductive, making the already reticent immigrant leaders even more hesitant to remain part of the committee. The sense that working in the committee involved cooperation with the Germans on one level or another became a growing problem, leading eventually to several resignations. The committee was gradually stripped of its immigrant participation, thereby exacerbating relations within the community.

The Coordinating Committee underwent a major realignment, co-opting respected native leaders (among them André BAUR, Juliette Stern, Marcel Stora, and Fernand Musnik), but it remained stigmatized in the eyes of the immigrant community, especially after the mass internments in Paris in May 1941. Thus, as the "Aryanization" of Jewish property took on serious proportions from the summer of 1941, as the newly established transit camp at Drancy began to intern thousands of Jews in squalid conditions, and as pockets of poverty deepened in the Jewish community, the organizing of relief and aid of different kinds remained divided among the Coordinating Committee, Amelot and its subsidiary bodies, and Solidarité. The Joint Distribution Committee provided considerable funds to the Coordinating Committee and to Amelot. Throughout the first half of the year, Dannecker expressed his overall dissatisfaction with this situation and continued his efforts for a more influential and cohesive committee.

The attitude toward participation in the Coordinating Committee reflected the divisions within the Jewish community. Although no significant resistance activity emerged during the first year and a half of the occupation, it was apparent that far more elements within the immigrant community and its organizations had gravitated to illegal activity and clandestine behavior, fearing the slightest association with the Germans. This was especially true for Solidarité. On the other hand, the Consistory and the Coordinating Committee, representing the more established sectors of the native community, continued to bide for time, adhered to the legalistic approach, and counted on the French authorities for support. These polar attitudes widened when Dannecker tried to establish a compulsory Jewish organization in the fall of 1941.

In the south of France, where the massive migration had increased the Jewish population to approximately 150,000, the needs were no less urgent than in the north, though without the oppressive Nazi occupation. Jews had flocked to the major cities—Lyons, Marseilles, Toulouse—and to hundreds of smaller cities. Former leaders of the community resettled in Lyons and Marseilles and gradually began to map out plans for relief. Here, too, the conflict and lack of trust that had characterized immigrant-native relations in the 1930s were revived, and certain aggressive positions of native leaders were reasserted. The Joint's diligent European director, Joseph SCHWARTZ, was instrumental in cutting through some of the mutual suspicion, and encouraged the Chief Rabbi of France, Isaïe Schwartz, to initiate an umbrella organization to solve the divisiveness and make efforts to ward off persecution.

At the end of October 1940, two weeks after the publication of the *Statut des Juifs*, which equally affected the Jews of the unoccupied zone, leaders of the major relief organizations met in Marseilles to establish the Commission Centrale des Organisations Juives d'Assistance (Central Commission of Jewish Relief Organizations; CCOJA). The CCOJA was to unite all the major relief organizations and to guarantee contacts with governmental and public authorities, to establish a communal fund, and to coordinate the various bodies within the community. Although it continued to function until the beginning of 1942, the CCOJA proved to be ineffectual. Once again, the division between immigrant organized relief (concentrated in the Fédération des Sociétés Juives) and native relief (centered in the Comité d'Assistance aux Réfugiés d'Allemagne, or Committee to Aid German Refugees) could not be easily circumvented; the different agencies maintained a mutual distrust and thus feared indirect funding from the Joint. Moreover, the individualistic mentality of French Jewry, nourished by generations of emancipation, was hesitant to succumb to the CCOJA's call for a new communal orientation.

In southern France, expressions of rebellion and outright opposition to the Vichy government among the general population were few and far between in 1941, even among the radical Left. This was true of the Jewish community as well. A sense of "wait and see" dominated their outlook and behavior. Notwithstanding the flood of antisemitic legislation initiated by the Vichy regime, trust in the leadership of France was still a basic postulate for the widest sections of the community, native and immigrant, and individual and community activity centered on coping with the daily difficulties. Nazi Germany was considered responsible for the anti-Jewish legislation, yet its awesome presence in northern France remained a distant reality. However, as the war progressed and the Nazi designs against the Jews became more extreme, opposition within the community grew. A case in point was the German-Vichy attempt to establish a compulsory umbrella organization for French Jewry in the fall of 1941.

Dannecker's original plan, following the strategy of the SD (Sicherheitsdienst; Security Service) in the Nazi-occupied territories from the beginning of the war, was seized upon by Vichy. In its reluctance to allow the SD control over the "Jewish question," Vichy proposed extending such an organization to the unoccupied zone as well. After months of negotiations between the French authorities and leaders of the Jewish organizations, the UGIF was established in late November 1941 and was to replace both the Coordinating Committee and the CCOJA.

Internal Jewish deliberations in the north pitted members of the Coordinating Committee against the immigrant leaders, who condemned the UGIF participants as collaborators with the Nazis and refused to join. In the south, native Jewry was split between members of the Central Consistory, who saw the racial definition of the organization as an affront to the French-Jewish symbiosis, and members of native relief organizations, who considered participation a necessity to safeguard the relief activity. Immigrant leaders, in particular Marc JARBLUM, were vociferous in their opposition and called for a rejection of the German-Vichy design. Nonetheless, the UGIF began to function in both zones, committed to preserving the welfare and relief activity, but severely compromised by the widespread opposition within the community.

The deportations that began in March 1942 jolted the community and sent thousands of Jews into a frenzy, looking frantically for refuge from the Nazis and the French police. Jews began to seek hiding places in thousands of French villages and rural communities, aided by the local population, while thousands more attempted to cross over the border to Switzerland. More than twenty-seven thousand Jews were caught and deported in the German *Aktionen* of that summer. Countless families were separated, and many were left homeless. Vichy's responsibility for this was considerable. It had allowed the German authorities to deport Jews from French internment camps in the unoccupied zone, clearly exposing its dependency and releasing significant public protests. The nature and extent of these events impelled more and more Jews to question their acceptance of a legalistic existence and accelerated the resistance tendencies in organizations in both north and south.

Buoyed by French protests and humanitarian actions, Jewish relief groups assumed a more active role in directing the population to seek alternative ways of existence and to cease all official contacts. This was especially so in the occupied zone, where the immigrant groups energetically advocated a bolder response to the authorities and some began to engage in forms of sabotage against German officers and institutions. As Jewish organizations turned to illegal activity—removing Jewish children to Christian homes and monasteries, forging identification papers and documents, aiding Jews in hiding and in crossing the border to Spain and Switzerland, and the like—tension mounted between these organizations and the centers of the UGIF in the north and south. The UGIF continued to uphold a legalistic orientation, although in the south, participant organizations had begun to operate on a basis that was partly legal and partly illegal. For some, like the OEUVRE DE SECOURS AUX ENFANTS (OSE), this pattern continued until the fall of 1943, when a direct Gestapo raid on a children's home showed the bankruptcy of the dualistic orientation.

French Jewry's predicament deteriorated still further in the wake of the German occupation of the south in November 1942. One of the first victims of this new situation was the Jewish community in Marseilles. Some two thousand foreign and native Jews were seized in a large-scale roundup at the end of January 1943, followed by minor roundups in Lyons and other southern cities. These events brought home to the Jewish organizations in the south the implications of the German occupation and, in contrast, the apparent benevolence of the Italian occupation of eight southern regions.

From November 1942, Jewish organizations of every persuasion in France went all out to capitalize on the protection from antisemitic legislation that the Italian authorities granted the Jews. As many as thirty thousand Jews had found their way into the Italian zone by September 1943, when they were confronted by the crude reality of a German takeover and an aggressive attempt to seize as many Jews as possible. Thousands were rounded up by the German net, but thousands avoided arrest by immediately going into hiding.

The lot of the Jews who remained under German occupation, in the north and south, was uneven during this period. For example, Parisian Jews enjoyed a certain relief after the traumatic days of July 1942. They did not experience another major roundup, but their numbers dwindled markedly as a result of constant dispersion outside the city into small villages and hamlets, and widespread hiding within its limits. By the summer of 1944, only fifteen thousand Jews lived openly in the capital, thousands of whom continued to receive relief in one form or another from Jewish organizations. Alongside material aid to the needy, care for orphaned children, and assistance to the thousands of internees in Drancy, armed resistance emerged in Paris from within a number of organizations, especially the units of Solidarité and the ARMÉE JUIVE, an armed unit composed of members of several youth movements.

In the German-occupied south, where Gestapo efforts to increase the lagging deportation count were supported by the French militia, Jews were often on the run, foreseeing the impending danger. A sign of the times could be detected in the community realignments: Jewish organizations were slowly mending their differences and joining forces.

The beginning of 1943 witnessed a rapprochement between the UGIF and the Central Consistory, while toward the end of the year a dramatic alliance took place between the Consistory and representatives of all the functioning organizations outside the orbit of the UGIF.

In 1944 the CONSEIL REPRÉSENTATIF DES JUIFS DE FRANCE (Representative Council of French Jewry; CRIF), an umbrella organization, was founded to coordinate resistance activity among the Jewish groups. This was a remarkable step on the part of Jewish leaders to set aside their distinct ideological differences and agree to consolidate measures for the community and to contribute to the overall French Résistance movement. The movement in this direction reflected an increasing consensus of opinion in the Jewish community, buttressed by the activities of the Armée Juive, which arranged border crossings to Spain and later took part in military operations against the German occupation in the north and south. Hundreds of Jews from these ranks lost their lives in military encounters with the Germans.

A divided community at the outset of the war, beset with political and social differences, French Jewry emerged severely depleted at liberation, but somewhat reoriented. It had lost some seventy-eight thousand Jews and harbored thousands of broken families in its midst, but it had also shown an ability to confront the catastrophe with diverse forms of aid and assistance. Facing the combined opposition of the Gestapo and the French authorities, the community resorted to traditional forms of relief throughout most of the war. In its struggle for existence, French Jewry had to reappraise its trust and confidence in the French authorities before it was able to overcome internal differences and open up new avenues of opposition and self-help. This emerged only in the latter part of the war, when the designs of its enemies had been extensively realized. The trend toward organizational unity would serve the community in good stead in the very difficult period of reconstruction that followed liberation.

Jews in France, individually and collectively, were continuously seeking new havens of rescue. As the demographic distribution of the community during the war attests, Jewish internal migration was extraordinary, and Jews were recorded in more than six thousand localities within France, a fact of considerable importance when assessing the overall number of victims and the assistance of local French people. Not always, as in the case of the Italian buffer zone, were their perceptive changes of location capable of foreseeing political developments, but this was part of the tragedy that they could not control.

BIBLIOGRAPHY

L'activité des organisations juives en France sous l'occupation. Paris, 1947.

Adler, J. *The Jews of Paris and the Final Solution: Communal Response and Internal Conflicts, 1940–1944.* New York, 1987.

Cohen, R. I. *The Burden of Conscience: French Jewish Leadership during the Holocaust.* Bloomington, 1987.

Kedward, H. R. *Resistance in Vichy France: A Study of Ideas and Motivation in the Southern Zone, 1940–1942.* Oxford, 1978.

Latour, A. *The Jewish Resistance in France (1940–1944).* New York, 1981.

Lazare, L. *La résistance juive en France.* Paris, 1988.

Marrus, M. R. "Jewish Leadership and the Holocaust: The Case of France." In *Living with Antisemitism: Modern Jewish Responses,* edited by J. Reinharz, pp. 380–396. Hanover, N.H., 1987.

RICHARD COHEN

After the Holocaust

Like many other Jewish communities in post-Holocaust Europe, French Jewry confronted the massive task of reconstruction with despair and trepidation. Parisian Jewry was weakened seriously by the loss of approximately fifty thousand members. Throughout France, Jews agonized over the disappearance of hundreds of small communities and the reduction of many large settlements to a mere handful of Jewish families.

However, in comparison with other European Jewish communities, the situation of French Jewry after liberation seemed far from hopeless. French Jews were in the unique position of having experienced the

Holocaust yet having survived in large enough numbers to reassert themselves after the war. The continuous influx of Jewish survivors fleeing DISPLACED PERSONS' camps and emerging from hiding—more than thirty-five thousand in the first three years after the war—meant that France would soon contain the most populous Jewish community on the Continent.

Of the many pressing problems facing the newly reconstituted community in the early days after the end of the war, three consumed most of its energy and interest: the restoration of spoliated property; the care and feeding of refugees; and the plight of orphaned and "adopted" children. The attempts at solution were checkered. Despite intense efforts by community leaders to petition government officials for restitution, French Jewry had only limited success in reclaiming the businesses, furniture, and apartments of deportees. More successful were the activities of the Comité Juif d'Action Social et de Reconstruction (Jewish Committee for Social Action and Reconstruction), which was able to feed and house nearly three-quarters of the forty thousand Holocaust survivors who sought refuge in France. Thanks to the efforts of organizations such as the Oeuvre de Protection des Enfants Juifs and the OEUVRE DE SECOURS AUX ENFANTS, nearly one hundred institutions were created to care for orphaned children and to reintegrate them into the community. While the French Jewish community was able to provide foster parents for orphans, however, it had little success in recovering Jewish children adopted by non-Jews during the war.

Postwar reconstruction involved more than simply responding to immediate needs. If French Jewry was to successfully confront the challenges raised by post-Holocaust Europe, it would have to accomplish two major tasks: to set about restructuring the Jewish community to ensure its survival and growth; and to seriously reevaluate deeply rooted beliefs concerning French-Jewish relations in light of the Vichy experience.

Despite elements of goodwill and repeated calls for unity, native and immigrant leaders quickly lapsed into prewar patterns of organizational behavior. However, the failure to create a unified communal structure did not preclude coordinated activity on specific issues. Pressured by the Joint Distribution Committee to coordinate its fragmented relief effort, in October 1949 the community formed the Fonds Social Juif Unifié (United Jewish Social Fund; FSJU), which soon emerged as the central agency for the collection of funds and the distribution of services among French Jewry. In leading French Jewish philanthropy from traditional reliance on individual acts of beneficence to a commitment to professional community service, the FSJU helped to forge communal solidarity and Jewish pride.

The CRIF served as the political arm of French Jewry and was an active participant in public debates on a number of important postwar issues of interest to the French Jewish community in the 1940s and 1950s. These included German rearmament, the prosecution of German war criminals, reparations for Holocaust victims, monitoring the activities of antisemitic organizations, and the passage of anti-racist legislation. Though CRIF's effectiveness in the political arena depended in large part on the policies of the French government, it clearly strengthened the community by developing what one observer called a *judaïsme musculaire,* that is, a willingness to assertively defend Jewish interests.

The success of the massive reconstruction effort waged by organizations such as the FSJU and CRIF attests to the significant transformations that French Jewry underwent in the late 1940s and early 1950s. Yet the community structure rested on weak ideological foundations, attitudes, and assumptions about Jews and France that had been shaped by prewar experiences and by contradictory responses to the events of World War II. Despite their public demands for the banning of anti-Jewish groups and demonstrations and their expressions of outrage at government leniency with regard to collaborators, most native Jews chose to define French wartime attitudes toward Jews in terms of the resistance of a minority to Nazism rather than in the collaboration or at least passive acceptance of the majority. Even immigrants who suffered the greatest losses in the Holocaust quickly fell prey to the national mythology surrounding the French Revolution and the Résistance that dominated French political discourse in the immediate postwar period.

Nowhere was the fragility of French Jewish consciousness more clearly revealed than in the community's response to the creation of the state of Israel. Aside from the obvious issue of financial support, there was little in communal discussions concerning the Jewish state that pointed to a distinctive French Jewish contribution to the new nation. Nor was there any interest in the question of how Israel could help to ensure the future of Jews in France. Most committed French Jews undoubtedly shared the sentiments of the journalist Bernard Kessler, who wrote in 1946: "Without a Jewish homeland in Palestine, Judaism will disappear sooner or later, either through persecution or through assimilation and conversion."

What was missing in this intense and important discussion, as well as in the response to postwar antisemitism, was a strong defense of a Jewish presence in France. Despite its impressive successes in creating new institutions and in rehabilitating the tens of thousands of broken men and women who returned from the Nazi extermination camps and emerged from hiding, French Jewry in the 1940s and early 1950s lacked confidence in its future. Though far from moribund, the French Jewish community seemed to be marking time, waiting, as it had done in the past, for a fresh infusion of immigrants, which in fact took place from the mid-1950s, with the influx of Jews from North Africa.

BIBLIOGRAPHY

Blumenkranz, B., ed. *Histoire des Juifs en France.* Toulouse, 1972.

Rabi (Rabinovitch, W.). *Anatomie du judaïsme français.* Paris, 1962.

Roland, C. *Du ghetto à l'occident: Deux générations yiddiches en France.* Paris, 1962.

Weinberg, D. "The French Jewish Community after World War II: The Struggle for Survival and Self-Definition." *Forum* 45 (Summer 1982): 45–54.

DAVID WEINBERG

FRANK, ANNE. [*This entry is divided into three parts. The first tells about Anne Frank's family and recounts the story of her life; the second describes her diary. The third part is about the Anne Frank House in Amsterdam.*]

Family. Otto Heinrich Frank (1889–1980) was born in Frankfurt, Germany. He grew up in an assimilated, liberal Jewish environment, attended high school, and trained for a while at Macy's department store in New York. During World War I he was a reserve officer in the German army. After the war Frank started his own business, with mixed success. In 1925 he married Edith Holländer, the daughter of factory owners in Aachen. The couple had two daughters, Margot Betti (born February 16, 1926) and Annelies Marie (born June 12, 1929), called Anne.

Soon after the Nazis came to power in January 1933 and the first anti-Jewish measures were announced, the Frank family decided to leave Germany. Otto Frank went to Amsterdam. He knew the city well from frequent visits and had several good friends there. After finding an apartment he brought over the rest of his family. He set up a company, Opekta, that made and distributed pectin for use in homemade jams and jellies. In 1938, together with Hermann van Pels, Frank started a second company, Pectacon, which specialized in the preparation of spices for sausage making. Van Pels, his wife Auguste, and their son Peter had recently fled to Amsterdam from Osnabrück in Germany.

Anne and Margot quickly adapted themselves to their new life. They learned Dutch and attended the local Montessori school. The Franks joined the liberal Jewish congregation of Amsterdam.

This relatively carefree existence came to an end on May 10, 1940, when the Germans invaded and occupied the Netherlands. The invasion was soon followed by anti-Jewish measures. That October a law was passed requiring all Jewish-owned businesses to be registered. With the help of non-Jewish friends and colleagues both Opekta and Pectacon were "Aryanized" on paper, and the businesses continued. Another law stipulated that Jewish children could attend only Jewish schools, and Anne and Margot switched to the Jewish Lyceum.

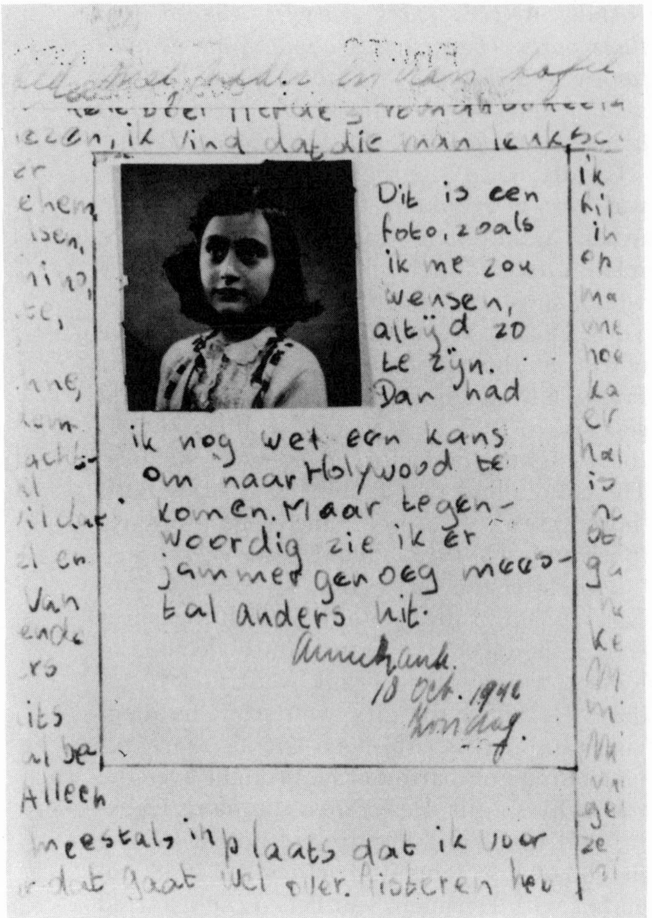
Dit is een foto, zoals ik me zou wensen, altijd zo te zijn. Dan had ik nog wel een kans om naar Holywood te komen. Maar tegenwoordig zie ik er jammer genoeg meestal anders uit.
Annefrank.
10 Oct. 1942
Zondag.

Photo and excerpt from Anne Frank's diary. [© 1988, Copyright by Cosmopress, Geneva & Anne Frank-Fonds.]

Meanwhile, Otto Frank, who had no illusions about the Nazis, had begun preparations to go into hiding, if this proved necessary. Little by little, the family's possessions were brought to the vacant annex to Frank's office at Prinsengracht 263. Four employees were informed of his plans and agreed to help: Victor Kugler, Johannes Kleiman, Elli Voskuijl, and Miep Gies (born Hermine Santrouschitz). Miep had worked with Otto Frank for years and had become his right hand. Born in Vienna, she had been one of the many thousands of Austrian children who after World War I were taken into Dutch foster homes to improve their health. Miep had stayed on, and in 1941 she married Jan Gies.

The Franks' hiding plans went into high gear on July 5, 1942, when Margot received a registered letter from the ZENTRALSTELLE FÜR JÜDISCHE AUSWANDERUNG (Central Office for Jewish Emigration), a Nazi bureau. Margot, then sixteen years old, was ordered to register for what the letter called "labor expansion measures." After consultation with the van Pels family, the Franks decided to go into hiding immediately. The next day they moved into the annex, followed a week later by the van Pels family and their fifteen-year-old son, Peter. On November 16, 1942, they were joined by an eighth *onderduiker* (lit., "one who dives under"), the dentist Fritz Pfeffer, who had fled from Berlin in 1938. These eight people were to spend two years living in a few cramped rooms made in an attic. As food and clothing became scarce and could be bought only with coupons, which Jews in hiding could not obtain, the four helpers in the office managed somehow to buy enough supplies to feed and clothe eight additional people, often at great risk to their own lives.

On August 4, 1944, the SD (Sicherheitsdienst; Security Service) in Amsterdam received an anonymous phone call—it has never been established from whom—with information about Jews in hiding at Prinsengracht 263. A police van immediately drove to the Prinsengracht, and the eight Jews were found and arrested. A policeman named Silberbauer demanded money and jewelry; to hide these he emptied an attaché case full of papers, which he threw on the floor. Among the papers was Anne Frank's diary. Also arrested were Kleiman and Kugler, two of the employees who had assisted the families. After the police left, Miep Gies and Elli Voskuijl went back to the annex to pick up many personal items, such as photographs, books, and other papers. A few days later all the furniture and clothing were hauled away from the annex, a customary procedure after an arrest. During the arrests Miep Gies had realized that Silberbauer, like her, came from Vienna. This may have been why he did not arrest her, although he made it clear that he suspected her as well of having helped the Jews. The next day Miep sought him out to see if there was a way the prisoners could be set free, but Silberbauer indicated there was nothing he could do. Kugler and Kleiman were taken to the concentration camp in Amersfoort, in the Netherlands. Kleiman suffered a hemorrhage of the stomach, and through the intervention of the Red Cross was sent home in September 1944. Kugler was able to escape during a transport in March 1945 and remained in hiding until the liberation of the Netherlands in May.

The Jewish prisoners arrived at the WESTERBORK transit camp on August 8, 1944. From there a full trainload of prisoners left for the extermination camps every week. On September 3 the last transport to leave Westerbork for AUSCHWITZ departed. According to the meticulously kept transport lists, there were 1,011 people on board, among them the Franks, the van Pels family, and Pfeffer. On arrival at Auschwitz-Birkenau, 549 of them were immediately gassed. Hermann van Pels was one of these. Edith Frank, her daughters Margot and Anne, and Auguste van Pels were interned in the Frauenblock. Pfeffer was the next to die. He is listed in the death book of the NEUENGAMME camp on December 20, 1944. Edith Frank perished at Auschwitz-Birkenau on January 6, 1945. It has not been established where and when Auguste van Pels died, but it is assumed that it was at the end of March or early April, somewhere in Germany or Czechoslovakia. Peter van Pels was one of the many thousands of prisoners who, because of the advancing Russian army, were put on DEATH MARCHES. He died shortly before the liberation in May 1945 in the MAUTHAUSEN camp in Austria.

Anne and Margot were sent to BERGEN-BELSEN at the end of October 1944. This camp filled up with thousands of prisoners from other camps that were being vacated as the Russians advanced. Housing, food, and medicine became totally inadequate, and many prisoners weakened from hunger and the cold. A typhus epidemic took many victims. Margot died of typhus around the beginning of March; Anne, who believed that both her parents had perished, died a few days later. Two sisters from Amsterdam who had been with the Frank sisters in both Westerbork and Auschwitz later stated that they had carried Anne's body from the sick barrack. She was buried in one of the mass graves at Bergen-Belsen. Otto Frank was the only survivor of the eight in hiding. The Soviet army liberated Auschwitz on January 27, 1945, and Frank returned to Amsterdam the following June. After Anne's death had been confirmed, Miep Gies returned to him the papers she had kept.

Diary. On June 12, 1942, her thirteenth birthday, Anne received from her father a red-checked diary. That same day, Anne wrote on the first page:

> I hope I shall be able to confide in you completely, as I have never been able to do in anyone before, and I hope that you will be a great support and comfort to me.

In letters to her imaginary friend, Anne painted a picture of herself and of her personal development in the context of the problems and fears of eight Jews trying to hide from deportation. The frightening news about the developments on the outside reached those in hiding through the radio and through their helpers. On October 9, 1943, Anne wrote:

> Dear Kitty, I've only got dismal and depressing news for you today. Our many Jewish friends are being taken away by the dozen. These people are treated by the Gestapo without a shred of decency, being loaded into cattle trucks and sent to Westerbork, the big Jewish camp in Drente. Westerbork sounds terrible: only one washing cubicle for a hundred people and not nearly enough lavatories. . . . It is impossible to escape; most of the people in the camp are branded as inmates by their shaven heads and many also by their Jewish appearance.
>
> If it is as bad as this in Holland whatever will it be like in the distant and barbarous regions they are sent to? We assume that most of them are murdered. The British radio speaks of their being gassed.
>
> Perhaps this is the quickest way to die. I feel terribly upset.

When Pfeffer arrived at the annex, Anne noted:

> Pfeffer has told us a lot about the outside world, which we have missed for so long now. He had very sad news. Countless friends and acquaintances have gone to a terrible fate. Evening after evening the green and gray army lorries trundle past. The Germans ring at every front door to inquire if there are any Jews living in the house. If there are, then the whole family has to go at once. If they don't find any, they go on to the next house. No one has a chance of evading them unless one goes into hiding. Often they go around with lists, and only ring when

> they know they can get a good haul. Sometimes they let them off for cash—so much per head. It seems like the slave hunts of old times. But it's certainly no joke; it's much too tragic for that. In the evenings when it's dark, I often see rows of good, innocent people accompanied by crying children, walking on and on, in the charge of a couple of these chaps, bullied and knocked about until they almost drop. No one is spared—old people, babies, expectant mothers, the sick—each and all join in the march to death.

Still, the *onderduikers* tried to lead a normal life. For Anne as well as Margot and Peter, this meant doing homework with the help of their old schoolbooks and new books borrowed from the library by Miep and Elli.

Fear of discovery created enormous pressure on those in hiding. During the day they could not move around or use the bathroom because not everyone in the office below was aware of their presence. The close quarters and constant tensions were often too much for Anne. On October 29, 1943, she wrote:

> I wander from one room to another, downstairs and up again, feeling like a song-bird whose wings have been brutally clipped and who is beating itself in utter darkness against the bars of its cage. "Go outside, laugh, and take a breath of fresh air," a voice cries within me, but I don't even feel a response any more; I go and lie on the divan and sleep, to make the time move quickly, and the stillness and the terrible fear, because there is no way of killing them.

Anne described the difficulties with her mother, her special relationship with her father, her sexual development, and her efforts to improve her character. She fell in love with Peter but later wrote about her disappointment in him.

Anne's diary is also a monument to the helpers who for two years struggled to obtain food and clothing and provided spiritual support:

> Our helpers are a very good example. They have pulled us through up till now and we hope they will bring us safely to dry land. Otherwise, they will have to share the same fate as the many others who are being searched for. Never have we heard one word of the burden which we certainly must be to them, never has one of them complained of all the trouble we give. They all come upstairs every day, talk to the men about business and politics, to the women about food and wartime difficulties, and about newspapers and books with the children. They put on the brightest possible faces, bring flowers and presents for birthdays and bank holidays, are always ready to help and do all they can. That is something we must never forget; although others may show heroism in the war or against the Germans, our helpers display heroism in their cheerfulness and affection.

On March 28, 1944, Anne heard over the British radio about a plan to gather diaries and letters about the war. "Of course, they all made a rush at my diary immediately," she wrote the following day. "Just imagine how interesting it would be if I were to publish a romance of the 'Secret Annex.' The title alone would be enough to make people think it was a detective story." On May 11 she wrote:

> Now, about something else: you've known for a long time that my greatest wish is to become a journalist some day and later a famous writer. Whether these leanings towards greatness (of insanity?) will ever materialize remains to be seen, but I certainly have the subjects in my mind. In any case, I want to publish a book entitled *Het Achterhuis* [The Annex] after the war. Whether I shall succeed or not, I cannot say, but my diary will be a great help.

Anne prepared a list of pseudonyms for possible publication: Van Pels became Van Daan, Pfeffer became Dussel, and so on.

Anne observed herself and her environment, made plans for the future, commented and criticized, and did not spare herself in that regard. In the high-pressure situation of the annex, she changed from a shy young girl to a young woman. Superficial comments about girlfriends and admirers made place for philosophical statements about herself and the world around her. One of the last entries in the diary is from July 15, 1944:

> That's the difficulty in these times: ideals, dreams, and cherished hopes rise within us, only to meet the horrible truth and be shattered. It's really a wonder that I haven't dropped all my ideals because they seem so absurd and impossible to carry out. Yet, I keep them, because in spite of everything I still believe that people are really good at heart. I simply can't build up my hopes on a foundation consisting of confusion, misery, and death. I see the world gradu-

> ally being turned into a wilderness, I hear the ever-approaching thunder, which will destroy us too, I can feel the sufferings of millions, and yet, if I look up into the heavens, I think that it will all come right, that this cruelty too will end, and that peace and tranquillity will return again. In the meantime, I must uphold my ideals, for perhaps the time will come when I shall be able to carry them out. Yours, Anne.

Apart from the diary, Miep had also saved a book of stories ("Stories and Adventures from the Annex") and the "Book of Beautiful Phrases." In this Anne had copied quotations that had pleased her.

Friends of Otto Frank's to whom he had shown some of the passages from Anne's diary persuaded him to find a publisher. After the historian Jan Romein published an article in which he related his emotions on reading parts of the diary, the publisher Contact approached Otto Frank, and *The Annex* appeared in June 1947 as edited by Frank, who had deleted several passages that he deemed either offensive or too personal. Several pieces from the "Story Book" were added to the diary.

The book went through many reprints. In 1950 it appeared in Germany and France, and in 1952 in England and the United States. For the American edition, Eleanor Roosevelt wrote in the preface: "This is a remarkable book. Written by a young girl—and the young are not afraid of telling the truth—it is one of the wisest and most moving commentaries on war and its impact on human beings that I have ever read."

The diary has been published in more than fifty editions; the total number of copies printed amounts to almost twenty million. Dramatic presentations have also reached a large public. The stage version by Albert Hackett and Frances Goodrich premiered on Broadway on October 5, 1955, and received the Pulitzer prize for the best play of the year. The film version followed in 1959.

Numerous other artists, including sculptors, painters, composers, and choreographers, have been inspired by Anne Frank. Many schools have been named after her. Anne's wish—"I want to live on, even after my death"—has become a reality. Throughout the world she has become a symbol of the millions of victims of the Holocaust. For many people, Anne's diary is the first confrontation with the Nazi persecution of the Jews. The influence of the diary is such that those who try to deny the Nazis' crimes also denounce the diary as a fraud. To counter such efforts, the RIJKSINSTITUUT FOR OORLOGSDOCUMENTATIE (Netherlands State Institute for War Documentation) in Amsterdam published in 1986 an annotated edition of both versions of Anne's diary, the earlier edition with passages deleted, and the later

The home of the Frank family in Amsterdam (Prinsengracht 263), where Anne and her family lived hidden in the attic for two years. The house is now a museum. [Anne Frank Stichting]

complete version. The English translation appeared in 1989.

After Otto Frank's death in 1980, Anne's papers went to the Rijksinstituut. The diary is on loan to the Anne Frank House, and is on display there. The copyright is owned by the independent Anne Frank Foundation in Basel.

The Anne Frank House. After the publication of *The Annex* many visitors found their way to the house at Prinsengracht 263, which was still being used as an office. In 1957 there were plans to raze the house to make room for a new building, but the public outcry prevented this action. The owner of the building then donated the house to the newly established Anne Frank Foundation on condition that the building be open to visitors.

The museum opened its doors in 1960. Besides the maintenance of the Annex, it has as its second goal the struggle against antisemitism and racism. It was Otto Frank's wish that the museum not become a memorial to Anne but instead contribute to an understanding of prejudice and discrimination. The Anne Frank Foundation maintains a documentation center on antisemitism and racist groups in Western Europe and the United States. It produces teaching aids and organizes traveling exhibits in various languages. The foundation has an office in New York City.

The number of visitors to the Anne Frank House continues to increase each year. In 1988 there were a total of 550,000 from around the world. The impact of Anne's diary has not diminished and continues to confront readers with the cruel truth: "Six million Jews were not murdered. One Jew was murdered, six million times over" (Abel Herzberg, survivor of Bergen-Belsen).

BIBLIOGRAPHY

Anne Frank Foundation. *Anne Frank in the World, 1929–1945.* Amsterdam, 1985.

The Diary of Anne Frank. Dramatized by F. Goodrich and A. Hackett. New York, 1956.

Frank, Anne. *The Diary of Anne Frank: The Critical Edition.* New York, 1989.

Frank, Anne. *The Diary of a Young Girl.* New York, 1952.

Frank, Anne. *Tales from the Secret Annexe.* New York, 1956.

Gies, M., with A. Gold. *Anne Frank Remembered: The Story of Miep Gies, Who Helped to Hide the Frank Family.* New York, 1985.

Schnabel, E. *Anne Frank: A Portrait in Courage.* New York, 1959.

JOKE KNIESMEYER

Translated from Dutch by Elly Dickason

FRANK, HANS (1900–1946), jurist and Nazi official; governor-general of POLAND from 1939 to 1945. When Hitler's Germany conquered Poland in September 1939, the eastern third of the country was occupied by the Soviet Union (in accordance with the secret terms of the NAZI-SOVIET PACT), the western third was annexed to the Third Reich, and the central region became a German-occupied territory known as the GENERALGOUVERNEMENT. Appointed governor-general was the legal expert of the Nazi party and Hitler's personal lawyer, Hans Frank, who henceforth played a major, albeit vacillating, role in implementing the racial policies that the Nazis pursued so relentlessly in eastern Europe.

Hans Frank graduated from a Munich *Gymnasium* in 1918. The young Frank displayed his commitment to militant nationalist and right-wing politics by joining the Epp Freikorps (a paramilitary group commanded by Ritter von Epp) in 1919 while he was pursuing the study of law at the universities of Kiel and Munich. In 1923 he passed his first-level exams, joined the SA (Sturmabteilung; Storm Troopers) and Nazi party, and took part in Hitler's ill-fated Beer-Hall Putsch in Munich. He fled briefly to Austria, then returned to Germany to finish his doctorate at the University of Kiel in 1924.

In 1926, Frank left the Nazi party in protest against Hitler's renunciation of German claims over the South Tyrol, only to rejoin a year later. His career in the party then flourished as he undertook the legal defense of various party members, most prominently in Hitler's many libel cases and in the 1930 Leipzig trial of three Nazi army officers. He also handled the very delicate matter of researching Hitler's family tree for possible Jewish ancestors.

After Hitler took power, Frank's usefulness rapidly diminished. He was given numerous honorific but powerless positions that helped to make plausible the charade of Hitler's "legal revolution." In 1933, he was appointed minister of justice for the state of Bavaria, and in 1934, minister without portfolio. From 1934 to 1941 he was president of the Academy for German Law, with the self-assigned task of reformulating German law on the basis of National Socialist principles. A middle-class intellectual who was never admitted to the inner circle of Nazi leaders, Frank remained oblivious to Hitler's open aversion to law, lawyers, and any procedures that threatened to curtail his own freedom of action. He came to prominence when Hitler appointed him head of the Generalgouvernement in October 1939.

Frank's ambitions in the Generalgouvernement, both to build up a strong power base for himself and to retain Hitler's favor, encountered almost constant frustration. Hitler's practice of presiding over a chaotic system of "institutional Darwinism"—leaving his various vassals to engage in a constant internal struggle for power and jurisdiction and keeping for himself the role of indispensable arbiter and pacesetter—was incompatible with Frank's mania for "unity of administration." While Frank managed to curtail the influence of the military and to reach an agreement for close cooperation with Hermann GÖRING concerning the economic exploitation of the Generalgouvernement, his efforts to control the activities of Heinrich HIMMLER's SS and police were totally futile.

As a result, Frank was torn between two opposing tactics. In his desire to build up his own domain, he inclined toward a pragmatic policy of economic stabilization, less arbitrary and oppressive treatment of the Poles, and their closer integration into the Third Reich. However, in response to contrary hints periodically emanating from Hitler, or in order to outbid his rival Himmler, Frank often veered suddenly to support policies of radical brutality and destructiveness, usually accompanied by bombastic pronouncements delivered with great rhetorical flourish. Thus, Frank vacillated between opposing and supporting the influx of Poles and Jews expelled from the "incorporated territories," between approving the self-sufficiency and rational exploitation of ghetto economies and encouraging the starvation and then mass murder of the Jews, between a genocidal repression of Polish culture and national consciousness and recruitment of Polish collaboration through assuring the Poles a place in the New Order.

Hans Frank in his prison cell in Nuremberg during his trial before the International Military Tribunal. [United States Army]

Ultimately, Frank's loyalty to Hitler and his own ambition could not be reconciled. He saw himself as the head of the model "crusader kingdom" of Germany's *Drang nach Osten* (drive to the east), while Hitler saw the Generalgouvernement as the racial dumping ground, the slave-labor reservoir, and finally the slaughter yard of the Third Reich. Since Himmler's views more closely approximated those of Hitler, Frank's defeat was inevitable. On March 5, 1942, the hapless Frank was summoned before a tribunal consisting of Himmler, Hans Heinrich LAMMERS, and Martin BORMANN, and stripped of all jurisdiction over racial and police matters. These were now to be the exclusive domain of Himmler's *Höherer SS- und Polizeiführer* (Higher SS and Police Leader), Friedrich Wilhelm KRÜGER.

Perhaps feeling himself free to play the fool, or hoping to force Hitler to relieve him from his humiliating position, Frank delivered a series of lectures at four German universities in the summer of 1942, denouncing the emasculation of German justice by the police state. He also sent Hitler a long memorandum criticizing SS policies in Poland. "You should not slaughter the cow you want to milk," he concluded. Hitler relieved Frank of all his party positions and forbade him to speak publicly within the Reich, but refused to accept his numerous letters of resignation. Thus Frank remained as governor-general until he fled before the Russian advance; he took with him the many volumes of his official diary that have since become a major source for historians of the Third Reich and an important document for the Nuremberg Military Tribunals. Frank was tried among the major war criminals in the NUREMBERG TRIAL, and hanged at Nuremberg.

BIBLIOGRAPHY

Fest, J. *The Face of the Third Reich.* New York, 1970.

Piotrowski, S. *Hans Frank's Diary.* Warsaw, 1961.

Präg, W., and W. Jacobmeyer, eds. *Das Diensttagebuch des deutschen Generalgouverneurs in Polen, 1939–1945.* Stuttgart, 1975.

Rich, N. *Hitler's War Aims: The Establishment of the New Order.* New York, 1974.

Wulf, J. *Das Dritte Reich und seine Vollstrecker: Die Liquidation von 500,000 Juden im Getto Warschau.* Munich, 1978.

CHRISTOPHER R. BROWNING

FRANK, KARL HERMANN (1898–1946), Sudeten German leader and later virtual ruler of the Protectorate of BOHEMIA AND MORAVIA. Frank served in the Austrian army in the latter part of World War I and then became a bookseller in his native Karlsbad, but failed in business. In 1933 he entered Sudeten German politics as propaganda chief under Konrad Henlein. He became a Sudeten German delegate in the Czech parliament in 1935, and in 1938, after the MUNICH CONFERENCE, deputy *Gauleiter* in the Sudetenland. In March 1939, following the German annexation of the remainder of Czechoslovakia, Frank served as state secretary to the Protectorate under Konstantin von NEURATH, with the rank of SS-*Gruppenführer.* In 1942 Frank

Karl Hermann Frank at his public hanging in Prague (1946).

manifested his vengefulness when the Czechoslovak village and inhabitants of LIDICE were destroyed after the assassination of Reinhard HEYDRICH. When Frank became virtual ruler of Czechoslovakia in 1943 as minister of state, he maintained the same policy of terror, particularly against Czech Jewry. At the end of the war he fled to the West, but the Americans extradited him to Czechoslovakia, where a Czech court sentenced him to death. He was executed by public hanging.

BIBLIOGRAPHY

Frank, E. *Karl Hermann Frank: Staatsminister im Protektorat.* Heusenstamm, West Germany, 1971.

LIONEL KOCHAN

FRANK, WALTER (1905–1945), Nazi historian. Frank was born in Fürth, and even as a young man developed a marked antisemitic outlook. This was reinforced during his student years at the University of Munich, where he came under the influence of Professor Alexander Von Müller, the pro-Nazi president of the Bavarian Academy of Sciences. Frank graduated in 1927 with a dissertation on the antisemite Adolf Stoecker and the Christian Social movement (published in 1928). His later historical writings were imbued with the same nationalist spirit; in *Nationalismus und Demokratie im Frankreich der Dritten Republik, 1871–1918* (published in 1933), he claimed to unmask the noxious role of the "international Jew" in French political life.

Frank first met Hitler in 1923, and after 1933 he advanced rapidly as professor and president of the Reichsinstitut für Geschichte des Neuen Deutschlands (Reich Institute for the History of the New Germany). He saw himself as the destined leader of German historiography, with the task of forming the soul of the nation in a Nazi spirit. In 1936 a special Research Department for the Jewish Question (Forschungsabteilung Judenfrage) was created within the institute and directed by Frank. Its publications included the notorious nine-volume *Forschungen zur Judenfrage* (Research into the Jewish Question; 1937–1944). Conflict developed, however, between Frank's institute and a rival institute under Nazi party auspices, the Institut des NSDAP zur Erforschung der Judenfrage. Frank's influence declined, especially after 1941, when Rudolf HESS, his patron, fled to England. Frank committed suicide in May 1945 at Gross-Brunsrode, near Brunswick.

BIBLIOGRAPHY

Heiber, H. *Walter Frank und sein Reichsinstitut für Geschichte des neuen Deutschlands.* Stuttgart, 1966.

LIONEL KOCHAN

FRANKFURT AM MAIN, German city, now part of the state of Hesse in the Federal Republic of GERMANY. Founded in Charlemagne's time, Frankfurt was for many years the site of the election and coronation of the German emperors, and in the fourteenth century it became an imperial free city, a status it retained until its annexation by Prussia in 1866. Jews first settled there in 1074, and over the course of time its Jewish community became one of the most important in Europe. In the nineteenth century, Frankfurt was a cultural center of the Jewish Enlightenment (Haskalah), as well as of Neo-Orthodoxy. It also played an important role in commerce, industry, and banking (the Rothschild Bank had its center in Frankfurt until the early twentieth century). Two of the outstanding personalities based in Frankfurt in the twentieth century were the philosophers Franz Rosenzweig and Martin Buber. In 1817 the city had a Jewish population of 3,300 (10 percent of the total); in 1930 it numbered 30,000 (5.5 percent); and in June 1933, 26,158. Frankfurt was one of the largest Jewish centers in Germany, second only to Berlin. In early 1933 it even had a Jewish mayor, Ludwig Landmann.

Following the Nazi rise to power on January 30, 1933, Frankfurt Jews were subject to physical assaults. The Nazis in the city did not wait for the official launching of the anti-Jewish BOYCOTT on April 1, 1933, to take boycott action against Jewish stores, and they persisted in such action after April 1, extending it also to German-owned stores with Jewish employees. Trade went down sharply in the Jewish stores, and many went bankrupt or were transferred to Nazi ownership. In the period from March to October 1933, 536 Jewish business enterprises in Frankfurt were closed. The new Nazi mayor dismissed all Jews employed by the city even before the enactment of the national law to that effect. (When the law was passed, the mayor had to reinstate employees who had seen active service in World War I, since the new law specifically exempted them from dismissal.) Following the example set by the city government, all public institutions gradually dismissed the Jews on their staffs—the hospitals, law courts, schools, university, and institutions of culture and the arts. When the NUREMBERG LAWS went into effect in 1935, Jews who had been frontline soldiers lost their exemption and were also discharged. Most privately owned commercial establishments also dismissed their Jewish employees.

As a result of the deterioration of economic conditions among the Jews, the two Jewish communities—the general and the "secessionist" Orthodox community—faced financial collapse. Their members, however, were willing to pay high community taxes and make substantial contributions in the form of cash or property, and thereby enabled the communities and welfare organizations to continue functioning. In fact, in response to the growing needs, a large welfare network was established. In 1935, forty-five hundred Jews were in need of help, almost 20 percent of the Jewish population. In addition to financial assistance or help in kind (mainly clothing and food), a vocational training program was set up, for the retraining of hundreds of youngsters of both sexes in productive occupations, trades, and agriculture.

Frankfurt's Jews—like Jews elsewhere in Germany—responded to their exclusion from society and cultural life by setting up their own cultural activities. In 1933 Martin Buber reactivated the Jüdisches Lehrhaus (Jewish Academy), which Franz Rosenzweig had established in the 1920s, with a varied program of lectures. A Jewish symphony orchestra was formed, as were other musical groups and theatrical troupes, and the Jews had a rich schedule of performances and exhibitions from which to choose, ranging from music to photography. A sports program was also organized, with thousands of youngsters participating. These activities were confined to special sports complexes; in 1935 a special swimming pool was allocated as the only one to which Jews were admitted (the community paid an annual fee for its use).

In 1937 Jacob Hoffmann, the leader of the Mizraḥi movement in Germany and the Orthodox rabbi serving the main community, was expelled to Hungary. Among the Polish Jews expelled from Germany on October 26, 1938, 2,000 were from Frankfurt. On October 31 they were allowed to return to the city, but were denied access to their homes, which in the interval had been sealed by the police. The community provided accommodation for them in school buildings and private houses, and the Jewish welfare agencies took care of them until they were able to return to their own homes. During the KRISTALLNACHT pogroms on November 9–10, 1938, five of the city's large synagogues and most of the small prayer houses were burned down. Gangs of rioters roamed the streets, ransacking and destroying Jewish stores, and also causing loss of life. In the following days, thousands of Jews were arrested in their homes, on the streets, and in the railway stations. For several days they were detained in a large public hall, and were then taken to BUCHENWALD (2,161 Jews) and DACHAU. Nazi propaganda stressed the point that the family of German diplomat Ernst vom Rath (whose assassination was the pretext for the pogroms) came from Frankfurt, and that the assassin, Herschel GRYNSZPAN, had been a student at the Frankfurt Yeshiva (rabbinical academy). The yeshiva building was destroyed by the Nazis.

In the wake of the pogrom and the ensuing riots and arrests, the Jews started fleeing from the city. In November 1938, 618 Jews left Frankfurt; in May 1939, 13,751 Jews (identified by religion) were left, half of the 1933 total; in addition, there were another 440 "members of the Jewish race," by Nazi definition, and 2,687 persons of "mixed blood." By the end of September 1941, the total number of "members of the Jewish race" had gone down to 10,592.

The Frankfurt municipality purchased properties from the Jewish community—belonging to both the main and the "secessionist" communities, which had merged in the wake of *Kristallnacht*—at a price much lower than their real value. The large synagogues, except for one, were torn down. The old Jewish cemetery was leveled, and from the other Jewish cemeteries all pieces of metal were removed, including the lettering on the tombstones, "for use in the war effort." The municipality had an official who was in charge of Jewish welfare, but in February 1940 a Gestapo officer in charge of "Jewish welfare" was appointed, representing both the Gestapo and the municipality; such a post existed only in Frankfurt. This officer, Ernst Holland, handled all affairs relating to Jews in the city, and supervised all the Jewish property and the operations of the Jewish institutions still in existence. His mandate was to reduce Jewish activities and save the costs involved, and to transfer Jewish property and financial assets to "Aryans." This involved, in part, evacuating Jews from their apartments and forcing them to move in with others or to find accommodation in the Jewish community buildings; in this way, the officer was able to transfer hundreds of Jewish apartments into German hands. On March 4, 1941, the Jews were put on forced labor, and this too was under the Gestapo officer's supervision. Between *Kristallnacht*—November 1938—and 1943, 715 Jews committed suicide in Frankfurt.

On October 19, 1941, the first transport of Jews left Frankfurt for Łódź, with 1,125 Jews on board the train. On November 11, 1,052 Jews were deported to Minsk, and on November 22, 902 Jews were sent to Riga. In another three transports (May 8 and 24, and June 11, 1942), 2,886 Jews were deported to eastern Europe; in three more transports (August 18, and September 1 and 15, 1942), 2,952 Jews were sent to THERESIENSTADT. On September 24 another 234 Jews were deported to the east. In 1943, 120 more Jews were deported, in six groups, to various destinations. On January 8, 1944, 56 Jews were sent to Theresienstadt. In June 1943 the post of officer in charge of Jewish welfare was abolished, since there was no longer any need for it.

After the war a new Jewish community was established in Frankfurt; it is now the second largest in Germany. The one remaining large synagogue in the Westend quarter is again being used for religious services. The Jewish community takes care of the cemeteries, but on several occasions Jewish cemeteries have been desecrated.

BIBLIOGRAPHY

Heuberger, R., and H. Krohn. *Hinaus aus dem Ghetto . . . Juden in Frankfurt am Main 1800–1950*. Frankfurt, 1988.

Kommission zur Erforschung der Geschichte der frankfurter Juden. *Dokumente zur Geschichte der frankfurter Juden, 1933–1945*. Frankfurt, 1963.

Schembs, H.-O. *Bibliographie zur Geschichte der frankfurter Juden, 1781–1945*. Frankfurt, 1978.

Wipperman, W. *Das Leben in Frankfurt zur NS-Zeit*. Vol. 1 of *Die Nationalsozialistische Judenverfolgung*. Frankfurt, 1986.

JACOB BORUT

FRANKFURTER, DAVID (1909–1982), medical student. Born in Daruvar, Croatia, Frankfurter was the son of the local rabbi, Dr. Moshe Frankfurter. In 1929 David Frankfurter began to study medicine, first at Leipzig and later at Frankfurt; he witnessed the Nazi rise to power and their persecution of the Jews in the first years of their rule. In 1934 he moved to Bern, Switzerland, to continue his studies, while maintaining his interest in the events taking place in Nazi Germany. The NUREMBERG LAWS, enacted in September 1935, strengthened his conviction that he had to make a move against the Nazis that would arouse the world's attention. In November of that year he began to follow the activities of Wilhelm GUSTLOFF, the National Socialist leader of Switzerland; on the evening of February 4, 1936, he shot and killed Gustloff at Davos, the famous resort town, and then surrendered to the police.

David Frankfurter.

Frankfurter's trial before a court at Chur, in the Graubünden canton, began on December 9, 1936. His action was received with great admiration by wide circles of the Swiss population, but Switzerland, apprehensive about its Nazi neighbor, did all it could to restrict the trial to its criminal aspect. The prosecution and the court both rejected the modest effort made by the defense to raise the issue of a young Jew's reaction to the Nazis and their antisemitic policy. Frankfurter was convicted and sentenced to eighteen years in prison.

On February 27, 1945, as Germany was on the verge of collapse in the war, Frankfurter applied for a pardon, which was granted on June 1. He was released, but was expelled from Switzerland and went to Palestine, where he settled in Tel Aviv.

It was only in September 1969 that Switzerland rescinded Frankfurter's banishment from the country, after friends had interceded on his behalf. His memoir of the events appeared in English (published in *Commentary*) in February 1950 and in Hebrew (*First of the Nazi Fighters*) in 1984.

BIBLIOGRAPHY

Frankfurter, D. "I Killed a Nazi Gauleiter: Memoir of a Jewish Assassin." *Commentary* 9/2 (1950): 133–141.

SHMUEL SPECTOR

FRANZ, KURT (b. 1914), SS officer; deputy commandant of the TREBLINKA extermination camp. Franz enlisted in the army in 1935, and on completion of his army service he volunteered for the SS, serving initially in the BUCHENWALD concentration camp. Late in 1939 he was transferred to the EUTHANASIA PROGRAM. In April 1942, after AKTION REINHARD had begun, he was sent to the BEŁŻEC extermination camp, with the rank of SS-*Oberscharführer.* In late August or early September of that year he was transferred to Treblinka as deputy to the camp commandant, Franz STANGL.

At Treblinka, Franz dominated daily life at the camp. He was the cruelest and most terrifying of the SS officers there; his handsome appearance earned him the nickname Lalka ("doll" in Polish) among the prisoners. He regularly toured the camp, reviewed the prisoner parades, and abused, struck, and shot prisoners at every opportunity and for the slightest infraction. Franz's work at Treblinka was rated "excellent," and as a result he was promoted to the rank of *Untersturmführer,* in June 1943. After the revolt at Treblinka that August, and with the cessation of the extermination activities there, Stangl left and Franz remained to dismantle the camp and obliterate the traces of the slaughter there. In late November 1943 the last Jews engaged in the demolition of the camp were killed.

After the war, Franz stood trial in his native Düsseldorf, together with nine other SS officers who had served at Treblinka. At this First Treblinka Trial (there were three trials, all conducted in Germany), held from October 12, 1964, to August 24, 1965, Franz was sentenced to life imprisonment.

BIBLIOGRAPHY

Arad, Y. *Belzec, Sobibor, Treblinka: Operation Reinhard Death Camps.* Bloomington, 1987.

Arad, Y. *Treblinka: Hell and Revolt.* Tel Aviv, 1983. (In Hebrew.)

YITZHAK ARAD

FREEMASONS, secret fraternal order. The Masonic movement, founded in England in 1717, admitted Jews to its lodges as early as 1732, first in England and later in the Netherlands, France, Germany, and other countries. The attitudes of European Freemasons toward Jews tended to be ambivalent. Until the 1870s the lodges opened their doors to Jews, but with the rise of political antisemitism in the 1880s, Freemasonry began to reject them. This was the main reason for the creation of Jewish fraternal lodges such as B'NAI B'RITH, whose German branch was founded in Berlin in 1885. The anti-Jewish views held in German Masonic lodges are borne out by the small number of Jews in their membership: in the Weimar period, for example, Jews constituted only 4 percent of the eighty thousand Masons registered in Germany.

The slogan "Jews and Freemasons" as a battle cry of right-wing organizations originated in Germany in the late 1840s, spreading from there to France, and later to the rest of the world. The belief that the Masonic lodges were a cover for a Jewish conspiracy to destroy Christianity and national traditional society was especially strong in Catholic circles. When an anti-Masonic world congress was convened in Trent, Italy, in September 1894, it was supported not only by notorious French antisemites such as Edouard Drumont, but also by Pope Leo XIII. In France, monarchist reactionaries propagated the idea that the Republic was a creation of Jews and Masons. The notorious antisemite Charles Maurras developed the doctrine of the four confederate states—Jews, Protestants, Freemasons, and aliens—who were responsible for undermining Christian society in a sinister plot to control the world. The legend of Ahasver, "the wandering Jew," was also associated in France with a conspiracy of Freemasons and Jews.

These ideas were repeated in the post–World War I antisemitic literature. Thus, the PROTOCOLS OF THE ELDERS OF ZION linked Jewish and Masonic conspiracies, arguing that the Freemasons were in the service of the "Elders of Zion." In Germany, pan-Germans and racists such as Dietrich Eckardt, Alfred ROSENBERG, Erich LUDENDORFF, and his wife, Mathilda Ludendorff, were the main figures spreading the anti-Masonic and antisemitic slogans, using the periodical *Auf gut Deutsch* (In Good German) as one of their vehicles. In Nazi Germany an anti-Masonic museum was established. All members of German lodges who had not left them until after January 30, 1933 (the date of the Nazi seizure of power), were not accepted in the Nazi party, and some were sent to concentration camps. The lodges were forced to dissolve themselves in September 1935, and their property was confiscated.

Since Freemasonry was considered an ideological foe of Nazism, a special section of the SD (Sicherheitsdienst; Security Service), II/111, dealt with it. Later, section VII B 1 of the REICHSSICHERHEITSHAUPTAMT (Reich Security Main Office; RSHA) performed the same function. In the SD analysis, Freemasonry was not only a part of the "Jewish problem" but also an autonomous ideology with political power, ruling the press and public opinion and motivating wars and revolutions. The SD believed that the Jews used Freemasonry, with its international links, as a means for achieving world domination. The Freemasons were able to operate openly on behalf of the Jews, who preferred to remain inconspicuous. In fact, Freemasonry's principles of racial equality and human progress served Jewish interests, since they paved the way for Jewish emancipation. Freemasonry's humanitarian goals of spreading toleration and humanist principles were interpreted as aiming to establish a world Jewish republic. Both the French Revolution, which had emancipated European Jewry, and World War I were perceived as combined Judeo-Masonic actions to destroy Russia and Germany, in order to install Jewish domination.

BIBLIOGRAPHY

Katz, J. *Jews and Freemasons in Europe*. Cambridge, Mass., 1970.

DAVID BANKIER

FREMDARBEITER. *See* Forced Labor: Fremdarbeiter.

FRENCH JEWISH ORGANIZATIONS, FEDERATION OF. *See* Fédération des Sociétés Juives de France.

FRENCH JEWISH SCOUTS. *See* Eclaireurs Israélites de France.

FRENCH JEWS, GENERAL COUNCIL OF. *See* Union Général des Israélites de France.

FRENCH POLICE (Police et Gendarmerie Françaises). The entire French police force, including the section serving in the German-occupied zone of FRANCE, functioned under the authority of the Vichy government in the region of the country that until November 1942 did not come under German occupation. Some one hundred thousand policemen served in the Vichy government police force, thirty thousand of them in Paris. They included men in the *gendarmerie* responsible for the provincial regions, as well as the special branches such as intelligence and the squads for suppressing Résistance activists.

In the fall of 1941 a special police section was set up to deal with Jewish affairs on behalf of the Ministry of the Interior, but it came under the supervision of the COMMISSARIAT GÉNÉRAL AUX QUESTIONS JUIVES (General Office for Jewish Affairs) in France, and its functions were officially restricted to intelligence and investigation.

In contrast to this large French police force, the German force numbered at most some three thousand police, whose performance was hampered by inability to speak French and unfamiliarity with the terrain in which they were stationed. Consequently, the Germans assigned to the French police the tasks of maintaining public order, preventing subversive activities, suppressing crime, and implementing the German anti-Jewish policy.

On July 16 and 17, 1942, thirteen thousand Jews were arrested in Paris, among whom were four thousand children, as well as old people and the handicapped and ill. They were concentrated mainly in the Vélodrome d'Hiver, a closed structure in which even minimal amenities had not been prepared, and lacking in toilet facilities. For this operation nine thousand French policemen were brought in, and they carried out the arrests.

More than ten thousand Jews whose names appeared on the lists of those to be arrested succeeded in leaving their homes in time, some because of warnings passed on by police officials out of humanitarian considerations. From the end of July 1942 agreements were signed between Carl Albrecht OBERG, *Höherer SS- und Polizeiführer* (Higher SS and Police Leader) in France, and René Bousquet, chief of the Vichy police, defining the authority of the French police and the amount of weapons and equipment they were allowed. The leaders of the Vichy government considered these agreements proof that despite the German occupation they had succeeded in maintaining the sovereignty of France and freedom of action regarding its citizens.

Until the summer of 1943, a policy of cooperation was maintained throughout France in keeping with the Oberg-Bousquet agreement with no particular difficulty. The police force carried out the registration of the Jews and the expropriation of their property and businesses, conducted mass arrests and *Aktionen*, and made sure that the Jews wore the yellow Jewish BADGE and that their identity cards were stamped with the word *Juif* ("Jew"). The police force was also responsible for the construction, operation, and guarding of concentration camps. In addition, they provided armed guards to escort the trains transporting Jews to the German border. Negligence, corruption, and neglect of sanitary and medical services were common in the concentration and transit camps under the responsibility of the French police. The special police section in Paris was active in the liquidation of the underground Communist partisan units, which included a large number of Jews.

In the summer of 1943, after recruitment notices were sent out to thousands of young Frenchmen for forced labor in Germany, groups of partisans became organized throughout the country and inflicted losses not only on the occupation forces but also on the French police. The French police services gradually stopped arresting Jews, and the French administration in the DRANCY concentration camp was replaced by the Gestapo under Alois BRUNNER.

In 1944, Joseph Darnand, head of the French fascist militia established during the previous year, was appointed chief of police in place of Bousquet, who had been dismissed. From then on the operations against the Jews were carried out by the brutal militia forces, which executed their tasks industriously and pitilessly against the Jews of France.

BIBLIOGRAPHY

Klarsfeld, S. *Vichy-Auschwitz: Le rôle de Vichy dans la solution finale de la question juive en France, 1942.* 2 vols. Paris, 1983, 1985.

Marrus, M. R., and R. O. Paxton. *Vichy France and the Jews.* New York, 1981.

Paxton, R. O. *Vichy France: Old Guard and New Order, 1940–1944.* New York, 1982.

LUCIEN LAZARE

FREUDIGER, FÜLÖP (1900–1976), Hungarian Jewish leader. Born in BUDAPEST to a well-to-do family ennobled by Emperor Franz Josef, Freudiger succeeded his father, Abraham, as the head of the Orthodox Jewish community of Budapest in 1939. As a founder and leading figure of the Orthodox RELIEF AND RESCUE COMMITTEE OF BUDAPEST in 1943 and 1944, he helped many of the illegal foreign Jewish refugees in HUNGARY. After the German occupation of the country on March 19, 1944, he was appointed to the Central Jewish Council (Központi Zsidó Tanács), the JUDENRAT of Budapest—a position he retained after the council's reorganization on April 22.

Through the intermediacy of Rabbi Michael Dov WEISSMANDEL of Bratislava, Freudiger established close contact with Dieter WISLICENY of the Eichmann Sonderkommando almost immediately after the occupation. He also received from Weissmandel a copy of the AUSCHWITZ PROTOCOLS (a report by two Auschwitz escapees), and disseminated information about the mass killings taking place at Auschwitz to Jewish and non-Jewish leaders in Hungary. By bribing Wisliceny, Freudiger succeeded in rescuing eighty prominent Orthodox Jews from various ghettos in Hungary. Partly with Wisliceny's aid, he and his family escaped to Romania, on August 9, 1944. Freudiger eventually settled in Israel, where his role in the Central Jewish Council and his escape were subjects of controversy. He served as a prosecution witness in the EICHMANN TRIAL in 1961.

BIBLIOGRAPHY

Diamant, S., and G. Link. "Report on Hungary, March 19–August 9, 1944." *Hungarian Jewish Studies* 3 (1973): 75–146.

RANDOLPH L. BRAHAM

FRICK, WILHELM (1877–1946), Nazi leader. Frick was one of Hitler's earliest followers. He studied law, earning the degree of D.Juris, and then joined the Munich Police Commission. He was dismissed from that post for taking part in Hitler's attempted coup in 1923 and sentenced to fifteen months' internment, but did not serve the full term, being released on his election to the Reichstag. In 1928, Frick became party whip of the Nazi Reichstag faction. He was the first Nazi to become a minister in a German provincial government (Thüringen), and through the conduct of his office presented a general outline of Nazi policy, earning a wide reputation by his purges of public officials, his incitements to antisemitism, and his Nazi-oriented policy in cultural affairs.

From January 30, 1933, Frick, as Reich minister of the interior, was responsible for the enactment of most of the racial laws, and he extolled them in his public appearances. After the creation of Heinrich HIMMLER's police department in his ministry, Frick gradually lost his control of the ministry's affairs; this eventually led to his replacement by Himmler in August 1943. Frick was then appointed *Reichsprotektor* (governor) of BOHEMIA AND MORAVIA, an appointment he held until the end of the war. The International Military Tribunal found Frick guilty of crimes against peace and humanity and of war crimes, and he was one of the major war criminals hanged on October 16, 1946.

BIBLIOGRAPHY

Bracher, K. D. *The German Dictatorship: The Origins, Structure, and Effects of National Socialism.* London, 1971.

UWE ADAM

Wilhelm Frick in his prison cell in Nuremberg, where he was held during his trial before the International Military Tribunal. [United States Army]

FRONT OF THE WILDERNESS GENERATION (Hazit Dor Bnei Midbar; HDBM), Zionist youth movement in the ŁÓDŹ ghetto, founded on August 14, 1940, by Aharon Jacobson. The official name of the group was Front Młodożydowski (Jewish Youth Front; FMZ), but Hazit Dor Bnei Midbar was the name by which they knew themselves. The latter was a biblical reference (to Isaiah and Jeremiah) alluding to the sufferings of the Israelites during the Exodus; this was the members' way of linking their suffering to the continuum of Jewish history. The nucleus of the group was made up of Zionist graduates of the Jewish vocational school in Łódź.

The HDBM's declared objective was to unify all the ghetto's Zionist youth movements in order to centralize mutual aid, education, and defense in face of the negative influences of the ghetto, which had been established on February 8, 1940. Members were not required to give up their political outlooks, but were told that their realization had to be postponed until after the war.

The movement had about four hundred members and was headed initially by a five-member command. In 1942, young people who had been deported from the surrounding towns joined the HDBM, and its command became a leadership composed of the Zionist youth movements members of Ha-Shomer ha-Tsa'ir, Gordonia, Ha-No'ar ha-Tsiyyoni, Ha-Tehiyya, and Betar. On September 22, 1943, the HDBM merged with Ha-No'ar ha-Tsiyyoni and the movement's name was changed to Hazit ha-No'ar ha-Tsiyyoni (Zionist Youth Front). After the merger a core of oppositionists to German policy, headed by Dov Lemberg, was organized in the HDBM.

The movement functioned until the last days of the ghetto. One of its leaders, Raphael Zelwer, attempted to assemble in AUSCHWITZ-Birkenau the survivors of the HDBM who had been deported there, organizing meetings until the remaining members were dispersed among other camps, where most of them perished.

BIBLIOGRAPHY

Bauminger, A. "Chazit Dor Bnei Midbar." *Yad Vashem Bulletin* 1 (April 1957): 29–31.

ARIEH BEN-MENAHEM

FSJF. *See* Fédération des Sociétés Juives de France.

FÜHRERPRINZIP ("leadership principle"), Nazi term referring to the creation of authority from above downward and of responsibility from below upward. A special characteristic of NATIONAL SOCIALISM was a religious veneration of the leader, a cult of the Führer. This was based on pseudo-Germanic ideas of order, authority, and hero worship, placing the leader and his followers in a military relationship of dominance and obedience. After Hitler became the leader of the National Socialist party in July 1921, its organizational structure became thoroughly authoritarian and defined by this principle. The function of the leadership principle combined the political-charismatic idea, racial criteria, and the bureaucratic-authoritarian concepts of the totalitarian order. The structure of all Nazi organizations, economic enterprises, and social institutions was also adapted to the leadership principle. The principle went on to be implemented outside Germany through the Nazi war policy, with its programs of racial persecution, territorial expansion, and exploitation of "inferior" races. The manifestation of the leadership principle in the organization of political and social life was intended to create a perfect monolithic state governing the extension of power to the lower echelons. Paradoxically, however, in order to achieve the supervisory functions of the totalitarian regime, the machinery of both party and state had to be expanded. This expansion hindered the full implementation of the *Führerprinzip*.

BIBLIOGRAPHY

Bracher, K. D. *The German Dictatorship: The Origins, Structure, and Effects of National Socialism.* London, 1971.

Wörtz, U. *Programmatik und Führerprinzip.* Nuremberg, 1966.

DAVID BANKIER

FUNK, WALTHER (1890–1960), Nazi economist and politician. Funk was born in East

Center: Walther Funk, finance minister of the Third Reich. At his right, in top hat, is State Secretary Fritz Reinhardt; at his left is Reich Minister Albert Speer. [National Archives]

Prussia and studied law and economics at the universities of Berlin and Leipzig. From 1922 to 1930 he was editor in chief of the *Berliner Börsenzeitung* (Berlin Stock Exchange Journal). An early member of the Nazi party, he joined in 1924 and became one of its leading figures. In 1931, Adolf HITLER appointed Funk to be his personal adviser on economic affairs. Funk was the party's liaison with the top figures in German industry, among them Emil Kirdorf, Fritz Thyssen, Albert Voegler, and Friedrich Flick.

Owing to Funk's initiative and influence, leading companies in the Reich, such as the chemical conglomerate I.G. FARBEN, made large contributions to the Nazi party treasury. It was also Funk who impressed upon Hitler the importance for the Nazi cause of German heavy industry and private enterprise.

Funk rose rapidly, as evidenced by the many offices he held. From 1933 to 1937 he was in charge of the German press and *Staatssekretär* (state secretary) of Joseph GOEBBELS's Propaganda Ministry, as well as a member of the board of the Reich Broadcasting System and vice-chairman of the Reich Chamber of Culture. In 1937 he was appointed minister of economics (succeeding Hjalmar SCHACHT in that post), and in 1939 he became president of the state bank, the Reichsbank. In the final years of the war, however, it was Albert SPEER who was the main influence in the Reich economy, despite Funk's wide range of activities in the field—a situation that illustrates the fragmentation of the assignments held by the top men in the Nazi hierarchy and the rivalry that prevailed among them.

In the NUREMBERG TRIAL Funk was found guilty of war crimes, crimes against peace, and crimes against humanity. He had taken part in the confiscation of murdered Jews' valuables and financial assets and their transfer to the SS. He was sentenced to life imprisonment, but was released in 1957 because of ill health.

BIBLIOGRAPHY

Neumann, F. *Behemoth: The Structure and Practice of National Socialism, 1933–1944.* New York, 1966.

Petzina, D. *Autarkiepolitik im Dritten Reich: Der nationalsozialistische Vierjahresplan.* Stuttgart, 1968.

Speer, A. *Inside the Third Reich.* New York, 1970.

ZVI BACHARACH

G

GALEN, CLEMENS AUGUST GRAF VON (1878–1946), Catholic bishop in Münster; one of the most prominent Catholic opponents of Adolf Hitler. In 1933 Galen became an archbishop, and at the end of World War II he was raised to the rank of cardinal.

When the Nazis came to power, Galen pledged his loyalty to the new regime, hoping that the Nazis would retrieve for Germany the honor lost in its World War I defeat. Before long, however, his support of the Nazis turned to opposition, on account of the anti-Catholic propaganda that they were conducting and the pagan concepts that he discovered in Alfred ROSENBERG's book *Der Mythus des 20. Jahrhunderts* (The Myth of the Twentieth Century; 1930). Galen launched a sharp attack against that book by the Nazi party's chief ideologue because of its racist views.

The single most significant act in the record of Galen's campaign against Nazism was his courageous denunciation of the EUTHANASIA PROGRAM; in a sermon he gave on August 3, 1941, he declared that euthanasia was simply murder. There is a widely held belief that Galen's public statements on the subject caused Hitler to put an end to the project (although the killing of the chronically ill was not completely abandoned). Some scholars believe that public opinion in Germany, at a time when the Third Reich's military success was at its height, had an effect on Hitler's decisions. The fact is, however, that no such public protest was made, by the churches or by any other German institutions, against Nazi policy on the Jews and the "FINAL SOLUTION." In the eyes of the Nazi leadership the archbishop's statements on euthanasia were tantamount to an act of treason; his life was saved only because Hitler did not want to clash openly with the Catholic church. Following the July 20, 1944, attempt on Hitler's life, Galen was imprisoned in the SACHSENHAUSEN camp. He was held there until the war came to an end.

BIBLIOGRAPHY

Lewy, G. *The Catholic Church and Nazi Germany.* New York, 1964.

ZVI BACHARACH

GAMZON, ROBERT (1905–1961), French partisan commander. Gamzon, who was born in Paris, founded the Jewish scout movement in FRANCE (ECLAIREURS ISRAÉLITES DE FRANCE), guiding it to become a pluralist organization attracting young Jews from different countries and backgrounds and with various shades of political opinion. In 1939 and 1940 Gamzon, who was an electronic-sound engineer, served as communications officer in the French Fourth Army headquarters. Following the French surrender in June 1940, Gamzon reestablished the Jewish scout movement's institutions in the cities of unoccupied France into which Jewish refugees were pouring, as well as in Algeria. He took the initiative in establishing children's homes, welfare centers, workshops, and agricultural training farms in the villages (the last so as to provide an

Robert Gamzon.

educational network for the Jewish youth). He also arranged courses in Jewish culture and tradition for youth instructors. In January 1942 Gamzon was appointed to the executive board of the UNION GÉNÉRALE DES ISRAÉLITES DE FRANCE (UGIF) in southern France and was active in the organization up to the end of 1943. In order to help Jews escape the Gestapo manhunts, Gamzon formed a clandestine rescue network in the summer of 1942 code-named "The Sixth" (La Sixième), which produced forged identity papers, found asylum for children and teenagers in non-Jewish private homes and institutions, and smuggled Jews of all ages across the borders into Spain and Switzerland. In May 1943 Gamzon, in his capacity as a member of the UGIF board, went to Paris, where he helped coordinate clandestine operations.

In December 1943, Gamzon (who by now had the code name "Lieutenant Lagnès") formed a Jewish partisan unit in the Tarn district of southwest France, which graduates of the village workshops and the Jewish scout movement came to join. By entering the command of the ARMÉE JUIVE, Gamzon helped unify all the Jewish armed organizations in France; he then took over command of the partisan unit he had set up in Tarn. This became, by June 1944, a trained and disciplined military unit of 120 men, affiliated with the Forces Françaises de l'Intérieur; the unit bore the name of Marc Haguenau, who had been the leader of "The Sixth" and had committed suicide when he fell into Gestapo hands. Following the orders of the underground district military commander, Gamzon received the parachute drops for Allied saboteurs and large quantities of light and medium arms for use in ambushing German patrols. On August 19, 1944, the Jewish scout unit seized a powerful German armored train, and on August 21 it liberated two cities, Castres and Mazamet.

In 1949 Gamzon settled in Israel together with a group of fifty graduates of the Jewish scout movement in France, who followed his lead.

BIBLIOGRAPHY

Latour, A. *Jewish Resistance in France (1940–1944).* New York, 1981.

Lazare, L. *La résistance juive en France.* Paris, 1987.

Michel, A. *Les Eclaireurs israélites de France pendant la seconde guerre mondiale.* Paris, 1982.

Pougatch, I. *Un bâtisseur: Robert Gamzon, dit "Castor soucieux," 1905–1961.* Paris, 1972.

LUCIEN LAZARE

GANZENMÜLLER, ALBERT (1905–d. after 1973), Nazi official; state secretary of the Reich Transportation Ministry from 1942 to 1945, a period during which the German railway system carried some three million Jews to extermination camps. Born in Passau, Ganzenmüller completed his studies in engineering and began work for the German RAILWAYS in 1928. He rose rapidly and entered the railway section of the Reich transportation ministry in 1937. Unlike many of his colleagues, Ganzenmüller was anything but an apolitical technocrat. He had been involved in paramilitary activities in Bavaria as a teenager in the early 1920s and joined the Nazi party and SA (Sturmabteilung; Storm Troopers) in 1931.

Following the German invasion of the Soviet Union in June 1941, Ganzenmüller volunteered for service in the east and was put in charge of restoring the system of the Main Railway Directorate East in Poltava in the bitter winter of 1941–1942. He was then appointed state secretary of the transportation ministry, at the age of thirty-seven.

While almost no internal documents of the German railways have surfaced that explicitly delineate its role in deporting Jews to the extermination camps, one fragment of correspondence of July or August 1942 between Ganzenmüller and Heinrich HIMMLER's adjutant, Karl WOLFF, has survived. It concerns the "special joy" of the SS over the state secretary's efforts in providing trains to deport five thousand of "the chosen people" from WARSAW daily to TREBLINKA and twice weekly to BEŁŻEC. Such documents provide only the slightest glimpse into the vital role of the German railways in carrying out the "FINAL SOLUTION."

After the war Ganzenmüller escaped to Argentina; he returned to Germany in 1955. An initial indictment against him was dismissed for lack of evidence in 1970. In 1973 he was finally brought to trial, in Düsseldorf, but he suffered a heart attack shortly after the proceedings began. The trial was never resumed.

BIBLIOGRAPHY

Hilberg, R. *Sonderzüge nach Auschwitz.* Mainz, 1981.

CHRISTOPHER R. BROWNING

GARDA DE FIER. *See* Iron Guard.

GAS CHAMBERS, method used by the Nazis for "efficient" mass murder. Both mobile and stationary gas chambers were put into use. The first recorded instance of mass murder by gas took place in December 1939, when an SS SONDERKOMMANDO used carbon monoxide to kill Polish mental patients. The following month, January 1940, Viktor BRACK, head of the EUTHANASIA PROGRAM, also decided on the use of pure carbon monoxide, having already tested it successfully. In the program's institutions, the facilities in which the gassing was performed were disguised as shower rooms, the steel tanks containing the gas being attached to the outer wall of the gas chambers.

After the inauguration of the "FINAL SOLUTION" in the summer of 1941, gas chambers were introduced as a method for the mass murder of Jews. The method was launched in December 1941 at CHEŁMNO, by SS-Sonderkommando Lange, using mobile vans that had been constructed and equipped for this specific purpose—a project that the REICHSSICHERHEITSHAUPTAMT (Reich Security Main Office; RSHA) had been working on since September of that year.

Unlike the method used for the euthanasia murders, the exhaust gas from the trucks was piped into the closed van. Depending on the size of the truck, forty to sixty persons could be gassed at a time. A total of twenty such mobile gas chambers were constructed, and most of them were used by the four EINSATZGRUPPEN deployed on Soviet soil.

The first stationary gas chambers that were to help facilitate the "Final Solution of the Jewish question" were put up at BEŁŻEC, in February 1942. Following several trial gassings with carbon monoxide cylinders and exhaust gas, the latter was chosen as the better alternative, since it was cheaper and did not require special supplies. The next month, regular killings commenced at Bełżec, by means of three gas chambers in a single wooden barrack. SOBIBÓR was next, in May, but here the installation was a brick building, with concrete foundations, that contained the gas chambers. The third and last of the AKTION REINHARD extermination camps in the GENERALGOUVERNEMENT was TREBLINKA, whose three gas chambers could be sealed hermetically (which was not the case in the other two extermination camps).

In the summer and fall of 1942 the capacity of the three extermination camps was greatly increased, both by enlarging the existing gas chambers and by adding new ones. Thus, in the ten gas chambers of Treblinka, twenty-five hundred persons could be put to death in a single gassing round, lasting an hour. The victims were forced to enter with their arms raised so that as many people as possible could be squeezed into the chambers. Babies and small children were thrown on top of the human mass. The tighter the chambers were packed, and the warmer the temperature inside the chamber, the faster the victims suffocated. All the gas chambers in the extermination camps were disguised as shower rooms; in Treblinka the Nazis went even further. By planting flower beds and creating what on the surface appeared to be a pleasant environment, they attempted to practice complete deception.

Each of the Aktion Reinhard killing centers operated in approximately the same way. When a transport arrived at the well-camouflaged station, a few of the victims were selected to form a Sonderkommando. A handful of victims with special talents were selected for work in the repair shops that serviced the camp SS staff and their Ukrainian helpers. The vast majority went through an assembly-line procedure, moving along the various camp stations, at which they surrendered any valuables left in their possession, undressed, and had their hair shorn. This procession culminated in the gas chambers, with the men of the transport being murdered first to prevent resistance. Once the victims were dead, the members of the Sonderkommando removed their bodies from the gas chambers and were responsible for their burial (and, later on, their cremation). After a time, the men of the Sonderkommando were killed as well, and were replaced by new victims from later transports.

In their search for a more efficient means of extermination, the Nazis experimented with other forms of poison gas, and also with electrocution. When the latter proved impractical, gassing experiments with ZYKLON B were made at the main camp of AUSCHWITZ, using Soviet prisoners of war, in preparation for the mass murder of Jews in the adjoining Birkenau camp. Zyklon B proved far superior to the diesel exhaust gas that had been used in the Generalgouvernement extermination camps, and Auschwitz camp commandant Rudolf HÖSS decided in its favor. A crystalline form of hydrogen cyanide, Zyklon B turned to gas immediately upon contact with oxygen, giving off deadly fumes that killed everyone in the gas chamber. Depending on weather conditions, primarily temperature and humidity, the murder operation in the

The large gas chamber at the Majdanek concentration camp. Together with other buildings, it is preserved as a Polish national memorial. [Geoffrey Wigoder]

Auschwitz-Birkenau gas chambers took from twenty to thirty minutes. According to Höss, "In all the years, I knew of not a single case where anyone came out of the chambers alive."

The existing gassing facilities at Auschwitz could not possibly meet the Nazis' requirements, and they were repeatedly enlarged. After an inspection of the Auschwitz-Birkenau facilities in the summer of 1942 by Reichsführer-SS Heinrich HIMMLER, the decision was taken to construct updated and more efficient crematoria, which were connected to the gas chambers in Birkenau. The J. A. Topf und Söhne company of Erfurt, Germany, was contracted to rebuild the facilities, a project that was completed in the spring of 1943. These units came into operation between March 22 and June 28 of that year. The use of the new combined gas chambers and crematoria considerably speeded up the murder process in Auschwitz, which soon became the Third Reich's main killing center.

In Lublin-MAJDANEK, mass murder by gassing was introduced in September 1942 with the use of carbon monoxide cylinders, which were replaced by Zyklon B in the spring of 1943. Although not primarily operated as mass extermination sites, some of the other major concentration camps also had gas chambers. One each was in operation in MAUTHAUSEN (beginning in the fall of 1941), NEUENGAMME (September 1942), SACHSENHAUSEN (mid-March 1943), STUTTHOF (June 1944), and RAVENSBRÜCK (January 1945). All of them used Zyklon B.

BIBLIOGRAPHY

Cohen, E. *Human Behavior in the Concentration Camp*. New York, 1953.

Gutman, Y., and A. Saf, eds. *The Nazi Concentration Camps: Structure and Aims; The Image of the Prisoner; The Jews in the Camps*. Proceedings of the Fourth Yad Vashem International Historical Conference. Jerusalem, 1984.

Kogon, E., et al., eds. *Nationalsozialistische Massentötungen durch Giftgas: Ein Dokumentation*. Frankfurt, 1983.

UWE ADAM

GAS VANS. Poison gas was used by the Nazis to murder many hundreds of thousands of people. Various methods were employed, one of them being gas vans. The first time that the Nazis used gas was in the EUTHANASIA PROGRAM, in which the victims were retarded persons, the mentally or chronically ill, and habitual criminals. They were put into hermetically sealed chambers, into which carbon monoxide gas was released from metal containers. The first experiment utilizing a gas van was made in 1940, at Kochanówka, near Łódź: mentally ill children were locked inside a sealed van and put to death by the same method.

In the early stages of the war with the Soviet Union, the EINSATZGRUPPEN (mobile killing squads) killed many thousands of people by shooting. But before long the men in these units complained about the "mental anguish" they suffered from having to kill women, children, and ill people. Their superiors at the REICHSSICHERHEITSHAUPTAMT (Reich Security Main Office; RSHA) in Berlin then began to look for an alternative method of murder, one that would reduce the mental stress to which the executioners were exposed.

The first to find such a method was Arthur NEBE, the commander of Einsatzgruppe B. His men had been killing mental patients by shooting and with explosives, but these procedures had not proved satisfactory. Consequently, he tried out a technique of killing them by channeling exhaust gas from a truck into a sealed chamber, and was able to report to Berlin on the success of the experiment. Nebe had been in charge of the Reichskriminalpolizeiamt (Reich Criminal Police Office) and of the RSHA's Kriminal Technische Institut (Police Forensic Institute), and he put the institute's chemists to work on more experimentation based on this method. The results led to a decision by the RSHA to introduce the exhaust-gas method for the killing of people.

Walter RAUFF, who was in charge of Section II D (Technical Affairs) of the RSHA, was instructed to implement the decision. The Gaubschatt firm in Berlin installed hermetically sealed vans on the chassis of large trucks, and the SD (Sicherheitsdienst; Security Service) workshop provided the specialized apparatus needed. As the workshop foreman, Harry Wentritt, described it at a postwar trial,

> A flexible exhaust pipe was installed at the truck's exhaust, with a diameter of 58 to 60 millimeters [2.26 to 2.34 inches], and a hole of the same size was drilled in the van floor; a metal pipe was soldered into the hole from the outside to which the flexible exhaust pipe was fixed. When the various parts were connected, the truck engine was started and the exhaust fumes were channeled into the van, through the pipe leading from the exhaust to the hole in the van floor.

When the first gas vans were ready, in September 1941, they were tried out in the SACHSENHAUSEN camp, the victims being Soviet prisoners of war. The second test was attended by two chemists of the Criminal Identification Institute, Dr. Walter Hees and Dr. Theodor Friedrich Leidig. Leidig gave the following description at a postwar trial in West Germany: "The van was opened; some bodies fell out, others were removed by prisoners. As our chemists had predicted, the bodies had the pinkish tinge typical of victims of carbon monoxide poisoning." Following the successful tryouts, more trucks were fitted with the new apparatus, and by June 23, 1942, twenty such vehicles were in operation, with ten others in various stages of preparation. Some of the trucks, made by the Saurer firm, were larger in size, with a capacity of fifty to sixty people, while others, made by the Diamond Reo firm, had a smaller capacity of twenty-five to thirty people.

The first gas vans were apparently put into use as early as November 1941. According to evidence given by Einsatzgruppen men, a gas van was used in the November 1941 *Aktion* in POLTAVA, in the Ukraine, and one in December 1941 in KHARKOV; also in December 1941, three vans were put into operation in the CHEŁMNO extermination camp. A memorandum submitted to Rauff by Willy Just of the SD, on June 5, 1942, attests to the effectiveness of the vans: "Since December 1941 . . . 97,000 persons have been processed [*bearbeitet*] with the help of three vans, without a single disruption." Some 320,000 persons were killed by this method in the Chełmno camp, most of them Jews.

GAS VANS

Fifteen gas vans were in operation in German-occupied Soviet territory, where the Einsatzgruppen put them at the disposal of their sub-units, the Einsatzkommandos. The commander of the SS and police for REICHSKOMMISSARIAT OSTLAND in Riga had one or two gas vans for use in Latvia and Estonia and in the area between these states and the eastern war front.

Four vans were operated in Belorussia, by the commander of the SD and SICHERHEITSPOLIZEI (Security Police; Sipo) in MINSK and by Einsatzkommandos 6, 7, 8, and 9. From evidence given by the drivers and the SS men who operated the vans it is possible to reconstruct how the killing was carried out and to learn about the victims. As a rule, the gas vans served to empty prisons that had filled up with Jewish prisoners—men, women, and children—most of whom had been caught while trying to hide or escape from *Aktionen.* In Borisov and Minsk the vans were used to kill the workers, most of them Jewish, who were employed by AKTION 1005 units to disinter and burn the corpses of Jews murdered in large-scale operations. Heinze Schlechte, the driver of a gas van that operated in Mogilev, estimated that in his van alone, five thousand to six thousand persons had been killed by the fall of 1942.

In Minsk, the gas vans were used to kill the Jews transported from the Reich and the Protectorate of Bohemia and Moravia, and in October 1943 they were used in the liquidation of the Minsk ghetto. One of the transports, carrying a thousand Jews from THERESIENSTADT, arrived in Minsk while the ghetto was being liquidated; it was diverted to Baranovichi, and two gas vans were dispatched in its wake to kill the Jews in the transport. A local Jewish resident, Dr. Zalman Loewenbuch, who was working in the Baranovichi railway station at the time, gave evidence of what he saw (quoted in the Baranovichi *Memorbuch*): "The trucks had huge doors which sealed hermetically. . . . In Russian the sealed vans were called *dushegubki*—killers of souls."

Einsatzgruppe C, in the Ukraine, had five or six vans at its disposal, two used by Sonderkommando 4a, two by Einsatzkommando 6, one by the SD and Sipo commander in Kiev, and, apparently, one by Sonderkommando 4b. As noted above, two vans were used in Poltava and Kharkov in November and December 1941. Anton Lauer, the commander of a Sonderkommando 4a sub-unit operating in the area, testified at a postwar trial:

> They [the trucks] entered the [Poltava] prison courtyard, and the Jews—men, women, and children—had to enter, straight from the prison cells. I was familiar with the inside of the vans; [it was lined] with aluminum sheets and had a wooden grating on the floor. The exhaust fumes were pumped in . . . the driver started the engine . . . then the doors were shut and the trucks left for a field outside Poltava, where the trucks came to a halt. . . . I saw that, too. . . . When the doors opened, a thick cloud of vapor was emitted, followed by a heap of contorted human bodies. . . . It was a frightful sight.

In late December 1941 and early January 1942, Sonderkommando 4a liquidated the remaining Jews of Kharkov by shooting and gassing them. Some Jews had gone into hiding, and when they were discovered they were taken to the Kharkov prison and then killed in gas vans together with the prisoners. A similar method of killing prisoners was used in Kiev, as recounted by former SS-Oberscharführer Wilhelm Findeisen, the driver of a gas van for Sonderkommando 4a, at a postwar trial: "The truck was loaded in the [Sicherheitsdienst] compound, and forty people were put in—men, women, and children. I had to tell them that they were being taken to work."

In the southern Ukraine, the Crimea, and Ciscaucasia (the Krasnodar and Stavropol territories), three or four gas vans were used by Einsatzgruppe D and its sub-units. By means of the vans, the Simferopol and Kerch prisons were emptied of Jews, the Jews of Sevastopol and Feodosiya were liquidated, the chronically ill and sick Jewish children in the large hospitals of the Kislovodsk and Mineralnye Vody spas were murdered, and the Jews of Piatigorsk and Cherkessk were put to death.

After several months of use in the Soviet Union, the gas vans were found to have technical deficiencies, and problems developed in their operation. In May 1942, Untersturmführer Dr. August Becker of the RSHA was sent on an inspection tour, in the course of which he visited all the Einsatzgruppen units. On his return to Berlin, he submitted a written report to the RSHA in which he singled out two major problems: (1) the mental stress on the SS men who had to unload the vans themselves, since they could not entrust prisoners with the task, lest they flee; and (2) the frequent breakdowns, caused by the poor condition of the Soviet roads. Becker's report was used as an exhibit (PS-500) by the prosecution in the postwar Nuremberg Trials.

Information on the use of gas vans in other places is scanty. One such place was SAJMIŠTE, a concentration camp in Yugoslavia. In March 1942 there were 7,000 prisoners in the camp, mostly Jewish women and children. At the request of the military governor and the SD in Serbia, an Einsatzkommando accompanied by a gas van and two drivers was assigned to the camp, and within a short while all the prisoners were killed. The only exceptions were non-Jewish women married to Jews, and their children. One of these women, a Swiss national named Hedwig Schönfein, gave evidence on these events before a postwar Yugoslav tribunal. When the murder of the Sajmište prisoners was completed, the SS commander, Obersturmbannführer Dr. Emanuel Schäfer, sent the following telegram to Berlin: "The drivers, SS-Scharführers Götz and Mayer, have completed their special assignment [*Sonderauftrag*], and they and the above-mentioned vehicles are therefore free to go back." Gas vans are also known to have been used in LUBLIN, where they were employed from time to time to kill Polish and Jewish inmates of the prison in the Lublin fortress. The vans then went to the MAJDANEK camp, where the corpses were burned in the camp crematorium.

After the war, Otto OHLENDORF, the commander of Einsatzgruppe D, testified at the SUBSEQUENT NUREMBERG PROCEEDINGS (Trial 9, The *Einsatzgruppen* Case, July 3, 1947–April 10, 1948) that Heinrich HIMMLER had given the order to kill Jewish women and children by gassing, and it was for this purpose that the vans were supplied. As it turned out, the gas vans did not meet the expectations that the Nazi leaders had had for them—to be an effective instrument for the trouble-free killing of masses of people. For that purpose, stationary gas chambers using hydrogen cyanide gas (ZYKLON B) proved speedier and more efficient. Still, the total number of victims of the gas vans was approximately 700,000, half of them in the occupied areas of the Soviet Union and the other half in the Chełmno extermination camp.

BIBLIOGRAPHY

Browning, C. R. *Fateful Months: Essays on the Emergence of the Final Solution*. New York, 1985.

Krakowski, S. "In Kulmhof: Stationerte Gaswagen." In *Nationalsozialistische Massentötungen durch Giftgas*, edited by E. Kogon et al., pp. 110–145. Frankfurt, 1983.

Spector, S. "Tötungen in Gaswagen hinter der Front." In *Nationalsozialistische Massentötungen durch Giftgas*, edited by E. Kogon et al., pp. 81–109. Frankfurt, 1983.

SHMUEL SPECTOR

GAULLE, CHARLES DE (1890–1970), French army officer, statesman, and political leader. An expert on intensive armored warfare, which he had anticipated, de Gaulle was one of the few French commanders to gain success against the German attack in the west in May 1940. On June 6, 1940, he was appointed deputy minister of war. Ten days later, de Gaulle was among the first who refused to go along with the surrender to Germany by French prime minister Philippe PÉTAIN. Arriving in London, de Gaulle announced the formation of a Free France Committee and called on French soldiers and civilians, wherever they might be, to join him. He sought to engage French forces in battles for the liberation of French colonies, even when this meant fighting against the French army that had remained loyal to the Vichy regime. This was the case in SYRIA AND LEBANON in June 1941, when the Free French fought alongside the British. On this occasion de Gaulle visited Palestine, from June 13 to 23. In the November 1942 battle for the liberation of North Africa, however, the Allied forces did not inform de Gaulle of their plans, preferring to entrust the civilian administration of Algeria to François DARLAN and the Vichy officials who surrendered to them. The anti-Jewish legislation that the Pétain government had introduced in Algeria remained in force until it was rescinded by de Gaulle in

October 1943, when he overcame his rivals and placed Algeria under Free French control.

In 1943 and 1944 the participation of French forces in the fighting grew increasingly prominent during the campaigns in Italy and France. When Paris was liberated in late August 1944, de Gaulle became premier of the Provisional French government. He abolished all the racial laws and took steps to ensure that the Jews' rights and property were restored. After the war, his efforts to institute a new constitution that would have provided for a presidential form of government failed, and he resigned from the government in 1946.

In May 1958, under the impact of the war in Algeria, de Gaulle returned as premier. This time he won a majority for the creation of a presidential form of government in France. He was elected president under the new constitution, retaining the post until 1969, when he resigned. Before World War II, de Gaulle wrote a book on the art of war; after the war he wrote three volumes of wartime memoirs, *The Call to Honor* (1955), *Unity* (1959), and *Salvation* (1960).

BIBLIOGRAPHY

Abitbol, M. *The Jews of North Africa during the Second World War.* Jerusalem, 1986. (In Hebrew.)

Aron, R. *De Gaulle before Paris: The Liberation of France, June–August, 1944.* London, 1962.

Aron, R. *De Gaulle Triumphant: The Liberation of France, August 1944–May 1945.* London, 1964.

Lacouture, J. *Le rebelle.* Vol. 1 of *Charles de Gaulle.* Paris, 1984.

LUCIEN LAZARE

Gen. Charles de Gaulle, second from right; Prime Minister Winston Churchill; Gen. Władysław Sikorski, second from left, prime minister of the Polish government-in-exile and commander in chief of the Polish armed forces. The photograph was taken somewhere in Great Britain.

GDAŃSK. *See* Danzig.

GEBIRTIG, MORDECAI (pen name of Mordecai Bertig, 1877–1942), Yiddish folk poet. Born in KRAKÓW to a poor family, Gebirtig attended a Jewish school only up to the age of ten. He became a carpenter and plied this trade for the rest of his life, even when he had gained great fame. At an early age he took an interest in theater, poetry, literature, and music, becoming acquainted with Yiddish literature as an amateur actor and through the Jewish workers' movement. In World War I Gebirtig worked as a medical orderly in a Kraków military hospital, where he heard the songs of the many peoples of the Habsburg Empire serving in its army—Czechs, Hungarians, Romanians, Ukrainians, Serbs, and Croatians. Gebirtig could not read music, and the tunes for his poems were composed by others; he wrote the lyrics after first learning the tune.

Gebirtig wrote of the simple Jewish folk, and his talent lay in his ability to give expression to the sentiments felt by the Jewish masses of eastern Europe. His poems, set to music, were performed in theaters, concert halls, and on the radio, and were sung at public meetings, by street singers, and by ordinary Jews. During World War II they were sung in the Kraków and other ghettos and in the concentration camps. In his lifetime Gebirtig wrote about one hundred poems.

Of the poems he wrote during the Holocaust period, fifteen to twenty are known; most of them were published in Kraków in 1946 in a special volume, *S'Brent (1939–1942),* with a foreword by Joseph Wolf. Wolf, who was a member of the Kraków ghetto underground from 1941 to 1943 and was close to Gebirtig, relates that Gebirtig was very pleased to hear from him that "S'Brent" (a poem Gebirtig had written in 1938, under the impact of the pogrom that took place that year in Przytyk) was highly popular with the young people in the ghetto, inspiring them to take up arms against the Nazis and serving as a slogan for their appeals to the Jewish population at large. Other settings for his poems were sung in the Kraków ghetto and also in the Warsaw ghetto theater, as revealed by an exchange of letters between Gebirtig and Diana Blumenfeld, an actress in the Warsaw ghetto. Just as his poems before 1939 had reflected the life of his people, those he wrote during the Nazi regime are a direct expression of pain, despair, hope, anger, and the desire for revenge.

Gebirtig's writings during the war cover three different periods, corresponding to his fate and that of the Jews of Kraków. First was the period from September 5, 1939, to October 24, 1940, which he spent in occupied Kraków. An outstanding example from this period is "S'Tut Vey," a song of rage and anger, in which he indicts the Poles who, despite the bitter fate they shared with the Jews at the hands of the joint Nazi enemy, could not help gloating over the sufferings of the Jews. Other poems from that period express both pain and hope. In the second period, from October 24, 1940 (when he had to flee from Kraków and took refuge in Lagiewniki, a nearby village), until the spring of 1942, Gebirtig wrote poems of revenge, such as "A Tog fun Nekome" (A Day of Revenge), as well as poems of hope and yearning. The third period covers the time Gebirtig spent in the Kraków ghetto, from April 1942 to June 4, 1942, the day he was killed. In that period his songs became somber, dominated by gloom and fear. He was then sixty-five years old, and in these last months of his life his spirits were raised by a report that the fighters of the underground had made "S'Brent" their anthem. In January 1943 or later, after Gebirtig's death, Gusta Dawidson DRAENGER, then in the MONTELUPICH PRISON, translated "S'Brent" into Polish. It became a folk ballad, sung in the ghettos and forests of occupied Poland and, after the war, by Holocaust survivors.

The 1946 Kraków edition of Gebirtig's writings, which contains nearly all his known work from the Holocaust period, cannot be regarded as definitive. The poem "Minuten fun Yiush" (Moments of Despair), which Gebirtig wrote a year after the war had started, was excluded, probably because it expressed the poet's momentary weakening of faith and his heretical thoughts about God.

In 1967, *Ha-Ayara Bo'eret* (The Town Is Burning) was published in Israel, containing a selection of Gebirtig's poems in Yiddish together with Hebrew translations. The book also contains photocopies of Gebirtig's manuscripts of poems from the Holocaust period, as well as an account of the manuscripts' history and how they were saved.

BIBLIOGRAPHY

Bauminger, A. *The Fighters of the Cracow Ghetto.* Jerusalem, 1986.

Kalisch, S. *Yes, We Sang: Songs of the Ghettos and Concentration Camps.* New York, 1985.

Niger, S. "Yiddish Poets of the Third Destruction." *Reconstructionist* 13/10 (June 27, 1947): 13–18.

Rubin, R. "Yiddish Folksongs of World War II: A Record of Suffering and Struggle." *Jewish Quarterly* 11/2 (Summer 1963): 12–17.

YEHIEL SZEINTUCH

GEHEIME STAATSPOLIZEI. *See* Gestapo.

GENDARMERIE, HUNGARIAN, police force, formally known as the Magyar Kiralyi Csendorseg (Royal Hungarian Gendarmerie), employed primarily for the maintenance of law and order in the Hungarian countryside. The gendarmerie was established under a law of February 14, 1881; during World War II it became a major force in protecting the regime against its opponents and implementing anti-Jewish policies. In the summer of 1941, units of the gendarmerie were involved in the roundup and deportation of nearly 18,000 Jews who were not Hungarian citizens. Most of these Jews were subsequently slaughtered near KAMENETS-PODOLSKI. In January and February 1942, gendarmerie units were also involved in the massacre of over 3,300 Serbs and Jews in and around Novi Sad (Hung., Újvidék). After the German occupation of HUNGARY on March 19, 1944, the gendarmerie became the major instrument of state power in the ghettoization and deportation of approximately 440,000 Jews.

The gendarmerie was under the overall command of the *Magyar Kiralyi Csendorseg Felugyeloje* (Superintendent of the Royal Hungarian Gendarmerie), a position that was held in 1944 by Lt. Gen. Gábor Faragho. The three thousand to five thousand gendarmes employed in the anti-Jewish operations served under Lt. Col. László FERENCZY. Ferenczy was nominally the liaison officer in charge of coordinating the operations of the

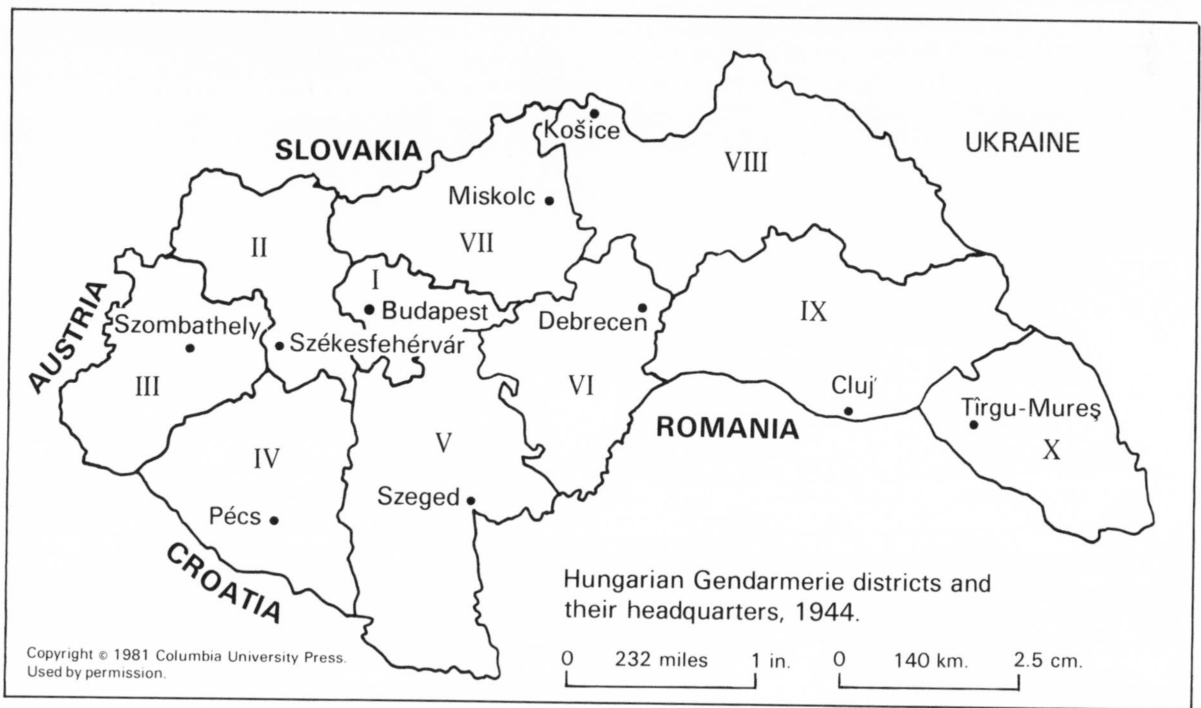

Hungarian Gendarmerie districts and their headquarters, 1944.

The Hungarian Gendarmerie round up the Jews of Bezdan and move them into the ghetto (1944). Bezdan is located 60 miles (96.5 km) northwest of Novi Sad in Yugoslavia, near the present Hungarian-Yugoslav border. During the war Bezdan was in the territory annexed by Hungary.

gendarmerie with the German SD (Sicherheitsdienst; Security Service) and with Adolf EICHMANN's Sonderkommando.

The gendarmerie operated on a territorial basis. There were ten district commands, each headed by a colonel, who played a crucial role in planning and implementing the anti-Jewish policy in the territory under his jurisdiction. The district commanders were actively involved in the conferences organized by the leaders in charge of the "de-Judaizing" process, including Ferenczy, László ENDRE, the representatives of the county and local administration, and the special advisers of the Eichmann Sonderkommando. For purposes of the anti-Jewish drive, Hungary was divided into six operational zones, each zone encompassing one or two Gendarmerie districts.

The ghettoization process began on April 16, 1944, in Zone I, which encompassed Gendarmerie District VIII, covering the areas of the TRANSCARPATHIAN UKRAINE and northeastern Hungary. This was followed by Zone II, encompassing Gendarmerie districts IX and X—the area of northern TRANSYLVANIA. These territories, closest to the eastern front, were inhabited largely by unassimilated Orthodox Jews. The gendarmes played a determining role in all aspects of the ghettoization, concentration, entrainment, and deportation of the Jews. During each of these phases, special investigative units of the gendarmerie were involved in expropriating the property of the Jews. These units were particularly active in the larger ghettos, usually established in the county seats, which also served as entrainment centers.

In each of these entrainment centers, the investigative units set up a *penzverde* ("mint"), a place where Jews were tortured into confessing where they had hidden their alleged valuables. The gendarmes' barbarous behavior during the interrogations as well as during the ghettoization and entrainment of the Jews has been highlighted in countless accounts by survivors. It shocked many decent Hungarians and even some of the Germans involved in the anti-Jewish drive. To ensure the effectiveness of the gendarmes, the "de-Judaizing" command saw to it that the anti-Jewish operations in a particular county were carried out by a gendarmerie unit from another part of the country, in order to prevent possible corruption or leniency based on personal contacts with the local Jews.

The gendarmerie served the pro-Nazi regimes of both Döme SZTÓJAY and Ferenc SZÁLASI until Hungary was liberated by Soviet troops on April 4, 1945. Shortly after the end of the war, the Provisional National Government of Hungary dissolved the gendarmerie by a decree of June 9, 1945, citing its prewar and wartime abuses.

BIBLIOGRAPHY

Braham, R. L. *The Politics of Genocide: The Holocaust in Hungary.* New York, 1981.

Hollos, E. *Rendorseg, csendorseg, VKF 2.* Budapest, 1971.

RANDOLPH L. BRAHAM

GENERALGOUVERNEMENT (General Government), administrative unit established by the Germans on October 26, 1939, comprised of those parts of POLAND that had not been incorporated into the Reich, an area with a total population of twelve million. The full official designation was Generalgouvernement für die Besetzten Polnischen Gebiete (General Government for the Occupied Areas of Poland), and it was only in July 1940 that the shortened name came into use. The Germans had used this name previously, when they occupied Poland in World War I and set up an administration there, also called the Generalgouvernement.

The Generalgouvernement area was divided into four districts, KRAKÓW, WARSAW, RADOM, and LUBLIN, which in turn were split into subdistricts. The administrative center was Kraków. In the summer of 1941, following the German attack on the Soviet Union, Galicia became the fifth district, adding between three million and four million to the population. Only a few Polish institutions were permitted by the Nazis to function, among them the bank that issued the country's currency; the POLNISCHE POLIZEI, or Polish Police, known as Granatowa (Blue), from their dark blue uniforms; and the Central Relief Committee, all of them operating under the strict supervision of the occupation authorities. Heading the Generalgouvernement was the governor-general, Hans FRANK. As of May 1940, Frank operated through the Generalgouvernement administration, headed by Josef Bühler. The SS and police were headed first by SS-Obergruppenführer Friedrich KRÜGER, and then by Wilhelm KOPPE.

The occupation authorities believed that the task of the Polish population of the Generalgouvernement was to obey the Germans and work for them. At first the Poles were regarded as a reservoir of manpower, to be exploited for the needs of the Reich. Later, the Germans considered a number of projects, such as the establishment of colonies, "Germanization," expulsion of the population of ZAMOŚĆ, and identification of those Poles who were *deutschstämmig* (of German origin).

The obedience of the Polish population was attained by extreme terrorization. For every

GENERALGOUVERNEMENT, January 1940

German killed by the underground, fifty to one hundred Poles were executed. Of exceptional cruelty were two terror actions that the Germans carried out. The first was Sonderaktion Krakau (Special Action Kraków) in November 1939, in which 183 staff members of schools and colleges in Kraków were arrested while attending a meeting with the German police. They were deported to SACHSENHAUSEN, from which many never returned. The other action took place in LVOV, where 38 Polish professors were executed shortly after the Wehrmacht entered the city.

The Germans destroyed Polish cultural and scientific institutions, and a large-scale program of plundering artistic and archeological treasures was instituted. In the economic sphere, the Poles were left only with small industries and work on the land. Heavy food quotas were levied on the villages, and trade in foodstuffs was prohibited, so as to restrict the urban population to the starvation diet provided by the food rations. As a result, the Poles engaged in widespread food smuggling.

The Ukrainians in the Generalgouvernement were intended by the Germans to provide a counterweight to the Poles. In contrast to the treatment that the Germans meted out to the population of the REICHSKOMMISSARIAT UKRAINE (Reich Commissariat for the Ukraine), which was exceedingly harsh, the Ukrainians in the Generalgouvernement received concessions and their living conditions even improved, in comparison with the prewar situation.

The Jewish population of the Generalgouvernement, numbering 1.8 million, were the victims of discriminatory decrees. Their property was confiscated, and they were drafted for forced labor. From early 1940, the Jews were imprisoned in ghettos, where they suffered from severe shortages and were isolated from the rest of the world. In the spring of 1942 the Germans began deporting the Jews from the ghettos to extermination camps in the Lublin district, and by 1944 all the ghettos in the Generalgouvernement were liquidated. By early August 1944 a part of the Generalgouvernement—the area between the Vistula and Bug rivers—was liberated by Soviet forces and the Polish National Liberation Council had been formed, with its center in Lublin. The rest of the Generalgouvernement was set free in January 1945, in the course of the Soviet army's winter offensive.

[*See also* Aktion Reinhard.]

BIBLIOGRAPHY

Gross, J. T. *Polish Society under German Occupation: The Generalgouvernement, 1939–1944.* Princeton, 1979.

Madajczyk, C. *Polityka III Rzeszy w okupowanej Polsce.* Warsaw, 1970.

Piotrowski, S. *Hans Frank's Diary.* Warsaw, 1961.

CZESŁAW MADAJCZYK

GENERALPLAN OST (General Plan East), the plans of the Nazis for the territories of eastern Europe. The term is mentioned in mid-1940 in documents of the Stabshauptamt (General Staff Main Office) of the REICHSKOMMISSARIAT FÜR DIE FESTIGUNG DES DEUTSCHEN VOLKSTUMS (Reich Commissariat for the Strengthening of German Nationhood). Shortly after his appointment as head of the planning section in the Stabshauptamt, as well as of the Zentralbodenamt (Central Lands Office), SS-Oberführer Professor Konrad Meyer-Hetling, in July 1941, submitted initial proposals for the settlement and regional planning of Polish territories that had been incorporated into the Reich. Describing these proposals as "preliminary suggestions for *Generalplan Ost*," he addressed them to Heinrich HIMMLER, who headed the Reich Commissariat for the Strengthening of German Nationhood. The final version of the plan was presented by Meyer-Hetling in an exhibition called "Planning and Construction in the East," and in a book of that title, published in Berlin in 1942.

The earliest mention of the Reich's plans for its eastward expansion was made by Reinhard HEYDRICH, in a speech in Prague in October 1941, on the occasion of his appointment as Reich Protector of BOHEMIA AND MORAVIA. The term *Generalplan Ost* as such does not appear in the speech, but its contents forecast the permanent takeover by Germany, in stages, of eastern Europe. Guidelines in this vein were also contained in a memorandum drawn up by Erhard Wetzel, the official in charge of racial policy in the political section of the Reichsministerium für die Besetzten Ostgebiete (Reich Ministry for the Occupied Eastern Territories). In February 1942, Wetzel identified Section III B of the REICHSSICHERHEITSHAUPTAMT (Reich Security Main Office; RSHA) as the source of *Generalplan Ost.* Wetzel had known since November 1941 that the RSHA, which also played a role in the "strengthening of German nationhood," was working on an overall plan for the territories in the east, according to which thirty-one million people were to be settled there. Adolf Hitler envisaged that within ten years, four million Germans would be settled in the east, with the number of such settlers (Germans and "Germanized") rising to ten million at a minimum within twenty years.

Wetzel's memorandum—presented as an "expert opinion"—was highly critical of the RSHA's plans and questioned the expertise of the plan's RSHA author. In his opinion, the figure given by the RSHA for the current population of the territories was too low, the estimate of the human reservoir available for settlement in the east was too optimistic, the racial makeup envisaged was not arrived at scientifically, and the proposal that western Siberia be earmarked for the resettlement of Poles, "who cannot be liquidated like Jews," Ukrainians, and others was against the interests of the Reich. Despite these reservations, however, Wetzel's memorandum supported the aim of *Generalplan Ost,* which was to transform central-eastern Europe into a German colony.

It seems clear that *Generalplan Ost* was formulated in late 1941 and early 1942, that it was considered as reflecting the views of Himmler, and that it was to be implemented after the war over a period of thirty years. The "settlement of the east" was to be carried out by ten million Germans moving there from German territories and from non-German countries in Europe that had a German population. The territories designated for settlement were the occupied areas of POLAND, the Baltic states, BELORUSSIA, the districts of ZHITOMIR and KAMENETS-PODOLSKI, a part of the VINNITSA district of the UKRAINE, the Leningrad district, the Crimea, and parts of the Dnieper basin.

The contemporary population of the areas that were to be resettled by Germans was estimated at 45 million, and the number of Jews among them at 5 million to 6 million. Of the 45 million, 31 million were classified as "racially undesirable" and were to be expelled to western Siberia, and a small number were to be put to work in the administration of the vast expanses of Russia.

According to *Generalplan Ost* as drawn up by the RSHA, 80 percent to 85 percent of the population of Poland, 64 percent of the population of the western Ukraine, and 75 percent of the population of Belorussia were to be expelled and resettled. The rest of the local population was to stay in place; most of them were to be Germanized, or, as Himmler put it, they would "either be absorbed or killed." The RSHA version of *Generalplan Ost* was an elaboration of Hitler's ideas of expelling and resettling elsewhere the population of Polish territories that were incorporated into the Reich.

The Stabshauptamt began active preparations for *Generalplan Ost* in late January of 1942, on Himmler's orders. With Meyer-Hetling in charge, the Stabshauptamt worked out a plan that laid down the legal and economic principles on which the future "reconstruction" of the east was to be based, and included the settlement of the Crimean peninsula. The project was to be completed within twenty-five years after the end of the war. The Polish areas that had been annexed to the Reich were to be completely Germanized; in the rest of Poland and in large parts of the Soviet Union, *Reichsmarken* (points of settlement) and *Siedlungsstutzpunkte* (settlement bridgeheads) were to be established.

In compliance with racist doctrine, priority would be given to agricultural settlement, and the urban population was to be kept at a minimum, especially in the north, where agricultural settlement was to consist of 90 percent to 95 percent of the population. Meyer-Hetling estimated that the costs of the project would amount to 45.7 billion reichsmarks. The funds would be provided by various sources—special tax levies on the conquered countries, credits, and the Reich state budget.

Himmler lost no time in reacting to the plan when it was presented to him. He demanded that the length of time allowed for its implementation be cut down to twenty years, and that Germanization also include the GENERALGOUVERNEMENT, LATVIA, and ESTONIA (for which the original version provided for "settlement points" and "bridgeheads"), in addition to the Polish territories that had been annexed. In September 1942 Himmler made reference in a statement to the establishment of settlement (i.e., colonization) bases as far afield as the Don and the Volga.

In late 1942 Meyer-Hetling followed up by presenting to Himmler an overall detailed plan, including a financial estimate. Again Himmler gave the subject his immediate attention, this time demanding that the area to be colonized in eastern Europe include the Generalgouvernement, the Baltic states, Belorussia, the Crimea (including KHERSON), and the Leningrad district. On Himmler's orders, Meyer-Hetling hastily revised and completed the plan, which now became the *Generalsiedlungsplan*, the master plan for the colonization of the east. In its new version, the area earmarked for settlement by Germans was larger than in the RSHA's version of *Generalplan Ost*.

In early 1943, Section III B of the RSHA arranged for a meeting at which consultations were held on the implementation of Meyer-Hetling's plan and further details that were to be incorporated into it. The area in which the plan was to be realized now comprised 270,000 square miles (700,000 sq km), of which 135,000 square miles (350,000 sq km) was cultivated land; in 1938 the entire area of the Reich was 225,000 square miles (583,000 sq km). Among the subjects that came up at the meeting was the transfer of the existing population in the area earmarked for German settlement: 6 million to 7 million people were to be moved from the Polish area incorporated into the Reich; 10 million from the Generalgouvernement; 3 million from the Baltic states; 6 million to 7 million from the western Ukraine; and 5 million to 6 million from Belorussia.

The Jews were singled out for "total removal" (i.e., extermination). In the first decade of the plan's operation, the "racially undesirable" population was to be removed, presumably to be followed, in the second decade, by the "politically undesirables." The Protectorate of Bohemia and Moravia was not included in the immediate plans of resettlement. After the battle of STALINGRAD, Himmler rapidly lost interest in having a definitive version of the plan drawn up. Also, following his proclamation of total war, Hitler ordered a halt on the planning of all postwar projects.

The work on *Generalplan Ost* and the *Generalsiedlungsplan* coincided with the period when massacres in eastern Europe were at their height, with millions of Soviet prisoners of war and millions of Jews being murdered. In 1941 and 1942 the loss of life in Poland and in the occupied areas of the Soviet Union ran to several million people. In addition, in that period a million Poles and two million Ukrainians were sent to the Reich on FORCED LABOR, and another two million Poles were subjected to forced Germanization in the areas that had become part of the Reich; in other occupied areas similar plans were in preparation. At this time the German authorities also embarked upon the settlement of Germans in several of the areas designated for that purpose in *Generalplan Ost*, encountering some resistance in that operation or running into difficulties arising out of the military situation. About thirty thousand German repatriates from Lithuania who had been waiting to be resettled in the Polish areas annexed to the Reich were directed to the southwestern part of Lithuania.

Between November 1942 and August 1943, Poles living in the southeastern part of the Lublin district (the so-called ZAMOŚĆ region) were expelled from their homes and replaced by Germans. This area was being prepared for complete or partial settlement by Germans, and was part of the territories that under *Generalplan Ost* were to be totally Germanized, resettled, or used for the establishment of colonization bases.

Germany was able to carry out, almost in full, the "Final Solution"—the murder of the Jews, whom the Nazis regarded as their main racial enemy. This operation cost the lives of millions of people. *Generalplan Ost* demonstrates that there were other plans based on racism that while not calling for extermination, provided for the expulsion of many populations, especially Slavs. These racist-motivated plans were only begun, and were to be fully executed after the Germans had won the war.

BIBLIOGRAPHY

Koehl, R. L. *RKFDV: German Resettlement and Population Policy, 1939–1945: A History of the Reich Commission for the Strengthening of Germandom.* Cambridge, Mass., 1957.

Madajczyk, C. "Generalplan Ost." *Polish Western Affairs* 3/2 (1962): 1–54.

CZESŁAW MADAJCZYK

GENOCIDE (from Greek *genos,* "race," and Latin *caedes,* "killing"), liquidation of a people. The term "genocide" was first introduced by Raphael LEMKIN, a Jewish jurist, who used it at a 1933 conference of jurists in Madrid and further defined and analyzed it in books that he wrote during World War II. On December 9, 1948, the United Nations General Assembly adopted a convention for "the prevention of genocide and the punishment of the organizers thereof."

The term, now widely used in legislation, international conventions, legal judgments, and scientific and general literature, is generally applied to the murder of human beings by reason of their belonging to a specific racial, ethnic, or religious group, unrelated to any individual crime on the part of such persons, the intention of the murderer or murderers being to cause grievous harm and destroy the specific group per se.

Lemkin pointed out that the crime of genocide need not mean the immediate and total destruction of the group; it may also consist of a series of planned actions designed to destroy basic components of the group's existence, such as its national consciousness, its language and culture, its economic infrastructures, and the freedom of the individual.

The United Nations Genocide Convention specifically mentions the following actions, which, when carried out against a national, ethnic, racial, or religious group in order to destroy that group, in full or in part, come under the rubric of genocide:

1. Killing persons belonging to the group
2. Causing grievous bodily or spiritual harm to members of the group
3. Deliberately enforcing upon the group living conditions which could lead to its complete or partial extermination
4. Enforcing measures designed to prevent births among the group
5. Forcibly removing children from the group and transferring them to another group

As indicated by this list of crimes, a close link exists between them and many of the crimes that the International Military Tribunal (IMT) at Nuremberg was empowered to deal with and that were defined as "CRIMES AGAINST HUMANITY." These crimes included murder, cruel treatment, and persecution on racial and ethnic grounds that were not directed against individuals or groups of individuals as such, but rather had the purpose of destroying the very existence of the group or groups to which the victims belonged. The IMT did not seek to determine the guilt of the accused brought before it for the crime of genocide, since that crime was not listed in the London Agreement under which the IMT was established, but the charge of genocide was included in the SUBSEQUENT NUREMBERG PROCEEDINGS and in several of the trials of Nazi criminals held in Poland. Among these were the trial of Amon GOETH, the liquidator of the Kraków and Tarnów ghettos and a commandant of the PŁASZÓW camp; and the case of Rudolf HÖSS, the commandant of AUSCHWITZ-Birkenau. In its verdict against Arthur GREISER, announced on July 9, 1946, a Polish court defined several of the crimes committed by the defendant against the Polish people as "genocide." These included:

1. Placing Poles in a special unlawful category with regard to rights of possession, employment, education, and the use of their native tongue, and applying a special criminal code to them
2. Religious persecution, having the characteristics of genocide, of the local population, by mass murder and the imprisonment of Polish clergy (including bishops) in concentration camps; reduction of the availability of religious facilities to a bare minimum; and destruction of churches, cemeteries, and church- owned buildings

3. Genocide-like actions against cultural and educational treasures and institutions
4. Humiliating the Polish people by treating them as second-rate citizens, and differentiating between the Germans as the "master race" and the Poles as the "servant race"

That court also found, on the basis of the evidence submitted to it, that the defendant had ordered or cooperated in actions designed to cause criminal harm to the lives, well-being, and property of thousands of Polish residents of the occupied area and had made it his objective to carry out a total genocide-like attack on the rights of small- and medium-sized ethnic populations, on their national identity and culture, and on their very existence.

The government of Israel joined the Convention on the Prevention and Punishment of Genocide, and on the basis of that convention enacted, in 1950, the Genocide Prevention and Punishment Law 5710-1950; the definition of genocide in that law follows that of the United Nations Genocide Convention. Israeli legislation also used that definition in another law, the Nazis and Nazi Collaborators (Punishment) Law 5710-1950. That law, first used against a Nazi criminal in the EICHMANN TRIAL, contains the definitions of crimes against humanity and war crimes as laid down in the London Agreement on the establishment of the International Military Tribunal, and it also contains the definition of "Crimes against the Jewish People." The latter is defined as applying to any one of the following actions, carried out with the intent of exterminating the Jewish people, totally or partially:

1. Killing Jews
2. Causing grievous bodily or mental harm to Jews
3. Placing Jews in living conditions calculated to bring about their physical destruction
4. Imposing measures intended to prevent births among Jews
5. Forcibly transferring Jewish children to another national or religious group
6. Destroying or desecrating Jewish religious or cultural assets or values
7. Inciting to hatred of Jews

Like the Polish definition in the Greiser case, and in other cases, the Israeli law mentions the concept of cultural genocide, but in the main it refers to the special form of crimes against humanity as contained in the NUREMBERG LAWS, and particularly to the specific form in which genocide was in fact carried out, especially against the Jewish people. The crime against the Jewish people was a crime against that people only, since it was committed against Jews only, and is *sui generis*. Nevertheless, in formal legal, as well as in social, terms, and in its political and moral aspects, the crimes against the Jewish people were also crimes against the principles of humanity and an offense against the whole of mankind, by seeking to remove from its midst one of its component parts.

The experts on the subject all agree that genocide is a component of the Holocaust, but it has been contended that the Nazi crime against the Jewish people was unique and extended far beyond genocide, by virtue of the planning that it entailed, the task forces allocated to it, the killing installations set up for it, and the way the Jews were rounded up and brought to extermination sites by force and by stealth; and above all, because of the stigma and charge of collective guilt with which the Jews as a whole were branded—of being a gang of conspirators and pests whose physical destruction must be carried out for the sake of society's rehabilitation and the future of mankind.

On November 4, 1988, President Ronald Reagan signed legislation that enabled the United States to become the ninety-eighth nation to ratify the United Nations Genocide Convention.

[*See also* "Final Solution"; Racism.]

BIBLIOGRAPHY

Bauer, Y. "Whose Holocaust?" In *Confronting History and Holocaust: Collected Essays, 1972–1982*, edited by J. N. Porter, pp. 35–45. Washington, D.C., 1983.

Harf, B. *Genocide and Human Rights: International Legal and Political Issues*. Denver, 1984.

Lemkin, R. *Axis Rule in Occupied Europe: Laws of Occupation, Analysis of Government, Proposals for Redress*. Washington, D.C., 1944.

Robinson, N. *The Genocide Convention.* New York, 1949.

MARIAN MUSHKAT

GENS, JACOB (1905–1943), head of the JUDENRAT (Jewish Council) in the VILNA ghetto. Gens was born in Illovieciai, a village in the Šiauliai district of LITHUANIA. In 1919, when Lithuania was fighting for its independence, he volunteered for the Lithuanian army. Sent to an officers' training course, he graduated as a second lieutenant, and was sent to the front to join the fight against Poles. He served in the army until 1924. (In the late 1930s, as an officer in the reserves, he was sent to a staff officers' course and promoted to captain.) In 1924 Gens enrolled in Kovno University, earning his living as a teacher of Lithuanian and of physical education in the Jewish schools of Ukmerge and Jurbarkas. Three years later, he became an accountant in the Ministry of Justice in Kovno. He completed his university studies in law and economics in 1935.

In July 1940, when Lithuania became a Soviet republic, Gens was dismissed from his post. A Zionist who was close to the Revisionists, Gens feared that he was in danger of being arrested in a campaign that was being waged against anti-Soviet elements, and he moved to Vilna, where he was not known. A Lithuanian friend who headed the municipal health department there helped him obtain work as an accountant in the department.

When the Germans occupied Vilna in late June 1941, his Lithuanian friend appointed Gens director of the Jewish hospital. At the beginning of September, when a ghetto was set up in Vilna, Anatol Fried, chairman of the Judenrat, who had become acquainted with Gens as a patient in the Jewish hospital, appointed Gens commander of the ghetto police. Gens set up the police force, organized it, and made it into an orderly and disciplined body. The Jewish police were assigned a role in the *Aktionen* that were conducted in the ghetto from September to December 1941, in which tens of thousands of Jews were killed. According to most of the evidence available, Gens, within the framework of his job, did his best to help the Jews. He became the predominant personality in the ghetto and its de facto governor. His direct contact with the German authorities, bypassing the Judenrat, added to his prestige among the Jews in the ghetto. Gens involved himself in affairs that had nothing to do with the police: employment, cultural activities, and other aspects of ghetto life.

In July 1942 the Germans dismissed the Judenrat and appointed Gens head of the ghetto administration and sole representative of the ghetto (*Ghettovorsteher*), thereby making official his de facto position. Gens promoted the idea of "work for life," meaning that the survival of the ghetto Jews depended on their work and productivity. He believed that efforts had to be made to gain time and keep the ghetto in existence until Germany was defeated in the war, and that this could be achieved by working for the

Jacob Gens.

Germans. He constantly sought to increase the number of Jews in such positions. In the last few months of the ghetto's existence, 14,000 out of the total ghetto population of 20,000 were employed inside or outside the ghetto. On one occasion, Gens was ordered by the Germans to send the Vilna ghetto police to the Oshmiany ghetto, to carry out a *Selektion* there and to hand over 1,500 children and women who were not employed. Instead, Gens delivered to the Germans 406 persons who were chronically ill or old. He justified this action to the Jews by claiming that if the Germans and the Lithuanians had done the selecting, they would have taken the children and the women, whom he wanted to keep alive for the sake of the future of the Jewish people.

Gens's attitude toward the ghetto underground was ambivalent. On the one hand, he maintained contact with the underground leaders and declared that when the day of the ghetto's liquidation arrived, he would join them in an uprising; but on the other hand, when the underground's activities endangered the continued existence of the ghetto, he opposed it, and he complied with a German demand to hand over to them the underground commander, Yitzhak WITTENBERG.

Once the process of liquidating the ghetto had been set in motion, in August and September 1943, Gens knew that his life was in danger. His Lithuanian wife and his daughter were both in Vilna, where they lived outside the ghetto. He had several offers from his Lithuanian relatives and friends to leave the ghetto and take refuge with them, but he refused, believing that in his role he was engaged in a mission on behalf of the Jewish people. On September 14, 1943, nine days before the final liquidation of the ghetto, Gens was summoned to the Gestapo. The previous day, he had been warned that the Germans were planning to kill him, and had been urged to flee. He replied that his escape would mean disaster for the Jews who remained in the ghetto.

Gens reported to the Gestapo on September 14, and at 6:00 p.m. he was shot to death in the Gestapo courtyard. News of his death reached the ghetto at once, and the Jews who were still alive mourned his passing. Gens's belief that if the ghetto were productive its Jews would be saved proved baseless; but under the terrible conditions prevailing at the time, he did his best, as he understood it, to save as many as possible.

BIBLIOGRAPHY

Arad, Y. *Ghetto in Flames: The Struggle and Destruction of the Jews of Vilna in the Holocaust.* Jerusalem, 1980.

Dworzecki, M. *Jerusalem of Lithuania in Revolt and Holocaust.* Tel Aviv, 1951. (In Hebrew.)

Friedman, P. *Roads to Extinction: Essays on the Holocaust.* Philadelphia, 1980. See chapter 14.

Korchak, R. *Flames in Ash.* Merhavia, Israel, 1946. (In Hebrew.)

YITZHAK ARAD

GEPNER, ABRAHAM (1872–1943), businessman and public figure; member of the WARSAW ghetto JUDENRAT (Jewish Council). Gepner was born in Warsaw, into a poor family; his father died when Abraham was still a boy, and his studies had to be cut short. Owing to his drive and diligence, he rose from errand boy to become the owner of a trading firm and a number of factories in the metals industry in Poland, with far-flung international ties.

Gepner was a fervent Polish patriot and in his youth was inclined to join the assimilationists. In 1912, when the Polish nationalists declared an economic boycott of the Jews, Gepner abandoned assimilation and became active in the Jewish community. For many years he played a leading role in the Association of Jewish Businessmen in Poland, serving as its chairman from 1935 to 1939. He was a member of the Warsaw city council, and became known for his generous support of orphanages and vocational training institutions and for his efforts to raise productivity. Gepner was known for his austere private life; he set himself the rule of tithing, contributing a tenth of all his income to charity and welfare.

When World War II broke out, Gepner was sixty-seven years old. He and Samuel ZYGELBOJM were the two Jews among the twelve hostages whom the Germans seized in Warsaw when they captured the city in October 1939. Gepner was a member of the Judenrat

Abraham Gepner.

from its inception and was close to Adam CZERNIAKÓW, the Judenrat chairman. From the beginning, Gepner assisted in organizing Jewish self-help, and when the ghetto was set up in November 1940, he was appointed head of the supply department (Zakład Zaopatrywania). This department had the task of supplying food and other essential items to the ghetto—under the prevailing conditions, a most delicate and responsible task. Gepner was not able to prevent hunger and mass deaths from starvation, but he had the ghetto population's confidence, and his organization was efficient (in relative terms); as a result, the supply organization was the target of far less criticism than the other Judenrat departments.

In the ghetto, too, Gepner was involved in aid and welfare; his main concern was children, and especially orphans. Early in the ghetto's existence, Gepner established contact with the Jewish political underground, lent support to the clandestine pioneer movements, and kept track of the latter's activities. He was in favor of youth movements and aided them even after the ŻYDOWSKA ORGANIZACJA BOJOWA (Jewish Fighting Organization; ŻOB) was established and preparations were under way for the ghetto uprising.

When the revolt broke out, on April 19, 1943, Gepner at first refused to take refuge in a bunker, but he gave in to his friends' appeals and together with his family went into the bunker of 30 Franciszkanska Street, where the staff of the supply department had gathered in the last days of the ghetto's life. On May 3 the Germans dragged Gepner, together with many others, out of the bunker and killed him. A letter he wrote on January 1, 1943, contains the following passage: "I have no regrets about staying in the ghetto, nor about any of the decisions that I made. Recently I reached the age of seventy, and remaining in the ghetto, together with my brothers and sisters, I regard as the most important step I took in my life. If I have succeeded in drying a single tear—that is my reward. I have a daughter living in the United States. Tell her that I served my people faithfully."

BIBLIOGRAPHY

Ringelblum, E. *Notes from the Warsaw Ghetto.* New York, 1974.

ISRAEL GUTMAN

GERMAN ARMAMENT WORKS. *See* Deutsche Ausrüstungswerke.

GERMAN VANGUARD, GERMAN JEWISH ADHERENTS. *See* Deutscher Vortrupp, Gefolgschaft Deutscher Juden.

GERMANY. The first few Jews to arrive in Germany came there in the wake of the Roman legions and settled in the cities along the Rhine. The earliest documents attesting to a sizable Jewish population are imperial edicts, dating back to A.D. 321 and 331, concerning the city Colonia Agrippensis (Cologne). There is no clear evidence, however, of an uninterrupted presence of a Jewish population in Germany after the Roman empire came to an end, and it is only from the tenth century, when Jewish merchants from Italy and France settled in Germany, that a continuous history of Jews in Germany is certain.

By the late Middle Ages the Jewish population of Germany was consolidated. The German Jewish community became one of the centers of spiritual creativity among European Jewry, and the cradle of Ashkenazic Jewry and the Yiddish language. In the economic sphere the Jews gained prominence in commerce (including trade with Near Eastern countries) and later primarily as moneylenders. This period, however, witnessed widespread persecution of Jews and, on occasion, the destruction, in various parts of Germany, of entire Jewish communities. The persecution of Jews, in most cases, was set against a background of religious and social ferment and political upheaval. The worst persecutions took place during the Crusades (especially the first Crusade, in 1096) and during the period of the Black Death (1348–1349). From the fifteenth century, and especially during the Reformation, the status of the Jews and of the role they played deteriorated, and they were expelled from most of the large German cities. Some of those expelled remained in Germany, taking up residence in hundreds of small communities, while others migrated to the newly emerging centers of Jewish population in the countries of eastern Europe. In the Age of Absolutism the situation of Jews improved, one of the reasons being the status and activities of the "court Jews" (*Hofjuden*), who were instrumental in enabling Jews to resettle in the large cities.

The economic rise of an elite Jewish group and the penetration into late eighteenth-century Jewish society of the ideas of the Enlightenment marked the beginning of the process of the social and political emancipation of the Jews, the struggle for which was waged throughout the nineteenth century and reached its goal, in formal terms, when Germany was unified in 1871. The drawn-out struggle for emancipation, and the new ideological trends that had emerged among German Jewry since the Haskalah (the Jewish Enlightenment movement) in the eighteenth century, had a very significant impact on Jewish communities in other parts of Europe and overseas. Among the important transformations that took place in German Jewry in the nineteenth century and that affected Judaism as a whole were the rise of the *Wissenschaft des Judentums* (the modern scholarly study of Judaism and Jewish history); the growth of new religious movements in Judaism—Reform, Conservative, and Neo-Orthodox; the rapid urbanization of the Jews; and their integration into modern society and economic life. In the nineteenth century the Jews of Germany made important contributions to cultural life, to social and political philosophy, to the economy, and even to political life. Among outstanding Jews were the poet Heinrich Heine; the fathers of socialism, Ferdinand Lasalle and Karl Marx; the bankers of the Rothschild and Bleichröder families; and the leaders of the National Liberal party, Eduard Lasker and Ludwig Bamberger.

The emancipation of the Jews, however, and their integration into the various spheres of German life, met with resistance from a sizable part of German society. By the 1870s this opposition led to politically organized ANTISEMITISM—which in its modern form also had RACISM as a basic ingredient. In the following two decades antisemitic political parties ran in elections and scored successes. The influence of these parties waned toward the end of the nineteenth century, but antisemitism continued to flourish in economic, social, and academic organizations. It also penetrated the major political parties in various ways and became a factor in the struggle between the national conservative and democratic socialist camps over the future political character of German society.

The rise of modern antisemitism, in addition to other factors, led to the establishment of political organizations among German Jewry in Imperial Germany. The most important organization established in this period (in 1893) for the defense of the Jews' civil rights was the CENTRALVEREIN DEUTSCHER STAATSBÜRGER JÜDISCHEN GLAUBENS (Central Union of German Citizens of Jewish Faith). It had been preceded by the non-Jewish Verein zur Abwehr des Antisemitismus (Association for Combating Antisemitism), founded in 1890. Also in the 1890s, during the Jewish national renaissance movement, the German Zionist Organization was formed. Before long, its leaders, including David Wolffsohn, Otto Warburg, Arthur Ruppin, and Max Bodenheimer, assumed leading posts in the World Zionist Organization. From the death of Theodor Herzl up to the end of World War I, the organizational center of the Zionist movement was located in Germany.

During World War I, antisemitism was again on the rise. Its most humiliating manifestation was the German High Command's decision in 1916, in response to the demand of certain sectors of public opinion, to take a special census of Jewish soldiers to determine whether the number of Jews serving in the armed forces, and especially the number in combat units, was in proportion to their percentage of the general population. The results of that census were not published.

Weimar Republic, 1918–1933. A new era in the history of German Jewry began when Imperial Germany collapsed and was replaced by the democratic regime of the Weimar Republic. The outstanding feature of this period was the polarization between the unprecedented integration of the Jews in every sphere of life, and the growth of political antisemitism among various organizations and political parties, especially in the immediate postwar years.

Important achievements by Jews were recorded in the theater (Max Reinhardt), in music (Arnold Schönberg), in the visual arts (Max Liebermann), in philosophy (Herman Cohen), and in science (Albert EINSTEIN). Among the Nobel prize winners in Germany up to 1938, 24 percent were Jews (nine Jews out of a total of thirty-eight). It was in political and public life, however, that the Jewish role was most prominent. Jews played an important role in the first cabinet formed after the 1918 revolution (Hugo Haase and Otto Landsberg), the Weimar Constitution was drafted by a Jew (Hugo Preuss), and Jews were conspicuously present in the abortive attempts to create radical revolutionary regimes, especially in Bavaria. The revolutionary government in Munich was headed by a Jewish intellectual, Kurt Eisner, and after his assassination, two other Jewish leaders, Gustav Landauer and Eugen Levine, assumed positions of major influence in the "Räterepublik" ("Soviet" Republic). Rosa Luxemburg, who was also assassinated, was a leader of the revolutionary Spartakusbund, which was one of the predecessors of the German Communist party.

In the following years as well, Jews held

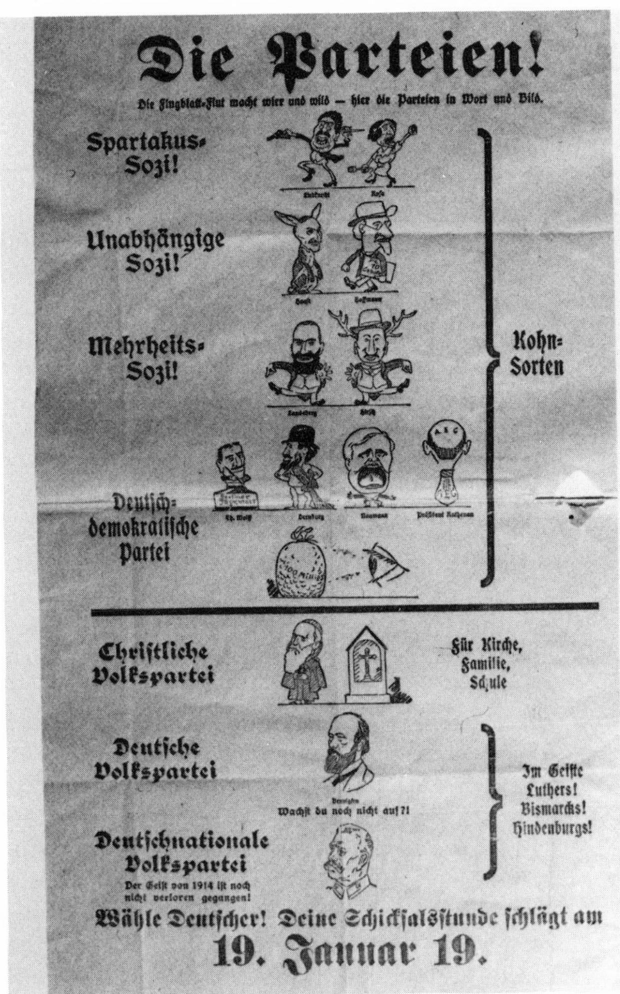

Political poster, Weimar Germany. [A Living Memorial to the Holocaust—Museum of Jewish Heritage, New York]

major political posts, primarily in the leadership of the democratic and socialist parties. The most prominent Jewish political figure was Walther RATHENAU, who served first as minister for economic affairs and then as foreign minister. Rathenau's murder by right-wing radicals in June 1922 was one of the dramatic high points of the antisemitic incitement that charged the Jews with responsibility for Germany's defeat in the war (the DOLCHSTOSSLEGENDE, or "stab-in-the-back" myth) and for the economic and social crises that struck the newly born republic after the war, reaching their climax in the terrible inflation of 1922 and 1923. The presence of Jews from eastern Europe (*Ostjuden*), who had immigrated to Germany before, during, and after the war, was also a favorite subject of antisemitic incitement.

Among the antisemitic movements and political parties, the most radical was the relatively small National Socialist party, which had been founded in Bavaria in 1919. Its platform included conspicuous paragraphs calling for the abolition of civil rights for Jews and far-reaching measures for eliminating Jews from various spheres of life. The propaganda speeches and publications of the party's leaders, especially those of Adolf HITLER, presented a radical antisemitic ideology that did not stop short of demands for the "total elimination of the Jews" and called for the *Ausrottung* ("extermination") of the Jews *mit Stumpf und Stiel* ("root and branch"). Despite the party's nationalist character, the antisemitism it advocated went beyond the confines of national categories, its ideology demanding a radical solution of the "Jewish question" in order to save all of human society. The National Socialist racial doctrine, which was based on the inequality of races and a Social Darwinist struggle for survival among them, regarded the Jews as a biological source of ideologies (including Marxism, democracy, and even Christianity) that defy the "natural order." As a result of the stabilization of the German economy and of the republic in 1924, the strength of the antisemitic parties went into a temporary decline and the number of their members in the Reichstag dropped from forty to fourteen.

According to the 1925 census, the Jewish population of Germany was 564,379, representing 0.9 percent of the total population. The great majority (377,000, or 66.8 percent) lived in six large cities, which also had the largest Jewish communities: BERLIN (with 180,000 Jews, a third of the entire Jewish population in the country), FRANKFURT, HAMBURG, Breslau, Leipzig, and Cologne. Approximately 90,000 Jews (16 percent) lived in the smaller cities, and 97,000 (17.2 percent) in over a thousand towns and villages with a population of less than 10,000. For the most part the Jews belonged to the middle class and were self-employed, in various branches of business and in the professions. The Jews' intensive participation in the life of German society accelerated the process of assimilation, which was manifested in the growing number of mixed marriages, secessions from the organized Jewish community, and conversions to Christianity. Thus, in 1927, 54 percent of all marriages of Jews were contracted with non-Jews, and in that year one thousand Jews are estimated to have opted out of Judaism, about half of them by conversion to another faith.

On the other hand, in the Weimar era the activities of the Jewish political, religious, and social organizations were maintained and even expanded. New organizations were added to the Centralverein, the Zionist Federation, the Orthodox and Liberal organizations, and the HILFSVEREIN DER DEUTSCHEN JUDEN (German Jews' Aid Society), which all had their beginnings before Weimar. The major new organizations were the REICHSBUND JÜDISCHER FRONTSOLDATEN (Reich Union of Jewish Frontline Soldiers); left- and right-wing Zionist parties such as the Jüdische Volkspartei, or Jewish People's Party; youth and sports organizations; student groups; and so forth. The Jewish communities retained the officially recognized legal status they had attained under the Kaiser; the innovations in the Weimar era were the establishment of Landesverbände Jüdischer Gemeinden (State Unions of Jewish Communities) and attempts to organize all of German Jewry into a nationwide body.

Religious and general Jewish studies taught in the rabbinical seminaries in Berlin and Breslau (founded in the nineteenth century) were broadened and intensified under the impact of the encounter with east European Jews and their culture. In fact, the influx of Jewish scholars and intellectuals from eastern Europe, coupled with the revival of Jewish consciousness among the established Jewish population, turned Germany in that period into a great center of modern Jewish scholarship and culture. As a result of efforts of Jewish thinkers and educators—men like Franz Rosenzweig and Martin Buber—large groups among the general Jewish population began to take an interest in Jewish learning, leading to the establishment of *jüdische Lehrhäuser* (institutes of Jewish learning) for adult Jewish education. A wide range of Jewish periodicals and Jewish publishing houses played an important role in Jewish life; two of the significant publishing projects undertaken were the five-volume *Jüdisches Lexikon* and the *Encyclopaedia Judaica* (of which ten volumes had appeared when its publication came to a halt in 1934).

The final years of the Weimar Republic, during which Germany was hard hit by the global economic crisis, were marked by the rise of the National Socialist party. Just before the crisis broke out, in 1928, the Nazis won only 3 percent of the vote; however, in the first elections that took place during the crisis, in September 1930, their share jumped to 18 percent, and in July 1932 to 37 percent of the vote. With 230 members in the Reichstag, the Nazis became the largest party—and retained that position in the next elections, in November 1932, despite a drop to 33 percent of the vote and 196 Reichstag members.

During those years, antisemitism came to have a profound effect on Jewish life. It was one of the central elements in the Nazi party's violent struggle for power, and its effect on the Jews was not confined to physical violence (desecrations of synagogues and Jewish cemeteries, and even attacks on individual Jews). Nazi political propaganda succeeded in making the "Jewish question" into a major issue in the Nazi struggle against the democratic regime. As a result, not only was the position of the Jews in German society impaired, but the Jews themselves underwent a crisis of Jewish consciousness and began to reexamine their Jewish identity.

From 1933 to 1938. In January 1933, on the eve of Hitler's rise to power, the Jewish population of Germany (including the Saar district, which two years later was reincorporated into Germany) numbered 522,000 Jews by religion; under the racist criteria established by the Nazis, which were to form the basis of their persecution of the Jews and to find formal expression in racist legislation, the number of Jews by race was 566,000.

On January 30, President Paul von HINDENBURG appointed Hitler Reich chancellor. This appointment was the outcome of a continuous economic and parliamentary crisis in which the democratic system of government became an authoritarian regime, on the basis of the emergency powers granted to the president by the constitution. As soon as Hitler was appointed, the National Socialist party and its paramilitary organizations—primarily the SA (Sturmabteilung; Storm Troopers) and the SS—launched a drive to seize, by violent means where necessary, all government and public institutions and to transform Germany into a totalitarian state. In the ensuing terrorist actions (as early as February and March 1933) against opponents of National Socialism, especially members of the Left political parties, liberals, and intellectuals, the Jews were a major target. Many Jews were subjected to public humiliation and were arrested; others were forced to quit their posts, especially at the universities and the law courts. Before 1933, the Nazis had called for the plundering of Jewish property and for a boycott of Jewish businesses and services; this was now adopted as the official policy of the ruling party. A climax was reached with the Anti-Jewish BOYCOTT of April 1, 1933, the first occasion on which the new regime openly took discriminatory action against a part of the country's citizens. It caused a deep shock to Germany's Jews and evoked a sharply hostile reaction from world public opinion.

The boycott was brought to a halt after a day had passed, but from April 7, anti-Jewish laws were enacted that in effect abolished the principle of equal rights for Jews, rights that had been established by the German constitution in 1871. The legal basis for these measures was the *Ermächtigungsgesetz* (Enabling Law), passed on March 24, 1933, which gave the government dictatorial powers first for a four-year period and subsequently for the life span of the Third Reich. The regime used this emergency law to abolish the democratic freedoms that had been in force under the republic and brought about the dissolution of Germany's independent political parties and organizations. The process of totalitarian *Gleichschaltung* ("coordination," that is, Nazification) led to the reorganization of all spheres of public and official life, including control of the media and all forms of publication, and a thorough and far-reaching purge of the civil and public service. In the March 5 elections, which nominally were still democratic and were held before the Enabling Law was passed, the Nazis received only 44 percent of the vote, as against the more than

90 percent support they achieved in the November 1933 referendum and later.

Anti-Jewish policy was put into effect on two parallel levels: by means of laws, decrees, and administrative terror; and by "spontaneous" acts of terror and incitement of the population to hostility against the Jews. The early anti-Jewish laws included the Law for the Restoration of the Professional Civil Service. The racist basis of that law was expressed by the ARIERPARAGRAPH ("Aryan Paragraph"), which became the foundation for all anti-Jewish legislation passed before the enactment of the NUREMBERG LAWS in the fall of 1935. Other laws passed at that stage restricted the practice of law and medicine by Jews; a special law mandated that the number of Jews in an educational institution must not exceed that proportional to their percentage of the population; and Jews were excluded from cultural life and journalism. The only exception to these laws applied to Jews who had served as frontline soldiers in World War I.

The main purpose of the legislation was to give formal expression to the ideology and policy of discrimination against and persecution of the Jews, but it was also meant to serve as a means of restraining "spontaneous" terror and stabilizing the status of the Jews in the National Socialist state. In particular, it was the conservative elements in the government coalition who in the second half of 1933 advocated such "stabilization," out of concern for the country's international standing and the adverse effect that unrestrained Nazi action against the Jews could have on efforts to restore the country's economy. Among the officials who warned of the impact that a foreign economic boycott might have on Germany was Hjalmar SCHACHT, head of the Reichsbank, and Foreign Minister Konstantin von NEURATH. Hitler spoke in a similar vein in July 1933, when he called for a curb on the revolutionary zeal and the need to direct it into channels designed to consolidate the foundations of the new regime.

The methods employed in the regime's terror campaign against its opponents consisted mostly of arrest and imprisonment in concentration camps. The percentage of Jews among the detainees was quite high, and they were singled out for particularly cruel and humiliating treatment, which in many instances resulted in death. Shocked by such terrorization and the overall onslaught on their position in the country, many Jews reacted with headlong flight, a wave of emigration that encompassed thousands of people. According to the census taken in June 1933, the Jewish population in Germany was 502,799 (by religion) or 540,000 (by race); these figures show that since January of that year about 26,000 Jews "by race" had left the country. By the end of 1933, 63,000 Jews had emigrated, according to retrospective statistics compiled in 1941 by the Reichsvereinigung der Juden in Deutschland (Reich Association of Jews in Germany).

Support of the German people for the regime's policy against the Jews was not uniform, and while there was broad recognition of the need to find a "solution" to the "Jewish question," there were also reservations about the violent methods being applied, as well as individual cases of solidarity with the Jews. However, few public protests were made by the leadership of institutions that were still relatively independent, such as the Protestant and Catholic churches; the objections raised to the persecution of the Jews referred primarily to the thousands of Christians of Jewish origin who were affected by the racist legislation.

Among the Jews, the reaction to what was happening was different on the individual and the organizational level. Although the Jews' social and political status had suffered a tremendous blow, their existing organizational network was scarcely touched—indeed, new organizations came into being. In this respect the situation of the Jews was in stark contrast to the prevailing trend of totalitarian *Gleichschaltung*, the purpose of which was to destroy the existing social and political fabric of German society and construct a homogeneous national society in its place. It was the exclusionary racist principle on which the policy toward the Jews was based—their separation and isolation from the general society—that made possible the continuing existence of the Jews' own institutions. Moreover, "alien" and "decadent" ideas and principles such as political pluralism and democracy, which were now beyond the pale among the general population, were still the rule in Jewish public life. This was, however, the freedom of the outcast, of a community that now seemed doomed to disappearance (at this stage of the Nazi regime) through emigration.

The mass emigration and the large number of suicides were manifestations of the crisis experienced by German Jewry as it saw the fundamental premises on which its existence had been based collapsing. At the same time, the organizational structure of German Jewry adapted itself to the changing conditions, and even intensified its varied internal activities. Prior to 1933 the Jewish communities had been entities recognized by public law—a status they retained under the Nazis, in that early stage—but no nationwide organization of communities of similar status had come into being. In 1932 a beginning was made with the formation of a loose national federation of existing Landesverbände (State Unions) of communities, which in the Third Reich made its first public appearance with a memorandum it published in May 1933. It was only in September of that year, however, that a truly representative and comprehensive national organization was established, which, in addition to the Landesverbände, included the major political bodies and the large communities. This was the REICHSVERTRETUNG DER DEUTSCHEN JUDEN (Reich Representation of German Jews), under the leadership of Rabbi Leo BAECK and Otto HIRSCH. Its major operational instrument was the Zentralausschuss, which had been formed even before the Reichsvertretung was formally constituted.

The Reichsvertretung, an umbrella organization, set itself the purpose of representing the Jews of Germany vis-à-vis both the authorities and Jews in other countries, assuming the leadership of the Jewish population and coordinating the wide range of new activities through which the Jews had attempted to cope with the changed situation. Prominent among these activities was the creation of an expanded network of educational institutions for youth and adults, especially through the work of the MITTELSTELLE FÜR JÜDISCHE ERWACHSENENBILDUNG (Jewish Center for Adult Education), founded and administered by Martin Buber. Other areas covered by the Reichsvertretung were vocational training and retraining, expanded welfare operations, economic assistance, aid in finding employment for Jews who had lost their jobs, and preparing for emigration. In the political sphere, it submitted memorandums to the authorities and published statements in the Jewish press in which it demanded safeguards for Jewish life, even under the existing circumstances. On several occasions, as when the Nazi newspaper *Der* STÜRMER (The Attacker) came out with a special issue on the blood libel—the accusation that Jews kill gentiles to obtain their blood for Jewish rituals—the Reichsvertretung did not hesitate to react with public protests.

The Jewish press at this time greatly increased in size and circulation. In 1934 the combined monthly circulation of national and community newspapers was 1,180,000. In the area of cultural activities, a special organization was founded in July 1933, the KULTURBUND DEUTSCHER JUDEN (Cultural Society of German Jews), which set itself the tasks of finding employment for the many Jewish artists and intellectuals who had been dismissed from their posts, and of serving as the cultural center for the Jewish population. Before long, the Kulturbund became one of German Jewry's largest and most proficient organizations.

The emergence of umbrella organizations did not remove from the Jewish scene the competition among different political and religious orientations for influence among the Jews and for representation in the community institutions. The main polarization was between the mainstream of German Jewry and the Zionist movement. The former was represented by the Centralverein and the Reichsbund der Deutschen Frontsoldaten, and its main purpose was to struggle for Jewish existence and the preservation of Jewish rights in Germany. The primary goal of the latter was gradually to prepare the Jews for a

Overleaf: In the autumn of 1935 a Dutch motorcyclist traveled from Bentheim (on the Dutch frontier) to Berlin by way of Hannover. During the trip he took photographs of the antisemitic signs he saw. (The Nazis had been in power less than three years.) Among the legends on the signs are: "Jews are not wanted in this place"; "The residents of this place want nothing to do with Jews"; "Jews enter this place at their own risk"; "The Jew is our misfortune. Let him keep away"; "Hyenas are scum and so are Jews"; "Jews get out!"

Juden nicht erwünscht
Das Kaufhaus hier gegenübe
gehört dem Juden
David Boas!
In Heisede
sind Juden
ungebetene Gäste
Juden
sind unerbetene
Gäste
Die
Einwohnerschaft de
Ortes wünscht keine
Umgang mit Jude
Juden
haben in Ahrberge
nicht's zu suche
Juden sind hier
nicht erwünscht
Juden
wandert in euer Lan
in unserm seid ihr doc
erkann
Die Einwohnerschaft des Ortes
wünscht keinen Umgang mit
Juden.
Juden
haut ab!
Wir wollen keine
Juden sehen.
Juden sind
unser Unglück.
Deutscher Kaufmann
Juden
nicht
erwünscht!
JUDEN — ACHTUNG
Der Weg nach
Palästina führt nicht
durch diesen Ort!
Juden
hier in Hildesheim
Umgang mit Juden
Ausschluss aus de
Dorfgemeinschaft

Die Rassenfrage ist der Schlüssel zur Weltgeschichte
Die Juden sind unser Unglück
Wer beim Juden kauft ist ein Volksverräter
Frauen und
Verderben
Juden sind in diesem Orte nicht erwünscht
In Heisede sind Juden ungebetene Gäste
Juden betreten diesen Ort auf eigene Gefahr
Der Jude ist unser Unglück er bleibe uns vom Leibe
Juden haut ab!
Juden sind unerbetene Gäste
Juden haben in Ahrbergen nicht's zu suchen.
Die Juden sind ungebetene Gäste
Deutscher Kaufmann
Juden nicht erwünscht!
uden sind hier
icht erwünscht
snabrück
65
Juden sind in diesem Orte nicht erwünscht
N.S.D.A.P. Ortsgruppe-Everloh-Amt NS. HAGO
Die Juden sind unser Unglück
Wer beim Juden kauft ist ein Volksverräter
Frauen und Mädchen die Juden sind Euer Verderben
DEM SCHAFFENDEN DEUTSCHLAND

new life in the national home in Palestine. By this time the Zionist movement had made substantial gains in Germany, especially among the young people. The He-Haluts pioneering movement had a strong base, and Recha Freier had established the YOUTH ALIYA organization.

All public activities by Jews were under the watchful eye of the authorities, mainly the Gestapo and the SD (Sicherheitsdienst; Secret Service), whose policy was to put restraints on any that were designed to encourage German Jews to stay in the Reich (mainly by the Centralverein and the Reichsbund der Deutschen Frontsoldaten). On the other hand the Zionist movement was able to carry on with relative freedom of action and with little interference. Notwithstanding National Socialism's sharp opposition to the Zionist movement's political aim of establishing a Jewish state, the Nazi regime at this time encouraged the work of the Zionists, believing that it promoted the emigration of Jews from Germany.

As far as official antisemitic policy was concerned, 1934 was a relatively uneventful year, and some of the Jewish emigrés living in difficult circumstances as temporary refugees in neighboring countries even decided to return to Germany. The restriction of Jewish rights now took the form of decrees and regulations issued by local authorities and professional organizations that applied in practice the principles enunciated in the 1933 anti-Jewish legislation.

The clash between the regime's tendency toward stabilization and consolidation as an authoritarian and totalitarian state and the still-existing revolutionary radicalism in the party ranks prompted Hitler, in June 1934, to stage a purge in which the top echelon of the SA, as well as other opposition leaders, were executed. One outcome of this confrontation was the strengthening of the conservative elements in the government, mainly among the army officers and the officials dealing with economic affairs; another was the rise of new centers of power, primarily the SS. The ongoing process of centralization resulted in the seizure of control over all police forces in the Reich by Heinrich HIMMLER, chief of the SS and the Gestapo. The effect of this development on the situation of the Jews was the establishment of special sections in the Gestapo and SD to deal with the "Jewish question."

In the wake of the sweeping victory in the Saar plebiscite in January 1935, which restored that district to the Reich, a new drive of violence against the Jews was launched. This time it took the form of a series of locally initiated actions (*Einzelaktionen*), accompanied by a high-powered campaign of incitement against the Jews in the press and in mass rallies, a campaign orchestrated by Joseph GOEBBELS and Julius STREICHER. A special feature of it was the denunciation and public humiliation of persons accused of having committed *Rassenschande* ("race defilement"), that is, sexual intercourse between Jews and "Aryans." The various German states passed anti-Jewish legislation of their own, for example, forbidding Jews to display the German flag and outlawing marriages between Jews and Aryans. It was in the smaller population centers that the Jews suffered most in this campaign, and as a result more and more Jews left their homes in the provinces and took up residence in the large cities.

The terror campaign reached its height in the summer of 1935 and was one of the factors leading to the enactment of the NUREMBERG LAWS in September of that year. These laws were designed to serve two purposes: to restore "law and order," and to meet the demands of radical party circles for implementation of the original antisemitic planks in the Nazi platform. The Nuremberg Laws were *Verfassungsgesetze* (constitutional laws), one of them the Reich Citizenship Law and the other the Law for the Protection of German Blood and German Honor, and they contained a new definition of the term "Jew," based on race. This was the definition on which all subsequent anti-Jewish legislation was based until 1943, when a final decree was enacted under which Jews were denied protection of the courts.

Secret government and party reports on the mood of the German population revealed that the reaction to the Nuremberg Laws was mixed. In wide circles it was believed that Hitler's statement describing the laws as a possible formal framework for the continued existence of the Jews in Germany meant that the laws were a solution of sorts, providing for racial and cultural segregation of the Jews from the German people and for their social isolation. Other circles, especially those with religious leanings and among the liberal bourgeoisie, expressed strong reservations and even criticism. Yet a third group, consisting mainly of radical Nazi party members, found the Nuremberg Laws too moderate, called for a more far-reaching solution of the "Jewish question," and, on their own initiative, continued anti-Jewish violence on the local level. The church leadership took no public stand on the Nuremberg Laws, despite the fact that the laws also affected thousands of converts, an issue that had confronted the churches from the moment the first anti-Jewish legislation was enacted in April 1933.

The SD's Section for Jewish Affairs was also reorganized in 1935, with Herbert Hagen as section chief and Adolf EICHMANN as his deputy. Henceforth, the section was to make persistent efforts to have exclusive charge of Jewish affairs in the Reich and beyond its borders.

The Jewish population and its leaders tried to cope with the deteriorating situation by intensifying and broadening their own activities in the social and economic spheres. In some Jewish quarters it was believed that under the situation created by the Nuremberg Laws the Jews would experience a kind of "group emancipation." The resulting status would safeguard certain civil rights of German Jews as a group, replacing the nineteenth-century Emancipation, which had endowed the individual Jew with equal civil and political rights. On the political level, the Reichsvertretung reacted by lodging protests and issuing a statement for publication by the Jewish press. Other Jewish reactions included a manifesto of August 1935 remonstrating against the rising tide of terror, and a special prayer written by Leo Baeck on the eve of the Day of Atonement. Both these protests led to punitive action by the Gestapo. In its memorandum reacting to the Nuremberg Laws, the Reichsvertretung gave expression to the sense of humiliation and insult aroused among the Jews by the laws, but it also saw in them a possible basis for some kind of continued autonomous Jewish existence in Germany.

In 1936, when the Olympic games were held in Berlin, there was a relative relaxation in public anti-Jewish activity. It seemed that the continued economic activities of the Jews and the consolidation of their newly established organizational and social structures had created a pattern of life that could be maintained even under a racist totalitarian regime. At that very time, however, a new antisemitic policy that was to have far-reaching consequences was being formulated for translation into practice during the following years. Hitler's secret memorandum on the FOUR-YEAR PLAN, which he wrote in August 1936, contained an ideological and political section in which he called for an all-out war against Judaism as a driving motive in Germany's future foreign policy and its preparations for the war against the Soviet Union that was sure to come within four years. The last part of this document contained the principles of the draconian punitive measures against the Jews that were to be the guidelines of future policy. In late 1936 and early 1937 the practical details of this radical policy were spelled out in documents drafted by the SD's Jewish section, for future application. The interim goals for the "solution of the Jewish question" were to include an intensified drive to eliminate Jews from the economy, and increased pressure for their emigration by such means as the "people's fury," that is, officially organized terror. The implementation of this policy on an informal basis was launched in the second half of 1937, mainly by the "Aryanization" (ARISIERUNG) of Jewish business enterprises. In this operation the SD contested the policies of other official agencies, especially the moderate pragmatic policy advocated by the Ministry for Economic Affairs; the struggle intensified when the minister, Hjalmar Schacht, was dismissed from his post in the fall of that year.

The year 1937 was a time of crisis inside the Third Reich, with signs of opposition to the regime manifested in various sectors of German society. One expression of the crisis was the sharpening conflict *(Kirchenkampf)* between the churches and the regime. Its most prominent manifestation was the German-language encyclical issued by Pope Pius XI, *Mit brennender Sorge* (With Burning

GERMANY—February 1938

Concern), which was distributed all over Germany. The encyclical denounced Nazi neo-paganism and the cult of racism, but it did not explicitly condemn the persecution of the Jews. The reactions of the regime varied, and included the staging of numerous show trials of clerics, who were imprisoned in concentration camps. According to secret official reports, by the end of the year the disapproval of and outright opposition to the regime were fast becoming a threat to its stability. These attitudes were especially prominent in conservative circles, with the churches and the army in the lead, but they were also evident among the workers. This was the background of the "crisis of the generals," which erupted in early 1938, and of the drastic changes introduced by Hitler in the top echelons of the army and the ministries of war and foreign affairs. Werner von BLOMBERG and Konstantin von Neurath fell from power, and Joachim von RIBBENTROP was appointed foreign minister, in preparation for a radicalized policy in both internal and foreign affairs.

This policy soon resulted in the annexation of Austria in March 1938, the Czech crisis and subsequent annexation of the Sudetenland in September of that year, the creation of the Protectorate of Bohemia and Moravia out of the occupied western part of Czechoslovakia in March 1939, and, finally, the invasion of Poland in September 1939, which marked the beginning of World War II. Of special significance was the declaration that Hitler made on January 30, 1939, which he was to repeat during the war on various public occasions and in closed meetings with party and army leaders: "If international-finance Jewry in Europe and elsewhere once again succeeds in dragging the nations into a world war, its outcome will not be the Bolshevization of the globe . . . but the annihilation of the Jewish race in Europe."

The year 1938 witnessed a significant stage in the further radicalization of the Third Reich's anti-Jewish policy, which was applied in the newly acquired territories. The radical policy took the form of a series of new laws and decrees, mass arrests of Jews, and a variety of "spontaneous" and official terror actions, the latter culminating in the pogrom of November 9–10. The first important step in this process was a law put into effect on March 28, 1938, that abolished the legally recognized status of the Jewish communities, a status they had been accorded in the nineteenth century. This was followed, on April 26, by a decree ordering the registration of Jewish property, and on June 15, by the arrest of 1,500 Jews and their imprisonment in concentration camps (the "June Operation"). Other anti-Jewish laws passed at this time forbade Jews to practice medicine (June 25), ordered male Jews to assume the name Israel, and female Jews, the name Sarah (August 17), forbade Jews to practice law (September 27), and stipulated that the passports of Jews be marked with a capital *J*, standing for *Jude* (October 5). In this period, and especially during the Czech crisis, there was a sharp rise in the number of "unofficial" terror actions taking place. They included the destruction of Jewish property, the expulsion of Jews, mainly from smaller population centers, and the desecration and destruction of synagogues, among them the main synagogue at Munich (June 9) and at Nuremberg (August 10).

On October 28, 1938, fifteen thousand to seventeen thousand Jews of Polish nationality were expelled from Germany. The Polish government refused to admit them into Poland, and for a considerable period of time they were trapped in the no-man's-land between the two countries. Their bitter fate caught the attention of public opinion all over the world (*see* ZBĄSZYŃ). On November 7, Herschel GRYNSZPAN, a Jewish youth whose parents were among the expelled Jews, shot Ernst vom Rath, a German diplomat in Paris. The Nazis used this act as the pretext for an organized pogrom against the Jews, which took place on November 9–10 in every part of Germany and in the areas it had annexed that year (Austria and the Sudetenland). In this pogrom, which came to be called KRISTALLNACHT, or "Night of Broken Glass" (so named from the shattering of the show windows of Jewish enterprises), hundreds of synagogues and thousands of Jewish businesses were burned down, destroyed, or damaged. Some thirty thousand Jews were put into concentration camps, and almost one hundred Jews were murdered.

The pogrom was followed by a collective fine of 1 billion marks imposed on the Jews and by a new series of harsh laws and regulations. Among these were a law providing for elimination of the Jews from the German economy (November 12); a regulation on the final expulsion of Jewish pupils from public schools, also on November 12; restrictions on the freedom of movement by Jews in public places (November 28); and a regulation ordering all Jewish newspapers and periodicals to be shut down (there were sixty-five newspapers and periodicals and forty-two organizational bulletins with a total monthly circulation of 956,000). All Jewish organizations were dissolved, leaving only the Reichsvertretung, the Kulturbund, and, temporarily, the Palestine Office of the Zionist organization. The only paper permitted to be published was the *Jüdisches Nachrichtenblatt*, the semi-official newspaper of the Reichsvertretung.

Classified reports by the Reich security services revealed that the reaction of the German public to the *Kristallnacht* pogrom, like that to the Nuremberg Laws, was not uniform. The disapproval voiced was on a much larger scale, but it focused primarily on the damage caused to German property and the German economy, and only in small degree on the moral aspect of the terror directed against the Jews and the destruction of their property. Once again the church leadership refrained from taking a public stand. A few individual clerics denounced the riots for their barbarity, which, they said, "contradicted the spirit of the Gospels." The underground German Communist party devoted an entire issue of its newspaper *Die Rote Fahne* (The Red Flag) to condemning the pogrom.

From 1938 to 1945. Before the end of November 1938 the Reichsvertretung resumed its activities, which centered mainly on intensifying the emigration of Jews from Germany and obtaining the release of those who had been imprisoned in concentration camps. It also proceeded to implement its earlier decisions to revise its organizational structure and its position within Jewish society and the National Socialist state, a process begun when the legal status of the Jewish communities was abolished in March 1938. By July that year all the Landesverbände of Jewish communities and the major Jewish organizations had decided to merge and to establish a new central organization, a nationwide Jewish community with a democratic constitution that would seek official recognition by the authorities. The name proposed for the new body was the Reichsverband der Juden in Deutschland (Reich Federation of Jews in Germany). Based on this initiative, which did not materialize in the wake of the November pogrom and its immediate repercussions, the Jewish leadership announced in February 1939 the formation of the Reichsvereinigung der Juden in Deutschland (Reich Association of Jews in Germany). The Reichsvereinigung regarded its main concerns as emigration, Jewish edu-

GERMANY—Kristallnacht, November 9, 1938

cation, and welfare. This development took place at a time when the authorities as well had an interest in the existence of a more authoritative, centralist Jewish organization. On July 4, 1939, a law was passed granting recognition to the Reichsvereinigung. This law, however, required that all Jews by race, as defined in the Nuremberg Laws, had to belong to the new organization. The Reichsvereinigung was put under the supervision of the Ministry of the Interior, which in practice meant that it was under the control of the SS.

In 1938 and 1939, emigration of Jews ("by race") from Germany reached new heights—49,000 in 1938 and 68,000 in 1939—despite the many difficulties that stood in the way, such as new restrictive entry regulations in the target countries, restrictions on immigration to Palestine, and the failure of the EVIAN CONFERENCE. Long before November 1938, the Reichsvertretung had recognized the importance of the role it had to play in emigration, and early that year it had set up a coordinating office for this purpose. The Reichsvereinigung kept up its efforts on behalf of Jewish emigration even after the war broke out, routing the emigrants through neutral Spain and Portugal to the Western Hemisphere, through the Soviet Union to East Asia, and through Italy and the Balkan states to Palestine by means of Aliya Bet ("illegal" immigration). These efforts came to an end in October 1941, when all Jewish emigration was prohibited.

As the agency with the sole responsibility for Jewish education, the Reichsvereinigung created a network which ensured that Jewish schooling was available wherever Jews lived in Germany and also supervised the training of teachers. The Kulturbund continued its activities and, indeed, added to them by taking over some of the functions of the Mittelstelle, those for adult education.

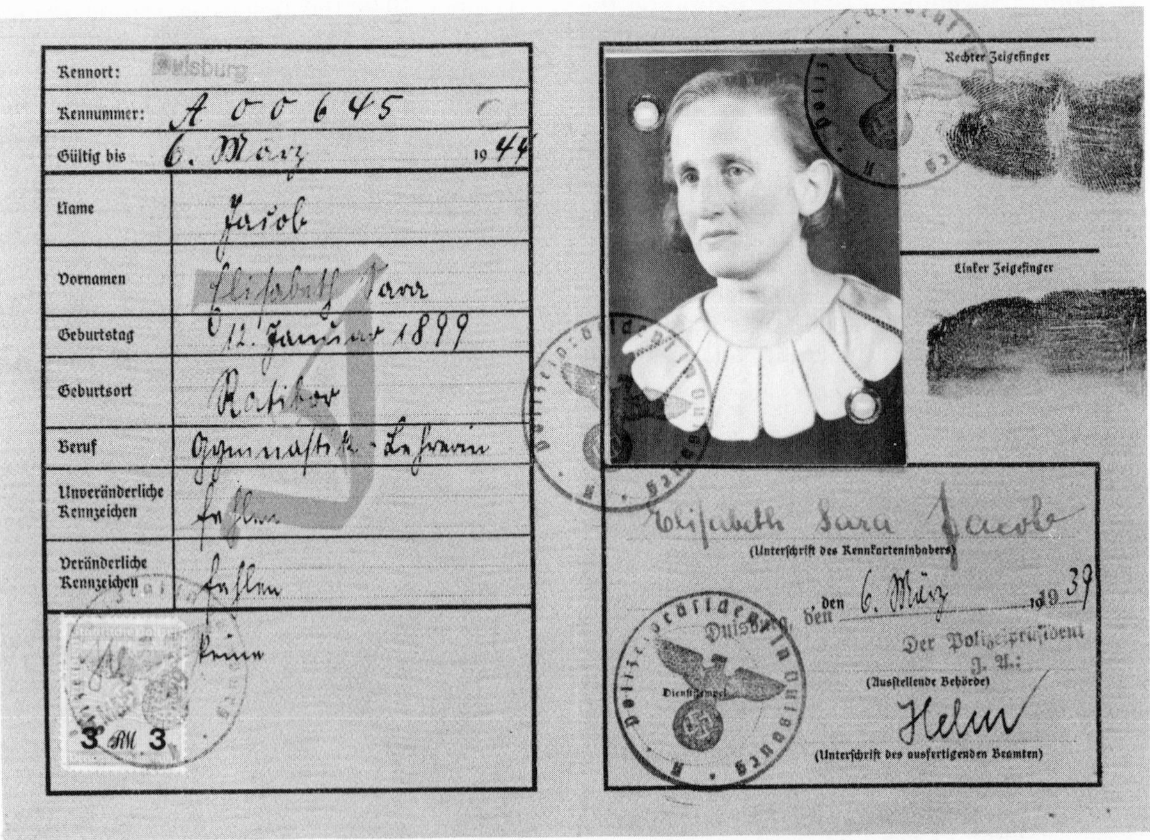

Kennort:	Duisburg
Kennummer:	A 00645
Gültig bis	6. März 1944
Name	Jacob
Vornamen	Elisabeth Sara
Geburtstag	12. Januar 1899
Geburtsort	Ratibor
Beruf	Gymnastik-Lehrerin
Unveränderliche Kennzeichen	fehlen
Veränderliche Kennzeichen	fehlen
	keine

3 RM 3

Rechter Zeigefinger

Linker Zeigefinger

Elisabeth Sara Jacob
(Unterschrift des Kennkarteninhabers)

Duisburg, den 6. März 1939

Der Polizeipräsident
I. A.:
(Ausstellende Behörde)

Dienststempel

(Unterschrift des ausfertigenden Beamten)

Jewish identity card in the German Reich. Note the large "J" printed on the left side. The card was issued to Elisabeth Sara Jacob, a gym teacher of Duisburg, on March 6, 1939.

With regard to social welfare, the Reichsvereinigung was confronted with enormous problems, owing to the fact that practically all German Jews had been deprived of their livelihood, that the average age of the Jews remaining in Germany was quite high, and that financing had to be found for the emigration of the growing number of would-be emigrants who had no means of their own. To deal with these problems the Reichsvereinigung gave its support to existing fund-raising institutions for mutual help, but its main source of funds was the revenue it obtained from a progressive tax imposed on Jews who still had property in their possession, including Jews who were about to emigrate. The Reichsvereinigung also continued to receive financial assistance from American Jewish welfare agencies, until America's entry into the war in December 1941.

As a growing number of countries became involved in the war, the Germans expanded their policy of Jewish persecution as it had evolved in Germany since 1933, applying it in the countries that occupied or that were under their influence. The form of this policy differed from one country to another, but its ultimate aim was the same everywhere—the "FINAL SOLUTION" of the "Jewish question." In Germany proper the outbreak of the war set off a new round of anti-Jewish decrees and regulations affecting nearly every sphere of the Jews' life. Among the first was a decree that prohibited Jews from leaving their homes after dark and placed certain sections of cities out of bounds to them. Another that reduced their allocation of rationed foods and restricted their purchases to certain shops and certain times of day. Other decrees, by the dozen, ordered the Jews to hand over their jewelry, radios, cameras, electrical appliances, and any other valuables in their possession. In September 1941 all Jews aged six and above were ordered to wear the *Judenstern* (the Jewish star; *see* BADGE, JEWISH), and Jews were no longer permitted to use public transportation. In contrast to the situation in most other countries of Europe, no ghettos were created in Germany, and the isolating of the Jews was achieved by imposing residential restrictions that forced them out of their homes and concentrated them in *Judenhäuser* ("Jewish buildings"). Jews who were declared "fit for work" were put on forced labor, and the practice of arresting individual Jews and sending them to concentration camps was continued. The persecution of the Jews by means of decrees and regulations was formally ended, in July 1943, by another decree that removed them from the protection of the law and placed them under the exclusive jurisdiction of the security services and the police.

The first deportations of Jews from Germany took place in February 1940, and affected Jews from Stettin (now Szczecin) and Schneidemühl (Piła) and their environs (*see* NISKO AND LUBLIN PLAN). These deportations were discontinued in the spring of that year, but in the summer, after the victory over France, the idea came up of deporting the Jews to Madagascar (*see* MADAGASCAR PLAN). In October 1940, in a single night, all the Jews of Baden, the Palatinate, and the Saar district—a total of 7,500 persons—were deported to France, most of them to the GURS camp, and from there to extermination camps in the east. In October 1941 the deportation of masses of Jews on a systematic basis was launched, a process that led to the liquidation of German Jewry. The majority of these transports had as their destination the Łódź and Warsaw ghettos in Poland, and the ghettos of Riga, Kovno, and Minsk in the German-occupied parts of the Soviet Union.

By then the mass murder of Jews by the EINSATZGRUPPEN was in full swing in the German-occupied Soviet territory; the first phase of the total annihilation of the Jews of Europe had begun. Some of the transports from Germany to these territories were liquidated upon their arrival in the ghettos (as in Riga and Minsk) during the course of local *Aktionen;* the other deportees, if they did not perish from epidemics and starvation, were deliberately killed. In 1942 and 1943, these German Jews were deported by the tens of thousands directly to the extermination camps, mainly to AUSCHWITZ. Some forty-two thousand Jews from Germany, mostly elderly people and those with "privileged status," were sent to the THERESIENSTADT ghetto; the majority either perished there or were deported to the extermination camps. Even before the systematic mass annihilation started, several hundred Jews were murdered

GERMANY — November 1942

between 1939 and 1941 inside Germany, within the EUTHANASIA PROGRAM.

The link of ideology and political policy with the destruction of the Jews in Europe in relation to the impending war was propounded by Hitler in public speeches (as of January 1939), in secret operational directives that he issued during the war, and in his last testament, dictated in April 1945. Most scholars believe that there was a close connection between the radicalization of the war that was inaugurated by the invasion of the Soviet Union and the beginning of the mass murder of the Jews, and that the *rassenideologische Vernichtungskrieg* (the racist and ideologically motivated war of extermination) deliberately coincided with the campaign against "Jewish Bolshevism" and its "biological sources," the millions of Jews in eastern Europe.

But despite its unique character, the Nazi extermination of the Jews should be seen as part of a larger concept, the racial revolution planned by the Nazis, which was to restructure the face of Europe by exterminating and subjugating entire sectors of the population and by uprooting millions of people from their homes, mainly in eastern Europe (*see* GENERALPLAN OST). During the war, in addition to the Jews, the Nazis also murdered GYPSIES, the chronically and mentally ill in Germany itself, Soviet prisoners of war, and intellectual and political elites in Poland and in the Soviet Union.

In practical terms, the policy toward the Jews in all its phases, both before the "Final Solution" and during its course, was shaped by the Third Reich's bureaucracy and police, and especially by the section for Jewish affairs, headed by Eichmann, in the REICHSSICHERHEITSHAUPTAMT (Reich Security Main Office; RSHA). Also taking part in the mass murder of the Jews or witnessing it were the tens of thousands who served in the Einsatzgruppen and millions of soldiers in the German occupation army; these were also the main sources that channeled information on the fate of the Jews to the German population.

The attitude of the German population to the "solution of the Jewish question" during the war years does not appear to have been different from that during the years preceding the war, but because of the far harsher treatment meted out to the Jews once the war began, the German people's reaction takes on a different meaning. The growing isolation of the Jews during the war, prior to their deportation, is reflected mainly in the absence of concern on the part of the German population to what was happening to the Jews. But even at that stage, particularly before the start of the mass deportations, there was pressure by various groups for a more extreme anti-Jewish policy in Germany, along the lines of the policy that had been introduced in Poland by this time. There were appeals for further restrictions to be imposed on the Jews in day-to-day life, for the introduction of the Jewish badge, and even for the expulsion and liquidation of the Jews. On the other hand, secret reports on public opinion in Germany at that time noted that there were reservations about the treatment of the Jews, especially with respect to the introduction of the yellow badge and the first deportations to the east, the more so after information had been received concerning the fate of the deportees and the mass murder of Jews in eastern Europe. These reservations were expressed primarily in the educated circles of the middle class, among religious Germans, and in the lower ranks of the clergy. As before, the church leadership did not protest. Only in 1943, when it seemed that a similar fate was in store for the thousands of German Jews who had hitherto been safe because they were living with their Christian spouses, and also for their (mostly Christian) descendants, was a public protest issued.

A stronger reaction to reports on the extermination of German Jewish deportees and of Jews from other countries was expressed after the defeat at Stalingrad and the massive air raids on German cities in 1943. On the whole, however, it appears that the majority of the German people maintained a passive attitude toward the fate of the Jews, and this was also true of the "conservative resistance" circles, led by army chiefs. The political plans drawn up by the participants in the 1944 plot against Hitler contain little reference to the Jews, and the leading figures in the conspiracy did not believe that there was room for the resettlement of Jews in Germany, or anywhere in Europe, for that matter. At the same time, there is evidence that thousands of Germans risked their lives and the lives of their families to extend help to Jews, thus saving some of the Jews who had gone into hiding.

Despite the progressive radicalization of the Nazi policy on the Jews, the Reichsvereinigung continued to function throughout the war years according to the policy that had crystallized when it was reorganized in 1938 and 1939. The new situation, and especially the onset of the mass deportations in 1940, created problems and posed unprecedented challenges to the Reichsvereinigung. The welfare needs, which in the past had been confined to a minority, now came to involve the great majority of the Jewish population in Germany. In addition to the regular subsidies that it made, the Reichsvereinigung had to provide emergency housing for the thousands of Jews who had been evicted from their homes, and particularly for the patients and inmates of medical institutions and old-age homes that had to be evacuated and turned over to the authorities. The Reichsvereinigung provided educational facilities to all German Jews, even after emigration and, later on, mass deportation, had thinned out the ranks of both students and teachers. Only in the summer of 1942 was the Jewish school system closed down, on orders issued by the Gestapo when the wave of deportations was at its height. The Reichsvereinigung also continued to run its training and retraining institutions, and to help support the agricultural training farms (*hakhsharot*) of the Zionist movements, which in the eyes of their participants were "the remaining islands of self-contained Jewish life" in Germany. These establishments, too, were gradually closed down in 1942 and 1943, during the mass deportations.

The Reichsvereinigung did not abandon its independent role as the responsible Jewish leadership, as demonstrated forcefully by its reaction to the first mass deportations from Germany in 1940 and to the Madagascar Plan broached that year. When Eichmann presented to the Reichsvereinigung leaders the plan for the expulsion to Madagascar of the European Jews, their response was that the only possible place for the mass settlement of Jews was Palestine. After the deportation of all the Jews of Baden and the Palatinate in October 1940, the Reichsvereinigung undertook a number of protest actions to which the Nazi authorities retaliated sharply, in part by arresting and murdering one of the organization's leading officers, Julius Seligsohn. From then on, until the liquidation of German Jewry, the leadership's activities in relation to the authorities were conducted in an atmosphere of growing terror, with some of the leaders arrested and deported to concentration camps. One of the first victims was Otto Hirsch, who perished in the MAUTHAUSEN camp in June 1941. In those years, a major concern of the Reichsvereinigung leadership vis-à-vis the authorities was to assert its rights of ownership of Jewish public property. Such property was gradually being sold, and the proceeds were one of the most important sources for the financing of the Reichsvereinigung's operations on behalf of the Jews remaining alive in Germany in the wake of the deportations.

Beginning in the fall of 1941, the procedure for the mass deportations usually consisted of rounding up Jews and taking them to special assembly points in the large cities. The RSHA planned the deportations, and the lists of the candidates for deportation were compiled by the Gestapo offices in the various districts and large cities. In some places the local Jewish community was ordered to distribute the deportation orders to its members. Contrary to an assumption prevailing among survivors for many years after the war and consequently found in research literature, the Reichsvereinigung did not participate directly in the deportations; this has been revealed in documents in its archives, which came to light only relatively recently. Many of the Reichsvereinigung leaders and staff were among the victims imprisoned and deported in June 1942 in retaliation for an attack on an anti-Soviet exhibition in Berlin by the underground Jewish Communist BAUM GRUPPE. During the retaliatory operation, hundreds of Jews from Berlin and elsewhere were executed.

At the end of January 1943, when the mass deportations were drawing to an end, two of the remaining leaders of the Reichsvereinigung, Leo Baeck and Paul EPPSTEIN, were transferred to the Theresienstadt ghetto. In February of that year a drive was made to round up the Jews who were still left in Berlin, working in war-essential industrial plants. Some of these Jews, who were married to gentile women, were saved when their wives staged public demonstrations in their behalf. Several months later, in July, after the deportations had come to an end, the liquidation of German Jewry was officially declared to have been completed; the offices of the Reichsvereinigung and the Berlin Jewish community were closed down and the remainder of the staff was deported. The semiofficial Jewish newspaper was also closed down. During the time it was published, it had served primarily as a source of information on emigration opportunities and on the ways and means of organizing emigration. When emigration was forbidden, the paper's main role was to inform the German Jews about decrees and orders issued by the authorities concerning Jewish affairs.

After the disbandment of the Reichsvereinigung in July 1943, the affairs of the approximately fifteen thousand Jews who were left in Germany (most of them because they were married to non-Jews) were put in the hands of an organization known as the Rest-Reichsvereinigung (Residue Reich Association). It had little authority and played a very modest role, but it remained in existence until the end of the war.

Conclusion. Of the 566,000 Jews (by race) who lived in Germany when Hitler came to power, some 200,000 fell victim to the Nazi extermination policy and some 300,000 were saved, mostly by emigrating from the country. (These and subsequent figures refer to Jews by "race" and are rounded off in thousands.) During the existence of the Third Reich, the surplus of deaths over births among the Jewish population of Germany (which had a rate of aging that was high even before 1933, and that rose further as a result of emigration) was 66,000.

The actual number of Jewish emigrants from Germany between 1933 and 1945 was 346,000. This figure includes 98,000 who emigrated to European countries conquered later by the Nazis; of these, an estimated 70,000 were deported during the Nazi occupation, together with Jews from the local population. Some 5,000 of these deportees survived the war. Approximately 137,000 Jews were deported directly from Germany, of whom about 9,000 survived. The figure of 200,000 German Jews who fell victim to Nazi extermination also includes several thousand Jews who were murdered in the Euthanasia Program or who committed suicide (most of the suicides occurred at the time of the deportations). In addition to the 20,000 Jews surviving the war in Germany (15,000 in the open, mostly MISCHLINGE, and 3,000 to 5,000 who had gone undergound), another 5,000 survived in the Theresienstadt ghetto and 4,000 in other concentration camps.

In the early stage of the war no Jews were sent to Germany on forced labor, but this policy changed in the final stages, during which tens of thousands of Jews were taken out of concentration camps and brought to Germany. They worked there under subhuman conditions, mostly in the armament industry and in the removal of debris in the German cities caused by the Allied air raids. The majority of these Jews soon lost whatever physical strength they had left and were sent back to the extermination camps, to be killed there; only a small number were left in Germany and liberated when the war ended.

During the last few months of the war, tens

of thousands of Jews were taken out of concentration camps in the east, where the war front was drawing near, and put on DEATH MARCHES to Germany. Those who survived the marches were put in concentration camps in Germany, Austria, and the Protectorate of Bohemia and Moravia. Many of them died there, after the camps were liberated, from exhaustion and the epidemics that broke out. In some of the concentration camps, such as DACHAU and BUCHENWALD, Jewish underground resistance groups were organized in the final months of the war, and shortly after liberation they formed the core of the She'erith ha-Peletah, or "surviving remnant," the seventy thousand to eighty thousand Holocaust survivors on German soil.

"The Third Reich has put an end to a thousand years of Jewish history in Germany." These prophetic words, uttered by Rabbi Leo Baeck as early as 1933, proved true to an unfathomably tragic extent.

[*See also* Education on the Holocaust: West Germany; Literature on the Holocaust: Germany; Reparations and Restitution; Trials of War Criminals: Germany *and* Postwar Dispensation of Justice in Germany; Youth Movements: Germany and Austria.]

BIBLIOGRAPHY

Adam, U. *Judenpolitik im Dritten Reich*. Düsseldorf, 1972.

Bracher, K. D. *The German Dictatorship: The Origins, Structure, and Effects of National Socialism*. New York, 1970.

Craig, G. *Germany: Eighteen Sixty-Six to Nineteen Forty-Five*. New York, 1980.

Genschel, H. *Die Verdrängung der Juden aus der Wirtschaft im Dritten Reich*. Göttingen, 1966.

Jäckel, E. *Hitler's Weltanschauung: A Blueprint for Power*. Middletown, Conn., 1972.

Jäckel, E., and J. Rohwer, eds. *Der Mord an den Juden im Zweiten Weltkrieg*. Stuttgart, 1985.

Krausnick, H., et al. *The Anatomy of the SS State*. New York, 1968.

Kulka, O. D. "Public Opinion in Nazi Germany and the Jewish Question," *Jerusalem Quarterly* 25 (Fall 1982): 121–144; 26 (Winter 1982): 34–45.

Kulka, O. D., and Mendes-Flohr, eds. *Judaism and Christianity under the Impact of National Socialism*. Jerusalem, 1987.

Mosse, G. L. *Germans and Jews*. New York, 1970.

Mosse, W., and A. Paucker, eds. *Entscheidungsjahr 1932*. Tübingen, 1965.

Niewyk, D. *The Jews in Weimar Germany*. Baton Rouge, La., 1980.

Paucker, A., ed. *Die Juden im Nationalsozialistischen Deutschland, 1933–1943*. Tübingen, 1986. (In German and English.)

Schleunes, K. *The Twisted Road to Auschwitz*. Urbana, Ill., 1970.

Strauss, H. "Jewish Emigration from Germany." *Leo Baeck Institute Year Book* 25 (1980): 313–358; 26 (1981): 343–409.

Walk, J. *Das Sonderrecht für die Juden im NS-Staat*. Karlsruhe, 1984.

OTTO DOV KULKA
and ESRIEL HILDESHEIMER

GERSTEIN, KURT (1905–1945), SS officer and head of the Waffen-SS Institute of Hygiene in Berlin who vainly tried to make known the reality of the "FINAL SOLUTION." Gerstein was born in Münster and qualified as a mining engineer. He joined the Nazi party in 1933 but combined party membership with adherence to the Confessing Church (Bekennende Kirche), for which he was dismissed from state service in 1936. After a period of imprisonment in a concentration camp, he was expelled from the party in 1938. Gerstein then took up the study of medicine. After the death of his sister-in-law under the EUTHANASIA PROGRAM, he resolved to learn more of the truth about the killing of mental patients in "euthanasia institutes." He volunteered for the Waffen-SS, and in 1941 was assigned to its hygiene institute as a contaminations expert.

Early in 1942, Gerstein was appointed to head the Technical Disinfection Department within the Health Technology section. In this capacity he worked with ZYKLON B (hydrogen cyanide). In August 1942, on an inspection visit to the extermination camps of TREBLINKA, SOBIBÓR, and particularly BEŁŻEC, Gerstein saw Zyklon B in operation. His sole desire, as he said, was to ascertain the facts of the machinery of destruction "and then shout them to the whole world."

Gerstein's first contact was with Baron Göran von Otter, a Swedish diplomat, whom Gerstein met by chance on the Warsaw-Berlin express train while returning from

Bełżec. Gerstein was also in contact with Bishop Otto DIBELIUS of the Confessing Church; Archbishop Cesare Orsenigo, the papal nuncio in Berlin; and members of the Dutch underground. His efforts to make known the facts of the mass murder had little success, although his reports have been shown to be accurate in all essential respects. After the war Gerstein was arrested by the French as a suspected war criminal and member of the SS. He committed suicide in his prison cell, apparently out of despair at his failure to have halted the mass murder, but it has also been suggested that he was killed by SS fellow prisoners.

BIBLIOGRAPHY

Franz, H. *Kurt Gerstein: Aussenseiter des Widerstandes der Kirche gegen Hitler.* Zurich, 1964.

Friedländer, S. *Kurt Gerstein: The Ambiguity of Good.* New York, 1969.

Hochhuth, R. *The Deputy.* New York, 1964.

Joffroy, P. *A Spy for God: The Ordeal of Kurt Gerstein.* New York, 1971.

LIONEL KOCHAN

GESTAPO (acronym of Geheime Staatspolizei; Secret State Police), the Prussian, and later the Third Reich's, secret state police and the Nazis' main tool of oppression and destruction.

The Prussian Gestapo (1933–1944). The Gestapo originated in the political department of the police headquarters in Berlin during the Weimar Republic. At that time, the department served the government of Prussia as a domestic intelligence agency. Later in the 1920s, the Prussian political police became a semi-official federal bureau of investigation, although a much less powerful one than the American FBI. When Adolf Hitler became the chancellor of Germany, Hermann GÖRING was made the interior minister of Prussia, thereby taking over the Prussian political police. Göring appointed Rudolf Diels its first executive director in his bid to consolidate Nazi power in Prussia.

Diels, a Prussian civil servant and fellow traveler with the Nazis, served as the necessary tool for transforming an intelligence organization serving a democratic state of law into a separate and executive police-intelligence apparatus of a totalitarian dictatorship. He helped purge "politically unreliable elements" and Jewish officials. He also established a semi-independent headquarters, the Gestapa (Geheimes Staatspolizeiamt), comprised of low-level but experienced Prussian bureaucrats. When Göring was made prime minister of Prussia on April 11, 1933, the Gestapa was separated entirely from the overall police structure.

The First Gestapo Law, of April 26, 1933, officially gave Diels the authority of an independent state political-police commissioner, although his field branches *(Staatspolizeistellen)* at first remained under the control of the Prussian provincial governors. The emergency regulations of February 28, 1933, gave the Gestapa complete freedom to impose "protective custody" (*Schutzhaft*) upon anyone it wanted, to prevent undesirable political activities, and to wiretap political suspects and follow all their activities. The torture and execution of prisoners without regular legal proceedings remained illegal, but it nevertheless often took place in makeshift SA (Sturmabteilung; Storm Troopers) and SS bunkers and concentration camps already in existence. Diels tried to gain control over the concentration camps. However, he eventually had to come to terms with the SA and the growing power of the SS, and to be satisfied with playing a major role in the camp system without controlling it. During 1933, SA and SS intrigues drove Diels to flee abroad for a time, but he reassumed his position in November of that year, accepting an honorary SS officer's rank.

The Second Gestapo Law, of November 30, 1933, made Göring head of the political police and Diels directly responsible to him. The secret police now became officially known as the Gestapo. It was free of legal or administrative lawsuits against its actions, and it assumed direct control over its field branches. Specially trained, ruthless bureaucrats produced regular intelligence reports on political and ideological "enemies of the Reich." In 1934, a Jewish Section was established in the Gestapa. Diels eventually managed to gain nominal control of the Prussian concentration camps; his efforts to gain such control, along with his efforts to centralize the political police, ultimately served the Nazis, who were the real masters of Germany.

The Gestapo under Himmler and Heydrich. Under Heinrich HIMMLER and Reinhard HEYDRICH, the Gestapo played an important role in the amalgamation of the SS and the police. First, Himmler established SS control over the political police and concentration camps in Bavaria in early 1933. Later he imposed the Bavarian model on all the German states, including Prussia, where as Göring's deputy he took over the Gestapo on April 20, 1934. He made Heydrich its director, and a group of low-ranking Bavarian political-police officials were made SS officers in allegiance to Himmler. Later in the year, Himmler was made the chief of all the political police in Germany.

Although throughout Germany the concentration camps came under the control of the SS, the Gestapo had the power to send its victims to them. Moreover, through a "political section" in the camps' headquarters, it could order that prisoners be released, tortured, or executed. Similar treatment awaited its victims in its own basements. To circumvent the criminal code that forbade torture and murder, the Gestapo adopted methods, tested in the DACHAU concentration camp, of fabricating natural causes of death or serving the inmates' families notice that the prisoners had been "shot while trying to escape."

In June 1936 Himmler officially became the chief of all the German police, his title being *Reichsführer-SS und Chef der Deutschen Polizei* (Reich Leader of the SS and Chief of the German Police). Now that he controlled both the concentration camps and the police, the amalgamation of the SS and police could be completed. Himmler set about reorganizing the police system. This whole process, which had Hitler's consent, helped him gain complete independence from the state and the Reich bureaucracy. Himmler set up two main branches of the police force, the ORDNUNGSPOLIZEI (Order Police; Orpo) and the Sicherheitspolizei (Security Police; Sipo). The Orpo was the "regular" police and included the Schutzpolizei (Protection Police—the uniformed officers), the Gendarmerie (rural police), the Feuerschutzpolizei (firefighting police), and various technical and auxiliary services. Sipo was composed of the Gestapo and the KRIMINALPOLIZEI (Criminal Police). The Gestapo and the field units (now renamed Staatspolizeileitstellen; state regional headquarters) took over all the German political-police agencies. After Himmler's takeover, the Gestapo grew enormously with the recruitment of personnel lacking the traditional qualifications for public service.

From the time of Himmler's takeover until September 1939, when the REICHSSICHERHEITSHAUPTAMT (Reich Security Main Office; RSHA) was established, the structure of the Gestapo stayed the same. Division I was responsible for organization and finance, including legal matters. Its director between 1935 and 1939 was Dr. Werner BEST, the SS lawyer and SD (Sicherheitsdienst; Security Service) executive who perfected the legal side of the Gestapo's circumvention of the criminal code and its other activities. Division II, under Heydrich's direct control, was the main body of the Gestapo. Under Heinrich MÜLLER, Section II 1 was charged with fighting the "enemies" of the regime, to which belonged the Communists, Social Democrats, the outlawed trade unions, monarchists, and anti-Nazi ultraconservatives. Special sections dealt with Austrian matters, Jews, other religious groups, FREEMASONS, and immigrants. The Gestapo intensified the regime's policies of segregation and emigration until 1938, in competition with the SD's radical and aggressive treatment of the "Jewish question." Division III was the counterintelligence unit (Abwehrpolizei), under an SD agent, Günther Palten, who had already penetrated the Gestapo in Diels's time. Between November 1937 and October 1938, special Gestapo-SD units were trained to terrorize and Nazify foreign countries. Following Adolf EICHMANN's initiative in driving many Jews from Austria later in 1938, Müller, with Eichmann as executive, assumed the overall control of the forced emigration of the Jews from all Nazi-controlled territories. After KRISTALLNACHT (November 9–10, 1938), the Gestapo became the main instrument of the regime's anti-Jewish policies.

The Gestapo during World War II (1939–1945). In 1939 the Gestapo, as part of the Sipo, was fused with the SD to form the RSHA. Thus, young, ruthless, and fanatical SD agents such as Eichmann became Gestapo officers; the academics, lawyers, and old-style Prussian civil servants, who had completed their transitional role, either were pushed aside or integrated themselves into the spirit and practices of the SS-infested civil service. With the creation of the RSHA, the Gestapo was expanded, with the border police now coming under its auspices. As with the rest of the RSHA and the SS, the Gestapo, with the onset of the war, took part in the enslavement of "inferior races," "pacifying" and subduing the occupied territories in the west, persecuting the Jews, and, finally, carrying out a major role in the "FINAL SOLUTION." It also continued its activities in the Reich itself. Throughout this period, the head of the Gestapo (Amt IV of the RSHA) was Müller, and the head of the Jewish section (IV B 4) was Eichmann.

The Gestapo's main tool remained the "protective custody" procedure, which was simplified and which allowed the Staatspolizeileitstellen freedom of action against "enemies of the Reich." These activities were carried out according to general or specific directives issued by Heydrich; by his successor, Ernst KALTENBRUNNER; by Müller; or by RSHA section chiefs such as Eichmann. The Gestapo did not even take the trouble to place Jews and GYPSIES in the category of "enemies of the Reich" but rather rounded them up, stole their propoerty, deprived them of their citizenship, and finally deported them. Such acts could be committed with impunity because the Gestapo was allowed to function outside the rule of law, acting instead in accordance with an "overall political mission." Its position above the law and its special mission were spelled out in an RSHA decree of April 15, 1940: "The powers required by the Gestapo for the execution of all measures necessary to their task stem not from specific laws and ordinances, but from the overall mission allotted to the German police in general and the Gestapo in particular in connection with the reconstruction of the National Socialist State" (Buchheim, in Krausnick, pp. 189–190).

In the occupied territories, each headquarters of the Befehlshaber der Sicherheitspolizei und des Sicherheitsdienstes (Commanders of the Sipo and SD; BdS) had a Gestapo representative (Amt IV of the BdS). They hoodwinked the Judenräte and took their members hostage, perfected a special jargon of deceit (SPRACHREGELUNG), and supervised the phasing out of the ghettos. They also maintained pressure on satellite countries to deport their Jews. Eichmann's Jewish section and his field representatives generally arranged the deportation to concentration and extermination camps. In particular, Eichmann maintained direct control over the special camp in THERESIENSTADT, and a special Sonderkommando under his command deported most of Hungarian Jewry to AUSCHWITZ in 1944.

Persecuting defenseless Jews and maintaining control through terror in Germany itself and in the occupied territories, the Gestapo relentlessly served Hitler and the goal of remaking the world in the Nazi image. Millions of Germans accepted the Gestapo in its initial phase, collaborated with it later, and supplied the military-organizational framework that made Gestapo atrocities possible.

BIBLIOGRAPHY

Aronson, S. *The Beginnings of the Gestapo System: The Bavarian Model in 1933.* Jerusalem, 1970.

Delarue, J. *The Gestapo: A History of Horror.* New York, 1964.

Krausnick, H., et al. *The Anatomy of the SS State.* New York, 1968.

SHLOMO ARONSON

GETTER, MATYLDA (d. 1968), mother superior of the Warsaw branch of the Order of the Franciscan Sisters of the Family of Mary, a Polish religious order that carried on educational work, mainly among orphans, and cared for the sick in hospitals. In 1942, Sister Matylda decided to accept all the Jewish children fleeing from the WARSAW ghetto who were brought to her and to shelter them in the order's many locations, but especially in its branch at Pludy, some 7.5 miles (12 km) outside Warsaw, on the right bank of the Vistula River.

It is estimated that Sister Matylda was instrumental in rescuing several hundred Jewish children from certain death. Her principal aim was not to gain new souls for the church, but to rescue human lives. She was accused by some of unnecessarily endangering the lives of the many non-Jewish orphans in the order's homes by harboring Jewish children in their midst. Her reply was that by virtue of the Jewish children's presence, God would not allow any harm to befall the other children. Special precautions were taken to remove the too obviously Jewish-looking children for temporary shelter elsewhere when Sister Matylda was alerted to possible Gestapo raids on the orphanages. When time proved too short for this, children with a more Jewish appearance would have their heads or faces partially bandaged, to look as though they had been injured. Sister Matylda was at the time an elderly person and ill with cancer. After the war, the children were released to their parents or relatives.

Sister Matylda Getter was posthumously recognized by YAD VASHEM as a "RIGHTEOUS AMONG THE NATIONS."

BIBLIOGRAPHY

Bartoszewski, W., and Z. Lewin. *Righteous among Nations: How Poles Helped the Jews, 1939–1945.* London, 1969.

MORDECAI PALDIEL

GHETTO. [*This entry gives a general survey of the Jewish ghettos in Nazi-occupied Europe. For detailed descriptions of the life and fate of the ghettos, see under individual cities and towns; some of the major ghettos were those of* Białystok; Kovno; Łódź; Minsk; Riga; Vilna; *and* Warsaw. *For information on Nazi-sponsored Jewish organizations in the ghettos, see* Judenrat *and* Jüdischer Ordnungsdienst. *On Jewish attempts to document their plight,* see Łódź Ghetto, Chronicles of the; *and* Oneg Shabbat. *Resistance in the ghettos is detailed in* Fareynegte Partisaner Organizatsye; Resistance; Jewish; Warsaw Ghetto Uprising; Żydowska Organizacja Bojowa; *and* Żydowski Związek Wojskowy.]

The word "ghetto" originally referred to a city quarter or street in which only Jews lived, confined and separated from the other parts of the city. The term had its origin in Venice, where in 1516 the Jews were forced into a closed quarter call the Geto Nuovo (New Foundry). Other Italian cities—with the exception of Leghorn (Livorno)—also put their Jews into ghettos, and the practice was adopted by towns in southern France that belonged to the pope; by several large cities in Germany; in Bohemia and Moravia; and in some Polish cities. The purpose of ghettoizing the Jews was to restrict contacts between them and Christians and to confine the Jews to certain economic activities. Inside the ghettos, the Jews lived their lives in accordance with their traditional customs. From the end of the eighteenth century, the forcible restriction of Jews to ghettos was gradually abandoned; the last ghetto to exist in Europe was the one in Rome, which came to an end in 1870, when papal rule of the city was terminated.

Separate city quarters, on a voluntary or compulsory basis, for both Jews and Christians existed in many Muslim countries until the twentieth century. For the most part, the Jews lived in separate quarters of their own free will and were not barred from residing in other parts of the city. In more recent times the term "ghetto" came to be applied to urban areas inhabited by blacks in the United States and South Africa and to quarters inhabited by any minority that was oppressed and living in slum conditions.

None of these forms of ghetto can be compared to the ghettos established by the Germans in the countries they occupied in World War II. These were not designed to serve as a separate area for Jewish habitation; they were merely a transitional phase in a process that was to lead to the "FINAL SOLUTION" of the Jewish question. The Nazi-instituted ghettos were, in fact, camps where the Jews were held under duress, with their internal life and organization imposed on them and enforced, through violent means, from the outside, by the Nazi regime. The ghettos were introduced after the outbreak of the war in the towns and cities of eastern Europe—in Poland, the Baltic states, and the occupied parts of the Soviet Union. The ghetto established in Amsterdam, which was not a closed ghetto; the houses in BUDAPEST marked as "Jewish" in the final stage of the war; and the THERESIENSTADT camp, near Prague, differed in their form and structure from the

A sign in the Kovno ghetto (1941). The Yiddish text reads: "JEWS! Contribute for the poor and the naked. Give used winter clothes and shoes that you no longer need. Do not begrudge, and give with an open hand." [Centre Commémoratif de l'Holocauste à Montréal; J. Glasrot Collection]

ghettos in eastern Europe, and are not included in this survey.

Nazi-instituted Ghettos during the War. There is no record of any general order having been issued for the establishment of ghettos, and it may be assumed that they were the result of local initiative. True, Reinhard HEYDRICH's directive of September 21, 1939, on the policy to be adopted toward the Jews in the occupied territories, stated that "the concentration of the Jews in the cities may require, for reasons of general police security, that orders be issued prohibiting Jews from entering certain parts of the cities; also, while taking into consideration the needs of the economy, Jews will not be permitted to leave the ghetto after a certain time in the evening, and so on." The directive, however, did not contain a specific order for the establishment of ghettos, and Heydrich apparently used the term to refer to the Jewish quarters existing at the time in Polish cities. At any rate, when Hans FRANK became responsible for the GENERALGOUVERNEMENT, he did not issue a general order providing for the creation of ghettos, as he did with regard to Judenräte (Jewish councils; *see* JUDENRAT), the Jewish BADGE, and the forced-labor system.

As a result, the ghettos in the various parts of occupied Poland were not set up at one and the same time, nor was there uniformity in the method of separating the ghettos from the outside world, or in the internal regimes of the ghettos. The first ghetto in Poland, in PIOTRKÓW TRYBUNALSKI, was started as early as October 1939, while the ghetto in ŁÓDŹ, Poland's second largest city (situated in the WARTHEGAU, the part of Poland that was annexed to the Reich), was closed on April 30, 1940, at which time it had a population of 164,000. The WARSAW ghetto, the largest in occupied Europe (Warsaw having contained Europe's largest Jewish community), was fenced in during November 1940; its population reached its maximum in March 1941, when it numbered 445,000. In LUBLIN and KRAKÓW the ghettos were established in March 1941, followed in April by RADOM, KIELCE, and CZĘSTOCHOWA, the remaining large cities of the Generalgouvernement. In Silesia, an area that was annexed to the Reich, Jews were locked into ghettos only at the end of 1942 and the beginning of 1943, at the time when its Jewish communities were about to be annihilated. The SOSNOWIEC ghetto was established in October 1942. When the German invasion of the Soviet Union was in full swing, in the latter part of 1941, ghettos were set up in the areas captured from the Soviet Union—in VILNA, in KOVNO, in the Baltic states, and in Belorussian towns. At the end of August 1941, the military administration in the Ukraine ordered that ghettos be established "in places with a relatively large Jewish population, primarily in the cities." In those towns and cities of eastern Europe in which the Jews constituted a majority of the population, the establishment of ghettos ran into difficulties and took time. In the Soviet areas the establishment of the ghettos was preceded by massacres, carried out by the EINSATZGRUPPEN; in some places, such as Vilna, the congregation of the Jews in a ghetto was planned as part of an operation, in which the next steps were to seize masses of Jews and to take them to sites that had been designated for their murder. In areas that had been part of the Soviet Union before World War II, the mass murder and annihilation of Jews were carried out as soon as the German army and the Einsatzgruppen reached the scene, and only a few ghettos were set up; the largest was in MINSK, the capital of Belorussia, which had a maximum population of 100,000.

Euphemisms, Brick Walls, and Barbed Wire. The Germans did not use the term "ghetto" in every instance in which they locked Jews into a separate quarter. In Piotrków Trybunalski they did use the term in the order for the establishment of such a quarter, as they did in Łódź, where it was officially called the Litzmannstadt ghetto (the Germans used the name Litzmannstadt for Łódź). In Warsaw, Kraków, and other places they referred to the ghetto as the *Jüdischer Wohnbezirk* (Jewish residential quarter), carefully avoiding the use of any other term.

The methods by which the ghettos were locked in and guarded took various forms. The Łódź ghetto was enclosed by a barbed-wire and wooden fence and, in some places, a brick wall, with guards posted on both the inside and the outside of the dividing line. The Warsaw ghetto was surrounded by an 11-mile (18-km) wall, with guards posted at the gates and patrolling the length of the wall; the Kraków ghetto was also behind a wall. The Łódź ghetto was hermetically closed, non-Jews being able to enter only by special permission and Jews unable to leave at all; there was hardly any smuggling in the ghetto, in either direction. In the Warsaw ghetto, on the other hand, smuggling went on throughout its existence, by way of the wall or checkpoints, and there was also infiltration by individuals into the ghetto. In medium-sized cities and towns, there were ghettos that Jews were permitted to leave at certain hours of the day only, to make food purchases, while in other places it was possible to move in and out without special difficulties. Piotrków Trybunalski, for example, did not have a fence and was not under guard, and hundreds of Poles were able to go back and forth, while the Jews had no difficulties in leaving. This situation, however, began to change at the end of 1941, and by the spring of 1942 the ghetto was locked in. When the deportations and the "Final Solution" were launched, most of the ghettos were put under lock and key. Under a decree issued in October 1941 by Hans Frank, chief of the Generalgouvernement, any Jew found outside the ghetto without permission was to be put to death; on the basis of this order, Jews from Warsaw—including women and children—were executed at the end of 1941. Nevertheless, the smuggling did not stop for as long as the ghettos remained in existence, despite the cost in human lives.

A ghetto and its administration required the provision of services and institutions in which Jews had had no previous experience. In their cynical propaganda, the Nazis often described the ghetto as a form of self-government, a sort of autonomy, that they had granted to the Jews. In addition to the Judenräte, which were created before the ghettos were established and without connection with them, the ghetto framework, as well as specific orders issued by the authorities, forced the Jews to organize a police force and postal services, to distribute food rations, and to provide work, housing, and health facilities—the kind of municipal and other services that had not previously been within the range of functions carried out by Jewish community organizations.

Reasons and Excuses. The German authorities justified the introduction of ghettos on various grounds: they were to prevent the spread of contagious diseases by the Jews, to combat Jewish profiteering and political rumormongering, and the like. Some of these claims were unfounded and partly invented as excuses for their actions. A number of scholars maintain that the ghettos were designed to serve as an indirect instrument of destruction, as a means of physically destroying the Jews by denying them the basic necessities of life, rather than by the use of lethal weapons. The situation in the two large ghettos—Łódź and Warsaw—seems to support this thesis. In 1941 and 1942, 112,463 persons died in the two ghettos of starvation and disease, which means that 20 percent of the population perished in the space of two years, while the birthrate was practically nil. Joseph GOEBBELS spoke of the ghettos as *Todeskisten* ("death crates"), and Hans Frank, in August 1942, stated: "Clearly, we are sentencing 1.2 million Jews [i.e., the Jewish population of the Generalgouvernement] to death by starvation; and if they do not die from hunger, we will have to adopt other anti-Jewish measures." When Frank made this statement he was already well aware of the "Final Solution" and its implications; previously he had said it would be worthwhile to exploit skilled Jewish laborers, who would be working practically for free. Senior Nazi officials in the Generalgouvernement had on several occasions suggested that Jewish food rations be increased to raise productivity. In the medium-sized cities the Jews in the ghettos suffered from severe shortages, from the hard labor forced on them, and from the overall intolerable conditions, but in many cases there was no death from starvation. It is correct to say that although the Nazis had no qualms about masses of Jews dying from hunger and shortages of other basic necessities, especially if they were not part of the needed labor force, no conclusive evidence exists that the ghettos were created for the purpose of the physical destruction of the Jews, or that in the course of time the Nazis sought to transform the ghettos into places where the total liquidation of the Jewish people would be carried out.

The "Final Solution" Implemented. The ghettos established in the cities housed not only the local Jewish population and those classified as Jews according to the racial laws, but also refugees from other towns and villages, near and far. Thus, by the time the Warsaw ghetto was enclosed, in November 1940, ninety thousand refugees had been added to the city's Jewish population. In addition to Polish Jewish refugees, Jews from Germany, Austria, and the Protectorate of Bohemia and Moravia were also brought to the ghettos; at the end of 1941, twenty thousand Jews from these countries were deported to the Łódź ghetto, and thousands to the Riga, Minsk, and Warsaw ghettos. The Łódź ghetto, at one stage, also took in Gypsies, who were housed in a special section. Some places had more than one ghetto, or the ghetto consisted of several separate parts. In most cases, two ghettos existed—one with a working population, the other for Jews whose annihilation was imminent. Such differentiation was instituted at an early stage, when the Einsatzgruppen were being deployed, as in Vilna. The procedure was also followed in the final stage of the liquidation of the ghettos; in Warsaw, for example, from the great deportation of the summer of 1942 until the final annihilation of the Jews in the city during the spring of 1943, there were three separate ghettos, or separate divisions of the ghetto. In Minsk, Jews brought in from western Europe were confined to a ghetto of their own.

The liquidation of the ghettos coincided with the beginning of the "Final Solution," in the spring of 1942. The last ghetto to be liquidated was that of Łódź, in the summer of 1944. On July 19, 1942, Heinrich HIMMLER issued an order for the physical destruction of the Jews of the Generalgouvernement by the end of the year: "After December 31, 1942, no person of Jewish origin must be found in the Generalgouvernement, with the sole exception of those in the concentration camps [*Sammellager*] in Warsaw, Kraków, Częstochowa, Radom, and Lublin." Another Himmler order, dated June 21, 1943, provided that "all Jews who may still be found in ghettos in the Ostland must be confined in concentration camps." Most of the Jews taken out of the ghettos were murdered in the extermination camps, and only a small percentage were put into concentration and forced-labor camps in the latter stages of the war. Himmler's orders also specified that "the presence of the remaining Jews in labor camps is also to be regarded as temporary; they will stay there only as long as there is a need for the work they do and they are physically able to perform it."

All the Jews of the occupied countries in eastern Europe were enclosed in ghettos, but when the territories in which ghettos had been established were liberated, in the Soviet Union, Poland, and Lithuania, not a single ghetto was left standing, in whole or in part.

BIBLIOGRAPHY

Blumenthal, N. *Conduct and Actions of a Judenrat: Documents from the Bialystok Ghetto*. Jerusalem, 1962. (In Hebrew and English.)

Blumenthal, N. *Documents from the Lublin Ghetto: Judenrat without Direction*. Jerusalem, 1967. (In Hebrew and English.)

Dobroszycki, L., ed. *The Chronicle of the Lodz Ghetto, 1941–1944*. New Haven, 1984.

Trunk, I. *Ghetto Lodz*. New York, 1962. (In Yiddish.)

Trunk, I. *Judenrat: The Jewish Councils in Eastern Europe under Nazi Occupation*. New York, 1972.

ISRAEL GUTMAN

GHETTO FIGHTERS' MUSEUM. *See* Museums and Memorial Institutes: Bet Loḥamei ha-Getta'ot.

GHETTO POLICE. *See* Jüdischer Ordnungsdienst.

GHETTOS, NUTRITION IN. The Polish ghettos received food supplies in two ways—from official and from unofficial sources. Official supplies were distributed on the basis of ration cards issued by the occupation authorities, a method that was introduced even before the Jews were confined to separate city quarters. Already at that early stage, the food rations allocated to the Jews were far short of those supplied to the rest of the population. (This entry will deal solely with the ghettos in Poland.)

When the ghettos were established, their supply departments were authorized to purchase food in specific quantities, according to allocations determined by the German authorities. In the GENERALGOUVERNEMENT these allocations were very meager and did not meet the minimum requirements. In the second half of 1941, the daily food ration received by Jews on the basis of their ration cards consisted of an average of 184 calories; in comparison, a person employed on light work requires 2,400 calories a day. In other words, the Jews received 7.5 percent of the normal quota of food. The Germans received the full ration, while the Poles were given 26 percent of their basic requirements.

The quantity and quality of the food rations for the Jews in the Generalgouvernement led to their physical extermination. Generalgouverneur Hans FRANK, in a speech on August 24, 1942, made the following statement: "In passing, may I say that we are sentencing 1.2 million Jews to death by hunger. It is obvious that if the Jews do not die from hunger, the execution of anti-Jewish orders will have to be speeded up."

In most of the ghettos of western Poland, in the areas that had been incorporated into the Third Reich, except for Łódź and a few other ghettos, the standard of nutrition was a little better than in the Generalgouvernement. At first, the daily food ration for the Jews contained 1,500 calories, with those who were employed on hard labor receiving 1,800 calories. This level of nutrition was planned for the people employed in the armaments industry and other branches of the economy that were of importance to the Reich, and was to be maintained until the time came for the liquidation of the Jewish population. In practice, however, the food ration in many of the ghettos in the incorporated areas was reduced to 513 calories per day, and 638 for those employed on hard labor.

Items supplied on the basis of ration cards were sold at a much lower price than they were on the free (black) market. The items supplied on the basis of ration cards were few in number: bread, 2.47 to 8.82 ounces (70–250 g) in the Generalgouvernement; a few potatoes; sugar, 8.82 ounces (250 g) per person per month; and sometimes also such items as jam, cabbage, and beets. Since the food supplied on the ration cards was far from enough, people of means tried to buy more food. This was easier to do in the ghettos of the Generalgouvernement than in the areas that had been annexed to the Reich. In the ghettos of the annexed areas there was no free, unfettered market where goods smuggled in by local peasants could be bought; the food that did reach the ghettos, in small quantities, had to be smuggled in at the risk of life. Such goods were more expensive in the ghetto than in the free market outside; in the Warsaw ghetto, bread cost 32 percent more and potatoes 25 percent to 73 percent more than in "Aryan" Warsaw.

Most of the Jews were impoverished, having been robbed of their possessions by the Germans and having lost their sources of livelihood when they were confined to walled-in ghettos, where there were no openings for work (this applied to 60 percent of the Jewish population). This meant that in the Generalgouvernement ghettos, only the relatively wealthy could afford to buy food on the black market; but even those who had not lost their source of income, or had accumulated savings, had to scale down their food purchases because of the high prices and the uncertain future they were facing.

For example, in December 1941, Warsaw Judenrat employees—who were regarded as having a privileged status—consumed an average of 1,665 calories per day; the various types of teamsters, 1,544; shopkeepers, 1,429; self-employed artisans, 1,407; unemployed professionals, 1,395; house superintendents, 1,350; employees of "shops" (ghetto workshops), 1,229; refugees in bunkers, 805; beggars, 785 calories.

In general, the Jews paid for their food purchases with the proceeds of the sale of their possessions on the "Aryan" side. As a result, the price of clothes and household goods declined the most. People who did not have any savings went hungry, or starved to death, despite the additional nourishment available in the soup kitchens; the latter, at a fairly low price, provided a calorie-poor soup (the nutritional value of one portion of soup in the Warsaw ghetto at the end of 1941 was 110 calories). At the height of their operation, the soup kitchens in Warsaw supplied 128,000 soup portions per day. In the first eighteen months of the ghetto's existence, 15 percent to 20 percent of its population starved to death. In other ghettos the situation was much the same, as shown by the statistics of the huge rise of the mortality rate and of diseases caused by hunger. Particularly hard hit was the Łódź ghetto, where a special currency was introduced in the Jewish quarter and Jews were not allowed to have regular money in their possession. In this way, the Jews in the ghetto were completely isolated economically, without means of smuggling, and were unable to purchase food to any appreciable extent. This caused the mortality rate in the Łódź ghetto to soar, from 0.96 percent in the prewar period to 3.92 percent in 1940, 7.57 percent in 1941, and 15.98 percent in 1942.

Some of the ghetto population, who were employed on jobs in German-operated factories and were housed in barracks (mainly in the period when the ghettos were being liquidated, beginning in mid-1942), had part of their food requirements provided to them by the management of these factories, the rations they received depending on the type of work they were doing. The official rations were close to starvation level and the workers were forced to obtain their own food, which became increasingly difficult during the liquidation of the ghettos, when unofficial supplies were drastically reduced.

The lack of food in the ghettos was sometimes exploited by the Germans to persuade the Jews to report for deportation of their own free will. In one period, Jews in Warsaw who volunteered for deportation were given 6.6 pounds (3 kg) of bread and 2.2 pounds (1 kg) of jam.

BIBLIOGRAPHY

Dobroszycki, L., ed. *The Chronicle of the Lodz Ghetto, 1941–1944.* New Haven, 1984.

Gutman, Y. *The Jews of Warsaw, 1939–1943: Ghetto, Underground, Revolt.* Bloomington, 1982.

Trunk, I. *Judenrat: The Jewish Councils in Eastern Europe under Nazi Occupation.* New York, 1972.

ZBIGNIEW LANDAU

GILDENMAN, MOSHE ("Uncle Misha"; d. 1958), partisan commander. A resident of the town of Korets in eastern Volhynia, Gildenman was an engineer by profession. After the Nazis' first *Aktion* in Korets on May 21, 1942, in which his wife and daughter died, Gildenman, together with his son, Simha, organized a rebel unit. On September 23 of that year, on the eve of the final liquidation of the Jews of

Moshe Gildenman.

Korets, Gildenman, Simha, and ten young men left for the forests, armed with two revolvers and a butcher knife. After wandering northward for about two weeks, they took in the survivors of an armed group of Jews in the Klesov area, together with whom they made their base in the wooded and swampy terrain north of the Sarny-Rokitno railway track. All of the unit members armed themselves with weapons taken in battles, attacked German farms and Ukrainian police centers, and took revenge on collaborators.

In late January 1943, the unit joined Gen. Aleksandr Saburov's partisan group. The resulting company that Gildenman formed was initially entirely Jewish, but as it grew the Jews became a minority. The company operated independently in the northern area of the Zhitomir district until its liberation in October 1943. Early that month, Gildenman rescued beleaguered units of the Thirteenth Soviet Army; he went on to volunteer for the Soviet army and served as a captain in the engineer corps until the end of the war. He subsequently described the exploits of his unit in articles and in books (*On the Road to Victory: Types of Jewish Partisans*, 1946; and *The Destruction of Korets*, 1949; both in Yiddish). In the early 1950s, Gildenman emigrated to Israel; he died in Rehovot.

BIBLIOGRAPHY

Suhl, Y. *They Fought Back.* New York, 1967. See pages 261–273.

Suhl, Y. *Uncle Misha's Partisans.* New York, 1973.

SHMUEL SPECTOR

GITTERMAN, YITZHAK (1889–1943), director of the American Jewish JOINT DISTRIBUTION COMMITTEE (the Joint) in POLAND, an organizer of Jewish welfare in occupied Poland, and an active member of the underground and the ŻYDOWSKA ORGANIZACJA BOJOWA (Jewish Fighting Organization; ŻOB). Born in Horonstopol, a town in the Ukraine, Gitterman at an early age aided in organizing support to refugees and victims of persecution. In World War I war refugees from towns in Galicia and Lithuania benefited from his assistance, which also included facilitating their emigration from war-torn Europe. In 1921 he was appointed head of the Joint in Warsaw and took part in the postwar rehabilitation of the Jewish population and the establishment of welfare institutions. He was deeply involved in the relief efforts designed to alleviate the grave problems caused by the economic crisis of 1926 and its disastrous effect on the position of the Jews. Gitterman created a network of institutions that provided interest-free loans, the Centralna Kasa Bezprocentowa covering every city and town in Poland. This became an important instrument in Polish Jewry's defense against economic discrimination and boycott. There were places where no organized Jewish community existed, but the loan institution was there, representing every public institution whose services were required by a Jewish community. In the 1930s Gitterman was able to slow down somewhat the rapid pauperization process of Polish Jewry through vocational retraining and the introduction of new occupations.

When World War II broke out, Gitterman made his way to Vilna, which had a large concentration of refugees, and set up aid operations. He was on his way to Sweden to appeal for help when the boat on which he was sailing was seized by the Germans on the high seas. Gitterman was interned in a prisoner-of-war camp and returned to Warsaw in April 1940. He lost no time in taking over responsibility for the major functions of the Jewish Self-Help Society (Żydowska Samopomoc Społeczna) and the Jewish Mutual Aid Society (Żydowskie Towarzystwo Opieki Społecznej). When the Joint's financial resources were exhausted, Gitterman and his associates in the Joint leadership turned to the Jews of Poland themselves with an appeal for financial contributions.

As soon as the Jewish underground was set up, it benefited from Gitterman's support. The Self-Help Society, in which Gitterman played a prominent role, also had an underground council, made up of the leaders of the political underground in the Warsaw ghetto. Gitterman took a direct part in underground activities, together with Emanuel RINGELBLUM (a close friend), in the clandestine cultural programs and in social work for the underground organizations and YOUTH MOVE-

MENTS. He was a member of the ONEG SHABBAT and Idische Kultur Organizacje (Yiddish Culture Organization) executive boards.

When the first reports came in of the mass murder of Jews in eastern Europe, Gitterman lent his support to the emerging ŻOB, and provided funds to the Białystok ghetto fighters for the acquisition of arms. When the ŻOB was established in Warsaw in October 1942, Gitterman joined its coordinating committee's financial subcommittee, whose main task was to obtain funds for the purchase of arms.

Gitterman was killed on January 18, 1943, the first day of the second *Aktion* in the Warsaw ghetto.

BIBLIOGRAPHY

Bauer, Y. *American Jewry and the Holocaust: The American Jewish Joint Distribution Committee, 1939–1945.* Detroit, 1982.

Ringelblum, E. "Yitzhak Gitterman." In vol. 2 of *Dziennik Warszawskiego Getta: Natatki i szkice (1942–1943)*, pp. 122–141. Warsaw, 1961.

ISRAEL GUTMAN

GLASBERG, ALEXANDRE (1902–1981), French priest, born a Jew in Zhitomir, in the Ukraine. Glasberg wandered about central Europe, converted, and became a priest in France. In 1940, after the German conquest of France, he established a charitable organization, Amitié Chrétienne (Christian Friendship), to help the victims of the anti-Jewish measures. Under the patronage of Cardinal Pierre-Marie Gerlier, the head of the Catholic church in France, Glasberg's organization set up shelter institutions that took in hundreds of Jewish prisoners who had been released from internment camps run by the French authorities.

When the mass arrests and deportations of Jews began in the summer of 1942, Glasberg turned his rescue efforts into clandestine operations. He cooperated closely with the Jewish rescue organizations, taking special care to ensure that no attempt was made to influence the religious convictions of the persons who were in the care of his institutions. In December 1942, when the Gestapo discovered his activities, Glasberg joined the French partisans, under an assumed name. After the war he played an important role in the operations of the Mosad Aliya (the organization that dealt with the "illegal" immigration of Jews into Palestine) in France and Iran.

BIBLIOGRAPHY

Lazare, L. *La résistance juive en France.* Paris, 1987.

Marrus, M. R., and R. O. Paxton. *Vichy France and the Jews.* New York, 1981.

Wellers, Z. G., A. Kaspi, and S. Klarsfeld, eds. *La France et la question juive, 1940–1944.* Paris, 1981.

LUCIEN LAZARE

GLAZER, GESJA (d. 1944), underground fighter in LITHUANIA. Before World War II Glazer was a member of the Communist party in KOVNO, and she spent years in jail and concentration camps on account of her party activities. When the Germans invaded the Soviet Union on June 22, 1941, Glazer fled to the Soviet interior. From Moscow she was

Gesja Glazer.

dispatched to Lithuania (dropped by parachute), where she became active in setting up an underground and partisan movement to fight the German invaders. On one occasion she entered the Kovno ghetto and, in the name of the Communist party, handed a pistol to the committee of the Antifascist Organization, in appreciation of its operations; she suggested that she would be prepared to lead fighting units of the Jewish underground into the Augustów forest and establish partisan bases there. According to her plan, the bases were to take in the entire membership of the ghetto underground.

After a week Glazer departed for the forest, remaining in touch with the ghetto underground until February 1944. She then left to take part in the VILNA underground operations. When she saw the German police closing in on her, Gesja Glazer committed suicide.

ISRAEL GUTMAN

Josef Glazman.

GLAZMAN, JOSEF (1913–1943), Jewish underground and partisan leader. Born in the town of Alytus, in southern LITHUANIA, Glazman was given a nationalist and traditional upbringing and was active in the Betar Zionist youth movement. In 1937 he was appointed Betar leader for Lithuania, retaining the post until July 1940, when the Soviets dissolved all Jewish political movements in the country. In the first phase of Soviet rule in Lithuania, from July 1940 to the end of June 1941, Glazman was one of the underground leaders of the Revisionist party. When the Germans occupied Lithuania, Glazman was in VILNA, where he was apprehended and sent on forced labor in nearby Reise. In early November of 1941 Glazman returned to the Vilna ghetto, where he organized an underground group made up of Betar members. In order to aid his underground activities he joined the Jewish ghetto police, and at the end of November 1941 he was appointed its deputy chief.

Glazman was one of the founders of the FAREYNEGTE PARTIZANER ORGANIZATSYE (United Partisan Organization; FPO) of the Vilna ghetto and participated in its founding meeting on January 21, 1942. He became the FPO's deputy commander and was also in charge of its intelligence section and commander of one of its two battalions. His official post as deputy chief of the ghetto police was of great help to the underground's operations. Glazman also took an active part in the ghetto's educational and cultural activities. In June 1942, when the ghetto administration was reorganized, Glazman left the police and was appointed head of the ghetto housing department within the JUDENRAT (Jewish Council).

Glazman's relations with Jacob GENS (chief of the ghetto police and, as of July 1942, ghetto head) were strained because of Glazman's underground activities and their differences over policy. At the end of October 1942, Glazman was arrested on Gens's orders and dismissed from his post. He was released in mid-December 1942 after spending several weeks in jail; at the end of June 1943 he was again arrested and sent to the Reise labor camp, on Gens's orders. His arrest was accompanied by a clash between FPO members and the ghetto police.

A few weeks later, Glazman was returned to the ghetto. In the wake of the WITTENBERG affair (July 15, 1943), Glazman left the ghetto, leading the first group of FPO members into the forest in order to establish a partisan base there. On the way they fell into a German ambush and in the ensuing fight the group lost a third of its men. At the end of July, Glazman and his men reached the Naroch Forest, where he formed the Nekama (Revenge) Jewish partisan unit of the partisan brigade commanded by Fyodor Markov. At the end of September the Soviet command decided to dissolve the Jewish unit. As a result of this decision the unit also lost most of its arms. Glazman and a group of his comrades went over to the Lithuanian partisan command.

At this time the Germans launched a determined drive against the partisans in the Naroch and Kozhany forests. Glazman and a group of thirty-five Jewish partisans tried to break through to the Rudninkai Forest in the south in order to join up with FPO members who had gone there from the Vilna ghetto. On October 7, 1943, Glazman and his men were encircled by a superior German force. In the fierce struggle that followed he and his comrades were killed; only one member of the group, a young girl, was saved.

BIBLIOGRAPHY

Arad, Y. *Ghetto in Flames: The Struggle and Destruction of the Jews in Vilna in the Holocaust.* New York, 1978.

Lazar, C., ed. *Josef Glassman.* Publications of the Museum of the Combatants and Partisans, 4/10. Tel Aviv, 1983.

Tushmet, L. *Pavement to Hell.* New York, 1972.

YITZHAK ARAD

GLIK, HIRSH (Hirshke; 1922–1944), poet and partisan in Lithuania. Born in Vilna, Glik began working at the age of fifteen. He joined the Ha-Shomer ha-Tsa'ir Zionist youth movement, and in 1935, when he was only thirteen, he began to write Hebrew poems. Later he wrote mostly in Yiddish; in the period preceding the war he was the most outstanding member of the Yungwald (Young People) group of young writers (named after the literary journal of that name). In 1940 he published poems in *Vilner Emes* (Vilna Truth) and in the Kovno *Naye Bleter* (New Bulletin).

When Vilna was occupied by the Germans at the end of June 1941, Glik and his father were among the Jews who were seized at random and taken to labor camps, to work in the peat deposits at Biała-Waka and Rzesza. Even there Glik continued to write prodigiously, and the Vilna Writers' and Artists' Association awarded him a prize for a play he wrote that dealt with the life of the Jews working in the peat bogs.

In early 1943, when the Biała-Waka camp was liquidated, Glik was moved to the Vilna ghetto. He joined the FAREYNEGTE PARTIZANER ORGANIZATSYE (United Partisan Organization; FPO), and continued his writing. At this time he wrote *Di Balada fun Broynem Teater* (The Ballad of the Brown Theater), a macabre work that describes the terrible suffering of the Jews in the Lukishko prison before they were sent to their death at PONARY. On September 1, 1943, the FPO unit to which he belonged was captured and Glik was deported to Estonia, where he was imprisoned first in the Narva camp and then in the Goldfilz camp. In the summer of 1944 Glik broke out from the camp together with eight other FPO men, but all were killed by the Germans while trying to make their escape.

Even in the camps Glik did not cease writing, and he recited his poems to his comrades. Among the poems he wrote there were "In Gehenem bay Leningrad" (In Hell near Leningrad) and "Der Fay fun Mototsikl," (The Five from Mototsikl), a sarcastic verse composition about the Narva camp commandant, as well as poems about Vilna and hiding places in the ghetto. None of these works survived.

Glik's poems are very musical, and during the Holocaust years he composed poems that were to be sung. Most of these were designed to raise morale among the Jews, to glorify the deeds of the partisans, and to strengthen the Jews' faith and hope in the future. He gained fame with his "Song of the Partisans," which began: "Zog nisht keynmol az du geyst dem letztn Veg" (Never say that you are on your last journey). Glik based the song on a tune by two Soviet Jewish composers, the brothers Dimitri and Daniel Pokras. It became the partisan anthem as soon as it was written, and was sung in many places under Nazi rule. After the war it was translated into numerous languages and became popular among Jews all over the world.

BIBLIOGRAPHY

Dworzecki, M. *Hirsch Glik: The Author of the Jewish Partisan Hymn.* Paris, 1966. (In Yiddish.)

Dworzecki, M. *Jewish Camps in Estonia, 1942–1944.* Jerusalem, 1970. (In Hebrew.)

Meisel, N. "Hirsch Glik: His Life and Works." In *Hirsch Glik: Songs and Poems,* pp. 11–40. New York, 1953. (In Yiddish.)

YEHIEL SZEINTUCH

GLOBKE, HANS (1898–1973), civil servant in the Reich Ministry of the Interior and coauthor of an official commentary on the NUREMBERG LAWS of 1935. Globke was born in Düsseldorf and studied law in Bonn and Cologne before joining the civil service in 1929, as ministerial councillor in the Prussian Ministry of the Interior. Before 1933 he belonged to the Catholic Center party, and he never joined the Nazi party.

Globke used his legal training in helping to draft the emergency legislation that gave Adolf Hitler dictatorial powers. He also worked on the legislation that dissolved the Prussian State Council and coordinated all Prussian parliamentary bodies (the Prussian Enabling Act of June 1, 1933). He achieved notoriety through a commentary that he wrote, together with Wilhelm STUCKART, on the racial legislation in the Nuremberg Laws and through his participation in drafting the Reich Citizenship Law (1935) and the Law for the Protection of German Blood and German Honor (1935). These laws excluded "persons of alien blood" and opponents of the regime from citizenship and the exercise of civil rights. They also aimed at the "biological separation" of Jews from "Aryans." Globke prepared later legislative instruments whereby all German Jews were required to adopt the middle name Israel or Sarah, and the Jewish-owned property of concentration camp victims devolved to the state (1944). During the war Globke worked with Heinrich HIMMLER in applying these Nuremberg racial laws in occupied Europe.

After the war, Globke was arrested but later released because he had been only a Nazi "fellow traveler." He became a Reichstag deputy for the Christian Democratic party and, in 1953, state secretary in the Chancellery of the Federal Republic and head of its personnel division. His association with the Nazis made him a target for widespread criticism, especially from East Germany. Although he offered to resign several times, he was always defended by Chancellor Konrad Adenauer, who accepted Globke's claim that he had in fact sought to alleviate the legal measures demanded by Hitler. Globke retired to Switzerland in 1963; he died in Bad Godesberg on February 13, 1973.

BIBLIOGRAPHY

Zaborowski, J. *Dr. Hans Globke, the Good Clerk.* Poznań, 1962.

LIONEL KOCHAN

GLOBOCNIK, ODILO (1904–1945), senior SS commander; a principal participant in the extermination of Polish Jewry. Born in Trieste to an Austrian-Croat family of minor officials, Globocnik was a contractor by profession. He joined the Nazi party in Austria in 1931 and the SS in 1934. His illegal activity on behalf of the party led to a number of short spells of imprisonment. Before the ANSCHLUSS (the annexation of Austria to Germany in 1938), Globocnik was already active in the formation of Nazi factory cells in the provinces, and in 1936 he was appointed provincial party leader in Carinthia. He earned rapid promotion in 1938, in March to SS-*Standartenführer,* and in May to state secretary and *Gauleiter* of VIENNA. He lost this position in January 1939 on account of illegal currency dealings, but was pardoned by Heinrich HIMMLER, and in November 1939 was appointed district *SS- und Polizeiführer* (SS and Police Leader) for the Lublin district of Poland and promoted to SS-*Brigadeführer und Generalmajor.*

In 1941 Himmler entrusted Globocnik with the planning and establishment of police- and SS-fortified strongpoints in Poland, and, in 1942, with the implementation of AKTION REINHARD. For this purpose Globocnik was

Odilo Globocnik.

put in charge of special SS troops subordinate only to Himmler. He used the camps of BEŁŻEC, SOBIBÓR, TREBLINKA, and MAJDANEK to carry out a fourfold task: the exploitation of the Jewish work force, the extermination of Jews, the acquisition of the real estate of the murdered Jews, and the seizure of their valuables and movable property. More than two million Jews were killed during Aktion Reinhard, and property to the value of 178 million reichsmarks was seized for the benefit of the Reich.

In August 1943, as a result of differences with other party and SS leaders, Globocnik, was transferred to Trieste. He was taken captive by British troops at the end of the war and committed suicide in May 1945.

BIBLIOGRAPHY

Arad, Y. *Belzec, Sobibor, Treblinka: The Operation Reinhard Death Camps.* Bloomington, 1987.

Hilberg, R. *The Destruction of the European Jews.* New York, 1985.

LIONEL KOCHAN

GŁÓWNA KOMISJA BADANIA ZBRODNI HITLEROWSKICH W POLSCE. *See* Documentation Centers: Main Commission for Investigation of Nazi Crimes in Poland.

GLÜCKS, RICHARD (1889–1945), SS officer. A native of Düsseldorf, Glücks served as an officer in World War I and then became a merchant. He joined the Nazi party only after its rise to power. In 1936 he became chief aide to Theodor EICKE, the *Inspekteur der Konzentrationslager* (Inspector of Concentration Camps), rising to the rank of SS-*Brigadeführer.* Shortly after the war broke out, Glücks was appointed as Eicke's successor and promoted to SS-*Gruppenführer.*

Under Glücks there was a sharp rise in the number of concentration camps and their imprisoned population. At the time he took charge, the camps' main function was to serve the war effort by utilizing masses of forced laborers, mostly from the German-occupied territories. A large number of non-Jews were among the concentration camp inmates, in addition to the Jews. All were put on hard labor, and a great many inmates perished in the camps, from starvation, disease, and ill-treatment.

Glücks was responsible for the establishment of the AUSCHWITZ camp, which was to become a major instrument for the implementation of the Final Solution. He was also responsible for the construction of the GAS CHAMBERS that helped serve this goal, and he had a part in the MEDICAL EXPERIMENTS that were being performed in the concentration camps.

In 1942, Glücks was put in charge of one of the units of the SS WIRTSCHAFTS-VERWALTUNGSHAUPTAMT (Economic-Administrative Main Office; WVHA), which was headed by Oswald POHL. At the end of the war, Glücks had the rank of SS-*Obergruppenführer.* He died in Flensburg in May 1945, apparently by committing suicide.

BIBLIOGRAPHY

Hilberg, R. *The Destruction of the European Jews.* New York, 1985.

Reitlinger, G. *The Final Solution: The Attempt to Exterminate the Jews of Europe, 1939–1945*. London, 1953.

DAVID HADAR

GOEBBELS, JOSEPH (1897–1945), Nazi leader. Goebbels was born in Rheydt, in the Rhine district, into a poor and pious Catholic family. Born with a clubfoot, he did not serve in the army in World War I; instead, he studied at the University of Heidelberg and earned a doctorate in literature and philosophy. After failing in his attempts to become a writer, Goebbels found ample room for his talents as a propagandist and speaker for the Nazi party, which he joined in 1924. At first he worked together with Gregor Strasser, a rival of Adolf HITLER, but before long he became one of Hitler's most ardent admirers and in 1926 was appointed *Gauleiter* of Berlin, his assignment being to win over the capital for the party. In 1928 he was elected to the Reichstag. Two years later he was also appointed the party's chief of propaganda, and it was he who ran the Nazis' stormy election campaigns from 1930 to 1933.

On March 13, 1933, soon after Hitler's accession to power, Goebbels was appointed minister of propaganda and public information. He imposed Nazification upon the country's artistic and cultural life, working through the branches of the ministry that he headed. He controlled the media (although he had to contend with some rivals in that regard), and it was at his prompting that "un-German" books were burned on May 10, 1933. Goebbels was also one of the creators of the "Führer" myth, an important element in the Nazis' successful bid for the support of the masses.

By the time the Nazi regime was firmly established, Goebbels's position was weakened and he also lost some of his standing in Hitler's eyes. Once the political forces that had opposed the Nazis were destroyed, Goebbels no longer had an "enemy" to fight (except for the Jewish "enemy"), and Hitler was angered by the frequent crises in Goebbels's marital life, fearing that they might cause damage to the party's image.

When the war broke out, Goebbels assumed a key role in psychological warfare (although in that field, too, he had rivals), and when the situation on the fronts took a turn for the worse, he again played a central part in the leadership. His ties with Hitler resumed their closeness, although the feelers that he put out to bring the war to a "political end" were disregarded, as, for a long while, was his demand for the "totalization" of the war. It was only in July 1944 that he was appointed to the coveted task of having responsibility for the total mobilization of the population for the war effort.

Joseph Goebbels.

When Hitler put an end to his life in the besieged capital, Goebbels refused to accept the post of Reich chancellor, to which he was appointed in Hitler's will. On May 1, 1945, on the morrow of Hitler's suicide, Goebbels and his wife, Magda, followed Hitler's example and also committed suicide in the Führer bunker, after first ordering the killing of their six children, aged four to twelve.

Joseph Goebbels, minister of propaganda, speaking before a crowd on April 1, 1933, the day of the economic boycott against the Jews of Germany.

Goebbels was the father of modern propaganda in a totalitarian state (a term that he coined), in which he made use of every available means. The propaganda he spread was remarkably replete with defamations, libels, and lies; he was convinced that people would believe the lies if only they were repeated often enough, and the bigger the lie, the better chance it had of being believed. Goebbels's propaganda always incited hate against some enemy. He was a radical and fanatic antisemite, but his hatred of Jews was also based on utilitarian considerations of exploiting antisemitism for the furthering of his propaganda aims.

Goebbels was relentless in depicting "the Jew" as an abominable creature and the principal enemy of the German people. It was Goebbels who conceived the idea of the KRISTALLNACHT pogroms in November 1938, and it was he who gave the event its flippant designation. Following these pogroms, he drastically reduced organized Jewish activities and freedom of movement in the sphere that he controlled. Once the war had broken out, the ministry he headed launched a concerted effort designed to aggravate living conditions for the Jews of Berlin. The first deportations of Berlin Jews to the Łódź ghetto, in October 1941, were carried out to fulfill an express promise that Goebbels had given to Hitler, to make Berlin *judenrein* ("cleansed of Jews") as soon as possible. In pursuit of this aim, Goebbels always kept in touch with Hitler and with the REICHSSICHERHEITSHAUPTAMT (Reich Security Main Office; RSHA). His diary contains specific mention of the destruction of the Jews; in an entry that he made in May 1943, when the extermination operation in Poland was at its height, Goebbels stated: "The nations that were the first to reveal the true face of the Jew will be the ones that will take the Jew's place in ruling the world."

[*See also* Propaganda, Nazi.]

BIBLIOGRAPHY

Bramsted, E. K. *Goebbels and National Socialist Propaganda, 1924–1945.* Lansing, Mich., 1965.

Frölich, E., ed. *Die Tagebücher von Joseph Goebbels: Sämtliche Fragmente. Teil 1: Aufzeichnungen, 1924–1941.* 4 vols. Munich, 1988.

Heimer, H. *Joseph Goebbels.* Berlin, 1962.

Lochner, L. P., ed. *The Goebbels Diaries, 1942–1943.* Garden City, N.Y., 1948.

Reimann, V. *Goebbels.* Garden City, N. Y., 1976.

Trevor-Roper, H., ed. *Final Entries, 1945: The Diary of Joseph Goebbels.* New York, 1978.

YEHOYAKIM COCHAVI

Amon Goeth.

GOETH, AMON LEOPOLD (1908–1946), SS officer. Born in Vienna, Goeth joined the National Socialist party in 1932. In 1940 he joined the SS, where he rose to the rank of SS-*Hauptsturmführer*. Goeth was assigned to the headquarters of the SS Command and to the Lublin police. Subsequently he was transferred to KRAKÓW, where he was in charge of liquidating the ghettos and labor camps at Szebnie, Bochnia, TARNÓW, and Kraków, among other places. From February 1943 to September 1944 Goeth commanded the concentration camp at PŁASZÓW, near Kraków. After the war he was extradited to Poland at the request of the Polish authorities and tried before the Polish Supreme Court, on a charge of committing mass murder during the liquidation of the ghettos at the Szebnie camp and at Płaszów. He was sentenced to death, and executed in Kraków.

BIBLIOGRAPHY

Proces ludobojcy Amona Leopolda Goetha przed Najwyższym Trybunalem Narodowym. Warsaw, 1947.

STEFAN BIERNACKI

GOGA, OCTAVIAN (1881–1938), Romanian national poet and one of the leaders of the antisemitic movement in ROMANIA. Goga developed his antisemitic philosophy under the impact of the nationalist conflict between the Romanians and the Hungarians in Transylvania, and the role (in the view of the Romanian nationalists) that the Jewish minority played in this struggle. He was convinced that the Jews in Transylvania were "irrevocably" pro-Hungarian; that they were the leaders of the anti-Romanian cultural conflict in the region, demonstrating loyalty to the Hungarian language and culture; and that, consequently, they were a corrupt, dangerous, and alien entity in the united Romanian state.

At the beginning of the 1930s, Goga formed the Partidul Agarar (Agrarian Party), which derived its main strength from farmers in Transylvania, but the party did not gain significant support. This political activity enabled Goga to express his hatred for the Jews as well as for the Hungarians. It brought him close to the thinking of "classic" Romanian antisemites such as Alexandru CUZA, and to support of the Nazis. Through the intervention of representatives of the National Socialist party, and in particular of Alfred ROSENBERG, Goga and Cuza established the Partidul National Crestin (Christian National Party) in 1935. It became the second most important antisemitic organization after the Totul Pentru (IRON GUARD).

The Nazis viewed the new party, and Goga himself, as constituting an upcoming force worth cultivating. The ceremony marking the amalgamation of the Liga Apararii Nationale Crestin (League of National Christian Defense) and Goga's tiny Agrarian Party was held in the cathedral of IAŞI, and Goga and Cuza undertook to implement a virulent antisemitic platform. Despite his loyalty to King Carol II and his support of the parliamentary system, when it came to antisemitism, Goga completely lost control of himself;

the national poet became the leader of an antisemitic movement dependent on Nazi Germany to support its efforts to achieve power. Its gang of hooligans, based on the Nazi model, spread havoc, attacking Jews and political rivals no less than did the Iron Guard. In his speeches and at mass demonstrations Goga always made reference to the "Jewish problem," describing the Jews as lepers who had spread throughout Romania.

At the end of 1937 Goga was appointed prime minister of Romania, and he devoted himself to implementing his antisemitic policies. His was the first Romanian government with a manifest antisemitic platform like that of the Nazis. During the forty days that he headed the government he did everything within his power to implement his principles, closing down the democratic newspapers, promulgating laws and regulations dismissing Jews from government posts, annulling work permits, and so forth. His most serious act was the passing, on January 22, 1938, of the Law for the Reexamination of Citizenship of the Jews, according to which the civil rights of one-third of Romania's Jewish citizens were annulled. Goga stated that "a new page in the history of Romania has been opened and it cannot be turned back." The following month, he was forced to resign by virtue of pressure brought to bear by France and Britain. He claimed that his resignation was a "victory of the Jews." After his death, Goga's wife, Veturia Goga, continued to play a leading role in the antisemitic movement, especially during the government of Ion ANTONESCU, through her influence on the Romanian dictator.

BIBLIOGRAPHY

Seicaru, P. *Poezia si politica: Octavian Goga.* Madrid, 1956.

Vago, B. *The Shadow of the Swastika: The Rise of Fascism and Anti-Semitism in the Danube Basin, 1936–1939.* London, 1975.

JEAN ANCEL

GOLDMANN, NAHUM (1895–1982), Jewish and Zionist leader. Goldmann was born in Lithuania and taken to Germany when he was five years old. He studied at German universities, obtaining doctorates in humanities and law. At the outbreak of World War I, he joined the staff of the German Foreign Ministry's Jewish section. With his friend, the philosopher Jacob Klatzkin, Goldmann formed Eshkol Publishing House for the publication of the *Encyclopaedia Judaica.* The encyclopedia's completion was prevented by Hitler's rise to power, and only ten volumes in German and two in Hebrew were issued. In the 1960s, Goldmann initiated the publication of the English-language *Encyclopaedia Judaica,* which appeared in 1971.

Forced to leave Germany when Hitler came to power in 1933, Goldmann settled in Switzerland and, at the end of that year, was elected chairman of the Committee of Jewish Delegations, which had come into existence after World War I to present the Jewish case at the Paris Peace Conference. In the summer of 1932 the leaders of the Committee of Jewish Delegations and of the AMERICAN JEWISH CONGRESS, aware of the significance of the Nazi menace, had called the first preparatory conference for the WORLD JEWISH CONGRESS (WJC). At that conference, warnings concerning the Nazi danger had been voiced by the WJC's future leaders Stephen S. WISE and Nahum Goldmann. The new organization, founded after several more preparatory conferences, in August 1936 called for the mobilization of the Jewish people and of democratic forces against the Nazi onslaught; the struggle for equal political and economic rights everywhere, particularly for the Jewish minorities in central and eastern Europe; and support for the Jewish national home in Palestine. The WJC was established as a worldwide Jewish representative body, democratically organized and based on the concept of the unity of the Jewish people.

Goldmann was elected chairman of the WJC's Administrative Committee and until 1939 was its representative at the League of Nations; from 1934, he also represented the Jewish Agency for Palestine at the league. In this capacity he led the WJC's efforts with governments and the League of Nations to obtain prolongation of the Minority Rights Agreement covering Upper Silesia (*see* BERNHEIM PETITION) and thereby prevent the application of Nazi discriminatory measures in that region. When the government of Octavian GOGA introduced anti-Jewish measures in ROMANIA in 1937, the WJC petitioned the League of Nations, whose condemnation of Romania led to Goga's resignation early in 1938. Before and after the ANSCHLUSS, the WJC repeatedly appealed to the League of Nations for protection of the Jews of Austria.

Goldmann represented both the WJC and the Jewish Agency at the ill-fated EVIAN CONFERENCE, held in 1938, of which he later wrote: "The Evian Conference is an irrefutable indictment of the civilized world in its attitude to the Nazi persecution of the Jews." To facilitate the immigration to Palestine of Jews from Nazi Germany, Goldmann, who proclaimed a Jewish anti-Nazi boycott (*see* BOYCOTTS, ANTI-NAZI), was instrumental in concluding the HAAVARA AGREEMENT between the Jewish Agency and Nazi Germany.

Goldmann moved to the United States in June 1940, and throughout the war worked for both the WJC and the Jewish Agency. With Stephen S. Wise, he tried to mobilize American Jewry and public opinion to help the Jews in Nazi-occupied Europe, keeping in close contact with WJC offices in Geneva and London, and through these offices monitoring the havoc wrought by the Nazis. When in August 1942 Dr. Gerhart Riegner (*see* RIEGNER CABLE), the WJC representative in Geneva, cabled news of the "FINAL SOLUTION," Goldmann and Wise broke the media silence on the mass annihilation of Jews and bombarded President Franklin D. ROOSEVELT and the administration with pleas for help. This activity led to a December 1942 collective Allied condemnation of the Nazi extermination policy toward Jews and a stern warning of retribution.

An Advisory Council on European Jewish Affairs, under Goldmann's chairmanship, was set up in New York with representative committees from eighteen European countries. Tens of thousands of individual parcels were sent to concentration camps, and tons of food and medicines to Jewish communities in occupied Europe. A far-reaching rescue program was submitted to the 1943 refugee conference in Bermuda (*see* BERMUDA CONFERENCE); a memorandum on Jewish aspects of relief and rehabilitation was submitted to the first session of the UNITED NATIONS RELIEF AND REHABILITATION ADMINISTRATION (UNRRA) in 1943; and in December 1943 a license was obtained from the United States Treasury to transmit funds to Europe for the rescue and assistance of persecuted Jews, a step leading to the eventual establishment of the WAR REFUGEE BOARD.

Nahum Goldmann (right) with Louis Lipsky, American Zionist leader, at the inaugural assembly of the World Jewish Congress in Geneva (1936). [World Jewish Congress]

At the 1944 WJC War Emergency Conference in Atlantic City, Goldmann presented the first comprehensive program for the postwar rehabilitation of the Jewish people, including calls for REPARATIONS AND RESTITUTION from Germany to Jews, use of heirless Jewish property for Jewish rehabilitation, and punishment of Nazi persecutors of Jews. With the end of war in Europe, Goldmann was in the forefront of the struggle for the admittance into Palestine of the survivors, and for the reconstruction of destroyed Jewish communities. As chairman of the Conference on Jewish Material Claims against Germany, which he created, he led the negotiations for restitution and indemnification to Israel and to individual victims of Nazi persecution.

Looking back on the years of the Holocaust, Goldmann said that the greatest tragedy of all was that both the Jews and the democratic world failed to realize the magnitude and the depth of evil that Nazism embodied. He acknowledged the failure of his generation to stand up to the challenge.

After the war, Goldmann was co-chairman

of the executive of the World Zionist Organization (1948–1956), its president (1956–1968), and president of the WJC (1953–1977). He published his recollections in *The Autobiography of Nahum Goldmann: Sixty Years of Jewish Life* (New York, 1969), *Mein Leben als deutscher Jude* (My Life as a German Jew; Munich, 1980), and *Mein Leben: U.S.A.—Europa—Israel* (Munich, 1981).

BIBLIOGRAPHY

Dränger, J. *Nahum Goldmann: Ein Leben für Israel.* 2 vols. Frankfurt, 1959.

Garai, G., ed. *Forty Years in Action: A Record of the World Jewish Congress, 1930–1976.* Geneva, 1976.

Kubowitzki, A. L. *Unity in Dispersion: A History of the World Jewish Congress.* N.p., 1948.

ELIZABETH E. EPPLER

GOMEL, city in BELORUSSIA. In the nineteenth century Gomel had a Jewish population of over twenty thousand (56 percent of the city's population). On the eve of World War II, fifty thousand Jews were living in the city, a third of the total population. The Germans occupied Gomel on August 19, 1941. In the two months that passed between the Germans' invasion of the Soviet Union and their capture of the city, many Jews succeeded in fleeing from Gomel into the Soviet interior. Once the city was in German hands, the military governor, Schwach, ordered the Jews to wear the yellow badge (*see* BADGE, JEWISH). Ten Jews were put to death on the pretext that they were "Bolsheviks and terrorists."

A ghetto was established in Gomel, divided into four parts. In addition, three camps were set up for Jews: the Monastyrsk camp, with eight hundred Jews; Novo-Lubiensk, with five hundred Jews; and Novaya Belitsa, with two hundred. The inmates of these camps did not receive any food rations. At a later stage a fourth camp was set up in Povski Bazarchik, for Jews from foreign countries; its inmates were employed in clearing mine fields near the front line.

According to a December 1941 report by an Einsatzgruppe (*see* EINSATZGRUPPEN), 2,365 Jews were executed for having given aid to

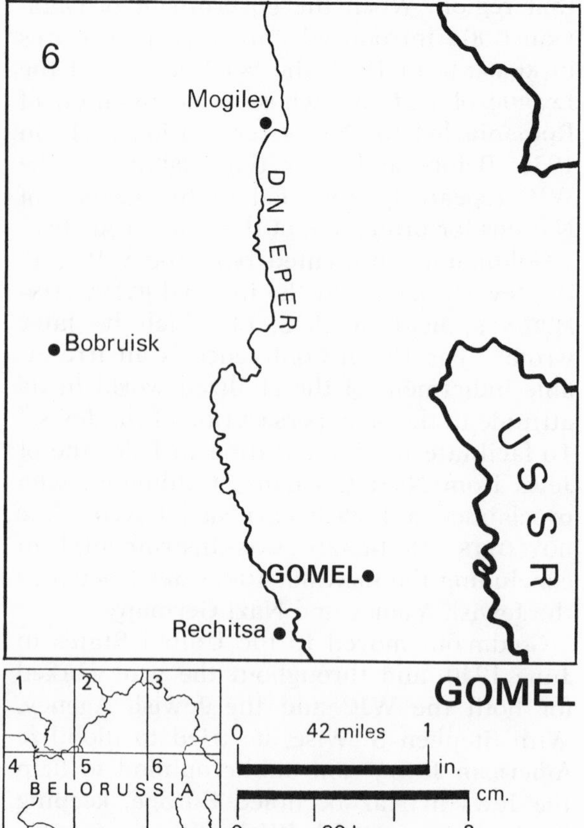

GOMEL

the partisans. They were apparently buried in military trenches near Leshtsinets on the way to Rechitsa. That same month, another 4,000 Jews from Gomel were put to death, in antitank ditches 5.6 miles (9 km) from Gomel, on the way to Chernigov. The women and children were gassed. These murders were most likely the work of Einsatzkommando 7b, commanded by Günther Rausch.

Gomel was liberated by the Soviets on November 26, 1943.

BIBLIOGRAPHY

Kahanovitch, Y. "Homel." In vol. 2 of *Jewish Mother-Cities,* edited by Y. L. Hacohen Fishman, pp. 187–269. Jerusalem, 1948. (In Hebrew.)

SHALOM CHOLAWSKI

GORDONIA. *See* Youth Movements.

GÖRING, HERMANN (1893–1946), Nazi leader. Göring was born in Rosenheim, Bavaria, the son of a wealthy family. In World War I he distinguished himself as a fighter pilot and commander of a renowned fighter squadron. He joined the Nazi party in 1922, was appointed commander of the SA (Sturmabteilung; Storm Troopers), and in November 1923 took part in the abortive Nazi putsch in Munich, in which he was wounded. In 1928, Göring was elected to the Reichstag on the Nazi ticket; he was elected Reichstag speaker in 1932. When Adolf HITLER came to power, Göring was appointed minister without portfolio, and then commissioner of aviation and Prussian minister of the interior. In April 1933 he became prime minister of Prussia and was one of the men responsible for the creation of the Gestapo. In the minds of many people, Göring was regarded as being behind the plot to burn down the Reichstag, in February 1933. In June 1934 he played a major role, together with Heinrich HIMMLER, in the liquidation of the SA leader Ernst RÖHM and his cohorts. Göring was appointed commander of the German air force (the Luftwaffe) in January 1935; this was followed by his promotion to *Reichsmarschall.* In 1936 he was put in charge of the FOUR-YEAR PLAN and given dictatorial powers in the economic sphere. From August 1939 Göring chaired the ministerial Reich Defense Council (Reichsverteidigungsrat), and on September 1, 1939, when war broke out, Hitler appointed him to be his successor.

As the person in charge of the country's economy, Göring was responsible for the confiscation of Jewish property in 1937. Following the KRISTALLNACHT pogroms, Hitler put him in charge of the "Jewish question," and Göring lost no time in accelerating the plundering of the Jews, imposing on them a collective fine of a billion reichsmarks. On January 24, 1939, he issued orders for the establishment of the ZENTRALSTELLE FÜR JÜDISCHE AUSWANDERUNG (Central Office for Jewish Emigration), on the model of Eichmann's operations in this sphere in Vienna. When Poland was occupied, Göring became involved in the expulsion of Jews from the western parts of Poland that were annexed to the Reich, and he set up the HAUPTTREUHANDSTELLE OST (Main Trusteeship Office East), to take charge of and administer confiscated Jewish property. On July 31, 1941, Göring ordered Reinhard HEYDRICH to "carry out all necessary preparations with regard to

Berlin. Generalfeldmarschall Hermann Göring reviews a parade of his regiment on Luftwaffe Day in March 1939. To his left is Generaloberst Wilhelm Keitel.

the Jewish question in the German sphere of influence in Europe." In the opinion of many scholars, this order was the first important document that set the "FINAL SOLUTION" in motion, and it establishes Göring's share in the responsibility for the extermination of the Jews of Europe.

As a result of the failures of the Luftwaffe in the Battle of Britain (1940–1941), its weak performance on the Soviet front, and its inability to defend Germany's skies, relations between Hitler and Göring soured. In the last few days of the Nazi regime, Göring lost whatever standing he had left, and was dismissed from all his posts and from the party; Hitler appointed Adm. Karl Dönitz in his place.

Göring was arrested by the Allies and was one of the defendants in the trial of major war criminals by the International Military Tribunal (the NUREMBERG TRIAL). He was sentenced to death, but on October 15, 1946, the eve of his scheduled execution, he poisoned himself in his prison cell.

BIBLIOGRAPHY

Bewly, C. *Hermann Goering and the Third Reich: A Biography Based on Family and Official Reports.* Toronto, 1962.

Fest, J. C. *The Face of the Third Reich: Portraits of the Nazi Leadership.* New York, 1970.

Irving, D. *Göring.* New York, 1989.

Manvell, R., and H. Fraenkel. *Goering: A Biography.* New York, 1962.

Mosley, L. *The Reich Marshal.* New York, 1975.

YEHOYAKIM COCHAVI

GORODENKA (Pol., Horodenka), town in Eastern Galicia. In the interwar period, Gorodenka was part of independent Poland; in September 1939 it was occupied by the Red Army, and like the rest of eastern Poland, was annexed by the Soviet Union, becoming part of the Ukrainian SSR. On the eve of World War II, Gorodenka had a Jewish population of four thousand. When the war broke out in September 1939, a large number of Jews from the German-occupied areas of western Poland took refuge there. Following the German invasion of the Soviet Union on June 22, 1941, a few dozen of the town's Jews escaped into the Soviet interior.

On July 2, 1941, units of the Hungarian army, which was allied with the Germans, entered Gorodenka. The local Ukrainian inhabitants began to attack the Jews, but the Hungarian troops tried to restrain them. The Ukrainian militia seized Jews in the streets for forced labor and abused them. In September of that year Gorodenka was put under direct German control, and the situation of the Jewish community became even worse. More Jews were seized for forced labor, fines were imposed, Jewish-owned apartments with all their contents were confiscated, and freedom of movement by Jews, inside and outside the town, was restricted.

In November a JUDENRAT (Jewish Council) was set up. Although forced to follow German orders, the Judenrat members did what they could to improve conditions in the community, establishing soup kitchens and intervening with the German authorities in an attempt to postpone anti-Jewish measures.

On December 4 and 5, Gorodenka's Jews were ordered to report to the Jewish school, ostensibly for vaccination, but actually to be sent to their death. A few skilled craftsmen were released; the rest of the twenty-five hundred who gathered were taken to a forest situated between the villages of Siemakowce

and Michalcze, 8 miles (13 km) from Gorodenka, and murdered there.

At the beginning of 1942 many Jews from small places in the vicinity were moved to the Gorodenka ghetto. The resulting overcrowding by far exceeded its capacity; many people died of starvation and disease. On April 13, another *Aktion* took place, and fourteen hundred persons were taken to the BEŁŻEC extermination camp; sixty Jews were murdered in the Gorodenka Jewish cemetery. In May and June several dozen Jews from Gorodenka were sent to the KOLOMYIA ghetto.

In July 1942 the liquidation of the ghetto began, with the murder of the remnants of the community in the town and of those Jews who had taken refuge in the nearby forests; some of the Gorodenka ghetto inhabitants were transferred to other ghettos in the area. Others fled to Tluste, hoping to find at least temporary asylum there, but most of these were murdered, together with the local Jews. After the liquidation of the Gorodenka ghetto some of the surviving Jews were taken to the JANÓWSKA camp in Lvov, and the rest to Bełżec.

Several dozen Gorodenka Jews escaped to the forests, and some of them joined the Soviet partisans. Many of those who reached the forest were killed by Ukrainian nationalists of the UKRAINSKA POVSTANSKA ARMYIA (Ukrainian Insurgent Army). Gorodenka was liberated by the Red Army on March 27, 1944. The few Jewish survivors eventually made their way to the West.

BIBLIOGRAPHY

Meltzer, S., ed. *Sefer Horodenka.* Tel Aviv, 1963. (In Hebrew and Yiddish.)

AHARON WEISS

GRÄBE, HERMANN FRIEDRICH (1900–1986), a "RIGHTEOUS AMONG THE NATIONS." Born in Solingen, Germany, Gräbe was a member of the Nazi party for a few months, but he later spoke out against the Nazi regime and served a short prison term. A construction worker, he was employed as a foreman at the Jung Company in Solingen. In October 1941 he was entrusted with setting up a branch of Jung in Zdolbunov, Volhynia,

Hermann Gräbe, seated at left, receiving a medal and certificate as a "Righteous among the Nations" from Aryeh Kubovy, chairman of Yad Vashem in Jerusalem (September 20, 1965).

for the construction and repair of buildings used by the railway directorate in the REICHSKOMMISSARIAT UKRAINE. Thousands of Jews were employed by Gräbe, and he insisted that his subordinates treat the workers properly. An intervention on his part with the Zdolbunov district commissar resulted in the cancellation of fines that had been imposed on the Jews; he also saved his Jewish employees from the *Aktionen* in Rovno in November 1941 and July 1942, not hesitating to intervene with the SD (Sicherheitsdienst; Security Service) commander in Rovno for this purpose.

Several dozen Jewish men and women were employed by Gräbe in the company's head office. In the summer of 1942, when they were seen to be in danger, they were given "Aryan" papers and sent to POLTAVA to work in what was purported to be a company branch; in actuality, it had been established by Gräbe without the authorization or knowledge of his employers, and it was maintained out of his own funds. In October of that year, alerted by his Jewish secretary, Gräbe went to Dubno, where he witnessed the murder of the city's Jews.

Gräbe saved the lives of dozens of Jews. At the NUREMBERG TRIAL, where he gave evidence on the crimes committed by the Nazis in Volhynia, his description of the slaughter of the Dubno Jews made a deep impression. This created widespread animosity against him in Germany, and with the help of Jewish organizations he emigrated with his family to the United States, settling in California. In 1966, Gräbe was invited to Israel to be presented with the "Righteous among the Nations" Award. There he planted a tree on the "Avenue of the Righteous" at Yad Vashem in Jerusalem.

BIBLIOGRAPHY

Spector, S. *The Holocaust of Volhynian Jews, 1941–1944.* Jerusalem, 1986. (In Hebrew.)

SHMUEL SPECTOR

GRAND MUFTI OF JERUSALEM. *See* Husseini, Hajj Amin al-.

GRAWITZ, ERNST ROBERT (1899–1945), Nazi official; head of the SS health services. The chief SS physician, in 1936 Grawitz was made head (*Reichsarzt*) of the SS health services, with the rank of SS-*Obergruppenführer*, and head of the German Red Cross. When implementation of the "FINAL SOLUTION" was officially approved in 1941, it was Grawitz who advised Heinrich HIMMLER on the use of GAS CHAMBERS.

As chief SS physician, Grawitz was among those responsible for carrying out different kinds of MEDICAL EXPERIMENTS on prisoners in the concentration camps, and by virtue of his rank in the SS he was administratively responsible for all these experiments. He was associated with almost every kind: survival experiments (testing how long a person can survive in severely adverse environmental conditions), healing experiments (involving infection with contagious and epidemic diseases, war wounds, and wounds from chemical warfare), and sterilization of women.

Grawitz committed suicide at the end of the war.

BIBLIOGRAPHY

Lifton, R. J. *The Nazi Doctors: Medical Killing and the Psychology of Genocide.* New York, 1986.

ZVI BACHARACH

GREAT BRITAIN. [*This entry consists of four articles:*

General Survey
Appeasement of Nazi Germany
Fascism in Great Britain
Jewish Refugees

The first is an overview of British and Anglo-Jewish history during the 1930s, and the second deals with British efforts to avert hostilities by the policy of appeasing Germany. The shifting fortunes of the British fascist movement are reviewed in the third article. British immigration policy toward Jewish refugees from continental Europe is the subject of the fourth article, which also discusses the efforts of British Jewry to aid the refugees.]

General Survey

At the outset of World War II, Britain's strategic interests were seriously overextended. With involvements stretching from East Asia through India, the Middle East, the Mediterranean, and to the North Sea, Britain was unable to defend the empire on its own. Since the beginning of the century, British politicians had been aware of the fundamental weakness underlying Britain's position. The huge manpower and material losses of World War I were still keenly felt, and until 1936 there was little public support for a serious rearmament program. Not surprisingly, British foreign policy attempted to appease potential enemies and win friends among neutral countries by making concessions to their demands. After the complete German takeover of Czechoslovakia, however (contrary to the agreement reached at the MUNICH CONFERENCE), Prime Minister Neville Chamberlain reversed his government's foreign policy based on appeasement and resolved to offer a mutual defense pact to Poland in order to deter German aggression against that state.

Militarily, Britain was too weak to present any meaningful threat to Germany. Rearmament had started late, and the British army was totally unprepared for war. When it broke out in September 1939, there were only two fully trained divisions in the United Kingdom. Other British troops were dispersed in the colonies, including almost seventeen thousand in Palestine. Despite the initial weakness of the army, Britain (together with its ally, France) declared war on Germany on September 3, 1939, two days after Germany invaded Poland.

The months that followed the declaration of war were popularly called the "phony war." Once Poland had fallen, there were no further German advances until May 1940. Britain was able to use this period to dramatically improve its fighting ability. Although the United States was technically neutral, President Franklin D. ROOSEVELT promised that American supplies would be available to Britain. The dominions—Canada, South Africa, Australia, New Zealand—and India also declared war on Germany. However, they were too far away from the main theater of action in Europe to make any significant contribution at this stage. When the fighting spread to North and East Africa and to Asia, the British dominions played a more active role.

Britain's most significant ally was France. Anglo-French strategy was based on a combined use of their navies to prevent German control of the seas—a vital consideration, since none of the belligerents was self-sufficient in natural resources.

In May 1940, the Germans moved against Belgium, Luxembourg, and the Netherlands and invaded France. Soon afterward, Italy joined the Axis and declared war on Britain. Despite German peace feelers and the fact that Britain was the only country in Europe still fighting Hitler, the British refused all negotiations. The successful evacuation of 200,000 British troops from France at Dunkerque, at the beginning of June 1940, enabled Britain to prepare for an expected German invasion of the British Isles. During this period of crisis the government of Neville Chamberlain was replaced by a national coalition led by Winston CHURCHILL. Churchill announced that Britain would continue fighting until the defeat of Germany.

The threat of an imminent German invasion lessened when, between August and October 1940, the Luftwaffe failed to defeat the Royal Air Force in the prolonged Battle of Britain. Nevertheless, the overall strategic situation had seriously deteriorated. The fall of France deprived Britain of the support of the French navy and of the substantial number of French troops in France, the Middle East, and North Africa. The entry of Italy into the war meant that the British could no longer safely transport soldiers or supplies to India via the Middle East. Italian forces in Libya attacked the large British bases in Egypt, but British forces managed to defeat the Italian thrust. As a result, German forces under Gen. Erwin Rommel were sent to North Africa to reinforce the Axis position.

British isolation during this period was alleviated by the growing willingness of the United States to support the British war effort. In March 1941, Roosevelt succeeded in having Congress pass the Lend-Lease Act, which allowed the administration to supply Britain with weapons under a leasing arrangement. The act recognized the importance for American security of an eventual British victory against Hitler. The growing political alliance between the two powers was given expression in the Atlantic Charter of August 14, 1941.

Throughout the late 1930s, Britain had attempted to strengthen its position in the Middle East by seeking the support of the independent Arab states. Although there were a number of differences between Britain and the Arab leaders, Britain decided that the conflict in Palestine was the most significant cause of Anglo-Arab disagreement. The 1939 British WHITE PAPER on Palestine, limiting Jewish immigration and the sale of land to Jews, and undertaking to establish a future independent Palestinian state with a large Arab majority, was in part an attempt to win Arab support in the inevitable war against Germany. Appeasement, however, failed in the Middle East, just as it had failed in Europe. The British had to threaten the use of force in Egypt to induce the government there to break off diplomatic relations with Italy after that power declared war against Britain. The Transjordan Frontier Force, which had been created by the British, proved unreliable in the Iraq campaign. A pro-Axis government rose to power in Iraq in April 1941, leading to the British occupation of that country shortly afterward. Syria and Lebanon were taken over by British and Free French troops in July 1941. These were holding operations, designed to prevent the emergence of a strategic threat to Britain's position in Egypt from the east. The main theater in the Middle East remained the battle of the Western Desert.

When the German air force lost the Battle of Britain, Hitler abandoned his plan for the invasion of the British Isles and turned his attention to the Soviet Union. On June 22, 1941, German troops invaded Russia on a broad front from the Baltic to Romania. Despite Churchill's strong anti-Communist beliefs, he immediately offered Joseph STALIN assistance in supplies and weapons. Hitler's decision to strike out eastward transformed the nature of World War II, and considerably relieved the pressure on Britain and on British positions in the Middle East. The Japanese attack on Pearl Harbor on December 7, 1941, and the official declaration of a state of war between the United States and Japan (followed soon after by the German declaration of war against the United States), meant that the war had become truly global. Britain was no longer fighting alone, or only in the Middle East.

By the beginning of 1942 a grand alliance, led by Churchill, Roosevelt, and Stalin, had been formed. A number of basic principles guided the joint Allied effort against the Axis. The war against Germany was given priority over the war in the Pacific, despite the rapid advance of Japanese forces during 1942. Given the disproportionately large number of troops fighting on the Russian front, Britain and America undertook to open a second European front against the Germans as soon as possible.

The three remaining principles of Allied policy toward Germany eventually had major implications for Allied policy on the relief and rescue of European Jewry. First, the blockade of occupied Europe was recognized as an essential weapon against the German war effort. It was central to British wartime strategy, and the British government refused all efforts to circumvent it. This included British opposition to the sending of relief supplies to the civilian populations under German control (although there were some exceptions). The second principle was that there would be no negotiations with Hitler. This was designed to reassure Stalin that Britain and America would not join with the Germans in a joint effort to destroy the Soviet Union. Although there were contacts with the Germans by means of neutral states and the International RED CROSS on various humanitarian issues, the principle of "no negotiations" prevented any serious consideration of German proposals for the ransom of Jews. The third principle was that the Allies would fight until the unconditional surrender of Germany and the Axis. This ensured that there would be no negotiations for a compromise peace and that the war would come to an end earlier.

The tide of war turned in late 1942. The halting of the German advance into Russia at Stalingrad in October, and the defeat of Rommel at El Alamein in November, marked the beginning of the eventual defeat of Nazi Germany.

World War II was a total war, both in its global spread and in the full mobilization of resources that it required. Its impact on domestic society, particularly in Britain, was far-reaching. As large numbers of men were enlisted in the army, women entered the work force in unprecedented numbers.

The important role played by organized labor in the war effort, and the central role of the Labour party in the coalition government, led to a new awareness of the importance of social-welfare policies. Britain had been a hierarchical society preoccupied with questions of class and status, dominated by Conservative politicians and badly affected by the mass unemployment of the Great Depression. War made the government and the civil service sensitive to public opinion and to demands for social reform. The first proposals for reform were published in the 1942 Beveridge Report, which formed the basis for

British social-welfare planning in the postwar period.

The desire for change was reflected in the results of the elections, held immediately after the end of the war in Europe. Despite the immense popularity of Churchill as a war leader, his Conservative party lost the elections in July 1945 to the Labour party.

World War II also transformed Britain's dependent empire. The occupation of colonies in East Africa by Italian forces and in Asia by the Japanese went far to destroy the mystique of European supremacy and British power. As was true for other European colonial powers, Britain was not able to reestablish her authority in a number of colonies even after the Japanese had been defeated. In other parts of the empire, most notably India, political concessions were granted to nationalist forces in order to secure their continued support during the period of Britain's great vulnerability. The revolution in the relations between Britain and its empire brought about by World War II led to the effective dissolution of the empire by the mid-1950s. Although the war ended victoriously, with British troops occupying large parts of central Europe, the human and material destruction suffered in Britain was immense. Added to the impact of World War I, from which Britain had barely recovered when World War II began, and to the loss of empire, the war marked the end of Britain's role as a great power.

[*See also* Yishuv.]

BIBLIOGRAPHY

Agar, H. *The Darkest Year: Britain Alone, June 1940–June 1941.* New York, 1973.

Collier, B. *The Defense of the United Kingdom.* London, 1957.

Longmate, N. *How We Lived Then: A History of Every-Day Life during the Second World War.* London, 1971.

Wasserstein, B. *Britain and the Jews of Europe, 1939–1945.* London, 1979.

Wheatly, R. *Operation Sea Lion: German Plans for the Invasion of England, 1939–1942.* Oxford, 1958.

Zweig, R. W. *Britain and Palestine during the Second World War.* Suffolk, England, 1986.

RONALD W. ZWEIG

Appeasement of Nazi Germany

Great Britain's policy toward Germany in the period between the two world wars, and particularly in the second half of the 1930s, may accurately be characterized as one of appeasement. "Appeasement" was originally a positive term, describing a desire and an effort to establish peace between antagonistic countries. After World War II, however, the term acquired a negative sense, being linked with capitulation and faintheartedness in the face of aggression. This negative meaning was a result of the association with British policy, particularly during Neville Chamberlain's term of office as prime minister from 1937 to 1940. The agreement signed by Chamberlain at the MUNICH CONFERENCE in September 1938 was considered *a posteriori* the lowest point of appeasement. It surrendered Czechoslovakia, a friendly and free country, to Adolf Hitler, whether out of cowardice or foolish blindness concerning Hitler's true aims.

Britain's appeasement policy was adopted many years before the Nazis' rise to power and their policy of aggression. It was a direct result of the peace agreements at the end of World War I, and in particular of the Treaty of Versailles with Germany. Even at the Versailles Conference, the harsh terms dictated to the Germans aroused misgivings among the British and Americans. Penetrating discussions centered on the question of whether to aim for a peace treaty in a spirit of appeasement or to insist on harsh terms. The latter option was accepted, a fact that produced a sense of guilt toward Germany among many of the politicians involved. In Britain and the United States, sympathy developed for Germany because of the injustices that were felt to exist in the peace treaty.

Appeasement toward Germany was also sustained by the traditional interest of Britain, as a nation dependent on international trade, in maintaining peace through commerce and the renewal of commercial ties in Europe, especially with Germany. During the Weimar Republic, however, the British did not succeed in overcoming the objections of the French, who, justifiably concerned with their security, were far more hostile to Germany and wished to restrict its capacity for economic and military recovery. Appeasement, which produced a willingness to change the conditions of the peace treaty, was supported in Britain by all the political parties. It had a following among the intellectual Left of the Labor party, which tended to discuss foreign relations in terms of political morality, and stressed among the wrongs done to Germany the inclusion of the Sudeten Germans in the new Czechoslovak republic against their wish and against their right to self-determination.

British politicians tended to see the Nazi rise to power as a result of the mistaken policy toward Germany, and their negative attitude to Nazi rule did not change their appeasement policy. Rather, as the danger of German strength grew, Britain increasingly sought to attain relief in the international arena through accords with Germany. Various initiatives were proposed in the British government for the economic appeasement of Germany: the granting of colonies in Africa, trade agreements, and even military agreements. Germany, however, adopted a policy of presenting *faits accomplis* that modified the terms of the peace treaty, such as the abolition of military restrictions and the entry of its army into the demilitarized Rhine region. It thereby denied Britain political compensation, in the form of international peace, for its steps.

Up to 1937 Britain practiced a policy of passive appeasement, accepting *a posteriori* unilateral actions taken by Hitler. Chamberlain, who became prime minister in May 1937, initiated a policy of active appeasement, advocating negotiations with the Germans on the modifications desirable for Germany and necessary for the removal of the threat and insecurity aroused by Germany in Europe. Chamberlain informed the Germans of his desire for change, while stressing as a basic condition that no international modification be made violently. However, when Hitler annexed Austria in March 1938 in violation of the peace treaty, the West limited itself to a protest. When it became clear that Hitler's next target was Czechoslovakia, Chamberlain took a series of steps aimed at preventing a German attack on it. Such an attack was liable to lead to war with France and the Soviet Union, Czechoslovakia's allies, and it also entailed the danger of an unavoidable British involvement.

Chamberlain attempted to prevent war through cooperation with Germany, in order to stabilize international relations with that country. The means of attaining cooperation was to compel Czechoslovakia to make far-reaching concessions to the Sudeten Germans, thus preventing any need for German action. The British and French demands on Czechoslovakia aggravated the relations between the Czechs and the Germans, and by mid-September 1938 a real danger of war seemed to be hovering over Europe. Chamberlain went to meet with Hitler in Germany. Prior to the talks, the British government had decided to accord autonomy to the Germans within Czechoslovakia, but at their meeting, Hitler and Chamberlain immediately agreed on the annexation of areas of Czechoslovakia to Germany. The Munich agreement was signed after two weeks of talks.

At that time, the attempt to appease Germany by putting pressure on an independent state was not seen in Britain as a base or treacherous act, but as a bold step to save Europe from war. The granting of self-determination to the Sudeten Germans "returning to their homeland," Germany, was seen as a just act. During the negotiations, however, when Hitler introduced new demands, other than those already agreed on, doubts intensified in various circles in Britain concerning the morality and even the utility of this act of appeasement. After the signing of the agreement, Alfred Duff Cooper, the First Lord of the Admiralty, resigned from the government, and Winston CHURCHILL, a longtime critic of appeasement, harshly criticized in Parliament the stupidity and danger of the Munich agreement. Both in Parliament and in the press, the agreement was attacked as a shameful capitulation that would encourage Hitler to further acts of aggression. Nevertheless, the government continued the appeasement policy, hoping to achieve international peace by encouraging Germany to take agreed-upon economic control over southeastern Europe.

When Hitler violated his pledges and occupied the rest of Czechoslovakia in March 1939, all were convinced that the policy of appeasement was a complete failure, and both morally and politically indefensible. Chamberlain was obliged to surrender to internal pressures and change his policy. He gave guarantees of support to Poland and Romania, which were expected to be Hitler's next victims. Nonetheless, he did not abandon hope of salvaging peace by maintaining contact with leading figures in Germany. Even after the German invasion of Poland, when an ultimatum had to be presented demanding that Germany retreat from Polish territory, and even when he was forced to declare war on Germany, Chamberlain did so with a heavy heart and without being entirely convinced of the need to fight. Thus, appeasement was accepted over a long period of time by the great majority of the British, and was embodied first and foremost in the personality and policy of Chamberlain.

Two arguments are presented for diminishing the personal culpability of Chamberlain. One stresses that Britain, as a world power with responsibilities outside the European continent, refused to accept commitments in a region where it had no interests. This was especially so since Britain's overseas empire opposed an involvement in Europe, which was liable to lead again into an expensive and, from the empire's viewpoint, superfluous war. Britain had no land army, and militarily, the British Empire's commitments throughout the world were a decisive consideration against war, which was seen as being beyond its military capacity, especially in view of the expiration of the treaty with Japan and the danger to the British Empire in the Far East. According to this argument, appeasement stemmed from Britain's interests in the Far East, the Mediterranean (particularly in Palestine), the North Sea, and the Atlantic Ocean. At a time of economic crisis, unemployment, and pacifism, when industry was just beginning to recover from the depression, the government refused to finance a comprehensive transformation of industry to the production of war materials, or to gamble on United States support. A strong psychological factor against war was the exaggerated military estimates of the German air force's capacity for destruction.

A second explanation of appeasement is connected with the mood then prevailing: the general changes in Britain's political culture as the empire began to decline and society experienced the rise of new social forces, some socialist, some pacifist, and some enthusiastically supporting the League of Nations as an alternative to any international struggle. The reaction against the aggressive jingoism of the pre–World War I period, and against the belief that Britain had the right to rule the world, aroused doubts and self-criticism, a retreat from excessive rigidity in the international arena, and tolerance even toward despotic regimes. The intellectuals of that period, especially of the Left, wished to rid themselves of narrow British approaches and to understand the desires of other peoples, especially of the Germans.

BIBLIOGRAPHY

Bruegel, J. W. *Czechoslovakia before Munich: The German Minority Problem and British Appeasement.* Cambridge, 1973.

Fuchser, L. W. *Neville Chamberlain and Appeasement.* New York, 1982.

Gilbert, M. *The Roots of Appeasement.* New York, 1966.

Mommsen, W. J., and L. Kettenacker, eds. *The Fascist Challenge and the Policy of Appeasement.* London, 1983.

HEDVA BEN-ISRAEL

Fascism in Great Britain

The first organization in Britain to possess a distinctively fascist title appeared in the 1920s and reflected the changing economic and social conditions that followed World War I. The British Fascisti was formed in 1923 and the Imperial Fascist League was established in 1928. The former, associated particularly with R. Lintorn Orman, had only a brief existence, but the latter, associated predominantly with Arnold S. Leese, continued its existence until Leese's death.

In the 1930s a number of small and short-lived organizations came and went, but with the formation of the British Union of Fascists (BUF) by Sir Oswald MOSLEY in 1932, FASCISM in Britain took an important step forward. Mosley viewed the BUF as a political vehicle through which his restless and impatient ambitions could be satisfied. However, developments in National Socialist Germany lost the BUF some support, as did its involvement in political violence. In these circumstances, the BUF became increasingly embroiled in the local politics of London's East End, and this development brought into the open the BUF's antisemitic ideology. It resulted also in violent clashes with antifascists, a conflict symbolized by the "Battle of Cable Street" in October 1936, in which the BUF and antifascist groups fought each other. Such developments in the East London campaign also helped to sideline the BUF. With the government's ban on the wearing of uniforms in public under the Public Order Act of 1936, the development of the BUF (whose hallmark was the wearing of a black shirt) was further hindered. Moreover, the recovery of the economy in the course of the 1930s did not assist the BUF's cause. Even so, Mosley's movement remained active until World War II, and Mosley continued to attract large crowds at public meetings.

The outbreak of World War II soon resulted in the restriction of fascist activity, although it never disappeared entirely. In early 1940 leading members of the BUF, including Mosley and key members of his organization such as Neil Francis Hawkins and Alexander Raven Thomson, were interned under Regulation 18B(1A), which permitted the government to detain persons who had had associations with enemy powers. Arnold Leese was among the other fascist internees.

By the end of the war, fascism in Britain had become equated with the excesses of National Socialist Germany. For some individuals, however, this situation brought no change in their political stance. Arnold Leese, supported by a legacy from H. H. Beamish, a racial nationalist who had founded the antisemitic group The Britons in 1919, retracted nothing and remained a committed fascist until his death in 1948. Through his postwar activity, evidenced in his newsletter, *Gothic Ripples*, Leese assumed an important role in securing the continuity of the fascist tradition in Britain. Mosley, by contrast, attempted to distance himself from the prewar days when he revived his activity in the Union Movement. But no success followed from this adjustment, and following his defeat in North Kensington in the 1959 general election, Mosley retreated from any direct personal involvement in British politics.

By the time of Mosley's death in 1980, however, important developments had taken place in the world of British fascism and the related political province of racial nationalism. When Arnold Leese died, the mantle of National Socialism in Britain fell upon Colin Jordan, who, like Leese, continued to proclaim Adolf Hitler's message. That political stance was a quick route to political obloquy and oblivion. Indeed, none of the fascist groups of the early 1960s managed to achieve any political clout. However, in 1967 various organizations that had attempted to perpetuate the fascist tradition united with racial nationalist organizations to form the National Front (NF).

The NF openly eschewed the designation of being a fascist group. But in view of its nationalism, its political authoritarianism, its opposition to Jews (the NF played its part in the spread of Revisionist ideology of the Holocaust), its opposition to black and Asian immigration (which it viewed as a Jewish plot to undermine Britain), and its involvement in violent street politics, not all commentators were persuaded that the NF had effectively discarded the fascist tradition. The political heyday of the NF, under the leadership of John Tyndall, occurred in the late 1960s and 1970s, but after its failure to achieve any political impact in the 1979 general election, the front split into opposing factions. Ten years later, the leaders of the organization, which continued to call itself the National Front, were still reorientating its political direction.

BIBLIOGRAPHY

Benewick, R. *The Fascist Movement in Britain.* London, 1971.

Lebzelter, G. *Political Anti-Semitism in England, 1918–1939.* New York, 1978.

Lewis, D. S. *Illusions of Grandeur: Mosley, Fascism, and British Society, 1931–1981.* Manchester, 1987.

Lunn, K., and R. C. Thurlow, eds. *British Fascism.* London, 1980.

Skidelsky, R. *Oswald Mosley.* London, 1975.

Taylor, S. *The National Front in English Politics.* London, 1982.

Thurlow, R. *Fascism in Britain: A History, 1918–1985*. Oxford, 1987.

COLIN HOLMES

Jewish Refugees

Between 1933 and 1945, Britain was an important country of refuge for Jews fleeing Nazi-controlled Europe. For many, Britain, with its liberal tradition of granting asylum to REFUGEES, was the preferred country of immigration. Others sought temporary refuge there while awaiting transshipment overseas. A third category looked to Britain as the entry point for the large number of territories in Britain's dependent empire. In relation to its population and its size, Britain gave shelter to a significant number of Jews during the Holocaust.

British immigration policy, like that of all other countries of refuge for Jews from Nazi-controlled Europe, evolved in response to events. The first wave of refugees arrived in Britain during the months following Hitler's rise to power in January 1933. Church groups, in particular the Quaker Society of Friends, were active on their behalf, and Parliamentary opinion was sympathetic to these first victims of Nazism. But the official attitude toward Jewish refugees was dictated by the determined adherence of the British government to its policy of nonintervention in Germany's internal matters. The humanitarian approach to the refugees, advocated by circles and organizations outside the government, was seen as harming Britain's political and economic interests. After the ANSCHLUSS in March 1938 the government's position toward refugees changed significantly, and Great Britain became a haven for a considerable number of refugees. At that time, the government announced that all refugees who were en route to other destinations, and all children whose maintenance could be guaranteed, would be permitted to enter Great Britain.

Immigration and the coordination of the means necessary for assisting refugees reached their pinnacle in the last year before the outbreak of World War II. Among the non-Jewish public there was a great deal of support for Jews who had escaped from the Third Reich. However, despite the prevailing generosity, many refugees discovered streaks of antagonism. Several trade unions assumed a threatening posture and even took action against the refugees. The fear of aliens was also spurred by a number of newspapers. The Jewish press stood at the forefront of efforts to mollify the fears and prejudices against the refugees.

Because Britain was not an immediate neighbor of Germany, the number of refugees arriving there shortly after the Nazi seizure of power was small; in December 1933 there were only three thousand, and in April 1934 only two thousand. Despite these low figures, the refugees who wished to enter Great Britain met with many difficulties, primarily because of the immigration laws of 1919 (the Aliens Law), whose statutes remained in effect until 1938. The authorities made no distinction between refugees and other immigrants, demanding financial guarantees on their behalf and pledges that they would remain in Great Britain only temporarily, either to arrange further transit or to receive some sort of preparatory training that would help them along their way. After the Anschluss, the limitations became stricter, with visas now required for all who wished to enter Great Britain.

However, the waves of refugees caused by the Anschluss in March 1938, the German occupation of the Sudetenland that October, and *Kristallnacht* in November all brought British immigration policy under renewed pressure. In part because of the activities of pro-refugee groups and members of Parliament, and in part because of the acute political embarrassment caused by the British campaign against Jewish immigration into Palestine, Britain responded by further liberalizing the regulations governing the entry of refugees. This was contrary to the practice of most other countries of refuge in the immediate prewar months. But with the outbreak of war in September 1939, all immigration into Britain and the British Empire from enemy or enemy-controlled territory was banned.

Jewish refugees continued to reach Britain after 1939, but in radically reduced numbers. Following the fall of France, Norway, Denmark, Belgium, the Netherlands, and other

Jewish refugee children arrive in Great Britain (1938).

countries, entry was permitted only from neutral countries. The difficulties of transport during wartime made even that limited inflow almost impossible. A number of Polish Jews arrived in units of the Polish army stationed in the United Kingdom. Later, as the tide of war turned, the restrictions on entry were partly lifted. According to estimates made by Jewish organizations after the war, a further ten thousand Jews were permitted entry between 1939 and 1945.

From an early stage, Jewish organizations in Great Britain addressed themselves to the refugee problem. In March 1933, Otto Schiff established the Jewish Refugees Committee (for a time called the German Jewish Aid Committee), which was the most important voluntary organization to deal with refugee aid. In April, Schiff and the chairmen of the BOARD OF DEPUTIES OF BRITISH JEWS and of the Anglo-Jewish Association (Neville Laski and Leonard Montefiore) met with the Home Secretary. They pledged that no refugee would become a public charge and that the Jewish community would ensure support of the refugees until they either had been integrated into British life or had emigrated to another country. Despite the enormous growth in the number of refugees, sufficient money was allocated for their upkeep by the Central British Fund and the COUNCIL FOR GERMAN JEWRY until the end of 1939, that is, as long as the pledge remained in force.

The Jewish Refugee Committee looked after the needs of the refugees—their maintenance, education and training, and further emigration. Its work was conducted through subcommittees for reception, accommodation, agricultural training, vocational training, education, emigration, assistance to academics and professional workers, information, and press. Special organizations were established to deal with aid to emigré students and academics who had lost their positions or had been prevented from continuing their studies for reasons of religion or race.

Eventually, more than 10,000 unaccompanied refugee children, most of them Jewish, reached Great Britain from central Europe. The 431 children who had come to Great Britain up to November 1938 were assisted by the existing Jewish refugee organizations and the Children's Inter-Aid Committee. In the wake of *Kristallnacht,* 9,354 refugee children, of whom 70 percent were Jewish, arrived between December 1938 and September 1939. Five main organizations assisted the young refugees: B'NAI B'RITH, the Women's Appeal Committee (which worked with YOUTH ALIYA in Great Britain), the Chief Rabbi's Religious Emergency Council (headed by Rabbi Solomon SCHONFELD), the Children's Inter-Aid Committee, and the Movement for the Care of Children from Germany. In March 1939 these last two groups merged and were incorporated into the Refugee Children's Movement (RCM), chaired by Lord Gorell. Apart from the main RCM body, local committees of the organization found and inspected homes, supervised the children, and arranged for their general, vocational, and religious education. The children were chosen by the children's emigration departments of the central Jewish organizations in Germany, Austria, and Czechoslovakia. An additional 500 children were brought to Great Britain as members of Youth Aliya groups, and 1,350 arrived as agricultural trainees.

The children were divided into two categories: those guaranteed by private sponsors, and those guaranteed by the RCM. In February 1939, the government insisted that sponsors post a fifty-pound bond for each child to cover his reemigration. The bonds were later paid for by the Lord Baldwin Fund, which was created to offer financial assistance to Jewish refugees from Germany. Once in Britain, the children were housed in reception camps and later taken to foster homes or hostels. After heated discussion, it was decided by the leaders of the Jewish organizations assisting the children to accept offers of hospitality in non-Jewish homes. The representatives of the Chief Rabbi's Religious Emergency Council, however, continued to warn against growing missionary attempts aimed at the children.

Unlike the RCM, which promoted the integration and assimilation of the children, the London office of Youth Aliya, under the leadership of Eva Michaelis Stern, strove to keep the children together. It therefore created a number of agricultural training centers where children lived collectively, studied, and worked. Many of the RCM children eventually requested to join these centers in search of companionship and values lacking in their foster placement surroundings.

Because of difficulties in distinguishing between Jews and non-Jews and between permanent residents and transmigrants in official statistics, it is not possible to ascertain the exact number of German Jewish refugees in Britain. It has been estimated that until the outbreak of the war more than 80,000 Jewish refugees reached Great Britain and some 55,000 remained there. In addition to the 10,000 children, there were some 14,000 women who entered the country as domestic help. In a special camp, Kitchener, in Richborough, Kent, some 5,000 people who needed immediate shelter were housed during an eighteen-month period from the end of January 1939. These 5,000 refugees had been released from concentration camps, or their internment had been deferred by the Nazis, who were willing to let them alone on condition that they leave Germany immediately. The Home Office gave them a group entrance visa and waived the normal regulations for passports and individual permits.

The government's decision, after *Kristallnacht,* to simplify the entrance procedures for refugees, and the subsequent large growth in their numbers, placed a great responsibility on the Jewish organizations and caused them difficulties of a magnitude for which they were not prepared. The major problem was financial. The organizations were still pledged to support the refugees, and this became such a great burden that they were forced to implement very strict criteria for the selection of those who would be allowed to enter, and had to turn away thousands of applicants. From early 1939 pressure was brought to bear on the government to share in the financing of the refugees, but it refused, resting on the principle, established at the EVIAN CONFERENCE, that all aid to refugees must come from private sources. However, owing primarily to the fear that the relief organizations might collapse, the government changed its policy. The change was gradual, and only after the outbreak of the war were the Jewish organizations released from their pledge.

British Jewry did all it could in the last year before the war to effect the release and rescue of as many Jews as possible from the Nazis. In addition to their generous contributions to the various funds, their aid to children, and their help in setting up the agricultural training centers, British Jews gave personal bonds that enabled thousands of refugees to make their entrance into Great Britain and guaranteed their support once they arrived. They also provided work as domestics for thousands of women and teenage girls, providing for them and, when necessary, for their children. Many volunteers worked in the relief organizations, whose proportions reached those of a government office.

With the outbreak of war, refugee children were evacuated, along with British schoolchildren and other vulnerable persons, to the Midlands and Wales. The treatment of refugees at this time became worse. Following the outbreak of hostilities, all Germans and Austrians in Great Britain, including Jewish refugees, were defined as "enemy aliens." All enemy aliens were examined before special tribunals, and some were interned. The tribunals were not always astute bodies, and Jews and pro-Nazi Germans were occasionally interned together. The fear of foreigners, the developments in the European war, and especially the anxiety (which increased after the fall of the Netherlands) about the activities of a supposed fifth column caused mass hysteria and open hostility toward the refugees. The government, with the full support of the public and the press, decided on the mass internment of aliens from Germany and Austria in the early summer of 1940. Within several weeks about thirty thousand were interned in camps, most of them Jewish refugees who unhesitatingly supported the Allies, and some of them older children. Later in the summer of 1940 the government took an additional step that had great ramifications: it deported aliens from Great Britain. Some eight thousand aliens were sent to CANADA and AUSTRALIA, and for this purpose ships badly needed for the war effort were used.

Only after the scandals and disasters resulting from the deportations (such as the sinking of the ship *Arandora Star* carrying deportees, with great loss of life) had taken place was severe criticism raised in public, and the injustice being done to the deportees—already victims of Nazism—and the folly of the policy became evident. Shortly thereafter, the government changed its policy, canceling the deportations and returning some of the deportees to Great Britain. Within a year almost all of the internees were released and were integrated into British society. Thousands of them joined the British army in the war against the Nazis.

BIBLIOGRAPHY

Bentwich, N. *They Found Refuge: An Account of British Jewry's Work for the Victims of Nazi Oppression.* London, 1956.

Berghahn, M. *German-Jewish Refugees in England.* London, 1984.

Gilbert, M. "British Government Policy towards Jewish Refugees: November 1938–September 1939." *Yad Vashem Studies* 13 (1979): 127–167.

Sherman, A. J. *Island Refugee: Britain and Refugees from the Third Reich, 1933–1939.* London, 1973.

Stevens, A. *The Dispossessed: German Refugees in Britain.* London, 1975.

Wasserstein, B. *Britain and the Jews of Europe, 1939–1945.* Oxford, 1979.

JUDITH TYDOR-BAUMEL, NANA SAGI, and RONALD W. ZWEIG

GREECE. A kingdom prior to 1924, Greece became a republic that year. In November 1935, following years of political turmoil after the end of World War I, an overwhelming majority in Greece voted in a plebiscite to restore the monarchy, and King George II returned to Greece from exile. At the 1936 elections, neither the Liberal party nor the Populists and their royalist allies received a majority. In the midst of the political stalemate, the king appointed Gen. Ioannis Metaxas as prime minister, although in the past the general had been involved in one of numerous military coups. Metaxas temporarily instituted a dictatorship in Greece. His regime manifested hostility toward liberalism, communism, and parliamentary government, and it evinced profascist tendencies. This ideological attachment to fascism was paralleled by an increase in trade with Germany. Despite Metaxas's admiration for the domestic policies of Nazi Germany and Fascist Italy, he did not disturb Greece's relationship with Great Britain, for he was wary of its sea power. Although he failed to make an alliance with Britain, a few days after the Italian occupation of Albania, in April 1939, Britain and France offered Greece a guarantee of its territorial integrity in the event that it chose to resist aggression.

At the outbreak of World War II in September 1939, Metaxas tried to maintain a position of neutrality. When Italy provoked Greece in August 1940 by torpedoing the cruiser *Elli,* anchored off the island of Tinos, Greece did not retaliate. Metaxas, however, refused to agree to Italy's humiliating ultimatum of October 28, 1940, that Greece give up its sovereignty, and Italy invaded Greece. The Italian force crossing the Albanian border met fierce opposition by the Greek army, led by its chief of staff, Gen. Alexander Papagos. Within a few days, the Italians occupied major towns in northern Epirus. The Greeks fought valiantly and drove the Italians back into Albania. The war reached a stalemate in the snowbound mountains of Albania and the Greeks were prevented from capturing Valona, the principal port in the south, which would have enabled the Greek forces to receive supplies by sea.

Metaxas died in January 1941, but the war continued. On April 6, Hitler intervened to secure his southern flank for the upcoming invasion of the Soviet Union, and his forces now also invaded Greece, by way of Yugoslavia and Bulgaria. The Greek army, aided by a small British force, was outflanked and unable to stop the German attack. As a result, Prime Minister Alexandros Koryzis committed suicide on April 18 and the Greek army and the king fled to Crete as the Germans closed in on Athens. Most of the British troops (forty-two thousand out of fifty-eight thousand) were evacuated from Greece. The intention of making Crete into a stronghold never materialized, and following the massive airborne German attack of May 20, 1941, and intense fighting, the island fell to the Germans. Many British soldiers became prisoners of war, including a large number of Palestinian Jewish soldiers abandoned in the Peloponnese. The remaining British and Greek fighting forces withdrew to Egypt. The Greek government-in-exile and King George set up their headquarters in London and, after disturbances in the Greek armed forces in the Middle East, moved to Cairo in March 1943.

Greece was divided into three zones of occupation. The Italians occupied Epirus, the Ionian islands, central and southern Greece from the Platona line southward, and ATHENS, with its strategic position. The Germans held central Macedonia and a strip of land at the eastern edge of Greek Thrace (which included Orestiás, Dhidhimótikon, and Souflion). The Bulgarians occupied Thrace. Gen. George Tsolakoglu was made prime minister in a puppet government subordinate to the

GREECE

Germans. He was succeeded by the civilians Constantine Logothetopoulos and Ioannis Rallis.

The Greek Communist party chairman, Nikos Zakhariadis, was imprisoned in DACHAU for the duration of the war, but the experienced and organized party from the Metaxas era succeeded in forming the resistance Ethnikon Apeletherotikon Metopon (National Liberation Front; EAM) in September 1941. Its military arm, the Ellenikos Laikos Apelethorotikos Stratos (Popular Greek Liberation Army; ELAS), was formed at the end of December 1941. The first guerrilla units arrived in the mountains early in the summer of 1942. The most important of the units was led by Athanasios Klaras, known as Aris Velouchiotis.

The main non-Communist resistance movement was the Ellenikos Dimokratikos Ethnikos Stratos (National Republican Greek League; EDES), led by the republican general Napoleon Zervas. EDES began its partisan activities early in the summer of 1942. Another republican resistance organization, Ethniki kai Koinoniki Apelethérosis (National and Social Liberation; EKKA), led by Col. Dimitrios Psarros, became militarily active in the spring of 1943.

That September, the Italian regime fell in Greece and the Germans took full control over the previous Italian zone. Some fifteen thousand Italian troops stationed in Greece transferred their allegiance to the Allies through British liaison officers who were attached to the Greek resistance movement.

In anticipation of the German defeat, British and American units infiltrated into Greece throughout 1944 to harass the retreating Germans and also to ensure an Allied presence after the liberation. The Germans evacuated Greece in September 1944, with the exception of RHODES, Crete, and some other islands, where the Germans surrendered only in May 1945. Following its liberation, Greece entered a long period of political turmoil. This erupted into a civil war that continued until October 1949, when the Communist forces conceded defeat to the monarchists.

Greek Jewry in the Holocaust. The major stages in the destruction of Greek Jewry include the deportation from Bulgarian-occupied Thrace and Macedonia in March 1943; the deportations from German-occupied SALONIKA and its environs from March to May 1943; and the deportations from the former Italian zone after Italy's surrender (September 1943), in March, April, and the summer of 1944. All the deportations took place after the Italians had recognized that the war was lost. This attitude, plus their antipathy to German brutality, caused Italian military and diplomatic personnel to aid as many Jews as possible to escape, either to the Italian-occupied zone or out of the occupied Balkans.

In April 1941 the Jewish archives and libraries in Salonika and Athens were confiscated by EINSATZSTAB ROSENBERG. During the spring and summer of 1941 Germany stripped Greece of its edible and cash crops and sequestered its natural resources. In the resulting famine of 1941 and 1942, which severely affected the Greek population, the Jews suffered especially. On July 11, 1942, nine thousand Salonikan Jewish males aged eighteen to forty-five were humiliated and later assigned to ORGANISATION TODT labor battalions within Greece; many died and others suffered from disease and exhaustion. The Jewish community sought to ransom the young Jewish laborers, but the communal leaders did not succeed in raising the needed sums. To compensate for the remainder, the famous Jewish cemetery of Salonika was expropriated, turned over to the municipal authorities, and destroyed.

The first Greek Jews to be deported were those of Macedonia and Thrace, which had been annexed by BULGARIA. In mid-February 1943, the Bulgarian minister of internal affairs, Petur Gabrovski, agreed to the deportation to the Reich of 20,000 Jews, including those of Macedonia and Thrace. The deportation was organized by Yaroslav Kalitsin, chief of the administrative section of the Komisarstvo za Evreiskite Vuprosi (Commissariat for Jewish Questions) in Bulgaria. He established three concentration points, at Radomir, Dupnitsa, and Gorna Dzhumaya. At 4:00 a.m. on March 4, 1943, the Jews of Thrace were arrested, interned for several days in tobacco warehouses, and sent by train to Bulgaria. Only some 200 Jews escaped the roundup, either by fleeing to the

Italian zone or by having been drafted into labor battalions. The remaining 4,100 were sent by train and barge to Vienna and then by train directly to TREBLINKA, where they were gassed on arrival.

The local population in the Bulgarian zone was completely cowed by savage German reprisals for acts of sabotage and dissent (beheading, mutilation, firing squads, and so on). Bulgaria was determined to repopulate the new territories with Bulgarian peasants, and it encouraged Greek migration to the German zone. Even so, some Jews who escaped the roundup were hidden or escorted to the partisans in the mountains. Many acts of kindness by non-Jews toward the deportees are recorded, along with acts of theft.

In the German-occupied zone, Dieter WISLICENY and Alois BRUNNER, representing the office of Adolf EICHMANN, orchestrated the deportations through the JUDENRAT (Jewish Council) headed by Chief Rabbi Zvi KORETZ, who was appointed its president in December 1942. During February 1943 the NUREMBERG LAWS were implemented through Dr. Maximilian Merton, adviser to the German military administration, and the Jews were mainly isolated in three ghettos: the Hagia Paraskevi district, the so-called 151 quarter, and the Baron de Hirsch transit camp, all in or near Salonika. From the last they were transported by train to AUSCHWITZ during March and April. Some 48,000 Jews were deported; 37,000 were gassed on arrival and 11,000 were selected for the labor camp. Between April 30 and May 8, 1943, the Jews of Dhidhimótikon, Orestiás, Florina, Veroia, and Souflion were arrested by the Germans. They were brought to Salonika, and shipped to Auschwitz on May 9. Most were gassed on arrival as part of the seventeenth Salonikan transport. The last transport from Salonika, which included the Judenrat (74 individuals), went to BERGEN-BELSEN in August 1943. The

Oberleutnant Kurt Waldheim (1) relaxing in 1943 at the Hotel Grande Bretagne in Athens with fifteen other German officers. [World Jewish Congress]

Wehrmacht supplied all the trains, at the command of Gen. Alexander Löhr of Army Group E.

The Greek leaders made numerous protests to the Greek government and the Italian and German occupiers. About one hundred and fifty Salonikan lawyers, after approaching Simonides, the Greek governor of Macedonia, appealed to the government in Athens to at least shift the goal of the deportations from Poland to a Greek island. The response was that the Germans would not allow it. Salonikan Jewish refugees in Athens, aided by Athenian Jews, tried to pressure the government. They were joined by the intellectual and religious leadership, especially Archbishop Damaskinos and the heads of the institutions of higher learning, who argued eloquently on behalf of the Jews. However, Dr. Constantine Logothetopoulos, who headed the government in 1943, wanted to settle the Greek Orthodox refugees of Bulgarian-occupied Thrace in the vacant Jewish quarters of Salonika. His halfhearted attempt to stop the deportations through a letter to the German plenipotentiary in Athens, Günther Altenberg, on March 23, 1943, arrived too late. On March 29, Athenian nongovernment leaders made an appeal, unprecedented in occupied Europe, to Prato, the political secretary of the Italian embassy, to halt the deportations of loyal Greek citizens. This too failed, because Salonika was in the German zone. The government of Ioannis Rallis protested to the Gestapo over the deportations, contributing to an atmosphere in which the Greek Jews were assisted by the population. In particular, Professor Nikolaos Louvaris, the minister of education and later of communications, expended considerable effort to save the Jews.

The officials in the Italian consulate in Salonika—consul Guelfo Zamboni, vice-consul Cavalliere Rosenberg, Stabila, Emilio Neri, Doefini, Merci, Mark Mosseri, and Valerie Torres—assisted Jews to escape to the Italian zone. All their efforts helped many hundreds of the three thousand Salonikan Jews to escape to Athens. More than three hundred held false Italian documents issued by the consulate.

The surrender of Italy brought under German control the remainder of Greek Jewry, which had hitherto enjoyed the protection of Gen. Carlo Geloso, the Italian police commander in Athens and administrator of southern Greece, and his successor, General Vecchiarelli. Under the direction of Wisliceny, with the assistance of SS general Jürgen STROOP, 800 Athenian Jews were arrested and deported to Auschwitz, along with Jews from smaller mainland towns who were arrested on March 24 and 25, 1944: Arta (352), Préveza (272), Patras (12 families), Chalcis (90), Volos (130), Larissa (225), Trikkala (50), Ioannina (1,860), and Kastoria (763). Most were gassed on arrival.

The Jews of CORFU were arrested on June 6, 1944; nearly 1,800 out of 2,000 were sent to Auschwitz, of whom 200 were selected for forced labor and the remainder gassed. On July 20, 1,700 Jews of Rhodes were sent by way of Piraeus to Auschwitz, where 700 were selected for forced labor and the rest killed. The 260 Jews of Canea were arrested on May 21, 1944, and the boat carrying them sank mysteriously; there were no survivors.

According to extant Auschwitz figures, at least 54,533 Greek Jews were transported there. Of these (for whom figures are available), 41,776 were sent immediately to the gas chambers and 12,757 (8,025 men and 4,732 women) were selected for forced labor, the orchestra, MEDICAL EXPERIMENTS (sterilization and experiments involving twins), and the SONDERKOMMANDO. Periodically, Greek Jews were assigned to the Auschwitz crematoria in 1943 and 1944. One group of 400, selected in the summer of 1944 to expedite the destruction of Hungarian Jews, refused the assignment, knowing that the punishment was death. The incident is reported by a number of Auschwitz survivors. Also in the summer of 1944, Albert Errera of Larissa, part of an ash-emptying detail, wounded his guards and escaped across the Vistula. Recaptured, he was tortured to death. One hundred and thirty-five Greek Jews, former officers in the Greek army, participated in (and perhaps instigated) the revolt that broke out on October 6–7, 1944 (or on September 9, according to some sources). Greek survivors claim responsibility for blowing up Crematorium III; nearly all those involved died singing the Greek national anthem.

By August 2, 1944, there were 292 Greek

A Jewish couple from Salonika wearing the Jewish badge.

men in Auschwitz I (the main camp), 929 men in Auschwitz II (Birkenau), and 517 men in Auschwitz III (Buna-Monowitz), in addition to 731 women. Most of the Salonika women and men selected for forced labor died subsequently from the cold, hunger, typhus, dysentery, and the cruelty of guards. Many committed suicide when they learned the fate of their families. The abovementioned 400 (or 435) Jewish prisoners, who were from Salonika, were gassed after refusing to serve in the Sonderkommando; and at least 135 Greeks died in the Sonderkommando revolt. Many of those who survived into 1945 left with the DEATH MARCHES of January 17 to MAUTHAUSEN, Bergen-Belsen, STUTTHOF, and other places. By the end of the war, the survivors numbered only in the hundreds. Fewer than 2,000 of the more than 54,000 deported returned to Greece.

In August 1943 about 300 Salonikan Jews were part of a contingent comprised of non-Polish-speaking Jews, sent to WARSAW to recycle the ruins of the ghetto. That October a second group of Salonikan Jews was sent to the Warsaw ghetto. Many died from starvation and disease. Shaul Senor, a Salonikan Jew from Palestine (later hanged for attempted escape), is credited with saving many sick prisoners. At the end of July most of the Greek Jews were transferred to Dachau. During the Warsaw Polish uprising of August and September 1944, the surviving Greeks participated in the fighting or hid in the bunkers. Many were killed by the Germans, and a few by antisemitic Poles who took part in the revolt. The Greeks split up to improve their chances of survival. Later, some re-formed as a unit and fought under a Greek flag. Only about 27 Greeks survived that revolt.

Greek Jews were active in the resistance in Greece both before and after the formation of organized fighting partisan units. The Greek resistance went through several stages. Soldiers who were demobilized after the war with Italy or the surrender of Greece to Germany formed militant bands in the mountains. They were organized and supplied by the British Middle East Command late in 1942, especially those in Epiros, who were republican or royalist (EDES, EKKA). Others fled to areas in central Greece (the Pindus and Olympic ranges) controlled by nationalist democratic forces with a strong Communist leadership (EAM/ELAS). Active military resistance against the Germans did not begin until well into 1943.

A number of Jewish communities survived in their entirety or in part. All the Jews of Agrinion (40) dispersed into the countryside, and the planned deportation of Zante (275) never took place. Most of the Jews of Thessaly and central Greece—Volos (750), Katerínē (35), Larissa (500), Trikkala (450), Kardhitsa (100 to 150), Chalcis (270), Athens (2,000), and Patras (200)—hid with neighbors, fled to the mountains, or escaped to Palestine by way of Turkey.

The Greek population in the Italian-occupied zone rallied to the support of the Jews, whom they publicly acknowledged as Greek citizens. The successive Greek governments protested, though ineffectively, against the deportations from the German zone in 1943. Leading intellectuals in Salonika and

Athens submitted protest letters; the Germans closed the University of Athens in retaliation for protests. The Greek Orthodox church, led by the metropolitan of Athens, Archbishop Damaskinos, resisted, by making formal protests; by issuing encyclicals to the clergy, calling upon them to protect Jewish refugees; by hiding Jewish children (over two hundred and fifty); and by issuing false baptismal certificates. More than six hundred Greek clergy were arrested and many deported as a result. The Athens police supplied forged papers. The foreign consulates of Spain, Turkey, and Italy protected any Jew who could remotely claim their citizenship. Those so saved numbered many thousands. The Greek underground hid Jews, smuggled them to unoccupied Greece, or transported them to Turkey. Their efforts also aided many of the Palestinian Jewish soldiers, trapped in Greece after the collapse of the British Expeditionary Force in 1941, to escape from the Germans.

STEVEN B. BOWMAN

The Postwar Period. In 1941 the population of the Greek Jewish communities (including that of Rhodes, which was annexed to Greece after World War II) was 77,178, with 56,000 living in Salonika. About 96 percent of Salonika's Jews died in the Holocaust; 1,000 returned after the war and another 1,000 emigrated to Palestine, France, or the United States. Today in Salonika a small Jewish community maintains a cultural center, a historical library, two synagogues, a cemetery, an old-age home, and an elementary school.

Most Jews in Greece now live in Athens. Although soon after the war 4,930 Jews lived there, as of the end of the 1980s there were slightly under 3,000. They maintain a synagogue, a Jewish museum, an elementary school, and a cemetery.

The majority of the Jews of Thessaly (Larissa, Trikkala, and Volos) survived the war in the mountains. After the war, there was a significant emigration to Israel and Athens from this area. These communities, as well as smaller communities such as those of Rhodes, Chalcis, Corfu, and Ioannina, are too small to support Jewish education, cultural activities, or many opportunities for prayer. Generally, the young people have left these places for Athens or the United States, and the older generation in these small urban communities throughout Greece is dying out.

No survivors returned from the Thracian deportation. A group of forty Jews who survived because they were sent on forced labor to Bulgaria emigrated to Israel after the war. Jewish life in communities like those of Serrai, Dráma, Xánthi, Komotinē, and Alexandroupolis ceased to exist after the Holocaust. The community of Zákinthos survived, with the exception of some thirty victims of starvation, but after the war most of the community settled in Israel.

After the war, the Kentriokon Israelitikon Symvoulion (Board of Jewish Communities in Greece), along with the American Jewish JOINT DISTRIBUTION COMMITTEE, helped rebuild synagogues, schools, clubs, and old-age homes throughout Greece. The Holocaust survivors returned to Greece penniless, and through the help of these organizations, were able to rehabilitate themselves.

The Greek government entrusted the Organization for the Assistance and Rehabilitation of Greek Jews with the task of recompensing the Jews and reallocating their lost property. Although the Greek Jewish survivors in Greece received reparations from West Germany, some seven hundred Greek Holocaust survivors in Israel received no compensation for the Nazi pillaging of their families' property.

YITZCHAK KEREM

BIBLIOGRAPHY

Avni, H. "Spanish Nationals in Greece and Their Fate during the Holocaust." *Yad Vashem Studies* 8 (1970): 31–68.

Ben, Y. *Greek Jewry in the Holocaust and the Resistance, 1941–1944.* Tel Aviv, 1985. (In Hebrew.)

Carpi, D. "Notes on the History of the Jews in Greece during the Holocaust Period: The Attitude of the Italians (1941–1943)." In *Festschrift in Honor of Dr. George S. Wise,* edited by H. Ben-Shahar et al., pp. 25–62. Tel Aviv, 1981.

Chary, F. B. *Bulgarian Jews and the Final Solution, 1940–1944.* Pittsburgh, 1972.

Molho, M., and J. Nehama. *The Destruction of Greek Jewry, 1941–1945.* Jerusalem, 1965. (In Hebrew.)

Molho, M., and J. Nehama. *In Memoriam: Hommage aux victimes juives des nazis en Grèce.* Salonika, 1973.

Novitch, M. *Le passage des barbares: Contribution à l'histoire de la déportation et de la résistance des Juifs grecs.* Nice, 1962.

GREISER, ARTHUR (1897–1946), prominent figure in the Nazi party and the Third Reich administration. Greiser was born in the town of Środa, in the Poznań (Ger., Posen) province; his father was a government official. In World War I Greiser served as an air force officer. After the war he spent some time in the Freikorps and then tried his hand at business, without much success. In 1924 Greiser was one of the founders of Stahlhelm (Steel Helmet), a nationalist association of former servicemen, in DANZIG. In 1928 he joined the Nazi party, and then the SA (Sturmabteilung; Storm Troopers); after a while, he switched to the SS. Greiser held various Nazi party posts in Danzig, was elected to the city senate, and was appointed its president in 1934, replacing Hermann RAUSCHNING. (Between the two world wars Danzig had the status of a free city, under international trusteeship.)

During the Polish campaign in September 1939, Greiser was appointed head of the civilian administration of Poznań. In October and November he became *Gauleiter* and *Reichsstatthalter* (governor) of the WARTHEGAU, the large Polish territory (which included the city of Łódź) that was incorporated into the Reich. Unlike the other governors of the Polish territorial units, Greiser was able to gain the support of persons with influence in the Reich Chancellery in Berlin and to maintain good relations with Heinrich HIMMLER. In 1942 he was appointed an SS-*Gruppenführer.* Greiser was determined to uproot the Polish population from the area under his administration, in order to speed up its "Germanization." His fanatic anti-Polish policy expressed itself in various forms, such as

At a festive gathering, Wilhelm Frick, Reich minister of the interior (seated to the left of the empty chair), inducts Gauleiter Arthur Greiser as *Reichsstatthalter* (governor) of the Warthegau. Greiser delivers his address in the old throne room of the Poznań castle (November 1939).

confiscating Polish property, restricting educational and cultural activities, "Germanizing" Polish orphans, and persecuting the Catholic church and the Polish clergy. His most severe action, however, was the expulsion of Poles and Jews from the territory. In the period from 1939 to 1945, some 630,000 Poles and Jews were removed or expelled from the Warthegau, and 537,000 VOLKSDEUTSCHE (ethnic Germans) were brought in from areas in the Baltic states, southeastern Poland, Romania, and the Soviet Union.

In 1945 Greiser was captured by the Americans in the Alps and extradited to Poland. During the trial of Hans BIEBOW in 1946, the former German commissar of the Łódź ghetto testified that Greiser had rejected appeals to improve the food rations of the Jews in the ghetto, and that his radical anti-Jewish attitude had served as a model to his subordinates. Greiser had praised the men of the German unit that from December 1941 operated the CHEŁMNO extermination camp in the area under his administration, the first of its kind in occupied Poland. Upon the conclusion of a *Sonderbehandlung* ("special treatment," that is, extermination) operation in which one hundred thousand Jews from the Warthegau had been killed, Greiser wrote a letter to Himmler proposing that the same treatment be meted out to Poles afflicted with tuberculosis, because they were endangering the health of the German population.

Greiser was tried in June and July 1946 by a Polish national tribunal and was sentenced to death. He was hanged in front of the house in Poznań that had served as his residence when he was governor of the Warthegau.

BIBLIOGRAPHY

Broszat, M. *Nationalsozialistische Polenpolitik, 1939–1945.* Stuttgart, 1961.

Proces Artura (Greisera): Przed Najwyższym Trybunalem Narodowym. Warsaw, 1946.

ISRAEL GUTMAN

GREYSHIRTS, South African national socialist movement founded in October 1933 by Louis Weichardt. Its original name was the South African Christian National Socialist Movement, which changed in May 1934 to the South African National Party. "Greyshirt" referred to the upper part of the uniforms worn by the militant sector, or advance guard, of the movement, which was responsible for maintaining order at political meetings and protecting the leader.

Although centered in Cape Town, the Greyshirt organization had cells throughout the country. The movement published a fortnightly bilingual newspaper, *Die Waarheid* (The Truth), from February 23, 1934, to July 29, 1938. Its monthly organ, *Die Blanke Front* (The White Front), appeared from July 1947 to May 1948.

Weichardt, an Afrikaner antisemite who had joined up to fight for Germany in World War I, fashioned the movement's racist, antisemitic, and fascist philosophy. Parliamentary politics and liberalism were attributed to "British-Jewish" contamination. The movement was eventually absorbed into the Reunited National Party, which defeated the Jan Smuts government in 1948. Weichardt subsequently became a senator.

[*See also* South Africa.]

BIBLIOGRAPHY

Roberts, M., and A. E. G. Trollip. *The South African Opposition, 1939–1945.* London, 1947.

Shimoni, G. *Jews and Zionism: The South African Experience (1910–1967).* Cape Town, 1980.

MILTON SHAIN

GROBELNY, JULIAN (1893–1944), Polska Partia Socjalistyczna (Polish Socialist Party) activist. From 1919 to 1921 Grobelny strove for the annexation of Silesia to Poland. Subsequently employed in Łódź, he was active in the organization of social assistance. In 1940 he joined Wolność, Równość, Niepodległość (Freedom, Equality, Independence), the right-wing faction of the Polish Socialist party, and was a member of the party's regional labor committee in the Warsaw suburbs (he was known by the code name "Trojan").

Under Grobelny's chairmanship, from January 1943, ZEGOTA, the Polish Council for Aid to Jews, greatly expanded its activity and in-

Julian Grobelny.

creased its budget. Grobelny was of great assistance to the large group of people in the organization's care, and he was particularly sensitive to the distress of the children.

Arrested in March 1944 and imprisoned, Grobelny developed tuberculosis and was admitted to the prison hospital. After about a month he was smuggled out by the Polish underground and went into hiding in MIŃSK MAZOWIECKI. After the liberation he became mayor of that town.

BIBLIOGRAPHY

Prekerowa, T. *Konspiracyjna Rada Pomocy Żydom w Warszawie, 1942–1945.* Warsaw, 1982.

TERESA PREKEROWA

GRODNO, city in the western part of BELORUSSIA. In the interwar period Grodno was part of Poland; in September 1939 it was occupied by the Red Army and annexed to the Soviet Union. Grodno had one of the oldest and largest Lithuanian Jewish communities, which took pride in its numerous social and cultural institutions and was a center of Zionism. One the eve of World War II, Grodno had a Jewish population of twenty-five thousand.

On the first day of their invasion of the Soviet Union, June 22, 1941, the Germans reached Grodno. As soon as they entered the city, they put all Jews aged sixteen to sixty on forced labor. In July of that year, eighty Jews belonging to the intelligentsia were put to death. Some time after the occupation, the Germans administratively transferred Grodno from Belorussia to the district of Białystok, and annexed it, in March 1942, to East Prussia.

On November 1, 1941, the Germans ordered the establishment of two ghettos, ghetto "A" for skilled workers and ghetto "B" for "nonproductive" Jews. The ghettos were the scene of educational, cultural, communal, and youth movement activities, with the participation of community leaders, educators, and members of Zionist youth movements.

Because of its location, between Vilna and Białystok, Grodno became a center for the Jewish underground. It was one of the first places to hear reports of the large-scale massacres at PONARY. At the beginning of 1942 an underground movement was founded in the Grodno ghetto, based on non-Zionist and Zionist youth movements (Ha-Shomer ha-Tsa'ir, Dror, Betar), the BUND, and the Communists. The pioneering Zionist movements wanted to fight inside the ghetto, whereas the Communists urged escaping from the ghetto into the forests. Mordechai TENENBAUM (Tamaroff) twice went to Grodno seeking to set up an underground that would encompass the whole gamut of movements, from the Revisionist Zionists to the Communists. Such cooperation was in fact achieved, and some of the underground activists were transferred to the Białystok ghetto.

On November 22, 1942, 2,400 Jews from Grodno were taken to AUSCHWITZ. While this *Aktion* was underway, Zerah Silberberg, one of the Ha-Shomer ha-Tsa'ir activists in the Białystok underground, went to Grodno to train the underground commanders and try to establish a common front of Zionist and non-Zionist youth movements.

A further 2,000 Jews were deported from Grodno at the end of November 1942; their destination was Kielbasin, a transit camp for onward deportation to extermination camps. A second transport of Jews from Grodno to Kielbasin followed in early December. The underground had a plan to assassinate the

German commander of ghetto "B," Streblow, but failed to carry it out. Five members of Dror and Ha-Shomer ha-Tsa'ir were sent to the forests; four found their death there and the one survivor returned to the ghetto, declaring that Jews without arms in their possession could not survive in the forest. The determination to stay in the ghetto and fight there gained in strength among the underground members, but some groups of Jews continued to escape into the forests. Several women members of the underground who had set up a workshop for forging documents were moved to Białystok on orders of the underground, to serve as liaison officers; they included Bronka Winicki (Klibanski), Hasya Belicka (Borenstein), Zila Schachnes, and Liza Czapnik. Two underground members, Motl Kuperman and Nahum Kravyets, set an ambush one night for Streblow, but they were shot before they could draw their guns. Another assassination attempt, by Shayke

Matus, whose target was the commander of ghetto "A" and Streblow's superior, Kurt Wiese, also failed.

In an *Aktion* that came to an end on January 22, 1943, 10,500 Jews were deported to Auschwitz. Many of the deportees jumped off the trains, and some of these made their way to the Białystok ghetto. The last group of Jews to be deported from Grodno, numbering some 500 persons, was taken to Białystok. The flight to the forests, mostly on an individual basis, continued in the winter of 1943, the destination being the nearby forests of Nacha and Augustów. These escapees were not accepted by the non-Jewish partisan units, and hunger and cold forced some of them to return to the Grodno ghetto. A number of young people from Grodno who had gone to Białystok left that ghetto for the forest in August 1943 and operated in the Knyszyn and Jasinowka areas under the name "White Furs," mainly taking revenge on local peasants who had collaborated with the Germans. The group finally managed to join a Soviet partisan unit, and fought with it up to the liberation.

Grodno was liberated by the Red Army on July 14, 1944. Approximately two hundred Jews were still alive, including partisans and persons who had survived locally or who came back to Grodno from other places in the Soviet Union.

BIBLIOGRAPHY

Rabin, D., ed. "Grodno." In vol. 9 of *Encyclopedia of the Jewish Diaspora: Memorial Books of Countries and Communities.* Jerusalem, 1973. (In Hebrew.)

SHALOM CHOLAWSKI

GROJANOWSKI REPORT, report on the murder of Jews in the CHEŁMNO extermination camp, composed in the Warsaw ghetto in the winter of 1942 by ONEG SHABBAT (the Ringelblum Archive). The report is based on the testimony given by Jacob Grojanowski, the first person to escape from the Chełmno camp.

Grojanowski was taken to Chełmno from Izbica, his place of residence, on January 6, 1942, together with a group of twenty-eight other Jews. In the extermination camp he was put to work burying the victims of the GAS VANS, together with Jews who had been brought to the camp from various other places in the area. The victims—men, women, and children—were Jews, with the exception of eight groups of GYPSIES, who were shipped to the camp in the course of Grojanowski's stay. Grojanowski managed to escape from the camp and make his way to the Warsaw ghetto, apparently in February 1942. His testimony contains an exact and detailed description of the extermination procedure followed in Chełmno—the deception practiced on the inmates up to the very last moment, their asphyxiation by exhaust gas in the special vans constructed for this purpose, the removal of the bodies from the vans by prisoners turned gravediggers, the cleanup of the van interiors following the murders, and the method of burying the corpses in pits. Grojanowski also describes the grim mental and emotional state of the men who were forced to handle the bodies, the sadism displayed by the murderers, and his own escape from the camp. On the basis of this testimony, Oneg Shabbat prepared a report on the Chełmno murders, in Polish and German. The Polish version was meant for the DELEGATURA (the representation, in Poland, of the POLISH GOVERNMENT-IN-EXILE), which passed it on to London, where it was received in March or April 1942. The German version was intended for distribution among the German people, in the hope that the information it contained would have some effect.

BIBLIOGRAPHY

Shaul, E., trans. "The Testimony of a Forced Grave-Digger: Jacob Grojanowski, Izbica-Kolo-Chelmno." *Yalkut Moreshet* 35 (April 1983): 101–122. (In Hebrew.)

ELISHEVA SHAUL

GROSMAN, HAIKA (b. 1919), underground activist and partisan. Born in BIAŁYSTOK, Grosman became a member of the Zionist youth movement Ha-Shomer ha-Tsa'ir at an early age. At the outbreak of World War II

Haika Grosman.

she moved to VILNA and helped to concentrate members of the pioneering Zionist youth movements in that city. Following the German invasion of the Soviet Union (June 22, 1941), Grosman returned to Białystok, where she became one of the organizers of the underground there. Posing as a Polish woman, she went on many underground missions to various cities and ghettos, including the Warsaw ghetto. She belonged to the "Antifascist Białystok" cell and, together with five other young women who posed as Poles—Marila Ruziecka, Liza Czapnik, Hasya Belicka (Borenstein), Ana Rud, and Bronka Winicki (Klibanski)—gave assistance to the Jewish underground and to the partisans who were then organizing themselves in the forests around Białystok. She participated in the Białystok ghetto revolt in August 1943 and was a member of a Jewish partisan unit that operated in the area.

After liberation, Grosman served as the Ha-Shomer ha-Tsa'ir representative in the institutions set up by the remnants of the Jewish population in Poland. She settled in Israel in 1948, joining Kibbutz Evron in western Galilee. Grosman became politically active in Israel and was a member of the Knesset (the Israeli parliament) from 1969 to 1981, and again from 1984. She is the author of *People of the Underground* (published in English as *The Underground Army,* 1988), which contains memoirs and chapters on the struggle of the Białystok Jews.

BIBLIOGRAPHY

Grossman, C. *The Underground Army: Fighters of the Bialystock Ghetto.* New York, 1988.

Syrkin, M. *Blessed Is the Match.* Philadelphia, 1976. See chapter 7.

ISRAEL GUTMAN

GROSSMAN, MENDEL (1917–1945), photographer in the ŁÓDŹ ghetto. Grossman commemorated the horrors of the Łódź ghetto in more than ten thousand pictures taken throughout the ghetto's existence. Since Jews were forbidden to photograph in the ghetto, he risked his life carrying out the task. He used his position in the ghetto's statistics department, where he received photographic materials and was permitted to keep a cam-

Mendel Grossman, the photographer of the Łódź ghetto, in his laboratory.

era. Upon the liquidation of the ghetto he was sent to the Königs Wusterhausen labor camp, where he secretly continued photographing, but not developing and printing. When the war front advanced and came closer, and the prisoners of the camp were taken out on the liquidation march, Grossman collapsed and died with his camera on him. The negatives of his photographs, hidden by him in the ghetto, were found and sent to Israel, but most of them were lost during the War of Independence. Those photographs that were saved were used in the book *With a Camera in the Ghetto* (New York, 1977).

BIBLIOGRAPHY

Ben-Menahem, A. "Mendel Grossman: The Photographer of the Lodz Ghetto." *Dappim: Studies of the Holocaust and the Jewish Resistance* 1 (1969): 279–288. (In Hebrew.)

ARIEH BEN-MENAHEM

GROSS-ROSEN, concentration camp established in the summer of 1940 as a satellite camp of SACHSENHAUSEN, in the vicinity of the granite quarry of Gross-Rosen, in Lower Silesia. On May 1, 1941, Gross-Rosen became an independent concentration camp; it remained in operation until mid-February 1945. Its commandants were, successively, SS-Obersturmbannführer Arthur Rödl, SS-Hauptsturmführer Wilhelm Gideon, and SS-Sturmbannführer Johannes Hassebroock. At first, the camp prisoners were put to work in the quarry, owned by the SS-Deutsche Erd- und Steinwerke GmbH (SS German Earth and Stone Works), and in the construction of the camp, which was speeded up in the summer of 1943. This was followed by the building of a large number of subcamps. The number of prisoners grew steadily, from 1,487 in 1941 to 6,780 in 1942, 15,400 in 1943, 90,314 in 1944 (not allowing for the fact that many prisoners were counted twice), and 97,414 on the eve of the camp's liquidation.

In its final stage Gross-Rosen had a prison population of 78,000 (52,000 men and 26,000 women), representing 11 percent of all the prisoners then in Nazi concentration camps. A total of 125,000 prisoners of different nationalities passed through Gross-Rosen; the number of victims who perished in the camp and in the evacuation transports is estimated at 40,000.

Jews represented the largest group among the victims in Gross-Rosen, and their proportion in the camp population was considerable, especially in late 1943 and early 1944. Beginning in late 1943, 57,000 Jews were brought there, including 26,000 women. The assignment of Jews to the camp, and their use as manpower for the German war economy, resulted from a reorganization of the SS methods for exploiting Jews and from the evacuation of the PŁASZÓW camp and of AUSCHWITZ-Birkenau. The Jews, among them a high proportion of women, were distributed among satellite camps outside the main camp.

The first Jewish prisoners to arrive in Gross-Rosen were sent there from DACHAU (48 Jews, on June 18, 1941) and Sachsenhausen (32 on August 13, 1941, 21 on September 18 of that year, and 94 on September 20). In 1942 small groups of Jews, totaling 100 persons, arrived, from the RADOM district, from the prison in TARNÓW, and from Sachsenhausen and BUCHENWALD. They were housed in Block 4, which was run by German convicts: G. Prill, A. Radtke, and P. Alt. Prill and Radtke were particularly brutal sadists and murderers.

The living and working conditions of the Jewish prisoners were extraordinarily harsh and inhumane. In addition to the backbreaking work in the quarry and the construction of the camp, they were exploited for special work assignments during what were supposed to be their hours for rest. The Jewish prisoners were not permitted to establish contact with one another, each prisoner being restricted to his own block. They were also denied medical attention. Before long their state of health had deteriorated and they were completely exhausted. The mortality rate was high, and by the end of 1941, 84 had died. Others became *Muselmänner* (*see* MUSELMANN), and in December 1941, 119 of these were victims of a EUTHANASIA PROGRAM *Selektion*. The high mortality rate continued in 1942. Prisoners classified as "disabled" were sent to Dachau. The last 37 Jewish prisoners were transferred to Auschwitz on October 16 of that year, in the course of an operation designed to remove Jews from all camps situated in the Reich. For a period of twelve months, Gross-Rosen was *judenfrei* ("free of Jews").

In October 1943 the influx of Jewish prisoners into Gross-Rosen was renewed, this time in larger groups and transports. The first such group consisted of 600 prisoners moved from the Markstadt labor camp to Fünfteichen, a new Gross-Rosen satellite camp, where they were put to work in Krupp factories. Another group of 600 Jewish prisoners was put at the disposal of I.G. FARBEN, to work in the factories at Dyhernfurth, where poison gas was to be produced. More groups came in March 1944, inaugurating an uninterrupted flow of Jewish prisoners that continued until January 1945. Additional Gross-Rosen satellite camps were put up to accommodate them.

Most of the Jewish prisoners were from Poland and Hungary, but others were from Belgium, France, Greece, Yugoslavia, Slovakia, and Italy. The Jewish prisoners of Gross-Rosen were distributed among over fifty satellite camps, designated as *Arbeitslager* (labor camps). Most were situated in Lower Silesia, and the rest in the Sudetenland and Luzyce. Some of these satellite camps were put up when Gross-Rosen took over a number of *Zwangsarbeitslager* (forced-labor camps) from Heinrich HIMMLER's special plenipotentiary for recruiting foreign labor in Upper Silesia, ORGANISATION SCHMELT. A total of twenty-eight such forced-labor camps were appropriated by Gross-Rosen, twenty-three in Lower Silesia and five in the Sudetenland. Of these, twenty were kept in operation as Gross-Rosen satellite camps, and the prisoners from the remaining eight camps were transferred to existing satellite camps. The following satellite camps were established in this way: Bunzlau I (for men); Dyhernfurth II (for men); Gräben (for women); Gräflich-Röhrsdorf (women); Grünberg (women); Hirschberg (men); Kittlitztbren (men); Langenbielau (women and men); Merzdorf (women); Neusalz (women); Peterswaldau (women); Waldenburg (men); Wolfsberg (men); Zillerthal-Erdmannsdorf; and five camps in the Sudetenland: Bernsdorf, Gabersdorf, Ober Altstadt, Parschnitz, and Schatzlar (all for women).

A second group of completely new satellite camps for Jews was put up when more transports came in at the demand of the armaments inspector for the Silesia military district (Wehrkreis VIII) and of the ORGANISATION TODT, and, later, upon the partial evacuation of the Płaszów and Auschwitz camps. Conspicuous among these camps were the twelve in the Sudetic Mountains that comprised the *Arbeitslager Riese* (Giant Labor Camp) complex, all for men: Dörnhau, Erlenbusch, Falkenberg, Fürstenstein, Kaltwasser, Lärche and Märzbachtal, Oberwüstegiersdorf, Säuferwasser, Schotterwerk, Tannhausen, and Wolfsberg. Established from April to June 1944, these camps were a manpower reserve for the construction of Hitler's subterranean home. They held 13,000 Jews, most of them from Hungary. The hard labor involved in building subterranean passages, roads, and so forth, together with the poor living conditions and total lack of hygiene, soon caused a large number of prisoners to become *Muselmänner*. A *Selektion* was made and 857 prisoners from these camps were sent to Auschwitz, on September 29 and October 19, 1944. The mortality rate in the *Arbeitslager Riese* complex was exceptionally high; extant records reveal that at least 3,068 prisoners died there.

Other satellite camps for Jewish prisoners were Bad Warmbrunn, Balkenhain, Friedland, Schertendorf, Grünberg, Brünnlitz, and Geppersdorf, whose inmates were employed in local armaments factories. The women, distributed over forty-two satellite camps, came mostly from Poland and Hungary. They arrived from Poland when Organisation Schmelt was disbanded (and fifteen satellite camps were transferred) and, in late 1944, when Płaszów, Auschwitz-Birkenau, and the Łódź ghetto were evacuated (the last via Auschwitz). They also came from Hungary in transports that first passed through Auschwitz-Birkenau. The women's camps (*Frauenarbeitslager*) taken over from Schmelt contained 6,000 to 7,000 women. The prisoners in thirteen of these camps were employed in textile factories; in one camp, in the aircraft industry; and in another, in an armaments factory. The regime in the women's camps was less harsh; out of 5,000 prisoners, only 58 died. The other satellite camps for women were put up at the following times:

the Grafenort satellite camp in March 1944; Christianstadt in June; Breslau-Hundsfeld, Guben, and Weisswasser, in July; Freiburg and Mittelsteine, in August; Görlitz, Liebau, Wiesau, and Ober Hohenelbe, in September; Birnbaumel, Hochweiler, Kurzbach, Sackisch, Schlesiersee, Halbstadt Kratzau (I and II), and Zittau, in October; and Brünnlitz and Saint Georgenthal, in November. More women's satellite camps were established in 1945: Langenbielau, Wüstegiersdorf, Gablonz, and Morchenstern. Tens of thousands of women were concentrated in these camps and put to work in armaments factories (the prisoners from eight camps); in the aircraft industry (five camps); in the radio industry (four camps); in the Organisation Todt, constructing trenches (four camps); in textile factories (two camps); and so on.

Before 1944 there were no large transfers of Jewish prisoners from Gross-Rosen to other concentration camps, and available records show only the transfer of some 200 *Muselmänner* to Auschwitz and of 400 prisoners to Buchenwald. There were, however, frequent internal transfers from one satellite camp to another to meet current requirements of the war economy, and, at a later stage, as part of the gradual liquidation of Gross-Rosen.

In the first phase of the evacuation—the last ten days of January 1945—the satellite camps on the eastern bank of the Oder were liquidated. The men's satellite camps located there (including Fünfteichen and Dyhernfurth, with their Jewish prisoners) were moved to the main camp. The prisoners in the women's camps, for the most part, were transferred to concentration camps deep inside the Reich. The prisoners were evacuated by foot, in what came to be known as DEATH MARCHES, in the cold of winter and without food. Many prisoners perished on those marches, but no accurate estimate can be made of their number. The ultimate fate of some columns of prisoners remains unknown.

The main camp, Gross-Rosen itself, was evacuated in early February 1945, and the remaining satellite camps thereafter. Although the prisoners in the main camp were evacuated by rail, the condition of the cars that were used (they normally carried coal) and the lack of food caused the death of many after a few days in transit. The prisoners of the satellite camps were evacuated on foot; those of the Bunzlau camp, for example, were on the march from February 12 to March 26, 1945, with 260 perishing en route.

During the evacuation of Gross-Rosen and the satellite camps, 3,500 Jews were moved to BERGEN-BELSEN (mostly women prisoners from the Birnbaumel, Christianstadt, Hochweiler, and Kurzbach camps); 5,565 were moved to Buchenwald; 489 to Dachau; 4,930 to Flossenbürg; 2,249 to MAUTHAUSEN (mostly from the *Arbeitslager Riese* network); and 1,103 to Mittelbau. The NEUENGAMME camp also took in a small number of women prisoners from Weisswasser.

Including the transfers made in 1944, a minimum of 19,500 Jewish prisoners were moved from Gross-Rosen to concentration camps in the Reich, that is, 35 percent of the total number of Jewish prisoners in Gross-Rosen. The fate of the other 37,500 has not been established so far; some of them, no doubt, were included in the evacuation. The number of Jewish prisoners in the Gross-Rosen camp complex who did not survive is unknown, except in the case of *Arbeitslager Riese.* About half of the Jewish prisoners in the satellite camps are known to have been left behind. The surviving prisoners in these camps were liberated by Soviet troops on May 8 and 9, 1945. Of the women's satellite camps, twenty were liberated; in thirteen of them, 9,000 women survived. In Langenbielau, 1,400 surviving Jews were recorded upon liberation; in Brünnlitz, 800 had survived; and in Waldenburg, 600.

Even from these incomplete data it is clear that a large proportion of the prisoners lived to see the Nazi regime's downfall. When the satellite camps were liberated, Jewish committees were formed in them that took the prisoners under their care, especially the many who were sick. They obtained food and clothing and assisted in the prisoners' repatriation to their countries of origin.

A large number of the former Gross-Rosen prisoners gathered in Dzierżoniów (Reichenbach), and on June 17, 1945, representatives of the Jewish committees of six Lower Silesian towns convened there and formed a district committee of Polish Jews. The purpose was to coordinate activities in behalf of the surviving Jewish population under the new social and political conditions.

BIBLIOGRAPHY

Gutman, Y., and A. Saf, eds. *The Nazi Concentration Camps.* Jerusalem, 1980.

Moldawa, M. *Gross-Rosen: Obóz koncentracyjny na Śląsku.* Warsaw, 1967.

ALFRED KONIECZNY

GROSSWARDEIN. *See* Oradea.

GRUENBAUM, ITZHAK (1879–1970), Polish Jewish and Zionist leader. Gruenbaum was born in Warsaw, studied law, and was a Zionist from an early age. He edited newspapers and periodicals in Polish, Yiddish, and Hebrew, was prominent in the radical wing of the General Zionist party, and fought for the secularization of Jewish life and the promotion of the Hebrew language. From 1919 to 1932 he was a member of the Sejm (the Polish parliament), where he fought for equal rights for Jews as citizens and as a national minority, and was one of the sponsors and organizers of the parliamentary National Minorities Bloc.

Itzhak Gruenbaum. [Israel Government Press Office]

In 1932 Gruenbaum moved to Paris, and a year later, after being elected a member of the Zionist Executive, he settled in Palestine. From 1933 to 1935 he headed the Jewish Agency's Immigration Department, and from 1935 to 1948, its Labor Department. That year he became a member of Palestinian Jewry's quasi government in the months preceding the establishment of the state. In the period of the provisional government (1948–1949), he was minister of the interior.

When World War II broke out in 1939, Gruenbaum took the initiative in establishing a Committee of Four in the Jewish Agency Executive, for assisting Polish Jewry, and became the committee's head. In January 1943, when the Jewish Agency's Joint Rescue Committee was created, he was elected its chairman. During the two years of the Rescue Committee's activities (1943–1944) Gruenbaum was the butt of harsh criticism, and there were calls for his resignation. This criticism was based on several grounds. First, Gruenbaum for a long time would not believe the reports that were coming in—with increasing frequency in 1942—of the systematic murder of the Jews and the existence of extermination camps. As a result, by the end of that year, when he delayed making public the RIEGNER CABLE (which, on the basis of information received from a reliable German source, confirmed the systematic extermination of the Jews), he was accused of deliberately hushing up these reports. Second, by early 1943 Gruenbaum despaired of the chances of any large-scale rescue efforts succeeding, and concluded that Palestine Jewry's main task was to prepare a haven of refuge in Palestine for those Jews who would survive; therefore, the needs in Palestine took priority over those of the Jews in the Diaspora. He was of the opinion that no public mourning over what was happening in Europe should take place in Palestine, and that the Zionist National Funds should not allocate money for rescue efforts.

Gruenbaum aired his views in no uncertain terms, in a manner that many found objectionable. A third complaint was that Gruenbaum was not devoting all his attention to rescue work because of the many posts he held, as head of a Jewish Agency department and a member of numerous committees. Gruenbaum's critics failed to realize that despite his opinions and his refusal to resign from his many other posts, he was exerting himself in behalf of rescue. He did this mainly by raising funds from sources other than the national funds, and by means of the far-flung correspondence he conducted with statesmen and institutions the world over, to solicit their support for the saving of Jews—even though he had little hope on that score. He initiated various ideas and proposals that he tried to implement, and advocated "rescue for rescue's sake," to any place in the world, and not necessarily in order to bring Jews to Palestine.

Gruenbaum's chairmanship of the Rescue Committee eventually became the great tragedy of his life. Subsumed in that tragedy were the severe censure to which he was exposed, the Rescue Committee's weak status and lack of authority, his strained relations with David BEN-GURION, his ongoing dispute with the religious political parties over his efforts for the separation of religion and state, the knowledge that his son Eliezer was a prisoner in Birkenau (and later in BUCHENWALD), and, above all, the destruction of Polish Jewry, which he had not been able to prevent.

After the war Gruenbaum's son was charged with having been a KAPO, but was cleared of the charge. He settled in Israel and fell in Israel's War of Independence, in 1948. During Palestinian Jewry's struggle with the British, Gruenbaum was arrested and interned for a time in Latrun, together with other Zionist leaders. When the state of Israel was declared, on May 14, 1948, Gruenbaum did not affix his signature to the Independence scroll, since he refused to leave besieged Jerusalem to attend the ceremony (which took place in Tel Aviv). As minister of the interior, Gruenbaum organized the elections to the constituent assembly (the First Knesset), but he himself was not elected. Thereafter he kept up his writing and Zionist activities, in which he stated his views, now strongly leftist.

BIBLIOGRAPHY

Porat, D. "Al-Domi: Palestinian Intellectuals and the Holocaust." *Studies in Zionism* 5/1 (Spring 1984): 92–124.

Prister, R. *Without Compromise: Yitzhak Gruenbaum, Zionist Leader and Polish Patriot.* Tel Aviv, 1987. (In Hebrew.)

DINA PORAT

GRÜNINGER, PAUL (1891–1972), local police commandant of the Saint Gall canton in Switzerland, on the Austrian frontier, who was responsible for assisting thousands of Jewish refugees.

After Austria's annexation by Germany in March 1938, the stream of Jewish refugees seeking to leave the Reich increased, and many sought to gain access to Switzerland. But at this critical juncture, the Swiss government closed its borders to Jewish refugees. Grüninger was instructed on August 18, 1938, to refuse entry to refugees fleeing Germany for racial reasons. Confronted by an unending wave of Jewish refugees at his border post, he defied his government's instructions and allowed all the Jews crossing the border at his

Paul Grüninger (left) in police uniform (February 15, 1934).

checkpoint entry into the country. As a cover-up, he predated official seals in the refugees' passports to indicate that their holders had entered the country prior to the August 1938 government ruling. Thus, from August through December 1938, when he was summarily suspended, Grüninger allowed some thirty-six hundred persons (according to the state prosecutor) illegal entry into Switzerland.

Alerted by the German legation in Bern, the Swiss government in January 1939 opened an inquiry into Grüninger's activities, and charges were filed against him. Found guilty of insubordination, he was sentenced in 1941 to a stiff fine and the forfeiture of all retirement and severance payments. Grüninger was later denied access to other suitable positions in the government and the private sector, and he was never fully rehabilitated by the Swiss government. In 1971, he received recognition from YAD VASHEM as a "RIGHTEOUS AMONG THE NATIONS."

BIBLIOGRAPHY

Häsler, A. A. *The Lifeboat Is Full: Switzerland and the Refugees, 1933–1945.* New York, 1969.

MORDECAI PALDIEL

GRYNSZPAN, HERSCHEL (1921–1943?), refugee assassin of a German diplomat in Paris. Born in Hannover of Polish nationality, Grynszpan fled to Paris in 1936. On November 7, 1938, having learned of the deportation of his parents from Germany to ZBĄSZYŃ, on the Polish frontier, he shot the third secretary of the German embassy in Paris, Ernst vom Rath, as a protest, and promptly surrendered to the police. When the diplomat died two days later, the Nazis launched the KRISTALLNACHT riots throughout the Reich.

In 1940, the Vichy government turned Grynszpan over to the Germans. Two years later, the Nazi authorities planned a great show trial, orchestrated by Joseph GOEBBELS, hoping to demonstrate Grynszpan's link with a Jewish conspiracy to plunge Europe into war. Grynszpan himself seems to have sabotaged this scheme by reviving a story he had fabricated about a homosexual liaison between the diplomat and his assassin. His manner of death has never been clarified, but he almost certainly did not survive the war.

Herschel Grynszpan being taken from police headquarters in Paris.

BIBLIOGRAPHY

Heiber, H. "Der Fall Grünspan." *Vierteljahrshefte für Zeitgeschichte* 5 (1975): 134–172.

Marrus, M. R. "The Strange Story of Herschel Grynszpan." *The American Scholar* 57 (1987–1988): 69–79.

Roizen, R. "Herschel Grynszpan: The Fate of a Forgotten Assassin." *Holocaust and Genocide Studies* 1/2 (1986): 217–228.

MICHAEL R. MARRUS

GUNSKIRCHEN, assembly camp for the Jewish prisoners from the MAUTHAUSEN concentration camp that went into operation in March 1945. It was situated in the vicinity of the town of the same name, which was close to Wels, a city in Upper Austria. In April 1945 the camp comprised seven unfinished huts and

Under the supervision of the Seventy-first Infantry Division of the United States Third Army, German soldiers, prisoners of war, remove dead victims from the Gunskirchen concentration camp. [United States Army]

two huts used as auxiliary structures. Administratively, the camp was separate from the Mauthausen camp network, and was utilized as an assembly point for Jewish prisoners only. The camp commandant was an SS-Obersturmführer Werner.

In the second half of April, some seventeen thousand to twenty thousand prisoners were brought from the tent camp that had been set up at Mauthausen, and from other camps. All of them were packed into the Gunskirchen camp. The prisoners already there had ceased to work; their weakness was such that they were close to death. There was one toilet for all the prisoners, and drinking water was distributed from a tank holding 396.4 gallons (1,500 l), brought to the camp once a day on a fire truck. The prisoners fought for a sip of water and even sold their daily bread ration in exchange for it. About twenty-five hundred people were compressed into each hut; as a result, the weak were crushed to death at night. Epidemics of typhus and dysentery were rife. The doctors among the prisoners were unable to offer assistance, for there were no medical facilities whatever, and the mortality rate in the camp increased daily. The food rations were even smaller than those in the tent camp at Mauthausen, and many prisoners were saved only by small supplements of food from the Red Cross packages that were distributed once or twice. A truck arrived daily in the camp to transport the day's corpses to a grave dug in the nearby forest. As the mortality rate increased, burial pits were dug in the camp's limited area.

On May 4, 1945, all the SS officers disappeared from the camp. The prisoners overran the food stores next to the kitchen and seized everything they could lay their hands on. On the following day, May 5, a United States Army Medical Corps unit arrived at the camp. It was littered with corpses, and those prisoners still alive were filthy, lice-infested skeletons. The American unit transferred the sick and the dying to a temporary hospital in nearby Wels. At the time of the liberation there were 5,419 survivors; an unknown number of prisoners had departed on the eve of the liberation. Seven communal graves were discovered in the camp, containing the remains of 1,227 victims.

BIBLIOGRAPHY

Adler, S. *In the Valley of Death: A Year in the Life of a Youth in a Concentration Camp.* Jerusalem, 1979. (In Hebrew.)

Eckstein, B. *Mauthausen: Concentration and Annihilation Camp.* Jerusalem, 1984. (In Hebrew.)

BENYAMIN ECKSTEIN

GURS, the first detention camp to be established in FRANCE, and one of the largest. The Gurs camp was situated in a locality of the same name, 50 miles (80 km) from the Spanish border and 10 miles (16 km) from the town of Oloron-Sainte-Marie, on the plateau overlooking the lower Pyrenees.

The Gurs camp was set up in April 1939, coinciding with the collapse of the Spanish republic, and the first prisoners to be detained in it were Spanish republican soldiers who had fled to France in the wake of Franco's victory; among them were Jewish volunteers of the International Brigade. In early 1940 some four thousand German and Austrian nationals—most of them Jews—were interned in Gurs, as well as leaders of the French Communist party who had denounced the war against Germany, in line with the NAZI-SOVIET PACT. Between October 22 and 25, 1940, four months after France had surrendered, the German authorities—in violation of the armistice with France—deported to Gurs the entire Jewish population of Baden and the Palatinate, as well as Jews from some locations in Württemberg. Some seventy-five hundred Jews were included in Aktion Bürckel, so named after Josef Bürckel, the *Gauleiter* of Alsace-Lorraine.

All the non-Jewish German nationals and pro-Nazis had been released from Gurs in mid-July 1940, shortly after the French defeat. The French Communists were set free at the end of October 1940; of the Jews, some two thousand were released in stages between November 1940 and August 1942, with the help of HICEM, and emigrated overseas.

Conditions in the camp were very harsh: the sanitary arrangements were primitive, there was a shortage of water, and all the detainees suffered constantly from hunger. In the winter of 1940–1941, 800 detainees died in epidemics of diseases such as typhoid fever

A view of the Gurs concentration camp.

and dysentery that broke out in the camp. A total of 1,187 detainees were buried in the Gurs cemetery; 20 of these were non-Jewish Spaniards and all the rest Jews.

Despite the harsh conditions in the camp, many cultural activities were conducted there, in various fields and on a very high level—concerts, theater performances, lectures, and exhibitions. There were also courses of instruction in Hebrew, French, and English, Jewish history, the Bible, and the Talmud, and thousands of prisoners attended religious ceremonies and prayer services on the holy days.

Six thousand Jewish prisoners were deported from Gurs to AUSCHWITZ-Birkenau and SOBIBÓR by way of the DRANCY camp, the first transport leaving Gurs on August 6, 1942, and the last in the fall of 1943; by December 29, 1943, no more than forty-eight Jews were left. The camp was liberated in the summer of 1944. The French poet Louis Aragon said of the Gurs camp: "Gurs is a strange sound, like a moan stuck in the throat."

BIBLIOGRAPHY

Krehbiel-Darmstaedter, M. *Briefe aus Gurs und Limonest, 1940–1943.* Heidelberg, 1970.

Marrus, M. R., and R. O. Paxton. *Vichy France and the Jews.* New York, 1981.

Rutkowski, A. "Le camp d'internement de Gurs." *Le Monde Juif* 100 (1980): 128–146; 101 (1981): 13–32.

Schramm, H. *Menschen in Gurs: Erinnerungen an ein französischen Internierlager (1940–1941).* Worms, 1977.

ADAM RUTKOWSKI

GUSEN, camp established in Germany as the first branch of the MAUTHAUSEN camp. Gusen was 2.8 miles (4.5 km) to the west of the main camp, near St. Georgen, and was put into operation on March 9, 1940. In its first two years, the Gusen camp maintained its own register of prisoners, but later they were listed and numbered together with the Mauthausen prisoners. From May 1940 to the end of that year, 5,000 prisoners were brought to Gusen, where they were put to work in local quarries and brickyards. During that period 1,507 prisoners died in the camp, their deaths recorded in the camp's separate register. In addition, 240 Polish officers and students were shot to death in Gusen, on orders of the Gestapo in Poland and in accordance

A general view of the Gusen concentration camp, which was liberated on May 5, 1945, by the United States Army. [United States Army]

with a list it submitted to the camp administration (which was commanded by SS-Hauptsturmführer Karl Chmielewski). The camp contained thirty wooden barracks and two stone buildings. At first, six of the barracks were used as a hospital; four more were designated as hospital barracks in the winter of 1943–1944. In 1943, railway lines were laid to the quarries and to the Messerschmitt and Steyr plants operating in the camp, which employed many of the prisoners in the manufacture of aircraft parts and machine guns.

A second camp, designated as Gusen II, was opened on March 9, 1944, with 10,000 prisoners, followed by a third, Gusen III, in December 1944, with 262 prisoners. Gusen II prisoners were engaged in the construction of underground passages leading to the armament plants' workshops; one of the passages —which was 4 miles (7 km) long, 26 feet (8 m) wide, and 23 feet (7 m) high—was completed, enabling Steyr to manufacture ball bearings there. No other passage had been completed by the end of the war.

Living conditions for the prisoners in the camps were extremely harsh. Driven by the camp staff, which was made up primarily of ex-convicts, the prisoners had to maintain a fast pace in their work, and those who were unable to keep it up were killed. In the period from October 1941 to May 1942, 2,151 Soviet prisoners were listed in the camp's register of death, in addition to prisoners of other nationalities.

Barrack No. 30 was an assembly point for prisoners who had been selected for killing by phenol injections. This was also where debilitated prisoners were beaten to death by the *Blockälteste* (barrack elder). From time to time groups of prisoners were taken to nearby Hartheim castle, to be killed in the gas chambers that had been set up there.

A total of 67,677 persons were imprisoned in the Gusen camps, nearly half of whom —31,535—were listed as having died there. The figure does not include at least 2,500 persons, mostly Jews, who died in the camps without having their deaths recorded, and the 2,630 Gusen prisoners who were taken to Hartheim to be gassed there.

The Gusen camps were liberated on May 5, 1945, by American troops, but the condition of some two thousand of the prisoners was so poor that they died at about the time the camps were set free. Chmielewski, who had been camp commandant up to 1942, was tried by a court in Ansbach after the war and sentenced to life imprisonment.

BIBLIOGRAPHY

Eckstein, B. *Mauthausen: Concentration and Annihilation Camp.* Jerusalem, 1984. (In Hebrew.)

Le Chêne, E. *Mauthausen: The History of a Death Camp.* London, 1971.

Marsalek, H., and K. Hacker. *Kurzgeschichte der Konzentrationslager Mauthausen und seiner drei grössten Nebenlager Gusen, Ebensee, und Melk.* Vienna, n.d.

BENYAMIN ECKSTEIN

GUSTLOFF, WILHELM (1895–1936), German leader of the Nazis in Switzerland. Gustloff was born in Schwerin. In 1917 he moved to Davos, Switzerland, for reasons of health. He joined the Nazi party in 1929 and in 1932 was appointed head of the party's AUSLANDSORGANISATION (Foreign Organization) in Switzerland.

Gustloff made special efforts to have the PROTOCOLS OF THE ELDERS OF ZION, an antisemitic forgery, widely distributed, causing Jewish circles in Switzerland to sue for libel the book's distributor, the Swiss Nazi party. Gustloff himself remained in the background, since as a foreigner he was in danger of being expelled from the country. His share, however, in the unrestrained anti-Jewish agitation being stirred up at the time was public knowledge. This caused David FRANKFURTER, a Jewish student, to ambush Gustloff at his home in Davos and shoot him to death, on February 4, 1936.

The Nazi regime made him a martyr, and at his funeral in Schwerin, Adolf Hitler himself eulogized Gustloff. Nazi propaganda claimed that the assassination was a conspiracy planned by "international Jewry," although in fact Frankfurter had acted on his own initiative. Because of the Olympic games, however, which were about to be held in Berlin, in August 1936, Nazi reaction to the assassination was restrained.

BIBLIOGRAPHY

Diewerge, W. *Der Fall Gustloff.* Munich, 1936.

Diewerge, W. *Ein Jude hat geschossen.* Munich, 1937.

Frankfurter, D. "I Killed a Nazi Gauleiter: Memoir of a Jewish Assassin." *Commentary* 9/2 (February 1950): 133–141.

DAVID HADAR

GWARDIA LUDOWA (People's Guard), underground army organization in occupied POLAND. Created in January 1942 by the Polska Partia Robotnicza (Polish Workers' Party; PPR), the Gwardia Ludowa was active in the GENERALGOUVERNEMENT and the areas of Poland annexed to the Reich. It was directed by a supreme command and had a staff that was divided into sections.

The organization's area of activity was broken down by districts and regions. In the spring of 1942 the first Gwardia Ludowa partisan units were formed according to the instructions of the heads of the PPR, and they commenced sabotage activities immediately. Various estimates for late 1943 put the organization's membership at fifteen thousand to twenty thousand; its scores of units directed and conducted military and sabotage actions.

In 1942 and 1943, Gwardia Ludowa units carried out about seventeen hundred military actions, according to the organization's records. In January 1944, the Gwardia Ludowa became the Armia Ludowa (People's Army), by order of the Krajowa Rada Narodowa (Polish National Council), an organization founded on January 1, 1944, by Communists and Communist sympathizers. Gen. Michał Zymierski, known as "Rola," was appointed commander of the Armia Ludowa, which retained the same organizational structure as that of the Gwardia Ludowa.

By the summer of 1944 the Armia Ludowa had about thirty-four thousand members. From January 1944 to January 1945, according to the estimates of its General Staff, Armia Ludowa forces carried out more than fifteen hundred military actions of different kinds, about half of them against German transport and communications.

Several units of Jewish partisans, which had initially operated independently, joined the ranks of the Gwardia Ludowa and the Armia Ludowa. The best known was Yehiel

A group of partisan fighters from Yehiel Grynszpan's unit attached to the Armia Ludowa.

Grynszpan's unit in the Parczew Forest (*see* PARTISANS). Originally an independent unit, it became a family camp (*see* FAMILY CAMPS IN THE FORESTS) and subsequently received aid from the Armia Ludowa.

The Gwardia Ludowa provided the ŻYDOWSKA ORGANIZACJA BOJOWA (Jewish Fighting Organization; ŻOB) in the WARSAW ghetto with a small quantity of arms, and during the WARSAW GHETTO UPRISING its units attempted several unsuccessful military holding actions outside the ghetto walls. In July 1944 the Armia Ludowa merged with the Polish army formed in the Soviet Union, which fought under the command of Gen. Zygmunt Berling together with the Soviet army. In this way the Polish army of the new Polish government was created.

[*See also* Armia Krajowa.]

BIBLIOGRAPHY

Ciechanowski, J. M. *The Warsaw Rising of 1944.* Cambridge, 1974.

Historia Polskiego Ruchu Robotniczego: 1939–1944. Vol. 4. Warsaw, 1984.

Korbonski, S. *The Polish Underground State: A Guide to the Underground, 1939–1945.* New York, 1969.

Wieczorek, M. *Armia Ludowa: Powstanie i organizacja 1944–1945.* 2 vols. Warsaw, 1979, 1984.

EUGENIUSZ DURACZYNSKI

GYPSIES, a people living in Europe from the fifteenth century, bound by a common language and culture, and—until the twentieth century—by a nomadic way of life. The Gypsies, also called Rom, were among the groups singled out by the Nazi regime for persecution.

While there are differences of opinion regarding their early history, it seems fairly clear that the Gypsies originated in India and were in Iran by the fourteenth century. By 1438, they had reached Hungary, and had entered Serbia and other Balkan countries. They then spread into Poland and Russia, and by the sixteenth century had reached Sweden and England. In Spain they settled in fairly large numbers at the same time. While some Gypsies became Muslims (in Bosnia, the Crimea, and elsewhere) or Orthodox (in Serbia), most European Gypsies became Roman Catholics, but kept many of their pre-Christian beliefs alongside their new religion. Split into many dialects, their language is only now becoming a written language, though Romany publications appeared in the Soviet Union in the early years of the Communist regime.

Prejudice and animosity toward Gypsies were and are widespread. Their professions were dictated by their wandering way of life; they were usually not allowed to obtain land in their adopted countries. Generally, they bought and sold horses and other animals, engaged in petty trade, and practiced arts such as silverwork, goldwork, and music. Fortune-telling, for which they gained a wide reputation, was usually a sideline. Gypsies were frequently accused of stealing and dishonesty, largely because of their living habits and language. Aggression was diverted toward them in a process of transference, to a certain extent similar to that applied to the Jews. On occasion, this animosity turned into murderous policies. Thus, the Prussian king, Frederick William I, decreed in 1725 that all Gypsies over eighteen were subject to killing. At the same time, their music and their poetry were the inspiration of famous artists, for example Franz Liszt. Although for different historical reasons, in many ways they shared with the Jews the doubtful honor of being the quintessential strangers in an overwhelmingly sedentary, Christian Europe.

With the advent of modern industrial society, the Gypsies were out of place in the eyes of the authorities. In 1899 Bavaria established a special office for Gypsy affairs; it was the center for anti-Gypsy policies in Germany until the Nazi period. In February 1929, the Munich office became a Central Bureau, with close ties to a similar office in Vienna. In 1929, regulations came into effect that enabled the police to coerce Gypsies, who had no permanent occupation, to work at forced labor. Similar regulations were operative in a number of other European countries.

The Gypsies occupied a special place in Nazi racist theories. According to a report submitted to Heinrich HIMMLER in 1941, there were some twenty-eight thousand Gypsies in Germany, and an additional eleven thousand in Austria. Most of these Gypsies belonged to the Sinti and Lalleri tribes. The basic attitude of the Nazi regime was extremely hostile; old prejudices and animosities were added to an ideal of a "pure" Nordic society that emphasized peasant life and sedentary habits. This stood in clear contradiction to the Gypsies' way of life. In the eyes of the regime, the Gypsies were "asocials" who did not fit into the new society that was to be built. While one could not very well doubt the Aryan parentage of the closely knit Gypsy families, they were also clearly "people of different blood" (*Andersblütige).*

With the advent of the NUREMBERG LAWS in September 1935, the interpreters of the decrees explicitly included the Gypsies, along with the Jews, in their regulations. In 1936, groups of Gypsies were delivered to the DACHAU camp as "asocials." At this time a racist ideologue, Dr. Robert Ritter, was empowered to set up a Research Office for the Science of Inheritance (Erbwissenschaftliche Forschungsstelle). In 1937 it became the Research Office for Race Hygiene and Population Biology (Rassenhygienische und Bevölkerungsbiologische Forschungsstelle). Dr. Ritter was to examine the Gypsy population from the Nazi point of view and propose solutions as to what to do with them.

According to Dr. Ritter and his co-workers, an examination of some twenty thousand Rom showed that over 90 percent were to be considered MISCHLINGE (of mixed blood). This solved the problem of having to deal with an Aryan minority; the Nazis simply denied that the Gypsies were Aryans. Ritter's proposals were to prevent Gypsies from mixing with people of "German blood," to separate "pure" Gypsies from *Mischlinge* Gypsies, and to perform sterilizations on the latter, while putting them in forced-labor camps. Both "pure" and *Mischlinge* Gypsies were considered "asocial"—work-shy individuals and aliens. Here the Nazis maintained an important element of continuity with traditional European discriminatory thought. According to Himmler's decree of December 14, 1937, "preventive" arrests could be made of persons who, while not guilty of any criminal act, "endangered the communality by their asocial behavior." Administrative regulations implementing this decree, which were issued on April 4, 1938, specified that it was directed against "beggars, vagabonds (Gypsies), prostitutes . . . without a permanent residence."

It soon became clear to the Nazis that this provision was too broad and could not be implemented at the time. Therefore, further regulation of March 1, 1939, classified Himmler's underlying ideas and his practical policies. As a basis for dealing with what he labeled "the Gypsy plague," he called for a separation between Gypsies and Germans, and between "pure" and *Mischlinge* Gypsies. The way of life of both latter categories would be regulated by the police.

Contrary to this provision, but in line with the general radicalization of Nazi racial policies, the fate of the German Gypsies became tied up with that of the Poles and Jews after the Nazi conquest of Poland. In September 1939, Reinhard HEYDRICH issued instructions projecting the removal of thirty thousand Gypsies from all of Germany to the GENERALGOUVERNEMENT, together with the removal of Poles and Jews from the newly occupied western Polish territories. This order may have been designed to remove all *Mischlinge* Gypsies from Germany. However, plans went amiss—with respect to the Gypsies as well as to the Jews and the Poles. In the end, in April 1940, the Nazi governor of the Generalgouvernement, Hans FRANK, received twenty-five hundred Gypsies, who were removed from the western territories to the Generalgouvernement. These Gypsies were mostly released in Poland.

Attitudes toward the Gypsies became more brutal as time went on. In the fall of 1941, 5,007 Austrian Gypsies of the Lalleri tribe were deported to the ŁÓDŹ ghetto. They were included among the victims of the mass murders committed against the Jews in the CHEŁMNO extermination camp in early 1942. No survivors are known. Three thousand more Austrian Gypsies were put into concentration camps at the same time.

In the meantime 18,922 (or roughly two-thirds) of the 28,607 German Gypsies had been classified by Ritter: 1,079 were defined as "pure," 6,992 as "more Gypsy than German," 2,976 as "half-breeds," 2,992 as "more German than Gypsy," 2,652 were "Germans who behaved as Gypsies," and 2,231 were still being investigated. From the Nazi point of view, and in light of the radicalization of Nazi racial policies, the "problem" was one of thoroughgoing clarification, which meant —in Nazi logic—murder on the one hand, control on the other. "Pure" Gypsies could not, by this logic, be excluded from society —that is, murdered. And so, on October 13, 1942, Himmler issued a clarification "relating to Gypsy chiefs," concerning pure "Sinti Gypsies for whom in the future a certain freedom of movement is to be permitted." *Mischlinge,* "who are good *Mischlinge* in the Gypsy sense, are to be reintroduced into racially pure Sinti Gypsy clans." The same would apply to the surviving Austrian Lalleri. For these "pure" or relatively "pure" Gypsies, there would be appointed nine chiefs *(Obmänner),* who would supervise the "certain freedom of movement" to be allowed their charges. According to a document of January 11, 1943, 13,000 Sinti and 1,017 Lalleri were to be considered under this lifesaving provision. As to the others, Himmler issued a clear order on December 16, 1942, indicating that they were to be sent to AUSCHWITZ, except for those who were "socially adapted," "former Wehrmacht soldiers," or "war industry workers in important positions." For these exempted categories, sterilization was proposed.

In reality, the distinctions were not that clear. The first large transport of Gypsies arrived in Auschwitz on February 26, 1943, and a Gypsy family camp was established in Birkenau. The number of Gypsies in the Auschwitz "Gypsy camp" is believed to have been about 20,000. Living, or rather existing, in the most indescribable conditions, a great many of them died from starvation, epidemics, and "medical experiments," such as Josef MENGELE's experiments with twins. On August 2, 1944, 2,897 Gypsies were gassed as part of the destruction of the Gypsy family camp. Practically all the women and children were killed, this being a time when the Hungarian Jewish transports had ceased arriving in large numbers and the gas chambers were available. Some of the men were sent to slave-labor camps or other concentration camps to do vital war work. Others were recruited into the Wehrmacht to clear away mines or perform other life-endangering functions, from which only a fraction returned.

It is unlikely that German statistics on Gypsies and "Germans wandering about in the Gypsy manner" were very accurate, nor need the documents regulating exceptions be taken literally. Auschwitz survivors have related stories of Gypsies—good Nazis and loyal Germans, some of officer rank—who were weeded out of German army units and sent to Auschwitz. Others, apparently, were not touched; it depended on the zeal of the local commander or the civilian party boss, and on his interpretation of the instructions. Nor were the Gypsies shipped to Auschwitz all German citizens. The order of December 16, 1942, mentioned above referred to "Gypsy *Mischlinge,* Rom Gypsies, and members of clans of Balkan origins who are not of German blood." Clearly, the Nazis got mixed up in the intricacies of their own language. What was meant, it seems, were non-Sinti Gypsies; members of the clans known as Rom were "of Balkan origins."

The total number of German and Austrian Gypsies deported to Auschwitz was 13,000. If one excludes the category of "Germans who behaved as Gypsies," Ritter's German Sinti "Gypsies" numbered 25,955. This number, combined with the roughly 11,000 Austrian Lalleri, made for a total of about 37,000. Of this total, 2,500 were deported to Poland in 1939 and 1940 and mostly killed later; 3,000 were interned in Austrian camps, and presumably mostly killed; 5,000 were sent to Łódź and gassed at Chełmno; and 13,000 were deported to Auschwitz and mostly killed there. This breakdown, totaling 23,500, leaves 13,500 unaccounted for. These probably are the 14,017 Sintis and Lalleri defined by Himmler as pure or nearly pure Gypsies who would be spared.

Before the dismemberment of Czechoslovakia, about thirteen thousand Gypsies lived in the territories that would constitute the Protectorate of BOHEMIA AND MORAVIA. About half escaped to SLOVAKIA before the Nazis began to deport Gypsies. Some four thousand were sent to Auschwitz between July 1943 and May 1944, and only a few hundred Czech Gypsies survived the war.

Information as to the fate of the Gypsies in

the rest of Europe is sketchy. According to one source, more than two hundred thousand were killed all over Europe (Zulch, 1979). This, however, may be an underestimate. In Yugoslavia, Gypsies were murdered together with Jews by the USTAŠA regime; possibly as many as ninety thousand were killed.

In the occupied areas of Europe, the Nazis generally interned Gypsies and later transported them to Germany or Poland for use as workers or to be killed. Apparently BULGARIA, DENMARK, FINLAND, and GREECE were the only countries where the Gypsies escaped this treatment. In the NETHERLANDS, Gypsies, like the Jews, were interned in WESTERBORK and from there sent to Auschwitz. Gypsies from LUXEMBOURG and BELGIUM were also sent to the notorious extermination camp.

Before the Nazi occupation, French authorities had already restricted the movement of Gypsies. After the defeat of FRANCE in June 1940, Gypsies from Alsace and Lorraine were interned in a camp at Schirmeck, where they were kept separate from "asocials" and "criminals." Shortly before Christmas 1941, they were deported. In unoccupied France, thirty thousand Gypsies were interned under the supervision of Xavier VALLAT and the Ministry for Jewish Affairs. Later, most were sent to camps in Germany, including BUCHENWALD, Dachau, and RAVENSBRÜCK, where between sixteen thousand and eighteen thousand perished. In Algeria as well, Gypsies were interned; seven hundred were restricted to the Maison Carrée area near Algiers.

Gypsies in ITALY, like the Jews, had a mixed experience. Often persecuted, many were also saved by the Italians. Before the war the authorities rounded up Gypsies and put them on islands off the mainland. Later, Gypsies in the Three Venices area were sent to Germany on forced labor or to extermination camps. Others, however, who managed to escape the Ustaša massacres in Croatia, were sheltered by the authorities. In the fall of 1943, when the Germans took over territories that the Italians had held in Yugoslavia and Albania, they interned the Gypsies and sent some to Buchenwald, MAUTHAUSEN, and other camps.

Although the Hungarians planned to intern Gypsies in labor camps as early as February 1941, the policy was never fully implemented. After the ARROW CROSS PARTY coup in October 1944, persecution of Gypsies began in earnest in HUNGARY. Germans and Hungarian collaborators rounded up Gypsies, deporting some together with Hungarian Jews. Reputedly, some thirty-one thousand Gypsies were deported within a few months and only three thousand returned. The sources for these figures, however, are not clear.

The large Romanian Gypsy population was not exposed to an outright extermination policy. According to a postwar Romanian People's Court, however, tens of thousands met their death through the expulsion. In 1941 and 1942, about twenty-five thousand Gypsies from the Bucharest area were sent to TRANSNISTRIA, and others were sent to the Ukraine.

Slovak Gypsies were treated somewhat better than those in the Protectorate. On January 18, 1940, along with young Jewish men, they were drafted into labor brigades. Orders issued in 1941 to expel them from their quarters in most towns and villages were carried out unevenly. Slovak fascists, however, murdered hundreds of Gypsies in pogromlike rampages.

Most Gypsies in Poland faced deportation to concentration and extermination camps. Beginning in September 1944, the majority of those remaining in the ghettos were killed. About twenty-five thousand persons, some two-thirds of the Polish Gypsies, died during the Nazi occupation.

In the Baltic States and the SOVIET UNION, Gypsies were murdered by the EINSATZGRUPPEN, who mentioned the killings in their reports. A report by the secret army field police (Geheime Feldpolizei), dispatched on August 25, 1942, stressed the need to "ruthlessly exterminate" bands of wandering Gypsies. Apparently, Gypsies were murdered along with Jews at BABI YAR near Kiev. In May 1943, Alfred ROSENBERG, the minister for the Eastern Occupied Territories, proposed that the Gypsies be concentrated in special camps and settlements. They were not, however, to be "treated as Jews." Himmler, in his order of November 15, 1943, said: "(1) Sedentary Gypsies and part Gypsies are to be treated as citizens of the country. (2) Nomadic Gypsies and part Gypsies are to be placed on the same level as Jews and placed in concentration camps. In cases of doubt, the police commanders will decide who is a Gypsy." The distinction between sedentary Gypsies and nomadic Gypsies was applied only in the Baltic states and the occupied areas of the Soviet Union. Some sedentary Gypsies in the latter were drafted into labor brigades or sent to concentration camps.

The Nazis' killing of wandering groups of Gypsies stood in contradiction to the notion that the "pure" Gypsies were the wandering ones, and should therefore be spared. Moreover, there is no evidence that the Germans tried to ferret out sedentary Gypsies, or even conducted special campaigns to find and register wandering Gypsies with the aim of murdering them.

What emerges is a seemingly confused picture. In the Reich, the Nazis murdered those whom they saw as *Mischlinge* while they mostly spared the "pure" Gypsies. In the rest of Europe they did not have a very clear policy, except that wherever they found wandering clans of Gypsies, they murdered them —as "asocials," as Otto OHLENDORF, commander of SS-Einsatzgruppe D, said at his trial. The fate of the Gypsies was in line with Nazi thought on the whole: Gypsies were not Jews, and therefore there was no need to kill all of them. Those Gypsies who were of "pure blood" or who were not considered dangerous on a racial level could continue to exist, under strict supervision. The *Mischlinge* were, as a matter of course, doomed to death. The difference between the fate of the Gypsies and that of the Jews is clear. The Jews were slated for total annihilation, whereas the Gypsies were sentenced to selective mass murder on a vast scale. Even today the Gypsies are still a persecuted minority, and research about their history in the Nazi period remains sketchy.

BIBLIOGRAPHY

Kenrick, D., and G. Puxon. *The Destiny of Europe's Gypsies.* London, 1972.

Porter, J. N., ed. *Genocide and Human Rights: A Global Anthology.* Washington, D.C., 1981. See pages 151–192.

Yoors, J. *Die Zigeuner.* Stuttgart, 1970.

Zulch, T., ed. *In Auschwitz vergast; bis heute verfolgt.* Hamburg, 1979.

YEHUDA BAUER

HAAVARA AGREEMENT, an agreement between the German economic authorities on the one hand and the Zionistische Vereinigung für Deutschland (German Zionist Federation; ZVfD) and Anglo-Palestine Bank on the other; the Hebrew word *haavara* means "transfer." The pact was signed in early August 1933 after three months of negotiations. It made possible the export of Jewish capital from Germany to Palestine in the form of goods, by either immigrants or investors, and also assisted Jewish emigration from Germany.

While the Jewish response to the Nazi persecution of German Jewry was principally aimed at the preservation of Jewish rights, as symbolized by the anti-Nazi BOYCOTTS, the Zionist interest focused primarily on the prospects of utilizing the crisis to attract immigration to Palestine. The main obstacle in the way of emigration from Germany was the German legislation banning the export of foreign currency. These laws had been enacted by pre-Nazi governments during the world economic crisis in order to stop the flight of capital, but some loopholes had been left that were soon grasped by German Zionist leaders, both in Germany and Palestine.

In May 1933 Chaim Arlosoroff, head of the Jewish Agency's Political Department, visited Germany. He concluded that massive immigration from Germany depended on the establishment of an internationally guaranteed liquidation bank that would dispose in an orderly manner of Jewish assets in Germany and transfer their equivalent to Palestine through the export of German products. Thus Germany would be compensated for the loss of foreign currency by the increase in its production and international trade. At the same time, a Jewish businessman from Palestine, Sam Cohen, made a private agreement with the German Ministry of Economics that allowed prospective immigrants to transfer their capital in the form of certain goods through Cohen's company, up to the limit of 3 million reichsmarks.

After the murder of Arlosoroff in Tel Aviv in June 1933, Cohen made a new pact with the German authorities that expanded the previous one. This time the ZVfD opposed the move and put pressure on both Cohen and the German officials to bring in the Anglo-Palestine Bank as trustee of the transferers. Under the combined pressure, the Transfer Agreement was concluded. It served as a basis for all subsequent understandings concerning "capitalist" immigration to Palestine, though various changes were introduced throughout the 1930s.

The pact provided for two separate categories of transferers: (1) immigrants who wished to transfer money in excess of 1,000 pounds sterling; (2) investors who wanted to invest money in Palestine but for the time being remained in Germany. This second category also permitted the transfer of contributions to the Zionist national funds, tuition money for students, and pensions. Two companies were established for the implementation of the accord: PALTREU (Palästina Treuhandstelle zur Beratung Deutscher Juden) in Berlin and Haavara in Tel Aviv. The first was a partnership of the Anglo-

Palestine Bank (represented by the Zionist movement's Palestine Office in Berlin) and the German Jewish banks of Max WARBURG and Oskar Wassermann; it received the deposits in reichsmarks and purchased the German products for export. The second was a subsidiary company of the Anglo-Palestine Bank that disposed of the imported goods in Palestine and reimbursed the immigrants accordingly, or acted as a trustee for investors who remained in Germany.

Zionist interest in the Transfer Agreement emanated from the aspiration to attract affluent immigrants to Palestine. The German motivation was threefold: (1) the desire to get rid of Jews; (2) economic interests, such as the promotion of production and creation of new jobs; (3) propaganda considerations aimed at undermining the anti-Nazi boycott in a particularly symbolic place, namely Palestine.

The agreement was sharply criticized by sectors of Jewish public opinion, notably in the Diaspora, as a breach of Jewish solidarity and a violation of the boycott. The official Zionist attitude claimed for a time that the agreement was a private arrangement between the German Zionists and the German government. This changed only in the summer of 1935, under the pressure of the Zionist labor movement, when Haavara alone emerged as a practical way to ensure immigration from Germany.

Until 1935 the agreement concerned only immigrants whose property exceeded 1,000 pounds. This sum was required by the British authorities in order to obtain a "capitalist" certificate (*Vorzeigegeld*), for immigration to Palestine. It was allocated in foreign currency by the German authorities, and in 1935 the *Vorzeigegeld* became an additional liability for the Haavara and depended on Haavara's capability to distribute German products. The Palestine market was small, and in order to overcome the problem of disposal, Haavara had to expand its activities to neighboring Arab countries.

Attempts were made to reach similar settlements with several countries of central and eastern Europe. The most successful was the arrangement with the Czech government, which made possible the importation to Palestine of a half-million pounds and the immigration of several thousand Jews on the eve of World War II.

The Haavara agreement functioned until a few months after the outbreak of the war, when it had to be stopped because of the economic blockade on Germany. In less than seven years it brought to Palestine about 8 million pounds sterling directly, and 6 million indirectly. Several thousand immigrants used its services, and many times more than this number benefited from the general increase in the country's absorptive capacity, thanks to the influx of German Jewish capital.

BIBLIOGRAPHY

Feilchenfeld, W., D. Michaelis, and L. Pinner. *Haavara-Transfer nach Palästina und Einwanderung deutscher Juden, 1933–1939*. Tübingen, 1972.

Gelber, Y. "Zionist Policy and the Transfer Agreement, 1933–1935." *Yalkut Moreshet* 17 (January 1974): 97–152; 18 (November 1974): 23–100. (In Hebrew.)

Krojanker, G. *The Transfer: A Vital Question of the Zionist Movement*. Tel Aviv, 1936.

YOAV GELBER

HA-BONIM. *See* Youth Movements.

HADASSAH WOMEN'S ZIONIST ORGANIZATION. *See* American Zionist Emergency Council.

HAGUE, THE (Du., 's Gravenhage), city in the NETHERLANDS; administrative center of the government. The Hague had its beginnings in the thirteenth century; Jews have been living there since the seventeenth century. In 1940 it had a population of a half million, with 18,000 Jews, representing 3.6 percent of the total. There were three Jewish communities: the large Ashkenazic community, with 17,379 members; the Portuguese community, with 200 members; and the relatively new Liberal community, to which seventy-five families belonged. The Ashkenazic community included a large number of eastern European Jews, concentrated, for the most part, in the coastal town of Scheveningen (which is part of The Hague). The Ashkenazic community and its religious societies had about ten synagogues. Dozens of Jewish organizations were active, including charitable and social-service institutions, leisure and sports clubs, and local branches of national bodies such as the Zionist Organization and Agudat Israel (the ultra-Orthodox Jewish movement). The Hague also had a Jewish home for the aged.

When the Germans occupied the Netherlands in May 1940, thirty Jews in The Hague committed suicide, among them a member of parliament and a member of the city council. The Germans established the main offices of their administration in The Hague; this meant that, unlike in the rest of the Netherlands, Jewish affairs were not exclusively in the hands of the Gestapo office in Amsterdam, but were also dealt with by SS-Sturmbannführer Franz Fischer, representing Section IV B 4 (Evacuations and Jews) of the REICHSSICHERHEITSHAUPTAMT (Reich Security Main Office; RSHA) in Berlin, headed by Adolf EICHMANN. The Jews of The Hague were subject to all the laws, regulations, and decrees that the German administration issued against the Jews of the Netherlands, but because of the city's status, its Jews were singled out for special treatment. Thus, about two thousand Jewish residents of The Hague who did not have Dutch nationality were forced to leave the city as early as September 1940 and look for accommodation elsewhere in the country.

In the early days of the occupation, The Hague was the scene of several anti-Jewish demonstrations organized by the NATIONAAL SOCIALISTISCHE BEWEGING (National Socialist Movement; NSB). On February 2, 1941, German Nazis tried to burn down the Great Synagogue, but the local fire department put out the flames. Following the February strike of Dutch workers protesting the deportation of Jews, the German administration tightened its control and did not permit antisemitic elements to riot.

Late in 1940 a Joodse Coördinatiecommissie (Jewish Coordinating Committee) was formed in order to determine the Jewish reaction to the anti-Jewish legislation. Chairing the committee was Lodewijk Ernst VISSER, the former president of the supreme court (he had been removed from his post), who lived in The Hague. Among the eight members of the committee were two other residents of The Hague—Jozef Emanuel Stokvis, a socialist member of parliament, and August David Belinfante, a lawyer—both of whom headed the committee's branch in The Hague. The Coordinating Committee first had its main office in Amsterdam, but when it ran into difficulties with the JOODSE RAAD (the Jewish Council, established on German demand), Visser decided to move the committee to The Hague (April 1941), with Henri Edersheim, an attorney, as director. Visser, who was also the chairman of the city's Jewish community board, called on the Jews to hold their heads high in response to the attacks on them, for, as he put it, "we are Dutch, but Dutch who for generations have maintained their unique identity." Accordingly, he decided that the synagogues would be kept open, despite the arson attempt that was made on the main synagogue.

In October 1941 the Coordinating Committee was closed down, and a local branch office of the Amsterdam Joodse Raad was set up in The Hague. Edersheim, who headed the office, went out of his way to collaborate with the Germans, establishing a close relationship with Franz Fischer, and putting Joodse Raad employees at Fischer's disposal to bring the Gestapo card index up to date, since it had proved unreliable during deportation operations.

On August 18, 1942, deportations of Jews from The Hague began, with 4,000 Jews summoned to travel by rail to the WESTERBORK camp. Only 1,200 responded to the summons. In The Hague no Jews were apprehended in the streets; the arrests were made in their homes, according to a list of addresses. The first such wave of arrests took place on August 22, and it mainly affected Scheveningen. Not all of the deportees were ordered to go straight to Westerbork; some were directed to move to Amsterdam. When the VUGHT camp was set up and the Jews were ordered out of all the Dutch cities (except Amsterdam), large numbers were commanded to report to the new camp, in April 1943.

Large-scale deportations were resumed in January 1943, when 1,000 Jews were sent to Westerbork. On February 18, forty-three Jewish boardinghouses were raided, and all their residents—together with other Jews, 780 in all—were taken to Westerbork. The Dutch police cooperated with the Germans at all times, and had a special section staffed by detectives who searched for Jews in hiding. Section IV B 4 also had a mixed German-Dutch team that searched for Jews, and it managed to seize 2,000 persons—Jews and Dutchmen who had helped them. This team was in touch with a Jew named Weinreb, who had begun by assuring Jews that, for a fee, he could arrange for them to make their way to freedom, and had later become an informant for the Germans.

A total of fifteen thousand Jews from The Hague were deported to the Nazi camps, and only a handful came back. Two thousand Jews stayed in The Hague and survived there, mainly by going into hiding. Jewish partners of mixed marriages were not deported, but they were put on forced labor.

Following the surrender of the German forces in the Netherlands, on May 5, 1945, The Hague was liberated and the Jewish community set about restoring its institutions; the first synagogue was reopened on May 17, 1945. In 1977 the Ashkenazic community consisted of twelve hundred persons; only a few were left from the Portuguese community. The Liberal community, on the other hand, had a membership of 125 families in the 1970s, and acquired the old Portuguese synagogue for its use.

BIBLIOGRAPHY

Houwaert, D. *Kehillo Kedousjo Den Haag.* The Hague, 1986.

Michman, J., et al., eds. *The Netherlands.* In *Pinkas Hakehillot; Encyclopaedia of Jewish Communities.* Jerusalem, 1986. See pages 238–260. (In Hebrew.)

Presser, J. *The Destruction of the Dutch Jews.* New York, 1969.

JOZEPH MICHMAN

HAHN, LUDWIG (b. 1908), SS officer. A native of the province of Schleswig-Holstein in northern Germany, Hahn studied law at the universities of Jena and Göttingen and earned a law degree. He joined the Nazi party in February 1930 and in April 1933 enrolled in the SS. In June 1935 he joined the SD (Sicherheitsdienst; Security Service), and held various senior posts in the Staatspolizei (State Police) in Hannover and Weimar. He became an SS officer in 1936, rose rapidly in rank, and by the end of 1938 was a *Sturmbannführer* (major).

Ludwig Hahn.

In September 1939 Hahn was the commander of an Einsatzkommando operating in Poland. In January 1940 he was appointed Sicherheitspolizei (Security Police; Sipo) and SD commander in Kraków, and in August of that year was posted to Bratislava as special representative of the *Reichsführer-SS* (Heinrich HIMMLER) and as senior police officer at the German legation in the Slovak capital.

Appointed Sipo and SD commander in WARSAW on August 1, 1941, Hahn was in charge of the deportation of Warsaw's Jews to TREBLINKA. He took part in suppressing the WARSAW GHETTO UPRISING and was responsible for the murder of thousands of Poles, mainly in the PAWIAK PRISON in Warsaw.

Hahn was posted to the western front in December 1944 and was appointed commander of the Einsatzgruppe active in the Moselle region of France. From there he was transferred to the Weichsel (Vistula) Army Group, commanded by Himmler, and then to the senior SS commander's staff in Dresden. In March 1945 he became senior Sipo and SD commander in Westphalia.

After the war, Hahn went into hiding under an assumed name. In 1949, when he was no longer in danger of being extradited to Poland, he resumed his own name and worked as an insurance agent. He was arrested in July 1961 but was released. Arrested again in December 1965, he was again released two years later, for reasons of health. Hahn was finally put on trial in June 1975, and on July 4 of that year was sentenced to life imprisonment.

BIBLIOGRAPHY

Gutman, I. *The Jews of Warsaw, 1939–1943: Ghetto, Underground, Revolt.* Bloomington, 1982.

SHMUEL SPECTOR

HALUTS YOUTH MOVEMENTS. *See* Youth Movements.

HAMBURG, GERMANY's second largest city and its largest port. Hamburg was founded in the ninth century and became a free city in the fourteenth century; it was a center of Germany's economic life, commerce, shipping, culture, and the arts. In 1871 it became a member state in the German Empire.

Spanish and Portuguese Jews first settled in Hamburg at the end of the sixteenth century, and Ashkenazic Jews in the early seventeenth century, in Altona and then in Wandsbek (both close to Hamburg); as time went on they also moved into Hamburg itself. In 1671 the three congregations united to form a single community. Hamburg was one of the first Haskalah (Jewish Enlightenment) centers and a pioneer of Reform Judaism. Orthodox Jewry in Hamburg was more moderate than elsewhere in Germany. In the latter half of the nineteenth century and the first three decades of the twentieth, the general atmosphere in Hamburg was favorable for its Jews, who were well integrated into the city's life and society.

The June 1933 census recorded Hamburg's Jewish population at 16,885 (1.5 percent of the total). It was the fourth largest Jewish community in Germany, with more than one hundred societies, institutions, charitable funds, and cultural, youth, and sports bodies. Of special significance were the three religious organizations in Hamburg—the Orthodox Synagogenverband (Union of Synagogues), the Reform Tempelverband, and the Conservative Neue-Dammtor Synagoge—all three cooperating within the framework of the community organizations. Jewish coexistence was also expressed by the joint participation of both the acculturated CENTRALVEREIN DEUTSCHER STAATSBÜRGER JÜDISCHEN GLAUBENS (Central Union of German Citizens of Jewish Faith) and the Zionists. In economic terms the Jews were prosperous and were entrenched in banking (an example was the Warburg Bank), commerce (department stores and international trading companies), shipping (for example, the company of Albert Ballin), and the academic profession. Until 1933 there were no serious antisemitic incidents in Hamburg, except for some instances of desecration of synagogues and cemeteries. Assimilation was widespread and the percentage of mixed marriages among Jews was very high (close to 40 percent, in 1933).

After the Nazi rise to power, when it became known that in Morocco the Jews had imposed a boycott on German goods, the Hamburg authorities asked the Jewish Community Board to intervene, which the board agreed to do without delay. On the day of the boycott, April 1, 1933 (*see* BOYCOTT, ANTI-JEWISH), the local Nazi paper came out with large headlines about the impending operation. According to many eyewitness accounts, however, in some parts of the city the population did not cooperate with the Nazis, and in some instances non-Jews demonstrated their solidarity with the Jews. People found it ridiculous that SA (Sturmabteilung; Storm

Troopers) patrols were posted at the entrance to shops owned by observant Jews, since these shops were closed in any case because of the Sabbath. A few weeks later, Jews were being dismissed from government posts, the judiciary, health institutions, and the university.

The new situation led to large-scale emigration by Hamburg Jews (five thousand in the period from 1933 to 1937), but it also called for the reorganization of communal institutions. The two schools maintained by the community—the Talmud Torah and the girls' school on Karolinen Street—took in hundreds of new students who had been forced to leave the public schools. New consulting and welfare organizations were set up, as well as cultural and sports clubs, some on a local basis, and others as branches of countrywide organizations. According to a list submitted to the state police by the chairman of the Jewish community, Dr. Max Plaut, in 1935 Hamburg had approximately one hundred Jewish institutions, including thirty-four social and cultural societies, thirteen branches of national organizations (one was the Zionist movement, which had eighteen local chapters), and eighteen synagogues, with a total of forty-three hundred seats.

The change in the social environment and the mass dismissals brought new faces into active community affairs. Among these, an outstanding figure was Dr. Leo Lipmann, who for many years had held a senior post in the Hamburg state finance department as a *Staatsrat,* or state councillor. In 1935 he was elected as one of the two chairmen of the community board and handled many of the community's financial affairs, especially in the final few years, when the community was dissolved and its property had to be sold. In April 1936, Dr. Joseph Carlebach, the rabbi of Altona, was appointed Chief Rabbi of Hamburg. The new chief rabbi, who was intimately involved in community affairs and in the 1920s had been principal of the Talmud Torah, became Hamburg Jewry's spiritual leader, in fact as well as in title. Max WARBURG, the banker, came to play an increasingly large role in the affairs of the community, as well as in national Jewish affairs. He was one of the leading members of the Reichsvertretung der Juden in Deutschland (Reich Representation of Jews in Germany) and chairman of the HILFSVEREIN DER DEUTSCHEN JUDEN (Relief Organization of German Jews). When the date for the election of a new community assembly drew near, in 1937, the various constituents came to an agreement on the composition of the assembly, without going through elections. The new assembly consisted of seven Liberals, five Orthodox, five Zionists, and four representatives of the Economic party; after a year it was disbanded by the authorities. In early 1938 the Jewish community lost its legal status and was renamed the Jüdischer Religionsverband Hamburg E.V. (Hamburg Jewish Religious Organization).

In the KRISTALLNACHT pogrom of November 1938, most of the Hamburg synagogues were vandalized. The central synagogue, on Bornplatz, was sold to the state and was torn down in 1939. The Tempel on Ober Street was also sold (it now serves as the North German Broadcasting Station). The Neue-Dammtor Synagoge was repaired, only to be completely destroyed by air attacks during World War II.

The disbanding of the various organizations, and the handing over of their assets to the community, had begun even earlier. The Jewish calendar published by the community orphan asylum on the eve of Rosh Hashanah (the Jewish New Year) 5698 (1938) mentions some fifty institutions. In the wake of *Kristallnacht,* the authorities ordered that the Jewish organizations be dissolved more rapidly; this process was further speeded up after the outbreak of the war. In April 1939 the two schools run by the community were merged. The unified school had a total attendance of 1,337 pupils and continued to receive financial aid from the state, in the amount of 180,000 reichsmarks. It existed until the second half of 1942. In November of that year the Hamburg Jewish community was attached to the northwestern district office of the Reichsvereinigung der Juden in Deutschland (Reich Association of Jews in Germany; the successor to the Reichsvertretung), which also included the Bremen and Hannover Jewish communities. Dr. Max Plaut was put in charge of the district office of the Reichsvereinigung.

That year deportations were already in full swing, and the community was dwindling. In the period from 1941 to 1945, seventeen transports of Jews left Hamburg for ŁÓDŹ, MINSK, RIGA, AUSCHWITZ, and THERESIENSTADT. Among the deportees were some of the community's leading figures: Rabbi Carlebach, who would not leave his flock, having chosen not to emigrate when this was still possible (he was killed in Riga in December 1941); Dr. Nathan, the community's legal adviser; Dr. Jonas, principal of the girls' school; Max Mendel, a member of the Hamburg Senate; and many more. More than three hundred members of the community committed suicide, eighty of them when the deportations were at their height, in the second half of 1941. In that year the city's Jewish population dropped from eight thousand to four thousand. By early 1943 only eighteen hundred Jews remained in Hamburg, most of them partners of mixed marriages; more Jews were to be deported before the war came to an end. In June 1943 the Jewish community was officially liquidated and its officers, too, were deported (Dr. Lipmann and his wife committed suicide before the deportation). The total number of victims is estimated at seventy-eight hundred. Hamburg's Jewish community was revived after the war and within two years grew to twelve hundred, but few of these Jews had lived there before the war. In 1960 a new community synagogue was consecrated in Hamburg.

BIBLIOGRAPHY

Freimark, P., ed. *Juden in Preussen—Juden in Hamburg*. Hamburg, 1983.

Gilbert, M. *The Holocaust*. New York, 1985.

Randt, U. *Carolinenstrasse 35: Geschichte der Mädchenschule der Deutsch-Israelitischen Gemeinde in Hamburg, 1884–1942*. Hamburg, 1984.

Wolfsberg, Y. "Altona, Hamburg and Wandsbek." In vol. 2 of *Jewish Mother-Cities*, edited by Y. L. Fishman, pp. 5–57. Jerusalem, 1948. (In Hebrew.)

ELIEZER DOMKE

"HARVEST FESTIVAL." *See* "Erntefest."

HASAG (Hugo Schneider Aktiengesellschaft-Metalwarenfabrik, Leipzig), one of the privately owned German industrial companies manufacturing armaments that employed concentration camp prisoners. HASAG was the third largest after I.G. FARBEN and the Hermann Göring Werke.

HASAG was founded in Leipzig in 1863 as a small lamp factory and became the Hugo Schneider Aktiengesellschaft in 1899, when it was converted into a metal products factory. In 1930 the company had about one thousand employees and an annual turnover of 5 million marks.

In 1932, Paul Budin, a member of the Nazi party and a *Sturmbannführer* in the SS, was appointed general manager of HASAG. His deputies were Dr. Georg Mumme, Hans Führer, and Gustav Hessen; Dr. Ernst von Schön was chairman of the board, and the shareholders included Hugo Zinsser, Ernst von Wildeneg, and Richard Koch.

Beginning in 1933 the company developed contacts with the infantry ordnance branch of the Wehrmacht High Command, and it became a regular supplier of ammunition to the infantry and the air force. In 1934 HASAG was classified as a *Wehrmachtsbetrieb* (a company working for the armed forces). By 1939 its annual turnover was 22 million marks and it employed thirty-seven hundred workers.

HASAG's status was raised to that of *Rüstungsbetrieb* (armaments company) in 1939. When the German armaments industry was reorganized in 1940, Budin was appointed the chairman of Special Committee II, which had the task of supervising the production in the Reich of light ammunition for the infantry and the air force. When Albert SPEER was appointed minister of armaments in 1942, the committee's range of responsibilities was broadened and Budin's stature also grew as a result. In 1944 HASAG was charged with the mass production of infantry rocket launchers and received Hitler's thanks for its achievements. HASAG-Leipzig was also singled out as an "Exemplary National Socialist Enterprise."

In Germany. During the war HASAG had eight plants in Germany, with two categories of workers. The first was that of civilian workers, men and women from all over Eu-

TABLE 1. *Work Force in the HASAG Camps on January 31, 1945*

AUSSENKOMMANDO NUMBER	LOCATION	NUMBER OF JEWISH MEN	NUMBER OF JEWISH (AND OTHER) WOMEN	TOTAL
3	Altenburg	52	2,616	2,668
24	Colditz	300		300
42	Flössberg	396		396
65	Leipzig	221	5,067	5,288
74	Meuselwitz	290	1,376	1,666
95	Schlieben	2,339	242	2,581
107	Taucha	426	1,256	1,682
Total		4,024	10,557	14,581

rope, especially the Slavic countries. Some chose to work for HASAG, but the majority were forced laborers (*see* FORCED LABOR). By 1941 HASAG was employing a large number of Polish and Croatian voluntary workers, and in subsequent years it also employed French and Russian workers. Special open camps were established in the vicinity of the plants for the Slavic workers, but they were kept under strict police surveillance. The pay for these workers was very low.

The second category was that of concentration camp prisoners. Beginning in the summer of 1944, labor camps were established next to each HASAG plant, all of them as *Aussenkommandos* (satellite units) of the BUCHENWALD camp. According to incomplete data based on the Buchenwald card index, the composition and size of the work force in the HASAG labor camps on January 31, 1945, were as shown in Table 1. In addition, according to an entry of August 5, 1944, HASAG employed 2,000 prisoners at Aussenkommando 53, Herzberg am Elster, in the manufacture of explosives.

The employment by the HASAG industries of such a large number of female forced laborers was determined by a number of factors:

1. The mechanization and automation of the production of small- and medium-size munitions enabled women to replace men in the assembly line.
2. Women cost less than men. HASAG paid the SS less for women prisoners, both in Germany and the GENERALGOUVERNEMENT.
3. HASAG's experience with Jewish forced labor showed that, all other things being equal, women's adaptability and resilience were much greater than men's. The average mortality rate was higher for men than for women.

Between twenty thousand and twenty-two thousand prisoners of different nationalities passed through the HASAG labor camps in Germany from their establishment until their final liquidation in April 1945. With the advance of the Allied armies, some of the prisoners were transferred to other camps. Others, who were put on DEATH MARCHES, were dispersed in many small groups, and therefore no estimate can be made of the number of prisoners who died or were killed en route. Between 70 percent and 80 percent of the Jewish prisoners in the HASAG camps in Germany may be presumed to have survived.

In Poland. Following the German invasion of Poland in September 1939, HASAG began operating in the RADOM district in the central part of that country. In 1940, on the recommendation of the Armed Forces High Command, HASAG was put in charge of the administration of the ammunition factories in Skarżysko-Kamienna, the Granat grenade factory in KIELCE, and the Rakow foundry in CZĘSTOCHOWA. The three plants were also classified as *Wehrmachtsbetriebe.* Early in 1943 HASAG acquired the plants from the Generalgouvernement, for a payment of 16.5 million zlotys (1.5 million reichsmarks).

After the German invasion of the Soviet Union in June 1941, HASAG became the

TABLE 2. *Average Number of Prisoners and Total of Jewish Prisoners in the HASAG Camps*

CAMP	PLACE	DATE OF ESTABLISHMENT	DATE OF LIQUIDATION	AVERAGE NUMBER OF PRISONERS	TOTAL OF JEWISH PRISONERS
HASAG-Skarżysko-Kamienna	Skarżysko-Kamienna	August 1942	August 1, 1944	6,000–8,000	25,000–30,000
HASAG-Granat	Kielce	September 2, 1943	August 20, 1944	500	800
HASAG-Apparatexbau	Częstochowa	September 22, 1942	January 16, 1945	5,000	7,000
HASAG-Częstochowianka	Częstochowa	June 1943	January 16, 1945	2,000	
HASAG-WARTA	Częstochowa	June 1943	January 16, 1945	2,000	4,000
HASAG-Rakow	Częstochowa	June 1943	January 16, 1945	500	

main supplier of ammunition to the Generalgouvernement. Figures show that on February 1, 1942, HASAG was the largest employer among the sixty-four *Wehrmachtsbetriebe* in the Generalgouvernement, with a work force of 13,850, mostly Poles. Of these, 10,267 worked at the Skarżysko-Kamienna factories, 1,379 at Granat, and 2,204 at the Częstochowa foundry.

In the spring of 1941, HASAG began transferring its Polish workers in the Generalgouvernement to its factories in Germany. In 1942, when absenteeism became rife among the Polish workers, HASAG set up two *Arbeitserziehungsanstalten* (labor training schools) in Skarżysko-Kamienna and Kielce. The prevailing shortage of workers led to an agreement between the Inspectorate of Armaments and SS-Obergruppenführer Friedrich Wilhelm Krüger, the *Höherer SS- und Polizeiführer* (Higher SS and Police Leader) of the Generalgouvernement, for the employment of Jews in the armaments industry. Under this agreement, signed on October 12, 1942, six forced-labor camps were established by HASAG in the vicinity of Radom. Jews from Poland, Austria, Czechoslovakia, Germany, and Hungary were imprisoned in them and put to work in armaments plants. The average number of prisoners in the HASAG labor camps and the total number of Jewish prisoners who passed through them are shown in Table 2. In late June 1943 the HASAG forced-labor camps held approximately 17,000 Jewish prisoners, 6,408 of them in Skarżysko-Kamienna.

For each Jewish prisoner in the labor camps HASAG paid four to five zlotys per day, less maintenance costs, into the account of Herbert Bötcher, the *SS- und Polizeiführer* for the Radom district. The prisoners' living conditions differed from one camp to another, depending on the attitude of the factory managers. In general, the policy of "Vernichtung durch Arbeit" (extermination through work) was applied, and in all the camps *Selektionen* were launched from time to time, culminating in the killing of all those who were no longer considered "fit for work."

From July 1944 until early 1945, HASAG transferred to Germany most of the equipment and raw materials it had in its factories in the Generalgouvernement, together with groups of Polish workers. After the final *Selektionen*, most of the remaining Jewish prisoners were also moved to HASAG factories in the Reich.

Paul Budin is assumed to have committed suicide, together with his wife, in April 1945, when he blew up the company's head office building in Leipzig. HASAG personnel were not put on trial at the SUBSEQUENT NUREMBERG PROCEEDINGS.

BIBLIOGRAPHY

Buchenwald—Mahnung und Verpflichtung: Dokumente und Berichte. Frankfurt, 1960.

Frey, H. *Die Hölle von Kamienna unter Benutzung des amtlichen Prozessmaterials.* Berlin, 1949.

Kaczanowski, L. *Hitlerowskie fabryki śmierci na Kielecczyznie.* Warsaw, 1984.

Rutkowski, A. "Martyrologia: Walkai zagłada ludności żydowskiej w dystrykcie radomskim podczas okupacji hitlerowskiej." *Biuletyn Żydowskiego Instytutu Historycznego* 15–16 (1955): 75–182.

FELICJA KARAY

HA-SHOMER HA-TSA'IR. *See* Youth Movements.

HASSELL, ULRICH VON (1881–1944), German diplomat and foreign-affairs adviser to the German anti-Nazi resistance. Hassell was born in Pomerania to an old, established north German family of public officials. He entered the Foreign Office in 1908, after studying law, and held a number of diplomatic posts abroad both before and after World War I; he was ambassador in Copenhagen (1926–1930), Belgrade (1930–1932), and Rome (from 1932 until his dismissal in 1938). In 1918 he joined the German National People's Party (Deutschnationale Volkspartei) and was initially sympathetic to the Nazis owing to his Prussian nationalist outlook. In 1933 he joined the Nazi party despite his contempt for its "vulgarity." He deplored Nazi adventurism abroad and foresaw disaster for Germany from the policy of Italian-German rapprochement and war against Britain and France.

Hassell was dismissed from his post when Joachim von RIBBENTROP became foreign minister in 1938. He now sought contacts elsewhere in Europe and associated himself with the German resistance of Ludwig Beck and Carl Friedrich Goerdeler. After the outbreak of war in 1939 he tried in vain to win the support of German generals such as Walther von Brauchitsch and Erwin Rommel for a negotiated peace. In the case of a successful coup d'état Hassell was to occupy the post of foreign minister in a Goerdeler cabinet. But in 1942 he was informed by a former colleague, Ernst von WEIZSÄCKER, that he had aroused the suspicion of the Gestapo. A few days after the failure of the July 1944 plot to assassinate Adolf Hitler, Hassell was arrested and sentenced to death; he was hanged in September 1944. After the war his diaries, *Vom anderen Deutschland: Aus den nachgelassenen Tagebüchern 1938–1944* (The Other Germany: From Posthumous Diaries, 1938–1944), which had been buried in the garden of his Bavarian home, were published. They are an invaluable source of information about the day-to-day activities of the German resistance.

BIBLIOGRAPHY

Deutsch, H. C. *The Conspiracy against Hitler in the Twilight War.* Minneapolis, 1968.
Hoffman, P. *The History of the German Resistance, 1933–1945.* Cambridge, Mass., 1978.

LIONEL KOCHAN

HAUPTTREUHANDSTELLE OST (Main Trusteeship Office East; HTO). The Haupttreuhandstelle Ost was established on October 19, 1939, by Hermann GÖRING in his capacity as the official responsible for the FOUR-YEAR PLAN. It dealt with the confiscation of Polish state property and the property of Polish citizens, including Jews, in the Reich and in the territories annexed to it. Shortly after the HTO's establishment, the confiscation of farms, forests, art treasures, and the property of Polish government offices and Polish political organizations was excluded from its purview.

The HTO, headed by Göring and managed by Max Winkler, had its head office in Berlin, with branches (*Treuhandstellen*) in Ciechanów, Katowice, and Poznań (the last with a sub-office in Łódź). District representatives (*Kreisvertrauensmänner*) of the HTO were appointed for the districts of Danzig–West Prussia, the Warthegau, and Ciechanów. They in turn had subdistrict representatives in Będzin, Bielsko-Biała, Chorzów, Cieszyn, Lubliniec, Sosnowiec, Żywiec, and, as of 1941, also in Białystok.

By 1942 the HTO had confiscated in the annexed territories over 200,000 factories, transport agencies, workshops, and commercial shops; over 290,000 plots of land; the contents of 500,000 apartments; and movable property and valuables worth several billion zlotys. The HTO also confiscated Polish state and private property in Germany, Austria, and other countries incorporated into the Reich, amounting to 270 million reichsmarks ($108 million).

The administration of the plundered property was handled partly by companies set up for this purpose, such as the Auffangsgesellschaft für Kriegsteilnehmer–Betriebe des Handels (Receiving Company for War Veterans–Commercial Shops). This company administered shops confiscated from their Polish or Jewish owners and staffed them with German war veterans. A similar role was played by the Grundstückgesellschaft (Real Estate Company), regarding residential houses and lots in the cities, and the Hotel und Gaststättengesellschaft (Hotels and Inns Company), regarding restaurants and hostelries. The confiscation of raw materials was handled jointly by the HTO, the Verwaltungs- und Verwertungsgesellschaft (Administration and Utilization Company), and the Treuhänder für Textilstoffe (Trusteeship Office for Textile Products), which operated in Łódź until the end of December 1939. Other companies functioning under the aegis of the HTO promoted German industry, labor, and trade in the annexed territories and also sought to integrate this economic activity into that of the rest of the Reich.

Agricultural land confiscated from Poles in the annexed areas was administered by the Ostdeutsche Landbewirtschaftungs—Ostland (East German Land Cultivation Authority—Ostland), later renamed Ostdeutsche Landbewirtschaftungs—Reichsland. In 1943 it administered 2,400 plots of land and 390,000 confiscated Polish farms. The same company also operated in France, on the basis of the experience and expertise it had acquired in Poland.

BIBLIOGRAPHY

Czubinski, A. "Poland's Place in Nazi Plans for a New Order in Europe in the Years 1934–1940." *Polish Western Affairs* 21 (1980): 19–46.

Luczak, C. *Polityka ekonomiczna Trzeciej Rzeszy w latach drugiej wojny światowej.* Poznań, 1982.

Madajczyk, C. *Polityа III Rzeszy w okupowanej Polsce.* Warsaw, 1970.

CZESŁAW LUCZAK

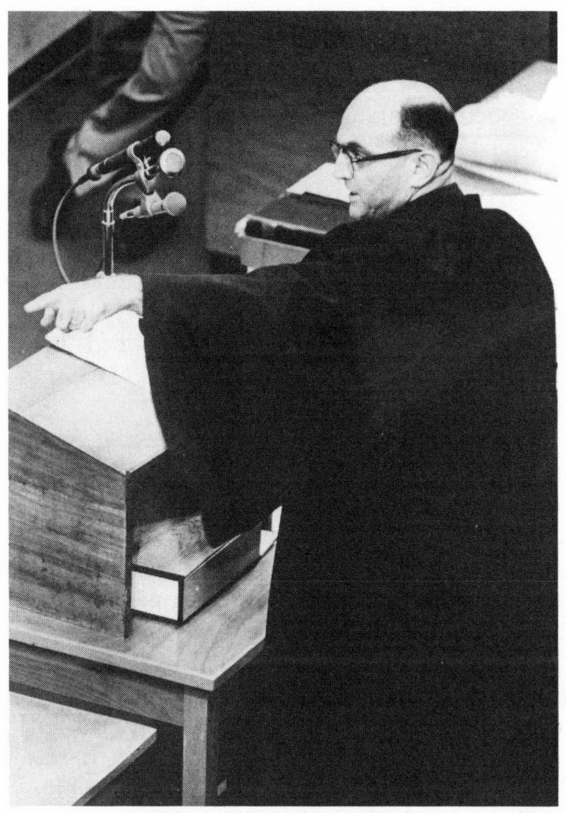

Gideon Hausner, Israeli attorney general and chief prosecutor at the Eichmann trial.

HAUSNER, GIDEON (b. 1915), Israeli jurist and public figure. Hausner was born in Lvov and settled in Palestine with his family when he was twelve years old. In Israel's War of Independence (1948–1949) he served as a military prosecutor and then as president of the military court in Jerusalem. He also taught at the Hebrew University Law School. From 1960 to 1963, Hausner was the legal adviser to the Israel government (the attorney general), and in that capacity he became the prosecutor in the EICHMANN TRIAL in Jerusalem. His opening speech was one of the highlights of the trial.

Hausner was active in the Progressive party and in the Independent Liberal party that succeeded it. He was a member of the Knesset (the Israeli parliament) from 1965 to 1981, and from 1972 to 1974 served in the cabinet as minister without portfolio. When he retired from political life he devoted himself to the commemoration of the Holocaust, becoming chairman of the World Council of YAD VASHEM and frequently lecturing on the

Holocaust in Israel and abroad. He is the author of *Justice in Jerusalem* (New York, 1966), a book on the Eichmann trial, which has been translated into several languages.

ISRAEL GUTMAN

HAUTVAL, ADELAIDE (b. 1906), French physician. Born into a Protestant family, Hautval studied medicine in Strasbourg and later worked in several psychiatric clinics in Strasbourg and Switzerland.

In April 1942, Hautval was arrested trying to cross without a permit from the occupied to the unoccupied zone in France in order to attend her mother's funeral. Awaiting trial in the Bourges prison, she vehemently protested to the Gestapo against the harsh treatment of Jewish prisoners incarcerated with her. In reprisal, she was transferred to the Romainville prison with other political detainees, and eventually sent as a doctor to AUSCHWITZ with a convoy of Jewish women, arriving there in January 1943. She reportedly bore a yellow badge attached to her overcoat, with the inscription "A friend of the Jews."

At Auschwitz, she helped hide a group of women afflicted with typhus on the top floor of her block and treated them as well as conditions allowed. She was later approached by SS-Hauptsturmführer Dr. Eduard Wirths, the garrison doctor (*Standortarzt*), and asked to practice gynecology. Aware of the sterilization experiments practiced in Block 10, Hautval accepted in order to gain a firsthand view of the Nazi procedure. She soon discovered that in this block Wirths was in charge of a team of doctors (Horst Schumann, Carl CLAUBERG, and Władysław Dering) who used women as guinea pigs, sterilizing them by means of X rays and ovariectomy (surgical removal of ovaries). These experiments were part of a large-scale plan: sterilization was intended to be applied (worldwide) to all half and quarter Jews who were left alive after the Nazi victory. Hautval expressed her complete opposition and refused to participate in these experiments (in which Dr. Josef MENGELE was also involved). She feared retribution, but was not punished.

Adelaide Hautval, who received the "Righteous among the Nations" award at Yad Vashem on April 17, 1965.

After her confrontation with Wirths, Hautval continued practicing medicine in the nearby Birkenau camp (Auschwitz II) as best she could until August 1944, when she was transferred to the women's camp at RAVENSBRÜCK. She survived and was liberated in April 1945.

A libel trial (*Dering* v. *Uris*) was held in London in 1964, at which Dering claimed that the author Leon Uris had slandered him in his book *Exodus*. At the trial, Hautval refuted Dering's claim that it was futile to refuse to obey orders in Auschwitz, maintaining that one could bypass SS commands to remove women's ovaries and still manage to avoid punishment. The presiding judge, Justice Frederick Horace Lawton, in his summation to the jury called Hautval "perhaps one of the most impressive and courageous women who have ever given evidence in the courts of this country."

Hautval received recognition by YAD VASHEM as a "RIGHTEOUS AMONG THE NATIONS" in 1965.

BIBLIOGRAPHY

Hill, M., and L. N. Williams. *Auschwitz in England: A Record of a Libel Action*. London, 1965.

MORDECAI PALDIEL

HAZIT DOR BNEI MIDBAR. *See* Front of the Wilderness Generation.

HDBM. *See* Front of the Wilderness Generation.

HEBREW LITERATURE ON THE HOLOCAUST. *See* Literature on the Holocaust: Hebrew Literature.

HE-HALUTS HA-LOHEM (Organizacja Bojowa Żydowskiej Młodzieży Chalucowej; Fighting Organization of Pioneer Jewish Youth in Kraków), Jewish underground organization. It was created in KRAKÓW in mid-August 1942, not in order to save lives but out of a desire "to die as Jews without the shame of dying as slaves." The initiative for its creation came from the pioneer youth movement Akiva, which was also the guiding force in its activity. Other members came from Dror, Ha-Shomer ha-Dati, Ha-Shomer ha-Tsa'ir, and the Pioneer Youth Organization (*see* YOUTH MOVEMENTS). He-Haluts ha-Lohem had about one hundred members.

The decision to form the organization was taken after the deportation of about six thousand of the Jews of Kraków in June 1942, after news had arrived of mass slaughter in parts of eastern Poland and the Soviet Union occupied by the Germans. At its head was a four-member command: Aharon LIEBESKIND, who was responsible for obtaining arms; Avraham Leibovich ("Laban"), a member of Dror, who was appointed treasurer; Shimshon DRAENGER, in charge of the "technical office" for forging official documents; and Manik Eisenstein, a member of the Pioneer Youth Organization.

He-Haluts ha-Lohem was in close contact with the ŻYDOWSKA ORGANIZACJA BOJOWA (Jewish Fighting Organization; ŻOB) in Warsaw, but it was autonomous in determining the timing and the place of the armed struggle. Its command had a unique conception of the system of opposition and fighting, the essence of which was transferral of the arena of action and struggle to the area outside the ghetto. The organization's fighters wished to hide their Jewish identity so that the responsibility for their actions would not be placed on the ghetto and thereby lead to the ghetto's liquidation. Only in January 1943 was their Jewish identity revealed, as a result of the "Cyganeria" action (see below).

There were several reasons for this method of struggle:

1. A sense of responsibility for the ghetto's fate was a consideration for precluding a link between the sabotage activities outside the ghetto and the ghetto residents.

2. The ghetto in Kraków was small. The GENERALGOUVERNEMENT ruler, Hans FRANK, did not want many Jews in Kraków, the capital and administrative center of the Generalgouvernement. From the June 1942 deportation until December 1942 the ghetto area was reduced twice, and it was finally divided into two ghettos, Ghetto A and Ghetto B. This prevented the creation of hiding places.

3. The Kraków ghetto population was small and unstable. After June 1942 many of the Jewish ghetto residents were not from Kraków, were strangers to the members of the local underground, and in some instances were considered unreliable.

4. The creation of a labor camp in PŁASZÓW, near the city, gave the Jews a sense of hope for survival. There was no feeling of "nothing to lose" and it was difficult to obtain support from the inhabitants of the ghetto, which was liable to be liquidated in the event of a revolt.

5. Since Kraków was the capital of the Generalgouvernement, there were many sabotage objectives, and it was possible to operate in the "Aryan" part of the city with a handful of men having a meager supply of weapons in their possession. The aim was to undermine the self-confidence of the authorities, to harm their position, and to injure as many Germans as possible.

Many preparations were made for the armed struggle. Forged documents were prepared by the "technical office" to ensure freedom of movement for members of the organization. Money was obtained for the purchase of arms by the sale of forged documents and by "expropriations" (forcible collection of money from rich Jews), and arms were acquired by attacks on German soldiers alone or in pairs, in the middle of the night on the city boulevards. Arms were purchased principally with the aid of the Polska Partia Robotnicza (Polish Workers' Party; PPR [Communists]). Efforts were made to find an ally to assist with the military and underground work and with arms, and the PPR was approached through Gola Mire, a member of the Polish Communist party. The number of members in He-Haluts ha-Lohem was increased by adding members from youth movements, principally Akiva and Dror, in cities close to Kraków. Through liaisons, He-Haluts ha-Lohem was organized into groups of five, each with a commander in contact with the principal command.

On September 20, 1942, the first group of five went out to the forests in the Rzeszów district. It had been promised aid by the PPR, which it was supposed to join so as to prepare the ground for the many who were to follow. The promised aid did not materialize, however, since the PPR had not yet begun activities in the forests, and contact with the PPR was terminated.

In October a group was sent to the forests in the Dębica area. Before it left, points were established in the small towns close to the forests, which were to serve as bases for those going there. This attempt too ended in failure and in battle losses. It was then concluded that the time had not yet arrived to leave for the forests, and that the organization should confine itself to opposition activities in Kraków itself and to organizing points of support in the directions of Warsaw and Lvov, where members could take refuge after carrying out their activities.

Until November 1942, operations within the ghetto consisted of attacks on German soldiers and Gestapo men, seizure of their weapons, and surveillance of informers in order to liquidate them. A second fighting organization, which operated in the ghetto and which was in touch with the PPR, carried out similar activities and also sabotaged German installations in the city and its surroundings.

During that period, the ghetto served as a base for operations outside the ghetto. After members of the command had been traced, the location was transferred to the "Aryan" part of the city, and members of the organization were dispersed outside the ghetto. In preparation for a large-scale operation, He-Haluts ha-Lohem renewed its contact with the PPR, and coordination was established with the command of the Jewish group. Most of the latter's members came from Ha-Shomer ha-Tsa'ir, and it operated in the framework of the PPR; a joint command was created for the two organizations in October and November of 1942. The date of the action was determined—December 22, 1942, just before Christmas, when the city would be flooded with German soldiers on holiday leave.

The targets of the action were cafés in the center of town where the German soldiers passed their time. Best known was the Cyganeria, which was attacked with homemade hand grenades. The Germans announced twenty dead and wounded. None of the attackers was injured, but about twenty He-Haluts ha-Lohem fighters, returning to their base in the deserted Jewish hospital, walked into a Gestapo ambush and were taken to the MONTELUPICH PRISON. Among those captured was command member "Laban"; Aharon Liebeskind was killed in combat in the headquarters apartment.

That action concluded the organization's operations in the city. Activity was renewed after the escape on April 29, 1943, of Shimshon DRAENGER and Gusta DRAENGER from the Montelupich prison, where they had been held since January 1943. On March 13 the remaining fighters, who had assembled in Bochnia after the Cyganeria action and who were to have gone out to the Wisnicz Forest, were arrested and brought to Montelupich.

The Draengers and Hillel Wodzisławski, a member of the command from Wisnicz, worked in the Wisnicz Forest to assemble the remaining fighters there. Their principal objectives were to offer defense and aid to save the survivors of the ghettos, and to take reprisals against farmers who handed over Jews. They also renewed publication of the underground journal *He-Haluts ha-Lohem*, which was the link among the forces scattered in the forest. It issued warnings to the Polish farmers, and described the history and problems of the ŻOB in Kraków. In November 1943, after the Draengers fell into German hands, the He-Haluts ha-Lohem organization ceased to exist.

Only fifteen members of He-Haluts ha-Lohem survived. Almost all of them emigrated to Israel.

BIBLIOGRAPHY

Dawidson, G. *Justina's Diary*. Tel Aviv, 1978. (In Hebrew.)

Hechalutz Halochem: Organ of the Chalutz Underground Movement in Occupied Cracow, August–October 1943. Naharia, Israel, 1984. (In Hebrew.)

Memorial Journal: In Honor of Jews from Cracow Who Perished, 1939–1945. New York, 1967.

Perlis, R. "The Hechalutz Fighting Resistance in Cracow." *Studies on the Holocaust Period* 2 (1981): 150–176. (In Hebrew.)

YAEL PELED (MARGOLIN)

HE-HALUTS YOUTH MOVEMENTS. *See* Youth Movements.

HELBRONNER, JACQUES (1873–1943), Jewish leader in Vichy FRANCE. The son of a distinguished lawyer, Helbronner was born in Paris. In 1927 he was appointed to the Conseil d'Etat (Council of State), in which he too became a noted lawyer. During the 1930s, Helbronner was an active member of the CONSISTOIRE CENTRAL DES ISRAÉLITES DE FRANCE (Central Consistory of French Jews), becoming its vice president. Deeply rooted in French society and culture, Helbronner was well qualified to represent the native French Jews, who maintained close contacts and associations with the French bureaucracy.

With the fall of Paris in June 1940, the Consistory joined other major Jewish organizations in the mass exodus to the unoccupied southern zone. Since the president of the Consistory had succeeded in leaving France, Helbronner quickly emerged as his successor, a choice no doubt reinforced by his close personal relations with the French chief of state, Marshal Philippe PÉTAIN. There is evidence that during the first year and a half of the occupation, Helbronner met privately with Pétain twenty-seven times and continued his adoration of the World War I hero, after whom he had named his own son. A sense of trust in the French leader and his principles helped shape the direction in which Helbronner guided the Consistory in the face of Vichy's anti-Jewish laws. Reasoned but impassioned pleas that invoked the spirit of the glorious French traditions and were directed to the "father of the homeland" (*père de la patrie*) characterized Helbronner's approach as president from the first official meeting of the Consistory after the armistice, in March 1941. In this same vein, Helbronner, who was seemingly the first Jewish leader in the south to learn of the intention to establish a compulsory Jewish organization (later to be called the UNION GÉNÉRALE DES ISRAÉLITES DE FRANCE, or UGIF), stood on principle and legal precedents and succeeded in negotiating a special status for the Consistory that kept it independent of the UGIF throughout the war. Simultaneously, he counseled Jewish leaders to refrain from joining the UGIF and pursued an active campaign against its supporters. Defying the racial and national definition of Jews propounded by Vichy, Helbronner continued to adhere to the Consistory's historical definition of Judaism as a religion alone.

Helbronner's leadership of the Consistory came under strong criticism from various sectors of the Jewish community in the wake of the mass deportations of Jews from the south of France in August 1942. Attacked for timidity and for disregarding the plight of foreign-born Jews in France, Helbronner persisted in upholding his elitist and legalistic orientation and remained at his post. Signs of a changing perspective appeared only after the German occupation of most of southern France in November 1942. Helbronner advanced the negotiations that had been taking place between members of the Consistory and the UGIF, and looked for ways to widen the scope of aid to the needy community. A telling blow, the roundup of native and foreign Jews in Marseilles in January 1943, impelled Helbronner to a clear act of reconciliation with the leaders of the UGIF and to cooperation with them. Throughout this trying period, Helbronner protested sharply to the French authorities against the deterioration of Jewish life in France and raised his voice against the arrests of the UGIF leaders in the summer of 1943. These protests seem to have contributed to his eventual arrest on October 19 of that year and to his deportation a month later, together with his wife, to AUSCHWITZ, where they were killed.

A man of sixty-eight when he assumed the presidency of the Consistory, Helbronner regarded himself as the spokesman of the Jews "of old vintage" (*de vieille souche*) and throughout the difficult years in Lyons he remained anchored in legalistic diplomacy. Encumbered by his trust and confidence in France and its head of state, Helbronner directed the Consistory on the path of least resistance, which began to change course with his deportation.

BIBLIOGRAPHY

Cohen, R. I. "French Jewry's Dilemma on the Orientation of Its Leadership (From Polemics to Conciliation: 1942–1944)." *Yad Vashem Studies* 14 (1981): 167–204.

Cohen, R. I. "Religion and Fatherland: The Central Consistory in France during the Second World War." In *Israel and the Nations: Essays Presented in Honor of Shmuel Ettinger*, edited by S. Almog et al., pp. 307–334. Jerusalem, 1987. (In Hebrew.)

Szajkowski, Z. *The Analytical Franco-Jewish Gazetteer, 1939–1945*. New York, 1966.

RICHARD COHEN

HELMRICH, EBERHARD, German who rescued Jews in Poland during the war. Helmrich had the rank of major. As head of a farm at the Hyrawka labor camp in DROGOBYCH (Pol., Drohobycz), Eastern Galicia, he had the task of supplying German army units with foodstuffs. Helmrich used this opportunity to employ Jewish men and women from the Drogobych ghetto, who constituted over half of the nearly three hundred workers on his farm—most with no previous farming experience. He protected them from deportation roundups, hiding some in his home and helping to release others already arrested, with the excuse that they were needed for the proper functioning of the farm.

Israeli consul general Michael Arnon, left, presents Eberhard Helmrich with the Yad Vashem Righteous among the Nations medal in New York (1968). [Paul Schumach, Metropolitan Photo Service Inc.]

Realizing that the Germans were planning the liquidation of all the Jews in his region, Helmrich devised a plan—together with his wife, Donata—by means of which he succeeded in spiriting about twelve Jewish girls out of Poland. Provided with false credentials that he himself helped manufacture, the girls were sent to Germany as Ukrainian and Polish housemaids with German families. Helmrich coordinated this underground operation with his wife over vast distances—between Drogobych and Berlin. Donata Helmrich looked after her charges, making sure that they were not placed as domestics near Ukrainian and Polish women, so that there would be no suspicion as to their origins.

When asked about their motivation, after the war, the Helmrichs answered: "We were fully aware of the risks and the clash of responsibilities, but we decided that it would be better for our children to have dead parents than cowards as parents. After that decision, it was comparatively easy. We figured that after we had saved two people, we'd be even with Hitler if we were caught, and with every person saved beyond that, we were ahead."

Eberhard and Donata Helmrich were recognized by YAD VASHEM as "RIGHTEOUS AMONG THE NATIONS."

BIBLIOGRAPHY

Boehm, E. H. *We Survived*. New Haven, 1949.

MORDECAI PALDIEL

HESS, RUDOLF (1894–1987), Nazi leader; a close aide of Adolf HITLER. In World War I,

Hess volunteered for service in the German army, serving first as an infantry officer and later as a pilot.

Hess was among the first to join the Nazi party, in 1920. He took part in the abortive November 1923 putsch, when Hitler tried to overthrow the Bavarian government, and was imprisoned in the Landsberg prison with Hitler, whom he helped to compose MEIN KAMPF. When the two were released in 1925, Hess became Hitler's personal aide and private secretary, a position he held until the Nazi rise to power, in January 1933. In April of that year, Hitler appointed Hess deputy leader of the Nazi party, and in December he was also named minister without portfolio; henceforth all the laws issued by the Nazi regime bore Hess's signature. A member of Hitler's inner circle, Hess was entrusted in 1938 with important missions relating to Germany's takeover of Austria and the Sudeten region of Czechoslovakia.

On the eve of World War II, Hess was a member of the Geheime Kabinetsrat (Secret Cabinet Council) and the Ministerrat für die Reichsverteidigung (Reich Ministerial Defense Council), two bodies with little influence. Hess's belief that he had been removed from the decision-making process, coupled with Hitler's intention to attack the Soviet Union, seem to have been among the factors that gave him the bold idea of flying to Britain. In May 1941 Hess took that step, in the hope that the impending invasion of Russia would persuade the British to make peace with Germany. No authoritative information has ever emerged as to whether Hess undertook his daring mission entirely on his own initiative, or whether he was inspired to do so by Hitler, directly or indirectly.

In the event, Hitler repudiated the attempt as soon as its failure was known. Hess was arrested when he landed in Britain and was held there until the end of the war. After the war he was one of the defendants at the main NUREMBERG TRIAL, together with the other leaders of the Nazi regime. In October 1946, Hess was acquitted of war crimes and crimes against humanity, but was found guilty of crimes against the peace; he was sentenced to life imprisonment. The Soviet judge in the trial had demanded that he be condemned to death.

From that time on Hess was held in the Spandau Prison in West Berlin, under the joint control of the United States, Great Britain, the Soviet Union, and France. At no time would the Soviets agree to his release, and for many years, until his death by suicide in August 1987, Hess was the sole inmate of the huge prison.

Rudolf Hess in his prison cell in Nuremberg during his trial before the International Military Tribunal. [United States Army]

BIBLIOGRAPHY

Bird, E. K. *The Loneliest Man in the World.* London, 1974.

Douglas-Hamilton, J. *Motive for a Mission: The Story behind Hess's Flight to Britain.* London, 1971.

Hutton, J. B. *Hess: The Man and His Mission.* London, 1970.

Leasor, J. *Rudolf Hess: The Uninvited Envoy.* London, 1962.

DAVID HADAR

HEYDRICH, REINHARD (1904–1942), head of the Nazi SICHERHEITSPOLIZEI (Security Police; Sipo), the SD (Sicherheitsdienst; Security Service), and, later, the REICHSSICHER-

HEITSHAUPTAMT (Reich Security Main Office; RSHA); key person in planning and executing the anti-Jewish policies of the Third Reich.

Heydrich was born in Halle, a provincial Saxon town, to a family of musicians. His father was an opera singer and the director of a conservatory. In his youth Heydrich was exposed to his father's cult of Richard Wagner, his mother's stern discipline, and the worship of the authority of the state and its rulers. He was also exposed to a (false) suspicion that he was partly of Jewish origin.

Commissioned as an ensign and trained as a signal officer, Oberleutnant zur See Heydrich was discharged from the navy in April 1931. A naval court of honor found him guilty of misconduct toward a female friend, whom he mistreated and whose reputation he further blemished during the court proceedings.

Frustrated by the rules of civil society, Heydrich, who initially had regarded the Nazi party with contempt, was introduced by a family friend to Heinrich HIMMLER. Himmler made him an intelligence officer and entrusted him in 1931 with the organization of the SS espionage and surveillance apparatus, the SD. Freed from the restraints of navy discipline and the civil code of behavior, and benefiting from his threatening mien and "Aryan" look, Heydrich gave full rein to his ruthlessness, cynicism, and ambition, combining them with loyalty to his new masters. Inquiry into his alleged Jewish ancestry showed the rumor to be false, but his superiors capitalized on the suspicion, which guaranteed his loyalty. As SD chief, Heydrich was entrusted with the information-gathering, blackmail, and intrigue needed to establish Himmler's control over the secret state police (GESTAPO) during the first years of the Nazi regime. He was assisted by able administrators such as Carl Albrecht OBERG. At the same time, Heydrich became executive director of the Bavarian political police, the nucleus of the Gestapo system under Himmler. The SD, together with the Gestapo, of which he later became executive director, was instrumental in establishing the Nazi terror apparatus and executing the leaders of the SA (Sturmabteilung; Storm Troopers) on June 30, 1934.

Heydrich played a role in purging the army high command in 1938, and also helped plant the false information that led to STALIN's purge of the Red Army's high command. Reflecting Himmler's fanatical race ideology, the SD developed into a political network of espionage and warfare, both ideological and practical, while suggesting increasingly radical solutions to the "Jewish question," such as pogroms and forced emigration. In 1936 Heydrich was made chief of the Gestapo and the KRIMINALPOLIZEI (Kripo), retaining separate control over the SD.

As Gestapo chief, Heydrich had unlimited power to confine to concentration camps "enemies of the Reich," among them Jews. He encouraged competition between the SD and the Gestapo, which under his aegis vied with each other to execute Hitler's Jewish policies. They also competed with other party elements, under Joseph GOEBBELS's influence, and with the SA. SD functionaries such as Adolf EICHMANN were encouraged to implement "solutions" to the "Jewish question," such as the assembly-line deportation organized primarily for Jews in Austria and Czechoslovakia.

In KRISTALLNACHT, the Goebbels-instigated pogrom of November 9 and 10, 1938, the SA and the Nazi party took the lead. Heydrich, however, assisted by Heinrich MÜLLER and using prepared lists, saw to it that thousands of Jews were arrested by the Gestapo and SS. On January 24, 1939, Hermann GÖRING established the Reich's ZENTRALSTELLE FÜR

Reinhard Heydrich.

JÜDISCHE AUSWANDERUNG (Central Office for Jewish Emigration), appointing Heydrich's subordinate Müller as its executive director. This transferred the implementation of the Reich's Jewish policy to the SS; from then on, Heydrich was the chief executor of this policy.

When war broke out in 1939, Heydrich was in charge of the EINSATZGRUPPEN. In a special ordinance of September 21, 1939, he ordered them to carry out the ghettoization and concentration of Polish Jews and the establishment of Judenräte (Jewish councils). He then unified the Gestapo and SD within the framework of the newly established RSHA, giving ruthless SD functionaries such as Eichmann complete executive power in their anti-Jewish actions. Heydrich was instrumental in such schemes as the NISKO AND LUBLIN PLAN and the proposed mass deportations to Madagascar (*see* MADAGASCAR PLAN). In 1941, prior to Hitler's assault on the Soviet Union, Heydrich concluded, apparently on Hitler's order, an agreement with the army high command securing military assistance for the Einsatzgruppen in Russia. Heydrich ordered the latter to implement the "special tasks" of immediate annihilation of the Jews and Soviet officials in the Russian areas soon to be occupied.

On July 31 of that year, Göring, possibly on Heydrich's initiative, charged him with the "final solution of the Jewish question" in the entire German sphere of influence in Europe. To carry out this task, Heydrich required the cooperation of the Reich's ministerial agencies, and to this end he convened a meeting of top officials at Wannsee, a Berlin suburb (*see* WANNSEE CONFERENCE), on January 20, 1942, to confirm the program for the planned extermination. Heydrich enjoyed direct access to Hitler and steadily increasing power, but it is debated to what extent he initiated the rationale and the methods adopted for the "final solution."

Late in 1941, Heydrich was rewarded for his anti-Jewish terror and extermination campaign by being appointed acting governor of the Protectorate of BOHEMIA AND MORAVIA. Attacked by Czech resistance fighters in an ambush near Prague, Heydrich died of his wounds on June 4, 1942. In retaliation, five days later the Germans destroyed the Czech village of LIDICE and killed all its male inhabitants.

[*See also* Aktion Reinhard.]

BIBLIOGRAPHY

Aronson, S. *Reinhard Heydrich und die Frühgeschichte von Gestapo und SD.* Stuttgart, 1971.

Calic, E. *Reinhard Heydrich.* New York, 1985.

Deschener, G. *Reinhard Heydrich: A Biography.* New York, 1981.

MacDonald, C. *The Killing of SS Obergruppenführer Reinhard Heydrich.* New York, 1989.

Wykes, A. *Heydrich.* New York, 1973.

SHLOMO ARONSON

HICEM, organization founded in 1927 by amalgamating three Jewish migration agencies: the New York–based HIAS (Hebrew Sheltering and Immigrant Aid Society); the Paris-based ICA (Jewish Colonization Association), founded by Baron Maurice de Hirsch; and the Berlin-based Emigdirect, an association founded in 1921 to centralize the work of organizations and local committees involved with Jewish immigration. The name HICEM is an acronym of HIAS, ICA, and Emigdirect.

The agreement called for the merger of all local branches of the three organizations outside the United States, while allowing HIAS to continue to deal with all matters pertaining to Jewish immigration to the United States. With the outbreak of World War II in 1939, the Paris-based HICEM was faced with ever-increasing applications to help service the emigration of Jewish refugees. Emigdirect had withdrawn from the agreement in 1934, and ICA, registered as a British philanthropic agency, was—owing to English wartime regulations—prohibited from using its funds outside the Sterling area. Thus, the HICEM budget was financed for a limited period solely by HIAS.

The German invasion of France prompted the closing of HICEM's European headquarters in Paris on June 10, 1940, and, after various temporary relocations in the south of France, a permanent European headquarters was reestablished in Lisbon, Portugal, on June 26, under HICEM's European director,

Dr. James Bernstein, with Ilja Dijour as secretary.

Portugal, unlike Spain, had an incorporated and officially recognized Jewish communal organization, and HICEM operated under the transparent guise of the immigration section of the local community. Local Jews, notably Professor Moses B. Amzalak and Dr. Augusto d'Essaguy, greatly aided the work of HICEM by helping it maintain and develop a cordial relationship with the authorities. Moreover, Portugal had a friendly relationship with Britain and the Allies, in contrast to Spain's links with the Axis camp; in addition, Lisbon was a neutral port that served as the only European continental point of departure for North and South America. This made Lisbon the natural place for HICEM to relocate its European headquarters. The move was duplicated by other Jewish organizations, such as the American Jewish JOINT DISTRIBUTION COMMITTEE (known as the Joint), and non-Jewish organizations, such as the AMERICAN FRIENDS SERVICE COMMITTEE and the Unitarian Service Committee.

HICEM's main activities were geared toward helping the refugees with information, visa applications, and transportation. Financial matters were generally handled by the Joint, both for the refugees and, to a great extent, for the HICEM budget. The relationship between these two Jewish organizations was often abrasive, especially between the United States headquarters of HIAS-HICEM and the Joint. This infighting focused on problems of prestige, credit, and jurisdiction. The Joint, a philanthropic organization of German Jewish background, entered into the field of Jewish immigration with the Nazi rise to power and the ensuing Jewish emigration from Germany, Austria, and Czechoslovakia. HICEM, which basically reflected an eastern European Jewish background, strongly protested this incursion into what it regarded as its sphere of activities and made it clear that, although its background was eastern European, it felt capable of dealing with the emigration of German Jews.

Further points of friction centered on the two organizations' approaches to dealing with the strictly restrictive immigration laws of the United States. HICEM maintained a far less legalistic approach to such questions as payment by the individual refugee for his own passage and the procurement of affidavits, while the Joint was much less flexible about these and other questions regarding United States currency and immigration regulations.

Nonetheless, a working arrangement was reached that helped solve some of the more pressing problems, such as ethnic quotas and insufficient transportation and accommodation. As a result, some ninety thousand Jews were able to flee Europe by way of Lisbon during the Holocaust.

BIBLIOGRAPHY

Avni, H. *Spain, the Jews, and Franco*. Philadelphia, 1974.

Bauer, Y. *American Jewry and the Holocaust*. Detroit, 1981.

YITZCHAK MAIS

HIGH COMMISSION FOR REFUGEES FROM GERMANY. *See* McDonald, James Grover.

HILFSVEREIN DER DEUTSCHEN JUDEN (Relief Organization of German Jews), organization established by German Jews in 1901 to engage in social welfare and educational activities among needy Jews. It remained in operation until 1941, and during the Nazi period it assisted German Jews trying to emigrate. The Hilfsverein was founded by an elite group of Jews, active in economic and cultural life, in order "to promote the moral, spiritual, and economic progress of our coreligionists," especially in eastern Europe and the Near East. One of its basic objectives was to spread the German language and German culture.

After World War I the Hilfsverein concentrated its efforts on Jewish refugees from eastern Europe who were stranded in Germany while trying to emigrate overseas. The experience accumulated in this period, and the institutions created, were utilized in the wake of the Nazi rise to power, when Germany's Jews were seeking to emigrate. Pressure by German Jews for such assistance began as early as March 1933, on the eve of the Boycott of April 1 (*see* BOYCOTT, ANTI-JEWISH). The help that the Hilfsverein was able to give encompassed all aspects of emigration: up-to-date information, based on reports received from hundreds of contacts abroad; vocational counseling; technical arrangements; bureaucratic formalities; and financial advice. Where necessary, the society provided grants to tide the emigrants over during the transitional period. At that juncture, the leading figure in the organization was Max WARBURG, and its practical operations were headed by the secretary-general, Mark Wischnitzer. When the Hilfsverein began to assist Jewish emigration from Germany, a clear division of responsibility was made between it and the Jewish Agency; the latter, through the Palästina-Amt (Palestine Office), dealt exclusively with emigrants to Palestine, while the Hilfsverein dealt with Jews seeking to emigrate elsewhere.

The lull in the pressure to emigrate, which lasted from the end of 1933 until early 1935, gave the Hilfsverein a breathing space that enabled it to improve its organizational setup and prepare some long-range planning. In the second half of 1935, prospects for the emigration of Jews from Germany took a drastic turn for the worse. Emigration to Palestine was severely curtailed, and few openings were left for the absorption of Jews in European countries. It was just at this time that the demand for emigration grew rapidly, as a result of the NUREMBERG LAWS published in September 1935. The Hilfsverein reacted by opening more branch offices in German cities, exploring new possibilities, and generally adapting itself to the growing needs, in part by accelerating cooperation with Jewish relief agencies abroad and with local committees in the target countries. Together with the American Jewish JOINT DISTRIBUTION COMMITTEE, the Hilfsverein drew up a four-year emigration plan, based on the premise of 25,000 emigrants per year (or, according to another version, 40,000), not including emigration to Palestine. At this point the Hilfsverein also became active in group migration and resettlement, which it felt represented a unique contribution to Jewish survival.

The sharp growth of anti-Jewish persecution in 1937, further exacerbated in the wake of the KRISTALLNACHT pogrom of November 1938, turned the Hilfsverein's work into an emergency operation. Even so, the principle of planned and organized emigration was not abandoned. Representatives of the society participated in the EVIAN CONFERENCE in the summer of 1938, presenting to the conference leaders a memorandum with detailed proposals for organizing and increasing emigration. In practice, however, the possibilities for emigration fell desperately short of the needs. The Hilfsverein continued to function as an independent agency until 1939, when it became a section of the Reichsvereinigung der Juden in Deutschland (Reich Association of Jews in Germany). In 1941, when emigration was prohibited altogether, that section, too, went out of existence.

BIBLIOGRAPHY

Rinot, M. *The German Jewish Aid Society: Its Formation and Struggle.* Jerusalem, 1972. (In Hebrew.)

Zentralausschuss der Deutschen Juden für Hilfe und Aufbau. *Arbeitsbericht für Hilfe und Aufbau.* 7 vols. Berlin, 1933–1938.

YEHOYAKIM COCHAVI

HILFSWILLIGE ("volunteer helpers"; abbr., Hiwis), designation applied to Soviet prisoners of war and Soviet civilians in the Nazi-occupied areas of the Soviet Union who volunteered for auxiliary services in the rear-echelon units of the German army, or were drafted into such services.

Even in the early stages of the campaign against the Soviet Union, the German army commanders realized that because of the wide expanses of the area under their control and the shortage of German manpower, they would have to resort to local recruits. Soviet citizens therefore came to be employed as auxiliaries, functioning as drivers, mechanics, fitters, coachmen, kitchen workers, porters, and so on. They served either as individuals or as members of a group (up to company size) attached to German units, mainly supply units operating in the rear.

Based on this successful experience, the

Germans gradually expanded the range of jobs on which Hiwis were employed; their conditions of service were formalized, they were given German uniforms, and their food and pay were made almost equal with those of German soldiers.

At the beginning of the winter of 1941–1942, guard units made up of Hiwis were added to the existing service units. These units were armed, and assigned to guard military objects in the rear. They grew rapidly in number and size (to battalion strength), and became known as OSTBATAILLONE.

BIBLIOGRAPHY

Dallin, A. *German Rule in Russia, 1941–1945: A Study of Occupation Policies.* New York, 1957.

SHMUEL SPECTOR

HIMMLER, HEINRICH (1900–1945), Reich Leader (*Reichsführer*) of the SS, head of the GESTAPO and the Waffen-SS, minister of the interior from 1943 to 1945, and, next to Adolf Hitler, the most powerful man in Nazi Germany. Himmler was born in Munich into a middle-class Catholic family; his father was a schoolteacher with authoritarian views. Educated at a secondary school in Landshut, Himmler joined the army in 1917 as an officer cadet, but he never saw service at the front. Later he studied agriculture and economics at the Munich School of Technology. He worked briefly as a salesman and as a chicken farmer in the 1920s. During this period he developed a close contact with the embryonic Nazi party. Himmler took part in the Hitler Putsch of 1923 at the side of Ernst RÖHM, joined Röhm's terrorist organization, the Reichskriegsflagge (Reich War Flag), and held various positions in the *Gau* (region) of Bavaria.

In 1926 Himmler became assistant propaganda leader of the Nazi party. He joined the SS in 1925 and in 1929 became its head. This personal bodyguard of Hitler, which at that time numbered some two hundred men, became under Himmler's leadership a key element in the power structure of the Nazi state. Himmler was elected a Nazi Reichstag dep-

Heinrich Himmler (right) talking to Obergruppenführer Sepp Dietrich (left), the commander (1933–1943) of the Leibstandarte Adolf Hitler (Adolf Hitler Bodyguard Regiment), on September 13, 1940. [Bildarchiv Preussischer Kulturbesitz]

uty in 1930, and immediately after the Nazi seizure of power in January 1933 was appointed police president in Munich and head of the political police throughout Bavaria. This gave him the power base to extend SS membership, organize the SD (Sicherheitsdienst; Security Service) under Reinhard HEYDRICH, and secure their independence from Röhm's SA (Sturmabteilung; Storm Troopers).

In September 1933 Himmler was appointed commander of all the political police units throughout the Reich (except Prussia). The following year, Hermann GÖRING appointed him deputy head of the Gestapo in Prussia. Himmler was instrumental in crushing the abortive SA putsch of June 1934, which eliminated Röhm and the SA as potential rivals for power and opened the way to the emergence of the SS as an independent force. The next stage in Himmler's ascendancy came in 1936, when he won control of the entire police force throughout the Third Reich, with the title of *Reichsführer-SS* and Head of the German Police. He created a state within a state, using his power to terrorize all opponents of the regime as well as his personal enemies. Himmler established the first concentration camp at DACHAU in 1933, and the further organization and administration of the camps continued to be the work of the SS.

Himmler was inspired by a combination of fanatic racism and a belief in occult forces. His concern for "racial purity" led to the encouragement of special marriage laws that would further the systematic procreation of children of perfect "Aryan" couples, and also to the establishment of the Lebensborn (Fountain of Life) institutions at which girls would couple with SS men, both selected for their perfect Nordic qualities. Himmler aimed to create an aristocracy of the "master race," based on the traditional virtues of honor, obedience, and courage. By recruiting "Aryans" of different nationalities into the Waffen-SS, he would establish a pan-European order of knighthood, owing allegiance to Hitler alone. These fantasies went hand in hand with Himmler's efficiency, utter lack of scruples, and competence in administration. He suffered, however, from psychosomatic illnesses that took the form of intestinal cramps and severe headaches. Himmler was squeamish, and on one occasion he almost fainted at the spectacle of a hundred Jews, including women, being shot to death on the Russian front. This helped lead to the introduction of poison gas as "a more humane means" of execution.

The war gave Himmler the opportunity to implement the other side of his program, that is, the elimination of Jews and Slavs as "subhumans." This made Himmler one of the greatest mass murderers in history. In October 1939 he was appointed *Reichskommissar für die Festigung des deutschen Volkstums* (Reich Commissar for the Strengthening of German Nationhood) and was also given absolute authority in the newly annexed part of Poland. This entailed responsibility for the replacement of Poles and Jews by VOLKSDEUTSCHE (ethnic Germans) from the Baltic states. By the time of the invasion of the Soviet Union in 1941, Himmler controlled all the organs of police and intelligence power, and through the SS he dominated the concentration and extermination camps in Poland. His Waffen-SS with its thirty-five divisions almost constituted a rival army to the Wehrmacht. He also controlled the political administration in the occupied territories. When he was made minister of the interior in 1943, Himmler gained jurisdiction over the courts and the civil service as well. He used these powers to exploit Jews and Slavs as slave laborers, to gas millions of Jews, and to institute pseudo-MEDICAL EXPERIMENTS on "asocial individuals" (Jews, Gypsies, and criminals), to determine their resistance to extremes of cold and decompression.

The killing of the Jews represented for Himmler the fulfillment of a mission. The "Final Solution" was the means to achieve the racial supremacy of the "Aryan" and purify the world of contamination by subhumans. His four EINSATZGRUPPEN in the east were the agencies of extermination when the SS established the extermination camps of BEŁŻEC, SOBIBÓR, and TREBLINKA in the spring of 1942. After the July 1944 bomb plot on Hitler's life, Himmler received even further advancement, as commander in chief of the Reserve Army and commander of Army Group Vistula.

Toward the end of the war, aware of the inevitable German defeat, Himmler made a number of gestures, apparently hoping to ingratiate himself with the Allies. He sanctioned negotiations in Budapest that would have allowed the release of Hungarian Jews in return for trucks supplied by the Allies. In November 1944, he tried to conceal the evidence of mass murder in the extermination camps and permitted the transfer of several hundred camp prisoners to Sweden. He also tried to initiate peace negotiations with the Allies through Count Folke BERNADOTTE, head of the Swedish Red Cross. Himmler ordered a cessation of the mass murder of Jews at this time, and proposed surrendering to Gen. Dwight D. EISENHOWER in the west while continuing the struggle in the east. This proposal infuriated Hitler, who stripped Himmler of all his offices. Even Adm. Karl Dönitz, who succeeded Hitler in the last days of the war as head of the German government, spurned Himmler's services. After the German surrender, Himmler assumed a false identity and tried to escape, but he was captured by British troops. He committed suicide on May 23, 1945, before he could be brought to trial as one of the major war criminals.

BIBLIOGRAPHY

Frischauer, W. *Himmler: The Evil Genius of the Third Reich.* London, 1953.

Kersten, F. *The Kersten Memoirs, 1940–1945.* New York, 1957.

Krausnick, H., et al. *Anatomy of the SS State.* London, 1968.

Manvell, R., and H. Fraenkel. *Heinrich Himmler.* London, 1965.

Smith, B. F. *Heinrich Himmler: A Nazi in the Making, 1900–1926.* Stanford, 1971.

Smith, B. F., and A. F. Peterson. *Geheimreden 1933 bis 1945 und andere Ansprachen.* Frankfurt, 1974.

LIONEL KOCHAN

Reich President Paul von Hindenburg (left) with Reich Chancellor Adolf Hitler (1933).

HINDENBURG, PAUL VON BENECKENDORFF UND VON (1847–1934), German army officer and statesman; president of Germany. Born in Posen (present-day Poznań), Hindenburg attended officers' school and served in the German army until 1911, retiring with the rank of general. At the outbreak of World War I, he was recalled to the army and appointed commander in chief of the eastern front, where his decisive victory over the Russians in the battle of Tannenberg earned him great fame. In 1916 he became chief of staff of the German army, with the rank of *Generalfeldmarschall* (General of the Army), his principal aide being Gen. Erich LUDENDORFF, who made the real decisions. Under the leadership of these two men the German high command put its stamp on all the internal political moves made by Imperial Germany in the final stages of the war, foiling all efforts to bring the war to an end by a compromise peace.

Nevertheless, Hindenburg remained a war hero in the eyes of many Germans, and this, in 1925, helped him to be elected the second president of the Weimar Republic, as the candidate of the right-wing parties. In the early part of his term of office, Hindenburg acted in strict compliance with the Weimar Constitution, which restricted presidential powers. From 1930, however, as a result of the economic crisis and the growing unemployment, democracy in Germany was shaken to the core and was no longer able to function properly.

Hindenburg's first term ended in 1932. Despite his age (he was eighty-five at the time), he decided to run again, this time as the candidate of the moderate left-wing and Center parties (except for the Communists), who all gave their support to the chancellor, Heinrich Brüning. But as soon as he was reelected, Hindenburg abandoned his supporters, dismissing Chancellor Brüning in May 1932 and appointing Franz von PAPEN in his place; Papen, who had bolted the Center party, had only the support of the right-wing parties (excluding the Nazis).

In the July 1932 elections, the Nazis gained the largest number of votes. Hindenburg, however, was not prepared to entrust Adolf HITLER with forming a cabinet, and used his powers to dissolve the Reichstag. The new elections, held in November 1932, did not change the political constellation in the Reichstag to any appreciable extent; the Nazis suffered some losses but remained the largest political party. Again Hindenburg refused to appoint Hitler chancellor, nominating Gen. Kurt von Schleicher to the post in December. When Schleicher failed in his efforts to create a broad popular base of support for his cabinet, Hindenburg finally gave in to the urgings of his close confidants and appointed Hitler the new chancellor, but not before extracting the agreement that the new cabinet would retain the moderate conservative-national character of its predecessor by giving its non-Nazi members a decisive majority. However, as soon as Hitler was installed, on January 30, 1933, he took complete control of the regime. The staged Reichstag fire persuaded the old president, on February 28, to sign a decree "for the protection of the people and the state" that put an end to the regime of the Weimar Republic and abolished basic civil rights as they had been in force in Germany. Thereafter, Hindenburg no longer played any real role in the political life of the country. He died on August 2, 1934, at the age of eighty-seven.

Mention should be made of Hindenburg's intervention concerning the Law for the Restoration of the Professional Civil Service, which was the Nazis' first anti-Jewish legislative act, designed to eliminate Jews from the German civil service. On Hindenburg's request, the new law was not applied to persons who had been front-line soldiers in World War I. This restriction was abolished when the NUREMBERG LAWS went into effect in September 1935.

BIBLIOGRAPHY

Dorpalen, A. *Hindenburg and the Weimar Republic.* Princeton, 1964.

Görlitz, W. *Hindenburg: Ein Lebensbild.* Bonn, 1953.

Hubatsch, W. *Hindenburg und der Staat: Aus den Papieren des Generalfeldmarschalls und Reichspräsidenten von 1878 bis 1934.* Göttingen, 1966.

Wheeler-Bennett, J. W. *Hindenburg: The Wooden Titan.* London, 1936.

DAVID HADAR

HIRSCH, OTTO (1885–1941), chairman of the REICHSVERTRETUNG DER DEUTSCHEN JUDEN (Reich Representation of German Jews). Hirsch was born in Stuttgart, the capital of Württemberg, and studied law. He joined the civil service, first on the municipal and later on the provincial level.

In 1919 Hirsch represented Württemberg at the Weimar National Assembly and the Paris Peace Conference. Active in Jewish affairs, he became one of the leaders of the CENTRALVEREIN DEUTSCHER STAATSBÜRGER JÜDISCHEN GLAUBENS (Central Union of German Citizens of Jewish Faith), and was among those of its members advocating that the Centralverein promote Jewish settlement in Palestine. Hirsch was on the committee that prepared for the establishment of the Jewish Agency, a Zionist organization; he also belonged to the Committee of Friends of the Hebrew University and the Provincial Council of Württemberg Jews, whose chairman he became in 1930. A meeting with Martin Buber aroused his interest in adult education, and on Hirsch's initiative a Lehrhaus (Bet-Midrash, or Jewish house of study) was established in Stuttgart, with Buber as one of its lecturers. Hirsch headed the Lehrhaus board together with Jews of various shades of opinion.

In 1933 Hirsch was among the founders of the Reichsvertretung (as of 1939 the Reichsvereinigung der Juden in Deutschland) and became its chairman. He played a major role in the Reichsvertretung's activities: economic aid to Jews, vocational training and retraining, expansion of the Jewish network of schools, and Jewish emigration. He also had a part in the establishment and operation of the Center for Jewish Adult Education, headed by Buber. Hirsch was a courageous representative of the Reichsvertretung vis-à-vis the German authorities. He guided the organization through its internal problems, successfully mediating between opposing views and conflicting demands. An authority on organization and budgeting, he was the liaison between the Reichsvertretung and Jewish aid organizations abroad, especially the British COUNCIL FOR GERMAN JEWRY and the American JOINT DISTRIBUTION COMMITTEE, gaining their full confidence as a representative of German Jewry.

In the summer of 1935 Hirsch was arrested for the first time, in connection with a sermon that the Reichsvertretung had prepared to be read out in all the synagogues of Germany on the Day of Atonement. Refusing to go into hiding at the time of the KRISTALLNACHT pogroms in November 1938, Hirsch was arrested for a second time and held for two weeks in the SACHSENHAUSEN concentration camp. On resuming his post, he focused most of his efforts on emigration and rescue. His plan was to establish transit camps for refugees in Britain and other countries; he hoped that this would facilitate and speed up the release of the many thousands of Jews who had been arrested in Germany and that it would bolster the rescue efforts. He held numerous meetings in Britain and the United States in 1938 and 1939 with representatives of aid organizations and government officials, and was the Reichsvertretung delegate to the EVIAN CONFERENCE.

On February 16, 1941, Hirsch was again arrested, and a few months later was taken to the MAUTHAUSEN concentration camp, despite the fact that his wife had obtained an entry visa for him to the United States. He was tortured to death in the camp, and his family was later informed by the camp administration that he had died on June 19, 1941. After the war, a memorial to Otto Hirsch was erected in his native city of Stuttgart and in Shavei Zion, a settlement in northern Israel founded by Jews from Württemberg.

BIBLIOGRAPHY

Marx, L. "Otto Hirsch: Ein Lebensbild." *Bulletin des Leo Baeck Instituts* 6/24 (1963): 295–312.

YEHOYAKIM COCHAVI

HIRSCHLER, RENÉ (1905–1944), Chief Rabbi of Strasbourg on the eve of World War II, prominent in welfare activity in Vichy France. Born in Marseilles, Hirschler became an important figure for Jewish youth in Alsace in the 1930s as the editor of *Kadimah*, a French-language periodical that both supported Zionism and advocated increased Jewish involvement in community affairs. Hirschler was instrumental in organizing the welfare structure for the thousands of Jews from Alsace-Lorraine who fled to the south of France with the outbreak of war in September 1939 or were evacuated to that region in the summer of 1940. Acutely aware of the needs of the Jewish refugees in the south, he also encouraged Isaïe Schwartz, the Chief Rabbi of France, to unite the various Jewish welfare societies in an umbrella organization. Herschler emerged as the chief figure in the Commission Centrale des Organisations Juives d'Assistance (CCOJA), established on October 30–31, 1940, in Marseilles. He called upon the community leaders and their constituents to build a strong and effective organization in anticipation of the dire days ahead, but his call fell on deaf ears, and notwithstanding his efforts, the CCOJA remained an insignificant body.

In early 1942, Hirschler turned his energies to establishing the Aumônerie Générale Israélite (Jewish Chaplaincy), which diligently served the Jews in French internment camps in the south of France. He developed a wide network of rabbis and laymen who traveled throughout the camps, assigned residences, hospitals, and so on, and offered both religious support and general relief. Although often at odds with the CONSISTOIRE CENTRALE DES ISRAÉLITES DE FRANCE, his supporting agency, Hirschler was undaunted in pursuing his relief goals, even to the point of overriding the chief rabbi's directives. His wide-ranging activity and forceful interventions with the authorities eventually led to his arrest, on December 22, 1943. Together with his wife and close collaborator, Simone Hirschler, he was deported to AUSCHWITZ on February 3, 1944, and perished there.

BIBLIOGRAPHY

Cohen, R. I. *The Burden of Conscience: French Jewish Leadership during the Holocaust*. Bloomington, 1987.

Cohen, R. I. "The Jewish Community of France in the Face of Vichy-German Persecution, 1940–1944." In *The Jews in Modern France*, edited by F. Malino and B. Wasserstein, pp. 181–204. London, 1985.

RICHARD COHEN

HIRSCHMANN, IRA A. (1901–1989), American business executive; vice president of Bloomingdale's department store in New York City from 1936 to 1946. In 1935 Hirschmann served as board chairman of the University in Exile (of the New School for Social Research), which offered positions to exiled German scholars.

In the summer of 1943, Hirschmann was asked by the Emergency Committee to Save the Jewish People in Europe of the BERGSON GROUP to investigate rescue possibilities in Turkey. After delays, he reached Ankara in February 1944 as the special attaché of the WAR REFUGEE BOARD (WRB) to the United States embassy. Hirschmann and Ambassador Laurence Steinhardt exploited Balkan fears of postwar Allied retribution to obtain rescue of or improved conditions for thousands of Jews in Romania, Bulgaria, and Hungary. Hirschmann also helped Steinhardt overcome Turkish reluctance to allow refugees to land in Turkey. Nearly seven thousand Jews reached Turkey and Palestine under the WRB's aegis during the tenures of Hirschmann and his successor, Herbert Katzki.

Hirschmann contributed to a spectacular success in March 1944 when he helped per-

Ira Hirschmann (third from right), special inspector general for UNRRA, visiting the Bergen-Belsen displaced persons' camp in June 1946.

suade the Romanian ambassador to Turkey, Alexander Cretzianu, to prevail upon the Romanian government to transfer the remaining forty-eight thousand Jews in TRANSNISTRIA to the Romanian interior. In June, Hirschmann interviewed Joel BRAND in Cairo and recommended that the Allies continue negotiations in order to win time for the Hungarian Jews. Hirschmann contributed to additional successes that summer, including the provision of baptismal certificates by apostolic delegate Monsignor Angelo Roncalli (later Pope John XXIII) for Hungarian Jews in hiding, the Romanian government's agreement to allow Hungarian Jews to escape secretly to Romania and continue to Turkey, and the Bulgarian government's August 31 decision to abrogate its anti-Jewish laws.

In May 1946, Hirschmann was appointed special inspector general for the UNITED NATIONS RELIEF AND REHABILITATION ADMINISTRATION (UNRRA) to examine the conditions of Jewish DISPLACED PERSONS in Germany. He described his experiences in *Lifeline to a Promised Land* (1946) and *Caution to the Winds* (1962).

BIBLIOGRAPHY

Feingold, H. L. *The Politics of Rescue: The Roosevelt Administration and the Holocaust, 1938–1945.* New York, 1980. See pages 285–291.

Wyman, D. S. *The Abandonment of the Jews: America and the Holocaust, 1941–1945.* New York, 1984. See pages 215–220.

DAVID SILBERKLANG

HISTORIOGRAPHY OF THE HOLOCAUST. The twelve years of the Nazi regime, from its rise in 1933 to its demise in 1945, represent the most tragic era in Jewish history. Of the total world Jewish population of eighteen million in 1939, one in three had been killed. Specifically, two of every three European Jews alive in 1939 were dead in 1945. Before the war, the Jew in the Greater German Reich suffered every indignity, losing his citizenship, his civil rights, and his property. As the Nazis occupied most of Europe, the danger to Jewry's very survival increased. The Jew was herded into ghettos and concentration camps, where he was beaten, starved, and overworked. With the "FINAL SOLUTION," the Nazis took the last right away from the Jew—his right to life. The survivors and the bystanders found themselves at a loss to explain this heinous crime perpetrated against an innocent people by an ostensibly civilized nation.

As with all epoch-making events, considerable attention has been focused on making the Holocaust comprehensible to scholars and laymen alike. Almost every methodology that could be used to analyze the destruction of European Jewry has been used, to one degree or another: those of history, political science, sociology, psychology, philosophy, and theology. Although not yet authoritative, Holocaust historiography has made considerable strides since the end of World War II. It is now both possible and desirable to summarize trends that have developed in the decades since 1945.

Research Trends. Overall, historians have approached the Holocaust in two ways: (1) a global approach, which tries to explain the Holocaust as a whole; and (2) a modular approach, which attempts to view the component parts of the Holocaust, preparing the ground for an eventual synthetic history. Historical studies may be divided into three periods: (1) an initial period, from the end of the war until the EICHMANN TRIAL; (2) a middle period, from the Eichmann trial to the mid-1970s, and, finally, (3) the period from the 1970s to the present. In each, different focuses and methodologies have been used.

In the initial period, writers concentrated primarily on collecting the facts in order to explain the Nazis' cold-blooded program of mass extermination and to chronicle its impact on the Jewish victims. Authors writing in this period made considerable use of documents from the Nuremberg war crimes trials, in addition to the few published sources then available, including the *Black Book,* published by the Jewish Black Book Committee in 1946. Significant contributions of this period included Léon Poliakov's *La bréviaire de la haine* (1951; published in English as *Harvest of Hate,* 1954) and Gerald Reitlinger's *The Final Solution* (1953). Both authors emphasize description of the events over evaluation, and may be seen as chroniclers trying to establish the facts. Both place heavy emphasis on the question of the number of victims. Poliakov, anticipating questions that attained crucial importance at a later date, dedicates separate chapters to Jewish resistance and to Nazi treatment of "inferior" peoples, that is, Slavs. Reitlinger's account covers neither issue systematically and suffers from an almost complete dependence on German documents, to the extent of repeating German evaluations of Jewish behavior *in extremis*.

The Eichmann trial renewed interest in the Holocaust, while also opening new sources for study. The period after the trial witnessed an increasing sophistication in Holocaust historiography. Some of the most important works on the Holocaust were published in the middle period (1960 to 1973), including Raul Hilberg's *The Destruction of the European Jews* (1961) and Nora Levin's *The Holocaust* (1973). Hilberg's book, now in a revised and definitive edition (1985), is a masterful reconstruction of the Nazi murder process as seen through the prism of the bureaucratic machinery created for the sole purpose of extermination.

In *The Destruction of the European Jews* Hilberg, like Reitlinger, made almost exclusive use of German documentation, despite the increasing number of Jewish documents, published and unpublished, that had become available during the late 1950s, especially in the evaluation of Jewish behavior. On this basis, Hilberg attempted to generalize about what he termed the Jewish "compliance reaction," whereby Jews are said to have almost completely cooperated in their own destruction. Similar conclusions by Hannah Arendt (*see* ARENDT CONTROVERSY) and Bruno Bettelheim stimulated considerable interest in the question of Jewish resistance (*see* RESISTANCE, JEWISH), the history of the Holocaust, and the nature of the Nazi regime. Numerous responses to the Hilberg-Arendt-Bettelheim thesis were published. One of the most immediate reactions to appear on the subject was Jacob Robinson's *And the Crooked Shall Be Made Straight* (1965), a detailed response to Arendt representing an almost line-by-line response to her assertions.

Although it languished in the late 1960s, interest in the Holocaust never completely ceased. Two unrelated events, the Yom Kippur War (October 1973) and the coincidental flourishing of collegiate-level Judaic studies in the United States beginning in 1970, led to further attempts at a synthetic account. Four such works have been published. Lucy S. Dawidowicz's *The War against the Jews* (1975), the most widely read, is essentially based on secondary sources. Dawidowicz was able to integrate a wealth of Jewish documentation for the first time. Nathan Eck's *The Holocaust of European Jewry* (1976) is similar to Dawidowicz, but is not as well known. Whereas Dawidowicz eschewed a global approach, preferring to concentrate on the key Jewish communities of Germany, Russia, and Poland, Eck attempted to provide a readable, chronologically organized, comprehensive account. However, significant historiographical issues, such as resistance, are lost in this approach, which also suffers from repetition. More recently, Yehuda Bauer has provided a concise college text in *A History of the Holocaust* (1982), while Martin Gilbert's *The Holocaust* (1985) has developed the use of Jewish documentation, in this case almost to the exclusion of German documents. Bauer and Gilbert also represent a concerted effort to view the Holocaust within the broader context of Jewish history.

Two interim surveys of Holocaust historiography have also been published. The first is Dawidowicz's *The Holocaust and the Historians* (1981), in which she initially seeks to explain why the history of the Holocaust has been virtually ignored by Anglo-American historians. Dawidowicz also studies the distortion of the Holocaust in Eastern Europe and, finally, tries to summarize the place of the Holocaust in Israel's historiography. More conscious of the interim nature of his conclusions is Michael R. Marrus, in *The Holocaust in History* (1987), an attempt to summarize the trends of Holocaust historiography in a thematic approach. Both of these summaries contribute to a clarification of the questions that have been studied since the end of World War II.

Methodological Issues. A number of issues have become the focus of intensive debate over the years. While some of these debates have been bitter and characterized by mutual accusations of falsification, others have been relatively mild. In general, passions have flared when issues relating to victims or survivors have been involved, although this has not always been the case. Basically, two types of disagreements have arisen, one concerning methodological problems and the other a variety of controversial questions raised by historians.

Undoubtedly, the most important methodological problem relates to the use of sources. Authors such as Hilberg have been accused of placing too heavy an emphasis on German or other non-Jewish sources, while ignoring or downplaying the significance of Jewish materials. Yet it must be remembered that although Jewish primary sources (existing chiefly in the form of diaries, testimonies, and postwar accounts of survivors) are great in number, they are considerably less extensive than the Nazi documentation. The historian's dilemma is that he has to document his assertions; his temptation is to study the subject from the perspective of his documentation. However, most of the individual victims left no records of their own, and such documents as did survive do not represent a systematic overview. The ONEG SHABBAT archive in the Warsaw ghetto, and the Białystok and Łódź ghetto archives, do contain systematic and almost full accounts of some aspects of ghetto life. In other major ghettos—those of Kraków, Lvov, Riga, and Vilna—and in most of the small ghettos, the Jewish records are more fragmentary.

One possible way to augment these written Jewish sources has been the use of oral histories or other ex post facto statements by survivors, who are interviewed with the intention of gleaning new or useful perspectives on historical questions. Oral history is, however, fraught with difficulties. Memory tends to fade over time, and it becomes increasingly difficult for the survivor to keep events in chronological order. The posing of leading questions by the interviewer, and the survivor's inability to verify assertions, for lack of other sources of information, also tend to lessen the usefulness of oral histories. Yet precisely because of this lack of verifying sources, oral histories have become an important element in Holocaust research; the truism that researchers must use care is even more relevant in this case.

Great care must also be taken in the use of terms. Terms such as "ghetto" or "concentration camp" conjure up for the reader an image that may be misleading. Thus, when using the term "ghetto," readers almost automatically picture a hermetically sealed, overcrowded, and dirty part of a city into which Jews were forced to move from their former residences. While this picture is accurate for all of the large ghettos and most of the smaller ghettos in Poland, Russia, and the Baltic republics, there also existed a number of so-called open ghettos that were not sealed. In a few cases they encompassed the areas where Jews had lived before the occupation, and from which they were not forcibly relocated. Even greater care must be taken with terms originating with the Nazis, since they were purposely misleading. *Aussiedlung*, which literally means "resettlement" in German, was used by the Nazis as a camouflage for deportation to extermination sites; *Sonderbehandlung*, literally "special treatment," meant expeditious murder (*see* SPRACHREGELUNG).

Historiographic Controversies. At least six questions raised by historians have become centers of significant controversy: the decision to implement the "Final Solution"; the role of Jews in the murder process; resistance; rescue; Jewish-gentile relations; and the response of the free world. Each has become the vortex of bitter debate, with many accusations and counteraccusations of distortion being leveled by one or another side.

Regarding the question of the nature and development of the Nazi plan for extermination, two schools of thought exist, the intentionalist and the functionalist. Intentionalists emphasize the role of Hitler's virulent antisemitism and generally posit a straight line from the Nazi *Machtergreifung* (seizure of power) to Auschwitz. They therefore tend to concentrate on ideological factors and the totalitarian nature of the Third Reich to establish what may be seen as a top-down theory for the emergence of the "Final Solution." Stated briefly, intentionalists view the "Final Solution" as the culmination of a Nazi plan that can be dated at least to 1933, if not earlier. In contradistinction, functionalists argue that the "Final Solution" was more an example of bureaucracy run amok, with neither pre-planning nor an initial murderous intent. They emphasize the fluid political situation in Germany during the entire Nazi era and the dynamic nature of Nazi policy regarding Jews.

Both schools have strengths and weaknesses. Most notably, the intentionalists have great difficulty in explaining the often contradictory policies carried out by the Nazis before extermination began en masse in 1941, while the functionalists can explain neither the ideological background of Nazi antisemitism nor the fixation with the pursuit of a racial millennium that animated the Nazis to place a higher priority on killing Jews than on winning the war. It is difficult to say at this time in which direction the study of the question is heading, although it appears that an eclectic position, adopting some of the arguments by both groups, is presently emerging.

Similarly contentious, but for different reasons, is the question of the role, if any, that Jews played in their own destruction. Here, the writings of a number of historians and scholars, including Hilberg and Arendt, have been interpreted as a slight on the victims and survivors. More specifically, Arendt, in *Eichmann in Jerusalem,* pointed an accusing finger at the leaders and workers of the Judenräte (*see* JUDENRAT), claiming that they assisted the Nazis in their goals. According to her argument, Jews would not have suffered more than they actually did if they had been completely leaderless, while without Judenrat assistance in effecting deportations and slave labor, more Jews might have survived. Hilberg, in *The Destruction of the European Jews,* wrote about a Jewish "compliance" reaction based on two thousand years of being a persecuted minority.

These apparent accusations led to a two-phased response: an initial apologetic response, and a response through scholarship, which seeks an objective evaluation of the facts. In the apologetic phase, works were written as impassioned defenses of the martyrs, seeking to disprove the accusations by documenting the heroic Jewish response to Nazi persecution. In the second, and still continuing phase, an attempt has been made to both depict and evaluate the behavior of the Jewish leaders and masses *in extremis.* Perhaps the most significant contribution to the study of this question is Isaiah Trunk's *Judenrat* (1972), which showed the way for much of the recent scholarship on the Holocaust. The application of social- and political-history techniques to the subject of Jewish response is the logical outcome of the debate, and forms the basis for almost all of the studies on the Holocaust produced in the 1980s.

The problem of Jewish resistance is an inherent part of questions regarding Jewish response to Nazi persecution. Here too, accusations of Jewish passivity led to an initially apologetic response, followed by a later emphasis on objective scholarship. Apologists attempted to defend the honor of the victims who stood accused of going to their deaths like sheep. Exemplifying this type of literature is Karl Shabbetai's *As Sheep to the Slaughter?* (1963), a response to young Israelis' comments about the victims, and Ruben Ainsztein's massive *Jewish Resistance in Nazi-occupied Eastern Europe* (1974).

However, if the history of Jewish resistance is ever to be clearly understood, it must be seen in the context of the trans-European resistance movement. Every European country, including Germany, produced some form of an anti-Nazi resistance movement, just as all of them produced collaborators and quislings. The objective study of the resistance is actually still in its infancy; the mythologized view of the brave Maquis that was popular during and after the war is now giving way to a more sophisticated view, in which both resistance and collaboration are viewed as competing responses to the reality of defeat and occupation. Similarly, as the study of Jewish resistance matures, the issue is no longer viewed as "death with dignity" versus "cowardly fatalism." Conditions for successful resistance, now finally being studied, point to the fact that the Jewish uprisings in ghettos and in extermination and concentration camps, as well as the existence of Jewish partisan groups in both eastern and western Europe, was nothing short of a miracle.

In short, the accusations about Jewish complicity in the murder process, coupled with the question of Jewish resistance, has led to an outpouring of research, including numerous significant contributions to the understanding of the Holocaust. These include, to name only a few, Shmuel Krakowski's *The War of the Doomed* (1984), Dov Levin's *Fighting Back* (1984), Yisrael Gutman's *The Jews of Warsaw* (1982), Yitzhak Arad's *Ghetto in Flames* (1978), and Richard I. Cohen's *The Burden of Conscience* (1987).

Although the Nazis created their racial theory based on the assumption of a Jewish threat to the "Aryan" world, inherent in which was the all-powerful and rapidly multiplying Jew, the reality was considerably different. European Jews constituted slightly more than 1 percent of the total European population, and only in Poland did they comprise as much as 10 percent of the population. The question of how non-Jews in various countries reacted to the extermination of their Jewish neighbors is thus a crucial one, and is fraught with considerable difficulty. As a result, the issue has not been given the attention it deserves. Here too, earlier works tended to emphasize what may be characterized as an all-or-nothing approach, either by placing all European gentiles into a monolithic camp that did not make any exertions on behalf of the threatened victims, or by absolving the gentiles of all responsibility through the blanket conclusion that everything that could be done to help the victims was done. Between these two extremes, scholarly opinion—now being formed in monographic studies—seems to lean toward a more complex understanding that a majority of the European population neither helped nor hindered the "Final Solution."

A minority of collaborators, varying in size from country to country, did help murder Jews, while another minority, smaller yet, actively risked life and limb to save some Jews. Examples of works on these topics include Susan Zuccotti's *The Italians and the Holocaust* (1987) and Michael Marrus and Robert Paxton's *Vichy France and the Jews* (1981); the latter is not primarily concerned with the French population, but rather with the policies and views of the collaborationist Vichy regime.

Within the context of the popular response to the persecution of the Jews, the attitude of specific altruists, known collectively as *hasidei umot ha-olam* (righteous gentiles), has been reviewed, for example by Philip Friedman in *Their Brothers' Keepers* (1957) and, more recently, by Nechama Tec in *When Light Pierced the Darkness* (1986). With the exception of the Danish people, who acted collectively, the "righteous gentiles" acted alone or in small groups, with little or no public support (*see* "RIGHTEOUS AMONG THE NATIONS"). The non-Jewish response cannot, therefore, be seen as one of European civilization's finer hours. Yet it must be noted that in more than half of the countries of Europe, 50 percent or more of the Jewish population survived.

The possible implications of the demographic facts of Jewish victimization and survival prompted Helen Fein to attempt a sociological investigation of the Holocaust, in *Accounting for Genocide* (1979). Using a synthesis of available secondary sources as a basis, Fein was able to develop a workable statistical model that could be used to predict whether or not a random Jewish community could survive. Such variables as prewar antisemitism, the type of Nazi occupation, and the number of Jews, as well as the extent of their integration, meant the difference between a 90 percent victimization rate in Poland (over 3 million Jews killed out of a prewar population of approximately 3.5 million), a 30 percent rate in France (about 100,000 out of 350,000), and the very nearly zero rate in Denmark (although 700 Danish Jews were deported, almost all survived the war).

Two related questions have also received considerable attention. One is the question of the response of the CHRISTIAN CHURCHES—Catholic and Protestant—to the murder of the Jews. As a result of the debate over Rolf Hochhuth's *The Deputy* (1964), a play in which Pope Pius XII is accused of callously watching the slaughter without making any effort to help Jews, the issue of church responses has now become interlocked with the response of the various national groups, as it should in fact be. Although specific evaluations differ, the consensus seems to be that in countries where proportionally more Jews survived, many did so because of the timely intervention of local clergy, while in countries where proportionally fewer survived, there tended to be a lack of such interventions.

Also related to the broader issue of intergroup relations under the impact of Nazism is the claim that, to a degree, non-Jews in many countries did not help Jews since they too suffered under the barbaric heel of the Nazis. Such a view has been particularly adopted by apologists, generally, though not exclusively, by those dealing with the thorny issue of Polish-Jewish relations. One author, Richard Lucas, has entitled his book on life in Nazi-occupied Poland *The Forgotten Holocaust* (1986). The implication is that since Poles too suffered grievously, they were absolved from trying to help their neighbors. It is true, of course, that the Nazis did persecute almost everyone—Poles, homosexuals, Gypsies, Jehovah's Witnesses, Communists, pacifists—the list could go on ad infinitum. Only one group, however, was marked by the Nazis for *Ausmerzung,* or total eradication: the Jews. As such there can be no comparison in suffering. To date the only readily available objective study on Polish-Jewish relations is Emanuel Ringelblum's *Polish-Jewish Relations during the Second World War,* the English translation (1974) of a study done by the Warsaw ghetto archivist.

One further area of study has become popular in recent years, and also very controversial: the question of the response of the free world to the Holocaust. This question is in fact comprised of two interrelated issues: the response of the governments, neutral or anti-Nazi, of the countries not within the Nazi sphere of influence; and the response of the Jewish communities in those countries. Most particularly, the actions and inactions of the United States and of American Jewry have come under close scrutiny. Attention has also been focused on the attitudes of Great Britain and Anglo-Jewry, the Palestinian YISHUV, and Switzerland.

Here again two positions exist, of accusers who point a finger of guilt, or at least of moral responsibility, at the entire free world, including the Jewish communities; and of those who maintain that all that could be done was done to rescue European Jewry. Both positions are nuanced and should not be seen as monolithic; those who accuse governments often defend the actions of Jewish communities, and vice versa. Although the issue is highly emotional and controversial, a consensus seems to emerge from works on the subject such as Henry Feingold's *The Politics of Rescue* (1970), Bernard Wasserstein's *Britain and the Jews of Europe* (1979), Monty N. Penkower's *The Jews Were Expendable* (1983), David Wyman's *The Abandonment of the Jews* (1984), and Dina Porat's *An Entangled Leadership: The Yishuv and the Holocaust* (1986; in Hebrew). This is a view that while the various governments probably could have done more to save European Jewry, the existence of a number of domestic factors —ranging from antisemitism to simple bureaucratic inertia—meant that what aid was given was invariably too little, too late. On the other hand, the free-world Jewish communities probably could not have effected changes in governmental policy, although they could have been more vocal in publicizing the plight of European Jewry. Removing the polemics from much of the writing on the free-world Jewish response leads to one clear and unfortunate conclusion: that the Nazis caught European Jewry in a murderous stranglehold at a time when world Jewry was politically powerless and racked by internal dissensions, and when there was no other group ready or willing to take up the case for the victims.

Conclusions. Several decades have passed since the end of World War II, and the significance of the Holocaust as a historic event is only now becoming widely recognized. As the survivors pass on and take their experiences with them, the Holocaust becomes "merely" one more event recorded in history books. Increasingly, Holocaust research is being undertaken by scholars who are personally unacquainted with the events. To an extent, this means a greater degree of scholarly dispassion, but it also implies that greater care is needed to ensure that the moral lessons of the "Final Solution" not be lost on future generations. Although it is premature to attempt to draw any long-term conclusions, one thing is clear from a review of the questions asked by scholars since the end of the war: while some questions have already been answered, many more have yet to be asked.

[*See also* Holocaust, Denial of the.]

BIBLIOGRAPHY

Arendt, H. "Social Science Techniques and the Study of Concentration Camps." *Jewish Social Studies* 12/1 (1950): 49–64.

Dawidowicz, L. S. *The Holocaust and the Historians*. Cambridge, Mass., 1981.

Edelheit, A. J., and H. Edelheit. *Bibliography on Holocaust Literature*. Boulder, 1986.

Esh, Shaul. "Words and Their Meaning: 25 Examples of Nazi Idiom." *Yad Vashem Studies* 5 (1961): 133–168.

Friedman, Philip. *Roads to Extinction*. Philadelphia, 1980.

Gutman, Y., and G. Greif, eds. *The Historiography of the Holocaust Period*. Proceedings of the Fifth Yad Vashem Historical Conference. Jerusalem, 1988.

Marrus, M. R. *The Holocaust in History*. New York, 1989.

Yad Vashem–YIVO Joint Bibliographic Series. 15 vols. Jerusalem–New York, 1960–1978.

ABRAHAM J. EDELHEIT

HITLER, ADOLF (1889–1945), Führer (leader) of the Third German Reich. Born in Braunau, Austria, the son of a customs official from a smallholder family, Hitler spent his youth in the country of his birth. From 1900 to 1905 he attended the intermediate grades of the *Realschule* (secondary school), which concluded his formal education. Hitler's father died in 1903. In 1907 Hitler took the entrance test for the Vienna Academy of Art's School of Painting, and failed. His mother died that year, of breast cancer; the doctor who treated her was a Jew named Eduard Bloch. In 1908 Hitler made Vienna his home, living on the orphan's stipend that he received. Antisemitism was rife in Vienna at the time. In Hitler's own words, the Vienna period of his life was formative and decisive in shaping his views, and especially his concept of the Jews; but it is not certain whether by then he was already an antisemite.

In 1913 Hitler moved to Munich. When World War I broke out in 1914, he volunteered for the Bavarian army. He served as a dispatch runner in Belgium and France, was promoted to private first class (lance corporal), and was awarded medals for bravery, one of them the Iron Cross, First Class, in 1918. That October he was temporarily blinded in a British gas attack, and in the military hospital at Pasewalk he learned of Germany's collapse. It was then and there, by his own admission, that Hitler decided to enter politics, in order to fight the Jews.

On his return to Munich, Hitler stated, in his first political document (written on September 19, 1919), that the final goal of antisemitism must be "the total removal of the Jews." He served as a political spokesman and agent for the Bavarian army, and in 1919 joined a small antisemitic party that in 1920 took the name Nationalsozialistische Deutsche Arbeiterpartei (National Socialist Workers' Party, or NSDAP; *see* NAZI PARTY). The party's 1920 platform called for all the Jews of Germany to be deprived of their civil rights and for some of them to be expelled. Hitler gained attention as a public speaker, and in 1921 became the party chairman, with unlimited powers. In November 1923 he headed an attempt to bring the government down by an armed putsch, known as the Munich (Beer-Hall) Putsch, for which he was sentenced in 1924 to five years' imprisonment in a fortress.

During his imprisonment in Landsberg, Hitler dictated the first volume of his book MEIN KAMPF (My Struggle). He was released after only nine months. In 1925 he reestablished the National Socialist party and created the Schutzstaffel (Protection Squad; SS) to serve as the party's fighting force. Several of the German states prohibited his appearance as a public speaker.

The second volume of *Mein Kampf* was published in 1926, a year after the first. Another book, written in 1928 but not published in his lifetime, appeared in 1961 as *Hitler's Second Book*. It contains Hitler's grounds for his antisemitism, based on the race theory (*see* RACISM). In the book, Hitler now promoted his antisemitism as the central aspect of his personal and political career.

Hitler aimed to use constitutional means

to gain a parliamentary majority in order to destroy the constitution by due process. In 1928 the National Socialist party ran in the Reichstag elections for the first time, receiving only 2.8 percent of the votes. The party began its rise in 1929, and in the 1930 elections it won 18.3 percent of the total vote. In 1932 Hitler was granted German citizenship, which enabled him to run in the presidential elections. He lost, against Paul von HINDENBURG, but received 36.8 percent of the vote. In the Reichstag elections of July 1932, the National Socialist party received 37.3 percent, the highest it ever obtained in free elections, and it became the largest political party represented in the Reichstag. But in the elections held in November of that same year, the party received only 33.1 percent of the vote, and Hitler failed in his attempt to seize control of the government.

On January 30, 1933, Hitler was appointed chancellor of a minority government. The conservative opponents of the Weimar Republic hoped to use him as a means to gain mass support while controlling him and his radical movement, but it was he who took control of the state apparatus and later the state power to establish a regime of terror.

Although his party held only three out of the eleven ministries, Hitler managed to set up a dictatorship. Following the Reichstag fire of February 27, basic civil rights were suspended and, after elections held on March 5, parliamentary rule was abolished by the *Ermächtigungsgesetz* (Enabling Law). This law transferred all legislative power from the Reichstag to the cabinet, where the conservatives held a solid majority. Eventually, by outmaneuvering them, Hitler became all-powerful. Antisemitic riots took place in March, culminating in the boycott of April 1, 1933 (*see* BOYCOTT, ANTI-JEWISH), and in a law, passed on April 7, that inaugurated the Jews' elimination from public life in Germany. On July 14, after the dissolution of the trade unions and the other political parties, the NSDAP became the only recognized party in the land.

After Hindenburg's death, on August 2, 1934, Hitler also became head of state and commander in chief of the Wehrmacht, and assumed the title of *Führer und Reichskanzler* (Leader and Reich Chancellor). He was now the dictator of Germany. The rearmament of the country was accelerated, as was the persecution of the Jews. The NUREMBERG LAWS were adopted on September 15, 1935, and many other decrees issued by Hitler or in his name led to the exclusion of the Jews from German society. By the end of 1937 about 150,000 Jews had left Germany, approximately one-third of the country's Jewish population.

After the ANSCHLUSS of Austria on March 13, 1938, nearly 200,000 Jews were added to the Reich. Although a quarter of them left the country within six months, at the end of 1938 Germany again had the same number of Jews that it had had in 1933. In October 1938, some 17,000 Jews of Polish nationality were expelled from Germany to Poland (*see* ZBĄSZYŃ). This was soon to be followed by the November KRISTALLNACHT pogrom.

Hitler's radical racial *Weltanschauung* was

Hitler at a *Reichsparteitag* in Nuremberg (1934).

combined with a Social Darwinism that saw the Jew as a source of danger to Germany and humanity, and as a central factor in the dynamic development of hostile ideological trends such as democracy, liberalism, and socialism. Even the Christian sources of ethnic political thinking in Western society were perceived by Hitler as manifestations of the infiltration of the Jewish spirit into western European civilization.

As early as the 1920s, in *Mein Kampf*, Hitler presented the Jews, or rather "international Jewry," as the world's foremost enemy:

> [The National Socialist movement] must open the eyes of the people concerning foreign nations and must over and over again recall who is the real enemy of our present world. In place of the insane hatred for Aryans . . . it must condemn to general wrath the evil enemy of humanity as the true creator of all suffering. . . . It must see to it that, at least in our country, the most deadly enemy is recognized and that the struggle against him, like an illuminating sign of a brighter epoch, also shows to the other nations the road of salvation of a struggling Aryan humanity.

On January 30, 1939, Hitler declared in the Reichstag that a new world war would lead to the destruction of the Jewish race in Europe. When the war began in Poland, on September 1 of the same year, the Germans embarked upon the destruction of Jews in that country, although for a while this was done in a haphazard rather than a methodical way. It was also at about this time that the systematic killing of the mentally ill with toxic gas was undertaken, on Hitler's orders (*see* EUTHANASIA PROGRAM).

In September 1939, Reinhard HEYDRICH told his assistants that Hitler had agreed to the expulsion of the Jews from Germany into the Polish territories annexed by the Reich. Hitler informed Alfred ROSENBERG that he wished to concentrate all the Jews from the territories under German rule in an area between the Vistula and Bug rivers. He told Hans FRANK on June 19, 1941 (three days before the attack on the Soviet Union), that the Jews would be dispatched from the GENERALGOUVERNEMENT, which would then serve only as a kind of Jewish transit camp.

The systematic killing of Jews (the "FINAL SOLUTION") began after the German invasion of the Soviet Union on June 22, 1941. According to Hitler's world view and his political strategy, the goal of the territorial expansion—to gain LEBENSRAUM ("living space") in the east—and the destruction of the Jewish people as the central ideological enemy were connected and were the focal point of the whole struggle.

The first massacres of Jews in the Soviet Union were carried out by the EINSATZGRUPPEN in June 1941; the killing was then extended to include the rest of the Jews of Europe. On several occasions Hitler reminded the public about his prophecy concerning the destruction of the Jews, and on April 2, 1945, he boasted that he had "exterminated the Jews of Germany and central Europe." His political testament of April 29, 1945, ended with a call for "merciless resistance to the universal poisoner of all nations—international Jewry." The following day he committed suicide in Berlin.

EBERHARD JÄCKEL

Decision Making and Jewish Policy. A fundamental tenet of Nazi ideology with regard to decision making was the so-called FÜHRERPRINZIP ("leadership principle"), which called for the exercise of absolute authority from above and absolute obedience from below. The iron discipline and maximum efficiency implied in this conception of decision making, the Nazis assumed, set them apart from the divisiveness and inefficiency of their supposedly chaotic predecessors, the democrats and liberals of the Weimar Republic. After 1933 many German institutions, including schools and universities, adopted the *Führerprinzip* to emphasize their allegiance to the new regime. Hitler was glorified by the principle because it made him the fount of all wisdom and the universal giver of orders. When historians and social scientists after the war were called upon to explain the functioning of the Nazi system, they found variations of the *Führerprinzip* a congenial component for their models of totalitarianism.

Scholars have subsequently discovered the decision-making process of the Third Reich to have been considerably more chaotic than the *Führerprinzip* would suggest. Hitler's work habits alone were too unsystematic to allow him to run a smoothly functioning decision-making apparatus. His interests, moreover, were not sufficiently broad for him to perform the role of a universal giver of orders. Only in matters of foreign policy, rearmament (and, after 1939, war), and the architectural reconstruction of Berlin was he able to concentrate his attention consistently and effectively.

Hitler's erratic work habits have long been known by scholars, but have not always been taken sufficiently into account in their analyses of the Nazi system. To be sure, Hitler was at times capable of working for weeks at a pace that left his aides exhausted, but these bouts of frenzied activity would be followed by weeks of lethargy. During these periods of lethargy, aides had difficulty prevailing on him to perform even the necessary routines of his office, let alone make important decisions. Albert SPEER's memoirs provide the most accessible evidence of Hitler's work habits, but they were already attested to by his private secretaries in interrogations conducted shortly after the war ended.

Hitler was not an effective delegator of responsibility. He did not generally assign subordinates to take responsibility for policy areas that, for whatever reason, he chose not to supervise himself. The result was often a competitive free-for-all among ambitious subordinates eager to demonstrate their competence to the Führer as well as to assure for themselves a position in the top ranks of the Nazi hierarchy. To secure these positions they had to be able to overcome rival claimants who sought the same powers and status. Those most successful in this fight for survival, such as Hermann GÖRING and Heinrich HIMMLER, wound up in charge of vast empires; those less able or less ambitious, like Alfred ROSENBERG or Wilhelm FRICK, had to be satisfied with occupying a less prestigious rung on the Nazi ladder.

Hitler's authority over these empire builders rested largely upon his unique personal qualities, the wellspring of his charismatic powers, and less upon his legal position at the top of a bureaucratic hierarchy. Although he rarely did so, Hitler could at any time intervene authoritatively in any of the innumerable disputes between his ambitious underlings. This was learned by Ernst RÖHM and the SA (Sturmabteilung; Storm Troopers) leadership during the June 1934 "Night of the Long Knives," in which Röhm and others were murdered on Hitler's orders. Hitler's powers, though not always exercised, have been called permanently potential: they could be exercised with unexpected and brutal swiftness. Indeed, the relationship of Hitler to his subordinates has been compared to the feudal relationship between lord and vassal.

Controversies about the Nazi decision-making process and Hitler's role in it have been particularly prevalent among scholars of the Holocaust. As it became clear to them during the 1960s that the *Führerprinzip,* at least as it was defined by the Nazis, did not reflect how most major decisions on Jewish policy in the Third Reich were actually made, an interpretive school arose. This school suggested that the rivalries between would-be claimants for control over Jewish policy were themselves an important radicalizing element in the persecutions of the Jews, propelling them from the ARIERPARAGRAPH ("Aryan clause") legislation (*see* ANTI-JEWISH LEGISLATION) of 1933 to the NUREMBERG LAWS of 1935, the "Aryanization" (ARISIERUNG) of Jewish-owned properties, and the DEPORTATIONS of 1938 and 1939.

Ultimately, in this view, it was the most radical claimants, Heinrich Himmler and the SS, who managed to outmaneuver their rivals and establish themselves, after the war broke out, as chief executors of a policy of mass murder. This interpretation suggests that the "Final Solution" and the AUSCHWITZ extermination camp that has become its symbol were the result of a radicalization process that, in the wake of the extraordinary Nazi military successes against the Soviet Union in the summer of 1941, was freed of all external constraints. Because they focus their analysis on how the Nazi system functioned in practice, these scholars have come to be called "functionalists." They see Hitler primarily as the legitimizer of the process of persecution, a process in which he only occasionally played a directing role, but one that he heartily endorsed and encouraged.

The "intentionalists," on the other hand, suggest that Nazi Jewish policy was from its beginning the product of long-term Nazi intentions. They point to utterances made by Hitler from the 1920s about the killing of Jews as evidence of his early intention to solve "the Jewish problem" by physical annihilation. Hitler and his minions, in their view, hid their ultimately murderous intentions until time and circumstances in 1941 were ripe for the "Final Solution" to be implemented. The escalation of the persecution of German Jewry during the years after 1933 was, accordingly, part of a clearly conceived design whose incremental unfoldings were realized only as circumstances allowed.

Neither the fundamentalists nor the intentionalists have managed to prevail in the debate, partly because the documentation that might allow either side to prove its argument is lacking, either because it was destroyed or because it never existed. Abundantly clear to both sides, however, is the fact that Hitler paid less attention to the details of Jewish policy than he did to foreign policy, rearmament, or war.

Although, as far as is known, Hitler never devoted one of his bouts of frenzied activity to the making of Jewish policy, it is instructive to observe his role at several critical turning points in the making of that policy. The notorious Nuremberg Laws of September 1935 and the infamous *Kristallnacht* pogrom of November 1938, both milestones in the escalating persecution of Jews, came about—at least in their timing—not as a result of long-range planning but by the accident of circumstance. In the case of the Nuremberg Laws, the underlying racist logic that Aryans and Jews should no longer be allowed to marry or have sexual relations was so much a part of Nazi ideology that civil servants in the Interior Ministry had long before prepared drafts of legislation to prevent such race mixing. However, Hitler's sudden decision at the 1935 Nuremberg party rally to present to his puppet Reichstag a law governing such mixing was the product of his need to fill an unexpected hiatus in the rally's agenda. The officials suddenly called upon to draft the concrete legislation were caught off guard, and had to improvise without the extensive files back at their offices in Berlin.

The circumstances leading to the *Kristallnacht* pogrom in November 1938, although different from those surrounding the creation of the Nuremberg Laws, demonstrate a similar inclination on Hitler's part to act impulsively. On November 7 a Jewish youth, seeking revenge for the deportation of his parents from Germany, shot and killed a German diplomat in Paris. This inspired Propaganda Minister Joseph GOEBBELS, eager to ingratiate himself with the Führer and to gain additional influence in Jewish policy, to propose to Hitler that the SA be set free all across Germany to wreak vengeance against the "Jewish crime in Paris." The result was a brutal night of murder, rioting, and looting. The decrees issued two days later served to complete the process of excluding Jews from German economic and cultural life. The Nazis announced those decrees as punishment, but in fact they had been ready for some time beforehand. Nevertheless, their sudden implementation was the result of Hitler's impulse. Thus was a significantly new stage in Nazi Jewish policy inaugurated.

Against this background it may be possible to understand more fully the decision in 1941 to implement the "Final Solution" by means of extermination camps established in eastern Europe. No single document with Hitler's signature calling for the mass murder of Jews has ever been found. This lack has sometimes been attributed to the chaotic way in which the Nazi system functioned, suggesting that the order could have been delivered orally, or even that by 1941 the system no longer required an order from Hitler to set the machinery of murder in action. Another possibility is that Hitler and the Nazi leaders deliberately tried to keep the order secret, either by delivering it orally or marking it "Destroy after reading." Alternatively, such a document might have been destroyed by an act or accident of war. There is no debate among scholars, however, about Hitler's responsibility for the decision to implement the "Final Solution," even if its execution was carried out largely by the elaborate SS machinery under the command of Himmler.

KARL A. SCHLEUNES

BIBLIOGRAPHY

Broszat, M. *Hitler and the Collapse of Weimar Germany.* Leamington, England, 1987.

Bullock, A. *Hitler: A Study in Tyranny.* London, 1974.
Fest, J. C. *Hitler.* London, 1974.
Flood, C. B. *Hitler: The Path to Power.* Boston, 1989.
Haffner, S. *The Meaning of Hitler.* New York, 1979.
Heiden, K. *Hitler: A Biography.* New York, 1975.
Jäckel, E. *Hitler's Weltanschauung: A Blueprint for Power.* Middletown, Conn., 1972.
Langer, W. C. *The Mind of Adolf Hitler.* London, 1972.
Maser, W. *Hitler: Legend, Myth, and Reality.* New York, 1973.
Schleunes, K. A. *The Twisted Road to Auschwitz.* Urbana, Ill., 1970.
Toland, J. *Adolf Hitler.* Garden City, N.Y., 1976.
Trevor-Roper, H. *The Last Days of Hitler.* London, 1971.
Waite, R. *The Psychopathic God: Adolf Hitler.* New York, 1977.

HITLERJUGEND (Hitler Youth; HJ), the National Socialist youth movement. The Hitlerjugend had its origins in the Jungsturm Adolf Hitler (Adolf Hitler Boys' Storm Troop), an SA (Sturmabteilung; Storm Troopers) offshoot founded in 1922. It changed its name to Hitlerjugend in 1926. Originally a boys' movement only, from 1928 it also admitted girls, into a separate organization that in 1930 became known as the Bund Deutscher Mädel (League of German Girls; BDM).

In 1931, Baldur von Schirach was appointed Reich Youth Leader (*Reichsjugendführer*) in the Nazi movement. Schirach's immediate goal was to bring the different youth organizations in the party under a single authority; these included, in addition to the BDM, the NS-Schülerbund (League of Nazi Students) and the Deutsches Jungvolk (German Young Folk), which inducted youngsters at the age of ten. Schirach achieved his goal when he was appointed *Jugendführer des Deutschen Reiches* (Youth Leader of the German Reich) in June 1933. By 1935, the HJ was a huge organization, comprising 60 percent of the country's youth.

The HJ admitted children at the age of ten; its membership was organized into two age brackets, from ten to fourteen and from fourteen to eighteen. The organizational chart devised by Schirach followed the military pattern, involving squads, platoons, and companies. The companies were within territorial formations based on the *Gau* (a term used for the territorial division of Germany for purposes of the NAZI PARTY), the *Untergau* (Lower *Gau*), and the *Obergau* (Upper *Gau*). They were all organized into the Gauverband (Association of *Gaue*) and subject to the authority of the Reichsjugendführung (Reich Youth Leadership). BDM affairs were handled by the *Reichsreferentin BDM* (Official in Charge of the BDM), who was given broad powers to execute her tasks.

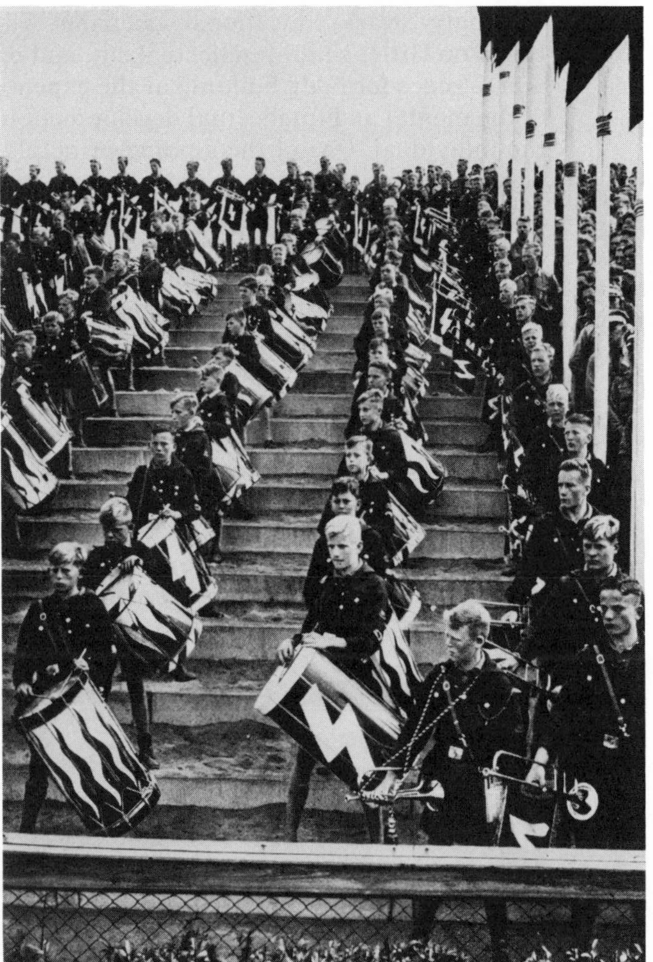

Hitler Youth at a *Parteitag* rally in Nuremberg (c. 1934).

The HJ and its organizational form were outgrowths of Hitler's ideology, in which the young generation represented the reserve manpower that would ensure the continued existence of the "Thousand-Year Reich." Accordingly, Nazi educational doctrine was based on Hitler's anti-intellectualism, and on a preference for body building at the expense of the mental and intellectual development of the individual. One of the guiding principles of Nazi education was to keep the young people in constant action and to constantly spur them to activism. This was the system to which a boy was subjected from the moment he entered the HJ until he became a soldier or an SS man. He was equipped not only with a uniform, but with a bayonet as well. When boys reached nineteen, they were drafted into the Reichsarbeitsdienst (Reich Labor Service), which stressed physical work and iron discipline, with thousands of the youngsters put to work on the land. As soon as they had completed the compulsory term in the Labor Service, the young men enlisted in the armed forces. This process enabled the Nazi party to control and supervise German youth from age ten to age twenty-one.

The objectives of the BDM were based on the Nazi ideal woman—in other words, the racist ideal. The values that were to be implanted in the girls by their training were obedience, performance of duty, self-sacrifice, discipline, and physical self-control. Two-thirds of the time the girls spent in the BDM was taken up with sports, and one-third with ideology. The main goal for which the girls were trained was to become mothers of genetically healthy children, whom they would in turn educate in the spirit of National Socialism. The BDM members were indoctrinated with "racial pride" and the consciousness of being "German women," who would shun any contact with Jews.

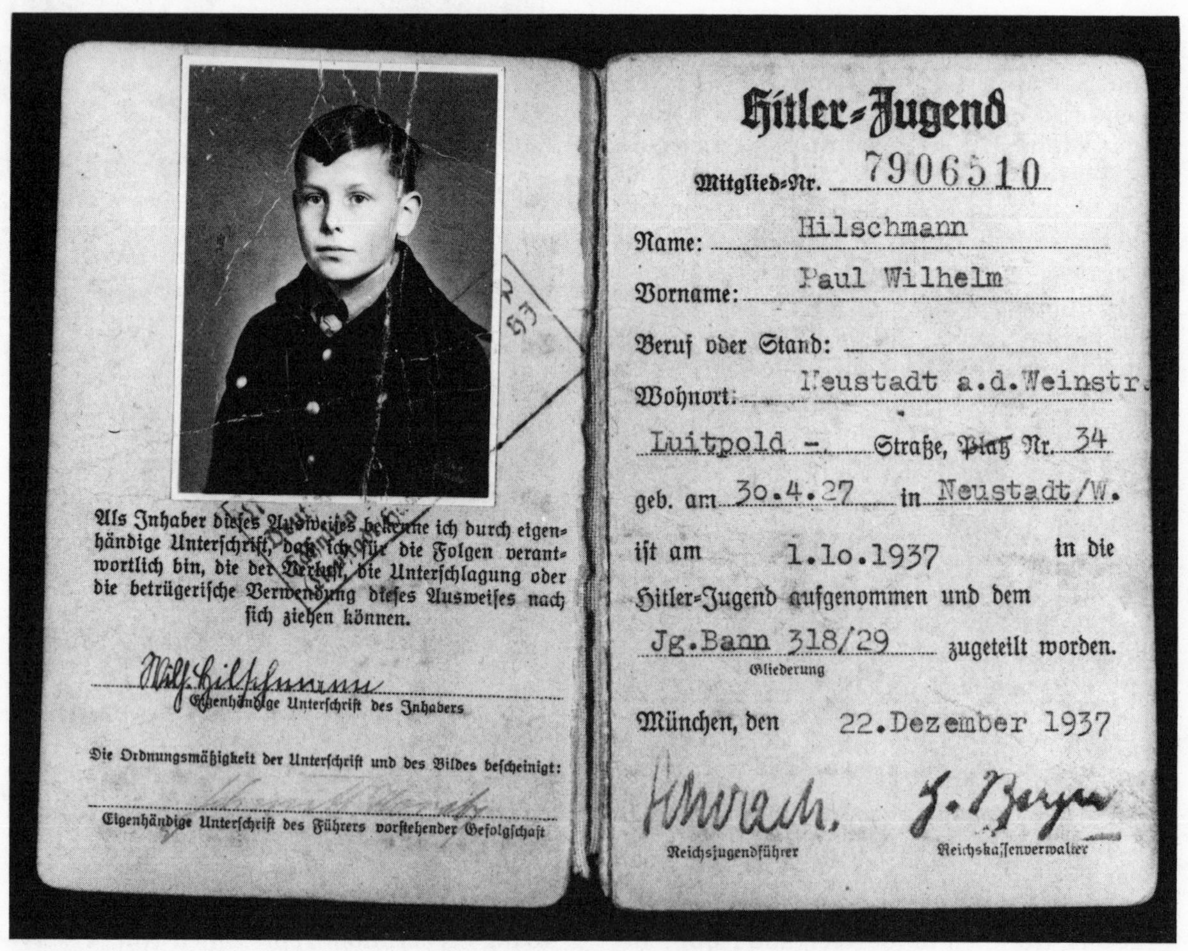

Als Inhaber dieses Ausweises bekenne ich durch eigenhändige Unterschrift, daß ich für die Folgen verantwortlich bin, die der Verlust, die Unterschlagung oder die betrügerische Verwendung dieses Ausweises nach sich ziehen können.

Eigenhändige Unterschrift des Inhabers

Die Ordnungsmäßigkeit der Unterschrift und des Bildes bescheinigt:

Eigenhändige Unterschrift des Führers vorstehender Gefolgschaft

Hitler-Jugend

Mitglied-Nr. 7906510

Name: Hilschmann

Vorname: Paul Wilhelm

Beruf oder Stand:

Wohnort: Neustadt a.d.Weinstr.

Luitpold - Straße, ~~Platz~~ Nr. 34

geb. am 30.4.27 in Neustadt/W.

ist am 1.10.1937 in die Hitler-Jugend aufgenommen und dem Jg.Bann 318/29 zugeteilt worden.
Gliederung

München, den 22.Dezember 1937

Reichsjugendführer   Reichskassenverwalter

Hitler Youth identification card. [A Living Memorial to the Holocaust—Museum of Jewish Heritage, New York]

During the war the BDM became increasingly involved in the war effort, at the expense of ideological training. Political and ideological indoctrination in the HJ played a much larger role than in the BDM. The activities in which the HJ members were engaged overshadowed the formal education they were receiving and estranged them from their families; quite often the youngsters became their family's Nazi propagandists—and ideological supervisors. The propaganda used for the implanting of Nazi ideas also drew on the mass media, and sophisticated methods were employed to gain German youth's support for the HJ ideals. The film *Hitlerjunge Quex* (Hitler Boy Quex) is a typical example of the Nazi style of brainwashing. Produced in 1933, the film tells the life story of a boy imbued with Nazi ideas.

Many of the young men who were converted to Nazi ideology during their membership in the HJ absorbed the poison of Jew hatred through their training and activities, and when they grew up became agents of the "Final Solution"—murderers by conviction.

BIBLIOGRAPHY

Klönne, A. *Hitlerjugend: Die Jugend und ihre Organisation im Dritten Reich.* Hannover, 1956.

Koch, H. W. *Hitler Youth: Origins and Development, 1922–1945.* New York, 1975.

Noakes, J., and G. Pridham, eds. *Documents on Nazism, 1919–1945.* New York, 1975.

Walker, L. D. *Hitler Youth and Catholic Youth.* Washington, D.C., 1970.

ZVI BACHARACH

HITLER YOUTH. *See* Hitlerjugend.

HIWIS. *See* Hilfswillige.

HLINKA, ANDREJ (1864–1938), Slovak cleric and political leader. Born in a village in northern SLOVAKIA, Hlinka became a Catholic priest and also a fanatic nationalist. The spiritual and secular Hungarian authorities alike were outraged by his propagandist activity, accusing him of violating the civil as well as the canon law; he was jailed and deprived by his bishop of priestly authority. During Hlinka's absence a new church was constructed in his village, and the villagers asked that Hlinka, as a native son, be permitted to consecrate it. In the clash that ensued with the local gendarmerie, dozens of people were killed or wounded. The incident made Hlinka's name known all over Europe and drew attention to the tribulations of the minorities living in the kingdom of Hungary.

When Czechoslovakia was founded as a republic in 1918, Hlinka welcomed it and supported Slovakia's joining the new state. Both he and the Slovak clergy, however, were troubled by the separation of church and state, and particularly by the laws that secularized education, taking the schools out of their hands. Disappointed by these developments, Hlinka decided to reestablish the Slovak People's Party (Slovenská L'udová Strana), originally founded in 1905, and lead

Andrej Hlinka.

it in a struggle for Slovak autonomy within the framework of the Czechoslovak republic. Before long, Hlinka and his party clashed with the authorities, whose policy was based on belief in a single Czechoslovak people. This policy—in addition to a sense that anti-Slovak discrimination existed in economic and cultural affairs and in the local Czechoslovak administration—antagonized many Slovaks and led them to support Hlinka's party, which was eventually named after him. The party platform, nationalist and Catholic-oriented, came to represent the voice of Slovak nationalism. Hlinka was not always able to force his views on his aides and advisers; the party became increasingly hard-line, and after 1935 some of its sectors were inclined to cooperate with extreme right-wing movements. The radicals in the party, especially the younger members, aspired to the dismemberment of Czechoslovakia, whereas Hlinka himself continued to adhere to the more limited demand for Slovak autonomy. When the German-sponsored Slovak republic was created in 1939, after Hlinka's death, his party became the predominant political force and his memory became the symbol of a Slovak national renaissance.

In his youth Hlinka had spread anti-Jewish propaganda, and his party too used antisemitism to attract followers; among the younger generation it became an unbridled incitement to violence. Hlinka himself assured the Jews that he disapproved of antisemitism and discrimination against Jews, calling on them to support the Slovaks' national struggle.

A fervent nationalist who was utterly devoted to his people, Hlinka is regarded as the outstanding Slovak personality of the twentieth century.

BIBLIOGRAPHY

Fagula, L. G. *Andrej Hlinka*. Bratislava, 1943.

Hoensch, J. K. *Die Slowakei und Hitlers Ostpolitik: Hlinkas Slowakische Volkspartei zwischen Autonomie und Separation, 1938–1939*. Cologne, 1965.

Jelinek, J. *The Parish Republic: Hlinka's Slovak People's Party, 1939–1945*. New York, 1976.

YESHAYAHU JELINEK

HLINKA GUARD (Hlinková Garda), the militia maintained by the Slovak People's Party in the period from 1938 to 1945; named after Andrej HLINKA.

The Hlinka Guard was preceded by the Rodobrana (People's Defense) organization, which existed from 1923 to 1927, when the Czechoslovak authorities ordered its dissolution. During the crisis caused by Hitler's demand for the Sudetenland (in the summer of 1938), the Hlinka Guard emerged spontaneously, and on October 8 of that year, a week after Hitler's demand had been accepted at the MUNICH CONFERENCE, the guard was officially set up, with Karol Sidor (1901–1953) as its first commander.

The guard was the Hlinka party's military arm for internal security, and it continued in that role under the autonomous government of SLOVAKIA in federated Czechoslovakia. It operated against Jews, Czechs, the Left, and the opposition. By a decree issued on October 29, 1938, the Hlinka guard was designated as the only body authorized to give its members paramilitary training, and it was this decree that established its formal status in the country. Hlinka guardsmen wore black uniforms and a cap shaped like a boat, with a woolen pom-pom on top, and they used the raised-arm salute.

Until March 14, 1939, when Slovakia declared its independence, the Hlinka Guard attracted recruits from all walks of life. On the following day, March 15, Alexander MACH became its commander, retaining the post up to the collapse of the pro-Nazi regime in Slovakia in 1945. Its functions were laid down in a series of government decrees: it was to be a paramilitary organization attached to the party, fostering love of country, providing paramilitary training, and safeguarding internal security. By assuming these tasks, the guard was meant to counterbalance the army and the police. In 1941 Hlinka Guard shock troops were trained in SS camps in Germany, and the SS attached an adviser to the guard. At this point many of the guardsmen who were of middle-class origin quit, and thenceforth the organization consisted of peasants and unskilled laborers, together with various doubtful elements. A social message was an integral part of the radical nationalism that it sought to impart.

In 1942, the Hlinka Guard joined the police and the storm troopers of the local German population in deporting Jews to camps in Poland. Over the course of time, the guardsmen prospered financially and their zeal abated. Leadership passed into the hands of elements close to the Hlinka party. A small group called Nas Boj (Our Struggle), which operated under SS auspices, was the most radical element in the guard. Throughout its years of existence, the Hlinka Guard competed with the Hlinka party for primacy in ruling the country. After the SLOVAK NATIONAL UPRISING in August 1944, the SS took over and shaped the Hlinka Guard to suit its own purposes. Special units of the guard (Pohotovostne Oddiely Hlinkovej Gardy) were employed against partisans and Jews.

BIBLIOGRAPHY

Jelinek, Y. *The Parish Republic: Hlinka's Slovak People's Party, 1939–1945.* Boulder, 1976.

Jelinek, Y. "Storm-Troopers in Slovakia: The Rodobrana and the Hlinka Guard." *Journal of Contemporary History* 6/3 (1971): 97–119.

Susko, L. "Hlinková Garda od svojho vzniku az po salzburske rokovanie (1938–1940)." *Zbornik Muzea Slovenskeho Narodneho Povstania* 11 (1969): 167–262.

YESHAYAHU JELINEK

HOLLAND. *See* Netherlands, The.

HOLOCAUST (Heb., *sho'ah*). The word "holocaust" is derived from the Greek *holokauston,* which originally meant a sacrifice totally burned by fire; it was used in the translation of 1 Samuel 7:9, "a burnt offering to God." In the course of time it came to be used to describe slaughter on a general or large scale, and, especially, various forms of the destruction of masses of human beings. In the 1950s the term came to be applied primarily to the destruction of the Jews of Europe under the Nazi regime, and it is also employed in describing the annihilation of other groups of people in World War II. The mass extermination of Jews has become the archetype of GENOCIDE, and the terms *sho'ah* and "holocaust" have become linked to the attempt by the Nazi German state to destroy European Jewry during World War II.

The use of the Hebrew word *sho'ah* to denote the destruction of Jews in Europe during the war appeared for the first time in the booklet *Sho'at Yehudei Polin* (The Holocaust of the Jews of Poland), published by the United Aid Committee for the Jews of Poland, in Jerusalem in 1940. The booklet contains reports and articles on the persecution of Jews in eastern Europe from the beginning of the war, written or verbally reported by eyewitnesses, among them several leaders of Polish Jewry. Up to the spring of 1942, however, the term was rarely used. The Hebrew term that was first used, spontaneously, was *hurban* (lit., "destruction"), similar in meaning to "catastrophe," with its historical Jewish meaning deriving from the destruction of the Temple. It was only when leaders of the Zionist movement and writers and thinkers in Palestine began to express themselves on the destruction of European Jewry that the Hebrew term *sho'ah* became widely used. It was still far from being in general use, even after the November 1942 declaration of the Jewish Agency that a *sho'ah* was taking place. One of the first to use the term in the historical perspective was the Jerusalem historian Ben-Zion Dinur (Dinaburg), who, in the spring of 1942, stated that the Holocaust was a "catastrophe" that symbolized the unique situation of the Jewish people among the nations of the world.

BIBLIOGRAPHY

Eliach, Y. "Defining the Holocaust: Perspectives of a Jewish Historian." In *Jews and Christians after the Holocaust,* edited by A. J. Peck, pp. 11–23. Philadelphia, 1984.

Tal, U. "On the Study of the Holocaust and Genocide." *Yad Vashem Studies* 13 (1979): 7–52.

URIEL TAL

HOLOCAUST ART. *See* Art of the Holocaust.

HOLOCAUST, DENIAL OF THE. Denying the Holocaust includes attempts to deny the fact that the extermination of the Jews by the Nazis ever took place; contentions that Jewish losses have been grossly exaggerated; denials that the Holocaust was the result of a deliberate policy; and the tendentious and trivializing claim that the Holocaust was not unique and that there had been precedents, even precedents that had served as models for the Holocaust.

Such attempts began even before the conclusion of World War II and have since been systematically spread, in various ways, in many countries. The phrase "denial of the Holocaust," however, should not be restricted to the false accusations or the distortions of historical fact that began to appear as early as 1945, with the collapse of the Nazi regime. It also refers to the suppression of facts and the disavowal and destruction of pieces of evidence that were an integral part of the murder action and its implementation. The German bureaucracy entrusted with the task of carrying out the different stages of the "FINAL SOLUTION" used a variety of euphemistic terms to cover up the mass killings. The transports of Jews to AUSCHWITZ-Birkenau—where some or all of them were destined to be killed in gas chambers—were accompanied by a document stating that they were to undergo "special treatment" (*Sonderbehandlung; see* SPRACHREGELUNG). SS men and police who handled the deportations and operated the extermination camps, such as the AKTION REINHARD teams, were sworn to secrecy and committed themselves not to reveal anything about their actions, even after their mission had been accomplished. In an address made by Heinrich HIMMLER in October 1943 to an assembly of senior SS officers in Posen (Poznán), the SS chief said that the mass murder of the Jews was an operation "of which we shall never speak publicly." In July 1943, Martin BORMANN issued an order in Adolf HITLER's name prohibiting public reference to the "total solution" (*Gesamtlösung*) that was under way, and instructing that the treatment of the Jews be described as their "collective draft for a planned labor program." During the last two years of the war, special SS units were formed whose task was to remove the corpses of Jews from the pits where they had been buried and to burn them, so as to eradicate all traces of the massacres that had taken place. Paul BLOBEL, the commander of the units formed to carry out AKTION 1005, testified at Nuremberg (in June 1947) that "in June 1942 Gruppenführer [Heinrich] MÜLLER instructed me to obliterate traces of the massacres carried out by the EINSATZGRUPPEN in the east."

Some of the Jewish victims were well aware of the Nazis' intention to deny the murders and their responsibility for them. The diarists of that period stated that they felt it their duty to make a written record of what was taking place, so that the world and the future generations would know the truth. Thus, Itzhak KATZENELSON, the poet who was imprisoned in the VITTEL camp in France and later killed at Auschwitz, wrote in his diary on the eve of his deportation:

> They will never believe. They will never believe that the people of Adolf Hitler set up a slaughterhouse and massacred seven million Jews. They won't believe it, and worse: they will pretend to accept the big lie which that loathsome people has spread throughout the war years: "We did not kill the Jews. The Jews died on the way when we were taking them to the concentration camps. This was what was ordained for them. . . . They succumbed because they were weak, a weak and feeble people." They invented these terrible lies for the sake of their allies, to serve as an excuse, an alibi.

Leib Langfuss, one of the Jews working for the SONDERKOMMANDO in Auschwitz, wrote (on pages that were found in the vicinity of the Birkenau crematoria) that even those who witnessed what was happening in the ghettos could only tell the truth that they knew, but that "the real truth is far more tragic and dreadful."

Those who deny the Holocaust exploit various versions and methods. The most extreme among them claim that the Third Reich authorities never planned to murder the Jews of Europe, that no extermination camps were built and operated, and that there is no truth to the allegations that a murder apparatus run by the Nazis exterminated five million to six million Jews by deliberate, sophisticated methods. Others do not resort to a total denial of the facts, but they deny that the murder was as thorough and as extensive as it actually was. Also to be included among those who seek to deny the whole truth of the Holocaust are revisionists, among them genuine scholars and historians, who do not disclaim proven facts, but seek to reduce the degree of responsibility that the top Nazi echelon and Hitler himself bore. They depict the Holocaust as an occurrence that was essentially no different from earlier mass slaughters, such as those perpetrated by Stalin in the Soviet Union, which even served the Holocaust as models.

According to the most extreme version, the Holocaust never took place and is to be seen as a Zionist-Communist fabrication designed to besmirch Germany's reputation. In *The Lie about Auschwitz,* Thies Christophersen, an SS man who had been stationed in one of the Auschwitz satellite camps, claims that there were no gas chambers in Birkenau; he had personally investigated such "rumors" during his stay in Auschwitz, and they turned out to have no basis in fact. Another German, Wilhelm Staeglich, a Wehrmacht officer who served in the Auschwitz area, also claims to know that no murder by gassing took place in the Auschwitz-Birkenau camp. (After the war, Staeglich was a judge in the Federal Republic for twenty years, until he was ousted.) According to these claims, a Zionist-Communist conspiracy concocted the Holocaust. The Communists, it is alleged, seek to undermine Germany, which constitutes the main obstacle to Communist expansion in Europe, while the Zionists want Germany and the rest of Europe to suffer guilt feelings toward the Jews so that the Zionists can exploit these feelings, materially and politically, for the promotion of their own aims. The anti-Zionist policies of the Communist camp have, however, made the charge of a "Zionist-Communist conspiracy" ludicrous, although the charge is still being raised, separately, against each of the "partners" in this "conspiracy." In some of the printed material put out by the revisionists, the claim is made that it was no accident that the extermination camps were situated in areas that are now under Communist control, where no reliable on-the-spot investigation can be made. These extreme revisionists are not deterred by the evidence given by Polish emigrants in the West, who cannot be suspected of sympathy with the regime in their native country —evidence that confirms the existence and operation of Nazi extermination camps on Polish soil. Nor are the revisionists impressed by the thousands of documents and testimonies given by victims of the Holocaust, as well as by men who were in charge of the murder operations; or by important public acts such as Pope John Paul II's praying on the murder sites and branding the murders as such. On the basis of the authentic documents and proven testimonies now available, it is possible to reconstruct almost everything that went on in the extermination camps, and to follow the tracks of every transport that reached them from every part of occupied Europe. To this large body of incontrovertible evidence the inveterate revisionists turn a deaf ear.

More sophisticated, and therefore more dangerous, is the partial denial—the attempt to undermine the validity of historical facts by casting doubts on the numerical data, the credibility of documents and witnesses, and so forth. Those who adopt this approach also aim at total denial of the Holocaust, but they believe it is easier to attain their objective by questioning the reliability of various details in the total historical picture. This method is deemed more effective, since it poses as a revisionist approach that examines each event on its own merits. This group of "partial revisionists" includes some who regard the total denial as ineffective and damaging, and others who believe that while the propaganda material circulated by the radicals addresses itself to the ignorant as well as to the extreme right, articles posing as respectable theoretical discussions will reach an intelligent sector interested in studying the subject.

One of the most widespread tactics in the writings of the revisionists is to question the legitimacy of the NUREMBERG TRIAL, which is attacked from various legal angles, some of them taken from critics who did not question the facts of the Holocaust. One major approach relates to the Soviet participation in the Nuremberg Trial and the ban on the introduction of crimes committed by the Soviets. This argument was raised by many critics of the International Military Tribunal, and the revisionists exploit it to cast doubt on the reliability of the many documents that served the prosecution as the basis for its case. In actuality, the documents collected for the trial and published in numerous volumes together with the proceedings of the trial represent one of the best-known, most widely circulated, and most credible source collections.

Another issue often raised by the revisionists is the number of victims. The radicals propagate the thesis put forward by a veteran Nazi, Wolf Dieter Rothe: "I am firmly convinced that not a single Jew was liquidated with the knowledge of the Reich government, of Adolf Hitler, who was then the Führer, and of the German people, simply because he was Jewish." In their attempt to refute the real number of victims and to sow doubt and confusion on this issue, the revisionists quote misleading prewar figures, or invent new ones, to demonstrate that the millions of Jews who were murdered during the war were a figment of the imagination. They have also proposed a variety of theories concerning the present whereabouts of the Jews from Nazi-occupied Europe. According to Paul Rassinier, a Frenchman who is one of the founders of the revisionist school, between half a million and a million Jews perished during the war, mostly as the result of the prevailing bad conditions and the Jews' inability to adapt to the changes that were taking place. Those who pursue this line of argument, however—that those Jews who died perished gradually—are faced with an irrefutable counterargument in the case of HUNGARY. There the Jews fell into the Nazis' clutches only in March 1944, and the destruction of most of the community was complete by early July of that year. Here a slow attrition cannot account for their disappearance. Rassinier "discovers" the millions of Jews who disappeared from Europe in various places. He claims, for example, that the masses of North African Jews who settled in Israel before and after its establishment as a state were not necessarily native North Africans but that many were Jews who had escaped from Europe. A prominent American revisionist, Arthur R. Butz, author of *The Hoax of the Twentieth Century*, claims that no more than 350,000 Jews are missing; some of them, according to Butz, lost touch with their relatives and are not really missing, and about 200,000 were executed by the German authorities on various grounds. Butz also "reveals" that large numbers of Jews entered the United States as illegal immigrants, assumed a new identity, and were swallowed up in the vast urban concentrations of America without leaving a trace.

Another piece of Butz's "evidence" that the figure of 6 million Jews who were murdered is nothing but a myth willfully spread by the Zionists is that YAD VASHEM (an institution that, Butz claims, was established for the very purpose of spreading the "trumped-up Jewish version" of the Holocaust, and has collected memorial pages for "every victim" of the Holocaust) has not been able to discover more than 2.5 million to 3 million names. Butz does not explain why the institution that purportedly has the task of spreading a myth did not also fabricate a few million names in order to produce the required figures.

Another target for the revisionists is the enormous wealth of material examining and documenting the Holocaust years and the Nazi crimes, down to the last detail—including official papers and thousands of diaries, testimonies, and memoirs. Very few events of historical dimensions have left behind such an enormous mass of documentation. The Nazis habitually put everything on paper, whatever the subject, even the most confidential issues, and although part of the documentation was destroyed in the last stages of the war, large quantities fell into the hands of the victorious powers. Contrary to the usual practice with official records, this material was not subjected to a long freeze before its release to the general public, and it has been readily available for research and publication. Among the most revealing documents are those from the war itself; the office diary kept by Hans FRANK, the head of the GENERALGOUVERNEMENT; a book written by Hitler in 1928 and shelved (*Hitler's Second Book*); the diaries of Joseph GOEBBELS; the speeches of Heinrich HIMMLER; and the minutes of the WANNSEE CONFERENCE on the implementation of the "Final Solution." Among the important sources of information from after the war are the statements made by the many thousands of Nazi criminals in their interrogations and during their court trials, and the autobiography and other notes of Rudolf HÖSS, the commandant of Auschwitz.

The revisionists become trapped in their attempts to explain or reject this huge accumulation of documents. The diaries and testimonies of Jews are rejected as not credible, because Jews are an interested party, and whatever they said or wrote down is dismissed as one big after-the-fact lie. Testimonies given by non-Jews, and documents forwarded from the occupied countries during the war (especially from Poland), which provide a record of the events that were taking place from non-Jewish and sometimes even anti-Jewish sources, are rejected as biased and written under pressure from Jews. The revisionists ingeniously exploit any contradiction or distortion in the documentation. Thus, when some witnesses let their imagination run free and incorrectly claim that the DACHAU concentration camp had working gas chambers, the revisionists pounce on this discrepancy to assert that if some details in the evidence given by witnesses are incorrect, then the whole story of the Holocaust must be nothing but a pack of lies. Generally, however, the revisionists realize that such wholesale denials on their part weaken their case, and so they concentrate on seeking to discredit particular aspects. For example, Robert Faurisson has argued that it was impossible to use ZYKLON B gas regularly in one place, as was the case in Auschwitz, and that therefore the story of the use of gas in Auschwitz is not true. An American colleague of Faurisson's, Reinhard K. Buchner, has sought to prove that it is impossible to cremate human bodies at the rate that this was done in the extermination camps, basing his conclusion on a comparison with the time it takes to cremate bodies in ordinary crematoria operating under normal conditions.

A vexing question in this denial of the Holocaust is the identity and nature of the people involved and their motivations. Another question is whether they know the truth and deliberately fabricate their web of lies. A careful analysis of their writings indicates that prominent revisionists know the truth. Their arguments carefully avoid the obvious weak points that could reveal them as liars, and the construction of their arguments discloses that they are aware of the truth, but are trying to distort and suppress it. Altogether, only a few dozen people are involved in this enterprise—writing books and articles, holding conferences, and quoting one another to create the impression that they represent a historical school. There are no historians among them: Butz is a professor of electronics; Faurisson was a professor of literature; Rassinier, a teacher of geography; some are journalists. They have an international organization of sorts coordinating their activities, distributing books and pamphlets from country to country and from continent to continent, operating cells in different countries, and establishing channels to reach various sectors of the population. One of the revisionists' major problems is obtaining serious academic status for their arguments and their publications, so as to gain entry to universities and colleges and capture the attention of students and educators. Their center in California specializes in these efforts. It conducts international conferences of revisionists and seeks to have them invited to prestigious universities. The revisionist *Journal of Historical Review* is published in Torrance, California, with a format like that of an authentic scholarly journal. Other centers of revisionist activities are in Sweden, Germany, France, England, Argentina, and Australia.

The revisionists' motivations are varied. Some are Nazi activists who are using the denial of the Holocaust to repair the Nazi image. Rassinier, and perhaps others like him, have joined because of their bitter hatred of communism and Communists, which is so extreme that it forces them to adopt an apologetic position on Nazism. Rassinier was formerly a Socialist, was himself a prisoner in a Nazi concentration camp, and at first recognized that the Holocaust had taken place; but his clash with communism became a deep-rooted phobia. Some of the revisionists are arch-antisemites who are ready to adopt any means to attack Jews. Most of them belong to neo-Nazi and neofascist movements, which have received little credence, largely because of the revelation of the horrors of the Holocaust. It is not surprising, therefore, that the present-day fascists and their sympathizers seek to hide or obliterate the truth about the Holocaust, which blocks their quest for power.

The writings of some reputable scholars and authors are utilized and recommended by the revisionists. One example is *The Origins of the Second World War*, by A. J. P. Taylor. This controversial book, written by a respected historian, apportions the blame for the outbreak of World War II in equal measure among all the parties involved in the conflict, and regards Hitler as just one more bad German leader; that in itself is seen by the revisionists as a support for their views. In his book

Der erzwungene Krieg (The Forced War; 1961), David Hoggan, who is scarcely a historian on a par with Taylor, tries to present a revisionist interpretation of the causes of World War II. David Irving's book *Hitler's War* propounds the view—completely baseless—that until the fall of 1943 Hitler had no knowledge of the mass murder of Jews, which was being carried out behind his back. The inference drawn is that neither Hitler nor some of his close confidants bear responsibility for the crime. Irving is a deliberate and consistent apologist for the Nazis and has contacts with the revisionists and their conferences. Professor Ernst Nolte, a respected German scholar and student of political movements, especially in the field of fascism, National Socialism, and totalitarian regimes, has made statements in his writings that contain elements taken from the revisionist trends and arguments. Of course, Nolte does not deny that there was a Holocaust, but he argues that Hitler had reason to be wary of the Jews. Some of them, like Chaim WEIZMANN, president of the World Zionist Organization and the Jewish Agency, had declared at the outbreak of the war that the Jews considered themselves part of the democratic camp that was fighting the Nazis and therefore the Jewish people had declared war on Hitler. Moreover, Nolte believes that the Holocaust was no different from other mass murders carried out in the twentieth century, the only unique feature being the use of gas for the murders. He points out that Hitler's massacres were preceded by those of Stalin and that these may have been not only a model, but also a motive for the Holocaust. The publication of Nolte's controversial ideas sparked a sharp and widespread debate in which many leading German historians participated; quite a few were inclined to justify Nolte's assumptions or even to agree with him. In Nantes, France, a doctoral dissertation justifying the denial of the Holocaust was submitted to the local university, and was approved. Because of public pressure, the approval of the dissertation was canceled, as was the academic degree awarded on its basis.

The historiography of the Soviet Union has seen no denial of the Holocaust as far as the facts are concerned. Soviet historians, however, refer to the victims as citizens of the Soviet Union or of the other states from which they came; the Soviets do not identify the Jewish victims as such, and do not make it unequivocally clear that the Jews were massacred only because they were Jews, not because they were Russians, Ukrainians, or citizens of the European countries. Soviet writings on the subject also overlook the role played by the peoples of the Soviet border regions in the persecution of the Jews, in collaboration with the Germans.

The arguments of the revisionists have won attention and acquired influence. In some quarters their impact may grow among young people who learn nothing about the Holocaust. It is natural that such persons, hearing about the Holocaust for the first time, refuse to believe that such incredible events could have occurred. Consequently, those who seek to deny that such events did take place, or to discredit them in one way or another, find a ready audience. Moreover, at some academic institutions the presentation of revisionist ideas has been legitimized by holding them forth as counterarguments to accepted historical facts concerning the Holocaust. The revisionists also claim the right to be given access to the media, and when no notice is taken of them, they complain that the principles of democracy and freedom of speech are being violated and that they are the victims of a conspiracy. In some instances, when the revisionists used provocative means to promote their ideas, their attempts failed. In California, for example, they announced in 1980 and 1981 that they would give a prize to any person who could prove that murder by gassing was committed at Auschwitz; they were brought to court and sharply reproved for their action. Some countries have outlawed the revisionists' publications. Revisionists have also been put on trial in some places, and in most cases, the judgment has gone against them. But there have also been instances when judicial authorities refused to take a clear stand on such issues as the murder methods used in the Holocaust or the dimensions of the Holocaust, on the ground that these are historical matters that a court of law is not competent to judge.

Attempts to deny the Holocaust have also led to vigorous counteraction. The denial attempts have had the unintended effect of arousing interest in the subject and a desire to learn more about the Holocaust and its meaning. They have spread awareness of the Holocaust and of the need to protect humanity from the scourge of racism and genocide.

[*See also* Historiography of the Holocaust.]

BIBLIOGRAPHY

Gutman, Y. *Denying the Holocaust.* Jerusalem, 1985.

Kampe, N. "Normalizing the Holocaust? The Recent Historians' Debate in the Federal Republic of Germany." *Holocaust and Genocide Studies* 2/1 (1987): 61–80.

Klarsfeld, S., ed. *The Holocaust and the Neo-Nazi Mythomania.* New York, 1978.

Kulka, E. *The Holocaust Is Being Denied: The Answer of Auschwitz Survivors.* Tel Aviv, 1977.

ISRAEL GUTMAN

HOLOCAUST EDUCATION. *See* Education on the Holocaust.

HOLOCAUST FILMS. *See* Films on the Holocaust.

HOLOCAUST LITERATURE. *See* Literature on the Holocaust.

HOLOCAUST MARTYRS' AND HEROES' REMEMBRANCE AUTHORITY. *See* Yad Vashem.

HOLOCAUST MEMORIAL COUNCIL. *See* U.S. Holocaust Memorial Council.

HOLOCAUST SURVIVORS. *See* Survivors, Psychology of; United States Army and Survivors in Austria and Germany.

HOME ARMY. *See* Armia Krajowa.

HOMOSEXUALITY IN THE THIRD REICH. In 1871, when the Prussian-dominated German Empire was established, the Reich penal code had a paragraph (para. 175) that classified homosexuality as "an unnatural form of licentiousness," carrying a prison term for persons caught in such an act. Under the Weimar Republic (1919–1933), the issue became a subject of free public discussion, and the Wissenschaftlich-Humanitäres Komitee (Scientific-Humanitarian Committee) was established for the defense of homosexuals. Even in that period the Nazi party denounced homosexuality in no uncertain terms, declaring it a deviation from normal sexual behavior that placed the main emphasis on the sensual, pleasurable element of sex life to the detriment of the natural increase in population, the nation's strength, and a proper family life. Sexual relations, according to the Nazi view, "serve the reproductive process, their purpose being the preservation and continued existence of the *Volk,* rather than the provision of pleasure to the individual." Homosexuality, in males and females, was not only an egotistic form of sex life; it also harmed the strength of the *Volk* and the race, and was therefore incompatible with the ideal of racial purity.

The wave of "protective custody" (*Schutzhaft*) of hostile political elements that was launched in the middle of March 1933 also included persons who were known for their activities in behalf of homosexuals. In 1935, paragraph 135 of the penal code was made more stringent when the promotion of friendship between males that was based on homosexuality, even without actual homosexual acts being performed, was made an offense. In August 1936 arrests were carried out in several large cities, in places where homosexuals were known to congregate. The attitude toward homosexuals was that they were asocial elements who should be put in prison. Persons who were found to be "recidivist" and "chronic" homosexuals were incarcerated in concentration camps.

The Nazi position on homosexuality, however, was inconsistent, and the approach to it was tactical in nature. Officially, homosexuality was sharply denounced, but its practice in certain Nazi circles was tolerated or ignored. This was the case with Ernst RÖHM, chief of the SA (Sturmabteilung; Storm Troopers) and a Hitler confidant, who was a known homosexual, as were several of his aides in the SA command. Political opponents took the Nazis to task over Röhm's homosexuality, but Hitler chose to ignore his close aide's sexual preference. It was only after the "Night of the Long Knives" (June 30–July 1, 1934), when Röhm and a group of his SA cohorts were murdered in the wake of a political confrontation in the Nazi leadership, that Röhm's homosexuality was mentioned as one of the reasons for his murder.

The charge of homosexuality was also used to get rid of prominent figures who were no longer regarded as desirable. Thus, in 1938, the chief of the general staff, Gen. Werner Freiherr von Fritsch, was dismissed from his post because he disagreed with Hitler's political and military plans. The official reason given, however, was that he had been discovered to be a homosexual—a libel invented by the Gestapo.

Under Nazi rule, tens of thousands of persons were punished on the charge of homosexuality. Thousands of them (some sources put the figure at ten thousand or more, but no precise figure is available) were imprisoned in concentration camps, where they had to wear a pink triangular patch (*rosa Winkel*). Many of the homosexuals imprisoned in the camps perished there. Shortly before the end of the war, some of them were set free and drafted into frontline service with the Wehrmacht. This step, of course, violated the Nazi principle on the issue.

Persecution of homosexuals was restricted to the Reich and the areas annexed to it. There is no evidence of Nazi-instigated drives against homosexuality in the occupied countries.

BIBLIOGRAPHY

Heger, H. *The Men with the Pink Triangle.* Boston, 1980.

Plant, R. *The Pink Triangle: The Nazi War against Homosexuals.* New York, 1986.

Rector, F. *The Nazi Extermination of Homosexuals.* New York, 1981.

ELISHEVA SHAUL

HORODENKA. *See* Gorodenka.

HORST WESSEL SONG, Nazi anthem. Horst Wessel (1907–1930) was a member of the SA (Sturmabteilung; Storm Troopers) who was shot dead by a Communist in a private vendetta. His killing was depicted by Nazi propaganda as a political assassination, and he became a Nazi hero and political symbol. The lyrics of a poem he published in 1929 in Joseph GOEBBELS's newspaper, *Der Angriff* (The Attack), set to the tune of a sailors' marching song, became the official song of the Nazi party and the second song of the Third Reich, after the national anthem, *Deutschland über Alles*. The lyrics were:

Die Fahne hoch!
Die Reihen dicht geschlossen,
SA marschiert
Mit ruhig festem Schritt.
Kameraden, die Rote Front und
Reaktion erschossen,
Marschieren im Geist in unsern Reihen mit.

Die Strasse frei den braunen Bataillonen!
Die Strasse frei dem Sturmabteilungsmann!
Es schaun aufs Hakenkreuz voll
Hoffnung schon Millionen.
Der Tag für Freiheit und für Brot bricht an.

Zum letzten Mal wird zum Appell geblasen!
Zum Kampfe stehn wir alle schon bereit.
Bald flattern Hitlerfahnen über allen Strassen,
Die Knechtschaft dauert nur noch kurze Zeit!

Banner up! With ranks tightly closed,
The SA marches with calm, firm step.
Comrades shot by the Red Front and
reactionaries
March with us in spirit.

Clear the streets for the brown battalions,
Clear the streets for the storm troopers.
Filled with hope, millions already look toward
the swastika.
The day of freedom and bread dawns.

Blow the roll call for the last time,
We all stand ready for the fight.
Soon Hitler flags will flutter over all streets,
Servitude will only last a short time longer.

DAVID BANKIER

HORTHY, MIKLÓS (1868–1957), regent of HUNGARY from 1920 to 1944. In 1919 Horthy was the military leader of the counterrevolutionary "white terror" campaign against the short-lived Béla Kun Socialist-Communist regime, and after the evacuation of the Romanian occupying forces, he became regent of the Hungarian kingdom (March 1, 1920).

Miklós Horthy (November 1938).

His initial, aggressively antisemitic regime was gradually moderated, especially after the debate on the first anti-Jewish *numerus clausus* (quota) laws (September 22, 1920). In general, Horthy's rule was characterized throughout by constant official and semiofficial antisemitism. Throughout the 1920s and 1930s, he conducted a conservative internal policy, relying on the traditional aristocracy and on certain modern capitalist elements, and was a widely popular leader. The main objective of his foreign policy was the revision of the Treaty of Trianon (concluded in Versailles in 1920, when Hungary ceded about two-thirds of its prewar territory), which brought him to an ever-growing cooperation with Hitler's Germany.

Between 1938 and 1941, Horthy authorized three increasingly harsh and comprehensive anti-Jewish laws. Nevertheless, in 1942 and 1943, while facing Hitler's challenge, he rejected German pressure to impose even harsher measures, such as the exclusion of Jews from all economic activities, enforcement of wearing the Jewish BADGE, ghettoization, and the deportation of all Jews to concentration and extermination camps.

After the German occupation of Hungary (March 19, 1944), Horthy nominated a government totally subservient to the Nazis, giving it unlimited authority for all anti-Jewish measures. Some 500,000 Jews never returned from the deportations. On July 7, 1944, with over 150,000 Budapest Jews and several thousand men in labor service still in the country, Horthy ordered the deportations stopped. On October 15, after an aborted armistice attempt, he was deposed by the Germans and replaced as head of state by Ferenc SZÁLASI, the leader of the fascist ARROW CROSS PARTY. After the war, the Allied powers allowed Horthy to go to Portugal, where he wrote his memoirs, which were published in 1965.

BIBLIOGRAPHY

Braham, R. L. "The Rightists, Horthy and the Germans: Factors Underlying the Destruction of Hungarian Jewry." *Jews and Non-Jews in Eastern Europe*, edited by B. Vago and G. L. Mosse, pp. 137–156. New York, 1974.

Fenyo, M. D. *Hitler, Horthy, and Hungary: German-Hungarian Relations, 1941–1944*. New Haven, 1972.

Katzburg, N. *Hungary and the Jews: Policy and Legislation, 1920–1943*. Ramat Gan, Israel, 1981.

Macartney, C. A. *October Fifteenth: A History of Hungary, 1929–1945*. New York, 1957.

ASHER COHEN

HORTHY OFFER, proposal made public by the Hungarian regent, Adm. Miklós HORTHY, in July 1944, recommending that several categories of Jews in HUNGARY be allowed to emigrate, primarily to Palestine. The public offer was made soon after Horthy halted the deportations of Jews from Hungary early that month, partly because of Allied pressure. The Swedes and the Americans in particular had appealed to Horthy to ameliorate the suffering of the remaining Hungarian Jews (in effect, the Jews of BUDAPEST), and among other steps had called for Hungarian permission to allow Jews to emigrate to Palestine. As a result, some ten days before he stopped the deportations, Horthy submitted his proposal to the Germans for their approval. The plan proposed that 1,000 children under the age of sixteen, plus 100 adult chaperons and an additional nine families per week, would emigrate to Palestine. Three weeks later, the Germans allowed the Hungarians to inform the western Allies and neutral nations of the offer.

The first news of the offer was sent to Haim Barlas, of the Jewish Agency delegation in Istanbul, by the head of the Palestine Office in Budapest, Moshe (Miklós) Krausz, on July 13. According to Krausz, 1,000 children, as well as 8,243 holders of immigration certificates to Palestine and their families, would be allowed to leave Hungary for Palestine. Four days later the Hungarian chargé d'affaires in Bern, Imre Tahy, informed Carl Burckhardt of the International RED CROSS about the offer in similar terms. He added two important clauses: Jews who had parents in Sweden or who maintained business relations with Sweden could go either to Palestine or to Sweden; and the Germans had agreed to the offer. In actuality, the Germans were not at all willing to allow substantial emigration from Hungary.

The British, the Americans, and the Jewish Agency took the offer at face value, and the Jewish Agency urged the western Allies to accept it. The official response of the Americans and the British to the offer was published on August 18, 1944:

> Because of the desperate plight of the Jews in Hungary and the overwhelming humanitarian considerations involved, the two governments are informing the government of Hungary through the International Red Cross that despite the heavy difficulties and responsibilities involved they have accepted the offer of the Hungarian government for the release of the Jews and will make arrangements for the care of such Jews leaving Hungary who reach neutral or United Nations territory, and also that they will find temporary havens of refuge where such people may live in safety. . . . The governments of the United Kingdom and the United States emphasize that in accepting the offer which had been made, they do not in any way condone the action of the Hungarian government in forcing the emigration of Jews as an alternative to persecution and death.
>
> (*New York Times*, August 18, 1944)

The United States was the motivating force behind this declaration, to which the British agreed primarily because of American pressure. Throughout the summer and fall, the United States sought to convince neutral governments in Europe and Latin America to provide a haven for any Jews who might succeed in leaving Hungary. Most of the Latin American countries eventually made only minimal concessions to this pressure. The Swiss and the Swedes, however, both promised to allow into their countries several thousand Jews. For their part, the British agreed to allow into Palestine those Jews who had immigration certificates. As a result, *Schutzpasse* (safe-conduct passes issued by the neutral governments), which had already surfaced in Budapest, were issued by the neutral representatives to tens of thousands of Jews there who were considered potential citizens of a number of neutral and Western countries, including Palestine. No Jews, however, would leave Hungary during the summer and early fall through the Horthy offer, owing to German opposition. With the ousting of Horthy on October 15 and his replacement by the ARROW CROSS PARTY regime of Ferenc SZÁLASI, the offer seemed to have lost its validity.

However, the repercussions of the offer continued to have an effect throughout the last months of the German occupation of Hungary. Shortly after the Arrow Cross coup, in a meeting between Friedrich Born, the International Red Cross representative in Budapest, and Edmund VEESENMAYER, the German plenipotentiary for Hungary, an offer similar to Horthy's was discussed. On October 23, 1944, as a result of this meeting, the Germans declared that they would allow Jews to leave Hungary, and on November 15, they set the number of emigrants at 8,000. Once again, none of these Jews were allowed to leave, but the mere discussion of emigration gave value to the *Schutzpasse* and contributed to the rescue activities in Budapest of neutral diplomats such as Raoul WALLENBERG, Carl LUTZ, and Born, as well as of the Zionist youth and the RELIEF AND RESCUE COMMITTEE OF BUDAPEST during the Szálasi regime.

BIBLIOGRAPHY

Vago, B. "The Horthy Offer: A Missed Opportunity for Rescuing Jews in 1944." In *Contemporary Views of the Holocaust,* edited by R. L. Braham, pp. 23–45. Boston, 1983.

ROBERT ROZETT

HÖSS, RUDOLF (1900–1947), camp commandant of AUSCHWITZ. Höss was born in Baden-Baden; his father was an officer in the German colonial army in southeast Africa. When World War I broke out Höss volunteered for service, even though he was underage. On his return to Germany after the war he joined the Freikorps in East Prussia, then the Rossbach Freikorps in the Baltic states, and later participated in terrorist actions against the French occupation forces in the Ruhr and against the Poles in the struggle for Silesia (1921).

In November 1922, Höss joined the Nazi party while attending a reunion of members of the Rossbach Freikorps in Munich. In June 1923 he was arrested in the Ruhr district and sentenced to a ten-year prison term, for participating in the murder by a Freikorps underground group of a German teacher who had collaborated with the French. By 1928 Höss was pardoned, and as soon as he was released he joined the Artamanen Society, a nationalist-*völkisch* group that advocated work on the land and settlement in the east, on Polish territory. Höss and his wife, Hedwig, who was also a member of Artamanen, worked for various groups of the society's *Arbeitsdienst* (labor service), which was a device for recruiting members for militant Nazi organizations, mainly the SS.

In 1933, on instructions from the Nazi party and local estate owners, Höss formed an SS cavalry unit that was based on the Sullentin estate in Pomerania. In June 1934 he joined the SS for active service, at the suggestion of Heinrich HIMMLER, who was one of the leaders of the Artamanen Society. From December 1934 until May 1938 Höss held various appointments in the administration of the DACHAU concentration camp, where he trained under Theodor EICKE, the first commandant of the camp. In May 1940 Höss was posted to Auschwitz, appointed *Obersturmbannführer,* and became the actual founder of the camp and its first organizer and commandant. In the summer of 1941, Höss began readying the camp under his command for the extermination of masses of human beings, and as of January 1942 he was at the helm of the killing operation in the installations set up for this purpose in Auschwitz-Birkenau.

A report on the extermination in Auschwitz that Höss wrote while under investigation after the war in a Kraków jail opens with the following words:

> In the summer of 1941—I cannot state the precise date—I was summoned by the adjutant's office to Berlin, to report to Reichsführer-SS [Chief of the SS] Himmler. Without his aide-de-camp present—contrary to his usual practice—Himmler said to me: "The Führer has ordered the 'Final Solution of the Jewish Question.' We, the SS, are charged with the execu-

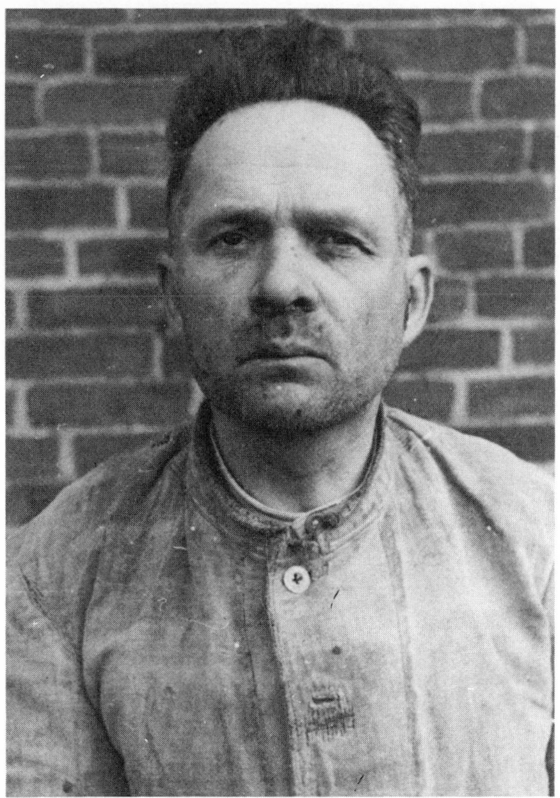

Rudolf Höss, former commandant of Auschwitz, during his trial in Poland.

tion of this task. I have chosen the Auschwitz camp for this purpose, because of its convenient location as regards transportation and because in that area it is easy to isolate and camouflage the camp. I first thought to appoint one of the senior SS officers to this task, but then I changed my mind because of the problems of the division of authority that such an appointment would run into. I am herewith charging you with this task. This is a strenuous and difficult assignment that calls for total dedication, regardless of the difficulties that will arise. Further practical details will be conveyed to you by Sturmbannführer Adolf Eichmann of the Reichssicherheitshauptamt, who will soon get in touch with you. The offices concerned will hear from him at the appropriate time. You must keep this order absolutely secret, even from your own superiors. After your talk with Eichmann let me know what arrangements you propose to be made."

On December 1, 1943, Höss was appointed chief of Section 1D of the SS WIRTSCHAFTS-VERWALTUNGSHAUPTAMT (Economic-Administrative Main Office; WVHA). In late June of 1944 he was sent back to Auschwitz, on a temporary assignment, to preside over the murder of the Jews of Hungary. In that operation—Aktion Höss, as it was named—430,000 Jews were brought to Auschwitz in fifty-six days, to be annihilated there. In recognition of his "outstanding service" in the concentration camps, Höss was awarded war crosses classes I and II, with swords. After the fall of the Reich, Höss assumed the name Franz Lang; he was released from a prisoner-of-war collection point and put to work in agriculture.

In March 1946 Höss was recognized, arrested, and handed over to the Polish authorities, in keeping with the agreement on the EXTRADITION OF WAR CRIMINALS. He was taken to Warsaw and from there to Kraków, where his case was investigated. In the Kraków jail where he was held in 1946 and 1947, Höss wrote an autobiography and a series of notes about the SS commanders in the concentration camp and those who were in charge of putting the "Final Solution" into effect, including a profile of Eichmann (published in English as *Commandant of Auschwitz: The Autobiography of Rudolf Hoess;* 1960). The supreme court in Warsaw sentenced Höss to death, and he was hanged in Auschwitz on April 16, 1947.

BIBLIOGRAPHY

Frankel, T. "The Good German of Auschwitz." *Midstream* 6/3 (Summer 1960): 16–24.

Tenenbaum, J. "Auschwitz in Retrospect: The Self Portrait of Rudolf Hoess, Commandant of Auschwitz." *Jewish Social Studies* 15/3–4 (July–October 1953): 203–236.

JOZEF BUSZKO

HOTEL POLSKI, hotel in Warsaw. In mid-1943 the Gestapo lodged in the Hotel Polski Jews holding citizenship papers of neutral—primarily South American—countries, who were to be exchanged for German nationals interned by the Allies.

Most of these papers were fictitious documents made out by consulates in Europe. Some Jews who had gone into hiding acquired the documents, at great cost. With the papers in their possession, they left their hiding places, despite warnings they were given by the underground and the great risk involved, because they felt that they could not hold out for long in their temporary refuge.

Eventually the Jews in the hotel were taken to the VITTEL camp (300 persons) or to BERGEN-BELSEN (2,000 to 2,500). Some of the people on the last transport, which was made up of 420 persons, were shot to death in the PAWIAK PRISON. The South American countries did not honor the documents issued by their consulates, and as a result 2,500 holders of such documents were deported to AUSCHWITZ, in the fall of 1943 and spring of 1944, where they perished. Several hundred Jews were saved, most of them candidates for exchange with German nationals interned in Palestine.

BIBLIOGRAPHY

Shulman, A. *The Case of Hotel Polski.* New York, 1982.

TERESA PREKEROWA

HTO. *See* Haupttreuhandstelle Ost.

HUGO SCHNEIDER AKTIENGESELLSCHAFT METALWARENFABRIK, LEIPZIG. *See* HASAG.

HULL, CORDELL (1871–1955), United States secretary of state from 1933 to 1944. Hull entered the State Department with little foreign-policy experience from his years in the House of Representatives (1907–1921 and 1923–1931) and Senate (1931–1933).

During the prewar years, Hull's interest lay in international trade and relations with Latin America. The former led him to oppose both an economic boycott of Germany and increased tariffs on German imports. His knowledge of the Nazi persecution of the Jews was limited, although he expressed his disapproval to German ambassador Hans Luther in May 1933. Generally, Hull declined to intercede in what he regarded as Germany's internal affair, but he supported the recall of the United States ambassador to Germany, Hugh Wilson, on November 15, 1938, in protest against KRISTALLNACHT. Throughout his tenure, Hull opposed any relaxation of American immigration regulations.

Hull presided over his department while its influence was declining during the war. He was preoccupied with laying the groundwork for a postwar United Nations, for which he received the Nobel Peace Prize in 1945, and he left rescue and refugee matters to his subordinates, particularly Breckinridge Long. When Treasury secretary Henry MORGENTHAU, Jr., confronted Hull, in December 1943, with the State Department's obstruction of information about and rescue efforts for Jews, he found Hull uninterested and uninformed. The subsequent creation of the WAR REFUGEE BOARD effectively took rescue activities out of the State Department.

Ill-health forced Hull to resign in November 1944. He was replaced by the more interested and energetic Edward R. Stettinius, Jr.

BIBLIOGRAPHY

Feingold, H. L. *The Politics of Rescue: The Roosevelt Administration and the Holocaust, 1938–1945.* New York, 1980.

Pratt, J. W. *Cordell Hull, 1933–1944.* 2 vols. New York, 1964.

Wyman, D. S. *The Abandonment of the Jews: America and the Holocaust, 1941–1945.* New York, 1984.

Wyman, D. S. *Paper Walls: America and the Refugee Crisis, 1938–1941.* Amherst, Mass., 1968.

DAVID SILBERKLANG

HUNGARIAN LABOR SERVICE SYSTEM. *See* Munkaszolgálat.

HUNGARY. [*This entry consists of an overview of Hungary's history and policies from the early 1930s to the end of World War II, followed by a history of Hungarian Jewry focusing on the Holocaust period.*]

General Survey

Following Adolf Hitler's rise to power in 1933, the Hungarian leadership became interested in forming an alliance with Nazi Germany. An alliance attracted Hungarian leaders for three main reasons: Nazi Germany offered Hungary a market for its agricultural goods; it would be a strong ally in the struggle for revision of the Treaty of Trianon, which had deprived Hungary of more than two-thirds of its territory and about 60 percent of its population after World War I; and it offered an element of political and ideological kinship, since Hitler's government was fascist and regent Miklós HORTHY's government was chauvinistic and authoritarian. As time passed, Hungary was drawn increasingly closer to Nazi Germany, but eventually elements in the Hungarian ruling circle sought a way to distance their nation from Hitler.

As early as 1923, the Hungarian racist Gyula Gömbös had established a mutual rapport with Hitler. Gömbös, who became Hungarian prime minister in 1932, resumed his personal relationship with Hitler after the Nazis came to power. Tangible cooperation between the two nations, however, began in the economic sphere. Germany wanted to expand its interests in east-central Europe, whereas Hungary eagerly sought markets for its agricultural surplus in the wake of the worldwide depression. Against this background, Germany soon became Hungary's foremost trading partner.

By the mid-1930s, political considerations began to rival economic interests in drawing the two countries together. Nazi Germany's growing strength and audacious behavior in the international arena whetted Hungary's appetite for the return of its lost territories and peoples. Understanding Hungary's revisionist desires, Hitler offered German support for territorial revision from 1937 onward. In return, Hungary offered Nazi Germany economic and political concessions.

With the 1938 Munich agreement, the courting of Hitler paid off, as Hungary received part of a former territory from Czechoslovakia. This convinced some Hungarian politicians that the Axis would play a leading role in Europe for the next several decades.

Gyula Gömbös (center), Hungarian racist and prime minister, at the Reich Chancellery with Adolf Hitler (left) and Hermann Göring (right) during a visit to Germany in 1934.

Others, however, harbored the traditional Hungarian fear of a strong Germany, which was exacerbated by the inherent brutality of the Nazi system. Count Pál Teleki, who became Hungary's prime minister in March 1939, retained this traditional fear to a certain extent. He tried to maintain some distance from Hitler and did not join the war effort in 1939. Teleki sought to strike a balance between Hungary's desire for territory and its desire for a degree of political independence.

Nazi successes in Poland and western Europe in the early stages of the war confirmed the belief of many politicians that to achieve their political goals, they should cooperate with Germany. Nevertheless, the long-standing traditions of fear of Germany and sympathy for Poland were not totally forgotten. During the first months of the war, the Hungarian government allowed more than one hundred thousand Polish refugees to find shelter in Hungary, which did not help it to ingratiate itself with Hitler.

Throughout the interwar period, one of Hungary's foremost desires had been for the return of TRANSYLVANIA, which was 33 percent Hungarian and about 55 percent Romanian. Hitler, who sought to dominate southeastern Europe, wanted to be the supreme judge of the fate of this area. In August 1940, the foreign ministers of Germany and Italy (Joachim von RIBBENTROP and Count Galeazzo Ciano) signed an agreement, the second Vienna Award, which allowed the Hungarians to take possession of northern Transylva-

HUNGARY

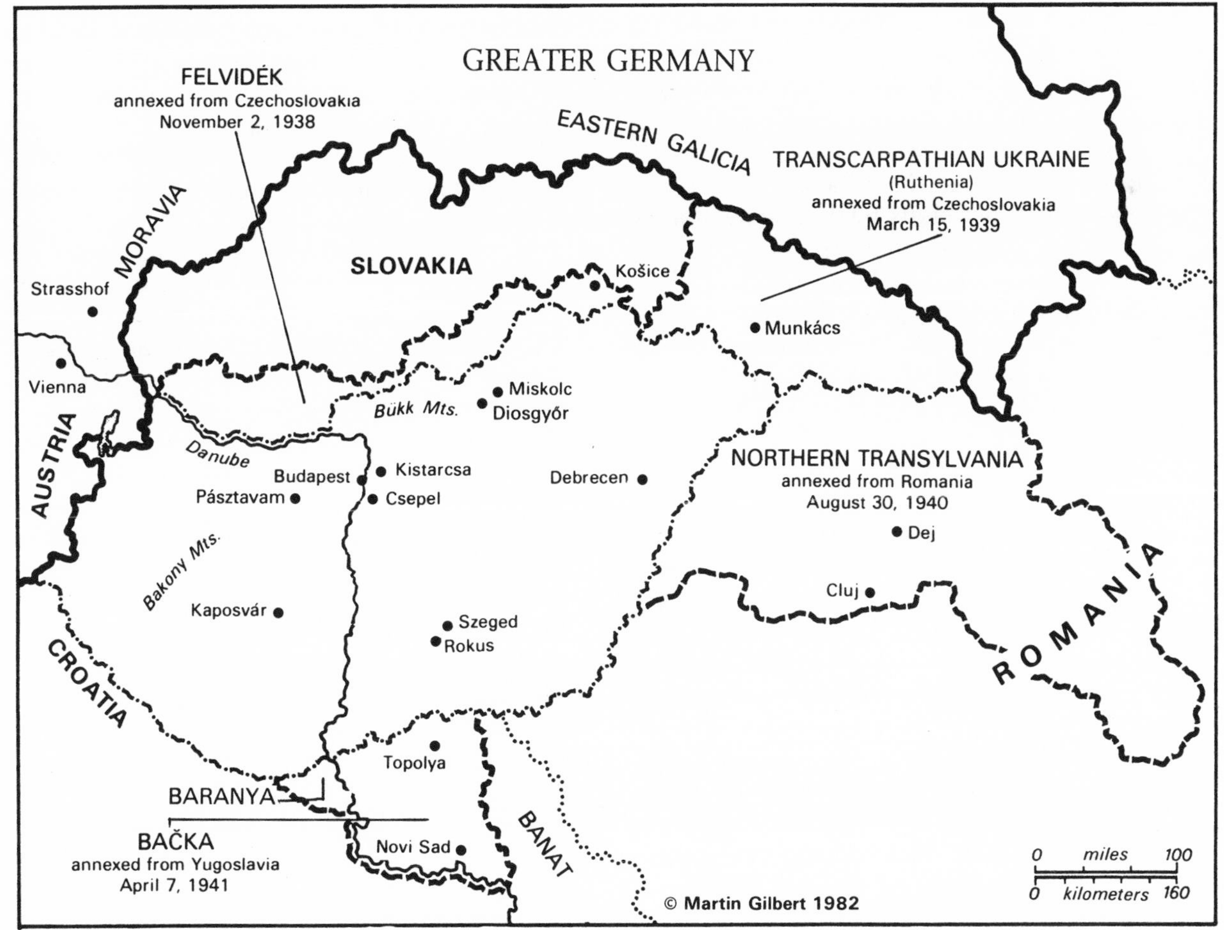

nia and its 2.5 million inhabitants. Most Hungarians regarded this as a major foreign-policy success.

Teleki, however, saw quite clearly that Hungary would have to pay a further price for northern Transylvania. Part of the price had been spelled out at the time of the award. Hungary was to allow the Nazi Volksbund to be the sole representative of the VOLKSDEUTSCHE (ethnic Germans) in Hungary. Soon afterward, through the Hungarian ambassador in Berlin, Döme SZTÓJAY, it also was made clear that Hungary was to integrate itself more fully into the new German order. On October 10, 1940, an accord was reached, calling for better coordination between Hungarian agricultural production and German needs. Moreover, Hungary was allowed to join the recently concluded Tripartite Pact binding Germany, Italy, and Japan. This sealed its formal military and political alliance with Nazi Germany.

Domestically, concessions were also made. The fanatic leader of the ARROW CROSS PARTY, Ferenc SZÁLASI, was released from prison; the ban prohibiting civil servants from joining extremist parties was lifted; and a new political party, which adhered strongly to the Nazi political platform, was formed.

In the first year of the alliance, three major foreign-policy decisions further subordinated Hungarian interests to those of Nazi Germany. In December 1940, as a show of its desire for a modicum of independence, Hungary signed a pact of "eternal friendship" with Yugoslavia, which, except for the Soviet Union, was its only neighbor not yet dominated by Hitler. But in March 1941, following a military coup there by anti–Tripartite Pact forces, Hitler decided to invade Yugoslavia. He offered Horthy territorial rewards if he would join the fray, and the Hungarians accepted. In the wake of the events, Teleki committed suicide, and the new prime minister, László Bárdossy, sent Hungarian troops to Yugoslavia a few days after the German attack. As a result, Hungary received territory with a population of over one million (36 percent Hungarian).

The second major decision was to join the Germans in their war against the Soviet Union. The bombing of several Hungarian towns, pressure from the German and Hungarian military, and the government's perception of domestic and foreign-policy considerations all combined to catapult the nation into the new offensive on June 26, 1941. In particular, the government feared that by not joining Romania and Slovakia, which were already fighting, Hungary would look bad to the Germans.

The last fateful move was the declaration of war on the United States in December 1941. This led to a British declaration of war on Hungary and the severance of all major links with the West. The ill-fated Hungarian declaration came while the Axis was suffering its first significant defeat in the Soviet Union. Hungary soon saw itself isolated, committed to a long war, and at the mercy of increasing Nazi coercion. Instead of being a partner, the nation was becoming more and more a satellite of Germany. In January 1942, the Germans pressed Hungary to send most of its troops to the Soviet Union, and the Hungarians complied.

Elements of the Hungarian ruling elite began to regard Bardossy as too subservient to Germany, and in March 1942 a new prime minister, Miklós KÁLLAY, was appointed by Horthy. A conservative politician, with neither personal nor political affiliations with Germany, he pursued a more cautious policy.

With the Axis defeat at STALINGRAD and with the debacle at Voronezh on January 13, 1943, when the Red Army broke through the Hungarian lines and caused the loss of 150,000 of the 200,000 Hungarian soldiers, Kállay began to work toward extricating Hungary from its alliance with Nazi Germany. No more troops were sent to the Russian front in 1943, and preparations were made to allow more political freedom at home. Peace feelers were put out to the West and a preliminary agreement was signed in Istanbul, stating that Hungary would change sides when British and American forces reached the Hungarian frontier. The Germans were aware of this change in attitude, but they were not inclined to intervene as long as Hungary maintained its economic agreements and as long as the British and United States armies were far from its borders. Still, as early as September 1943, the German general staff prepared a contingency plan for the military occupation of Hungary.

The Hungarian Gendarmerie, which after the German occupation of Hungary on March 19, 1944, became the major instrument of state power in the ghettoization and deportation of approximately 440,000 Jews.

At the end of the year, as a gesture of goodwill toward the Allies, Hungary tried the officers responsible for the massacres that had taken place in January 1942 in the Délvidék region. At the same time, plans were made to welcome the American and British envoys, and Horthy personally requested the withdrawal of Hungarian troops from the Soviet Union.

With the Red Army approaching the Carpathian Mountains, Hitler decided to move against Hungary in March 1944. On March 18, he invited Horthy to Germany and told him of the imminent occupation. Because Horthy feared that if he did not comply Romania would take part in the occupation, the Hungarians did not resist the Germans. On March 19 German soldiers entered Hungary, and a government that the Nazis considered reliable was set up under the former Hungarian ambassador in Berlin, Sztójay. Horthy himself withdrew from public affairs, and various "experts" arrived from Germany to put Hungary back on a pro-German course.

Sztójay's government began carrying out the directives of the German plenipotentiary, Edmund VEESENMAYER. All anti-Nazi parties and politicians were eliminated. After some hesitation, the government also mobilized 300,000 soldiers to try to thwart the advance of the Red Army, which was less than 62 miles (100 km) from the Hungarian border.

In August, Horthy replaced Sztójay with Gen. Géza Lakatos. Lakatos's government continued the earlier policy of seeking a way for Hungary to pull out of the war. This was complicated by Romania's successful reversal at the end of the month. On the one hand, the Romanian example bolstered the anti-German forces in Hungary, while on the other, it worsened their diplomatic position and contributed to actual fighting on Hungarian soil. After a few failed attempts to extricate Hungary from the war, through contacts with only the western Allies, a secret Hungarian armistice delegation arrived in Moscow on October 1. A preliminary agreement was reached, according to which Hungary would give up territories gained through its alliance with Germany and would turn against the Nazis.

On October 15, 1944, Horthy decided to carry out his planned change of course. The announcement was made, but the Germans had made contingency plans. They blocked Horthy's move, taking his son Miklós (Nikki) prisoner and threatening Horthy with the latter's death if the reversal were carried out. The Germans replaced Horthy with the Arrow Cross party leader Szálasi, and Arrow Cross men took over strategic positions throughout the country.

Total chaos seized Hungary. The Arrow Cross began a reign of terror, plundering, pillaging, and murdering. Szálasi promised to send 1.5 million soldiers to the Russian front, intending to draft all males and females between the ages of twelve and seventy into the army or labor brigades. The Nazis and the Szálasi government proposed to follow a scorched-earth policy. Factories were dismantled and sent to Germany, along with livestock. Many train cars and a large part of the precious-metal reserves in the National Bank of Hungary were also dispatched to Germany. The population was ordered to retreat with the fascist troops in the direction of Germany. Whatever could not be sent to Germany was to be destroyed. In November, political prisoners were turned over to the Nazis, who sent them to concentration camps, where most of them died.

As the Red Army overran Hungary, a handful of complete troop formations went over to the Soviets; tens of thousands more Hungarians dodged conscription and deserted from the army. To stem the tide, Szálasi decreed summary trials and executions. Signs of active opposition also increased by November, when the Soviets had taken two-thirds of the country. The Magyar Front (which had been formed in May under the leadership of the Social Democrat Arpad Szakasits) and the Committee of Liberation (headed by Endre Bajcsy-Zsilinsky and Lt.-Gen. János Kiss), which incorporated the Front in November, made plans to foment armed resistance. But before they could put their plans into operation, Bajcsy-Zsilinsky and Kiss were captured by the Arrow Cross and executed. The Rákosi brigade fought the Germans in the Carpathians, and the Petőfi group resisted in Slovakia. Several smaller groups, like Szir, Marot, and Laci, committed acts of sabotage in the capital. Similar groups functioned in the Bukk and Bakony mountains. But on the whole, even at this late date, organized Hungarian armed resistance was negligible.

In January 1945, a Hungarian armistice was signed with the Soviet Union. On January 17 Pest fell to the Red Army, and less than a month later Buda followed. By April 4, 1945, no more Germans were fighting in Hungary.

[*See also* Gendarmerie, Hungarian; Trials of War Criminals: Hungary.]

BIBLIOGRAPHY

Fenyo, M. D. *Hitler, Horthy, and Hungary: German-Hungarian Relations, 1941–1944.* New Haven, 1972.

Lacko, M. *Arrow Cross Men, National Socialists, 1935–1944.* Budapest, 1969.

Macartney, C. A. *A History of Hungary, 1929–1945.* New York, 1957.

Ranki, G. *1944: Marcius 19.* Budapest, 1978.

Sakmyster, T. L. *Hungary: The Great Powers and the Danubian Crisis, 1936–1939.* Atlanta, Ga., 1980.

Vago, B. *The Shadow of the Swastika: The Rise of Fascism and Anti-Semitism in the Danube Basin, 1936–1939.* London, 1975. See pages 115–154.

GYÖRGY RANKI

Jews during the Holocaust

According to the census of 1941, Hungary had a Jewish population of 725,007, representing 4.94 percent of its total population of 14,683,323. Of the country's Jews, 401,000 lived in Trianon Hungary (Hungary according to the Treaty of Trianon, which deprived it of much of its territory); more than 67,000 in the Felvidék (Upper Province), the area acquired from Czechoslovakia in November 1938; 78,000 in Carpathian Ruthenia (*see* TRANSCARPATHIAN UKRAINE), the territory acquired from Czechoslovakia in March 1939; 150,000 in northern TRANSYLVANIA, the area acquired from Romania in August 1940; and 14,000 in the Délvidék, the area conquered from Yugoslavia in April 1941. In addition, there were approximately 100,000 converts and Christians of Jewish origin, who were racially identified as Jews according to a 1941 law and subjected to the anti-Jewish measures, although they occasionally had certain privileges exacted of the government by the Christian churches.

Jewish settlement in the area of what is now Hungary goes back to Roman times. In the modern period, the Jewish community of

Hungary became highly integrated into the economic and cultural life of the country. Especially from the second half of the nineteenth century until World War I, Hungarian Jews became willing partners in the struggle of the Magyars (Hungarians) to strengthen their language and culture in a land populated by diverse minority groups. As a result most Hungarian Jews felt very Hungarian, especially those living in the truncated area left to Hungary by the Treaty of Trianon at the close of World War I. For the most part, this Hungarian national identification remained quite firm despite the increased antisemitism that marked the interwar years, and it continued to influence the response of Hungarian Jews to their evolving situation during World War II.

The "Jewish question," which came to the fore during the counterrevolution that followed the short-lived proletarian dictatorship of Béla Kun (1919), acquired a special momentum during the 1930s. Demands for its solution emanated from a variety of pro-Nazi rightist political parties and movements and from the heads of the Christian churches. The anti-Jewish climate was fanned by the mass media, especially the largely German-financed press. In addition, the Honvédseg, the Hungarian armed forces, was one of the most radical and aggressive hotbeds of antisemitism in Hungary. Shortly after the ANSCHLUSS, Hungary adopted the first major anti-Jewish law (May 1938), which restricted the Jews' role in the professions and the economy to 20 percent. The second anti-Jewish law (May 1939) further restricted the Jewish role in the economy to 6 percent and identified the Jews in racial terms—a process that culminated in the racial law of 1941, which resembled the NUREMBERG LAWS. Hungary also introduced (1939–1940) a unique labor service system designed for Jewish men of military age: the MUNKASZOLGÁLAT, which was under the command of the Honvédseg. The Jews in the service were not allowed to bear arms or, after a while, to wear military uniforms. Once drafted, they

A group of Jews from the forced-labor camp in Bogdany, a town about 3 miles (5 km) north of Budapest (1941). [Beth Hatefutsoth]

were organized into battalions and companies and assigned primarily to war-related work projects. These included building and repairing roads, clearing forests, digging trenches, and building tank traps, at home and along the fronts in the Ukraine and Serbia. Close to forty-two thousand Hungarian Jews perished in these mobile forced-labor units before the German occupation of Hungary on March 19, 1944.

Prior to the occupation, Hungarian Jewry also suffered as many as eighteen thousand other casualties. Of these, around seventeen thousand were "alien" Jews seized by the Hungarian authorities in July and August 1941 and deported to a site near KAMENETS-PODOLSKI, where the majority of them were massacred, together with the indigenous Galician Jews, by SS troops under the command of SS-Obergruppenführer Friedrich JECKELN. More than one thousand Jews were murdered in Novi Sad (Ujvidék) and other areas of the Délvidék region in January and February 1942 by Hungarian military and gendarmerie units "in pursuit of partisans." Except for these tragedies, the Hungarian Jews continued to live in safety, although considerably restricted in their civil rights and economic opportunities, until the German occupation. Miklós KÁLLAY'S government (March 1942 to March 1944) consistently rejected the repeated German demands that Hungary emulate the other Nazi-dominated countries in Europe by implementing the "FINAL SOLUTION" program. It was for this reason, among others, that the Jewish leadership pinned its hopes on the conservative aristocratic regime, mistakenly convinced that Hungary, a member of the Axis, would retain its sovereignty to the end.

These illusions were shattered when the Third Reich, aware of the Kállay government's "secret" efforts to have the western Allies extricate Hungary from the war, decided to intervene militarily. Kállay was replaced by the pro-German Döme SZTÓJAY. The occupation forces included a Sonderkommando (Special Commando) headed by Adolf EICHMANN, which provided guidance and technical assistance for the speedy implementation of the "Final Solution" program. The quisling regime adopted an avalanche of anti-Jewish decrees and placed the instrumentalities of state power at the disposal of a special "de-Judaizing" group, which included László BAKY and László ENDRE, the notorious antisemites serving as undersecretaries of state in the Ministry of the Interior. This group also included László Ferenczy, the gendarmerie officer in charge of the roundup, concentration, entrainment, and deportation of the Jews.

On April 15, 1944, leading antisemites, including Endre, established the Zsidókérdest Kutató Magyar Intézet (Hungarian Institute for the Researching of the Jewish Question), under the direction of Zoltán Bosnyák in Budapest. Advised and guided by SS-Hauptsturmführer Heinz Ballensiefen, a Nazi expert on anti-Jewish propaganda, the institute was modeled after the Institut zum Studium der Judenfrage, Berlin (the Rosenberg Institute). According to the bylaws, its task was "to study the Jewish question in Hungary in a systematic and scientific manner, to collect and scientifically process the related data, and to inform Hungarian public opinion about the Hungarian and general Jewish question." To further this goal, the institute published the newspaper *Harc* (Battle), which was modeled after Julius STREICHER'S *Der* STÜRMER (The Attacker).

The anti-Jewish decrees provided, among other things, for the isolation, marking, plundering, ghettoization, concentration, and deportation of the Jews. The isolation of the Jews, which began with the imposition of travel restrictions and the confiscation of telephones and radios, was completed with their marking: after April 5, when the compulsory wearing of the yellow badge (a 3.8 × 3.8 inch, or 9.65 × 9.65 cm, Star of David) was introduced (*see* BADGE, JEWISH), the Jews became easy targets for the antisemites. This measure was followed by the confiscation and expropriation of Jewish-owned businesses, industrial enterprises, financial establishments, and professional offices. Jews were deprived of their personal property, including their valuables, bank accounts, and jewelry. Although the decree for the ghettoization of the Jews was published only on April 28, the Jews of Carpathian Ruthenia and northeastern Hungary were ordered into ghettos on April 16, the first day of Passover. They were ordered at the crack of dawn to pack and leave their homes within a half hour. Their homes were usually looted shortly after the owners' transfer.

In the rural areas, the Jews were normally first ordered into the local synagogues or community centers, and a few days later transferred to ghettos in the county seats. In some cities, the ghettos were established in the Jewish sections; in others, in brickyards or idle factories; in still others, the Jews were compelled to "set up camp" in neighboring forests under the open sky. The ghettos were hermetically sealed and were guarded by both local policemen and gendarmes brought in from other parts of the country. Internally, each ghetto was administered by a Zsidó Tanács (Jewish Council), which usually consisted of the traditional leaders of the communities. The Jewish councils were associated with the Central Jewish Council in Budapest, which was headed by Samu STERN, leader of the Budapest Neolog (Reform) community and a counselor to the royal court. The ghettos were short-lived, lasting only from two to six weeks. In addition to suffering from the horrible conditions, including the lack of food and adequate sanitary facilities, the Jews, especially those perceived as well off, were subjected to barbaric treatment by police and gendarmes searching for "hidden wealth."

The entrainment and deportation of the Jews proceeded according to a territorial order of priority. Because of the rapidly deteriorating military position of the Axis (the Soviet forces were about to cross the Romanian frontier), the "de-Judaizers" proceeded at lightning speed, focusing first on the liquida-

In the spring of 1944 the Jews of Kőszeg, a town in western Hungary near the Austrian border, were rounded up by the Hungarian Gendarmerie and ghettoized in a building that was formerly used for grain storage. Jews from the ghetto were tortured by the gendarmerie on June 18 so that they might reveal where they had hidden valuables. On July 4 the Jews were all deported to Auschwitz. The photo shows the deportation.

A stream of Hungarian Jewish refugees, survivors of the Holocaust (1946). [JDC Archives, New York]

tion of the largely Orthodox and Hasidic Jewish communities of Carpathian Ruthenia and northeastern Hungary. Then there followed the entrainment and deportation of the Jews of northern Transylvania, who in turn were followed by those living in the northern, southern, and western parts of the country.

The 434,351 Jews who were deported mostly from the countryside ended up in AUSCHWITZ. (In contrast to this figure, cited in László Ferenczy's report, Edmund VEESENMAYER, the German plenipotentiary in Hungary, cited the number of deportees as 437,402.) They were deported between May 15 and July 9, 1944, from fifty-five major ghettos and concentration centers, in 147 trains composed of hermetically sealed freight cars. Most of the Hungarian Jews were gassed in Birkenau shortly after their arrival. By July 7, when Miklós HORTHY halted the deportations (the "de-Judaizers" continued their operations for two days, liquidating the Jewish communities in western Hungary and around the capital), Hungary was already *judenrein* ("cleansed of Jews"), with the exception of BUDAPEST. A few transports, with about 21,000 Jews from the southern part of Hungary, were directed to STRASSHOF, near Vienna, to be "put on ice" pending the outcome of Zionist-SS negotiations (*see* RELIEF AND RESCUE COMMITTEE OF BUDAPEST). Most of these Jews survived the war.

The anxiety-filled but relatively safe period for Budapest's Jewry—confined since June 1944 to living in special buildings designated with a yellow star (*csillagos házak*)—ended on October 15 of that year. On that day the Hungarian Nazis, the ARROW CROSS PARTY, came to power with the aid of the Germans in the wake of Horthy's unsuccessful attempt to extricate Hungary from the war. Thousands of Jews, mostly women, were force-marched to Hegyeshalom and its environs near the Reich to build fortifications for the defense of Vienna. Most of them were first concentrated in the Óbuda brickyards. Terror was rampant, with armed Arrow Cross gangs roaming the streets, robbing and killing Jews. Many of the victims were taken to the banks of the Danube, where they were shot and thrown into the river. Early in December, during the Soviet siege of Budapest, close to seventy thousand Jews were ordered into a ghetto that was established in the Jewish section, near the Dohány Street synagogue. Although relatively short-lived (it was liberated on January 17–18, 1945), the ghetto suffered horribly. Thousands died as a result of disease, starvation, and the cold.

The plight of the Jews during the Arrow Cross era was eased by the heroism of many. It was at this time that the young Zionist pioneers saved many lives by forging and distributing various types of documents, and by supplying the ghetto with food. Similar rescue activities were undertaken by the representatives of the neutral states, above all Raoul WALLENBERG of the Swedish legation and Carl LUTZ of the Swiss legation. Many Jews, especially children, owed their lives to the activities of those associated with various Christian orders and agencies of the International RED CROSS, headed by Friedrich Born.

The Hungarian Jewish community lost 564,500 lives during the war, including 63,000 before the German occupation. Of the 501,500 casualties of the post-occupation era, 267,800 were from Trianon Hungary—85,500 from Budapest and 182,300 from the provinces—and 233,700 from the territories acquired from Czechoslovakia, Romania, and Yugoslavia during the period from 1938 to 1941.

[*See also* Youth Movements: Hungary.]

BIBLIOGRAPHY

Braham, R. L. *The Politics of Genocide: The Holocaust in Hungary.* 2 vols. New York, 1981.

Braham, R. L., ed. *Hungarian Jewish Studies.* 3 vols. New York, 1966–1973.

Katzburg, N. *Hungary and the Jews: Policy and Legislation, 1920–1943.* Jerusalem, 1981.

Lévai, J. *Zsidósors Magyarországon.* Budapest, 1948.

RANDOLPH L. BRAHAM

HUSSEINI, HAJJ AMIN AL- (1895–1974), Grand Mufti of Jerusalem; one of the most prominent Arab leaders in Palestine and the Middle East. Husseini was born in Jerusalem, into a well-connected and wealthy family from whose ranks, for many generations, had come religious leaders and public personalities. During World War I Husseini was an officer in the Turkish army. In 1920 he helped to organize and incite the anti-Jewish riots that took place in Palestine; he was sentenced to fifteen years in prison, but was pardoned. The following year the British appointed him mufti (Muslim religious head) of Jerusalem, and in 1922 he was elected head of the Supreme Moslem Council, a British-created body. Husseini gradually became the top leader of the Palestinian Arabs, a status he achieved by exploiting his clerical position and his family connections, as well as by using terror against his rivals and by taking the most radical and uncompromising position against the settlement of Jews in Palestine. At the beginning of the Palestine riots of 1936 to 1939, Husseini was elected chairman of the Arab Higher Committee. The British outlawed that committee in October 1937 and disbanded the Supreme Moslem Council, but they let Husseini flee the country for Lebanon, where he remained until October 1939.

The story of Husseini's ties with the Axis powers, and especially with Nazi Germany, covers only a fraction of his far-flung political activities, but it has been the subject of much speculation and a variety of interpretations. Some believe that Husseini's collaboration with the Germans was designed to obtain support for Arab national goals from a power that seemed to have very good prospects of winning the war and that had no colonial past in the Middle East. According to this view, Husseini mainly sought a strong ally to replace the consistent support he had had from the British in the 1920s and 1930s.

Others link Husseini's sympathy for Nazi Germany to his enthusiasm for its policy on the Jews, and particularly its plan for the "FINAL SOLUTION." Husseini did not confine himself to the struggle against a Jewish national home in Palestine, but set "world Jewry" as the target of his fight, because in his opinion the solution of the "Palestine question" depended upon a solution of the entire "Jewish question."

Some go further and perceive a general ideological affinity between the totalitarian Fascist and Nazi theories and Islam, as conceived by Husseini. Hitler's unchallenged position of central leadership and authority may have appeared to Husseini to have much in

Hajj Amin al-Husseini, mufti of Jerusalem, inspecting troops in Bosnia (1943).

common with the all-embracing leadership that the caliph had exercised in the Muslim world, and it may have inspired him to seek a similar position of leadership for himself. Most importantly, National Socialism's world view corresponded to Husseini's Pan-Arabic policy (and also to his Pan-Islamic views for the more distant future). Paradoxically, this basic ideological affinity may account for Husseini's relatively small success with the Nazi and Fascist leaders; his global ambitions, even though restricted to Muslims, had a negative effect on government circles in Berlin.

Husseini made his first approach to the Nazis immediately after their victory in the March 5, 1933, elections, when he called on the German consul in Jerusalem to congratulate him on the new regime. It was only in late 1937, however, after he had broken with Britain and had launched an open struggle against British policy in Palestine, that Husseini made concrete proposals to the Germans for collaboration with them. Prior to the outbreak of the war, Husseini sent two emissaries to Berlin; the first, in December 1937, was Dr. Said Abd-al-Fattah Imam, and the second, in May 1939, was a close confidant, Awni-bey Abd-al-Hadi. Both asked for German aid, in the form of financial support and military arms, for the Arab rebellion in Palestine; they also sought public German support for the independence of Arab countries. Official German reaction to these requests was reserved, but Adm. Wilhelm CANARIS, chief of the ABWEHR, gave financial support for the Arab uprising in Palestine from 1936 to 1938. Later, too, the Abwehr—as well as the REICHSSICHERHEITSHAUPTAMT (Reich Security Main Office; RSHA) and the SS—displayed more interest in Husseini's ambitions than did the German Foreign Office.

When World War II broke out Husseini, together with other exiles from Palestine, fled to IRAQ. There he contributed much to the planning and organization of the pro-Nazi revolt headed by Rashid Ali al-Kailani, in April 1941. Husseini also engaged in propaganda activities among the nationalist fascist circles in Iraq who in early June of that year launched a pogrom against the Jews of Baghdad.

When the revolt in Iraq was quelled, Husseini lost his Middle Eastern base and went into exile, first in Fascist Italy and then in Nazi Germany. From October 1941 to the end of the war, Husseini linked his fate to that of the Axis powers. His first meeting with Benito MUSSOLINI took place on October 27, 1941, and with Adolf Hitler, on November 28, 1941. He maintained regular contact with the German Foreign Office, as well as with the top echelons of the SS and the Gestapo, which appointed special liaison officers for these contacts and paid Husseini and his entourage a monthly stipend of tens of thousands of reichsmarks. Husseini was also in touch with the Japanese authorities. Throughout this period he operated on two major levels simultaneously: pursuing Arab national political goals and lending his support to the "Final Solution."

In his efforts on behalf of the Arab cause, Husseini did not separate the national goals from his own personal ambitions. He sought to gain recognition as the undisputed leader of the Arabs of Palestine and the whole of the Middle East, and eventually, as the spokesman of all the Muslims of the world. For this purpose he set himself three goals: (1) the issuance of a German-Italian joint declaration recognizing the independence of the Arab countries and their unity in a federation; (2) the establishment of a center for pro-Axis propaganda and sabotage, under his control, in one of the Arab countries; and (3) the formation of an Arab army, wearing Arab national insignia, that would fight together with the Axis forces, and whose military objectives would be determined in consultation with himself.

Husseini made a special effort to obtain the joint declaration, only to have one disappointment after the other. Its first version, officially published in October 1940, was nothing more than an expression of general support for the Arab cause, and contained no provision recognizing the independence of Arab states or their unity. A second version, which came much closer to the text that Husseini had in mind, was contained in a letter that the German foreign minister, Joachim von RIBBENTROP, sent to Husseini on April 28, 1942. This, however, was a secret and personal letter, and was addressed both to the "Grand Mufti of Palestine" (Husseini) and to Rashid Ali al-Kailani, Husseini's rival for Nazi favor, whom Ribbentrop referred to as the "prime minister of Iraq." The declaration in the letter, moreover, related only to "Arab states suffering under the yoke of British oppression," which meant that it did not cover even the mufti's minimal program.

Husseini's proposal to establish a Nazi-Fascist propaganda and sabotage center was intended to enable him to restore, with the help of German and Italian bayonets, the support base that he had lost in Iraq. In order to convince his interlocutors in Berlin and Rome of the feasibility of his proposal, Husseini presented himself as chief of a secret organization, the Arab People's Party, which, he claimed, had had branches in all the Arab countries since its founding in Iraq, in the summer of 1940. The Germans had justifiable doubts about the effectiveness of this organization (of whose existence there is no clear-cut evidence). Still, the mufti did succeed in linking himself with the German intelligence network in the Middle East, whose outstanding contribution was to give a precise advance warning of the timing of the Allied invasion of North Africa in November 1942, as well as information about its objectives.

The Italians too came to realize Husseini's potential for intelligence assistance. In September 1942 the chief of Italian intelligence, Gen. Cesare Ame, drew up with Husseini a plan for the establishment of an intelligence and sabotage center in Libya, to be headed by Husseini. The British victory at Al-Alamein, in October and November 1942, put an end to that plan. In the fall of 1944 the Germans made another gesture to indicate their interest in an Arab intelligence and sabotage center (even though they do not seem to have had any confidence in its possible effectiveness). In October 1944 they dropped five parachutists (three Germans and two Arabs) over Jericho, and in November, four parachutists—all Arabs—over Mosul in Iraq. Most of them were caught; the Arabs among them were all Husseini supporters who had been in his entourage in Palestine and Iraq.

Husseini's plan to form an Arab national legion, within the structure of the Axis forces, also failed to gain much of a response. In late 1941 the Deutsch-Arabische Lehrabteilung (German-Arab Training Section) was created, under the German general Helmuth Felmy, with its base at Cape Sounion (Cape Colonna) in Greece. By the end of 1942 it consisted of no more than 130 men. The mufti made efforts to enlarge this unit, and called for the establishment of regular Arab formations, which would fight under his command and under the Arab flag. He also complained about Muslim units being sent to fight in the Caucasus rather than in the Western Desert, seeing this as a waste of their potential propaganda value. On this occasion, too, the mufti sent one of his confidants to act as a liaison officer between the Muslim population in the Caucasus and the German command. It was only in November 1944 that an announcement was published on the establishment of an Arab Legion in Germany, which would wear a patch with the words "Free Arabia" and would be manned by Arab students in Germany, Arab volunteers, released Arab prisoners of war, and soldiers who had previously served in the French Foreign Legion. This plan, too, existed for the most part only on paper.

It so happened that Husseini made his contribution to the Axis war effort in his capacity as a Muslim, rather than as an Arab leader, by recruiting and organizing in record time, during the spring of 1943, Bosnian Muslim battalions in CROATIA comprising some twenty thousand men. These Muslim volunteer units, called Handjar (Sword), were put into the Waffen-SS, fought Yugoslav partisans in Bosnia, and carried out police and security duties in Hungary. They participated in the massacre of civilians in Bosnia and volunteered to join in the hunt for Jews in Croatia. A German general named Berger was the special liaison officer between Husseini and the SS. The Germans made a point of publicizing the fact that Husseini had flown from Berlin to Sarajevo for the sole purpose of giving his blessing to the Muslim army and inspecting its arms and training exercises.

Husseini also helped boost the fighting morale of the OSTBATAILLONE, Muslim auxiliary units of the Wehrmacht that had been formed in early 1942 and had fought bravely against the Soviet army. They had been recruited among the Tatars in the Crimea and Caucasia and among Muslim volunteers in prisoner-of-war camps whose ethnic origins were in Turkistan, Azerbaijan, and other parts of Central Asia. The ethnic leaders and officers of these Ostbataillone attended training courses at the Islamic Institute that Husseini had established in Dresden for this purpose. One of the men who underwent this training was Ahmed Osenbashli, leader of the Tatars in the Crimea and the Volga region, who was the German candidate for the post of mufti in the Muslim areas of the Soviet Union. Husseini also appointed a chief imam for the Turkish units of the Ostbataillone, Mullah Mussayev Uthman.

Other plans hatched by Husseini were not adopted. One such proposal was to appoint a grand mufti for the German-occupied areas, to counterbalance the mufti of the Soviet areas, based in Tashkent. Husseini also proposed that an Islamic training center be established with an integrated military, religious, and political training program, the graduates of which would serve as soldier-preachers in the various Muslim units.

The postwar demand by Jewish representatives to put Husseini on trial as a war criminal was based, in part, on his role in the "Final Solution" of European Jewry. Husseini's men attended SS training courses and even visited the SACHSENHAUSEN concentration camp. At an early stage the mufti was aware of the enormous extent to which the Jews of Europe were being exterminated. He tried to persuade the Axis powers to extend the extermination program to include the Jews of Palestine, the Middle East, and North Africa. As part of his general struggle against world Jewry, Husseini repeatedly proposed that the Luftwaffe bomb Tel Aviv. From late 1942 to early 1943, when the Axis forces were about to evacuate Libya, he asked that Tripoli be "purged" of its Jews and that their property be confiscated.

When Husseini found out that efforts were under way to save Jews by means of various barter arrangements, he did all he could to foil them. He appealed to the foreign ministers of Romania, Bulgaria, and Hungary, to the German Foreign Office (Ribbentrop), and to the RSHA (Heinrich HIMMLER) to cancel emigration permits given to Jews, on the ground that letting them leave these countries for Palestine would not only impair Arab interests but would also harm the war effort. The proper solution, he argued, would be to send these Jews "to a place where they would be under strict supervision," such as Poland—that is, to exterminate them. German Foreign Office correspondence on this issue reveals that the mufti's pressure had a considerable influence on German thinking. Adolf EICHMANN was the mufti's most devoted ally in trying to persuade the Foreign Office to delay the negotiations on rescue arrangements for as long as possible. These delaying tactics usually achieved their goal.

In late 1943 the mufti, as part of his propaganda drive against the Jewish people and the Jewish religion, established the Arab Institute for Research into the Jewish Question in Berlin, for which the Germans provided the financing. This was an Arab version of a similar institute in Frankfurt, inspired by Alfred ROSENBERG, which the mufti inspected in the spring of 1943.

Although there was ample evidence to declare Husseini a war criminal, the Allies made no effort to arrest him and to put him on trial after the war. The British and the French were deterred from doing so by Husseini's prestige in the Arab world—which persisted in spite of his political failures—

and by their concern that his arrest and trial might compromise their long-standing interests in the Middle East and North Africa. The United States and the Soviet Union did not want to risk their own chances of gaining a foothold in that area. In 1946 the Yugoslav government asked for the mufti's extradition as a war criminal, but the chairman of the Arab League and the government of Egypt succeeded in having that demand tabled. In the British Parliament and the UNITED STATES DEPARTMENT OF STATE, the issue was taken off the agenda for "technical reasons." The argument was that Husseini could not be regarded as a war criminal because he was not the national of an enemy state (Germany or Italy) and had not been on active service in the Axis forces.

When the war ended Husseini was arrested in France, but in June 1946 he managed to escape and was given asylum in Egypt. In the autumn of 1948 he formed the All-Palestine Government in Gaza, but it did not gain any real influence. During the rest of his life he resided in various Arab capitals, primarily in Beirut.

BIBLIOGRAPHY

Carpi, D. "The Mufti of Jerusalem: Amin el-Husseini and His Diplomatic Activity during World War II (October 1941–July 1943)." *Zionism* 9 (1984): 285–316. (In Hebrew.)

Cooper, E. "Forgotten Palestinian: The Nazi Mufti." *American Zionist* 68/4 (March–April 1978): 5–39.

Hirszkowicz, L. *The Third Reich and the Arab East.* London, 1966.

Nevo, J. "Al-Hajj Amin and the British in World War II." *Middle Eastern Studies* 20/1 (January 1984): 3–16.

Nicosia, F. *The Third Reich and the Palestine Question.* London, 1985.

Pearlman, M. *Mufti of Jerusalem: The Story of Haj Amin el-Husseini.* London, 1947.

Schechtman, J. B. *The Mufti and the Fuehrer: The Rise and the Fall of Haj Amin el Husseni.* New York, 1965.

IRIT ABRAMSKI-BLIGH

I

IAŞI (Ger., Jassy), regional capital of northeastern ROMANIA. In 1565, Iaşi became the capital of Moldavia. The presence of Jews there was first mentioned in the fifteenth century. A Jewish community was established in Iaşi in the sixteenth century, and the town was known for its rabbis, its Jewish intellectuals, its Jewish theater, and its Zionist activity. In 1930, 35,462 Jews lived in Iaşi, and their numbers increased to 51,000 after Jews were excluded from the surrounding villages and towns in 1941. The city was known as a center for antisemitic activity; the Jews there suffered from pogroms initiated by Romanian students in 1899 and 1923. In 1923 the Christian National Defense League was created, headed by the progenitor of modern antisemitism in Romania, Alexandru CUZA. It was the forerunner of the IRON GUARD, founded in 1930.

When Ion ANTONESCU came to power, Iaşi was proclaimed the "capital of the Iron Guard" (September 8, 1940), and organized persecutions of the city's Jews began—arbitrary arrests, oppression, extortion, property confiscations, seizure of businesses and factories, staging of trials of suspects charged with belonging to the Communist party, and the like. In November 1940 two of the splendid synagogues were destroyed on the orders of members of the Iron Guard. The leaders of the anti-Jewish agitators included priests who belonged to the Iron Guard. The Jews tried to defend themselves; the heads of the community did not hesitate to lodge complaints about the acts of the "Legionnaires" (another name for the Iron Guard), and in several quarters the Legionnaires who came to carry out pogroms were beaten. In defiance of an express order, the Jewish merchants refused to open their shops and factories on the Day of Atonement, 1940. The principal activity of the Iron Guard members in the city between September 1940 and January 1941 centered on the "struggle" to acquire the shops and houses owned by the "Yids." The heads of the Jewish community bribed the heads of the Iron Guard, and first and foremost their leader, Ilie Vlad Sturza, so that quiet reigned in Iaşi during the Iron

Annexations from June to September 1940: (1) Bessarabia and (2) N. Bukovina to USSR; (3) N. Transylvania to Hungary; (4) S. Dobruja to Bulgaria.

On June 29, 1941, 2,430 Jews from Iaşi were brought to the railway station and packed into freight cars, which were then locked and sealed and the windows boarded over. The prisoners in the train were not given food or water, and the heat and overcrowding were unbearable. After making many stops for removal of the dead bodies, the train arrived at Călăraşi, 63 miles (101 km) southeast of Bucharest—a distance of about 265 miles (428 km) from Iaşi—on July 6, having traveled six days and seven nights. The survivors were billeted in the yard of an army camp and were assisted by the local Jewish community. On August 30, 980 survivors of the original 2,430 were returned to Iaşi.

The dead bodies were thrown out of the train along the tracks at each of the stops. Here, local Romanian farmers rummage among the bodies for clothes and other valuables, including gold teeth.

Guard's revolt against Antonescu and its attempt to seize power (January 21 to 23, 1941).

On the eve of the war against the Soviet Union, Iaşi was an assembly point of Romanian and German army units, and the tension between non-Jews and Jews increased. Pogroms in the city were organized by members of the Romanian Special Intelligence Service, the liaison office with the German army, the heads of the Romanian military and civil authorities in the city, and Romanian and German army units stationed there. Following the circulation of rumors that Jews had signaled to Soviet planes which bombed the city, assaults on the Jews began on the eve of June 28, 1941, with the participation of Romanian and German soldiers, policemen, and many residents. Thousands were killed in their homes and on the streets, and thousands more were arrested by Romanian and German army patrols and brought to police headquarters. In the homes of Christians, crosses and icons appeared, as well as signs reading: "Here live Christians, not Yids."

On June 29, 1941, dubbed "Black Sunday" by the Jews, of the thousands of Jews assembled in the courtyard of the police headquarters, many were shot by Romanian soldiers; 4,330 of the surviving Jews, as well as Jews collected from all parts of the city, were placed in closed cargo vans and crowded into train cars; 2,650 of them suffocated or died of thirst. Many lost their sanity. On July 2, the police reported to Antonescu that more than 8,000 Jews had been killed in the disturbances. The court that tried the Romanian war criminals in 1948 determined that over 10,000 Jews had been murdered in Iaşi.

BIBLIOGRAPHY

Carp, M. *Pogromul dela Iaşi.* Vol. 2A of *Cartea Neagră.* Bucharest, 1948.

Karetki, A., and M. Covaci, eds. *Zile insingerate la Iaşi, 28–30 Iunie 1941.* Bucharest, 1978.

Lavai, T., ed. *Romania,* vol. 1. In *Pinkas Hakehillot; Encyclopaedia of Jewish Communities.* Jerusalem, 1969. See pages 141–176. (In Hebrew.)

Zaharia, G. "Quelques données concernant la terreur fasciste en Roumanie (1940–1944)." In *La Roumanie pendant la Deuxième Guerre Mondiale: Études,* pp. 9–36. Bucharest, 1964.

JEAN ANCEL

IEQJ. *See* Institut d'Etude des Questions Juives.

IGCR. *See* Intergovernmental Committee on Refugees.

I.G. FARBEN (IGF), German limited company that was a conglomerate of eight leading German chemical manufacturers, including Bayer, Hoechst, and BASF (Badische Anilin- und Sodafabrik), which were the largest such firms in existence at the time. As early as World War I these firms had established a "community of interests" (*Interessengemeinschaft;* hence the initials I.G.), which merged into a single company on December 25, 1925, constituting the largest chemical enterprise in Europe and, indeed, the whole world. Its share capital in 1926 was 1.1 million reichsmarks; its turnover increased from 1.2 million reichsmarks in 1926 to 3.1 billion in 1943. On the German market IGF had a monopoly, and it was the country's largest single exporter. The first chairman of its board was Dr. Karl Bosch, who had previously been the chief executive officer of BASF.

Costly innovations, such as the production of synthetic fuel from coal and of synthetic rubber (Buna) from coal or gasoline, persuaded IGF, at the time the economic crisis came to an end, that the company ought to establish close ties with Hitler. At an early stage Hitler had become aware of the opportunity for Germany to become independent of imports of raw materials, by means of the production processes in IGF's possession. In order to be profitable, the new IGF products needed an assured market, and Hitler indicated that he would be ready to give guarantees for the purchase by the state of these products, in appropriate quantities. At a meeting of leading German industrialists with Hjalmar SCHACHT, Hermann GÖRING, and Heinrich HIMMLER, held on February 20, 1933, IGF contributed 400,000 reichsmarks to the Nazi party, the largest single amount in the total sum of 3 million reichsmarks raised at this meeting by German industrialists for the Nazi party's election campaign. Notwithstanding the presence on the IGF board of several Jewish members, and the fact that even after 1933 Nazi propaganda continued for a time to attack IGF as an example of an international Jewish firm that was exploiting its workers, the contacts between IGF's management and the government became increasingly close, since the products of the great chemical conglomerate were an indispensable element in the Nazi rearmament program.

The FOUR-YEAR PLAN, proposed by Hitler in 1936, which intended to put the entire German industry on a war footing, further enhanced IGF's influence. A member of its board, Carl Krauch, was given a leading position in the organization headed by Göring that had the task of implementing the Four-Year Plan. By this time the company was also adapting itself to the regime's ideological requirements; in 1933 Bosch had still objected—although in vain—to the removal

Heinrich Himmler (front, left), with Walter Dürrfeld and other I.G. Farben representatives, during Himmler's March 1941 inspection of the Auschwitz plant. [YIVO Institute for Jewish Research]

of Jewish scientists from the company and from various scientific institutions, but by 1937 no Jews were left in the IGF executive or on its board of directors. The majority of the board members joined the Nazi party. By means of economic and political blackmail, IGF took over important chemical factories in the areas annexed to the Reich or occupied by it. Bosch resigned his post as chief executive officer in 1935 and was instead elected chairman of the board. His successor as chief executive officer was Hermann Schmitz, a member of the BASF board. After Bosch's death (April 26, 1940), Krauch took his place as board chairman, adding this position to the different posts he held in the Four-Year Plan administration. More than anyone else, Krauch personified the link between private industry and the growing government involvement in economic life during the Nazi period.

In connection with the economic preparations for the forthcoming war against the Soviet Union, the IGF board, with government support, decided to establish an additional Buna works and installations for the production of synthetic fuels. The board decided on AUSCHWITZ, in Upper Silesia, as the place where the new installations were to be located, not only because of its convenient closeness to the railway and to coal mines but, primarily, because the concentration camp then being constructed on the site offered the company up to ten thousand prisoners for work on the construction of the new plant. Board members Otto Ambros and Heinrich Bütefisch were responsible for the Auschwitz plant in their capacity as the officers in charge of Buna and gasoline, respectively. Dr. Walter Dürrfeld became general manager. At first, the plant management protested against the maltreatment of the prisoners working in the plant and their poor physical condition, but Dürrfeld eventually went along with the SS policy, in order to speed up the work. In the middle of 1942 a new section of the concentration camp (Auschwitz-Monowitz) was established, close to the site of the IGF works, to house the prisoners working there and thereby save the time-consuming daily march from and to the main camp. The prisoners' performance, however, never came close to IGF expectations and was always considerably inferior to that of free workers. The Buna production never got started—in part because of the Allied air attacks—and only small quantities of synthetic fuel were actually produced. ZYKLON B gas, used in Auschwitz for the killing of Jews, was a product of DEGESCH, a firm in which IGF had a decisive share.

In the SUBSEQUENT NUREMBERG PROCEEDINGS, which were tried by the Nuremberg Military Tribunals, the United States, as the occupying power, conducted trials against (among others) the top officers of three major industrial concerns—Krupp, Flick, and I.G. Farben. In the IGF trial the accused were the chairman of the board, Carl Krauch, and several of his associates, including Dürrfeld. The major charges were: (1) preparing and waging aggressive war; (2) crimes against humanity, by looting the occupied territories; and (3) enslaving and murdering civil populations, prisoners of war, and prisoners from the occupied territories. All the defendants were acquitted of the first count; nine were found guilty of the second; Krauch, Fritz ter Meer (the board member responsible for the entire Buna production), Ambros, Bütefisch, and Dürrfeld were found guilty of the third. Against the last four defendants, the decisive factor was their role in the construction of the Auschwitz installations. The tribunal did not find the IGF board criminally involved in the poison-gas deliveries made by the DEGESCH company. The sentences imposed on Ambros and Dürrfeld were the most severe (eight years each). By 1951, however, all the IGF officers convicted had been released from prison.

Under Allied Control Council Law No. 9, of November 30, 1945, IGF assets were seized by the Control Council, which in turn handed them over to the four occupying powers, instructing them that installations for the manufacture of war material were to be destroyed, certain plants were to be appropriated as war reparations, and the entire conglomerate was to be broken up. The IGF plants existing in the Soviet zone of occupation were nationalized. In the Western zones, however, no change of ownership took place in the end. Basically, the conglomerate was broken up into its original three major component parts—Bayer, BASF, and Hoechst—whose balance sheet, by the end of the 1950s, already exceeded that of the original IGF. The final IGF Liquidation Act, of January 21, 1955, removed all the remaining restrictions

The Subsequent Nuremberg Proceedings. Trial 6, The I.G. Farben Case, May 8, 1947–July 30, 1948. Fritz ter Meer, the highest-ranking scientist on the I.G. Farben managing board, being sentenced to seven years' imprisonment for his part in the Auschwitz operation.

The Subsequent Nuremberg Proceedings. Carl Krauch, Nazi plenipotentiary for chemical production, who praised the efficiency of the Auschwitz solution of the labor problem, being sentenced.

imposed by the Allies; many of the former top officers of IGF, including Ter Meer and Ambros, were soon again in leading positions in the German chemical industry.

A court of the Federal Republic of Germany in a 1953 decision established the principle that a Jewish prisoner who had been forced to work for IGF in Monowitz had a right to sue the company for compensation. In the wake of this decision and after prolonged negotiations, the residual company—I.G. Farben in Liquidation—agreed to put 27 million deutsche marks at the disposal of the Jewish Material Claims Conference to cover the claims of all Jewish forced laborers and prisoners who had been compelled to work at Monowitz. The payment was described as having been made on a purely voluntary basis and was not to be interpreted as an admission of guilt. IGF did not pay any compensation to non-Jewish forced laborers and prisoners.

[*See also* Forced Labor.]

BIBLIOGRAPHY

Borkin, J. *The Crime and Punishment of I.G. Farben.* New York, 1979.

Ferencz, B. *Less Than Slaves: Jewish Forced Labor and the Quest for Compensation.* Cambridge, Mass., 1979.

The I.G. Farben Case. Vols. 7 and 8 of *Trials of War Criminals before the Nuremberg Military Tribunals under Control Council Law No. 10.* Washington, D.C., 1952.

FALK PINGEL

IMMIGRATION TO PALESTINE. *See* Aliya Bet; Exodus 1947; HICEM; Mauritius; St. Louis; Struma; Yishuv; Youth Aliya.

IMT. *See* Trials of War Criminals: Nuremberg Trial.

INSTITUT D'ETUDE DES QUESTIONS JUIVES (Institute for the Study of the Jewish Problem; IEQJ), anti-Jewish institution that existed in FRANCE from 1941 to 1943. The IEQJ was founded in May 1941, and financed by the German occupation authorities. Its purpose was to encourage anti-Jewish propaganda under a French label.

The institute, headed first by René Gérard and then by Paul Sézille, engaged in general anti-Jewish propaganda, in promoting the "Aryanization" of French economic and cultural life, and in encouraging the French population to inform on Jews and hand them over to the authorities. Its most significant operation was the exhibition "Le Juif et la France" (The Jew and France), which was housed in the Palais Berlitz and opened on September 5, 1941. Aimed at demonstrating to the public in visual form the destructive and disastrous role that Jews and "Judaizers" had played in French history, the exhibition had widespread success. In Paris alone, five hundred thousand persons attended it, before it moved on to Bordeaux and Nancy. Apart from this, the institute also spent much effort and money on the publication and distribution of anti-Jewish literature, especially the bimonthly *Le Bulletin* and *Le Cahier Jaune,* both modeled on Julius STREICHER's *Der* STÜRMER.

In May 1942 the COMMISSARIAT GÉNÉRAL AUX QUESTIONS JUIVES was entrusted (by Pierre LAVAL) to Louis DARQUIER DE PELLEPOIX, an event implying that closer collaboration with Nazi designs had been adopted by the highest echelons of French officialdom and making the IEQJ superfluous and indeed embarrassing, from the German point of view. In June 1942 the institute's director, Paul Sézille, decided to attach it to Darquier's commissariat. Within its new framework, the institute (renamed the Institut d'Etude des Questions Juives et Ethno-Raciales, or Institute for the Study of Jewish and Ethno-Racial Problems) was headed by Georges Montandon, an anthropologist who tried to uncover Jews by means of physical criteria. The institute was officially inaugurated on February 24, 1943, but, except for Montandon's spurious research, it existed on paper alone, and by July of that year it had disappeared altogether.

BIBLIOGRAPHY

Billig, J. *Le Commissariat général aux questions juives, 1941–1944.* 3 vols. Paris, 1955–1960.

Billig, J. *L'Institut d'étude des questions juives, officine française des autorités nazies en France: Inventaire commenté de la collection de documents, provenant des archives de l'Institut conservés au C.D.J.C.* Paris, 1974.

Cotta, M. *La collaboration, 1940–1944.* Paris, 1964.

Marrus, M. R., and R. O. Paxton. *Vichy France and the Jews.* New York, 1981.

Polonski, J. *La presse, la propagande et l'opinion publique sous l'occupation.* Paris, 1946.

ADAM RUTKOWSKI

INTERGOVERNMENTAL COMMITTEE ON REFUGEES

INTERGOVERNMENTAL COMMITTEE ON REFUGEES (IGCR), committee created at the EVIAN CONFERENCE in July 1938 with the intent of solving the growing problem of REFUGEES in Europe. Its first director, George Rublee, an American lawyer, approached the German government to negotiate the orderly transfer of Jews, with their property, in order to facilitate resettlement. In December 1938, Rublee began negotiations with Dr. Hjalmar SCHACHT, president of the Reichsbank. After Schacht's dismissal the following year, Rublee continued negotiations with Helmuth Wohlthat, an official of the Reich Ministry of Economics. The Rublee-Wohlthat plan that emerged envisaged the establishment of a trust fund, based on Jewish property in Germany, to finance the eventual departure of 400,000 Jews from the Reich. The plan also called for the creation of an international corporation, the Coordinating Foundation, to assist in the project. Though most Jewish organizations opposed the plan, labeling it Nazi blackmail, it was supported by President Franklin D. ROOSEVELT and by several prominent Jews.

The Coordinating Foundation was established in July 1939. However, the outbreak of war put an end to its activities. The attempts of the IGCR to find places of refuge, particularly in undeveloped countries, were also unsuccessful. In the first years of the war the IGCR, now directed by Sir Herbert Emerson, ceased to function in all but name. At the BERMUDA CONFERENCE of April 1943, a decision was made to revitalize the IGCR and grant it greater authority and financing. The reorganization of the committee dragged on for months, and the ineffective IGCR played only a minor role in the rescue of refugees.

During the postwar years the IGCR fulfilled an important role in the resettlement of DISPLACED PERSONS. In June 1947 it was disbanded, and its functions were assumed by the International Refugee Organization.

BIBLIOGRAPHY

Bauer, Y. *American Jewry and the Holocaust.* Detroit, 1981.

Feingold, H. L. *The Politics of Rescue: The Roosevelt Administration and the Holocaust,* 1938–1945. New York, 1982.

Wyman, D. S. *The Abandonment of the Jews.* New York, 1984.

Wyman, D. S. *Paper Walls: America and the Refugee Crisis, 1938–1941.* New York, 1968.

ARIEL HURWITZ

INTERNATIONALE BIBELFORSCHER VEREINIGUNG. *See* Jehovah's Witnesses.

INTERNATIONAL MILITARY TRIBUNAL. *See* Trials of War Criminals: Nuremberg Trial.

INTERNATIONAL RED CROSS. *See* Red Cross, International.

IRAQ. The Jewish community of ancient Babylonia—whose territory was part of what is now Iraq—dates back to the period of the First Temple. For hundreds of years the Jews of Babylonia constituted the largest and most important Jewish community in the world, containing the leadership of the Jewish people as a whole.

In the late 1920s the Jewish community of Iraq numbered some 120,000, most of them living in Baghdad (90,000) and Basra (10,000), and the rest in Mosul, Kirkuk, Sulaimaniyah, Irbil, and various small towns and villages, representing 2.5 percent of the total population (25 percent of the population of Baghdad). By the 1930s, the community was well organized and played an active part in the economy and the general life of the country—more so than the Jews of other countries in the East.

A critical juncture in the situation of the Jews occurred in October 1932, when the British Mandate came to an end and Iraq declared its independence. This was a turn for the worse, which was exacerbated with the death of King Faisal I, in September 1933. In the eight years that followed Faisal's death, Iraq experienced five military coups. Iraqi nationalism was on the rise and consolidating its strength, and it was marked by hatred of foreigners and members of the minorities. One of the manifestations of this attitude was the brutal slaughter of the Assyrian Christian minority in Iraq, in the summer of 1933.

The internal upheavals taking place in Iraq coincided with the Nazi rise to power in Germany, Nazi propaganda in Iraq, and the growing tension in Arab-Jewish relations in Palestine. In October 1932 Fritz Grobba, an Orientalist, was appointed German minister to Baghdad, and he succeeded in skillfully adapting Nazi propaganda to the Iraqis' expectations. The German legation acquired an Iraqi daily, *Al-Alim al-Arabi,* which, beginning in October 1933, serialized Hitler's book MEIN KAMPF, and published propaganda pieces praising the fascist regimes. Members of the intelligentsia and army officers were invited to Germany as guests of the Nazi party. Radical nationalist organizations inspired by fascist ideology were established, such as the Arab Cultural Society, in 1931, and the Mutana Ibn Hartha Society in 1935 (the latter named after the commander of the first Muslim force that invaded Iraq). In 1938 the Al-Futuwwa youth organization sent a delegate to the Nuremberg Nazi party rally, and in turn hosted the Hitler Youth leader Baldur von Schirach in Baghdad. In 1939 all students attending secondary schools, as well as their teachers, were obliged to join Al-Futuwwa, and its membership grew to sixty-three thousand. It was this movement that produced the men who were to stage the pogrom against Baghdad Jews in 1941.

The Arab riots that took place in Palestine between 1936 and 1939 gained wide publicity in Iraq, thanks to efforts made by Palestinian and Syrian exiles and refugees who came to Iraq after participating in them. In October 1939 they were joined by the mufti of Jerusalem, Hajj Amin al-HUSSEINI.

Official discrimination against Jews was introduced in Iraq in 1934, when dozens of Jewish civil servants were dismissed from the ministries of economic affairs and transportation. In 1935 an unofficial *numerus clausus* (quota) made its appearance in government schools. Jews who wanted to travel to Palestine ran into bureaucratic problems and had to pay a deposit of 50 dinars, to be held until their return to Iraq; as time went on, the sum of this compulsory deposit grew to 3,000 dinars. In February 1936, some three hundred Jewish officials—most of them holding senior posts—were dismissed. That same year, when the Arab riots broke out in Palestine, physical assaults on Jews were launched. On the eve of the Jewish New Year in 1936, three Jews were murdered. A few days later, on the Day of Atonement, a bomb was thrown into a Baghdad synagogue, and only by pure luck was a catastrophe averted. Anti-Jewish incitement in the form of demonstrations, newspaper articles, and posters became commonplace. A Jewish-owned newspaper, *Al-Hassad,* was closed down in 1938. Antisemitic incidents grew in violence and frequency, culminating in the Baghdad pogrom.

German victories in Europe in the early years of World War II raised new hopes among the Iraqi nationalist movement. On April 1, 1941, four colonels (dubbed the "Golden Square"), led by Rashid Ali al-Gaylani, a lawyer by profession and a radical nationalist, seized power in the country and established a pro-Nazi "government of national defense." In the two months that the pro-German government was in power, the Jews lived with fear and terror in their hearts. No blood was shed, but the war against the British, who had reoccupied Iraq to prevent Nazi control, also singled out the Jews as its target, and the presence of Germans made itself felt in the country. Anti-British and anti-Jewish propaganda was disseminated in the media and at public assemblies. Anti-Jewish demonstrations took place in Baghdad, Mosul, Kirkuk, Irbil, and Amara, often ending in violence. Much money was extorted from the Jewish community, and considerable Jewish property was confiscated to service the needs of the war against the British. Jews were arrested and tortured on charges of spying for the British and giving signals to British aircraft hovering over Baghdad. Police duties and the maintenance of public order were put into the hands of Al-Futuwwa members, organized into armed gangs under the name of Ketaib a-Shabab (Youth Battalions). These battalions were under the authority of the nationalist lawyer and translator of *Mein Kampf* Yunis es-Sebawi, a government minister holding several portfolios, including those of propaganda and internal security, who was pro-Nazi and radically antisemitic. In Baghdad the Ketaib took over two Jewish schools and launched attacks on Jews and violent break-ins to Jewish houses.

The great pogrom and slaughter of Jews in Baghdad and the pillage of Jewish-owned stores in Basra took place after officials of the Rashid Ali regime had fled and before another regime had been installed in its place. Basra was taken by the British on May 16, 1941, but in order to interfere as little as possible with Iraq's internal affairs, the British forces were encamped on the outskirts of the city. This situation was exploited by mobs that on May 19 broke into the commercial quarters to pillage and destroy Jewish shops and businesses. No loss of life was recorded.

Baghdad was taken by the British on May 30, and here too the British troops stayed outside the city. That same day Rashid Ali, the mufti Husseini, and their close associates escaped to Iran. The only member of the pro-Nazi regime to stay behind was es-Sebawi, who appointed himself military governor. According to some versions, es-Sebawi planned the organized slaughter of Jews. He held power, however, for a few hours only, and was replaced by a Committee of Public Order. The rioting began on the Jewish Festival of Weeks (Shavuot), June 1, 1941, when Iraqi soldiers, frustrated by their defeat at the hands of the British, encountered a group of Jews in festive attire at the Al-Har bridge; the Jews were on their way to welcome Abdul Illah, the pro-British regent, on his return to the capital. The soldiers were joined by a mob, and within a few hours the rioting spread to various other parts of the city. Leading the mobs were the Ketaib a-Shabab, which had been trained by es-Sebawi. All this happened at a time when actual control was in the hands of the British. The rioting mobs were made up of Muslims from the lower classes, a few Christians who guided the mob to the Jewish houses, and Bedouin from outside the city. The police took no action, and the Committee of Public Order apparently intervened only when it seemed that the riots might spread and endanger non-Jewish property as well. In all, 179 persons were killed in the riots and 2,118 were injured; 242 Jewish children were orphaned. The number of persons whose property was looted was put at 48,584. Unspeakable brutalities were committed in the pogrom: rape, murder, and the crushing of body organs of babes in arms, women, and men, young and old. Synagogues were profaned and Torah scrolls defiled.

Once a permanent government was installed, order was restored. On June 8, a commission of inquiry into the events was appointed; its findings called for the punishment of the leaders of the rioting. Pro-Nazi elements were arrested and exiled, and the

Jews were even awarded a rehabilitation grant. Nevertheless, the pogroms had created a new situation, as far as the Jews were concerned. True, the traditional Jewish leadership still believed that the 1941 pogroms had been an exceptional occurrence and that the Jews had to integrate into Iraqi society. The leadership was also influenced by the promise of easy enrichment held out by the economic boom that followed the British victory. It even withheld publication of the inquiry commission's report. The Jewish youth, however, looked for new paths to follow. Most of the young people turned to Zionism, and the first Jewish youth organizations, such as Youth for Rescue, Unity and Progress, and the Society of Free Jews, were founded; in April 1942 a Hagana organization came into being, with the help of Jewish emissaries from Palestine. Some of the Jewish youth joined the Communist party, whose prestige had risen, especially after the great victories that the Soviets had scored in the war. Both the Zionist movement and the Communist party operated as underground organizations.

There were more sporadic attacks on Jews in Iraq during the war years, in remote places. Thus, on December 17, 1942, eight Jews were murdered in Sandur, in the Kurdish area of northern Iraq, by Arabs from a neighboring village. The murderers were not punished.

BIBLIOGRAPHY

Goldstein-Meir, A. "Pogroms against the Jews of Baghdad." *Pe'amim* 8 (1981): 21–37. (In Hebrew.)

Hirszowicz, L. *The Third Reich and the Arab East.* London, 1966.

Kazaz, N. "The Influence of Nazism in Iraq and Anti-Jewish Activities, 1933–1941." *Pe'amim* 29 (1986): 48–71. (In Hebrew.)

Kazaz, N. "The Report of the Government Committee of Investigation of the Occurrences of 1–2 June 1941." *Pe'amim* 8 (1981): 47–59. (In Hebrew.)

IRIT ABRAMSKI-BLIGH

IRGUN BERIT ZION (United Zion Organization; IBZ), secret Zionist organization founded in KOVNO, Lithuania, at the end of 1940. Its goal, at the time it was founded, was to foster Jewish national culture and Zionism, which was jeopardized after the incorporation of Lithuania into the Soviet Union earlier that year. The emphasis was on "general" Zionism, the founders of IBZ disapproving of the proliferation of organizations in the Jewish community at the time.

The activists in the organization, including its founder and first leader, Shimon Grau, came from among the older former students of the Hebrew secondary schools, which had been closed down by order of the Communist authorities. Some of the pupils, but not all, had belonged to Zionist youth movements, mainly to Ha-No'ar ha-Tsiyyoni, Maccabi ha-Tsa'ir, and Bnei Akiva. Under Soviet rule, during 1940 and 1941, the organization operated on the basis of underground cells and never had more than one hundred members. Its main activities were the publication of a Hebrew magazine, *Nitsots* (Spark), at regular intervals, and the operation of study groups. Later, when Lithuania was under German occupation and the Jews of Kovno were ghettoized, IBZ also sought to recover the Hebrew books that the Soviet authorities had confiscated.

IBZ was at its most successful in 1943, when it numbered from 150 to 200 members, most of the newer ones between the ages of twelve and fifteen. The members were enrolled in permanent organizational units—companies, battalions, and the like—which bore Hebrew names such as He-Atid, Nili, and Ma'apilim. In the three years of its existence in the ghetto IBZ was headed, at various times, by Yitzhak Shapira, Avraham Melamed, and Aryeh Cohen. In addition to *Nitsots,* which became a monthly in the ghetto, IBZ produced other publications, such as *Shalhevet* and the almanac of the Ma'apilim battalion. Its main emphasis was on ideological and educational activities.

IBZ did not discourage those of its members who were set on escaping from the ghetto to join the partisans or to go into hiding in the villages. In the final months of the ghetto's existence, IBZ concentrated on preparing hideouts in the ghetto, but these did not stand the test when it came during the liquidation of the ghetto in July 1944, and many IBZ members met their death there. The remaining members, together with the

A group of Irgun Berit Zion members in Kovno. Standing, left to right: Lalka Kilson, Shlomo Frankel-Shafir, Sarah Petrobolski, Zerubavel Rosenzweig. Seated, left to right: Sasha Gurewitz, (?), Fima Shtrofan.

other survivors of the ghetto, were sent to concentration camps in Germany, mainly to DACHAU and KAUFERING. Even there, some IBZ members continued to publish *Nitsots*, until their liberation in April 1945. Four months earlier, the IBZ in the camps had united with the underground Masada organization from ŠIAULIAI and with other Zionist groups into a new framework that they called Hitahdut ha-No'ar ha-Yehudi (Jewish Youth Association). Some fifty IBZ members survived the war; most of them settled in Israel.

BIBLIOGRAPHY

Levin, D. *Between a Spark and the Flame*. Ramat Gan, Israel, 1987. (In Hebrew.)

DOV LEVIN

IRON GUARD (Garda de Fier; also called Totul Pentru Țară, "All for the Fatherland"), Romanian fascist and antisemitic movement. It was established in July 1927 by Corneliu Codreanu under the name of Legiunea Arhangehelului Mihail (Legion of the Archangel Michael), which was changed to Iron Guard in 1929. An extremist antidemocratic movement, the Iron Guard gained support among college and high school students, and its activity marked a milestone in the annals of the Jews of ROMANIA. On December 9, 1927, during a convention of Christian students in ORADEA MARE, a pogrom took place in which five of the city's synagogues were destroyed and twenty-eight Torah scrolls were desecrated and burned; in CLUJ, eight synagogues were destroyed and forty-six Torah scrolls defiled. Acts of vandalism also occurred in other Transylvanian cities, as well as in IAŞI. The members of the Iron Guard—who were also called "Legionnaires"—were organized into paramilitary units and operated in party cells.

Before long, the Iron Guard became a fascist movement with original Romanian characteristics, based on Christian mysticism, the cult of death, antidemocratic principles, absolute obedience to the "leader," and rejection of the parliamentary system of government. It also aimed at excluding Jews from all spheres of the country's life, abrogating their civil rights, and, if possible, "purging" Romania of their presence, out of the belief that Jews were the major cause of the crises besetting Romanian society. The Iron Guard leaders succeeded in turning their organization into a mass movement by exploiting the peasants' devotion to the Christian faith and fanning their antisemitism, which the movement's leaders depicted as an integral part of that faith—an ideology that gained them the support of the clergy in the rural, as well as the urban, areas.

Close ties with the Nazis came relatively late, only in 1936, and the Iron Guard leaders prided themselves on having anticipated their Nazi friends, mainly on the issue of Jew-hatred. The growth of the Iron Guard's power was also facilitated by the leniency with which it was treated, and by the support given by various Romanian governments to antisemitic movements—sometimes in the form of financial subsidies—in the hope that the governments could exploit these movements when the need arose.

Under pressure from France, its patron power, the Romanian government dissolved the Iron Guard at the end of 1933. The movement reacted by launching a murderous political terror campaign, in the course of which it assassinated two prime ministers and dozens of other political adversaries. Despite its official dissolution, the Iron Guard took part in the 1937 elections (the last democratic elections held in Romania), under the name Totul Pentru Țară; the election results made it the third largest political party in the country. In 1938 King Carol II banned all political activity, by which ruling Iron Guard activities were also outlawed. On a visit to Germany, the king realized that the Iron Guard had become the most powerful pro-Nazi element in Romania and was a threat to his regime, and he ordered the execution of its leaders, including Codreanu.

In the summer of 1940 the king became reconciled with Horia SIMA, Codreanu's successor, and appointed him to the Cabinet. On September 6 of that year, Ion ANTONESCU and Sima formed a National Legionary government, which put into practice parts of the Iron Guard's antisemitic platform. The members of the movement, within the government as well as outside it, set up a regime of terror in the country against their political adversaries and against the Jews. Their major goal was to strip the Jews of their property and eliminate them from economic and cultural life; to achieve their purpose they applied both racist legislation and violence. Romania's ties with Nazi Germany and Fascist Italy were greatly strengthened, and the country's leaders went out of their way to please Nazi emissaries in Romania. From January 21 to 23, 1941, Horia Sima staged a coup against Antonescu, which failed because the army remained loyal and because Hitler too supported Antonescu and ordered Nazi units in Romania to place themselves at the prime minister's disposal. The abortive coup was accompanied by anti-Jewish riots in Bucharest in which 123 Jews were killed. The Iron Guard leaders took refuge in Germany, where they became bargaining cards for the Germans in their dealings with Antonescu.

In December 1944, following Romania's surrender, the Nazis formed a Romanian government-in-exile in Vienna, made up of Iron Guard men, with Sima at its head. When the war ended the Iron Guard leaders dispersed all over the world, mainly to Spain and Portugal. They were able to avoid being tried as war criminals, since during most of the war they had not been in Romania and were not there when the Antonescu regime committed its great crimes against the Jewish people. These included the annihilation of the Jews of BESSARABIA and BUKOVINA, the massacre of the Jews of ODESSA, and the deportation of Jews to TRANSNISTRIA. Groups of former Iron Guard men are to be found in Spain, the United States, Canada, and some countries in Latin America.

BIBLIOGRAPHY

Codreanu, C. Z. *Eiserne Garde.* Berlin, 1939.

Palaghita, S. *Garda de Fier: Spre reinvierra Romaniei.* Buenos Aires, 1951.

Patrascanu, L. *Sous trois dictatures.* Bucharest, 1946.

Vago, B. *The Shadow of the Swastika: The Rise of Fascism and Antisemitism in the Danube Basin, 1936–1939.* London, 1975.

JEAN ANCEL

ISRAEL. *See* Yishuv.

ITALY. [*This entry consists of three articles. The first is a general survey of Italy and Italian Jewry in the Fascist era. The second article deals with the concentration camps set up in Italy by the Fascist regime and used later by the Nazis. The third focuses on the aid offered to Jews during the Holocaust by the Italian people.*]

General Survey

The Italian Jewish community is the oldest continuous settlement of the European Diaspora; its annals span well over twenty centuries. The emancipation of Italian Jewry, first granted in the kingdom of Sardinia in 1848 and extended to the whole of the Italian peninsula by 1870, was a unique achievement, in both its positive and its negative aspects: in the security, opportunities, and acceptance accorded the Jewish minority on the one hand and in the progressive erosion of Jewish identity on the other. Jews were fully integrated into Italian society and politics and had access to careers in the diplomatic corps, the civil service, and the army—careers generally closed to them elsewhere in the West.

Until 1936, fourteen years after Benito MUSSOLINI's seizure of power, antisemitism on the peninsula was a marginal phenomenon, isolated from the mainstream of Italian life, and the clerical campaign against the Jews (1883–1903) served only to increase the isolation of the Catholic church from the political life of the kingdom. On the other hand, the post-risorgimento period was marked among Jews—at least up to 1938—by progressive assimilation, ever-increasing secularization, widespread intermarriage, and a sharp drop in the Jewish birthrate. Assimila-

tion was facilitated by several factors particular to Italy (at least in their convergence): the numerical insignificance of the Jewish nucleus (about one tenth of one percent of the total population); the virtual absence of Jewish immigration from eastern Europe; the liberal ideology of the Italian state; the "universalistic" nature of Italian nationalism itself (which, until 1938, was defined in cultural and not in "racial" terms); and, last but not least, a curious blend of respect for individual Jews and disregard for Judaism as a religion and as an ethical system, a combination that subtly encouraged irreligion and apostasy among Italian Jews.

Countercurrents of Jewish revival surfaced in the first two decades of the twentieth century, with the emergence of Zionism, the formation of a school of historical studies at the Rabbinical College of Florence, the Pro Cultura circles, the proliferation of Jewish periodicals, and the founding of a Jewish youth movement. These manifestations of Jewish "separatism" gave rise to criticism, given the liberal assumption that emancipation would be followed by the disappearance of the Jewish minority. The advent of FASCISM gave a fresh impetus to this criticism, largely owing to Fascist suspicions of Jewish internationalism and the danger it was believed to represent to the "monolithic unity" of the future Fascist state. Mussolini himself repeatedly denounced "Jewish" Bolshevism and "English" Zionism in his newspaper *Il Popolo d'Italia* between 1919 and 1922; he also warned the Italian Jews not to stir up antisemitism in the only country where it had never existed, adding that the "New Zion" of Italian Jewry was not in Palestine, but in Italy.

The Fascists Seize Power. The Fascist seizure of power on October 30, 1922, evoked a certain alarm among the leaders of Italian Jewry, owing as much to Mussolini's previous invectives against the Jews as to the general enthusiasm that the March on Rome aroused among foreign antisemites. Simultaneously, charges of antisemitism were leveled against the new regime in the international Jewish press; and on March 26, 1923, the president of the World Zionist Organization, Chaim WEIZMANN, repeated these charges in a public speech in New York. The Fascist reaction was swift; immediately after the March on Rome, a member of the Italian government assured the Chief Rabbi of Rome, Angelo Sacerdoti, that Fascism was entirely free from antisemitic tendencies. A year later Mussolini received Sacerdoti in order to repeat these assurances as publicly and as emphatically as possible:

> As Dr. Sacerdoti in the ensuing conversation drew the Hon. Mussolini's attention to the fact that the antisemitic parties abroad desire in some fashion to find an accession of strength to their antisemitic policy in an alleged antisemitic attitude on the part of Italian Fascism, on which they wish to model themselves, His Excellency declared formally that the Italian government and Italian Fascism have never had any intention of following, nor are following, an antisemitic policy, and further deplore that foreign antisemitic parties should desire to exploit in this manner the spell which Fascism exercises in the world.

This public declaration was followed by a confidential remark about the kindred movement in Germany: "I have refused to receive Hitler, and the Bavarian papers have accused me of being a tool of the Jews; when they hear what I am telling you now, they will say that I have myself become a Jew."

The evolution of Fascist policy toward the Jews may be divided into four periods: (1) a "honeymoon period" of outwardly cordial relations, during which some sort of symbiosis developed between the regime and Italian Jewry (1922–1932); (2) a transitional phase of ambivalent posturing, during which Mussolini performed a "balancing act" between Hitler's Germany and the Western democracies (1933–1936); (3) a six-year span of increasingly violent antisemitism, beginning with racist propaganda and culminating in discrimination and persecution (1937–1943); and (4) the final period of German domination, during which Hitler's Jewish-affairs experts applied the "Final Solution" of the Jewish problem to the German-occupied part of the Italian peninsula (1943–1945).

Cordial Relations. In the decade following the March on Rome, the civil and religious rights of the Jewish minority were respected. Mussolini publicly condemned racism and antisemitism, had cordial talks with Zionist leaders, and encouraged (up to a certain point) the activities of the Italian Zionist Federation, despite his objections to Jewish "separatism." It was during this phase that the Fascist dictator began to use the Jews as a vehicle for the extension of Fascist power at home and for the expansion of Fascist influence abroad. This policy found expression in the most important act of Fascist legislation regarding the Jews before the racial laws of 1938: the establishment in 1930 and 1931 of the Union of Italian Jewish Communities, as an officially recognized representative and administrative body, by a series of royal decrees that gave a coherent and unified legal status to Italian Jewry and provided a stable financial base for Jewish religious, cultural, and charitable activities. By the same decrees, the Jewish communities of LIBYA and RHODES were aggregated to the union and placed under its jurisdiction, thereby accelerating their Italianization and "Fascistization."

Transitional Phase. Hitler's rise to power in 1933 marked the beginning of a reorientation. For the next three years, until the outbreak of the Spanish Civil War, Mussolini alternated declarations and acts in favor of the Jews with (strictly unofficial) antisemitic moves and expressions of sympathy for the German position. The Ethiopian war gave rise to fresh polemics against "international Jewry," accused of being the occult power behind Anglo-French "sanctionism." Throughout this transitional phase, however, no alteration in the favorable legal status of Italian Jewry was either effected or contemplated, and no anti-Jewish measures, official or unofficial, were taken by the regime. Mussolini even tried to win laurels as a mediator between Jews and Germans. He also called for the establishment of a Jewish state in Palestine and had "cordial" talks with the Zionist leaders, Chaim Weizmann, Nahum Sokolow, and Nahum GOLDMANN. As late as July 1936 his agents made advances to Zionist leaders.

Antisemitism Increases. German-Italian intervention in Spain put an end to these ambivalent developments. After the German-Italian rapprochement of October 1936, the evolution of the Jewish question in Italy was determined by the exigencies of Axis policy, despite the fundamental conflict of interest between the Axis partners and the divergence of views on Hitler's doctrine of Nordic superiority (which had anti-Italian as well as anti-Jewish implications). In the fall of 1936 Mussolini launched an antisemitic press campaign that, unlike previous anti-Jewish polemics, was explicitly directed against Italian Jewry as a whole. The promulgation of discriminatory legislation was delayed because of the need to prepare Italian public opinion, the desire to avoid a premature clash with the Vatican, continued friction between Rome and Berlin, and a lingering fear of negative repercussions in the Western democracies. When the racial laws were finally issued in the autumn of 1938, it was clear to all concerned that Mussolini had burned his bridges with the West and committed himself to the Rome-Berlin Axis.

With Italy's entry into World War II on June 10, 1940, new anti-Jewish measures were decreed and the anti-Jewish press campaign was intensified. However, though side by side, the two allies never marched in step, and this was again reflected in the field of Fascist Jewish policy. Given his military and economic dependence on the Germans, Mussolini could not back away from his anti-Jewish legislation, nor could he mitigate his racist ideology. On the other hand, the Jewish question outside Italy served the Fascists as a means of asserting what little freedom of action from their Axis partners they were able to maintain. Together with genuine expressions of spontaneous humanitarianism, this eminently political consideration explains why the Italian-occupied territories in FRANCE, YUGOSLAVIA, and GREECE became havens of refuge for persecuted Jews. It also explains why Mussolini, while approving of security measures against hostile Jewish elements, would never agree to the deportation of Italian citizens to the east. Hitler was determined to impose his anti-Jewish obsession on the whole of Europe, including Italy; but until Italy's surrender to the Allies, he was not prepared to jeopardize relations with Rome on a question of extending the "Final Solution" to the Italian sphere of influence. It was only after the Italian armistice with the Allies on September 8, 1943, that he decided to treat the part of Italy under German control as conquered as well as occupied territory, and to include Jews of Italian nationality in the "racial" measures from which they had hitherto been exempt.

"Final Solution" Applied to Italy. In assessing the impact of the German occupation on the Holocaust in Italy, three basic facts must be borne in mind. First, there was the geographical distribution of Italian Jewry. Ever since the expulsions of 1492 and 1541, Italian Jewish life had been confined to the north of the country, that is, the part of Italy that came under German control. Second, there was Hitler's decision (taken against the advice of his experts) to restore Mussolini to power in 1943. Since the success of the anti-Jewish policy depended largely on Italian cooperation, the creation of a Fascist puppet republic had the effect of facilitating the implementation of the "Final Solution" in Italy. And third, there was Hitler's change of mind with regard to the projected occupation of the Vatican. Of all the decisions taken by the German dictator after the Italian "betrayal," this was the only one that benefited the Jews, for it enabled the Catholic church to save thousands of Jewish lives.

Fascist antisemitism was neither a logical development of the Fascist creed nor a logical extension of the racial measures adopted in Africa after the Ethiopian campaign. It was, however, a logical consequence of Mussolini's alliance with Hitler; it was implicit in Fascism because the Rome-Berlin Axis was implicit in the "totalitarian" pretensions of the movement, with particular reference to the Fascist pursuit of empire. The Fascist race laws were neither an original Italian creation (as Mussolini asserted) nor a slavish imitation of the German model (as his opponents claimed) but an unsuccessful attempt to adapt the German racial theories to Italian conditons. The result was a watered-down version of Hitler's NUREMBERG LAWS that antagonized Italian and Western opinion, displeased the Germans, and alienated the Cath-

Jewish forced laborers in the town of Gorizia, on the Yugoslav border, 23 miles (37 km) northwest of Trieste (September 1942).

The memorial at the Ardeatine Caves, outside Rome. Here, on March 24, 1944, the Germans massacred 335 men and boys (of whom 78 were Jews) in retaliation for the killing of thirty-three German SS police by Italian partisans in Rome on the previous day, March 23. The victims were taken to the caves and made to wait outside while groups of three were taken inside, forced to kneel, and shot in the back of the head.

olic church. Far from strengthening the Axis alliance, it added a new dimension to the conflict of interest between the two countries. Worse still, it marked the beginning of a rupture between the Fascist regime and the Italian people, as well as the end of the idyll between Italy and the Holy See.

Between September 15, 1943, and January 30, 1944, at least 3,110 persons of Jewish "race" were shipped from Italy to AUSCHWITZ, 2,224 of whom are known to have perished in the Holocaust. Between February and December 1944, at least another 4,056 were deported to the east on orders from Friedrich Robert Bosshammer, Adolf EICHMANN's Jewish-affairs expert in Italy; 2,425 of these are known to have lost their lives. About 2,700 Italian Jews were deported from areas outside of Bosshammer's jurisdiction—837 from Trieste to Auschwitz, Ravensbrück, and Bergen-Belsen, in which places all but 77 met their end; over 1,800 from Rhodes to Auschwitz, where 1,622 of them died; and at least 82 from foreign countries under German rule, only 9 of whom survived the war. At least 44 were deported for reasons unconnected with their "race"; 25 of these are known to have lost their lives. There were 387 deportees whose date of departure has not yet been ascertained; and 334 of them are known to have perished. In addition, at least 173 Jews were murdered on Italian soil between the Italian armistice and the collapse of the Fascist republic, including 78 who were butchered at the Ardeatine Caves near Rome on March 24, 1944, in retaliation for the ambush of an SS detachment in Rome. As late as April 26, 1945, three days before the collapse of Hitler's hold on Italy, 6 Jews (all of them foreigners) were killed by the SS at Cuneo; and at least 119 persons of Jewish "race" perished in Italian prisons and internment camps during the twenty months of the German occupation.

Collaboration and Aid Given. At the trial of Eichmann in 1961, it was stated that "every Italian Jew who survived owed his life to the Italians." But while it is true that most of the

Jewish survivors were saved by Italian "Aryans" of all classes, it is no less true that such "successes" as Bosshammer was able to achieve were largely owing to (willing or unwilling) Italian collaborators. Thousands of Jews were arrested and interned by the Fascist police to be deported and killed by Himmler's subordinates. Others were denounced by Italian agents of the SS; still others were tracked down by Fascist squads headed by notorious thugs. Not a few Jews had their hiding places betrayed by Italian civilians who were motivated by greed, the Germans having offered rewards for the denunciation of Jews. There were even a few renegade Jews who made common cause with the enemies of their people, the most notorious being Celeste di Porto, a Roman Jewish woman who turned over dozens of fellow Jews to the Italian agents of the SS for 5,000 lire each.

At the time of the Italian armistice there were some 44,500 Jews in Italy and Rhodes, about 12,500 of them foreigners. By the end of the war, at least 7,682 of these had perished in the Holocaust. Of the 8,369 deportees who have so far been identified, only 979 returned to Italy after the war, including a baby born at Bergen-Belsen. In addition, at least 415 Jews survived imprisonment or detention in Italy proper, and a few leaped to freedom while on their way to the extermination camps.

But although approximately four-fifths of the Jews of Italy survived the war, Italian Jewry suffered a blow from which it is unlikely to recover in the foreseeable future. Thousands had abandoned the community, and some six thousand had emigrated; many of those who remained were physically and spiritually broken. The habit of Jewish life had been interrupted, and in many places its very setting had disappeared. Italian Jewry remains only a shadow of its former self.

BIBLIOGRAPHY

Carpi, D. "The Origins and Development of Fascist Anti-Semitism in Italy (1922–1945)." In *The Catastrophe of European Jewry,* edited by I. Gutman and L. Rothkirchen, pp. 283–298. Jerusalem, 1976.

Michaelis, M. *Mussolini and the Jews: German-Italian Relations and the Jewish Question in Italy, 1922–1945.* Oxford, 1978.

Zuccotti, S. *The Italians and the Holocaust: Persecution, Rescue, and Survival.* New York, 1987.

MEIR MICHAELIS

Concentration Camps

Before the outbreak of World War II, concentration camps, as an institution for the systematic isolation and liquidation of political opponents, did not exist in Italy. Persons suspected of being engaged in hostile actions against the Fascist regime were restricted to residence in remote villages, chiefly in the central or southern parts of the country. Political prisoners who had been tried and sentenced served their terms in regular prisons or special wings of such prisons.

This situation changed on the eve of Italy's entry into the war (June 10, 1940), with mass arrests of the foreign nationals among the Jews who had not complied with the expulsion order issued in 1938. Men, women, and children were thrown into jail with no charges brought against them, and were often held under appalling conditions. Three months later, on September 4, the Ministry of the Interior ordered forty-three concentration camps to be established, for the imprisonment of enemy aliens and of Italians suspected of subversive activities. Among the prisoners in these camps were thousands of Jews who were foreign nationals or stateless persons, and 200 Italian Jews who were known to oppose the Fascist regime.

With respect to the prisoners' physical safety and living conditions, there was no comparison between the concentration camps in Italy and those set up by the Nazis in Germany and in the countries they occupied. In the Italian concentration camps, families lived together; there were schools for the children and a broad program of social welfare and cultural activities. For the most part, the work imposed on the prisoners involved only services required for the camp itself. As time went on, more camps were set up, for Allied prisoners of war; one of these camps, Fossoli di Carpi, later became a concentration and transit camp for thousands of Jews who were designated for deportation.

The fall of the Fascist regime on July 25, 1943, and Italy's surrender to the Allies on September 8, 1943, were dramatic turning points. King Victor Emmanuel and the prime minister, Pietro BADOGLIO, fled to the south; the army disintegrated; and the country was divided into two, the south in the hands of the Allies and the central and northern parts in the hands of the Germans. For many Jews, who had been imprisoned in Fascist concentration camps, this meant liberation, since most of the camps were situated in the southern districts that were the first to be set free. This included the largest camp, at FERRAMONTI DI TARSIA. On the other hand, the bulk of the Jewish population of Italy, which for historical reasons was concentrated in Rome and the north, was caught in the German-occupied part. It was in this section that the Fascist satellite state, the Italian Socialist Republic, was set up.

After the north fell under German rule, seizures of Jews took place in all the major cities, where the Jews were still living peacefully in their homes. The German raiding parties had lists of the names and addresses of the Jews and were assisted, passively or actively, by the Italian Fascist armed forces. In Rome, the Germans cordoned off the Jewish quarter, and in a single day—October 16, 1943—arrested more than one thousand persons. Similar actions took place in Trieste (October 9), Genoa (November 3), Florence (November 6), Milan (November 8), Venice (November 9), Ferrara (November 14), and other places. After being held in local jails for a while, the Jews were confined to concentration camps, usually in Fossoli and Bolzano; from there, when a certain number of prisoners had been collected, they were deported to extermination camps, mainly to AUSCHWITZ.

The Fascist satellite state under Mussolini at first contented itself with issuing a declaration of principles, which laid down that "the members of the Jewish race" were aliens who "in this war are regarded as belonging to an enemy nation." Before long, however (on November 30, 1943), this declaration was followed up by an order from the minister of the interior, G. Buffarini Guidi, requiring all Jews, without exception, to be put in concentration camps and their property to be confiscated. Other orders in this vein, issued by various branches of the Fascist government, dealt mainly with procedural matters regarding the confiscation of Jewish property. But these did not affect the situation of the Jews, who by then had either abandoned their property and fled for their lives or had been imprisoned in concentration camps or deported to eastern Europe. In Italy, the Germans—who bore the main responsibility for actions against the Jews and, for the most part, also carried them out—carefully abstained from issuing special anti-Jewish decrees, such as the wearing of the yellow badge (*see* BADGE, JEWISH) or the establishment of ghettos and Judenräte (Jewish councils). They concentrated on seizing Jews, imprisoning them in jails or special concentration camps, and deporting them from Italy.

This last period, from September 8, 1943, to April 1945, can be described as the period of the manhunts for Jews. In these manhunts, more than 20 percent of Italy's Jews (who numbered thirty-seven thousand on the eve of the German occupation) were imprisoned in jails and concentration camps in Italy, and kept there for weeks or months prior to being deported to the extermination camps. The conditions that prevailed in transit and concentration camps were not uniform. Some were under German command from the beginning, others had a mixed German-Italian command, and a third group was handed over to the Germans by their original Italian commands. Some were labor camps; others were transit camps where the Jews were held pending deportation. In one camp, San Sabba, near Trieste, killings took place and a crematorium was set up.

The Fossoli camp, established in 1940 to house prisoners of war, was located near the town of Carpi, 12.5 miles (20 km) north of Modena. In the initial stage it consisted of several large barracks, surrounded by a triple-apron barbed-wire fence and guard towers. Following Italy's surrender, Fossoli was handed over to the Germans and soon began to be filled with Jews—individuals and families; men, women, and children—who had been seized in their homes during the systematic manhunts and designated for deportation. Also held in the camp, in barracks of their own, were political prisoners and Italian army personnel who refused to serve under the flag of the Fascist satellite state. The number of persons belonging to either of these groups varied according to the type of transport that was being readied, either Jewish transports (which went chiefly to Auschwitz, though one transport of Jews, nationals of neutral countries, was sent to BERGEN-BELSEN) or those of political prisoners, which went mainly to MAUTHAUSEN.

Initially, the camp was able to hold 800 prisoners, but by the end of 1943 its capacity was enlarged. Between November 1943 and the end of 1944, at least 3,198 Jews are known to have passed through Fossoli—in other words, more than a third of the number deported from Italy. Fossoli was at all times under the command of German officers, who were assisted by SS men and Fascist militia.

Conditions in the camp were a strange mixture of callousness, starvation, and violence on the one hand, and, on the other, some "humane" habits that did not exist in other German camps. The Jewish prisoners lived together in several barracks, men and women separately; they were allowed to take care of the children, even the infants and those who were without parents. The few possessions that the prisoners had brought along were not confiscated, nor did they have to wear prison garb.

The Bolzano camp was established by the Germans in late 1943 or early 1944 in Gries, a suburb of Bolzano. It had the largest capacity of all the concentration camps in Italy, housing as many as three thousand prisoners at a time. The Jews in the camp never numbered more than 20 percent of the prisoner population. Beginning in early August 1944, most of the prisoners and the entire administrative staff of the Fossoli camp were moved to Bolzano; Fossoli was no longer regarded as safe because of the advancing front line and the rise of partisan operations in the area. Several transports left Bolzano for Auschwitz (the last on October 24, 1944) and then for concentration camps in Germany (RAVENSBRÜCK and Flossenbürg). The last transport from Bolzano apparently left on January 25, 1945; thereafter, no more than eight hundred prisoners remained, including several dozen Jews. The Germans had planned to deport them on February 25, 1945, but they missed the opportunity: the Alpine passes were being bombed from the air, disrupting all traffic with Germany. The prisoners, who were already on their way there, were taken back to Bolzano, where they remained until they were liberated at the end of April 1945.

In its layout and established procedures, Bolzano resembled a typical German labor camp, more than any other camp in Italy. On arrival, the prisoners had to go through the usual routine: their hair was shaved, their possessions were confiscated, and their clothes were exchanged for prison uniforms. Every prisoner had to sew a triangular patch on his or her clothing displaying a registration number. The patches were in different colors—red for dangerous political prisoners, pink for ordinary political prisoners or military personnel, yellow for Jews.

The prisoners were put on hard forced labor inside and outside the camp, working in the fields, making railway repairs, digging tunnels near the camp, and so on. Only the political prisoners classified as "dangerous" were not put to work, for security reasons, and were restricted to their block.

Escape attempts were rare, one reason being that the German South Tyrol minority was hostile to all Italians and especially to Italian Jews. The few prisoners who did escape from the camp and were caught by these local inhabitants were handed over at once to the camp guards and executed, after undergoing cruel torture. An organized escape attempt, through a tunnel that was dug in the block of the dangerous political prisoners, was also doomed to failure.

The La Risiera di San Sabba camp was not an extermination camp in the standard meaning of the term, but it had a crematorium that was used for burning the corpses of prisoners who had been executed or had died under torture. The original structure had been built at San Sabba, near Trieste, in 1913 by the Austrian authorities who were then in control of the area, to serve as a plant for separating rice from chaff (hence the name Risiera). This large structure also contained a furnace and a high chimney, for drying the rice. By the 1920s the structure was no longer in use for its original purpose and was only temporarily occupied, from time to time, by Italian army units.

After the Italian surrender to the Allies, Trieste became part of a special district, separate from the rest of Italy, that was put under the direct and exclusive control of the German security authorities—the Adriatisches Küstenland Operationszone (Adriatic Coastal Area Operational Zone). Two notorious SS officers, Odilo GLOBOCNIK (who was a native of Trieste) and Franz STANGL, operated in this zone at different times.

Shortly after they had taken control of the area, the Germans seized the abandoned structure and made it into a transit camp, bringing Slovenian partisans there for questioning, torture, and execution. Also brought to La Risiera were political prisoners and Jews, for questioning and detention pending their dispatch to the north. Commandants of the camp, successively, were SS-Obersturmbannführer Christian WIRTH (from the fall of 1943 to May 1944) and SS-Obersturmbannführer Dietrich Allers, who had been director of the German euthanasia campaign in 1939 (June 1944 to April 1945). The camp staff was all German, except perhaps for a few Ukrainian auxiliaries. In the period of its existence, more than twenty thousand prisoners passed through La Risiera. Several thousand persons were murdered—generally by having their skulls cracked with heavy clubs—and their bodies were burned in the crematorium (which had been constructed by enlarging the old furnace and also utilizing the existing chimney). Several dozen Jews were among those killed at La Risiera, and their bodies, too, were cremated; some six hundred and fifty were deported to Auschwitz or, as of the end of 1944, to camps in Germany. The last transport left the camp on January 11, 1945.

Apart from these three camps—Fossoli, Bolzano, and San Sabba—the main assembly points for Jews in Italy were in Mantua, in a building that had belonged to the Jewish community; in the San Vittore prison in Milan; and in Borgo San Dalmazzo.

BIBLIOGRAPHY

Baccino, R. *Fossoli.* Modena, 1961.
Folkel, F. *La Risiera di San Sabba.* Milan, 1979.
Levi, P. *Survival in Auschwitz.* New York, 1959.
Liggeri, P. *Triangolo rosso.* Milan, 1963.
Michaelis, M. *Mussolini and the Jews: German-Italian Relations and the Jewish Question in Italy, 1922–1945.* London, 1978.

DANIEL CARPI

Aid to Jews by Italians

During World War II the Italians, more than most other peoples in Europe, extended aid to the Jews. These rescue efforts took different forms and sprang from a variety of motives. The period during which they occurred may be divided into three different stages.

In the first stage, from the beginning of the war to mid-1942, the Italian authorities, and particularly Foreign Ministry officials, gave protection to Jews of Italian nationality living in German-occupied territories or in countries in the German sphere of influence. Particularly outstanding in their range and forcefulness were the actions taken by the Italians in occupied FRANCE, where there were fifteen hundred Jews of Italian nationality, and in TUNISIA, where they numbered fifty-five hundred. Jews were also protected in SALONIKA and in satellite states in the Balkans and the Danube basin. With these actions the Italians safeguarded their own interests, maintaining their presence and their social and economic position, since more often than not it was Italian Jews living in these areas who served these interests, especially in the Mediterranean countries. Moreover, in this period the Italians were still on an equal footing with the Germans and were not prepared to tolerate discrimination of their nationals, irrespective of the "race" to which they belonged.

The second stage extended from mid-1942 to September 1943. During this period, the Italians witnessed the arrest, roundup, and deportation to the east of entire Jewish populations in France, Belgium, and Greece, and saw with their own eyes the unspeakable atrocities committed against Jews in CROATIA. Moreover, rumors of what was happening in eastern Europe had come to their attention. Many of the Italian military personnel and Italian diplomats serving in these places were outraged, and persuaded their superiors in the Foreign Ministry and the General Staff in Rome to give aid to Jews, regardless of their nationality, who were seeking asylum in the Italian zones of occupation. As a result a genuine rescue operation was launched in areas under the supervision or control of the Italian army: in Dalmatia-

Croatia, where five thousand Jews found refuge; in southern France, where approximately twenty-five thousand had gathered (the Germans cited a figure of fifty thousand); and in ATHENS and the Greek islands, where thirteen thousand Jews had congregated. In this way, at least forty thousand Jews who were not Italian nationals were given refuge in the Italian-occupied areas. The Italians treated these Jews in a humane manner and did not hand them over to the Croats, the Vichy police, or the Germans, despite unceasing demands and protests.

The Germans, in particular, brought tremendous pressure to bear upon Italy, on different military and diplomatic levels—all the way up to Mussolini—to have the Jews handed over to them. On at least two occasions, Mussolini was ready to yield to the German pressure, and he even gave his agreement to surrender the Jewish refugees from Croatia. But the high-ranking diplomats and officers in his entourage who would have had to implement this order refused to do so, and by various means succeeded in thwarting this act.

Italian diplomats who distinguished themselves in this effort included Luigi Vidau, Leonardo Vitetti, Luca Pietromarchi, Giuseppe Bastianini, and Blasco Lanza d'Ajeta in Rome; Giuseppe Castruccio, Guelfo Zamboni, and Pellegrino Ghigi in the Italian mission in Athens; Vittorio Zoppi, Alberto Calisse, Gustavo Orlandini, and Gino Buti among the diplomats serving in France; and Vittorio Castellani in Croatia. Among the army officers, Generals Giuseppe Pièche, Giuseppe Amico, Carlo Avarna di Gualtieri, Mario Roatta, Carlo Geloso, and Mario Vercellino were prominent. Also outstanding in this effort was Guido Lospinoso, an Italian police inspector serving in southern France. In addition, during this period thousands of Jews infiltrated into Italy itself, especially from Yugoslavia and with the assistance of the Italian military, and found refuge there from their persecutors.

The third and last stage was ushered in on September 8, 1943, when the Italian government surrendered to the Allies. From then on, until the day of liberation, the Jews were hunted down mercilessly in every place. In this period of endless terror, during which every Jew was in danger of his life, each Jew, whether an Italian or an alien, was in desperate need of help from the Italian people. In most instances the Jews were given such help, by people from all walks of life. On the other hand, Italy had its collaborators with the Germans, the men of the Fascist Black Brigades and the volunteers of the Italian SS. These men represented a constant threat to the Jews, for they did not have the slightest compunction about helping the Germans to round up the Jews, question them, and deport them to their deaths. There were also informers among the Italians.

The great majority of the people of Italy, however, including a substantial part of the Italian clergy, gave aid to the Jews and helped them go into hiding, in the homes of "Aryan" friends, in remote villages, and in monasteries. It was thanks to this aid, as well as to other possibilities (such as crossing into Switzerland or to southern Italy, which had already been liberated by the Allies), that the greater part of the Jews of Italy were saved.

BIBLIOGRAPHY

Carpi, D. "Notes on the History of the Jews in Greece: Attitude of the Italians (1941–1943)." In *Festschrift in Honor of Dr. George S. Wise*, pp. 25–62. Tel Aviv, 1981.

Carpi, D. "The Rescue of Jews in the Italian Zone of Occupied Croatia." In *Rescue Attempts during the Holocaust.* Proceedings of the Second Yad Vashem International Historical Conference, edited by Y. Gutman and E. Zuroff, pp. 465–526. Jerusalem, 1972.

Poliakov, L., and J. Sabille. *Jews under Italian Occupation.* Paris, 1955.

Zuccotti, S. *The Italians and the Holocaust: Persecution, Rescue, and Survival.* New York, 1987.

DANIEL CARPI

IVANO-FRANKOVSK. *See* Stanisławów.

J

JABOTINSKY, VLADIMIR (Zeev; 1880–1940), Zionist leader and author. Jabotinsky was born in Odessa, studied law in Italy, and became a journalist and writer. He was one of the founders of the Jewish battalions in World War I and fought in their ranks. In 1920 he was sentenced to jail for participating in the defense of Jerusalem during bloody riots that took place in the city, but was pardoned. Jabotinsky was a member of the Zionist Executive but resigned. In 1925 he established the Revisionist movement, becoming its leader and the head of Betar, the Revisionist youth movement. From 1936 he was also supreme commander of Irgun Tseva'i Le'ummi.

Vladimir Jabotinsky. [Central Zionist Archives, Jerusalem]

When Hitler came to power in Germany, it was Jabotinsky's view that Nazi antisemitism was "the most significant component" in the Nazi party's collective soul. Like other Jewish leaders, however, he did not consider Hitler's MEIN KAMPF a blueprint for extermination, although he was not at all optimistic about the Nazi regime and did not exclude the possibility that it would maintain itself for a long time. Jabotinsky was inclined to regard the Hitler regime as based on weak foundations resting solely on Jew-hatred, and incapable of realizing its dream of a Greater Germany. The Third Reich, he thought, was "no more than a trite episode in the story of Jewish suffering." Jabotinsky felt that the Nazis' aim was to gain the support of the *petite bourgeoisie* (lower middle class) and the German intelligentsia by destroying the role played by the Jewish merchants and the Jewish intelligentsia. When the anti-Nazi boycott movement was launched (*see* BOYCOTTS, ANTI-NAZI), Jabotinsky assumed that it would turn international public opinion against the Nazis and might lead to Hitler's downfall. Consequently, he was strongly opposed to the

HAAVARA AGREEMENT, which was intended to facilitate the emigration of Jews from Germany and enable them to take out part of their assets.

All his life Jabotinsky believed in a theory of antisemitism that he had developed, following in the footsteps of Theodor Herzl and Max Nordau. According to this theory there were two kinds of antisemitism: the "subjective antisemitism of people" and the "antisemitism of objective reality." The latter was represented by Polish antisemitism, which was the most threatening and foreshadowed a "social earthquake"; on the other hand, the antisemitism found in Germany, Romania, and Hungary was "subjective antisemitism," a form of virulent animosity with its ups and downs. But even when it is on the rise only a minority pursues it actively, while the rest are pulled along. This antisemitism is flexible, and when its protagonists are ordered to cease and desist, they obey.

There is no truth to the widely held belief that Jabotinsky foresaw the extermination of the Jews, from either "subjective antisemitism" or "antisemitism of objective reality." In his opinion, the solution to the question of the Jews of Europe lay in "evacuation": the transfer, within ten years, of 1.5 million Jews from eastern Europe to Palestine—on both banks of the Jordan—so as to save them from the ongoing erosion of their social and economic status. The deterioration of the situation of the Jews following KRISTALLNACHT caused Jabotinsky to revise his "Ten-Year Plan," and he called for the immediate emigration to Palestine of a million Jews. He did not expect a second world war to break out; when Hitler occupied Prague in March 1939, Jabotinsky said that war between the great powers was impossible, except for a war between Japan and the Soviet Union. When war did begin, he realized that he had erred in not foreseeing it, but he doubted that the war would widen and (in January 1940) expected that the warring powers would enter negotiations.

Jabotinsky kept careful track of the Nazi massacres of Jews in Poland that the Jewish Telegraphic Agency was reporting, while the general press was ignoring some of these reports. He collected the reports, but did not revise his theory of differentiating between "objective" and "subjective" antisemitism—despite his finding that the loss of life suffered by the Jews was higher than that of the combined losses of the Polish and German armies (except for the losses in actual combat) and that the agony the Jews were experiencing was worse than that of any other people.

After war had broken out, Jabotinsky concentrated mainly on raising the demands of the Jewish people, as conceived by the Zionist Revisionist movement, and obtaining the recognition of these demands as war aims by the Allies that were at war with Hitler. The Lublin Reservation project (*see* NISKO AND LUBLIN PLAN) was in his eyes a "confused improvisation" by the Germans that might vanish from the scene, but that might also develop into a broad solution. Jabotinsky's estimate of the Nazi murders in Poland was that they did not exceed the usual pattern of pogroms; hence his demand that after the war the Jews of Poland be granted equal rights, but that the Allied powers had to realize that Poland alone could not be expected to bear the whole burden of the Jewish problem on its shoulders. In sum, Jabotinsky did not consider Nazi antisemitism as a new phenomenon, but rather as part of nineteenth-century German antisemitism, a tradition that claimed adherents from Arthur Schopenhauer to Houston Stewart CHAMBERLAIN, which political parties had turned into a political doctrine. On the eve of his death Jabotinsky was of the belief that most of the Jews of Europe would survive.

Jabotinsky died when the war had been in progress for only eleven months. At that point, only a very few envisaged the possibility of a holocaust on the scale that in fact took place.

BIBLIOGRAPHY

Jabotinsky, V. *The Jewish War Front.* London, 1940.

Schechtman, J. B. *The Vladimir Jabotinsky Story.* 2 vols. New York, 1956, 1961.

JOSEPH HELLER

JÄGER, KARL (1888–1959), SS officer. Jäger was born in Schaffhausen, Switzerland, and engaged in commerce. He joined the Nazi

Karl Jäger. [National Archives]

party in 1923 and the SS in 1932. Beginning in 1935 he served in Ludwigsburg, Ravensburg, and Münster, successively. In Münster, where he was assigned in 1938, he was appointed chief of the SD (Sicherheitsdienst; Security Service). After serving in the occupied Netherlands for a time, Jäger was appointed commanding officer of Einsatzkommando 3 in Einsatzgruppe A, which was attached to an army corps in northern Soviet Russia. He later became commander of the Sicherheitspolizei (Security Police) and SD for the General Commissariat of LITHUANIA in Kovno, with the rank of SS-*Standartenführer.*

In this capacity, Jäger was in charge of the extermination of Lithuanian Jewry, as witnessed by the reports that he submitted. In a report dated December 1, 1941, Jäger stated: "There are no more Jews in Lithuania, except for those in three small ghettos, ŠIAULIAI, KOVNO, and VILNA." In another report, of February 9, 1942, Jäger summed up the killings accomplished by the unit under his command: 136,421 Jews, 1,064 Communists, 653 mentally ill persons, and 134 others. Among the 138,272 victims there were 55,556 women and 34,464 children.

In the fall of 1943 Jäger was reassigned to Germany and was appointed chief of police in Reichenberg, in the Sudetenland. When the war ended he succeeded in assuming a false identity and became a farmer. In April 1959 he was arrested, and on June 22 of that year he committed suicide in his cell.

BIBLIOGRAPHY

Krausnick, H., and H.-H. Wilhelm. *Die Truppe des Weltanschauungskrieges: Die Einsatzgruppen der Sicherheitspolizei und des SD, 1938–1942.* Stuttgart, 1981.

YAACOV LOZOWICK

JANÓWSKA, labor and extermination camp situated in the suburbs of LVOV, in the Ukrainian SSR. In September 1941 the Germans set up a factory on Lvov's Janówska Street, to service the needs of the German army. Soon after, they expanded it into a network of factories as part of the DEUTSCHE AUSRÜSTUNGSWERKE (German Armament Works), a division of the SS. From their inception, these factories used the Jews of Lvov as forced labor; in September 1941, 350 Jews were employed there, and by the end of October their number had risen to 600. At that point the factories' status underwent a change: the area in which they were located became a restricted camp, enclosed by barbed wire, which the Jews were not permitted to leave. In 1942 the labor in the camp was intensified and its inmates were employed in metalwork and carpentry. They were also given jobs with no practical purpose, such as digging trenches and moving loads from one place to another, in order to break the prisoners in body and spirit before dispatching them to their death.

At the beginning of November 1941, the Germans asked the Lvov JUDENRAT (Jewish Council) to supply more workers for the camp, but the Judenrat chairman, Dr. Joseph Parnes, refused to comply. As a result, he was executed. In the wake of an *Aktion* against the Jews of the city in March 1942, several hundred more Jews were put into the camp. When the mass deportation of Jews from Eastern Galicia to the BEŁŻEC extermination camp began during that month, the role of the Janówska camp changed: from time to time, groups of Jews from towns and villages in the area were interned there before being sent on to their death. Inside the camp, *Selektionen* classified some as fit for work; these stayed behind, while the others were dispatched to Bełżec. Later in the spring of that year the camp was enlarged and took on the character of a concentration camp, with beatings and killings, starvation and disease becoming the lot of its prisoners. In an effort to ease their plight, the Lvov Judenrat, together with the prisoners' families, organized a committee that sent food to the camp. Only a fraction of it reached the prisoners, however, the bulk being confiscated by the camp staff.

Following *Aktionen* in Lvov in the summer of 1942, thousands more Jews were put into the camp. By mid-1943 Janówska, while still functioning as a labor camp, was being turned into an extermination camp. Fewer prisoners were employed in the factories inside the camp and in the city and the length of stay of newcomers was shortened, most being taken directly to places of execution on the city outskirts. In the middle of May 1943 over six thousand Jews were murdered. The harassment and killing of Jews were directed by the exceptionally cruel German camp commanders and staff, among them Obersturmführer Fritz Gebauer, Untersturmführer Gustav Wilhaus, Hauptscharführer Joseph Grzimek, and Obersturmführer Wilhelm Rokita.

Despite the reign of terror in the camp, there were cases of mutual help and even efforts at organizing resistance. In particular, the prisoners tried to help those who were ill, so that they would not be put to death immediately. In the middle of 1943, attempts were made to form resistance groups in the camp. Underground activists among the prisoners smuggled in arms with the help of prisoners whose place of work was on the outside; the aim was to offer armed resistance when the camp was about to be liquidated. The liquidation did in fact begin in November 1943, and it has been suggested that the Germans advanced the date in order to preempt a general uprising in the camp. While the Jewish underground did not have the time to organize such an uprising, there were instances when prisoners at-

The Janówska camp orchestra played while the inmates set out to work and when they returned. It was established by the Germans, who amused themselves by mocking and humiliating the inmates.

tempted armed resistance while being taken to the execution sites. On November 19, a revolt broke out among the group of prisoners known as Sonderkommando 1005 (*see* AKTION 1005), who had the task of collecting and cremating the bodies of the victims. Several of the guards were killed and some among the Sonderkommando escaped, although most were caught and executed.

No precise figures are available on the number of Jews who perished in the Janówska camp, but it is estimated that tens of thousands of Jews from Lvov and Eastern Galicia met their death there.

BIBLIOGRAPHY

Kahana, D. *Lvov Ghetto Diary*. Jerusalem, 1978. (In Hebrew.)

Schoenfeld, J. *Holocaust Memoirs: Jews in the Lwow Ghetto, the Janowski Concentration Camp, and as Deportees in Siberia*. Hoboken, 1985. See pages 125–153.

Wells, L. *The Janowska Road*. New York, 1963.

Zadereczki, T. *When the Swastika Ruled in Lvov: The Destruction of the Jewish Community as Seen by a Polish Author*. Jerusalem, 1982. (In Hebrew.)

AHARON WEISS

JAPAN. Japan's policy toward the Jews during the Hitler era was anomalous. A full partner in the Berlin-Rome Axis, and greatly influenced by Nazi propaganda, Japan had its own influential "experts on Jewish affairs" who wrote as well as translated antisemitic works and sponsored antisemitic fairs that were subsidized by the German Ministry of Foreign Affairs. Yet the fifteen thousand or so stateless Russian Jews living in eight communities of northern China and Manchuria under Japanese control were granted legal status. Within this status, the Jewish refugees were recognized as one of the Manchurian nationalities and were enabled to carry out their autonomous community affairs within the laws of the country. As part of this, the Japanese government officially recognized their Zionist organization. Moreover, during this period, Japan provided a haven from Hitler's clutches for about seventeen thousand Jewish refugees from Germany, Austria, and Poland, in SHANGHAI.

At a secret Five Ministers' Conference on December 6, 1938, only a few weeks after the KRISTALLNACHT pogrom, when thousands of central European Jews were seeking refuge, Japan formulated a pro-Jewish policy enabling thousands of Jews to immigrate to the Japanese-occupied sector of the International Settlement in Shanghai, without visas or papers of any kind. This was at a time when the world's doors were virtually closed to Jewish refugees.

This singular behavior can be explained by the influence on Tokyo of Japanese "experts on Jews": middle-echelon officers in the Japanese army and navy, such as Col. Senko Yasue and Capt. Koreshige Inuzuka. Yasue, Inuzuka, and their dozen or so colleagues sincerely believed the canard, found in the PROTOCOLS OF THE ELDERS OF ZION and other antisemitic books, that world Jewry had conspired to bring about the downfall of the Russian, German, and Austro-Hungarian empires during World War I and wielded decisive financial and political power on the international scene, especially in Western countries such as the United States and Great Britain.

To the Japanese "experts," the validity of the notion of the Jews as rich, influential financiers was confirmed by the one Jew familiar to every Japanese: Jacob Schiff, the head of Kuhn, Loeb and Company, a New York–based banking firm. With the help of the Jewish banking firm M. M. Warburg and Company, of Germany, and of Sir Ernest Cassel in England, Schiff floated four crucial loans for Japan during the Russo-Japanese War (1904–1905). Schiff was the first Westerner to be honored by the emperor, and his name became a household word in Japan.

Throughout the 1920s and 1930s, Inuzuka, Yasue, and their fellow "experts on Jews" wrote books containing such statements as:

> The Bolshevik Revolution is part of the Jewish plot. . . . Zionism seems to be the goal of the Jews, but they actually want to control the world's economy, politics, and diplomacy. . . . The Jewish plot must be destroyed by force. . . . The Jews are responsible for the American and European control of the Chinese Nationalist government. . . . The Jews control the American press and thereby public opinion, turning it against Japan. . . . They are responsible for the immorality of the Japanese youth.

The existence of such antisemitism among the Japanese, who were barely aware of the existence of Jews, can be understood only in light of Japan's painful process of modernization in the late nineteenth and early twentieth centuries. Along with industrial, technical, and military innovations came the inevitable flood of Western concepts, which were in direct conflict with Japan's ancient culture and traditional values. The sacrosanct nature of family and nation headed by a revered emperor was antithetical to democracy's emphasis on the individual. Especially disturbed were the ultranationalists, both military and civilian, who resented this "intrusion" from the West. Imbued with the agrarian myth of an earlier, more innocent age, they sought, unsuccessfully, to hinder technological progress, which must inevitably lead to social acculturation as well. Like their counterparts in Russia, Germany, and even the United States, they truly believed in the canards of the *Protocols* or *The International Jew*, which portrayed the Jew as the ultimate cause of international and domestic problems. In the minds of the less sophisticated Japanese, it appeared only logical that since Jews controlled the United States and Britain, which represented the West, the Jews and the West were synonymous. Thus, antisemitic books were written with "Jew" in the title, but nowhere in the entire text were Jews mentioned.

In contrast to the Western tradition of antisemitism, however, the Japanese lacked two millennia of hatred of the Jews as "perpetrators of deicide," and this gave their antisemitism its peculiarly Japanese pragmatic twist. Japanese ultranationalists intended to apply the Western version of antisemitism and "Jewish power" to Japan's "New Order" in East Asia. But while writing the most vicious antisemitic works, in practice they inspired Japan's pro-Jewish policy and personally treated Jews well.

The transition from theory to practice began to take shape after Japan occupied Manchuria in 1931 and 1932. Yasue, Inuzuka, and their dozen or so colleagues were leaders of the military and civilian political clique, known as the Manchurian faction, that pushed for the Manchurian takeover. Its goal was the development of Manchuria and its vast resources, which were vital to Japan's defense. Two to three billion dollars were required to finance the Manchurian project, and their assumption was that if Japan treated the Jews in East Asia well, the Jews in turn would convince their rich and influential co-religionists in the United States to emulate Schiff's loans.

Moreover, these Russian or Sephardic Jews, or German refugees, residing peacefully under benign Japanese rule, would also, through their influential fellow Jews, mitigate America's negative policy toward Japan. After Japan occupied Manchuria, and especially after the start of hostilities with China in 1937, United States policy toward Japan was extremely harsh and inflexible. For example, in 1938 the United States established an embargo against Japan that withheld scrap iron and oil crucial to Japan's industrial and military needs. The Japanese also looked on the refugees from Germany as potential hostages and as possessing the scientific knowledge necessary for Manchurian development. At the same time, to counterbalance the Soviet Jewish "homeland" in nearby Birobidzhan, these Jewish inhabitants of Manchuria would be offered a Zionist state of their own.

Around 1936, Gisuke Ayukawa, the industrialist member of the Manchurian faction, formulated his plans for the industrialization of Manchuria, to be underwritten by American capital. Thus, the pro-Jewish policy received a further stimulus. It came to full fruition at the Five Ministers' Conference of 1938, which resulted in an open-door policy for central European refugees fleeing to Shanghai and opened an era of goodwill toward Jews that lasted until the outbreak of the war in the Pacific, on December 7, 1941.

The first beneficiaries of the pro-Jewish policy were the stateless Russian Jews living under Japanese hegemony in Manchuria, who suffered from White Russian antisemitism and from economic pressure exerted by the Japanese during the early 1930s. Though many were impelled to leave for the freer economic atmosphere of Shanghai and Tientsin, those who remained finally achieved legal status and protection. None other than Colonel Yasue was made the liaison between the Japanese authorities and the Jews. He promptly closed *Nash Put,* the White Russian antisemitic newspaper, and in 1937 he helped organize the first of three annual Far Eastern conferences of Russian Jewish communities. These conferences were attended by a thousand delegates, and the Zionist flag flew alongside the flags of Japan and Manchuria, while uniformed members of the Zionist youth movement Betar joined Japanese soldiers in standing guard. In 1941 Yasue went to Palestine, where he was inscribed in the Golden Book of the Jewish National Fund. He is remembered fondly by Jews of that era—all this while pseudonymously writing books such as *The Jewish Control of the World* and translating the *Protocols of the Elders of Zion.*

At the same time, Captain Inuzuka served as his counterpart in Shanghai, where he headed the Bureau of Jewish Affairs and tried to effect his goal of a Jewish settlement in Shanghai, instead of in Manchuria. His objectives came somewhat closer to fruition with the arrival of the Jewish refugees from 1938 to 1941. They were permitted entry into Shanghai despite efforts by the Western members of the governing body of the International Settlement, including the United States and Britain, to keep them out.

In November 1940, soon after the signing of the Tripartite Pact between Germany, Italy, and Japan, and to the consternation of the German Ministry of Foreign Affairs, Inuzuka broadcast a pro-Jewish message on the Tokyo radio, in which he contrasted Japan's favorable treatment of the Jews with that of the Nazis. At the same time, under a pseudonym, he published a translation of the *Protocols,* lauded by the same unwitting Germans.

Then, in early 1941, when more than a thousand Polish Jewish refugees found themselves stranded in Kōbe, Japan, with Curaçao visas of questionable validity and expired Japanese transit visas, Foreign Minister Yotsuke Matsuoka (the former governor of Manchuria) approved the extension of their transit visas (*see* RESCUE OF POLISH JEWS VIA EAST ASIA). This was just prior to his trip to Berlin to cement relations with Hitler. With the approach of war, the Japanese relocated the Polish refugees—among them writers, artists, Socialist leaders, Talmudic students, and rabbis—to their sector of Shanghai. For his help in providing this new home, the Union of Orthodox Rabbis of the United States and Canada sent an inscribed silver cigarette case to Captain Inuzuka (which was to help him obtain release from a trial of war criminals in Manila after the war).

With the beginning of the war in the Pacific, the Japanese became more susceptible to Nazi influence. The "pro-Jewish" Bureau of Jewish Affairs was disbanded, and Inuzuka was shipped to the Philippines. By February 18, 1943, the Japanese finally gave in to German demands to set up a ghetto for the Jews. Only the German, Austrian, and Polish refugees were relocated, to a ghetto of 2 square miles (5 sq km), which included thousands of Chinese. Because of Japan's sensitive relationship with the Soviet Union, the three thousand to four thousand stateless Russian Jews remained free, as did the few hundred Sephardic Jews (the wealthy ones were interned as British "enemy nationals").

While the ghetto posed great economic and psychological hardship, in no way did it resemble its European counterparts. Although Japanese soldiers, with the help of unarmed Pao Chia (Jewish auxiliary police), guarded entry to and exit from the ghetto, no walls or even barbed wire surrounded it. The Japanese authorities generally left the community alone—with all its cultural, religious, and educational activities intact—and engaged in no random torture or shooting, along Nazi lines. Thus, the refugees lived in relative peace throughout the war, though with not too much to eat. Only if a refugee required a pass to leave the ghetto for business or medical reasons would he possibly encounter trouble with the Japanese officials. Okura might throw one in jail, or Ghoya, who called himself "King of the Jews," might slap or even kick the refugee standing on line one minute, and behave like a gentleman the next. But unlike the Americans, with their stringent wartime communication laws, the Japanese never prevented the sending of money by Jewish organizations via neutral countries to support most of the indigent refugees in Shanghai. By the end of 1943, in response to pressure by the VA'AD HA-HATSALA (Rescue Committee of United States Orthodox Rabbis), the United States permitted such money transfers, and conditions improved for the refugees.

The Japanese, even in the midst of war, were still under the illusion of a potent "Jewish power" in the United States. They tried several times, unsuccessfully, to send out peace feelers to the United States by means of unsuspecting Jews in Shanghai or Tientsin. Ironically, throughout the period of the Holocaust, it was this type of Japanese antisemitism that served to protect, rather than hurt, some Jews.

[*See also* Sugihara, Sempo.]

BIBLIOGRAPHY

Kranzler, D. "The Japanese Ideology of Antisemitism and the Holocaust." In *Contemporary Views of the Holocaust,* edited by R. L. Braham, pp. 79–107. Boston, 1983.

Kranzler, D. "Japanese Policy toward the Jews, 1938–1941." *Japan Interpreter* 11/5 (1977): 493–527.

Kranzler, D. *The Japanese, the Nazis, and the Jews.* New York, 1976.

DAVID KRANZLER

JARBLUM, MARC (1887–1972), Jewish leader in Vichy France. Born in Warsaw, Jarblum came to Paris at the age of twenty and soon became a central figure in Po'alei Zion, a Socialist Zionist movement. In the interwar period he was also active in various immigrant organizations, while maintaining close ties with the French Socialist movement. After the fall of France, Jarblum attempted to coordinate welfare activity in the occupied zone and supported the creation of the Commission Centrale des Organisations Juives d'Assistance, attempting unsuccessfully to make it the political representative of the Jewish community in France. Jarblum found himself at odds with the French-born Jewish leaders and often condemned their lack of concern for the immigrant Jews in France. When the UNION GÉNÉRALE DES ISRAÉLITES DE FRANCE (UGIF) was proposed, he immediately opposed it, led the campaign against its creation, and refused to be nominated to its council.

Following the deportations from France in the summer of 1942, Jarblum channeled the activities of the FÉDÉRATION DES SOCIÉTÉS

Marc Jarblum speaking before a displaced persons' demonstration in the Bergen-Belsen camp that called for free immigration to Palestine.

JUIVES DE FRANCE into "illegal" welfare work, though the federation continued to maintain an official position within the UGIF. He also encouraged Jews to flee to the Italian zone after November of that year, when the south of France was conquered by Germany and Italy; he himself was pursued by the Nazi-sponsored French militia and the SS for his anti-Vichy activity and escaped to Switzerland in spring 1943. While in Switzerland, Jarblum collected funds for Jewish organizations in southern France to enable them to extend their illegal work and free themselves from the UGIF's guardianship. Various projects to save Jewish children, either by hiding them in France or by helping them escape to Spain, were high on the list of his priorities. Jarblum survived the war and continued his Zionist activity in France before immigrating to Israel in 1955. His writings include *La lutte des Juifs contre les Nazis* (1945).

BIBLIOGRAPHY

Bauer, Y. *American Jewry and the Holocaust: The American Jewish Joint Distribution Committee, 1939–1945.* Detroit, 1981.

Cohen, R. I. *The Burden of Conscience: French Jewish Leadership during the Holocaust.* Bloomington, 1987.

Weinberg, D. H. *A Community on Trial: The Jews of Paris in the 1930s.* Chicago, 1977.

RICHARD COHEN

The former priest Miroslav Filipović-Majstorović, a member of the Jasenovac camp staff, in his Ustaša uniform.

JASENOVAC, the largest concentration and extermination camp in CROATIA. Jasenovac was in fact a complex of several subcamps, in close proximity to each other, on the bank of the Sava River, about 62 miles (100 km) south of Zagreb. The women's camp of Stara Gradiška, which was farther away, also belonged to this complex.

Jasenovac was established in August 1941 and was dismantled only in April 1945. The creation of the camp and its management and supervision were entrusted to Department III of the Croatian Security Police (Ustaška Narodna Služba; UNS), headed by Vjekoslav (Maks) Luburić, who was personally responsible for everything that happened there. Scores of Ustaše (Croatian fascists) served in the camp; the cruelest was the former priest Miroslav Filipović-Majstorović, who killed scores of prisoners with his own hands.

The Jasenovac camp.

Some six hundred thousand people were murdered at Jasenovac, mostly Serbs, Jews, GYPSIES, and opponents of the USTAŠA regime. The number of Jewish victims was between twenty thousand and twenty-five thousand, most of whom were murdered there up to August 1942, when deportation of the Croatian Jews to AUSCHWITZ for extermination began. Jews were sent to Jasenovac from all parts of Croatia—from Zagreb, from Sarajevo, and from other cities and smaller towns. On their arrival most were killed at execution sites near the camp: Granik, Gradina, and other places. Those kept alive were mostly skilled at needed professions and trades (doctors, pharmacists, electricians, shoemakers, goldsmiths, and so on) and were employed in services and workshops at Jasenovac. The living conditions in the camp were extremely severe: a meager diet, deplorable accommodations, a particularly cruel regime, and unbelievably cruel behavior by the Ustaše guards. The conditions improved only for short periods—during visits by delegations, such as the press delegation that visited in February 1942 and a Red Cross delegation in June 1944.

The acts of murder and of cruelty in the camp reached their peak in the late summer of 1942, when tens of thousands of Serbian villagers were deported to Jasenovac from the area of the fighting against the partisans in the Kozara Mountains. Most of the men were killed at Jasenovac. The women were sent for forced labor in Germany, and the children were taken from their mothers; some were murdered and others were dispersed in orphanages throughout the country.

In April 1945 the partisan army approached the camp. In an attempt to erase traces of the atrocities, the Ustaše blew up all the installations and killed most of the internees. An escape attempt by the prisoners failed, and only a few survived.

BIBLIOGRAPHY

Romans, J. *Jews of Yugoslavia, 1941–1945: Victims of Genocide and Freedom Fighters.* Belgrade, 1982.

Sindik, D., ed. *Secanja Jevreja na logor Jasenovac.* Belgrade, 1972.

MENACHEM SHELAH

JASSY. *See* Iaşi.

JDC. *See* Joint Distribution Committee.

JECKELN, FRIEDRICH (1895–1946), SS commander. Born in Hornberg, Jeckeln joined the Nazi party in the 1920s; by 1930 he was an SS-*Obergruppenführer.* Following the German invasion of the Soviet Union in June 1941, Jeckeln was appointed *Höherer SS- und Polizeiführer* (Higher SS and Police Leader; HSSPF) on the southern front, which included the occupied areas of the Ukraine. On September 1, 1941, the units under his command slaughtered at least fourteen thousand Hungarian Jews who had been deported to the KAMENETS-PODOLSKI area. From July to October of that year they participated in the massacre of the Jews of Kiev at BABI YAR and in the mass killings at ROVNO and DNEPROPETROVSK. On October 11, Jeckeln was appointed HSSPF on the northern front and in Ostland, which encompassed the Baltic countries (Lithuania, Latvia, and Estonia) and parts of Belorussia. Jeckeln was in charge of the annihilation of the Jews of RIGA in November and December 1941, including the Jews from Germany and Austria who were sent to that city in the last months of 1941. In Aktion Sumpffieber (Operation Malaria), carried out in early 1942, the anti-partisan units under his command in Belorussia liquidated many ghettos and slaughtered tens of thousands of Jews.

Friedrich Jeckeln.

After the war, Jeckeln was arrested by the Allies and handed over to the Soviet Union. He was tried in Riga before a Soviet military court, which sentenced him to death by hanging on February 3, 1946. The sentence was carried out immediately.

BIBLIOGRAPHY

Hilberg, R. *The Destruction of the European Jews.* New York, 1986.

Krausnick, H., and H. Wilhelm. *Die Truppe des Weltanschauungskrieges: Die Einsatzgruppen der Sicherheitspolizei und des SD, 1938–1942.* Stuttgart, 1981.

YITZHAK ARAD

JEFROYKIN, JULES ("Dika"; 1911–1987), Jewish resistance leader in Vichy France. The son of Israel Jefroykin, a prominent figure in the eastern European Jewish community in interwar France, Jules Jefroykin, together with Simon LEVITTE, was instrumental in organizing the Mouvement de la Jeunesse Sioniste (Zionist Youth Movement; MJS) in the winter of 1941–1942. Open to Jewish youth of every persuasion, the MJS spearheaded cultural and social work in southern France, both officially and clandestinely. Jefroykin later became the JOINT DISTRIBUTION COMMITTEE's representative in southern France and was, with Maurice Brener, responsible for diverting the Joint's funds to "illegal" work. Jefroykin also participated in the underground operations of the Organisation Juive de Combat, most daringly in efforts to smuggle Jewish children and youth across the Pyrenees into Spain.

BIBLIOGRAPHY

Avni, H. "The Zionist Underground in Holland and France and the Escape to Spain." In *Rescue*

Attempts during the Holocaust. Proceedings of the Second Yad Vashem International Historical Conference, edited by Y. Gutman and E. Zuroff, pp. 555–590. Jerusalem, 1977.

Bauer, Y. *American Jewry and the Holocaust: The American Jewish Joint Distribution Committee, 1939–1945.* Detroit, 1981.

RICHARD COHEN

JEHOVAH'S WITNESSES (Ger., *Bibelforscher,* or "Bible Students"), religious sect organized in Germany as the Internationale Bibelforscher Vereinigung (International Bible Students' Association), affiliated with the Watchtower Bible and Tract Society of New York, Inc., whose main task is to distribute the sect's printed material. In 1933 the sect had about twenty thousand members in Germany.

The Jehovah's Witnesses' faith is based on an eschatological doctrine; in every generation they expect the "end of days," which will be inaugurated by a great trial of all people who do not belong to the sect. The "end of days" will be preceded by political catastrophes, such as war, revolution, or economic crisis. Obviously, the Nazi policy of persecution and war could be interpreted as heralding the approach of the "end of days."

While the Witnesses were among the early victims of Nazism, their initial attitude toward the Nazi regime was ambivalent. There is no evidence of concrete action on their part against the regime in its early period. In Bavaria the sect was outlawed in April 1933, and other provinces followed suit. Relations between Nazi Germany and the Catholic church seem to have been a decisive consideration for this step, in view of the extremely tense relationship between the sect and the Catholic church. An additional consideration was the existence of a tight international organization of Witnesses, and their refusal to officially renounce religious meetings, Bible evenings, and the recruitment of new members. The day after Prussia issued its prohibition of the sect (June 24, 1933), a convention of the Witnesses in Germany was still able to declare that essentially it had no quarrel with the National Socialist government, and in principle shared its hostile attitude toward Bolshevism and the church, and its antisemitism. It was only when the Witnesses refused to make the "Heil Hitler" salute, and, beginning in 1935, to serve in the army, that the sect's officials and large parts of its membership adopted a clear posture of opposition to the regime. This led to the first wave of arrests of Witnesses in 1936 and 1937, which in many cases led to imprisonment in concentration camps. An international convention of the Witnesses, held in Lucerne, Switzerland, in September 1936, reacted by issuing a resolution condemning the entire Nazi regime. Although at the time the sect's leading officials in Germany were under arrest, it found a way of distributing the text of the "Lucerne Resolution" among its members in Germany (as it did in the rest of the world). More large-scale waves of arrests were recorded after the outbreak of the war, and again in 1944.

At all times, however, the Witnesses in the concentration camps were a relatively small group of prisoners (not exceeding several hundred per camp) and mostly of German nationality. As a rule the Witnesses imprisoned in the camps refused to renounce their convictions. Even though they could obtain their release, or could have escaped imprisonment in the first place, by signing a declaration that they would no longer be active on behalf of their organization, most of the Witnesses refused to do this. Inside the concentration camps the Witnesses were a relatively compact group, supporting one another and conspicuous by the order, cleanliness, and discipline that they maintained in their barracks. Their helpfulness also benefited other groups. The Witnesses' behavior, however, was determined by their religious beliefs; they did not cooperate with the illegal political groups, and refused to try to escape from the camps or to offer active resistance to the SS.

At first, the SS used special methods of harassment, their purpose being to break up the Witnesses' internal solidarity. The SS also sought to keep the Witnesses apart from other prisoners lest they gain new converts to their faith. At a later stage, the SS made a conscious effort to disperse the Witnesses in the camps and thereby to break up their cohesive groups. Finally, the SS exploited the Witnesses' exceptional behavior for its own purposes. On Heinrich HIMMLER'S orders, for example, it was permitted to use the Witnesses for gathering mushrooms and fruit outside the camp, since there was no danger of their trying to escape or attacking the SS. As a result of this change in SS policy, the situation of most of the Witnesses in the concentration camps was changed for the better.

BIBLIOGRAPHY

"The Holocaust: Why Did God Allow It? Will Those Dead Return?"*Awake!* (8 April 1989): 1–20.

King, C. E. *The Nazi State and the New Religions: Five Case Studies in Non-Conformity*. Vol. 4 of *Studies in Religion and Society*. New York, 1984.

FALK PINGEL

JEWISH AGENCY FOR PALESTINE. *See* Yishuv.

JEWISH ANTIFASCIST COMMITTEE (Evreiski Antifashistski Komitet), Soviet Jewish institution founded in 1942 that functioned in the SOVIET UNION throughout World War II and until 1948. Its offices were first in Kuibyshev (to which several government ministries had moved in October 1941, when the battle of Moscow began) and later in Moscow. It was one of several antifascist committees that were part of the Soviet Propaganda Office (Sovinformbiuro).

In 1938, in the wake of KRISTALLNACHT, Soviet Jewish personalities were recruited to take part in Soviet antifascist propaganda. In August 1941, following the German invasion, a public meeting was held in Moscow (and broadcast on Soviet radio) in which the unity of the Jews of the Soviet Union with their Jewish brethren the world over was upheld. Among those who addressed the meeting were the actor Shlomo Mikhoels, director of the Moscow Jewish Theater, and the writers Peretz Markish, David Bergelson, Ilya EHRENBURG, and Shmuel Marshak. The meeting was followed, in September through November of that year, by an effort to establish an Anti-Hitler Jewish Committee, initiated by Henryk Erlich and Wiktor Alter, BUND leaders from Poland who had taken refuge in the Soviet Union and had been jailed but subsequently released. This attempt, which was unsuccessful, went through various phases and its full story is yet to be revealed; Erlich and Alter were rearrested at the beginning of December, and were put to death.

In April 1942, Moscow announced the formation of several antifascist committees, among them the Jewish Antifascist Committee—the only one to speak on behalf of a national group. The committee addressed itself to the Jews of the world—with American Jewry as its main target—and called on them to join the struggle against Nazi Germany. Its appeals made use of Jewish themes, Jewish symbols, and the names of Jewish personalities. During the war, some one hundred Soviet Jews lent their names to these appeals. Heading the committee was an executive council made up of twenty prominent Soviet Jews from all walks of life. Shlomo Mikhoels was the council's chairman, and its active members included the poet Itzik Fefer and the journalist Shakhno Epshtein, who was the committee's secretary and editor of its newspaper, EYNIKEYT.

The committee's declared purpose was to disseminate antifascist propaganda, primarily among world Jewry, but its members and leaders did not disregard the current needs of the Soviet Jewish population. From time to time distinctively Jewish topics were raised, such as the return of the Jews to the liberated areas of Europe and their resettlement there; antisemitism among the non-Jewish Soviet population; and the difficulties encountered in the effort to revive Jewish culture. A major issue that came up for discussion was the murder of Jews by the Nazis and the Jewish fight against the Nazis. The committee was one of the first organizations to document the Holocaust and the heroism of Jewish resistance, setting up a special subcommittee for this purpose. *Eynikeyt* published reports, articles, and testimonies on the murder of Jews in German-occupied Soviet territory, and it had a regular feature on Jewish soldiers who had distinguished themselves in the Red Army. The committee maintained contact with the Soviet Government Commission for

Members of the Jewish Antifascist Committee. Far left: Itzik Feffer, Yiddish poet, executed in 1952 during Stalin's anti-Jewish purges. Third from left: Shlomo Mikhoels, actor and manager of the Moscow Jewish Theater, killed by the Soviet secret police in 1948. Far right: Peretz Markish, Yiddish writer, executed in 1952 during the anti-Jewish purges. [Ben-Zion Goldberg]

the Investigation of Nazi Crimes, and its major enterprise was compilation of the *Chernaia kniga* (The BLACK BOOK OF SOVIET JEWRY), which aimed to document the fate of the Jews in the occupied areas of the USSR. Ilya Ehrenburg was the first to oversee this project, followed by another writer, Vasily Grossman; the book, however, was not published in the Soviet Union, owing to the change in Soviet policy after the war. The Jewish Antifascist Committee maintained contact with Jewish organizations and prominent Jews outside the Soviet Union, and it supplied material relating to the Holocaust to Jewish institutions and newspapers abroad. These contacts reached their high point when Mikhoels and Fefer visited the United States, Canada, Mexico, and Great Britain in 1943. Efforts to arrange a visit to Palestine of a delegation from the committee did not succeed.

When the war was coming to an end, and in the immediate postwar period, the committee, on its own initiative, submitted proposals to the Soviet authorities concerning the restoration and expansion of Jewish cultural institutions and activities, and the creation of new possibilities for the settlement of Jews. In 1944 it proposed the establishment of a Soviet Jewish republic in the Volga region, from which the German population had been removed, or in the Crimea, from which the Tatars had been expelled. All these plans came to nothing. The committee also supported the renewed settlement of Jews in the Jewish Autonomous Oblast of Birobidzhan.

During its existence, the committee was regarded as the central Jewish institution in the Soviet Union, a representative body to which Jewish requests for advice and support could be directed. Many Soviet Jews also saw in it an appropriate repository for complaints and for the expression of their hopes and expectations. Mikhoels, its chairman and moving spirit, was asked for help by Jews in personal affairs as well as matters of Jewish public interest. The committee kept in contact with Yiddish writers, both native Soviet Jews and those who were refugees in the country. Throughout its existence, but especially from 1944–1946, the committee served as a meeting place for Jewish writers, artists, soldiers, and partisans, and from 1943 to 1948 it had a regular evening program on literature and art.

The Soviet authorities had an ongoing interest in the existence of a specifically Jewish institution and supported the committee's worldwide information and propaganda campaign. This kept the committee in existence even after the war come to an end. Gradually, however, the discrepancy between the official purpose for which the committee had been created and the hopes that some Soviet Jews pinned on it widened, while the oppressive character of the Soviet regime and the cold war increased. The authorities were also taken aback by the enthusiasm displayed by part of the Soviet Jewish population over the establishment of the state of Israel and the arrival of its diplomatic representatives in Moscow. As a result, the committee's activities were curbed and eventually, in November 1948, it was abolished. Earlier, in January 1948, Shlomo Mikhoels had been killed in Minsk, on STALIN's orders. Before long, most of the committee members were imprisoned. The more prominent among them were put to death in the course of Stalin's anti-Jewish campaign (1949–1952).

BIBLIOGRAPHY

Altshuler, M. "The Jewish Antifascist Committee in the USSR in the Light of New Documentation." *Studies in Contemporary Jewry* 1 (1984): 253–291.

Redlich, S. *Propaganda and Nationalism in Wartime Russia: The Jewish Antifascist Committee in the USSR, 1941–1948*. Boulder, 1982.

SHIMON REDLICH

JEWISH ARMY. *See* Armée Juive.

JEWISH BADGE. *See* Badge, Jewish.

JEWISH BRIGADE GROUP, a brigade group of the British army, composed of Jewish volunteers from Palestine, that was formed in September 1944 and fought in the Italian theater of war from March to May 1945.

The origins of the brigade can be traced back to the earlier stages of World War II. Upon the outbreak of hostilities, Chaim WEIZMANN, as president of the World Zionist Organization, offered the British government the full cooperation of the Jewish people in the war effort, and began negotiations on the creation of a Jewish fighting force within the British army. The British were at first reluctant, but in the summer of 1940 they changed their minds, hoping to achieve by the formation of a Jewish force greater support in American public opinion for a policy of assistance to isolated Britain. In October 1940 the War Cabinet decided to establish such a force, amounting initially to one division. Most of the recruits were to come from the neutral United States and from refugees. Palestine would provide this division with a nucleus of commanding staff to safeguard its national-Zionist character.

The actual talks with Weizmann on the establishment of the division were put off until the American presidential elections in November 1940, and then they dragged on inconclusively until March 1941. In the interval the war situation changed considerably. The threat of invasion to the British Isles receded, while the Middle East and the Balkans became Britain's principal theater of war. The British generals in the Middle East were apprehensive of the likely Arab reaction to the establishment of a Jewish division, and Winston CHURCHILL was persuaded by his ministers and generals first to postpone the execution of the War Cabinet decision for a few months, and then to cancel it altogether in October 1941.

With the occupation of Europe by the Nazis and the imminent entrance of the United States into the war, the whole idea of a Jewish formation within the British army had to be modified. It was now completely based on volunteering in Palestine. In July 1940 the British renounced their earlier idea of mixed Jewish-Arab units, and accepted the principle of Jewish companies in most ancillary corps of the ground forces. At the same time,

A party given by Jewish Brigade Group soldiers in Nijmegen, 12 miles (19 km) south of Arnhem, for Jewish children who had been hidden in monasteries and Christian homes (1946). [Beth Hatefutsoth]

the Jewish Agency agreed to cooperate in the recruitment of 2,500 individuals for ground crews of the Royal Air Force and in the formation of Jewish Auxiliary Military Pioneer Corps companies. In September 1940, the British responded to another Jewish request and created the Jewish infantry companies known as the "Buffs" and several Jewish anti-aircraft and coastal artillery batteries as a part of the garrison in Palestine, where they officially promised these units would serve.

About three thousand of the volunteers who had enlisted at the beginning of the war were dispatched in early 1941 to Greece. About one hundred were killed in action and seventeen hundred were captured by the Germans in the campaigns of Greece and Crete. The remainder were evacuated to Egypt. Under the growing threat to Britain's position in the Middle East, enlistment increased in the spring of 1941.

The recruitment campaign reached its peak in July 1942, when German general Erwin Rommel's troops arrived at El Alamein in Egypt and the British position in the Middle East seemed to collapse. Under pressure from American and local public opinion, the British on August 6, 1942, declared the establishment of the Palestine Regiment, consisting of three Jewish battalions and one of Arabs. The low status of the Palestine Regiment disappointed the YISHUV (the Jewish population in Palestine); recruitment began to dwindle, and many soldiers asked for transfer into ancillary units, which at least served nearer the front lines in Egypt and the Western Desert, and sometimes participated in the fighting.

The news of the extermination of the Jews in Europe, which reached Palestine in November 1942, had little influence on enlistment in the army. Eighty percent of the thirty thousand recruits joined the army in the first half of the war, and only one-fifth enlisted in the following years. The Holocaust had more impact within the ranks, particularly among the soldiers of the infantry battalions and artillery batteries stationed in Palestine. Against the official stance of the Jewish Agency, they now demanded to be dispatched out of the country and sent to the front, where they would be able to take their revenge on the Nazis and assist the surviving remnant of European Jews upon its liberation. The demand persisted throughout 1943, and was nourished by the news of the participation of Jewish transport and engineers' companies in the landings in Italy and their assistance to the liberated Jewish inmates of FERRAMONTI DI TARSIA and other camps, as well as to refugees who crossed the Adriatic from Yugoslavia.

New Zionist proposals in the summer of 1943 for the creation of a fighting force were not connected with the Middle East and its sensitive equilibrium between Arabs and Jews, and the British were this time more responsive. Though the generals still had several misgivings, moral considerations carried more wieght than before. It seemed unjustifiable to deny the Jews the right to revenge and fight their oppressors, when the Allies were doing practically nothing to stop the mass murder. Churchill exercised all his personal authority in favor of accepting the Zionist proposal and urged his colleagues to approve it. On July 3, 1944, the British War Cabinet decided that although the formation of a Jewish division was not feasible on practical grounds, the creation of a brigade should be immediately and positively examined.

The cabinet decision opened the way to intensive talks, culminating in an official communiqué by the War Office on September 20, 1944, announcing the formation of the Jewish Brigade Group. Brigadier Ernst Benjamin was appointed its commanding officer, and the Zionist flag was officially approved as its standard.

The three infantry battalions of the brigade assembled near Alexandria; in early November they sailed for Italy. The brigade took part in the early stages of the final Allied offensive in Italy in April 1945 and then was withdrawn for reorganization. Its casualties at the front totaled fifty-seven killed and about two hundred wounded (including non-Jewish personnel). Although the brigade was not the first Jewish unit to take part in combat, it was the first and only Jewish formation to fight in World War II under the Jewish flag, recognized as representing the Jewish people.

After the termination of hostilities, the brigade was stationed in Tarvisio, near the border triangle of Italy, Yugoslavia, and Austria. Several missions set out from Tarvisio to eastern Europe and to the DISPLACED PERSONS' camps in Austria and Germany, and soon the brigade became a source of attraction for the surviving Jewish youth from all over the continent. During its two months' sojourn in the region, about one hundred fifty thousand Jews were smuggled to Tarvisio, where they were hospitalized and fed by the soldiers until their eventual transfer by the Jewish transport units to the refugee centers farther south.

In July 1945, the brigade moved to Belgium and the Netherlands. About one hundred and fifty soldiers were clandestinely dispatched to conduct organizational and educational work in the displaced persons' camps, to organize the BERIḤA stations in Austria and Germany, and to assist in the preparations for "illegal" immigration to Palestine. Other soldiers concentrated on illegal arms purchase for the Hagana (the Jewish underground military organization in Palestine). Despite last-moment attempts by the Jewish Agency to prolong the brigade's existence, the British were determined to disband it according to their demobilization plan, and this was accomplished in June and July of 1946.

Thirty thousand Jews volunteered in Palestine for service in the British army between 1939 and 1946. They sustained 700 fatalities; 1,769 were taken prisoner; several thousand were wounded; and 323 were decorated or mentioned in dispatches. Five thousand served in the Jewish Brigade.

[*See also* Resistance, Jewish.]

BIBLIOGRAPHY

Casper, B. M. *With the Jewish Brigade.* London, 1947.

Gelber, Y. *History of Volunteering.* 4 vols. Jerusalem, 1979–1984. (In Hebrew.)

Penkower, M. N. "The Struggle for an Allied Jewish Fighting Force during World War II." In *Contemporary Views of the Holocaust,* edited by R. L. Braham, pp. 47–75. Boston, 1983.

Rabinowitz, L. *Soldiers from Judea: Palestinian Jewish Units in the Middle East, 1941–1943.* New York, 1945.

YOAV GELBER

JEWISH CENTER FOR ADULT EDUCATION. *See* Mittelstelle für Jüdische Erwachsenenbildung.

JEWISH CENTER IN ROMANIA. *See* Centrala Evreilor.

JEWISH CENTER IN SLOVAKIA. *See* Ústredňa Židov.

JEWISH COUNCIL. *See* Judenrat.

JEWISH COUNCIL IN THE NETHERLANDS. *See* Joodse Raad.

JEWISH FIGHTING ORGANIZATION. *See* Żydowska Organizacja Bojowa.

JEWISH GHETTO POLICE. *See* Jüdischer Ordnungsdienst.

JEWISH HISTORICAL INSTITUTE. *See* Documentation Centers: Żydowski Instytut Historyczny.

JEWISH LABOR COMMITTEE (JLC), organization formed in New York City in 1934 to represent Jewish trade union interests, mainly in the then predominantly Jewish needle trades. Rapidly recognized as a major American Jewish organization, it took an active part in the movement to boycott German goods, and was the most outspoken of all Jewish organizations in the struggle to increase the number of Jewish refugees allowed to enter the United States.

Through its close ties to the Jewish Labor BUND in Poland, the JLC was the first group to receive news of the massacre of Polish Jewry, in May 1942. It was able to use its contacts with the POLISH GOVERNMENT-IN-EXILE to send funds to the Bund underground. The JLC also used its strong position in the American trade union movement to enlist the support of the American labor leadership to pressure the United States government to aid in the rescue and relief of European Jewry. Having easy access to the large numbers of Jewish workers at their factories, the JLC was able to mobilize large numbers of Jewish workers for demonstrations. Among these was the work stoppage on December 2, 1942, which was called to commemorate the Jewish people who had been massacred in Europe. This event was intended to create pressure for American intervention to save European Jewry.

The JLC often found itself working closely with the ultra-Orthodox VA'AD HA-HATSALA because of the readiness of both groups to take steps that were illegal to aid or rescue the beleaguered Jews in Europe. As one of the major American Jewish organizations, the JLC participated in all the joint rescue endeavors of the American Jewish community, and was critical of the failure of the short-lived Joint Emergency Committee for European Jewish Affairs (comprising various leading United States Jewish organizations) to carry out a forceful struggle for rescue. The JLC was at first a participant in the AMERICAN JEWISH CONFERENCE, but left when the conference accepted to membership the pro-Communist Jewish People's Fraternal Order.

BIBLIOGRAPHY

Finger, S., ed. *American Jewry during the Holocaust.* New York, 1984.

ARIEL HURWITZ

JEWISH MILITARY UNION. *See* Żydowski Związek Wojskowy.

JEWISH PHILOSOPHICAL AND THEOLOGICAL RESPONSES TO THE HOLOCAUST. The overwhelming reality of the destruction of European Jewry has, of necessity, elicited a wide variety of philosophical and theological reflections. Contemporary thinkers have sought to give some response to the radical happenings associated with this event, either through recycling, often with special emphases, classical "answers" to the problems of theodicy and human suffering, or through innovative conceptual analyses. All of these responses remain problematic.

Traditional Answers. Jewish history is no stranger to national calamity, mass death, and immense human suffering. In response the Jewish tradition has, with varying degrees of success, formulated a series of replies that seek both to explain what has happened and to comfort the victims. Though perhaps the least appealing from the modern perspective, the ascription of the tragedy to the sinfulness of the Jews is historically primary among these theological paradigms, and the most deeply rooted in the biblical sources. Given this explanation, the horrific actuality of Auschwitz raises no special dilemmas for faith: the Jews were untrue to their covenantal obligations and God responded by punishing them. There is no need to look further for reasons, or to question either God's existence or the reality of the Jews' covenantal faith. As an explanation applied to the events of the 1930s and 1940s specifically, this accusation has taken three forms among the more Orthodox Jews. The first lays the general charge of infidelity and sinfulness against the Jews but eschews further specificity (the view of Rabbi Isaac Hutner); the second causally connects the Holocaust with the rise of Reform and other non-Orthodox forms of Judaism (the view of Rabbi Elhanan Wasserman, among others); the third cites Zionism as the culprit because it sought to reject the Exile, not being content to wait on God's messianic redemptive act (the position of Rabbi Joel Teitelbaum). All three forms of this response are problematic, not least because of the sort of God they picture, that is, one who would find it necessary for a million Jewish children to be murdered for any or even all of these "sins."

Four other biblically grounded doctrines or models that have been called into service to respond to the annihilation of European Jewry are (1) the *Akeda*—the Binding of Isaac; (2) the "Suffering Servant" of Isaiah; (3) *Hester Panim*—the "Hiding" of God's countenance; and (4) Job. The *Akeda* paradigm likens the victims to Isaac, innocent victims who are sacrificed (unlike the biblical Isaac) as a test of faithfulness. Bearing no sin, free of all imputation of guilt, they die as an act of ultimate fidelity to Jewish tradition, to Torah, to the God of Israel. This paradigm has long been hallowed in Jewish life. Its appositeness with regard to the Nazi extermination camps, however, is questionable, not least because the SS are not Abraham and their victims not martyrs in the classical sense of having freely chosen their fate.

The Suffering Servant model, drawing primarily on Isaiah 53, has also found a significant place in post-Holocaust reflections. Like the *Akeda*, it is an appealing form of response and explanation because it lays no blame on the victims, seeing their suffering rather as a vicarious, if mysterious, means by which God balances the forces of creation and brings salvation to the wicked while assuring His special love, even sharing in the suffering of the righteous victims whom He rewards in the hereafter. As employed in modern times (by Hasidic leaders, by Abraham Joshua Heschel, by the Orthodox thinker Eliezer Berkovits, and by the Reform theologian Ignaz Maybaum, among others) to answer the theological dilemma, it has been criticized, not least because it evokes a doctrine of vicarious suffering, which itself needs to be deciphered. Moreover, it raises the difficult question of why God—and what sort of God—would require such sacrifices to regulate His universe.

Hester Panim, appealing to the Divine hiddenness, is explained in the Bible as being due to sin (as in Dt. 31:17–18) and also and quite differently as a mysterious, inexplicable happening for which no clear reason can be given (as in Psalm 44, Psalm 13, Is. 8:17, and Is. 45:5). This concept is connected in some theological accounts to God's quality of "long-sufferingness"; that is, His gracious toleration of the sinner means that He must allow sin to occur, which necessarily creates victims. This "explanation" ultimately falters, for it explains one conundrum, the reality of evil, by creating another—Divine hiddenness. Thus, when employed by contemporary theologians in response to Auschwitz (as for example in Martin Buber's *Eclipse of God*), it explains too little.

Finally, the Job paradigm, while widely invoked and appealing because Job is known not to be a sinner, appears both theologically and methodologically unsatisfactory. Whereas the biblical Job is protected by God as a condition of this test (see Job, "Prologue"), the Jewish people in our time knew no such protection. Nor, again, did the Divine reveal itself in an unambiguous theophany after the "test," confirming His existence and control of the cosmos (even if in a manner that transcends human understanding), as He did to Job. However, this issue is complex, for some credit the creation of the state of Israel as such a theophany, even though it is not an "unambiguous" revelation as occurs in the book of Job.

Modern Responses. In contrast to these well-worked replies to calamity, other Jewish thinkers have creatively, if not altogether satisfactorily, responded to the Holocaust with original and thought-provoking explanations. The most extreme, if also the least satisfactory, has been that offered by Richard Rubenstein in *After Auschwitz* (1966). Rubenstein argued that the Holocaust decisively disproves the existence of God and proves the bankruptcy of traditional Jewish theology. The universe is absurd, without meaning or purpose, and in such a universe it is not surprising that obscenities like Auschwitz exist. Accordingly, Jews should turn away from their ancient theological myths of transcendence and salvation and recognize instead a new immanent, naturalistic system of values, which alone can provide what happiness and solace there can be in this world. As developed by Rubenstein, however, this thesis is riddled with logical and methodological difficulties that undermine its coercive force.

Another approach is the "free-will defense," a revised version of a classical argument that sought to account for the existence of human evil in God's creation. Here evil is logically legitimized through the contention that for human beings to be free and hence majestic, they must also be free to sin and hence create evil consequences for others (see especially the employment of this thesis in the works of Eliezer Berkovits and Arthur A. Cohen). Not God but human beings are the cause of evil. This view too lacks complete plausibility, for it fails to grapple sufficiently with alternative metaphysical possibilities, for example, the possibility that God could have created a world with freedom and less or no evil; or that He could have at least created human beings with a stronger disposition toward good and with a more receptive capacity for moral education.

The third novel position concerning the Holocaust has been advanced by Emil Fackenheim, who has argued that it should be understood as a new occasion of Divine revelation. God was at Auschwitz, though we cannot understand exactly what He was doing there. And out of the cataclysm has emerged a new 614th commandment (in addition to the traditional 613 commandments): "Jews, do not give Hitler a posthumous victory." By speaking of this commandment, Fackenheim intends to convey that Jews should understand themselves as being under a sacred obligation to survive so as to ensure that Hitler, with his genocidal frenzy aimed at the Jewish people, does not ultimately succeed. Above all, this commandment entails both Jewish survival and the dialectical obligation that Jews are "forbidden to despair of the God of Israel, lest Judaism perish." Philosophical difficulties, however, ensue from adopting this position, and revolve around certain elemental problems in Fackenheim's notions of revelation and commandment.

An even more radical position has been proposed by Irving (Yitzchak) Greenberg. He has made the observation that the Holocaust shattered the covenant between God and Israel. Describing the terms of the traditional covenantal relationship as a "suicide mission" that can no longer be commanded, even by the Almighty, Greenberg advances the provocative thesis that while the old terms of Israel's relation to God are at an end, Israel has now voluntarily entered into a new and more equal relationship with God as a result of what took place. This sidesteps the reason why the Holocaust happened and focuses instead on the proper post-Holocaust response to be adopted by the Jewish people. While it is an intriguing proposal, the logic of the position, especially its use of basic theological terms and concepts such as "covenant," "commandments," "revelation," and "God," is open to interrogation, as is the centrality it gives to Hitler in defining a post-Holocaust Jewish theology.

Moving in a still more novel direction, Arthur A. Cohen, in *The Tremendum: A Theological Interpretation of the Holocaust* (New York, 1981), has suggested that the only way to resolve the many fundamental theological issues emerging from the Holocaust is to redefine God, that is, to recognize that our older notion of the Divine, replete with all the omni-predicates (omniscience, omnipotence, and so on), is mistaken. There is a God, but He does not have the power to interfere in human affairs, as previous generations have thought. Our understanding of Him as the all-powerful providential orderer of history and nature has to be scrapped and a more modest conception of Divinity substituted in its place. But this raises the question as to whether God is still God if He is no longer the providential agency in history. And even if one could defend this minimalizing conceptualization in general philosophical terms, can such a "reduced" divinity be the God of Torah and covenant, of prayer and redemption—the God of Israel?

There are, finally, those who have championed silence as the most appropriate response to the genocidal horrors of our time: not the silence of the agnostic, but rather the silence of those who have wrestled with the abyss, of those who, having pushed reason to its limits, recognize the limits of reason.

BIBLIOGRAPHY

Berkovits, E. *Faith after Auschwitz.* New York, 1973.

Berkovits, E. *God, Man, and History: A Jewish Interpretation.* New York, 1959.

Berkovits, E. *With God in Hell.* New York, 1979.

Cohen, A. A. *Arguments and Doctrines: A Reader of Jewish Thinking in the Aftermath of the Holocaust.* New York, 1970.

Cohen, A. A. *The Tremendum: A Theological Interpretation of the Holocaust.* New York, 1981.

Fackenheim, E. *God's Presence in History: Jewish Affirmation and Philosophical Reflections.* New York, 1972.

Fackenheim, E. *The Jewish Return into History: Reflection in the Age of Auschwitz and a New Jerusalem.* New York, 1978.

Fackenheim, E. *To Mend the World.* New York, 1982.

Greenberg, I. "Religious Values after the Holocaust: A Jewish View." In *Jews and Christians after the Holocaust,* edited by A. J. Peck, pp. 63–86. Philadelphia, 1982.

Katz, S. T. *Post-Holocaust Dialogues: Critical Studies in Modern Jewish Thought.* New York, 1983.

Maybaum, I. *The Face of God after Auschwitz.* New York, 1976.

Rubenstein, R. L. *After Auschwitz: Radical Theology and Contemporary Judaism.* Indianapolis, 1966.

STEVEN T. KATZ

JEWISH POLICE. *See* Jüdischer Ordnungsdienst.

JEWISH RESCUE COMMITTEE. *See* Pracovná Skupina.

JEWISH RESISTANCE MOVEMENT IN FRANCE. *See* Armée Juive.

JEWISH SCOUTS, FRENCH. *See* Eclaireurs Israélites de France.

JEWISH YOUTH FRONT. *See* Front of the Wilderness Generation.

JEWISH YOUTH MOVEMENTS. *See* Youth Movements.

JODENVEREENIGING VAN BELGIE. *See* Association des Juifs en Belgique.

JODL, ALFRED (1890–1946), German military commander; Hitler's chief adviser on strategy and operations throughout World War II. Born in Würzburg, Bavaria, Jodl served in World War I mainly in staff assignments. After the war, he served until 1938 as *Chef der Abteilung Landesverteidigung* (Head of the Defense Department) in the General Staff. On August 22, 1939, he was appointed *Chef des Wehrmachtführungsstabes im OKW* (Chief of the Armed Forces High Command Operational Staff), a post he held until the end of World War II. In this capacity he directed, under Adolf HITLER and Field Marshal Wilhelm KEITEL, all the campaigns except that against the Soviet Union, which was conducted by the Oberkommando des Heeres (Army High Command; OKH), and countersigned many orders to shoot hostages and to execute other war crimes contrary to international law. He was promoted in 1940 to the rank of general of artillery, and in 1944 to *Generaloberst* (senior general).

On May 7, 1945, Jodl signed, by order of

Alfred Jodl, general in the German High Command, arriving at Lüneburger Heide to surrender to the British (May 1945). [National Archives]

Adm. Karl Dönitz, Hitler's successor, the general capitulation of the German armed forces at Reims, France. He was sentenced to death for war crimes by the International Military Tribunal (*see* NUREMBERG TRIAL) on October 1, 1946, and was hanged on October 16.

During Jodl's imprisonment in Nuremberg, he dictated a number of memoranda, including "Betrachtungen über den Einfluss Hitlers auf die Kriegsführung" (Reflections on Hitler's Impact on the Conduct of War). Though a stout believer in Hitler's genius, Jodl came to believe while in prison that he had in fact been exploited by the Nazi leader.

BIBLIOGRAPHY

Brett-Smith, R. *Hitler's Generals.* San Rafael, Calif., 1977.

Jodl, L. *Jenseits des Endes: Leben und Sterben des Generaloberst Alfred Jodl.* Vienna, 1976.

Kriegstagebuch des OKW. Frankfurt, 1961.

JEHUDA L. WALLACH

JOINT BOYCOTT COUNCIL (JBC), American organization founded in 1936 to coordinate Jewish anti-German boycott groups. In March 1933, boycott actions against Germany were undertaken in the United States, with the Jewish War Veterans of the United States of America taking the initiative. The campaign, however, was conducted by several organizations, each acting individually, a situation that resulted in lack of coordination and duplication of efforts. The first committee to be established was set up by Abraham Coralnik, a Yiddish journalist, and was called the American League for the Defense of Jewish Rights. Three months later the American Jewish Congress set up its own boycott committee, and when the JEWISH LABOR COMMITTEE was founded in 1934, it too engaged in boycott activities. In 1936, the Jewish Labor Committee's boycott committee joined forces with that of the American Jewish Congress, forming the Joint Boycott Council in order to coordinate activities.

The league that Coralnik had founded—now headed by Samuel Untermyer—did not join the JBC; it had become a general American rather than a Jewish organization, and had changed its name to the Non-Sectarian Anti-Nazi League to Champion Human Rights. The two bodies—the JBC and the league—continued to function independently of each other.

Throughout its existence, the JBC was headed by Dr. Joseph Tennenbaum, who proposed the pro-boycott resolution passed by the World Jewish Congress in 1936. When the B'NAI B'RITH lodges in Germany were closed down, in January 1939, the parent organization in the United States also joined the JBC. The council kept up its work up until the end of 1941, when the United States entered the war.

[*See also* Boycotts, Anti-Nazi.]

BIBLIOGRAPHY

Gottlieb, M. "The Anti-Nazi Boycott Movement in the United States: An Ideological and Sociological Appreciation." *Jewish Social Studies* 35/3–4 (July–October 1973): 198–227.

Gottlieb, M. "In the Shadow of War: The American Anti-Nazi Boycott Movement." *American Jewish Historical Quarterly* 62/2 (December 1972): 146–161.

DAVID H. SHPIRO

JOINT DISTRIBUTION COMMITTEE (JDC; full name, American Jewish Joint Distribution Committee; also known as the Joint), American Jewry's overseas relief and rehabilitation agency, founded in 1914. As early as 1930, the JDC's European director, Bernard Kahn, had foreseen the need for mass emigration of German Jews, but the decrease in income of American Jews following the 1929 economic crisis and the inbuilt German Jewish ideology of the JDC's lay leaders, who could not conceive of a catastrophe of the kind that befell German Jewry after 1933, prevented proper preparation for what then happened. Nevertheless, once the calamity came about, the JDC became a major factor in an overall effort to help German Jews find new bases for economic survival in Germany. At the same time, it aided in the emigration of those who could not stay there in what it hoped would be an organized exodus. The JDC supplied between 28.7 percent and 36.3 percent of the budget of the ZENTRALAUSSCHUSS DER DEUTSCHEN JUDEN FÜR HILFE UND AUFBAU (Central Committee of German Jews for Relief and Reconstruction) between 1934 and 1937 —a sum equivalent to $4.6 million. This was about 64 percent of the total expenditure of the JDC in those years. The rest went mainly to support the eastern European communities, which were in a far worse economic situation than even German Jewry during the first years of Hitler's regime. The JDC also funded HICEM, the Jewish emigration organization, as well as helping to support emigration directly.

The committee's leaders from 1914 to 1937 were Felix M. Warburg, born in Hamburg (his son, Edward M. M. Warburg, was to become the leader in later years), and Paul Baerwald, also originally a German Jew. However, as time went on, professional fund-raisers played an increasingly central part in the JDC's operations, especially Joseph C. Hyman in the early 1930s, and after him Moses A. Leavitt. During World War II, the central figure was Joseph J. SCHWARTZ, who became head of the JDC's European operation.

During the Holocaust, the JDC maintained three types of policies: (1) the central office in New York followed American official policy to the letter; (2) Schwartz, in neutral Lisbon, stretched that policy so that the JDC's operations in Europe verged on, and sometimes went beyond, the boundaries of legality (in American terms); (3) the JDC's local offices in Nazi-occupied Europe often became foci of self-help and underground activity, and even supported armed resistance. Expenditures

Distribution of basic food products (milk, flour, fats) to the needy Jewish population of Żelechów, about 50 miles (80 km) northwest of Lublin, by the Joint Distribution Committee.

came to $12.29 million in 1938–1939, and $11.9 million in 1940–1941. The decrease was due to the American Jews' disinterest in what was happening in Europe, despite strenuous fund-raising efforts by the JDC. In 1942, the crucial year of the Holocaust, the committee had $6 million at its disposal for European relief, but funds could no longer be transferred to Europe except under crippling conditions. In Switzerland, which could have been the main center for distribution of funds, the JDC nominated Saly MAYER, who was to resign soon from the presidency of the Federation of Swiss Jewish Communities (Schweizerischer Israelitischer Gemeindebund; SIG) as its representative. But in 1942–1943, owing to disagreements between the American and Swiss governments, no funds could be transmitted to that country. Global expenditures increased in 1943 to $8.9 million, to $14.8 million in 1944, and to $26.8 million in 1945, but by that time most of European Jewry had been murdered, though the funds helped some of those who had a chance of survival.

The JDC funds were used to provide aid to French Jews, partly by means of the UNION GÉNÉRALE DES ISRAÉLITES DE FRANCE and partly through underground channels, among them the FÉDÉRATION DES SOCIÉTES JUIVES DE FRANCE. Orphanages, hospitals, and public kitchens were supported by JDC funds. Schools, theaters, and study groups received JDC aid, as did efforts to help Jews obtain false identity papers and cross international borders. Small groups of surviving Jews were supported in Berlin in 1944, and the remnants of the community in Zagreb were helped. Parcels were sent to a number of concentra-

A meeting in Paris (1939) of the heads of the Joint offices in Europe, chaired by Morris C. Troper of New York, the European director of the JDC. On September 9, 1940, Troper addressed the board of directors of the JDC in New York as follows: "[The Jews in Europe] have nothing to look forward to except starvation, disease, and ultimate extinction. . . . Ours is the sacred task of keeping our brethren alive—if not all, then at least some. . . . The problem is one and indivisible for all the Jews of the world." [JDC Archives, New York]

tion camps and to the ghetto of Theresienstadt; aid was sent to the so-called Jüdische Soziale Selbsthilfe (directed by Michael Weichert) in Kraków during the late stage of the war, a controversial social-aid operation under German surveillance.

Until the United States entered the war, in December 1941, the JDC sent food and money by various means to Poland (after the American entry into the war, the committee was forbidden to help "enemy" countries). Several thousand Jews were evacuated from Lithuania to East Asia, largely with JDC support. In Warsaw, a very active JDC committee under the leadership of Yitzhak GITTERMAN raised funds (against the instructions it received from New York, but with Schwartz's tacit approval) by promising repayment in dollars after the war (these promises were later honored). Children's centers, hospitals, and house committees providing social, cultural, economic, and moral support were established under the JDC's supervision in the Warsaw ghetto. Educational efforts were made on a large scale, again by the JDC. Finally, the JDC office in Warsaw provided funds for armed resistance, both in Warsaw and in Białystok.

Owing again to the initiative of a local JDC leader, Gisi FLEISCHMANN, the JDC became a very active participant in the attempts to rescue Slovak Jewry. From Switzerland, Mayer could not supply the large sums that were needed in Slovakia, because he did not receive them from New York or from the committee's European office in Lisbon, but some funds were sent and others raised locally. Some Polish Jews were smuggled into Slovakia, where the JDC supported work camps that were to provide relative safety for their inmates. In Hungary, after the March 1944 occupation of that country by the Germans, the JDC supplied large sums of money. These funds were used to establish children's shelters (later under international protection) and were given to neutral diplomats to provide aid to Jews. Raoul WALLENBERG received the money he needed from the JDC, as did Carl LUTZ, the Swiss vice-consul in Budapest. In Hungary, particularly in late 1944, when the fascist SZÁLASI government took over (October 15), the JDC's help became crucial in saving the remnants of Hungarian Jewry until Budapest was liberated.

The JDC supplied large sums of money, channeled through Switzerland, to aid Romanian Jewry. Wilhelm FILDERMAN, the acknowledged leader of the Jewish community in Romania, was also the JDC representative. JDC funds also went to save what was left of the Bessarabian and Bukovina Jews who had been expelled to the southern Ukraine (TRANSNISTRIA) in 1941.

The JDC's operations, on the whole, were the main way in which American Jewry aided their European brethren during the Holocaust. Some of this was not actually American help but locally organized actions using the name of the Joint. In sum, the various aspects of the JDC's material succor aided a large number of Jews and helped an undetermined number of them to survive.

After the war, the conscience of American Jews was aroused, and self-accusations were made regarding what had not been done during the Holocaust. Perhaps as a result of this, the JDC, working together with the (Zionist) Jewish Agency, the United HIAS Service, and other organizations, became the central Jewish agency supporting survivors in the DISPLACED PERSONS' camps in Germany, Austria, and Italy, and in Poland, Hungary, Romania, and elsewhere. Between 1946 and 1950, the sum of $280 million was spent (compared to $169 million between 1914 and 1945), and quantities of food to augment the official rations; clothing, books, and school supplies for children; cultural amenities; religious supplies; and much more were provided. Vocational training centers were aided, and after the establishment of Israel in May 1948 the JDC became responsible for bringing immigrants there. Until 1949, it also supported the social activities in the detention camps that the British had set up in Cyprus. The JDC's work with survivors terminated with the closing of the last displaced persons' camp (Föhrenwald) in 1957, and with the committee's participation in the Claims Conference (*see* REPARATIONS AND RESTITUTION), which received and administered German reparation funds to Holocaust survivors after 1953. Without the JDC, the survivors' fate would have been much harder than it was.

BIBLIOGRAPHY

Bauer, Y. *American Jewry and the Holocaust: The American Jewish Joint Distribution Committee, 1939–1945.* Detroit, 1981.

Bauer, Y. *My Brother's Keeper: A History of the American Joint Distribution Committee, 1929–1939.* Philadelphia, 1974.

YEHUDA BAUER

JOINT RESCUE COMMITTEE (also known as the Committee for the Jews of Occupied Europe), a committee within the Jewish Agency established by the institutions of the YISHUV, the Jewish community of Palestine, to find ways of helping the Jews of Europe during the war.

When World War II broke out, a four-man committee was set up by the Jewish Agency in Jerusalem, made up of members of the Executive—Itzhak GRUENBAUM, Moshe Shapira, Eliyahu Dobkin, and Dr. Emil Schmorak. Known as the "Committee of Four" or the "Committee for Polish Jewry," its task was to gather the reports that were coming in from the Jews in the Polish ghettos and to extend aid to these Jews, by obtaining immigration certificates to Palestine for them, sending them food parcels, and maintaining contact with them. Before 1942 the aid provided by the committee (which operated together with a body representing Polish Jewry) was modest and was extended primarily to veteran Zionists and to relatives of Jews living in Palestine. At the end of 1942, when it became clear that systematic physical extermination of Jews was being carried out in Europe, the Jewish public in Palestine demanded that a body be set up that would represent the entire Yishuv, with the authority and means to serve as the central agency for the rescue efforts.

As a result, in January 1943 the board of a Rescue Committee was appointed. It consisted of twelve members: the original four, together with Bernard (Dov) Joseph, also a member of the Jewish Agency executive board; Itzhak Ben-Zvi, Shlomo Zalman Shragai, and Yehoshua Suprasky, all three members of the Va'ad Le'ummi, the National Council of Jews in Palestine; Binyamin Mintz and Rabbi Isaac Meir Levin, representing the religious movement Agudat Israel; and Joseph Klarman and Zvi (Herman) Segal, of the nationalist Revisionist party. Itzhak Gruenbaum was appointed chairman of the board. A council was also elected consisting of thirty members, most of them representing the various immigrants' associations, as well as institutions and political parties. The three-man secretariat consisted of Maximilian Apolinary Hartglas (the last chairman of the Zionist organization of Poland) as political secretary; Avraham Haft, a member of Kibbutz Deganya Aleph, as treasurer; and Joseph Kleinbaum as secretary-general.

From the very beginning, the committee was subject to public attack because of its composition. Its members had many other responsibilities and could not devote all their time to the rescue efforts. Moreover, it had no authority of its own, since the operations of other departments of the Jewish Agency deprived it of any real power. Public demonstrations and petitions were handled by the Va'ad Le'ummi, and other Agency bodies gathered information. These misgivings about the committee were shared by all of its members except for the five who were on the Jewish Agency executive board.

The committee's chairman, Itzhak Gruenbaum, was the target of especially severe criticism and was repeatedly called upon to resign. In 1942, Gruenbaum refused to lend credence to the reports of systematic murders and extermination camps. By early 1943 Gruenbaum despaired of the success of any large-scale rescue efforts, in view of the Yishuv's lack of resources and the indifference displayed by the Allies, and he stated that the Yishuv's main role was to establish in Palestine a place of refuge for those Jews who survived the war. He did not hesitate to speak his mind in no uncertain—and even provocative—terms, as when he stated that the needs of Palestine and of the Yishuv took priority over the needs of the Diaspora. Nevertheless, Gruenbaum collected large sums of money for the rescue efforts from non-Agency sources, and he conducted a far-flung correspondence with statemen and organizations in many parts of the world, urging them to participate. He also came up with a variety of ideas and proposals for saving Jewish lives and for bringing Jews out of Europe, although not necessarily to Palestine.

The tense relations between Gruenbaum and David BEN-GURION, the chairman of the Jewish Agency, made it difficult for Gruenbaum to carry out his function as chairman of the Rescue Committee, and contributed to the committee's lack of any real power. Its activities remained primarily marginal: it collected information, sounded out new ideas, dispatched cables, and appealed for aid. Most of the Yishuv's rescue efforts were carried out by other bodies, such as the Mosad le-Aliya Bet (Organization for "Illegal" Immigration), by leading figures in the Hagana (the underground Jewish army) and Histadrut (the Trade Union Federation), and by Yishuv representatives in Istanbul and Geneva. The operations of these institutions and individuals were confidential and therefore not known to the public at large, leaving the Rescue Committee as the only target for the Yishuv's profound dissatisfaction with the modest rescue efforts in 1943 and 1944.

Nevertheless, the committee remained in existence for a year and a half, mainly because the participating organizations realized that the situation in Europe was far too complex for any one of them to operate on its own, and also because of the high respect that they had for Gruenbaum's integrity and personal stature. In June 1944 the Revisionist representatives on the committee were dismissed, their party was conducting its own fund-raising for rescue operations, and their relations with the Yishuv's official institutions were deteriorating. In 1945 the Rescue Committee's main efforts were devoted to aiding the war refugees. As the time drew near for the establishment of the Jewish state, the committee ceased its operations.

BIBLIOGRAPHY

Gruenbaum, Y. *In the Days of Destruction and Holocaust, 1939–1945.* Jerusalem, 1950. (In Hebrew.)

Morgenstern, A. "The Jewish Relief Committee Attached to the Jewish Agency, 1942–1945." *Yalkut Moreshet* 13 (June 1971): 60–103. (In Hebrew.)

Porat, D. *An Entangled Leadership: The Yishuv and the Holocaust, 1942–1945.* Tel Aviv, 1986. (In Hebrew.)

DINA PORAT

JOODSE RAAD, the Jewish Council (JUDENRAT) in the NETHERLANDS, in existence from 1941 to 1943. The Joodse Raad was established in the wake of the riots caused by Dutch Nazi units in the Jewish quarter of Amsterdam in early February 1941, and of the ensuing clashes between Jews and non-Jews. One of the means to which the Germans resorted to reestablish order according to their needs was the creation of a Judenrat, on the model existing in other occupied countries. A German official on the staff of Arthur SEYSS-INQUART, the Reichskommissar for the Netherlands, summoned three Jews to his office, one of whom was Abraham ASSCHER, a well-known public figure (the other two were rabbis). Asscher agreed to set up a seventeen-member Judenrat for Amsterdam, with the aid of his close friend David COHEN.

Most of the men invited by Asscher and Cohen to join the Joodse Raad had worked with them for years in various Jewish institutions. Professionals and wealthy businessmen were in the majority, and the others were representatives of the Ashkenazic and Sephardic communities; religious leaders and Socialists were a very small minority. The day after receiving the German "invitation," the prospective members held their first meeting, on February 13, 1941. One of those present, Dr. Isaac Kisch, expressed his misgivings about the establishment of a Joodse Raad and spoke of the risks that the Jews would be taking if they agreed to set up such a body. Kisch was a member of the Jewish Coordination Committee, which the Jewish community organizations had formed at the end of 1940 to deal with problems created by the occupation and the German authorities' anti-Jewish policy. The chairman of that committee, Lodewijk Ernst VISSER, was totally opposed to the policy of cooperation with the Germans that Asscher and Cohen were advocating, and argued that the Jews should not negotiate with the Germans but should call on the

Dutch administration to protect the Jews as Dutch nationals. The co-chairmen of the Joodse Raad, Asscher and Cohen (especially the latter), were of the contrary opinion that the Jews had to accept the facts that the Germans were in power in the Netherlands, that it was they who determined policy toward the Jews, and that only by cooperating with them would it be possible to exert influence and gain some concessions. Within a short while Asscher had the opportunity of testing the validity of this view. When Dutch workers went on strike in February to protest Nazi brutalities, he appealed to employers to help prevent the strike from spreading to their own enterprises, and was permitted to go on the local radio station to call on the Jews to calm down.

The Joodse Raad rapidly became a strong, authoritative body, mainly owing to its large and efficient staff—the staff of the Comité voor Bijzondere Joodse Belangen (Committee for Special Jewish Affairs), which Asscher and Cohen had formed in 1933 to aid Jewish refugees from Germany. The Joodse Raad's prestige also benefited from its success in obtaining a permit to publish a weekly for the Jewish population, *Het Joodse Weekblad* (The Jewish Weekly). For a while the Germans considered setting up a national Jewish body to represent all the Jews of the Netherlands, and giving it legal status. At the end of 1941, however, Seyss-Inquart decided to have the Amsterdam Joodse Raad deal with all Jewish affairs in the country without changing its name or giving it such status. This decision also meant that the Jewish Coordination Committee had to be disbanded. While that committee cooperated with the Joodse Raad in some areas, it was basically at odds with it, with Visser attacking Asscher and Cohen for taking (in his view) too submissive a line toward the Germans.

Expansion of Activities. In the course of 1941, the range of the Joodse Raad's activities grew and its staff took on the size of a government department. The main cause of this phenomenal growth was the anti-Jewish policy of the occupying authorities. The Jews were dispossessed of their businesses and livelihood, and their economic contacts were restricted to other Jews; as a result, a large part of the community was in need of financial assistance. Public institutions and parks were placed out of bounds, and the Jews had to expand their existing institutions or create others from scratch.

Some one thousand Jewish companies and societies were dissolved or broken up in 1941; in most instances their property was confiscated and their obligations were passed on to the Joodse Raad. An umbrella organization, financed by the Joodse Raad, was founded to include all social-welfare agencies. Another expansion of the Joodse Raad's size and responsibilities was caused by the exclusion, in the summer of 1941, of all Jewish children from public schools. At first, local government authorities assumed the task of establishing schools for the Jewish children, but since these authorities required the Joodse Raad's advice and assistance, the council created a special bureau for this purpose. After the first school year was over, the entire Jewish educational system was put into the hands of the Joodse Raad, and all the teachers in the system became its employees. In February 1942, its educational network consisted of 111 schools in 36 cities, with a staff of 758 teachers and a student body of 14,500. The staff of the central school administration also dealt with school buildings, teaching aids, and supervision. Apart from its responsibilities for education and social welfare (which included supervision of hospitals and their staff), the Joodse Raad also was in charge of food distribution to the Jews of Amsterdam and the issuance of various types of certificates, such as travel permits. This meant a corresponding growth in the size of the staff; at its height, it numbered seventeen thousand. Some of these workers were unpaid, their employment by the council providing assurance—for a while—that they would not be sent to labor camps and from there deported to Poland.

Taxes and Money Collection. Even before the Joodse Raad was created, a finance committee for Jews in the Netherlands had been formed, under the auspices of the Committee for Special Jewish Affairs. On German orders, that finance committee was taken over by the Joodse Raad. Shortly after the occupation of the country in May 1940, the finance committee imposed a "voluntary" tax on all Jews in order to fund educational and other activities. It also determined the amount to be paid by

The Joodse Raad. Seated at the far left is Abraham Asscher, co-chairman; next to him is Professor David Cohen, co-chairman. Chief Rabbi Philip Frank is seated sixth from the left.

every Jew out of his income and his financial assets. By the time the committee was taken over by the Joodse Raad, the tax had become compulsory; anyone who did not pay was not issued a "gray card." This card, certifying that the bearer had fulfilled his financial obligation, had to be produced by every Jew who applied to the Joodse Raad for aid. The substantial sum of 6 million gulden was collected in this manner.

On August 8, 1941, the Germans published an order according to which all Dutch Jews had to deposit their money in a single bank, Lippmann-Rosenthal—a Jewish bank that became a de facto extension of the German administration. From then on, all contributions to the Joodse Raad had to be paid through this bank. On January 1, 1943, all individual Jewish accounts were abolished and their balances were absorbed into a single general account, from which the Joodse Raad received a monthly allocation to cover its expenses. According to its section, monthly costs for the four permanent outlays—education, organizations, welfare, and general expenses—amounted to 945,000 gulden. As of that month, however, the German administration demanded that the Joodse Raad also finance the monthly allocations that individual account-holders had hitherto been permitted to withdraw; these added up to 600,000 gulden a month. This meant that the council required over 1,500,000 gulden a month to meet its obligations. The German administration, however, transferred only 800,000 gulden a month and was generally late with that. The Joodse Raad's expenditures therefore had to be reduced by nearly 50 percent.

The "Final Solution." In summer 1941 the German authorities in the Netherlands embarked on preparations for the "Final Solution" and assigned new tasks to the Joodse

Raad. Of these, the most difficult to implement was the concentration in Amsterdam of Jews from the rest of the Netherlands (except for those who were taken to the VUGHT camp) and the supplying of Jews to the labor camps that were being set up. The German administration ordered the Joodse Raad to provide it with lists of all unemployed Jews—after first depriving many Jews of their work permits so as to render them unemployed. The council also had to deal with the administrative aspects of moving Jews to the labor camps, the latter ostensibly being run by the Dutch authorities. The fact that the Joodse Raad agreed to select the candidates for the labor camps caused great resentment among Jews. Both the men who were sent to the camps and the families they left behind suffered severely. Especially after April 1942, conditions in the camps were harsh, and Jewish laborers were treated worse than the non-Jewish unemployed.

On May 3, 1942, the yellow badge (*see* BADGE, JEWISH) was introduced in the Netherlands, with the Joodse Raad actively participating in its distribution. On June 26 of that year, the council was told of the deportations to eastern Europe, where, it was explained, the deported Jews would be asked to perform "police duties in German labor camps." In order to turn the Joodse Raad into an effective instrument in the operation, the Germans promised its staff that "until further notice" they would be exempt from the deportations. As it turned out, however, the Joodse Raad could not force the Jews to report for the transports of their own free will. The German and Dutch police had to seek them out and arrest them, using for this purpose lists based on the council's card index.

Throughout the period of the deportations, the Joodse Raad sought to keep up its educational and social-welfare functions, but in practice most of its efforts were related to the deportations. It attempted to negotiate the release of Jews, either as members of its staff or on the basis of documents it submitted to the Nazis trying to prove that the persons threatened were "Aryans" or were making an essential contribution to the German war effort. The Joodse Raad also tried to help Jews who were about to be deported, mainly by providing them with warm clothing.

For about ten months it was found possible to fill the trains that left the WESTERBORK transit camp for the extermination camps in Poland without touching the Joodse Raad staff to any appreciable extent. But their turn came. In May 1943, the Joodse Raad leaders were told to provide a list of 7,000 of the council's employees and their families (some 40 percent of the total protected staff) for deportation to the east. Once again the leaders gave in. In a single day, a small select team drew up a list of candidates for deportation, filled in the individual "invitations" to report for expulsion (over David Cohen's signature), and had runners deliver them to the victims. However, only about 10 percent of the candidates reported at the specified time and place, indicating that the Joodse Raad no longer had control over the Jews.

The reaction of the German administration came the very next day (May 26), when a major raid was launched in the old Jewish quarter of Amsterdam and its vicinity. On June 20 a similar raid was made in other parts of the city inhabited by Jews; 8,850 Jews were seized in the two raids and taken to Westerbork. What remained of the Joodse Raad continued to function until September 29, 1943, when most of the remaining Jews—numbering some two thousand persons—were taken to Westerbork. Asscher and Cohen, the two chairmen, were among them, and in Westerbork they were informed that the Joodse Raad had ceased to exist.

After the war, when members of the Joodse Raad returned to the Netherlands, both the surviving Jewish public and the Dutch authorities raised grave accusations against them. Cohen and Asscher were arrested and were to stand trial. The trial, however, never took place, partly because of evidence that came to light of the enormous role played by non-Jewish administrators in the crimes against the Jews. A "court of honor" that the Jews set up found Asscher and Cohen guilty on five counts: (1) the very establishment of the Joodse Raad; (2) the publication of a weekly paper that disseminated their course of action; (3) the giving of instructions concerning the deportations to eastern Europe; (4) the participation in handing out the yellow badge; and (5) the selection of 7,000 names for deportation. The sentence, issued in 1947, was intended to bar the two from serving in any honorary post in a Jewish institution. In 1950 the Union of Ashkenazic Congregations quashed the sentence.

BIBLIOGRAPHY

De Jong, L. *Het Koninkrijk der Nederlanden in de Tweede Wereldoorlog.* Vols. 4–8. The Hague, 1972–1978.

Herzberg, A. J. *Kroniek der Jodenvervolging.* Amsterdam, 1978.

Michman, J. "The Controversial Stand of the Joodse Raad in the Netherlands." *Yad Vashem Studies* 10 (1974): 9–68.

Michman, J. "The Controversy Surrounding the Jewish Council of Amsterdam." In *Patterns of Jewish Leadership in Nazi Europe, 1933–1945.* Proceedings of the Third Yad Vashem International Historical Conference, edited by Y. Gutman and C. J. Haft, pp. 235–258. Jerusalem, 1979.

Michman, J., H. Beem, and D. Michman, eds. *The Netherlands.* In *Pinkas Hakehillot; Encyclopaedia of Jewish Communities.* Jerusalem, 1985. See pages 79–138. (In Hebrew.)

Presser, J. *The Destruction of the Dutch Jews.* New York, 1969.

JOZEPH MICHMAN

JOYCE, WILLIAM ("Lord Haw-Haw"; 1906–1946), British fascist; broadcaster of Nazi propaganda from Germany to the British Isles during World War II.

Joyce was born in New York into an Irish family. His father was a Catholic and his mother a Protestant. The family became American nationals, but returned to Ireland in 1909. Joyce's parents were loyal British subjects and educated him to be the same. In 1921 they moved to England, and Joyce engaged in university studies in London.

In 1923 Joyce joined a small group of anti-Communist British fascists. He became a member of the British Union of Fascists (BUF) when it was founded in 1932, under the leadership of Sir Oswald MOSLEY. By virtue of his talents and zeal, Joyce was put in charge of the party's political propaganda machine, and achieved a reputation as a fiery speaker who aroused audiences with his radical ideas. He failed to be elected to a local council in London and fell out with Mosley, whose anti-Jewish policy he considered too moderate. For these reasons, and also because of the current financial crisis, in 1937 Joyce left the BUF. Together with former member of Parliament John Beckett, who had also broken with the BUF, he established the National Socialist League. The league was close to German Nazism; Joyce admired Adolf HITLER, and aspired to escalate the struggle against capitalism and the Jews. It remained a small group of extremists and made no impression on the political life of Britain.

In August 1939, on the eve of the outbreak of war, Joyce decided to go to Germany together with his second wife. Shortly after the war began, he began to make propaganda broadcasts, including attacks on the Jews, to Britain on behalf of the Germans, in the program "Germany Calling," which attracted many listeners. Estimates differ as to the impact of these broadcasts. Some observers claim that the British public considered them a kind of wartime entertainment, while others have suggested that the broadcasts helped to spread defeatist rumors, arguing that they always included a certain amount of genuine information together with falsehoods and provocations. The nickname "Lord Haw-Haw" originated in the British press before Joyce's true identity was known. He was hated by the British people and considered a traitor. Joyce himself wrote the majority of the material he broadcast.

During the war Joyce was granted German citizenship, and after the defeat of the Nazis he tried to escape under an assumed name, but he was discovered and arrested at the end of May 1945. He was brought to Britain and charged with treason in time of war. In his defense Joyce argued that he was not a British national, that he was an American citizen by birth, and that during the war he had received German citizenship. However, it was discovered that in 1933 Joyce had applied for and received a British passport, claiming British nationality; that the validity of the passport had been extended; and that he had used it to travel to Germany. The trial evoked tremendous public interest. He was found guilty, and in January 1946 he was executed.

Joyce's last public statement was: "During

my life and at my death I fought against the Jews, who were the cause of the war and who represent the forces of evil."

[*See also* Great Britain: Fascism in Great Britain.]

BIBLIOGRAPHY

Cole, J. A. *Lord Haw-Haw—William Joyce.* New York, 1965.

West, R. *The Meaning of Treason.* London, 1952.

JACQUELINE ROKHSAR

JUDENRAT [*This entry is a survey of the Jewish councils created by the Nazis to administer the internal life of the ghettos of eastern Europe and the regional Jewish populations in western Europe. See also* Ghetto; *for more information about specific Judenräte, see the headings in the encyclopedia by country and place. See in addition the biographies of individual heads of Judenräte.*]

The name "Judenrat" (pl., Judenräte) refers to the Jewish councils established on German orders in the Jewish communities of occupied Europe. Judenräte were first instituted in occupied Poland, on instructions issued by Reinhard HEYDRICH on September 21, 1939, and through an order promulgated by Hans FRANK, the head of the GENERALGOUVERNEMENT, on November 18, 1939, and subsequently in other countries conquered by Germany. The Judenräte did not have a uniform structure; some of them held authority in one location only, while others administered Jewish communities throughout a district or even an entire country. The role played by the Judenräte in Jewish public life during the Holocaust is one of the most controversial issues relating to the period; some historians believe that the institution of the Judenrat had a debilitating effect on the inner strength of the Jewish communities, whereas others maintain that the Judenräte reinforced the Jews' power of endurance in their struggle for survival.

On the basis of Heydrich's instructions of September 21, Judenräte were set up over the course of a few weeks in September and October 1939 in the communities of central and western Poland. The guidelines stipulated that the Judenräte would be fully responsible for the implementation of German policy regarding the Jews and would be made up, "as far as possible, of influential people and rabbis." In this way, the Jewish communities had forced on them a body whose function was to receive German orders and decrees and be responsible for carrying them out. The inclusion of prominent personalities in the Judenräte had a dual purpose: to ensure that

Members of the Kovno Ältestenrat (Council of Elders). Dr. Elchanan Elkes is in the center.

The Judenrat of the town of Checiny, 9 miles (14.5 km) southwest of Kielce, in Poland. The German army entered the town on September 5, 1939. On September 13, 1942, the ghetto was liquidated and the remaining Jews deported to Treblinka.

German orders were implemented to the fullest possible extent, and to discredit Jewish leadership in the eyes of the Jewish population.

Under Frank's order, in places where the Jewish population did not exceed ten thousand the Judenrat was to have twelve members, and in the larger towns or cities it was to consist of twenty-four members. The councils were to be elected by the members of the community and were themselves to elect their chairman and vice-chairman. The process of electing the Judenräte and their two top officers was to be completed by December 31, 1939; the results were subject to the approval of the German *Kreishauptmann* (chief district official) or, in the cities, of the German *Stadthauptmann* (chief city official). This last provision meant in effect that the elections provided for in Frank's order were quite meaningless, and that the Germans never did intend to have the Judenräte's composition determined by elections. German intervention in the process, however, was not absolute, and on a number of occasions active members of the Jewish community had a say in determining the composition of the council. In some cases, Jewish activists refused to join the Judenrat, because they were suspicious of the use that the Germans would make of the institution. Generally, however, local Jewish leaders did become members of the councils. This corresponded to the wishes of the Jewish population, which felt that it was precisely the traditional leaders of the community who were best equipped to represent it vis-à-vis the German authorities in the critical and perilous situation that had arisen. Thus, paradoxically, the two conflicting purposes, of the Jews and the Germans, ensured that in the

Members of the Kraków Judenrat.

early stages of their existence, the Judenräte preserved the continuity of local leadership. However, even in the first councils to come into being, some of the members had no previous experience in public affairs.

Decisions on Implementation. Once the Judenräte were established, the Germans lost no time in presenting them with urgent tasks: drafting people for forced labor, taking a census of the Jewish population, evacuating apartments and handing them over to Germans, paying fines or ransoms, confiscating valuables owned by Jews, and so on. In most cases, the Judenrat members tried to delay the administrative and economic measures that the Germans were imposing, or at least to alleviate them. However, the traditional methods employed by Jews for dealing with the authorities, such as lobbying officials and utilizing personal contacts, were not applicable under the new conditions. The Judenräte did try to exploit the rivalry among the various branches of the German administration in order to lighten the burden imposed on the Jews, but their success here was minimal.

The Judenräte believed that by complying with the German demands they would impress upon the Nazis the vital importance to the Germans of the Jewish community. In this way they hoped to avert or moderate some of the blows, to gain time, to ward off or delay collective punishments, and perhaps even to persuade the Germans to reconsider their policy in view of the benefit they could derive from the Jews, as a reservoir for the manpower the Germans sorely needed; in the meantime, the Jews hoped, the war would end in a German defeat. It took a while before these theories and assessments were put to the test—until the mass deportations of 1942, when the true nature of German policy became increasingly obvious.

Providing Basic Needs. Judenrat members were also involved in providing the community with its basic needs. The German invasion of Poland, and subsequently of other countries, destroyed the existing Jewish economic structure, which even before the war had been shaky. Jewish society had always included groups requiring public assistance, but the problems created by the German occupation were of unprecedented dimensions. Various measures imposed upon the Jewish community caused a further deterioration of their economic condition. Tens of thousands of Jews were displaced from their homes and became refugees, without a place to live or a source of food. Jews were no longer covered by the general public services and required their own health services and public institutions, such as homes for the aged, orphanages, and, in part, educational institutions. In coping with this daily struggle for the survival of the community, the Judenrat members drew upon their experience gained in Jewish welfare activities before the war, even though there was no comparison between conditions in the two eras. The Judenrat's efforts to ease the plight of the Jewish population were among of the ways in which it sought to counter the Nazi policy of starving the communities and breaking their power of resistance. Even in that first stage, however, some of the Judenrat activities were not without instances of protectionism, favoritism, misuse of positions of public trust for personal advantage, and so on. Such practices caused bitter resentment in the communities and were harshly criticized.

More functions were imposed upon the Judenräte by the Germans with the ghettoization of the Jews of occupied Poland and, following the invasion of the Soviet Union, the Jews of other countries of eastern Europe. The Judenräte were made responsible for transferring Jews from their homes into the areas allotted for the ghettos, for providing accommodation in the ghettos for the new inhabitants, for maintaining public order in the ghettos, and for preventing smuggling. Some of these duties were carried out by the Jewish police (*see* JÜDISCHER ORDNUNGSDIENST).

Under ghetto conditions, which separated the Jews from the general population, the hardships became much worse. Large sections of the Jewish community faced starvation. It was the Judenrat's responsibility to distribute the food rations permitted by the Germans, but usually these did not constitute even the barest minimum needed for survival. In a number of ghettos, the Judenräte sought to obtain more food by buying provisions on the black market or on the "Aryan" side, or by bartering products manufactured in the ghetto. The Judenräte also established organizations for mutual help, thereby providing some relief from the suffering.

Self-Help. As a result of starvation, overcrowding, and the lack of basic sanitary facilities, diseases spread in the ghetto. The Germans held the Judenrat responsible for ensuring that contagious diseases did not cross the ghetto borders, but they regarded the growth of the death rate in the ghettos as a welcome addition to their own measures taken against the Jews. The Judenrat, for its part, set up hospitals and clinics and organized other forms of medical aid in order to reduce, as much as possible, the dimensions of the diseases and epidemics. In many ghettos, community forces other than the Judenrat waged war on starvation and disease through such unofficial frameworks as political organizations and youth movements. In Poland, the Żydowska Samopomoc Społeczna (Jewish Self-Help Society), an organization recognized by the Germans, sought to provide help to the needy. In some cases the Judenrat and the voluntary organizations cooperated with one another, but there was friction between them when the Judenrat wanted to exercise supervision over all welfare and medical-aid operations among the Jewish population.

Beginning in 1940, the Judenräte were given the task of providing forced labor for the camps that were being set up, first in occupied Poland and later in other occupied areas. This was a fundamental change from the Judenrat's previous assignments. It did not mean sending people on forced labor in or near their place of residence, where they could return in the evening to their community and family; it meant total separation and transfer to remote locations where a much harsher regime was in force—a regime that many prisoners could not endure for long.

Compliance or Refusal. The Judenräte had to make a decision whether to comply with this German demand. In most instances they did supply the required quota of able-bodied young men as workers for the labor camps, causing friction with the community when the latter had to be seized on the streets for deportation to the camps. In the initial stages of forced-labor deportations, the Judenräte tried to maintain contact with the members of their community imprisoned in the camps, sending them food, clothing, and medicines, but when German policy took a turn for the worse, the contact was broken off. In some cases councils refused to supply quotas for the labor camps. When Joseph Parnes, chairman of the Judenrat in LVOV, refused to send men to the JANÓWSKA camp, he forfeited his life.

As time went on, however, and Nazi policy

approached the next phase, that of mass extermination of Jews, the Judenräte had very little room left for maneuvering between the needs of the Jewish population and the demands made by the Germans. Judenrat members had to confront the question of where to draw the line—to decide whether compliance with German orders was still to be regarded as a contribution to the community's struggle for survival. On this issue there were bitter discussions within and outside the Judenräte. The decisions taken by the council members and the answers they gave to this crucial question differed in substance, and also depended on the specific moment when they had to be made. It is these decisions and answers that form the basis for value judgments of the Judenrat.

The pattern of behavior of Judenrat members falls into four categories:

1. Refusal to cooperate with the Germans, even with regard to economic measures or other relatively mundane issues;
2. Acquiescence with extreme measures of a material nature, such as the seizure of property, but absolute refusal to hand over human beings;
3. Resignation to the destruction of parts of the Jewish community, on the assumption that this would enable other segments to be saved;
4. Compliance in full with all German orders, without any consideration for their effect on the Jewish public, and with concern only for one's own personal interests.

Isaiah Trunk, in his 1972 study on the Judenrat, provides data on the fate of 720 Judenrat members in eastern Europe, summarized in Table 1. These figures show that close to 80 percent of Judenrat members died either before the mass *Aktionen* took place or in the course of the deportations to extermination camps. In very many cases, they lost their lives as a result of their failure to comply with German orders. The conduct of 146 Judenrat chairmen, the first to be appointed to their posts in the Generalgouvernement, is shown in Table 2, a summary of data in Aharon Weiss's 1977 study.

It can be seen that in the first phase of the Judenrat's existence, the chairmen looked after the interests of their community and did not give in to German pressure. Those who followed—that is, those who assumed their posts after the original chairmen had been dismissed or killed—were, for the most part, German appointees, and their conduct in office shows a different pattern. For that final phase, Table 3 summarizes data (in Weiss's study) on 101 communities in the Generalgouvernement.

The outstanding feature of these data is the sharp rise in the figures that indicate obedience to the Germans and yielding to their pressure. Whereas in the first phase the Judenrat chairmen (or at least some of them) had been responsible Jewish leaders, their successors were less sensitive to public interests; in the final stages of mass extermination and relentless terror, these Judenrat chairmen almost invariably carried out Nazi orders.

In their search for ways to prevent, slow down, or reduce the onslaught upon their communities, many Judenräte adopted a pol-

TABLE 1. *Fate of 720 Judenrat Members in Eastern Europe*

	NUMBER	PERCENTAGE
Relinquished their membership	21	2.9
Were removed from the Judenrat or arrested	13	1.8
Were murdered before the deportations to extermination camps	182	25.3
Went to their death during the deportations (either murdered on the spot or deported)	383	53.2
Committed suicide	9	1.2
Died a natural death	26	3.6
Survived	86	12.0
Total	720	100.0

TABLE 2. *Conduct of 146 Judenrat Chairmen in the Generalgouvernement*

	NUMBER	PERCENTAGE
Extended help to the community, refused to carry out economic measures, warned of *Aktionen* that were being prepared	45	30.8
Resigned from their posts because they could not accept Nazi policy	11	7.5
Were dismissed by the Germans after failing to carry out orders	26	17.8
Were killed by the Germans after refusing to hand over members of the community	18	12.3
Committed suicide	5	3.4
Maintained contact with the underground	2	1.4
Died at beginning of term	4	2.7
Were replaced by the Jews themselves	1	0.7
Opinions differ on their conduct in office	13	9.0
Complied with German orders	21	14.4
Total	146	100.0

icy of "rescue by labor." The Judenrat members who supported this policy saw in it one of the few realistic alternatives they had to convince the Germans of the importance, for Germany, of the continued existence of the community. And, as the war went on and the economy required additional manpower, certain German circles, on both the central and the local level, were inclined to utilize Jewish manpower. These were primarily officials in charge of the production of arms and other military equipment and supplies. Their view was not a deviation from the "Final Solution" policy; it represented no more than a pragmatic consideration dictated by the prevailing conditions. But there were Judenräte that saw in such German needs openings that could be exploited to save Jews. The Judenräte that applied this policy were in fact resigned to the hopelessness of trying to save their entire community, but they felt they might salvage a part of it. Prominent among

TABLE 3. *Conduct of 101 Later Judenrat Chairmen in the Generalgouvernement*

	NUMBER	PERCENTAGE
Helped the community, refused to comply with economic decrees, warned of impending *Aktionen*	16	15.8
Could not accept Nazi policy and resigned from their posts	4	3.9
Were dismissed by the Germans for failing to carry out orders	8	7.9
Were killed by the Germans after refusing to hand over members of the community	2	2.0
Committed suicide	1	1.0
Maintained contact with the underground	1	1.0
Died a natural death	1	1.0
Opinions differ on their conduct	7	7.0
Complied with German orders	61	60.4
Total	101	100.0

members who supported this line were Mordechai Chaim RUMKOWSKI of Łódź, Jacob GENS of Vilna, Moshe MERIN of SOSNOWIEC, in Eastern Upper SILESIA, and Efraim BARASZ of BIAŁYSTOK.

Resistance. Relations between the Judenrat and the Jewish underground and fighters' organizations in the ghettos were highly complex and did not follow a uniform pattern. A substantial number of Judenräte were opposed to the idea of armed resistance or of fleeing to the forests to join the partisans. Some council members believed that underground activities in the ghetto would endanger the entire community and hasten its liquidation, in view of the rule of "collective responsibility" that the Nazis had introduced. This was the background to the tension in many ghettos where the Judenrat and the underground competed for influence. In some places, feelings ran high enough for violent clashes to erupt: in WARSAW, where the ŻYDOWSKA ORGANIZACJA BOJOWA (Jewish Fighting Organization; ŻOB) attacked the Jewish police, and in VILNA, where a dispute erupted over the Yitzhak WITTENBERG affair. In Eastern Upper Silesia, Judenrat chairman Moshe Merin waged all-out war against the underground; similar situations existed in Kraków and other places.

Some Judenräte did not have a clear-cut position on the issue of resistance. They accepted the presence of an underground and even gave it help, but argued that if active resistance were offered prematurely, it would interfere with the Judenrat's policy, the main purpose of which was to gain time in the hope that developments in the war situation would bring rescue for the Jews. While supporting the concept of resistance, they felt it should be implemented only when it was clear that the community was about to be liquidated. This was the position held by Efraim Barasz, chairman of the Judenrat in Białystok.

In other ghettos, such as those of KOVNO and (at one period) MINSK, Judenrat members assisted the underground without reservations of any kind. There were also instances when Judenrat members headed underground activities and took a leading part in uprisings. Dov Lopatyn, the Judenrat chairman in LACHVA, was one of the leaders of the uprising there, in which the whole community took part; in DIATLOVO, the Judenrat members organized a partisan unit; and council members played a central role in the uprising in TUCHIN.

National and Local Function. As the war progressed and German power increased, the Germans and their allies continued to establish Judenräte. The problems facing these Judenräte had much in common with those of eastern Europe. But there were also differences, which depended on local conditions, on the structure of the Jewish communities and the standing of their leaders, and on the policies pursued by the German government and the governments of the satellite and German-protected states. Thus, for example, in the areas of eastern Europe where the Germans exercised direct control, the Judenräte were local institutions and, for the most part, had no contact with one another. In other parts of Europe, the councils were set up as country-wide institutions, and this affected the way they functioned, their relations with the Germans and the local governments, and their ties with the Jewish population.

Germany. In 1933, when the Nazis came to power in GERMANY, the Jews, on their own initiative, established an umbrella organization, the REICHSVERTRETUNG DER DEUTSCHEN JUDEN (Reich Representation of German Jews), a voluntary federation of Jewish communities and large organizations. Its purpose was to deal with the major problems that German Jewry was facing under the Nazi regime. In 1939 the Reichsvertretung became the official central organization of the Jews, with its name changed to the Reichsvereinigung der Juden in Deutschland (Reich Association of Jews in Germany). It was headed by the same men who had been the leaders of the Reichsvertretung, Rabbi Leo BAECK and Otto HIRSCH.

Until recently, the prevailing opinion of scholars was that the change from a voluntary to a centralist and compulsory organization had been instigated by the Germans to facilitate the implementation of their steadily hardening policy toward German Jewry. A large number of scholars considered that the Reichsvereinigung was the prototype of the Judenräte which the Germans were to set up in the areas they occupied during the war. Current research, however, has revealed that the changeover from Reichsvertretung to Reichsvereinigung was largely initiated by the Jewish leadership itself, which sought to strengthen its influence on the Jewish population in view of the Nazi decision, in 1938, to abolish the legal status of the Kultusgemeinde (local Jewish community organizations). Coincidentally, the Germans were also interested in establishing a central Jewish body—their purpose indeed being to turn it into an instrument for implementating measures against the Jews that was more efficient and easier to control than its predecessor. In due course, the Germans were to apply the same principles in the creation of the Judenräte.

Other Countries. In FRANCE, a central Judenrat, the UNION GÉNÉRALE DES ISRAÉLITES DE FRANCE (UGIF), was set up on November 29, 1941. It consisted of two branches, one in German-occupied northern France and the other in Vichy France, in the south. All other political and public Jewish organizations were closed down, though most continued to operate as independent bodies under the cover of UGIF departments, which enabled them to combine their legal functions with their clandestine aid and rescue operations. The UGIF was headed by prominent prewar Jewish leaders who took no part in the arrest, imprisonment, and deportation of Jews, and who tried to ease the overall lot of the French Jews.

In BELGIUM, the order for the establishment of a Judenrat was announced on November 25, 1941. It was named the ASSOCIATION DES JUIFS EN BELGIQUE (AJB), and the Chief Rabbi of Belgium, Solomon Ullman, was appointed its chairman. The AJB, with local branches in the Belgian cities, was charged with setting up a register of the Jewish population that the Germans planned to use in drafting Jews for forced labor and for deportation. Most of the time the AJB complied with the orders it was given by the Germans, thus causing bitter resentment and resistance among the Jews. In the summer of 1942, Judenrat members delivered to the Jews German notices ordering them to report for forced labor—in actuality, a cover for deportation to "the east." As a result, other Jews who had been working for the Judenrat decided to resign. The phenomenon of AJB members giving in to German decrees repeated itself in 1943 and 1944, but there were also many AJB people who established ties with the Jewish underground and general Jewish organizations during that period and who made their contribution to the resistance and rescue efforts.

The Germans established a Judenrat, the JOODSE RAAD, in the NETHERLANDS in early 1941. Its authority was restricted at first to Amsterdam, but within a short time was extended to the entire country. David COHEN and Abraham ASSCHER, two veteran leaders of the community, were appointed as the Judenrat heads. In the first phase of its existence, the Joodse Raad organized services needed by the community, but it was also charged with various tasks that served German measures against the Jews, such as registering the Jewish population of the country. In summer 1942 the Joodse Raad was ordered to draw up lists of persons who were to be sent "to work in the east." Following a sharp internal debate, the council agreed to provide the Germans with 7,000 names. For this action and for other instances of compliance with German orders, the Judenrat in the Netherlands was severely criticized at the time, and also in the postwar years.

In SLOVAKIA, a central Judenrat, the ÚSTREDŇA ŽIDOV (Jewish Center), was set up in September 1940, with headquarters in the capital, Bratislava, and branches in other cities. It was the only institution authorized to represent the Jews, and its officers were well-known public figures. The council sought to provide the Jewish population with essential services, give aid to the needy, create employment, and establish vocational training courses. Following the 1942 deportations from Slovakia, it increased its activities in the labor camps, setting up workshops and organizing construction crews, with the object of demonstrating that the Jews played a vital role in the country's economy. Some members were inclined to submit to German demands; one of these was Karel Hochberg, who wielded considerable influence in the Ústredňa Židov. During the deportations an underground group, the PRACOVNÁ SKUPINA (Working Group), was formed within the council, under the leadership of Gisi FLEISCHMANN and Rabbi Michael Dov WEISSMANDEL, who did not belong to the latter. In addition to their official duties in the Ústredňa Židov, the

An Ústredňa Židov (Jewish Center) workshop in Slovakia for vocational retraining.

Pracovná Skupina members initiated aid and rescue efforts, in the course of which they made contact with elements outside Slovakia; it was they who put forward the so-called EUROPA PLAN, a proposal for rescuing the surviving remnants of European Jewry.

A central Judenrat for HUNGARY was instituted in Budapest in March 1944, under the name of Zsidó Tanács (Jewish Council). Its chairman was Samu STERN, a leader of the Neolog (progressive Judaism) movement in Hungary and the president of the Jewish community in Pest. Local councils were formed in other Hungarian cities. Both the central and local councils in Hungary complied with the administrative and economic measures that were imposed on the Jews. Researchers of the Holocaust in Hungary stress that the Judenrat members gave no warning to the communities in which they operated of the dangers in store for them, although they themselves were well aware of what had happened to the Jews in other countries under German occupation. The legalistic-traditional approach of the Hungarian Judenrat leaders was unsuitable for the conditions that prevailed in the Holocaust era: they expected that Hungarian political forces would rally to their defense, but these, for the most part, turned their backs on the Jews. The Judenrat members in Hungary have been accused of failing to exercise proper leadership of the community in that grim period.

In ROMANIA, the CENTRALA EVREILOR (Jewish Center) went into operation in Bucharest at the beginning of 1942, with branches in various Romanian cities. The Union of Jewish Communities (Federatia Uniunilor de Comunitati Evreesti), which until then had administered Jewish community life in the country, was disbanded. Nandor Ghingold, a baptized Jew who was totally unknown among the Jewish population, was appointed chairman of the council, which was directly subordinated to Radu LECCA, the Romanian official in charge of Jewish affairs. The council operated in four areas: preparing surveys of the Jewish population, drafting Jews for forced labor, collecting fines imposed on the Jews, and organizing welfare assistance. The Germans kept track of the council's activities and exerted pressure on the Romanian government to use it in a manner designed to weaken the public standing and influence of Dr. Wilhelm FILDERMAN, who had been the head of the Union of Communities, and of other traditional Jewish leaders. The attempt failed, and Filderman and the other veteran leaders worked to block the designs of the Germans and the Romanian antisemites. The Centrala Evreilor, on the other hand, did not gain the recognition of the Jewish population.

In GREECE there was no overall Judenrat per se. The Germans took SALONIKA on April 9, 1941, two months before all of Greece was occupied (on June 2) and divided among Germany, Italy, and Bulgaria. The Gestapo immediately seized some of the Jewish community leaders of Salonika—whom they considered possible sources of resistance—and appointed Shabbetai Shealtiel, an employee of the Jewish community association, as head of a newly constituted community board. The board was ordered to supply men for forced labor and to implement anti-Jewish economic measures. It complied with these demands.

Shealtiel proved to be inefficient, and in December 1942 he was dismissed and the Chief Rabbi of Salonika, Zvi KORETZ, was appointed in his place. From this point on, the board lost all autonomy, rapidly assumed the characteristics of a Judenrat, and was forced to carry out German orders to the letter. When deportations from Salonika to the extermination camps in Poland were launched in March 1943, Koretz tried to stop them, appealing to the Greek authorities to intervene on behalf of the Jews, but his efforts failed. Opinions differ as to Rabbi Koretz's actions; some historians point to the exertions he made to assist the Salonika community in critical days, while others emphasize his submission to German pressure.

Historical View. Research on the Judenrat phenomenon has been gradually abandoning the earlier indiscriminate condemnation of the Judenräte, and there is now a sharper discernment of the various elements that made up their activities. This view of the Judenrat takes into account the different phases that Nazi policy on the "Final Solution" went through and the changes that took place in the composition of the Judenräte, and examines the effect of these changes on the conduct of Judenrat members. Efforts have been made to understand the Judenrat by ascertaining how it used its limited authority—given to it by the Germans with the sole aim of enabling it to carry out German orders—for the good of the Jewish population; to what extent it achieved a fair distribution of the burden among the Jews; how it acted during the mass deportations to the extermination camps; the attitude of Judenrat members toward the deportations before it was known what fate awaited the deportees, and their actions once that fate was discovered; how the Judenrat viewed rescue efforts and the underground. An objective assessment of all these elements permits a more realistic and accurate historical evaluation of the Judenrat.

BIBLIOGRAPHY

Bauer, Y., and N. Rotenstreich, eds. *The Holocaust as Historical Experience: Essays and Discussion.* New York, 1981.

Friedman, P. "The Messianic Complex of a Nazi Collaborator: Moses Merin of Sosnowiec." In *Roads to Extinction: Essays on the Holocaust,* edited by Ada J. Friedman, pp. 353–364. Philadelphia, 1980.

Gutman, Y., and C. J. Haft, eds. *Patterns of Jewish Leadership in Nazi Europe, 1933–1945.* Proceedings of the Third Yad Vashem International Historical Conference. Jerusalem, 1979.

Klein, B. "The Judenrat." *Jewish Social Studies* 22/1 (1960): 67–84.

Trunk, I. *Judenrat: The Jewish Councils in Eastern Europe under Nazi Occupation.* New York, 1972.

Weiss, A. "Jewish Leadership in Occupied Poland: Postures and Attitudes." *Yad Vashem Studies* 12 (1977): 335–365.

AHARON WEISS

JÜDISCHER CENTRALVEREIN. *See* Centralverein Deutscher Staatsbürger Jüdischen Glaubens.

JÜDISCHER ORDNUNGSDIENST (Jewish GHETTO police, referred to by the Jews as the "Jewish police"), Jewish police units established by the Germans in certain places in the areas under their occupation. A relatively short time after their establishment, the Judenräte (Jewish councils) in eastern Europe were ordered to organize these units, usually in anticipation of the ghettoization of the Jews.

Whereas the JUDENRAT itself, although also

Jewish police in Lublin.

created on German orders, often contained elements of voluntary association, the Jewish police came into being only on German orders. There was no precedent in the life of the Jewish community for the existence of a Jewish police force, and no indication that independent initiative by Jews in any way played a part in the establishment of the ghetto police.

The Germans set guidelines according to which the Judenrat was to recruit the police personnel—physical fitness, military experience, and secondary or higher education. In practice, these guidelines were not always observed. Formally, the Jewish police constituted one of the Judenrat departments, but from the very beginning many Judenräte were apprehensive about the police department's public character and the way it would function. They suspected that the Germans would have direct supervision of the police and use it for the implementation of their policies. Aware of this danger, many Judenräte sought to establish their own means of controlling the police and the standards of its behavior, and tried to attract to the police young Jews who would be trustworthy. At first, some of the recruits did indeed believe that joining the police gave them an opportunity to serve the community. But there were other reasons for joining. Belonging to a protected organization, provided immunity from being seized for forced labor. Police service also offered greater freedom of movement and possibilities of obtaining food.

A study of the records of over one hundred Jewish police officers in the GENERALGOUVERNEMENT reveals that the Judenräte did not succeed in their efforts to ensure that the police had public credibility. Seventy percent of the men who served in the police force had taken no part in political and community life before the war, and some 20 percent were refugees and strangers to the ghetto population; only 10 percent had participated in community affairs in the prewar period. The Germans themselves often made sure, when the police was set up, that it would be headed by men who would blindly follow their orders. Some circles in the ghetto population who were not associated with the Judenrat regarded the Jewish police from the outset as an alien body and a potential danger to the community. In many places, youth movements and Jewish political parties did not permit their members to enlist in the police.

The size of the Jewish police force was not fixed but depended on the size of the Jewish community. Thus, in Warsaw the Jewish police at first numbered 2,000, in Lvov 500, in Łódź 800, in Kraków 150, and in Kovno 200. There was no uniform structure for the police units. In the large ghettos, the commanders held officer rank and the units were made up of subdivisions and district stations. The policemen were identified by the different caps they wore and by the unit's designation inscribed on their armband, the yellow badge that they, like all other Jews, had to wear (*see* BADGE, JEWISH). In the small ghettos where the police consisted of a few men only, no such organizational differentiations were made.

Jewish police in the Warsaw ghetto.

Police Duties. The duties carried out by the Jewish police can be divided into three categories:

1. Duties in response to specific German demands as conveyed to the police by the Germans, via the Judenrat
2. Duties related to the Judenrat's activities among the Jews that were not directly related to German demands
3. Duties related to the Jewish population's needs

The first two categories included collecting ransom payments, personal belongings and valuables, as well as taxes; fetching people for forced labor; guarding the ghetto wall or fence and the ghetto gates; escorting labor gangs who worked outside the ghetto; and, as time went on, conducting random seizures of persons to be sent to labor camps and participating in the roundup of Jews for mass deportations.

The exclusion of the Jewish population from public services and their isolation in ghettos created serious problems. In the early stage of its existence, the Jewish police attended to sanitary conditions and assisted in the distribution of food rations and aid to the needy. It also helped in the control of epidemics, and the settling of disputes—all this, of course, in addition to complying with German demands. The ghetto population appreciated the Jewish police for these public-welfare activities. However, already at this stage, there were instances of corruption and misconduct among the police.

Dilemmas. As time went on, the role of the Jewish police in alleviating living conditions in the ghetto was considerably reduced. The mass deportations to extermination camps, beginning in 1942, affected the families of the men serving in the police, their friends, acquaintances, and fellow Jews, and they had to decide whether or not to stay at their posts. Many decided to quit the force, some in an overt manner, so as to express their identification with their families and with the Jewish population as a whole. Most of the Jewish policemen who made such a decision were subsequently included in the transports that left for the extermination camps. But there were also Jewish police who stayed on their jobs up to the final phases of the ghettos' existence, submitting to German pressure and obediently following orders. At that stage the Jewish police took on a different complexion. Directly intervening in its administration, the Germans recruited new men into the force, both as officers and rank and file, who had no commitment at all to the Jewish population. Among the new Jewish police personnel were many refugees with no ties to the surviving remnants of the local Jewish community, as well as men of dubious reputation. In numerous ghettos where the Judenrat was not prepared to submit blindly to German orders, it was the Jewish police who gained in strength, to the extent that it was able to control the Judenrat or simply take its place.

The Underground. The attitude of the Jewish police toward the ghetto underground took on three different forms:

1. The most common relationship was one of tension. In several ghettos—such as those of BĘDZIN, SOSNOWIEC, KRAKÓW, and WARSAW—the Jewish police tried to do away with the underground (which is not to say that all members of the police in these places took part in such efforts). In Warsaw, in August 1942, during the mass deportations, the Jewish police commander, Joseph Szerynski, was attacked by the underground and seriously wounded. His successor, Jacob Lejkin, was assassinated in October of that year, on orders of the ŻYDOWSKA ORGANIZACJA BOJOWA (Jewish Fighting Organization; ŻOB).

2. There were instances when the Jewish police followed a policy of nonintervention in the activities of the underground that sometimes took on the form of "benign neglect."

3. In some ghettos, such as that of KOVNO, the Jewish police gave active help to the underground, and some policemen were also members of clandestine organizations.

Conclusion. When the war ended, the conduct of the Jewish police in the ghettos came under investigation by groups of survivors. In Munich (which was in the American zone), forty Jewish policemen were found guilty of improper conduct and were ostracized by the Jewish public. In Israel, several policemen were charged under the Nazis and Nazi Collaborators (Punishment) Law; a few were convicted but most were acquitted, the courts taking into account, *inter alia*, the extraordinary circumstances under which the Jewish policemen in the ghettos had had to function.

BIBLIOGRAPHY

Trunk, I. *Judenrat: The Jewish Councils in Eastern Europe under Nazi Occupation.* New York, 1972. See pages 475–569.

Weiss, A. "The Relations between the Judenrat and the Jewish Police." In *Patterns of Jewish Leadership in Nazi Europe, 1933–1945.* Proceedings of the Third Yad Vashem International Historical Conference, edited by Y. Gutman and C. Haft, pp. 201–217. Jerusalem, 1979.

AHARON WEISS

JUD SÜSS. *See* Films, Nazi Antisemitic.

JURISPRUDENCE IN NAZI GERMANY. *See* Law and Judiciary in Nazi Germany.

KACZERGINSKI, SHMARYAHU (Shmerke; 1908–1954), Jewish writer, poet, and partisan. Kaczerginski attended the Talmud Torah (religious school) in Vilna and then received vocational training, becoming a lithographer. While still at school he wrote poems and stories, and in the late 1920s was one of the founding members of Yung-Vilne (Young Vilna), a group of modernist Yiddish writers. He was arrested a number of times for his activities among the underground Communist youth. His revolutionary poems became popular folk songs in Poland, and prior to World War II he published poems, stories, a novel (*Yugnt on Freyd* [Youth without Joy]), and articles. He was also a correspondent of *Morgn Frayhayt,* the New York Yiddish daily.

After the German invasion of the Soviet Union in June 1941, Kaczerginski tried unsuccessfully to escape to the Soviet interior, and for a year he roamed about Vilna, posing as a deaf-mute. In the spring of 1942 he entered the Vilna ghetto and took an active part in its cultural life and the education of the youth. He directed the programs of the Yugnt Klub, a club for youth of school age. He also joined in the preparations for the formation of the FAREYNEGTE PARTIZANER ORGANIZATSYE (United Partisan Organization; FPO), the ghetto's movement for armed resistance to the Nazis. The poems that Kaczerginski composed at the time relate to these activities. Some of them became popular in the ghetto and have survived, such as the lullaby "Shtiler, shtiler" (Softly, Softly) and "Yugnt-Himen" (Youth Anthem). In addition to poems, Kaczerginski wrote articles and lectured extensively to ghetto audiences. His writings include an essay on the poet Abraham SUTZKEVER and a 300-page monograph on Chaim Grade, the Yiddish poet and novelist.

The Germans made use of Kaczerginski in sorting out valuable books (*see* EINSATZSTAB ROSENBERG) in the library of Vilna's Yivo Institute for Jewish Research (YIVO) for confiscation by them. The library was situated outside the ghetto; this enabled Kaczerginski to establish contacts for obtaining arms and smuggling them into the ghetto, and also to save books and manuscripts from the Germans. Together with Sutzkever and others, Kaczerginski saved some eight thousand items in the Vilna ghetto archives, among them the diary of Herman KRUK. This collection is now in the possession of YIVO in New York.

On September 12, 1943, Kaczerginski, together with a group of FPO members, succeeded in leaving the ghetto clandestinely. For ten months, until the liberation of Vilna (July 13, 1944), he served with the partisans of the Voroshilov Brigade in the Naroch Forest. The brigade commander appointed Kaczerginski and Sutzkever official historians of the partisan movement in the region; their task included interviewing partisans and recording their statements on the partisan operations. Among those they interviewed were Jews who had taken refuge in the forest or were serving in the brigade. The impression made by these encounters is reflected in poems and stories about partisans that Kaczerginski wrote, especially in 1943.

Shmaryahu Kaczerginski.

He also made translations from Russian into Yiddish.

In 1948 Kaczerginski published a collection of 250 Yiddish poems that had been composed in the ghettos and the camps, including notes on the fate of the authors, music to about 100 songs, and his own introduction. This is still the largest and most important collection of its kind. In 1950 Kaczerginski emigrated to Argentina, where he lost his life in an airplane accident.

BIBLIOGRAPHY

Kaczerginsky, S. *Songs of the Ghettos and Concentration Camps.* New York, 1948. (In Yiddish.)

Kalisch, S. *Yes, We Sang: Songs of the Ghettos and Concentration Camps.* New York, 1985.

Niger, S. "Yiddish Poets of the Third Destruction." *Reconstructionist* 13/10 (June 27, 1947): 13–18.

Rubin, R. "Yiddish Folksongs of World War II: A Record of Suffering and Struggle." *Jewish Quarterly* 11/2 (Summer 1963): 12–17.

YEHIEL SZEINTUCH

KAHN, FRANZ (1896–1944), Czechoslovak Zionist leader, born in Plzeň (Pilsen), in Bohemia. In 1916, while serving as a captain in the Austro-Hungarian army on the Russian front, Kahn was wounded and lost his left arm. After World War I he became active in the Zionist Tekhelet-Lavan (Blue-White) movement, and completed his law studies. In 1921, when the Zionist Organization of Czechoslovakia moved its headquarters to Moravská Ostrava, Kahn also moved to that city as the organization's secretary, and later became one of the leaders of Zionism in the country. At the end of 1938, following the MUNICH CONFERENCE and the truncation of Czechoslovakia, Kahn returned to Prague and was co-opted to the Zionist Action Committee.

Franz Kahn.

When BOHEMIA AND MORAVIA were occupied by the Germans in March 1939, Kahn, unlike other members of the Zionist leadership, refused to abandon Protectorate Jewry and save himself by leaving the country; nor did he seek to exploit his privileged status as a disabled war veteran. He did arrange for his son and daughter to immigrate to Palestine. As the son of an American citizen, Kahn could have applied for repatriation to the United States, but he refused to affix his signature to such a request. He believed that this step might bar him from representing the Jews vis-à-vis the Germans, which he felt to be his duty, despite the loathing he felt whenever he had to meet with Germans.

In January 1943, Kahn and his wife were moved to the THERESIENSTADT camp. He did not join the camp's Ältestenrat (Council of Elders), but accepted the post of director of the cultural section and devoted himself to work among the youth in the camp. The many efforts made to rescue Kahn, by Nahum GOLDMANN and Stephen S. WISE in the United States, and by Chaim WEIZMANN and Moshe Shertok (Sharett) in London and Jerusalem, were of no avail. In October 1944 he was deported to AUSCHWITZ, as were most of the other Jewish leaders in Theresienstadt and their families, although as a rule, disabled war veterans in Theresienstadt were not subject to further deportation. That same month he was killed in Birkenau.

BIBLIOGRAPHY

Bondy, R. *"Elder of the Jews": Jakob Edelstein of Theresienstadt.* New York, 1989.

Dagan, A., ed. *The Jews of Czechoslovakia: Historical Studies and Surveys.* Vols. 2, 3. Philadelphia, 1971, 1984.

SEEV GOSHEN

KAIDAN. *See* Kėdainiai.

KAISERWALD (Latv., Meza-Park), concentration camp in LATVIA. Kaiserwald was set up in March 1943 in a recreation village near RIGA. Its first inmates were several hundred German convicts. From June 1943 the majority of the Jews expelled from Riga were sent to Kaiserwald. In November of that year, the remainder of Latvian Jewry was taken to Kaiserwald from the liquidated ghettos of Riga, LIEPĀJA, and DVINSK, as were survivors of the VILNA ghetto. A few Jews from the Riga ghetto were sent to labor camps to work at the Lentta factory, the Strazdenhof (Strazdemuiza) camp, the German government railways (the Reichsbahn), and German military and police bases such as the Heeres Kraftfahrpark (the military vehicle maintenance services) and the Armeebekleidungsamt (the military clothing stores). Over the course of time these camps were brought under the jurisdiction of the Kaiserwald camp, and all the Jews living on Latvian soil were incarcerated there. In 1944, thousands of Jewish women were brought to Kaiserwald from Hungary, as was a group of Jews from ŁÓDŹ. In March of that year there were 11,878 inmates in the camp and its subsidiaries, 6,182 males and 5,696 females. Only 95 were non-Jews. A small number of Jewish children who had succeeded in escaping the *Aktionen* lived in the camp unofficially.

The Kaiserwald camp was planned to exploit the labor potential of the inmates. The majority worked in factories, mines, and farms. A large group of women worked in the gigantic A.E.G. (Allgemeine Elektrizität Gesellschaft; the German industrial electric corporation), and a few Jews were employed in the camp kitchen, clothing stores, workshops, and medical services. Kaiserwald's organization was like that of the other concentration camps: uniform clothing, identification numbers, separate housing for men and women, hard labor, rigid discipline, and brutal punishment. The inmates suffered from hunger, cold, and overcrowding. The camp commandant was an SS-*Obersturmführer* named Zauer.

In July 1944, as the Soviet army approached the Latvian border, the Germans began gradually to evacuate the inmates. Prior to the evacuation, vicious *Aktionen* were carried out in which thousands of Jews who were unfit for work—the ill, the frail, and the young—were put to death. In one of the subsidiary camps of Kaiserwald, all the Jewish prisoners who had been convicted of offenses during their internment were put to death. In another, all the Jews except those between the ages of eighteen and thirty were massacred. The evacuation was completed in September 1944, except for a few dozen Jews left by the Germans to perform various tasks. The evacuees were transferred by ship and train to the STUTTHOF camp near Danzig, and in the course of time were dispersed among a number of camps inside Germany.

BIBLIOGRAPHY

Levin, D., ed. *Latvia and Estonia*. In *Pinkas Hakehillot; Encyclopaedia of Jewish Communities*. Jerusalem, 1988. (In Hebrew.)

ESTHER HAGAR

KÁLLAY, MIKLÓS (1887–1967), Hungarian statesman. The scion of an ancient family of the nobility, Kállay held leading positions in various governments. He succeeded László Bárdossy as prime minister on March 9, 1942, and held this position until March 19, 1944, when the Germans occupied the country. A number of anti-Jewish measures were adopted during Kállay's tenure; for example, tens of thousands of Jewish men in the Hungarian labor service system (MUNKASZOLGÁLAT) were assigned to the Ukrainian front, where many of them were subsequently killed. Yet he successfully resisted the Third Reich's pressures on Hungary to resolve its "Jewish problem." After Italy's attempt to break away from the Germans in 1943, he tried to find an honorable way out of the war, and this induced the Germans to occupy Hungary. Kállay found haven in the Turkish legation, but he was compelled to leave his refuge following the fascist ARROW CROSS PARTY coup of October 15, 1944. He was subsequently deported to MAUTHAUSEN. After the liberation of the camp, Kállay went to Rome, and in 1951 he settled in New York. In 1954 he wrote *Hungarian Premier: A Personal Account of a Nation's Struggle in the Second World War*, which tells of his term of office.

Miklós Kallay (right) with Joachim von Ribbentrop. [National Archives]

BIBLIOGRAPHY

Braham, R. L. *The Politics of Genocide.* New York, 1980.

Katzburg, N. *Hungary and the Jews: Policy and Legislation, 1920–1943.* Ramat Gan, Israel, 1981.

Macartney, C. A. *October Fifteenth: A History of Hungary, 1929–1945.* New York, 1957.

RANDOLPH L. BRAHAM

KALMANOWITZ, ABRAHAM (1891–1964), rabbi of Tiktin, Poland. Kalmanowitz played a leading role in the rescue from Vilna to Shanghai of the Mir yeshiva (rabbinical academy) and in the activities of the VA'AD HA-HATSALA of the Orthodox rabbis in the United States. After the outbreak of World War II he escaped to Vilna, and from there he went to the United States in early 1940. Immediately upon his arrival in America, he assumed a leadership role in the Va'ad ha-Hatsala and traveled to numerous cities to raise funds for its work. After the United States entered World War II, he maintained contact with and sent relief to the hundreds of rabbis and yeshiva students stranded in Shanghai, by means of clearance arrangements via Uruguay and Argentina. Kalmanowitz was recognized for his expertise in influencing government officials and political leaders. He was also known for the fact that on several occasions he publicly rode vehicles on the Sabbath to stress the urgency of the predicament of European Jewry under Nazi rule.

BIBLIOGRAPHY

Kranzler, D. *Thy Brother's Blood.* Brooklyn, N.Y., 1987.

Zuroff, E. "Rescue Priority and Fund Raising as Issues during the Holocaust: A Case Study of the Relations between the Vaad Ha-Hatzala and the Joint, 1939–1941." *American Jewish History* 68/3 (1979): 305–326.

Zuroff, E. "Rescue via the Far East: Attempt to Save Polish Rabbis and Yeshivah Students, 1939–1941." *Simon Wiesenthal Center Annual* 1 (1984): 153–184.

EFRAIM ZUROFF

KALTENBRUNNER, ERNST (1903–1946), Nazi politician. Born in Ried im Innkreis (Upper Austria), Kaltenbrunner attended school in Linz. After studying chemistry and law in Prague and elsewhere, he practiced as a lawyer. He joined the National Socialist party and the SS in 1932. In 1934 and 1935, Kaltenbrunner was imprisoned in Austria on a charge of high treason. He headed the SS in that country from 1935 until 1938.

After the ANSCHLUSS, Kaltenbrunner, now an SS-*Gruppenführer,* was promoted to the post of under secretary of state for public security in the Ostmark (as Austria was renamed by the Nazis). He remained there until 1941, and at the same time was a member of the Reichstag. Together with Gauleiter Josef Bürckel, Kaltenbrunner was responsible for the ZENTRALSTELLE FÜR JÜDISCHE AUSWANDERUNG (Central Office for Jewish Emigration) in Vienna, headed by Adolf EICHMANN. Up until Eichmann's transfer to Prague in April 1939, 150,000 Jews emigrated from Austria. After the attempt on Reinhard HEYDRICH's life on May 27, 1942, Kaltenbrunner was appointed head of the REICHSSICHERHEITSHAUPTAMT (Reich Security Main Office; RSHA). Heydrich died on June 4, and Kaltenbrunner was formally named his successor as

Heinrich Himmler visiting the Mauthausen concentration camp in April 1941. From left: Himmler; Sturmbannführer Franz Ziereis (1905–1945), commandant of Mauthausen from August 1939 to May 1945, when the camp was liberated; and SS-Gruppenführer Ernst Kaltenbrunner.

chief of the Sicherheitspolizei and the SD (Sicherheitsdienst; Security Service) on January 30, 1943.

In addition to Heinrich HIMMLER, Kaltenbrunner was one of the main initiators of AKTION REINHARD and bore much of the responsibility for the implementation of the "FINAL SOLUTION" from 1942 to 1945, although few contemporary documents record his activities in this connection. The same holds true for his participation in the EUTHANASIA PROGRAM. This may be partly attributed to Himmler's growing tendency to reserve the credit for himself. There exists evidence, however, of Kaltenbrunner's role as instigator of the deportation from THERESIENSTADT in the spring of 1943 of Jews unfit for work, and of Bulgarian Jews in the summer of 1943. In 1945 Kaltenbrunner took as his personal adjutant an SS officer who in 1941 had been responsible for the murder of at least sixty thousand Jewish men, women, and children in Lithuania.

Because of Kaltenbrunner's personal reserve, many of his department heads appeared to be more important than they actually were in the power structure of the RSHA. This may have been connected with Kaltenbrunner's belief that, in contrast to many of his subordinates, he had a very real chance to survive after the end of the war. Even at Nuremberg (*see* NUREMBERG TRIAL), he attempted to play the part of someone who "had absolutely no idea." Nevertheless, on October 9, 1946, the International Military Tribunal sentenced him to death by hanging, and the sentence was carried out on October 16.

The so-called Kaltenbrunner reports are a collection of reports on the Gestapo interrogations conducted after the attempt on Hitler's life of July 20, 1944. They were drawn up for Martin BORMANN, on Kaltenbrunner's orders, by an ad hoc RSHA unit headed by SS-Obersturmbannführer Walter von Kielpinski. According to the historian Hans-Adolf Jacobsen, they were the result of "thousands of investigations" carried out by some four hundred RSHA officials operating in eleven groups—the Sonderkommandos 20 Juli—who took part in suppressing the attempted coup.

BIBLIOGRAPHY

Black, P. R. *Ernst Kaltenbrunner: Ideological Soldier of the Third Reich*. Princeton, 1984.

Krausnick, H., and H. Wilhelm. *Die Truppe des Weltanschauungskrieges: Die Einsatzgruppen der Sicherheitspolizei und des SD, 1938–1942*. Stuttgart, 1981.

HANS-HEINRICH WILHELM

KAMENETS-PODOLSKI, city in the Ukrainian SSR where mass killings of Jews, mostly from HUNGARY, took place in August 1941. Shortly after Hungary declared war on the Soviet Union, on June 27, 1941, a plan was devised by Ödön Martinides and Árkád Kiss, two leading officers of the National Central Alien Control Office (Külföldieket Ellenórzó Országos Kozponti Hatosag; KEOKH), the agency with jurisdiction over foreign nationals living in Hungary, to "resettle" the Polish and Russian Jews in the Hungarian-administered part of "liberated" Galicia. Under Decree No. 192/1941, adopted on July 12, and a subsequent secret directive of the KEOKH, a drive was begun to deport "the recently infiltrated Polish and Russian Jews in the largest possible number and as quickly as possible." Among the "alien" Jews rounded up that month were also a considerable number of Hungarian Jews who could not prove

Bodies of Jews massacred at Kamenets-Podolski.

their citizenship simply because their papers were not immediately available. Other Hungarian Jews were merely caught up in the maelstrom. In the TRANSCARPATHIAN UKRAINE, an area inhabited by Orthodox and Hasidic Jews, many Jewish communities were uprooted in toto. Since the Jews were rounded up at great speed, usually under cover of darkness, very few of them could take along adequate provisions.

The "alien" Jews were packed into freight cars and taken to Körösmező, near the Polish border. From there, they were transferred across the border at the rate of about 1,000 a day. By August 10, approximately 14,000 Jews had been handed over to the SS. An additional 4,000 were transferred by the end of the month, when the operation was completed. From Körösmező the Jews were first taken to KOLOMYIA, and then marched in columns of 300 to 400 to Kamenets-Podolski. Their fate was decided on August 25 at a conference held at the Vinnitsa headquarters of the *Generalquartiermeister-OKH*, where SS-Obergruppenführer Friedrich Jeckeln assured the conferees that he would complete the liquidation of the Jews by September 1, 1941. The *Aktion* took place on August 27 and 28 near the city and claimed (according to Jeckeln's Operational Report USSR No. 80) 23,600 Jewish lives—the first five-figure massacre in the Nazis' "FINAL SOLUTION" program. Of these, 14,000 to 18,000 Jews were from Hungary; the remainder were local.

BIBLIOGRAPHY

Braham, R. L. "The Kamenets Podolsk and Delvidek Massacres: Prelude to the Holocaust in Hungary." *Yad Vashem Studies* 9 (1973): 133–156.

RANDOLPH L. BRAHAM

KAMINSKI BRIGADE. *See* Russkaya Osvoboditelnaya Armiya.

KAPLAN, CHAIM AARON (1880–1942), author of a WARSAW ghetto diary. Born in a village near Baranovichi, Belorussia, Kaplan became the principal of a Hebrew school in Warsaw. He kept a detailed personal diary (starting apparently in 1933) written in Hebrew, which is one of the rare original documents of its kind that has survived the Nazi era. It describes the decline of Jewish Warsaw and the Holocaust period in general. The diary, as Kaplan put it, became "my soul brother, my colleague and companion." Until the beginning of World War II it was a private personal account; but when the war broke out the diary changed its character, and in addition to his own experiences and troubles, Kaplan recorded the story of the Jews of Warsaw, his own speculations on future developments, the behavior and policies of the Germans as they unfolded before his eyes, and his opinions about the Poles.

Kaplan had a penetrating mind and a sharp eye, and his diary faithfully reflects the events of most of the ghetto's existence. The war diary begins on September 1, 1939, and ends on August 4, 1942, the day when the mass deportation was at its height. Kaplan evidently made his final entry a day or two before his own deportation to TREBLINKA. "When my end comes—what will happen to the diary?" reads the last sentence.

Kaplan's war diary was discovered almost intact after the war on a farm outside Warsaw, preserved in a kerosene can; the notebooks were legible and in good condition. The diary was published in Hebrew (*Megilat Yisurin, Yoman Geto Varsha—September 1, 1939–August 4, 1942,* with introduction and notes by A. I. Katsh and N. Blumental; Tel Aviv and Jerusalem, 1966) and in two English editions. The second contains all the pages of the diary that were recovered (*The Warsaw Diary of Chaim A. Kaplan,* translated and edited by A. I. Katsh; New York, 1965, 1973).

BIBLIOGRAPHY

Gutman, Y. *The Jews of Warsaw, 1939–1943: Ghetto, Underground, Revolt.* Bloomington, 1982.

ISRAEL GUTMAN

KAPLAN, JOSEF (1913–1942), a leader of the WARSAW Jewish underground and a founder of the ŻYDOWSKA ORGANIZACJA BOJOWA (Jewish Fighting Organization; ŻOB). Kaplan was born in Kalisz, in western Poland, into a poor family and a strict religious atmosphere. Early in his youth he was drawn to secular education and culture and joined the Ha-Shomer ha-Tsa'ir Zionist youth movement in the town. In the late 1930s he was one of the leaders of that movement in Poland. During the first few days of World War II, in September 1939, Kaplan joined the flood of refugees to the east, and took charge of the illegal border-crossing point at Lida on the Polish-Lithuanian border. At the beginning of 1940 he returned to Nazi-occupied Poland from Vilna (which in the meantime had been incorporated into Lithuania), in order to take charge of the underground Ha-Shomer ha-Tsa'ir movement. From that moment on, Kaplan devoted all his time to the underground. He consolidated the movement's structure in the various ghettos and ensured the continuation of agricultural training even on a clandestine basis; he published and distributed underground newspapers, and was his movement's representative in the overall Jewish underground organizations and institutions.

Josef Kaplan.

In the spring of 1942, Kaplan embarked upon the formation of a Jewish body that would fight against the Nazis. He took part in the activities of the Antifascist Bloc in Warsaw and, in July of that year, in establishing the ŻOB in Warsaw. On September 3, 1942, in the midst of the mass deportation of Jews from Warsaw, the Nazis caught Kaplan in the act of preparing forged documents for a group of fighters who were about to join the partisans, and he was killed.

Kaplan kept a diary, but it was not preserved. Irena ADAMOWICZ, who knew him well, described him in the following terms: "The activist who had been likable but quite average turned into a great man, very strong . . . and very calm. He was an excellent organizer and an ideal underground operator, painstaking and resourceful in all humdrum day-to-day affairs, and with a clear and inspiring approach to matters of principle, of life and death."

BIBLIOGRAPHY

Gutman, Y. *The Jews of Warsaw, 1939–1943: Ghetto, Underground, Revolt.* Bloomington, 1982.

Gutman, Y. *The Revolt of the Besieged: Mordehai Anilevitch and the Uprising of the Warsaw Ghetto.* Merhavia, Israel, 1963. (In Hebrew.)

ISRAEL GUTMAN

KAPLINSKI, HIRSCH (Zvi; 1910–1942), underground leader and partisan commander. Born in DIATLOVO (Zhetl), in the NOVOGRUDOK district of Poland, Kaplinski was the secretary of the local Tarbut (Zionist-oriented) school and took an active part in Zionist and Jewish public life in the town. After World War II broke out, he served as a sergeant in the Polish army and then joined the underground in the Diatlovo ghetto. His parents, wife, and son were killed in the second *Aktion,* on August 5, 1942; together with comrades Kaplinski escaped from the ghetto to the Lipiczany Forest.

Kaplinski was a founder and commander of the Jewish partisan battalion known as the "Kaplinski Battalion." Consisting of 120 men, it was later incorporated in the Borba (Struggle) unit, as a company. The battalion took punitive action against peasants who had collaborated with the Nazis, fought the German militia in Mirovshchina, Zykovshchina, Nakryshki, and Mutsevichi, blew up bridges, and collected captured arms (in the Ruda-Jaworska battle).

During the German attack on the Lipiczany Forest, on December 10, 1942, Kaplinski was ambushed while on his way to division headquarters, and in the course of the fight was severely wounded. Apparently, the Russian partisans whom Kaplinski asked for help disarmed and killed him.

BIBLIOGRAPHY

Kahanovich, M. *The War of the Jewish Partisans in Eastern Europe.* Tel Aviv, 1954. (In Hebrew.)

Kaplinski, B. *Pinkas Zetel [Zetel Record]; A Memorial to the Jewish Community of Zetel.* Tel Aviv, 1957. (In Hebrew.)

SHALOM CHOLAWSKI

KAPO (from Ital. *capo,* "chief," "boss"), term used in the Nazi CONCENTRATION CAMPS for an inmate appointed by the SS men in charge to head a *Kommando* (work gang) made up of other prisoners. The term "Kapo" is sometimes also used for any prisoner who was given an assignment and collaborated with the Nazis, and, beyond that, for any Nazi collaborator. In the German-occupied countries and in the camps, however, only the "bosses" of prisoner work gangs were referred to as "Kapos."

Generally, the Kapo was not a skilled worker, and his job was to escort the prisoners to their place of work and ensure that they performed their tasks properly and met the quotas. But work as such was not the major objective in the concentration camps; the real purpose was to break the prisoners in mind and spirit. The Kapo, therefore, became the instrument by which a regime of humiliation and sheer physical cruelty was imposed upon the prison population. At the workplaces, the work gangs were split up into smaller groups, each headed by a *Vorarbeiter* (foreman) responsible to the Kapo.

In 1942 there was a slight improvement in the regime prevailing in the camps, because the Germans became interested in exploiting the prisoners' productive capacity, which meant that they had to treat them better. In many instances, the Kapos—

especially those who were political prisoners in the camps—pretended to be strict with the prisoners, when in fact they tried to handle them as moderately as possible. At all times a deep gulf divided the rank-and-file prisoner from the Kapo and other supervisors, affecting the human relationship between them and the conditions under which they lived. The Kapos' clothing was relatively warm, they had enough to eat, and they enjoyed their own reserved section in the prison barrack (the "block"), whereas such amenities were privileges unthinkable for the regular prisoners. In many instances Kapos mistreated prisoners in a criminal fashion and were put on trial after the war.

BIBLIOGRAPHY

Cohen, E. A. *Human Behavior in the Concentration Camp.* New York, 1953.

Glicksman, W. "Social Differentiation in the German Concentration Camps." *YIVO Annual* 8 (1953): 123–150.

Kogon, E. *The Theory and Practice of Hell: The German Concentration Camps and the System behind Them.* New York, 1950.

ISRAEL GUTMAN

Col. Herbert Kappler of the German army, in custody. Kappler carried out the massacre of Italian civilians at the Ardeatine Caves near Rome on March 24, 1944. [National Archives]

KAPOSVÁR, capital of Somogy county, in southwestern Hungary. In 1941, it had a Jewish population of 2,346, representing 7.1 percent of the total. The community was headed by Ödön Antl, who also served as the chairman of the sixteen-member JUDENRAT (Jewish Council) that was established after the Jews were ordered into a ghetto in May 1944. The ghetto was located in and around Berzsenyi and Kanizsai streets, the central thoroughfares of the community. Toward the end of June, the ghetto population was transferred to an artillery barracks near the railway lines. The barracks, which served as the main entrainment center, already "housed" the slightly more than 2,500 Jews brought in from the smaller towns and rural communities in Somogy county. The liquidation of the ghetto took place when 5,159 Jews were deported to AUSCHWITZ, on July 4, 1944. In 1946, Kaposvár still had 439 Jews, representing 1.3 percent of the population. Many of them were survivors who had moved into the city from neighboring rural communities.

RANDOLPH L. BRAHAM

KAPPLER, HERBERT (1907–1978), official in the Nazi SD (Sicherheitsdienst; Security Service). When he was sent to ROME in 1939, Kappler was an SS-*Obersturmbannführer.* As head of the SD in Rome, he cooperated closely with the Italian Fascist police. In 1944 he became head of the Gestapo in Rome.

Kappler began to play a more significant role after September 8, 1943, when the Germans took over the control of Rome. That month he helped organize the rescue of Benito MUSSOLINI by SS commandos. He planned and executed the deportation of about ten thousand Jews of Rome after the extortion of their gold. During the night of October 15–

16, 1943, the *Aktion* started, and 1,259 Italian Jews were arrested. On October 18, 1,007 were sent to AUSCHWITZ; only about 10 came back alive.

On March 23, 1944, Italian partisans killed thirty-three Germans with a bomb on Via Rasella in Rome. An order was received from Adolf Hitler to kill 10 Italians for each German soldier. Kappler, together with Pietro Caruso, the chief of the Italian police, was responsible for selecting the victims. People arrested on the spot, political prisoners, and Jews were sent to the Ardeatine Caves near Rome, shot in the neck in small groups, and buried under the sand; the entrances were subsequently sealed by exploding charges. Altogether, 335 Italians were killed at the Ardeatine Caves, among them seventy-eight Jews.

After the war Kappler was held by the British and then handed over to Italian authorities in 1947. He was put on trial before an Italian military tribunal and given a life sentence. In 1977, he fell ill and was taken to a hospital in Rome, from which he managed to escape. He died a year later in his own home in Germany.

BIBLIOGRAPHY

Michaelis, M. *Mussolini and the Jews: German-Italian Relations and the Jewish Question in Italy, 1922–1945.* Oxford, 1978.

Piscitelli, E. *Storia della resistanza romana.* Bari, 1965.

Zuccotti, S. *The Italians and the Holocaust: Persecution, Rescue, and Survival.* New York, 1987.

SERGIO I. MINERBI

KARAITES. The Karaites were members of a Jewish sect that emerged in the eighth century in Babylon, and spread from there to the countries of the Middle East. In the thirteenth and fourteenth centuries Karaites migrated to the Crimean peninsula. The Lithuanian prince Vytautus (Witold) the Great (r. 1386–1430) moved hundreds of Karaites from the Crimea to the north and settled them in Troki, Lutsk, and Galich (Pol., Halicz). From the early nineteenth century Karaites in Russia demanded equal rights, and several of their scholars (such as Abraham Firkovich) claimed that their origins were not Jewish. In the second half of the nineteenth century this claim was accepted; the Karaites were accorded the same rights as the Russians, and were integrated into society, serving in the tsar's army and in government service. In the Civil War that followed World War I, Karaite officers fought in the White Army against the Bolsheviks. After the Bolshevik victory they emigrated to the West, settling in Warsaw, in Berlin, in France, and in Italy.

Between the two world wars, 9,000 Karaites lived in the Soviet Union, mostly in the Crimea (6,500). In eastern Poland there were Karaites in Troki (300), Vilna (200), Lutsk (50), and Galich (40 families). A few families lived in Ponevezh in Lithuania, in Riga in Latvia, in Warsaw and its vicinity, in Berlin (18), in France (250), and in Italy (a few score).

The Nazis first came up against the problem of the Karaites when they published the regulations for enforcement of the NUREMBERG LAWS. The heads of the small Karaite community in Berlin asked the authorities to exempt them from the regulations; on the basis of their legal status in tsarist Russia, they claimed that they were not of Jewish origin. After examination of the claim, on January 5, 1939, the Reichsstelle für Sippenforschung (Reich Agency for Investigation of Families) determined that the Karaite sect should not be considered part of the Jewish religious community with regard to those regulations, and that the racial classification of the Karaites should be decided not according to their attachment to a specific people, but according to their personal genealogy. That document became an edict, and from then on it served the Nazi authorities as the basis for dealing with the Karaites.

After the outbreak of World War II the Germans again encountered Karaites, first in occupied France, and then in occupied areas of the Soviet Union. The COMMISSARIAT GÉNÉRAL AUX QUESTIONS JUIVES (General Office for Jewish Affairs) in Vichy France required Karaites to be registered as Jews. But on the basis of memoranda and opinions of the heads of the Orthodox church there, the Karaites attempted to prove that they were not of Jewish origin. The journal of the UNION GÉNÉRALE

DES ISRAÉLITES DE FRANCE (General Council of French Jews) claimed that the Karaites were Jews, but eventually instructions arrived from Berlin to accept the Karaites' position.

In the USSR the first Germans to come across the Karaites were the EINSATZGRUPPEN. Although at that time the origins of this sect were not clear to the Nazis, the Einsatzgruppen attacked them in several localities, for instance in Kiev, where more than two hundred Karaites died at BABI YAR. When approaching the Crimea, the Einsatzgruppen sought clarification from Berlin, and received instructions not to harm the Karaites, since they were not of Jewish origin.

When members of the Nazi civilian government established their authority in the occupied areas of the USSR, they also met the Karaites. The heads of the Generalkommissariat of Lithuania encountered Karaites in Troki and in Vilna, among them the chief religious authority of the Karaites, Seraya Shapshal. The Generalkommissariat wrote to the REICHSKOMMISSARIAT OSTLAND, which passed on the inquiry to the Ministry for the Occupied Territories in the East, located in Berlin. An exchange of letters, opinions, and position papers ensued, containing frequent references to the edict of the Reich Agency for Investigation of Families. In those documents it was again decided that the Karaites were of Turkish-Mongolian extraction, and had adopted the Jewish religion from missionaries in the Kuzari kingdom in the eighth and ninth centuries. In the late summer of 1942 the Nazis addressed separate inquiries to Jewish scholars in three ghettos: Professor Meir Balaban and Dr. Ignacy SCHIPER in Warsaw, Selig Hirsh Kalmanowitz in Vilna, and Dr. Leib Landau and Dr. Yaakov Schall in Lvov. Wishing to save the Karaites from the fate of the Jews, the scholars expressed the opinion that the Karaites were not of Jewish extraction.

In May 1943 the Ministry for the Occupied Territories in the East finally determined that the Karaites were not part of the Jewish religious community, and that their origin was Turkish-Tatar-Mongolian. The determination of origin had been made, it was claimed, on the basis of racial examinations carried out among different groups of Karaites. The ministry demanded that the Karaites be treated like Turks and Tatars, in order not to anger those peoples. Politically, it was hoped that decent treatment of the Karaites would gain the sympathy of the Turks and Tatars, which the Germans needed at that time, since they were in general retreat from the USSR following the fall of STALINGRAD and the withdrawal from the Caucasian front. The ministry decision saved the Karaites from the fate of their Jewish brethren—annihilation in the framework of the "FINAL SOLUTION" to the Jewish problem.

In the second half of 1944 the problem of the Karaites again arose, when the heads of the SS realized that about five hundred to six hundred of the sect were serving in the Waffen-SS and the Tatar division of the German army. These must have been Karaites who served in the Crimea, in local government and police, and in various auxiliary army units, and who were retreating to the west. Their families settled in the vicinity of Vienna, and there, together with the Crimean Tatars, they created the Association of Tatars and Karaites from Crimea, an organization with social objectives.

The fact that Karaites were serving in the army disturbed SS circles, and correspondence began on this matter between the heads of Heinrich HIMMLER's personal staff and the head office of the SS responsible for the Waffen-SS. Again the question of the Karaites' religion and origin was raised, and the decision of the Ministry for the Occupied Territories in the East was again accepted. The political reasoning was also reendorsed: the Karaites must not be harmed because of their blood relatives, the Turks and the Tatars. The Jewish religion of the Karaites annoyed the SS circles, and it was therefore recommended not to publicize Karaite activity in the army. On December 7, 1944, Himmler approved these conclusions and recommendations, and the Karaites continued to serve in the German army until its surrender in early May 1945.

The relationship of the Karaites to the "Rabbanite" (non-Karaite) Jews is not easy to determine, in view of the dearth of evidence. Certainly, it was not uniform. In Lutsk the Karaites cooperated in the cruel treatment of the local Jews, and in Vilna and Troki they furnished precise lists of the members of their community, thereby frustrating an attempt to save hundreds of "Rabbanite" Jews who had obtained forged Karaite certificates. Those Jews were caught and killed. In other localities the Karaites helped the Jews, even providing original certificates and saving individual Jews.

After the war the number of Karaites in the USSR decreased. In 1959 there were 5,727 Karaites, mostly in the Crimea, and a minority in Lithuania (Troki, Vilna) and in the western Ukraine (Lutsk, Galich). In Poland there were about 600 Karaites in Warsaw, Szczecin (Ger., Stettin), and Silesia. A few hundred lived in Germany, France, and Italy, and several hundred in the United States. The largest community of Karaites (several thousand) is in Israel, and is of Egyptian origin.

BIBLIOGRAPHY

Friedman, P. "The Karaites under Nazi Rule." In *On the Track of Tyranny: Essays Presented by the Wiener Library to Leonard G. Montefiore, O.B.E., on the Occasion of His Seventieth Birthday*, edited by M. Beloff, pp. 97–123. London, 1960.

Green, W. P. "The Nazi Racial Policy Towards the Karaites." *Soviet Jewish Affairs* 8/2 (1978): 36–44.

Spector, S. "The Karaites in Nazi-Occupied Europe as Reflected in German Documents." *Pe'amim* 29 (1986): 90–108. (In Hebrew.)

SHMUEL SPECTOR

KARSKI, JAN (real surname, Kozielewski; b. 1914), Polish non-Jew who brought information on the Holocaust to the West. Born in Łódź, Karski completed his studies in demography at Lvov University in 1935 and worked in the Polish Foreign Office. After the occupation of Poland in September 1939, he joined the Polish underground and was a courier for the POLISH GOVERNMENT-IN-EXILE.

In 1942 Karski was sent on a mission to London, the headquarters of the government-in-exile, to transmit a report on the situation in occupied Poland, and in particular on the situation of the Jewish population there. To be able to give authentic testimony, Karski twice visited the WARSAW ghetto, where he met with two Jewish leaders, Menahem Kirschenbaum of the General Zionists and Leon FEINER of the BUND. They asked him to inform world leaders of the desperate situation of Polish Jewry.

In November 1942 Karski arrived in London, transmitted the report to the Polish government, and met with Winston CHURCHILL and other statesmen, journalists, and public figures. Basing itself on Karski's report, the Polish government-in-exile called on the Allied governments in December of that year to take steps that would compel Germany to halt the massacres of the Jews.

Following this mission, Karski left London for the United States. There he met with President Franklin D. ROOSEVELT and other statesmen, and tried to arouse public opinion against the massacres being carried out by the Germans. After the war, he remained in the United States.

Karski wrote a book about his experiences, *The Story of a Secret State* (1944). In 1982 he was awarded the title of "RIGHTEOUS AMONG THE NATIONS" by YAD VASHEM.

BIBLIOGRAPHY

Gilbert, M. *Auschwitz and the Allies*. New York, 1981.

Laqueur, W. *The Terrible Secret*. London, 1980.

ELISHEVA SHAUL

KASSA. *See* Košice.

KASZTNER, REZSŐ (Rudolf or Israel; 1906–1957), journalist, lawyer, and Zionist leader. Kasztner was a Labor Zionist activist, first in his hometown of Cluj and then, after the annexation of Transylvania by HUNGARY in 1940, in Budapest. In early 1943 he became the vice chairman, in fact the guiding spirit, of the RELIEF AND RESCUE COMMITTEE OF BUDAPEST of the Zionist movement, under Ottó KOMOLY. The committee maintained contact with the Slovak PRACOVNÁ SKUPINA (Working Group), which included Gisi FLEISCHMANN and Rabbi Michael Dov WEISSMANDEL; through it with Poland; and with a group of Palestinian emissaries in Istanbul, among whose founding members were Haim Barlas, Menachem Bader, and Venja Pomerantz.

The committee was well aware of the Holocaust in Poland and elsewhere, and tried to spread information about it, which was disbelieved in spite of the accounts of Polish Jewish refugees arriving in Hungary after 1942. In 1943 the committee was instrumental (through the work of Joel BRAND) in smuggling refugees from Poland and Slovakia into Hungary. Despite internal dissensions, the committee tried to prepare for the eventuality of German occupation, even attempting to organize armed resistance. Such resistance, however, proved illusory in Hungary, owing to pervasive anti-Jewish hostility on the part of the population, the lack of any local anti-German resistance, and the fact that most young Jewish men were compelled to serve in the labor service system (*see* MUNKASZOLGÁLAT) under Hungarian army control.

When the Germans occupied Hungary in March 1944, the committee made contact with the SS group in charge of the future extermination program under Adolf EICHMANN. Similar contacts had led to ransom negotiations in Slovakia, where the Jewish negotiators believed they had resulted in the rescue of the remnant of Slovak Jewry and had led to the negotiations of the EUROPA PLAN. Kasztner believed that in Hungary, the only avenue for rescue was negotiation with the Germans. Consequently, sums of money were paid to the SS, and Joel Brand was sent to Istanbul in May to negotiate the release of large numbers of Jews in return for trucks and other materials (the operation was called "Blood for Goods"). Brand was accompanied by Andor (Bandi) Grosz, a quadruple agent who served German, Hungarian, and other masters.

Historians differ as to the seriousness of the proposal brought by Brand, but there is no doubt that it was originally formulated by Heinrich HIMMLER himself. When Brand was detained by the British and could not return as promised, his wife, Hansi, and Kasztner took over direct negotiations with Eichmann. At the end of June, a train with 1,684 Jews chosen by a committee headed by Komoly and Kasztner left Hungary, ostensibly for Spain or Switzerland; it was, however, directed to the BERGEN-BELSEN camp, where these Jews were interned. On the train were Kasztner's family and friends from Cluj, but in the main the group consisted of representatives from all political and religious factions, as well as wealthy people who had paid large sums subsidizing the others. Kasztner's idea was that this exodus would serve as a precedent for undoing the murder program, and that more trains would follow. However, none did.

In July an SS officer, Kurt BECHER, received Himmler's permission to negotiate with Kasztner. As a result, Brand's negotiations were continued with the JOINT DISTRIBUTION COMMITTEE representative in Switzerland, Saly MAYER, on the Swiss border. The first meeting, on August 21, 1944, led to Himmler's order to refrain from deporting the Jews of Budapest, and 318 Jews in Bergen-Belsen from the "Kasztner train" were released to Switzerland. In December of that year the remainder of the Bergen-Belsen internees were also sent to safety, and Becher became obligated to the Jews by his contacts with Kasztner. At Kasztner's prodding, he intervened in favor of the Budapest Jews. Becher appears to have acted from a variety of motives, but the outcome was an increase in Himmler's willingness to make some lifesaving gestures here and there, against the background of the approaching German defeat. The Jewish negotiators utilized the Germans' illusion that there might exist a possibility for negotiating with the West for a separate peace.

After the war, Kasztner was called to Nuremberg (*see* NUREMBERG TRIAL) to help the investigators in their work with Nazi criminals. His written testimony in favor of Becher undoubtedly helped to save the latter from a closer investigation into less savory aspects of his wartime career. (Becher had served in some notorious SS units in the Russian campaign in 1941 and 1942. He had confiscated the Manfred Weiss industrial concern, resulting in a huge sum paid to the SS, in return for allowing some members of the Weiss-Chorin family to escape to Lisbon.) Kasztner also testified in favor of other Nazis, such as SS-Obergruppenführer Hans Jüttner, chief of the SS-Führungshauptamt (SS

Jews from the "Kasztner train" arriving in Switzerland (1944). [Weiss family]

Operational Main Office), who had made the rather meaningless gesture of disapproving of the death march from Budapest in November 1944. Kasztner's line seems to have been one of *noblesse oblige*: once the war was over, any Nazi who had made a gesture or taken action in favor of Jews should be recognized for it.

In 1954, Kasztner brought a suit against one Malkiel Grünwald, who had accused him of being a traitor and causing the deaths of many Jews. The trial, in Israel, became instead a trial of Kasztner himself. Shmuel Tamir, Grünwald's attorney, steered the trial in the direction of an indictment of the Mapai Labor party, which had placed Kasztner on its list of candidates for the Knesset elections. The judge, Benjamin Halevi, accepted most of Tamir's arguments and summed up the court's opinion of Kasztner by accusing him of having "sold his soul to the devil." This referred both to the negotiations with the Nazis and to the train, which was seen as an avenue of rescue for Kasztner's relatives and friends and a German sop to Kasztner in return for his refraining from warning Hungarian Jewry of the impending disaster. The Israeli Supreme Court was debating Kasztner's appeal when he was murdered by nationalist extremists who took Halevi's words literally. In a final verdict, the court exonerated Kasztner from all accusations except the charge that he had helped Nazis to escape from justice.

Given the conditions in Hungary at the time, negotiations with the Nazis were in actuality the only way in which Jews might have been saved. The train could just as well have arrived in Auschwitz, and perhaps by

Rezső Kasztner (left) and Ottó Komoly (1944). [Peretz Revesz]

putting his relatives on it, Kasztner persuaded many others to board it; in any case, he saw this as a breakthrough for future rescues. In the winter of 1944–1945, when he was already safe in Switzerland, Kasztner voluntarily returned to Germany, and with Becher went to Berlin to try and save the Jewish remnants in the concentration camps. His intervention was possibly instrumental in securing the surrender of Bergen-Belsen to the British without the bloodbath that could have taken place there.

The most difficult problem is the charge that he did not warn Hungarian Jewry. Kasztner was totally unknown, was not in control of the Hungarian Jewish Council (Zsidó Tanács), and was in no position to warn anyone. In Cluj, where he was known, a rescue committee composed of important local citizens failed to convince all but a very few to escape for their lives to neighboring Romania, a mere ten miles away. Kasztner's tragic figure has been the subject of plays and stories, and continues to engender heated controversy.

BIBLIOGRAPHY

Bauer, Y. *American Jewry and the Holocaust: The American Jewish Joint Distribution Committee, 1939–1945*. Detroit, 1981.

Bauer, Y. *The Holocaust in Historical Perspective*. Seattle, 1978.

Biss, A. *A Million Jews to Save: Check to the Final Solution*. Cranbury, N.J., 1975.

Kasztner, R., ed. *Der Bericht des jüdisches Rettungskomitees aus Budapest, 1942–1945*. Budapest, 1946.

YEHUDA BAUER

KATYN, town near Smolensk, in the USSR, in the vicinity of which Polish officers were murdered in large numbers. According to data in the possession of the POLISH GOVERNMENT-IN-EXILE, at the beginning of 1940 the Soviet Union held as many as 15,000 Polish prisoners of war, of whom 8,300 were officers. They had been taken prisoner by the Red Army in the second half of September 1939 and were interned in three camps: at Kozelsk, Starobelsk, and Ostashkov. Toward the end of 1940 there were reports that the three camps had been disbanded. Repeated requests for information on the fate of the prisoners made by the Polish government-in-exile to the Soviet Union in 1941 and 1942 were of no avail.

On April 13, 1943, the Germans announced that mass graves had been discovered in the Katyn forest, in their area of occupation, containing the bodies of thousands of Polish officers who had been shot in the head from behind. The Germans charged the Soviet authorities with murder and appointed a multinational medical commission to probe the matter. In May 1943, the commission reported that the graves contained the bodies of 4,143 officers, of whom 2,914 were identified by documents in their uniforms. It was the commission's opinion that the men had been shot to death in the spring of 1940. The Soviet authorities flatly rejected these charges made by a German-appointed commission; they claimed that the murder had been the work of Germans when they had occupied the area in July 1941.

In mid-April of 1943, when the Polish government-in-exile demanded that an investigation of the Katyn killings be made by the

International Red Cross, the Soviet Union reacted by severing relations with the government-in-exile, on April 25. This step was to have far-reaching effects on relations between the Soviet Union and Poland. In November of that year, several months after the Red Army had liberated the area, the Soviet Union appointed an inquiry commission of its own, which charged that the Katyn murders had been committed by the Germans. A United States congressional inquiry in the early 1950s concluded that the NKVD (Soviet secret police) was responsible, and most Western historians now believe that the massacre was ordered by the Soviet authorities. On March 8, 1989, the Polish government officially accused the NKVD of perpetrating the massacre.

BIBLIOGRAPHY

Fitzgibbon, L. *Katyn: A Crime without Parallel.* New York, 1971.

Mackiewicz, J. *The Katyn Wood Murders.* London, 1951.

SHMUEL KRAKOWSKI

KATZENELSON, ITZHAK (1886–1944), poet, playwright, and educator. Katzenelson was born in Korelichi, in the district of Minsk, Russia, where his father was a writer and teacher. In 1886 the family moved to Łódź. Katzenelson began writing poetry at an early age, and throughout his life he wrote in both Yiddish and Hebrew. His first book of Hebrew poems, *Dimdumim* (Twilight), appeared in 1910; earlier, in 1908, he had begun to write comedies in Yiddish, which he himself translated into Hebrew. Several of his Yiddish plays were performed in Łódź even before World War I. In 1912 he founded a theater, Ha-Bimah ha-Ivrit (The Hebrew Stage), in Łódź and took it on tours of cities in Poland and Lithuania. Before World War I Katzenelson undertook the creation of a network of Hebrew schools in Łódź, from kindergarten to high school, which functioned until 1939. He was the author of textbooks, biblical plays, and children's books. Beginning in 1930 he belonged to the Dror movement in Łódź and to the He-Haluts movement, the latter operating a training kibbutz (Kibbutz Hakhsharah) in Łódź.

Union Calendar No. 792

82d Congress, 2d Session - - - - - - - House Report No. 2505

THE KATYN FOREST MASSACRE

FINAL REPORT

OF THE

SELECT COMMITTEE TO CONDUCT AN INVESTIGATION AND STUDY OF THE FACTS, EVIDENCE, AND CIRCUMSTANCES OF THE KATYN FOREST MASSACRE

PURSUANT TO

H. Res. 390

AND

H. Res. 539

(82d Congress)

A RESOLUTION TO AUTHORIZE THE INVESTIGATION OF THE MASS MURDER OF POLISH OFFICERS IN THE KATYN FOREST NEAR SMOLENSK, RUSSIA

DECEMBER 22, 1952.—Committed to the Committee of the Whole House on the State of the Union and ordered to be printed

UNITED STATES
GOVERNMENT PRINTING OFFICE
26668 WASHINGTON : 1952

Title page of the Congressional report on the Katyn Forest massacre. The report concluded: "This committee unanimously finds, beyond any question of reasonable doubt, that the Soviet NKVD (People's Commissariat of Internal Affairs) committed the mass murders of the Polish officers and intellectual leaders in the Katyn Forest near Smolensk, Russia."

Katzenelson's work in the interwar period was based on his sense that Jewish life in the Diaspora was incomplete; this belief also motivated his participation in cultural and other public affairs in those years. Such feelings appear in his works in the form of somber symbols of death, boredom, and silence. In his Yiddish play *Tarshish,* Katzenelson

Itzhak Katzenelson.

deals with the roots of antisemitism in Poland and with the utter hopelessness of Jewish life on Polish soil.

In late November 1939 Katzenelson fled from Łódź to Warsaw, where he lived and wrote (in Yiddish) until April 20, 1943, the day following the outbreak of the WARSAW GHETTO UPRISING. Then, for several weeks, he was in hiding on the "Aryan" side of Warsaw. In May the Germans discovered his real identity, but since he held a Honduran passport he was sent to the VITTEL camp in France, where he stayed for a year, keeping up his writing. In April 1944 he and his surviving son were deported to their death in AUSCHWITZ.

Katzenelson's work clearly reflects the shifts in the situation of the Warsaw ghetto; indeed, his literary output of that period reflects the events that were taking place. From the very first day of his stay in the ghetto, he contributed to the underground press and participated in educational and cultural activities—teaching in the high school and in the underground seminars conducted by Dror, founding and directing a Yiddish dramatic troupe and a Hebrew theater circle, advising the elementary-school teachers, involving himself in the cultural program of the orphanages, and so on. By public readings from his works, through the Bible study groups that he organized, and with the help of his close ties with Dror, Katzenelson was able to convey to the public his thoughts and feelings, as expressed in his poetry, plays, essays, and lectures. In this way his literary creations came to have an impact on day-to-day life in the ghetto.

Katzenelson spent much of his time in translating sections from the biblical prophetic books into Yiddish, for his reading public, and in writing plays for children or about children's life in the ghetto. In the first nineteen months of the Nazi occupation of Warsaw, Katzenelson sought to strengthen the ghetto population's resilience by interpreting contemporary reality in the light of the past history of the Jewish people—consoling them and offering the hope that "this too shall pass"—until the terrible truth dawned on him that the Nazis were aiming at the total destruction of the Jewish people.

In February and March of 1942, the mood of his writings became sharply more pessimistic, as reports came in of the mass murder being committed in the CHEŁMNO camp. After that, his writing addressed itself to the confrontation with death—the death, as he expected, of all the Jews of Poland. For the next two years, Katzenelson was the elegist of the Jewish people that was being driven to its death and also the prosecutor on its behalf, calling for the indictment of Western Christian civilization and for the punishment of the Germans, as a nation, for their crimes. Katzenelson's comprehensive reaction to the events finds its expression, above all, in the poem *Dos Lid funem Oysgehargetn Yidishn Folk* (The Song of the Murdered Jewish People; English ed., 1980), written in Vittel during the last year of his life. The poems that he composed in his last year in the Warsaw ghetto attempt to define and depict the essence of Jewish heroism (*Dos Lid vegn Shloyme Zhelichowski* [The Poem about Shlomo Zhelichowski] and *Dos Lid vegn Radziner* [The Poem about the Radzin Rebbe]). In that same year, he also elegized his wife and two of his sons, who had been deported to TRE-

BLINKA in the mass deportation of the summer of 1942 from the Warsaw ghetto.

Two days before that deportation was begun, Mordechai TENENBAUM hid portions of Katzenelson's works, together with the Dror archive, in a subterranean hideout; of the works that he composed in the Vittel camp, the Holocaust researcher Miriam Nowitz was able to save a part. The Ghetto Fighters' Museum (BET LOḤAMEI HA-GETTA'OT) at Kibbutz Loḥamei ha-Getta'ot in Israel is named after Itzhak Katzenelson. It has made extensive efforts to collect his manuscripts and to translate his works into English and other languages, and has published three editions of his writings, consisting mostly of his last writings, consisting mostly of Hebrew translations of his Yiddish works and the Hebrew works that he wrote in the Holocaust period. Katzenelson's *Vittel Diary* was published in English (Tel Aviv, 1964).

BIBLIOGRAPHY

Even-Shoshan, S. *Yitzhak Katzenelson: Holocaust Mourner*. Naharia, Israel, 1964. (In Hebrew.)

Frank, M. Z. "Yitzhak Katzenelson, Martyred Poet." *Jewish Frontier* 30/9 (October 1963): 15–19.

Liptzin, S. *A History of Yiddish Literature*. New York, 1972.

Szeintuch, Y. "The Work of Yitzhak Katzenelson in the Warsaw Ghetto." *Jerusalem Quarterly* 26 (Winter 1983): 46–61.

Szeintuch, Y. *Yitzhak Katzenelson: The Last Writings in Hebrew and Yiddish from the Warsaw Ghetto and the Vittel Camp*. Jerusalem, 1989. (In Hebrew.)

Szeintuch, Y., ed. *Yitzhak Katzenelson: Yiddish Ghetto Writings; Warsaw, 1940–1943*. Naharia, Israel, 1984. (In Yiddish.)

YEHIEL SZEINTUCH

KATZMANN, FRITZ (1906–1957), SS officer. Katzmann joined the Nazi party in 1928 and the SS in 1930, eventually rising to the rank of SS-*Gruppenführer* and police lieutenant general. From November 1939 until August 1941 he was the SS and Police Leader of the RADOM district; he then became SS and Police Leader of the region of Galicia, overseeing the implementation of the "FINAL SOLUTION" for the Jews of that area. It was in the period of his command (which lasted until the fall of 1943) that most of the Jews of Eastern Galicia were murdered, with Katzmann bearing direct responsibility for the crime. In a report to his superiors dated June 30, 1943, he gave a detailed description of how he and the men under his command had purged the area of practically all the Jews who had lived there, either killing them on the spot or deporting them to forced-labor and extermination camps. Katzmann's report also referred to Jewish resistance in his area. In 1944 he became SS and Police Leader in Wehrkreis (military district) XX, with headquarters in DANZIG.

After the war, Katzmann went into hiding under an assumed name; he died in 1957. Nothing else is known of his fate.

BIBLIOGRAPHY

Hilberg, R. *The Destruction of the European Jews*. 3 vols. New York, 1985.

AHARON WEISS

KAUFERING, network of subsidiary camps of the DACHAU concentration camp in Germany. From June to October 1944, fifteen such subsidiary camps (eleven for men and four for women) were established around the village of Kaufering, about 25 miles (40 km) southwest of Munich. The inmates were used as part of the Jägerstab program, Albert SPEER's plan to bring Jewish slave labor to Germany to build underground fighter-aircraft factories inaccessible to Allied bombing attacks. The central camp administration was situated near Kaufering, about 4 miles (7 km) north of Landsberg. The commandant was subordinate to the commandant of Dachau.

The inmates of the Kaufering camps lived in huts half buried under the ground. Inadequate food, the absence of medical care, maltreatment, and extremely hard work for construction firms and armament industries caused a soaring death rate.

The first prisoners were Lithuanian Jews who arrived in June 1944. They were followed in October by large transports of Hungarian, Polish, Czechoslovak, and Romanian Jews, most of whom came from AUSCHWITZ. There are no exact statistical data as to how many

One of the subsidiary Kaufering camps was located at Landsberg, 3 miles (4.8 km) south of Kaufering. At this camp, called Lager No. 3, a Polish Jew who had been a prisoner for seven months looks at the bodies of his comrades, killed by the Germans. In an attempt to destroy the evidence the Germans had poured gasoline over the bodies and set them on fire (May 1, 1945). [United States Army]

prisoners were transported to Kaufering, how many perished there, or how many lived to see the liberation. Jules Jost, a French prisoner who helped keep the camp records, stated after the war that he had registered about twenty-eight thousand Kaufering inmates. At the beginning of December 1944, the fourth camp (No. IV) was put under quarantine because of an epidemic of typhus, and it became the sick bay for all the Kaufering camps.

A week before the liberation by American military units, evacuation of the Kaufering prisoners to Dachau and its subsidiary work camp at Allach began. When the Americans arrived on April 27, 1945, the camps were found abandoned, and many of the huts had been burned down by the SS guards. A few prisoners who had hidden in the woods returned to show the liberators burial pits containing thousands of bodies, and to bear witness to the crimes committed in these camps.

BIBLIOGRAPHY

Ervin-Deutsch, L. "About Those Who Survived and Those Who Died." *Dachau Review* 1 (1988): 116–156.

BARBARA DISTEL

KAUNAS. *See* Kovno.

KĖDAINIAI (Yi., Keidan), town located in the central part of the Lithuanian SSR. Jews lived in Kėdainiai beginning in the fifteenth century; from the sixteenth to the eighteenth century the town was an important trading center. On the eve of World War II it had a

Jewish population of three thousand, many of whom were truck farmers.

On June 24, 1941, two days after the German invasion of the Soviet Union, Kėdainiai was occupied. Only a few Jews managed to flee to the interior of the country. Upon the arrival of the Germans, the town's Lithuanian inhabitants began to harass and murder the Jews. At the end of July a ghetto was set up in Smilga Street, where all the Jews had to live; they were also forced to pay a heavy ransom. Two weeks later the Jews were taken to a nearby horse farm, where they were held under appalling conditions. On August 28, all the Jews—men, women, and children—were killed by firing squads made up of Lithuanians and men of Einsatzkommando 3. One of the Jews attacked two members of a firing squad, dragged them into a ditch, and choked one of them to death, but was himself immediately shot and killed.

Kėdainiai was liberated in the fall of 1944. Only 150 of its Jews survived, including those who had fled to the interior of the Soviet Union. After the war, a memorial was erected on the site of the execution.

BIBLIOGRAPHY

Chrust, J., ed. *Keidan Memorial Book.* Tel Aviv, 1977. (In Hebrew.)

DOV LEVIN

KEITEL, WILHELM (1882–1946), head of the Oberkommando der Wehrmacht (Armed Forces High Command; OKW) from 1938 to 1945. During World War I, Keitel fulfilled staff assignments and administrative duties in the Reichswehr. In 1934 he became closely associated with the Nazi party and advanced rapidly in his military career. When Hitler assumed personal command of the armed forces in February 1938, Keitel was appointed to the new post of chief of staff of the OKW, a post he held until the final surrender of Germany on May 8, 1945. In 1940 he was made a field marshal. Owing to his servile admiration for Hitler, Keitel was nicknamed by many German officers "Lakeitel" (from *Lakai,* "lackey").

Wilhelm Keitel in his prison cell in Nuremberg during his trial before the International Military Tribunal. [United States Army]

Keitel signed a number of orders for the shooting of hostages, as well as for the wholesale murder of prisoners of war and civilians in occupied territories, including the notorious KOMMISSARBEFEHL and the *Nacht-und-Nebel-Erlass* (Night and Fog Decree; *see* NACHT UND NEBEL). After the July 20, 1944, attempt on Hitler's life by military conspirators, Keitel became a member of the "Court of Honor" (*Ehrengerichtshof*). This court stripped many high-ranking officers of their rank, leading to death sentences for them. On May 8, 1945, Keitel signed the document for the unconditional surrender of Germany.

At the NUREMBERG TRIAL, Keitel claimed that as an army officer he had served only to carry out orders of the state, but the tribunal declared that the defense of "superior order" did not apply to violations of international law. On October 1, 1945, Keitel was found guilty on all four counts of the indictment: conspiracy to wage a war of aggression; waging a war of aggression; war crimes; and crimes against humanity. He was sentenced to death and hanged on October 16, 1946. Keitel's memoirs, *In the Service of the Reich,* were published in 1979.

BIBLIOGRAPHY

Davidson, E. *The Trial of the Germans.* New York, 1967.

Görlitz, W., ed. *Generalfeldmarschall Keitel: Verbrecher oder Offizier? Erinnerungen, Briefe, Dokumente des Chefs OKW.* Göttingen, 1961.

JEHUDA L. WALLACH

KHARKOV, second-largest city in the Ukrainian SSR. According to the 1939 census, the city had a Jewish population of 130,200, one-sixth of the total. In the summer of 1941, when the Germans were approaching the city, many of its inhabitants fled, including the bulk of the Jewish population. Kharkov was captured by the Germans on October 23, 1941, and became the headquarters of the German Sixth Army; it was under a military government throughout the German occupation and was not part of REICHSKOMMISSARIAT UKRAINE.

All the decrees concerning the city, including those affecting the Jews, were issued by the military government. Thus, on November 3, 1941, the military government announced the meager food rations, of which Jews were to receive only 40 percent; for example, the daily bread ration was set at 150 grams (5.25 oz), but Jews received only 60 grams (2 oz). Every day, hostages were taken, and, according to orders issued by the rear headquarters of Army Group South (to which the military government was subordinated), most were Jews; they were shot or hanged. On November 26, Sonderkommando 4a arrived in Kharkov, headed by Paul BLOBEL, and this meant the murder of more Jews. They were seized in groups from streets and houses; taken to the Hotel International, where they were tortured; and then murdered, mostly in GAS VANS.

On December 14, 1941, in an announcement published over the signature of the military governor of Kharkov, the city's Jews were ordered to assemble on the site of a nearby tractor plant by December 16. The plant was situated 7.5 miles (12 km) from Kharkov, and the Soviets had moved all its equipment to the east before their retreat. In order to terrorize the Jews, Sonderkommando 4a murdered 305 Jews, on the pretext that they had been spreading false rumors. The sheds in which the prisoners were housed had no doors, windows, or heating facilities, and the winter of 1941–1942 was severe. The number of people who were crowded in exceeded the sheds' capacity several times over. The prisoners were not permitted to fetch water or food and had to bribe the guards in order to obtain these basic needs. They were forbidden to leave the sheds at night, though there were no sanitary installations inside. There were many deaths from cold, disease, and hunger.

Only three weeks after the establishment of this ghetto, the liquidation of the Jews of Kharkov was set in motion. On the first day, "volunteers" were called for work in Poltava and Lubny, located west of Kharkov. The 800 men who reported for the trip were taken by truck to the Drobitski Ravine (Drobitski Yar), a nearby site, where they were murdered in pits that had been prepared in advance. In the following days more Jews were taken to the same ravine, by truck or on foot, and murdered. Gas vans were also used for killings. The mass slaughter was carried out by men of Sonderkommando 4a, assisted by members of German Police Battalion 314 and Waffen-SS

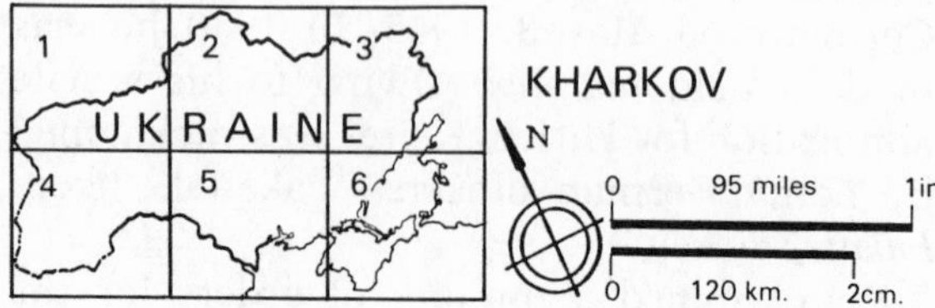

soldiers, who were probably from an SS Totenkopf (Death's-Head) unit (*see* TOTENKOPFVERBÄNDE).

A report issued by the special committee that after the war investigated Nazi crimes in Kharkov and opened the burial pits in the Drobitski Ravine stated that 15,000 people had been murdered there. However, according to evidence given at the trial of the officers and men of Sonderkommando 4a by the intelligence officer of the German Sixth Army (to which the Sonderkommando had been attached), the actual number of victims, as he had heard it from Blobel himself, was 21,685. This figure includes all the Jews killed from the beginning of the German occupation until early January 1942, when the liquidation of the Jews of Kharkov was completed.

The city was liberated on February 16, 1943, reconquered by the Germans, and liberated again on August 23. Only a few Jews survived; they had gone into hiding with the help of local inhabitants.

BIBLIOGRAPHY

Ehrenburg, I., and V. Grossman, eds. *The Black Book of Soviet Jewry*. New York, 1981.

SHMUEL SPECTOR

KHERSON, capital of the oblast (district) of the same name in the Ukrainian SSR. Kherson was founded in the eighteenth century. Jews lived there from the very beginning, and on the eve of World War II they numbered more than 15,000, out of a population of 167,108.

On August 19, 1941, Kherson was captured by the Germans; two-thirds of its Jewish population had by then been evacuated or had fled the city on their own. In the first few days of the occupation, the Jews were ordered to form a "Jewish committee," which was to register all the Jews from August 24 to 27. On August 25, the Jews were ordered to wear a Jewish star (*see* BADGE, JEWISH) on their chests (a yellow badge in the form of a Shield of David); they were also forced to hand over to the German administration all the money and valuables in their possession. When the registration was completed, the Jews were all concentrated in a ghetto. Between September 16 and 30, 1941, the five thousand Jews of Kherson were taken to an antitank ditch outside the city and murdered there.

The Kherson oblast contained the Jewish autonomous subdistricts of Kalinindorf, Stalindorf, and Nay Zlatopol. There were Jewish kolkhozes (collective farms) in these subdistricts, successors to the Jewish agricultural settlements that had been established there in the second half of the nineteenth century. On the eve of World War II, the three subdistricts had a Jewish population of thirty-five thousand, most of them farmers.

The fate of the Jews living in the kolkhozes can be deduced from the course of events in the Stalindorf subdistrict. In the second half of September 1941, *Aktionen* took place, and groups of Jewish men were murdered in several kolkhozes. Heavy collective fines were imposed on the Jews. They were robbed of their belongings, and the community property of the kolkhozes was confiscated. Early in the spring of 1942 the Jewish farmers were told to sow potatoes and grow vegetables for the German administration. In April, many Jewish men were drafted and put into eight labor camps, to work on the construction of the Dnepropetrovsk-Zaporozhye highway. The old men, women, and children left behind in the kolkhozes were rounded up and killed on May 29. On December 5, 1942, all the men were put into the Lyubimovka camp, where they were murdered or died as a result of hard labor and disease.

The Kherson region was liberated in mid-March 1944. Surviving Jewish farmers who returned, expecting to rehabilitate their farms, found them occupied by Russians and Ukrainians. The appeals that Jews made to the authorities in Kiev to restore the Jewish autonomous subdistricts were rejected, and when the war ended they were officially abolished.

SHMUEL SPECTOR

KIDDUSH HA-HAYYIM (lit., "sanctifying Life"), Hebrew term used during the Holocaust to refer to spontaneous, as well as planned, Jewish responses to the deadly objectives of Nazi Germany and its supporters by various means of resistance. The term is attributed to the European religious Zionist leader Rabbi Yitzhak Nissenbaum (1868–1942), who wrote, in the early months of the Warsaw ghetto: "This is the hour of *Kiddush ha-Hayyim* and not of KIDDUSH HA-SHEM by death. Formerly, our enemies demanded our soul, and the Jew sacrificed his body in sanctifying God's Name. Now the enemy demands the body of the Jew. This makes it imperative for the Jew to defend it and protect it."

The considerations and stimuli for *Kiddush ha-Hayyim* responses were varied and complex. For some they represented acts that sustained the morale of the individual, the family, and the community. For others, *Kiddush ha-Hayyim* was a new form of traditional Jewish response to crisis or a natural extension of genuine piety and belief. The psychologist Bruno Bettelheim, himself a prisoner in Dachau and Buchenwald in 1938 (whose harsh views on the passive response of Jewish victims have aroused indignation), states that expressions of *Kiddush ha-Hayyim* were the instinctive attempts of the victim to protectively insulate himself within the boundaries of "private behavior." In this manner, the person rejects traumatic forces that threaten the integrity and stability of the personality. This response, against unequal massive terror and the methods of its perpetrators, who sought to destroy the Jews, expressed the intention of the victim to live to the fullest, and, in the words of the Israeli Holocaust scholar Shaul Esh, "this often meant to live Jewishly." In raising the falling spirits of his flock in Zelichowo in June 1942, Rabbi Avraham Shalom Goldberg entreated: "Every Jew who remains alive sanctifies the Name of God among many."

There were numerous attempts to maintain independent Jewish community life in the face of hostility, intimidation, and risk. An early expression of group integrity and self-respect was the article "Wear the Yellow Badge with Pride," by Robert Weltsch, the editor of the Zionist *Jüdische Rundschau*, appearing in Berlin in April 1933. This audacious challenge to Jews to strengthen their ethnic and national commitments galvanized community efforts in Germany to enrich the internal Jewish fabric of their communities not only in terms of physical rescue efforts but also in the spiritual, cultural, and educational domains. Jewish and general education in independent school networks, cultural institutions, and YOUTH MOVEMENTS were activated in order to cope with entire populations who were suddenly disenfranchised educationally and professionally in their communities. Newspapers, at first tolerated and eventually prohibited, served as an important means of communication in the attempt to resume dignified communal life.

Though spiritual resistance included every

type of nonviolent act by secular as well as believing Jews who responded in terms of their own traditions, *Kiddush ha-Hayyim* is generally associated with the *Kiddush ha-Shem* world of belief, faith, and the Jewish life cycle. Roughly sketched calendars projected the Jewish religious year and the candle-lighting times for the Sabbath and festivals. They marked traditional days of joy and mourning. In the absence of Jewish ritual objects and facilities, the daily, weekly, monthly, and yearly events were commemorated symbolically. A glass of water could substitute for the mikva (ritual pool for immersion). Stale bread crumbs would serve instead of Sabbath wine and loaves. Potato peels would briefly provide the fuel for candles for Sabbath festivities. Scraps of prayers and study texts from the Talmud were circulated among camp inmates. The age-old tradition of rabbinic responsa to questions of Jewish law produced a genre of Holocaust responsa literature. The best known of these are in Rabbi Efraim Oshry's *Mi-Ma'amakim* (New York, 1949, 1963, 1969) and *Divrei Efraim* (New York, 1949), Rabbi Zvi Hirsh Meisels's *Mekadshei ha-Shem* (Chicago, 1955), and Rabbi Yehiel Weinberg's *Sifrei Esh* (Jerusalem, 1961–1969). They reflect the attempts of Jews of faith to continue to cling to ritual and tradition despite, or perhaps in response to, the declared objectives of Nazi Germany to destroy not only Jews but Judaism.

Kiddush ha-Hayyim, by means of benevolent acts toward others and steadfast faith in God (who is seen as suffering together with his people), is also conceived as the necessary catalyst for *tikkun* (reconstruction) within destruction in a rare work of rabbinic Hasidic theology written during the Holocaust. Rabbi Kalunimus Kalmish Shapiro, the Hasidic leader of Piaseczno, wrote in the Warsaw ghetto following Rosh Hashanah (New Year) of 1941: "When we undergo today these sufferings . . . we have to believe that out of our vast affliction will evolve a new creation by way of renewed penitence and good deeds."

The *tikkun* theme is central to Rabbi Issachar Shlomo Teichthal, who pleaded with the Jewish remnant in Hungary, in *Em ha-Banim Semeha* (Budapest, 1943), to dedicate itself to the return and rebuilding of the land of Israel. Only by re-creating an autonomous Jewish homeland—the ultimate reaffirmation of the sanctity of life for the Jew, the Jewish people, and the God of Israel—can the martyrdom of the Holocaust have any meaning. "If we shall move and ascend to Zion we will restore the Jewish souls who were murdered in acts of *Kiddush ha-Shem.* They with their lives will have compelled us to return to the estate of our forebears."

BIBLIOGRAPHY

Esh, S. "The Dignity of the Destroyed: Toward a Definition of the Period of the Holocaust." *Judaism* 11/2 (Spring 1962): 99–111.

Oshry, E. *Responsa from the Holocaust.* New York, 1983.

Rudavsky, J. *To Live with Hope, to Die with Dignity.* Lanham, Md., 1987.

PESACH SCHINDLER

KIDDUSH HA-SHEM (lit., "sanctifying the Name [of God]"), Hebrew term that was used in postbiblical Jewish history to denote exemplary ethical conduct and that became applied to religious martyrdom. A Jew who consciously chose to offer his own life for the sake of his faith was considered a *kadosh* ("holy one"), sanctified as a martyr.

The long epoch of Jewish martyrdom emerged during the periods of Greek domination in the second century B.C. and the subsequent persecutions of the Roman era. The religious faith of the Jews was repeatedly tested during the Middle Ages under both Muslim and Christian rule. The chronicles of the period depict acts of *Kiddush ha-Shem* by entire communities in England, France, and Germany, especially in the wake of the Crusades. Acts of martyrdom punctuated Jewish history from the fifteenth to the nineteenth century in the precarious world of ghettos, inquisitions, expulsions, and pogroms in Europe. In most instances the choice of accepting *Kiddush ha-Shem* was voluntary, with various options made available by the hostile surrounding society and even by Jewish law.

The Holocaust eliminated the element of choice for the victim. Religious (conversion), ideological, or economic means could not influence the racial definitions and the fate of the Jews. Rabbi Shimon Huberband, a member of the secret ONEG SHABBAT group in the WARSAW ghetto, invoked the Jewish religious legal authorities Maimonides and Rabbi Moshe Sofer (the Ḥatam Sofer) in broadening the definition of *Kiddush ha-Shem*: a Jew murdered by non-Jews, whether from religious motives or for criminal reasons, is considered a *kadosh*.

Numerous eyewitness reports describe *Kiddush ha-Shem* scenes in which the *Viddui* (the confessional) and the final *Shema Yisrael* ("Hear O Israel"; Deuteronomy) were recited in public and death was faced with dignity, love, and even joy. Among the many rabbinic responsa emerging from the Holocaust was the answer of Rabbi Efraim Oshry in the Kovno ghetto concerning the proper text for the blessing traditionally recited by Jews about to undergo martyrdom: "Blessed are you, Lord, who has added holiness to our life through His commandments and commanded us the command to sanctify His Name in public." Among the many ritual artifacts discovered in the ghettos and camps were prayer books and notes inscribed with this text, evidently to be utilized prior to the expected moment of martyrdom.

Among the most remarkable eyewitness reports is the final plea by the eminent scholar of pre-Holocaust Jewry, Rabbi Elchanan Wasserman, sent to his death in Lithuania.

> Evidently they consider us righteous in Heaven, for we have been chosen to atone with our bodies for all of Israel. If so, we must repent now, at this very spot. Time is short. If we repent we shall be able to save our brothers and sisters in America. The NINTH FORT [where the Jews of Kovno were executed] is close. Let us remember to be faithful in sanctifying the Name. We shall walk erect. Let us not, Heaven forbid, inject impure thoughts that would invalidate our sacrifice. We are about to fulfill the most critical of all commandments: *Kiddush ha-Shem*. The very fires that shall consume our bodies will in turn spark the renewal of the Jewish people. (quoted in Eliav)

BIBLIOGRAPHY

Eliav, M., ed. *I Believe: Testimonies of the Life and Death of Believers during the Holocaust.* Jerusalem, 1969. (In Hebrew.)

Gottfarstein, Y. *Kiddush Hashem over the Ages and Its Uniqueness in the Holocaust Period; Jewish Resistance during the Holocaust.* In Proceedings of the Conference on Manifestations of Jewish Resistance, pp. 453–482. Jerusalem, 1971.

Huberband, S. *Kiddush Hashem: Jewish Religious and Cultural Life in Poland during the Holocaust.* New York, 1988.

Schindler, P. "The Holocaust and Kiddush Hashem in Hassidic Thought." In *Religious Encounters with Death,* edited by F. E. Reynolds and E. N. Waugh, pp. 170–180. London, 1977.

PESACH SCHINDLER

KIELCE, district capital in southeast POLAND, situated north of Kraków and south of Radom. The Jewish community of Kielce was established in 1868, but it was only at the turn of the century that many Jews began moving there from the neighboring townships. By 1921 the Jews in the city numbered 15,550, about one-third of the total population. According to the 1931 census, the number of Jews in Kielce was 18,083; in 1939 it was estimated at 24,000.

The city was captured by the Germans on September 4, 1939, a few days after the outbreak of World War II, and anti-Jewish atrocities began immediately: expropriations, heavy fines, forced labor, the taking of hostages, beatings, and killings. The first head of the JUDENRAT (Jewish Council) was Dr. Moses Pelc, who was soon sent to AUSCHWITZ for refusing to cooperate with the Germans in the execution of their policies. He was replaced by the industrialist Hermann Levy, who served the Germans until the liquidation of the ghetto, when he was murdered by Hans Geier, an SS officer, in September 1942.

The Kielce ghetto was established early in April 1941 in accordance with an official order issued by Stadthauptmann Hans Drechsel, the German civilian administrator of the city. The number of Jews grew when 1,000 Jews deported from Vienna were brought to Kielce, as well as several thousand from neighboring small towns and more distant areas around Poznań and Łódź. By the end of 1941 there were 27,000 Jews in the Kielce ghetto. The able-bodied males were used by the Germans as laborers in the local stone quarries. Others worked in the ghetto

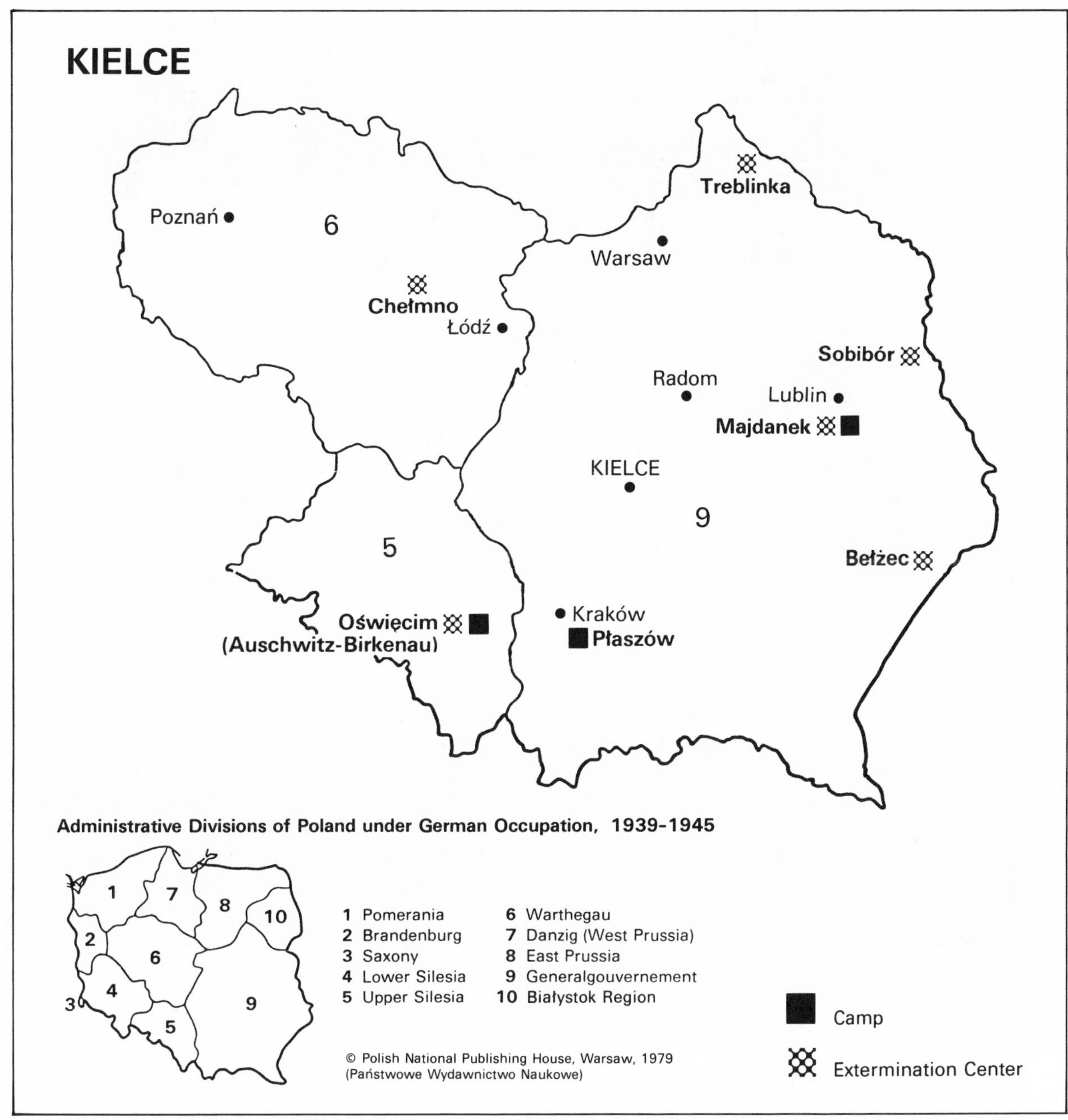

Administrative Divisions of Poland under German Occupation, 1939–1945

as tailors, shoemakers, and carpenters, and at other trades. Between April 1941 and the mass *Aktionen* of August 20 to 24, 1942, some 6,000 Jews died of hunger, cold, and typhus within the ghetto confines.

In January 1942 seven Jews were shot for trying to leave the ghetto. Several other executions had taken place in the preceding summer, especially of activists and community leaders. Under the command of two SS officers, Hauptsturmführer und Kriminalkommissar Ernst Karl Thomas and Hauptmann Hans Geier, the liquidation of the ghetto began, on August 20. It lasted until August 24, when all the Jews, with the exception of two thousand who were young and healthy, were loaded on freight trains and sent to TREBLINKA. The sick Jews and the children of the Jewish orphanage had been killed by the Germans before the deportation. Some five hundred Jews managed to escape.

The remaining two thousand Jews of Kielce were placed in three labor camps in Kielce: HASAG-Granat (quarries, workshops, and mu-

Jewish refugees, survivors of the Kielce pogrom, waiting to leave Poland (July 1946).

nitions), Henryków (carpentry), and Ludwików (foundry). A projected revolt, to be led by David Barviner and Gershon Levkowitz, was aborted by an informer. In August 1944 the surviving inmates were sent to BUCHENWALD or Auschwitz. The last surviving group, consisting of forty-five Jewish children, was taken to the Jewish cemetery and killed there by the Germans.

When the Soviet army captured Kielce on January 16, 1945, only two Jews remained of what had once been a twenty-thousand-strong community. However, during the eighteen months that followed, about one hundred and fifty Jews—former residents who had survived the camps or were hiding in the forests, and Jews who had never lived in Kielce—gradually gathered in the former Jewish community building at No. 7 Planty Avenue. Most of them lived on funds sent by the JOINT DISTRIBUTION COMMITTEE, forming a kibbutz and waiting for an opportunity to go to Palestine.

The hatred of the Poles toward the Jews was so intense that whenever a former Jewish resident appeared in town he was greeted with the words: "What? You are still alive? We thought that Hitler killed all of you." Rumors spread that masses of Jews would soon return to reclaim their former houses and belongings. The incitement culminated at the end of June 1946 when a woman ran through the streets shouting that the Jews on Planty Avenue were killing Polish children and drinking their blood. Another rumor was spread that a Polish boy had been killed in the basement of the community building and his blood used to make matzoth.

On July 1, mobs began gathering around the building. When the police were called in all they did was to confiscate the few licensed weapons that the Jews had. Appeals to the church dignitaries were dismissed with the excuse that they could not intercede for the Jews because the latter had brought communism into Poland. On July 4 the mob attacked and massacred forty-two Jews and wounded about fifty more. The central Polish authorities in Warsaw sent in a military detachment and an investigation committee. Order was quickly restored, and seven of the main instigators and killers were executed. The missing Polish boy was soon found in a nearby village.

Thus, the thousand-year history of the Jews of Poland came to an ignominious end with a medieval-style pogrom, an event that touched off a mass migration of hundreds of thousands of Jews from Poland and other countries of eastern and central Europe who had somehow survived World War II and the Holocaust.

In 1946 the tomb with the names of the forty-two victims that had been erected in the Kielce Jewish cemetery was destroyed by the local Poles. It was rebuilt in 1987, when the chairman of the Kielce Society in New York, William Mandel, also erected an iron fence around the cemetery. The monument for the forty-five children killed in 1944 was rebuilt as well.

BIBLIOGRAPHY

Citron, P. *The Kielce Book: The History of the Kielce Community from Its Foundation to Its Destruction.* Tel Aviv, 1958. (In Hebrew.)

Stockfisch, D. *About Our House Which Was Devastated.* Tel Aviv, 1981. (In Hebrew and Yiddish.)

SINAI LEICHTER

Manfred von Killinger.

KIEV. *See* Babi Yar.

KILLINGER, MANFRED VON (1886–1944), German diplomat; ambassador to ROMANIA from 1941 to 1944. In World War I, Killinger served as a torpedo boat commander. He joined the Nazi party in 1928 and rose rapidly in the SA (Sturmabteilung; Storm Troopers). Though he was made *Reichskommissar* for Saxony in 1933, he narrowly escaped execution during the bloody purge of leading SA men on June 30, 1934 (the "Night of the Long Knives").

Killinger began rebuilding his political career by joining the Foreign Office, and in 1940 was made a roving troubleshooter for eastern European affairs. In this capacity he visited the capitals of Germany's new eastern European allies, urging them to request German advisers and making no secret of the Third Reich's interest in the way they treated their Jews. His major success was in Slovakia, where he advised the ouster of the relatively independent-minded foreign minister, Ferdinand Ďurčanský, in favor of the pro-German Vojtech TUKA as foreign minister and Alexander (Saňo) MACH as interior minister. Subsequently, Killinger was made German ambassador to Slovakia, where he installed the system that brought in Dieter WISLICENY as adviser for Jewish affairs.

In December 1940, Killinger left Slovakia to become the German ambassador to Romania. Again German advisers quickly followed, including Gustav RICHTER as consultant for Jewish affairs. Given his SA background, it is not surprising that Killinger had numerous quarrels with the SS. His relations with Richter became especially strained when the latter, without keeping Killinger informed, reached an agreement with the Romanian government in July 1942 concerning the deportation of Romanian Jews to Poland. The ensuing squabble gained time for the Romanians, who eventually backed out of the deportation agreement. Killinger committed suicide in Bucharest in 1944 to avoid capture by the Russians.

BIBLIOGRAPHY

Broszat, H. "Das Dritte Reich und die rumänische Judenpolitik." *Gutachten des Instituts für Zeitgeschichte* 1 (1958): 102–183.

Browning, C. R. *The Final Solution and the German Foreign Office: A Study of Referat D3 of Abteilung Deutschland, 1940–1943.* New York, 1978.

CHRISTOPHER R. BROWNING

KISHINEV (Rom., Chişinău), capital of the Moldavian SSR. From 1918 to 1940 and again from 1941 to 1944 it was the capital of BESSARABIA, in ROMANIA. Jews lived in the town from the eighteenth century, and by the late nineteenth century they made up half its population. They fell victim to pogroms in 1903 and 1905. The community was a cultural center for the Jews of Bessarabia and Romania, with a rabbinical academy (yeshiva), a Yiddish newspaper, Hebrew and Yiddish schools, and Zionist and Socialist activities. In 1930 the 41,405 Jews living there constituted over 36 percent of a total population numbering 114,896. Under Soviet rule, from July 1940 to July 1941, the number of Jews in the city increased to an estimated 60,000.

On June 22, 1941, with the German invasion of the Soviet Union, Kishinev's town center was severely bombarded by German and Romanian planes. Thousands, including many Jews, died in the bombing and the resulting conflagrations. The disorderly flight of the Soviet authorities caused panic among the Jews, who were seen by the Romanian majority in the city as supporters of the Communist regime. There was no official evacuation of the Jews, although some fled to the east on their own initiative and at their own risk. Kishinev and the surrounding villages were inhabited mainly by Romanians who viewed the entry of the Romanian and German armies as a liberation and not as an occupation. Thousands of Jews from Kishinev and from nearby towns were cruelly slaughtered by Romanian farmers or executed by Romanian soldiers while attempting to flee.

The annihilation of the Jews of Kishinev was carried out in several stages. With the entry of the Romanian and German units, an

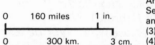

Annexations from June to September 1940: (1) Bessarabia and (2) N. Bukovina to USSR; (3) N. Transylvania to Hungary; (4) S. Dobruja to Bulgaria.

unknown number of Jews, estimated by Matatias Carp (1946) at ten thousand, were slaughtered in the streets and in their homes. After the establishment of the ghetto, about two thousand Jews, mainly members of the liberal professions (doctors, lawyers, engineers) and local Jewish intellectuals, were systematically executed by Einsatzkommando 11a of Einsatzgruppe D. Members of the Romanian army and police force took part in some of these executions as auxiliaries.

After the wave of killings, the eleven thousand remaining Jews were concentrated in the ghetto, created on July 24, 1941, on the order of the Romanian district ruler and the German Einsatzkommando leader, Paul Zapp. The inhabitants of the ghetto were robbed, tortured, conscripted for forced labor, and executed. The Jews of central Romania attempted to assist their brethren in the ghetto, sending large amounts of money by illegal means. A committee was formed to bribe the Romanian authorities so that they would not hand the Jews over to the Germans.

On August 7, 500 Jewish men and 25 Jewish women were sent to work in the Ghidighici quarries; within a week about 325 of them had been killed by Romanian soldiers. That fall, on the Day of Atonement (October 4), the military authorities began deporting the remaining ghetto Jews to TRANSNISTRIA, by order of the Romanian ruler, Ion ANTONESCU. One of the heads of the ghetto, the attorney Shapira, managed to alert the leaders of the Jewish communities in Bucharest, but attempts to halt the deportations were unsuccessful. The first group was taken by the Orhei-Rezina road toward the Dniester River. The property of all the deportees was plundered by their escorts and by the representatives of the Romanian National Bank, and most of the Jews of the first group were murdered while crossing the river. The deportations continued throughout October. Hundreds of Jewish corpses littered the roadsides leading to the Dniester. On October 31, the last convoy of 257 deportees left the ghetto. The community was not completely liquidated, however, since some Jews had found places of concealment in Kishinev and its vicinity or elsewhere in Romania. In May 1942, the last 200 Jews in the locality were deported. Kishinev was liberated in August 1944. At that time no Jews remained in the locality.

BIBLIOGRAPHY

Carp, M. *Legionarii şi rebeliunea*. Vol. 1 of *Cartea Neagră*. Bucharest, 1946.

Istoriia Kishineva (1466–1966). Kishinev, 1966.

"Kishinev." In *Rumania*, vol. 2, edited by J. Ancel and T. Lavi, pp. 411–416. *Pinkas ha-Kehillot; Encyclopaedia of Jewish Communities*. Jerusalem, 1980. (In Hebrew.)

Mircu, M. *Pogromurile din Basarabia*. Bucharest, 1947. See pages 17–24.

JEAN ANCEL

KISTARCSA, camp located 9 miles (5.6 km) northeast of Budapest. Before the Nazis occupied Hungary, Kistarcsa was an internment camp. With the start of the DEPORTATIONS from Hungary in the spring of 1944, it became a transit camp from which Jews in the Budapest area were sent onward for annihilation, primarily to AUSCHWITZ.

During the 1930s, the regent, Adm. Miklós HORTHY, interned left-wing political opponents (among them Jews) in facilities at the Kistarcsa, Topolya, and Csepel camps. After the outbreak of World War II, Jewish refugees who managed to obtain legitimate papers were also held in these camps. The five buildings of the Kistarcsa camp, originally meant to house 200 prisoners, soon became overcrowded with 2,000 Jews.

When the Nazis occupied Hungary on

Jews rounded up by the SS and taken to the Kistarcsa camp (after 1944).

March 19, 1944, the SS began rounding up Jews. They were first held in railway stations in various Budapest suburbs, and from there transferred to the Kistarcsa camp. During the Nazi occupation, the SS took over the camp, but it was administered directly by the Hungarian police. By all accounts, the camp commandant, István Vasdenyei, was humane and did whatever he could to ease the plight of the Jews under his control. He cooperated with the Jewish relief organizations, the Magyar Izraeliták Pártfogo Irodaja (Welfare Bureau of Hungarian Jews), the Országos Magyar Zsidó Segito Akcio (National Hungarian Jewish Assistance Campaign), and the Orthodox Nepasztal (People's Table), which cared for the inmates.

The first transport of 1,800 Jews left the camp for Auschwitz on April 29, 1944. Adolf EICHMANN and his commando sent eighteen more trainloads of roughly similar size from Kistarcsa to Auschwitz before Horthy declared the cessation of deportations on July 7 of that year. Furious at Horthy's intervention, Eichmann attempted to dispatch another train on July 15. Acting on information from Vasdenyei, Horthy turned back the transport before it reached the Hungarian border. On July 19 Eichmann sent his underling Franz Nowak and a special team of deportation experts to the camp. Among the Hungarians present were László BAKY, the Hungarian secretary of state, and Pál Ubrizsi, the commandant of the Rokk Szillard jail. They sent 1,200 Jews to Auschwitz on what was the last deportation train from Kistarcsa. About 1,000 Jews remained in the Kistarcsa camp until it was dismantled on the Day of Atonement, September 27, 1944, and its inmates sent to various labor camps in Hungary.

BIBLIOGRAPHY

Braham, R. L. *The Politics of Genocide: The Holocaust in Hungary.* New York, 1981.

Lavi, T., ed. *Hungary.* In *Pinkas Hakehillot; Encyclopaedia of Jewish Communities.* Jerusalem, 1986. (In Hebrew.)

ROBERT ROZETT

KLAIPĖDA. *See* Memel.

KLAUSENBURG. *See* Cluj.

KLOOGA, subcamp of the VAIVARA camp in northern ESTONIA, near TALLINN. The Klooga camp was created in the summer of 1943, and was one of the large labor camps in Estonia. It held about two to three thousand male and female Jewish prisoners, most of whom arrived in August and September of 1943 from the VILNA ghetto; a minority came from the KOVNO ghetto and elsewhere. There were also about one hundred Soviet prisoners of war in the camp. The two camps at Klooga, the men's camp and the women's camp, were about 600 yards apart. Each had a large two-story building housing the Jewish prisoners. Barbed-wire fences enclosed the entire camp as well as the two internal camps, which were guarded by German and Estonian SS men.

The camps in Estonia, including Klooga, were created for exploitation of the local natural resources, assistance to the German war effort, and construction of fortifications against the advancing Soviet army. Three shifts of prisoners worked in the cement and brick works and in the sawmills at Klooga; part of the production was used for building fortifications, and part was sent to Germany. Other prisoners worked in a factory producing wooden clogs for the camp prisoners.

Conditions for the Jewish prisoners were extremely harsh, particularly for those transporting bags of cement from the factory to the train station. The prisoners received 7 to 9 ounces (200–250 g) of bread, a pint (0.5 l) of soup, and a limited quantity of water daily, and were obliged to work even when they were sick. The camp elder and most of the Jewish Kapos appointed by the camp commandant treated the other prisoners humanely and tried to help them. The Jewish underground in the camp had about seventy-five members, organized into groups of five. Most had belonged in the past to the underground in the Vilna ghetto. According to several accounts, the underground managed to obtain a few pistols, but failed in its attempts to establish contact with partisans and to organize an escape. In view of the frequent transfers of prisoners from camp to camp, the underground was unable to form a solid

Corpses of slain prisoners from the Klooga camp stacked for burning, as found by Soviet troops in September 1944.

core and leadership, hence the absence of organized resistance when the camp was liquidated. A number of escape attempts by individuals were successful; others failed, and the escapees were caught and executed.

As the Soviet army advanced through Estonia in July and August of 1944, the transfer of the prisoners in the Estonian camps to the STUTTHOF concentration camp in Germany began, via the Baltic Sea. In mid-September, while Jewish prisoners were still in the camps of Klooga and Lagedi, the German front in Estonia collapsed. On September 18, five hundred of the prisoners were shot at Lagedi.

Early on September 19, Klooga was surrounded by German and Estonian SS men. Toward midday they began to take groups of prisoners from the camp to a nearby forest for execution, beginning with the men's camp. Some of the men tried to hide inside the camp, but most were found and shot. Others tried to flee from the execution site. Approximately twenty-four hundred Jews and one hundred Soviet prisoners of war died in this slaughter. A few days later, on September 28, when the Soviet army liberated Klooga, they found the corpses of the slain stacked for burning. Eighty-five of the prisoners, who had managed to hide within the camp or escape to the nearby forests, survived.

BIBLIOGRAPHY

Dworzecki, M. *Jewish Camps in Estonia, 1942–1944.* Jerusalem, 1970. (In Hebrew.)

YITZHAK ARAD

KNOCHEN, HELMUT (b. 1910), SS and SD (Sicherheitsdienst; Security Service) officer. A native of Magdeburg, Knochen studied history and English at the universities of Leipzig and Göttingen and worked as a teacher and editor. He became a member of the Nazi party in 1932, joined the SS in 1936, and entered the SD administration. In 1937 he became an officer in the SS, rose rapidly in rank, and was promoted to *Standartenführer* in 1942.

In 1940 Knochen was appointed a senior commander of the Sicherheitspolizei (Security Police) and SD in Paris, and two years later, in 1942, his area of jurisdiction was extended to include all of occupied northern France, as well as Belgium. In this post he was in charge of rounding up French Jews and deporting them to concentration camps and extermination camps; he was also responsible for the execution of many Frenchmen. Following the liberation of France by the Allied forces, Knochen was posted to the Leibstandarte-SS "Adolf Hitler" (Adolf Hitler SS Bodyguard Regiment) of the Waffen-SS.

In June 1946 a British military court in the British zone of Germany sentenced Knochen to death for the murder of British pilots who had been taken prisoner. The sentence was not carried out, however. That October he was extradited to France, brought to trial there, and again sentenced to death, in 1954. In 1958 the sentence was commuted to life imprisonment. President Charles de GAULLE granted Knochen a pardon in 1962 and he was sent back to Germany, where he retired in Baden-Baden.

BIBLIOGRAPHY

Marrus, M. R., and R. O. Paxton. *Vichy France and the Jews.* New York, 1981.

SHMUEL SPECTOR

Erich Koch.

KOCH, ERICH (1896–1986), Nazi party functionary and governor of occupied territories. Born into a working family in Elberfeld, in the Rhineland, Koch graduated from a commercial secondary school and became a railway clerk. In World War I he served as a private, and when the war was over he fought in the ranks of the Freikorps—irregular volunteer units—against the French.

Koch was among the first to join the Nazi party (his membership card was No. 90). In 1928 he was appointed *Gauleiter* of East Prussia, and in 1930 was elected as one of East Prussia's Reichstag deputies. When the Nazis came to power he also became the *Oberpräsident* (governor) of the region.

In 1941 Koch was appointed *Reichskommissar* of the Ukraine and governor of the Białystok district over the objections of Alfred ROSENBERG, the minister of occupied territories in the east, who wanted exclusive jurisdiction in the area. Through these appointments Koch came to govern extensive territories, ranging from Königsberg on the Baltic to the shores of the Black Sea. His treatment of the inhabitants of these territories was exceedingly harsh and cruel; his aim was to implement the ideas of Hitler and Himmler regarding the total subjugation of the Slav peoples. Koch frequently went over Rosenberg's head, although Rosenberg was nominally his superior.

After the war, Koch lived for several years in Schleswig-Holstein, under an assumed name. He was arrested by the British occupation forces and extradited to Poland in 1950. In 1959 he was put on trial in Warsaw, and on March 9 of that year was sentenced to death by hanging. Owing to his poor state of health, however, Koch was not executed. He spent the rest of his life in a Polish prison until his death in November 1986.

BIBLIOGRAPHY

Orłowski, S., and R. Ostrowicz. *Erich Koch przed polskim sądem.* Warsaw, 1959.

Reitlinger, G. "Last of the War Criminals: The Mystery of Erich Koch." *Commentary* 27/1 (January 1959): 30–42.

SHMUEL SPECTOR

KOCH, ILSE. *See* Koch, Karl Otto.

KOCH, KARL OTTO (1897–1945), commandant of concentration camps. Koch was born in Darmstadt, where he attended a commercial secondary school and became a bank clerk. Toward the end of World War I he was wounded and captured by the British, and was a prisoner of war until October 1919. In 1930 he became a member of the Nazi party and a year later joined the SS. He held senior command posts in the Sachsenburg, Esterwegen, and Lichtenburg (Prettin) concentration camps in 1934, and the following year was appointed commandant of the notorious COLUMBIA HAUS, a prison in Berlin. In 1936 Koch was commandant of the Esterwegen and SACHSENHAUSEN concentration camps; in May 1937 he married Dresden-born Ilse Köhler (1906–1967). On August 1 of that year Koch was appointed commandant of the newly established BUCHENWALD camp, and promoted to SS-*Standartenführer*. His wife was made an SS-*Aufseherin* (overseer) in the camp commanded by her husband. Before long she became notorious for her extreme cruelty to the prisoners and for her nymphomania, which she vented on the SS guards in the camp.

In September 1941 Karl Otto Koch was appointed commandant of MAJDANEK, then a Soviet prisoner-of-war camp run by the Waffen-SS in Lublin. Under his tenure the camp was greatly enlarged, and civilian prisoners, including Jews, were brought in. Crematoria were constructed, and there was an enormous rise in the number of prisoners killed. In July 1942, after a mass outbreak from the camp, Koch was suspended and put on trial before an SS and police court in Berlin, but was acquitted in February 1943. He then held administrative posts in postal-service security units, only to be arrested again in August of that year on charges of embezzlement, forgery, making threats to officials, and "other charges." The last apparently referred to murders for which he was responsible that went beyond existing orders, and to his hobby of collecting patches of tattooed human skin and shrunken human skulls; Ilse was also arrested as an accomplice to her husband. It was she who selected the living prisoners whose skin she wanted, after they were killed, for her own collection and for use in making lampshades. In early 1945 Karl Otto Koch was sentenced by the Supreme Court of the SS (*Oberste SS- und Polizeigericht*) in Munich, and in April of that year he was executed.

Karl Otto Koch, commandant of the Buchenwald concentration camp. From the album of Ilse Koch. [National Archives]

Ilse Koch was acquitted and went to Ludwigsburg to live with her two children and her husband's stepsister. She was arrested by the Americans on June 30, 1945, tried in 1947, and sentenced to life imprisonment. In 1949 she was released under a pardon granted by Gen. Lucius D. Clay, the military governor of the American zone in Germany. Under pressure arising out of hearings held by a United States Senate committee, she was immediately re-arrested upon her re-

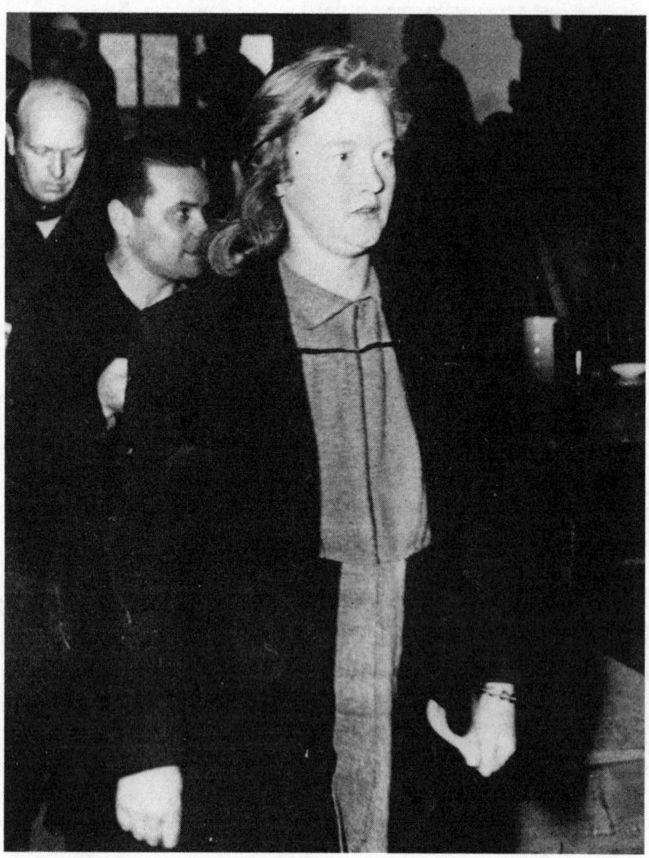

Ilse Koch ("the Bitch of Buchenwald"). [National Archives]

lease, and in January 1951 was again sentenced to life imprisonment, by the *Landesgericht* (State Court) in Augsburg. In September 1967 she committed suicide in her prison cell.

BIBLIOGRAPHY

Burney, C. *The Dungeon Democracy*. London, 1945.

Smith, A. L., Jr. *Die "Hexe von Buchenwald": Der Fall Ilse Koch*. Cologne, 1983.

SHMUEL SPECTOR

KOGON, EUGEN (1903–1987), journalist and political scientist; prisoner in the BUCHENWALD concentration camp. Kogon studied economics and sociology in his native Munich, as well as in Florence and Vienna, and earned a doctor's degree in law and political science. A Catholic, he was critical of the church, a view reflected in the articles he published in various (mostly Catholic) Austrian magazines; he also acted as adviser to the Christian trade unions in Austria.

Kogon's anti-Nazi positions led to his arrest when the Nazis marched into Austria in 1938, and, in 1939, to his imprisonment in Buchenwald. For several years he was on hard labor of different types. In 1943 he became the medical clerk in the camp, remaining in that post until April 1945. From this vantage point Kogon was able to gain insight into the MEDICAL EXPERIMENTS being performed on the prisoners. Prompted by the humane instincts that he retained throughout the years of his imprisonment, Kogon tried to use his position to alleviate sanitary conditions in the camp and save the lives of individual prisoners. He cooperated with the underground in the camp (most of whose leaders were German Communists). Kogon was one of forty-six Buchenwald prisoners whom the Gestapo planned to kill on the eve of liberation, but he managed to be smuggled out of the camp in a locked container on April 12, 1945. Once outside, he put pressure on the camp commandant, by means of a fabricated threatening letter, to behave properly. He also persuaded American troops who were approaching the camp to liberate it without delay.

After the liberation, Kogon drew up a report on Buchenwald for the Psychological Welfare Branch at the Allied Forces Headquarters. He later elaborated his report into a book that became the first comprehensive description of the Nazi concentration camps, *Der SS-Staat: Das System der deutschen Konzentrationslager* (1946; published in English as *The Theory and Practice of Hell: The German Concentration Camps and the System behind Them*, 1950). Containing the first fundamental analysis of the concentration camps, the book has since gone through several editions and has been translated into many languages. Among other things, it analyzes from sociological and psychological perspectives the means used by the SS to divide the prisoners into various groups and thereby facilitate control over them.

In 1946 Kogon helped found the journal *Frankfurter Hefte*, and he remained one of its editors and contributors until his death. His articles dealt mostly with the nature of Nazism and the development of the Federal Republic of Germany. From 1951 until his retirement in 1968, Kogon was a professor of political science at the College of Engineering in Darmstadt. Politically, he was active on behalf of the European Movement, which advocated a united Western Europe, serving as chairman of the German European Union from 1949 to 1953. He was also chairman of the German Political Science Association.

Basing his efforts on his idealistic humanist convictions, Kogon continued to call for the complete investigation and publicizing of the nature and meaning of Nazism and its racist ideology. As he stated in *Nationalsozialistische Massentötung durch Giftgas* (Nazi Mass Murder by Poison Gas; 1983), which he coedited, "Thought and action securely anchored in humanity provide the only protection against the racist mania and all its consequences; humanity is also the source of the right normative perceptions on which all existential decisions should be based. This applies to the individual, to society, and to the State."

BIBLIOGRAPHY

Des Pres, T. *The Survivor: An Anatomy of Life in the Death Camps.* New York, 1976. See pages 155–162.

FALK PINGEL

KOLBE, MAXIMILIAN (1894–1941), Polish monk, philosopher, priest, and Catholic saint. Kolbe was born in Zduńska Wola, in the Łódź district. His Christian name at birth was Raymond; at the age of seventeen he entered the Franciscan order and became Friar Maximilian. In 1912 he went to Rome to study theology and philosophy. He founded the Order of the Knights of the Immaculata in 1917, and was ordained a priest the following year; he returned home in 1919. In Poland, which by then had gained independence, Kolbe served as a priest; in 1927 he founded the City of the Immaculata (Pol., Niepokalanow), a center near Warsaw that was to disseminate the Catholic faith in the spirit of the Virgin Mary. By 1939 the number of the faithful at the center, followers of Kolbe, had grown to seven hundred. In 1930, in spite of being afflicted with tuberculosis, Kolbe went to the Far East, together with several assistants, to establish a Catholic mission. Located at Nagasaki, Japan, the mission was modeled on the Niepokalanow Center in Poland. Kolbe named it Mugenzai no Sono (Jpn.; Garden of the Immaculata). In 1936 Kolbe was summoned back to Poland, where he was appointed head of the Niepokalanow Center and its operations. His special interest was the center's publications network, which included a monthly, a youth magazine, and a popular newspaper, *Mały Dziennik* (Small Daily). Kolbe was very active in disseminating his religious views and his social ideas in speech and writing, and he gained a reputation for his piety and devotion.

Early in the German occupation, Father Kolbe was arrested and removed from Niepokalanow, but by December 1939 he was allowed back to his "city," where he set up an institution for the care of refugees from Poznań and its environs and, it was reported, also extended help to Jewish refugees. In February 1941 Father Kolbe was again arrested, and put into the PAWIAK PRISON. Three months later he was deported to the AUSCHWITZ extermination camp. According to eyewitness accounts by other prisoners, Father Kolbe remained true to his faith and sought to bring comfort to many other victims. In July 1941, a prisoner from Kolbe's block succeeded in escaping from the camp, and as punishment the SS decided to execute every tenth prisoner in the block. Standing in line next to Kolbe was a Polish workingman by the name of Gajowniczek, to whose lot it fell to be one of the victims. When the man cried out, "What will happen to my wife, to my children?" Kolbe stepped out of the line and declared that he wanted to take Gajowniczek's place. The Germans agreed, and Kolbe was moved to a starvation cell, where he was later put to death with a phenol injection.

In 1971 the Vatican proclaimed the beatification of Father Kolbe (a step below sainthood), and in October 1982 he was canonized as a saint of the Catholic church. Since 1971, and with greater intensity after his canonization, a debate has raged in Poland, Austria, the United States, and Britain concerning Kolbe's personality and work. It was claimed that while Kolbe was to be admired for what he did in his life and for his act of self-sacrifice, he had also been contaminated with antisemitic views, and the newspapers that he published had an anti-Jewish slant.

The ensuing examination of these claims showed that the newspapers published under Kolbe's supervision, and especially the daily, which had had a wide circulation, did indeed have a strong antisemitic flavor. While Kolbe had tried to restrain the daily's extreme antisemitism, his own letters and writings had an antisemitic tone, and he had justified the exclusion of the Jews from the Polish economy. Kolbe's brand of antisemitism was not racist, and he preached that the Jews should convert; some of his expressions against Jews and Freemasons, however, were quite extreme, and his writings contain references to the PROTOCOLS OF THE ELDERS OF ZION.

BIBLIOGRAPHY

Ricciardi, A. *St. Maximilian Kolbe: Apostle of Our Difficult Age.* Boston, 1982.

Saint Louis Center for Holocaust Studies. *Saint Maximilian Kolbe: An Interdisciplinary Interfaith Learning Project.* Saint Louis, 1984.

Treece, P. *A Man for Others: Maximilian Kolbe, Saint of Auschwitz, in the Words of Those Who Knew Him.* San Francisco, 1982.

ISRAEL GUTMAN

KOLDICHEVO, concentration camp established early in the summer of 1942 on a farm of the same name. It was located 11 miles (18 km) from BARANOVICHI, on the highway to Novogrudok, Belorussia (which in the interwar period belonged to Poland). In November 1942 a crematorium was constructed in the camp, and 600 corpses were incinerated there.

The Koldichevo camp was used for imprisoning Polish and Belorussian members of the underground and Jews from Gorodishche, Diatlovo, Novogrudok, Stolbtsy, and Baranovichi. The Jews were put into stables, in a separate part of the camp. The commandant of the camp was Fritz Jörn, an SS-*Hauptscharführer.* During the period from 1942 to 1944, twenty-two thousand persons—mostly Jews—were murdered in Koldichevo. One of the prisoners in the camp, Dr. Zelik Levinbok of Baranovichi, managed to supply medicines in large quantities to the partisans, with the help of a local peasant who was his patient. Eventually, Levinbok himself, together with his wife and eight-year-old son, managed to escape and join the partisans. There was a Jewish underground in the camp, headed by Shlomo Kushnir, a shoemaker. Its members had two guns and four hand grenades, and a Jewish prisoner in the camp who was a chemist manufactured a quantity of acid, to be used in self-defense.

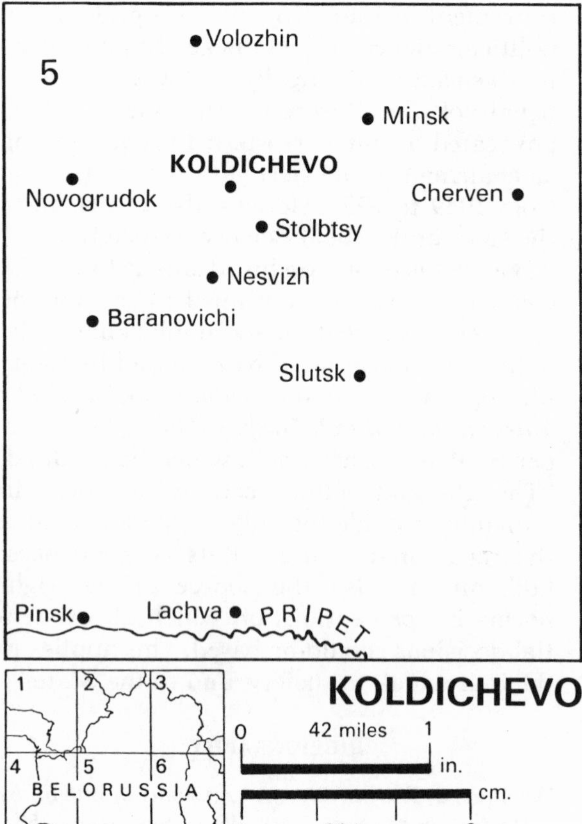

By means of tools that they obtained, the prisoners breached a wall. They practiced moving slowly and crawling on all fours, sewed cloth onto the soles of their shoes, and equipped themselves with knives. On March 17, 1944, a stormy night, they broke out from the camp, having first poisoned the watchdogs. Twenty-four prisoners were recaptured, but seventy-five escaped to the partisans; most joined the unit of Tuvia BIELSKI.

BIBLIOGRAPHY

Baranowicze Memorial Book. Tel Aviv, 1953. (In Hebrew.)

SHALOM CHOLAWSKI

KOLOMYIA (Ger., Kolomea; Pol., Kołomyja), city in the western part of the Ukrainian SSR, on the Prut River. Jews lived in Kolomyia from the sixteenth century. Between 1772 and 1918 it was part of Austrian-held Galicia, and in the interwar period it belonged to Poland. At the beginning of 1939 the city's Jewish population was about fifteen thousand; they were joined in September 1939 by thousands of Jewish refugees from the German-occupied parts of Poland. On September 17, 1939, Kolomyia was occupied by the Red Army and incorporated into the Soviet Union.

When the Germans invaded the Soviet Union, in June 1941, several hundred Kolomyia Jews fled to the east. On June 30 the Soviet army withdrew from the city, and three days later, on July 3, Hungarian troops entered (Hungary was an ally of the Germans). In those three days Ukrainian nationalists staged a pogrom against the Kolomyia Jews; when the Hungarians took over, the Hungarian military governor managed to restrain the Ukrainians. In the first half of July many anti-Jewish measures were imposed; for example, the Jews had to wear a badge with a Star of David (*see* BADGE, JEWISH), their property was confiscated, their freedom of movement was restricted, and they were put on forced labor.

The city came under direct German administration on August 1, and the anti-Jewish policy became more severe. On August 19 the Jews were ordered to pay a large ransom and to hand over their valuables. Also in August, a JUDENRAT (Jewish Council) was set up, headed by Mordechai Horowitz, who stayed in that post up to the end of 1942. Opinions of Horowitz are contradictory: many survivors stress his devoted efforts on behalf of the community, while others point out that he complied with all the demands made by the Germans for payments in money or in kind.

On October 12, the first large-scale *Aktion* took place in Kolomyia. The Germans and the Ukrainian police rounded up some 3,000 Jews, jailed them, and a few days later killed them in huge ditches that were located in a grove near Sheparovtse, a village 5 miles (8 km) from the city. Again, on November 6, hundreds of Jews were seized and murdered in the same place. On December 23, all the Jews who had foreign passports were ordered to report

to the Gestapo; 1,200 Jews responded to the order, and they were all taken to Sheparovtse and killed there. On January 24, 1942, the Germans arrested 400 Jewish intellectuals. They were first tortured and then killed.

A ghetto was established in Kolomyia on March 25, and over 18,000 persons were crowded into it. Many succumbed to the intolerable conditions, starvation, and disease. Despite all the difficulties, however, educational and cultural activities were organized for the ghetto inhabitants. On April 3 and 4 approximately 5,000 people were deported from the ghetto to the BEŁŻEC extermination camp, and another 250 were killed in the ghetto alleys. At the end of April more Jews were brought into the ghetto from a number of neighboring towns, including Kuty, Kosov, and Zabolotov. In an *Aktion* on September 7, 1942, 7,000 Jews were taken to Bełżec and another 1,000 were murdered inside the ghetto. Sporadic killing went on up to October of 1942. On October 11 another *Aktion* was undertaken, in the course of which children were removed from the orphanage and included among another 4,000 persons deported to Bełżec. In the latter half of that month the chairman of the Judenrat, Mordechai Horowitz, committed suicide. In an *Aktion* on November 4, 1,000 Jews were driven to Sheparovtse and shot to death there. On January 20, 1943, the remnants of the community, numbering some 2,000 persons, were rounded up and concentrated in a few houses in the ghetto; on February 2 the ghetto was definitively liquidated and the last of its inhabitants murdered at the Sheparovtse killing ground.

On March 29, 1944, Kolomyia was liberated by the Soviet army, and several dozen survivors came out of their hiding places. A few days later the Germans launched a counterattack and came so close to the city that the survivors had to flee; they were not able to return until August. Some of the surviving Jews of Kolomyia crossed the border into Romania in order to make their way from there to Palestine. Others went west, to Poland, and from there continued on to Palestine and other destinations.

BIBLIOGRAPHY

Bickel, S., ed. *Kolomyia Record.* New York, 1957. (In Hebrew.)

Noy, D., and M. Schutzman, eds. *Kolomeyer Memorial Book.* Tel Aviv, 1972. (In Hebrew.)

AHARON WEISS

KOLOZSVÁR. *See* Cluj.

KOMMISSARBEFEHL (Commissar Order), order issued by the German army to kill the political commissars in the Red Army who fell into German hands. The guidelines that Hitler gave the Wehrmacht for the attack on the Soviet Union (Operation "Barbarossa") ordered it to plan the attack not only from its military aspects but from the ideological aspect as well. Thus, the attack was to include the physical destruction of the bearers of the Communist idea and the political activists of the Soviet state establishment.

On June 6, 1941, two weeks prior to the invasion of the Soviet Union, the Oberkommando der Wehrmacht (Armed Forces High Command; OKW) issued the *Kommissarbefehl.*

> It must be expected that the treatment of our prisoners by the political commissars of all types, who are the true pillars of resistance, will be cruel, inhuman, and dictated by hate. . . . Therefore, if captured during combat or while offering resistance they must on principle be shot immediately. This applies to commissars of every type and position, even if they are only suspected of resistance, sabotage, or instigation thereto.
>
> According to the Directive for the Conduct of the Troops in Russia, . . . in their capacity as officials attached to enemy troops, political commissars . . . will not be recognized as soldiers; the protection granted to prisoners of war . . . will not apply to them. After having been segregated they are to be liquidated. . . .
>
> Commissars seized in the rear area of the army group . . . are to be handed over to the Einsatzgruppen or Einsatzkommandos of the Sicherheitspolizei [Security Police].

The order was signed by Gen. Walter Warlimont and its issue was authorized by Gen. Wilhelm KEITEL, the OKW chief of staff. It was based on the Order on Jurisdiction in the Operation "Barbarossa" Area of May 13, 1941, which gave the army and the SS wide powers and facilitated the establishment of a regime of terror and tyranny in the Soviet territories occupied by the Germans.

The *Kommissarbefehl* and the order of May 13 were both in violation of international conventions on the treatment and rights of prisoners of war and civilians in occupied territories. Together with other orders of the same type, it made the Wehrmacht an accomplice in the Nazi war crimes committed in the Soviet Union. A few days after the *Kommissarbefehl* was issued, Field Marshal Walther von Brauchitsch, chief of the Oberkommando des Heeres (Army High Command), issued guidelines giving every officer the authority to decide on the execution of commissars who had been made prisoners of war. Commissars were executed as soon as they were identified as such, whether on the front, when they were taken prisoner, or in prisoner-of-war camps in the rear. In the summer of 1941 Keitel ordered that all copies of the *Kommissarbefehl* that had been distributed to the various army headquarters be destroyed, in an effort to remove evidence implicating the army in war crimes.

BIBLIOGRAPHY

Dallin, A. *German Rule in Russia, 1941–1945: A Study of Occupation Policies.* New York, 1957.

Jacobsen, H. "The Kommissarbefehl and Mass Executions of Soviet Russian Prisoners of War." In *The Anatomy of the SS State,* edited by H. Krausnik et al., pp. 505–535. New York, 1968.

Reitlinger, G. *The SS: Alibi of a Nation.* New York, 1981.

YITZHAK ARAD

KOMOLY, OTTÓ (also Nathan Kahn; 1892–1945), Hungarian Jewish leader. Komoly was born in BUDAPEST and studied engineering. During World War I, he became a highly decorated officer. An active Zionist, he was elected deputy chairman of the Hungarian Zionist Federation late in 1940. Toward the end of 1941, he was drawn to the activities of Rezső (Rudolf) KASZTNER, who was trying to form a committee around Social Democrats and Liberal Jews to help Jewish refugees arriving in HUNGARY. Although the committee did not really coalesce, Komoly, Kasztner, Samuel Springmann, Joel BRAND, and several other Zionists continued to proffer aid to the refugees.

Following a suggestion by the YISHUV's recently organized rescue committee under Itzhak GRUENBAUM, the RELIEF AND RESCUE COMMITTEE OF BUDAPEST was formally established, with Komoly and Kasztner at its head, early in 1943. In his capacity as a leader of the committee, Komoly took part in relief work and in attempts to smuggle Jewish refugees into Hungary. In the committee's major achievement, about eleven hundred Polish Jews were brought to Hungary through the Tiyyul ("Excursion"; the code name for the operation of smuggling Polish Jews into Hungary) from Poland. With the help of Orthodox Jewish elements, Zionist youth movement members, and the PRACOVNÁ SKUPINA (Working Group), the Relief and Rescue Committee began to send messengers to Poland in the spring of 1943 to locate surviving Jews. Once found, they were smuggled to safety in Hungary, usually by way of Slovakia. This rescue work gained momentum in the autumn of 1943 and continued until the German occupation of Hungary in March 1944.

After the Germans entered Hungary, Komoly focused on efforts to convince the more moderate elements of the Hungarian leadership to protect the Hungarian Jews. As a head of the Relief and Rescue Committee, he also played a role in the Brand mission, the "Kasztner train," and other negotiation attempts between Hungarian Jews and the Nazis.

From the summer of 1944 until his death in January 1945, Komoly strove to help Jews through his contacts with neutral diplomats in Budapest. In September of that year, Friedrich Born, the representative of the International RED CROSS in Hungary, appointed Komoly head of Section A, the Red Cross department established to help Jewish children. Together with Born and members of the Zionist youth movement, Komoly set up children's houses under international protection, beginning in the summer of 1944 and continuing more intensively after the ARROW CROSS PARTY coup of October 15, 1944. After that month, Section A expanded its activities to include provision of food and other supplies for the Jews of Budapest. As head of the Relief and Rescue Committee and Section A, and because of his contacts, Komoly emerged as a central figure in the rescue activities in Budapest during the Arrow Cross reign of terror.

Apparently because of his rescue activities, the Arrow Cross executed Komoly, shortly before the conquest of Budapest by the Red Army. He was posthumously awarded the Hungarian Order of Freedom. In Israel, Moshav (cooperative settlement) Yad Natan was named after Komoly.

BIBLIOGRAPHY

Cohen, A. *The Halutz Resistance in Hungary, 1942–1944.* New York, 1986.

Rozett, R. "Child Rescue in Budapest, 1944–1945." *Holocaust and Genocide Studies* 2/1 (1987): 49–59.

Vago, B. "Budapest Jewry in the Summer of 1944: Otto Komoly's Diaries." *Yad Vashem Studies* 8 (1970): 81–105.

ROBERT ROZETT

KOPPE, WILHELM (1896–1975), a senior SS commander in occupied POLAND. Born in Hildesheim, Koppe served in the German army in World War I and then was a merchant and shopkeeper.

In August 1930 Koppe became a member of the Nazi party, and in 1932 he joined the SS. The following year, he was elected to the Reichstag. Rising rapidly in the SS, he was made a *Brigadeführer* in August 1934 and a *Gruppenführer* in September 1936.

On October 26, 1939, Koppe was appointed *Höherer SS- und Polizeiführer* (Higher SS and Police Leader; HSSPF) in the WARTHEGAU (the Poznań region), a post he held until November 9, 1943. Koppe was one of the leading figures in the establishment of the CHEŁMNO extermination camp, where 320,000 people were killed, and in the liquidation of the ghettos in the Warthegau. In January 1942 he was promoted to *Obergruppenführer,* and in November 1943 he became the HSSPF in the GENERALGOUVERNEMENT.

After the war, Koppe lived in West Germany under an assumed name (Lohmann) and worked as a factory manager. His real identity was discovered in 1961, and he was arrested and brought to trial in West Germany. The proceedings against him were discontinued in 1966, and he was released on medical grounds.

BIBLIOGRAPHY

Datner, S. *Wilhelm Koppe: Nieukarany zbrodniarz hitlerowski.* Warsaw, 1963.

Hilberg, R. *The Destruction of the European Jews.* 3 vols. New York, 1985.

SHMUEL KRAKOWSKI

Janusz Korczak and some of his young wards.

KORCZAK, JANUSZ (pen name of Henryk Goldszmit, 1878 or 1879–1942), physician, writer, and educator. Korczak was born in Warsaw, the son of an assimilated Jewish family. His father was a successful attorney who became mentally ill when Korczak was eleven; this was a heavy blow to the family's financial situation, and a trauma that cast its shadow over Korczak throughout his life.

Even while still a student of medicine at Warsaw University, Korczak was drawn to circles of liberal educators and writers in Poland. When he entered medical practice, he did his best to help the poor and those who suffered the most; at the same time he began to write. His first books, *Children of the Streets* (1901) and *A Child of the Salon* (1906), aroused great interest. In 1904 he was drafted into the Russian army as a doctor, and was posted to East Asia.

Both as doctor and as writer, Korczak was drawn to the world of the child. He worked in a Jewish children's hospital and took groups of children to summer camps, and in 1908 he began to work with orphans. In 1912 he was appointed director of a new and spacious Jewish orphanage in Warsaw, on Krochmalna Street. Throughout his life, his partner in his work was Stefania Wilczyńska, a superb educator, the daughter of a wealthy Jewish family who dedicated her life to the care of orphans and greatly influenced Korczak and his career as an educator. In the orphanage, Korczak studied the secret depths of the child's soul, and it was in the orphanage that he made practical application of his educational ideas.

Korczak called for an understanding of the emotional life of children and urged that children be respected. A child was not to be regarded as something to be shaped and trained to suit adults, but rather as someone whose soul was rich in perceptions and ideas, who should be observed and listened to within his or her own autonomous sphere. Every child, he maintained, has to be dealt with as an individual whose inclinations and ambitions, and the conditions under which he or she is growing up, require understanding. In several of his books—such as *King Matthew the First* (1923), *When I Am Small Again* (1925), and the short theoretical work *The Child's Right to Respect* (1929)—Korczak stressed the social conflict between child and adult in a situation when power and control are in the hands of the adult, even when the adult does not understand or refuses to understand the child's world, has no respect for the child, and deliberately deprives the child of his or her due. In Korczak's view, "to reform the world" meant "to reform the educational system."

In 1914 Korczak was again called up for military service in the Russian army, and it was in military hospitals and bases that he wrote his important work *How to Love Children.* After the war he returned to Poland—now independent—and to his work in the Jewish orphanage, but he was also asked to take charge of an orphanage for Polish children and to apply there the methods he had introduced in the establishment on Krochmalna Street. The 1920s were a period of intensive and fruitful work in Korczak's life. He was in charge of two orphanages (where he also lived), served as an instructor at boarding schools and summer camps and as a lecturer at universities and seminaries, and wrote a great deal. In the late 1920s, he was able to put into effect his longtime plan to establish a newspaper for children as a weekly added to the Jewish daily in the Polish language, *Nasz Przegląd*; it was written by children, who related their experiences and their deepest thoughts.

In the mid-1930s, Korczak's public career underwent a change. Following the death of the Polish dictator, Józef Piłsudski, political power in the country came into the hands of radical right-wing and openly antisemitic circles. Korczak was removed from many of the positions in which he had been active, and he suffered great disappointment. As a result, he took a growing interest in the Zionist effort and in the Jewish community in Palestine. He visited Palestine twice, in 1934 and 1936, showing particular interest in the state of education, especially the cooperative educational achievements of the kibbutz movement; but he was also deeply impressed by the changes he found in the Jews living there. On the eve of World War II, Korczak was considering moving to Palestine, but his idea failed to reach fruition.

From the very beginning of the war, Korczak took up activities among the Jews and Jewish children. At first he refused to acknowledge the German occupation and heed its rules; he refused to wear the yellow badge (*see* BADGE, JEWISH) and as a consequence spent some time in jail. When, however, the economic situation took a sharp turn for the worse and the Jews of Warsaw were imprisoned in the ghetto, Korczak concentrated his efforts on the orphanage, seeking to provide the children there with food and the basic conditions of existence. He was now an elderly and tired man and could no longer keep track of the changes that were taking place in the world and in his immediate vicinity, and he shut himself in. The only thing that gave him the strength to carry on was the duty he felt to preserve and protect his orphanage, where old rules continued to apply: it was kept clean, the duty roster was observed, there were close relations between the staff and the children, an internal court of honor had jurisdiction over both children and teachers, every Sunday a general assembly was held, there were literary evenings, and the children gave performances. Polish friends of Korczak's reported that they went to see him in the ghetto and offered him asylum on the Polish side, but he refused, not prepared to save himself and abandon the children.

During the occupation and the period he spent in the ghetto, Korczak kept a diary. At the end of July 1942, when the deportations were at their height—about ten days before he, the orphans, and the staff of the orphanage were taken to the UMSCHLAGPLATZ—Korczak wrote the following entry: "I feel so soft and warm in the bed—it will be hard for me to get up. . . . But today is Sabbath—the day on which I weigh the children, before they have their breakfast. This, I think, is the first time that I am not eager to know the figures for the past week. They ought to gain weight (I have no idea why they were given raw carrots for supper last night)."

On August 5, the Germans rounded up Korczak and his two hundred children. A witness to the orphans' three-mile march to the deportation train described the scene to the historian Emanuel RINGELBLUM as follows: "This was not a march to the railway cars, this was an organized, wordless protest against the murder! . . . The children marched in rows of four, with Korczak leading them, looking straight ahead, and holding a child's hand on each side. . . . A second column was led by Stefania Wilczyńska; the third by Broniatowska (her children bearing blue knapsacks on their backs), and the fourth by Sternfeld, from the boarding school on Twarda Street." Nothing is known of their last journey to TREBLINKA, where they were all put to death.

After the war, associations bearing Korczak's name were formed in Poland, Israel, Germany, and other countries, to keep his memory alive and to promote his message and his work. He became a legendary figure, and UNESCO named him "Man of the Year." Books and plays have been written about Korczak, and his own writings have been translated into many languages.

BIBLIOGRAPHY

Arnon, J. "The Passion of Janusz Korczak." *Midstream* 19/5 (May 1973): 32–53.

Korczak, J. *Ghetto Diary*. New York, 1978.

Lifton, B. J. *The King of Children: A Biography of Janusz Korczak*. New York, 1988.

Olczak, H. *Mister Doctor*. London, 1965.

Perlis, Y. *Janusz Korczak: Exemplary Life*. Naharia, Israel, 1982. (In Hebrew.)

ISRAEL GUTMAN

KORCZAK-MARLA, ROZKA (1921–1988), underground fighter and partisan. Korczak-Marla was born in Bielsko, Poland, and until the outbreak of World War II lived in Płock. At that time she went to VILNA, where she joined the leadership of the left-wing Zionist movement Ha-Shomer ha-Tsa'ir, with Abba KOVNER and Vitka Kempner. When Vilna's Ghetto No. 1 was liquidated and forty thousand Vilna Jews were killed, Korczak-Marla agreed with Kovner that the surviving Jews should offer armed resistance in the ghetto. Kovner made this proposal at a meeting of the movement's activists that Korczak-Marla attended. His proposal was approved at the meeting, and was followed by a manifesto drafted by him and published on January 1, 1942. Korczak-Marla was active in the FAREYNEGTE PARTIZANER ORGANIZATSYE (United Partisan Organization). After Yitzhak WITTENBERG's self-surrender to the Germans, when a decision was made to leave the ghetto for the forests, Korczak-Marla was among those who went to the Rudninkai Forest. There, the creation of autonomous Jewish partisan units was initiated.

Rozka Korczak (left) with Abba Kovner and Vitka Kempner (later Mrs. Kovner) as partisans after the liberation of Vilna in July 1944.

In July 1944 Korczak-Marla returned to

Vilna, which by then had been liberated, and she immigrated to Palestine on December 12, 1944. She joined Kibbutz Eilon and reported to the Jewish leaders on the Jewish resistance movement and the atrocities committed during the war. Later, she moved to Kibbutz Ein ha-Horesh, together with a group of ex-partisans that also included Kovner and Kempner. Korczak-Marla took part in educational projects and in the work of MORESHET, the memorial museum named after Mordecai ANIELEWICZ. She helped to establish the Holocaust studies centers at Givat Haviva and Yad Mordecai.

A book by Korczak-Marla, *Lehavot be-Efer* (Flames in the Ashes), was published in 1964.

BIBLIOGRAPHY

Kowalski, I. *Anthology of Armed Jewish Resistance, 1939–1945.* Vol. 1. See pages 484–485. Brooklyn, N.Y., 1986.

NILI KEREN

KORETZ, ZVI (d. 1945), Chief Rabbi of Salonika. Born in Rzeszów, Galicia, Koretz graduated from the Vienna Rabbinical Seminary and later studied at the Berlin Hochschule für die Wissenschaft des Judentums, an academy for Jewish studies. His appointment as Chief Rabbi of Salonika in 1933 reflected the victory of modernizers who wanted a Western, liberal rabbi to represent their community. The resulting communal split never healed, and Koretz's first term was marked by open clashes. The government headed by Ioannis Metaxas urged his reappointment in 1938.

The Germans imprisoned Koretz in Vienna from May to December 1941 for alleged anti-German propaganda, but in December 1942 they made him president of the Salonika Jewish community. He presided efficiently, and perhaps naively, over the deportations in March and April 1943. Deported to Bergen-Belsen with the JUDENRAT (Jewish Council) in August, he died of typhus in May or June of 1945 and was buried in Tröbitz, in Germany.

BIBLIOGRAPHY

Ben, J. "Jewish Leadership in Greece during the Holocaust." In *Patterns of Jewish Leadership in Nazi Europe, 1933–1945.* Proceedings of the Third Yad Vashem International Historical Conference, edited by Y. Gutman and C. J. Haft, pp. 335–352. Jerusalem, 1979.

Eck, N. "New Light on the Charges against the Last Chief Rabbi of Salonica, Dr. Zvi Koretz." *Yad Vashem Bulletin* 17 (December 1965): 9–15.

Recanati, D. *Salonika Memorial.* Vol. 1. Tel Aviv, 1972. (In Hebrew.)

STEVEN B. BOWMAN

KORHERR, RICHARD (b. 1903), German statistician employed, in his professional capacity, in the destruction of the Jews. Born in Regensburg, Korherr graduated from his academic studies with honors, and before long began to publish statistical works that earned him high praise. In 1928 he joined the staff of the Reich Bureau of Statistics, transferring in 1930 to the Bavarian Bureau of Statistics. The Bavarian prime minister appointed him chairman of the board of Reich und Heimat (Reich and Home), a government-sponsored society. Korherr's book *Geburtenrückgang* (Decline in the Birth Rate) was well received; Benito MUSSOLINI personally translated it into Italian, and it also appeared in a Japanese translation. The 1936 edition of the book had a foreword by Heinrich HIMMLER.

For a time in the early 1930s, Korherr was unemployed; from 1935 to 1940 he was director of the Würzburg municipal bureau of statistics and also lectured at the local university. As of 1934, and thereafter concurrently with his job in Würzburg, Korherr was in charge of the section of statistics and demographic policy in the headquarters of Rudolf HESS, then the deputy Führer. In 1937 and 1938 Korherr published *Untergang der alten Kulturvölker* (Decline of the Historical Civilized Peoples), and in 1938 an atlas, under the title *Volk und Raum* (People and Space). In May 1937 Korherr joined the Nazi party, but he did not become a member of either the SA (Sturmabteilung; Storm Troopers) or the SS.

On December 9, 1940, Korherr was appointed chief inspector of the statistical bureaus of the *Reichsführer-SS und Chef der*

Deutschen Polizei and of the REICHSKOMMISSARIAT FÜR DIE FESTIGUNG DES DEUTSCHEN VOLKSTUMS (Reich Commissariat for the Strengthening of German Nationhood), both jobs under Himmler. Korherr wrote numerous memoranda on a variety of statistical problems. In December 1942 he began processing data for the "FINAL SOLUTION" of the "Jewish question" in Europe, a task in which he was assisted by a Dr. Simon, a Jew who was the statistician of the Reichsvereinigung der Juden in Deutschland (Reich Association of Jews in Germany). Korherr also availed himself of material supplied by Adolf EICHMANN's section in the REICHSSICHERHEITSHAUPTAMT (Reich Security Main Office; RSHA).

Korherr was the author of the document that came to be known as the *Korherrbericht* (Korherr Report), whose subject was the extermination of the Jews of Europe; in 1943 and 1944 he updated the report every three months. In his trial in Jerusalem, Eichmann stated that the *Korherr Report* had served him in the planning stages of the extermination. Information on the number of Jews enabled the Nazis to determine the size of the team they would need to organize the liquidation of the Jews in a specific place or specific country, the number of railway cars that would be required, and the final destination of the victims, the extermination camp. Korherr's acquaintances described him as a technocrat, totally dedicated to his job, who was always trying to become close to Himmler, an effort in which he was not always successful.

After the war Korherr tried to diminish the importance of the report that bore his name. In evidence that he gave on July 13, 1951, at the trial of Alfred Filbert, commander of Einsatzkommando 9, Korherr claimed that the statistical data in his report were false, because they had been based on inflated figures given in the Einsatzgruppen reports. Thanks to the recommendation he received from Dr. Simon—whose life he had saved—Korherr was given a post by the West Germany Ministry of Finance, but he was dismissed from his job following the publication, in 1961, of Gerald Reitlinger's book *The Final Solution*, in which the *Korherr Report* figured prominently.

BIBLIOGRAPHY

"The First Unabridged Publication of the Two 'Korherr Reports.'" In *The Holocaust and the Neo-Nazi Mania*, edited by S. Klarsfeld, pp. 165–210. New York, 1978.

Wellers, G. "The Numbers of Victims and the Korherr Report." In *The Holocaust and the Neo-Nazi Mania*, edited by S. Klarsfeld, pp. 139–161. New York, 1978.

HANS-HEINRICH WILHELM

KOŠICE (Hung., Kassa), city in southeastern Slovakia; part of the territory annexed by HUNGARY on November 11, 1938. The first thirty-two Jewish families reached Košice in 1843; in 1930 the Jewish population of the city was 11,191, and by 1944 it had increased to 11,830. The number of Jews rose owing to the arrival of refugees from Poland and Slovakia during the earlier years of World War II, but the increase was tempered by the loss of the significant number of Jewish men from Košice who were drafted into the MUNKASZOLGÁLAT (Hungarian Labor Service System) beginning in the summer of 1940.

On the day the Germans occupied Hungary (March 19, 1944), their troops entered Košice. The city was designated as part of the first anti-Jewish operation zone (for the purpose of deportations, Hungary was divided into six zones). Late that month the authorities took as hostages about one hundred prominent Jews to ensure the Jewish community's cooperation. In mid-April a ghetto was set up in Košice and surrounded by a fence built by the Jews. On April 28 there was a major drive to incarcerate the Jews in the ghetto, under the direction of the mayor of Košice, Sándor Pohl, and the chief of police, György Horvath. During the concentration and subsequent deportation, the police acted with brutality. Jews from nearby towns and villages, as well as some of Košice's Jews, were concentrated in two brickyards located at the edge of the city. Altogether, more than twelve thousand Jews were held in the brickyards and the ghetto.

During the deportations, which began on May 15, 1944, all the Jews were sent to the brickyards. From there they boarded trains headed for AUSCHWITZ. Three transports left Košice, each with about four thousand Jews, the last departing on June 2, 1944. Two-thirds of the deportees from the city—some eight thousand individuals—were gassed immediately upon their arrival in Auschwitz. On May 17, the Zsidó Tanács (Jewish Council), which included Dr. Dezső Berger, Jenő Ungar, Igniac Spira, and Dr. Akos Kolozs, tried to blunt the blow that had befallen the community. They asked the head of the Košice Jewish Women's Association, Mrs. Samuel Gotterer, who was the wife of a severely wounded World War I veteran, to address a plea to the wife of Adm. Miklós HORTHY, the Hungarian regent. Her letter beseeched the Horthys to exempt children under the age of eighteen, women over the age of fifty, and men over the age of sixty from the transports that were allegedly destined for labor centers in the east. Her plea fell on deaf ears. During the rest of the deportations from Hungary, which lasted until early July of 1944, Košice was the point where the Hungarian authorities handed over the Jewish deportees to the Germans.

After the war some four hundred fifty Jews returned to Košice from the camps; about three thousand survived the war in Hungarian labor units, in the underground, or in the Czechoslovak Eastern Army, which fought alongside the Soviet army. The city, along with the surrounding area, which had been annexed by Hungary, was incorporated into the reestablished Czechoslovakia. In the middle of the 1960s, only thirteen hundred Jews were left in Košice.

BIBLIOGRAPHY

Braham, R. L. *The Politics of Genocide.* New York, 1981.

ROBERT ROZETT

KOSSAK-SZCZUCKA, ZOFIA (maiden name, Szatkowska; 1890–1968), Polish Catholic writer. Kossak-Szczucka's novels were in the main historical, among them *Krzyżowy* (The Crusaders) and *Złota Wolność* (Golden Freedom). During the German occupation of Poland, she led the Catholic underground orga-

Zofia Kossak-Szczucka.

nization, Front Odrodzenia Polski (Polish Resistance Front), which conducted social and educational activities and, from 1942, assisted Jews. In September 1942, Kossak-Szczucka helped found the Tymczasowy Komitet Pomocy Żydom (Temporary Committee for Aid to Jews). That December the committee became the Rada Pomocy Żydom (Council for Aid to Jews), known as ZEGOTA. Kossak-Szczucka then moved to the Społezna Organizacja Samoobrony (Civic Self-Defense Organization), where she continued to care for Jews in hiding. In September 1943 she was arrested under an assumed name, and the Germans did not identify her. She was interned in AUSCHWITZ until July 1944, and wrote a chronicle of this period, *Z otchłani* (From the Abyss). After the war she settled in Great Britain, returning to Poland in 1957.

BIBLIOGRAPHY

Bartoszewski, W., and Z. Lewin, eds. *Righteous among the Nations: How Poles Helped the Jews.* London, 1969.

Prekerowa, T. "The Just and the Passive." *Yad Vashem Studies* 19 (1988): 369–378.

TERESA PREKEROWA

KOVEL (Pol., Kowel), town in Volhynia, now in the Ukrainian SSR; in the interwar period it belonged to Poland. On the eve of World War II Kovel had a Jewish population of 13,200, about half the total population of 27,677. After 1939 the number of Jews grew, since many Jews from the German-occupied parts of Poland took refuge in Kovel. The Germans entered the town on June 28, 1941. In the first few days of the occupation, 1,000 Jews were seized and killed. The local Ukrainian authorities were hostile to the Jews and harassed them by withholding food supplies, electricity, and water, among other measures. At the end of July the Jews had to surrender all their Torah scrolls, which were then burned in public. This was followed by the confiscation of valuables in Jewish possession and the imposition of a collective fine.

On May 21, 1942, two ghettos were established in Kovel. One, in the new part of the town, held eight thousand persons—people who were working and had special passes, as well as their families. The other was in the old part, where six thousand persons were billeted, none of them with passes in their possession. The second ghetto was surrounded by police on June 2, and in an operation that went on for three days, all the inhabitants were taken out and killed. The turn of the other ghetto, where the workers lived, came on August 19. Many of the Jews tried to flee and hide, but they were caught and forced into the Great Synagogue; on the synagogue walls they inscribed their last wills and their call for revenge. On October 6, 1942, the liquidation of the Kovel Jews was completed.

At the beginning of May 1942 two emissaries of the underground in Warsaw, Frumka PLOTNICKA and Tema Sznajdermann, had succeeded in entering Kovel. On their return to Warsaw, they reported on resistance groups in the Kovel ghetto who had smuggled out arms from warehouses and passed them on to Soviet partisans active in the area. The hostile attitude of the partisan unit's commander foiled the resistance groups' efforts to leave the ghetto and go into the forests, and only a few succeeded in doing so.

Kovel was liberated on July 6, 1944, after a prolonged battle in which the town was destroyed. In the following days about forty Jews converged on Kovel, coming out of the forests and other hiding places.

BIBLIOGRAPHY

Belar, B. *Pincas Kowel.* Buenos Aires, 1951. (In Yiddish.)

Leoni-Tsuferfin, E. *Kovel: A Book of Testimonies and Memoirs for Our Community Which Was Mowed Down.* Tel Aviv, 1957. (In Hebrew.)

SHMUEL SPECTOR

KOVNER, ABBA (1918–1988), underground leader and partisan commander, one of the architects of the BERIḤA, poet, and writer; influential figure in Israel's cultural and political life.

Kovner was born in Sevastopol, Russia, attended a Hebrew secondary school in VILNA, and studied plastic arts; from his youth he was a member of the Ha-Shomer ha-Tsa'ir Zionist youth movement. During the period when Vilna was the capital of the Lithuanian SSR (1940–1941), he was active in the underground. When the city was captured by the Germans at the end of June 1941, Kovner, together with a group of his comrades, found temporary refuge in a Dominican convent on the outskirts of the city. On returning to the ghetto he learned of the massacres of the Jews, came to the realization that resistance was the only response, and decided to apply himself to the creation of a Jewish fighting force. At a meeting of the He-Haluts movement in Vilna, held on the night of December 31, 1941, a manifesto that Kovner had drawn up was read out. It stated (in part): "Hitler plans to kill all the Jews of Europe . . . the

Abba Kovner in Vilna (July 1944).

Jews of Lithuania are the first in line. *Let us not go like sheep to the slaughter.* We may be weak and defenseless, but the only possible answer to the enemy is resistance!" This was the first time that the mass killing of Jews by the EINSATZGRUPPEN was analyzed as being part of a master plan for the destruction of European Jewry, and also the first time that Jews were urged to offer organized fighting resistance to the Nazis.

On January 21, 1942, a Jewish combat organization, the FAREYNEGTE PARTIZANER ORGANIZATSYE (United Partisan Organization; FPO), was founded in Vilna, made up of youth movements and the various political parties. Kovner was a member of the FPO leadership, and in July 1943, when its first commander, Yitzhak WITTENBERG, fell into the Nazis' hands, Kovner took his place (using the *nom de guerre* "Uri"). During the final deportation from Vilna in September 1943, he directed the FPO's operations and the escape of the ghetto fighters into the forests. In the Rudninkai Forest (*see* PARTISANS), Kovner commanded a Jewish unit made up of Vilna ghetto fighters, as well as the Jewish camp's "Revenge" battalion.

After liberation, Kovner became one of the architects of the Beriḥa escape movement and was the moving spirit in the Organization of Eastern European Survivors. This was a supra-partisan organization comprising various Zionist factions that called for the unity of all forces, a call based on "the lesson of the Holocaust" and the dangers still threatening the Jewish people. In July 1945 Kovner arrived at the JEWISH BRIGADE GROUP base camp at Treviso, Italy, where he addressed an assembly of Jewish soldiers and, in moving and penetrating words, described the Holocaust and the Vilna uprising.

Kovner arrived in Palestine in the second half of 1945, on a short visit, in order to solicit support and resources for revenge operations in Europe against persons who had carried out murders or had been responsible for them. On his way back to Europe he was arrested by the British and returned to Palestine, where he spent some time in jail. After his release in 1946, Kovner joined Kibbutz Ein ha-Horesh, together with his wife, Vitka Kempner (who was also his partner in the underground and in the fighting), and a

Jewish partisans from Vilna who fought in the Rudninkai Forest return to Vilna after the city's liberation (July 14, 1944). Standing fourth from the left is Abba Kovner.

group of former partisans. During the Israeli War of Independence (1947–1949), Kovner was the education officer of the Givati brigade and produced the brigade's publication, *Battle Page.*

When the War of Independence came to an end, Kovner went back to his kibbutz and devoted his time to writing. He published two volumes of prose writings in the Panim el Panim (Face-to-Face) series and issued collections of his many poems, among them the partisan poems *Ad Lo Or, Mi-Kol ha-Ahavot,* and *Ahoti ha-Ketanna.* In 1970 he was awarded the Israel Prize in Literature. Kovner was chairman of the Israel Hebrew Writers' Association and the founder of MORESHET (the institute for Holocaust research in Givat Haviva, Israel) and of the Mordecai ANIELEWICZ Communities House. He shaped the character of the contents of Beth Hatefutsoth, the Nahum Goldmann Museum of the Jewish Diaspora, in Tel Aviv. A collection of his statements on current issues was published in the book *Al ha-Gesher ha-Zar* (1981).

BIBLIOGRAPHY

Arad, Y. *Ghetto in Flames: The Struggle and Destruction of the Jews in Vilna in the Holocaust.* Jerusalem, 1980.

Kovner, A. "A First Attempt to Tell." In *The Holocaust as Historical Experience: Essays and a Discussion,* edited by Y. Bauer and N. Rotenstreich, pp. 77–94. New York, 1981.

Kovner, A. "The Mission of the Survivors." In *The Catastrophe of European Jewry,* edited by I. Gutman and L. Rothkirchen, pp. 671–683. Jerusalem, 1976.

ISRAEL GUTMAN

KOVNO (Lith., Kaunas; Pol., Kowno), city in central LITHUANIA, situated at the confluence of the Neman and Neris rivers; founded in 1030 by Koinas, a Lithuanian prince, and named after him. In 1795 Kovno was part of the Polish-Lithuanian territory that was annexed by Russia, and from 1842 it was a district capital. Between 1920 and 1939 Kovno was the capital of independent Lithuania; in 1940 all of Lithuania was incorporated into the Soviet Union.

For the Jews of eastern Europe, Kovno was an important spiritual and cultural center. It was the site of the famous Slobodka yeshiva (Slobodka was a suburb of Kovno; its Lithuanian name is Vilijampole), and was also renowned for its extensive Zionist activities and for its Hebrew school system, ranging from kindergartens to teachers' training colleges.

In 1939 approximately forty thousand Jews lived in Kovno, constituting nearly one-quarter of the city's total population. During the Soviet rule, from 1940 to the German invasion in 1941, the Hebrew educational institutions were closed down and most of the Jewish social and cultural organizations were liquidated; of the city's five Yiddish dailies, only one remained in existence, becoming an organ of the Communist party. On June 14, 1941, a week before the German invasion, hundreds of Jewish families were rounded up and exiled to Siberia, among them factory owners, merchants, public figures, and Zionist activists and leaders.

Establishing the Ghetto. Kovno was occupied on the third day of the invasion, June 24, 1941. Several thousand Jews escaped from the city and made for the interior of the Soviet Union, some of them losing their lives during their flight. Even before the German entry into the city, bands of Lithuanians went on a rampage against the Jews, especially those living in the Slobodka suburb. The murder of Jews continued when the Germans occupied the city and took charge of

When the Germans occupied Kovno on June 24, 1941, they saw bands of Lithuanians seizing Jews in the streets and beating them to death. Here, Lithuanians beat Jews while German soldiers watch.

the killings. Thousands of Jews were moved from the city to other locations, such as the Seventh Fort (one of a chain of forts constructed around Kovno in the nineteenth century), where they were first brutally mistreated by the Lithuanian guards and then shot to death. A total of ten thousand Jews were estimated to have been murdered in June and July of 1941.

When a civilian administration was set up by the Germans, with SA-Brigadeführer Hans Kramer as city commissar, it issued a whole range of anti-Jewish decrees. The Jews were given one month to move into the ghetto that was being established. The area earmarked consisted of two parts (the "small ghetto" and the "large ghetto"), both situated in Slobodka, on either side of the main thoroughfare. A barbed-wire fence, with posts manned by Lithuanian guards, was put up around the ghetto, the gates of which were also watched by German police.

Aktionen and Punitive Decrees. When the ghetto was sealed off in August 1941, it contained 29,760 Jews. In the following two and a half months, 3,000 Jews—men, women, and children—were killed. On October 28 the "big *Aktion*" was staged, in the course of which 9,000 persons (half of them children) were taken to the NINTH FORT and murdered there. The *Aktionen* were then discontinued and a prolonged period of relative calm set in, which lasted up to March 1944. Of the 17,412 Jews now left in the ghetto, most of the adults were put on forced labor, mainly in military installations outside the ghetto. They were under constant, unbearable pressure and harassment. Two thousand Jews, most of them skilled artisans, were organized into "brigades" and put on jobs related to the war effort. Another 4,600 Jews worked in the ghetto workshops, where no Germans or Lithuanians were in attendance. Instead of wages, the Jews were given food rations, which in fact were on a starvation level. To stay alive, the ghetto inhabitants sold off their remaining possessions and used the proceeds to buy the food that was being smuggled into the ghetto at great risk.

During the so-called quiet period, there was a recovery of sorts among the Jews and their nourishment improved. This is not to say that the period was free of punitive measures and unpleasant surprises. In February 1942 the Jews were ordered to hand in all the books, other printed materials, and manuscripts in their possession; in August of that year the synagogues were closed down and public prayer services were outlawed. The bureau of education and the schools—which had continued to function—were now ordered closed (except for the vocational-training schools), and the bans on bringing food into the ghetto and being in possession of cash were strictly enforced. Hundreds of people were deported to RIGA or sent to work camps in various parts of Lithuania.

Internal Administration. Life inside the ghetto was administered by the Council of Elders of the Kovno Jewish Ghetto Community (Ältestenrat der Jüdischen Ghetto Gemeinde Kauen), chaired by Dr. Elhanan ELKES, a well-known physician and public personality, with Leib Garfunkel, a lawyer and veteran Zionist leader, acting as his deputy. Most of the members of the Kovno Ältestenrat were chosen for their posts through direct elections by the Jewish community members. Forced labor and the maintenance of public order were the responsibility of the Jewish police, which had a complement of about 150 men. Appointments to the police and supervision of the force were in the hands of the Ältestenrat. A department of health, welfare, culture, and the like was maintained by the Ältestenrat, providing various services to the ghetto population and running public institutions such as a hospital and medical clinic, a home for the aged, a soup kitchen, a school, and an orchestra. There were concerts, lectures, literary evenings, and other cultural events. After public education was prohibited, it was in fact kept up under the cover of the vocational-training schools. Even in the ghetto, Kovno Jews maintained their tradition of Torah study and of cultural and educational activities and mutual help, over and above the facilities and functions sponsored by the Ältestenrat. The political parties were also active, in the first instance by trying to locate their members and come to their aid. This led to the formation of Matsok (the Hebrew acronym for Zionist Center Vilijampole, Kovno), which was headed by several members of the Ältestenrat and its staff. They maintained contact with the anti-Nazi underground that existed in the ghetto. The Ältestenrat departments also provided substantive aid to the members of the underground who left the ghetto to join the partisans in the forests. In this, as well as in other social and communal aspects, the Kovno ghetto was an unusual phenomenon that has no parallel in the annals of the behavior of Jews under Nazi occupation.

Ghetto into Concentration Camp. Under an order issued by Heinrich HIMMLER on June 21, 1943, it was decided to impose a concentration camp regime upon the surviving Jews of the REICHSKOMMISSARIAT OSTLAND ghettos. In the autumn of 1943, the Kovno ghetto became a central concentration camp, KL (for *Konzentrationslager*) Kauen. Four thousand inhabitants of the ghetto were transferred to small camps, situated in Kovno's suburbs or its vicinity, in places such as Aleksotas, Šančiai, Palemonas, KĖDAINIAI (Keidan), and Kaišiadorys. On October 26, 1943, 2,800 Jews were moved to work camps in Estonia. An exceptionally cruel blow was dealt to the ghetto on March 27, 1944, when 1,800 persons—infants, children, and elderly men and women—were dragged out of their homes and murdered. Also executed were 40 officers of the Jewish police, killed for having given direct aid to the anti-Nazi underground in the ghetto; among those put to death were Moshe Levin, the police chief, and his deputies Yehuda Zupovitz and Ika Grinberg. The remaining police became a JÜDISCHER ORDNUNGSDIENST (Jewish ghetto police) under the direct control of SS men. The Ältestenrat was abolished, and Dr. Elkes was appointed *Judenältester* (senior Jew), a position devoid of any real authority, although he retained his moral authority among the Jews.

Anti-Nazi Underground. Groups of young people belonging to the Zionist YOUTH MOVEMENTS, such as IRGUN BERIT ZION and especially Ha-Shomer ha-Tsa'ir, He-Haluts ha-Tsa'ir, and Betar, resumed their activities, with the emphasis on the struggle against the Nazis. A substantial impetus to their decision to engage in such underground activities was given by Irena ADAMOWICZ, a Polish woman who acted as an emissary for the underground movements in the Warsaw and Vilna ghettos and visited Kovno in July 1942. The Communists were also quite active in the anti-Nazi struggle, through the Antifascist Struggle Organization, which was headed by Haim YELIN. Members of this organization sought to acquire arms and also to establish contact with the Soviet partisans in the forests. In the summer of 1943 the Zionists and the Communists established a joint body, the General Jewish Fighting Organization (Yidishe Algemeyne Kamfs Organizatsye; JFO), whose purpose was to organize operational cells and facilitate their departure from the ghetto so that they could join the partisans. At its height, the JFO had about six hundred members. Some were given military training, including instruction in the use of arms, by officers of the Jewish police. In September 1943 the JFO established a direct link with the partisan movement in Lithuania thanks to the help of a Jewish woman parachutist, Gesja GLAZER ("Albina"), who made a secret visit to the ghetto. The new connection enabled the JFO to send armed teams of members to the Augustów forests to set up partisan bases there. The cost of this venture was heavy. Out of a hundred JFO members who took part, ten were shot to death, fifteen died in prison, and fourteen were taken to the Ninth Fort.

At the end of 1943, 170 JFO members, split into eight groups, left the ghetto in trucks that they had secretly obtained from their Lithuanian drivers, and made for partisan bases in the Rudninkai Forest, south of Vilna (which was nearer than the Augustów Forest). Most of them joined the Kovno battalions of the Lithuanian partisan movement. Altogether, some 350 Kovno Jews, most of them members of the JFO, left the ghetto in order to join the partisans. About 100 of them met their death en route or were killed in action.

Liquidation of the Ghetto. On July 8, 1944, as the Red Army was approaching Kovno, the German authorities embarked upon the transfer of the Jews to concentration camps inside Germany. Many Jews went into hiding, in underground bunkers that they had prepared for just this purpose. The Germans used bloodhounds, smoke grenades, and firebombs to force the Jews out into the open; in the process, some 2,000 Jews died, by choking or burning, or as a result of the explosions. Only 90 were able to hold out in the bunkers and live to see the Red Army enter Kovno (on August 1, 1944). About 4,000 Kovno Jews were taken to Germany, the majority going either to the KAUFERING or the STUTTHOF concentration camps. In October 1944 they were joined by a number of Kovno Jews who had been held in camps in Estonia. When the camps were liberated, nearly 2,000 Kovno Jews had survived; together with those who had held out in various hiding places in Kovno and the vicinity, they accounted for 8 percent of the 30,000 Jews who had made up the original population of the ghetto.

After the war, the survivors were joined by Kovno Jews who came back from the Soviet interior. In 1959, 4,792 Jews were living in Kovno, approximately 2 percent of the city's population. Until 1951, Kovno had a Jewish orphanage and a Jewish school (this was the last such school to exist in the Soviet Union). Many of Kovno's Jews emigrated to Israel.

BIBLIOGRAPHY

Arad, Y. "The Judenräte in the Lithuanian Ghettos of Kovno and Vilna." In *Patterns of Jewish Leadership*, pp. 93–112. Jerusalem, 1979.

Bar-on, Z. A., and D. Levin. "The History of an Underground." *In Dispersion* (Winter 1964–1965): 155–168.

Brown, Z. A., and D. Levin. *The Story of an Underground: The Resistance of the Jews of Kovno (Lithuania) in the Second World War*. Jerusalem, 1962. (In Hebrew.)

Garfunkel, L. *The Destruction of Kovno's Jewry*. Jerusalem, 1959. (In Hebrew.)

DOV LEVIN

KOVPAK, SIDOR ARTEMEVICH (1887–1967), Soviet partisan commander in World War II. Kovpak was born in the village of Kotelva, in the Poltava district. During the Civil War he was a partisan fighter for the Reds, and he subsequently fought under Vasily Chapayev in the Red Army. Between the two world wars, Kovpak was employed in party and administrative offices, and in 1940 he was the mayor of the Putivl municipality in Sumy Oblast (district).

As the Germans drew near to the Sumy district in late September of 1941, Kovpak and Semyon Rudnev organized a partisan battalion that developed into a division. On October 26, 1942, at the head of his fifteen hundred fighters, Kovpak set off on a combat expedition to the west, and in early 1943 he reached northern Volhynia; in the second half of that year he conducted combat expeditions through Volhynia and Polesye. On June 12, 1943, he went on an expedition to the Carpathian Mountains, with two objectives: to demonstrate a Soviet presence in Eastern Galicia, where the UKRAINSKA POVSTANSKA ARMYIA (Ukrainian Insurgent Army) was in power, and to blow up oil installations in the Drogobych region. On his way, Kovpak liberated Jews from the Skalat labor camp, and a group of young people joined the division as a Jewish company under the command of veteran Jewish partisans. After bloody battles, the division was obliged on its way back to split into small groups. Many died during the retreat, and only part of the division reached the assembly point in northeastern Volhynia.

In January 1944, Kovpak was wounded and flown to the hinterland. He was twice awarded the Soviet medal for heroism, and was promoted to the rank of major general. His division was named the "Kovpak First Ukrainian Partisan Division," and placed under the command of Lt. Col. Petro Vershigora. On January 5, 1944, it began a campaign through Volhynia, Eastern Galicia, the Lublin district, Brest-Litovsk, and Pinsk. At the end of the campaign it was dismantled. In 1947 Kovpak was appointed deputy chairman of the Supreme Soviet of the Ukrainian SSR. His account of his partisan activities was published in *Our Partisan Course* (1965).

BIBLIOGRAPHY

Armstrong, J. A. *Soviet Partisans in World War II.* Madison, Wis., 1964.

Vershigora, P. P. *Liudi s chistoi sovest'iu.* Moscow, 1966.

SHMUEL SPECTOR

KOWALSKI, WŁADYSŁAW (1895–1971), Pole who saved Jews during the Holocaust. A retired colonel in the Polish army at the time of the German occupation, Kowalski was the WARSAW representative of the Dutch-based Philips concern. Nazi Germany's interest in the Dutch-owned company facilitated the mobility of its foreign representatives, affording Kowalski freedom of circulation in all parts of Warsaw, including the closed-off Jewish ghetto. His first opportunity to help Jews took place outside the ghetto, on the "Aryan" side, when he encountered Bruno Borl, a ten-year-old boy wandering the streets of Warsaw in September 1940, seeking food and shelter. Taking the boy home, Kowalski fed him and provided him with a new identity and a home with friends.

This led to a series of bolder undertakings. Two brothers named Rubin, a lawyer and a dentist, were helped to find a new location after their hiding place was uncovered by an informer. Exploiting his freedom of movement, Kowalski smuggled seven Jews out of the Warsaw ghetto in February 1943 by bribing the Polish guards at the gates, and found safe havens for the Jews on the "Aryan" side. In November of that year he helped a family of four move from the Izbica area to a safer place with friends in Warsaw. He also offered refuge to twelve Jews in his Warsaw home. Roman Fisher, a construction worker whom Kowalski had rescued, built an underground shelter with material that Kowalski surreptitiously brought with him inside heavy suitcases. From late 1940 until August 1944, Kowalski paid for the upkeep of those of his charges for whom he had arranged hiding places. The group hiding in his home was kept busy manufacturing toys that Kowalski sold in the market, thus helping defray maintenance costs. After the suppression of the WARSAW POLISH UPRISING in October 1944, and the forcible evacuation of all the Warsaw residents by the Germans, Kowalski converted a basement in a ruined building into a bunker and hid there along with forty-nine Jews. Their daily ration consisted of three glasses of water, a modicum of sugar, and vitamin pills. They stayed hidden for 105 days; by the time they were liberated by the Russians in January 1945, they were reduced to eating fuel. More than fifty Jews benefited from Kowalski's help during the occupation period.

In 1947, Kowalski married one of the Jewish women he had rescued, and they emi-

Władysław Kowalski (standing), speaking at a special ceremony held at Yad Vashem in Jerusalem on October 30, 1967, for "Righteous among the Nations" living in Israel. From left to right: Apolonia Oldak (Poland), Kowalski, Katriel Katz, of the Yad Vashem directorate, and Supreme Court Justice Moshe Landau. At the far right: Malvina Czismadia (Hungary) and Stefan Raczyński (Poland).

grated to Israel in 1957. In 1963 he was recognized by YAD VASHEM as a "RIGHTEOUS AMONG THE NATIONS."

BIBLIOGRAPHY

Bartoszewski, W., and Z. Lewin, eds. *Righteous among Nations: How Poles Helped the Jews, 1939–1945*. London, 1969.

MORDECAI PALDIEL

KRAKÓW, city in southern POLAND; the third largest in the country and one of the oldest. Kraków is mentioned from the eighth century; in the eleventh century it became the residence of the Polish princes. Between 1320 and 1596 it was the capital of the kingdom of Poland.

From the early fourteenth century, Kraków was one of the most important Jewish communities in Europe. In 1495 the Jews of the city were expelled to Kazimierz, a new town being built nearby that eventually became a quarter of Kraków, and the history of the Jews in the two places became closely intertwined. In 1867 Jews were given the right of residing in every part of the city.

Beginning in the Middle Ages, Kraków was an outstanding center of Jewish learning and culture in Europe. During the Swedish invasion (1655–1657) the Kraków Jewish community underwent much suffering, but after the city was liberated the community gradually regained its strength. From 1815 to 1846 Kraków and its environs constituted a free republic, and the Jewish community flourished. Subsequently, in the period from 1846 to 1918, when the city was part of Austrian-ruled Galicia, the Jewish community grew and progressed further, with a thriving cultural and social life. In independent Poland (1918–1939) Jewish life flourished in Kraków

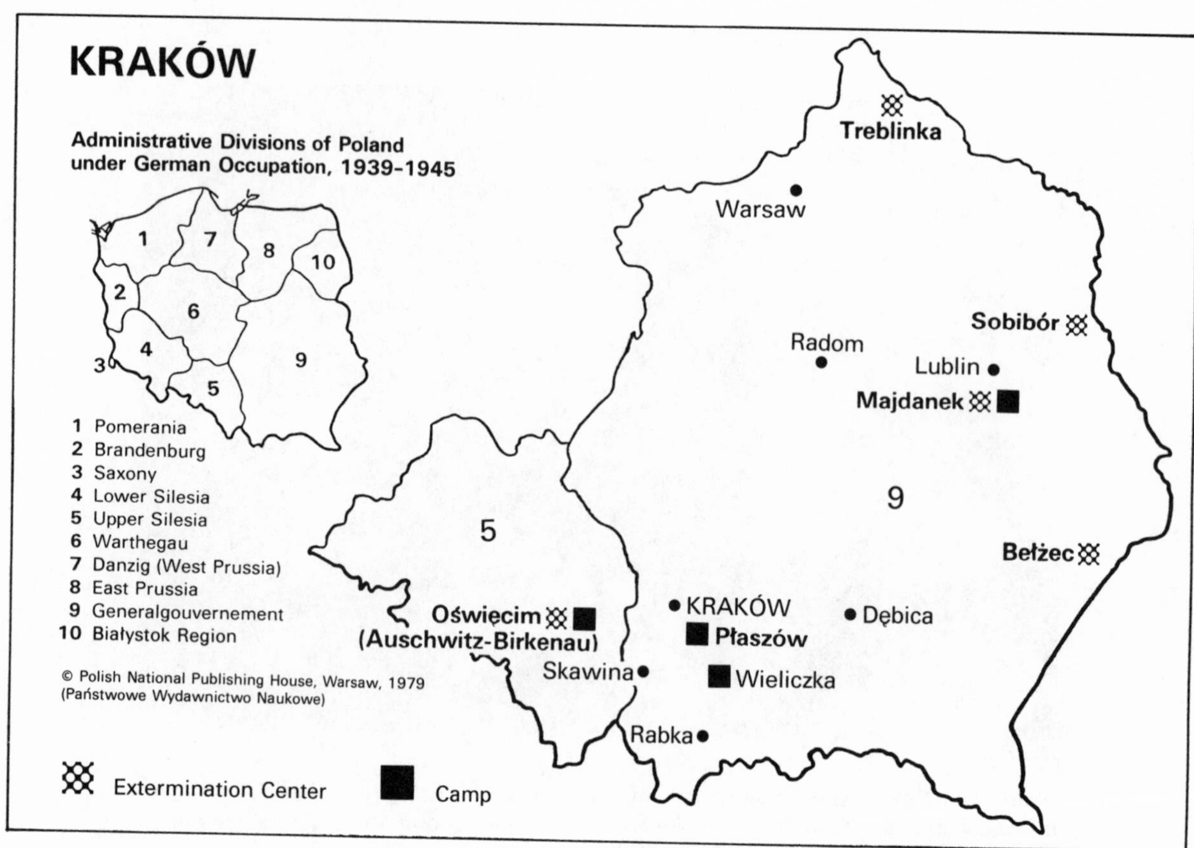

more than ever, although in the years preceding the outbreak of World War II the Jewish community suffered from the increase of antisemitism in the country.

In 1540, Kraków had a Jewish population of 2,100; in 1772, 4,000; in 1880, 20,000 (one-third of the total); in 1900, 25,000; and in 1921, 45,000. By 1939 the number of Jews had grown to 60,000, out of a total population of about a quarter of a million.

Nazi Occupation. Kraków was occupied by the German army on September 6, 1939, and the persecution of the Jews was launched without delay. It was organized mainly by Einsatzkommando 2 of Einsatzgruppe I, commanded by Obersturmbannführer Max Grosskopf. On October 26 the occupation authorities declared Kraków the capital of the GENERALGOUVERNEMENT (the territory in the interior of occupied Poland). As a result, the persecution of the Jews was intensified. It was in Kraków that the Generalgouvernement issued all its anti-Jewish decrees.

A Jewish committee was organized in the early stage of the occupation, and on November 28 it was declared a JUDENRAT (Jewish Council). The chairman of the Judenrat was Dr. Marek Bieberstein, with Dr. Wilhelm Goldblatt as his deputy. In the summer of 1940 both men were imprisoned by the Gestapo and Dr. Artur Rosenzweig was appointed chairman. On December 5 and 6, the Germans conducted a sweeping terror operation in the Jewish quarters, mainly to raid Jewish property. Several synagogues were burned down on this occasion.

On May 1, 1940, a decree was issued placing the city's boulevards and major squares out of bounds to Jews. That same month the expulsion of Kraków Jews to neighboring towns was launched; by March 1941, forty thousand Jews had been expelled and no more than eleven thousand were left in the city. While the expulsions were taking place, the victims were robbed of all their property.

The Ghetto. On March 3, 1941, the Kraków district governor, Otto Wachter, published a decree on the establishment of the ghetto, to be located in Podgorze, a section in the southern part of the city. The ghetto was

Moving into the Kraków ghetto.

sealed off on March 20, within a wall and a barbed-wire fence. It covered an area of no more than 656 by 437 yards (600 × 400 m), bisected by Limanowskiego Street. In addition to the Kraków Jews, several thousand Jews from neighboring communities were also packed into the ghetto, mainly from Skawina, Wieliczka, and Rabka. In late 1941, eighteen thousand Jews were imprisoned in the ghetto. The worst problems were the overcrowding (four to five persons to a room) and the poor sanitary conditions.

Several organizations were active in the ghetto in efforts to alleviate the plight of the population. The more important were the Jüdische Soziale Selbsthilfe (Jewish Social Self-Help Society), later called the Jüdische Unterstützungsstelle (Jewish Aid Agency), and the Centralne Towarzystwo Opieki nad Sierotami (Federation of Associations for the Care of Orphans; CENTOS).

The Germans established several factories in the ghetto to exploit the cheap manpower that was available among the imprisoned population. Several hundred Jews were also employed in factories situated outside the ghetto, and they were daily escorted to and from their work.

On March 19, 1942, the Germans launched what they called an *Intelligenz Aktion,* a terror operation directed at the intelligentsia in the ghetto. Some fifty prominent Jews were seized in this operation and were taken to AUSCHWITZ, where they were killed.

Deportations. At the end of May 1942, the Germans began deporting Jews from the ghetto to the extermination camps. On May 28 the ghetto was hermetically sealed off and the *Aktion* was launched. Taking part were special detachments of the Gestapo, the Schutzpolizei (regular uniformed police), and a Waffen-SS unit stationed at Dębica. The *Aktion* continued until June 8, and when it ended six thousand Jews were deported to the BEŁŻEC extermination camp; three hundred were shot to death on the spot. Among the victims were the poet Mordecai GEBIRTIG and the Judenrat chairman, Artur Rosenzweig, who had refused to carry out the Germans' orders. The Judenrat was liquidated, and in its place the Germans put up a Kommissariat, headed by David Guter.

Following this *Aktion* the ghetto area was reduced by half, although it still had a population of twelve thousand. In mid-October 1942 the Jewish Kommissariat was ordered to compile a list of four thousand ghetto inmates for yet another deportation. When the order was ignored, the Germans launched a second *Aktion,* on October 27 and 28, in which they employed their usual terror tactics to round up seven thousand Jews for de-

Jews of Kraków forced to dig a pit while under armed guard.

portation. In addition, they shot six hundred Jews on the spot. Most of the deportees were sent to Bełżec, and the rest to Auschwitz. In the course of this *Aktion* the hospital, the home for the aged, and the orphanage, all situated on Jozefinska Street, were liquidated. When the *Aktion* was over the ghetto area was further reduced, and what remained was cut in two. The first part, known as "A," contained the Jews who were working, and the second, "B," the rest of the ghetto prisoners.

On March 13, 1943, the residents of part "A," two thousand in number, were transferred to the PŁASZÓW camp; the following day, March 14, an *Aktion* took place in which part "B" was liquidated. Some twenty-three hundred Jews were taken to the Auschwitz-Birkenau extermination camp and killed there in the gas chambers, and seven hundred Jews were killed on the spot. Of the Jews who were transferred to Płaszów, only a few hundred survived.

The Resistance Movement. From its inception, the Kraków ghetto had underground organizations operating in it, of which the more prominent were the Akiva and Ha-Shomer ha-Tsa'ir Zionist YOUTH MOVEMENTS. In the initial stage the underground operations concentrated on education and mutual help. The Jewish underground also published a newspaper, *He-Haluts ha-Lohem* (The Fighting Pioneer). In October 1942 the Żydowska Organizacja Bojowa (Jewish Fighting Organization), a united underground organization independent of the Warsaw ŻOB, was formed. It set itself the goal of conducting an armed struggle against the Nazi occupiers.

Heading the organization were Zvi BAUMINGER, Aharon LIEBESKIND, Gola Mira, Shimshon DRAENGER, and Gusta (Justyna) DRAENGER-Dawidson. The Jewish Fighting Organization decided not to prepare for an uprising inside the ghetto, whose restricted space offered no chance at all for an armed struggle, and instead to move the fighting to the "Aryan" side of Kraków. Some ten operations were launched outside the ghetto, the most famous being the attack on the Cyganeria café in the center of the city, which was frequented by German officers. Eleven Germans were killed in this attack and thirteen wounded.

Attempts were also made to engage in partisan operations in the vicinity, but these encountered difficulties caused by the group's isolation and the hostile attitude manifested by the local units of the ARMIA KRAJOWA (the Polish Home Army), which did not take kindly to Jewish partisan operations. The Jewish underground suffered heavy losses, and in the fall of 1944 its remnants decided to cross the border into Slovakia and from there to make their way into Hungary. This plan succeeded, and members of the Kraków Jewish Fighting Organization continued their resistance operations in Budapest, where they joined up with the Ha-No'ar ha-Tsiyyoni (Zionist Youth) organization.

On the "Aryan" side of Kraków, a branch of ZEGOTA (Rada Pomocy Żydom, or Council for Aid to Jews) was active from the spring of 1943. It was headed by Stanisław Dobrowolski, a Polish Socialist Party activist. The Jewish representative in the branch, Miriam Hochberg-Peleg (whose underground alias was Maria Marianska), made tireless efforts in behalf of the Jews in the ghetto. The Zegota branch aided several hundred of the Kraków Jews who escaped.

After the war about four thousand survivors of the ghettos and concentration camps, most of them former residents of Kraków and its vicinity, settled in the city, remaining there for a short while. In 1946 thousands of Jews who had fled to the Soviet Union at the beginning of the war and were now returning to Poland made their home in Kraków, whose Jewish population rose to ten thousand. Several Jewish institutions were established, including a branch of the Jewish Historical Commission (the forerunner of the Warsaw ŻYDOWSKI INSTYTUT HISTORYCZNY, or Jewish Historical Institute), which was headed by Josef Wulf and Michał Maksymilian Boruchowicz (Borwicz). Most of these Jews emigrated from Poland between 1947 and 1951, under the impact of the antisemitic waves that struck the country. After 1968 only a handful of Jews were left in Kraków.

BIBLIOGRAPHY

Dawidson, G. *Justina's Diary.* Naharia, Israel, 1978. (In Hebrew.)

Karol, Z. "Cracow." In vol. 2 of *Jewish Mother Cities,* edited by Y. C. Cohen-Fischmann, pp. 284–354. Jerusalem, 1948. (In Hebrew.)

Pankewicz, T. *The Cracow Ghetto Pharmacy.* New York, 1987.

Peleg, M., and M. Benzvi. *Outside the Walls of the Ghetto in Occupied Cracow.* Jerusalem, 1986. (In Hebrew.)

SHMUEL KRAKOWSKI

KRAMER, JOSEF (1906–1945), commandant of the BERGEN-BELSEN camp. Kramer was born in Munich. He joined the Nazi party in 1931, and a year later became an SS man. His concentration camp career began in 1934, in DACHAU, where he was at first a guard, but his advance was rapid and he held senior posts in a number of concentration camps, including SACHSENHAUSEN and MAUTHAUSEN. For several months in 1940 he served as aide-de-camp to Rudolf HÖSS, the commandant of AUSCHWITZ. From April 1941 to May 1944, Kramer was commandant of the NATZWEILER camp. He was promoted to the rank of *Hauptsturmführer* in 1942. In May 1944 he was again posted to Auschwitz, and was put in charge of the gas chambers and crematoria in Auschwitz II–Birkenau. On December 2 of that year he was appointed commandant of Bergen-Belsen. Following his arrival there, Bergen-Belsen officially became a concentration camp, and conditions deteriorated sharply.

When the camp was liberated, Kramer was arrested by the British and put on trial, together with forty-four other members of the camp staff, among them fifteen women. The trial, which took place in Lüneburg, lasted from September to November 1945. Kramer was sentenced to death, as were ten others of the accused, and was executed on December 12, 1945.

BIBLIOGRAPHY

Phillips, R., ed. *Trial of Josef Kramer and Forty-Four Others: The Belsen Trial.* London, 1949.

SHMUEL KRAKOWSKI

KRASNODAR, capital of Krasnodar Krai (territory) in Northern Caucasia, in the Russian Soviet Federated Socialist Republic. In 1926 the total population of Krasnodar was about 174,000 and its Jewish population was 1,746, which presumably had increased by 1941. By

the time the city was occupied by the Nazis on August 9, 1942, thousands of refugees from the southern part of the Ukraine and the Crimea, Jews and non-Jews, had flocked into Krasnodar, in an effort to escape from the Germans.

In the wake of the German army, Sonderkommando 10a of Einsatzgruppe D entered the city. On August 16 an officer of that unit went to the home of a Jewish professor, Vilik, and put him in charge of the Jewish population of the city. The following day, Professor Vilik was told to inform the Jews that they must report for registration. A few weeks later the Jews were ordered to assemble at a certain point in Krasnodar. From there they were taken outside the city and killed, some by means of GAS VANS. Seven thousand persons, mostly Jews, were murdered by the men of Sonderkommando 10a.

Krasnodar was liberated by the Soviet army in February 1943. From July 14 to 17, 1943, a trial was held there of thirteen Soviet citizens who had served in a Sonderkommando 10a auxiliary unit and had participated in the mass murder (*see* TRIALS OF WAR CRIMINALS: KRASNODAR TRIAL).

SHMUEL SPECTOR

KREMENCHUG, city in the central Soviet Ukraine; it is a port on the Dnieper, a railway junction, and a center of metal, machine, textile, and food industries. Kremenchug was founded in the sixteenth century, and Jews first settled there at the end of the eighteenth century. In 1926 it had a Jewish population of 28,969, out of a total of 60,000. On the eve of the Holocaust its Jewish population was 40,000, out of a total population of 90,000.

Kremenchug was occupied by the Germans on September 9, 1941. Many of the Jews had fled the city or had been evacuated by the Soviet authorities, and only nine thousand were left when the Germans came. Even in the first few days of the occupation, the Germans and Ukrainian police harassed and mistreated the Jews. The Jews had to wear on their sleeve a badge (*see* BADGE, JEWISH) with a Star of David, they were under curfew after 5:00 p.m., they were prohibited from making purchases in the shops, and they were put on forced labor, to clean and repair the city streets. When a church was reopened in Kremenchug, on September 25, Jews in large numbers sought to convert, and the mayor and two clerics extorted large sums of money from them in exchange for the con-

version. The following day the Jews were ordered to report for a roll call, but only thirty-five hundred Jews, together with one hundred families of mixed marriage, answered the call. On September 27 the Jews were ordered to move into a camp consisting of wooden barracks in Novoivanovka, a suburb. The conditions were hardly bearable, and the Jews were not even allowed to prepare cooked food.

The killing of the Jews of Kremenchug was launched on September 28. The Jews were taken from Novoivanovka to pits, previously dug by prisoners of war, on the way to the village of Peschanoye. On the first day sixteen hundred Jews were murdered, and by November 7 all those who had been concentrated in Novoivanovka were dead. Most of the remaining fifty-five hundred Jews who had gone into hiding were turned over to the Nazis by local Ukrainians and were also murdered. A small group of professional men, mostly doctors, were retained for a while, pending their replacement. They were killed in January 1942.

Kremenchug was liberated by the Soviet army on November 29, 1943.

SHMUEL SPECTOR

KRIMCHAKS, Jews who settled in the Crimean peninsula, apparently as early as the second century B.C. In their dress and housing the Krimchaks followed the customs of their Tatar neighbors, and for everyday conversation they used a Jewish-Tatar dialect. In the 1926 census the Krimchaks accounted for 6,383 out of a total Jewish population in the Crimea of 42,000. Before the October Revolution they were mostly merchants and artisans, and subsequently suffered in the Sovietization of the country's society and economy.

When Einsatzgruppe D arrived in the Crimea in the wake of the German army, it encountered the problem of the peninsula's heterogeneous population, in ethnic and religious terms. Not knowing whether to include the KARAITES and Krimchaks in the "FINAL SOLUTION," the Einsatzgruppe commander, Otto OHLENDORF, in September 1941 asked

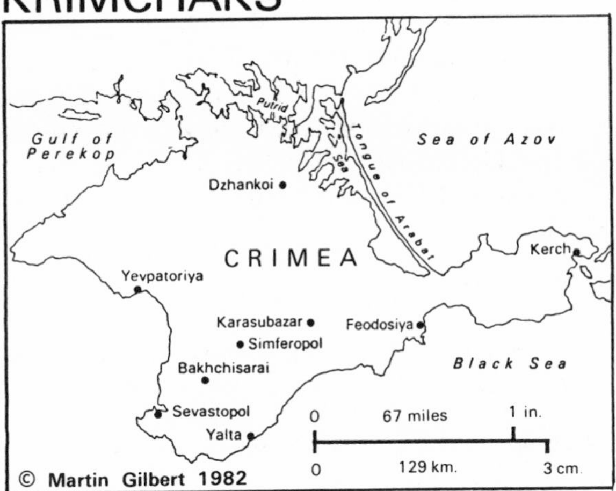

the REICHSSICHERHEITSHAUPTAMT (Reich Security Main Office; RSHA) in Berlin to decide the issue. The problem went all the way up to Heinrich HIMMLER, who ordered that the Krimchaks be included in the murder program, while the Karaites were to be exempt.

Between October 30 and November 16, 1941, the German army completed the occupation of the Crimea, with the exception of Sevastopol, which held out until July 3, 1942. In the first few weeks following the conquest, Einsatzgruppe D men rounded up the Jews, including the Krimchaks, and killed them. The following are the data on the murder of the Krimchaks, derived from various sources, mostly German. In SIMFEROPOL, which had the largest concentration of Krimchaks (2,500 in the 1926 census), 1,500 Krimchaks were murdered, on December 9, 1941. In Karasubazar (now Belogursk), the ancient Krimchak center, the murder of Krimchaks took place on November 10, 1941. In Bakhchisarai, some 40 Krimchak families were killed on December 13, 1941. In Yevpatoriya, the Krimchaks were murdered on November 24, 1941, together with the other Jews in the town. In Feodosiya 1,052 Jews were murdered subsequent to November 16, 1941, among them all the Krimchaks who had been living there. In Kerch, 7,000 Jews, including Krimchaks, were murdered between December 1 and 3, 1941.

According to routine reports submitted by the Einsatzgruppen, 2,504 Krimchaks were murdered in the period from November 16 to December 15, 1941. It may be assumed that this does not include all the Krimchak victims, and that additional Krimchak Jews, in groups and individually, were murdered at a later date. About 70 percent of the Krimchak population appears to have been killed in the Holocaust. When the war was over, only about 1,500 Krimchaks were left in the Crimea.

BIBLIOGRAPHY

Loewenthal, R. "The Extinction of the Krimchaks in World War II." *American Slavic and East European Review* 10 (1951): 130–136.

Spector, S. "The Destruction of the Krimchak Jews during the Nazi Occupation." *Pe'amim* 27 (1986): 18–25. (In Hebrew.)

SHMUEL SPECTOR

KRIMINALPOLIZEI (Kripo), the German criminal police. In the Third Reich, punishable offenses with a political aspect were handled by the GESTAPO, rather than by the criminal police. Until 1936 the criminal police was part of the administration of the *Länder,* the territorial divisions making up the Reich. As part of the centralization of the police introduced that year by Heinrich HIMMLER, the criminal police of all the *Länder* were incorporated into the Prussian criminal police. The following year (1937), the latter became the Reichskriminalpolizeiamt (Reich Criminal Police Bureau). Together with the Gestapo, the bureau became part of the Hauptamt Sicherheitspolizei (Security Police Main Office), which in turn, with the SD (Sicherheitsdienst; Security Service), was incorporated into the REICHSSICHERHEITSHAUPTAMT (Reich Security Main Office; RSHA) in 1939, with Reinhard HEYDRICH as its first chief. Kripo became the RSHA's Section V, with Arthur NEBE as section chief.

Within the borders of the Reich, Kripo officers wore plain clothes, but when they were on duty in German-occupied countries they wore SS uniforms—including those among them who did not belong to the SS—and SS insignia corresponding to their civilian ranks. The duties they performed in the occupied countries related to nonpolitical crimes, as in the Reich, but from time to time they were called on by the Gestapo to assist it in its operations against Jews and political opponents.

BIBLIOGRAPHY

Best, W. *Die deutsche Polizei.* Darmstadt, 1941.

Krausnick, H., et al. *Anatomy of the SS State.* London, 1968. See pages 127–301.

ADALBERT RÜCKERL

KRISTALLNACHT ("Crystal Night" or "Night of the Broken Glass"), pogrom conducted throughout Germany and Austria on November 9 and 10, 1938. It was officially presented as a spontaneous outburst provoked by the assassination of the third secretary of the German embassy in Paris, Ernst vom Rath, by a seventeen-year-old Polish Jew, Herschel GRYNSZPAN. The name *Kristallnacht* comes from *Kristallglas* (beveled plate glass) and refers to the broken shopwindows of Jewish stores.

The riots came as the culmination of assaults made upon the Jews in Germany and Austria following the ANSCHLUSS in March 1938, in which almost all elements of the Nazi regime had participated. Hermann GÖRING, who was responsible for the implementation of the economic FOUR-YEAR PLAN, had made practical and legal preparations for the "Aryanization" (*see* ARISIERUNG) of Jewish property; other decrees and laws affected the Jews' public and personal status and increased their segregation from the general public. Using administrative "infractions" committed by Jews and "unemployment" of Jews as pretexts, the GESTAPO and the SS under Heinrich HIMMLER and Reinhard HEYDRICH launched massive arrests of Jews, who were imprisoned in the concentration camps of DACHAU, BUCHENWALD, and SACHSENHAUSEN. Beginning in July 1938, these camps were readied to receive an even greater number of Jews. Functionaries of the National Socialist party, the *Gauleiter*, and the SA (Sturmabteilung; Storm Troopers) instigated local assaults on Jewish businesses and synagogues.

The authorities increasingly took to coercing Jews to leave the German Reich, disregarding the obstacles to emigration that had become obvious through the meager results of the EVIAN CONFERENCE. More and more indi-

Ruins of the Fasanenstrasse synagogue in Berlin. [Leo Baeck Institute, New York]

vidual Jews and entire groups were forcibly expelled, mainly from Austria and from Czechoslovakia after the latter had been truncated by the MUNICH CONFERENCE. The catalytic development was the deportation of about 17,000 Polish Jews who were driven into a no-man's-land between the two countries on October 28, 1938, following a ploy of the Polish government intended to deprive Polish Jews of the right of return from countries under German rule. The greatest number of the deportees were left stranded near the border town of ZBĄSZYŃ. Herschel Grynszpan's parents were in this group, and news of their plight drove the desperate youth to his act of revenge.

Following his shooting of vom Rath on November 7, an inflammatory editorial appeared in the *Völkischer Beobachter,* the official Nazi organ, and sporadic anti-Jewish rioting started on November 8. On the afternoon of November 9, vom Rath died. The same evening, Joseph GOEBBELS harangued the "old fighters" of the party who had gathered in Munich at their annual commemoration of Hitler's abortive putsch of November 8 and 9, 1923. Apparently with Hitler's consent, Goebbels hinted that this was the hour for action against the Jews. That night, instructions were conveyed to all parts of the country. In accordance with the orders, the crowds were encouraged by the SA to participate in the atmosphere of outrage. Mass frenzy broke out: synagógues were destroyed and burned, shopwindows of Jewish-owned stores were shattered, the shattered glass covering the sidewalks, and the demolished stores were looted. Jewish homes were assaulted, and in many places Jews were physically attacked. About 30,000 Jews—especially those who were influ-

Aftermath of *Kristallnacht* on Potsdamerstrasse in Berlin.

ential and wealthy—were arrested, often with the help of previously prepared lists, and were thrown into the three above-mentioned concentration camps, where they were treated with great cruelty by the SS. This was the first time that riots against the Jews of Germany had been organized on such an extensive scale, accompanied by mass detention. Though the violent onslaught was officially terminated on November 10, in many places it continued for several more days. In Austria it started only on the morning of November 10 but was especially fierce; arrests were widespread, and 4,600 Viennese Jews were among those sent to Dachau.

Heydrich's orders for the arrests were dispatched to the state police and the SS only after midnight, when the action was already in full swing. Heydrich, together with Himmler and Göring (who had not been present at the Munich celebration), were taken by surprise by Goebbels's initiative. Himmler ordered the SS to remain in their billets and not to take part in the rioting, while Heydrich forbade looting, but to no avail.

The burning of the synagogue in Siegen, a city 49 miles (79 km) east of Cologne.

In a provisional assessment, Heydrich reported to Göring on November 11 that 815 shops, 29 department stores, and 171 dwellings of Jews had been burned or otherwise destroyed, and that 267 synagogues were set ablaze or completely demolished (in fact, this was only a fraction of the number of synagogues actually destroyed). The same report refers to thirty-six Jews killed and the same number severely injured, but later it was officially stated that the number killed was ninety-one; in addition, hundreds perished in the concentration camps.

The pogrom was followed by administrative and legal orders issued with a fourfold object: to complete the process of "Aryanization" to the benefit of the government's disrupted revenues; to expedite the Jews' emigration; to isolate the Jews completely from the general population; and to abolish the still quasi-autonomous organization of the REICHSVERTRETUNG DER DEUTSCHEN JUDEN (the representative body of German Jewry) and other official Jewish institutions. These proposed developments were inaugurated at a representative meeting on November 12 called and presided over by Göring, who announced that Hitler had charged him with the implementation of the Reich's Jewish policy. In the ensuing discussion, the damage to Jewish property was estimated at several hundred million reichsmarks, and the insurance payments due to owners of 7,500 demolished stores came to 25 million reichsmarks.

Decisions taken on economic issues included a fine of one billion reichsmarks imposed on the Jewish community under the pretext of reparation for the murder of vom Rath, and confiscation by the state of the insurance payments, while at the same time making the Jewish store owners liable for the repairs. "Aryanization" was to be implemented along the lines already practiced by Hans Fischböck, the Austrian minister of

Kristallnacht in Baden-Baden. On November 10, 1938, Jewish men were rounded up by the police and marched through the city.

commerce. On Heydrich's suggestion, it was decided to coordinate the Jews' emigration through a ZENTRALSTELLE FÜR JÜDISCHE AUSWANDERUNG (Central Office for Jewish Emigration) to be established in Germany along the lines of the one developed by Adolf EICHMANN in Austria. Some of the economic measures were announced the same day; additional steps, including those aimed at undermining the Jews' status, were promulgated during the following months. The Kristallnacht prisoners surviving in the concentration camps were released early in 1939 for immediate emigration or for the "Aryanization" of their property, often for both.

The sharp reaction to the Kristallnacht outrage that was expressed by the Western press and public did not affect the Nazis. When President Franklin D. ROOSEVELT recalled the United States ambassador, Hugh Wilson, as a protest and declared his deep shock, the German ambassador in the United States was recalled home as well, because of "American interference in internal German affairs." Public pressure did, however, force most of the western European governments to admit more refugees, especially children.

Göring, who had persuaded Hitler to put him in charge, now handled the Reich's Jewish policy together with Himmler, and Goebbels's aspirations to play a decisive part were thus thwarted. The methods of the SS and of the SD under Heydrich became policy. While this conclusion about the result of the outbreak is generally accepted, historians differ in their opinions about its cause. Some hold that Goebbels exploited circumstances by improvisation, and others maintain that the assault was premeditated; probably both methods were involved. In any case, Kristallnacht was a turning point. It was the Nazis' first experience of large-scale anti-Jewish violence, and opened the way to the complete eradication of the Jews' position in Germany.

BIBLIOGRAPHY

Graml, H. *Der 9. November "Reichskristallnacht."* Bonn, 1955.

Kochan, L. *Pogrom: 10 November 1938.* London, 1957.

Schleunes, K. *The Twisted Road to Auschwitz: Nazi Policy toward German Jews, 1933–1939.* Chicago, 1970.

Thalmann, R., and E. Feinermann. *Crystal Night, 9–10 November 1938.* London, 1974.

Yahil, L. "Jews in Concentration Camps in Germany prior to World War II." In *The Nazi Concentration Camps.* Proceedings of the Fourth Yad Vashem International Historical Conference, edited by Y. Gutman and A. Saf, pp. 69–100. Jerusalem, 1984.

LENI YAHIL

KRÜGER, FRIEDRICH WILHELM (1894–1945), senior SS commander in occupied Poland. Born in Strasbourg, Krüger served in the German army in World War I. He became a Nazi party member in 1929, joining the SA (Sturmabteilung; Storm Troopers) in 1930 and transferring to the SS in 1931. The following year he was elected to the Reichstag, and in January 1935 he was promoted to the rank of *Obergruppenführer*. From October 4, 1939, to November 9, 1943, Krüger was the *Höherer SS- und Polizeiführer* (Higher SS and Police Leader) in the GENERALGOUVERNEMENT. As such, he was responsible for the liquidation of all the ghettos in the Generalgouvernement and for the operation of the BEŁŻEC, SOBIBÓR, and TREBLINKA extermination camps, where 1,720,000 Jews were murdered.

In May 1942, Krüger was given the additional title of Secretary of State for Security (*Staatssekretär für das Sicherheitswesen*) in the Generalgouvernement administration, and also became "Himmler's Representative for the Strengthening of Germandom in the Generalgouvernement." In the latter function he was responsible for the expulsion of 110,000 Poles from the ZAMOŚĆ area and the settlement of Germans in their place.

In May 1944, Krüger was appointed commander of the "Prinz Eugen" Division of the Waffen-SS, which fought against the partisans in western Yugoslavia. On May 9, 1945, the day after Germany's surrender, he committed suicide.

Friedrich Wilhelm Krüger. [National Archives]

BIBLIOGRAPHY

Birn, R. B. *Die Höheren SS- und Polizeiführer: Himmlers Vertreter im Reich und in den besetzten Gebieten.* Düsseldorf, 1986.

Krausnick, H., et al. *Anatomy of the SS State.* London, 1968.

SHMUEL KRAKOWSKI

KRUK, HERMAN (1897–1944), chronicler of the VILNA ghetto. Born in Płock, Poland, Kruk as a young man joined a Jewish socialist youth group that was close to the BUND. Under the influence of the Russian Revolution he joined the Polish Communist party, but was soon disillusioned by the party's stand on Jewish issues. In the 1920s, he found his way back to the Bund and was active in Tzukunft, the Bund's youth movement. Moving to Warsaw, he devoted himself primarily to educational and public activities, helped establish workers' libraries, contributed to *Volkstzeitung*, the Bund newspaper, and became one of the leaders of the movement in Poland.

In September 1939, when the Germans invaded Poland, Kruk fled from Warsaw and made his way to Vilna, which in October came under Lithuanian control. A large number of refugees from Poland had gathered there, and Kruk helped to organize their everyday life. Meanwhile, Lithuania was annexed by the USSR, in August 1940. With the help of the Bund, Kruk obtained a visa to the United States, but the Soviet authorities did not permit him to leave. In June of 1941, when the Soviet Union was invaded and German forces were approaching Vilna, Kruk decided to stay in the city under German rule and to record the events that were taking place. At the beginning of his diary, he wrote:

> I don't have the strength to become a wanderer once again. I am staying . . . and since I am staying and will be a victim of fascism, I will at least take up my pen and write the city's chronicle. There is no doubt: Vilna will be occupied, the Germans will make it fascist, the Jews will be put into a ghetto, and I shall record all these events.

Kruk's diary, written in Yiddish, is one of the most important documents relating to the Vilna ghetto. Not all of it has been saved—some pages are missing—but what survives gives an accurate description of the events in the ghetto and the lot of the Vilna Jews under Nazi occupation. The first entry in the diary is dated June 23, 1941, the evening of the German entry into Vilna; and the last, July 14, 1943, about two months before the ghetto's final liquidation. Kruk was active in the affairs of the ghetto and had a close relationship with its administration and its chairman, Jacob GENS. With a sharp eye for the developments unfolding before him, he recorded in his diary direct and undistorted information on the history of the ghetto, the deportation and extermination process, the ghetto's day-to-day life, the struggle for existence, the cultural activities, and the ghetto's underground and its relations with the JUDENRAT (Jewish Council). His own position faithfully reflected the Bund's attitude; at times he criticizes the Judenrat for its actions and at times he justifies it.

Kruk established and managed the ghetto library. He was also employed by EINSATZSTAB ROSENBERG, a Nazi agency that, among other activities, collected documentary material from the Vilna headquarters of YIVO, the Yidisher Visenshaftlikher Institut (Institute for Jewish Research), for transfer to Germany. Together with other Jewish employees of the agency, Kruk managed to smuggle into the ghetto valuable documents and thereby save them from being dispatched to Germany. His diary was typewritten, in three copies, and these were placed in different hiding places. One of the copies was discovered after the war by the poet Abraham SUTZKEVER, who gave it to YIVO in New York, where it was published as *Tagbuch fun Vilner Geto* (1960).

When the ghetto was liquidated, in September 1943, Kruk was deported to the KLOOGA concentration camp in Estonia. He continued to keep his diary in the camp. Some parts written during this period were eventually brought to Israel and handed over to MORESHET, a Holocaust research institute near Hadera, and were published. The last entry in the diary was made on September 17, 1944. The following day, Kruk was killed by the Nazis in the Lagedi concentration camp in Estonia.

BIBLIOGRAPHY

Arad, Y. *Ghetto in Flames.* New York, 1982.

Korczak, R. *Flames in Ash.* Merhavia, Israel, 1946. (In Hebrew.) Contains sections of Kruk's diary.

YITZHAK ARAD

KRUMEY, HERMANN (b. 1905), SS official. Born in Mährisch-Schönberg, Moravia, Krumey joined the SS after the ANSCHLUSS with Austria in 1938. From November 1939 to May 1940 he served in the Waffen-SS as an *Obersturmbannführer,* in the Posen (Warthegau) headquarters of the *Höherer SS- und Polizeiführer* (Higher SS and Police Leader). Between May 1940 and March 1944 he was a member of the Sicherheitspolizei (Security Police) in Łódź.

In the summer of 1941, Krumey was sent from Łódź to Croatia to take part in concentrating Jews in camps. In 1942 he helped arrange at least six transports from the ZAMOŚĆ area to AUSCHWITZ. He also assisted in deporting the Jews of Łódź to extermination camps, and in deporting Poles farther east.

Krumey entered HUNGARY with the occupation forces on March 19, 1944, as a leading member of Adolf EICHMANN's Sonderkommando (Special Commando). In this capacity, he played an important role in organizing Hungary's JUDENRAT (Jewish Council), the Zsidó Tanács, and in laying the groundwork for the destruction of Hungarian Jewry. In June 1944, in the wake of negotiations between Eichmann and the RELIEF AND RESCUE COMMITTEE OF BUDAPEST, close to twenty-one thousand Jews were transferred to STRASSHOF, a concentration camp in Austria. Krumey became the head of the Sonderkommando assigned there. Most of these Jews survived the war.

He was arrested by the Allies in Italy in May 1945, but was not prosecuted. Rezső (Rudolf) KASZTNER, the Zionist leader involved in the negotiations with the SS in Hungary, signed an affidavit on Krumey's behalf on May 5, 1948, and Krumey was released. He was again arrested in 1960, and after a trial in Frankfurt in 1965 was condemned to five years' hard labor, on February 3. Following an appeal by the prosecution, a new trial was held in 1968–1969, and Krumey was condemned to life imprisonment on August 29, 1969. The conviction was upheld by the Federal Court (*Bundesgerichtshof*) of Karlsruhe on January 17, 1973.

BIBLIOGRAPHY

Biss, A. *A Million Jews to Save: Check to the Final Solution.* Cranbury, N.J., 1975.

Brand, J., and A. Weissberg. *Desperate Mission: Joel Brand's Story.* New York, 1958.

RANDOLPH L. BRAHAM

KRUPP VON BOHLEN UND HALBACH, GUSTAV (1870–1950), German industrialist and armaments manufacturer. Born into a leading family of bankers, Krupp studied law at Heidelberg before entering a diplomatic career on the staff of a number of German embassies. Through marriage he entered the Krupp family firm in 1906, becoming president in 1909. He was a member of the Prussian State Council between 1921 and 1933 and from 1931 was president of the Reich Union of German Industry (Reichsverband der Deutschen Industrie). Although initially reputed to be an opponent of Hitler, Krupp in May 1933 accepted office in the governing body of the Adolf-Hitler-Spende (Adolf Hitler Fund) in Berlin, which made generous contributions to the Nazi party and the SS. This resulted in economic benefits for Krupp, particularly in the facilities offered to the firm's enterprises in occupied eastern Europe, where extensive use was made of the FORCED LABOR of Jews, Poles, and Russian prisoners of war. An estimated 70 percent to 80 percent of the labor force of 100,000 died as a result of the inhuman treatment. At a large fuse factory at Auschwitz, Jews were worked to a state of collapse and then gassed.

Gustav Krupp von Bohlen und Halbach.

At the end of World War II, Krupp was arrested as a major war criminal on charges of complicity in preparing a war of aggression, but he was not brought to trial, on grounds of ill health. He was also found unfit to plead at the Krupp Case, held in 1947 and 1948 (the tenth of the twelve trials constituting the SUBSEQUENT NUREMBERG PROCEEDINGS), at which the defendants were accused of plundering and of exploiting forced labor.

BIBLIOGRAPHY

Batty, P. *The House of Krupp*. New York, 1967.

Ferencz, B. *Less than Slaves*. Cambridge, Mass., 1979.

LIONEL KOCHAN

KUBE, WILHELM (1887–1943), Nazi party functionary and governor of occupied territories. Born in Głogów (Ger., Glogau), Silesia, Kube was one of the earliest members of the Nazi party and held various posts in the party hierarchy. In 1928 he became *Gauleiter* of the east German province of Ostmark, and in 1933, *Gauleiter* of the west German province of Kurmark. From 1924 to 1928, and again in 1933, he was a Nazi deputy in the Reichstag and in the Prussian Landtag (provincial legislature); in the latter body he was also chairman of the Nazi caucus. In 1933 Kube was appointed *Oberpräsident* (governor) of the Brandenburg-Berlin district. Because of his quarrels with party leaders and suspicions of embezzlement on his part, he was removed from all his posts.

In 1941 Kube was appointed *Generalkommissar* (governor) of Belorussia, which formed part of REICHSKOMMISSARIAT OSTLAND. Headquartered in Minsk, he fell out with the senior SS and police commanders, and attacked them for their mass murder and "scorched-earth" actions against the local population. He also demanded that there be no more transports of Jews from the Reich to the Minsk ghetto. Kube's charges and complaints were not motivated by humanitarian considerations; rather, he felt that these actions by the SS and the police were being carried out over his head and therefore that they weakened his authority. He put his complaints and protests in writing, in a letter to the Führer's bureau.

Wilhelm Kube.

On September 22, 1943, Kube was killed by a bomb planted under his bed by his maid, a Soviet partisan who had been assigned to the post.

BIBLIOGRAPHY

Hilberg, R. *The Destruction of the European Jews*. New York, 1985.

SHMUEL SPECTOR

KULMHOF. *See* Chełmno.

KULTURBUND DEUTSCHER JUDEN (Cultural Society of German Jews), organization engaged in promoting culture and the arts among the Jews of GERMANY between 1933 and 1941. The idea of establishing a cultural society for German Jews was put forward in the spring of 1933; its purposes were to enable the Jewish population to maintain the

Dr. Kurt Singer conducting an orchestra and choir in a performance in Berlin of Handel's *Israel in Egypt* (February 1937). [Bildarchiv Abraham Pisarek, Berlin]

cultural life to which they were accustomed, and to alleviate the distress of the thousands of Jewish theatrical artists and musicians who had been thrown out of their jobs when the Nazis came to power. The concept of an organization of this kind was the brainchild of a young theater director, Kurt Baumann, but the moving spirit in planning and running it was Dr. Kurt Singer, a medical doctor and musician who had been the director of the Berlin Opera. Singer headed the Kulturbund during the first five years of its existence, its most flourishing period. Joining Singer in the organizing team, at his invitation, were Julius Bab, an expert on the theater, and Werner Levie, as administrator. After consultations with the representative bodies of German Jewry, the organizing team applied to the German authorities, and the Prussian Ministry of Culture appointed Hans Hinkel—the head of its theater committee and a veteran Nazi cultural-affairs activist—as the society's supervisor. The Gestapo, on the other hand, was hesitant about accepting the society's existence. It gave its approval only when the words *deutscher Juden* were eliminated from the title (the society instead became known as the Jüdische Kulturbund, or Jewish Cultural Association), and it put the society's operations under surveillance.

In October 1933, the theater company organized by the Kulturbund in Berlin staged its first play, Gotthold Lessing's *Nathan der Weise* (Nathan the Wise). At about this time a symphony orchestra, an opera, a cabaret group, and a permanent lecture program were launched. The number of persons joining the society as members and subscribers was lower than the organizers had expected—some 18,000 out of the 160,000 Jews who made up the Berlin Jewish community.

On the model of the Berlin group, cultural societies on a regional and local level were established by Jewish communities all over the country. The more important of the regional organizations were the Rhein-Ruhr society, based in Cologne, which ran a regular theater; the Rhein-Main group, based in Frankfurt, which had an orchestra that also played outside its own region; and the Bavaria Cultural Society, based in Munich. The outstanding local societies were in Breslau, which ran an extensive program of musical activities; Mannheim, whose director, Karl Adler, managed to put all Jewish cultural and educational activities under one roof; and Hamburg, whose theater company also appeared regularly out of town. The membership of the societies in the medium-sized and small communities was proportionately much larger than in Berlin (indeed, usually twice as large).

In April 1935, thirty-six Jewish cultural societies, with seventy thousand members, were active in the Reich, and they organized themselves under an umbrella organization, the Reichsverband der Jüdischen Kulturbünde (Reich Association of Jewish Cultural Societies), centered in Berlin. This enabled the regional and local societies to improve their activities, facilitated the rational use of the existing artistic resources, and made possible the operation of a central professional training center that could influence the policies upon which the societies based their work. The German authorities also had an interest in the existence of a countrywide association, from both the administrative and the political aspects.

Hinkel, in the meantime, had been transferred to Joseph GOEBBELS's Ministry of Propaganda, from which he now supervised the Reich Association. The demand by the Nazis for overall supervision grew stronger, especially since the Gestapo, which also had a hand in the supervision, wanted a nationwide organization to be utilized for speeding up Jewish emigration.

Another organizational change was made in the wake of the November 1938 KRISTALLNACHT pogrom. On orders of the authorities, the umbrella organization, which had been a federation of independent societies, was transformed into a centralized body in charge of all Jewish cultural activities, including those that the local and regional societies had been carrying out on their own. These included the remaining publishing houses (most of the Jewish publishing houses had been closed down) and the editorial offices of the one newspaper, the *Jüdisches Nachrichtenblatt*, that the Jews were allowed to publish. In its new form the Kulturbund maintained its operations, mostly in the field of entertainment, on a modest scale. These were important to the Jewish population, whose conditions of life had come increasingly to resemble life in a ghetto. This remained the situation until the Kulturbund itself was closed down, in September 1941, on the eve of the deportations of eastern Europe.

Among the institutions maintained by the cultural societies were the following: four theater companies (the central theater in Berlin, a youth theater that was also based in Berlin and became a traveling troupe, and companies in Cologne and Hamburg); four symphony orchestras; two opera companies (one in Berlin and the other a traveling opera, also based in Berlin); a number of choirs (the largest, at Mannheim, consisted of one thousand singers); many chamber orchestras; entertainment groups and lecturers; and mixed groups that visited even the smallest, most out-of-the-way communities and entertained them with song and music, recitations and games. All these activities—which also included exhibitions—gave moral support to the persecuted Jews and helped to sustain their spirits.

The question of the Jewish content of its activities preoccupied the Kulturbund from the very beginning. The point at issue was whether it should aim at maximum integration with the culture of the majority in the country—which was what most of the Jewish public expected and most of the organization's leaders demanded—or whether it should be an instrument for heightening Jewish consciousness and for Jewish spiritual regeneration. This latter was what the Zionists advocated and, in their view, was what the Jews of Germany desperately needed. Another significant factor was the ban on the use of German cultural resources that the supervising authorities were gradually imposing on the Jews. At first, the view that prevailed emphasized integration into German culture, although important cultural events of Jewish content also took place, such as the presentation of Stefan Zweig's *Jeremiah* by the Berlin Jewish Theater at the beginning of its second season. But this trend changed as time went on.

The growing hostility to which the Jews were exposed and the need to protect themselves from its debilitating moral effect, together with the realization that it was not a passing phase through which they were living, reinforced the view that it was the cultural society's task to enrich the Jewish population's Jewish experience. Efforts were made, beginning in 1936, to include in the program of theater performances the works of Jewish playwrights, especially from eastern Europe or Palestine; and the writing of original Jewish plays and musical works was encouraged and supported. As a result, the Jewish component in the programs rose steadily. These efforts, however, had only partial success, and did not always meet with a positive response from the Jewish public. The transformation of the organization from a "Jewish Cultural Society" into a "Society for Jewish Culture" could not be successfully accomplished under the conditions prevailing at the time it was undertaken. Moreover, the mounting difficulties that the Jews had to cope with just to keep alive did not serve to encourage their interest in matters of the spirit.

Nevertheless, at a time of persecution and despair, the Kulturbund was a spiritual support for the German Jews, strengthening the ties of individual Jews with the Jewish people and with their faith, and giving them pride in their Jewish identity. In that sense, the society's activities were a form of moral resistance to the hostile regime.

BIBLIOGRAPHY

Cochavi, Y. *Armament for Spiritual Survival.* Naharia, Israel, 1988. (In Hebrew.)

Freeden, H. "A Jewish Theatre under the Swastika." *Leo Baeck Institute Yearbook* 1 (1956): 142–162.

Freeden, H. *Jüdisches Theater in Nazideutschland.* Tübingen, 1964.

YEHOYAKIM COCHAVI

KUTORGIENE-BUIVYDAITĖ, ELENA (1888–1963), a "RIGHTEOUS AMONG THE NATIONS." Born in Šiauliai (until 1917, Shavli) in Lithuania, Kutorgiene completed her medical studies at Moscow University in 1912 and was then employed as an ophthalmologist in a hospital in Moscow. In 1922 she returned to Lithuania, worked in medical institutions in KOVNO, was active in the OEUVRE DE SECOURS AUX ENFANTS, a Jewish welfare organization for children, and established close relations with Jewish doctors.

During the German occupation of Lithuania, Kutorgiene concealed Jews in her home in Kovno and found other places of concealment for them as well. She established close ties with the underground movement of the Kovno ghetto; the meetings that both she and the local partisans held with the commander of the ghetto underground, Haim YELIN, took place in her home. Kutorgiene helped the underground to obtain arms, sought out hiding places for underground activity, and disseminated anti-Nazi literature. Her son Viktoras assisted her. She kept a diary, *Yoman Kovno* (Kovno Diary), sections of which have been published in the USSR and in Israel, in the journal *Yalkut Moreshet*. She also hid the writings of Yelin and of his brother Meir in her home in Kovno.

Elena Kutorgiene-Buivydaitė.

Following the city's liberation, in August 1944, Kutorgiene worked on the Special Government Commission for the Investigation of War Crimes. After the war she was awarded the Order of Lenin for her extensive social and medical activity, and the Medal for Work during the Great Patriotic War; in 1958 she received the honorary title of Outstanding Doctor of Lithuania. In 1982 she was awarded the title of "Righteous among the Nations" by YAD VASHEM in Jerusalem.

BIBLIOGRAPHY

Kutorgiene, E. "Kovno Diary." *Yalkut Moreshet* 17 (January 1974): 31–72.

HAYA LIFSHITZ